FUNDAMENTALS OF CHILD DEVELOPMENT

FUNDAMENTALS OF CHILD DEVELOPMENT

Harry Munsinger
UNIVERSITY OF CALIFORNIA, SAN DIEGO

HOLT, RINEHART AND WINSTON, INC.
New York Chicago San Francisco Atlanta
Dallas Montreal Toronto London Sydney

Library of Congress Catalog Card Number: 71-122549
ISBN: 0-03-078605-3
Printed in the United States of America
234567890 071 9876543

TO MY WIFE, KIM

All the world's a stage,
And all the men and women merely players:
They have their exits and their entrances;
And one man in his time plays many parts,
His acts being seven ages. At first the infant,
Mewling and puking in the nurse's arms.
Then the whining school-boy, with his satchel
And shining morning face, creeping like snail
Unwillingly to school. And then the lover,
Sighing like furnace, with a woeful ballad
Made to his mistress' eyebrow. Then a soldier,
Full of strange oaths and bearded like the pard,
Jealous in honour, sudden and quick in quarrel,
Seeking the bubble reputation
Even in the cannon's mouth. And then the justice,
In fair round belly with good capon lined,
With eyes severe and beard of formal cut,
Full of wise saws and modern instances;
And so he plays his part. The sixth age shifts
Into the lean and slipper'd pantaloon
With spectacles on nose and pouch on side,
His youthful hose, well saved, a world too wide
For his shrunk shank; and his big manly voice,
Turning again toward childish treble, pipes
And whistles in his sound. Last scene of all,
That ends this strange eventful history,
Is second childishness and mere oblivion,
Sans teeth, sans eyes, sans taste, sans every thing.

AS YOU LIKE IT

PREFACE

An introductory text should attempt to settle ambiguous issues and disputed questions; the methods by which these decisions are made and the biases that guide them should be stated. In my particular case I have tended toward experimental as opposed to observational evidence when both are available, to human rather than animal studies when both are available, and to theory rather than empirical fact when both are available. Unfortunately, these happy intersections rarely occur; in most instances I included experimental and observational material, animal and human work, and both theory and raw facts. The book represents a series of compromises among scientific rigor, good teaching doctrine, and currently popular notions of child development. The compromises were necessary because it is impossible, given our present state of knowledge about development, to present anything like a finished picture of the child. Instead, we glimpse only faint outlines of where we may be and find occasional signposts placed by giants of the past. To build a clear, coherent picture from these scant data would be science fiction; thus, the present text paints the happy confusion and healthy conflict that is child psychology.

First, the development of fundamental human processes—perception, learning, personality, cognition, motivation, and social behavior—is outlined. My aim was to sample a representative set of research studies and to present them within a theoretical frame. Unfortunately, the particular theory changes as we progress from topic to topic. The central theme is a progression from direct one-to-one reflexive actions early in the infant's life (for example, sucking and crying) to complex symbolic relations (for example, language and thought) later in his existence. This transformation from reflexive reaction to thought is the heart of development. I have placed heavy emphasis on the biological, cognitive, and personal growth of children.

I have ordered topics along a chronological base paralleling rapid or important changes in the growing child. The book is separated into two main sections. The first eight chapters outline the development of the individual child; they cover basic processes. The second eight chapters treat the interacting child; they outline relations between the child and his family, school, and culture. Each chapter mentions a little history, some methods, and the main theories concerning various problems. Examples are selected for their relevance, not necessarily because they are famous or first.

THE INDIVIDUAL CHILD

Part One of this text considers biological substrate, sensory input, operations, and performance. Chapter 1 deals with genetics—the general principles and methods of modern genetics, including behavior genetics, the nature-nurture controversy, and the biochemistry of RNA and DNA. Chapter 2 considers the problems of human growth—the physiological and behavioral manifestations of the growth process. Particular attention is given to the prediction of physical maturity and the effects of growth on other processes, for example, self-concepts.

The section on sensory input, Chapter 3, concerns sensation—the development of our basic sensory abilities. Methods of sensory psychology are discussed; a simple example of a signal-detection experiment is presented, and various sensory abilities of the young infant are outlined. Chapter 4 treats perception: how we give meaning to our sensory information. The notion of object perception, the criteria of a dimension, theories of perception, and work on reading are outlined.

Under operations, Chapter 5 considers the various problems of learning; classical conditioning, operant conditioning, emotional learning, and learning to learn are discussed. Chapter 6 treats the growth of thinking. The theory of Piaget, on the concrete operational period, is presented, along with concept formation, computer simulation of thought, and some logical models of children's thinking.

The last two chapters concern the child's performance. Chapter 7 outlines the development of motivation; basic drive theory, the notion of learned drives, anxiety, and curiosity motivation are considered. Chapter 8 outlines modern notions of decision processes and choice. Choice among well-defined outcomes is discussed, along with the problem of conflict reduction of post-decisional dissonance, and preference.

THE INTERACTING CHILD

Part Two covers infant-mother relations and the child's interactions with family, culture, and society. Chapter 9 concerns early maternal influences: normal foetal growth, the types of prenatal influences to which the foetus might be exposed, and the effects of maternal health and prematurity on later development. Various behaviors of the embryo, foetus, and newborn are described. Chapter 10 examines the unique effects of early experience on later development. Notions of critical periods versus initial experience and of maternal deprivation and maternal separation are detailed.

Chapter 11 treats sensory integration—the various stages of early infant development, with particular attention to the work of Piaget. Chapter 12 covers parent-child relations. Two bipolar factors are proposed, love-hate and permissive-restrictive. The four combinations of these home atmospheres produce very different children. Next comes interactions between the child and his culture. Chapter 13 describes the growth of language, with close attention given to the work of Chomsky and Brown on language theory and the types of grammars young children develop on their way to adult speech. Chapter 14 considers the measurement of intelligence. Various tests of mental abilities—for example, those for the infant, the preschool child, the adult, and special tests—are examined along with the methodological problems of testing. Notions of creativity are also covered.

The final group of chapters treats social influences. Chapter 15 covers the child's social relations, the growth of play, dreams, and his notions of reality connected with play. The theory of games is briefly reviewed and applied to some simple situations. A variety of social influences are collected and their effects on the growing child outlined (the church, television, books, and the press).

Chapter 16 presents a more integrated picture of the child. Models of personality are outlined, some types of pathologies are discussed, and the defense mechanisms of the child are considered.

The plan of the book will enable an instructor to cover first the individual processes of the child—for example, genetics, growth, motivation, association, thinking, sensation, and perception—and then consider the more complex interactions of the child—for example, with the mother, the family, his culture, and society. Alternatively, the instructor may choose to follow a more chronological sequence; in this case he can alternate between the section on the individual child and the section on the interacting child—in this case, first genetics and growth, then paranatal influences and early experiences; after this would come sensation and perception followed by sensory-motor integration and parent-child relations. The next section could outline association and thinking and cover language and complex intellectual and creative processes. The following section could present motivation, emotion, and will, to be followed by the social relations of the child and his personality development. This sort of flexibility should appeal to a wide variety of teaching styles.

SPECIAL FEATURES OF THIS TEXT

1 The structure of each chapter should help the student learn. Each chapter begins with a map of where it is going and ends with a comprehensive summary. In addition, each paragraph is summarized in a single sentence printed next to it. These summary sentences are designed to give the student some warning of what is coming and to serve as a convenient review.

2 Remarks are included in each chapter which outline controversial issues. These may be omitted in a short course; for a more advanced course, the critical discussions may stimulate further discussion and thinking by the students.

3 Complete references are included for each chapter so that the student can read original work for himself if he is curious or requires additional information.

4 Further readings on each chapter are suggested.

5 A companion book of readings (*Readings in Child Development*), coordinated with the text, is available. These studies have been selected to examine critical problems in some detail. Each reading is introduced by a short discussion of why the research study was done, its importance, the main results, and any faults it may contain. Each chapter is introduced by a discussion of the issues covered and their relevance to the studies in the chapter.

6 A booklet of examination questions has been compiled for the instructor. Twenty to 25 multiple-choice questions of graded difficulty are presented for each chapter.

TO THE STUDENT

For a full appreciation of the ideas in this book, the student should (1) look at the end-of-chapter summary for an overview of the chapter; (2) read quickly through the summary sentences in the margin; (3) read each summary sentence and the paragraph associated with it; and (4) review each summary sentence to make sure it is understood. If the student does not then know what the summary sentence means, he should (5) reread the paragraph next to it. Finally, when reviewing for exams, he should read the summary sentences carefully and see if he can recall what was said in the paragraph.

ACKNOWLEDGMENTS

The writing of this book is primarily the result of discussions with my colleagues and students of development; its strength and insights must be shared with them. I owe a special debt to William Kessen who showed me the complications and happy complexities of children and the English language. I am indebted to the hundreds of students of children whose ideas I have combined into a collage about the child.

Particular thanks are due Tom Davies and Jane Mayo of Holt, Rinehart and Winston. The quality of my text owes much to their patience, foresight, and taste.

In addition to sources noted in the figure legends, credit is due the following for permission to reproduce or adapt material:

Figure 1.1. From *A history of embryology* by Joseph Needham. © Joseph Needham 1959. By permission of Abelard-Schuman Limited.

Figure 1.11. From "Genetics and intelligence: A review," by L. Erlenmeyer-Kimling & L. F. Jarvik. *Science*, 1963, **142,** 1477–1479. Copyright © 1963 by the American Association for the Advancement of Science.

Figure 2.2. From Boyd, E. *Growth of the surface area of the human body,* Child Welfare Monograph #10. University of Minnesota Press, Minneapolis. © 1935 University of Minnesota.

Figures 3.3 and 3.6. Reprinted from *The process of human behavior* by Mandel Sherman, M.D., Ph.D., and Irene Case Sherman, Ph.D. Copyright 1929 by W. W. Norton & Company, Inc. Copyright renewed 1956 by Mandel Sherman.

Figure 3.4. From Hershenson, M. Visual discrimination in the human newborn. *Journal of Comparative and Physiological Psychology,* 1964, **58,** 270–276. Copyright 1964 by the American Psychological Association and reproduced by permission.

Figure 4.2. From "The origin of form perception," by Robert L. Fantz. Copyright © 1961 by Scientific American, Inc. All rights reserved.

Figure 4.7. Reprinted with the permission of the publisher from R. F. Street, *A gestalt completion test.* New York: Teachers College Press, Copyright 1931.

Matrix, page 145. From *The developmental psychology of Jean Piaget* by John H. Flavell, Copyright © 1963, by Litton Education Publishing, Inc., by permission of Van Nostrand Reinhold Company.

Figure 6.7. From Kendler, T. S., & Kendler, H. H. Reversal and non-reversal shifts in kindergarten children. *Journal of Experimental Psychology,* 1959, **58,** 56–60. Copyright © 1959 by the American Psychological Association, and reproduced by permission.

Figures 6.8 and 6.9. From Kendler, H. H., & Kendler, T. S. Vertical and horizontal processes in problem solving. *Psychological Review,* 1962, **69,** 1–15. Copyright © 1962 by the American Psychological Association, and reproduced by permission.

Figure 7.1. From Kessen, W., & Leutzendorff, A. M. The effect of non-nutritive sucking on movement in the human newborn. *Journal of Comparative and Physiological Psychology,* 1963, **56,** 69–72. Copyright © 1963 by the American Psychological Association, and reproduced by permission.

Figures 7.2 and 7.3. From Harlow, H. F. On the meaning of love. *American Psychologist,* **13,** 1958, 673-685. Copyright © 1958 by the American Psychological Association, and reproduced by permission.
Figure 7.4. From Miller, N. E. Theory and experiment relating psychoanalytic displacement to stimulus-response generalization. *Journal of Abnormal and Social Psychology,* 1948, **43,** 155-178. Copyright 1948 by the American Psychological Association, and reproduced by permission.
Figure 7.7. From Miller, N. E. Studies of fear as an acquirable drive: I. Fear as motivation and fear-reduction as reinforcement in the learning of new responses. *Journal of Experimental Psychology,* 1948, **38,** 89-101. Copyright 1948 by the American Psychological Association, and reproduced by permission.
Figure 7.11. From "Emotion" by George Mandler, from *New Directions in Psychology* by Roger Brown, E. Galanter, G. Mandler, & E. H. Hess. Copyright © 1962 by Holt, Rinehart and Winston, Inc.
Figures 7.12 through 7.17. From Munsinger, H., & Kessen, W. Uncertainty, structure, and preference. *Psychological Monographs,* 1964, **78,** 1-24. Copyright © 1964 by the American Psychological Association, and reproduced by permission.
Tables 8.3 and 8.4. From *The authoritarian personality* by T. W. Adorno, et al., pp. 283, 285. Copyright 1950 by The American Jewish Committee. Reproduced by permission of Harper & Row, Publishers, Inc.
Table 8.5. Reprinted with permission of The Macmillan Company from "The authoritarian personality—A methodological critique," by H. H. Hyman & P. B. Sheatsley. In R. Christie & M. Jahoda (Eds.), *Studies in the scope and method of the authoritarian personality.* Copyright 1954 by The Free Press.
Figure 9.1. From *Human embryology* by W. J. Hamilton, J. D. Boyd, & H. W. Mossman. Copyright 1952, The Williams & Wilkins Co., Baltimore, Maryland 21202, U.S.A.
Table 9.1. From *Biography of the newborn* by M. S. Gilbert. Copyright 1938, The Williams & Wilkins Co., Baltimore, Maryland 21202, U.S.A.
Figures 10.5 through 10.8. From Harlow, H. F. "On the meaning of love," *American Psychologist,* **13,** 1958, 673-685. Copyright © 1958 by the American Psychological Association, and reproduced by permission.
Figure 10.9. From "Affectional responses in the infant monkey," by H. F. Harlow & R. R. Zimmerman. *Science,* 1959, **130,** 421-432. Copyright © 1959 by the American Association for the Advancement of Science.
Figure 10.12. From Harlow, H. F. "On the meaning of love," *American Psychologist,* **13,** 1958, 673-685. Copyright © 1958 by the American Psychological Association, and reproduced by permission.
Figure 12.1 and Table 12.1. From Glidewell, J. C. *Parental attitudes and child behavior,* 1961. Courtesy of Charles C Thomas, Publisher, Springfield, Illinois.
Figure 12.3. From Radke, M. J. *The relation of parental authority to children's behavior,* Child Welfare Monograph #22, University of Minnesota Press, Minneapolis. Copyright 1946 by the University of Minnesota.
Table 13.1. Reprinted with permission of The Macmillan Company from *Social psychology* by R. Brown. Copyright © 1965 by The Free Press.
Tables 14.3 and 14.5. From Anastasi, A. *Individual differences.* New York: Wiley, 1965.
Table 14.6. From Guilford, J. P. The structure of intellect. *Psychological Bulletin,* 1956, **53,** 267-293.
Table 15.1. Reprinted with permission of The Macmillan Company from *Children who hate* by F. Redl. Copyright 1951 by The Free Press, a Corporation.
Figure 16.2. From Goodenough, F. L. *Anger in young children,* Child Welfare Monograph #9, University of Minnesota Press, Minneapolis. Copyright 1931 by the University of Minnesota.

CONTENTS

Preface ix
Acknowledgments xiii

PART ONE

The Individual Child

1 **Genetics and Development** 3
Conceptions of Human Development; Modern Genetics; Biochemical Genetics; Behavior Genetics

2 **Human Growth** 29
The Establishment of Developmental Norms; The Development of Motor Abilities; Body Build and Personality

3 **Sensory Abilities** 53
The Notion of Threshold; Detection Theory as a Model of the Process; Basic Sensory Abilities

4 **Perceptual Growth** 78
Views of Perceptual Development; Perceptual Learning; Observation of the Newborn; Whole-Part Perception; Values and Perception; Perceptual Changes in the Adult

5 **Learning** 104
Basic Components of the Learning Situation; Association; Reinforcement; Complex Processes in Learning; Learning to Learn

6 **Thought** 130
Stages of Children's Thought; The Development of Symbolic Representation; The Nature of Preoperational Thought; Concrete Opera-

tions; Logical Groupings in Cognitive Behavior; An Association Theory of Thinking; Concept Attainment; Individual Styles of Concept Attainment; Computer Simulation and Reasoning

7 **Motivation and Emotion 160**
Primary Drives; Secondary (Learned) Drives; Physiological, Social, and Cognitive Factors in Emotion

8 **Will 192**
Choice, Preference, and Judgment; Conflict; The Development of Morality; Prejudice and the Authoritarian Personality

PART TWO

The Interacting Child

9 **Paranatal Influences 215**
Predeterminism; Neural Mediation of Behavior; Stages of Prenatal Development; Prenatal Influences; The Birth Process

10 **Early Experience 236**
The Use of Animals; Birth; Postnatal Experience; The Role of Infant Experience in Psychosexual Development

11 **Sensory-Motor Integration 264**
Piaget's Conception of Development; The Sensory-Motor Period: Special Developments

12 **Parent-Child Relations 286**
Dimensions of Parent-Child Interaction; Antecedents of Aggression; Social Class Differences; Mother-Child Relations; Family Composition

13 **Language 308**
Early Vocalizations; The Acquisition of Language; Theories of Syntax; Individual Variation in Language Skills

14 **Intelligence and Creativity** 331

The Development of Intelligence Tests; Reliability and Validity; The Constancy of IQ; Intelligence Tests; Learning Ability and Intelligence; "Culture-Fair" Intelligence Tests; Creativity and Productive Thinking; Facilitating and Inhibiting Factors in Creativity

15 **Social Relations** 358

Infant Social Relations; Play; Children's Peer Relations; Mass Media and Children; The Child in School

16 **Personality** 389

Problems of Development; The Self-Concept; Theories of Personality Development; Social Learning and Imitation; Mechanisms of Defense; Abnormal Development; The Treatment of Personality Disorders

Glossary 425
Index 447

PART ONE
THE INDIVIDUAL CHILD

1 GENETICS AND DEVELOPMENT

To you your father should be as a god;
One that composed your beauties, yea, and one
To whom you are but as a form in wax
By him imprinted and within his power
To leave the figure or disfigure it.

A MIDSUMMER NIGHT'S DREAM

This chapter outlines four conceptions of human development, considers the possibility of inheriting acquired characteristics, presents the fundamentals of Mendelian genetics, and covers more modern notions of quantitative genetic determination. A discussion of genetic information transfer, mechanisms that produce variability in human beings, and a look at the genetic basis of intelligence and abnormal behavior follow.

CONCEPTIONS OF HUMAN DEVELOPMENT

Four conceptions of man exist: predeterminism, preformationism, environmentalism, and interactionism.

Views concerning the relative influence of heredity and environment on the growing child have taken many forms. Preformationism, the earliest explanation, suggested that everything in the embryo is formed simultaneously. Growth, according to this view, was merely expansion of the preformed man; there was no theory since all "development" occurred at conception. A more reasonable explanation of age changes was proposed by the predeterminists, who believed that preset biological factors determine the child's development. The role of environmental effects was ignored. A third group, the empiricists, placed the environment in complete control. They assumed that all children are pretty much alike at birth and that individual differences result from various learning experiences. Recent conceptions of the nature-nurture controversy suggest that both genetic endowment and environmental influences must be considered in understanding man. Developmental psychologists are now interested in learning how the mechanisms work.

Preformationism asserts that embryos are miniature adults and that no age changes occur; Wolff demonstrated that these propositions are false.

Preformationism is an old idea. In the late seventeenth century a lively controversy erupted between the supporters of preformationism and predeterminism. Both groups appealed to scientific evidence for support of their arguments. The Dutch preformationist Anton van Leeuwenhoek (1677), inventor of the compound microscope, reported that he had observed "animalcules" (see Figure 1.1) in sperm. However, preformationism becomes an absurd theory if we consider the following: (1) If all animals are preformed, then the embryos of reptiles, birds, and mammals should be different during their early stages of development. In fact, they are remarkably similar. (2) If embryos are preformed, then each should be complete as soon as it is visible at all, and its shape should not change over time. If the shape of the embryo changes over time, it cannot be preformed. If no age changes are found, preformationism is upheld; if changes occur, predeterminism could be accepted. Through a compound microscope, Kaspar Wolff (1759) observed the development of chicken eggs over successively longer periods of incubation. Wolff, who looked primarily at the development of blood vessels, reported seeing a homogeneous mass transformed into islands separated by empty spaces. He next reported a red liquid and spaces covered with membranes. Finally, he noted, these membranes became blood vessels. Wolff described a similar series of changes

FIGURE 1.1

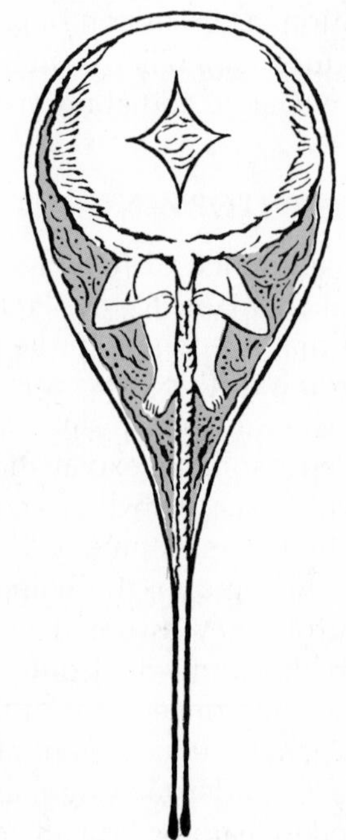

Hartsoeker's drawing of a human spermatozoon according to van Leeuwenhoek. (From Needham, 1959.)

for the chick's intestine. These systematic observations of developmental change marked the end of preformationionism as a serious theory of development.

Predeterminism assumes that biologically preset mechanisms determine development.

The demise of preformationism invited alternative conceptions of development. Biologically preset mechanisms had been proposed by many. Darwin (1859) considered heredity the primary controller of man and natural selection of the fittest (by some criterion) the primary mechanism of change. Hall (1883), a champion of Darwin's theory of evolution and the founder of child psychology in America, supported this conception of the child. He used the phrase "ontogeny recapitulates phylogeny" (child development reflects the course of evolution) to explain development. Hall expected to find the same behavior in young children and lower animals. Predeterminists preached the notion of preset behavioral and physical maturation. Hall was fond of illustrating preset biological maturation in children with the example of the frog. During its development from the tadpole state, the frog first grows a tail. This tail is later absorbed as the growing frog uses the tissue in the development of its back legs. If the tail is lost before the legs are formed, they develop abnormally. For Hall this example was clear evidence of preset sequential stages and pointed out the disadvantage of skipping a prior stage. The analogy, however, assumes that frogs' legs and children's minds follow similar rules of growth.

Terman (author of the Stanford-Binet Intelligence Test) and Gesell supported a predeterminist position.

Through Hall's influence predeterminism became a dominant theory of development. In addition to his own efforts, several of Hall's students made important contributions. Louis Terman (1916), who developed the Stanford-Binet Intelligence Test, believed intelligence to be the fulfillment of maturational forces; he felt that the best way to understand a child's development is to describe his current status compared with that of his peers. The notion of comparing a child with others of the same age was a major advance. Arnold Gesell (1941) also believed that the first step in understanding human development is to establish the normal course of growth for each age and the variation to be expected.

Watson introduced the notion of environmentalism; he captured the imagination of democratically disposed American psychologists.

At the turn of the twentieth century, a new conception of man emerged. Environmentalism (Watson, 1913) dominated American psychology for half a century. Behaviorists preached the doctrine that proper training could make any sound human neonate into any type of man. The notion had enormous appeal to democratically disposed Americans. As an alternative to racial prejudice, environmentalism remained popular long after scientific evidence failed to support the theory. This view fostered a strong interest in learning theory among American psychologists.

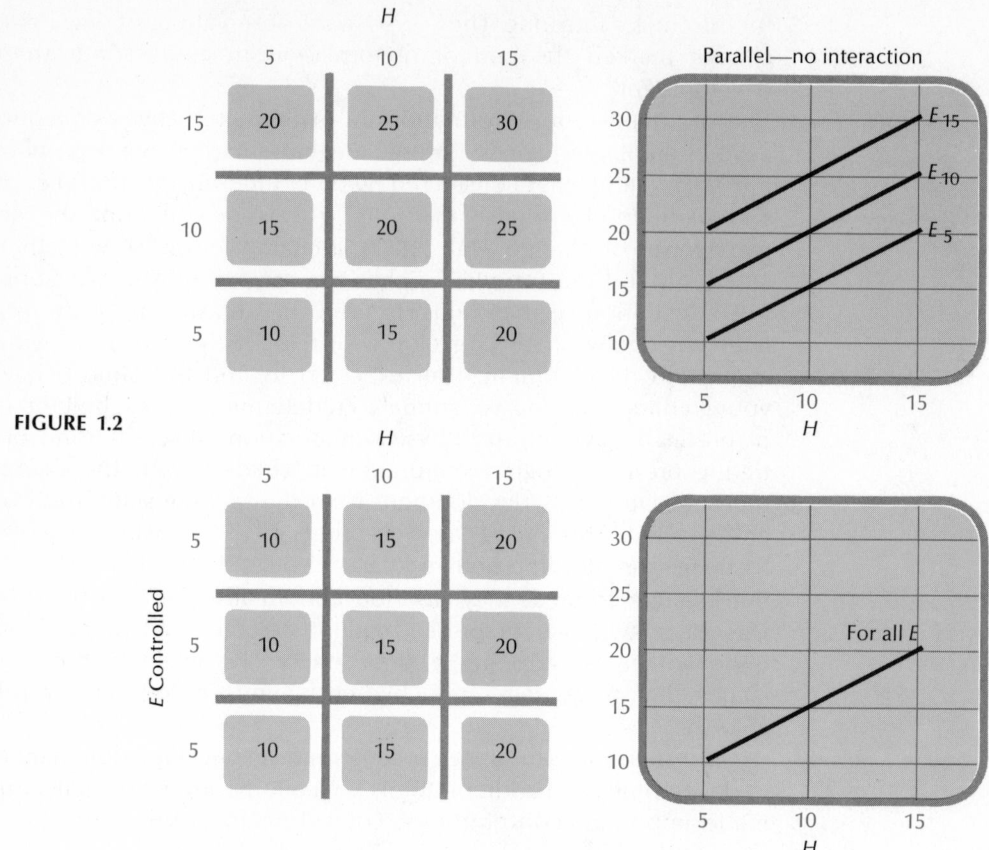

FIGURE 1.2

Additive model. According to this model, if either heredity or environment is constant, all variation among individuals results from the other variable. This is not true in fact. When we limit environmental effects, an organism develops abnormally [light-deprived rats in Hebb's experiments (1937) either could not see at all, or were very deficient in pattern vision]. Twin studies show that even when the environment *and* heredity are controlled, there is still unexplained variation. This extra variance is accounted for by interaction; it also contradicts a simple additive model.

Modern notions of development stress the joint influence of heredity and environment (see Figures 1.2, 1.3, 1.4).

Evidence has accumulated against a circumscribed view of development. No longer do we consider *only* hereditary or environmental influences in trying to understand age changes. A sophisticated conception of development includes the joint influence of genetics and environment. We need to understand *how* a genotype (the genetic endowment of the organism) and environmental influences combine to form a phenotype (the measurable physical characteristics of an organism). There are many ways to model the joint influence of heredity

FIGURE 1.3

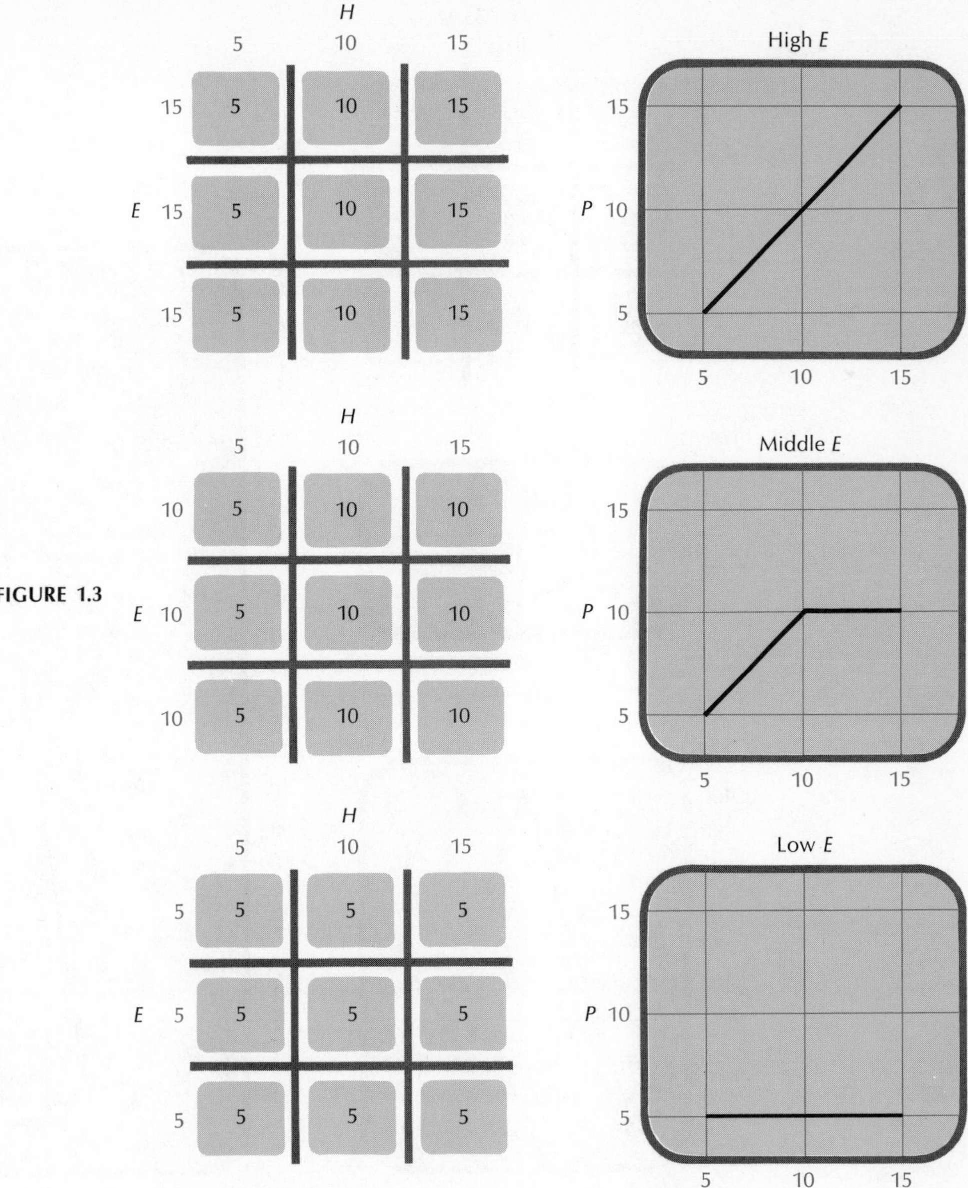

Interaction with limits. The limit model shows two things. (1) If the environment is rich enough, then hereditary determination is the controlling factor and the organism will reach its full potential; (2) if the environment is poor, then genetically superior individuals will not reach their full potential. The environment simply gives the organism a chance to reach his full genetic potential; this notion is called predeterminism.

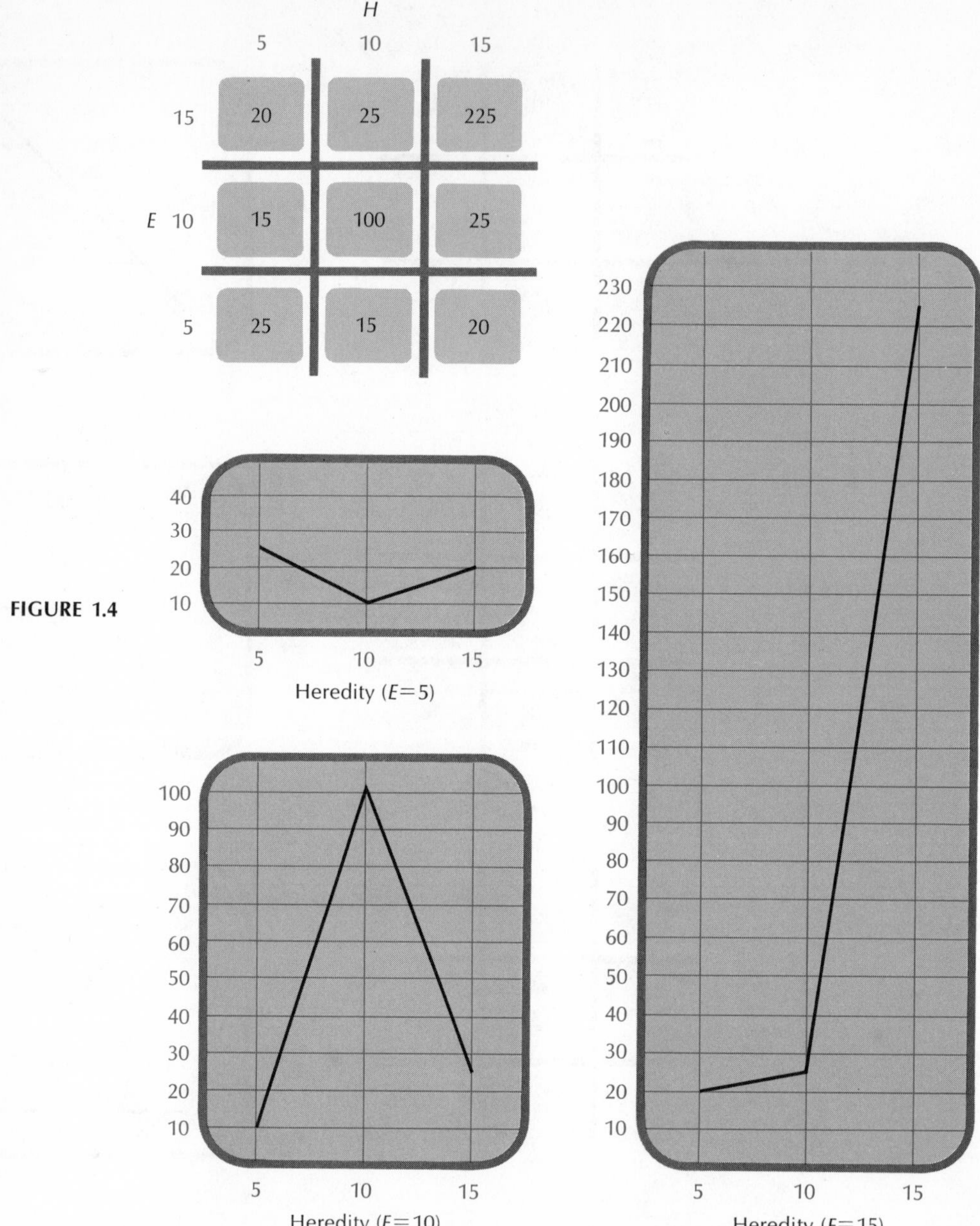

FIGURE 1.4

Interaction model. Suppose that heredity and environment interact such that a *mismatch* between levels of heredity and environment makes for an additive model of joint effects, while a *match* between the two will result in multiplicative effects. This model postulates that the very *process* of development is changed by a match or mismatch between heredity and environment.

and environment. Among these are (1) a simple addition of their effects, (2) a slightly more subtle model of development that assumes each factor can limit growth, and finally (3) a model which suggests that unique combinations of genetic endowment and environmental influence have differential effects. An additive model assumes that control of the development of an organism may come from either genetic or environmental factors and that the particular source of these effects makes no difference. In contrast to this simple view is the deprivation model, which assumes that either variable may limit development. Finally, an interaction approach assumes that unique combinations of hereditary influences and environmental effects produce differential growth rates; this model implies the existence of an optimum environment for the development of each unique genetic endowment.

A simple additive model of genetic-environment effects is wrong; selection among other models requires further work.

Figures 1.2, 1.3, and 1.4 show different diagrams of the joint effects of genetic and environmental influences. The simple additive model (Figure 1.2) predicts that under either constant environmental or genetic conditions, all differences among individuals will be due to the other factor. This statement is factually wrong. There is good evidence that a limitation of environmental influences will drastically limit development of a biological process and not just lower its over-all value. For example, monkeys raised in the dark (Riesen, 1947) never learned to see. A choice among the remaining models must await further research. At the moment, it is important to understand the general notion of interaction and what implications it holds. Most educators follow the theory that rich environments do less to limit the child than poorer ones (Figure 1.3); this approach is probably the safest if we have no good idea of what an optimum match between the environment and hereditary influences might be (Figure 1.4). However, if we could get a good measure of the child's ability, we should be able to place him in the optimum growth range.

MODERN GENETICS

Mendel introduced the gene and outlined rules of combination.

Modern genetics began when Gregor Mendel published a small paper in 1867 describing his work on the heritability of color in the sweet pea. This monk's brilliant work, lost to the world for almost fifty years, contained several important principles. Mendel's basic rules were that (1) inherited characteristics are produced by genes, which are transmitted unchanged from one generation to the next; (2) in each individual these genes are found in pairs, and if the two genes in a pair are different in their effects, one gene dominates the other; (3) when seeds are formed in any individual, the members of each pair of genes segregate independently of all other pairs; (4) single-gene sex cells mate, so that one gene comes from each parent to the offspring.

Early studies of genetics restricted environmental variation and thus missed evidence for interaction.

Early conceptions of genetic development ignored environment, so these rules and the evidence in support of them favored a predeterminist position. They do provide an adequate description of color heritability in the sweet pea. However, Mendel did not study heritability of traits over a wide range of environmental conditions (for example, temperature, humidity, light, or altitude). Current evidence suggests that the environment interacts with genetic characteristics to produce a phenotype. The important point in understanding interaction is to note that the size of chrysanthemums from genetically different clumps vary by different amounts as a function of altitude. To demonstrate an interaction we need at least two different genetic factors and two environmental influences. We must show that a phenotypic characteristic (such as size) varies as a function of environmental conditions, and that the way in which the phenotypic characteristic (size) changes is different for various genetic strains.

An example of genetic-environment interaction is color variation in the Himalayan rabbit.

Gene-environment interaction in the animal kingdom is shown by the hair color of Himalayan rabbits compared with that of ordinary white rabbits. The hair color of the extremities of Himalayan rabbits varies with the temperatures they experience early in maturation. This variation in coloring does not occur in other strains of rabbits. Thus, temperature and genetic strain of rabbit interact in determining hair color. We have the necessary and sufficient conditions for interaction—hair color (phenotype) changes as a function of temperature for genotype A (Himalayan), while for genotype B (white rabbit) hair color does not vary as a function of temperature. When we describe an interaction model of development, we assume an effect of the genotype, an effect of the environment, *and* an interaction between the two, all of which combine to form a particular phenotype. Our task is to understand the mechanisms involved.

Acquired characteristics

The notion that acquired characteristics can be inherited was proposed by Lamarck. The idea currently exists as a political doctrine.

An ancient controversy flourished in genetics concerning the effect of parents' acquired skills or deficiencies on the genetic endowment of their children. If a parent became a musician or mathematician or thief, would his children be genetically inclined and skilled in music or mathematics or thievery? The belief that acquired characteristics could be genetically transmitted came to be called Lamarckianism, after the biologist Lamarck (1914). This conception of genetics was successfully challenged when Weismann (1889) showed that although the rest of the body changes with age, the germ cells do not vary unless subjected to unusual conditions such as radiation, heat, or physical pressure. Genes may change by direct physical influences, but they are not ordinarily transformed. Although genetic trans-

REMARKS: COMMENTARY

The relative importance of genetic endowment and environmental influence has been decided from several views, most of them not scientific. For example, in the United States the widespread belief that all men are created equal has a political base. Any demonstration that genetic factors can permanently influence an individual's development runs counter to this belief. The racial and cultural excesses of the Nazi regime, with its support of genetic determination, has caused mankind to look askance at all suggestions of genetic determination. We see a strong flavor of the doctrines of genetic superiority in any such suggestion. Unless there is overwhelming evidence for genetic determination, we are unlikely even to suggest its existence. For this reason, many arguments in this chapter are intended to demonstrate that traits do indeed have a genetic base. It will be some time before a completely objective approach can be taken to this touchy problem. A way out is to study the mechanisms by which genetic traits are transmitted. This does not require taking a stand on whether the trait in question is more strongly genetically determined or environmentally influenced. In any event, since it is unlikely that eugenics (improvement of man by controlled breeding) will be politically or emotionally feasible within the next few hundred years, we should probably concentrate on finding ways to manipulate environmental influences on a person. We will gain some control over development and have a better chance of raising the general level of intelligence and adjustment if we do.

mission of acquired characteristics has recurred as a political idea, it is not a scientific explanation. The genetic inheritance of offspring is not affected from generation to generation by the particular experiences of the parents. Only direct action upon the germ cells can change genetic potentials.

Mechanisms of cell production

During germ cell production (meiosis) chromosomal pairs separate to ensure the correct number of genes in a mated cell; gene separation does not occur during regular cell production (mitosis).

In cell production we assume that the *mechanisms* of heredity are essentially the same from one species to another, though they have been investigated more completely in corn, sweet peas, and fruit flies than in humans. During the normal growth process (mitosis), each member of the 23 chromosome pairs splits, forming two new cells; each new cell contains the full complement of 23 pairs of chromosomes. In this way the genetic information originally deposited in the cell is left intact for later expression (see Figure 1.5). However, in the special case of production of sex cells (meiosis) this process is altered, as shown in Figure 1.6. In the case of sex cell production, each chromosome pair is reproduced and then each single chromosome migrates to a separate daughter cell, producing four

FIGURE 1.5

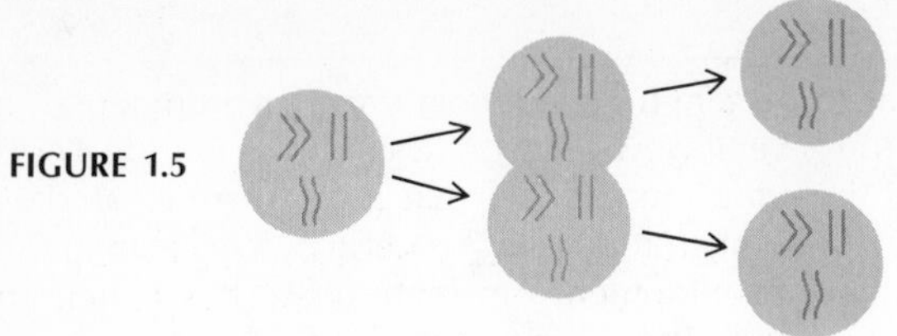

Mitosis (cell replication). During normal cell replication the complete genetic code (both pairs of each chromosome) are reproduced and enter the new cell.

cells instead of two as in normal cell growth. This process leaves each daughter cell with only half the required pairings of genes for normal growth; two sex cells (one from each partner) must unite to maintain the correct complement of 23 *pairs* of chromosomes. One chromosome for each pair is supplied by the mother and another by the father, producing an individual who is a blend of the characteristics of both. By receiving 23 chromosomes from the father and 23 from the mother, individuals may be produced from generation to generation with an enormous array of different characteristics. The number of different individuals this process can produce is on the order of 8×10^6; except for identical twins, no two individuals will ever have the same genetic endowment. This process guarantees various combinations of genetic material, contributing to wide individual differences and indirectly to our survival. There is good reason to believe that species which produce large variation in their kind are more likely to survive drastic changes in the environment.

The rule of segregation says that genetic material is not altered by association with other genes in the chromosome.

The rule of independent assortment explains the enormous variability of heredity.

There are two rules that govern the process of genetic transmission—segregation and independent assortment. To understand the notions of segregation and independent assortment, consider a simple example. If genes acted like liquids, mixing (conception) would change their makeup. However, genes behave like marbles; they can be poured into a single container at conception and retrieved intact at maturity (for sex cell production). Segregation refers to the integrity of the individual marbles; independent assortment means that you can take one marble without bringing others along. However, genes are linked into sets. This linkage places a major limitation on independent assortment. During crossing-over, parts of chromosomes are interchanged. The

FIGURE 1.6

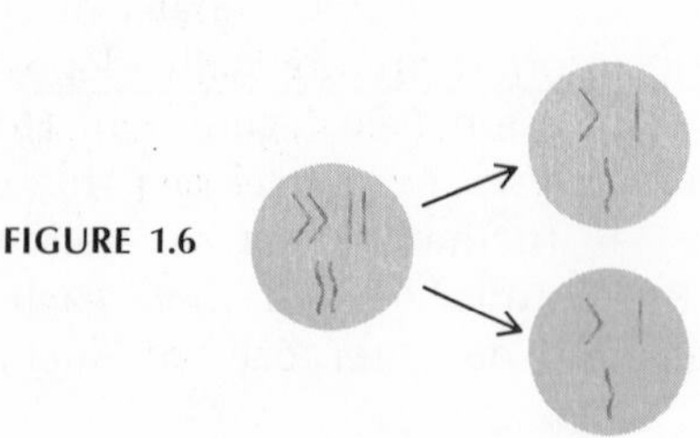

Meiosis (sex cell production). Half the genetic code from a mitotic daughter cell goes to each new sex cell. During conception a complete new genetic code (23 pairs of chromosomes) is produced by combining male and female sex cells. (This figure shows meiosis for one of the two daughter cells illustrated in Figure 1.5.)

interchange is restricted to linked sets, rather than single genes. Crossing implies the switching of parts of a chromosome from one pairing to another, as shown in Figure 1.7. The ends of a chromosome pair break from the remainder of the molecule and become reattached to the opposite member of the chromosomal pair. A crossover does not disrupt the genetic code, but it does change the composition of the

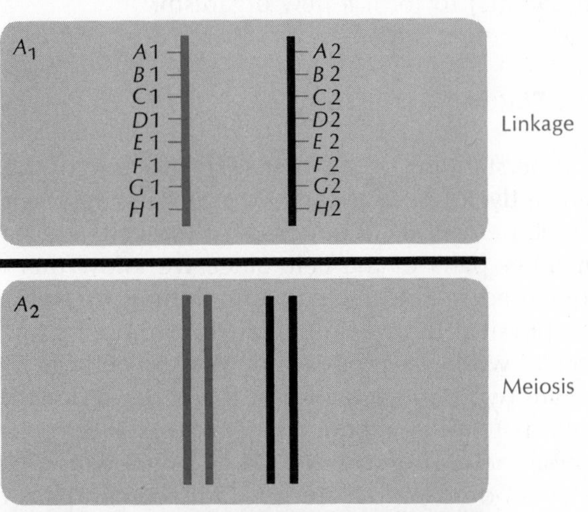

FIGURE 1.7

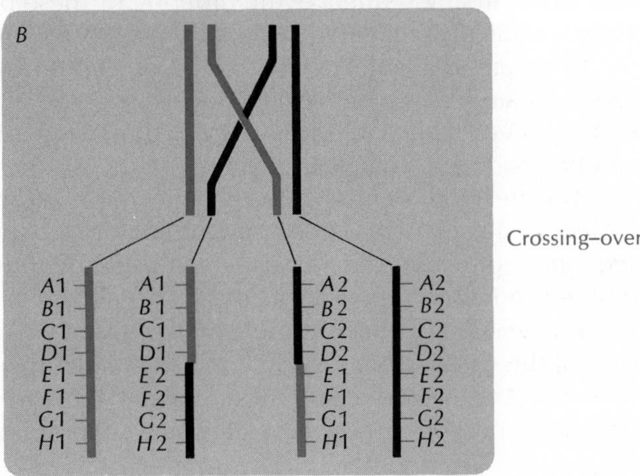

Linkage results because certain alleles of the chromosome are on the same member of the pair. Crossing-over results during meiosis when the top or bottom part of the member of the chromosomal pair becomes detached and is reattached to the other member of the pair. This process requires that both tops become separated and reattached to the opposite members.

particular chromosomal pair; traits are switched from one member to another. Another mechanism of change is mutation of chromosomes. Mutation may occur through the action of heat, radiation, or through other direct influences on the germ cell; almost all mutations are lethal. Most genetic variation can be accounted for by the random segregation of pairs of chromosomes and the combination of two germ cells (two parents) to form a new organism.

BIOCHEMICAL GENETICS

The Watson-Crick hypothesis assumes the DNA molecule is a double helix which controls its own reproduction and protein synthesis.

Our understanding of the molecular structure of the gene has increased significantly in recent years. Deoxyribonucleic acid (DNA) comprises about 40 percent of the nucleus of the cell, and it seems to be absent from other parts of the cell. Since we know that all genetic material is contained in the nucleus, this finding strongly suggests that DNA is the physical basis of inheritance. A model showing how hereditary processes work was proposed by Watson and Crick (1953). They believe there are two basic activities of the gene: self reproduction and determination of protein production. The Watson-Crick hypothesis postulates a double-helix structure for DNA, as shown in Figure 1.8. DNA is a long chain of organic materials. Only certain pairs can occur, but they may occur in any sequence; the ordering of these pairs constitutes the code in which the genetic information is stored. Since the ingredients for DNA are available in the cell, it is hypothesized that the helix separates and new chemical materials become attached to the free endings (see Figure 1.8). In this way two new identical DNA molecules can be produced from one original.

Biologists assume that genetic information is coded on the DNA molecule by sequences of chemicals.

The next problem is how genetic information is coded on the molecule. The genetic code must ultimately be specified in terms of *sequences* of chemicals. The code can use only four "letters" (the four different possible chemicals in the DNA molecule). It is assumed that the arrangement of these four chemicals, placed in any order along the sites of the chromosome, could contain 50 times more information than is in the Encyclopedia Brittanica. Several tentative codes have been proposed; none has received conclusive support.

Inheritance

Major-gene transmission occurs when one gene controls a phenotypic characteristic.

Basically, there may be two modes of inheritance—a simple one, where the trait is based on one or two genes (major-gene inheritance), and a second type where traits show continuous variations in amount (polygenetic inheritance). The process of major-gene transmission includes the following: (1) inherited characteristics are produced by

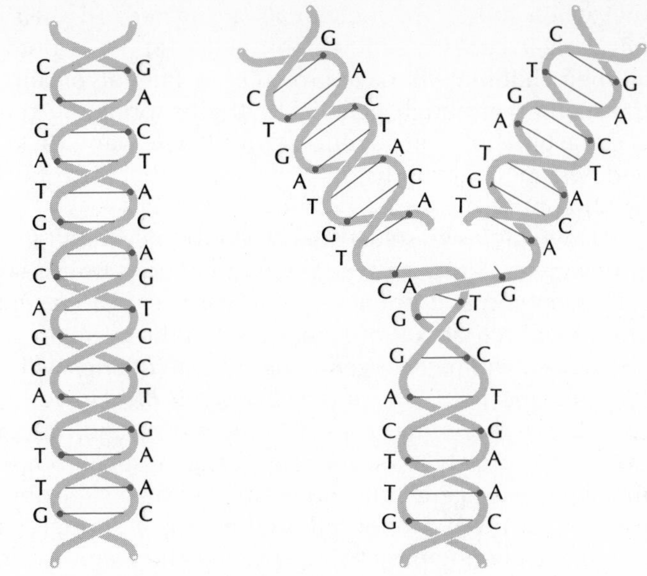

FIGURE 1.8

The Watson-Crick model of DNA. The helix on the left is how DNA appears during its normal state. The model on the right has become detached at the top and is in the process of reproducing itself. (Reproduced from Dobzhansky, 1962.)

genes and passed along unchanged from one generation to another; (2) genes are found on pairs of chromosomes in each individual; (3) genes in a chromosome pair differ in their effects; (4) one gene of a pair dominates the other; and finally, (5) during egg or sperm formation, members of each pair of chromosomes segregate independently, with one member of each chromosome pair coming from each parent. In the case of human beings, the original 23 pairs of chromosomes split; each sex cell contains 23 *single* chromosomes.

Dominant genetic characteristics occur in phenotypic traits. The only way to know whether a particular person is homozygous (identical genetic pairs) or heterozygous (different genetic pairs) is through controlled breeding.

Consider eye-color transmission. For simplicity we include only two colors—blue (*b*) and brown (*B*). Assume (*B*) is dominant; whenever it occurs the child will have brown eyes. Thus, the phenotypic characteristic of *bB* and *BB* is the same. If the mother and father are both blue-eyed (*bb*), all of the children will have blue eyes. Also, if both the father and mother have brown eyes and are homozygous (*BB,* the same gene in both parts of the chromosome), all the children will have brown eyes. However, there are two more complicated examples to outline. First, when one parent is a homozygous brown-eyed individual (*BB*) and the other is a homozygous blue-eyed individual (*bb*). This condition is shown in Matrix 1 of Figure 1.9. Notice that when these two individuals are mated, all their children receive *bB* as their genetic endowment. Since brown is dominant over blue, all their children will have brown eyes. Phenotypically they will be like their father, although genetically the offspring are different. This suggests a principle of genetic study. If we want to know the genetic endowment of any individual, we must either (1) know his past heredity or (2) control his future breeding.

Selective breeding uncovers homozygous recessive traits (if they exist).

How might we selectively breed to uncover an individual's genetic endowment? Suppose we take two children from Matrix 1, who have (*bB*) genotype and phenotypic brown eyes. The results of this mating are shown in Matrix 2 of Figure 1.9. On the average, one quarter of the individuals will receive genotype *bb,* one quarter will receive genotype *BB,* and one half will receive genotype *Bb.* However, phenotypically we will see three quarters with brown eyes and one quarter with blue eyes, since brown is a dominant characteristic. From this result we see that a recessive gene trait shows up phenotypically only in homozygous persons (*bb*). We cannot tell on the basis of a single mating whether a dominant phenotypic characteristic is the result of homozygous (*BB*) or heterozygous (*Bb*) gene combinations. Matrices 3 and 4 of Figure 1.9 show the results of second-generation (F_2) matings and allow us to differentiate the phenotypic characteristics into those that contain pure (*BB*) or mixed (*Bb*) genes. All of the offspring of the mating in Matrix 3 would show brown eyes, although their genetic endowments are different. Matrix 4 shows exactly the same situation as Matrix 2; we find three quarters with phenotypic brown and one quarter with phenotypic blue, which tells us again that the first generation was heterozygous. It takes detailed analysis over several generations to uncover the genotypic characteristics of individuals. Notice that we must control successive matings of the generations. The analysis becomes even more complex if we choose a trait that can be affected by environmental influences and if we allow these influences to interact with the genetic endowment.

Sex is controlled genetically by one chromosome (XY).

One of the clearest examples of genetic effects is sex determination. Of the 23 pairs of chromosomes, one pair controls the organism's sex. All ova from the female contain an *X* chromosome, while approximately half the sperm contain *X* chromosomes and the other half contain *Y* chromosomes. When a sperm with an *X* chromosome unites with an ovum, the result is a female (*XX*), but when a sperm with a *Y* chromosome unites with an ovum, the result is a male (*XY*). The *X* or *Y* chromosome of the sperm completely determines the sex of the offspring. Medical research has become interested in this fact, for if there were some way to separate *X* and *Y* sperm, it would be possible, through artificial insemination, to produce males or females on order. Since a *Y* sperm is more likely to penetrate the ovum than an *X* sperm,

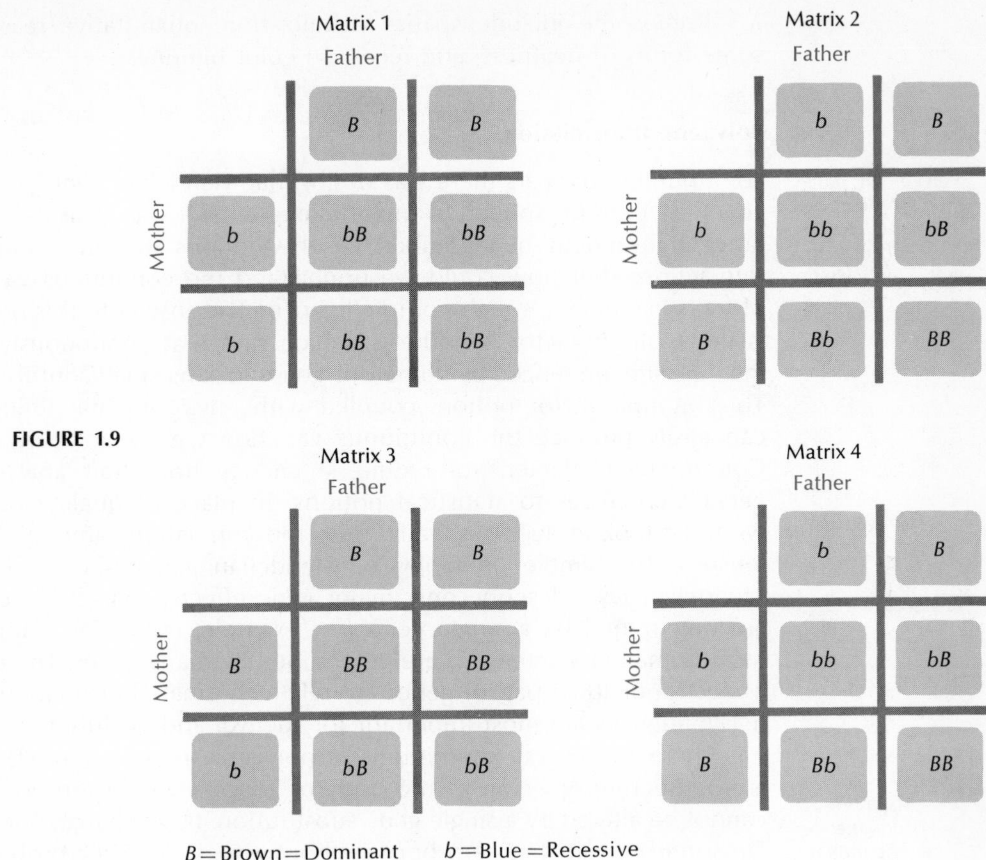

FIGURE 1.9

The possible combinations of brown- and blue-eyed parents. Note that one homozygous (*BB*) and one homozygous (*bb*) parent produce heterozygous (*bB*) brown-eyed children (Matrix 1), while heterozygous (*bB*) parents produce homozygous (*BB*), and (*bb*) and heterozygous (*bB*) children (Matrix 2). Matrix 3 shows the results of combining heterozygous parents; they produce homozygous (*BB*) and heterozygous (*Bb*) children, all brown-eyed. Matrix 4 shows the same result as Matrix 2, but the mother and father are reversed. The principle from this illustration is that only homozygous recessive traits show in the phenotype.

there are more males than females born—about 107 males for every 100 females. Because of their higher susceptibility to disease, males die younger and at a higher rate than females, so the abundance of males is gradually depleted: late in life, males are outnumbered. Few of the inherited traits in man are linked to the *Y* chromosome (probably because the *Y* chromosome has so few genes). Traits linked to the

X chromosome include spatial visualization, quantitative reasoning, some forms of deafness, and recessive color blindness.

Polygene transmission

Polygenetic transmission describes the combined effects of many genes on a single trait.

For a number of years there was doubt that Mendelian conceptions of genetics could be applied to quantitative traits. It was clear that qualitative traits could be described by the notions of genes and their interactions, but how could we understand the continuous variation of traits like height, weight, or intelligence? The answer to this problem is the multiple-factor hypothesis, which says that continuously varying traits are influenced by numerous genes making small contributions. This multiple-factor notion, coupled with environmental influences, can easily produce the continuous variation we see in many traits. Continuous characteristics require a change from trait analyses of genetic processes to statistical notions. In place of qualitative traits we must look at averages, variations, and correlations among characteristics. The simple principles of Mendelian genetics do not hold. Mendelian laws describe only major gene effects, characteristics that are determined by a single gene (for example, eye color). However, most human characteristics are determined by many genes. The effects of each individual pair of genes are relatively small, but their cumulative influences are most important for survival and evolution.

Polygene theory makes several assumptions: (1) dominance; (2) genetic interaction; (3) genetic environment interaction; and (4) genetic effects can be simulated by environmental effects.

There are several assumptions of polygene transmission. (1) There is no structure or organ of the body or process within the body that cannot be altered by a single gene substitution. If we change one gene, *Drosophila* (fruit flies) are born without wings. A major problem of modern genetics is to learn more about how structures change as a function of particular genes and combinations of genes. (2) There is no necessary one-to-one correspondence between the presence of a gene and the manifestation of its effect. This results from two things: genetic interaction and dominance, which we have already discussed. Genetic interaction appears when combinations of genes result in different phenotypic characteristics than one would expect of the separate genes. (3) Interaction with the environment can produce phenotypic variation. Recall that a Himalayan rabbit raised under cold conditions will have dark fur, while another raised under warm conditions will have white fur. (4) The effects of a gene can be produced (without the gene) through environmental interference at an appropriate time during the development of the organism. This is true even in the complete absence of the particular gene. For example, the eye color of fruit flies can be changed by proper environmental influences. (5) Different genes may have indistinguishable phenotypic effects. For example, there are two different genes that produce exactly the same syndrome of deafness, head movement, and circling behavior in mice. (6) Most genes have multiple effects on phenotypic characteristics. Nearly all the gene substitutions mentioned above are multiple in their effects, and many lower the individual's viability.

Mechanisms of variability

Three mechanisms which produce individual differences are conception, crossing-over, and mutation.

There are three common mechanisms for producing individual differences genetically: conception, crossing, and mutation. The most important mechanism is combining of genes from the male and female during conception. We noted before that the various combinations of 23 chromosomes are astronomical. This statistical mechanism accounts for a large proportion of individual differences. Crossing-over of chromosomal parts also results in different combinations of traits. Another relatively minor effect results from genetic mutation, which occurs through physical influences on the genetic material. Although mutations are almost always destructive, there is strong speculation that they may account for the formation of new species.

Differential rate of reproduction accounts for most genetic change.

Differential rates of reproduction account for most of the adaptive changes within species, and this modern conception of natural selection replaces the theory of survival of the fittest. Thus, differential reproduction increases the genetic frequency of groups with high reproductive rates.

BEHAVIOR GENETICS

Animals are used in genetics research because they are inexpensive, have short gestation and life cycles, and are easy to understand compared with human beings.

Much of the research in behavioral genetics has been conducted with animals, because they are cheaper, they may be inbred with little fuss, they have short gestation and life cycles, and their actions are easier to understand than more complex human behavior. This does not face the fundamental question: How applicable is research with animals to children and adults? The usual answer is that animal research gives us clues, so that we can use it as a guide in our search for human understanding. However, it is only suggestive.

Inbreeding (mating litter mates) and selective breeding (breeding high with high and low with low) are the main tools of behavioral genetic analysis.

There are two major methods of study in behavioral genetics: inbreeding and selective breeding. The logic of inbreeding studies is simple: By strict breeding within a group of animals over several generations genetic variation is assumed to approach zero. There is almost no likelihood that two different inbred strains will develop exactly the same genetic endowment. Therefore, we can tell a great deal about which traits are genetically influenced by subjecting different inbred strains to identical environmental conditions. Under the same environmental influences any variations which occur between the two species must be the result of genetic variations or interactions between the different genetic endowments and the environment. In addition to inbreeding, a number of studies have tried to selectively breed for particular characteristics by inbreeding animals that show a great deal of the trait and also inbreeding those that show almost none of the trait. If we can change the average score and lower the number of common scores between two groups by inbreeding, we have strong evidence that the trait is genetically influenced (see Figure 1.10).

Inbred strains differ in aggressiveness, activity, maternal behavior, and learning ability, among other traits.

Inbred strains of animals have been found to differ on a wide variety of traits, including aggressiveness, activity, sex drive, maternal behavior, and learning abilities. For example, Tryon (1940) bred "maze bright" and "maze dull" rats in an effort to determine the genetic base of animal intelligence. Later studies showed that the differences between groups were due to emotional differences, error tendencies, and brain biochemistry.

Human research in behavior genetics

Several stages of knowledge exist about genetics.

There are various stages of knowledge concerning hereditary mechanisms. At the most advanced level we know a trait is due to one gene located on a known region of one chromosome. Our knowledge of human genetics is not at this stage, although we are approaching that level for some sex-linked characteristics. At a lower stage of knowledge genes can be assigned to specific chromosomes, but not to definite locations. In human genetics this stage has been reached for the sex chromosomes. At a third stage of knowledge we can distinguish between the effects of a single gene and several genes. Finally, at the lowest stage of knowledge, we resort to the methods of statistical genetics to understand conditions controlled by many genes. Research with twins has proven to be valuable in helping to clarify these conditions.

Twins are used almost exclusively in human genetic studies.

Almost all genetic research with human beings has involved the use of twins. The logic to this is simple: Monozygotic (identical) twins have the same genetic makeup, while dizygotic (fraternal) twins are no more alike genetically than other siblings. Thus, any differences between identical twins must be due to environmental influences, while differences between fraternal twins must be due to both heredity and environment. If we assume that environmental influences are no more different in the case of identical twins than in the case of fraternal twins of the same sex, we can subtract the interpair difference between identical twins, that is, the differences between the characteristic of one identical twin and the other, from the interpair difference between fraternal twins. The difference between these interpair differences of

FIGURE 1.10

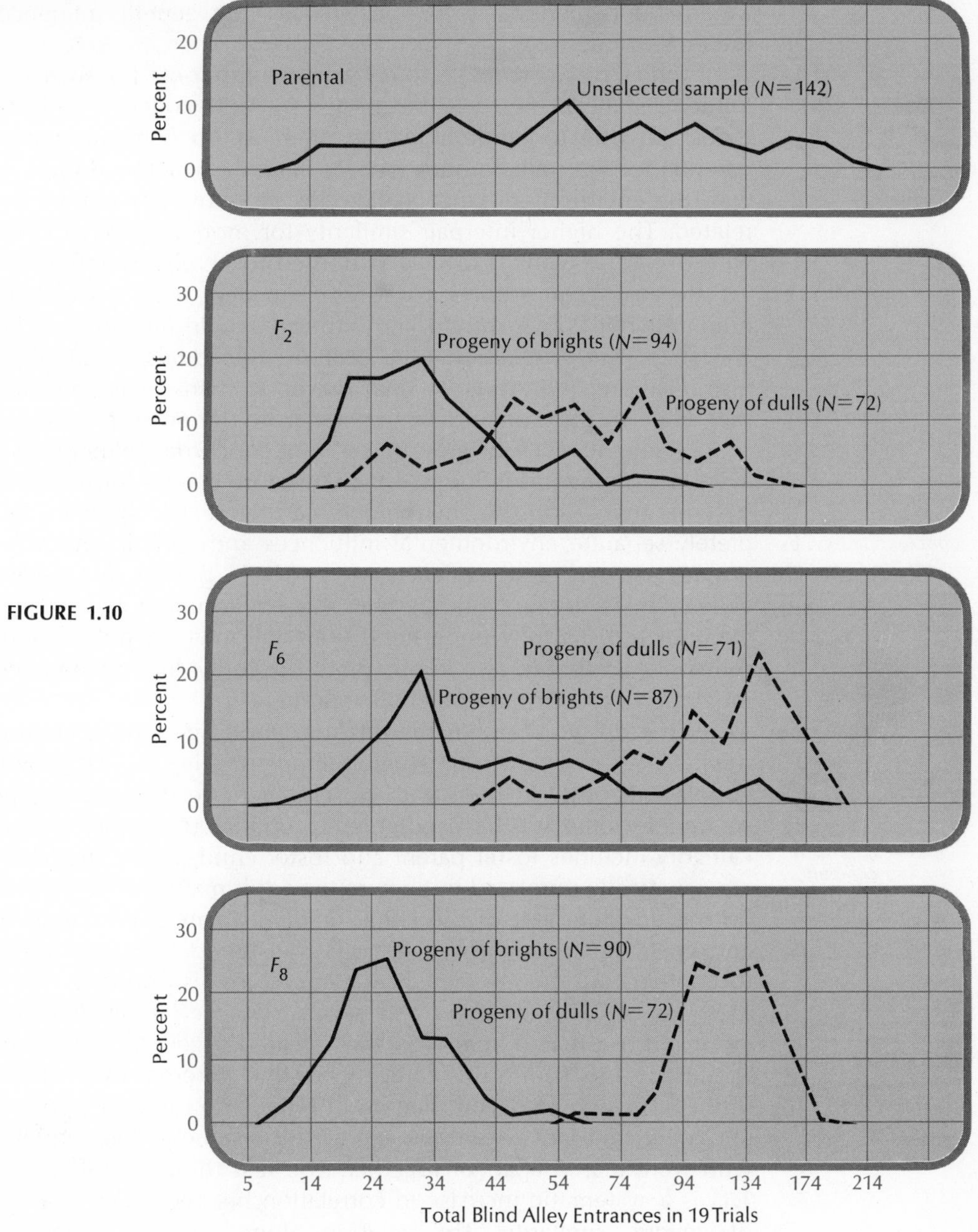

Error scores made by animals of successive generations. The vertical axis shows the percent of any one generation making the number of errors indicated on the horizontal axis. Note that the single distribution of scores forms two separate distributions over successive generations. (From Tryon, 1940.)

fraternal and identical twins must result from genetic influences and interaction effects.

Twin studies make four assumptions.

Studies of twins make four basic assumptions: (1) environmental influences are of the same magnitude for both fraternal and identical twins; (2) due to random mating, there is no correlation (between parents) for the traits in question; (3) hereditary factors do not interact with the environment; and (4) heredity and environment are not correlated. The higher interpair similarity for monozygotic as contrasted with dizygotic twins is usually attributed to hereditary influence.

Concordance is higher for identical than fraternal twins.

Because twin studies constitute a widely used research tool in human genetics, we should know their possible limitations. The concordance (the correlation of a trait in individuals) is usually much higher among monozygotic than dizygotic twins; it is generally held that some of this concordance comes from the environment.

Only random assignment of twins to various environments will unconfound genes and environment.

As genetic relations grow closer, trait concordance increases. However, environmental influences may be more similar for identical than fraternal twins, and the environment can interact with genes. To completely separate environmental influences and genetic endowment, it is necessary (1) that subjects are randomly placed into cells of an experimental design and (2) that the environment is systematically manipulated. To fully understand the relations of genotype and environment, we should also know about the individual's genetic endowment prior to our experimental treatment.

The relation between genetic overlap and IQ correlations strongly suggests genetic effects on intelligence.

What do we know of the relation among genotypic endowment, intelligence, and environmental influences? Figure 1.11 shows how correlations of IQ increase with closer genetic relations among people. At one extreme we have completely unrelated people. The second category includes foster parent and foster child, where the individuals are genetically unrelated but where the adult may have some influence on the development of the child. Our third category contains parent and child; here genetic influence is transferred from one generation to another, but environmental influences are also present. The fourth category contains brothers and sisters. This set is divided into two groups, those reared apart and those reared together. Twins comprise the final class. Within this category we find fraternal twins (twins that result from two eggs and may be of either the same or opposite sex) and identical twins (from one egg with the same genetic endowment) who were reared apart or together. The first thing to notice in Figure 1.11 is a systematic increase in correlation between IQ's as a function of genetic similarity. This relation alone suggests a very strong genotypic influence on intelligence. However, before we conclude that all intelligence is genetically determined, remember that the experiences to which each individual was exposed also increase in similarity with the genetic relation. In those few cases where this is not true, that is, for siblings reared apart versus siblings reared together, we find that siblings reared apart have a lower mean correlation than siblings reared together. This suggests that both genetic endowment and environmental factors influence intelligence. Furthermore, in the case of fraternal twins, those of opposite sex have a lower mean correlation than those of the same sex, again suggesting that differential treatment of the sexes has an influence on IQ. (However, remember that sex is genetically determined.) Finally, in the case of identical twins, those reared apart showed a lower mean correlation than those reared together (environmental influences can differentiate identical genetic endowments). Thus, intellectual level is not unalterably fixed by genetic constitution; rather, its expression in the phenotype results from the fulfillment of patterns laid down by the genotype under given environmental conditions.

FIGURE 1.11

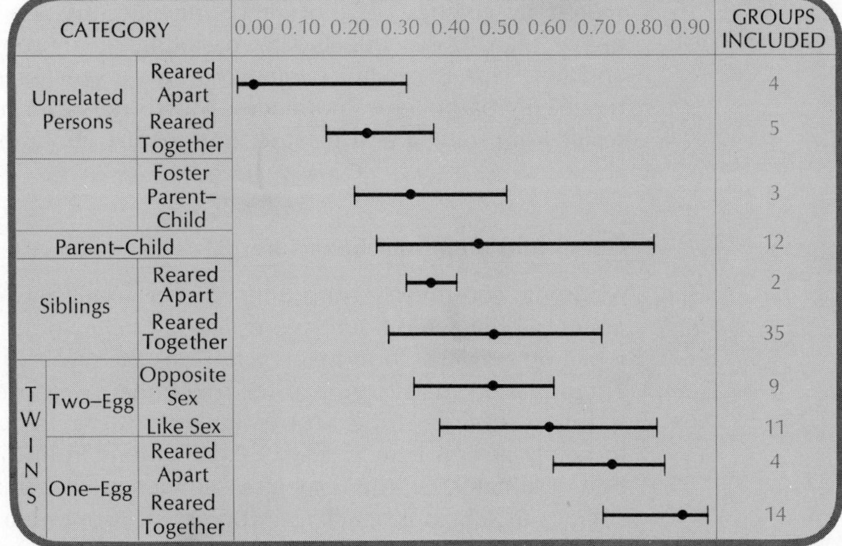

Correlation coefficients for "intelligence" test scores from 52 studies. Some studies reported data for more than one relationship category; some included more than one sample per category, giving a total of 99 groups. Over two thirds of the correlation coefficients were derived from I.Q.'s, the remainder from special tests (for example, primary mental abilities). Midparent-child correlation was used when available, otherwise mother-child correlation. Medians are shown by dots intersecting the horizontal lines (which represent the ranges). (From Erlenmeyer-Kimling & Jarvik, 1963.)

Individual differences result from genetic variation, environmental variation, and the interaction of these factors.

In summary, individual differences result from the nonuniform action of environmental stimuli upon nonuniform organisms. Characteristics of the organism vary as a joint function of environmental encounters and genes. Nonidentical twins given the same environmental influences will be different because of their genotypic endowment. The same genotypic endowment in diverse environments will result in different phenotypes because of environmental influences.

The conspicuous excess of very low intelligence suggests two factors, genetic variation and environmental trauma, are at work.

Statisticians have known for a long time that the distribution of measured intelligence fits a normal curve, except at the extreme lower end. There is a conspicuous excess of very low IQ individuals when compared with the expected theoretical value [around 20 times as great (Figure 1.12)]. Karl Pearson (1896), the famous British statistician of the last century, suggested that the excess of severe retardation represents pathogenic influences (disease, birth trauma) which have lowered the IQ of individuals who would, without these influences, have developed higher IQ's. Pearson also pointed out that the IQ's scored by siblings of idiots and imbeciles (IQ below 40) are much higher than those collected from siblings of morons (IQ between 50 and 60). This is exactly what we would expect if severe retardation represents pathogenic influences. Most idiots and imbeciles probably result from trauma and disease, not genetic limitation.

Genes and abnormal behavior

The relation of genetics to abnormal behavior is cloudy; it is clear that abnormality runs in families.

A strong controversy surrounds the relation between genetics and abnormal behavior. Some see psychotic behavior as primarily genetic, while others view abnormal reactions as the result of early experiences. There is a decided tendency for functional psychoses (schizophrenia) to run in families. Studies consistently show that frequency of psychosis in family groups is in excess of expectations from the general population. Estimates of the expected incidence of schizophrenia among siblings of schizophrenics is 5–10 percent if both parents are free from schizophrenia, 8–18 percent if one parent is schizophrenic, and 45–68 percent if both parents are schizophrenic. These numbers are far in excess of the general population, where the incidence of psychosis is less than 1 percent. Expectancies based on other categories of relations (half-siblings, grandchildren, nephews, nieces, and first cousins) are all above the general population figure, and they change in proportion to the degree of genetic relation. The observed high frequencies of schizophrenia in family groups, in the absence of any discernible common factor in the environment, strongly suggest that genetic factors are significant.

FIGURE 1.12

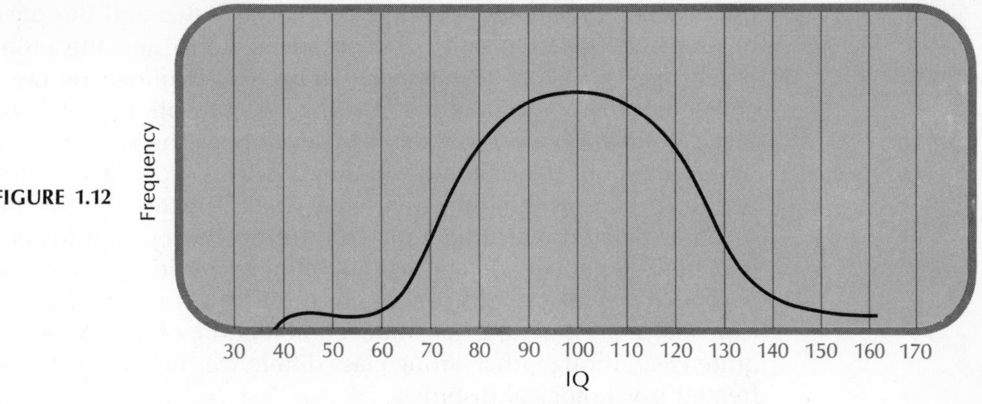

Approximate normal bell-shaped distribution showing the excessive number of cases at the lower end of the IQ distribution. Pearson suggested that these defective cases result from natural genetic causes and from destructive effects of birth and environmental influences during the early years.

Schizophrenia occurs in about 70 percent of identical twins and in only 10 percent of fraternal twins.

Kallman's (1953) extensive study of nearly a thousand pairs of twins and several thousand of their close relatives showed that both members were schizophrenic in approximately 69 percent of identical twins, while the corresponding frequency for fraternal twins (from two different eggs) was 10 percent. Slater (1953), in a smaller study, reported similar results—schizophrenia occurred in both members for 70 percent of his pairs of monozygotic twins as compared to 14 percent for dizygotic twins. Whatever the precise estimates may be, there is a strikingly higher risk of schizophrenia among monozygotic than among dizygotic twins when one member of each pair is psychotic.

Heredity is important in positive social development (smiling).

Heredity also plays a significant role in the development of positive and negative social responses. Identical twins show greater concordance than fraternal twins in both fear and smiling during their first year of life; heredity is a reasonable explanation. Smiling and fear of strangers are important prototypes of much later social behavior. A smile is the first expression of pleasure with another person. Fear of strangers is the first expression of anxiety and withdrawal from others. Smiling binds an infant to his parent, and later other human beings. Children of schizophrenic mothers do not show this positive hereditary reaction.

Mental illness is related to social class. Psychoses afflict the lower classes, while middle and upper classes are plagued by neuroses.

Behavioral differences among social classes may have a partially genetic origin. Differences among social strata of the United States with respect to mental illness are quite large. In the lowest class we find 800 percent greater prevalence of *psychosis* than in the upper class (Hollingshead & Redlich, 1958). These studies also show that *neuroses* were 360 percent more frequent in the upper strata than in the lowest. A relation exists between social status and the prevalence of mental retardation and between social status and the problem of psychosis. The hierarchy of social strata is determined by the reward characteristics of occupations. Matings occur within social strata, so that a correlation among abilities is developed. The selective influence of a common denominator—money—collects comparable levels of various abilities within the same social strata. The tendency for neuroses to be associated with upper classes and psychoses with lower classes may reflect genetic determination, differences in the availability of psychiatric services, differences in the stress to which people are exposed, ego structure, or some combination of these factors. It is quite clear, though, that strong class differences do exist with regard to treated psychological disorders.

SUMMARY

1 This chapter opened with four conceptions of human development. The ancient doctrine of preformationism was shown to be false, and the attribution of development either to heredity (predeterminism) or learning (environmentalism) alone is too narrow.

2 A middle ground of interaction between genetic endowment and environmental influences more fully describes the facts.

3 Three models of interaction were outlined. The additive model implies too simple a picture of the developing organism, and the notion of limits does not take into consideration the advantageous effects of optimal matching of the environment with the particular capabilities of an individual. A two-state model, which assumes an additive effect when there is a mismatch between the environment and genetics and a multiplicative effect when there is a match between characteristics of the world and the person, describes the processes.

4 A discussion of the mechanisms of cell production pointed out the differences between mitotic production of cells for growth and replacement and the production of germ cells through meiosis. The primary difference was the manner in which the chromosomes segregate—in mitosis there is a complete splitting of all 46 chromosomes with a complete complement of 23 pairs going to each new daughter cell; in meiosis the chromosomes do not duplicate, and only 23 single chromosomes are present in each daughter cell.

5 A distinction was made between major gene determination, which follows the classic rules of Mendelian genetics, and polygene determination, which must be studied with statistical techniques.

6 Examples of the problems and advantages of twin studies were presented, showing that the concordance of traits among individuals is a direct function of their genetic relation.

7 Several suggestive studies of genetic influences upon abnormal behavior were presented.

8 The general principle of this chapter should be the understanding that a significant amount of interaction can be expected among genes and environmental influences. Simple solutions to the complex problems of genetic and environmental influences are doomed to failure.

FURTHER READINGS

Fuller, J. L., & Thompson, W. R. *Behavior genetics.* New York: Wiley, 1960.

Sinnott, E. W., Dunn, L. C., & Dobzhansky, T. *Principles of genetics* (5th ed.). New York: McGraw-Hill, 1958.

REFERENCES

Darwin, C. *Origin of the species.* London: Murray, 1859.

Dobzhansky, T. *Mankind evolving.* New Haven: Yale University Press, 1962.

Erlenmeyer-Kimling, L., & Jarvik, L. F. Genetics and intelligence: A review. *Science,* 1963, **142,** 1477–1479.

Gesell, A., & Thompson, H. Twins T and C from infancy to adolescence: A biogenetic study of individual differences by the method of co-twin control. *Genetic Psychology Monograph,* 1941, **24,** 3–121.

Hall, G. S. The contents of children's minds. *Princeton Review,* 1883, 249–272.

Hebb, D. O. The innate organization of visual activity: I. Perception of figures by rats reared in total darkness. *Journal of Genetic Psychology,* 1937, **51,** 101–126.

Hollingshead, A., & Redlich, F. *Social class and mental illness: A community study.* New York: Wiley, 1958.

Kallman, F. J. *Heredity in health and mental disorder.* New York: W. W. Norton & Company, 1953.

Lamarck, J. B. *Zoological philosophy: An exposition with regard to the natural history of animals.* Translated by H. Elliot. London: Macmillan, 1914.

Leeuwenhoek, A. van. 1677. Observations concerning little animals, etc. *Philosophical Transactions,* London, Vol. II. P. 82.

Mendel, G. 1867. Letter to Carl Nageli. In M. Gabriel & S. Fogel (Eds.), *Great experiments in biology.* Englewood Cliffs, N.J.: Prentice-Hall, 1955.

Needham, J. *A history of embryology.* New York: Abelard-Schuman, 1959.

Pearson, K. Mathematical contributions to the theory of evolution, regression, heredity and panmixia. *Philosophical Transactions,* 1896, **187A,** 253–318.

Riesen, A. H. The development of visual perception in man and chimpanzee. *Science,* 1947, **106,** 107–108.

Slater, E. *Psychotic and neurotic illness in twins.* London: Her Majesty's Stationery Office, 1953.

Terman, L. *The measurement of intelligence.* Boston: Houghton Mifflin, 1916.

Tryon, R. C. Genetic differences in maze-learning abilities in rats. *39th yearbook, Part I. National Society for the Study of Education.* Chicago: University of Chicago Press, 1940. Pp. 111–119.

Watson, J. B. Psychology as the behaviorist views it. *Psychological Review,* 1913, **20,** 158–177.

Watson, J. D., & Crick, F. H. C. A structure for deoxyribose nucleic acids. *Nature,* 1953, **171,** 737–738.

Weismann, A. *Essays upon heredity and kindred biological problems.* Vol. I. F. B. Poulton, S. Schönland, & A. E. Shipley (Eds.). Oxford: Clarendon Press, 1889.

Wolff, K. F. 1759. *Theoria Generationis.* From J. Needham, *A history of embryology.* New York: Abelard-Schuman, 1959.

2 HUMAN GROWTH

If I do grow great, I'll grow less;
for I'll purge, and leave sack,
and live cleanly as a nobleman should do.
I HENRY IV

A child's personal development is affected by his body. If he is strong, healthy, and active, he will be competent in physical activities and socially attractive to others. Favorable social reactions affect how the child views himself; his personal growth is positively influenced by his physical being. If, however, the child sees his body as weak, sickly, and undesirable, his social and personal adjustment will suffer compared to his more physically attractive peers.

Physical characteristics are important social influences. When we attempt to describe another person we begin with his sex, age, height, weight, body build, coloring, and general attractiveness. Physical characteristics affect us when we see another person, and they color our self-concept. To understand the relations between physical and personal development we must know something of the principles that govern body growth, the sequencing of response patterns, the relations among motor abilities, and the specific effects of physical factors on personality development.

THE ESTABLISHMENT OF DEVELOPMENTAL NORMS

Norms are useful for locating extreme cases of development and charting the course of normal physical growth.

As a first step in the study of human growth, investigators collected descriptions of normal development. These norms are not intended to explain the growth of behavior; they are useful in locating extremes and charting the progress of the normal and exceptional child. The normal child falls near the middle (average) of a distribution of characteristics obtained from a representative sample of children. The term "normal" does not imply ideal. For example, the average boy reaches sexual maturity at around 14 years of age, but several studies indicate that early-maturing boys have social and psychological advantages over their later-maturing peers (Mussen & Jones, 1957).

Gesell produced some of the first developmental norms for children.

Developmental norms happened to be established by investigators convinced that most behavior results from predetermined genetic mechanisms. They felt the best way to study development was to outline maturational sequences. Gesell (1954) established norms for the development of early motor and sensory-motor behavior. He photographed infants under standard conditions and outlined the "typical behaviors" characteristic of children at various ages. These developmental norms were an attempt to chart the course of human growth by significant landmarks which would signal normal, exceptional, or retarded development in the individual child.

Predeterminism implies that genetics rules; an environmental position suggests that stimulation can change the child. Modern notions of interaction consider both factors.

A predeterminist view of development stresses the maturational (genetic) "readiness" of children, while an environmental view of human growth is concerned with the conditions necessary to produce "readiness" in children not yet performing a particular response. Growth norms give little indication of what to do with children outside the "normal" range. There is no problem with the child who is maturing rapidly and who seems brighter than average, but what of the slow child? Do we just shake our heads and say, "That is the way maturation determined his growth"? Many workers say no; the child can be helped once we understand the mechanisms that control growth (for example, nutrition, hormones). Strict predeterminism implies fatalism; it allows little room for modification or improvement (except through eugenics). Norms are helpful in determining the course of development, but we must look beyond norms to the mechanisms involved if we want to influence growth processes.

Some principles of growth and motor development

Infants grow from their heads toward their lower extremities, and motor control proceeds from the large muscles toward smaller peripheral ones.

Several principles emerge from research on physical growth. First is the cephalo-caudal progression of behavior—growth and motor development proceed from the head toward the lower extremities. The infant's head most closely approximates its adult size; his legs least approximate their final size. The first motor control occurs in the muscles that move the head; later, shoulder, arm, and abdominal muscles and finally leg muscles are controlled. Figure 2.1 shows the relative proportions of the child from 15 months to maturity. A second principle of motor development is the proximo-distal growth of behavior; motor development proceeds from the central axis of the body outward toward the periphery. The baby's early responses are gross bodily movements from the shoulder; his arm and hand cannot function separately. Only near the end of the first year can the infant make independent finger movements or oppose his thumb and finger. Also, development proceeds from general to more specific response patterns, and from gross to refined control.

The newborn possesses complex reflexive patterns; the young infant modifies these patterns to meet events.

Table 2.1 lists some early behaviors available to the newborn and young infant. The newborn shows only reflexive activities, but these are often highly integrated response patterns. The infant shows increased chaining or serial learning of motor responses as he develops. He becomes more efficient as he practices various motor activities. Inappropriate sequences drop out, and those that remain are smoother and more effective in accomplishing his purpose. The 18-month-old walks for practice, the two-year-old walks toward a goal.

TABLE 2.1 **Responses Available to the Newborn and Young Infant**

Eye Responses

(1) *Opening and closing of eyelids*—spontaneously and in response to a variety of external stimuli. The closing of the eyes is usually a bilateral response, but more pronounced on the stimulated side.

(2) *Pupillary response* (widening or narrowing of the pupils in response to light)—narrowing upon going to sleep and widening upon awaking. The pupillary response of the second eye is coordinated with the reactions of the stimulated eye.

(3) *Pursuit* (following a visual stimulus) and *saccadic* (quick, jerky fixations as occur in adult reading) movements occur in the very young infant.

(4) *Nystagmus* (rapid, restricted-in-scope eye-movement oscillations) may appear spontaneously or be evoked by thermal stimulation or rotation in the neonate.

(5) *Coordinate, compensatory eye movements* occur spontaneously; when the newborn's head is moved quickly in one direction, eye movements in the opposite direction are elicited.

(6) *Coordination of eyes*—eyes often move together, but not in well-coordinated movements.

(7) *Convergence* of two eyes occurs in some infants; some indication of *accommodation* varying with convergence of the eyes. The newborn does not accommodate or converge his eyes.

(8) *Eye position in sleep* is most frequently the upward and divergent position found in adults.

(9) *Tear secretion* has been observed during crying and upon irritation of the nasal membranes; tear secretion is unusual in the newborn.

Facial and Mouth Responses

(1) *Opening and closing mouth*—closed during sleep, opened after quinine application and as a part of yawning and coughing.

(2) *Lip movements*—licking, compressing lips, pursing lips in response to tactual stimulation.

(3) *Sucking* occurs spontaneously (possibly caused by stomach contractions) or in response to tactual and taste stimuli.

(4) *Smiling* occurs spontaneously after feeding or in response to tickling under chin.

(5) *Pushing objects from mouth*—strong solutions of salt and quinine are rejected.

(6) *Yawning* has been observed some five minutes after birth; it is a common response.

(7) *Grimaces* (including twisting the mouth, wrinkling the forehead) have been observed as spontaneous behavior and in response to noxious stimuli.

TABLE 2.1 Responses Available to the Newborn and Young Infant *(Continued)*

Oral Responses

(1) *Crying,* usually accompanied by activity of the arms and legs, seen spontaneously and in response to stomach contractions, cold, pain, bright lights, loud noises, holding the nose, and hampering the neonate's movements. These stimuli do not invariably evoke crying.

(2) *Swallowing* occurs in all normal newborn infants. *Gagging* may be elicited by noxious smells or tastes and by touching the back of the tongue or the tonsils. *Vomiting* has been observed.

(3) *Coughing* occurs within the first hour of life. *Sneezing* may occur spontaneously or in response to noxious olfactory stimuli.

(4) *Cooing* and *holding the breath* have been reported.

Head Movements

(1) *Upward and downward movements*—upward head movements can be evoked by placing the newborn on its stomach, holding its nose, or flashing a bright light before its eyes. Downward or ventral movements occur less frequently than upward movements.

(2) *Turning face to side* appears in response to tactual stimuli (such as nose cleaning), a touch on cheek, a dim light, the source of sound (in a few infants). Turning the face from side to side occurs during hunger or crying periods or when the infant is placed on his stomach.

(3) *Head shudder* in response to "bitter" stimuli.

(4) *Balancing head* in response to changes of bodily position (even when subjects are blindfolded); reported as early as two days of age.

Head and Arm Responses

(1) *Closing hand*—in response to tactual stimulation of fingers and palm. Many neonates are able to support their own weight momentarily by reflex grasping (discussed in some detail later in this chapter).

(2) *Arm flexion* can be evoked by a prick with a pointed instrument or by a sudden slight "tap" against the hand.

(3) *Rubbing face*—in response to noxious stimuli on nasal membranes—also appears spontaneously.

(4) *Startle response of arms*—in response to almost any type of intense, sudden stimulation. Hands are thrown outward with an associated tremor of the arms.

Trunk Reactions

(1) *Arching the back* frequently follows pinching the nose.

(2) *Twisting* of the trunk accompanies squirming. When the head is rotated, the shoulders and pelvis twist in the same direction.

(3) *Abdominal reflex*—in response to a needle as a stimulus.

Reproductive Organ Response

(1) *Cremasteric reflex* (raising of the testes) occurs in response to irritation of the inner thigh.

(2) *Penis erection*—noted by several investigators shortly after birth.

Foot and Leg Responses

(1) *Knee jerk and Achilles tendon reflex* present in most newborn infants.

TABLE 2.1 Responses Available to the Newborn and Young Infant *(Continued)*

(2) *Flexion of the leg*—elicited by stimulating the foot or leg tactually or with a noxious stimulus.

(3) *Extension of the leg* in response to a gentle push. This extension thrust is strong enough to support some infants' weight on the first day. Extension of the leg accompanied by dorsal flexion of the foot, the reverse of usual adult coordination.

(4) *Protective reflex*—when one stimulates one foot or leg the free foot almost invariably comes up and pushes against the source of stimulation.

(5) *Kicking* consists of pedaling and simultaneous extension or flexion of both legs; usually occurs during crying.

(6) *Stepping movements* occur when the newborn is held upright with the feet touching some surface.

Coordinate Responses of Many Body Parts

(1) *Resting and sleeping position*—the legs are flexed, the fists closed, the upper arms are out straight from the shoulders with the forearms flexed at right angles so they lie parallel to the head. The fists may lie below the chin (as in foetal life).

(2) *Backbone reflex* consists of the concave bending of a side that is stroked or tickled; the leg of the concave side is extended while the leg of the convex side is flexed. This same response occurs when the newborn is held in the air by a hand under one side.

(3) *Lifting the head and rear quarters* simultaneously appears in older infants; tendency toward such behavior in the newborn.

(4) *"Fencing position"* is observed when the newborn's head is rotated; the arm toward which the face is rotated extends, the other flexes; the legs do likewise.

(5) *"Springing position"*—when the infant is held upright and inclined forward, the arms extend forward and the legs are brought up.

(6) *Startle response,* often called the Moro reflex or "fear reaction," consists of throwing the arms apart, spreading the fingers, extending the legs, and throwing back the head; may be followed by crying, depending on the intensity and duration of the stimulus. This response may be evoked by loud noises, falling, hot or cold stimuli, and other sudden and intense types of stimulation; has also been observed in the absence of any type of external stimulation, being similar in these cases to the startle pattern demonstrated by adults in dropping off to sleep.

(7) *Creeping* movements have been observed when the newborn is placed in a prone position. The legs and arms are drawn under the body and the head is lifted; each pair of extremities alternates in movement.

(8) *Bodily jerk* appears in response to loud noises; the arms and legs flex strongly and jerk upward.

From this summary it can be seen that the newborn's repertoire of motor responses is considerable and that the behavior patterns demonstrated are sometimes quite complex. The naïve observer does a grave injustice to the newborn by reporting its motor responses as limited to crying, sucking, and waving of the arms and legs. Some of the motor responses summarized above have been extensively studied or have an interesting history of theoretical conjecture; a more detailed discussion of these behavior patterns is presented in the following sections. See Graham, Materazzo, and Caldwell (1956) for a battery of test procedures especially designed to differentiate normal and traumatized infants. These procedures include tests and ratings of vision, muscular tension, general irritability, pain thresholds, and over-all maturation.

SOURCE: Adapted from a classification by Dennis (1934), based on 80 scientific reports.

FIGURE 2.1

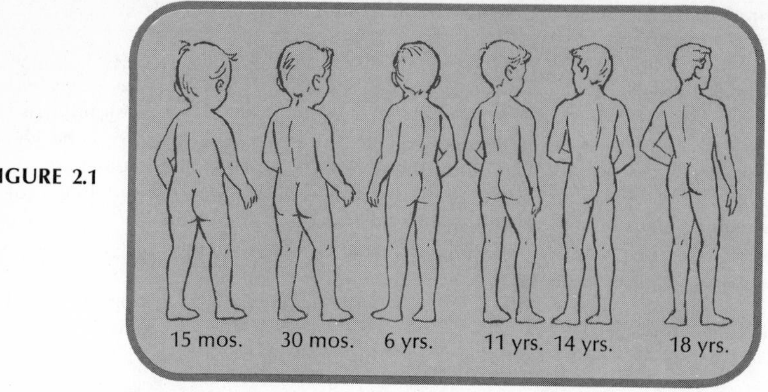

Changes in body proportions with growth, from 15 months to 18 years. The drawings are of the same boy at six ages, all adjusted to the same height. (From Bayley, 1956.)

FIGURE 2.2

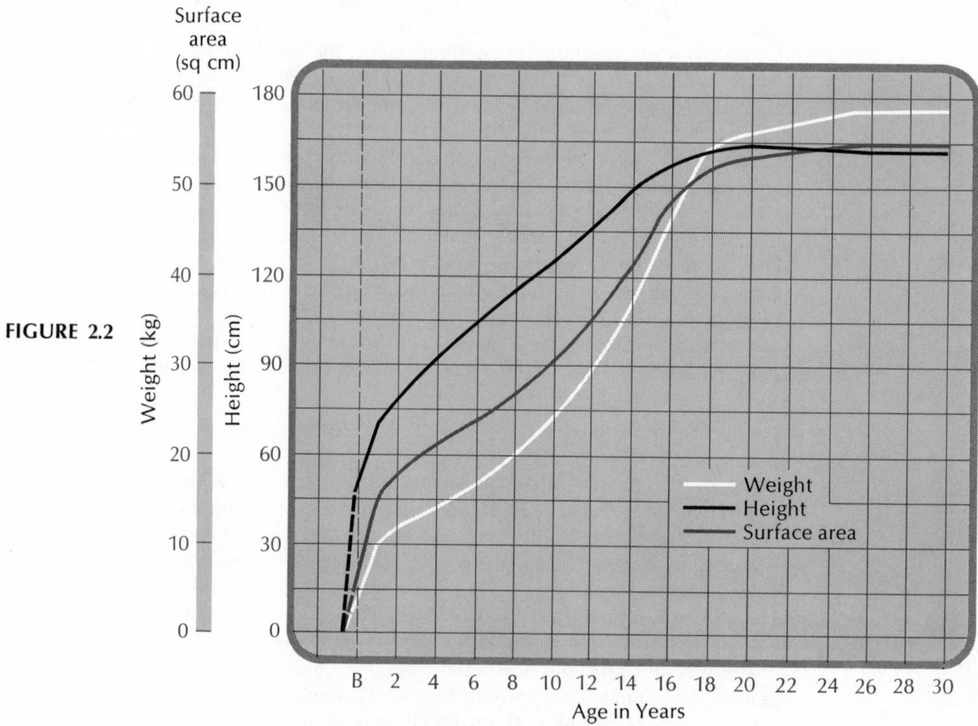

Growth curves for height, surface area, and weight drawn according to Quetelet's figures. (From Boyd, 1935.)

Physical growth

Boys are heavier than girls; first-born babies are lighter.

There are systematic differences in birth weight which favor males; they are about 4 percent heavier and 2 percent longer than their female peers. In addition, first-born infants are smaller than later siblings, although these differences fade with age.

Three commonly used measures of physical growth (weight, body area, and height) are highly correlated.

Three measures of growth are commonly taken: weight (a three-dimensional measure), body area (a two-dimensional measure), and length (a one-dimensional measure). All three scores show similar growth trends (see Figure 2.2). There are no seasonal variations in growth rate of length; however, several investigators have found that preschool children are more likely to gain weight during the fall and summer months and are less likely to gain weight during the spring and winter months. These seasonal variations in weight are probably related to illnesses.

The ratio of lower-limb length to total body length is a good measure of maturity; longer legs indicate greater maturity.

The ratio of lower-limb length to total length is a good indicator of physical maturity; it shows that girls are more mature than boys (girls' lower limbs are relatively longer in relation to their total length than are boys') even by eight weeks of age. Length is a good measure of general growth, while weight is a more sensitive measure of nutritional adequacy. During childhood, weight increases faster than height.

Different systems of the body show varying patterns of growth.

Various patterns of physical growth are shown in Figure 2.3. One is called the neural curve; it indicates growth trends for the brain, spinal cord, and eye. Rapid growth of the nervous system occurs during infancy, while little change occurs in childhood or maturity. A second pattern of growth characterizes sexual characteristics during infancy and childhood; there is a striking series of changes at puberty. Another pattern of growth describes the body (length of arms, size of chest, height, and weight). Somatic growth is rapid at first, then declines during infancy; a second rapid-growth period occurs during puberty.

THE DEVELOPMENT OF MOTOR ABILITIES

Three stages exist in the infant's motor development: (1) lifting the chin changes his perceptual world, (2) sitting up changes his perspective, and (3) walking changes his world.

Various stages of development occur as the child relates to his environment. These stages coincide with the infant's skill in climbing and exercising; physical growth makes him more and more independent of gravity. At first the infant can move only his arms and legs against gravity; his neck and trunk are bound by it. During the first month some control over gravity occurs when he begins to lift his chin. The next step comes at two months; the baby can push his chest off the floor with his back and stomach muscles and the help of his arms. The infant's perceptual field becomes much more varied once he can lift his head. However, in those cases where the infant is carried on the

FIGURE 2.3

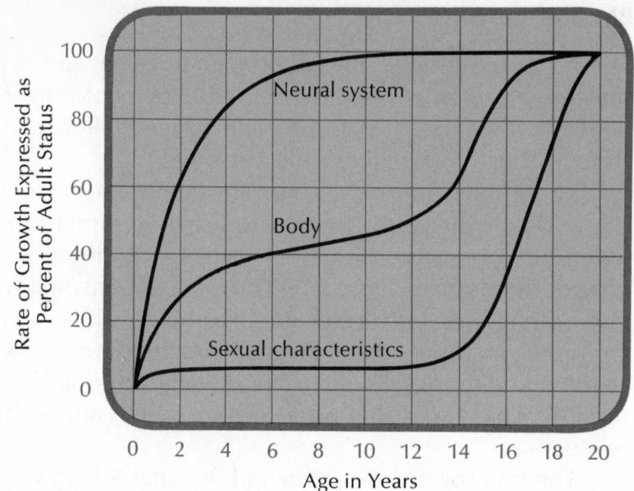

Relative patterns of physical growth in the human body during postnatal life. The upper curve demonstrates growth in the neural system; the middle curve illustrates growth of the body; the lower curve shows the development of sexual characteristics. (After Scammon in Jackson, 1928.)

mother's back—his perceptual world is already complex. Next, the infant learns to turn from his back to his stomach and over again. At about seven months he can maintain a sitting position, which gives him another perspective. He is curious, but cannot reach things. Creeping and crawling follow sitting (at about 10 months). At one year the infant can pull himself into a standing position; almost immediately he starts moving around the crib holding onto its edge. He has again enlarged his perceptual field. In another three months he walks. Table 2.2 and Figure 2.4 show these sequences of motor activities.

Norms are useful, but wide individual differences exist among normal children.

Table 2.2 is useful for parents and others who want to know whether a child's motor development is coming along normally. It must be understood, however, that there are wide individual differences in the age at which particular behaviors appear; some children "walk alone" before the end of the first year, while others may not start to walk until after 18 months. Also, the average performance among groups of children varies from one study to another due to sampling fluctuations. For these reasons, parents should not be alarmed if their child is a few months behind the norms in his motor development. Only wide deviation from the average should cause concern.

TABLE 2.2 The California Infant Scale of Motor Development

Test Items	*Age (months)*
Head erect—vertical	1.9
Head erect and steady	2.9
Turns from side to back	3.4
Sits with support	3.5
Holds head steady	3.6
Beginning thumb opposition	4.1
Sits with slight support	4.6
Turns from back to side	5.0
Partial thumb opposition	5.1
Sits alone momentarily	5.7
Pulls to sitting position	6.2
Rolls from back to stomach	7.0
Complete thumb opposition	7.6
Partial finger prehension	7.8
Sits alone with good coordination	8.5
Fine prehension with pellet	9.3
Raises self to sitting position	9.4
Pulls to standing position	10.5
Stands up	10.6
Walks with help	11.6
Sits down	12.5
Stands alone	12.5
Walks alone	13.0
Walks upstairs with help	20.3
Walks downstairs with help	20.5
Walks upstairs alone; marks time	24.3
Walks downstairs alone; marks time	24.5
Jumps off floor; both feet	28.0

SOURCE: From Bayley, 1935.

Some specific motor abilities

Six sequential stages exist in walking: (1) reflex, (2) static, (3) transition, (4) deliberate, (5) heel-to-toe progression, and (6) mature walking.

There are six stages in the development of walking in the child (see Figure 2.5): (1) reflex stepping in the newborn, (2) a static phase when subcortical activity is inhibited by the developing cerebral cortex, (3) the transition stage, (4) deliberate stepping movement, (5) heel-to-toe progression, and (6) mature, erect locomotion. The stability of an infant depends upon his body weight, center of gravity, and the area enclosed by his two feet. Children take their first steps from a broad base; their knees are slightly flexed to lower their center of gravity and their arms are raised for better balance. As the infant matures, his knees are straightened, his feet come together, and his arms are no longer used for balance.

FIGURE 2.4

The motor sequence. (Adapted from Shirley, 1933.)

FIGURE 2.5

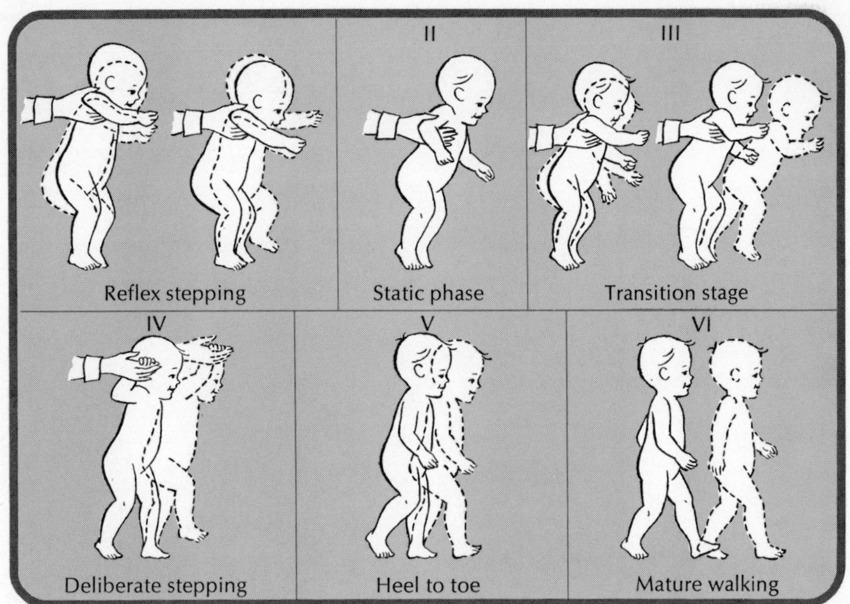

Developmental phases in erect locomotion. I. Newborn posture with reflex stepping movements which become somewhat more prevalent during the first three weeks. II. Inhibition, or static phase. This is characterized especially by better head control, as well as suppression of reflex stepping reactions. III. Transition stage, noted for up-and-down movements of the body and stepping motions which are noticeably different from those of the newborn. IV. Deliberate stepping while supported. V. Heel-toe progression. VI. More mature, well-integrated locomotion. (From McGraw, 1943.)

Handedness is usually established by two years of age; however, some children use different hands for various tasks.

Handedness, or laterality, is not apparent until the child is approximately 2 years of age. During the early years children are ambidextrous; by the second year a majority have developed a preference for the right hand. Most five-year-old children have established a consistent preference for one or the other hand. However, this preference varies somewhat; a child may eat with his right hand, write with his left, bat left-handed, and throw right-handed. Also, right-handedness does not necessarily imply dominance of the right eye or the right foot.

Cerebral dominance was assumed to explain handedness; however, training is now believed to be the determinant.

A cerebral-dominance theory was once widely accepted to explain handedness; now it is considered only speculation. This theory suggests that if the left side of the brain is dominant, then the individual will be right-handed; if the right hemisphere is dominant, he will be left-handed. Many people believed that damage was done to the child by changing his preferred hand. Several authors attributed stut-

FIGURE 2.6

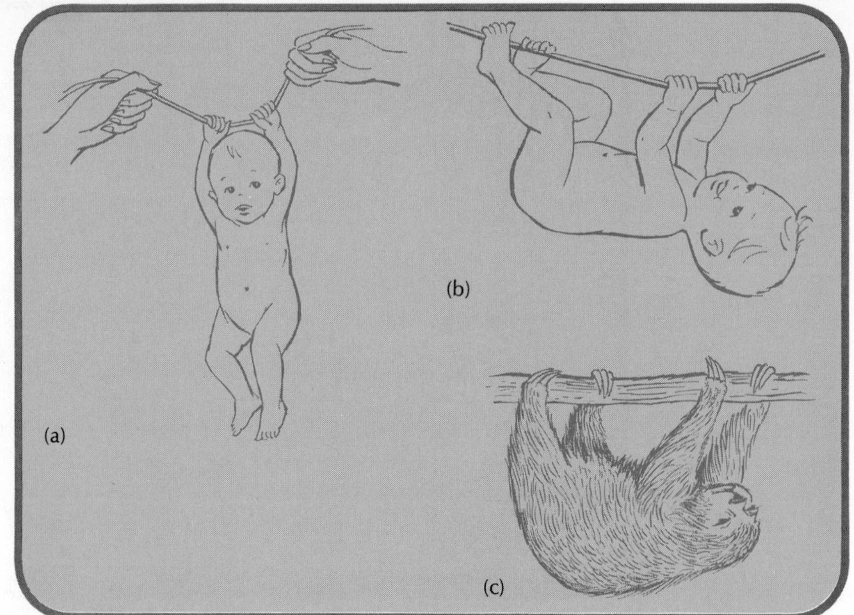

Grasp reflex in a prematurely born four-week-old twin (weight 6.7 pounds). (a) Arm suspension from the palmar grasp reflex. (b) Arm suspension with simultaneous leg suspension from palmar and plantar grasp reflexes. The grasp reflex in the human infant is similar to that of the sloth *(Choloepus didactylus)* as shown in (c) or of the monkey as discussed in the text.

tering and reading difficulties to changes in handedness (usually from left to right). If such an effect exists, it is much more likely to be a function of *how* the child is changed. Heredity may have something to do with laterality, although the evidence for social learning is quite strong. Early prehistoric tools were designed for left- as well as right-handed individuals; only later did right-handed implements predominate. Evidence for social learning shows that (1) hand preferences show cultural variations, (2) they develop gradually, (3) they show fluctuations before becoming firmly established, (4) they differ from task to task, and (5) they are remarkably susceptible to training.

Neonates possess a reflex grasp that can support about 90 percent of their weight.

At birth the human infant possesses a reflex grasp that shows two general phases—hand closure upon stimulation of the palm and reactions of the hand, arm, and shoulder to strain. Between birth and 24 weeks of age most infants can support about 90 percent of their weight with this grasp reflex (see Figure 2.6). After six months the

FIGURE 2.7

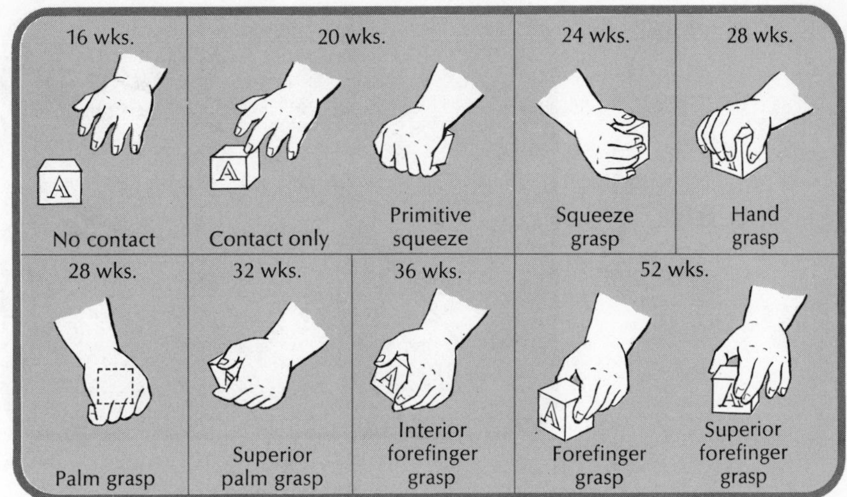

Types of grasping behavior in the human infant in the first year of life—from primitive squeezing, through crude palming, to the development of fingertip and forefinger grasping. (Adapted from Halverson, 1931.)

reflex gradually disappears. Probably the grasp reflex is analogous to the still-functional reflex of infant monkeys, who cling to their mothers' backs. Since the mother needs both hands to climb, the baby monkey must support himself.

Infants shift from crude palming to finger-thumb opposition during the course of grasping small objects.

The systematic changes in how infants grasp small objects are shown in Figure 2.7. The earliest approaches are gross shoulder and elbow movements. With further development (24–28 weeks) we see a crude palming pattern in which the thumb is inactive. Next comes a period (32–50 weeks) during which fingertip and forefinger grasping develops; this is followed by the growth of normal prehension with opposition of the thumb and forefinger.

Three factors contribute to increased motor abilities: (1) increased speed, (2) increased strength, and (3) a specific ability associated with handling balls and other small objects.

Interrelations among motor abilities

There are three basic factors in the development of motor behavior in childhood: an increase in speed, an increase in strength, and a specific factor associated with handling small objects (balls). Rate of nerve conduction increases until about age 13 (Figure 2.8), probably accounting for some of the increase in speed. However, most of the change is probably due to learning. Boys are slightly superior to girls in their speed of reaction. In a study of nursery school children, Koch (1934)

FIGURE 2.8

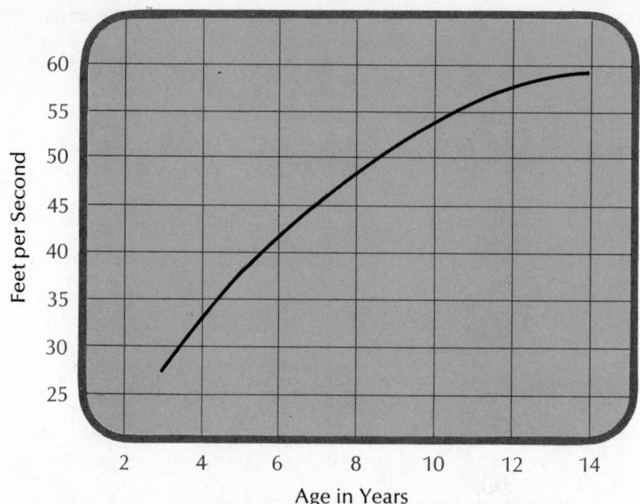

Rate of neural conductance as a function of age; with increasing maturity, rate of impulse conductance increases. This result probably explains some of the decrease in reaction time and increase in speed of movement with age. However, a good deal of the increased speed and flexibility is due to better coordination of perceptual and motor functions.

found that both aggressiveness and emotionality were attributed to children who perform tasks very quickly.

Until puberty boys are stronger than girls.

Both motor coordination and strength increase with age. Until puberty boys are stronger than girls, but during this period strength is temporarily equal, because girls mature earlier. Boys regain their mastery two years later. Grip strength is an increasing function of age, with boys superior to girls from three to ten years.

Children's motor skills are unrelated because of differential abilities, practice, and interest.

Is a child who is strong also faster or does he have more endurance? Is a child who is inferior in ball handling also bad at broadjumping, riding, and similar activities? The relations among motor abilities are much higher during infancy than in later childhood. Low intercorrelations in later childhood suggest that (1) differential opportunities for practice of various skills are available, (2) there is no general motor achievement factor, and/or (3) the interests of the child lead him to perform particular skills exceptionally well.

Motor skills depend on maturity, imitation, practice, and coaching.

Motor skills depend on several interrelated processes: neuromuscular maturity, opportunity to observe and imitate other children, availability of equipment, and the opportunity to experiment. If a child lacks opportunities for exploration and practice, or if he is inhibited in his locomotor activities (overprotected), his motor abilities will be poor. Gutteridge (1939) observed motor development of 1973 children between two and seven years of age. She made observations of several motor activities: climbing, jumping, sliding, tricycling, hopping, galloping, skipping, throwing, bouncing, and catching balls. Some established norms are given in Table 2.3.

TABLE 2.3 The Course of Development of Four "Typical" Skills in Childhood

Climbing—an activity already well established for half the children at three years, with gradual increments in skill until 92 percent of the children are proficient at six years. Early in the fourth year most of the children had climbed as high as opportunity permitted.

Jumping—a motor skill well developed in 42 percent of the children at three years, 72 percent at four and one-half years, and 81 percent at five years.

Tricycling—an accomplished skill among 17 percent of the two-year-olds and 63 percent of the three-year-olds. At four years almost 100 percent are skillful, stunting and using the tricycle for all kinds of imaginative variations.

Ball throwing—before two or three years almost no skill. At four years about 20 percent rated as throwing well. Between five and five and one-half years 74 percent can throw well. The earliest method of throwing a ball includes mass movements of all the body. Gradually the movements become more specialized and the use of two hands gives place to the use of one hand in a "clean throw." This latter illustrates both the mass-to-specific and the bilateral-to-unilateral trends in motor development.

Two classes of motor skills exist: (1) those developed by all children (walking) and (2) special skills acquired only through training (skiing).

There are two general classes of motor skills: special skills only acquired through training (for example, skiing) and phylogenetic skills developed by all children (for example, walking). Phylogenetic skills turn up in their own good time as a result of maturation; training or lack of experience have only minor effects on them (see Figure 2.9). On the other hand, those skills acquired only through training are strongly influenced by early practice. Whether training is started early or late, the quality of the training, the abilities of the child, and his motivation all affect the acquisition of complex motor skills.

Early practice has little effect on phylogenetic skills, which all children develop, but early practice helps special skills.

McGraw (1935) studied variations in the maturation and learning of several skills. She trained one fraternal twin (T) on a variety of motor skills from the age of 21 days to 22 months. The control twin (C) received no special training except for regular tests of motor ability (which constitute very minimal experience). The trained twin advanced greatly at some skills. He was an accomplished roller skater before he was two. His superiority occurred in areas of uncommon skills; he showed no superiority in the phylogenetic skills which all children acquire.

FIGURE 2.9

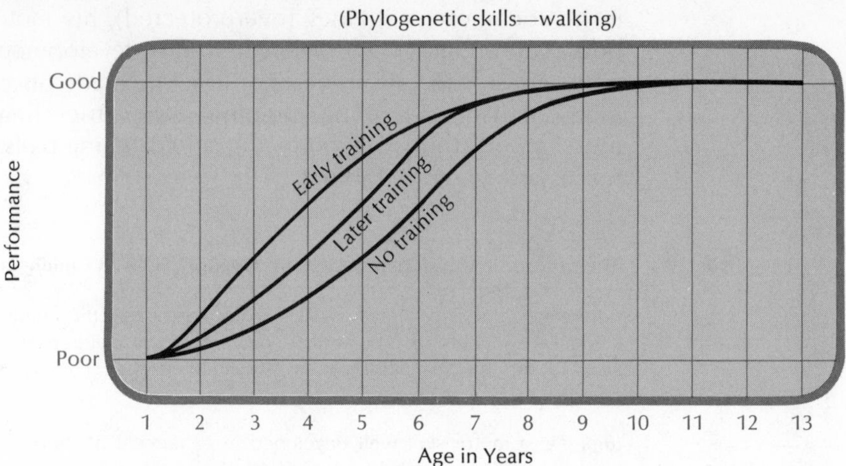

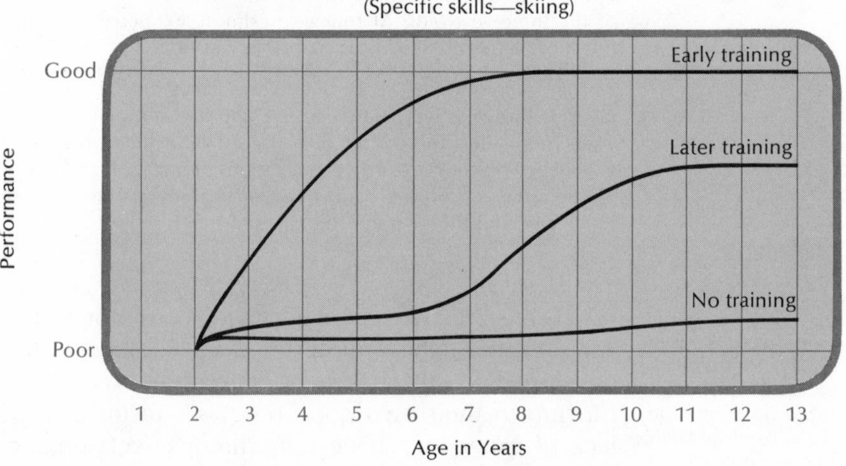

The effects of early, late, and no training on phylogenetic (for example, walking) and special (for example, skiing) skills of the child. Notice that little or no training produces relatively minor and short effects on phylogenetic skills but long-lasting effects on special skills.

Deprivation of early practice has little effect on phylogenetic skills.

Deprivation of early experience also has little effect on maturationally based skills. Swaddling (wrapping an infant with narrow bands of cloth on a board) is an accepted cultural practice in the Near East, the Balkans, Poland, and Russia. Armenian children who have been securely bound on a wood cradle in the darkest corner of the room for a year show retarded coordination at first, but they rapidly improve and suffer no permanent effects of the early restriction. Their social responsiveness and general motor behavior are equal to those of unswaddled children of the same age. The use of cradle boards during the first year of life, with the resultant lack of bodily contact and loss of opportunity for practice, makes little or no difference in the age at walking. Dennis and Dennis (1940) studied various groups of Hopi Indians, noting that in some villages infants were placed on a cradle board shortly after birth and remained there for the first few months of their lives while other Hopi infants were reared in the same fashion but without a cradle board. There were no differences in the age at which the two groups of children walked.

BODY BUILD AND PERSONALITY

Early and late physical maturity differentially affects boys and girls.

Boys and girls reach physical maturity at quite different rates. Girls of 11 and 12 are taller and heavier; they reach physical maturity about two years before their male peers. This differential rate of maturity brings obvious problems; girls are interested in dating and dancing earlier than their male peers. Investigators at the University of California studied the effect of early and late maturing on boys' later personality characteristics (Mussen & Jones, 1957). They used x-rays of the bones of the hand and knee as criteria of physical maturity. (The x-ray is a reliable and easy measure of general physical maturity, and it correlates quite well with other difficult-to-obtain measurements.) From an original sample of 90, 16 early-maturing and 16 late-maturing boys were studied intensively at age 14. The more mature boys were heavier, taller, and more active than their late-maturing peers. The physically retarded boys were long-legged, of slender build, and weak. They were also rated by adults as less physically attractive, less muscular, and more childish. They sought attention more often and were more tense.

Early-maturing boys have positive images of themselves, while late-maturing boys see themselves in a more negative light.

Early-maturing boys possess a clear advantage in social-sexual relations for several years. Their drives and interests match their feminine age mates. Late-maturing boys, on the other hand, must wait to catch up in height and weight with their peers. They undergo long periods of social disadvantage; they are also likely to feel immature and irresponsible because they are not good athletes. Mussen and Jones (1957) gave Thematic Apperception Tests to the early- and late-maturing boys when they were 17 years of age. In this test each boy was shown a series of pictures and asked to tell a story about each one. The storyteller is assumed to project his own needs and ideas into the character of the story, and his hero's actions are supposed to show how the child sees himself. Early-maturing boys see the hero as desirable, while late-maturing boys describe the hero in negative terms (imbecile, weakling). The hero is also disapproved of by his parents or by authorities in the late-maturing boys' stories. Physically advanced boys possess positive self-concepts, describing the hero as aggressive and domineering.

Sheldon proposed three body types: (1) the barrel-chested endomorph, (2) the muscular mesomorph, and (3) the thin ectomorph.

Sheldon (1954) developed three basic classifications of the human body: (1) the barrel-chested, big-bellied person who receives a high endomorph rating; (2) the muscular, broad-shouldered, narrow-hipped person who rates high on mesomorphy; and (3) the long, lean individual with large external body surface in relation to his total weight who obtains a high score on ectomorphy. Others have discovered differential social reactions to these various types of body builds. Brodsky (1954) used five silhouettes of males representing endomorph, endomesomorph, mesomorph, ectomesomorph, and ectomorph; he constructed a questionnaire that asked, for example, "Which of this group of five men is most aggressive? which one least aggressive?" He asked 75 men to rate the pictures. More than one-third of the respondents said that the endomorph would make the worst soldier, poorest athlete, poorest professor in philosophy, least successful military leader, and poorest university president. They also felt that he would be least aggressive, drink a lot, not be preferred as a personal friend, and that he would be selfish. The mesomorph was seen more favorably. The subjects said he would make the best athlete, the most successful military leader, and the best soldier. They felt the mesomorph is a man who would assume leadership, be elected leader, and be self-sufficient. The ectomorph is less socially desirable than the mesomorph, but he is seen in a more favorable light than the endomorph. The ectomorph was judged likely to have a nervous breakdown before the age of 30, eat the least, smoke three packs of cigarettes a day, not be self-sufficient, hold his liquor worse, and make a poor father. He is a socially acceptable neurotic. These are characteristic reactions to different physiques; in the context of early- and late-maturing boys, the more mesomorphic body build of the early-maturing boys suggests why they are more popular.

Children with well-developed motor skills have better social positions than their more clumsy peers.

Muscular skills are important in the history of mankind; our civilization has grown because man has the unique thumb-forefinger opposition necessary to develop and use complex tools. Also, motor skills are highly influential in the social development of children, particularly in play. Children with well-developed motor skills are more socially acceptable; good motor skills enhance their social position and help them assume leadership.

Ratings of boys' body builds and personality traits are correlated; boys with mesomorphic bodies are seen as more aggressive. None of these relations holds for girls.

Walker (1963) studied children's body build and their associated behavior as judged by nursery school teachers. He assumed that there are important associations between physique and bodily activities among preschool children. Girls were more often rated endomorph, boys more often mesomorph. In general, the boys rated as endomorphs were judged self-assertive, revengeful, and delinquent; mesomorphs were seen by their teachers as easily angered, quarrelsome, ambitious, energetic, and noisy. The ectomorphs were described as introverts—nonobjectionable neurotics. They were not self-assertive, noisy, or social, and they did not attack others; they daydreamed a lot and were not energetic. Almost none of these correlations held for girls, probably because physique is not so important for *little* girls' self-conceptions (a fact that changes drastically during puberty).

REMARKS: THEORY

The growth of a child is self-stabilizing; there is a strong tendency for his growth rate to return to its natural curve after being slowed by disease or starvation. Tanner (1963) suggested that the regularity of growth of children's height matches a self-stabilizing hypothesis. He showed that following severe disease or acute malnutrition, with an accompanying slowing of the growth rate, the body grows faster for a short period to catch up. During the catch-up period the child's growth may reach two or three times its normal rate.

The phenomenon of "catch-up" can be seen immediately after birth. For example, suppose the child is genetically destined to be large, but his intrauterine environment is restricted by a small mother. The newborn will be smaller at birth, but his rate of growth will increase substantially immediately after birth and continue at the higher rate until he catches up to his genetic potential.

The "target seeking" of human growth seems to be regulated by internal neural mechanisms which keep track of the rate of normal growth and also the difference between this normal pattern and the actual growth of the individual. If the discrepancy between the expected growth pattern and the actual pattern becomes larger, the rate of growth is increased to make up the difference. As the difference between the expected and the actual pattern of growth is lessened, the rate of growth is correspondingly slowed. Tanner proposed that there is a mechanism in the central nervous system which knows the expected size of the organism. The actual size of the body is monitored by means of a substance produced proportionately to the increase in body size. The relation between the indicator substance and expected body size is monitored, and the rate of growth is adjusted to be proportional to this relation. This simple mechanism can explain the normal growth curve and the catch-up of growth after starvation or disease.

Baby biographies were the earliest method of studying children.

Several methods have been used to study human growth. The earliest method was the baby biography. The first known biography of a child was commissioned by the court of France and was a diary describing the growth and behavior of young Louis XIII. Teidemann (1787) probably deserves credit for publishing the first scientific biography; he recorded his own son's behavior through infancy. A baby biography is exactly what the name suggests—an account of the day-to-day growth and behavior of a child. The baby biography presents an enormous amount of interesting and relevant data; it can be collected and presented in a relatively short period. During the early stages of child study, when there were few explicit hypotheses or well-established methods of study, the baby biography made good sense. The description of a single subject over time highlights the variables that need explanation. However, since only one subject is studied, the behavior may be unique to that particular child. We need other cases for comparison. The method of baby biography has been carried to its logical end by Barker and Wright (1951) in their book *One Boy's Day.* They followed a single boy around all day, recorded his every word and action, described the context of his action, and pointed to the goal of his action. They tried to record everything the child did without influencing him. They recorded every observable movement the child made (for example, walking down the street, kicking a stone, looking at the sky, whistling), and each observer also taped impressions of what they thought the child was doing (for example, his goals, the context of the action). They tried not to select, but recorded everything the child did for posterity. Biographies are an interesting way of generating hypotheses, but theories cannot be tested with them. To test theories we must first decide what are appropriate observations and then form groups that differ only in terms of these variables. Information from a single case is fruitful for suggesting hypotheses, but we must go beyond the single case to know whether the mechanisms and processes we propose can explain the behavior of other subjects under other conditions.

Three other methods are used in child psychology: (1) the longitudinal, (2) the cross-sectional, and (3) the mixed design.

In addition to the baby biography, there are three other methods used in the study of growth: the observation of a single group of children over an extended period of time (longitudinal), the simultaneous observation of several groups of children of different ages (cross-sectional), and a combination of both these methods (mixed). With the longitudinal method one knows the children are comparable from one age to another because they are the same children. Any differences as a function of age can be attributed to maturation and experience; they cannot be the result of poor sampling (genetic or historical differences). The main problems with longitudinal research are its expense and the time required. A longitudinal study of motor development from ages three to ten obviously requires seven years. The cross-sectional method can sample several *different* groups of children at various ages between three and ten to produce comparable information in a relatively short time. In the case of the longitudinal method all variation over ages is the result of maturation and experience. However, in the case of the cross-sectional method there is additional variation due to the different samples of children used at the various age levels.

Cross-sectional designs confound age variation with historical variation (children born at different times may experience different events).

Variation between groups (the fact that different groups may not be matched) can produce spurious age differences in cross-sectional studies. For example, suppose one group in our sample is much brighter than the others; the results from that group will confuse our findings; or suppose our older groups have a history of trauma (for example, war). We will not know whether differences are due to age changes, genetic differences, or historical variation. Also, the precision of measurement is lower for different groups of children than for the same group measured several times. Consequently, small developmental changes may be overshadowed by between-group variation.

The mixed design combines the best features of cross-sectional and longitudinal analyses. It requires that several groups be followed longitudinally for a short time.

The third method (mixed) combines the best features of both longitudinal and cross-sectional designs. To perform a "mixed" experiment, suppose groups of children ranging in age from three to nine years are selected (for example, three, five, seven, and nine years). Each group is measured immediately and then followed for two years (for example, the three-year-olds until they are five, the five-year-olds until they are seven, and so on). In this way longitudinal data are produced in just two years. The question of adequate sampling can be checked—the five-year-old group is compared with the three-year-old group (when these children are five) to see if the findings are congruent. If the samples are representative, the three-year-old group at five years of age will look like the five-year-old group at five years of age.

Observational studies usually rely on correlations to describe their findings. Correlations describe the co-variation of scores on two factors.

Most observational studies are analyzed by the method of correlation. The basic property of a correlation is quite simple: It tells you something of the relation between two variables. If a correlation is positive, a child who scores *high* on one trait will also score *high* on the other. On the other hand, a negative correlation tells us that a *low* score on one trait will be associated with a *high* score on another trait. If there is no correlation between two traits, scores on one are independent of scores on the other. A curvilinear relation between two variables suggests that both low and high values of the variable *B* are related to low values on variable *A,* while intermediate values of variable *B* are related to high values of *A*. Figure 2.10 shows scatter plots of the four possible relations.

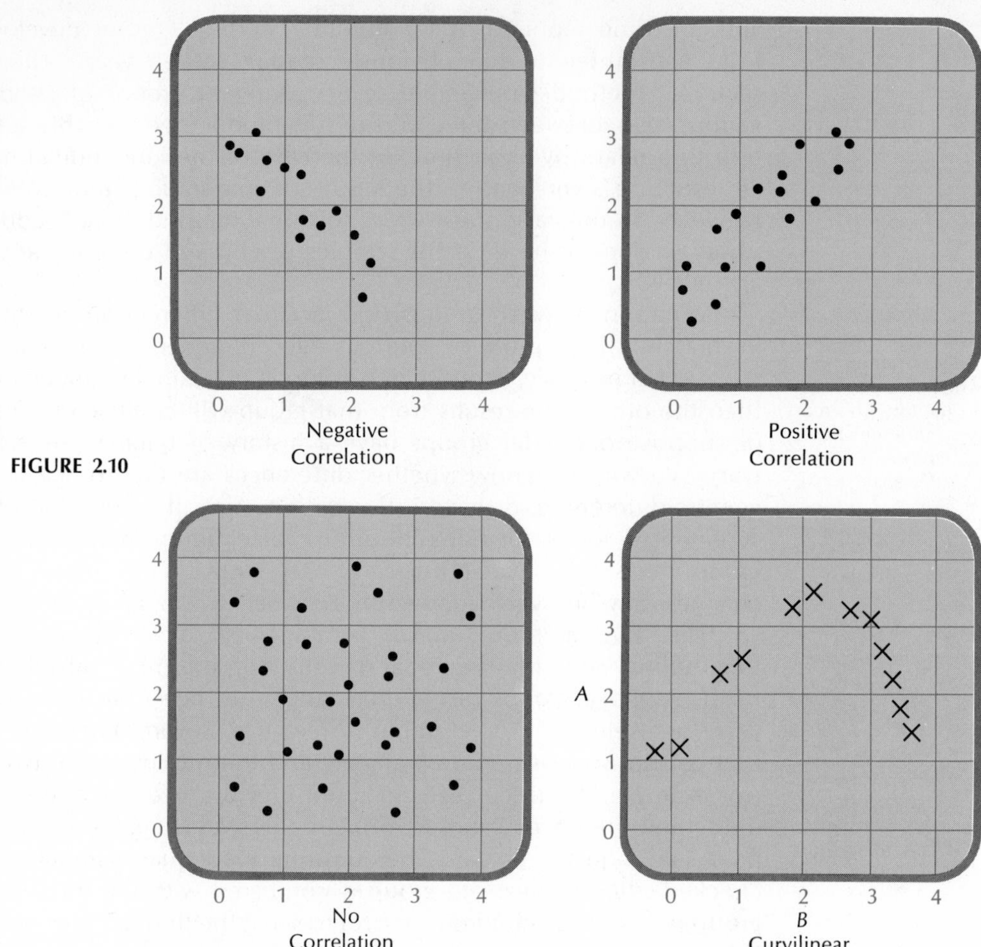

FIGURE 2.10

Four types of correlations between two variables. A negative correlation shows that high scores on one variable are related to low scores on the other variable, while a positive correlation shows that high scores on one variable are associated with high scores on the other variable; no correlation shows no relation. A curvilinear relation tells us that both high and low values of variable *B* are related to low values of variable *A*, while intermediate values of *B* are related to high values of *A*.

SUMMARY

1 As a first step in the study of development, investigators collected descriptions of normal growth. Although these norms do not explain human growth, they are a convenient reference against which to compare the child's development.

2 The major principles of growth are the cephalo-caudal progression of behavior from the head to the lower extremities and the proximal-distal development of behavior from the medial plane of the body toward the periphery.

3 Growth rate may be modified by diet, disease, or the normal "catch-up" mechanisms of the human organism. There is good reason to believe that the growth of the child is regulated by target-seeking mechanisms in the central nervous system.

4 The development of motor abilities in the young child is controlled by a few factors; later, the child's motor abilities are affected by the complex interaction of abilities, opportunities for practice, and motivation for a particular skill.

5 Motor abilities are interrelated early in the child's life, but they are independent later.

6 The type of body build the child develops affects how he is seen by others and how he views himself. In general, the early-maturing boy is seen as more positive both by himself and others, while the late-maturing boy is viewed in more negative ways. The opposite effects are found for early- and late-maturing girls.

FURTHER READINGS

Bayley, N. The development of motor abilities during the first three years. *Monograph of the Society for Research in Child Development,* 1935, No. 1.

Gesell, A. The ontogenesis of infant behavior. In L. Carmichael (Ed.), *Manual of child psychology* (2nd ed.). New York: Wiley, 1954. Pp. 335–373.

Thompson, H. Physical growth. In L. Carmichael (Ed.), *Manual of child psychology* (2nd ed.). New York: Wiley, 1954. Pp. 292–334.

REFERENCES

Barker, R. G., & Wright, H. F. *One boy's day.* New York: Harper & Row, 1951.

Bayley, N. The development of motor abilities during the first three years. *Monograph of the Society for Research in Child Development,* 1935, **1,** 1.

Bayley, N. Individual patterns of development. *Child Development,* 1956, **27,** 45–74.

Boyd, E. Growth of the surface area of the human body. *Institute of Child Welfare Monographs,* 1935, **10,** 114.

Brodsky, C. M. *A study of norms for body form-behavior relationships.* Washington, D.C.: Catholic University of America Press, 1954.

Dennis, W. A description and classification of the responses of the newborn infant. *Psychological Bulletin,* 1934, **31,** 5–22.

Dennis, W. Infant development under conditions of restricted practice and of minimum social stimulation. *Genetic Psychology Monograph,* 1941, **23,** 143–191.

Dennis, W., & Dennis, M. G. The effect of cradling practices upon the onset of walking in Hopi children. *Journal of Genetic Psychology,* 1940, **56,** 77-86.

Gesell, A. The ontogenesis of infant behavior. In L. Carmichael (Ed.), *Manual of child psychology* (2nd ed.). New York: Wiley, 1954. Pp. 335-373.

Graham, F. K., Matarazzo, R., & Caldwell, B. Behavioral differences between normal and traumatized newborns. *Psychological Monographs,* 1956, **70,** 427-458.

Gutteridge, M. A study of motor achievements of young children. *Archives of Psychology,* 1939, **34,** No. 244.

Halverson, H. M. An experimental study of prehension in infants by means of systematic cinema records. *Genetic Psychology Monographs,* 1931, **10,** 107-286.

Jackson, C. M. Some aspects of form and growth. In Robbins, W. J., Brody, S., Hogan, A. G., Jackson, C. M., & Green, C. W. *Growth.* New Haven, Conn.: Yale University Press, 1928.

Koch, H. A multiple-factor analysis of certain measures of activeness in nursery school children. *Journal of Genetic Psychology,* 1934, **45,** 482-487.

McGraw, M. B. *Growth: A study of Johnny and Jimmy.* New York: Appleton-Century-Crofts, 1935.

McGraw, M. B. The neuromuscular maturation of the human infant. New York: Columbia University Press, 1943.

Mussen, P., & Jones, M. C. Self-conceptions, motivations, and interpersonal attitudes of late- and early-maturing boys. *Child Development,* 1957, **28,** 243-256.

Sheldon, W. *Atlas of men: A guide for somatotyping the adult male at all ages.* New York: Harper & Row, 1954.

Shirley, M. M. The first two years. II. Intellectual development. Minneapolis: University of Minnesota Press, 1933.

Tanner, J. M. The regulation of human growth. *Child Development,* 1963, **34,** 817-847.

Teidemann, D. (1787) Record of an infant's life. In F. L. Soldan, *Teidemann's record of infant life. An English version of the French translation and commentary by Bernard Perez.* Syracuse, N.Y.: Bardeen, 1890.

Walker, R. N. Body build and behavior in young children: II. Body build and parents' ratings. *Child Development,* 1963, **34,** 1-23.

3 SENSORY ABILITIES

> Light seeking light doth light of light beguile:
> So, ere you find where light in darkness lies,
> Your light grows dark by losing of your eyes.
> Study me how to please the eye indeed
> By fixing it upon a fairer eye,
> Who dazzling so, that eye shall be his heed
> And give him light that it was blinded by.
>
> LOVE'S LABOUR'S LOST

Historically, psychologists have drawn a distinction between sensation (usually considered a simple, peripheral process) and perception (a more complex central activity). The distinction may be made on various grounds: (1) the differences between the sensory end organs, in more direct contact with physical energy of the external world, and the higher centers of the brain, where more central perceptual processes occur; (2) the relative simplicity of the relations between the stimulus energy and the response of the organism (simple functions for sensory processes, but more complex in the case of perceptual processes); and (3) the appearance of the processes at different stages in the development of the organism (sensory attributes make their appearance early in the life of the infant, while perceptual abilities occur later in the maturing child).

We are concerned with the basic sensory abilities of the infant.

Two issues grow from these distinctions: (1) What are the infant's basic sensory abilities? and (2) How does he combine these simple abilities to form complex perceptual objects? Sensory abilities of the neonate are explored in this chapter, while the more advanced perceptual processes of the child are outlined in the next.

We need to understand sensitivity and develop a model of how the child decides whether a stimulus is present or not.

To study sensory abilities we need to understand the notion of sensitivity and develop a model of how the human observer may decide whether a sensation is present or absent. Sensory abilities are the qualitative experiences of the organism (for example, red, bright); they are associated with sensory systems and reflect the infant's awareness of various classes of physical energy (for example, wavelength, intensity). Sensitivity to physical energies is the infant's basic contact with the world; he must integrate these sensations into perceptions, then combine these perceptions to form a coherent picture of the world.

THE NOTION OF THRESHOLD

Early conceptions of sensitivity assumed a threshold above which we are aware of stimuli and below which we ignore them.

Early conceptions of sensitivity centered on the notion of threshold; the observer was assumed to be aware of stimuli above threshold and unaware of stimuli below it. One view of sensitivity assumed that a stimulus initiated neural impulses which produced a message in a brain center (Bartley, 1958). Size of the central effect changed with stimulus intensity, receptor state, neural adaptation, and the level of background neural noise. If the central effect on a given trial was greater than a certain minimum, the brain center would discharge, yielding a response (for example, "I hear it," or a change in activity). The stimulus intensity necessary to produce this effect was the threshold. However, many factors—stimulus strength, receptor sensitivity, neural efficiency, and noise level—were assumed to vary randomly from trial to trial, yielding an approximately normal distribution of momentary thresholds. The average of this distribution was taken to represent the best value of the stimulus threshold. Various psychophysical methods were developed for systematically taking and treating these data in order to measure the "typical" value of the threshold and its variation.

REMARKS: METHOD

To measure an infant's sensory ability we assume that his responses adequately reflect his sensitivity. Also, we assume that the verbal responses of a child measure the same processes assessed by reflexive or conditioned responses in an infant. The equivalence of these measures of sensitivity (verbal and nonverbal) can be known once we have a comprehensive model of perceptual development. With a model we can see whether principles found using verbal and nonverbal procedures enter into related theoretical statements. If they do, we are justified in assuming the two measurement procedures sample related perceptual processes. For the moment, their equivalence remains a strong assumption. The particular response used depends on the capabilities of the observer. In the case of the newborn we might use the startle reaction, or looking time. In the young child differences in limb movement, ocular orientation, or classical conditioning might be used, and in the older child we can obviously use verbal reports. The particular response is irrelevant as long as two responses exist. With two responses we can generate quite elegant experimental paradigms for assessing an infant's sensitivity to sensory attributes. The comparability of responses remains an empirical question.

Newer notions of sensitivity include signal-to-noise ratios and decision criteria.

Newer conceptions of sensory systems emphasize the ratio of signal energy to background noise (irrelevant stimuli) rather than the absolute amount of physical energy of the stimulus. The notions of signal, noise, and a decision criterion are now proposed to measure the sensitivity of an observer. In addition to receptor sensitivity, the observer's criterion (how he separates those times when he will say yes from those times when he will say no) also affects his response to stimulation. There is reason to believe children have difficulty maintaining a stable criterion. Variable criteria produce underestimates of sensitivity. Children with variable criteria would appear insensitive when compared with observers who maintain a more stable criterion, even though both have equal sensitivity. Many reported variations between children and adults may be the result of other factors—response biases or criterion changes—and not reflect sensory development at all.

The typical sensory experiment includes stimulus and no stimulus trials on which the observer is required to say yes or no.

A typical experimental situation takes the form of a yes-no detection task. This situation is characterized by a well-defined time interval during which a signal may be presented or not, and the child is required to indicate whether a sensation was present or not. There is usually no sharp change between a child's reporting a sensation and his not reporting it, nor is there sharp discontinuity in reporting differences between sensations. These changes are small and continuous, and appropriate methods are required to measure them accurately. To measure sensitivity we need reliable presentation equipment, a plan for recording responses, and appropriate methods for treating data.

Classic procedures of estimating threshold varied signal strength from high to low and low to high to balance the observer's biases.

In the classic procedures signal strength was varied over a relatively wide range; at some point along this quantitative variation the infant's response changed. To balance the serial errors of estimation found in measurements of absolute thresholds, both high-to-low and low-to-high changes in amount of stimulation were used. In going from high-to-low stimulus values the observer tends to overestimate, while going from low-to-high stimulus values produces an underestimation. By balancing these two effects we produce a less biased estimate of the observer's sensitivity. The physical energy that resulted in 50 percent responses to the stimulation, averaged over both the ascending and descending trials, was considered the absolute threshold.

Difference thresholds require two stimuli that vary in similarity; the observer must say they are the same or different.

In the case of the difference threshold two stimuli are required, each producing a central excitation that varies randomly. By trying several different values of s_1, we may determine the stimulus difference necessary to displace one mean enough to give us 75 percent "greater" judgments, and we may call this value the difference threshold. The value of a difference threshold depends on the size of variations in excitation just mentioned; the difference threshold is a measure of sensory variability.

To measure difference thresholds in an infant we first habituate him to one stimulus and then change it. If the habituated response reappears, the infant sees the difference.

The experimental arrangement for measuring difference thresholds in infants is somewhat changed from that used for estimating absolute thresholds. For the difference threshold we again need an appropriate response from the infant. However, after finding an appropriate indicator we present the infant with *repeated* stimulation until his response to the stimulus fades and finally disappears. Following habituation of the infant's response to the original stimulus (to some arbitrary level of response probability—for example, 50 percent), we change the signal by a specified amount. When the change is large enough to elicit a response a significantly larger portion of the time (for example, 75 percent), we have defined the difference threshold for that particular set of stimuli. By differential responding the infant is telling us he can discriminate the two stimuli. An alternative procedure may be used when the infant is mature enough to allow classical conditioning (see Chapter 5). In this more traditional experimental situation we may associate different responses to the two stimuli and use the two conditioned responses as indicators of s_1 or s_2.

DETECTION THEORY AS A MODEL OF THE PROCESS

Detection theory provides a good analysis of sensitivity. It assumes the infant has decision rules, a criterion, and statistics.

Detection theory provides a convenient analysis of the process that generates sensations (stimuli the infant perceives) and noise (stimuli he does not perceive). A specific example will introduce, without undue formalism, many of the conceptions of decision theory that are relevant to the present discussion and will serve as a convenient referent. The general problem may be understood through a set of questions: Given a particular sensation, what response should the infant make? What is a good response, and how may we analyze it? While presenting this example we will discuss three concepts: *likelihood ratio, decision rule,* and *criterion.*

Deciding whether a signal was present or not is analogous to a game in which three dice are thrown and you are told their sum.

Consider the following game. Three tetrahedral dice are thrown. Two of the dice have one, two, three, or four spots appearing on the sides (noise). The third (odd) die has no spots on two sides and two spots on the remaining two sides. You do not observe the throw of the dice, but are told the total number of spots that appear. Your task is to decide whether the odd die shows zero spots (noise) or two spots (stimulus). What strategy might you use to play this game? You might decide to say "zero" or "two" randomly. However, if you want to be correct as often as possible, you must formulate a strategy.

To make a decision about the game you need a decision rule based on statistics about the dice.

How can you make intelligent decisions about the number of dots on the odd die, given only the total of all three dice and some statistical information about the frequencies of the possible combinations? Assuming your aim is to maximize the number of correct decisions, the best policy for our particular example is to say "zero" for those totals *below* six and to say "two" for those totals *above* six. The number six is indeterminate, and you should alternately guess "zero" and "two" when the total is six. This is true because the likelihood of the total's being six is the same, given either zero or two as the outcome for the third die. For the totals seven through ten, the probability of that number given two is higher than the probability of that number given zero. Similarly, for the totals less than six their probability is greater given zero than the probability of that same number given two.

The ratio of two probabilities (likelihood ratio) is a good means of deciding whether to say yes or no to a particular observation.

The ratio of these two probabilities—the probability of a particular total given that the odd die is two and the probability of that same total given that the odd die is zero—is called the likelihood ratio (because probabilities are sometimes called likelihoods, and this number is the ratio of two probabilities). The decision rule that maximizes the percentage of correct decisions suggests you say "two" when the likelihood ratio exceeds one and say "zero" otherwise. When the likelihood ratio is exactly one, you must decide on some other basis. If a decision rule is stated in terms of likelihood ratio, it always has the same form: Do something if the likelihood ratio is above a certain value and do something else if the ratio is below that value. The only thing that is changed by the objectives (goals) of the decision-maker is the value of the number (called the criterion) that divides the likelihood ratio continuum into two parts.

There are three necessary parts of a sensory experiment: (1) stimuli, (2) sensations, and (3) responses.

There are three necessary parts to a sensory experiment: (1) some possible states of the world (stimuli), (2) information about these possible states (sensations), and (3) a decision (response). In the typical detection situation, the states of the world are the presence or absence of a signal. The observer (child) attends to a display, or listens over earphones, during defined intervals to obtain the information he will use to make a decision. Finally, the child responds to information about the state of signal present or signal absent by making a differential response to indicate his decision. The observer is fallible, since some of his decisions are wrong. We assume that the state of the world "signal plus noise" and the state of the world "noise" produce different distributions of information (sensations) and that the observer uses these distributions to determine the likelihood ratios on which to base his response (see Figure 3.1). Specifically, we assume there is a background of noise present in the perceptual system (both from internal neural firing and external input) that allows the observer to accumulate a "noise" distribution. A second distribution is accumulated over the first several trials of the experiment (or during a practice session). This second distribution represents both signal and noise and is displaced by some amount from the distribution of noise alone. The task of the observer is to accumulate distributions of noise and signal plus noise, compare a sensation to these two distributions, and make a decision

FIGURE 3.1

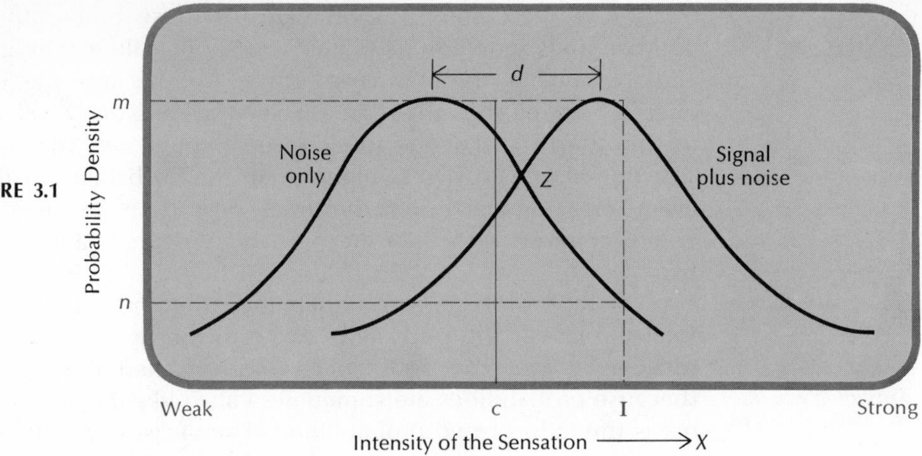

Assumed mental distributions of noise and signal plus noise. The line *X*, which is related to the sensory input, is the observer's "decision axis." He adjusts his criterion (c) to some point along this axis of sensations. The likelihood ratio (corresponding to some sensory input level such as I) is the ratio of the probability that the sensation comes from signal plus noise at point I to the probability that the sensation comes from noise alone at point I. (*m/n* is the ratio in this example.) The likelihood ratio will be equal to one at the point of intersection of the two distributions (*Z*). The value *d*, the difference between the means of the two sensation distributions, reflects the strength of the stimulus. As the stimulus becomes stronger, the difference between the two distributions of possible sensations to the stimulus will grow.

on the basis of these comparisons. When a particular sensation occurs on a given trial, he compares the sensation with his mental estimates and makes a decision about whether it was more like a sensation from the distribution of noise or the distribution of signal *and* noise. The responses an observer may use are determined by the experimenter. Usually they are in 1:1 association with the possible states of the world, and it is easy to score them as correct or incorrect. The average number of correct and incorrect responses constitute our data.

Several factors affect the outcome of a detection experiment: (1) the signal strength, (2) the probability of signal and noise, and (3) the payoff matrix.

Several factors may affect the outcome of a detection experiment. For the moment we consider only the *a priori* probability of stimulus presentation—whether the stimulus is to be presented half the time, less than half, or more than half the time—and the physical values of the signal. In the typical experiment the energy of the signal is held constant while the sensitivity of the observer is estimated at various response criteria. The child's response criterion may be varied by changing the payoff matrix (rewards and punishments), by giving verbal instructions to the child, or by varying the *a priori* probability of occurrence of the states of the world.

Representation of decision outcomes

There are different types of errors and correct decisions.

In any decision situation, a single response is either correct or incorrect. A decision-maker's performance is evaluated by looking at the *average* number of correct and incorrect decisions he makes. There are at least two types of correct decisions he can make and two types of error (see Figure 3.2). In general, when we decrease the probability of one kind of error we increase the chance of other kinds. It is impossible to increase the probabilities of both correct decisions simultaneously. Most decision processes are less than perfectly accurate. Sometimes one type of error is as costly as another; here the decision-maker's goal is simply to maximize the percentage of correct responses. In other situations one type of error may be particularly unacceptable. Here the goal of the decision-maker should be to minimize these particular errors, even if it means increasing other types of errors and lowering the total percent correct.

In a detection situation there are four outcomes: (1) a hit, (2) a correct rejection, (3) a false alarm, and (4) a miss.

In a yes-no task there are usually two possible stimuli and two possible responses. The process may be represented as a two-by-two matrix, with a particular trial represented by the intersection of one stimulus alternative and one response alternative [see Figure 3.2 (Green & Swets, 1966)]. Here, *n* is the occurrence of noise alone, *s* is the occurrence of signal and noise, *N* is the response "stimulus absent," and *S* is the response "stimulus present." Correctly saying "stimulus present" is called a *hit,* and correctly responding "stimulus absent" is called a *correct rejection.* On the other hand, saying that a stimulus is present

FIGURE 3.2

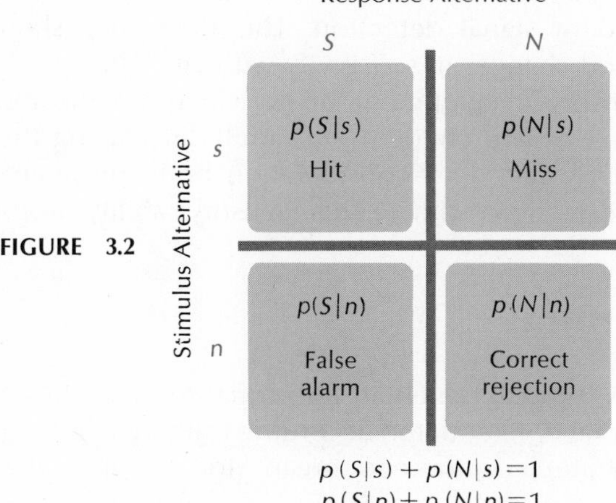

The stimulus-response matrix of the yes-no procedure. (From Green & Swets, 1966.)

when in fact it is absent is a *false alarm,* and failure to detect a stimulus when it is present is a *miss.*

Application to development

The simple detection situation can be applied to neonates by finding a suitable response and presenting stimuli systematically.

How may these procedures be applied to the study of an infant's sensitivity? First we must find a suitable response of the infant or child to the particular stimulus in question. Assume we use a conditioned response. A series of discrete trials at some signal energy should be presented in a counterbalanced order. Half the trials should contain no signal at all, and the other half should contain a signal strong enough so our infant will respond about 75 percent of the time. Note that this procedure is directly analogous to the experimental structure of the usual yes-no paradigm employed with adult observers. We may use the infant's conditioned responses to indicate whether we are to classify a particular trial as "Yes, I perceive it" or "No, I do not." Once we have divided the subject's responses into two classes, we are in a position to construct the two-by-two matrix of hits, misses, false alarms, and correct rejections. From this matrix we can derive a measure of the infant's sensitivity.

Signal-detection analyses avoid contamination of sensitivity and judgment.

The major advantages of signal-detection theory are these: First, we avoid the problem of contamination of the observer's sensitivity by a shifting criterion. The method of signal detectability insures that our measure of sensitivity, derived from both hit rate *and* false alarm rate, is independent of any particular criterion the infant happened to use in deciding the presence or absence of a stimulus. Signal-detection procedures also eliminate the problem of correcting for guesses. Correcting for chance guessing has been a continuing problem in the study of individual sensitivity and has no other satisfactory solution.

Studies that have not used these methods may reflect sensitivity changes, judgment changes, or both.

Unfortunately, most studies that use children as subjects have not utilized the method of signal detection. This deficiency should be recalled when we find changes in sensitivity with age. The age changes may be due to sensory development or they may be the result of differing criteria used by the children and adults in making their decisions. Only when we take into consideration both the infant's hits and false alarms can we estimate his sensory ability accurately.

BASIC SENSORY ABILITIES

Three criteria are used to determine a sense: (1) a separate receptor,

The sensory systems through which an individual receives information about his world can be differentiated according to three criteria: (1) the presence of a separate receptor end organ (for example, the eye),

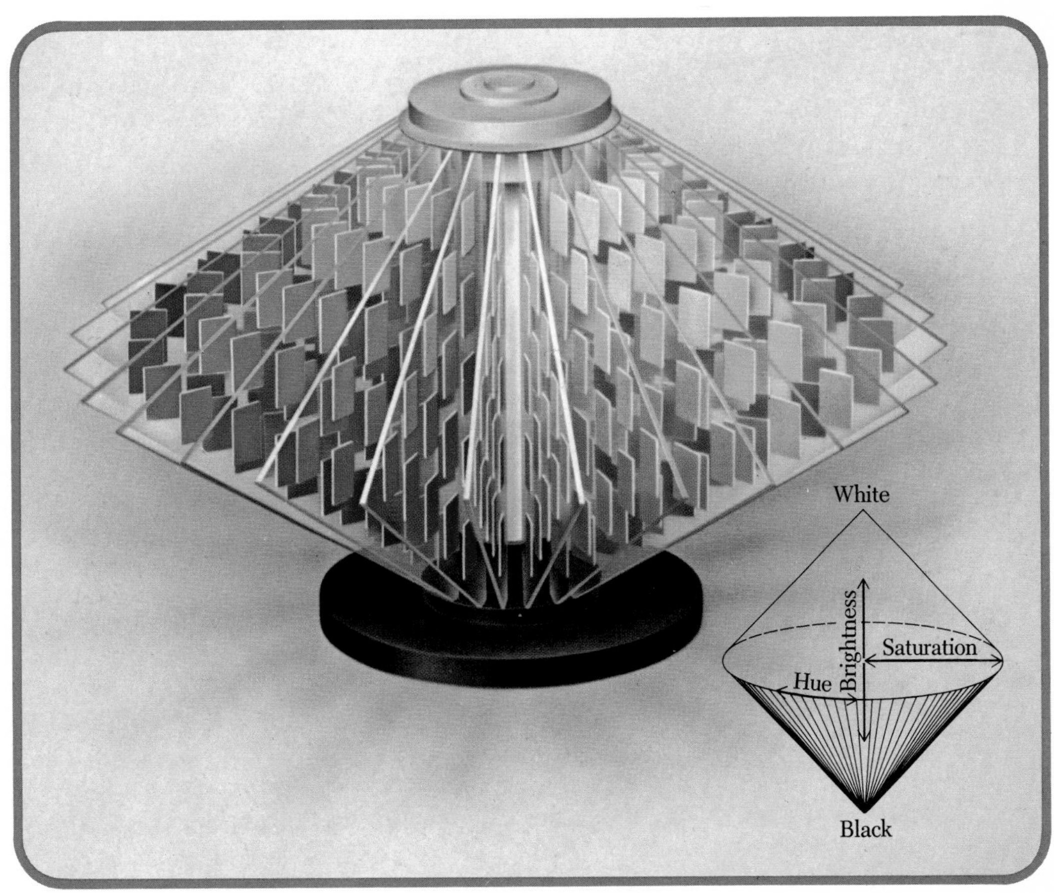

PLATE 1 A color solid showing the three dimensions of color sensitivity—hue, brightness, and saturation. The diagram in the lower-right corner illustrates the gradual change in brightness from black to white along the central axis. (See p. 62.)

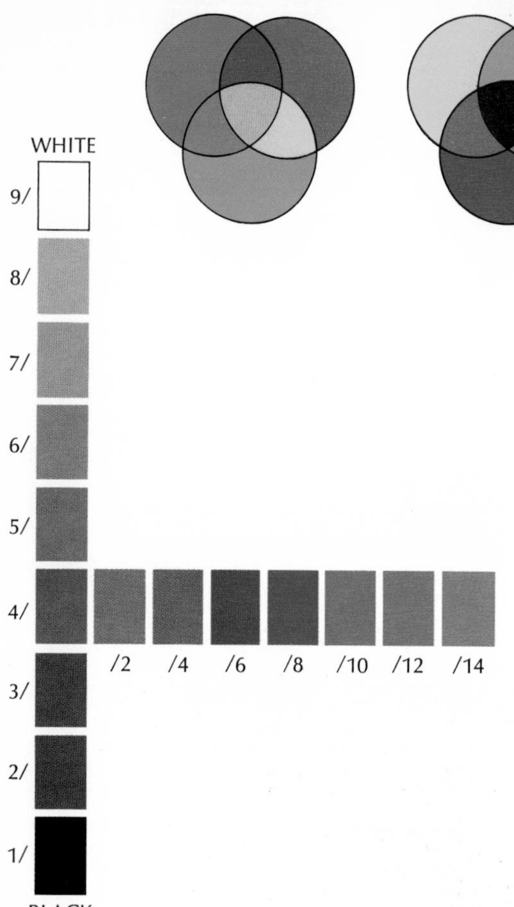

PLATE 2

Color mixtures. Additive mixtures (*left*) occur when the three primary colors are blended (overlap); they can produce all the colors seen by a human observer. Subtractive mixtures (*right*) can produce primary colors from the combination of other hues (canceling). Additive mixtures can be described by *logical union*, subtractive by *logical intersection*.

(*Vertical scale*) The brightness range from black to white. The steps are numbered according to a standard (Munsell) system of notation. (*Horizontal scale*) The saturation range from a hue approaching gray to a "pure" red.

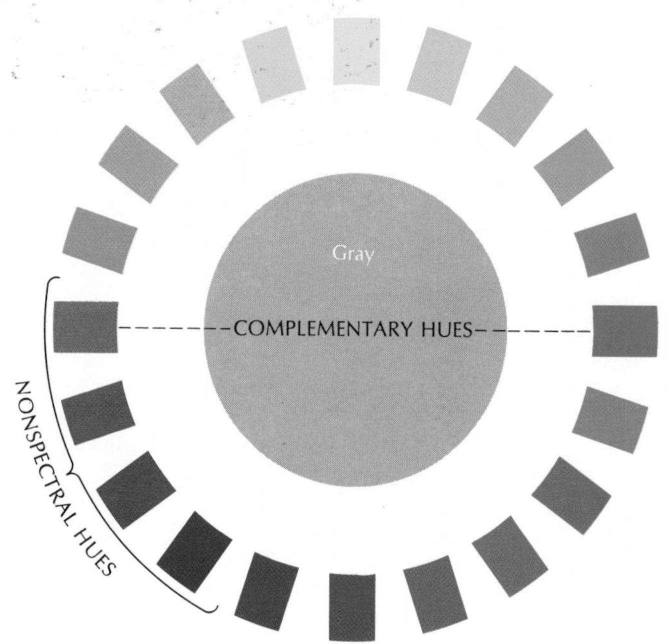

A color circle. The circle consists of spectral and nonspectral hues. The diameters of the circle connect complementary hues which, when mixed, produce gray. (See p. 64.)

(2) unique physical energy, and (3) special psychological experience.

(2) the existence of a single physical energy that ordinarily stimulates that end organ (for example, light), and (3) the availability of a unique sensory experience from that stimulation (for example, color). Any sensory system also includes a transducer (to change the physical energy into neural impulses), a transmission network of neural fibers (to carry the message and perhaps modify it by initial processing), and a central processing area (to make major computations, comparisons, and decisions). These complex systems produce our various sensory experiences.

On the basis of these criteria, we differentiate eight senses.

Using the criteria of a separate sensory end organ, unique perceptual experience, and appropriate physical energy, we can differentiate eight senses (see Table 3.1). The relation between the physical energies and their associated psychological experiences (for all eight senses) are discussed on the following pages. Particular attention is paid to the abilities of the newborn and young infant, since once he matures we will be interested in his perceptual abilities, including form perception, object constancy, size constancy, and the growth of person perception (these subjects are covered in the next chapter). There are three questions to consider for each sense modality: (1) What is an adequate stimulus (the physical energy that activates a receptor)? (2) What are the receptors that introduce the organism to a particular source of environmental energy exchange (the transducers of mechanical, electrical, or light energy into impulses that can be transmitted by neural cells)? (3) What are the sensory qualities of experience?

TABLE 3.1 The Eight Senses of Children

Sensory System	*Usual Physical Energy for the Sense*	*Sensory End Organ*	*Sensation*
1. Vision	Light energy of appropriate frequency	Eye	Color, brightness
2. Audition	Air vibrations	Ear	Pitch, loudness
3. Olfaction	Volatile substances	Olfactory receptors in nose	Pungent, sharp, sweet
4. Taste	Soluble substances	Taste receptors on tongue	Sweet, bitter, sour, salt
5. Touch	Physical displacement of the skin	Skin receptors	Object next to the skin
6. Movement	Acceleration and deceleration of the head	Semicircular canals in middle ear	Head and body changing position
7. Pain	*Any* strong stimulation. Tissue damage	Free nerve endings	Hurt
8. Temperature	Thermal activity	Thermal receptors in the skin	Warm, hot, cold

Vision

Neonates' sensitivity is studied by a variety of methods.

Investigators have studied the visual acuity of newborn infants by the following methods: conditioning the newborn to respond differentially to various visual stimuli, observing the tonic neck reflex (abrupt jerking back of head) in response to different light intensities, studying visual fixation, pursuit, and convergence movements in response to different visual stimuli (including colors), and observing general bodily activity, crying, heartbeat, and respiration under various conditions of illumination.

The newborn seems sensitive to brightness, he can coordinate his eyes a few days after birth, and he learns to fixate accurately in about four weeks.

The newborn infant is sensitive to most types of visual stimulation. For example, in a study of 944 infants by Peterson and Rainey (1910), 839 responded to light stimulation during the first week of life. Pratt, Nelson, and Sun (1930) reported similar results with 24 newborn infants; they presented flashes of light to the infants and found that 95 percent reacted to the stimulation. Although the neonate reacts to visual stimulation, a sustained visual fixation pattern is not present at birth; it appears in a few hours and reaches maturity in four or five weeks (Ling, 1942). Not only does the newborn infant not fixate but he cannot coordinate his eyes immediately after birth. His eye coordination improves rapidly during the first 36 hours (see Figure 3.3); the rapid improvement in eye coordination during visual fixation requires experience, indicating that both maturational and learning mechanisms are at work. The development of visual pursuit in infancy occurs in the following sequence: fixation, horizontal following, vertical following, and circular following (Jones, 1926; Morgan & Morgan, 1944). With increasing age visual pursuit movements improve in frequency and precision (McGinnis, 1930).

Adults see brightness, hue, and saturation.

The adult's subjective visual color field is a three-dimensional array. The basic psychological attributes of color vision are hue (related to the wavelength of light), brightness (related to the intensity of light), and saturation (very saturated colors are rich, full colors, while less saturated ones are pale). This set of relations may be represented by a color solid (see Plate 1). The psychological experience of color is not perfectly correlated with the physical variable of frequency. The tapering shape of the solid reflects the fact that maximal saturation is produced only at moderate levels of brightness. The relations among hue, saturation, and brightness are complex; they tell us little about the underlying processes.

Hershenson (1964) showed that neonates are sensitive to the dimension of brightness.

Hershenson (1964) has demonstrated that newborn infants are sensitive to brightness differences and that brightness is an ordered dimension. He used the newborn infant's ability to fixate in different spatial locations shortly after birth to measure brightness sensitivity. Working with an elaborate apparatus, including a 35 mm camera, infrared

FIGURE 3.3

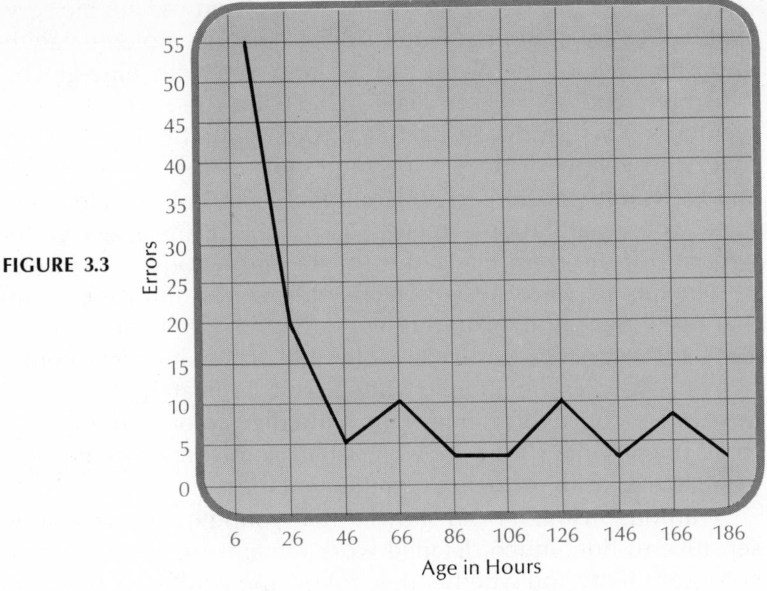

Coordination of the eyeballs of the newborn infant in following a light, shown as a function of age. (Adapted from Sherman & Sherman, 1929.)

photography, and special projection equipment, he showed that the newborn has a strong preference for an intermediate amount of brightness, compared with a very bright or a very dim light (Figure 3.4). There is no evidence concerning the newborn infant's sensitivity to saturation.

FIGURE 3.4

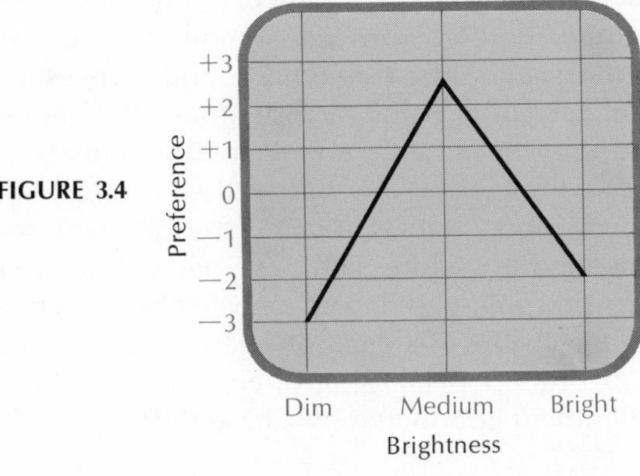

Curvilinear relation between neonate's preference and brightness of lights. (From Hershenson, 1964.)

All colors can be produced by mixing three primary colors.

Every hue has its complement, a color that can be mixed with the standard in an appropriate ratio to yield gray; complementary hues are opposite each other on the color circle—red with blue-green, yellow with blue, and so on (see Plate 2). Varying the ratio of two complementary colors produces a series of desaturated colors. Mixing a little blue with yellow decreases the saturation of the yellow but does not change its hue. Mixtures of noncomplementary colors yield intermediate hues whose saturation depends upon (a) the nearness of the components on the color circle and (b) the saturation of the components. In general, any mixture falls nearer the center than the components that make it up (the mixture is less saturated). There are many different ways to produce a particular color. All the colors experienced by a human observer (including white) may be matched by appropriate mixtures of only three hues. No particular color is required, but the three primary hues must be as far apart as possible on the color circle (see Plate 2) without being complementaries.

Although we believe that infants are sensitive to color, we know little about the laws which describe color combinations in infants.

Although Fantz (1958) showed that young infants are differentially sensitive to hue, much detailed work remains on how infants develop color sensitivity and whether they follow the adult laws of color mixing. If the adult color laws describe a newborn's experience, this implies that the laws are part of our biological organization. On the other hand, color may be learned at some later date through experience. These studies remain to be done, although the technique would be relatively simple. Using the detection situation, the infant could be tested for differential sensitivity to any particular color. Mixtures of colors could be developed and compared to the originals. Using the adult laws of color mixture, we could predict which mixtures should be seen as identical to other pure colors. If the neonate follows our expectations, then we know that the laws of color vision are genetically determined.

We agree that infants see colors, but evidence about neonates is ambiguous.

There is good agreement that infants react to color, but evidence on the extent of color vision in the newborn is ambiguous. Different hues must be equated for brightness, since infants can tell if one stimulus is brighter than another. However, stimuli have been matched by adults; as a result, we cannot be sure whether differences in infants' color preferences reflect color vision or brightness differences. With this ambiguity, we think the infant's ability to discriminate colors is limited but improves with age; by the end of the second year he can easily distinguish four colors (Staples, 1932). Twenty-seven percent of newborn infants respond to white light, 24 percent to yellow, 21 percent to green, 20 percent to red, and only eight percent to blue (Pratt, Nelson, & Sun, 1930). Notice, however, that the decreasing reactions to color also reflect decreasing brightness of the hues. In a rather ingenious experiment conducted by Chase (1937), a moving area of color was projected against either a colorless field equated for brightness or a background of another color. Monochromatic filters, equated so that there were no perceptible differences in brightness (for adults) were used to produce the colors. Both colors and background were projected upon a screen above the infant's head as he lay on his back. The infant's eyes following the moving area of color was considered evidence that he could distinguish the moving color from the background. Twenty-four infants between 15 and 70 days of age could discriminate perfectly between red and green, red and yellow-green, red and blue-green, yellow-green and blue-green, and green and yellow-green. These same infants failed to follow a colorless filter with a 25 percent darker spot in the center or a blue-green filter with a 24 percent darker spot in the center, suggesting that they were responding to color and not brightness. However, before we accept color vision in newborns, the brightness of various hues must be determined for their eye. If the newborn possesses only rod vision (no color cones), the brightness differences of various wavelengths (matched for adult spectral sensitivity) are on the order of six to eight. This order of brightness difference could easily be detected by newborn infants and would appear to reflect color vision.

The absolute threshold for color in the infant is unknown; adults are most sensitive to yellow.

We know very little about the absolute thresholds for hue in the infant (the amount of any pure wavelength that must be mixed with white light to produce a just perceptible experience of hue). With adults, we find that at 400 and 650 nanometers (the blue and red parts of the spectrum) the minimum increase necessary for a discernible difference in hue is much larger than in the intermediate wavelengths, around 500 nanometers (yellow). These results should be duplicated with infants and newborns to tell us whether spectral sensitivity differences are genetically determined by the structure of the eye or are learned through experience.

We also need information about the effect of interrupted light stimulation and light fusion in the infant.

Another area needing study is the effect of interrupted light stimulation on subjective brightness perception in the child. His eye may be stimulated by turning a light on and off very rapidly; at slow rates, a simple alternation of light and dark is seen. This experience changes to coarse and then to fine flicker as the on-off rate is increased. At some point he will experience a uniform brightness (critical fusion frequency, CFF). The judged brightness of the fused field corresponds to the amount of energy in the lighted sector corrected by the amount of time in which it is off. (With a light-dark ratio of 1:1, the fused field will appear half as bright as the illuminated sector.) This relation is known as the Talbot-Plateau effect. The CFF is an index of the discriminatory ability of the visual system. It increases with the intensity of light and is higher for cones than for rods. Little is known about the early course of development of the critical fusion frequency. However, McFarland, Warren, and Karis (1958) showed that the CFF steadily decreases from age 13 on. In general, for maximum CFF, light flashes should be of very short duration compared with the dark portion of the interval. The optimum light-on duration should comprise about 10 percent of the interval.

Studies of neonatal acuity suggest that young infants are comparable to an adult with 20/200 vision on the Snellen chart (20/20 is normal).

Forman, Cogan, and Gellis (1957) used optokinetic nystagmus as a method of measuring the acuity of the very young infant (under five days). Optokinetic nystagmus is obtained when a striped visual field is rotated about the infant's head. His eyes follow the field until they reach their maximum lateral movement; the eyes then quickly move back laterally and begin to follow the field again. This procedure allows the investigator to determine the minimum separation between lines (stripes in the visual field) which will elicit the lateral movement and quick return of the eyes. The notion is that when nystagmus first appears the infant is just beginning to differentiate lines from the background; we can thus measure the acuity of his visual system. When

FIGURE 3.5

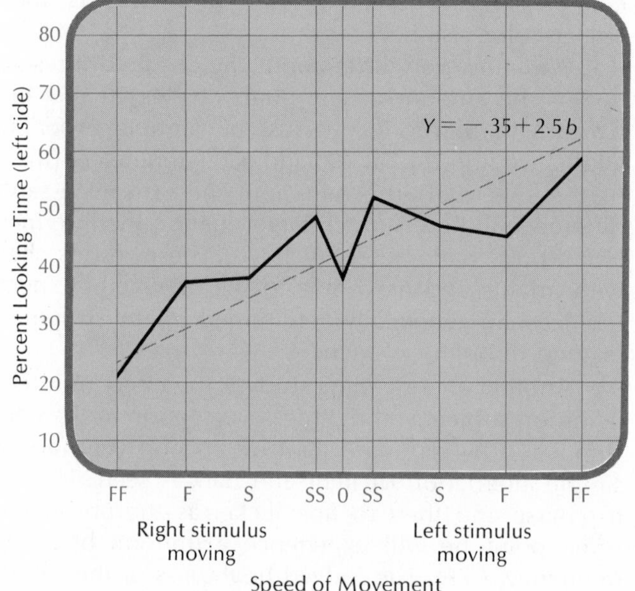

Amount of time spent looking at the left stimulus over several levels of speed of movement of the field. The infants were 24 weeks of age. The figure shows that the children look more at the faster-moving stimulus and that they are sensitive to movement by 24 weeks of age. (Silfen & Ames, 1964.)

five-day-old infants were tested, 93 percent of the cases produced nystagmus when stripes were 33.5 minutes of visual angle. [This result agrees with Fantz (1961).] When the width was 11 minutes of visual angle there was no response. The larger value reflects 20/200 vision in the notation of a Snellen chart (20/20 is considered normal), suggesting that the neonate has poor visual acuity but can see.

Infants are sensitive to amount of movement in their visual field.

Silfen and Ames (1964) found that infants (24 weeks of age) are sensitive to visual movement. They measured the amount of time infants looked at a moving versus a stationary field and found the results shown in Figure 3.5. This figure indicates that infants look more at the right side of their visual field (they were given a choice of looking to the left or right) when the right side is moving, and they look more to the left when that side is moving. In addition, the infants looked longer to the side that moved faster. These results show that infants are sensitive to movement, and to differences in rate of movement, by 24 weeks of age. In other studies, Silfen and Ames showed that infants as young as 16 weeks are sensitive to movement; however, their differential sensitivity was much less than in the case of their older peers. The 16-week-old infants could not differentiate the various rates of movement; they responded either to movement or no movement.

Audition

Sound includes amplitude and frequency.

Physical energy for audition is represented by two independent components—the frequency and the amplitude of vibration. These two physical dimensions are directly related to psychological phenomena—frequency to pitch and amplitude to loudness. The frequency of a sound is defined by the number of pressure changes per second; intensity is proportional to the square of pressure. In the adult interactions between pitch and loudness produce a third psychological experience—volume. Although the auditory mechanism of the newborn infant is sufficiently well developed to be functional, he probably hears little in his early postnatal hours; the middle ear is obstructed with fluid. Electric bells, wooden bells, tuning forks, and many other items have been used to test the hearing of newborn infants (Pratt, Nelson, & Sun, 1930), who respond about half the time to these auditory stimuli.

The infant responds to pitch, intensity, and duration of sound a day after birth.

We do know that the neonate responds differentially to three dimensions of auditory stimuli: pitch, intensity, and duration (Stubbs, 1934). The movements of neonates increase with increases in sound intensities, and they also respond with progressively more activity to tones of higher pitch within the frequency range of 128 to 4096 cycles per second. The neonate's response also increases as the duration of the stimulus is lengthened. However, we know little about the course of this sensitivity over age.

Olfaction

Neonates habituate to smells, and they show differential sensitivity to varying concentrations of odor.

Early investigators reported differential responses in infants to markedly different odors. They reported vigorous sucking in response to some odors and facial grimaces and turning away in response to strong, unpleasant odors like ammonia. However, these differences were highly variable (Pratt, Nelson, & Sun, 1930). Later work by Lipsitt, Engen, and Kaye (1963) on developmental changes in the olfactory threshold of the neonate sheds new light on this phenomenon. Utilizing a psychophysical technique to assess odor perception in the newborn, Lipsitt and associates reported that differential responsiveness of newborns to different olfactory stimuli does occur. They also suggested that the neonate's response to successive stimulation of single odors changes: Sensory adaptation occurs. Their study of absolute threshold used a graded set of seven steps of asafetida (a gum resin of various oriental plants of the carrot family). If no response was obtained to the weakest of the seven solutions, the next strongest solution was administered, and so on, until the infant's response threshold had been obtained for that day. This was done repeatedly at 24-hour intervals with a no-odor trial occurring before each odor administration. The responses the infants made to the different olfactory stimuli (general body activity and respiration) were recorded. Ten newborn infants were given this ascending scale of odor stimuli on four consecutive days, beginning with the first day of life. The results show a decreasing threshold of sensitivity; the infant reacted to a smaller and smaller percent solution over the four successive days, with most of the drop occurring from day one to day two. Whether this effect may be attributed to maturation or to learning cannot be known from Lipsitt's study, since it did not include a group of infants tested on day four only.

Taste

Taste receptors are not simply salt, sour, sweet, and bitter; complex neural codes tell us the flavor of foods.

Adult taste sensations have been analyzed into four basic ingredients: sweet, sour, bitter, and salt, because these four flavors represent differentially sensitive areas of the tongue. However, there is a good deal of recent evidence which indicates that taste receptors are not as simple as our four-sensation model suggests (see Remarks: Theory). Rate of firing from a single nerve fiber in the tongue of the cat in response to different concentrations of salt solution and pure water shows that both water and salt, and in some cases other substances, stimulate the same nerve fiber. This is contrary to our original assumption of four different kinds of receptors. Probably the code of several different nerves gives us a particular sensation of taste and not the specific nerves which are active.

Infants prefer sweet, salt, sour, and bitter in that order.

Little research on infants' taste exists, partly because of the difficulty of specifying the stimulus and partly because of the confounding of taste and smell (most taste experiences are a combination of these two senses). Also, taste is of relatively minor importance when compared with sight or hearing. Certain items are known: Sweet is the preferred taste for infants, as measured by the presence or absence of sucking (Pratt, Nelson, & Sun, 1930). Even in the very early days after birth, infants show increased sucking responses to sugar and produce what adults believe are signs of pleasure. Sweet tastes disrupt the infant's pulse and breathing less than other sensations. Next in the hierarchy of preference comes salt. The infant's breathing and circula-

REMARKS: THEORY—PHYSIOLOGY AND SENSORY QUALITY

Originally we thought that taste qualities included only sweet, salt, sour, and bitter; this assumption led to a search for specific taste buds associated with these qualities. The simple notion that experienced quality is closely related to physiological structure derives from the doctrine of *specific nerve energies,* formulated early in the nineteenth century by Sir Charles Bell and Johannes Müller (Murphy, 1949). The doctrine says that we are aware only of the state of our nerves, not of external stimuli. Any stimulation of the taste buds gives rise to experiences of taste. It was simple to infer that some taste buds should produce the experience of sweet, others of salt, sour, or bitter.

We now know there are not specific receptors for each taste quality. Some receptor cells respond only to a few chemicals, while others respond to several primary tastes. Advances in electrophysiology have made it possible to record the nerve impulses from a single taste nerve fiber (isolated from the bundles of such fibers that make up a nerve). As a solution, such as sugar, increases in concentration, there is a corresponding increase in the number of impulses fired by the nerve fiber. Other taste substances will also produce impulses in the same fiber but at different thresholds. In the rat, for example, thresholds based on the minimum concentration of the substance that can be detected can be arranged in order from low to high for the following substances: quinine, hydrochloric acid, sodium chloride, potassium chloride, and sucrose. The taste mechanism reacts most readily to quinine (bitter) and is least sensitive to sucrose (sweet).

Impulses in the nerve fibers for taste alone do not indicate which of several substances was applied to the tongue. How do we account for the fact that different substances taste different? We must use some sort of "code," which includes the frequency of stimulation in neighboring fibers and the relative amounts of parallel activity in units that happen to be more sensitive to one kind of stimulation than to another (Pfaffmann, 1964). While the doctrine of specific nerve energies is still appropriate, it must not be allowed to misguide us into oversimplified theories of the relation of phenomenal experience to activity in our nervous systems.

tion are disrupted by sour and bitter solutions compared with his reaction to either sweet or salt. Infants make grimaces of dislike and disgust when they are offered quinine solutions. However, these reactions may result from higher sensitivity to quinine (bitter) than to sugar (sweet).

Touch

Touch is mediated by any differential gradiant on the skin—either pressure or lifting of an object.

Sensitivity to touch is mediated by a variety of transducing receptors in the skin. For a long time the adequate stimulus for touch was thought to be pressure against the skin. Now we think that any displacement, including that produced by lifting an object attached to the skin [a decrease in pressure (Woodworth & Schlosberg, 1954)] can produce the sensation of touch. Observations of this sort led to a gradient theory of touch which proposes that receptors are mechanically stimulated by distortion or stretching of the surface of the skin. The magnitude of stimulation must vary with the pressure gradient at any given point.

Touch is active during the third month of foetal life around the mouth and face.

Reactions to touch have been observed in the third month of *foetal* life (Hooker, 1952). Touch sensitivity follows a cephalo-caudal course of development; it begins in the nose and mouth area and moves toward the lower regions. Sucking and head turning in the direction of contact is another response system associated with touch. The closer we touch to the mouth area, the more likely we are to produce head turning and reflexive sucking in the foetus or neonate. The response is stronger when an infant is awake than when he is asleep. The turning and sucking response is also more vigorous following strong rather than weak stimulation. Six months following birth, the infant has a well-differentiated sense of where tactile stimulation is applied. Before that time, except in the mouth region, we find an undifferentiated increase in total activity to touch, but little localization.

Balance—Kinesthesis

Kinesthesis and balance help us maintain our posture through space.

Kinesthesis is the sense of where we are and how we are moving. These effects are detected by sense organs in the joints and muscles and by balance organs in the inner ear. It is convenient to differentiate these two types of information: We call feedback from the musculature and joints kinesthesis, while reserving the term balance for the organs which register our relation to gravity and motion. If we stumble, we promptly make corrective movements. The kinesthetic sense organs in muscles and joints give us feedback—they tell us where we are. This feedback from the kinesthetic sense is so rapid that corrective actions are often taken before we are aware that something has happened.

We know that babies do not like to be dropped.

Relatively little work has been done on the effect of moving children's bodies through space. Watson (1925) maintained that suddenly dropping an infant produces fear; he concluded that fear of falling is inborn. Later studies indicate this is not true for all infants. Probably an infant's response is a joint function of autonomic reactivity, personal security, and prior experience with falling.

People become dizzy because their semicircular canals habituate to continued rotation.

Bodily rotation affects three semicircular canals; these canals are filled with endolymph, which is displaced when the head accelerates. The amount of displacement is related to the rate of acceleration; when a person is accelerated slowly or at a moderate rate, information from the canals says he is changing speed slowly. When acceleration becomes more extreme, the response is also more vigorous. Most people become dizzy and lose their balance following rapid rotation, due to habituation of the balance centers. Reflex eye movements following body rotation are responsible for the apparent spinning of the world when we stop (these eye movements are called nystagmus). Ballet dancers have known for a long time how to overcome the effects of rapid body rotation. The trick is to keep the visual world stable and stimulate the semicircular canals (the canals respond only to *changes* in speed; they give no sensation of continued movement). To stabilize the visual world, a dancer focuses her eyes on a single spot while her body is rotating; when she must, she moves her head rapidly and immediately stops to focus her eyes on another spot. Rapid movement and stopping plus focusing on a spot will stabilize the visual world and keep the semicircular canals stimulated—resulting in no dizziness!

Pain

Pain is a combination of tissue injury and anxiety.

Pain is a difficult sensation to define, although everyone knows it from personal experience. A sharp or dull unpleasant hurt describes the experience; pain results from damage to an area with free nerve endings. There are parts of the body without nerve endings; these areas are insensitive to pain. One such area is the cortex of the brain—although there are blood vessels in the brain that do contain free nerve endings; these vessels probably account for headaches.

Pain is difficult to study without confounding touch; to avoid this problem, use radiant heat.

Pain is a difficult sensation to study; it is almost always confounded with touch. The only practical method of studying pain without touch is to focus a beam of intense light onto the forehead or some other sensitive area of the body. The heat will eventually cause pain, depending on the intensity of the light, without the accompanying sensation of touch.

Newborns are insensitive to pain compared with infants and children.

The response to pain is less in newborns (particularly if they are premature) than in older children. That infants are relatively insensitive immediately after birth (McGraw, 1943) has led some individuals to speculate that birth itself adapts (makes insensitive) the baby's receptors. Others have suggested that the brain centers responsible for localization of pain are inadequately developed in the neonate. A single painful stimulation of the newborn often produces no response. However, normal newborns respond to repeated painful stimuli by attempting to withdraw their whole body or by crying (Figure 3.6). The first response to pain is crying, and it occurs early in infancy. The birth cry is not from pain; it is a reflex following the infant's first breath. By the time an infant is six months old his reaction to pain is specific and localized; he responds to pain by moving the appropriate limb and not his whole body.

Thermal sensitivity

Thermal sensitivity includes both warm and cold receptors.

It is not at all clear that the sensations of warm and cold are two ends of the same continuum. Obviously, heat is a single physical dimension, but two factors lead us to think warm and cold are not a single sensory dimension: (1) their thresholds are different and (2) spots on the skin that are sensitive to warmth are not necessarily sensitive to cold. In addition, we can produce paradoxical cold by stimulating cold receptors with a warm stimulus. The sensation of warmth can be transmitted either by contact or radiation.

Body heat is regulated by sensing mechanisms in the skin; we can cool the blood externally and kill an animal without changing its heat transfer.

The detection of external thermal conditions and body temperature regulation are intimately connected. For example, animals may be cooled by pumping their blood into an external cooling system while they are in a room of normal temperature. They experience no shivering or other symptoms of cold. In fact, one can lower blood temperature until the heart stops beating without getting any body reaction to the chilling. Under ordinary conditions the animal is warmed or cooled by heat exchange through its skin. However, when this process is bypassed there is no sensation of cooling, and the animal may die without even realizing he is losing heat.

Infants prefer milk at about body temperature, although they can be trained to like warmer or colder food.

The newborn infant is responsive to thermal changes; sharp deviations from his own body temperature (too warm or too cold) tend to increase his level of activity. The test mothers make to determine the temperature of an infant's formula (applying milk to the inside of the wrist) is adequate only because he is fairly insensitive. Jensen (1932) tested the preferences of 17 newborn infants for milk of various temperatures by measuring their sucking; increases in rate were assumed to indicate preference. A total of 450 stimulations were given. The range of individual preferences for warm milk was 120 to 150 degrees F. For cold stimuli the range was 41 to 50 degrees F. Preferences tended to remain constant for each infant during the tests. Pratt, Nelson, and Sun (1930) studied the responses of 21 newborn infants to a cold cylinder (average temperature 52 degrees F) applied to the forehead

FIGURE 3.6

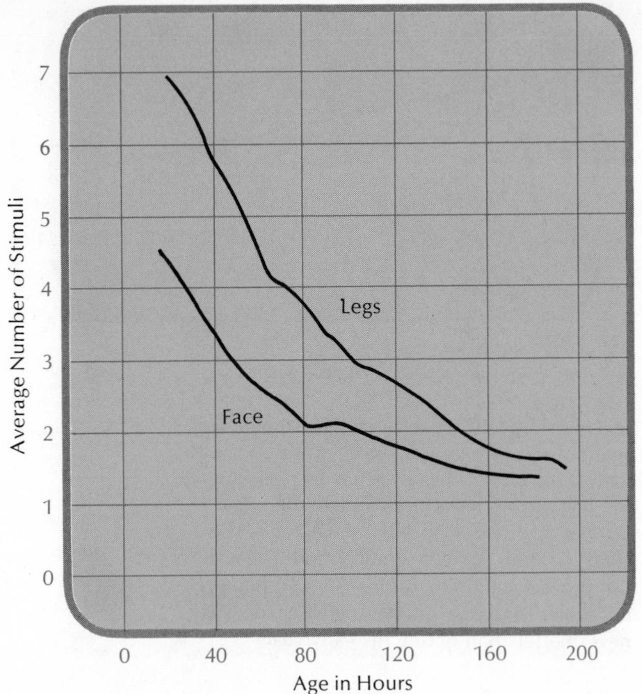

Number of pain stimuli applied to face and leg which are necessary to produce a response from infants of different ages. Note that newborns need many more stimuli. (Adapted from Sherman & Sherman, 1929.)

and the inside surface of the neonate's leg. The neonates responded to 93 percent of these stimulations; over half of the responses to cold stimulation on the forehead involved head movements, while about three fourths of the responses to leg stimulation involved flexion or extension of the legs.

Developmental trends in sensitivity

Age trends in sensitivity show a rapid development during the first few weeks of life and then a gradual decline.

The newborn's sensory abilities are well developed at birth; he can *detect* the same simple stimuli as an adult. During an early period in his life (the first few days) he is relatively insensitive. Following this initial period his sensitivity increases rapidly, in many cases exceeding that of the adult (Pollack, 1963). Following this initial increase in his sensitivity (see Figure 3.7) the infant gradually becomes less sensitive to physical changes in his environment. This fact contradicts our usual notion that adults are more sensitive to their surroundings than are

FIGURE 3.7

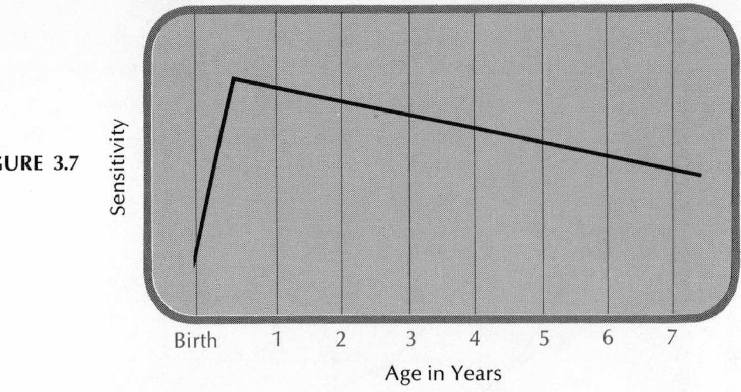

The general trend of sensitivity to stimuli over age; note that there is a rapid increase in sensitivity after birth, which reaches its peak during the first year. Following this peak there is a gradual decrease in sensitivity with age. The child is able to perceive much more because he can process multidimensional stimuli; however, his ability to detect simple energy changes is never better than during his early years.

children. The infant's sensitivity (sensation) decreased with age, but the ability of the infant and child to use information received from his senses (perception) increases rapidly during these same years. The net effect is that, although the child loses some of his sensitivity, he is better able to handle perceptual problems because he requires less information from his senses; the child is able to supply missing information from his own past experience.

SUMMARY

1 A distinction should be made between sensory abilities (simple peripheral processes) and perceptual abilities (more complex central activities).

2 The notion of sensitivity is basic to an understanding of sensation. Estimates of sensitivity in the infant result from two different processes—receptor functions and decision processes; both factors must be considered.

3 There are various response measures that may be used in studying sensory abilities in the neonate and young child. Central among these are conditioned responses, physiological measures of bodily activity, and ocular orientation.

4 The theory of signal detection presents the most adequate model of decision processes and sensory functioning available. The reader should understand the notions of likelihood ratio, decision rule, and criterion.

5 There are eight basic senses. These are differentiated by a unique (1) sensory end organ, (2) physical energy, and (3) psychological experience associated with each sense.

6 The newborn is sensitive to brightness and several hues, but seems insensitive to saturation.

7 He is also sensitive to pitch, loudness, and duration of tones.

8 Lipsitt has shown that the neonate can differentiate concentrations of various smells and shows heightened sensitivity over time.

9 Our classification of tastes into four is much too simple. There must be a complex code which tells us the particular taste we are experiencing.

10 The foetus is sensitive to touch and shows a cephalo-caudal growth in this ability.

11 The only thing we know of balance is that young infants do not like to be dropped.

12 The infant's sensitivity to pain is low immediately after birth, but gradually increases and becomes more differentiated. At first, the baby shows only a gross response to injury, but with age he tends to move the particular area that is hurt.

13 The trend in infants' sensitivity is: A low initial value followed by sharply increasing sensitivity; after this sensitivity increase there is a gradual decline into the adult years. Older children seem more sensitive than their younger peers because the older child's *perceptual* abilities compensate; he requires less information to make the same decision.

FURTHER READINGS

Geldard, F. A. *The human senses.* New York: Wiley, 1953.

Riesen, A. H. Receptor functions. In P. H. Mussen (Ed.), *Handbook of research methods in child development.* New York: Wiley, 1960.

REFERENCES

Bartley, S. H. *Principles of perception.* New York: Harper & Row, 1958.

Chase, W. P. Color vision in infants. *Journal of Experimental Psychology,* 1937, **20,** 203-222.

Fantz, R. L. Pattern vision in young infants. *Psychological Record,* 1958, **8,** 43.

Fantz, R. L. The origin of form perception. *Scientific American,* 1961, **204,** 5, 66–72.

Forman, J. J., Cogan, D. G., & Gellis, S. S. An apparatus for grading the visual acuity of infants on the basis of opticokinetic nystagmus. *Pediatrics,* 1957, **19,** 1088–1092.

Green, D. M., & Swets, J. A. *Signal detection theory and psychophysics.* New York: Wiley, 1966.

Hershenson, M. Visual discrimination in the human newborn. *Journal of Comparative and Physiological Psychology,* 1964, **58,** 270–276.

Hooker, D. *The prenatal origin of behavior.* Lawrence, Kan.: University of Kansas Press, 1952.

Jensen, K. Differential reactions to taste and temperature stimuli in newborn infants. *Genetic Psychology Monograph,* 1932, **12,** 361–479.

Jones, M. C. The development of early behavior patterns in young children. *Journal of Genetic Psychology,* 1926, **33,** 537–585.

Ling, B. A genetic study of sustained visual fixation and associated behavior in the human infant from birth to six months. *Journal of Genetic Psychology,* 1942, **61,** 227–277.

Lipsitt, L., Engen, T., & Kaye, H. Developmental changes in the olfactory threshold of the neonate. *Child Development,* 1963, **34,** 371–376.

McFarland, R. A., Warren, A. B., & Karis, C. Alterations in critical flicker frequency as a function of age and light-dark ratio. *Journal of Experimental Psychology,* 1958, **56,** 529–538.

McGinnis, J. M. Eye-movements and optic nystagmus in early infancy. *Genetic Psychology Monograph,* 1930, **8,** 321–430.

McGraw, M. B. *The neuromuscular maturation of the human infant.* New York: Columbia University Press, 1943.

Morgan, S. S., & Morgan, J. J. B. An examination of the development of certain adaptive behavior in infants. *Journal of Pediatrics,* 1944, **25,** 168–177.

Murphy, G. *Historical introduction to modern psychology.* New York: Harcourt, Brace & World, 1949.

Peterson, F., & Rainey, L. H. The beginnings of mind in the newborn. *Bulletin Lying in Hospital of New York City,* 1910, **7,** 99–122.

Pfaffmann, C. Taste, its sensory and motivating properties. *American Scientist,* 1964, **52,** 197–206.

Pollack, R. H. Contour detectability threshold as a function of chronological age. *Perceptual and Motor Skills,* 1963, **17,** 411–417.

Pratt, K. C., Nelson, A. K., & Sun, K. H. *The behavior of the newborn infant.* Columbus, O.: Ohio State University Press, 1930.

Sherman, M., & Sherman, I. C. *The process of human behavior.* New York: Norton, 1929.

Silfen, C., & Ames, E. Visual movement preference in the human infant. *Eastern Psychological Association paper,* 1964.

Smith, J. M. The relative brightness values of three hues for newborn infants. *University of Iowa Studies in Child Welfare,* 1936, **12,** 91–140.

Staples, R. The responses of infants to color. *Journal of Experimental Psychology,* 1932, **15,** 119–141.

Stubbs, E. M. The effect of the factors of duration, intensity, and pitch of sound stimuli on the responses of newborn infants. *University of Iowa Studies in Child Welfare*, 1934, **9,** No. 4, 75–135.

Watson, J. B. *Behaviorism* (rev. ed., 1930). New York: Norton, 1925.

Woodworth, R. S., & Schlosberg, H. *Experimental psychology*. New York: Holt, 1954.

4 PERCEPTUAL GROWTH

Beauty is bought by judgment of the eye,
Not utter'd by base sale of chapmen's tongues.
LOVE'S LABOUR'S LOST

In this chapter, three views of perceptual development are outlined and the problems of studying infant perception are explored. Some empirical findings are reviewed concerning depth perception, form perception, and the effects of set on seeing. Finally, recent work on tachistoscopic recognition and the differentiation of letters is presented along with motivational influences on perception.

Perception is an intermediate stage of information processing between sensation and cognition.

Most theorists consider perception an intermediate stage in the transmission of information from sensory end organs to the central processes of cognition. Perception is a necessary step in the development of processes which, when joined in coordinated sequences, form the thinking apparatus of the normal adult. Perception is the link between innately given organization of the senses and more complex cognitive processes.

The infant is capable of fairly complex perceptions.

The infant is capable of more complex perceptual operations than we thought possible a few years ago; he is sensitive to brightness, color, texture, and some complex stimuli, and these abilities can be influenced soon after birth. Fantz (1963) showed that infants stop looking at familiar stimuli and shift their attention to novel objects of the same complexity.

VIEWS OF PERCEPTUAL DEVELOPMENT

Predeterminism (genetic determination) and environmentalism (experience) were

Explanations of newborn perception range from Diety to DNA. The nativist believes in genetically determined perceptual abilities—that the human newborn is capable of seeing order in his universe from the moment of birth. On the other hand, the empiricist maintains that the *early explanations of perceptual development.*

newborn learns his perceptual abilities through experience. Modern conceptions stress interaction; both primitive innate mechanisms and learning are involved in perceptual development.

Mueller proposed a nativistic theory of perception in his doctrine of the specific energy of nerves.

Johannes Mueller [1948 (1838)] formally proposed a nativistic theory of perception. His notion of the specific energy of nerves assumed that the mind can have direct contact only with the states of nerves and not with external bodies. Mueller believed that because spatial relations are preserved in the arrangement of the optic nerve fibers, the mind directly perceives the spatial relations of the retinal image—a very precise statement of a pre-established harmony among retinal cells, nerve fibers, perceptual processes, and the external world. This belief in nativism had been proposed by Descartes [1927 (1650)] as innate ideas and by Kant [1929 (1781)] as *a priori* intuitions.

Predeterminism was also proposed by Gestalt psychologists, who believed that the mind's structure determines how we see.

The nativist position on perceptual development was also supported by members of the Gestalt school (Wertheimer, 1958), who claimed that the organization of perceptual objects is given by the physiological structure of the nervous system; the perceptual objects and the rules that produce them are genetically determined. The Gestalt school articulated several rules of perception (see Figure 4.1A): (1) nearness—things that are close together in the perceptual field are seen as a unit; (2) similarity—items in the perceptual field that are alike are seen as a unit; (3) good continuation—lines that continue a contour in a straight line or project a curve are viewed as a unit; and (4) good form—there are certain forms that are particularly good perceptual objects (for example, squares, circles, triangles). These forms tend to reduce the size of illusions when one is imbedded within a form (see Figure 4.1B).

FIGURE 4.1A

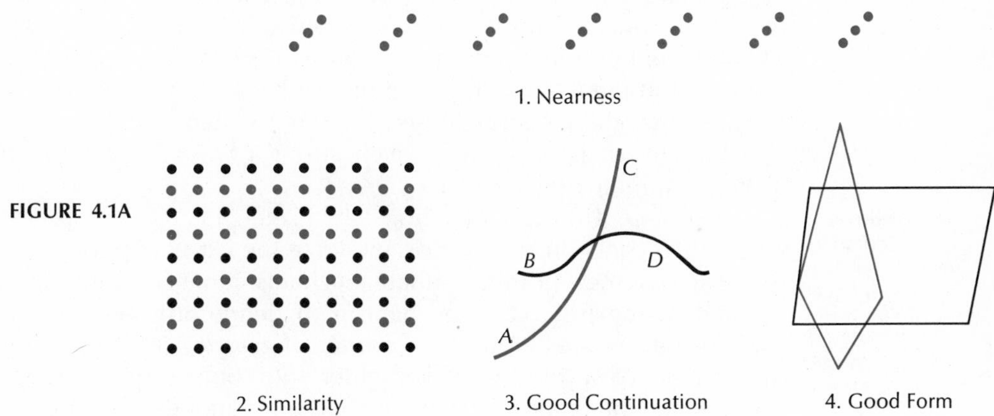

Examples of four principles of perceptual organization proposed by the Gestalt school of perception.

FIGURE 4.1B

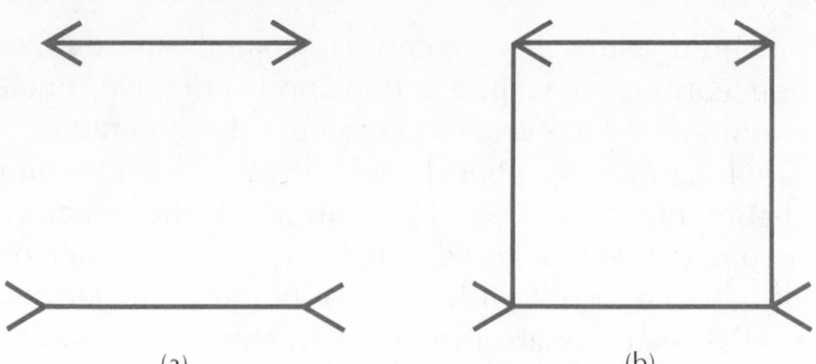

The Mueller-Lyer illusion (a) and the same illusion (b) embedded in a good figure (square). Notice that the illusion creates the perception of a longer second line when compared to the top line in (a), but the good form of the square cancels the illusion and the sides appear to be of equal length.

British empiricism championed the association of ideas as an explanation of perceptual development.

On the side of *tabula rasa* (blank mind) stands a long line of British empiricists, from Hobbes [1948 (1651)] through Locke [1948 (1690)]. In support of empiricism, it was pointed out that we align the fovea with any object that comes under attention, so that each retinal point can be associated with an intensity and a particular sensation of movement. We learn that *B* is between *A* and *C* because (in continuous movements) the signs are experienced in the order *A, B, C.* This empirical view of perceptual development says that we must learn discriminations among items and also that we must learn to group sensations to form perceptual objects. For example, we learn that four equal straight lines connected at right angles form the perceptual object we call a square. Empirical views of perceptual development say that the most important determinant of growth is experience; they feel that little or nothing is predetermined by genetic endowment. Explanations of how the child comes to see are left to theories of learning; the mechanism of association is given strong priority. The next chapter outlines stimulus-response associations.

Hebb and Piaget assume primitive genetic mechanisms and interaction with the world are necessary for learning to see.

Two recent theorists (Hebb, 1949; Piaget, 1950) have proposed an alternative conception that may integrate the extreme positions. These theorists assume a primitive innate mechanism that separates figure and ground. Using this basic mechanism to define attributes, the infant, by moving his eyes along the contour of a form, is assumed to learn the *orders* of attributes which enter into object perception. Thus, through the interaction of an innate figure-ground mechanism, learning, and eye movements the infant constructs his world.

Line detecting mechanisms

Research shows the existence of innate mechanisms for detecting slope and movement.

The nativism-environmentalism issue is complex; work by Hubel and Wiesel (1963) shows that the innate mechanisms of slope and movement detection require postnatal stimulation to continue functioning. Newborn kittens reared with their eyes closed for two months showed no electrical activity in those cells which normally detect line slope. The innate structure was lost during the period of disuse. How much stimulation is required to maintain the mechanisms is not known; it is clear that some patterning of light is required to maintain structures that develop from innate mechanisms.

PERCEPTUAL LEARNING

Theories of perceptual learning include sensory enrichment, motor response, and the acquired distinctiveness of cues.

Other notions of perceptual learning say that all improvement in perceptual abilities comes about through *enrichment* of the stimulus by the addition of associations. There are several subclasses of the enrichment theory; some are cognitively oriented and others response oriented. Some cognitive theories view perception as unconscious problem-solving (Bruner, 1957) while others see perceptual growth as the development of schemata (Piaget, 1950). Response-oriented theories of perceptual development may also be divided into two types. One response theory proposes that perception reflects the world by making a motor copy of it. Hebb (1949) and Piaget (1950) are similar but propose sensory-motor activity instead of motor activity as the important determiner of perceptual development. However, the most popular response theory of perceptual development goes under the title of acquired distinctiveness of cues. The notion is that two items which are similar become unique by acquiring distinctive associations. For example, two hues that are similar may be differentiated by associating one with a dress and the other with a sailboat. The theory assumes that the acquisition of differential associations makes each stimulus more unique.

The theory of acquired distinctiveness assumes that we add associations to stimuli to increase their discriminability.

The theory of acquired distinctiveness of cues assumes that the perceptual environment is sparse; the only way to differentiate stimuli is to add to their information content by collecting associations. However, the opposite seems to be the case: Perceptual systems collect an enormous amount of information. Perception is the reduction of information; the problem is to filter important information from noise and irrelevant stimuli. The task for the infant and child is to choose the important or distinctive features of perceptual input and to make his decision on this basis. A good example of this occurs in the study by Gibson, Pick, Osser, and Hammond (1962), which explored distinctive and irrelevant features of letters for children of varying ages. Their results demonstrated that young children do not attend to the correct differentiating features of the letters; only older children differentiate and attend to the proper features. Distinctive features are invariant; they do not change under minor transformations of the stimulus. For example, a c is curved in a particular direction whether it is red, blue, written, typed, small, or large. It is this sort of feature that the child must find and appreciate before he can learn to see.

OBSERVATION OF THE NEWBORN

Perceptual development was speculated about for centuries; now, students of seeing watch the neonate and infant.

Speculation and debate on the origins of perception is an ancient hobby. Early sources of information were the armchair or the experimental observation of adults. However, these inappropriate procedures have recently been supplanted by direct observations of the newborn and young infant. Investigators stopped speculating about development of the perceptual system and started examining infant perception. Assessment of perception in the newborn and young infant is complicated by the limitation of available response patterns; traditional psychophysical methods, requiring verbal instructions and responses, are inappropriate. Techniques must be developed which take into consideration the restricted capabilities of the newborn. Sucking, ocular orientation, heart rate, skin conductance, conditioned responses, and limb movement are now used as indicators of perceptual sensitivity. Only long-term gains in understanding will tell us if the infant's responses adequately mirror his perceptions.

We learn a good deal about the neonate's visual world by measuring his ocular orientations.

Information about the stimulus at which the newborn is looking can provide valuable insights into his perceptual world. The early world of the infant probably consists of simple attributes and a few innate perceptual abilities. From this base he constructs other perceptual processes by grouping sets of attributes into objects. We need to know: (1) what are his innate abilities and (2) what attributes can he see?

To ascribe a dimension to infant perception we must find differences among three levels of a stimulus dimension.

Before we can make sense of experiments with neonates, we must establish some criteria by which we may know that a baby is sensitive to a *dimension* and is not merely responding to an *attribute* of the stimulus. Before we can know that an infant is sensitive to a dimension, he must show us that he possesses an ordering of sensory attributes. It is entirely possible to find differences between pairs of stimuli and yet know nothing about whether the infant can order them.

For example, the infant may be sensitive to only one particular level of brightness, and he may ignore all others. If we tested this infant we would find that he makes differential responses when that level of brightness is compared to several others, but we would find no differences among the other levels of brightness. From these results we should conclude that the infant is sensitive to *one* level of brightness. Our hypothetical example is exactly what we find in many cases of newborn perception. However, we persist in talking about dimensions of sensitivity. Only when the investigation has determined that infants can differentially respond to *three* separate stimuli can we say anything about a dimension. In all other cases where there are less than three objects and less than three differences among objects, we can only say that the infant is interested in one of the objects to the exclusion of the others.

Fantz showed that infants are differentially sensitive to complex patterns.

Fantz (1958, 1961) conducted a series of pioneer experiments to determine whether visual organization and patterning are present in very young infants. His response measure was differential looking time. For example, four black and white patterns (horizontal stripes, bull's-eye, checkerboard, and gray patch) were presented (with gray as a standard) in random order (Fantz, 1958). The objects were each compared with a standard gray field (presented simultaneously). Fixation required that the corneal reflection (a reflected image of the stimulus) appear in the center of the newborn's pupil. Preference was determined by recording the length of fixation for each of the stimulus objects. The subjects were 30 human infants observed at weekly intervals from one to 15 weeks of age. Differential preferences were found when the ages were combined.

There are many confounded variables that must be eliminated before we can say whether the infant is sensitive to pattern, form, color, lines, or angles.

From this evidence, the author suggested that infants one week old are capable of pattern and form perception. The data do show that infants respond differentially to stimuli, but to say they possess form perception is a large step. These data show only that the neonate is sensitive to *some* difference between the stimuli. He may be sensitive to the number of lines, the number of angles, the length of the line, the brightness, the acuteness of the angle, or any number of other variables on which they differ. We need to use stimuli that differ only in pattern; if the infant reacts differentially to them, we can say something about form perception.

Fantz showed that infants prefer to view a regular face or a scrambled face rather than a pink and black oval.

In another study (Fantz, 1961), 49 subjects, four days to six months of age, were presented three flat objects painted black on a pink background (see Figure 4.2). The first object was a face painted in black; in the second the features were rearranged and scrambled; the third stimulus was an oval with a solid patch of black equal in area to that covered by the features on each of the other two stimuli. All

FIGURE 4.2

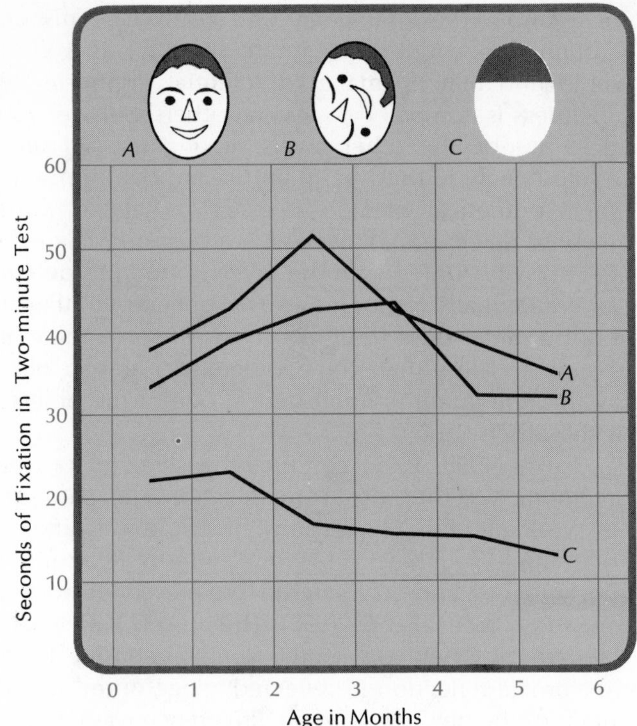

Fantz' test of pattern preference in infants. The lines show infants' fixation in seconds toward the face, the scrambled face, and the black and white oval. Young infants prefer complex stimuli as opposed to a simple oval, but do not differentiate faces. (From Fantz, 1961.)

possible pairs of these three stimuli were presented to the infants. For all age levels, the infants looked most at the real and scrambled patterns and infrequently at the control pattern. Preferences were consistent, but not strong, and other evidence suggests we interpret these data cautiously.

Hershenson showed that differential preferences for faces do not exist among newborns.

Hershenson (1964) attempted to replicate this study of preferences for *artificial* faces and found no significant preferences in newborns. Preference for the schematic human face apparently is not present in newborns, but may develop at a relatively early age. These discrepant results suggest we exercise great care in how we collect and analyze observations of infants.

REMARKS: THEORY AND METHOD

The basic procedure of the stimulus-preference method is to present stimulus objects simultaneously in all possible combinations of two (Torgerson, 1958). The resulting choices reflect (at least) ordinal relations among the stimuli along the dimension to which the infant is responding. Position preferences are corrected by counterbalancing the side on which each stimulus appears or by presenting the stimuli according to optimum orders which control order of presentation, side of presentation, and spacing of stimuli (Ross, 1934). If the infant fixates on one object significantly more than on another, a preference has been found. Although differential preference indicates that the infant is capable of discriminating between the two stimuli shown as a pair, the finding of no preference, unfortunately, does not indicate inability to discriminate. As is always the case with negative results, we cannot then conclude that no difference exists between the two stimuli.

There is a second problem if the infant does not look at both stimuli in each combination. The question is, must he actively compare the stimuli before we can write about discrimination or is it enough to assume that the infant has already looked at both of them through peripheral vision and is fixated on the one in which he has some interest? A careful investigator should assure himself that the infant has looked at *both* stimuli before making inferences about pair preferences. The task of determining the aspects of stimulus structure that correlate with the infant's response set can be simplified by using unidimensional stimuli. We never know for certain that an infant is responding to the particular dimension we chose to manipulate. A partial solution to this dilemma involves the study of *patterns* of responses in a wide variety of situations and the building of models of the perceiving infant. By discovering consistent patterns in the structure of the infant's response to stimuli, we may gradually define a set of dimensions that are optimal—optimal in the sense of requiring few dimensions to describe the widest possible set of stimuli to which the infant is exposed.

Now that interest in infants' perception is growing, we need to separate the factors that contribute to seeing.

Fantz stimulated our present interest in the nature of infant perception, and the preference method is a valuable tool for the study of perceptual development. However, the results of these early experiments illustrate the necessity of using proper experimental designs and scaling procedures. Designs used so far allow us to say only that the newborn or young infant shows differential sensitivity to stimuli. More analytic questions concerning what the infant sees and how he orders his world are not answered. Following these demonstrations of differential sensitivity, we need to apply techniques that will tell us what dimensions the infant perceives and how he comes to know objects.

The newborn cannot adjust his visual focal length.

Haynes, White, and Held (1965) showed that the newborn is unable to adjust the focal length of his lens. This handicap has implications for all of the research discussed. Infants who showed differential preference were focused to some extent upon the stimulus; those who did not may have been unable to differentiate the stimuli, or the stimuli may have been out of focus. The image may have been presented too far from the subjects or too near their eyes for clarity. We need to replicate those studies which produced negative results, to see if infants are more perceptive than we now believe. We must first measure the infant's focal plane (the distance from his eye where images are in focus) and then place the stimulus material in that plane; this guarantees that the baby can at least see our stimuli. To understand the newborn's perceptual constructions, we must be subtle; we need to consider what type of evidence we receive from differential preference scores and what criteria are necessary in order to infer that ordered dimensions exist in the infant's perceptual world.

The stimulus-preference method

An infant's preference among three or more stimuli can tell us a good deal about his visual world.

Hershenson (1964) studied fixation preferences for 36 newborns (between the ages of two and four days) along three stimulus dimensions—brightness, complexity, and organization. Using an elegant photographic technique and film sensitive to infrared light, he examined each infant under semidark conditions with stimulus materials projected onto viewing screens. The total proportion of time spent looking at each of the stimuli was computed. He used three levels of brightness in increasing logarithmic steps and found significant differences for *all three pairs* of brightness levels. This is a necessary and sufficient condition for an inference of dimensionality. Any outcome weaker than this (in terms of either fewer levels of the stimulus or fewer pairs of stimuli significantly different from each other) will *not* allow the inference of an ordered dimension. Hershenson found significant preference for the least over the most complex checkerboard pattern. A monotonic relation might exist between complexity and preference; however, the necessary *three* significant differences were *not* found.

Hershenson showed that newborns prefer intermediate brightness and simple checkerboards.

In order to test preferences for organization, three stimuli were used [similar to those of Fantz (1961)]—a photograph of a female face, the same face with the features moved into different positions, and finally the same face with all the elements randomly arranged. The light-dark ratio was the same for all faces, and the degrees of complexity were matched for two. There was no systematic preference over the entire set, suggesting that newborn infants are not sensitive to "facial" organization. Hershenson's results indicate that newborns respond differentially to checkerboards and that a brightness dimension exists. Only three stimuli were used in the study, so the exact nature of the function relating preference and brightness cannot be specified. In general, the newborn prefers an intermediate amount of brightness, rejecting lights that are either very dim or very bright; also, he looks longer at less complex checkerboards.

Increasing the visual complexity of the infant's environment decreases and then increases his visual searching.

Newborns and infants are capable of discriminating among various stimuli, but the significance of this ability for subsequent visual and cognitive development is an open question. An experiment relevant to this problem was performed by White (1963). Using a group of infants under special institutionalized care, he measured the amount of time they spent visually exploring. Following this base period of measurement, the complexity of the environment was increased for some infants but not for others. Those infants exposed to a more complex environment decreased their visual exploration at first; later, these same infants substantially increased their visual activity to the point where it surpassed the visual exploration of infants who had not been exposed to the more complex environment. The infants exposed to a more complex environment were apparently overwhelmed at first with sensory information. They reacted by restricting their exploration and sampling from the environment. Finally, after learning enough about their new environment to begin understanding it, they explored their environment more than the infants who had not received extra stimulation. The investigators did not show that the stimulated infants were able to perform other tasks better than the control infants, and we do not know how long the differential effect of visual exploration might be expected to last.

Depth perception

Depth perception can be measured by means of the visual cliff. Infants who crawl see depth.

A method for the study of depth perception was developed by Walk and Gibson (1961). Models of the visual cliff have been constructed which allow studies of young infants (see Figure 4.3). For human infants, a small table is constructed with a center board one foot wide elevated one inch from the glass surface of the table. An irregular pattern of tile is placed directly under the glass on one side of the center board; the same pattern covers the floor 40 inches below the glass on the other side. Raised boards prevent the infant from accidentally falling off the table. The visual cliff apparatus offers the infant a choice between what appears to be a very small drop on one side of a center board or a much larger drop on the other side. A strong sheet of glass extends from the center board across both sides to control for auditory, olfactory, and echolocation cues (and to catch the adventurous infant). A mother stands alternately at the deep and shallow side, attempting to persuade the infant to come her way. Infants six months or older consistently refuse to cross the deep side; they almost always cross the

FIGURE 4.3

A "visual cliff" used to test perception of depth in infants. The infant shows depth perception by not crawling over the deep end of the glass panel from the centerboard. The cliff shows that children perceive depth by the time they are six months old.

shallow side. The effectiveness of the visual cliff as a test of depth perception depends on the locomotor ability of the infant and his willingness to exercise this ability in a strange environment. Within these limitations, the results show that infants possess depth perception by the age of six months, since they refuse to descend onto the deep side of the cliff.

Monocular infants also see depth by six months.

To determine the importance of binocular vision in depth perception, Walk and Dodge (1962) tested a monocular infant on the visual cliff. The monocular infant discriminated depth; he would not cross to the deep side even when coaxed by his mother. Monocular cues are thus adequate for a primitive depth perception. Binocular disparity (images from two eyes which are interconnected to form a single view) and convergence are not necessary for the perception of depth in the young infant, although they do contribute to more precise depth perception in older children. Six-month-old infants possess adaptive depth perception. At the moment we know little about the developmental history of the trait (when it appears, whether the experience of falling is necessary, or how infants develop it).

Size and shape constancy

The visual system somehow considers the relation between distance from the retina and plane of view to correct visual distortions.

The perceived size of objects remains constant even when their distances and corresponding retinal images vary—for example, a man does not seem to shrink as he walks away from us. Furthermore, as the viewing angle of an object, and its corresponding retinal image, varies, the object is still seen as the same shape (see Figure 4.4). Size and shape constancy are often investigated by manipulation of stimulus size and distance from the observer. The problem of size constancy is to understand how the perceptual system estimates distance and uses this estimate to give us a size-invariant percept at varying distances. The retinal projection of an object varies directly with the distance of the object from the observer. The farther the object is from the observer, the smaller is its retinal projection. If this process were not corrected, objects would appear to grow smaller as they moved away, and people would expand as we walked toward them. However, there is a corrective mechanism in the perceptual system which takes into account the estimated distance from the observer to the object and corrects the retinal projection to give us a more stable representation of the world.

The usual procedure for studying constancy is to match a variable stimulus with some standard.

The usual technique for studying constancy requires that a comparison stimulus be matched to a standard. With this design a large number of variables may be studied (for example, the angle between the comparison and standard stimulus—the distance of the stimuli from the observer).

Infants of 60 days possess shape constancy.

Bower (1966) studied shape constancy in human infants between 50 and 60 days of age. He conditioned infants by reinforcing them for moving their head to the left following presentation of a board turned

FIGURE 4.4

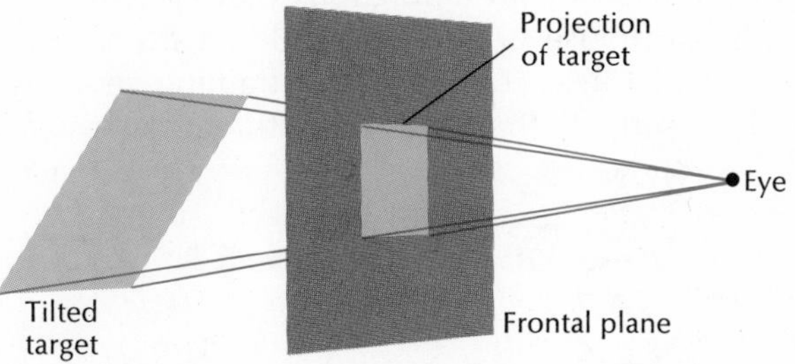

Frontal plane projection of a target lying in a tilted position with reference to the eye. Naturally, such a projection may be of a different size and shape than the target, but will compare to the shape of the image projected onto the retina. (From Bartley, 1958.)

45 degrees from the infant's frontal plane. (The center of rotation of the board lay in the infant's medial plane.) Following conditioning to the initial stimulus, he presented the infants with either (1) the original stimulus in its original position, (2) the original stimulus in a position parallel to the infant's plane, (3) a trapezoid in the frontal plane whose retinal projection was equal to the original stimulus at a 45-degree plane, or (4) the trapezoid at an angle of 45 degrees. The mean number of responses elicited by the four presentations were (1) the original stimulus, 51; (2) the same stimulus in a different orientation, 45; (3) the stimulus that projected a retinal shape identical with the original, 29; and (4) the trapezoid at 45 degrees, 26. Apparently, young infants possess a well-developed notion of shape constancy. They respond to the shape of an object, and they can recognize it in new orientations. The young infant does not respond directly to retinal shape; he is able to compute invariances in the shape after several rotations which allow him to perceive the "same" shape in another plane.

Perceptual set

Ambiguous perceptual stimuli are assimilated into previous sets.

If a series of figures is followed by an ambiguous picture, the perceptual set, induced by the series of training pictures, will lead children to see the ambiguous figure like the training figures (see Figure 4.5). Children from preschool age to second grade participated in an experiment (Reese, 1963), in which it was hypothesized that young children who are not able to use verbal mediation would not be influenced by the training figures as much as would older children. Three series of six drawings each—human faces, animals, and inanimate objects—were shown to the children. Each group received one of the nonambiguous series followed by an ambiguous picture (which could be interpreted as either a mouse or a man). Children from each age level saw each series of pictures. Following the training sessions, the children were asked to sort all the cards into three classes: animals, people, and

FIGURE 4.5

Rat-man ambiguous figure like that used by Reese (1963).

objects. The results showed that a perceptual set was not present at the youngest age levels but that older children classify ambiguous pictures as animals if they were trained with an animal series or as men if they had viewed the people series or as inanimate objects if they had been given that series during training. These results illustrate the influence of cognitive factors on children's perceptual abilities. If perceptual functions vary with age, we want to know whether the variation is related to changes in the child's perceptual or cognitive abilities. In this case perceptual set seems best explained by changes in conceptual abilities.

Older children have little trouble recognizing figures no matter what their orientation; however, younger children recognize figures better if they are upright.

Ghent (1961) investigated the extent to which the recognition of realistic figures is related to age. She reports that three- and four-year-old children recognize significantly more figures when they are "right side up" than when they are in other positions; this difference decreases with age. With older children (seven-year-olds) recognition is equally good in all orientations. She also reported that preschool children consistently prefer certain orientations of nonrealistic figures as being "right side up." Ghent, Bernstein, and Goldreber (1960) showed unrealistic figures to preschool children for short durations (1/25 of a second). This short exposure prevents overt eye movements so that preferences cannot be related to visual scanning of the stimulus. (Children showed the same preferences when they were allowed unlimited exposure.)

Stress and incorrect hypotheses lead to misperception of ambiguous pictures.

Other studies have tried to find variables responsible for the differential difficulties young children experience in classifying ambiguous figures. Evidence indicates that stress produces premature closure, (early structuring of ambiguous figures), thus making correct recognition more difficult (Smock, 1958). Also, Potter (1966) showed that prerecognition hypotheses (wrong ones) are maintained in an ambiguous task, often resulting in delayed recognition of familiar stimuli.

Maccoby and Hagan showed that older children can attend differentially to relevant and irrelevant stimuli; younger children cannot.

Maccoby and Hagan (1965) investigated the effects of distraction on children's selective attention and recall. They used children from first through seventh grades; half the groups were presented pictures on distinctively colored backgrounds and listened to low notes of music that were played at random intervals while the remaining groups received only the pictures. Recall of the relevant background increased regularly with age, while recall of the irrelevant pictures showed no systematic change with age. The random musical notes affected children's recall of the relevant colors but did not affect their recall of the irrelevant pictures. Irrelevant information was not affected by the random notes; this suggests that young children are unable to separate relevant and irrelevant input. Older children are better able to separate relevant from irrelevant information; therefore, they show better retention of relevant information and lower retention of irrelevant information under the distraction condition (when they are overloaded). For older children, high recall of relevant information was associated with low recall of irrelevant information. Older children were better able to retain the background colors, but they lost the irrelevant pictures in the process. The younger children paid attention to the irrelevant pictures; as a result, they were not as able to attend selectively to the relevant background colors.

WHOLE-PART PERCEPTION

Whole-part perception is related to the child's age, the names available, the stimulus, and their interaction.

Young children usually react to an entire stimulus rather than to its separate parts (see Figure 4.6). This is particularly true of unfamiliar stimuli. However, older children can attend to both the whole figure *and* to its component parts. We can formulate a rule: if the internal parts of a stimulus are not distinctive, only older children will differentiate it. However, if the parts are distinctive and the younger child knows the names of parts of the stimulus, he is likely to categorize parts rather than a whole. Very young children cannot recognize both the whole and the parts; however, this ability develops with age (Elkind, Koegler, & Go, 1964). The stimulus is seen as whole or parts depending

FIGURE 4.6

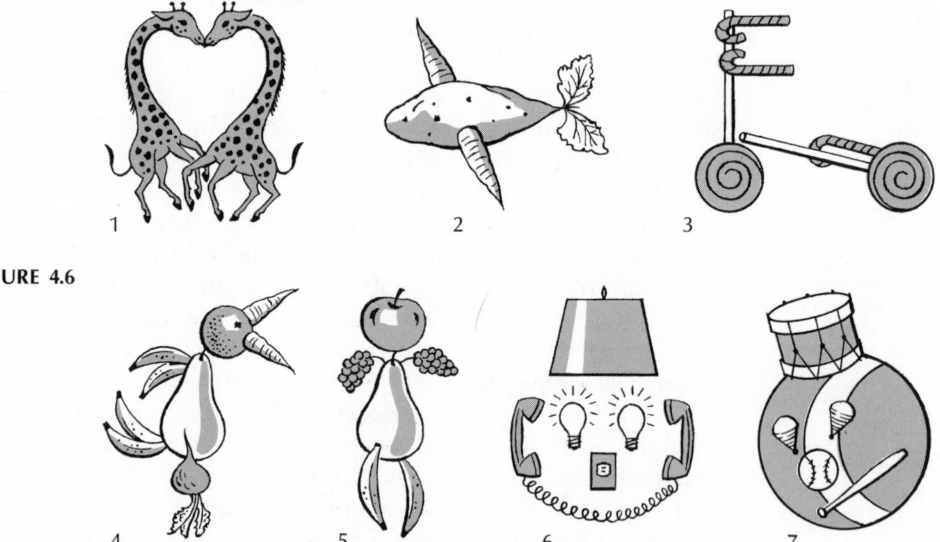

Drawings used in the study of part-whole perception. The figure shows stimuli in which there are meaningful parts that make up the composite whole. Children were tested for their perception of both parts and wholes. Young children see the entire figure, while older children see both the figure and its component parts. (From Elkind, Koegler, & Go, 1964.)

FIGURE 4.7

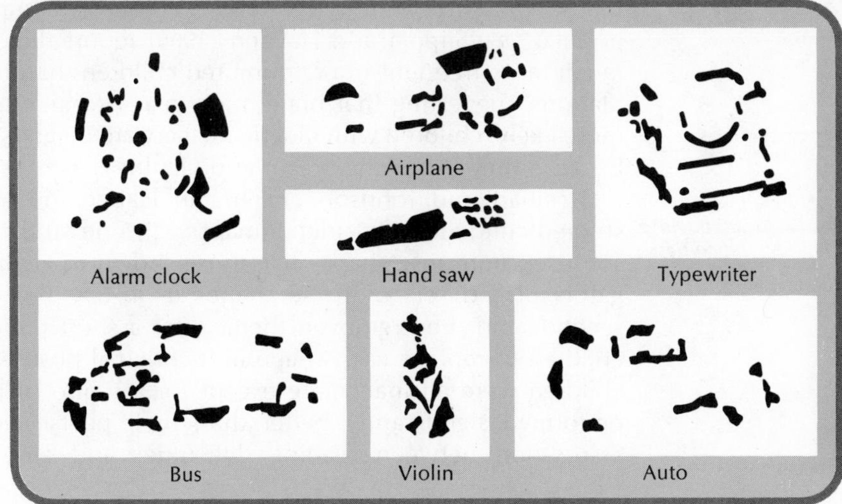

Dot patterns from the Street Gestalt test. Young children have great difficulty seeing the patterns as objects, while older children and adults are better able to perceive the objects. The name attached to the pictures helps our recognition and identification of the various forms. (From Street, 1931.)

upon (a) the age of the observer, (b) the type of stimulus, and (c) the names available to the child. Older children, well-differentiated stimuli, and parts with common names produce part perceptions; younger children, undifferentiated stimuli, and uncommon parts produce whole perceptions.

Older children require fewer cues to recognize a picture than their younger peers.

Compared with older children, the four- or five-year-old requires many more clues in order to recognize an object; the stimulus must be more redundant. Thus, if a ten-year-old is shown the series of pictures in Figure 4.7, he is likely to perceive them correctly (for example, as a clock or bus). The four-year-old child requires many more hints before he will recognize any pattern. With increasing age, less stimulus support is necessary for the child to recognize objects.

Eidetic imagery

Eidetic imagery (photographic memory) is rare at any age; however, it is more frequent among children diagnosed as brain damaged.

Eidetic imagery is very similar to popular conceptions of photographic memory—the ability to evoke an extremely clear image of an absent object or event. Individuals who possess eidetic imagery are able to report with remarkable accuracy even minor details of an event or picture from their past; they are able to reproduce a mental image of the picture during the reporting. Eidetic imagery is rare at any age, but there is some evidence that it declines after the age of about nine and that it is less frequent in Western countries as compared with African populations. Siipola and Hayden (1965) report that eidetic imagery is much more frequent in brain-injured children than in the normal populations, suggesting that brain injury may produce eidetic imagery, *or,* more likely, children with eidetic imagery are diagnosed as brain injured because they experience reading difficulties.

Eidetic imagery is also associated with reading difficulties.

Zelhart and Johnson (1959) and Haber and Haber (1964) have studied children with eidetic imagery. In one study Zelhart and Johnson used nonsense shapes like those shown in Figure 4.8. The investigators placed sets of these shapes in a 4 × 4 checkerboard for 30 seconds and then removed them. After a short period they asked the children to replace each shape in its original position. The third-grade children were all inaccurate except for a group of poor readers, who performed significantly better than their peers—suggesting again an association between reading difficulties and eidetic imagery. Why

FIGURE 4.8

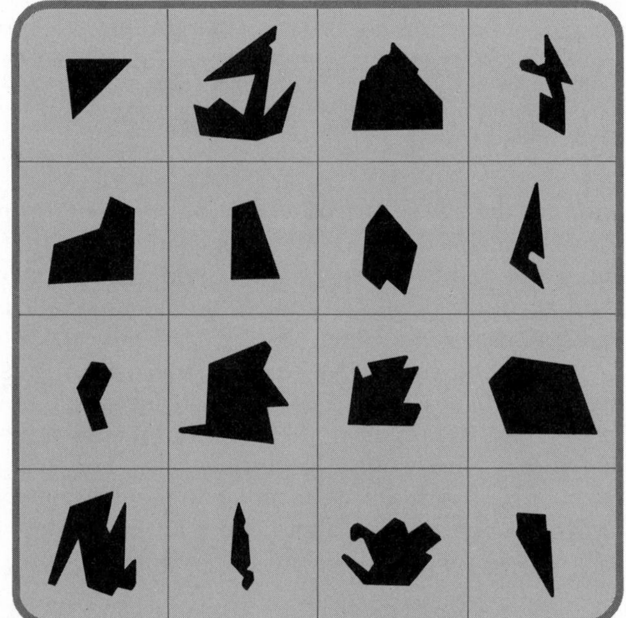

Nonsense shapes of differing association values. These forms were used as tests for eidetic imagery (photographic memory). Zelhart & Johnson found that children with eidetic imagery could replace each form in the correct square; this task was almost impossible for the average child (Zelhart & Johnson, 1959).

eidetic imagery is associated with reading problems is not at all clear. One possible reason is that children with eidetic imagery depend on their memory; as a result, they do not form the general rules and transformations which would allow them to understand the complex process of reading. If this is true, the way to overcome reading difficulties among children with eidetic imagery would be to teach them basic transformational grammar (see the chapter on language). Another problem might be their inability to erase one image to pay attention to another.

Haber and Haber showed that children with eidetic imagery do perform simple transformations on the image; they are not simply storing.

Haber and Haber (1964) reported that from 151 children tested in an elementary school in New Haven, Connecticut, 12 cases (8 percent) showed eidetic imagery. They were far above their peers in abilities to produce images and to report them accurately. However, after the memory trace failed, their recall was little better than that of their peers. They reported that the children with eidetic memory produced some interpolations and transformations on their images. This means the children were coding and storing the pictures and not just reporting a visual image from the retina. Also, the children reported that they could move their eyes and the movement did not produce lasting images.

Eidetic imagery is rare and a mixed blessing.

These results suggest that only a few children possess eidetic imagery, and it is a mixed blessing. Children with eidetic imagery may not learn to read.

Tachistoscopic recognition

When exposed to a stimulus for only a few milliseconds children see simple figures more accurately than complex ones.

Munsinger (1965) performed studies concerning the development of tachistoscopic recognition for abstract forms of varying complexity. In his first study four children ranging in age from four and one-half to five years of age and eight college adults served as subjects. Using a two-field mirror tachistoscope, a device which allows precise control of the exposure duration of stimuli, the subjects were tested for their recognition accuracy on sets of four stimuli. He found that recognition accuracy is higher for simple than for more complex figures for both adults and children. Children require longer exposure durations than adults to recognize either simple or complex shapes. Furthermore, both adults and children improved their recognition accuracy with no external feedback.

Children and adults have different rates of shape recognition.

Apparently, perceptual learning in the child and adult depends on an internal information feedback mechanism that does not require external validation. The results of this study indicate that children and adults have different rates of learning to recognize simple figures as opposed to more complex forms. Two distinct processes seem to contribute to shape recognition in adults and children. For simple figures there is a perceptual process that immediately presents a percept to the subject. When figures are more complex a process of guessing and partial processing of information occurs. This sampling or partial processing allows recognition of a complex figure, since many parts of the figure are unique and sufficient for a differential recognition. However, the sampling procedure does not allow efficient development of a single category for each form.

Adding symmetry (mirror image) to figures increases the recognition accuracy of children and adults.

A second study by Munsinger and Forsman (1966), using essentially the same procedure, varied the amount of information in the stimulus in two ways. In one case the information in the stimulus was varied by increasing the number of independent parts of the figure. In another condition the left half of the figure was a mirror image of the right, thereby producing redundancy. The findings of both studies were similar. Younger children require longer exposure durations to recognize figures than do older children and adults. Simple figures are easier to recognize than are complex figures. Adding symmetry (mirror image) to a figure increases the ease of recognition of the simple figures for both younger children and adults but does not help in the case of complex figures. This result suggests that children of four or five years of age and older are sensitive to redundancy (symmetry) in the stimulus and are able to use redundancy in perceptual recognition tasks.

Letter-word perception

Children confuse letters that overlap spatially.

Gibson, Pick, Osser, and Hammond (1962) analyzed the critical perceptual features of letters. They tried to find the features of letters which serve to differentiate one from another, and they wanted to know how children confuse letters. They supplied 87 four-year-old children with a standard letter (for example, *k*) which appeared for one second. Then the children were shown six letters (for example, *k, s, a, w, y, o*). Their task was to match the standard letter with one of the six. Two lists were used, one in which the letters had little spatial overlap and another with considerable overlap. The children made many more errors trying to match the confusable set of letters (those with considerable spatial overlap) than in matching the set that could be easily discriminated; more confusion occurred between a *q* and a *g* than between a *c* and an *l*. Their judgment time was also longer for the confusable set of letters.

Three dimensions describe how children see letters: (1) curved versus straight, (2)

Analysis of the children's errors showed three different features of their confusions. The strongest feature was straight and curved lines. Children confused straight letters with other straight lines and curved letters with other curved lines; they did not confuse straight with curved *obliqueness, and (3) complexity.*

lines. The relative obliqueness of letters was also important; oblique letters were confused with each other. Complexity was the final confusion feature. A simple letter *l* was not often confused with a complex letter *k*, but simple letters were confused with other simple letters and complex letters with other complex letters.

Confusion among letters occurs often from slant.

Next, Gibson and associates studied the ability of four-year-olds to discriminate among letters (see Figure 4.9). Sets of forms were constructed which followed the rules of letter construction. The rules

FIGURE 4.9

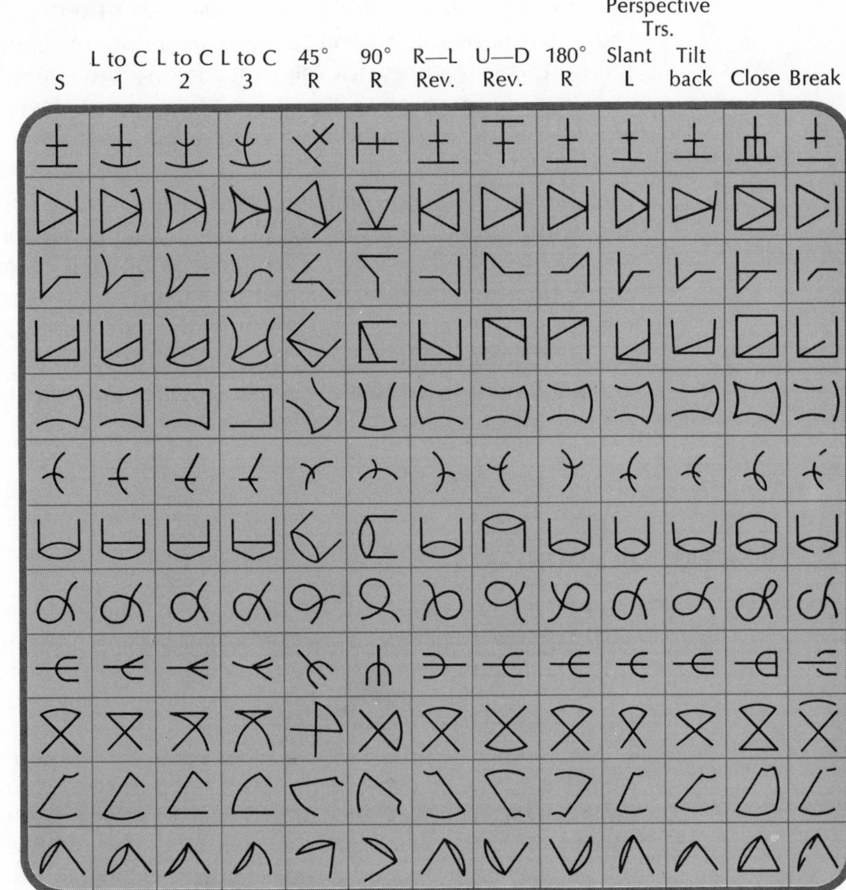

Stimuli used in the Gibson, Pick, Osser, and Hammond (1962) study. The standard stimulus is shown on the left; various transformations of the standard are displayed after it. Breaking or closing a figure produced few errors, but rotation of the figure was confusing to children of all ages. Errors decreased over age for most of the stimuli.

were: number of strokes, straight versus curved lines, and symmetry versus asymmetry. In addition, they transformed each of the standard stimuli by either changing a line to a curve, rotating or reversing the shape, changing the perspective, or breaking the figure. When children were required to match the sample to a standard, confusion errors decreased with age. Breaking or closing a figure resulted in few errors. Slanting to the left or slanting to the right caused many errors, and this effect decreased only slightly with age. Symmetrical figures were confused less than asymmetrical ones. Gibson and associates concluded that the child learns the abstract features of letters by the time he is four. He learns the critical features of graphemes, and is beginning to ignore those features not relevant for distinguishing them.

Children must learn relevant and irrelevant cues.

The common characteristic of perceptual development in young children is the differentiation of relevant and irrelevant stimulus features. In the studies of whole and part perception the younger child sees wholes; with age, he learns to differentiate the stimulus into wholes and component parts. In the studies of tachistoscopic recognition the task of the subject is to pick those parts of each complex figure which allow him to differentiate them. In learning to recognize letters the child must pay attention to features invariant over transformations and ignore features that are not invariant. With increasing differentiation and greater ability to select correct features and reject incorrect features of the stimulus, the child grows perceptually.

REMARKS: COMMENTARY

Moore (1965) has taught three-year-olds to read and write by letting them interact with a "talking typewriter" for a half hour each day. The "talking typewriter" is an electric typewriter connected to a computer; it corrects the child, answers his questions and tutors him in new sequences and words. The children were rewarded only by their curiosity—the satisfaction of learning and exploring new things. Moore and several other psychologists [for example, Hunt (1961) and Bruner (1966)] believe that the very young child can profit from early stimulation, and, in fact, the three-year-old may be in a better position to learn to read than his older peer. This controversy is by no means settled; there are no easy answers. At the moment there is good reason to believe that the very young child can learn to read if he is approached properly. However, if stringent demands are placed on him, his self-concept and ability to try new things may be harmed. The trick is to expose the child to new things but not to be disappointed if he shows no immediate improvement. When he is prepared the child's mind will grow; only by exposure can we find the correct time.

VALUES AND PERCEPTION

The value of an object can affect its perceived size.

Social values are associated with objects through experience. Once this occurs, these values affect our perceptions. For example, children from poorer homes, when matching sizes of coins from memory, tend to overestimate the size of coins more than children from well-to-do homes (Bruner & Goodman, 1947). A further study of this problem used nursery school children divided into two groups (Lambert, Solomon, & Watson, 1949). Children in one group learned to turn a crank to receive a poker chip. When the child inserted the poker chip in a slot he received a piece of candy. The assumption was that candy enhances the value of a chip; the increased value should cause the children to overestimate the size of the chips. Both the control and experimental groups of children overestimated the chips by 5 percent in a pretest. After ten days of rewarded learning with poker chips, the experimental group increased its overestimation to 13 percent (a significant gain) while during the same period the control group's estimates did not change. As further evidence of the importance of learned values on perception, the experimental group underwent extinction of the chip-candy association. Following the extinction period, during which they turned the crank and received chips, but the chips could no longer be exchanged for candy, their size estimation of the chips returned to the initial value. Reinstatement of value to the poker chip by further reward again led to overestimation.

PERCEPTUAL CHANGES IN THE ADULT

Adults and children adapt to inverted and colored perceptual fields; the changes occur in the coordination of sensory and motor inputs.

Experience can influence even the well-developed perceptual world of the adult. Studies by Kohler (1964) demonstrate that the mature adult can adapt his perceptions if for several weeks he wears lenses that distort his visual field. Suppose the glasses invert his world, so that he sees everything upside down. After a few weeks, the person begins to notice that the world close to him is right side up, although distant objects are still upside down. Kohler's experiments also show that a subject can adjust to other changes in his environment. If we put blue on the left and yellow on the right side of each lens, in a few weeks the world appears normal again. Apparently when a person looks to the right the perceptual system adds a complement of blue and when he looks to the left, a complement of yellow. When the colored glasses are taken off the world is colored (the complement of the originals); when the inverting glasses are taken off the world appears wrong and the subject must relearn up and down. The human being has great flexibility built into his perceptual system; the system allows changes as a function of sensory-motor coordination and experience. The changes may even occur very late in development if the experience is extensive.

SUMMARY

1 Three views of perceptual development have attracted the attention of psychologists: (1) nativism—all perceptual organization is innately determined; (2) empiricism—the learning of elementary associations can account for all our perceptions; (3) interaction—both innate organizing mechanisms (for example, sucking, looking) and learned associations among events contribute to perceptual development in the infant and child.

2 There are three major ways of observing the neonate's perceptual abilities: (1) ocular orientation—exactly where the neonate is looking from moment to moment; (2) pair preference—measurement of the amount of time he spends looking at each of two items; (3) counting of the total amount of visual exploration by the infant.

3 The development of depth perception may be studied by placing an infant on a "visual cliff" apparatus. If he goes over the deep side, we assume he is not aware of depth; almost all six-month-old infants show good depth perception.

4 Size and shape constancy results from the observer's ability to compensate for transformations of distance and point of view. Bower showed that the ability exists in very young infants.

5 The type of experience one receives just before viewing an ambiguous figure strongly affects what he sees. This phenomenon (called perceptual set) is not well developed in the young child.

6 Eidetic imagery is commonly called photographic memory; it is the ability to produce an extremely accurate mental image of a past event. Although the ability is rare, it does exist in young children.

7 Studies of tachistoscopic recognition (very brief exposure duration) show that adults are more accurate than children, that complex figures are more difficult to see than simple figures, and that adding redundancy to simple figures helps their recognition. However, redundancy does not help the recognition of complex figures. Two mechanisms are operating—one which processes a few items of information and another which handles complex materials by partial processing and guessing.

8 In differentiating among letters children use three attributes: (1) the number of strokes in the letter; (2) whether the letter is straight or curved; and (3) whether it is symmetrical or asymmetrical.

9 The value we place upon an object affects our perception of its size. For example, children's judgments of coin size are affected by their past experience with money. Also, reward associated with chips affected children's judgments.

10 The adult's perceptual system, although remarkably stable, can be changed by prolonged experience, such as the wearing of lenses that distort his visual field.

FURTHER READINGS

Gibson, E. J., & Olum, V. Experimental methods of studying perception in children. In P. Mussen (Ed.), *Handbook of research methods in child development.* New York: Wiley, 1960. Pp. 311-373.

Bartley, S. H. *Principles of perception.* New York: Harper & Row, 1958.

REFERENCES

Bower, T. G. R. Slant perception and shape constancy in infants. *Science,* 1966, **151,** 832-834.

Bruner, J. S. On perceptual readiness. *Psychological Review,* 1957, **64,** 123-152.

Bruner, J. S. *Toward a theory of instruction.* Cambridge: Harvard University Press, 1966.

Bruner, J. S., & Goodman, C. C. Value and need as organizing factors in perception. *Journal of Abnormal and Social Psychology,* 1947, **42,** 33-34.

Descartes, R. 1650. The passions of the soul. In R. M. Eaton (Ed.), *Selections.* New York: Scribner, 1927.

Elkind, D., Koegler, R. R., & Go, E. Studies in perceptual development: II. Part-whole perception. *Child Development,* 1964, **35,** 81-90.

Fantz, R. L. Pattern vision in young infants. *Psychological Records,* 1958, **8,** 43-47.

Fantz, R. L. The origin of form perception. *Scientific American,* 1961, **204,** 66-72.

Fantz, R. L. Pattern vision in newborn infants. *Science,* 1963, **140,** 296-297.

Ghent, L. Form and its orientation: A child's-eye view. *American Journal of Psychology,* 1961, **74,** 177-190.

Ghent, L. Bernstein, L., & Goldreber, A. M. Preference for orientation of form under varying conditions. *Perceptual and Motor Skills,* 1960, **11,** 46.

Gibson, E. J., Pick, A., Osser, H., & Hammond, M. The role of grapheme-phoneme correspondence in the perception of words. *American Journal of Psychology,* 1962, **75,** 554-570.

Haber, R. N., & Haber, R. B. Eidetic imagery: I. Frequency. *Perceptual and Motor Skills,* 1964, **19,** 131-138.

Haynes, H., White, B. L., & Held, R. Visual accommodation in human infants. *Science,* 1965, **148,** 528-530.

Hebb, D. O. *The organization of behavior.* New York: Wiley, 1949.

Hershenson, M. Visual discrimination in the human newborn. *Journal of Comparative and Physiological Psychology,* 1964, **58,** 270–276.

Hobbes, T. 1651. Humane nature. In W. Dennis (Ed.), *Readings in the history of psychology.* New York: Appleton-Century-Crofts, 1948.

Hubel, D. H., & Wiesel, T. N. Receptive fields of cells in striate cortex of very young, visually inexperienced kittens. *Journal of Neurophysiology,* **26,** 1963, 994–1002.

Hunt, J. McV. *Intelligence and experience.* New York: Ronald, 1961.

Kant, E. 1781. Critique of pure reason. In T. M. Greene (Ed.), *Selections.* New York: Scribner, 1929.

Kohler, I. The formation and transformation of the perceptual world. (Trans. by H. Fiss) *Psychological Issues,* 1964, **3.**

Lambert, W. W., Solomon, R. L., & Watson, P. D. Reinforcement and extinction as factors in size estimation. *Journal of Experimental Psychology,* 1949, **39,** 637–641.

Leibowitz, N., Waskow, I., Loeffler, N., & Glaser, F. Intelligence level as a variable in the perception of shape. *Quarterly Journal of Experimental Psychology,* 1959, **11,** 100–112.

Locke, J. 1690. An essay concerning human understanding. In W. Dennis (Ed.), *Readings in the history of psychology.* New York: Appleton-Century-Crofts, 1948.

Maccoby, E. E., & Hagan, J. W. Effects of distraction upon central vs. incidental recall: Developmental trends. *Journal of Experimental Child Psychology,* 1965, **2,** 280–289.

Moore, O. K. The responsive environments project and the deaf. *American Annals of the Deaf,* 1965, **110,** 512–522.

Mueller, J. 1838. The specific energies of nerves. In W. Dennis (Ed.), *Readings in the history of psychology.* New York: Appleton-Century-Crofts, 1948.

Munsinger, H. Tachistoscopic recognition of stimulus variability. *Journal of Experimental Child Psychology,* 1965, **2,** 186–191.

Munsinger, H., & Forsman, R. Symmetry, development, and tachistoscopic recognition. *Journal of Experimental Child Psychology,* 1966, **3,** 168–176.

Piaget, J. *The psychology of intelligence.* (Trans. by M. Piercy and D. E. Berlyne) New York: Harcourt, Brace & World, 1950.

Potter, M. C. On perceptual recognition. In J. Bruner, R. Oliver, & P. Greenfield, *Studies in cognitive growth.* New York: Wiley, 1966.

Reese, H. W. "Perceptual set" in young children. *Child Development,* 1963, **34,** 151–159.

Ross, R. T. Optimum orders for the presentation of pairs in the method of paired comparisons. *Journal of Educational Psychology,* 1934, **25,** 375–382.

Siipola, E. M., & Hayden, S. D. Exploring eidetic imagery among the retarded. *Perceptual and Motor Skills,* 1965, **21,** 275–286.

Smock, C. D. Perceptual rigidity and closure phenomenon as a function of manifest anxiety in children. *Child Development,* 1958, **29,** 237–247.

Street, R. F. *A gestalt completion test: A study of a cross-section of intellect.* New York: Teachers College, 1931.

Torgerson, W. S. *Theory and method of scaling.* New York: Wiley, 1958.

Walk, R. D., & Dodge, S. S. Visual depth perception of a 10-month-old monocular human infant. *Science,* 1962, **137,** 520–530.

Walk, R. D., & Gibson, E. J. A comparative and analytical study of visual depth perception. *Psychological Monographs,* 1961, **75.**

Wertheimer, M. Principles of perceptual organization. In D. C. Beardslee & M. Wertheimer (Eds.), *Readings in perception.* Princeton, N.J.: Van Nostrand, 1958.

White, B. L. The development of perception during the first six months of life. Paper presented to the American Association for the Advancement of Science, 1963.

Zelhart, P., & Johnson, R. C. An investigation of eidetic imagery. *Western Psychological Association Paper,* San Jose, Calif., 1959.

5 LEARNING

O, what learning is!
ROMEO AND JULIET

There are several recurring models of the child's mind. One position views it as a bundle of associations loosely connected by bonds (learning); another sees it composed of structures and rules (cognition). Correlated with theories of association versus structure is the categorization of children as passive receivers or active makers of their world. Those who assume an association theory of development usually see the child as a passive recipient of environmental effects, while the structuralist gives the child a more active role.

Interest among psychologists is shifting from association to perception and thought.

Until recently American psychology was dominated by association theory; how the child formed an associative bond was the dominant theme. Interest in perception and thinking has revived the study of complex cognitive processes. Rather than simply asking if the child can associate events, we now consider the more interesting question: What are the strategies that guide the child in his learning and what mental structures has he acquired that will help him in this particular learning situation? The child transfers solutions and strategies from one task to another; he never finds a problem completely new—except in the case of the neonate, and possibly not even there. The notion of structures and strategies that can apply to any learning situation is a powerful new conception of children's learning.

Learning describes the infant's association of simple events while cognition describes the child's mental functioning.

The association of two events in the child's mind is a basic example of how experience affects development. Association of experiences is the first process that transforms the reflexive infant into the child who possesses intentions, goals, and a semiformal logical system. Learning theorists look for a single set of laws to explain all the results of experience. However, developmental psychologists, fascinated by the notion of stages, are willing to proliferate a variety of mechanisms.The many mechanisms proposed could easily exist in an organism gaining more and more complex symbolic capabilities. During his first month the infant probably operates as a simple stimulus-response (association) theory would predict. However, by eight months of age he is beginning to separate means and goals into different classes. This separation of drive (goals) and instrumental responses (means) suggests the operation of different learning processes. Mediation theory proposes the existence of a set of internal processes that allow the infant to apply experience gained in previous learning situations to the current problem. A mediator may be simply the acquired distinctiveness of one stimulus or all the complexity of language. We will look at several mechanisms of mind.

Association shows simple one-to-one connections; cognition does not.

Early sections of this chapter cover areas of development in which the association hypothesis is more appropriate—simple motivation and learning. For other topics we need to consider structures and rules; these are processes that show no direct one-to-one connection between stimuli and responses (see Figure 5.1). This shift should neither frighten nor confuse the reader. Distinctions will become clear as we consider in detail the development of language and thinking in later chapters. Three basic theoretical notions of learning are discussed in this chapter: (1) classical conditioning—the association of a conditioned stimulus and an unconditioned stimulus (*S–S*); (2) instrumental learning—the connection of a stimulus with a response (*S–R*); and (3) operant behavior—the control of responding by reinforcement contingencies (*R*-Reinforcement). In addition, learning to learn is discussed within a

FIGURE 5.1

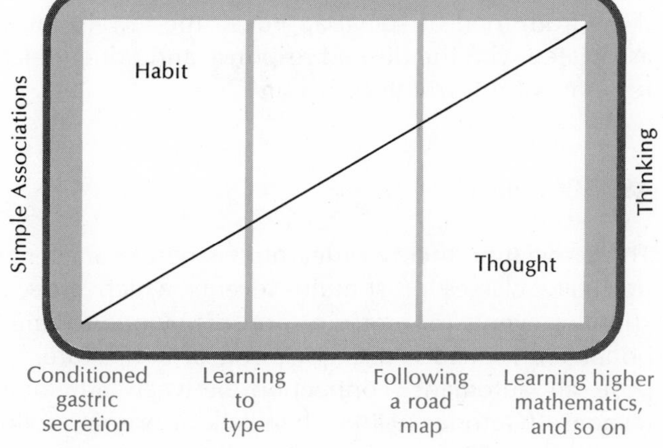

The scaling of learning tasks according to degree of understanding involved. Most learning involves a mixture of habit and thought.

discrimination learning situation; the implications of each type of learning are outlined, along with the effect of fear on learning and how the child forms concepts.

BASIC COMPONENTS OF THE LEARNING SITUATION

The four components of a learning situation are drives, stimuli, responses, and reinforcement.

There are four basic components in the typical learning situation: *drives, stimuli, responses,* and *reinforcements;* various theories make different uses of them. These four events, in combination with the child's cognitive structures, determine what he learns and how it is stored. *Drives* are of three types—the primary needs of physiological deficit, the secondary drives associated with primary needs, and cognitive motivations. Examples of primary drives include hunger, thirst, sexual excitement, and pain. The best example of a secondary drive is love of money. In addition to these physiologically based needs and associated drives, the child possesses cognitive motivations to know and understand the world; curiosity and achievement motivation are powerful forces. *Stimuli* must be attended and differentiated by the child. He must be able to discriminate the stimulus that is rewarded from the stimulus that is not rewarded. In many situations the only way we know whether a child has learned something is when he make a *response*. There is every reason to believe that the child can learn perfectly well without making an overt response; however, we cannot usually measure learning without some overt act. Children learn certain stimulus-response associations and not others because some stimuli signal reward and others do not. *Reinforcement* may be anything from food to social approval; the reward must be systematically associated with the desired response and not correlated with undesired responses for learning to occur.

ASSOCIATION

Associations may be between stimuli and stimuli (S–S), stimuli and responses (S–R), or ideas (I–I). Associations may form automatically, or only following drive reduction.

The association theory of learning is best characterized by models that postulate classes of stimulus events which are connected to other stimulus events (or motor responses) by one-to-one bonds. How these bonds are formed is a major point of conjecture. Some theorists propose an automatic connection between attended stimuli and the response (Guthrie, 1940); others talk of learning following drive reduction (Hull, 1952; Mowrer, 1960); still others propose a system of expectations and attentions (Tolman, 1932). The simple elegance of stimuli and responses in one-to-one correspondence gives the theory wide appeal.

Classical conditioning

Classical conditioning describes association between stimuli.

Classical conditioning is a good example of stimulus-stimulus association (see Figure 5.2). Classical conditioning requires four sets of events: (1) *US*—an unconditioned stimulus (a stimulus that elicits a reflexive response); (2) *CS*—a conditioned stimulus (a neutral stimulus to be associated with the unconditioned stimulus); (3) *UR*—an unconditioned response (a response elicited by the unconditioned stimulus); and (4) *CR*—the conditioned response (a displacement and modification of the unconditioned response in anticipation of the unconditioned stimulus). The optimum ordering of these events is shown in Figure 5.3.

Classical conditioning accounts for emotional learning.

As an example of classical conditioning, suppose we want to teach a small boy to fear white fur (Watson, 1928). In the formal language of classical conditioning, we could use a loud noise (buzzer) as the unconditioned stimulus, since this elicits fear in the young child; fear of the buzzer is the unconditioned response. White fur can be used as the conditioned stimulus, and anxiety associated with the white fur would be the conditioned response. The ordering of these events is very important. The optimum order for obtaining classical conditioning dictates that the *CS* appear first; the *US* should follow by about ½ second. Shortly after this event the *UR* will appear. When conditioning

FIGURE 5.2

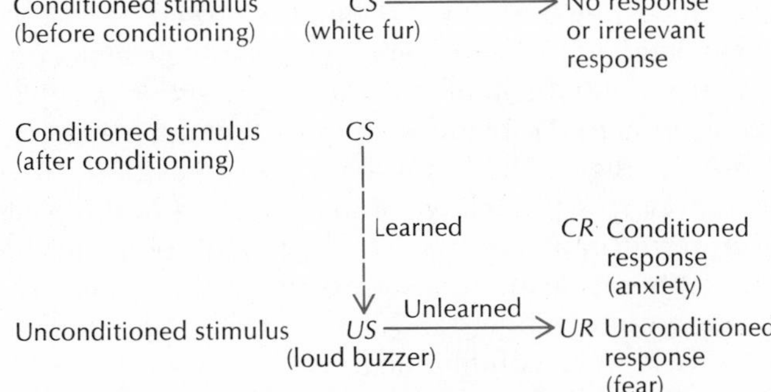

A diagram of classical conditioning. The association between the unconditioned stimulus and the unconditioned response exists at the start of the experiment; it does not have to be learned. The association between the conditioned stimulus and the unconditioned stimulus-conditioned response is learned. It arises through the pairing of the conditioned and unconditioned stimuli. The conditioned response resembles the unconditioned one, though they need not be identical.

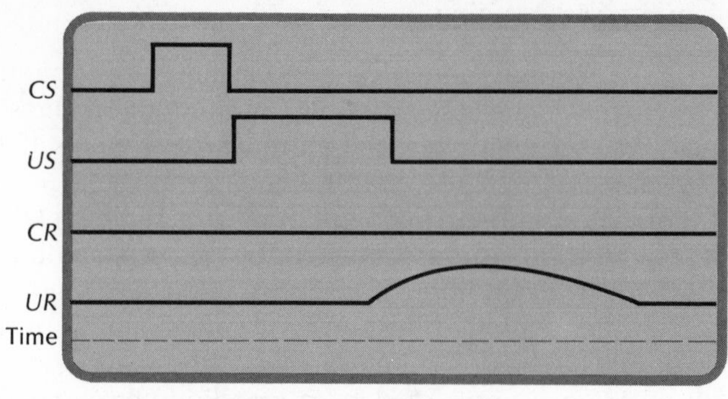

FIGURE 5.3

The optimum ordering of events to obtain classical conditioning. The *CS* (conditioned stimulus) should precede the *US* (unconditioned stimulus) by ½ second. The *US* will elicit an *UR* (unconditioned response). Repeated pairings of the *CS* and *US* will produce an association between them. To test for conditioning we eliminate the *US* on some trials; if the *CR* appears in response to the *CS* alone, we have classical conditioning.

has occurred the *CR* will appear without the *US*. (We test for conditioning by eliminating the *US* and looking for the *CR* following the *CS*.) By presenting the white fur with the buzzer, fear becomes automatically associated with fur. By employing simple classical conditioning, a previously neutral stimulus can take on either positive or negative value (love or fear). Problems with toilet training may be understood through this paradigm. The association of a previously neutral stimulus (the bathroom) with feelings of inadequacy (mother yelling when he fails) can result in a conditioned fear of bathrooms in the young child.

To establish classical conditioning we must associate a neutral stimulus with an unconditioned stimulus and present to other groups either (1) the unconditioned stimulus, (2) the conditioned stimulus, or (3) nothing.

When is learning first possible in the infant? To answer this question we must understand the control groups necessary to be sure we have classical conditioning. We need four types of groups: (1) an experimental group, which receives both the conditioned stimulus and the unconditioned stimulus (complete classical conditioning situation); (2) a control group that receives only the unconditioned stimulus (to test for pseudoconditioning—the sensitization of the child to any stimulus by presenting him with many unconditioned stimuli); (3) another control group that receives only the conditioned stimulus (to show that the conditioned stimulus is really a neutral stimulus); and (4) a maturation group, which receives nothing until the test period (to show that maturation alone has no effect).

Lipsitt & Kaye established classical conditioning in the

Lipsitt and Kaye (1965) used a loud 15-second tone as the conditioned stimulus and the insertion of a nipple into the infant's mouth after one second as the unconditioned stimulus. A control group of *first three days of an infant's life.*

infants received both the conditioned stimulus (tone) and the unconditioned stimulus (nipple), separated by 30 seconds, to control for possible increases in responsiveness and to make sure the conditioned stimulus was neutral. These investigators combined two control groups (testing the *CS,* and possible activation by receiving the *US*) into a single group. They did not include a maturation control group which received nothing until the testing period. All the infants received five trials with the conditioned stimulus alone, followed by 24 training trials on the same day. On every fifth trial the conditioned stimulus was presented alone. The percentage of trials on which sucking occurred when the conditioned stimulus alone was presented increased systematically with trials for the experimental group. For the control group responsiveness increased initially and then leveled off. This study indicates that classical conditioning can be established in the first three or four days of life, suggesting that the newborn infant starts immediately to order his environment.

Marum successfully conditioned newborns using shock as the unconditioned stimulus.

In another study, Marum (1963) successfully conditioned newborns to a tone, using shock as the unconditioned stimulus. Training was administered during the first four days of life, with 25 trials given each day. A sensitization control group received only the unconditioned stimulus and also functioned as a control for maturation. There is ample evidence that neonates can be conditioned.

The processes of conditioning include acquisition, extinction, and spontaneous recovery.

Figure 5.4 shows the course of acquisition, extinction, and spontaneous recovery for a conditioned response. Acquisition of a conditioned response occurs when the *CS* is repeatedly paired with the *US.* Extinction, the gradual disappearance of a response, occurs when the *CS* is presented several times to the infant without the occurrence of

FIGURE 5.4

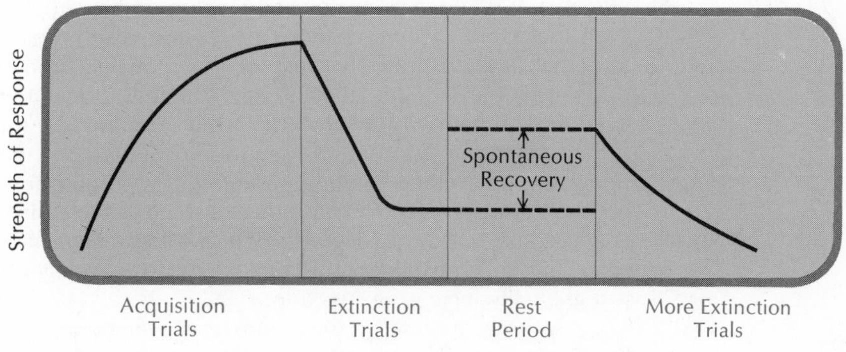

A schematic diagram of the course of acquisition, extinction, and spontaneous recovery. Within limits, the longer the rest period, the greater the degree of spontaneous recovery. A rest period occurs when the child is removed from the experimental situation for an interval (from a few minutes to several days).

the *US*. Spontaneous recovery is an increase in the strength or probability of occurrence of the conditioned response following extinction and a rest period. Spontaneous recovery is thought to occur because (1) the child becomes fatigued during extinction trials; (2) his drive becomes partially satiated through presentation of the *US* (for example,

REMARKS: THEORY—ALL-OR-NONE VERSUS INCREMENTAL LEARNING

In recent years a controversy has developed concerning how simple associations are formed. It had been assumed that stimulus-response connections were formed gradually; this was called the *incremental* position. More recently the view has been advanced that a stimulus-response association is formed in an *all-or-none* fashion; it forms all at once rather than gradually.

The new position was illustrated by Rock (1957). He set up a situation in which a number of paired items were to be memorized; any pair not learned in one trial was replaced by a new pair, so that only one trial, that is, all-or-none, learning was possible. He found that it took the same number of trials to learn a list in this manner, where gradual learning was not possible, as in the conventional experiment in which the same pairs are repeatedly reinforced until all are learned.

While there were some difficulties in the design of Rock's experiments, they called attention to the possibility of all-or-none learning, and later experimenters and theoreticians have shown both the possibilities and limitations of this model. In many experimental situations the all-or-none model does indeed yield a good fit to the data.

The assumptions of the all-or-none model are illustrated in Figure 5.5. Each of the eight small graphs at the top of the figure represents the probability of a correct response as a function of the number of trials for an individual subject. Each subject begins at the same initial level, and following each trial there is some chance that his response probability will jump from its initial level to unity. Because of the probabilistic nature of the process, different subjects learn, that is, jump to unity, on different trials; learning occurred on trial two for subject one but not until trial four for subject eight. If data are combined from a large group of subjects, all behaving in an all-or-none way, an average curve representing the proportion of correct responses per trial for the group would produce a smooth, increasing function. The large graph at the bottom of Figure 5.5 shows that even for our sample of eight subjects, the probability of a correct response averaged over these subjects is a gradually increasing function.

It is too early to settle the controversy over all-or-none versus incremental learning. It may well be that some types of learning are continuous in nature, while others follow an all-or-none rule. Defenders of the incremental position (Postman, 1963) have disagreed with the all-or-none assumption; this controversy will stimulate heat and light for some time to come.

FIGURE 5.5

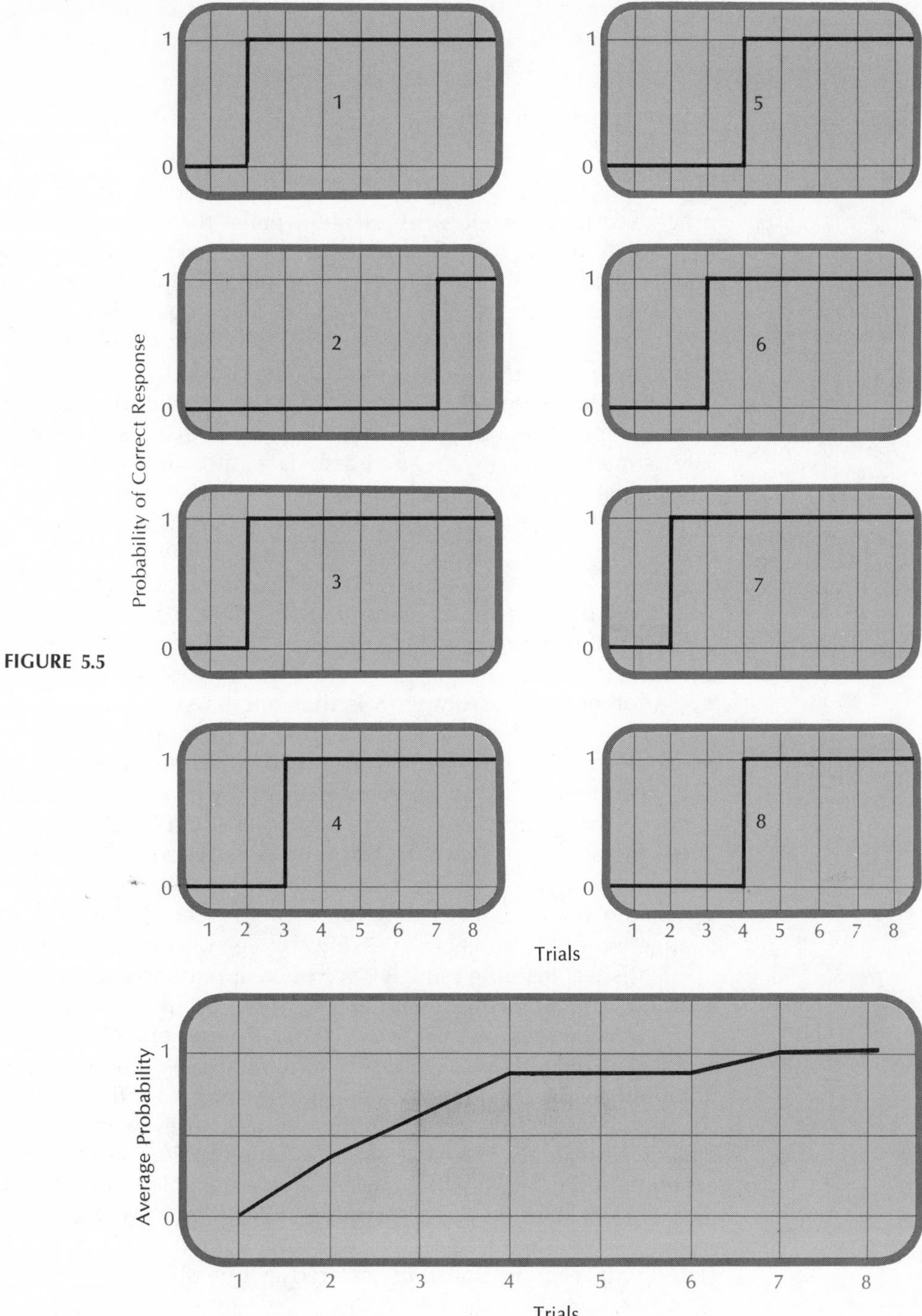

All-or-none learning curves. The graphs represent the probability of a correct response for each of eight subjects. Because individual subjects learn on different trials, the learning curve averaged over all eight subjects shows a gradually increasing function.

food) during the learning process; and (3) he forgets some fraction of the extinction process during the rest period.

Paired-associate learning

The association of stimuli and response is studied most often using the paired-associate technique.

Students of learning have used the paired-associate technique as another way to study simple connections between events. The usual procedure is to develop lists of item pairs; the task of the subject is to produce the second item of the pair (the response) when the experimenter shows him the first item (the stimulus). The subject may receive feedback by seeing the correct response following his own performance, or he may be told "right" or "wrong" following his response. Several mathematical models of this process are currently available.

The one-element model of paired-associate learning assumes (1) unitary stimuli, (2) all pairs are equally difficult, and (3) all-or-none learning.

The one-element paired-associate model makes the assumption of unitary stimuli, or a stimulus that the subject treats as a whole; therefore, stimuli used in a paired-associate situation should be clearly discriminable—for example, letters or numbers. A second assumption of the model is that all *S–R* pairs are equally difficult to learn. The experimenter usually makes this assumption tenable by randomly assigning response items to each stimulus. The one-element model assumes an all-or-none theory of associative learning (see Remarks: Theory), which implies that an association is either learned completely or not at all.

Mathematical theories of learning assume the subject never forgets a learned association and that he is guessing until he learns.

Another basic assumption is that once a stimulus-response association has been formed, it is available to the subject throughout the remainder of the experiment. This means that the subject should produce a correct response on every trial following the trial on which he connects the proper response to a particular stimulus. During the period when the subject is trying to learn, he is assumed to be guessing. His guessing strategy must be separated from his learning of associations. When the model fails to describe some aspect of the data, we may change either the subject's guessing strategy or the rules of the model.

Using statistical models of learning, one can test for rote association or insight.

Statistical learning models have been applied to children's concept learning. The following treatment borrows from Bower and Trabasso (1964) and Suppes and Ginsberg (1962). Suppes and Ginsberg used 5- and 6-year-old children, who were required to learn numbers in binary notation. In organizing their data the investigators first analyzed the six stimuli used to represent concepts as if they were independent, making the situation analogous to a simple paired-associate learning experiment. In this way the data became amenable to analysis in terms of a one-element statistical learning theory. In a second analysis the stimulus sets were treated as concepts, with the three stimuli associated with each response considered as one stimulus. In this second method of analysis learning was viewed as involving an association between the common properties of the stimuli that determine the concept and the response to that concept.

Using binary numbers as stimuli, Suppes and Ginsberg showed that young children learn by rote association.

Subjects in the experiment were 29 elementary school children, 15 from grade one and 14 from kindergarten classes. On each trial a stimulus was presented and the child made one of two possible responses. The stimuli (printed symbols on 8½ × 11 inch cards) were presented one at a time. Three stimuli represented the numeral four in binary notation and the remaining three represented the numeral five. The responses used were "four" for the stimuli representing four and "five" for those representing five. The equivalent binary numbers are, of course, 100 and 101, but since young children are familiar with some combinations of zeros and ones, other symbols were used in place of zeros and ones. Examples of the stimuli used and their numerical equivalents are given in Table 5.1. The first statistics calculated from the data were mean learning curves. There were no significant differences between the percentage of correct responses for kindergarten and grade one subjects. The data from both grades were combined and presented in terms of proportion of errors. (See Figure 5.6.)

TABLE 5.1 Stimuli and Equivalent Arabic Numerals Used in Learning Trials

Stimuli	*Numerals*
Γ**	4
Γ*Γ	5

SOURCE: From Suppes & Ginsberg, 1962.

Several parameters (for example, c, g) must be estimated from the data before applying a statistical model.

An extensive number of predictions may be developed from the theory of paired-associate learning (Atkinson, Bower, & Crothers, 1965). We assume that in a paired-associate experiment each item may be represented by one stimulus element, which may be in one of two states—conditioned to the correct response or not conditioned. In the one-element learning model, if the stimulus is unconditioned and the trial is reinforced, the stimulus becomes conditioned to the correct response with probability c and remains unconditioned with probability $1 - c$. The learning parameter (c) is estimated by the following method. A guessing parameter (g) is first obtained by assuming the child guesses correctly with probability $1/N$, where N is the total number of possible responses:

$$E(\text{average}) = \frac{1-g}{c}.$$

From the data of Bower and Trabasso (1964), we first use the obtained average number of errors (1.45) to produce

$$1.45 = \frac{1 - \frac{1}{2}}{c}$$

Solving this equation gives

$$c = .50/1.45 = 0.344.$$

We then use the parameters to predict the proportion of correct responses, errors, and so on.

We then insert our estimate of c into the expression $(1 - c)(1 - g)$ to predict the proportion of incorrect responses on trial n for $n = 1, 2, \cdots, 10$. For example, the observed frequency of incorrect responses on trial two was 96, so the observed proportion incorrect on that trial equals 96/290 = 0.331. The value 290 comes from the total number of subject-item sequences (29 subjects × 10 items). This value compares favorably with the predicted proportion:

$$(1 - c)(1 - g) = 0.656(0.500) = 0.328.$$

We decide among theories of learning by computing statistics from several theories.

From these and similar comparisons, Suppes and Ginsberg (1964) concluded that the one-element paired-associate model gives a satisfactory description of many statistical aspects of their data. This does not allow us to conclude, however, that the learning occurs in the fashion assumed by the model. Several alternative models should be applied to these data and conclusions about learning based on that model which generates the best description.

FIGURE 5.6

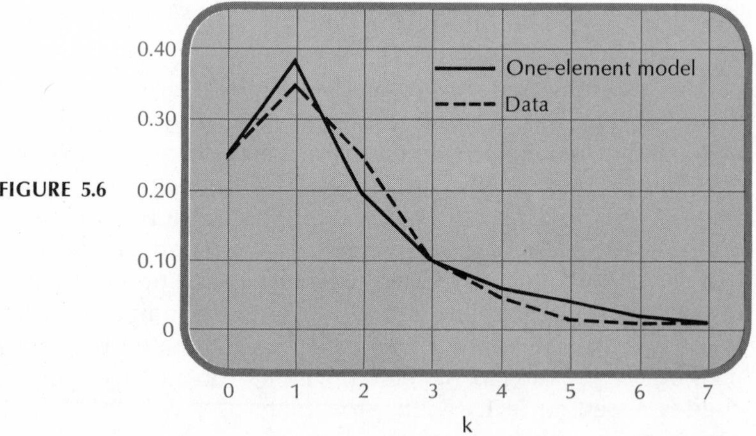

Distribution of T_N, the total number of errors per subject-item sequence. Note the good correspondence between predictions and data. (From Atkinson, Bower, & Crothers, 1965.)

Most theories of learning make simplifying assumptions that reduce their generality and power.

Mathematical theories of association are well-developed models whose aim is to generate a set of statistics that describe simple learning situations. The agreement of obtained and predicted results reflects the adequacy of the model. However, before we accept a model as a description of learning, we must consider the types of situations to which it has been applied and the assumptions we have made to simplify mathematical exposition. Most models of association assume that the subject has no strategy for learning the particular associations. The subject is assumed randomly to connect stimuli and responses until he hits upon the correct pairings. With young children this is a reasonable assumption, but with older children and adults there is ample evidence that strategies and bizarre associations between stimuli and responses are adopted. Also, once the subject has learned the association, there is the problem of performance. Mathematical theories of learning do not consider the influence of motivation. This is particularly relevant when stringent criteria are used to assess learning. The child may know the correct response, but before the stringent criteria are achieved he may miss an item because of boredom, curiosity, or momentary inattention. These factors should be included in our models.

The assumption of unitary stimuli is a gross simplification of perception.

The assumption that all stimuli and responses may be considered single elements is a gross simplification of the perceptual process. In many experiments these assumptions are met, but only by severely restricting their generality. Little work on perceptual learning has been done, although the theory of stimulus sampling is about perceptual learning.

Whether learning is all-or-none or incremental is a function of task and age.

If responses are well integrated, stimuli clearly differentiated, and stimulus-response pairings random, the subject appears to behave in an all-or-none fashion in learning. There is reason to believe, however, that children may show incremental learning in complex situations when the elements of the solution are not clear. In learning the concept of multiplication, for example, the child may not simply select relevant cues and associate them with the response. The whole problem of how the child progresses beyond the simple connecting of events and becomes able to form logical structures remains unsolved by these models.

Mathematical theories of learning are steppingstones to more adequate models of the mind.

Theories of learning are among the best examples of mathematical models available; they deserve careful study. Furthermore, the theory of stimulus sampling is a good model for the study of perceptual learning. The theories are restricted and make strong assumptions about the learning process, but they should not be rejected on these grounds. The present models are steppingstones toward more comprehensive theories. They should be judged by their fruitfulness in generating further models and not by their current generality or sophistication.

Operant behavior

Operant learning examines response as a function of reinforcement.

Simple stimulus-stimulus association cannot account for all the changes that take place during a child's development. Operant behavior is more complex; it concerns how the child's performance is influenced by association with reinforcement. No specific stimulus is required. Another difference between classical and operant behavior is the method used to elicit a response. In classical conditioning the response is elicited reflexively by an unconditioned stimulus. In operant behavior the experimenter must wait for an infant to produce a response voluntarily and then follow it with reinforcement. Following successive reinforcements, the child produces the response with increasing frequency. An operant response sets the occasion for reinforcement and occurs in the absence of specific, identifiable stimuli. Specific discriminative stimuli may be introduced into the operant situation to control the child's production of a response. For example, a response may be followed by reinforcement when a green light is on and not be followed by reinforcement when a red light is on. Operant procedures are used in a wide variety of clinical situations. Many behaviors can be manipulated by following the desired response with either positive reinforcement or the removal of negative reinforcement.

REINFORCEMENT

Effects of reinforcement

Resistance to extinction is greater following more or larger reinforcement.

Partial reinforcement produces greater resistance to extinction.

Resistance to extinction is positively related to the number of previously reinforced trials (see Figure 5.7). Other variables—for example, percent of trials followed by reinforcement, and the amount of reinforcement per trial—also influence extinction.

Children who receive partial reinforcement (only sometimes does reinforcement follow the response) resist extinction longer and respond faster than do children who receive reinforcement after every response. Partial reinforcement leads the child to perform the response for longer periods with no further external support. Bijou (1957) studied performance of preschool children using a ball-dropping technique with trinkets as rewards. Both groups received a total of six trinkets, but one group received 100 percent reinforcement, that is, a reinforcement every time the child made a response, while the other group received 20 percent reinforcement, two out of every ten responses were reinforced. The 20 percent reinforcement group made significantly more responses during a three and one-half minute extinction period than did the 100 percent reinforcement group.

FIGURE 5.7

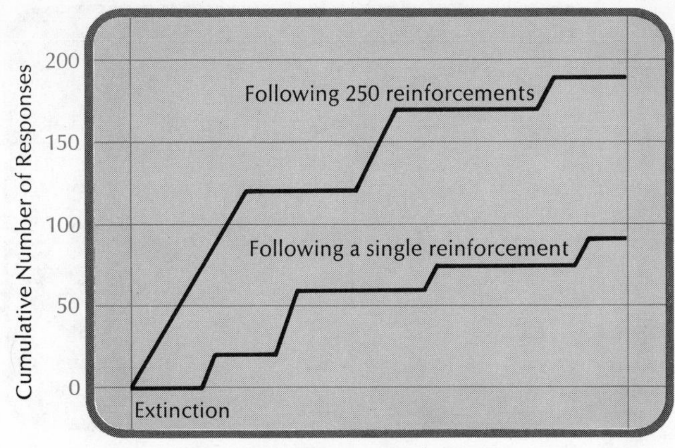

Cumulative curves during extinction. Curves of extinction of operant responses in the rat are plotted following a single reinforcement and following 250 reinforcements. The response is that of bar-pressing to obtain food. The plot shows the cumulative number of responses; every response raises the height of the curve, and the curve levels off when responses cease. (After Skinner, 1938.)

Young children respond more quickly when reinforcement is delayed, but they learn faster when reinforcement is immediate.

Other studies have considered the differential effect of immediate and delayed rewards (see Figure 5.8). Kindergarten and first grade children respond more *rapidly* in a situation in which reinforcement is delayed seven seconds than in a task with immediate reinforcement after a correct response, but they learn the immediately reinforced task better (Lipsitt & Castaneda, 1958). Rapid responding under the delayed condition is probably due to frustration, which tends to energize behavior.

A variety of reinforcing events exist; among them are social approval, candy, and toys.

Consumable, manipulable, and social tokens are all effective rewards for children. However, the strength of a reward depends on the social class, age, and drive level of the child. Specifically, lower class children tend to prefer tangible reinforcements (candy, toys) whereas middle and upper class children will learn equally well—or better—when reinforced by social approval. In addition, older children perform for social approval and the opportunity to be correct, whereas younger children prefer tangible rewards. The type of reward preferred and the ability to wait for a larger reward are both related to developmental maturity; the ability to delay gratification characterizes the socialized child.

FIGURE 5.8

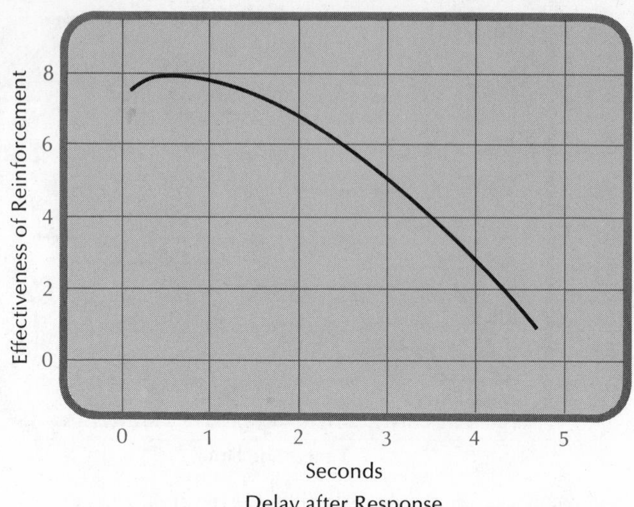

The effect of delay of reinforcement on the strength of an operant response.

Partial reinforcement leads to persistence, immediate reinforcement to quicker learning.

These rules are relevant to children in their natural setting. Consider the following examples: If you want a child to persist at a particular task, use a partial reinforcement schedule; give the child a trinket or social approval only occasionally. If you want a child to learn a task quickly, you should present the reward immediately after his response. The laws of learning suggest specific procedures to follow when you are interested in a particular goal.

Nonreinforcement and punishment

Nonreinforcement leads to extinction while punishment leads to suppression of the response. The consequences of these events are quite different.

Behavior may be modified either by nonreinforcement (extinction) or by punishment (suppression) of a response. However, the consequences of these widely used forms of control are quite different. A response may be eliminated from the repertoire of the child by nonreinforcement; in time he will come not to respond at all if he is not rewarded. On the other hand, if the same response is suppressed by punishment, it will reappear again as soon as the threat of punishment is removed (see Figure 5.9). When threat is removed the child will produce the original response with its original vigor (Estes, 1944). Suppression has only a short-term influence on behavior, and it produces undesirable side effects. Punishment increases the child's arousal level, resulting in heightened activity and less sensitivity to external cues. Punishment limits the child's learning and attentional abilities. Finally, punishment elicits aggression from the victim.

Nonreinforcement is the most efficient system for controlling children's behavior.

An efficient system for controlling the child's behavior involves removing those reinforcements that attract the child toward undesirable behavior, (parental attention) and channeling his activities into new directions by other reinforcements (social interaction). Fear and punishment emotionally arouse children, narrow their attention, and elicit aggressive responses. Extinction of the undesired response by removal of reinforcement is a more effective system for changing behavior.

Social conditioning

Social reinforcement (attention

In addition to the usual primary and secondary reinforcements (food, and lights associated with food), another class of events has attracted

FIGURE 5.9

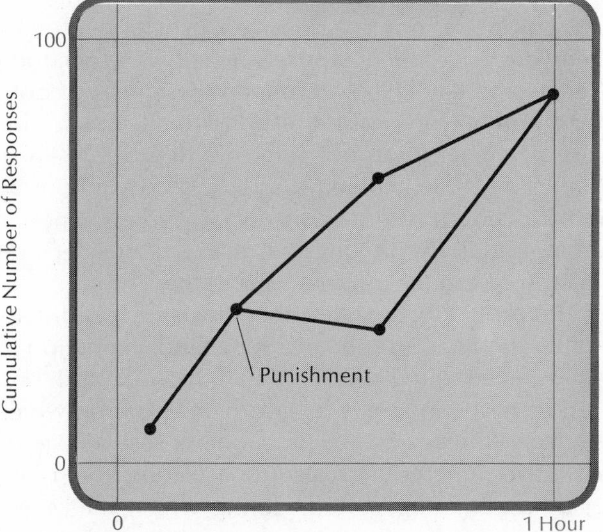

Cumulative curve of responses. Two cumulative curves showing that punishment only suppresses responding and does not produce extinction. At first the response rate decreased in the animals that were slapped; however, after a few trials (with no further punishment) their rate of responding increased, and they eventually produced as many responses as their unpunished peers. These findings strongly suggest that punishment is not an effective method for controlling behavior. The unwanted behavior will reappear as threat of punishment is removed. Effective control of behavior can be gained through extinction and then replacement of the old response.

from another) follows most of the rules of reinforcement.

considerable attention. The control of behavior by attention from another person has been extensively studied; reinforcement of responses by social interaction follows the same rules as do other types of reward. When social reinforcement is delayed, there is slower learning; intermittent social reinforcement leads to the same speed of acquisition but a higher resistance to extinction. The stronger the attraction of the reinforcing agent, the faster learning progresses—a child will perform better if social reinforcement comes from a valued peer rather than from a stranger. Finally, the more social reinforcements presented to a child, the stronger is his learning. However, social learning does *not* show the úsual pattern of deprivation effects (the longer a child is deprived of a primary reinforcer, the stronger is its attraction). Gewirtz and Baer (1958) assumed that social reinforcers might follow the principles of deprivation; they showed that children deprived of social interaction are more responsive to social reinforcement than are children who have been exposed recently to social interaction. However, Walters and Ray (1960) examined the effects of both social deprivation and emotional arousal on responsiveness to social reinforcement. They used a stranger to arouse some children while socially isolating others. Walters and Ray showed that arousal was important, but social isolation was not, in influencing social responsiveness to others in a reinforcing situation, proving that fear and not deprivation controlled the children in the Gewirtz and Baer study.

Brackbill showed that intermittent reinforcement leads to normal learning and higher resistance to extinction.

Brackbill (1958) tested the effects of two different social reinforcement schedules on the learning and extinction of smiling in eight infants aged three and one-half to four and one-half months. She used three periods—(1) a base period during which the experimenter stood motionless and expressionless just above the infant's face for eight five-minute intervals (to ascertain the base level of smiling); (2) a conditioning period, during which the experimenter reinforced the infant's smile (by speaking softly, picking the baby up, and fondling him); and (3) an extinction period similar to the base period. Infants were randomly divided into two groups. One group received reinforcements every time they smiled. The other group received reinforcements for every smile on the first few trials, then were gradually given reinforcements for every other smile (2:1), for every third smile (3:1), and finally only after four smiles (4:1). Both groups conditioned at about the same rate, but the intermittent reinforcement group—those receiving reinforcement after two or three or four smiles—showed greater responsiveness during the extinction period.

Infant vocalizations can be increased by social conditioning.

Another study of social conditioning was conducted by Rheingold and Gewirtz (1957). They manipulated vocalizations in three-month-old infants with the following procedure: There were two base-line days, during which no reinforcement was given to the infant, followed by two conditioning days (nine three-minute periods each day), during which the infant was reinforced for vocalizations. Reinforcement was a smile, vocal sounds, and a light touch to the infant's abdomen by the experimenter. Finally, there were two days of extinction, similar to the base-line days. The number of vocalizations increased significantly (see Figure 5.10) during the two conditioning days and decreased to the original level of vocalization during the two extinction days. Unfortunately, there was no "sensitization" control group; the increase in vocalizations may have been due to general excitation of the infant by repeated presentations of the reinforcing stimulus. In such a control group, the reinforcing stimulus would have been administered on a noncontingent basis (the same number of reinforcements, but not necessarily following a vocalization).

Weisberg showed that the social conditioning of infant vocalizations is due to contingent reinforcement and not activation.

To correct this deficiency, Weisberg (1963) divided 33 three-month-old infants into the following six groups: (1) no experimenter present, (2) experimenter present but not responding, (3) noncontingent social stimulation (a pseudoconditioning control), (4) noncontingent nonsocial stimulation, (5) contingent social stimulation (similar to the Rheingold & Gewirtz study), and (6) contingent nonsocial stimulation.

FIGURE 5.10

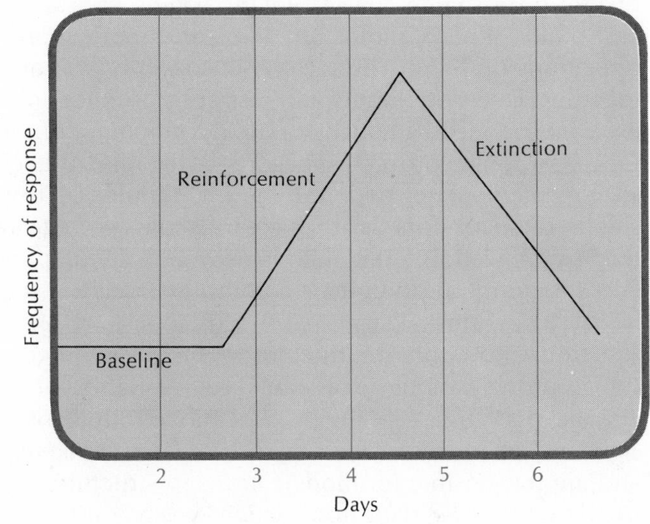

The effects of social reinforcement and extinction on infants' smiling.

In the noncontingent groups reinforcement was given randomly four times a minute. Social stimulation consisted of two seconds of rubbing the infant's chin, an open-mouthed smile, and the word "yea." Nonsocial stimulation consisted of a door chime. The contingent stimulation groups were on 100 percent reinforcement. All infants were placed in the experimental situation for two days of adaptation. Results showed that group one (a control for the presence of the experimenter) did not differ from group two (where the experimenter was present but not responding) in vocalization. The two pseudoconditioning groups showed no increase in vocalizations. Compared with the infants' vocalization rates in the presence of the unresponsive adult, vocalization was significantly higher for the contingent social reinforcement group. No effect was found for nonsocial stimulation. When social reinforcement was withdrawn during the extinction phase, the infants' rate of vocalization decreased significantly, although not to the original level. This well-controlled study demonstrates that the increased rate of vocalization was due to its association with social reinforcement and not to sensitization or pseudoconditioning.

COMPLEX PROCESSES IN LEARNING

Piaget believes that the infant comes into the world with a few reflexes and builds complex cognitive structures from them.

When Piaget (1952) observed his own children in their first three years of life, he assumed that an infant begins with a few innate reflexes and builds sensory-motor functions and more sophisticated cognitive operations on them. These early sensory-motor coordinations (binding together of sensory inputs and response productions to reach a simple external goal) lead gradually to the development of symbolic processes. Once symbolic processes become available, the child can actively search, manipulate, and test his environment. This active searching stands in sharp contrast to his earlier passive registration of memory traces (association). The child is now an inquiring scientist—given certain simple inputs, he builds a complex model of the world.

Piaget distinguishes between content, structure, and function.

In his writings, Piaget makes a basic distinction between structure, function, and content. Structure is the set of integrated interconnections among various ideas, abilities, or habits of the infant (which change over time and with experience). In contrast, functions are unchanging processes present in the early makeup of the organism and are responsible for modifications in structure. The contents of the mind are the raw data from which we may infer structure and function. The content is irrelevant in itself and becomes important only when we interpret it within our theoretical notions.

Piaget believes that the infant organizes his world by assimilation (taking input into existing structures) and accommodation (making new structures).

Piaget believes the newborn has two basic functions by which he organizes the world and maintains this organization in a state of equilibrium. The first function is assimilation, through which the infant fits environmental events into already existing cognitive structures. Assimilation results in no change in structure, no matter how inappropriate the classification. Accommodation, on the other hand, forces the infant to develop a new cognitive structure. Accommodation occurs when the repertory of the infant contains no category appropriate to handle a given sensory input. When the infant is presented a new sensory input, he must either develop a new category for it (accommodation) or distort the sensory information to fit existing categories (assimilation).

Accommodation is learning to call a flying squirrel a mammal while assimilation is calling the flying squirrel a bird.

To illustrate: A child familiar with flying animals will have available the category bird. The first time this child sees a flying squirrel, he is quite likely to call it a bird; he assimilates the flying squirrel into his already existing category of bird. He obviously distorts some properties of the object in making this classification. However, he may learn that it has no feathers or wings and is actually gliding. The child should then develop a new cognitive structure (through accommodation) in which to classify flying animals other than birds. Let us consider an example from a younger age. The first time an infant comes into contact with a ring, he will make a series of exploratory assimilations; he will stick it in his mouth, chew it, grasp it with his fingers, and suck on it. The ring is categorized under the class of things to be sucked and chewed. Later, the infant will begin to develop new ways of responding to the ring—throwing and twirling, for instance. At first, the young infant approaches every new object according to his category of "things to be mouthed." By a series of trials, he will gradually accommodate by developing new systems of behavior to encompass the ring.

A schema can be either a structure, a class of similar actions, or the operation which underlies actions.

A third major notion of Piaget's theoretical system is the "schema." A schema is (1) a cognitive structure, (2) a class of similar actions or thoughts, and (3) a category or underlying operation which subsumes a collection of similar action sequences. A schema may be all the means by which one can take a cookie from a jar, or it may be the class "dogs." Schemata are developed through experience. During a primary circular reaction, the child repeats the same act over and over—the action seems to generate itself (for example, sucking). Later, such simple events become linked and form a set of more complex operations (means) which the infant or child may use to order and understand his world. Piaget believes that schema may be developed separately to a point and then combined to form a superordinate schema through a process he calls reciprocal assimilation. Piaget stresses the integration of sensory-motor abilities in the development of intellect. This does not mean that Piaget is interested in motor skills. Instead, he is primarily concerned with the coordination of information from the various senses into a common picture of the world. Sensory-motor means the coordination of visual and kinesthetic information.

The functions of assimilation and accommodation don't change with age, only their relations.

In Piaget's "grand design," assimilation and accommodation are always interrelated. These two processes form an equilibrium (cognitive balance) in the developing organism. The functions of assimilation and accommodation do not change with the development of the organism; only their relations change systematically with age and experience. Piaget sees the basic development of the child shifting gradually from an early egocentric involvement in self (where the processes of assimilation and accommodation are undifferentiated and antagonistic) to a final stage of equilibrium and objectivity (in which assimilation and accommodation are separate and complementary). The various "stages" between these extremes may be represented by a differentiation of the two processes.

LEARNING TO LEARN

Children learn how to learn and thus change their association abilities.

Children learn how to learn. They do this by discovering strategies and rules in one situation and applying them in others. The ability to transfer a rule from one problem to another distinguishes the mature problem-solver from the naïve child. An example will illustrate rule learning and transfer. Suppose a child is brought into a room, seated at a low table, and told that he may win a large number of chips which will entitle him to a prize. He is shown three objects; two of the objects are alike and the third is different. The solution is to note that the two objects which are alike never conceal a chip, while the "odd" object always conceals a chip. The child's task is to look at the three objects and then tip over one to find the chip. He is allowed to keep the chip if he finds it. If he picks the wrong object, he may look at all three objects again, but is not allowed to correct his response. The first few problems puzzle the child. He has no particular notion of the rule to follow; he will respond randomly or by position preference until some hypothesis occurs to him. Very young children continue to respond randomly for many trials, and infants cannot learn this task. However, children over five can produce hypotheses after a few trials; they begin to pick the correct object—the "odd" one—more often. They learn a rule which allows them to solve a problem without previous experience with that particular example. They learn to transfer the rule "it is the odd one" from a situation in which they are presented with two spools and a wrench to another situation in which they are given a choice among two oranges and an apple. The ability to form these simple rules and transfer them from one situation to another distinguishes the concrete-operational child from the simple, sensory-motor infant.

Discrimination learning

Discrimination is the ability to tell stimuli apart.

Learning to differentiate the correct and incorrect stimuli from sets of items constitutes a major task for the child. He must learn to differentiate dogs from cats, houses from barns, trees from birds, and letters from each other. Psychologists have studied the process of distinguishing one item from another in relatively simple situations.

Psychologists have studied simultaneous and successive discrimination.

Two types of discrimination learning have been studied with children—simultaneous discrimination, in which both stimuli are presented at the same time, and successive discrimination, in which first one stimulus is presented and then (on the next trial) the other. Simultaneous presentation is more effective when the stimuli are quite similar, whereas successive presentation is more effective when the child's response to the discrimination is complex. For example, suppose we take two groups of fourth grade children and teach half the children in each group to differentiate among similar stimuli (pink and maroon), while the other children in each group are taught to differentiate among distinctive stimuli (red and blue). One group of children responds to the stimuli directly, while children in the other group respond to a button away from the colors. The stimuli are also presented for either simultaneous or successive discrimination (Jeffrey, 1958).

Under separate response conditions successive discrimination is easier; under connected response conditions simultaneous discrimination is easier.

The results (see Figure 5.11) show that when the locus of response was separate from the stimulus, successive discrimination was easier to master than simultaneous discrimination, presumably because in successive discrimination only one item is present at a time and the child is less likely to be confused about which button corresponds to which color. However, when the child was allowed to point to the colors, simultaneous discrimination was easier to master than successive discrimination. Touching one of the colors is a simpler response than pressing a button away from the stimulus, thus allowing the child to take advantage of the simultaneous presentation to compare the confusable stimuli. This suggests that a difficult response is more confusing to the child in the simultaneous than in the successive presentation of items. There was little or no difference between the similar and the distinctive cues in the simultaneous-presentation condition. Similarity of stimuli does not lead to confusion when the child can directly compare the alternatives. However, successive presentation of the similar stimuli made them much more difficult to learn than were

FIGURE 5.11

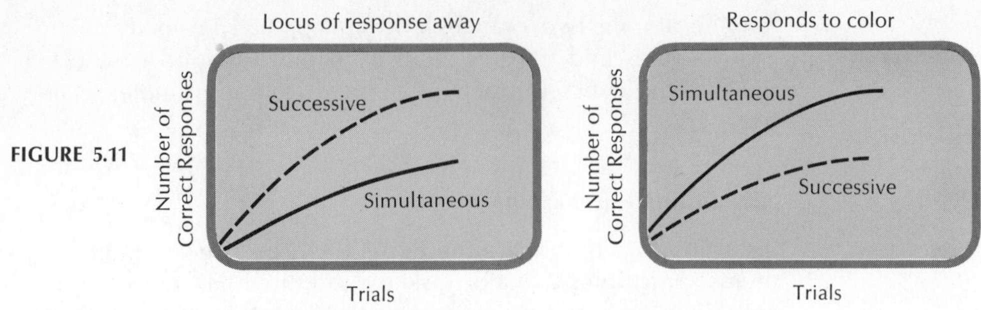

Simultaneous and successive discrimination learning in the child. The results show that simultaneous discrimination is more difficult than successive discrimination when the locus of response is away from the stimuli (left figure), while the opposite result occurs when the response is to the stimuli.

the more distinctive stimuli. It is only when the child must make absolute judgments—as are necessary with successive presentation—that similarity hinders him.

Concept formation

Concept learning is the association of several stimuli to a single response.

Concept learning is characterized by the association of a common response to several stimuli. The association may be on the basis of common elements, a rule, or some arbitrary characteristic of the stimulus set. The type of learning process used is a function of the child's level of development. Kendler and Kendler (1959) found that fast-learning subjects could reverse their response to the same dimension more easily than they could shift to another dimension; the opposite was true for slow learners. The Kendlers inferred that fast-learning children utilize a central conceptual process in the original discrimination (such as greater than, redder than, or square versus circle), while the slow learners make the discrimination by stimulus-response associations.

Bright children are more insightful about and more confused by complex stimuli (when the concept is really simple).

Osler and Fivel (1961) showed that bright children display more insightful learning than do their less intelligent peers. They used intelligent and dull children; half the children in each group worked with simple stimuli and half with complex stimuli. In each case the concept to be attained was the same (the number "two"). The complex stimuli generated many more possible hypotheses than the simple ones, interfering with the performance of the bright subjects. Although the complex stimuli made it more difficult for the bright children to solve the concept, they did not affect the dull children. The main characteristic that distinguishes the retarded child from the normal or superior child is not ability to learn simple associations or discrimination problems but ability to learn how to learn—to solve concept formation problems where he must extract the correct one from among several hypotheses.

SUMMARY

1 As a child matures he shifts from simple learning (the substitution of a conditioned stimulus for an unconditioned stimulus) through operant conditioning (production of a specific, reinforced response) to complex concept learning.

2 The child learns to learn; he formulates rules to describe his world. Classic theories of learning treat the child as a pale shadow of himself. They view the infant as a passive receiver of stimulus-response associations. However, the child is an active seeker after information.

3 The very young infant (before eight months of age) may fit the passive stimulus-response model, but the older child builds his own complex view of the world. The contingencies we present to him are no longer simple or direct (as the learning theorists would have us believe). On the contrary, even the simple situations we present to the older child are treated as complex, problem-solving situations to which he brings strategies, questions, and a history (Weir, 1964).

4 We cannot understand or predict how the child will perform by considering only simple stimulus-response theories. In the next chapter we see the young child as a model builder who develops his own internal representations of the world.

FURTHER READINGS

Hilgard, R. *Theories of learning.* New York: Appleton-Century-Crofts, 1956.

Spiker, C. C. Research methods in children's learning. In P. H. Mussen (Ed.), *Handbook of research methods in child development.* New York: Wiley, 1960. Pp. 374–420.

REFERENCES

Atkinson, R. C., Bower, G. H., & Crothers, E. J. *An introduction to mathematical learning theory.* New York: Wiley, 1965.

Bijou, S. W. Patterns of reinforcement and resistance to extinction in young children. *Child Development,* 1957, **28,** 47–54.

Bower, G. H., & Trabasso, T. R. Concept identification. In R. C. Atkinson (Ed.), *Studies in mathematical psychology.* Stanford, Calif.: Stanford University Press, 1964. Pp. 32–94.

Brackbill, Y. Extinction of the smiling response in infants as a function of reinforcement schedule. *Child Development,* 1958, **29,** 115–124.

Estes, W. K. An experimental study of punishment. *Psychological Monographs,* 1944, **57,** No. 263.

Gewirtz, J. L., & Baer, D. M. The effect of brief social deprivation on behaviors for a social reinforcer. *Journal of Abnormal and Social Psychology,* 1958, **56,** 49–56.

Guthrie, E. R. Association and the law of effect. *Psychological Review,* 1940, **47,** 127–148.

Hull, C. L. *A behavior system.* New Haven, Conn.: Yale University Press, 1952.

Jeffrey, W. E. Simultaneous and successive presentation of stimuli in discrimination learning with children. *American Psychologist,* 1958, **13,** 333.

Kendler, T. S., & Kendler, H. H. Reversal and nonreversal shifts in kindergarten children. *Journal of Experimental Psychology,* 1959, **58,** 56–60.

Lipsitt, L. P., & Castaneda, A. Effects of delayed reward on choice behavior and response speeds in children. *Journal of Comparative and Physiological Psychology,* 1958, **51,** 65–67.

Lipsitt, L. P., & Kaye, H. Change in neonatal response to optimizing and nonoptimizing sucking stimulation. *Psychonomic Science,* 1965, **2,** 221–222.

Marum, K. D. A study of classical conditioning in the human infant. Unpublished M.A. thesis, Brown University, 1963.

Mowrer, O. H. *Learning theory and behavior.* New York: John Wiley & Sons, Inc., 1960.

Osler, S., & Fivel, M. Concept attainment: I. The role of age and intelligence in concept attainment by induction. *Journal of Experimental Psychology,* 1961, **62,** 1–8.

Piaget, J. *The origins of intelligence in children.* New York: International University Press, 1952.

Postman, L. One-trial learning. In C. N. Cofer and B. Musgrave (Eds.), *Verbal behavior and learning.* New York: McGraw-Hill, 1963.

Rheingold, H. L., & Gewirtz, J. L. The conditioning of vocalizations in infants using an adult's social response as reinforcer. *American Psychologist,* 1957, **12,** 392.

Rock, I. The role of repetition in associative learning. *American Journal of Psychology,* 1957, **70,** 186–193.

Skinner, B. F. *The behavior of organisms.* New York: Appleton-Century-Crofts, 1938.

Suppes, P., & Ginsberg, R. Application of a stimulus sampling model to children's concept formation with and without an overt correction response. *Journal of Experimental Psychology,* 1962, **63,** 330–336.

Tolman, E. C. *Purposive behavior in animals and men.* New York: Appleton-Century-Crofts, 1932.

Walters, R. H., & Ray, E. Anxiety, social isolation and reinforcer effectiveness. *Journal of Personality,* 1960, **28,** 358–367.

Watson, J. B. *Psychological care of infant and child.* New York: W. W. Norton & Company, Inc., 1928.

Weir, M. W. Developmental changes in problem solving strategies. *Psychological Review,* 1964, **71,** 473–490.

Weisberg, P. Social and nonsocial conditioning of infant vocalizations. *Child Development,* 1963, **34,** 377–388.

6 THOUGHT

How well he's read, to reason against reading!
LOVE'S LABOUR'S LOST

This chapter presents Piaget's notions about children's thinking during the periods of preoperational and concrete-operational development. These phases in the growth of intellect, characterized by the development of sign-significate differentiation and logical operations, occur between two and ten years of age. The features of preoperational thought, the development of signs, and the several logical groupings of the period of concrete operations are covered. Examples of some groupings are given, followed by a discussion of children's concept attainment. A final section covers computer simulation of the development of thought.

STAGES OF CHILDREN'S THOUGHT

Piaget believes that children's thought is characterized by realism and animism.

Piaget proposed two intellectual traits which characterize children's thought: realism and animism. These tendencies grow from the child's egocentrism; he cannot differentiate himself from the world. The infant is also unable to discriminate clearly between psychological and physical events; human experiences—thoughts, feelings, wishes, and so on—constantly get confused with objective reality. The child tends to see psychological events such as thoughts, dreams, and names as physical entities; Piaget calls this realism. A complementary form of egocentrism is the tendency to give physical objects and events psychological attributes, to endow them with life or consciousness; this is animism.

Young children believe thought and speaking are the same; they confuse names and objects.

Young children are inclined to identify thought with the act of speaking (thought as an event rather than a psychological process). For the young child a name is also an essential part of its referent, the name of the sun is a physical part of the sun itself. Dreams are also regarded as substantial entities, located external to the child, and only later are they seen as subjective and internal.

Piaget studies children's thoughts by a series of "clinical" questions.

In one study (Flavell, 1963) the experimenter asked the child a series of questions about dreams, taking care, whenever possible, to avoid suggestion. "You know what a dream is?" "You dream sometimes, at night?" "Then tell me where the dreams come from." "While you dream, where is the dream?" "What do you dream with?" And so on. The following protocol illustrates features of the first stage:

> **Metr (5:9):** "Where does the dream come from?—I think you sleep so well that you dream.—Does it come from us or from outside?—From outside.—What do we dream with?—I don't know.—With the hands? . . . With nothing?—Yes, with nothing.—When you are in bed and you dream, where is the dream?—In my bed, under the blanket. I don't really know. If it was in my stomach (!) the bones would be in the way and I shouldn't see it.—Is the dream there when you sleep?—Yes, it is in the bed beside me." We tried suggestion: "Is the dream in your head?—It is I that am in the dream: it isn't in my head (!). When you dream, you don't know you are in the bed. You know you are walking. You are in the dream. You are in bed, but you don't know you are.—Can two people have the same dream?—There are never two dreams (alike).—Where do dreams come from?—I don't know. They happen.—Where?—In the room and then afterward they come up to the children. They come by themselves.—You see the dream when you are in the room, but if I were in the room, too, should I see it?—No, grown-ups (*les Messieurs*) don't ever dream.—Can two people ever have the same dream?—No, never.—When the dream is in the room, is it near you?—Yes, There!" (*pointing to 30 cms. in front of his eyes*) (Piaget, 1929, pp. 97–98).

Young children believe anything is potentially alive; finally, they come to know that only animals and plants live.

Another study concerned the types of objects the child will classify as alive. The sequence shows a gradual restriction of the objects that a child is willing to believe live. A complementary investigation was devoted to the child's attribution of consciousness—thought, feeling, intentionality, and so on—to various types of objects. The questions were: "If I pull off this button, will it feel it?" "Does the sun know it gives light?" "Would a table feel it if I were to prick it?" Piaget suggested there are four stages: (1) Almost any object is potentially conscious, given the right conditions. For example, a stone may normally be considered nonsentient, but will "feel it" if it is moved. Piaget appears to have found no children willing to assert that all objects are at all times conscious. (2) The potentiality for consciousness is generally attributed only to objects that regularly possess some kind of movement, whose special function is movement, and so on. Thus, a bicycle and the wind may know how to feel, but a stone cannot. (3) Only objects capable of spontaneous motion are conscious; the sun and wind can be, but no longer the bicycle. (4) Finally, the child attributes consciousness only to people and animals. The following is an interesting example of spontaneously expressed animism:

> We hung a metal box from a double string and placed it in front of Vel, in such a way that, on letting go of the box, the string unwound making the box turn round and round. "Why does it turn?—Because the string is twisted.—Why does the string turn too?—Because it wants to unwind itself.—Why?—Because it wants to be unwound (it wants to resume its original position, in which the string was unwound).—Does the string know it is twisted?—Yes.—Why?—Because it wants to untwist itself, it knows it's twisted!—Does it really know it is twisted?—Yes. I am not sure,—How do you think it knows?—Because it feels it is all twisted" (Piaget, 1929, pp. 175–176).

THE DEVELOPMENT OF SYMBOLIC REPRESENTATION

The period between sensory-motor development (0–2 years) and logical thought (about 13 years) is characterized by the growth of symbols.

The growth of preoperational thought occurs roughly in the time span bound by the last stage of sensory-motor development (approximately two years of age) and the period of concrete operations (around six years of age). In the beginning of this period, the infant possesses only sensory-motor abilities, but near the end he is capable of symbolic manipulations and logical operations. Preoperational thought is action-based and limited in scope, whereas concrete-operational thought shows logical processes at work. To appreciate the development of a sensory-motor infant into a child with preoperational thought and symbolic representations, we need to understand how the infant comes to possess symbolic representations and to think logically.

The primary requirement for the development of symbols is the differentiation of signs and significants.

The basic requirement for the development of representation is the ability to differentiate signs (words, symbols) from their significates (objects, relations). Once the child develops symbol capability, he may use signs to stand for events of the world. Although the young infant (one year) seems capable of very primitive sign-significate differentiations, it is only much later that he can easily evoke a sign (image) to represent a perceptually absent event. Because of this symbolic function, preoperational thought differs dramatically from simple sensory-motor behavior. Sensory-motor infants can link only successive actions or perceptual states. However, with the development of symbolic abilities, the infant can simultaneously grasp a sweep of separate events. He can recall the past, represent the present, and anticipate the future in a single symbolic process. The ability to differentiate signs from significates and to develop relations among those signs generates a more powerful and flexible cognitive structure than anything available to the sensory-motor infant. These symbolic abilities mark the transition from a simple passive receptor of events to a thinking, organizing, active child who builds models of the world.

Bruner (1960) suggests that the child uses three modes of symbolization during development: (1) *enactive representation*—the use of motor responses to stand for objects or relations; (2) *iconic representation*—the use of images to signify events; and (3) *symbolic representation*—the use of arbitrary signs (language) to represent things. There is a progression through these stages of representation, although adults may use all of them at varying times. He believes that language is not essential to thought but amplifies the process by systematizing it.

REMARKS: THEORY

Why does the infant not stay a simple, sensory-motor organism? That question plagues developmental psychology. One answer derives from the speculations of Hebb (1949) on perceptual learning. Hebb believes that when the same sensory-motor act is performed over and over, characteristics of these sensory and motor events are represented by neural traces. These representational neural patterns fire in a rapid sequence (as a cell assembly or phase sequence), allowing the organism to model and anticipate reality. These internal neural events are the first stage of symbolic representation. Once the infant begins internally to represent complex sets of sensory-motor events, he needs a simplifying rule by which to order happenings. He must develop a notion of what goes with what. This ordering process allows structuring of the world and permits generalizations to other events. The child learns to learn, and to solve problems; he begins to think. He develops techniques and rules for gathering, processing, storing, and retrieving information. He learns to ignore the specific instance and to remember and operate on the more general characteristics of the world. Common perceptual elements lead eventually to common conceptual groupings.

Hebb (1949, p. 70) writes on how perceptual integration may occur:

> The answer is not simple; perceptual integration would not be accomplished directly, but only as a slow development, and, for the purposes of exposition, at least, would involve several distinct stages, with the first of which we shall now be concerned.
>
> The general idea is an old one, that any two cells or systems of cells that are repeatedly active at the same time will tend to become "associated," so that activity in one facilitates activity in the other.

He goes on to outline how a series of cells may fire repeatedly in close contiguity and thereby develop a potentiating "cell assembly." The cell assembly is the equivalent of a schema in Piaget's formulation.

Munsinger & Kessen proposed that the child is: (1) sensitive to complexity, (2) limited in his abilities, (3) learns rules to structure the world, and (4) prefers to operate within his abilities.

Munsinger and Kessen (1966) proposed a model of how the child structures environmental variability. The propositions of their model were three: (1) complexity—human beings are sensitive to stimulus complexity; (2) limit—there is an upper limit on the capacity of human beings to process environmental information; (3) structuring—human beings are able to break through this limitation on their capacity to process independent environmental events through the development of rules that reduce the effective stimulus complexity. As another view of this problem, assume that children respond to cognitive complexity. In the limiting case, the unrealistic one in which there is no organizing structure, cognitive complexity is a simple function of stimulus complexity. However, even for unsophisticated human beings (the newborn infant at the extreme), rules are available that allow some coding or processing of stimulus complexity. Thus, we can think of cognitive complexity as a joint function of stimulus complexity and cognitive structure. Assume that human beings prefer an intermediate level of cognitive complexity. If stimulus complexity increases, with no concurrent increase in cognitive structure, the child's cognitive input will increase and he will be confused. However, by learning rules to simplify stimulus complexity the child can grow to handle increased information—and he will prefer it. This mechanism is a building block for a general model of intellective development. As a child learns to structure his world, he turns toward higher levels of stimulus complexity. This simple notion can be used to understand the child's preference for more complex events as he develops. It is the basis of curiosity.

THE NATURE OF PREOPERATIONAL THOUGHT (FLAVELL, 1963)

Preoperational thought is egocentric.

Preoperational thought is primitive, confused, and rigid; it is the infant's initial attempt at thinking. What sort of primitive characteristics does it possess? A major feature is its egocentrism. Representations of the preoperational child are egocentric, as the sensory-motor actions of the infant are egocentric. Preoperational thought stands somewhere between the socialized adult and the Freudian unconscious. This egocentrism is seen dramatically when the child must simultaneously look at a three-dimensional display from position *A* and represent the appearance of the display from position *B* (say from behind it). A common response of the preoperational child is to describe his own perspective (Figure 6.1). Suppose a preoperational child is shown the three-dimensional display of mountains pictured in Figure 6.1. The child's response when asked to draw them from position *Y* when he

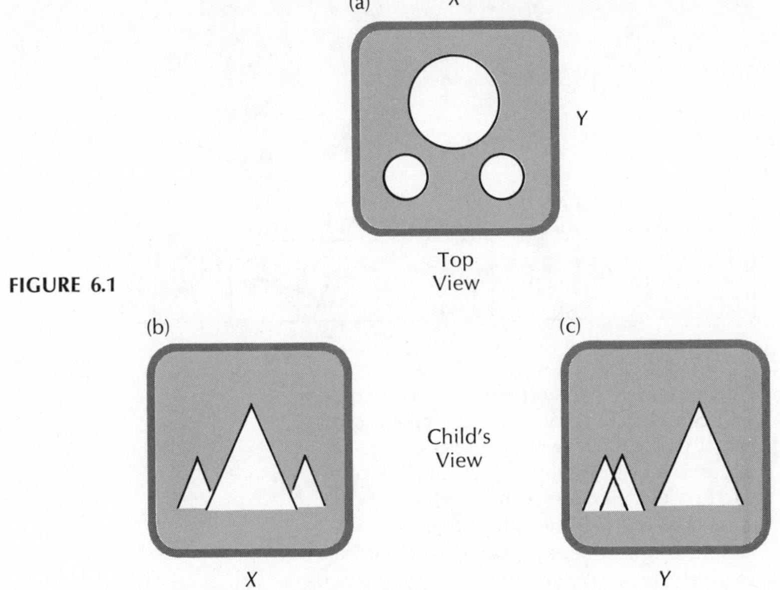

FIGURE 6.1

If a preoperational child is shown the three-dimensional display, shown in (a) from the top view, and asked to draw it from his position at *X,* he will draw the view shown in (b). However, if he is asked to draw the same display (still standing at *X*) from the imagined position *Y,* he will *not* produce (c) but will again draw the view from *X* (Figure 6.1b).

is at *X* will be the same as asking him to draw them from position *X.* He cannot take the position of another or imagine that the view might change. The preoperational child feels no need to justify his reasoning by logic or to look for internal consistency in his thoughts. Only through a long series of social interactions does he emerge as an interpersonal being.

The preoperational child cannot consider more than one perceptual event at a time.

A second characteristic of preoperational thought is centration. The preoperational thinking of children concentrates on a single feature of an object to the neglect of other important aspects. The preoperational child distorts his reasoning processes because he cannot decentrate (consider other features of the situation that would compensate for the distorting effects of a single dominant perceptual factor). He attends to superficial features of events, understanding only those characteristics which attract his attention. For example (see Figure 6.2), while admitting that two identical containers

FIGURE 6.2

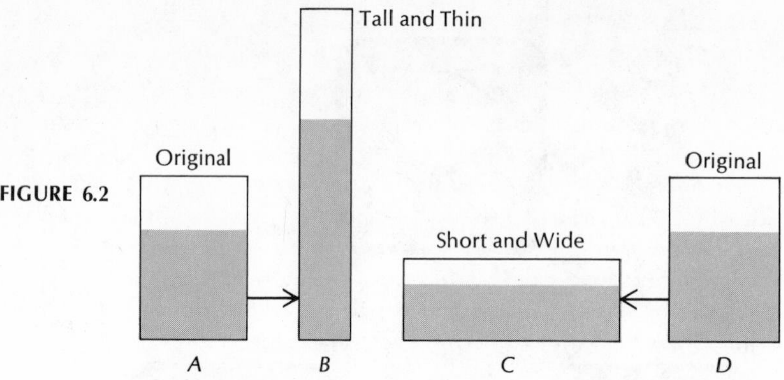

Preoperational children (before about 7 years of age) concentrate (center) on one aspect of the tall jar or the short, wide jar; they either say the new vessel contains less, if they are centered on the thinness or the shortness, or that it contains more, if they are centered on the tallness or the wideness, than the original jar. The inability to consider two factors characterizes the preoperational child.

have the same quantity of liquid (*A* and *D*), he will deny this equivalence in quantity after the contents of *A* are poured into a tall, thin container (*B*), while he watches, or into a short, broad container (*C*). He may assert that content *B* is now greater than *A*. In this situation, he centers solely on the height of *B* and therefore says it contains more liquid because it is tall, or else he centers on the width of the column of liquid in *B* and says that it contains less because it is thin. The preoperational child characteristically fails to consider, *jointly*, height and width. He does not understand that the height of *B* is compensated by its width. The preoperational child has a very limited capacity for processing information from several sources simultaneously, and as a result he neglects the compensating processes which lead to invariance of quantity or weight under changes in shape.

The preoperational child concentrates on static states rather than dynamic transformations.

A third characteristic of preoperational thought is the child's attention to static states rather than to transformations. He responds to successive patterns rather than to the transformations by which one state changes into another. Experiments in which liquids are poured from one jar to another may be used to explore this process. These problems contain an initial state *A*, some transformation, and a final state *B*. The transformation (pouring *A* into *B*) is lost for the preoperational child. He is not able to base his judgment on changes. Preoperational thought is superficial and rigid; it attends to this or that static condition but is not able to link successive states into a coherent sequence. This process reflects a limitation on the ability of the young child to handle complex information processing. He selects from the world a few simple events to code and store. The first events are steady-state phenomena. Later, he develops more complex processing rules and so is able to include the transformation from state *A* into state *B*. With these more powerful rules comes a gradual understanding of logically coherent systems and the notion of conservation.

The preoperational child cannot reverse his logic.

A final characteristic of preoperational thought is its nonreversibility. Reversibility—like equilibrium, to which it is closely related—is a complex notion. A cognitive organization is reversible if one can generate a path of thought, perhaps a few steps of reasoning about some transformation of a display, and then at some point along the trail reverse direction and find the original point of departure. If a thought process is not reversible, the child cannot regain the beginning state of the logical process once he has carried out part of the chain. Nonreversible thought processes cannot combine various transformations into a single organized system. The preoperational child cannot see that each change has an inverse (that one change may compensate for another) and that these compensating changes assure an underlying invariance for the whole system. By contrast, a reversible thought sequence is flexible and can correct for irrelevant changes by considering several characteristics of the situation simultaneously. The perceptually oriented processes of early preoperational thought are not reversible; they follow single events. For example, in the liquid problem the preoperational child cannot understand that conservation of quantity is insured because there exists an inverse transformation which will reproduce the original state (pouring the liquid from the flat, wide jar *C* back into the taller glass *A*). These two transformations exactly cancel each other, showing that the quantity of liquid has remained the same. Because of his nonreversibility, the preoperational child is constantly faced with contradictions.

CONCRETE OPERATIONS

The interval between sensory-motor and logical processes is characterized by two stages: preoperational thought and concrete operations.

The preoperational child's thought processes are more sophisticated than those of the sensory-motor infant. The preoperational child is capable of symbolic representation instead of only direct action. Piaget has subdivided the transition between sensory-motor and logical thought into two phases—the period we have just discussed, with the development of signs, and the stage of concrete operations, which develops in school. The main difference between the preoperational and the concrete-operational child concerns the stability and integration of his cognitive system. The child who has concrete operations possesses a solid, flexible, consistent cognitive structure. He does not fall into the perplexing contradictions of the preschool child.

An operation may be adding, classifying, or dividing.

What sort of cognitive process might be an operation? Basically, any process that is an integral part of an organized system—adding, subtracting, multiplying, dividing, or setting terms into correspondence within classes—is a logical operation available to the concrete-operational child. Consider a simple example: Suppose we have a set of marbles. The child may consider these sets of similar things, thus forming classes. He may also combine these classes—a logical operation of union—to form a superordinate class. The concrete-operational child can use relations of asymmetry and symmetry (*A* is the father of *B; A* is the brother of *B*) and he can combine them into new relations. From a set of asymmetrical, symmetrical, and equality transformations, the concrete-operational child can produce transitivity.

Why classification systems become organized is our fundamental problem.

Why do these operations come together into a total system? Piaget (1949) argues that they must necessarily gather, because one cannot understand the notion of class without understanding the implications of a classification system. He believes that the single class is only an abstraction from the total system. This statement guarantees that one needs the notion of total classification systems, but it does not explain why or how the child comes to develop it. One may borrow a page from learning theory, an explanation from heredity, or talk about equilibrium and equilibration; but whatever the explanatory mechanism, it seems clear that we must postulate some system of superordinate hierarchies in order to understand the preschool and the school child. This little question is the very heart of cognitive development. Once we know how a superordinate system is formed, we will know how the child develops intelligence from simple associations.

The preoperational child is centered on one perceptual event; the concrete-operational child considers more than one.

Consider an example of how possession of concrete operations might influence a child's understanding of liquids poured into different-shaped vessels. Recall that the preoperational child sees the appearance of things as their ultimate reality. He centers attention on the end state of a transformation, is unduly impressed by the magnitude of either height *or* width of the fluid, and errs according to the perceptual dominance of one of these characteristics. Domination by one perceptual event (with little or no systematic reference to other events) is the fate of the preoperational child. On the other hand, the operational child devotes much more attention to transformations; he can coordinate and reverse his cognitive processes. He approaches a problem quite differently. The concrete-operational child sees the transformation of *A* to *C* as an instance of the total system of possible transformations of *A* to C_1, *A* to C_2, *A* to C_3, · · · , *A* to C_n. Also, these possible transformations can be in the opposite direction, C_1 to *A*, C_2 to *A*, and so on (liquid obtained from the original vessel may be poured back). Similarly, the child of concrete operations understands that increases in height may be compensated by decreases in width. The older child possesses a crucial operator which the younger does not. The concrete-operational child brings to bear a system of potential operations on the specific instance at hand, and by so doing he can see the specific state as one of a set of possible alternatives.

The structures of concrete operations

Piaget believes that logical systems are good models of the child's mind.

The sensory-motor and preoperational processes of development may be represented by a probabilistic system, but concrete operations should be modeled by a logical computing machine that manipulates abstract structures. Piaget (1949) argues that mathematical-logical structures *are* models of the actual organization and processes of cognition in childhood. Logical structures constitute ideal patterns toward which all living systems evolve, and they provide us with useful criteria of how thought is organized. When Piaget says that the child possesses logical class addition, he means that the child's thought has certain formal properties—reversibility, associability, composition, tautology, and so on—as these are defined in logical algebra. He infers from the child's behavior a cognitive structure which has these properties. These logical systems and the rules governing their relations make up the theoretical model, the pattern of cognitive interrelations. This system of logic is not a wholly accurate model of the child; he often makes irrational or illogical steps during his development. The logic should be seen as an ideal toward which the child develops rather than a description of the actual processes of thought in the young child.

Kessen believes we must know our assumptions about the world; otherwise, we predetermine the theories and data we produce.

Kessen (1965) posed several questions for any theory of cognitive development. These questions seem particularly relevant to the use of logic and mathematics as models of the child. He suggested that before we make statements about cognition, we must be very clear about our own explicit or implicit epistemological assumptions (our assumptions about *how* we know). Kessen believes that the assumptions we make about how we know prejudge the kinds of data and theories we can generate. His suggestion of an antidote is neither the operationism of the 1940s (define everything in concrete terms) nor the empiricism which flourished in psychology following Watson's (1919) destruction of Mind (gather facts and they will lead us to understanding). Instead, he prescribes a thoughtful consideration of the broad range of questions subsumed under philosophical notions of theory construction, data collection, and epistemology. Unless we make explicit our assumptions about how we know, we will follow only our own jumbled, tangled web of presuppositions and prejudgments about the state of knowledge and find in our theories the implicit assumptions we have fallen into without thought. Explicit assumptions are helpful; hidden assumptions are only traps.

Groupings as concrete operations

Groupings are classifications of elements.

A grouping is a classification of a set of elements. The properties of composition, associativity, identity, and reversibility hold true. Several groupings of logical classes proposed by Piaget (Flavell, 1963, pp. 173–187) follow.

LOGICAL GROUPINGS IN COGNITIVE BEHAVIOR

Piaget proposed eight groupings as models of a child's thinking; the evidence for some groupings is sparse.

How do all of these groupings function in the analysis of human intellective behavior? They are presumed to be a model of how the child functions during the concrete-operational period. To make the model complete, Piaget should have not only asserted that the logical-mathematical structures are intended to be models but also developed theorems from the logical sets and collected data to establish relations between model and child. However, the data needed to make this 1:1 correspondence exist only in part. He seems to have divided his approach into two major sections—first, the logical operations that might be available to the child and, second, the empirical evidence. In many ways his approach is formally analogous to (1) the problem of a computer program which has the capacity to perform certain logical operations and (2) the problem of computer simulation, in which one tries to write a computer program to describe the behavior of a particular child.

Piaget proposed several possible models of thought but did not explain how to know which describes the child.

Piaget has done much more about writing logical programs than he has about the simulation of a child. His logical groupings were not derived from watching children think. For example, it turns out that Piaget has no empirical evidence relating to the concrete operations of groupings or of relations. These groupings were invented because they describe logically possible cognitive structures, not ones which have been seen. This is a fruitful area in need of further work. At the moment, a structural model for cognition is more a frame of reference than anything like a precise statement of thought. The experimental data necessary to support the logical system as a model of cognition exist only in fragments. However, the analogy of a logical-mathematical theory as a model of cognition has suggested several experiments. As an example, we may analyze the properties of Grouping III and see that a basic component is the ability to find the logical product or intersect of two overlapping classes. We can then devise studies to see if children (at appropriate ages) can in fact handle problems involving class multiplication. The existing experimental evidence on each of the logical groupings is reviewed, along with the properties of the groupings.

Grouping I—Primary addition of classes

Primary addition of classes possesses composition, associativity, general identity, and reversibility.

The basic properties of class addition (and all the other groupings) are as follows: (1) *Composition*—the product that results from combining any element with any other by means of a defined operation is itself an element in the class system: $(a + a' = b)$ and $(b + b' = c) \rightarrow (a + a' + b' = c)$. (2) *Associativity*—the sum of the series of elements is independent of the way they are grouped: $a + (b + c) = (a + b) + c$. (3) *General identity*—there is one and only one element—the identity element—that, when added to any other element whatsoever, leaves the other element unchanged. Piaget defines this element somewhat arbitrarily as the equation $0 + 0 = 0$ (the sum of two null classes). (4) *Reversibility*—for each and every element there is one and only one element, called its inverse, which yields the identity element when added to the former. The inverse of $a + a' = b$ is $-a-a' = -b$.

The addition of classes is Grouping I.

Considerable evidence is available concerning Grouping I. Piaget and Inhelder (1941) have shown that the ability to add classes is present in the concrete-operational child, but not in the preoperational child. The child with concrete operations can develop rough classifications, combine elementary classes into superordinate classes, and reverse this process by decomposing higher-order classes into their components.

The question about wooden and brown beads is a good example of Group I classification.

As an example suppose a child is presented with 20 wooden beads (see Figure 6.3), 17 brown and three white, and is asked, "Can you make a longer necklace with the brown beads or with the wooden beads?" (That is, is brown smaller than wooden.) The younger child (preoperational) tends to assert that the brown beads would make the longer necklace, because there are only three white ones. Piaget interprets this and similar kinds of behavior as suggesting that the young child does not have a completely reversible system of class operation. The experimenter has established beforehand that the child knows all the beads are wooden. When his attention is directed toward the brown beads, however, the fact that all the beads are wooden fades from awareness and only the white beads remain for comparison. The preoperational child is working at the perceptual level.

FIGURE 6.3

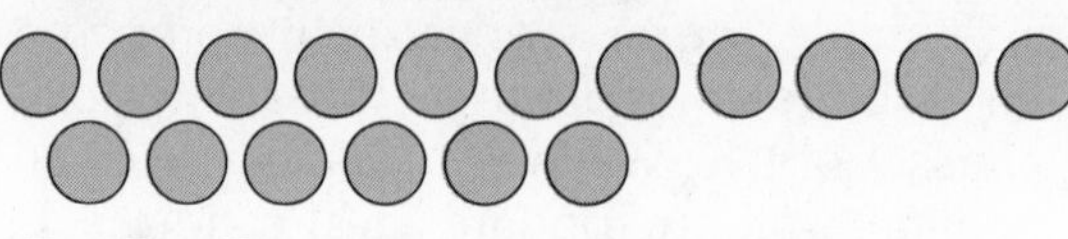

The experimental situation presented to a child to test for primary addition of classes. The preoperational child says there are more brown beads than white ones; the correct answer to the question is that there are more *wooden* beads—since all the beads are wooden. The confusion here may be linguistic. These studies should be replicated using perceptually available information and nonverbal methods. If the child persists in saying that there are more brown beads than wooden beads, then he does not understand addition of classes.

Grouping II—Secondary addition of classes

Operations associated with Grouping II concern class hierarchies.

Operations contained in Grouping II pertain to class hierarchies of the form $a + a' = b$ and $b + b' = c$. In these hierarchies the primary classes a, b, and c each refer to a single class, whereas the secondary classes a', b', and c' denote an unspecified number of classes of the same rank as the corresponding primary class. That is, a' does not refer to the single class with rank a but refers to all the complementary classes under b. As a specific example, suppose a is the color blue; then a' could be all the other visible colors and b would constitute the class "visible colors." Then b' could be the set of spectral energies of other frequencies and c could be the class of all electromagnetic energies.

The classification of one set of objects in several ways is an example of hierarchical grouping.

The only evidence we may cite on this ability is from a set of papers by Piaget and Inhelder (1959), which shows that the child is able to classify a given set of objects in several different ways. Such reclassification results precisely in equations of the type described in Grouping II.

Grouping III—Multiplication of classes

The multiplication of classes is Grouping III; here the intersection of classes (urban, Negro, poor) is the product.

Classes can be multiplied and divided as well as added and subtracted. Suppose we take a class of people, d_1, and divide it into subclasses according to skin color (a_1 = white, b_1 = black, c_1 = yellow). Note here that although $a_1 + b_1 + c_1 = d_1$, the subclasses a_1, b_1, and c_1 are of the same class rank. Similarly, we can take the same class of people called d_2 and subdivide them according to where they live (a_2 = urban, b_2 = suburban, c_2 = rural). Once these two series are constituted, one can logically multiply a member of one series by a member of the other. The result of this multiplication is the logical product of *intersect* (the largest class with the two members comprised in common). Thus, one can perform operations like ($a_1 \cap a_2$), the class of people who are both white and who live in the city, ($c_1 \cap b_2$), people who are both yellow and who live in the suburbs, etc.

The ability to complete a three by three matrix is an example of Grouping III.

Several relevant experiments are available for Grouping III. For example, Piaget and Inhelder (1959) have studied the simple operation of 1:1 correspondence, the fundamental process of all Grouping III operations. Also, they have performed a series of experiments in which the child is presented with a horizontal row of pictures of different forms which meet at right angles with a vertical column of differing colors (see Figure 6.4). The child's task is to determine which picture should be placed at the intersect of these two vectors. Since the picture in question will be in both a row and a column, it must contain both class attributes, for example, a red square. The mastery of this simple matrix problem comes at the level of concrete operations.

Grouping IV—Co-univocal multiplication of classes

Grouping IV involves the multiplication of one set with many others.

The formalized multiplication of groups established in Grouping III involves 1:1 correspondences between each of the component members of two or more series of classes. There is a second kind of class multiplication called co-univocal (one to many), in which one member of one series is set in correspondence with several members of each of one or more additional series.

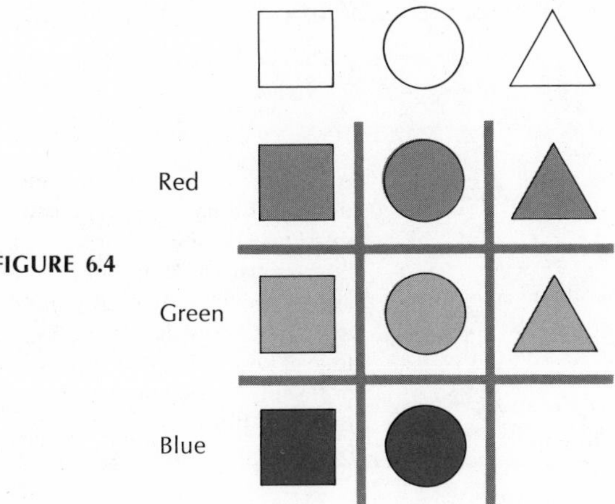

FIGURE 6.4 Univocal multiplication of classes. The child's task is to construct the intersections of form and color. For example, the first intersection should produce a red square, the second a red circle, and so on. If the child can combine the characteristics of a row and a column into a single class, he understands simple multiplication of classes.

There is no evidence related to Grouping IV.

There is no known evidence on Grouping IV. However, on Grouping V, the core of operations on relations, there is the whole problem of seriation itself—the building of elements into a transitive asymmetrical series.

Grouping V—Addition of asymmetrical relations

The addition of asymmetrical relations involves the notion of transitivity and seriation.

Groupings I through IV contain operations performed upon logical classes, whereas the remaining groupings involve operations performed upon the relations which exist between two or more classes. Piaget describes a number of different kinds of relations. Grouping V is specifically concerned with asymmetrical relations (*A* is smaller than *B*, higher than *B*, equal to *B*, etc.) whose compositions are transitive. Transitivity implies that if *A* is smaller than *B* and *B* is smaller than *C*, then *A* is smaller than *C*. Asymmetrical relations denote ordered differences between terms—differences, because smaller than *A* indicates a way in which *B* differs from *A*; ordered, because the differences go in a special direction ($A < B$ is not equal to $A > B$). Grouping V describes the logical addition and subtraction of these order differences. The groupings for relations parallel closely the groupings for classes.

The problem of transitivity has been studied extensively; children of the concrete-operational stage know $A > B$; $B > C$; therefore, $A > C$.

Piaget and Inhelder (1941) have studied this problem extensively. Usually the child is presented three objects of different shapes and allowed to compare only two objects at a time (Figure 6.5). The younger child does two unusual things in this task. First, for a set of three objects $A < B$, $B < C$, he is willing to form a complete ordered set after having established only that $A < B$ and $A < C$. Also, he is not at all sure that $A < C$ is guaranteed from knowledge only about $A < B$ and $B < C$. The child's major difficulty stems from an inability to understand that each item of an asymmetrical series must be considered in terms of both the direct (larger than) and the inverse (smaller than) relational operation—in terms of the reversibility of the relation.

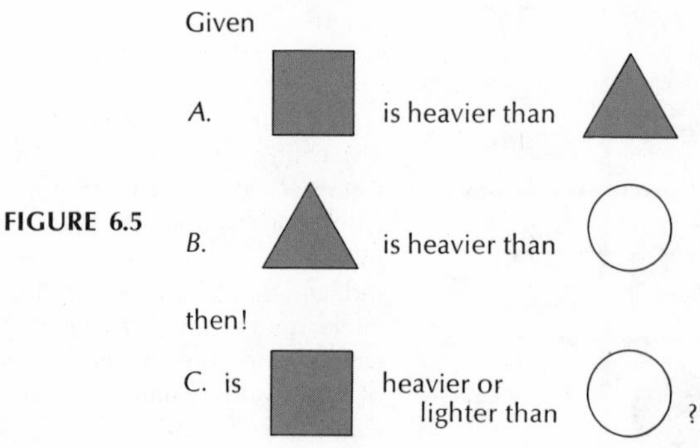

FIGURE 6.5 A design for the study of transitivity—addition of asymmetrical relations—among concrete-operational children. Before the age of about 7, children believe that the knowledge of *A* less than *B* and *B* less than *C* does not imply logically that *A* is less than *C*. After the age of 7, they begin to make this logical leap.

Grouping VI—Symmetrical relations

Symmetrical relations (brother of) are basic to Grouping VI.

Grouping VI treats the additive composition of several types of symmetrical relations. Consider the symmetrical relations found in a genealogical hierarchy. If *x, y,* and *z* are male members of the hierarchy, we may define relations of the following type:

$x = x$	Identity
$x \overset{a}{\leftrightarrow} y$	Where $\overset{a}{\leftrightarrow}$ means brother of
$x \overset{a'}{\leftrightarrow} z$	Where $\overset{a'}{\leftrightarrow}$ means first cousin to.

There are few data about Grouping VI.

There is little experimental evidence on this grouping, and what exists deals exclusively with the acquisition of the symmetric property itself—brother of, enemy of, foreigner to, etc. All the data are imprecise observations.

Grouping VII—Univocal multiplication of relations

Grouping VII involves the multiplication of two or more orders simultaneously.

This grouping involves the 1:1 multiplication of two or more series simultaneously. Consider the following matrix. (From Flavell, 1963.) Each pair of letters (A_1A_2) signifies an object of some given weight and volume. The horizontal arrows $\xrightarrow{a_1}$ $\xrightarrow{a_1'}$ represent differences in

Increasing volume ↑

A_1A_2' $\quad a_1 \quad$ $A_1'A_2'$ $\quad a_1' \quad$ and so on

A_1a_2 $\qquad\quad$ A_1a_2

A_1A_2' $\quad a_1 \quad$ $A_1'A_2'$ $\quad a_1' \quad$ and so on

A_1a_2' $\qquad\quad$ A_1a_2

→ Increasing weight

weight between the objects, while the vertical arrows $\uparrow a_2$ denote volume differences. With these asymmetrical relations, we can perform multiplicative compositions. We can multiply a weight relation by a volume relation to obtain a relation of both weight and volume.

Data relevant to Grouping VII come from asking the child to find boxes for several dolls.

The data relevant to this grouping involve an operation analogous to the 1:1 correspondence of unseriated elements already described for Grouping III. Suppose the child is given eight dolls of differing size and eight boxes of differing length; he is asked to arrange the toys and boxes so that each toy finds its own box. If the toys ascend in size from A to H and the boxes from 1 to 8, the correct 1:1 correspondence between toys and boxes would be $A1, B2, \cdots, H8$ (Figure 6.6). The ability to form such relational correspondences is achieved in the concrete-operational period. The development of the skill closely parallels the ability to construct single asymmetrical series.

Children have difficulty understanding asymmetrical and equality transitivity; this may be related to their need to obtain positive confirmation.

We noted earlier that the preoperational child has difficulty handling transitivity of asymmetrical relations ($A < B$ and $B < C$ implies $A < C$). He has the same difficulty with equality relations. Given a set of equal weight objects that vary in size and color, the young child can empirically establish $A = B$ and $B = C$ and yet still doubt that $A = C$. This may well be related to a notion of Hovland's (Hunt, 1962) that children need positive confirmation of a particular hypothesis. Enumerating the set of logical possibilities and eliminating items from this set is apparently not as compelling to the child as direct verification of a particular logical instance by positive feedback.

Grouping VIII–Co-univocal multiplication of relations

Grouping VIII concerns one-to-many-groupings.

This grouping deals with one-many groupings of the genealogical type. It is concerned with the multiplication of asymmetrical relations and symmetrical relations that define the classes of father of, cousin of, etc.

The data relating to Grouping VIII are sparse and inconsistent.

There is almost no evidence related to Grouping VIII. The method used is primarily clinical, and the procedure is modified to fit the individual child (Piaget & Inhelder, 1959). Questions are varied as the experimenter sees fit in order to test hypotheses concerning the nature of the child's reasoning. The data are extracted on a qualitative basis, and variations in procedure make quantitative treatment difficult. Piaget reports his results so that they are inseparable from his theory. Reduction of the original protocols is done by postulating cognitive systems. He treats the observed responses as indices of these underlying systems.

The preoperational child is perceptually bound, the concrete-operational child conceptually controlled.

Several studies (Piaget & Inhelder, 1959) investigated the ability of the child to deal with simple parts of set theory, classification, and the verbalization of class properties and relations. They reveal that in each area of behavior the child is initially dependent on the immediate perceptual elements of the situation; only gradually, as a formal operational system develops and becomes integrated, are responses determined by an internal system. In several studies Piaget and Inhelder found the young child's class criterion would drift with the elements before him at the moment. Eventually, however, the child was able to hold one criterion in mind. The criterion became similarity of objects rather than their spatial proximity. Also, Piaget and Inhelder found that children refuse (at first) to construct a singleton class. Apparently, they conceive of class as a *collection* of objects. Later, their operations on

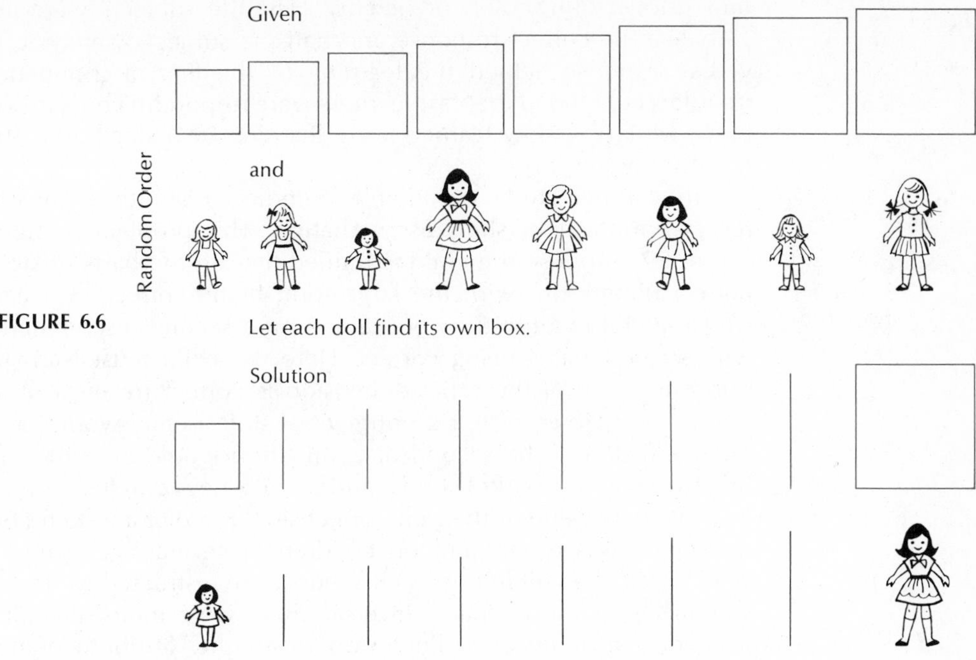

FIGURE 6.6 Multiplication of relations.

regular classes are extended to the single case, showing that the formal interrelations of the cognitive system, rather than the physical properties of a class element, now control behavior. Treatment of the null class shows a similar development. There is an initial refusal to construct a null class because children believe a class must be a collection of real objects. Later, a class is adequately specified for the child by the formal device of stating a criterion for membership.

AN ASSOCIATION THEORY OF THINKING

Association theories of thought propose three stages of development: (1) reflexive, (2) reflexive and mediational, and (3) mediation between stimuli and responses.

An associationistic interpretation of development suggests that the child passes through three stages: Until he is about three, he is controlled by simple stimulus-response associations; around four he is partially a stimulus-response organism and partially a symbolic organism; after five, the child is capable of symbolic mediation. Kendler and Kendler (1962) proposed these stages and used a discrimination situation to test their notions. The stimuli varied in three ways: form (circle, cube, and space), color (white and black), and size (½ in., 1 in., and 2 in.). The children were trained to discriminate along one particular dimension (form, color, or height). Half the subjects were asked to verbalize the correct response and half the subjects were not. Using a verbal response helped the learning of the first discrimination. The Kendlers concluded that fast learners were responding on a mediational basis, while the slow learners were learning by a single-unit stimulus-response association.

Kendler & Kendler investigated this notion using reversal and non-reversal shift paradigms.

In another study (Kendler & Kendler, 1959) they considered a reversal-nonreversal shift discrimination. This problem is outlined in Figure 6.7. Suppose the child is trained first on the basis of size as the correct dimension (with the large form being correct). For a *reversal* shift the child would then be trained on a second discrimination task with small squares being correct. Here the child must learn that the opposite value of the same dimension is correct (reversal of a single dimension). However, for a nonreversal shift a child would be trained on size first, and the second discrimination would be on the basis of brightness (black-white); he is shifted to a new dimension instead of just to a new value of the same dimension. Kendler and Kendler (1962) performed this experiment on children of several ages (three to ten years). Half the children in each group were instructed to describe the stimuli aloud for 10 trials. Reversal shifts were more difficult (going from one attribute of a dimension to another attribute of the same dimension) for nursery school children when compared with older children. Figure 6.8 shows the percentage of children who responded in a reversal-shift manner as a function of age. The Kendlers' proposition suggests that children should show more symbolic mediation as they mature; the child who mediates should be more able to respond

FIGURE 6.7

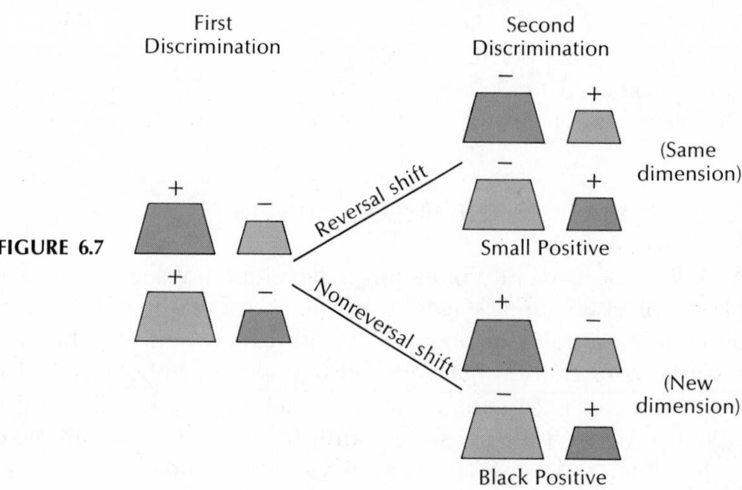

Examples of a reversal and a nonreversal shift.

FIGURE 6.8

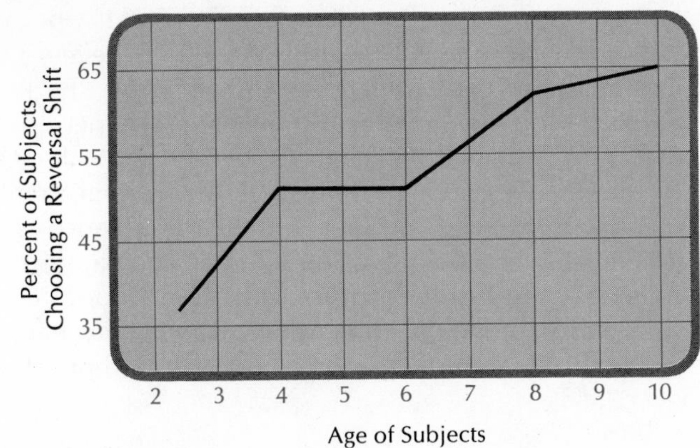

Percentage of children responding in a reversal shift manner as a function of age.

with a reversal shift than a child who cannot mediate. Their data are consistent with this interpretation.

According to Kendler's theory, the reversal shift should be easy for older children.

Figure 6.9 shows a schematic representation of the mediation and simple *S–R* interpretation of reversal and nonreversal shift learning. Notice that the reversal shift should be easy for the child who mediates, while the child who responds with simple associations should

FIGURE 6.9

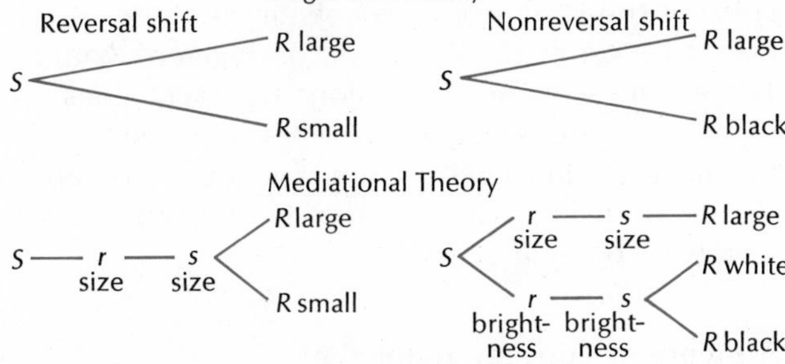

A single-unit and mediational *S–R* analysis of a reversal and nonreversal shift. The single-unit *S–R* analysis of discrimination learning says that the child produces different responses to each aspect of the stimulus and that he must extinguish one response before he can produce another (in the reversal case). In the case of mediational theory, however, the reversal merely requires that the child look at another value of the dimension of size to make the correct response. Reversal should be easy for children who mediate.

have some difficulty handling a reversal shift—he would first have to extinguish his original response and then develop another. However, in the nonreversal situation both children should be about equal. Verbalization had no effect on the children's performance; this suggests that verbal mediators may not be the critical factor. Other studies (Smiley & Weir, 1966) show that the younger child tends to prefer one dimension over another, and their preferences shift with age. These differences might explain the Kendler and Kendler findings. It is possible that the results of this study come from chance assignment of subjects to particular dimensions which they happen to prefer. This factor should be taken into account when replicating these studies.

CONCEPT ATTAINMENT

Concept identification experiments use sets of stimuli which are classified by some rule; the task of the child is to discover that rule.

Experiments on concept identification have the following structure (Atkinson, Bower, & Crothers, 1965): The experimenter develops a set of stimulus patterns that may be classified in various ways; he classifies them by some rule and then sets out to teach the rule to a subject. The patterns may be displayed in several different ways—all at once, segregated, allowing the subject to sample a subset of them, or one at a time. Following presentation of a single or several patterns, the subject is asked to classify the items. Suppose that the patterns of stimuli are constructed from binary (two-valued) dimensions, for example, the color of the stimulus, its shape, and its size. The particular dimension may take on two values—red and green would be values of color. These values of the dimensions represent cues to the concept. Some of the cues are relevant and others are irrelevant. The subject's task is to find the valid cues. A cue is valid if we can correctly classify the stimuli by using values of that dimension. Cues may be either completely or partially valid.

A theory of concept attainment

Concept experiments require the child to find relevant and irrelevant cues.

The basic problem facing a subject solving a concept identification task is learning which cue is relevant for the classification. Presumably, once he has identified that cue, he will attend to it and neglect the irrelevant cues. We will assume that he randomly selects single cues for testing. If the selected cue leads the child to a correct response, we assume that he keeps using that cue until it leads to an incorrect response. When it leads to an incorrect response, the subject replaces that cue in the sampling pool and randomly selects another (replacement of the cue leads to a stationary probability of sampling the correct cue, a simpler procedure mathematically). Since the dimensions we are using have only two values, the probability of his being correct is one half. A relevant cue always allows a correct response. Since some cues in the situation are more obvious than others, and the subject is more likely to attend to them, we shall assign weights (w) representing their distinctiveness.

We may define the parameter

$$C = \frac{w_r}{w_r + \Sigma w_i}$$

where w_r represents the weight of the relevant cue and w_i the weights of the irrelevant cues. Thus, C represents the probability, when the subject selects an attribute, that he will select w_r, the relevant cue. We will assume that the subject may be in one of two states—a solution state, denoted S, and a nonsolution state, denoted $\bar{S}$. When in state S, of course, the subject is attending to the relevant cue, and when he is in $\bar{S}$, he is attending to an irrelevant cue. We also assume that the subject begins the experiment in state $\bar{S}$. Learning consists of making a transition, on some trial, from the state $\bar{S}$ to the solution state S. The theory predicts that if a subject is in state $\bar{S}$ at the beginning of trials one, two, three, four, and five, makes an error on trial five, and enters state S, he will stay there throughout the remaining trials.

Mathematical theories of concept attainment assume a child can learn a new concept only after a mistake.

Notice that this transition to solution can occur only when the subject makes an error and then selects the relevant cue. We shall assume that the probability of an error on a trial when the subject is in state $\bar{S}$ is q, and the probability that the relevant cue is selected following the error is c. The probability of the joint event making an error and selecting a relevant cue is qc, which is the probability (on any given trial) that the subject who starts that trial in state $\bar{S}$ ends the trial in state S. This model of concept attainment is similar to the one-element model of paired-associate learning with the exception that concept learning is assumed to occur only following an error. Analyses of concept attainment data may be applied to paired-associate data, and vice versa.

Analysis of data prior to solution of the problem

Prior to solution the child is assumed to guess.

A subject can be in only one of two states, S or $\bar{S}$. We assume he begins a series of trials with a correct response probability of p and that he stays at this level during a randomly determined sequence of trials. Following the occurrence of an error, the subject may select the correct cue. He then shifts to the solution state and his responses are always correct.

The responses a subject makes before solution should be independent.

The second major assumption of this concept-attainment model is that prior to the solution, responses are statistically independent. This assumption says that the conditional probability of a success is the same whether the previous response was correct or not, and the same is true for an error. We will define an error as a one and a success as a zero to generate sequences of ones and zeros. To test the independence of the subject's responses, we must compare two conditional probabilities. One is that of success conditional upon a success in the previous trial. The other is the probability of success conditional upon the occurrence of an error on the previous trial. The test for independence of trials asks whether these two conditional probabilities are equal. If they are, the probability of success on any trial is independent of the response on the previous trial.

Several experiments with simple tasks and young children show that prior to solution they behave independently from trial to trial.

Consider a simple experiment (Suppes, 1963). The problem is similar to the familiar oddity problem used with animals, in which the subject is required to pick the odd one of three examples. The subjects were seven and eight year old children. On each trial the child was shown three standard dot-dash patterns immediately above the response keys, as shown in Figure 6.10. At the top of the screen the child was shown three stimuli in a horizontal row, with two of the stimuli the same and one different. Thus, for the display in Figure 6.10, response three is correct. The response position of a given dot-dash pattern changed from trial to trial in a randomized fashion. The results of this study are shown in Figure 6.11. There is almost no evidence of learning prior to the solution; perfect performance occurred after the first correct response.

INDIVIDUAL STYLES OF CONCEPT ATTAINMENT

Cognitive activity includes the input, storage, and transformation of data.

There are significant individual differences in conceptual styles of young children. Cognitive activity may be classified into at least three different processes that occur in the following sequence: (1) the initial categorization of external information, (2) the storage of this coded infor-

FIGURE 6.10

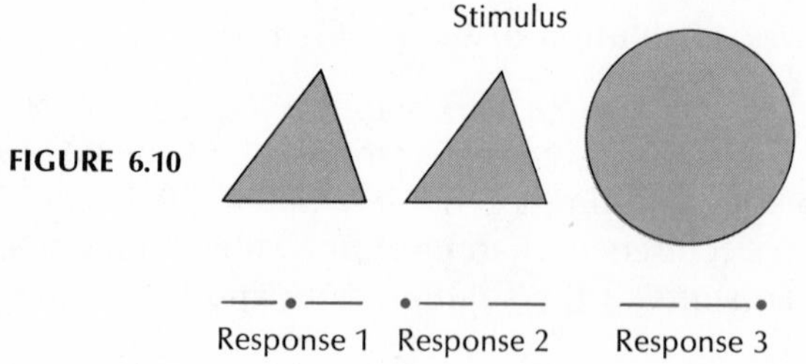

Typical stimulus display in pattern experiment.

FIGURE 6.11

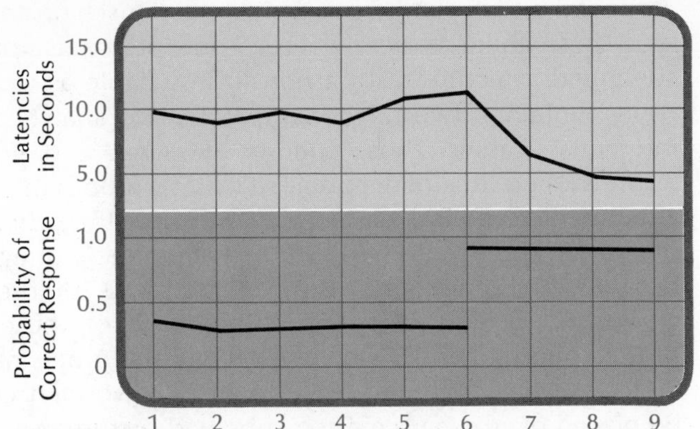

Learning curves for proportion of correct responses and mean latencies in seconds for pattern experiment ($N = 25$). The results show that the latencies of responding decrease dramatically following the solution of the problem, and the probability of being correct jumps from 50 to 100 percent in one trial. Both results agree completely with the predictions from a simple concept-learning model.

mation, and (3) the imposition of transformations upon the encoded data. Evidence from several directions indicates that differences between cognitive productions of children of various ages may be attributable to changes in the availability of rules of reasoning and storage capacity. However, other factors may also contribute to these differences. For example, differences in the kind of stimuli that are initially selected for labeling—(analytic or relational)—may affect concept formation (analytic responses occur when the child attends to component parts of a stimulus; relational responses are those in which the child attends to relations between stimuli).

Kagan showed that some children analyze stimuli while others attend to relations between stimuli.

Using a conceptual style test, Kagan, Moss, and Sigel (1963) studied children from the first through fifth grades. They tested for analytic concepts (those that involve a differentiated part of the total stimulus) and relational concepts (those that involve a functional relation between stimuli). The investigators found consistent tendencies for children to analyze visually presented stimuli on the basis of objective similarity. Analytic responses increased with age while relational responses decreased. This developmental change in analytic-reflective preference has implications for the types of concepts children can learn easily. Lee, Kagan, and Rabson (1963) chose a group of boys who produced a high number of analytic responses and another group who produced a low number of analytic responses on the conceptual-style test. These children were given a concept-acquisition task. The stimuli contained a picture, with a nonsense syllable as a response. The concepts contained two relational classes, two analytical classes, and two inferential classes. Those children who had a preference for analytic responses on the conceptual-style test found the analytic concept-attainment responses easier, and so on for the other groups.

Age and intelligence affect concept attainment.

Osler and Fivell (1961) studied the effects of age and intelligence on concept attainment. They divided 180 children into three age groups—6, 10, and 14 years. Within each of these age groups, half of the children had IQ's below 109 and the others had IQ's above that figure. All the children were shown two wooden cubes which could be placed over a marble. Each cube had pictures on the side (examples of the concept) to help them locate the marble. The older and more intelligent children made fewer errors. Osler and Trautman (1961) also varied the stimulus complexity of concepts at two levels of intelligence. They reasoned that increasing the number of irrelevant dimensions would suggest many hypotheses to more intelligent children and the extra hypotheses would probably interfere with their attainment of concepts. In the first set, with few alternative hypotheses, pairs of numbers were placed at random. In the second set, two objects were used—pictures cut out of children's books, which had a variety of irrelevant dimensions, i.e., color, form, object, class. Children were 6, 10, and 14 years of age; each age level was divided into those with IQ's below and those above 109. Increasing the number of irrelevant stimulus dimensions confused children with superior intelligence without affecting those with normal IQ's.

COMPUTER SIMULATION AND REASONING

Computer programs can simulate human thought; they manipulate symbols to produce novel solutions.

It is no longer necessary to argue that computers can be used to simulate thinking or to explain in general terms how simulation can be carried out. Computer programs have been written and tested that perform interesting symbol-manipulating problem-solving tasks somewhat like human subjects. They play chess and checkers, find proofs, compose music, balance assembly lines, design motors, memorize nonsense syllables, and form concepts. Computers are quite general symbol-manipulating devices that can be programed to perform many nonnumerical as well as numerical symbol manipulations. Programs can be written that use these symbol manipulations to perform tasks that in human beings require thinking and learning. These programs may be regarded as theories—in a completely literal sense—of the corresponding human processes (Newell, Shaw, & Simon, 1958). These theories may be tested by comparing the symbol behavior of the computer with the symbol behavior of the human subject when both are performing the same problem-solving or thinking task.

A program to play chess would include rules for moves, goals, priorities, and a decision device.

How might we use a computer to play chess? We might compute all possible continuations from a given position and then choose the one that leads to checkmate of the opposing king. However, even the fastest computers cannot carry out this enormous task in a reasonable amount of time. We must use rules, but which ones? In most beginning chess manuals there are maxims: "Control the four center squares." "Always make sure your king is safe before you attack," "Do not attack the opposing position unless your own position is developed," etc. How may we make these into principles to be used to control a machine? Several independent goals may be derived: (1) king safety, (2) material balance, (3) center control, (4) development, (5) king-side attack, and (6) promotion of pawns. The ordering of the goals is important, because the machine tries to achieve them in that rank. It will look first to see if the king is safe, and if not, how to protect it; then it will check the next goal, etc. Associated with each goal is a set of rules for generating moves relevant to that goal. For example, when the machine is trying to control the center of the board, it will first propose moving pawn to queen four, then to king four, then will propose moves that may prevent the opponent from making these two key moves, then propose moves that prepare for making these moves, etc. When the move generator has proposed something, the machine does not automatically do it but first evaluates it in the light of the over-all goals of the program. When the machine has a move with which all the goals agree, the move may be made. However, there may be better moves. The machine has the problem of choosing the "best" move. One solution is to set a lower bound for an acceptable move, and to execute the first acceptable play which the move generators produce.

The General Problem Solver is a set of operations that can minimize differences, transform inputs, and solve general logical problems.

Another program is called the General Problem Solver. It is not general in the sense that it will solve every type of problem. It obviously will not. It is called general because it will accept problems that are set in a specified but fairly general form. Because the method it employs makes no specific reference to the subject matter of the particular problem it is solving, the General Problem Solver is a system of methods believed to be those commonly used by intelligent college subjects. Before these general methods can be applied to any particular set of problems, the problem-solver must be taught the rules that apply to that particular domain. The General Problem Solver will not prove theorems unless instructed in the rules of proof. Thus, in any particular problem set the sources available to the General Problem Solver must include information about the task environment as well as its own repertory of methods.

The General Problem Solver will solve problems like the missionaries and the cannibals.

We introduce the General Problem Solver by means of a simple example, the problem of the cannibals and the missionaries. There are three missionaries and three cannibals on the bank of a wide river which they want to cross. There is a boat on the bank which will hold only two persons. All six members of the party know how to paddle it. The only difficulty is that cannibals are partial to a diet of missionaries. If, even for a moment, one or more missionaries are left alone with a larger number of cannibals, the missionaries will be eaten. The problem is to find a sequence of boat trips which will get the entire party across the river without the loss of any missionaries. Suppose we encounter this problem for the first time. We are endowed with certain abilities which enable us to tackle the problem. We might or might not solve it, but we would at least think about it. Of what would this thinking consist? How would we bring to bear our general problem-solving abilities?

The General Problem Solver abstracts states, differences, and uses operators to remove or minimize differences.

We must abstract from the problem those things which match our general methods. We have some people and a boat on this side of the river and we want them on that side. Stated abstractly, we have a state of affairs and we want a different state. Moreover, we can describe both states and we can describe the differences between what we have and what we want. In this case, the difference between the given and the desired is a difference in physical location. Our men are on one side and we want them on the other. Our experience tells us that boats are useful for reducing differences in location. So we begin to consider the possible sequences of boat loading that will get our party across the river without casualty. It should be clear from this formulation of the problem what part is played in our solution by general problem-solving techniques and what part by our knowledge and experience with the particular domain. A general-solution technique is to characterize the given and desired situation, to find the difference between them, and to search for means (implements or operators) that are relevant for removing differences of these kinds. A knowledge of the task and our experience tell us the given and desired sets and what kinds of operators might be relevant for getting from here to there.

Table 6.1 shows one set of moves which solves the missionary-cannibal problem.

One solution is given by the following sequence of moves. Let *x* stand for a missionary, *o* for a hungry cannibal. *S* for a state, and an *M* for a move. We may use the arrow $\longrightarrow$ with *x*'s and *o*'s over it to symbolize the direction of the boat (*B*) trip. Assume that the entire party starts on the left side of the page, and we want them all to end

TABLE 6.1 One Solution to the Cannibals and Missionaries Problem

Step	Left side	Move	Right side
S 1.	xxxoooB		
M 2.	xxoo	ox →	
S 3.	xxoo		Box
M 4.	xxoo	x ←	o
S 5.	xxxooB		o
M 6.	xxx	oo →	o
S 7.	xxx		Booo
M 8.	xxx	o ←	oo
S 9.	xxxoB		oo
M10.	xo	xx →	oo
S11.	xo		Bxxoo
M12.	xo	xo ←	xo
S13.	xxooB		xo
M14.	oo	xx →	xo
S15.	oo		Bxxxo
M16.	oo	o ←	xxx
S17.	oooB		xxx
M18.	o	oo →	xxx
S19.	o		Bxxxoo
M20.	o	o ←	xxxo
S21.	ooB		xxxo
M22.		oo →	xxxo
S23.			Bxxxooo

up on the right side (outside the bellies of the cannibals). A possible sequence of steps is given in Table 6.1.

Computer simulation of development should prove fruitful.

At the moment there exists little or no simulation of the process of development. In principle there is every reason to believe that the application of simulation techniques would prove fruitful.

SUMMARY

1 Piaget sees the young child's thought characterized by animism (the attribution of consciousness to all things) and realism, (the consideration of all psychological things as physical). Both processes result from the child's egocentrism.

2 The child proceeds from preoperational to concrete-operational thought by the development of signs and significates.

3 Preoperational thought is primitive, confused, and rigid relative to the more sophisticated concrete-operational thought. Preoperational thought is characterized by egocentrism, centration, attention to states, and nonreversibility.

4 Concrete-operational thought is capable of symbolic representation, the basic logical operations of addition, multiplication, conservation, and attention to transformations.

5 An association theory of thinking suggests that the child goes through three stages: First, he is a stimulus-response learner, then he is both *S–R* and mediational, and, finally, he is capable of symbolic thought.

6 Concept-attainment theories suggest that prior to finding a solution, the child produces random responses at the chance level; after solution he makes no more mistakes.

7 Individual styles of cognitive functioning cause various developmental changes. Children increase their analytic perception of events with age; these individual differences determine the type of concept which is easy for the child to solve.

8 A computer program that performs certain operations is a good analogue of child and adult functioning. There are programs that play chess, solve problems, and think.

FURTHER READINGS

Flavell, J. *The developmental psychology of Jean Piaget.* Princeton, N.J.: Van Nostrand, 1963.

Hebb, D. O. *The organization of behavior.* New York: Wiley, 1949.

Hunt, E. B. *Concept learning: An information processing approach.* New York: Wiley, 1962.

REFERENCES

Atkinson, R. C., Bower, G. H., & Crothers, E. J. *An introduction to mathematical learning theory.* New York: Wiley, 1965.

Bruner, J. *The process of education.* Cambridge: Harvard University Press, 1960.

Flavell, J. *The developmental psychology of Jean Piaget.* Princeton, N.J.: Van Nostrand, 1963.

Hebb, D. O. *The organization of behavior.* New York: Wiley, 1949.

Hunt, E. B. *Concept learning: An information processing approach.* New York: Wiley, 1962.

Kagan, J., Moss, H. A., & Sigel, I. E. The psychological significance of styles of conceptualization. In J. C. Wright & J. Kagan (Eds.), Basic cognitive processes in children. *Monographs of the Society for Research in Child Development,* 1963, **28,** No. 2, 73–124.

Kendler, H. H., & Kendler, T. S. Vertical and horizontal processes in problem solving. *Psychological Review,* 1962, **69,** 1–15.

Kendler, T. S., & Kendler, H. H. Reversal and nonreversal shifts in kindergarten children. *Journal of Experimental Psychology,* 1959, **58,** 56-60.

Kessen, W. Questions for a theory of cognitive development. Paper read at the 40th anniversary of the Institute of Child Development, University of Minnesota, 1965.

Lee, J. C., Kagan, J., & Rabson, A. Influence of a preference for analytic categories upon concept acquisition. *Child Development,* 1963, **34,** 433-442.

Munsinger, H., & Kessen, W. Stimulus variability and cognitive change. *Psychological Review,* 1966, **73,** 164-178.

Newell, A., Shaw, J. C., & Simon, H. A. Elements of a theory of human problem solving. *Psychological Review,* 1958, **65,** 151-166.

Osler, S. F., & Fivell, M. W. Concept attainment: I. The role of age and intelligence in concept attainment by induction. *Journal of Experimental Psychology,* 1961, **62,** 1-8.

Osler, S. F., & Trautman, G. E. Concept attainment: II. Effect of stimulus complexity upon concept attainment at two levels of intelligence. *Journal of Experimental Psychology,* 1961, **62,** 9-13.

Piaget, J. *The child's conception of the world.* New York: Harcourt, Brace & World, 1929.

Piaget, J. *The psychology of intelligence.* London: Routledge & Kegan Paul, 1950 (1947).

Piaget, J. *Traité de logique.* Paris: Colin, 1949.

Piaget, J., & Inhelder, B. Le developement des quantités chez l'enfant. Neuchatel: Delachaux et Niestle, 1941.

Piaget, J., & Inhelder, B. *La genèse des structures logiques élémentaires: Classifications et seriations.* Neuchatel: Delachaux et Niestle, 1959.

Smiley, S. S., & Weir, M. W. The role of dimensional dominance in reversal and nonreversal shift behavior. *Journal of Experimental Child Psychology,* 1966, **4,** 296-307.

Suppes, P. Mathematical concept formation in children. Address to the American Psychological Association, Philadelphia, 1963.

Watson, J. B. *Psychology from the standpoint of a behaviorist.* Philadelphia: Lippincott, 1919.

7 MOTIVATION AND EMOTION

Music oft hath such a charm
To make bad good, and good provoke to harm.
MEASURE FOR MEASURE

The concept of motivation is used to explain three factors of behavior: (1) the instigation of a response, (2) the energization of a response, and (3) the direction of that response. The traditional theory of motivation postulated primary physiological drives and their reduction as the basic answer to these questions; however, recent notions of curiosity and its relation to thought give an alternative view. Classic theories of motivation assume that the instigation of a response results from strong painful stimuli (external stimuli), homeostatic need (internal stimuli), or instinct. The strength of the response, according to classic theories, is related to the intensity of the internal or external stimulation. A response is more vigorous as the stimulation becomes stronger. Traditional theories of motivation handle the direction problem by assuming that any event which reduces drive (decreases stimulation) is a positive reinforcer, and that organisms prefer reinforcing agents or events associated with them.

Basic physiological needs describe the infant's motivation; however, children are curious.

While the simple model of primary drives adequately describes the motivation of a young infant, it cannot explain the variety of goals found in the child. Early stages of infant development are governed by primary biological drives and instinctive behaviors (hunger, thirst, temperature regulation, and CO_2 sensitivity); only later does the baby develop an active interest in the world. In addition to his new ability to manipulate symbols, the child shows curiosity (an increased interest in environmental events) not because events reduce primary drives but because they contain information. The transition from biological drive to interest in information marks a major change in behavior. He is no longer tied to tissue deficits; he is free to explore, play, and imitate. This chapter considers the basic biological processes and then outlines a model of curiosity and other "cognitive" drives.

PRIMARY DRIVES

Primary drives are unlearned and increase following deprivation.

A primary drive is unlearned; it is characterized by increased activity following deprivation. For example, if an infant is not fed for several hours, he becomes increasingly agitated; he requires food or an instinctive inhibition of distress (Kessen & Mandler, 1961) before he will quiet. In addition to primary drives, the infant is equipped with a variety of instinctive response systems which are triggered by appropriate external stimulation. These include sucking, head turning, and temperature regulation. For example, the infant's activity level increases in cool temperatures, while contentment and quiescence come with increases in temperature (within limits).

Sucking is a prewired instinctive system which inhibits infant distress.

Sucking is a basic, instinctive, organized reponse system elicited by appropriate external stimulation. Kessen and Leutzendorff (1963) showed that sucking is an inhibitor of distress and will quiet the newborn even when sucking is not followed by food. They photographically recorded the newborn's movement before and after nonnutritive sucking. To observe the effects of nonnutritive sucking on the newborn's activity, they put an ordinary hospital nipple, stuffed with sterile cotton, over a finger and inserted the nipple into the infant's mouth. As a control for tactual contact and to insure that the response to sucking was not an undifferentiated response to any sort of stimulation, each newborn was also stimulated by stroking his forehead with a hospital diaper. The results are shown in Figure 7.1. It is clear that nipple stimulation sharply decreased the amount of infant movement while stimulation of his forehead by rubbing with a diaper slightly increased the amount of movement the babies showed.

Infants are active before feeding, inactive following nursing.

A clear example of the relation between drive state and energization of behavior is seen in the infant's activity level before and after feeding. The pattern is quite characteristic—before feeding he is active; during and immediately after feeding there is a sharp drop in his activity. The infant stays at this low level for about an hour and then slowly becomes active again. If he is on a four-hour schedule, he will cry in four hours; if he is on a three-hour schedule, he reaches his peak of activity three hours after being fed. This is a modifiable phenomenon, as Marquis (1931) showed when infants were switched from three- to four-hour schedules. The babies were able (within a few days) to adjust to the new schedule.

FIGURE 7.1

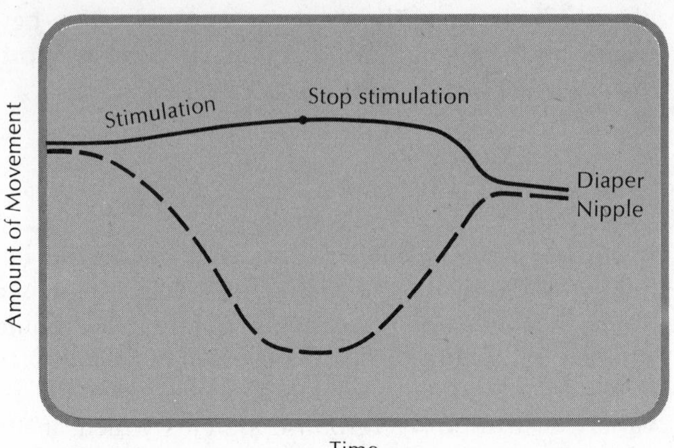

The amount of body movement neonates display following sucking on a nipple or being stroked on the forehead with a diaper. The results clearly show that sucking is an innate inhibitor of distress. (From Kessen & Leutzendorff, 1963.)

Feeding is not an important factor in the attachment of infant monkeys.

In his well-known studies of infant monkeys, Harlow (1958) showed that primary drive reduction (feeding) is not a very important factor in their motivational life. He reared several infant monkeys on surrogate mothers (see Figure 7.2). The surrogate was made from a block of wood covered with sponge rubber and sheathed in tan terrycloth. A light bulb behind "her" radiated heat. The result was a soft, warm, and tender mother with infinite patience, who never scolded, struck, or bit her baby in anger. Harlow believed he had engineered a superior monkey mother, although this position was not held universally by

FIGURE 7.2

A typical response of an infant monkey to a fear-producing stimulus in the presence of the cloth mother substitute. The infant clings to the cloth mother regardless of which mother fed him. (From Harlow, 1958.)

FIGURE 7.3

A typical fear response of an infant monkey in a strange environment. (From Harlow, 1958.)

monkey fathers. He also designed another surrogate mother with less than maximum contact comfort. The second surrogate was made of wire mesh, a substitute entirely adequate to provide postural support and nursing capability; she also was warmed by radiant heat. Her body differed, according to Harlow, in no essential way from the other mother surrogate other than in the quality of the contact comfort offered. However, there were obvious differences in terms of facial characteristics, which cannot be considered completely irrelevant.

A surrogate that furnishes contact comfort is more attractive to infants than a wire mother that lactates.

For each infant monkey a feeding bottle was attached to one of the mothers. Different groups of infants were fed on either the wire or the terrycloth mother surrogate. However, even when fed by the wire mesh mother, the infants spent almost all their time clinging to the terrycloth surrogate. This result strongly suggests that body contact and not the primary reward of feeding elicits the young monkey's affection for his mother. The finding casts strong doubt on the hypothesis that mother attachment is mediated through secondary reinforcement value of the mother derived from primary drive reduction. This hypothesis was proposed by proponents of learning theory to explain the infant's attachment to his mother. There are several mechanisms that mediate mother-child attachment. Among these are feeding, warmth, contact comfort, and familiarity; of these variables, contact comfort seems to be the strongest.

Dollard and Miller assumed that frustration leads instinctively to aggression.

Dollard and Miller (1950) proposed that our instinctive reaction to frustration is aggression. They assumed that natural selection had generated this connection because it is effective in dealing with frustration. Early studies supported their general notion: Frustrated rats attacked other rats in the same cage, and the response generalized (see Figure 7.4). However, Barker, Dembo, and Lewin (1941) showed that frustration may have other consequences than aggression; their classic study of the effects of frustration on children showed that regression is another mode of adjustment to frustration. The children did not aggress against the frustrating situation. Barker and his associates arranged for

FIGURE 7.4

Displacement of aggression. One rat strikes another; when the first rat is removed, the aggressive response generalizes to an "innocent" doll. (From Miller, 1948b.)

FIGURE 7.5

Prefrustration situation. The prefrustration situation contained many interesting toys in which the children became engrossed; following the early play period, a barrier was introduced between the interesting toys and the child. The children could then play only with the simple toys outside the barrier. Figure 7.6 shows the frustration situation. (From Barker, Dembo, & Lewin, 1941.)

children to play with very complex and attractive toys (see Figure 7.5); after they had become interested, the children were taken from the attractive toys and given other toys for their play. The experimenters obtained premeasures on the children's ability to play with these neutral toys. The result of the frustration—placing a barrier between the children and the nice toys so they could see them but not play with them (see Figure 7.6)—was to decrease the children's level of play. They interacted with the neutral toys at a much simpler level following frustration and engaged in a good deal of escape or barrier-attacking actions.

Frustration produces either aggression or regression.

Frustration produces aggression *or* regression. The factors that mediate the child's choice between these two responses to frustration are complex. For one thing, the types of models the child sees affect his choice; the amount of anxiety produced by aggressive responses (his inhibitions and morality) also controls his aggression. We consider these topics in Chapter 8.

FIGURE 7.6

Frustration situation. The barrier between the children and the toys produced primarily regression to an earlier form of behavior and not aggression against the barrier, as had been proposed by the frustration-aggression hypothesis. The children played with the simple toys on their side of the barrier, but the style of play and the complexity of their interactions deterioriated following frustration. (From Barker, Dembo, & Lewin, 1941.)

REMARKS: THEORY

Freud (1916) changed our conception of sex in motivation and emotion. He saw erotic elements in behavior not usually considered sexual. Sexual urges are important because if they do not find gratification in their original form, they change goals. Sexual urges can be repressed by the ego; they then become available in various disguises. We can sublimate the basic energy of our libido. Freud proposed successive stages of libidinal or motivational organization. During the first year, the oral stage, when the mouth is a primary region of gratification, the infant is interested in receiving; during the second and third years, the anal stage, he is primarily concerned with gaining control over bodily functions—to develop competence. The third stage is labeled the phallic period. It is characterized by the child's intrusion into the lives of others as he develops aggression. Freud's final stage of child development is labeled *genital;* it is characterized by the development of sensitivity to others. The interpersonal relations that create love and good will among individuals appear. Freud also included the death wish to explain the destruction of war, the aggressive instincts of the individual, and the neurotic hates to which man is prone.

Libido theory is about human motivations; however, it subordinates all strivings, except aggression, to the urge of pleasurable stimulation (the libido). Several neo-Freudians (Horney, 1939; Fromm, 1947) have argued that the course of child development does not follow instinctual energies alone. They see the relations between the parent and child as a crucial factor in the growth of human relations. The part played by motivation can be understood if we consider how various motives (aggression, hate, security) become attached to important human beings in the child's life. Fromm emphasized the child's need for self-esteem and for the esteem of other significant persons. When the child's conduct brings approval, he experiences happiness; when it meets disapproval, he falls into anxiety. The child's own feeling of competence is also a major determiner of personality development and the management of motives. Many of the child's later motivations and emotions result from the complex interaction of ego, drives, and the libido. The child is not only a pleasure-seeking creature, he is complex and contradictory. The child grows from simple instinctive control of behavior to more cognitive control of his goals. This change represents a major shift in motivation; it occurs when the child is competent to develop goals through internal symbolization during the last parts of the sensory-motor stage (18 months to two years).

SECONDARY (LEARNED) DRIVES

Learned drives and reinforcements are important determinants of behavior, according to learning theory.

A major proposal of learning theories concerns secondary drives and secondary reinforcement. The addition of "learned drives" and "learned reinforcers" is important to classic theories of motivation. A good example is classical conditioning, in which an initially neutral stimulus (conditioned stimulus) is associated repeatedly with an effective stimulus (unconditioned stimulus). Through stimulus substitution, the originally neutral conditioned stimulus acquires the motivational and/or reinforcing properties of the unconditioned stimulus. For example, see the study by Watson and Raynor (1920) discussed later in this chapter; they associated white fur with a loud noise. The infant (Albert) soon formed a connection between a previously neutral stimulus (*CS*—white fur) and an aversive stimulus (*US*—loud noise). As a result, he came to fear white fur; this is a clear example of negative secondary drive produced by classical conditioning.

Secondary reinforcements are strengthened by association with primary reinforcement.

Various learning factors are assumed to explain the effects of secondary drives and reinforcers on behavior; among these is the strength of the primary drive associated with the secondary drive. (The stronger a primary drive, the stronger a secondary drive.) Another factor that affects the strength of secondary drives is the number of pairings with a primary drive. (The more pairings, the stronger an association becomes.) A third factor that influences secondary drive strength is the delay between primary drive and the stimuli associated with it. The optimal interval between primary and secondary drive stimuli is about one half second. [The secondary drive stimulus (*CS*) must appear first.] Any deviation from this optimal interval will decrease the association and thus the strength of the secondary drive. Secondary drives extinguish. The best way to postpone extinction is to use a partial schedule, to follow secondary drive stimuli with primary drive stimuli only part of the time.

Learning theorists assume that secondary drives increase following deprivation (this is not true).

It has been suggested that secondary drives also are influenced by deprivation. By analogy with primary drives which increase in strength following withdrawal of a reinforcer, some people believe social reinforcement increases in effectiveness following a period of social deprivation. An experiment by Gewirtz and Baer (1958) seemed to support this notion. In their experiment, one group of children played for 20 minutes in a stimulating environment while children from a second group were placed for 20 minutes in a blank room with no toys or people. Following "satiation" or "deprivation," the children were taken into a standard play situation. In the play situation an experimenter recorded the number of dependency responses, the number of times the children asked questions, and the number of times the children initiated social interaction with the experimenter. They found a large difference in the number of child-initiated social interactions with the experimenter. The deprived children (those in a blank room for a period of time prior to the play situation) were more socially aggressive and interested in contacts with the experimenter than were the satiated children. The authors suggest that the deprived children had a "greater need" for secondary social reinforcement. However, before we accept this simple drive theory explanation of social reinforcement, consider the following alternative. Walters suggested that the difference between the isolated and the nonisolated children could be due to the emotionally arousing nature of isolation. In a test of their interpretation, Walters and Parke (1964) examined the effects of arousal and isolation on responsiveness to social reinforcement. They found that arousal accounted for most of the variation in children's behavior; social isolation, with arousal controlled, accounted for none of the responsiveness to social reinforcement shown by children.

Fear as a learned drive

Fear can be classically conditioned.

A classic experimental study by Watson and Raynor (1920) concerns the learning of fear by a little boy (Albert). Albert was not afraid of rabbits, Santa Claus masks, or other white fuzzy objects prior to the experiment. Following the systematic association of a white rabbit and a loud bell, sounded immediately behind him (Albert was afraid of loud noises and cried every time the bell was rung), he became fearful even when the rabbit alone was presented. After several days of conditioning, Albert would neither look at the rabbit nor play with it. He also feared a Santa Claus mask and would not eat if a kitten or a fox fur was brought into the room. The association of fear to a previously neutral object and generalization of the learned fear to other objects supplies a basic model of emotional learning. Watson did not report the therapy to which he exposed Albert, but through "counterconditioning" the learned fear could be reduced. Watson did mention that, while eating, Albert would allow the rabbit to be much closer than at other times. By pairing the object of fear and positive reinforcement—eating or drinking—children can be taught to overcome a learned fear.

Miller showed that classically conditioned fear can be used to produce other learning.

A more systematic study of the acquisition of fear was performed by Miller (1948a). He demonstrated that learned fear can be a powerful motivater. By placing a small harness on their backs, he showed that rats will pull with a force of about 50 grams for food if they are hungry; however, these same animals, in a strong fear-producing situation, will pull with a force of 200 grams. Miller assumed that fear produces random behavior at a high level. He defined fear as a learned drive; shock and its consequent pain was the unlearned drive. His general question was, if fear is reduced (if a secondary, acquired drive is reduced) by the animal escaping to a position of relative safety, will the random response that produced the fear reduction be learned without additional motivational or reinforcing support? We know that when primary drives are reduced they reinforce the behavior that reduced them. Is the same true of learned drives?

Miller used electric shock as the unconditioned stimulus for fear.

Miller used a box with black and white compartments separated by a middle door. The box had a grid on the floor. Each animal was placed in the box to see if it was innately afraid of it. If any animal showed "freezing" or other fearful behavior it was discarded. The second step was to place each animal in the white box and shock it with 500 volts at 60 cycles/second for 10 seconds. After the animal was shocked, the middle door separating the black and white compartments was opened and the rat was allowed to escape to the black box. Each animal was given 16 trials in this fashion. During the third stage, each rat was given several trials, with no shock, while the experimenter opened the door. This procedure tested whether the animal was motivated by fear alone. Miller found that all the animals immediately jumped from the white to the black side. During stage four, the experimenter hooked up a small wheel which would open the door when a rat turned it. The animals were required to learn to turn the wheel to open the door for themselves. All animals concentrated their activity around the door. They would stand up, sniff, bite the bars, crouch, and run. Finally, through trial and error, each animal turned the wheel which opened the door. The rats became more skilled with each trial until, when dropped into one side of the cage, they would immediately run to the wheel, turn it, and jump into the other side. At this point, the experimenter deactivated the wheel and activated a bar to open the door. During stage five, again without shock, the rats learned to open the door by pressing the bar. The animals stopped going to the wheel (extinguished) and began searching for another way to open the door. After several trials, when dropped into the white part of the cage they would immediately go to the bar, press it, and jump over into the black side (see Figure 7.7).

FIGURE 7.7

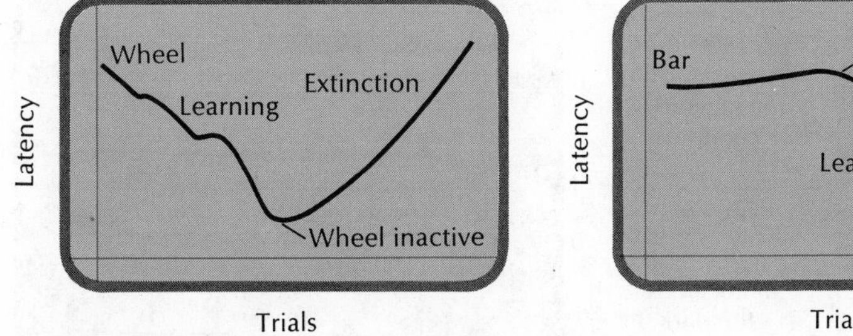

Graphs showing, first, the amount of time required for rats to turn a wheel which opened a door and then, when the wheel was no longer effective, their transfer to a bar-pressing response to open the same door. The rats were motivated and reinforced by learned fear of the white box. (From Miller, 1948a.)

Mild amounts of shock produce no conditioned fear.

In another study (Miller, 1948a), animals were given only 90 volts of shock. They showed no tendency to learn either wheel-turning or bar-pressing on subsequent trials. Another group was given 540 volts of shock. These animals learned slightly faster than the rats given 500 volts. These data strongly support the notion that fear is an acquirable drive which can be learned on the basis of classic conditioning; also, when reduced, fear results in the retention of that behavior which produced relief.

Fear of pain and bodily harm increase with age, while fear of strange persons, falling, and noise decrease after two years of age in children.

A number of studies have described the fears of early childhood. The child's fear of noise, falling, animals, sudden motion, or strange objects and persons increases until about two years of age and then decreases. Fear of pain, the dark, and bodily harm increases steadily with age (Jersild, 1935). The infant and younger child fear tangible events and situations in their immediate environment (see Figure 7.8). As the child grows older and his perceptual and intellectual powers increase, his fears change. Older children fear potential or imaginary dangers they did not recognize before. With increasing age, we find an increase in fear of imaginary creatures, the dark, and being left alone. At the same time, the child's wider experience and understanding make him more able to handle threatening situations, making him less fearful of tangible objects, noise, and falling. These fears are

FIGURE 7.8

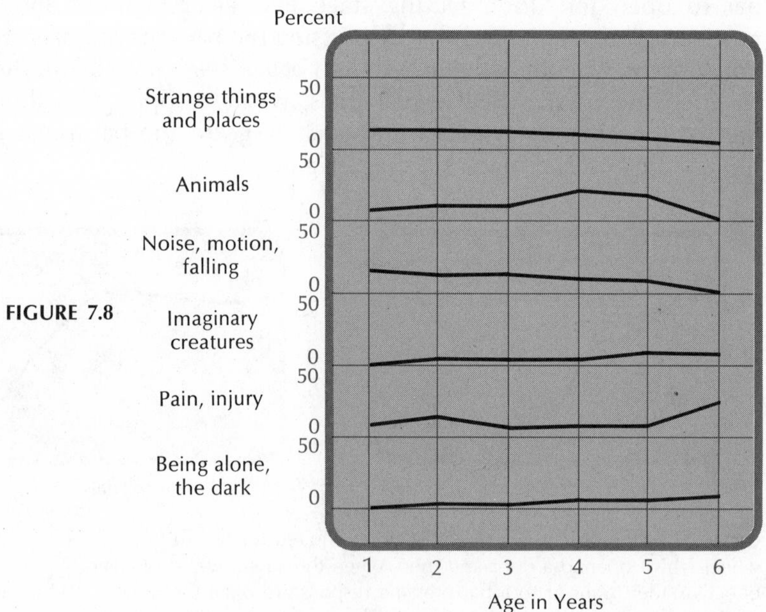

Situations in which children show fear.

replaced by abstract and improbable fears as the child matures; his expression of fear also becomes more subtle and complex.

Punishment and fear

Anxiety facilitates learning simple tasks and hinders learning complex tasks.

Anxiety is a nonspecific experience of fear. The effects of anxiety on learning have been carefully studied. Specifically, the relation between problem complexity and children's anxiety has received considerable attention. Studies of high- and low-anxious children performing simple and complex tasks show that for simple tasks there is a direct relation between the child's fear and his performance—anxious children condition faster than do their less fearful peers. An example will explain the complications generally found in more complex situations. In this particular study (Castanada, Palermo, & McCandless, 1956) 37 children were used. Half the children measured high on a children's scale of anxiety while the other half measured low on the same scale. Five

REMARKS: THEORY

The main findings from studies relating anxiety and learning show that fear facilitates simple learning and hinders complex learning; however, there are complications. For example, interruption seems to help performance of low-anxious children, while high-motivation conditions ("You are doing poorly," "Work faster," "You are failing," "This is a test," and so on) produce poorer performance among high-anxious children. Three interpretations of these effects have been offered; they are known as enhanced drive, irrelevant learning, and decreased perceptual abilities.

The notion of increased drive suggests that in simple tasks, such as conditioning, performance is a direct function of drive; however, in complex tasks where there are many competing responses, increased drive means it takes longer for the child to extinguish an incorrect response in his habit family hierarchy and move down the list far enough to find a correct response.

The association of irrelevant responses suggests the child is learning to worry and is producing emotional responses or other competing acts which interfere with the relevant task.

The notion that perceptual abilities are decreased by anxiety is summed up in the old maxim: blind with fear. The assumption is that anxious children do not pay attention, or have decreased discrimination capacity, and therefore cannot learn because the stimuli are not perceived.

Whatever the outcome of this controversy, it is clear that the level of anxiety associated with a task is strongly associated with learning efficiency. A good rule is that students in need of motivation profit from some anxiety; however, most students are highly motivated, and anxiety can only hinder their performance in the complex task of understanding.

pushbuttons were available to the children. Centered above the buttons were five lights. The children were each required to learn a series of light-button combinations, that is, to learn which button turned on which light. The complexity of the relation between buttons and lights was varied. The simple task provided a one-to-one relation between buttons and lights, while in the most difficult task a random relation between the lights and buttons was used. For simple tasks, anxious children learn faster than more relaxed children. However, in the complex condition the relaxed children learned faster. This reversal of performance in the two groups is an interaction between task complexity and subject anxiety (see Remarks: Theory).

Studies by Ruebush and Sarason and Palola showed that task, anxiety, and instructions interact to determine a child's performance.

A study by Ruebush (1960) provides another example of the relation between anxiety and performance. He presented children with a series of embedded figures (pictures embedded in other pictures). Again the relaxed children were superior to the anxious ones on the most difficult task; performance of the two groups was similar on the middle task, and on the third task—the easy one—anxious subjects were superior. Anxious students are superior to relaxed ones in simple learning situations; however, this ranking is reversed in a more complex situation. Studies by Sarason and Palola (1960) showed that instructions which reduce the stress upon a child influence his performance in a test situation. They found that relaxed instructions facilitate the performance of anxious children but are detrimental to the performance of secure children. We must consider not only the task complexity but also both the amount of stress inherent in the learning situation and the anxiety level of the child. Both frustration and anxiety lower the child's general information-processing ability. When his processing system is loaded with internal stimulation (fear) little capacity remains for handling external inputs.

Punishment will suppress a response but not eliminate it from a child's repertory.

The differential effects of punishment depend on whether we are trying to suppress a particular response or to change the child's behavior. A provocative experiment by Estes (1944) suggests that punishment is an ineffective way to suppress a response. He first produced a conditioned response in rats. After a series of reinforcements the animals had a strong habit established. Reinforcement was then withdrawn. Extinction (the number of times the rats responded without receiving food) was studied under two conditions. One group of rats was allowed free access to the lever, while rats in the other group were slapped vigorously as they approached the lever. The first group received only nonreinforcement, while the second group was punished in addition to the nonreinforcement. Immediately after punishment the rats in the second group decreased their rate of response dramatically; however, after a short interval of no further punishment these same animals increased their rate of response above the unpunished group. Both groups produced the same total number of responses. Punishment does not erase a habit; it only suppresses responding for a time.

However, punishment is effective for teaching discriminations among events.

However, in the case of differentiation between one response and another (the typical discrimination-learning situation) punishment is an effective training device. Brackbill and O'Hara (1958) found that kindergarten children learn a position-alternation sequence (*l, r, l, r, l, r*) faster under both positive and negative reinforcement than in response to either one alone. The children in their study were made to return candy to the experimenter following an incorrect response and were given a piece of candy for each correct response. Returning candy following an incorrect response was assumed to be a punishment, although this was not necessarily correct. Stevenson, Weir, and Zigler (1959) obtained the same result in an experiment with five-year-old children learning a discrimination. The children received a small trinket for each correct response and were required to return one for each incorrect response. The "punishment" and reward procedure was superior to reward alone. Meyer and Seidman (1960) studied the effects of verbal rewards or punishments versus mechanical rewards on learning the concept of "larger" in four-, five-, nine-, and ten-year-old children. Stimuli were pairs of blocks in the shape of cylinders. One group was told "right" for correct responses and nothing for incorrect responses. Another group was told "wrong" for incorrect responses and nothing for correct responses. A third group was told "right" for correct responses and "wrong" for incorrect responses, and a final group heard nothing but a buzzer after correct responses. The order of learning in the preschool children was (1) "right" and "wrong," (2) buzzer, (3) "wrong," and (4) "right." For older children the ranking was (1) "wrong," (2) "right" and "wrong," (3) buzzer, and (4) "right."

Social reinforcement

Stevenson examined the effects of age, sex of experimenter, and sex of child on social reinforcement responsiveness.

Stevenson (1961) examined the effects of the child's age and sex and the sex of the experimenter on social-reinforcement effectiveness. He found that women are usually more effective with boys than with girls, while men have a significantly greater effect with girls than with boys. The Oedipal situation described by Freud predicts exactly this relation. Freud wrote that during the early years, when the mother is the principal caretaker, she becomes a love object for infants of both sexes. Assuming this relation generalizes to other females, Stevenson expected that females would be more effective as social reinforcement for two- and three-year-old children than would males. According to

Oedipal theory, girls shift their love from the mother to the father as they grow older; boys do not change their love object. For a boy, the mother is still positive, but he comes to view his father as a rival. According to Freud, this shift for girls occurs in the four- to seven-year age range (during the Electra conflict). As children mature, they must resolve the Oedipal/Electra conflict and their patterns of responsiveness may shift again. During this latency period, from seven to eleven years, girls are assumed to identify with their mothers while boys identify with their fathers. In this period men should be more effective as social reinforcers for boys and women as social reinforcers for girls.

Using a simple marble-dropping game, he tested various persons' control of children's behavior.

Stevenson tested these notions using both sexes as subjects at three age levels—three to five years, six to seven years, and nine to eleven years. The children played a simple game in which marbles were counted as they fell into a bin. Either a female or a male experimenter made supportive comments during the child's performance. Children were tested individually. One minute was used as a base condition to determine how fast each child naturally played a marble-dropping game. Next came five minutes during which the male or female experimenter made supportive statements about the child's performance. The measure used to test social-reinforcement effectiveness was the average increase in responses during each minute of marble dropping following the one-minute base period. Women should have been more effective than men in changing the performance of very young boys and girls (three to five years); in the six- to seven-year range, adults of the opposite sex should be more effective; during the nine-to-eleven age range boys reinforced by men should show performance increase, due to identification, and girls tested by women should also show increased activity.

Women control young children, and they continue to control older boys; however, males do not increase their effectiveness, as is predicted by Freudian theory.

The results are presented in Figure 7.9. The first two hypotheses were partially confirmed. In the three- to five-year age range women significantly increased the rate of response of children while men slightly decreased it. With six- to seven-year-old subjects the women experimenters significantly increased the performance of the boys while there was no increase on the part of the girls who were socially reinforced by women. However, the reinforcement of girls by men was not significantly more effective than the results of boys socially reinforced by men. The third hypothesis was not confirmed. In fact, the opposite results occurred; at nine to eleven years boys were more influenced by women and girls by men. There are several explanations for this result. It may be that Stevenson merely picked the wrong age for the Oedipal solution (it may be that the latency period extends longer than we thought) or, alternatively, it may be that children in American culture do not solve the Oedipal situation. Another possi-

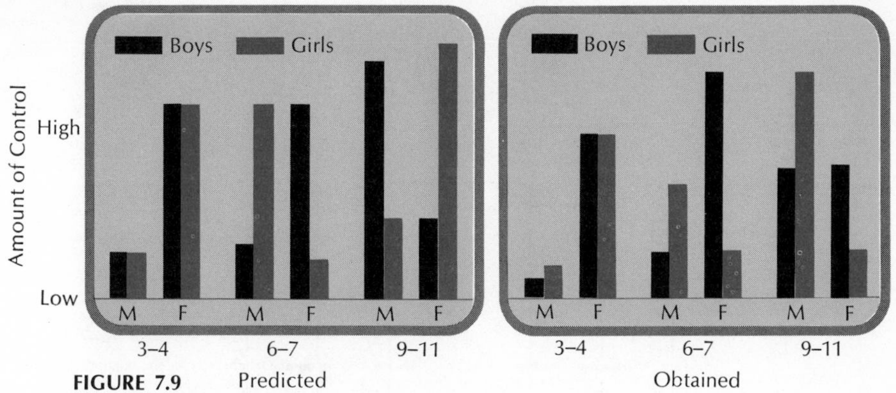

FIGURE 7.9

Predicted and obtained effectiveness in controlling the behavior of children by male and female experimenters making supportive statements. The predictions are from Freud. The results support his early stages, but the later age levels are contradictory.

bility is that the Oedipal situation is confounded by later experiences; for example, most teachers are women, and girls are more used to receiving supportive comments than are boys. At the moment, we cannot know what the answer is. It is clear, however, that opposite-sex parents have a strong role to play in children's socialization.

PHYSIOLOGICAL, SOCIAL, AND COGNITIVE FACTORS IN EMOTION

As the infant matures, his emotions are based more on social context.

As the infant matures, he shifts from an early dependence on biological reinforcement toward more cognitive control of his behavior. The total context of behavior now controls feelings; physiological, social, and cognitive factors influence his emotions. Following this excursion into sociology and physiology we examine curiosity.

Since the days of James (1890) we have believed that bodily changes follow the perception of an exciting fact and that our conscious experience of these bodily changes is emotion. Some writers have even speculated about the variety of different emotions available (see Figure 7.10). However, these speculations should be accepted as just that; there is no evidence that the infant's reactions to different situations can be judged with accuracy, given that the situation is not available for the observer to use in his judgment (Sherman & Sherman, 1929). This suggests that the variety of infant emotions are only projections of our own feelings. In fact, the only reaction that appears

FIGURE 7.10

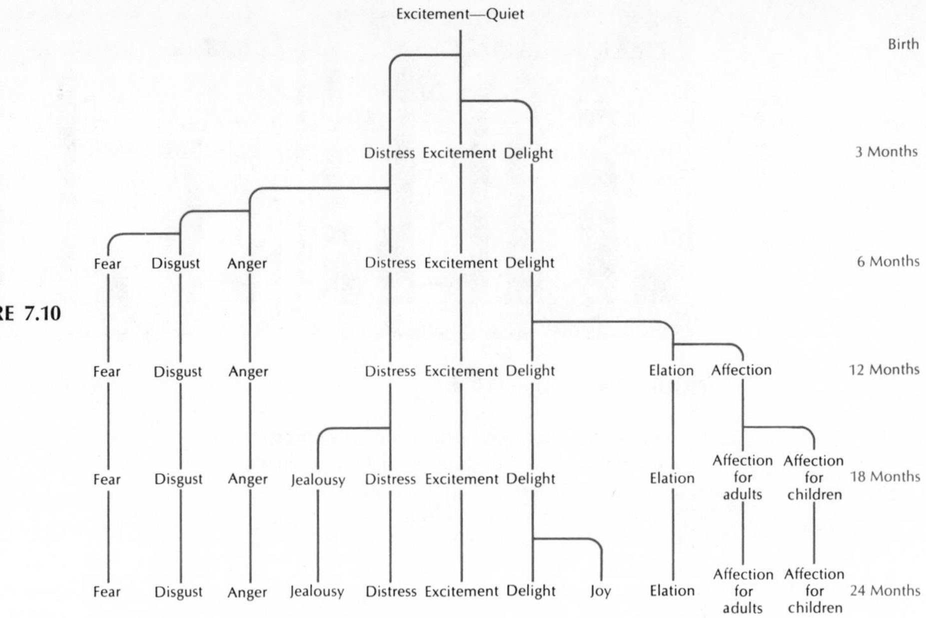

The approximate ages of differentiation of the various emotions during the first two years. These various emotions are mere speculation; they are impossible to accurately judge without a social context on which to base the decision. (From Bridges, 1932.)

in all infants as an unlearned response to fright is the startle reflex—which also appears in adults. Young infants do not show a variety of differing activities as a result of various emotional states; they are active or quiet.

James proposed that we have a particular bodily state and our later awareness of that state is emotion.

Since we are aware of a variety of feelings and emotional states, it should follow from James's proposition that various emotions should be accompanied by a variety of different bodily states. However, a formidable number of studies have searched for the physiological differentiators of our emotions, and the results are generally negative. All our emotional states are characterized by the same general pattern of sympathetic nervous system excitation.

Recent studies suggest we experience physiological arousal and our cognitive structure tells us what we are feeling.

This ambiguous situation has led several recent investigators to suggest that cognitive and social factors are the major determinants of emotional states. Suppose a general pattern of sympathetic excitation is characteristic of all emotional states; we might interpret and identify this stirred-up state in terms of the perceptual-cognitive situation. Our emotional state must be a joint function of our sympathetic nervous system and the cognitive situation. Cognition exerts a steering function (a framework in which one understands and labels his own feelings). Usually, cognition and physiology are related. Imagine a man walking down a dark alley. A figure with a gun suddenly appears. The perception-cognition (figure with a gun) and his physiological state (aroused) are both related by his knowledge of dark alleys and guns. The state is labeled fear. To study these two processes (cognition and arousal), we need circumstances in which the physiological and cognitive processes are somewhat independent. We need a situation in which we can manipulate the state of physiological arousal and (independently) the extent to which the subject has an appropriate explanation for his bodily state. We need to create situations in which different cognitive explanations may be derived, even though the various groups all have the same physiological state.

Physiological arousal alone produces "as if" emotion.

Physiological arousal alone is apparently not sufficient to induce "true" emotion. Experiments by Cantril and Hunt (1932) and Landis and Hunt (1932), in which patients were injected with adrenalin and then asked to introspect, showed that 71 percent of their subjects reported physical symptoms with no emotional overtones, while only 29 percent reported some emotion. The majority of those describing emotions labeled them "cold" or "as if" emotions—"feel like I was afraid" or "as if I were happy." They were neither happy nor afraid, only "as if."

Schachter and Singer studied physiological arousal and social context independently; they found both influence our emotions.

Another experiment was cast as a study of vitamin supplements and vision (Schachter & Singer, 1962). As soon as the subject arrived, he was told he would be given an injection of vitamin compounds to test their effects on vision. He was further told that the compound was harmless but that some people got mild feelings from it. The subjects were then injected, depending upon the condition, with either epinephrine (adrenalin) or a saline solution (a completely neutral material with no side effects at all). Some subjects were informed of the effects of epinephrine, another group was misinformed about the effects, and a third group was told nothing. Our hypothesis suggests that when a subject is in a state of physiological arousal without adequate explanation, cognitive and social factors can lead the individual to attach various emotional labels to his arousal. To examine this notion, two quite different emotional states were induced—euphoria and anger. Subjects were individually placed either with a stooge trained to act euphorically or a stooge trained to elicit anger. Under the euphoric condition, the stooge did funny things. Under the angry condition, the stooge and the subject took a questionnaire. The stooge constantly interrupted the subject and made misleading remarks. Two measures of the subjects' emotions were obtained. They were observed through one-way glass, and they completed self-reports on their moods at the moment.

When a person is aroused and has no explanation, he will label the state in terms of a social context.

The major findings of the experiment support the notion that when a person is in a physiological state of arousal for which he has no explanation, he will label the state in terms of his social situation. By manipulating the cognitions of an individual in an aroused state we can manipulate his emotions. Following the injection of epinephrine, those subjects who had no explanation for their bodily state reported and behaved as though they were angry or euphoric, according to the situation. If, however, the subject has an explanation for his state of physiological arousal, he will not label his state in terms of the cognitions available. Those subjects injected with epinephrine and then told precisely how they would feel were immune to the effects of the manipulated cognitions (see Figure 7.11). In the angry conditions, these subjects did not report or show anger. In the euphoric conditions, they reported themselves as less happy than subjects with identical bodily states but no adequate knowledge of why they felt that way. These results give good support to the proposition that when a state of sympathetic activation exists for which no immediate appropriate explanation is available, human subjects can be manipulated into states of euphoria, anger, or amusement. Emotional states are a composite of autonomic arousal and surrounding social-cognitive factors. Either factor alone cannot adequately describe the situation.

Adrenaline is associated with passive stress, while noradrenaline produces aggression.

Our emotions are related to the balance of adrenaline and noradrenaline (Funkenstein, King, & Drolette, 1957). Adrenaline is related to passive stress reactions while noradrenaline produces aggressive behavior. In response to frustration, some persons bottle up emotions while others express their anger. The "anger-in" person has an excess of adrenaline over noradrenaline while the reverse is true of "anger-out" adults. There is an abundance of adrenaline during early childhood, and only later do we shift toward a balance. It is not clear, however, why some individuals express anger while others repress it. Physiological processes may be basic, although there were significant differences in parent-child relations between the two groups. Adults who express anger believed that their mother was warm and their father authoritarian, while adults who internalized anger viewed both parents as affectionate. The process is complex. Psychological processes may determine the direction of anger expression and physiological processes sustain the direction.

Love is a neglected emotion.

One of our most important emotions has been neglected by psychology—love. McDougall (1926) wrote on the relation of sex and love; he believed sex to be an intimate part of love. Freud claimed that love is usually expressed in sexual terms, although love of

FIGURE 7.11

Schematic representation of an experiment with adrenaline and different expectations. Subjects injected with adrenaline gave a different emotional reaction to the stooge who is making "whoopee," depending upon whether or not they were given appropriate expectations of what the injection would do to them. The visceral reactions, involving organs of the body cavity, were not the only ones produced by adrenaline. (From Mandler, 1962.)

parents toward the child is surely not sexual (at least not at first). The child needs love, but the more general question—how a child learns to give and receive love—is unanswered by psychological experiment or theory. We need to receive love before we can develop a capacity to love others. Interpersonal love requires the ability to feel emotion, to express it to another, and to receive feedback from that expression. The male-female relation is particularly complex; femininity of women, masculinity of males, and their mutual role expectations are important.

Curiosity and cognitive change

Curiosity explains how children change from reflex to thought.

The infant develops from a simple sensory-motor creature capable of associating concrete events and motor actions to a sophisticated thinking being who can manipulate signs into novel combinations. Why does this occur? Investigators of widely divergent views have considered the problems of cognitive organization and development of rules. What are the motivational properties that lead the child to formulate rules and interpret environmental variations? The phenomena of cognitive behavior which must be explained are easy to describe in a general way. The adult human's response to environmental events is neither a simple function of states of the world (a stimulus) nor a direct result of states of the organism (a drive). In order to understand even the simplest cognitive processes, attention must be directed to stimuli, drives, *and* the structure of the person, that is, to the rules by which he orders the world. Theoretical systems developed to explain cognitive development include motivational, associationistic, and structural models.

Harlow and Butler showed that monkeys are curious.

Harlow (1953) and Butler (1953) performed several ingenious demonstrations of curiosity in higher primates. Harlow showed that a monkey, if given a relatively simple puzzle, will take it apart hour after hour with little or no rest, and without primary reinforcement. Butler demonstrated that a monkey will work to open a window so he may see out of a black box, suggesting that looking itself is reinforcing. Anyone who has turned on a television set can agree with this. Harlow assumed that primates have a basic curiosity drive which impells them to approach and investigate their environment.

Associationistic theories of motivation (e.g., Skinner) believe behavior is controlled by external events.

Opposed to the motivational notions of curiosity are associationistic theories of cognitive change, best represented by the writings of Skinner (1938). He believes all behavior is controlled by variations in the reinforcement contingencies of external events. He proposes that even the most complex cognitive events, such as language, are learned on the basis of reinforcement. The previously mentioned study by Rheingold and Gewirtz (1957) was intended to support this position. However, to change the rate of babbling of an infant and to teach the complex rules of grammar surely require different processes.

Assume the infant is (1) sensitive to complexity, (2) limited in ability, (3) learns rules, and (4) prefers to work within his abilities.

Against the variety of this background, consider a more neutral model to describe the development of cognition. We begin with four propositions: (1) Human beings are sensitive to the complexity of environmental events; (2) there is a limitation on the ability of human beings to process separate environmental events; (3) it is possible to escape this restriction on processing ability through rules derived from past experience; (4) human beings prefer to receive the number of events that matches their ability to process—they do not want to be bored by few events nor overcome by many, but instead prefer an intermediate level of complexity.

Miller reported that children and adults have restricted abilities to process information.

The notions of sensitivity to complexity and limits on processing ability have been demonstrated clearly in a series of experiments (Miller, 1956). Subjects were shown a set of random dots simultaneously for a very short duration. They were to guess the number of dots. Up to about six dots, children and adults were perfect in their estimation. However, above six they began making errors, first systematically overestimating and then systematically underestimating number. A limit on processing is reflected in the shift from perfect perception of six alternatives to inaccurate estimation of seven or more events. Analogous limitations on the number of alternatives that can be held in memory and the number of accurate absolute judgments the subject can make among a set of events place the notion of limited human processing capacity on a firm base.

Our limit is in terms of groups, not items.

The relation of complexity and preference is basic to this discussion. The child has a limited capacity to process information, but he is constantly presented with more events than he is able to process. His only recourse is to develop rules that simplify the events so he may understand them. By simplifying the world (grouping it), a child or adult appears to change his processing limit; however, the limit is in terms of "groups," and we can never break through it. The human capacity to process sensory information is limited; if sensory events are grouped, then the number of groups becomes the limiting factor. If we can develop a rule by which 50 objects can be grouped, for example, if they are in rows of ten, then the 50 objects can be processed easily as five rows of ten each. Grouping is a simple example of the development of rules.

Learning to read presents a clear case of coding; the child progresses from single letters to words and then sentences.

Another clear case comes when the young child learns to read. He begins by processing letters; at this stage each letter is a complex perception. His next step is to learn groups of these letters—words. Once words are learned, the child must group the words into sentences. The complex structuring of letters into words, words into sentences, and sentences into thought characterizes the development of rules. Obviously, the neonate cannot read complex English language, nor for that matter can the five-year-old. The adult has learned to group and process what is very difficult for the child even to understand.

Children develop rules to group the world and thus prefer more and more environmental complexity.

This analysis suggests that as we develop rules to simplify the world, our interest in events will systematically shift toward a preference for more complex stimulation. By grouping, the child is able to handle more events; as a result, what was complex before is now simple. Therefore, he must constantly look for new events to order. This interest in new, or more complex, events is the basis of curiosity.

Children's preference for complexity increases with age.

Consider some evidence for these notions. Suppose we vary the predictability of sequences of letters (Table 7.1). We might use the same letter repeated over and over (simple), then the same word repeated over and over, a short passage of prose, then a passage that looks a bit like English but contains no grammar, and finally a series of random words and a series of random letters (complex). These

TABLE 7.1 Sequence of Letters and Words of Varying Predictability (Complexity)

Predictability of Letters and Words	*Set I*	*Set II*	
Redundant letters	DDDDDD DDDDDD DDDDDD DDDDDD DDDDDD DDDDDD	YYYYYY YYYYYY YYYYYY YYYYYY YYYYYY YYYYYY	(*simple*)
Redundant words	Current Current Current Current Current	Include Include Include Include Include	
Prose	A short time at Alexandria is fine	He made life long friends there	
Fourth-order phrases	Students always the next room are	On my rug is deep with snow	
Third-order phrases	Happen to see Europe again is that	Trip to the end is coming here	
Second-order phrases	Him and substance was a piano is	Is that game since he lives in school	(*intermediate*)
First-order phrases	Want square chimney the wants	Especially much was said cake	
Random words	Obeisance cordial dip long bed hammer	Forget lethargy fluted watch attend	
Third-order words	Birs grocid ponde nome the	In no ist lat why cratict froure	
Second-order words	Incore st be S deamy thall	On ei are antsoutinys T	
First-order words	Tocro li rgwr nmielwis eu	Ll bnesebya tht eei the	
Random letters	Ffjccyk cqagx ydalm bixz xmrfj	Sjoml rxklr jffjuj zlp wofckeyj	(*complex*)

sequences of letters and words provide increasing unpredictability; they vary from simple to complex. From the propositions we discussed earlier (sensitivity to complexity, a limit on the ability to process environmental events, the side-stepping of this limit by the learning of rules, and preference for complexity at or near the child's ability to process), we can make simple statements about his preferences for these sequences of letters and words. Assuming that as a child matures he develops more and more sophisticated processing rules, we would expect the younger child to prefer simpler strings of letters and words; as he matures, he should systematically shift his preference toward more complex strings.

Children and adults prefer neither simple nor complex strings of letters and words.

Munsinger and Kessen (1964) presented these stimuli to third grade and sixth grade children and to college adults for preference judgments. Their results are shown in Figure 7.12. The assumption that all subjects prefer neither the very simple letters and words nor the very complex strings but would like an intermediate level of complexity was confirmed. In addition, the assumption that the adults, with their more sophisticated coding rules, would prefer more complex stimuli than the third and sixth grade children was also confirmed. In a related series of studies, responses to sets of random forms varying in number of sides (see Figure 7.13) showed the same systematic relation between preference and complexity (Munsinger & Kessen, 1964). The adults (Figure 7.14) stated a low preference for very simple figures, a high preference for an intermediate level of complexity of the figures, and a low preference for complex figures.

Preference for environmental complexity is determined by the stimulus and our rules for grouping.

Preference for complex events is jointly determined by two characteristics: (1) the amount of complexity in the stimulus itself and (2) the rules by which a person processes environmental events. There are several ways to change a person's coding rules. We might select subjects with experience in the production and evaluation of form and ask them to state their preference, or we might give people a series of training trials. Both experiments were performed by Munsinger and Kessen (1964). The first study used a group of art students. The art students were shown the random forms and asked to state their preference. They have a good deal of past experience with the production and evaluation of forms; their cognitive structure (rules)

FIGURE 7.12

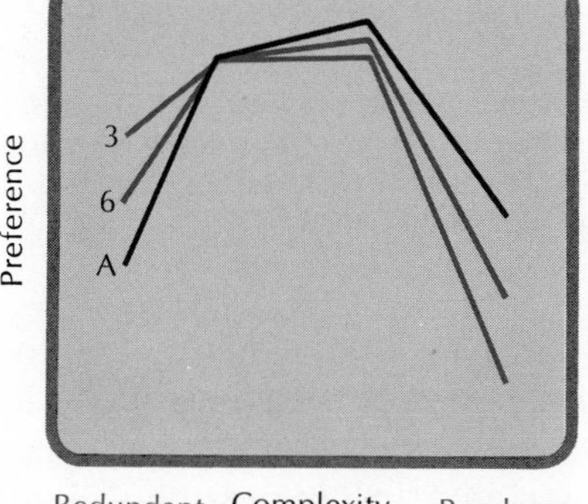

The relation between complexity of strings of letters and words and preference of children and adults. The results show that younger children prefer strings of letters and words, while older children and adults prefer more complex strings of letters and words for reading. (From Munsinger & Kessen, 1964.)

FIGURE 7.13

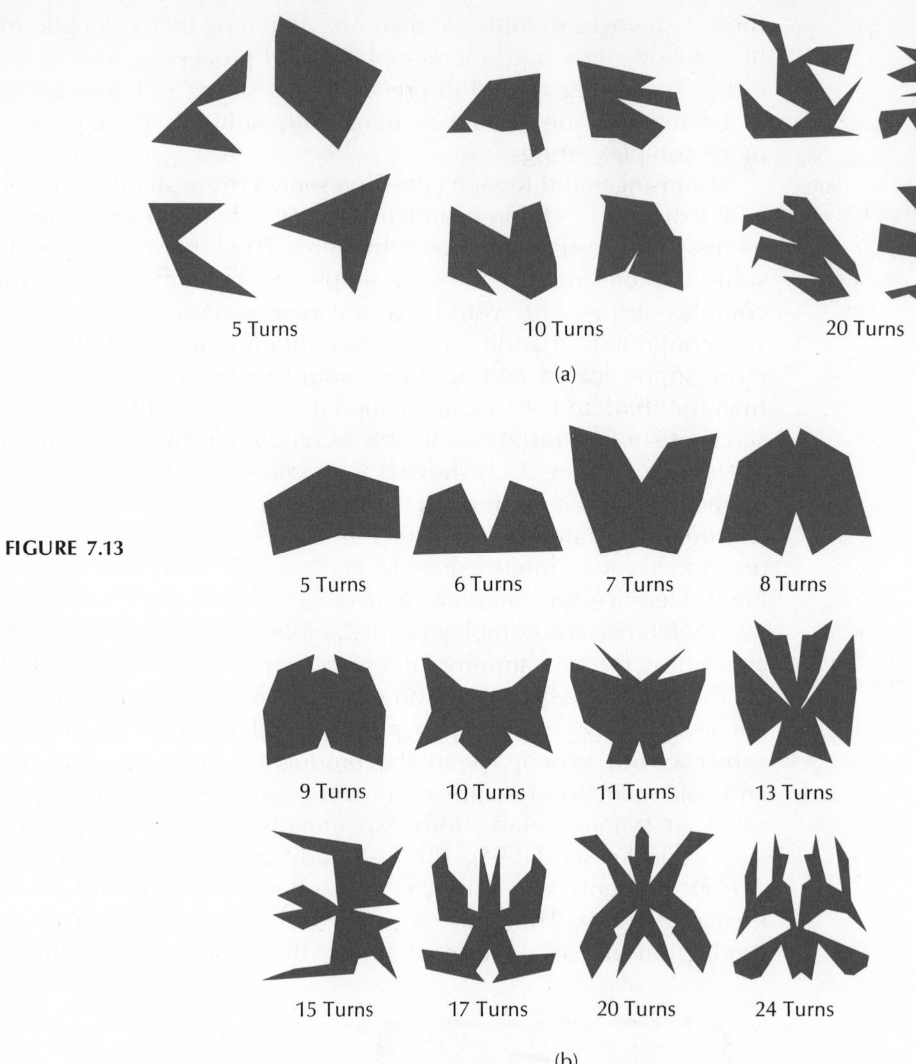

(a) Sets of 5-turn, 10-turn, and 20-turn asymmetrical figures used in studies of stimulus complexity. (b) Twelve symmetrical random shapes used in studies of stimulus complexity of independent turns from 5 to 24. (From Munsinger & Kessen, 1964.)

for the handling of form are more effective than the rules of unsophisticated college students. The art students prefer a high level of complexity as compared with college sophomores. Figure 7.15 shows that art students prefer complex figures, a confirmation of our expectation about the relation between stimulus complexity, coding rules, and

FIGURE 7.14

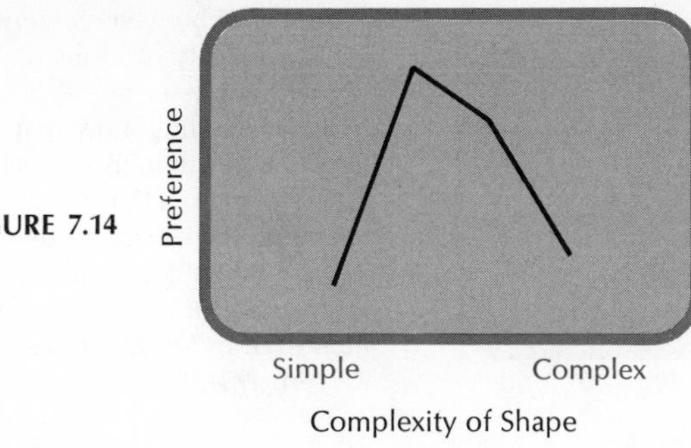

The relation between adults' preference for shapes and the complexity of the forms. The results support the conclusion that adults prefer neither too little nor too much information input, but will choose an intermediate level of stimulation which is at or near their ability to process. (From Munsinger & Kessen, 1964.)

preference. Moreover, students exposed to a series of random forms should learn rules about them. A group of undergraduates were exposed over and over again to the same set of random forms. Following experience, they preferred more complex forms (see Figure 7.16).

We can change children's preferences for complexity either by introducing rules or stimulus structure.

Another way of manipulating preference is to change the structure of the stimulus by introducing rules. Structure may be introduced into random forms by making them bilaterally symmetrical. This reduces the complexity (unpredictability) of the form by one half, for if we know the left side of a bilaterally symmetrical form, we can immediately predict the other half with no additional information. A series of symmetrical forms was shown to subjects for preference judgments (see Figure 7.13). The results (Figure 7.17) supported the conclusion that symmetrical forms (which are more easily coded) lead subjects to be interested in higher complexity forms.

Children (1) are sensitive to complexity, (2) learn rules, and (3) use these rules to process and prefer more complexity.

These studies support the following conclusions: (1) human beings are sensitive to the complexity of events; (2) they prefer stimulation at or near their ability to process complexity; (3) through experience, they can learn rules by which to simplify events; (4) these rules shift their preference toward more complex events; (5) by gradually grouping complex events (through rule learning), the child can shift from an understanding of very simple events to a knowledge of and interest

FIGURE 7.15

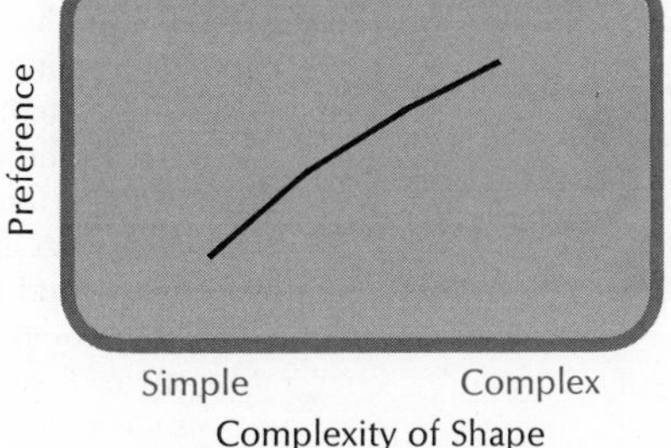

The relation between preference and complexity of stimuli among art students. The results suggest that art students, who have complex rules that allow the coding and processing of visual stimulation—can handle more information input and are drawn toward complex forms. (From Munsinger & Kessen, 1964.)

FIGURE 7.16

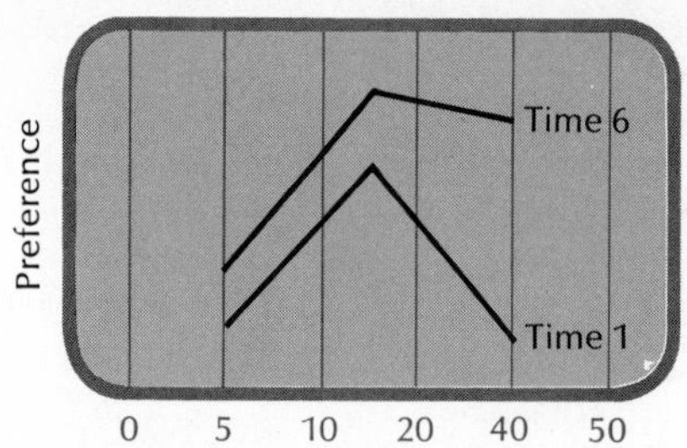

The relation between preference and complexity of forms plotted separately for first and sixth trials. The results show that exposure to stimulus variability allows the formation of rules for more efficient processing; as a result, subjects shift toward preference for more complex input. (From Munsinger & Kessen, 1964.)

in complex happenings. By this simple process of grouping and shifting toward more complex events, the child masters his world. He begins as a passive automaton, shoved and pulled by instincts; he ends as an active problem-solver and model-builder who is curious about more and more complex events.

Achievement motivation

Achievement motivation assumes children are driven to meet some external standard.

The assumption that children are driven by concern for meeting standards of excellence is called achievement motivation. This cognitive motivation is assumed to underlie such activities as scientific interest, artistic effort, and business achievement. The original test of achievement motivation was developed by McClelland (1955). He produced one situation in which students were expected to feel relaxed and another situation in which students were expected to feel motivated and at the same time believe they had failed at the assigned task. The task was a test of their imaginative skills. The relaxed group was told they were taking the test to help in its development. However, the aroused group was told that the test would determine their standing in a university; they were also given false forms which showed they had failed. The students were presented four pictures and asked to tell

FIGURE 7.17

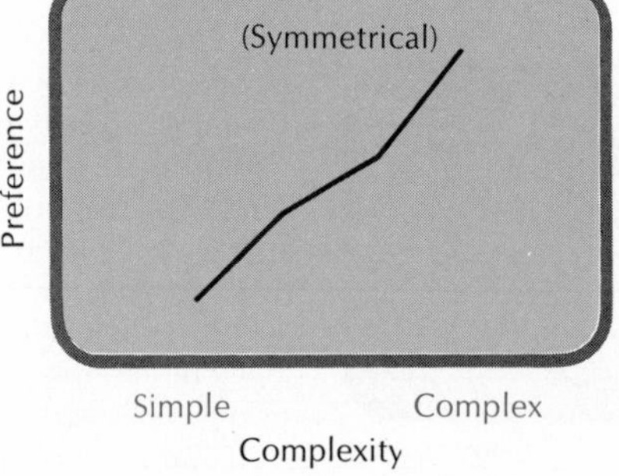

The relation between preference and complexity of forms (with structure added). The results show that symmetrical structure reduces the stimulus information and allows subjects to process, and therefore prefer, more complex forms. (From Munsinger & Kessen, 1964.)

a story about each. McClelland assumed that students who were aroused would tell stories about achievement, while students who were relaxed would say little about achievement. The results supported this notion. Then McClelland gave the test to another group of students. He found that they varied in the amount of achievement motivation they exhibited. He hypothesized that all students have a characteristic level of achievement motivation. Table 7.2 shows the results of individual variation and the levels of excitement (relaxed, neutral, and aroused) on the achievement motivation test. The scores are idealized.

Winterbottom found that mothers of high-achievement motivation children demand their children do new things.

Winterbottom (1953) obtained achievement motivation scores from 29 boys aged eight to ten years. In addition, she asked their mothers questions about how children should be raised and what kind of independent action they expected. Each mother was asked to tell when she expected her children to (1) know their way around the city, (2) try new things for themselves, (3) do well in competition, and (4) make their own friends. As one would expect, mothers of high-achievement motivation children expected them to perform earlier than mothers of low-achievement children. The primary demands were for the children to do new things—the demands to take over routine tasks were no different between low- and high-achievement children. These studies showed a correlation between the stated achievement demands of mothers and the achievement interests of their sons.

TABLE 7.2 Invented Scores Showing Ideal Effects of Situation and Personality

Absolute Scores on the Achievement Motivation Test	*Relaxed*	*Orientations Neutral*	*Aroused*
15			
14			
13			A
12			B
11			C
10			D
9		A	E
8		B	F
7		C	G
6		D	
5	A	E	
4	B	F	
3	C	G	
2	D		
1	E		
0	F		
−1	G		
−2			

Rosen and D'Andrade found that mothers of high-achievement boys are warm and understanding.

To test this proposition more directly, Rosen and D'Andrade (1959) visited 40 families (20 high-achievement boys and 20 low-achievement boys). Each son was asked to build a tower of blocks. The parents were allowed to look on and give directions, but could not touch the blocks. Each parent was asked to estimate how high he thought their son could build the blocks (parents' level of aspiration). Aspirations were higher among high-achievement parents than among low-achievement parents. The boys were then blindfolded, and each began to build towers while the parents gave him directions. Mothers of high-achievement boys were warm and encouraging; fathers of low-achievement boys were authoritarian and demanding. This was the only difference between the groups.

Our earlier notions of tissue deficit and primary drive have given way to social and cognitive theories of motivation.

Motivation is a complex issue; early notions of primary needs derived from tissue deficits have given way to the rich formulations of curiosity, achievement motivation, and secondary drives and reinforcement. The infant enters his world with a few primitive instincts; he differentiates these drives (through association and cognitive development) into taste, esthetic appreciation, and a variety of emotions.

SUMMARY

1 Motivation accounts for three aspects of behavior: the instigation of a response, the direction of a response, and the energization of a response.

2 Primary drives are unlearned physiological deficits that result in distress; reduction of the drive (reinforcement) is accomplished by repairing the tissue deficit.

3 Secondary drives are learned associations between previously neutral cues and primary drives. The strength of the secondary drive is controlled by the strength of the associated primary drive, by the number of pairings of the cues with the primary drive, by the timing of the pairings, and by their schedule.

4 Punishment results in fear and related emotional states; it is not an effective way to suppress a response. However, in conjunction with positive reinforcement, it is very effective in teaching discriminations between correct and incorrect responses.

5 Anxiety facilitates the learning of simple tasks but interferes with the solution of complex tasks.

6 Freud's Oedipal hypothesis suggests that very young children are attracted to their mothers, that slightly older children are attracted to the opposite-sexed parent, and that even older children (11-year-olds) are attracted to the same-sexed parent. Stevenson supported the first two propositions, but the third was disconfirmed.

7 Children are curious; curiosity is a complex function of the learned abilities of the child, the amount of information in the environment, and the limits on the child's processing capacity. Children learn to code information and travel in this manner from simple to more complex stimulus input by their curiosity.

8 High-achievement motivation is related to warm affection from the mother and early demands for independence among boys. Low-achievement motivation is related to harsh, critical demands from the father.

FURTHER READINGS

Nebraska symposium in motivation. Lincoln: University of Nebraska Press, 1953-present.

Mowrer, O. H. *Learning theory and behavior.* New York: John Wiley & Sons, Inc., 1960.

REFERENCES

Barker, R. G., Dembo, T., & Lewin, K. Frustration and regression: An experiment with young children. *University of Iowa Studies in Child Welfare,* 1941, **18.**

Brackbill, Y., & O'Hara, J. The relative effectiveness of reward and punishment for discrimination learning in children. *Journal of Comparative and Physiological Psychology,* 1958, **51,** 747–751.

Bridges, K. M. B. Emotional development in early infancy. *Child Development,* 1932, **3,** 324–341.

Butler, R. A. Discrimination learning by rhesus monkeys to visual exploration motivation. *Journal of Comparative and Physiological Psychology,* 1953, **46,** 95–98.

Cantril, H., & Hunt, W. A. Emotional effects produced by the injection of adrenalin. *American Journal of Psychology,* 1932, **44,** 300–307.

Castanada, A., Palermo, D. S., & McCandless, B. R. Complex learning and performance as a function of anxiety in children and task difficulty. *Child Development,* 1956, **27,** 327-332.

Dollard, J., & Miller, N. E. *Personality and psychotherapy.* New York: McGraw-Hill, 1950.

Estes, W. K. An experimental study of punishment. *Psychological Monographs,* 1944, **57,** No. 263.

Freud, S. *A general introduction to psychoanalysis.* New York: Liveright, 1916 (1935).

Fromm, E. *Man for himself.* New York: Holt, Rinehart and Winston, 1947.

Funkenstein, D. H., King, S., and Drolette, M. E. *Mastery of stress.* Cambridge: Harvard University Press, 1957.

Gewirtz, J., & Baer, D. M. The effects of brief social deprivation on behaviors for social reinforcers. *Journal of Abnormal and Social Psychology,* 1958, **56,** 49–56.

Harlow, H. Mice, monkeys, men, and motives. *Psychological Review,* 1953, **60,** 23–32.

Harlow, H. On the meaning of love. *American Psychologist,* 1958, **13,** 673–685.

Horney, K. *New ways in psychoanalysis.* New York: Norton, 1939.

James, W. *The principles of psychology.* New York: Henry Holt, 1890.

Jersild, A. T. Studies of children's fears. *Child Development Monographs,* 1935, No. 20.

Kessen, W., & Leutzendorff, A. M. The effect of non-nutritive sucking on movement in the human newborn. *Journal of Comparative and Physiological Psychology,* 1963, **56,** 69–72.

Kessen, W., & Mandler, G. Anxiety, pain, and the inhibition of distress. *Psychological Review,* 1961, **68,** 396–404.

Landis, C., & Hunt, W. A. Adrenalin and emotion. *Psychological Review,* 1932, **39,** 467–485.

Mandler, G. Emotion. In R. Brown, E. Galanter, E. Hess, & G. Mandler (Eds.), *New directions in psychology.* New York: Holt, Rinehart, & Winston, 1962.

McClelland, D. C. (Ed.). *Studies in motivation.* New York: Appleton-Century-Crofts, 1955.

McDougall, W. *Outline of abnormal psychology.* New York: Scribner, 1926.

Marquis, D. P. Can conditioned responses be established in the newborn infant? *Journal of Genetic Psychology,* 1931, **39,** 479–492.

Meyer, W. J., & Seidman, S. B. Age differences in the effectiveness of different reinforcement combinations on the acquisition and extinction of a simple concept learning problem. *Child Development,* 1960, **31,** 419–429.

Miller, G. A. The magical number seven, plus or minus two: Some limits on our capacity for processing information. *Psychological Review,* 1956, **63,** 81–97.

Miller, N. E. Studies of fear as an acquirable drive: I. Fear as motivation and fear-reduction as reinforcement in the learning of new responses. *Journal of Experimental Psychology,* 1948, **38,** 89–101(a).

Miller, N. E. Theory and experiment relating psychoanalytic displacement to stimulus-response generalization. *Journal of Abnormal and Social Psychology,* 1948, **43,** 155–178(b).

Munsinger, H., & Kessen, W. Uncertainty, structure, and preference. *Psychological Monographs,* 1964, **78** (Whole No. 586), 1–24.

Rheingold, H., & Gewirtz, J. The conditioning of vocalizations in infants using an adult's social response as reinforcer. *American Psychologist,* 1957, **12,** 392.

Rosen, B. C., & D'Andrade, R. G. The psychosocial origin of achievement motivation. *Sociometry,* 1959, **22,** 185–218.

Ruebush, B. K. Interfering and facilitating effects of test anxiety. *Journal of Abnormal and Social Psychology,* 1960, **60,** 205–212.

Sarason, I. G., & Palola, E. G. The relationship of test and general anxiety, difficulty of task and experimental instructions to performance. *Journal of Experimental Psychology,* 1960, **59,** 185–191.

Schachter, S., & Singer, J. E. Cognitive, social and physiological determinants of emotional state. *Psychological Review,* 1962, **69,** 379-399.

Sherman, M., & Sherman, I. C. *The process of human behavior.* New York: Norton, 1929.

Skinner, B. F. *The behavior of organisms.* New York: Appleton-Century-Crofts, 1938.

Stevenson, H. W. Social reinforcement with children as a function of CA, sex of E, and sex of S. *Journal of Abnormal & Social Psychology,* 1961, **63,** 147-154.

Stevenson, H. W., Weir, M. W., & Zigler, E. F. Discrimination learning in children as a function of motive-incentive conditions. *Psychological Report,* 1959, **5,** 95-98.

Walters, R. H., & Parke, R. D. Emotional arousal, isolation, and discrimination learning in children. *Journal of Experimental Child Psychology,* 1964, **1,** 163-173.

Watson, J. B., & Raynor, R. Conditioned emotional reactions. *Journal of Experimental Psychology,* 1920, **3,** 1-14.

Winterbottom, M. R. The relation of childhood training in independence to achievement motivation. University of Michigan: Abstract on University microfilm, publication No. 5113. Cited by D. C. McClelland et al., *The achievement motive.* New York: Appleton-Century-Crofts, 1953.

8 WILL

> Our wills and fates do so contrary run
> That our devices still are overthrown;
> Our thoughts are ours, their ends none of our own.
>
> HAMLET

The will is an ancient, abandoned notion in human psychology; James (1890) included a chapter in his famous book *Principles of Psychology,* which described how human beings judged events, made choices among alternatives, solved conflicts, and formed attitudes. A period followed during which the notions of choice, judgment, and conflict were neglected either as too complex, nebulous, and uncertain or as irrelevant to our understanding of human behavior. However, there is strong evidence that these topics are major human activities; they are among our most characteristic acts. This chapter covers modern notions of choice, preference, and judgment; a simple theory of conflict and its resolution is introduced. The processes of postdecisional conflict are studied (Festinger, 1957). Following these aspects of will, conceptions of children's morality and the development of attitudes and prejudices are outlined.

CHOICE, PREFERENCE, AND JUDGMENT

Choice reflects the joint effects of perception, thinking, and judgment.

Choice reflects the joint effects of perception (awareness of the objects of choice), thinking (analysis of the objects' meaning), and decision-making. We first develop a simple theory of choice among well-defined sets of alternatives, presenting Luce's (1959) choice axiom and some of its empirical implications (see Remarks: Theory). Luce's axiom of choice implies certain constraints upon the child's preferences for objects. The particular "drive" served by the choice is not relevant to our derivations nor does it enter into our empirical tests of the axiom.

Discrimination (a perceptual process), choice (a judgmental process), and preference (a motivational process) are often confused.

Choice is a common theme running through a variety of psychological problems. Discrimination and preference are always involved in a choice. The discrimination is among stimuli, whereas the preference is for outcomes of the choice. *Discrimination* requires the subject to say one item is different from another, and *choice* requires him to produce one response rather than another. Preference, on the other hand, is related to a child's goals, values, and needs; it is intimately tied to choice and discrimination. Most theorists ignore the problem of preference and write only about choice. We must be clear in talking about preference (a motivational problem), choice (a decisional problem), or discrimination (a perceptual problem).

Discrimination, choice, and preference should be studied separately.

Discrimination can be studied by using an obvious preference for a particular item (a child's wanting candy) and structuring the responses so that on any particular trial he may choose only one response (which will lead to candy if he is correct). This is the usual situation in discrimination-learning studies. Choice may be studied in any situation in which two or more responses are available to the subject; he must decide to produce one response or the other. A choice does not necessarily show preference for a particular stimulus or response used, since we can define rules for choice which are independent of the child's goals or wishes. For example, we may ask him to choose the heavier of two weights. He will be able to make decisions using this rule without telling us anything about his preferences for the weights. The child is telling us he prefers to be correct; this in no way reflects his preference for the objects (weights) of the experiment. We can assume a one-to-one correspondence between the subject's choices and his preferences only when he is given the object of his choice as the payoff and has been given no "rule" to guide his decision.

The choice experiment

The choice experiment includes well-defined alternatives, an observer, and rules which define the variables of interest.

Choice experiments include a set of well-defined alternatives (stimuli, objects, goals, responses, and so on) and an observer who must choose from among the set. By instructions or training we alert our subject to the appropriate dimension or attribute of the stimuli on which to base his judgments. In general, the subject is presented with various subsets of the alternatives for choice. The presentation schedule may be determined either by random selection without replacement or by optimization—that is, balancing the stimuli for side, order, and distribution of presentation (Ross, 1934). The datum for analysis is the alternative selected by the child when presented each set. We will assume in our model that the child's choices (over successive presentations) are independent. This implies that his choice on trial n is not influenced by

REMARKS: THEORY

All models of choice make a fundamental assumption—transitivity. There are three types of logical transitivity—weak, moderate, and strong. To illustrate, suppose we have three items—*A, B,* and *C.* Assume *A* is chosen over *B* 70 percent of the time and *B* over *C* 60 percent of the time. The statements we can make about the probability of our subject's choosing *A* over *C* depend upon whether we assume weak, moderate, or strong transitivity. Under weak transitivity we can say only that he will choose *A* over *C* 50 percent of the time; under moderate transitivity we can make the statement that his choice of *A* over *C* will be $\geq$ the smaller of the other two proportions (in this case, 60 percent), while under strong transitivity we can say that his choice of *A* over *C* will be $\geq$ the larger of the two probabilities (in this case, 70 percent).

There are two distinct kinds of transitivity in children. One is the *concept* of transitivity as presented in the works of Piaget [1950 (1947)], while the other notion of transitivity only implies something about the pattern of a child's preferences. Piaget makes the strong assumption that the child understands the notion that $A < B$ *and* $B < C$ implies $A < C$. This type of transitivity does not become available to the child until he is six or seven. However, to argue that there is no point in doing studies of choice before seven years of age is wrong; theories of choice do not say anything about the child's *concept* of transitivity. Choice models require only that the responses of children satisfy the constraints of transitivity. Whether they understand the process is irrelevant. This more general type of transitivity is satisfactory for our purposes and probably occurs much earlier in the life of the child.

his choice on trial $n-1$ or the order in which the various presentation sets occur.

We can minimize sequential dependencies among responses by having the observer make his choices over several days.

We can minimize sequential dependencies by measuring the various choices among the objects once a day. This requires that the child produce his choices on several successive days to obtain reliable estimates. However, by spreading our measurements over several days, developmental changes may occur which will influence our pattern of results. A good compromise might be to spread our measurements over several days and compare the results obtained during the first few days with those from later days. If no systematic differences occur, then the technique of measurement over several days was successful. If there are systematic differences, then more subjects should be measured, with somewhat less time between successive measurements. An iterative system such as this should result in an optimum compromise between the sequential dependencies that occur when the child is presented frequently with the same choice objects and the developmental changes that occur over substantial time intervals.

LUCE'S CHOICE MODEL (LUCE, 1959)

We now consider a choice axiom; it is a simple assumption with substantial support.

Suppose that a subject repeatedly chooses from among three alternatives (*A, B,* and C). Sample choice proportions are given in Table 8.1.

TABLE 8.1 Prediction of Pairwise Data from Triad

Choice Proportions	*Reduced Set*	*Normalized Proportions*
A 0.40	*A* 0.40	*A′* 0.40/0.70 = 0.572
B 0.30	*B* 0.30	*B′* 0.30/0.70 = 0.428
C 0.30		
A + *B* + C = 1.00	*A* + *B* = 0.70	*A′* + *B′* = 1.000

Suppose we now remove C and ask the child to choose between *A* and *B*. We would like to be able to predict the probability of his choosing *A* over *B* on the basis of our triad choice data. A sensible intuition might suggest the following: We delete alternative C and multiply *A* and *B* percentages by a factor, using the sum of their percentages in the triad (1/.70), which will make *A′* and *B′* add up to one. We will call this procedure normalizing the *A* and *B* scores; it is one version of Luce's choice axiom. The axiom predicts various relations among choice probabilities as we change the number of alternatives involved in the decision, and it assumes that the ratio of the likelihood of choosing *A* to the likelihood of choosing *B* is a constant, regardless of the number and composition of the other alternatives in the set presented for choice. This assumption is called *the constant ratio rule.* The example in Table 8.1 shows how the constant ratio rule operates. The ratio *A′/B′* is the same as the ratio *A/B,* which we obtained from the choice among three objects.

RESPONSE BIASES

The usual experimental practice in testing choice is to use easily discriminable stimuli and in testing discrimination to use preferences that are obvious, such as hungry men preferring food to no food. In these extreme cases the confounding of preference and discrimination are fairly well controlled. However, there is a more deeply confounded problem than the interlocking of preference and discrimination. Children often—in fact, almost always—exhibit preferences among responses as well as outcomes. To keep our terminology straight, we will speak of response preferences as biases among responses.

A striking example of response bias is the position habits of young children; biases occur whenever discrimination is difficult or when the differences among outcomes are slight.

Transitivity first constrains a child's preferences.

We may speculate about the age at which these constraints occur among children's choices. A reasonable expectation would suggest that pair choices would begin to follow the constraints of transitivity quite early and that triad and ranking data would show lawful relations only later. This simple prediction is generated by assuming that children can compare only a few events at a time. Presumably the pair choices offer fewer events to compare than the more complex selections. On the other hand, the nonsymbolic child may not be able to conceptualize relations among events that are not perceptually present. If this assumption is correct, we would expect the young child to show transitivity among three items more often when they are presented at the same time (triads) rather than when only pairs are presented (possibly the nonsymbolic child cannot abstract a ranking from pairs). This question remains unanswered.

The various methods of collecting choices (ranking, ratings, pair choices, and so on) often produce different data.

Two difficulties are associated with the application of models of choice. One problem occurs because there are many different ways in which stimuli can be presented to a child for choice. We can ask him to select the best of k stimuli (a subset of all n stimuli), to rank all n stimuli, to sort them into different categories, to assign qualitative ratings or quantitative estimates, to separate pairs of stimuli into classes representing equal similarity, to rank order the distances between pairs of stimuli, and so on. At the moment there is no clear theory to describe the various activities a child may be asked to carry out. We should not be surprised to find that different methods of data collection produce different results.

Gathering enough observations can be a problem. Using groups is an unsatisfactory solution.

The second problem concerns the difficulty of collecting data in a choice experiment. Most of the theories assume that choices are made by individuals. To obtain choice percentages from a single individual we must ask him to make the judgments many times. Except for cases involving imperfect discrimination, the subject's successive choices will be highly dependent. The child is likely to remember the response he gave last time and simply give it again. If you ask him 100 times which of two items he prefers, he is likely to think you are crazy. A frequently used solution to this problem is to ask groups of children to make only a few choices each. The theoretical probability is then estimated from the proportion of children who choose i over j when the pair ij is presented. The theory can be tested by seeing if the group proportions satisfy the constraints of the product rule or the constant-ratio rule. Careful analysis of the choice theories shows that the group average results are of questionable status (recall the problem with group learning curves and all-or-none versus incremental associative strength). It is not difficult to show that although individual subjects may conform to the axiom, the group average of these same subjects may not satisfy the axiom.

CONFLICT

Conflict occurs when the child's tendencies to approach and avoid an object are equal.

Conflict occurs when there is a balance between the child's approach and avoidance tendencies. When a child is exposed to either a positive or a negative stimulus, he experiences no conflict; he will approach the positive goal or avoid the negative goal. Only when the positive and negative values of a *single* goal are equal will the child be in conflict. There are several types of conflict (see Figure 8.1).

Conflict situations include approach–approach, avoidance–avoidance, approach–avoidance, and double approach–avoidance.

A simple type of conflict that is fairly easy to resolve is the approach–approach situation, in which both goals are positive and the child must choose between the two mutually exclusive alternatives. A second conflict situation, one that is much more difficult to resolve, is the avoidance–avoidance situation, in which both alternatives are negative. In this situation the child must choose one or the other negative goal. Finally, we come to the most difficult and interesting

FIGURE 8.1

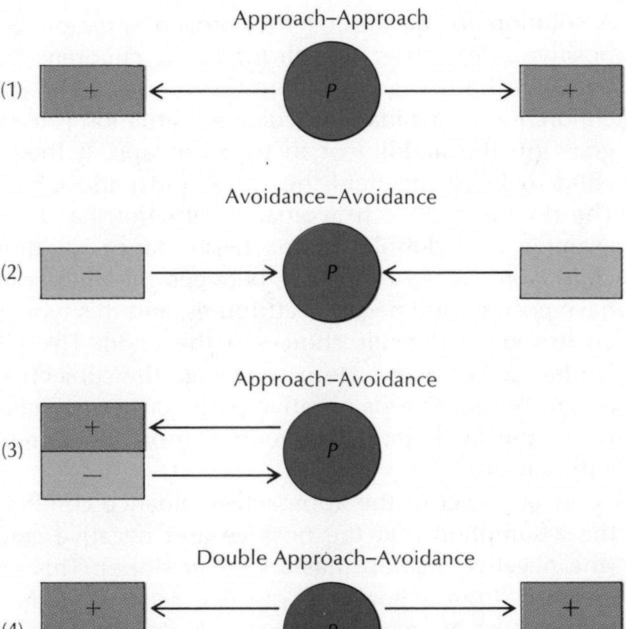

Four types of conflict. The circles represent people in conflict. The boxes containing + and − signs represent objects with positive or negative values. The arrows (vectors) have three properties: direction (toward or away from the object), strength, and point of application.

conflict situation—the approach-avoidance problem. This conflict is most representative of everyday choices. In the single approach-avoidance situation, the child must decide whether he wants to choose one alternative, with its positive and negative aspects, or whether he would rather not choose at all. Suppose he is trying to decide whether or not he wants to pet a dog. The positive aspect is, of course, petting the dog; the negative aspect is fear of strange animals. The other alternative is not to pet the dog; then we receive neither the positive nor the negative goal. The double approach-avoidance situation is even more complex and difficult to resolve. Here the child must choose between two mutually exclusive alternatives which are both positive and negative. An example might be a choice between buying an ice cream cone and spending money, or saving money and not having the ice cream.

Solutions to conflict

Solutions to approach-avoidance situations include not choosing, leaving the field, and reevaluating the situation so there is no conflict.

A solution to the approach-approach situation entails going to one positive side. This is difficult for young children; they tend to vacillate between the two goals before they choose. The preferred solution by children to an avoidance-avoidance situation is to stay away from both goals (in the middle) or to try to escape. If there is no way for the child to leave the field, he will avoid choosing as long as possible. The double approach-avoidance situation has been well studied. An example of a double approach-avoidance situation would be if the child were forced to choose between his mother and his father. Both have positive and negative attributes, and this type of problem presents an extremely difficult choice to the child. The child may solve the conflict in two ways. He may change the subjective value of the goal, either the positive or negative parts, or he may choose not to choose (leave the field altogether), either through suppression, repression, or withdrawal.

The approach-avoidance conflict model assumes that the positive and negative gradients have different slopes.

The power of the approach-avoidance conflict model stems from the assumption that the positive and negative gradients are different (the negative gradient has a steeper slope). This means that if one is far away from a goal, the positive aspects of the goal are more attractive (the approach gradient is higher), but as one approaches the goal, the negative gradient increases faster than the positive one (see Figure 8.2). The differential slope of the two gradients implies a point in many situations at which the positive approach tendencies and the negative avoidance tendencies balance. At this point, conflict occurs. The child vacillates at the intersection of the positive and negative gradients. If the two gradients do not cross, there is no conflict.

FIGURE 8.2

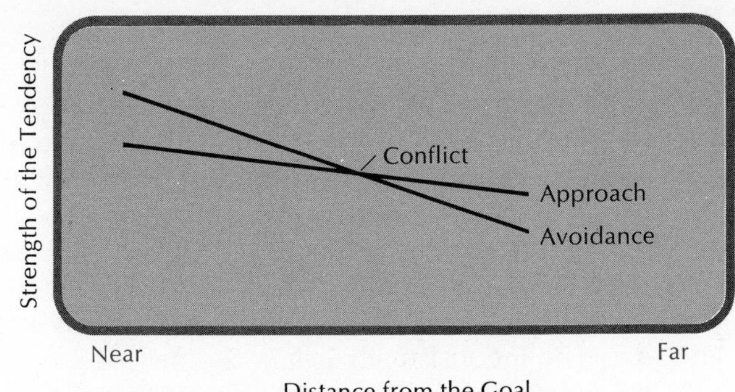

The approach-avoidance gradient model; it postulates that the slope of the positive and negative gradients are different. The negative gradient is assumed to have a steeper slope. Thus if one is far from the goal, the positive aspects will appear more attractive, while when one approaches the goal, the negative aspects will become more and more powerful. The differential slope of the two gradients produces a point of equality, which is the point at which conflict occurs.

One solution to any conflict situation entails raising or lowering one of the two gradients so they do not meet. This may be accomplished either by rationalization, reassessment of the goals, or through some other defensive mechanism that would allow the child to change the value of a goal. The child may also ignore negative aspects of the goal in reaching his decision. Once the child has committed himself to a goal, postdecisional processes begin working to reduce any residual doubt about the choice. Most children report they like the goal they have chosen.

Cognitive dissonance

Cognitive dissonance occurs when the child finds a difference between his present state and his desires.

Cognitive dissonance is a state of tension which motivates the child's efforts to achieve balance among his various wishes. Dissonance is a disequilibrium between the present state of the world and the child's wishes. A typical example is when a child chooses one object over another and then, after receiving the object, has second thoughts about his choice. This postdecisional conflict must be resolved if the child is to remain happy. Dissonance theory has emphasized some interesting kinds of inconsistency, some new aspects about the magnitude of inconsistency, and some interesting ways of reducing inconsistency.

Joining a new group and then wishing you had not is an example of dissonance.

As an example, suppose a child has just joined a new group. He may not really like the new group, but he is lonely, having just moved into the neighborhood, and he likes the idea of having playmates. Suppose he now finds a new friend who thinks the group he has just joined is not a good one. How will the child view his commitment to the group? If he had been very happy—or very unhappy—with the group in the beginning, he would not be in much conflict. But recall that he was ambivalent and joined out of loneliness instead of attraction toward the group. The child took an action inconsistent with his attitudes. The inconsistency lies in the pair of propositions—I chose to join this group; this group is not very good.

The greater the difference between our original desire to make a commitment and our new desire not to make it, the greater our dissonance.

The dissonance is generated by the child's commitment to an action he thought might be interesting, and now thinks he would like to avoid if he could, but he cannot. The greater the difference between the original desire to make the commitment and the now lower desire to be in the situation, the greater the dissonance. If the action cannot be accounted for by factors other than a favorable attitude, then there is a strong need to make the attitude favorable. Dissonance theory says that once we have taken a particular action, we make our attitudes congruent with that action. If we cannot justify our action on the basis of attitude, we change our attitudes to justify the action.

Subjects who perform a boring task for no external justification are most likely to feel cognitive dissonance (and change their attitudes to relieve the dissonance).

Consider some research inspired by dissonance theory. Festinger and Carlsmith (1959) asked subjects to perform a tedious task for one hour (place 12 spoons on a tray, empty the tray, and then refill it). At the end of this phase of the task all the subjects were told that the experiment was a study in set—the effects of expecting the task to be interesting and exciting. The subjects were then separated into three groups and were given the following different treatment conditions. One group (control) was asked to rate the procedure they had just gone through on a scale of interest and scientific importance. The other two groups of subjects rated the experiment after they had been given further instructions. Subjects in one of the latter groups were asked if they would like to serve as confederates of the experimenter to tell other subjects that the task had been fun and exciting (they were offered one dollar for this service). Subjects in the other experimental group were offered 20 dollars for the same task. Following these offers, both experimental groups rated the experiment for interest and scientific usefulness. The expectation from dissonance theory is that subjects who are offered one dollar and accept the task will have a more positive attitude about the task than will those who accept 20 dollars for the confederate's job. The one-dollar group has little external justification for their behavior and therefore must make the task seem more important and interesting than it really is to relieve their dissonance. The mean ratings were −.45 for the control group, +1.33 for the one-dollar group, and −.05 for the 20-dollar group. This outcome is difficult to predict from reinforcement theory and is not obvious on commonsense grounds. This type of prediction is a hallmark of the dissonance theorist.

The more work required, the more likely one is to feel something is desirable.

Another determinant of dissonance, besides the adequacy of payment to take an inconsistent action, is the amount of work associated with the action. If the child has to undergo a particularly difficult initiation to get into a group, he is more likely to feel that the group is valuable than if it was relatively easy to enter. Many people overvalue those things they have suffered to obtain. The Puritan ethic reflects this fact.

The more trouble one has, the more attachment one has to a group—for example, fraternity initiations.

A reasonable way to test this notion is to assign subjects randomly to conditions of difficult and easy initiation and then measure their evaluations of the experience following initiation. This will rule out self-selection and allow us to know the result of initiation alone. Aronson and Mills (1959) performed this experiment: College women volunteered to engage in a discussion of sex with the understanding that the session was a study in group dynamics. All the women were interviewed and asked whether they felt they could talk freely. Those in the control condition were accepted if they said they could talk freely. Those in the experimental conditions were given further tests. They were required to take an embarrassment test. For those assigned to a severe condition, the test involved reading aloud a list of obscene words before the male experimenter. Those in the mild condition were asked to read some sex-related materials. All subjects were told they had passed the test. They all then listened to a taped discussion of the secondary sex behavior of animals. The discussion was dull and banal. Then they were asked to rate the discussion on interest and intelligence. The expectation was that the more severe initiation would produce a more positive rating of the group discussion. Results supported this hypothesis.

Dissonance would not work if a child believed he was a liar with poor luck and bad judgment.

The unexpressed premises in all dissonance experiments contain notions such as, "I say what I believe"; "I do what I want to do"; "What I choose is better than what I reject." The manipulations used by these theorists would not cause dissonance in a person who believes he is a liar with bad luck, poor judgment, and no will power!

The stronger the values in conflict, the more dissonance is generated.

One determinant of dissonance is the relative value of the ideas involved. The stronger the value of two ideas in conflict, the greater the dissonance. There are many elements in the person's cognitive field which add to produce conflict. To predict the magnitude of dissonance, we must be able to count all these items; this is a difficult measurement problem. The dissonance theorist has not addressed himself to it in any consistent manner.

Alternative explanations include relief after a severe initiation and real interest from the added information.

There are various alternative hypotheses that may explain the results obtained in cognitive dissonance experiments. Consider the women who went through a severe initiation and then gave high ratings to the boring discussion that followed. Perhaps the recorded discussion was pretty lively because these women with additional experience could see where the discussion might go. Another possible interpretation is that the women were relieved by an intellectual discussion after their severe initiation.

Dissonance studies usually lose subjects from critical cells of the design.

There are also methodological problems connected with research in cognitive dissonance. In most of the experiments several subjects refuse to complete the study. Subject dropout is a serious problem, since those who drop out of the experiments shift the results in favor of dissonance theory. Consider the Festinger and Carlsmith experiment as an example. There is no reason why the control subjects, who simply rate the experiment, should refuse to complete that task. Which ones will refuse? Those offered one dollar in payment for their services as accomplices are more likely to refuse than those offered 20 dollars. Also, those who found the task extremely dull are more likely to refuse than those who found it only mildly dull. If we lose subjects from the one-dollar condition who feel that the task is dull, we keep more subjects who think the task is interesting. This is exactly the result proposed by dissonance theory. Dropouts do occur, and they do affect results. In the Festinger and Carlsmith study there were 11 dropouts; seven came from the one-dollar condition!

THE DEVELOPMENT OF MORALITY

Freud believed children develop a superego while Piaget proposed that morality is primarily cognitive.

How a child comes to know moral principles fascinates psychologists; Freud (1949) suggested that the main ingredient of moral development is the acquisition of a superego that tells children what to do and what not to do. This simple theory assumes that guilt is the main point of morality. However, Piaget (1950) ascribes more to morality than restriction by guilt. He believes there are strong cognitive aspects to morality; one comes to know and understand the features of moral acts.

According to Freud, the superego makes the ego feel guilty when we transgress.

How does the superego function? It gives us resistance to temptation. It also gives us shame for inadequacy, guilt for transgressions against the law, and feelings of self-esteem for virtue. There are two kinds of moral strictures: One, represented by guilt, is self-punishment we feel when we transgress. The other, represented by shame, is when we fear being caught or are actually caught. Guilt results from a difference between the ego and our ego ideal; the larger this discrepancy, the larger our feeling of guilt. The difference between our ego and our ego ideal can be reduced *either* by changing our behavior *or* the ego ideal, a point often missed by individuals who feel guilty. Somehow, they feel it is their behavior that must be changed when it may be that their ego ideal is unrealistic.

The superego comes from the incorporation of parents' standards.

How does the superego develop? It comes from the parents; it is the residue of years of dependency. It is not the parents' actions that are incorporated into the superego but their standards. According to Freud, the superego develops following the resolution of the Oedipal situation. Recall that the Oedipal situation places the little boy in sexual lust after his mother and in competition with his father. The resolution of this dilemma comes when the little boy gives up his lust for the mother and identifies with the father. This period of latency is supposed to occur because the little boy fears castration by the father and feels inadequate about possessing his mother. The boy then identifies with his more powerful father and takes him for an ego ideal. The case for the little girl is more difficult. Girls are not fearful of castration; they think it has already happened. They envy the penis of the father, and they turn away from the mother toward the father in hopes of possessing and controlling his penis. In time, their desire for the father's penis is supposed to be supplanted by desire for a child; however, what ends the Electra complex? Freud (1925) suggested that it just wears off. In addition, he suggested that women do not have a well-developed superego!

Parents who use little punishment tend to produce the strongest conscience in their children.

What determines the strength of the superego? Sears, Maccoby, and Levin (1957) obtained accounts of mothers' child-rearing practices from interviews. Recall that these data are bound to be somewhat unreliable and distorted. However, they give us some hint about the mechanisms of conscience development. Sears and his associates asked the mothers if there were times when the child was naughty; if there were such occasions, what did the child do about it? If he came to tell his mother about his bad behavior, they felt he had a strict conscience; if he did not, they felt he had little conscience. They found that physical punishment is negatively related to strength of conscience; those parents who used little physical punishment produced children with a stronger conscience (children who are not punished are more likely to confess their transgressions). Sears reported that mothers who withdraw love are most likely to develop a strong conscience in their children.

Piaget believes morality is the understanding of rules.

Piaget (1960) presents both a theory of moral development and experimental evidence for his theory. A good example of moral development and role-playing in children occurs in the game of marbles. Marbles can be complicated and variable. The variability is, however, entirely within a framework of rules. This point should be clear; the game is not a trivial sensory-motor exercise. It has elders, codified rules, legality of execution, and many other aspects of human society. We can compare it to society on a smaller scale. Piaget learned the basic operations of the game and then analyzed the behavior of children, differing in age, when they participate in the game. He discovered information about age differences in rule behavior by playing a game with children. But he does this as a novice wishing to learn the game, not as an adult questioning and intimidating the children.

Piaget finds four stages in morality: (1) motor, (2) egocentric, (3) cooperation, and (4) codification of rules.

From his analysis of children's behavior while playing, Piaget finds systematic changes in how they practice rules and their awareness of what rules are about. He finds four stages in the child's *use* of rules and three stages in his *consciousness* of them. In the child's practice of rules, stage 1 is called the motor or individual stage, stage 2 is denoted the egocentric stage, stage 3 is a time of cooperation, and stage 4 is when codification of the rules occurs. Concerning the child's consciousness of rules, stage 1 is a time when the child regards all rules as examples; in stage 2, however, he regards all rules as "sacred" and emanating from adults; finally, in stage 3, he comes to regard rules as stemming from mutual consent. The stages coordinate with age levels. Piaget does not rigorously analyze his data. He relies on insight and compelling arguments to carry his theories.

Kohlberg has expanded and clarified Piaget's stages.

Kohlberg (1966) has derived a developmental process of morality with three levels and six stages (see Table 8.2). In comparing Kohlberg's and Piaget's theories we find many similarities. Both see the child progressing from motor operations to an egocentric view, then to a stage of mutual cooperation, and finally to a state in which legal aspects of the game—either marbles or life—are codified, studied, and practiced with great relish and duty.

TABLE 8.2 Kohlberg's Developmental Stages of Morality

Level 1: Premoral	
Stage 1	Obedience and punishment orientation
Stage 2	Naively egoistic orientation
Level 2: Conventional Role Conformity	
Stage 3	"Good boy" orientation
Stage 4	Authority and social order-maintaining orientation
Level 3: Self-Accepted Moral Principles	
Stage 5	Contractual legalistic orientation
Stage 6	Conscience or principle orientation

Kohlberg showed that children in America and Taiwan progress through the same stages of morality.

Kohlberg used the cross-cultural method to test his stage theory. He conducted studies on five different cultures but reported only those on American and Taiwanese children. In these two quite divergent cultures children progress through the same (predicted) stages. Piaget's compelling arguments and Kohlberg's cross-cultural study lend support to their developmental process of morality.

Hartshorne and May showed that children's awareness of rules and their use of rules are not related.

What is the relation between consciousness of rules and their practice? Hartshorne and May (1928, 1929, 1930) found a low correlation between awareness of rules and children's practice of these same rules. They studied cheating and rediscovered facts which are well known to all children but forgotten by most adults: "Noncheaters" are simply more "cautious" rather than more "honest." It is wrong to be caught, not wrong to cheat. They also found, among the same children, that cheating in some classrooms was very high while cheating in others was very low. Apparently children have no internal morality against cheating; the external forces against cheating merely varied from one classroom to the next. They concluded that any "moral education" that does occur in school has no effect on the conduct of the child. Schools are almost totally ineffective at producing morality in children. The reasons for this stem from the artificiality of our educational system in relation to the child. Cheating is also compounded by an emphasis on grades.

Piaget believes that cheating is the natural result of our competitive school system.

Cheating is a defensive reaction demanded by our educational system. The system isolates the individual against the natural preference for cooperation with peers and condemns him to work against his comrades, each of whom will theoretically be trying to curry the master's favor by winning good marks, or for the purpose of winning good marks.

Parents function as models for children's moral behavior.

Cheating is by no means the only factor hindering children's moral education. Another factor is the child's well-developed sense of "fairness," Mischel and Liebert (1966) point out how the adult (acting as a model) influences the child's acquisition and transmission of moral criteria; they used young children (approximately seven to eleven years of age). An adult (*M*) alternated with the children in a game of bowling. The experimental treatments involved discrepancies between the performance criteria used by the adult to reward himself and to reward the child. They presented four conditions: (1) both the adult and the child were on a (stringent) high-achievement-for-reward criterion; (2) the adult rewarded himself for low achievement but the child only for high achievement; (3) both the adult and child were on a low-achievement criterion; and (4) the adult rewarded himself for high achievement and the child for low. Following this learning situation each child was required to teach the game and the reward system to another, younger child. It was noted how well the child adhered to the original criterion and how well he transmitted the criterion to the younger one.

Experiments show that children adopt high moral criteria only if their model is consistent.

The results showed that (1) if both the model and child received high-reward criteria, then the child adhered to these and transmitted them to the younger child; (2) if both had low-reward criteria; then the child neither adhered well to those criteria nor did he transmit them to the younger child; (3) if there was a discrepancy, the child did not adhere well to the criterion originally imposed upon him, but he did learn to use differing criteria for others than he used for himself.

Children are aware of the difference between what adults say and what they do.

All of this merely shows that the child is acutely aware of a discrepancy between what is "morally right," as told to him by parents and teachers, and the actual behavior exhibited by others. The child does note discrepant behavior. These conflicts produce the low correlation between a child's awareness of rules and his use of them.

Live models have longer effects on children's behavior than symbolic models.

This last point raises another question. Do children learn better from live models (humans) or from symbolic models (stories read to them)? Bandura and Mischel (1965) asked this question. They classified groups of children into those who preferred immediate rewards and those who preferred delayed but more substantial rewards for good behavior. They then split each group into three sections and submitted them to three different conditions: (1) training to accept the reward situation opposite that originally preferred (by the use of live models); (2) the same training but with the use of symbolic models; and (3) a control group that received no training. The live model was a woman who demonstrated the behavior she wished the child to learn. The symbolic model appeared in stories that demonstrated the desired behavior. The results showed that children learn better from live models than from symbolic models. Both models produced substantial modifications in the children's behavior pattern, but these modifications were more stable over time in the children exposed to the live model.

Mischel and Grusec studied the effects of reward and control on children's learning.

Mischel and Grusec (1966) studied the effects of control and reward on children's learning. Control describes the amount of authority exercised by the teacher over a pupil's life. Reward indicates the amount of positive reinforcement used by the teacher to encourage learning. Control is negative while reward is more positive.

Children learn rules under reward or control; however, they practice or transmit rules only under reward conditions.

Mischel and Grusec found that reward and control produce different effects when children are "taught" aversive behavior (waiting some time before they can play) or neutral behavior (marching around the room). Aversive behavior was never rehearsed by the child unless control was very high. On the other hand, reward strongly affected the transmission of behavior from one child to another. Apparently the child learns rules under either reward or control; however, his use of these rules (transmission to others) is contingent only on reward or very high levels of control. Unless the things we teach children are aversive, motivation should be by reward and not by control. Then the child will learn the desired rules *and act on them.*

PREJUDICE AND THE AUTHORITARIAN PERSONALITY

The Authoritarian Personality *study investigated correlations among prejudices.*

Attitudes toward others may be independent—a person may hate Jews and yet be a fine father—or attitudes and beliefs may co-vary—a person may hate Jews, be a weak father, and kick dogs. *The Authoritarian Personality* (1950) was a study of how traits co-vary with anti-Semitic feelings. Most of the data for the study were collected in the form of questionnaires given to over 2000 subjects.

Adorno and associates produced a scale of eight anti-democratic attitudes.

The Authoritarianism Scale measured eight correlated antidemocratic characteristics: (1) conventionalism—a rigid adherence to middle class values; (2) submission—a submissive attitude toward moral authorities; (3) aggression—a tendency to reject people who violate rules; (4) antiintraception—opposite of imagination; (5) stereoptypy—a belief in mystical determinants of the individual's fate; (6) power—a preoccupation with the dominance-submission dimension; (7) destructiveness—a hostility toward human nature; and (8) projectivity—the belief that dangerous things go on in the world.

There are high interrelations among the scales.

Each subscale correlates with the total score; thus, there is little reason to maintain the various subparts. The items within each part correlate as high with items from other scales as they do with items in the same scale. There is good evidence that the total Authoritarian Scale is reliable.

They also conducted interviews about the family relations of their subjects.

In addition to administering the scales, the researchers gathered information from interviews. They asked such questions as, "What was the power relation between your mother and your father?" The prejudiced person had a consistently more favorable impression of himself than did the unprejudiced person. Individuals who are prejudiced report that they have many sexual contacts and easy conquests, while the individual who is unprejudiced reports he is shy or retiring about sexual activities. The prejudiced person says his father was great and his mother was marvelous; the unprejudiced person says that his father was OK but gave too much advice or that his mother was too controlling.

They believed that reports by prejudiced people are glorified and biased.

One interpretation of these data is to assume that the two groups are telling the truth; the prejudiced group really is superior. However, the authors of *The Authoritarian Personality* did not think so. They believed that reports by unprejudiced people are accurate but that reports by prejudiced people are glorified and biased. We can doubt the truth of many statements by the prejudiced individuals simply on the grounds that people are not that good.

The authoritarian individual denies what he does not like and idealizes what remains.

There are two ways to handle ambivalence. We can differentiate it into those parts we like and those parts we do not like—the mother is warm but she controls too much. Or we can deny that part we do not like and idealize what remains. Apparently, the prejudiced person idealizes his parents while the unprejudiced individual is more realistic; he partitions his parents into that part he likes and that part he does not like. The prejudiced person keeps himself clear of ambivalence by denying those things which are bad about himself and his parents.

The authoritarian personality has a strong drive for status.

The authoritarian individual has a strong concern for status; he wants to make something of himself and his family. There is a strong wave of insecurity in the families of prejudiced individuals; they insist on trying to turn their children into little ladies and gentlemen. How does one do that? By using strict discipline in no uncertain terms. Strong, aggressive impulses are derived from this strict discipline, but the child is not allowed to express them directly. Instead, he finds other outlets for his aggressive impulses. His outlet is to project his hostile impulses onto others and then to reject those others; he directs the hostility he feels toward his parents into the more socially acceptable channel of hate and prejudice toward Negroes and Jews.

The sample was biased, and they used retrospective interviews; however, the results seem consistent and reliable.

There are problems with this study: The samples of subjects used were by no means representative; the authors selected only individuals who belonged to a group. Biased sampling can affect the relations among variables. However, Horowitz (1947) showed that the intercorrelations among different kinds of prejudice (in children) increase with age and grade in school. Apparently, the more structured a child's mind (the older he is), the more consistent are his attitudes and prejudices. If he is prejudiced, he will reject many types of individuals as he grows older, purely on the basis of increased cognitive consistency.

Another problem with the authoritarian scales is that people tend either to agree or disagree with everything—this should be controlled.

Other methodological problems are associated with the F Scale. For one thing, people have tendencies either to agree or disagree with all the propositions on a test. Since all items on the F Scale are answered in the same direction, people who agree with anything on a test will score high in authoritarianism even though they are only showing response acquiescence (a tendency to agree with all statements). Others, who do not agree with the content of any test, are likely to show a high democratic attitude (not at all related to their feelings). The best way to handle this problem is to use some items that state the proposition in one direction and an equal number that states the proposition in the opposite direction. In this way agreement and rejection of all test items will be balanced; only those persons who read the items and answer on the basis of content will receive high or low scores. Others will receive a middle score.

TABLE 8.3 **Mean Wechsler-Bellevue IQ Score for Each Quartile of the Ethnocentrism Scale (Psychiatric Clinic, Men and Women). (High scores on ethnocentrism are related to low scores on intelligence)**

Form 45 E Scale Quartiles	*Range on E*	*N*	*Mean IQ*
Low quartile	10–24	8	125.3
Low middle quartile	25–36	5	117.8
High middle quartile	37–50	13	113.9
High quartile	51–70	11	107.3
		37	114.9

SOURCE: From Adorno, Frenkel-Brunswik, Levinson, & Sanford, 1950.

Authoritarianism is associated with low economic status and low education.

Authoritarianism is associated with low economic status and low education (see Tables 8.3, 8.4, and 8.5). It may be that individuals score high on the E Scale because they are not well educated or do not have economic advantages. Of the various negative correlations, education is strongest; individuals with more education lack prejudice.

The studies are correlational—they say nothing about cause and effect.

What are the conclusions derived from these criticisms? First, the studies are correlational—they say nothing about cause and effect relations. Also, we have the problems of sampling and response bias. It may be that authoritarianism is caused by educational, intellectual, or economic factors.

Studies of children's prejudices confirm the major findings of the adult study.

One of the more interesting parts of the study of authoritarianism is its development in children. The original data were collected by recall from adults and thus are suspect. However, Frenkel-Brunswik (1953) directly observed prejudice in children and adolescents. She reported confirmation of most of the original findings. Children who are severely treated during their childhoods become more authoritarian. She reported that after the age of 10, children's personalities tend to fall into patterns similar to those of adults. Ethnocentric youngsters tend to display aggression, rigidity, cruelty, superstition, projection,

TABLE 8.4 **Mean Number of Years of Education for Each Quartile of the Ethnocentrism Scale (Psychiatric Clinic, Men and Women). (High scores on ethnocentrism are related to low education)**

Form 45 E Scale Quartiles	*Range on E*	*N*	*Mean Years of Education*
Low quartile	10–24	29	13.8
Low middle quartile	25–36	28	12.7
High middle quartile	37–50	27	11.8
High quartile	51–70	28	11.2
		112	12.4

SOURCE: From Adorno, Frenkel-Brunswik, Levinson, & Sanford, 1950.

TABLE 8.5 Agreement with F Scale Items and Education. (In percents)

	College N = 217	High School N = 545	Grammar School N = 504
Agree that:			
The most important thing to teach children is absolute obedience to their parents.	35	60	80
Any good leader should be strict with people under him in order to gain their respect.	36	51	66
Prison is too good for sex criminals. They should be publicly whipped or worse.	18	31	45
There are two kinds of people in the world: the weak and the strong.	30	53	71
No decent man can respect a woman who has had sex relations before marriage.	14	26	39

SOURCE: From Hyman & Sheatsley, 1954.

denial of weakness, and power orientation; they also tend to dichotomize the sex roles. The discipline of these ethnocentric children was strict, rigid, and punitive. Unprejudiced children see their parents as positive *and* negative; prejudiced children are compelled to view their parents as wholly good in spite of obvious feelings that at times they are wholly bad. Prejudiced children think it is the duty of parents to discipline their children.

Prejudice is related to early family experiences; children who deny their feelings project them onto others.

These developmental studies support the original conception that authoritarian personality traits are related to early family experiences. Prejudiced children tend to deny their own feelings of ambivalence; as a result of this denial they project their feelings of hatred and anger onto others. Once they project the hostility onto others, it is legitimate to reject these "hostile others." The answer to this problem is somehow to bring their denied feelings into consciousness. This could be done by psychotherapy. But, how can we produce enough therapists to handle the many people who are prejudiced? A better way would be to change the restrictive, hostile child-rearing practices that produce denial in the first place.

SUMMARY

1 Choice experiments imply preferences among outcomes and discrimination among stimuli that make up the set. Only when the items of choice are given to the subject and no instructions are given as to how he is to choose can we talk about preference. Usually the child makes choices among stimuli that he may or may not prefer; his preference is only for outcomes.

2 Luce's axiom implies that the ratio of choosing *A* over *B* is independent of the number of items involved in the choice set.

3 Conflict occurs when the child is drawn to and repelled by an item simultaneously. This conflict occurs only at the point where his positive approach and negative avoidance tendencies balance. Conflicts occur because a person's approach gradient has a flatter slope than his avoidance gradient. The only solutions to conflict are to leave the field (avoidance-avoidance) or to revalue one of the gradients so they no longer intersect.

4 Cognitive dissonance results from ambivalence following a decision; usually, the child is not entirely satisfied with his choice. In this case he will tend to overvalue his choice and undervalue the alternative. If he has worked particularly hard for the chosen item, he will value it even more. The more valuable the items involved in a choice, the higher is the cognitive dissonance generated by a decision.

5 Freud's conception of morality pits the child's superego against his libido. The stronger a child's superego, the more moral is his behavior. Discrepancy between the child's ego ideal and his behavior produces guilt feelings; either his behavior or his ego ideal may be changed to decrease guilt. Guilt is the fear of doing something wrong; shame is the fear of being caught doing something wrong.

6 Piaget sees the child passing through several stages of moral development: (a) the motor or individual stage; (b) the egocentric stage; (c) the time of cooperation; and (d) the stage of codification of rules. There is good support for these conceptions in the work of Piaget and in the cross-cultural studies of Kohlberg.

7 The authoritarian personality is a syndrome of correlated traits and attitudes toward others. Authoritarian individuals tend to overvalue their own worth and to reject their aggressive impulses. They project these impulses onto others and then reject these others because they are seen as aggressive and fearful. The child who develops prejudice is reared in a rigid and punishing manner by his parents.

FURTHER READINGS

Festinger, L. *A theory of cognitive dissonance.* New York: Harper & Row, 1957.
Piaget, J. *The moral judgment of the child.* New York: Free Press, 1960.
Luce, R. D. *Individual choice behavior.* New York: Wiley, 1959.

REFERENCES

Adorno, T. W., Frenkel-Brunswik, E., Levinson, D. J., & Sanford, R. N. *The authoritarian personality.* New York: Harper & Row, 1950.

Aronson, E., & Mills, J. The effect of severity of initiation on liking for a group. *Journal of Abnormal and Social Psychology,* 1959, **59,** 177-181.

Bandura, A., & Mischel, W. Modification of self-imposed delay of reward through exposure to live and symbolic models. *Journal of Personality and Social Psychology,* 1965, 698-705.

Festinger, L. *A theory of cognitive dissonance.* New York: Harper & Row, 1957.

Festinger, L., & Carlsmith, J. M. Cognitive consequences of forced compliance. *Journal of Abnormal and Social Psychology,* 1959, **58,** 203-210.

Frenkel-Brunswik, E., & Havel, J. Prejudice in the interviews of children: I. Attitudes toward minority groups. *Journal of Genetic Psychology,* 1953, **82,** 91-136.

Freud, S. *An outline of psychoanalysis.* New York: Norton, 1949.

Hartshorne, H., & May, M. A. *Studies in the nature of character.* (3 vols.) New York: Macmillan, 1928-1930.

Horowitz, E. L. Development of attitude toward Negroes. In T. M. Newcomb & E. L. Hartley (Eds.), *Readings in social psychology.* (1st ed.) New York: Holt, Rinehart and Winston, 1947.

Hyman, H. H., & Sheatsley, P. B. The authoritarian personality—A methodological critique. In R. Christie & M. Jahoda (Eds.), *Studies in the scope and method of the authoritarian personality.* New York: Free Press, 1954.

James, W. *Principles of psychology.* New York: Henry Holt, 1890.

Kohlberg, L. Moral education in the schools: A developmental view. *School Review,* 1966, **74,** 1-30.

Luce, R. D. *Individual choice behavior.* New York: Wiley, 1959.

Mischel, W., & Grusec, J. Determinants of the rehearsal and transmission of neutral and aversive behaviors. *Journal of Personality and Social Psychology,* 1966, 197-205.

Mischel, W., & Liebert, R. Effects of discrepancies between observed and imposed reward criteria on their acquisition and transmission. *Journal of Personality and Social Psychology,* 1966, 45-53.

Piaget, J. *The psychology of intelligence.* London: Routledge & Kegan-Paul, 1950 (1947).

Piaget, J. *The moral judgment of the child.* New York: Free Press, 1960.

Ross, R. Optimum orders for the presentation of pairs in the method of paired comparisons. *Journal of Educational Psychology,* 1934, **25,** 375-382.

Sears, R. R., Maccoby, E. E., & Levin, H. *Patterns of child rearing.* New York: Harper & Row, 1957.

PART TWO
THE INTERACTING CHILD

9 PARANATAL INFLUENCES

An I had but a belly of any indifferency, I were simply the most active fellow in Europe: my womb, my womb, my womb, undoes me.

II HENRY IV

In the Western world we begin a child's age at birth; the Chinese, however, are wiser—they add a year. This difference reflects an important oversight: Significant and often irreversible effects occur during intrauterine existence. Paranatal influences are events that affect the growing organism before, during, and immediately following birth. This chapter covers various issues that concern behavioral embryologists; it outlines the very early stages through which an infant passes, the types of prenatal influences to which he is sensitive, and the effects of premature birth on his later development.

Four issues related to early behavior are: (1) What are the first responses? (2) When does the central nervous system begin to work? (3) Do early responses approach or avoid stimulation? (4) Are the units of behavior structures or elements?

There are four basic issues in the early beginnings of behavior: (1) What are the first foetal responses? (2) At what point does receptor stimulation elicit motor reactions (activity of the central or peripheral nervous system)? Muscles respond to direct electrical stimulation long before they respond to receptor stimulation (spontaneous behavior appears before responsive behavior). (3) Do the earliest responses of the organism approach or avoid stimulation? And (4) are the units of development structures or elements? Are the first responses integrated, general responses that become individualized and differentiated as development proceeds, or are they specific reflexes that become integrated into more general response patterns?

PREDETERMINISM

Our answer to predeterminism

Is behavior predetermined or are the infant's first responses learned? The answer depends on the species we are using and the type of *depends on the subject used and the response measured.*

response we observe. In addition, there are problems with using mammalian subjects: The embryo of a mammal must be taken from the uterus while the mother is under anesthesia. This procedure raises serious questions about the embryo's health. Furthermore, once it is taken from the uterus, the embryo begins to die; it is impossible to observe the same embryo over time. This is particularly true for human embryos, where we depend upon abortions for our observations. Fish, amphibia, and birds have the advantage of permitting repeated observations on the development of the same individual (the eggs can be observed many times), but they may have little relevance to early human behavior.

Four methods of studying early behavior are used: (1) observation of embryos at various ages, (2) special stimulation, (3) experimental manipulation, and (4) surgical intervention.

Four major methods used to study embryological development include: (1) the observation of embryos at various stages of development; (2) the use of special stimulation during these various stages; (3) experimental manipulation of activities or circumstances while the organism develops—for example, Carmichael reared Amblystoma (salamander) with chloretone to immobilize them and looked at the effects of this immobilization upon their later development; and (4) surgical interference and observation of behavior following regeneration of the surgically altered system. Observation only gives us the gross outlines of behavior; we must rely on accidental and spontaneous internal stimulation to elicit responses. The use of special stimulation gets around this point; but what happens to the foetus as a result of our external stimulation: Is he developing at a different rate? We can test this by stimulating one group and not another. Any differences between these two groups would be attributable to differential early stimulation. We discover more about behavior and development if we experiment; however, this is usually impossible, since the human foetus dies soon after abortion. Also, there has been no surgical intervention on the human foetus, since it does not live long enough to heal, and the ethical problems involved in growing human foetuses in test tubes remain to be resolved.

Coghill showed that the behavior of amphibians follows their physical maturation.

Several investigators have studied predeterminism—the dependence of behavioral development upon anatomical maturation. Coghill (1929) used amphibians in his experiments; their anatomical maturation always precedes their behavior. Also, the behavior of amphibians follows the same developmental sequence as their anatomical maturation. This suggests that anatomical development (maturation) determines amphibian behavior. Coghill found cephalocaudal progression of development (from the head toward the tail). First he observed complete immobility, then a c-flexion as the animal went into a tight coil, next an *s* reaction, with the head turned in one direction and the tail in the other, and finally a repeated *s* reaction, controlled by a built-in neuromuscular sequence. He also found proximodistal progression of motor activity; the organism started moving in the middle, next to its central core, and the behavior developed in the limb buds later. Coghill's work was interpreted as strong support for predetermined development based on innate patterns of behavior that unfold automatically. Behavioral structures were assumed to directly reflect the maturation of anatomical structures.

Carmichael showed that immobilization of salamanders for short periods does not affect their behavioral development.

Carmichael (1954) worked with salamanders and frogs. He immobilized larvae with chloretone before they began to move. He kept them immobilized for five days while control animals were swimming freely. When he washed the chloretone away, the immobilized animals could swim as well as the control animals, suggesting that maturation is sufficient for their behavior. Inhibition of normal "practice" did not affect the behavior. However, there are limits to the length of time animals can be immobilized without serious effects. Matthews and Detwiler (1926) found that when salamanders are immobilized for a longer period (13 days), they fail to swim properly and never recover completely.

Kuo used the chick embryo and showed that external stimulation is important in determining early behavior.

Kuo (1932) strongly objected to Coghill's assertion that behaviors are determined by anatomical growth of the nervous and skeletal systems. He also objected to the concept of instinct; almost every response pattern characteristic of a species is exercised systematically before birth. The locomotor pattern of birds can be traced to its beginnings in the movements of the wing buds and leg buds. The chick embryo bobs its head very early, and this movement later develops as the pecking response. Kuo believed that the species-specific characteristics of behavior are a joint function of the prenatal environment (uterus or shell) in which the organism grows and the genes that govern its development. He assumed that organism-environment interaction is programmed in the sense that the maturation of structures and behaviors in a rigid, well-defined environment brings about the specific controlling conditions necessary for growth. If something goes wrong with the developmental sequence, understandable and predictable consequences follow. Kuo used the domestic chicken as his subject and found evidence for organism-environment interaction throughout the embryonic phase. He reported that the first movements of the chicken are started by extraembryonic movements.

Sperry showed that surgical rotation of lizard eyes changes visual perspective; the operated lizard saw up and down reversed.

Sperry (1951) showed quite clearly that some behaviors are dependent on anatomical development. He surgically rotated the eyes of lizards and frogs. He showed that surgical reversal of the eye results in reversal of the sensory-motor reactions to movement in the visual field. If the operated lizard sees something moving in front of him, he will react as if the object were behind him. The reversal cannot be overcome. Sperry also surgically rotated the eye and severed the optic nerve in another group of lizards. The animals were blind for about four weeks while the fibers regenerated from the retinal stump and established connections to the brain. The sensory-motor responses recovered, but the reversal of the retina and the resultant reversal of behavior occurred in the newly recovered fibers, suggesting that the optic nerve regenerates in a genetically determined pattern. Following the operation, connections were regenerated in the same prefixed manner regardless of whether the retina was upright or reversed; the reflexive associations formed by the ingrowing optic fibers established the same predetermined pattern without regard to the adaptiveness of the end result.

However, how relevant are these studies to man?

A serious criticism of all these data concerns their relevance to man. It may be quite true that amphibia have an instinctive, built-in maturational sequence for swimming, but it is not at all clear that instinctive behaviors control the development of man, particularly his higher characteristics (his language, perceptual abilities, concept formation, and personality). Sperry's results cannot be generalized to human beings. Anatomical regeneration itself is much less pronounced in the human; moreover, there is evidence from Kohler (1964) that man can accommodate to reversal of his visual field. The relation between anatomical arrangements of the nervous system and behavior of organisms becomes much more flexible as we study more complex organisms.

NEURAL MEDIATION OF BEHAVIOR

The first movement observed in the embryo is a heartbeat.

The first movement in an embryo is the heartbeat. This muscle responds to direct electrical stimulation long before the organism responds to stimulation of receptors. This finding suggests that muscles are well developed long before the neuromuscular connections have matured. Spontaneous movement occurs long before responsive action. Behavior begins when the foetus responds to stimulation. Hooker (1952) showed that the human foetus first reacts to stimulation about the mouth and face; sensitivity later develops over the body in a cephalocaudal direction.

Approach or avoidance of stimulation?

Embryos approach or avoid stimuli depending on where and how they are stimulated.

Do the organism's first movements in response to stimulation take him toward or away from the stimulus? Before birth, stimulation leads to contraction of the contralateral muscles, producing movement away from the point of stimulation. This reaction changes at birth; hunger appears, and we now see approach to stimulation around the mouth region. The intensity of the stimulation and the region stimulated both determine whether we produce approach or avoidance. We usually observe the foetus approach light touch and avoid intense stimulation. If he is stimulated about the mouth the neonate will approach, if he is stimulated on a limb he will avoid. The foetus avoids most strong stimulation; after he is born the infant approaches contact about the mouth region and avoids contact to other parts of his body. Later, the infant will approach his mother for contact comfort and will begin to avoid very intense stimulation (pain) to any part of his body. Between these extremes the type and area of stimulation determines approach or avoidance.

Structures versus elements

Cephalocaudal progression describes development.

Coghill believed that the early responses of the organism develop from an integrated whole, while more specific responses emerge through individuation. He argued by analogy with the anatomical development of the trunk and the extremities, which begin as buds and then differentiate. Carmichael's (1934) observations on the development of the guinea pig did not confirm Coghill's laws of behavior. The cephalocaudal progression was upheld, but the progression of responses from whole to parts showed an opposite trend in many cases. It is difficult to tell whether this contradiction is due to the subject used (amphibia versus mammals), the observer's bias, or the types of methods used.

Kuo showed that the size of a response (element or structure) is related to stimulus intensity.

Kuo observed chickens to see whether one finds integrated response structures that use a great deal of the embryo's musculature or only small, specific responses. He found that the type of response is a function of stimulus intensity. As stimulation becomes more intense, more of the embryo's musculature is involved; light tactual stimulation involves limited responses, while more intense stimuli evoke a generalized pattern which might be called integrated or disorganized, depending upon how one expects it to be. Hooker (1952) characterized the response of human embryos to a light touch as stereotyped, and yet other observers have seen complex, organized responses in the human embryo during the latter portion of the embryonic phase. This point of contradiction shows the difficulty of using subjective judgments and observations as techniques of measurement. When the measure is objective and easy to specify, disagreement vanishes.

STAGES OF PRENATAL DEVELOPMENT

Our main source of information about embryological behavior is surgical obstetrics.

Our main source of information about the foetus is surgical obstetrics. Therapeutic abortions, and natural accidents, supply the surgeon with many opportunities to observe and record embryonic and foetal reactions. From these observations under natural and sometimes controlled conditions we have come to a rough understanding of early behavior development. Behavioral embryology is a recent science with ancient beginnings. Most of what we know about prenatal development has been discovered during the past few decades. The following section covers the stages of prenatal development and the effects of various factors on this development. The period of intrauterine growth may be separated into three phases: germinal, embryonic, and foetal.

The germinal phase

The germinal phase covers early growth of the fertilized egg; the phase ends when the fertilized egg implants in the uterine wall.

During this period, which covers the first two weeks of the organism's life, the fertilized egg multiplies rapidly. Growth consists largely of cell division and differentiation into embryonic and extraembryonic tissue (that is, differentiation between the organism and the placenta). At the end of the germinal phase the collection of cells is implanted in the uterine wall. The germinal phase can only be estimated from the time of last menstruation.

The embryonic phase

During the embryonic phase three main tissue layers develop.

During the next six weeks all the basic structures of the body are formed. Cells collect to develop the embryo; in the course of early cell multiplication, three layers are formed. The outer layer (*ectoderm*) produces the sense organs and nervous system. The intermediate layer (*mesoderm*) becomes the skeleton, muscular structures, and circulatory system. The inner layer (*endoderm*) gives rise to our digestive organs. During the first two weeks the organism migrates down the Fallopian tube (where fertilization occurred) to the uterus; there it becomes attached to the spongy uterine wall. From this time (two weeks) until the end of the eighth week, the organism is called an *embryo*.

Growth and differentiation are extremely rapid during the germinal and early embryonic phases.

Following genetic codes, cell differentiation and multiplication continue. By the third week the embryo is $\frac{1}{10}$ inch long, the "heart" tubes begin to pulse, the brain has two lobes, and the spinal cord is formed. Growth is extremely rapid; by the end of the fourth week the embryo is nearly $\frac{1}{4}$ inch long (10,000 times larger than a fertilized egg). Within the first month, a transparent envelope forms around the embryo. Fluid fills this amniotic bag; it grows with the organism, giving it a highly satisfactory package in which to live (see Figure 9.1). Inside the sac the embryo is warm, protected, moist, and has enough room for movement without undue disturbance of his mother. At first the amniotic sac is covered with hundreds of *villi* (rootlike fingers that collect food from the uterine wall and deliver it to the foetus through a primitive tube or stalk). Later in the embryonic period most of the villi degenerate; the remainder develop into the placenta. The primitive stalk becómes the umbilical cord; two arteries carry blood

FIGURE 9.1

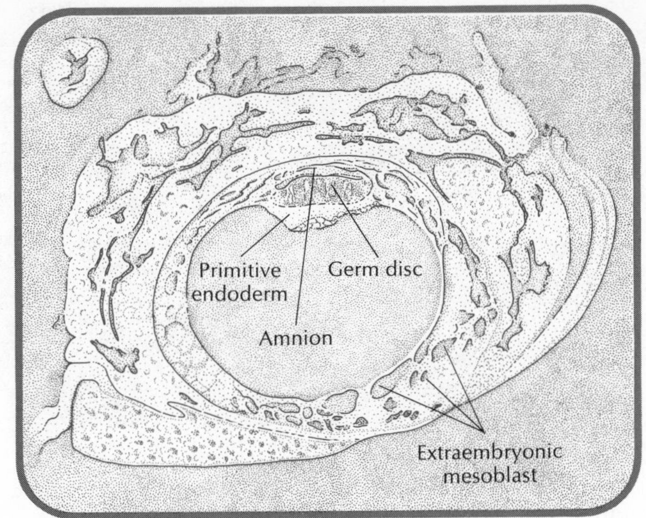

A schematic representation of human implantation at around 12 days. (Adapted from Hamilton, Boyd, & Mossman, 1952.)

from the infant to the placenta and one vein carries oxygenated blood back to the infant. The placenta provides an interchange of nourishment, gases, antigens, and waste materials for the growing organism. It also serves as a barrier to prevent some harmful substances from reaching the embryo and foetus.

During the second month, all remaining body structures are formed.

During the second month the remaining body structures are formed. By the eighth week the embryo has developed a reasonably human appearance (see Figure 9.2); he possesses the external organs of an adult —arms, legs, muscles, and hands and feet with recognizable fingers and toes. He is ugly and only about an inch long, but he lives. His heart beats, he secretes some digestive juices, and his arms and legs move. The remaining changes are primarily in size and proportion.

The foetal period

The foetal period covers the interval from three months to birth.

Between the third month and birth, size increases from 7 or 8 mm. to 50 cm. Proportions also change; the head is nearly half the total length of the foetus at the end of the second month but will be only a quarter of his length at birth (see Figure 9.3).

Between three and five months we see increased activity.

At around three months, the foetus becomes active; however, his mother will not feel his kicks for another month or two. Hooker (1952) observed surgically removed foetuses and he charted their behavioral development under various stimulus conditions. He obtained a response

FIGURE 9.2

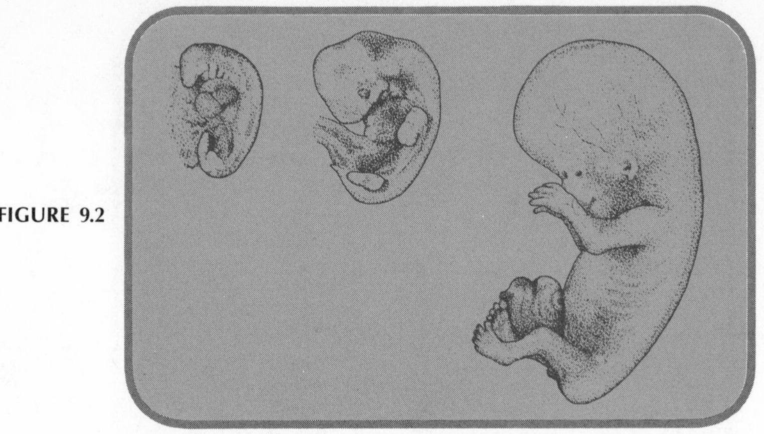

An embryo of 28 days (*left*), 40 days (*center*), and 60 days (*right*). Magnifications are, respectively, 6, 2, and 2.

FIGURE 9.3

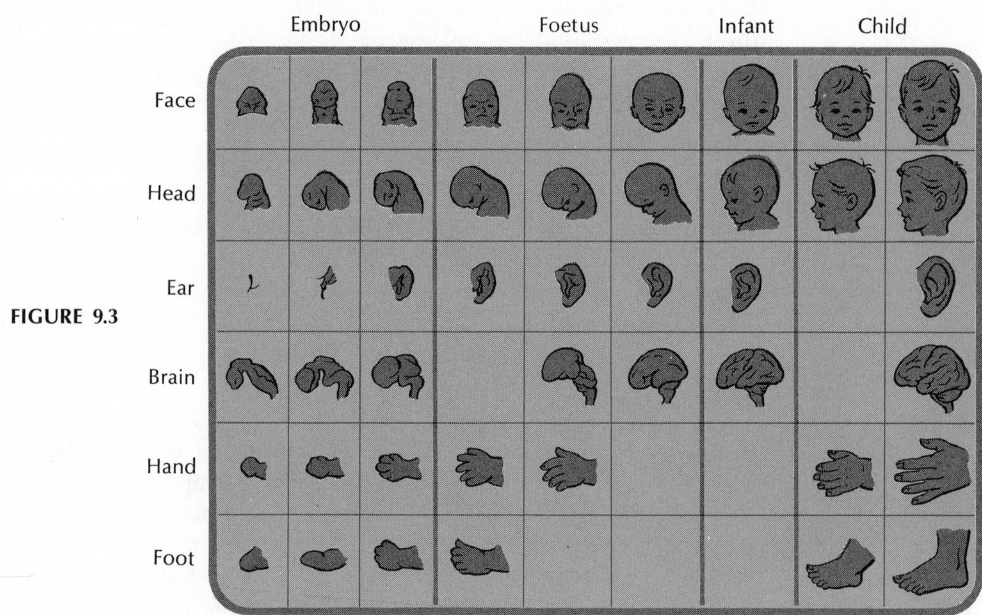

Change in proportions during the development of the human face, head, ear, brain, hand, and foot. (From University of Illinois, 1950.)

to stimulation as early as seven weeks; it was a generalized, body response rather than a specific movement to the stimulus (touch with a hair). The foetus produces spontaneous movements during the third month. Different parts of the foetus become active during the fourth month. Movements in response to touch also become more coordinated. By 14 weeks the foetus displays all the movements of a newborn infant, except respiration and vocalization. He reaches half his birth height and increases his weight six times during the fourth month. During the fifth month we see a marked increase in activity; movement becomes vigorous and the mother often feels periods of kicking and turning. The foetus shows periods of sleep or activity. Hair, eyelashes, and nails develop and his skeleton begins to calcify. Reflexes are easier to elicit and more definite; the five-month-old foetus moves his lips in a manner resembling sucking.

During the sixth month the foetus begins to breathe.

During the sixth month the foetus begins to "breathe"; he takes amniotic fluid into his lungs but does not drown. He receives adequate oxygen from the placenta until birth. During his sixth month the foetus grows to around 14 inches and weighs about a pound and one quarter. Buds for his permanent teeth form, his lids may open, and his eyes move. The grasp reflex becomes strong enough to support his weight. The foetus cannot usually survive alone at this stage; his systems could function, but neural control is not available to sustain life.

The seven-month-old foetus can survive if given proper medical attention.

Between seven months and birth the foetus grows in size, and his functions mature. Babies born in their seventh month have a fair chance of survival if good medical facilities are available. If he survives, the premature infant will not match the normal-term baby (of the same conceptual age) for many months; his growth and behavior will show evidence of immaturity and deficit (Lubchenco *et al.,* 1963).

TABLE 9.1 Timetable of Prenatal Development

First Month

Fertilization; descent of the ovum from the Fallopian tube into the uterus.
Early cell division and formation of embryonic ball.
Formation of the three embryonic layers—ectoderm, endoderm, and mesoderm.
A special layer forms in the uterus which becomes the placenta.
Another layer of cells forms the amniotic sac around the embryo.
The heart tube forms and begins to pulse; blood circulates about the embryo.
The nervous system begins to develop—the early neural tube forms.
The intestinal tract, lungs, liver, and kidneys begin to develop.

Second Month

The embryo increases from ¼ inch to about 1½ inch in length.
Bones and muscles begin to form.
The face and neck begin to take on human form.
The brain develops very rapidly.
Limb buds form and grow. Sex organs begin to appear.

TABLE 9.1 Timetable of Prenatal Development *(Continued)*

Third Month

The foetus continues sexual differentiation; male organs show rapid development.
Buds of the temporary teeth are formed.
The digestive system becomes active and the stomach secretes fluids.
The liver and kidneys begin to function.
Spontaneous movement of the arms, legs, and fingers is possible.

Fourth Month

Lower parts of the body show accelerated growth rate.
Hands and feet become well formed; the skin appears dark red.
Finger closure is possible.
Reflexes become more active.
Foetus begins to stir and move his arms and legs.

Fifth Month

Skin structures begin to attain final form.
Sweat and sebaceous glands are formed and begin to function.
Fingernails and toenails appear.
Foetus is now about one foot long.
He weighs about one pound.
If aborted, he would breathe for a short time and then die.
Neural maturation is inadequate for prolonged life.

Sixth Month

Eyelids, which have been fused closed, now open.
The eyes are completely formed.
Taste buds appear on the tongue and in the mouth.
If born, the six-month foetus would live for a short time.

Seventh Month

The foetus is now capable of extrauterine life.
Cerebral hemispheres cover almost the entire brain.
He can emit a variety of reflex responses (startle, grasp, swimming).
The foetus is generally about 16 inches long and weighs about three pounds.
If born, he can breathe, cry, and swallow.
He is very prone to infections, however.

Eighth and Ninth Months

Final preparations are made during these months.
Fat is deposited for later use.
Activity is greater; the foetus can change his position.
Periods of activity alternate with periods of quiet.
His organs step up their activity.
Foetal heart rate increases to become quite rapid.
Digestive system continues to work.
Finally, uterine contractions expel the foetus into the world.

REMARKS: METHOD

Can a mother's thoughts affect her child? Early folklore suggested that the feelings and dreams of a mother were transmitted to her baby inside the womb. Later, scientific opinion disagreed with this notion; it was pointed out that mother and child are separated by a placental barrier, there are no neural connections between mother and child, and the embryo (foetus) is housed in an insulated environment (the amniotic sac).

However, recent evidence strongly suggests that the mother's thoughts, and in particular her emotional states, are transferred to the foetus by the interchange of hormonal secretions through the placental barrier. The placental barrier is not a barrier after all. A host of complex chemical and physical influences affect the embryo and foetus during residence.

Separating the effect of prenatal influences from genetic predispositions is difficult. For example, mothers who are emotional obviously produce genetically emotional children. Is the child's emotionality the result of genetic factors alone, or is it also influenced by increased hormonal secretions during his intrauterine existence? The only way to separate these factors is through artificial transplantation of embryos. This transplantation has been done with animals. Emotional and nonemotional strains of animals are first inbred. Then half the embryos from high-emotional mothers are transplanted to low-emotional mothers; the reverse transplant is carried out for half the low-emotional animals. In this way the embryos grow in either high- or low-emotional mothers independent of their genetic background. If the genetic factors produce all differences in emotionality, there will be no differences between genetically emotional animals left in their own mothers and peers who were transplanted to low-emotional mothers (Figure 9.4A). However, if there is an interaction, then animals left in their high-emotional natural mothers should be exceptionally emotional in comparison with the genetically emotional animals who were implanted in the low-emotional mothers. The results of these types of experiments show there is usually an interaction (Figure 9.4B) between the genetic endowment and the intrauterine environment. Figure 9.4C shows what would be the results if there were only independent effects of genetics and intrauterine influences but no interaction.

PRENATAL INFLUENCES

The foetus is both independent of and dependent on his mother.

In uterine existence the foetus is dependent on his mother for nutrition, warmth, metabolic exchange, protection, and oxygen. At the same time, he is a somewhat independent system; he merely removes from the mother's system the food and other supplies he needs and returns to her his own waste products. He is somewhat independent of the mother's emotional and physical system, and at the same time quite dependent on it for his life. This unique interrelation has profound effects upon the embryo and foetus.

FIGURE 9.4

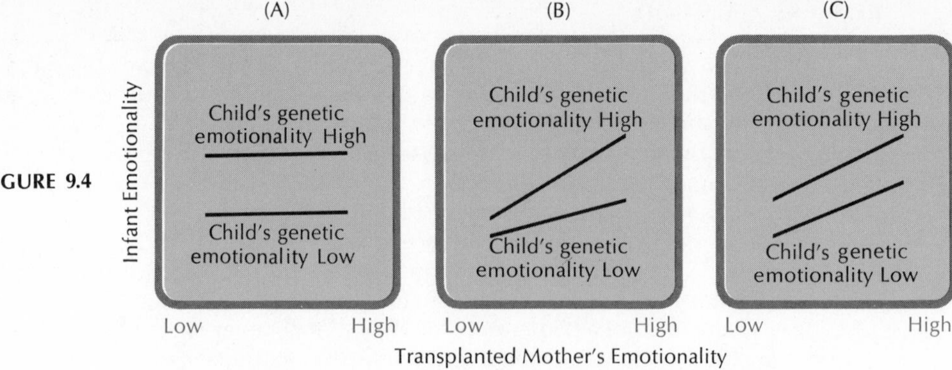

(A) shows the results if all differences are produced by genetic differences: there is no environmental effect and no interaction. (B) shows the effect of interaction between genetics and environment, while (C) shows both genetic and environmental effects but no interaction. The typical result is (B).

Prenatal life is full of potential hazards; many problems that result from prenatal influences show up only later.

Prenatal life contains hazards; specific damage and indirect effects from environmental deficiencies threaten the developing foetus. It is difficult to know the precise causes of many congenital effects. There is always confounding of genetic influences and prenatal influences from the environment (see Remarks: Method). In addition to this confusion, many malformations are not manifest until some time after birth; in particular, the functioning of the central nervous system cannot be assessed until long after birth. Many congenital malformations are lethal. Among the infants who survived, from a sample of 6000 pregnancies, seven percent developed malformations by the time they were one year of age. Less than half these problems were suspected at birth.

Maternal emotions

Gross chemical changes in maternal circulation affect the foetus.

There has been a long controversy in the annals of pediatrics concerning the influence of maternal emotional states on the growing foetus. Predeterminists supported the view that, since there are no neural connections between the mother and the child, the emotional state of the mother cannot affect the infant's development. Although there are no neural connections, gross chemical changes in the mother's circulatory system are transmitted through the placental barrier to the foetus, thus producing an interaction between the emotional state of the mother and the development of the foetus (Montagu, 1962).

Active mothers produce active foetuses.

Mothers with active autonomic indicators (high heart rate, high respiratory rate, and/or variability in heart and breathing rate) produce active infants. Also, infants of mothers who are emotionally disturbed exhibit hyperactive autonomic nervous functions at birth. Taken together, these data suggest that the mother can transmit emotional states to the foetus. Remember, we are dealing with an interaction; infants of emotionally disturbed mothers, with hyperactive autonomic nervous systems, probably inherit autonomic hyperactivity. Foetal emotionality must be the joint result of genetic hyperactivity and maternal emotional states.

When mothers are emotional, they increase their babies' activity by several hundred percent.

Studies at the Fels Institute showed increases of several hundred percent in foetal body movements during maternal emotionality. In one group, activity increased by a factor of six, and heart rate increased 22 beats per minute; these changes persisted for several weeks. Emotional mothers are likely to produce slim neonates, and the infants are likely to be hyperactive. The infants of emotional mothers are more irritable, cry more often, empty their bowels frequently, and are generally difficult. Forty percent of mothers with hyperactive babies experienced emotional stress during pregnancy (Montagu, 1962). A variety of infant problems have been attributed to maternal emotional disturbance; however, the evidence is not clear. Most babies are normal, even if their mothers were emotional during pregnancy.

Maternal nutrition

Maternal nutrition has a profound effect on the growing foetus.

The mother's nutrition is particularly important during pregnancy; malnutrition is the single most important environmental factor in poor infant development. Both the quantity and quality of maternal nutrition is important, since she must not only maintain herself but also supply the growing foetus.

Nutritional deficiency results in prematurity, lowered vitality, and death of the foetus.

Food deficiencies have been studied extensively; low birth weight, prematurity, lowered vitality, rickets, and death have been attributed to inadequate maternal diet. Usually, poor diet is not present only during pregnancy. Often the undernourished pregnant woman has a long history of malnutrition; the combination of poor maternal development and inadequate food supply compound the problem (Montagu, 1962). The incidence of brain malformation and other difficulties is greater in the lower classes, where the diet is poorer, than in the upper classes. This result is confounded with genetic factors, but some differences can be attributed to nutritional influences.

Cretinism results from iodine deficiency.

Cretinism, a mental and physical deficiency, is caused by a lack of iodine during pregnancy. Iodine deficiency is now rare; in less medically sophisticated societies and in geographically unique places (certain parts of Switzerland, for example) the incidence of cretinism was quite high. The cause is known; the cure is a small amount of iodine. However, other similar nutritional deficiencies may remain to be discovered.

Inadequate maternal nutrition impairs the size and health of infants.

Inadequate maternal diet also impairs the size and general health of newborns; a total of 284 cases showed that when the mother's diet was "excellent or good" 95 percent of the infants were in good or excellent condition at birth, while when the mother's diet was "poor to very poor" only eight percent of children were in good or excellent condition. Of the remainder, 30 percent were in fair condition and 62 percent in very poor condition (Burke, Stevenson, Worchester, & Stuart, 1949).

Drugs

Drugs of all types (unless specifically prescribed by a physician who is aware of pregnancy) must be avoided.

Members of our society consume enormous amounts of drugs, most of them to relieve minor pain or nervous tension. Many drugs are safe for adults, but their effect on the foetus is often unknown. As a result, we occasionally seen an outbreak of congenital abnormalities, which later is traced to a specific drug taken by pregnant mothers. The thalidomide disaster is only the best known of several such instances. Great numbers of deformed infants were born to mothers who had taken an apparently harmless tranquilizing drug. This tragedy stimulated public interest and led to increased attempts at drug control, but there will probably be more outbreaks. The only effective safeguard is elimination of all drugs that are not necessary to life during pregnancy. There are a number of drugs known to affect development of the foetus. Deafness may be traced to the mother's use of quinine as a treatment for malaria. Addiction to morphine can occur in the newborn of addicted mothers. Large doses of barbiturate given during delivery to ease the mother's pain may asphyxiate the baby, leading to later infant defects.

Smoking

Smoking tobacco increases prematurity and foetal heart rate.

Tobacco smoke contains nicotine, carbon monoxide, collidine, pyridine, and various tar products; there are large differences between babies of smoking and nonsmoking mothers. Two clear relations are known: increased prematurity (double the rate among smoking as compared to nonsmoking mothers) and reduced birth weight for full-term offspring of smoking mothers. Maternal smoking also increases the foetal heart rate; we do not know if this has subsequent effects on the development of the foetus (Montagu, 1962).

Maternal infections

Many infections can be transferred to the foetus; results depend on the developmental stage.

Many parents used to expose their young daughters to viruses to immunize them against later infection. Their reasoning is as follows: Viruses can affect the development of the foetus at critical periods by crossing the placental barrier. For example, during the first three months of foetal life, German measles produce cataracts, deafness, and other sensory defects in the foetus. Smallpox, chicken pox, measles, and mumps can be transmitted to the foetus with detrimental effects. The obvious solution is to immunize a girl long before she becomes a mother; if she becomes pregnant and is still susceptible to these infections, strict care must be exercised. The best solution is early immunization by vaccination.

Maternal sensitization: Rh factors

Maternal sensitization to the infant's antigens (Rh incompatibility) can result in miscarriage, abortion, or death for the infant.

There are genetically determined differences in blood types; certain types are incompatible when they occur in a mother and her child. If the child's blood contains a substance that makes it agglutinate (clump) in response to certain serums and the mother's blood lacks the substance, the child is called Rh positive and the mother Rh negative. The Rh positive foetus produces substances, called antigens, which pass into the mother's circulation (during the birth process, when the placenta is broken). Toxic antibodies are manufactured in the mother's blood and passed back to the next foetus. These antibodies can seriously damage the foetus, if he is Rh positive, by destroying his blood cells and preventing normal oxygen distribution. Rh incompatibility can have the tragic consequences of miscarriage, abortion, stillbirth, or death shortly after birth. If the child survives, he may be mentally defective due to brain damage from inadequate oxygen supply. Rh incompatibility can occur only when the mother is Rh negative and the father Rh positive. Even then it may occur only about half the time; since Rh factors are genetically determined, not all children of Rh positive men are Rh positive.

The first-born of an Rh-incompatible couple is almost always healthy. However, the probability of damage to subsequent Rh positive babies is substantial. A new drug is available that can be given to mothers immediately after delivery to counteract the serious problems likely to occur during later pregnancies. This treatment is strongly advised for all Rh-incompatible couples. The only other treatment available is complete blood exchange of affected foetuses, a difficult and dangerous process.

The incidence of Rh incompatibility is about 1 in 200.

The incidence of Rh incompatibility between mother and infant in the total population is approximately one in 200. However, the rate is obviously higher among Rh-incompatible couples. Women planning marriage should determine the blood types of themselves and their prospective husbands to be aware of possible dangers to their children.

Maternal age

Women between 20 and 30 years of age produce the healthiest children.

Advances in medical care have made pregnancy and childbirth much safer for both mother and child; however, mothers under 20 and over 30 years of age experience differential difficulties and produce more abnormal children than do women between 20 and 30. Early pregnancies are often disrupted by immaturity; by middle age, degeneration of the musculature and the reproductive apparatus and changes in the woman's hormonal system complicate pregnancy (Montagu, 1962). The incidence of defective children is much higher (especially among first-born infants) for very young and for older women. Mongolism, (Down's syndrome) occurs much more frequently among infants of mothers over 40 than among the children of younger women. Penrose (1934) has reported that the incidence of Mongoloid children among mothers under 30 is less than one in 2000; after this age, every five years triples the risk. Maternal age (that is, if the mother is very young or middle aged) also affects the probability of anencephaly (lack of cortex), hydrocephalus (dilation of the cerebral vesicles, leading to an enlarged brain, mental deficiency, and early death if not treated), congenital dislocation of the hip, miscarriage, and stillbirth. Neonatal death is more frequent among babies of very young and of older mothers.

Other influences

Large doses of X-rays can produce abortion or damage the foetus

Many physical factors can affect the growing foetus; for example, massive doses of X-rays will produce abortion or foetal malformation. Also, if the amniotic cavity is too small, pressure on the foetus can cause deformation during his growth.

Timing of the influence

When an influence occurs is as important as what it is; the particular organ or tissue that is growing most rapidly is most affected by the influence.

When an event occurs is often equal in importance to *what* the event is. For example, during the first eight weeks, the embryonic period, all the major structures of the baby are formed. If trauma occurs during this period it will have far-reaching effects on the organism; if the same influence occurs later, it will have a more specific effect (see Table 9.2). The effects of German measles are very different if contracted during the fifth or sixth week, when the primary fibres of the optic lens are

TABLE 9.2 The Origin of Acquired Congenital Defects

Paranatal Influence	*Embryonic Life*	*Foetal Life*	*Birth*
Infections			
German measles	"Siamese	Anomalies such as an-	In late pregnancy stage
Mumps	twins"	encephalus, club foot,	specificity in relation
Influenza	Cataract	and hernia may arise	to anomalous develop-
		early in foetal life.	ment is no longer sharply defined.
Chemical			
Diabetes	Deafness	Others like cerebral	"Mental retardation"
Hypoxia	Mongolism	palsy and hydrocepha-	may have its beginning
(oxygen deficiency)	Cleft palate	lus may have their onset	in the months before
Rh incompatibility	Heart defect	in midpregnancy.	or after birth or even during the early years of infancy.
Physical			
Trauma		These periods of gesta-	
Uterine anomaly		tion need further study.	
Placental malfunction			

SOURCE: Ingalls, 1960.

developing, as opposed to the eighth or ninth week of foetal life, when the organ of Corti is undergoing differentiation. In the first case, blindness results, while in the second the infant will be deaf. Ingalls (1960) reported many cases of congenital abnormality which resulted from specific factors at specific times; he has inferred from clinical and laboratory evidence the various effects of different factors and their timing (Table 9.2). He reported that trauma during the fourth week may result in loss of limbs, while trauma in the sixth week may develop heart defects. More remains to be known, but many defects that were called genetic or simply "cause unknown" are now thought to result from maternal trauma or deficiency at a specific time.

THE BIRTH PROCESS

Birth occurs about 280 days following conception.

Birth occurs about 280 days after conception, but there is considerable variation. Prior to birth, preparations are made: Placental activity slows and it begins to detach from the uterine wall. Uterine contractions begin, and late in the process the amnion breaks, releasing its fluid. If the birth is normal, the foetus will approach the birth canal head first; he will emerge, followed by the amnion and placenta—the "afterbirth." During the birth process foetal oxygen supply is curtailed and his body temperature drops. The infant's head is much larger than the birth canal; his head is elongated and the birth canal expanded during passage. After a short interval the infant's head and the birth canal will both regain their shapes.

Difficult labor, instrument delivery, or anoxia may produce later mental deficiency.

Birth is viewed by some as an event of enormous psychological significance. The infant is thrust from a calm, quiet, peaceful environment into a stimulating world. The many speculative hypotheses about birth are not testable, but there are measurable consequences of birth injury. Birth trauma may seriously affect the child's physical and intellectual status. Very difficult labor, instrument delivery, and anoxia may produce central nervous system damage with consequent motor and mental defect. Cerebral palsy, a motor defect dependent on pathological abnormalities in the brain, sometimes results from birth injury or oxygen loss. During birth, the infant requires a continuous oxygen supply; if it is delayed for several minutes, he may experience degenerative brain changes with subsequent retardation. Infants traumatized at birth are less sensitive to painful stimulation, less mature in their motor integration, and respond inadequately to visual stimulation (Graham, *et al.,* 1956). Traumatized infants are hyperactive, irritable, and muscularly tense.

Premature birth

Premature birth produces primarily sensory and cognitive effects, not physical change.

The premature infant is extremely vulnerable; he is not fully prepared for extrauterine existence. Premature births are usually precipitous or unduly long and thus subject the infant to additional stress. Comparisons of the early development of premature and full-term babies reveal that the lighter a baby's birth weight, the greater is his chance of neurological or behavioral defect (Lubchenco *et al.,* 1963). At 40 weeks of age, eight percent of premature infants (as compared with only 1.6 percent of normal children) show neurological defects, primarily in motor functioning. The long-term consequences of prematurity are not found in physical growth; rather, the premature infant is more likely to show sensory defects and a lower IQ than his full-term sibling. The premature infant is also more likely to have speech difficulties and poor motor coordination. He will tend to be either hyperactive or quiet and to be more shy and dependent upon his mother.

Many personality effects are the result of parental concern.

Many personality characteristics of the premature infant are not the direct result of premature birth, although a shorter prenatal period and possible birth injury can account for some of his difficulties.

Many effects of prematurity are due to interactions with his parents. The premature child is usually overprotected; his parents are afraid of harming the delicate little creature. Emotional problems may prevent the optimum use of his intellectual abilities. An unusually difficult birth, premature birth, or disturbance during pregnancy can result in brain damage which can lead to motor or mental defects; however, most children born under these abnormal circumstances still grow up naturally.

The birth cry

The birth cry is reflexive breathing, not anxiety.

The first behavior of the newborn is usually a loud cry. The birth cry has captured the interests of poets, novelists, and philosophers, who have described it as "a cry of wrath" or "the newborn's first feeling of inferiority when faced with reality"; physiologists report that the birth cry is only a reflexive response to the newborn's first breath. It is a mechanical sound produced by respiration; it marks the onset of breathing. Early students of behavior felt that the birth cry might reflect an emotional state, but infant crying cannot be reliably differentiated: Nurses, psychology students, and medical students show little agreement in judging the emotional content of infants' crying when the stimuli evoking crying are not seen (Sherman & Sherman, 1929).

Only by seeing the context of an emotion can we judge the particular state of the infant or child.

Most people judge the emotional behavior of an infant in terms of the situation that produced the reaction. There are abundant data on the characteristics of newborn infants' crying. It usually lasts about two hours out of every 24. The greatest amount of crying occurs when the caretaker is too busy to give much attention to the infant; the crying of one infant does not stimulate other infants around him. The amount of crying changes with feeding time; it is greatest right before he is fed.

Sleep

Sleep changes from intermittent to longer periods of wakefulness and sleep as the infant matures.

It is difficult to give a good definition of sleep without resorting to notions of attention and consciousness, and it is particularly difficult to define sleep in the newborn. However, the newborn's activity is lowest between his various nursing periods. There is a sharp drop in activity after nursing, followed by a general increase in bodily activity as the next feeding period approaches. With increasing age, the periods of sleep increase in length. At the same time, however, the total number of hours that the infant sleeps in a day decreases as he grows older.

SUMMARY

1 There are four basic issues in the study of early behavior: (1) Is early behavior predetermined? (2) When do neural mechanisms and receptor functions first mediate responses? (3) Do the early responses of the organism approach or avoid stimulation? (4) What are the units of behavior?

2 There are three stages in prenatal growth. The first period (the germinal phase) covers two weeks. During this time the fertilized egg increases in size and differentiation and travels down the fallopian tube to become implanted in the uterus. The second phase (the embryonic period) sees production of the three main tissue layers—(mesoderm, endoderm, and ectoderm). The main organ systems are also begun. At the end of eight weeks the third stage of development begins (the foetal period). Differentiation of structures and functions occurs from now until birth.

3 A variety of prenatal influences affect the embryo and foetus Among these are maternal emotions (emotional mothers produce more active babies and more abnormal infants), maternal nutrition (poor nutrition leads to a higher instance of infant death), drugs (some drugs adversely affect the embryo and foetus), smoking (smoking increases the probability of stillbirth and prematurity among infants), maternal infections (German measles adversely affect the embryo and foetus), Rh factors (Rh positive infants are incompatible with Rh negative mothers), maternal age (very young and much older women should not produce children). Finally, the timing of an effect has differential results; those structures growing most rapidly during a particular trauma are most affected.

4 The birth process has been viewed by some as a great trauma for the infant. There is little evidence for this supposition; however, the effects of trauma during the birth process may appear later as sensory and mental retardation.

5 Premature infants show more emotional and intellectual difficulties than their more patient peers. This is probably the joint result of overprotection and trauma.

6 The birth cry is a reflexive reaction to breathing and does not reflect anxiety by the neonate.

FURTHER READINGS

Hooker, D. *The prenatal origin of behavior.* Lawrence, Kansas: University of Kansas Press, 1952.

Montagu, A. *Prenatal influences.* Springfield, Ill.: G. Thomas, 1962.

REFERENCES

Burke, B. S., Stevenson, S. S., Worchester, J., & Stuart, H. C. Nutrition studies during pregnancy. Relation of maternal nutrition to condition of infant at birth: A study of siblings. *Journal of Nutrition,* 1949, **38,** 453–467.

Carmichael, L. An experimental study in the prenatal guinea-pig of the origin and development of reflexes and patterns of behavior in relation to the stimulation of specific receptor areas during the period of active fetal life. *Genetic Psychology Monographs,* 1934, **16,** 337–491.

Carmichael, L. The onset and early development of behavior. In Carmichael, L. (Ed.), *Manual of child psychology* (2nd Ed.). New York: Wiley, 1954.

Coghill, G. E. *Anatomy and the problem of behavior.* Cambridge: Cambridge University Press, 1929.

Graham, F. G., Matarazzo, R. G., & Caldwell, B. M. Behavioral differences between normal and traumatized newborns. *Psychological Monographs,* 1956, **70.**

Hamilton, W. J., Boyd, J. D., & Mossman, H. W. *Human embryology.* Baltimore: Williams and Wilkins, 1952.

Hooker, D. *The prenatal origin of behavior.* Lawrence, Kan.: University of Kansas Press, 1952.

Ingalls, T. H. Environmental factors and teratogenesis. In Wolstenholme, G. E. W., & O'Connor, C. M. (Eds.), *Ciba Foundation symposium on congenital malformations.* London: Churchill, Ltd., 1960.

Kohler, I. The formation and transformation of the perceptual world. (Trans. by H. Fiss) *Psychological Issues,* 1964, **3.**

Kuo, Z. Y. Ontogeny of embryonic behavior in Aves: I. The chronology and general nature of the behavior of the chick embryo. *Journal of Experimental Zoology,* 1932, **61,** 395–430.

Lubchenco, L., Horner, F. A., Reed, L., Hix, I. E., Jr., Metcalf, D., Cohig, R., Elliot, H., & Bourg, M. Sequelae of premature birth. *American Journal of Diseases of Children,* 1963, **106,** 101–115.

Matthews, S. A., & Detwiler, S. R. The reaction of Amblystoma embryos following prolonged treatment with chloretone. *Journal of Experimental Zoology,* 1926, **45,** 279–292.

Montagu, A. *Prenatal influences.* Springfield, Ill.: G. Thomas, 1962.

Penrose, L. S. The relative aetiological importance of birth order and maternal age in mongolism. *Proceedings of the Royal Society,* 1934, **115b,** 431–450.

Sherman, M., & Sherman, I. C. *The process of human behavior.* New York: Norton, 1929.

Sperry, R. W. Mechanism of neural maturation. In S. S. Stevens (Ed.), *Handbook of experimental psychology.* New York: Wiley, 1951. Pp. 236–280.

University of Illinois. *The miracle of growth.* Urbana, Ill.: University of Illinois Press, 1950.

10 EARLY EXPERIENCE

If I had a thousand sons, the first humane principle I would teach them should be, to forswear thin potations and to addict themselves to sack.

II HENRY IV

Events that occur early in the infant's life exert a strong influence over his later development. Freud (1949), Piaget (1950), and Hebb (1949) all looked at early experiences to explain later events. Because the infant has few well-established reactions and only limited intellectual abilities, early environmental events exert strong influences on his later development. The young infant lacks symbolic capacity and knowledge gained from previous experience, either of which could provide a way of handling early encounters. As a result of this helplessness, the young infant is inordinately impressed by early events. In addition, critical periods exist during which certain events exert dramatic effects on his later growth.

Initial experience and critical periods must be differentiated.

In this chapter, we first cover the general notions of initial experience and critical periods. Next, we outline immediate postnatal effects, paying particular attention to the relation between mother and child, and we discuss (through several stages of development) what is known of the effects of early events. Finally, we consider the role of infant experience in psychosexual development, with particular emphasis on the work of Freud.

THE USE OF ANIMALS

Factors that influence early experience include: (1) age, (2) duration of experience, (3) type of experi-

There are human constraints that make some experimental studies impossible; ethical considerations often eliminate the experimental method. No one would seriously consider depriving children of all sensory input for two years to study the effects of prolonged sensory isolation. However, animal studies, which offer good experimental

REMARKS: THEORY

The simplest assumption about early experience suggests that the earlier an event occurs, the stronger is its influence. This notion produces a simple decreasing relation between the amount of influence from an event and the time of its occurrence following birth (see Figure 10.1). An alternative to this simple relation is the concept of critical periods. Critical periods are intervals in the development of an organism during which he is particularly sensitive to certain classes of events (see Figure 10.2). However, a little thought will convince the reader that these seemingly diverse positions about early experience are equivalent: The proposition that early events are most important is a critical-period hypothesis (the critical period is, simply, immediately after birth!).

There are at least three important kinds of critical periods: (1) In the anatomical development of the embryo, there are critical periods during which the growth of certain organs (for example, the brain) is vastly accelerated. Intervention (infection or trauma) during these formative stages has strong effects on later growth; the effects are most pronounced on those organs growing at the fastest rate. (2) Critical periods also occur in the socialization of young animals. For example, wild animals learn to live with human beings if the animals and people are together during a critical time. [In puppies this period is between three and seven weeks (Scott, 1958).] However, if such experience occurs only before or after this period, the animal remains undomesticated. (3) Finally, critical periods occur in the learning of motor, perceptual, and intellectual skills. These critical stages are most clearly articulated in Piaget's conceptions of cognitive development and are covered in detail in Chapter 7.

ence, (4) behavior measured in the adult, (5) method of testing, and (6) genetics.

control, may be substituted. In studying animals (and infants) there are seven factors that influence the results of early experience. (1) The age of the child when experience is given: There are critical periods in development when a particular experience has inordinate effects. (2) The age of the child when he is tested for the effects of early experience: We may test shortly after the experience, a month later, or two years following the influence. (3) The duration or quantity of the experience given to a child: Larger amounts of early experience usually produce greater effects. (4) The type of experience given: Electric shock and early feeding produce different results. (5) The type of behavior measured in the adult: The particular response measure may change the effect of early experience. For example, handling may affect the infant's fear response but not influence his ability to learn simple associations. (6) The method of testing for persistence of an effect: Do we test for the effect by resistance to extinction in a learning experiment or by ability to relearn? (7) The genetic makeup of the child (emotionality, sex, for example).

FIGURE 10.1

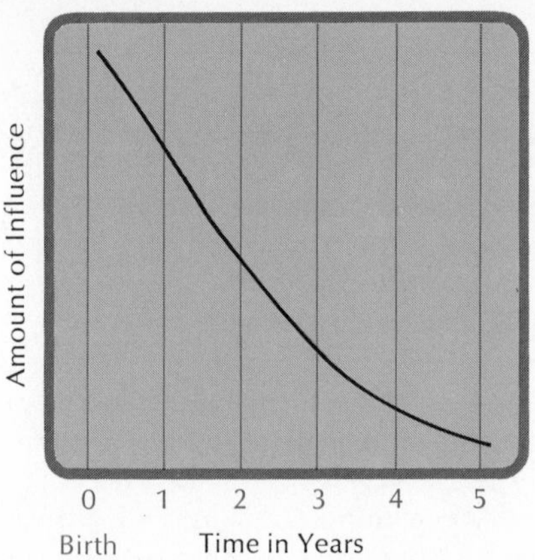

The early-experience hypothesis suggests that earlier events have more effect on the development of an organism.

Animals have shorter lives, they can be used ethically in experiments, and they show some of the same processes as human beings.

One major advantage of the use of animals is that they have relatively short life spans and can thus be studied over several generations in a short time. Also, they can be deprived and manipulated with fewer ethical problems. In this way it is possible to determine the relative effect of sensory and social deprivation, or the role of mother surrogates. Age factors, preseparation relations, and maternal substitution can be studied with animals as subjects. The major disadvantage of animal studies is that their results may not be comparable to what we would find from the same experiments on human infants. The comparability of processes that occur in the human and simpler animal must be established before we can generalize from animals to human infants.

FIGURE 10.2

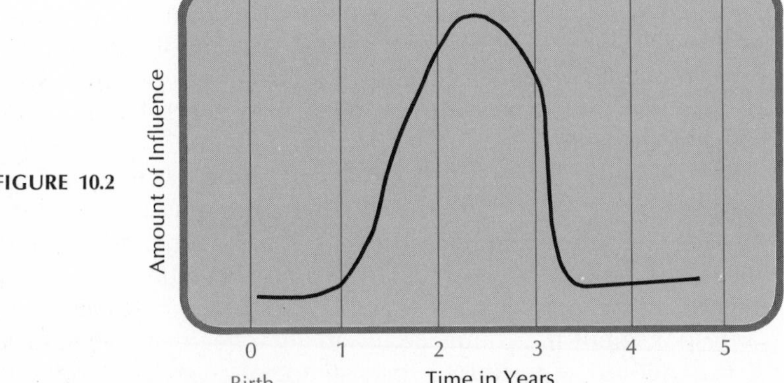

The critical-period hypothesis suggests that there is a time in the individual's developmental history when events are of particular importance. Before and after this period, events have little or no effect.

The results of carefully controlled animal studies must be compared and contrasted with comparable studies of "naturally occurring experiments with human infants." Also, more complex animals (monkeys) are more likely to resemble the human infant than are rats.

BIRTH

The major problem during birth is an adequate oxygen supply.

Birth is a major event; since it is the first extrauterine influence on the infant's life, proponents of initial experience have stressed its importance. While there is considerable evidence showing that birth injuries (from difficult labor, instrumental delivery, obstetrical mishandling, oxygen loss, or hemorrhaging) may produce central nervous system damage and affect the child's later physical and intellectual status, speculation about the birth process does not help us understand a child's later personality. There is some evidence of critical periods during birth. Slightly before, during, and immediately after birth, the child is particularly vulnerable to oxygen loss. Prolonged loss of oxygen supply (five to seven minutes) can produce degenerative changes in brain cells with subsequent retardation. Studies on the effect of anoxia (oxygen loss) on brain development show that traumatized infants are less sensitive to painful stimulation, are not as responsive to normal stimulation, are more irritable, are less mature in motor integration, and exhibit more muscular tension and rigidity than their normal peers (Graham, *et al.,* 1956).

Premature infants do not mature as well as their full-term peers.

Since the premature infant is not fully developed, he is less able to cope with extrauterine life than the normal, full-term newborn; birth is often traumatic for the premature baby. Studies comparing the early development of premature and full-term infants show a strong relation between weight at birth and later development of the infant. Lighter birth weight is associated with mental and neurological defects. These defects are not necessarily due to physiological factors. The family atmosphere in which a premature child develops is often different from that of the full-term baby—since the premature infant is so small, everyone is overprotective of him during his early growth. This suggests there may be a critical period for birth itself.

POSTNATAL EXPERIENCE

Hebb suggested that the early stimulation to which an animal is exposed influences his later abilities.

Hebb's (1949) speculations on sensory development have generated a number of experimental studies about the effect of early isolation on later perceptual abilities. In early studies, groups of rats were reared in the dark as infants and then tested as adults (Hebb, 1937). The results supported Hebb's prediction that dark-reared rats would have more difficulty learning size and brightness discriminations than do rats exposed to light during their early development. The deprived rats did not develop basic sensory mechanisms required for pattern vision and thus were not able to discriminate. Hebb (1947) reported a second study in which he compared (1) rats blinded at birth with rats blinded at maturity and (2) rats reared in cages with rats reared as pets. The late-blinded and pet-reared rats were superior in performance to the early-blinded and cage-reared groups on a measure of rat intelligence [a very complex alley maze (Hebb & Williams, 1946)].

Both sensory enrichment and sensory deprivation affect later abilities.

These studies indicate that the early visual experience of rats has a strong effect on their adult behavior, as has the early deprivation of light. The findings stimulated interest in studying the effects of sensory enrichment and sensory deprivation on perceptual-cognitive development. Hymovitch (1952) attempted to replicate Hebb's results, but found no differences between early- and late-blinded groups of rats. He did find significant differences between a group of rats raised in a free environment (that is, with visual and motor enrichment during infancy) and groups reared under various conditions of deprivation. The group raised in a free environment was superior in solving maze problems.

Enriched visual and motor experience produces superior rats.

Forgays and Forgays (1952) conducted a similar series of studies. They reported that a group of rats with enriched early experience (reared in the presence of playthings) performed better on a complex alley maze than did three other groups of animals. One group of animals had free experience without playthings, a second group was reared in small cages within a bare environment and given visual experience only, and the third group was raised in small isolated cages with no visual or motor experience. The investigators concluded that the superior performance of the rats who had playthings resulted from the enriched visual and motor experience. However, it could have been deprivation which caused the differences.

Early enrichment is better than later enrichment; both are superior to the normal environment of rats.

Forgus (1954) also found that rats given extensive early visual experience with geometric forms learned to discriminate the forms at maturity faster than did a group with no prior visual or motor experience with the forms. In subsequent studies Forgus (1955) found that rats given early visual experience with objects learned a maze faster than a group which had neither visual nor motor experience with objects. Apparently the observed importance of early visual and motor experience depends upon the requirements of the test situation. Forgus (1956) compared a group of rats that received early enriched visual experience (exposure to geometrical forms) with a group that received the same visual experience at maturity, and with another group that received only normal visual experience. He found that the group with early enriched experience was superior in visual discrimination to the group given enriched experience later and that both of these groups were superior to the normal control group. Walk (1958) reported that rats which received both visual and motor experience in infancy were superior on a visual task to rats that received only enriched visual experience. Gibson and Walk (1956) gave early perceptual enrichment (visual triangles and circles) and deprivation (darkness) to different groups of rats. They found the enriched group to be superior in discrimination ability.

Studies using dogs and chimpanzees show the same results.

In addition to studies with rats, several other investigators have used dogs, chimpanzees, and doves. Studies using dogs are consistent with the results on rats. Thompson and Heron (1954) found significant differences in problem-solving ability as a result of early experience; they emphasized the importance of perceptual rather than motor experience. Chow and Nissen (1955) varied early experience in chimpanzees, giving them either diffused or patterned lights, and then tested the animals for interocular transfer—the ability to solve a problem with either eye—on discrimination tasks. Those animals that received patterned light stimulation showed immediate transfer from one eye to the other, while the group of animals that received diffused light stimulation (white light which contains no contours or lines) did not show transfer. Reisen (1947) varied the early-light experience of groups of chimpanzees, using complete darkness, darkness combined with periods of diffused light, periods of pattern light, and periods of normal visual experience. He reported that the behavioral effects of complete darkness and diffused light were essentially the same in severity, while the periods of patterned light and of normal visual experience interspersed with dark-rearing produced only a transient visual deficiency. Studies with light-deprived chimpanzees suggest that early visual experience is most important and has the most pronounced effect upon monkeys and men.

Young children experience difficulty identifying simple forms with their hands.

The only relevant data concerning early experience and problem-solving in human beings concerns the tactual identification of hidden objects (Page, 1959). The results indicate that young children experience difficulty identifying simple geometric forms, suggesting that geometric abstractions are not understood until the more primitive perceptual images obtained from visual sensory systems are developed.

Congenitally blind individuals function at a very primitive level when their sight is restored by corneal transplantation.

Von Senden [1960 (1932)] reported a series of clinical investigations of congenitally blind persons who were given sight late in life through corneal transplantation. Although many of the cases are not well reported, the general findings are these: Shortly after the congenitally blind person gains his sight, he cannot perform a simple circle-triangle discrimination. Although the patients were perfectly capable of making this discrimination on the basis of tactual cues, they could not recognize a circle or a triangle visually. All the patients could report brightness changes, so the visual system seemed to be functioning at a primitive level. After a long series of trials, they learned to discriminate a triangle from a circle. Many of the patients reported looking for a curved versus an angular part. When these patients were later tested on a triangle-square discrimination they could not differentiate the objects. Changing the color of light in which a patient was seeing a circle-triangle pair interfered with his discrimination. These results support Hebb's assumption that only the ability to make simple figure-ground discriminations exists without experience; pattern perception is produced by the building of simple figure-ground differentiations into more complex perceptual mechanisms through experience.

Maternal separation and maternal deprivation

Maternal separation involves mother loss; maternal deprivation is lack of interaction.

Maternal separation implies a physical distance between mother and child, while maternal deprivation suggests an insufficiency in their relation. Separation need not lead to deprivation if an adequate mother-surrogate is provided. Conversely, deprivation does not imply separation, since the child may be living with his own mother but experience only minimal interaction. The effects of maternal deprivation (social isolation) show up shortly after birth. Sensory stimulation is of major importance to the infant; perceptual deprivation affects him almost immediately. Through interaction he learns to comprehend the world. On the other hand, the lack of a single mother has no effect until the infant is about seven months, since he usually does not differentiate his own mother from other human beings until around that age. Any adequate mother-surrogate can be substituted before the infant shows stranger anxiety (fear of strange persons); after this critical period the child will not accept a stranger as caretaker. The effects are most marked if separation occurs when the infant is between six and 24 months of age in those infants who enjoy good preseparation relations with their mothers.

Infants under seven months respond to maternal separation with calm; children over seven months protest.

Schaffer and Callender (1959) studied 76 children between three and 51 weeks of age who were hospitalized (and therefore separated from their mothers) for an average of 15.4 days. They found two distinct reactions: Children over seven months of age protested when separated from their parents. They developed feeding difficulties and were excessively dependent on their parents after reunion. Infants below six months of age showed no protest. Strangers were accepted with no change in the infants' responsiveness. Adjustment to different feeding schedules occurred with minor difficulty in the young infants. After reunion with their parents, the younger infants engaged in quiet preoccupation with their surroundings and in unfocused scanning of the environment. The older children realized their environment had

REMARKS: THEORY

Imprinting is a particularly strong attachment that is formed between the young of several species (ducks, geese, chickens, and some mammals) and the first object they see which moves, makes noise, or is colored somewhat like their natural mother. There are genetic tendencies to prefer certain types of stimuli when imprinting; however, these natural preferences can be overcome by strong experience during a critical period (Hess, 1959). Studies of wild mallards show that their critical period for imprinting is between eight and 24 hours following hatching. Before eight hours there is little retention of the attraction, and after 24 hours there is no indication that the bird can be attached to any particular object.

There are several differences between imprinting and simple association. Among these are: (1) Learning a visual discrimination is quicker and more stable when practice trials are spaced, but imprinting is more rapid following massed trials. (2) Recency of experience is more effective in learning; for imprinting, primacy is more important. (3) The administration of punishment increases the effectiveness of imprinting (following) while aversive experience leads to avoidance learning. (4) Finally, chicks and ducklings under the influence of meprobamate (a tranquilizer) are able to learn a color-discrimination problem at their normal rate; however, the administration of meprobamate reduces imprinting to zero.

changed drastically, while the younger children were unaware of what had happened. The younger children were not making a better adjustment; they simply did not know there was a problem!

Good maternal relations cause a more severe reaction to separation.

The effects of preseparation experiences on the child's reaction to maternal deprivation or separation were studied by Spitz and Wolf (1946), who concluded that loss of the mother following a stable mother-child relation leads to mild or severe depression, while separation following a poor relation results in better adjustment. Emotional stability is lowest in those infants who, after being together with the mothers for some time, are subsequently deprived of that relation. These studies suggest that a good mother-child relation results in more severe maternal-separation anxiety for the child than a poor mother-child relation. Studies concerning the replacement of a mother are scanty and inconclusive.

Evidence about human personality disorders is retrospective.

All the evidence we have from clinical studies of human personality contains an inherent defect—the studies are necessarily retrospective. They start with a disorder and work backward, tracing the experience of the individual as he, his relatives, and his associates recall them. Details are lost and the story is often so confused that it requires a generous exercise of intuition on the part of the investigator to make a coherent picture of the results. Evidence obtained by retrospection does not exclude other possible causes of personality disorder. However, through the use of primates (which are relatively close to humans in their play, family behavior, and mother-infant attachments) we can experimentally investigate some hypotheses. Monkeys display many of the same interaction patterns as humans; the results of changes in their early relations should have profound implications for human development.

Harlow experimentally studied the effects of maternal separation and deprivation on monkeys.

Harlow's (1958) investigations of emotional development in primates grew from his efforts to produce and maintain a colony of sturdy, disease-free animals for use in research programs. By separating the infants from their mothers a few hours after birth and placing them in a fully controlled physical-care regime, he hoped to produce a high rate of survival and be able to remove the animals for testing without maternal protest. Following separation of the infant from its mother, the baby was alone in a bare wire cage in a large room where other infants were housed. Each monkey could see and hear others of his kind but could not make direct physical contact. Fifty-six animals were raised in this manner. Only later did Harlow realize that the separated monkeys were emotionally disturbed, as well as sturdy and disease-free.

Maternal separation is traumatic for an infant; sexual behavior is most disturbed.

Early studies involved separation of four monkey mother-infant pairs for a three-week period and measurement of the infant monkeys' behavior before, during, and after separation (Harlow & Zimmerman, 1959). All the mothers and infants showed emotional disturbance following separation (see Figure 10.3). However, the infants' disturbances were much more intense and enduring than those of the mothers. Harlow found many behavior abnormalities in these monkeys that rarely occur in animals born in the wild and brought to the laboratory, even though the latter may be housed in individual cages for years. The laboratory-born monkeys (separated from their mothers) sat in cages staring into space, circled in a stereotyped manner, clasped their heads in their hands and arms, and rocked for long periods. They often developed compulsive habits (such as pinching the same patch of

FIGURE 10.3

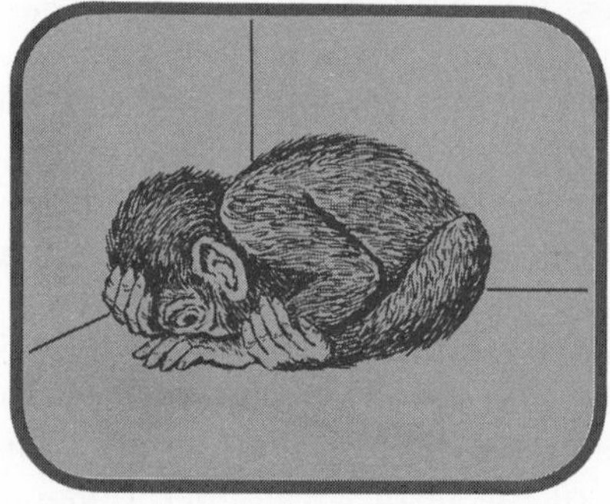

A depressed infant monkey who has been separated from his mother. (After Harlow & Zimmerman, 1959.)

skin). Occasionally an animal would chew on his body until it bled. Six two-year-old animals were individually observed. A most striking difference between the artificially reared animals and a control group was found in their sexual behavior. The laboratory-born animals did not lack sexual drive, since the males approached females and the females displayed the usual sexual-presentation response. However, they were unable to carry through the sexual act. The severity of affliction of the animals reared in the cages became more apparent as they grew older. They paid little attention to animals in neighboring cages; those caged with companions sat in opposite corners and did not interact. No complete heterosexual behavior ever occurred between the males and females, even though they were together for as long as seven years.

Harlow raised infant monkeys with terrycloth and wire mothers; he showed that feeding has little to do with mother-infant attachment.

Following these initial experiences with monkeys raised without mothers, Harlow performed a series of experiments on the relations between monkey mothers and infants. The infant monkeys developed strong attachments to terrycloth blankets given them after separation from their mothers. Harlow decided to build a surrogate mother, a wooden body covered with terrycloth, and to perform mother-infant experiments using surrogates instead of natural mothers. Two surrogate mothers were constructed, one covered with terrycloth and the other with wire mesh (see Figure 10.4). Bottle holders were installed in the upper portion of each surrogate to feed the infant. Both mothers

FIGURE 10.4

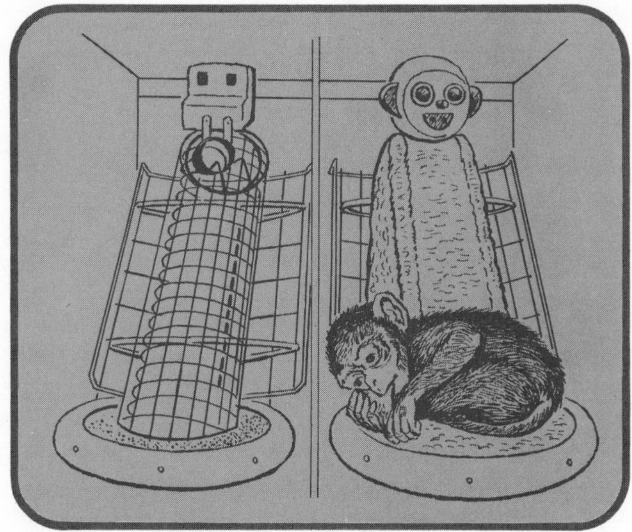

Wire and cloth mother surrogates. (After Harlow, 1958.)

FIGURE 10.5

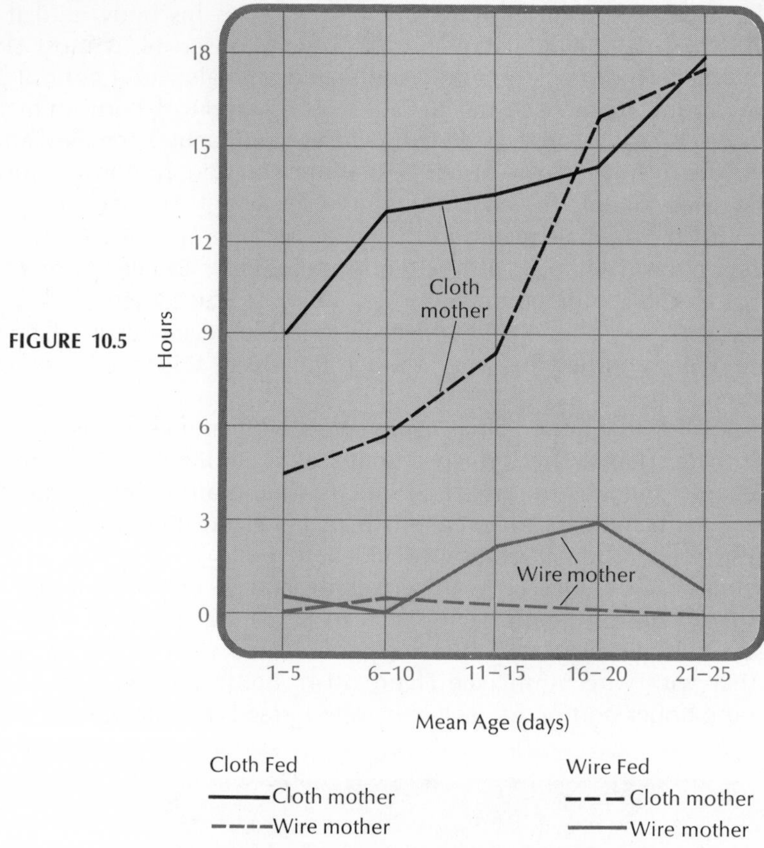

Time spent on cloth and wire mother surrogates. Short-term effects show that the infants spend their time on the terrycloth mother surrogate no matter which surrogate feeds them —a clear rejection of the reinforcement-theory explanation of infant-mother attachment. (From Harlow, 1958.)

provided the basic requirements for nursing (45-degree angle, bottle, and a place to grasp), but the terrycloth mother also provided contact comfort. Harlow's initial experiment investigated the effect of nursing on mother attachment; the cloth mother and the wire mother were placed in different cubicles attached to the infant's living cage. Eight infant monkeys were placed in individual cages with the surrogates; four infant monkeys were fed on the wire mother and four on the cloth mother surrogate. The infants fed on the wire and the cloth mother surrogates had similar performance scores across a wide variety of

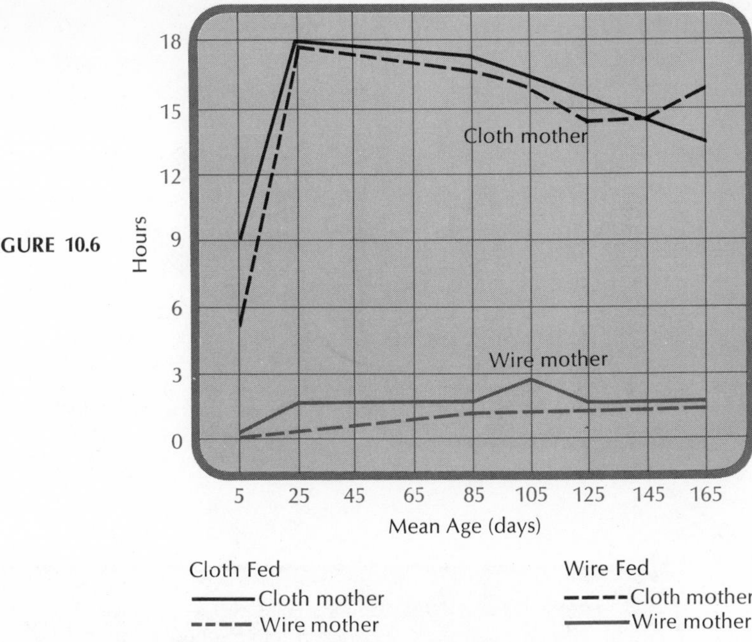

FIGURE 10.6

Time spent on cloth and wire mother surrogates. Long-term effects show that the infant monkeys spend their time on the terrycloth mother surrogate no matter which surrogate feeds them—a clear rejection of the reinforcement-theory explanation of infant-mother attachment. (From Harlow, 1958.)

tasks. However, all the infants spent most of their time clinging to the terrycloth mother; they virtually ignored the wire mother. The only time an infant approached the wire mother was during feeding time. Figures 10.5 and 10.6 show the short- and long-term effects of contact comfort and nursing on mother-infant attachment. The assumption of learning theorists that secondary reinforcement derived from feeding is a major factor in mother-infant attachment is wrong.

Cloth mothers are able to calm an infant's fear; wire mothers are not.

The amount of time spent on the mother might not reflect attachment as much as a comfortable sleeping platform. However, other tests showed that the cloth mother was more than a comfortable bed. A study of fear in the infant monkeys showed their selective maternal attachment. A typical fear-producing stimulus is shown in Figure 10.7. The data on differential responses under both feeding conditions are given in Figure 10.8. It is quite clear that a cloth mother is the preferred surrogate, regardless of the feeding situation. In addition to these data

FIGURE 10.7

Typical fear stimulus. (After Harlow, 1958.)

FIGURE 10.8

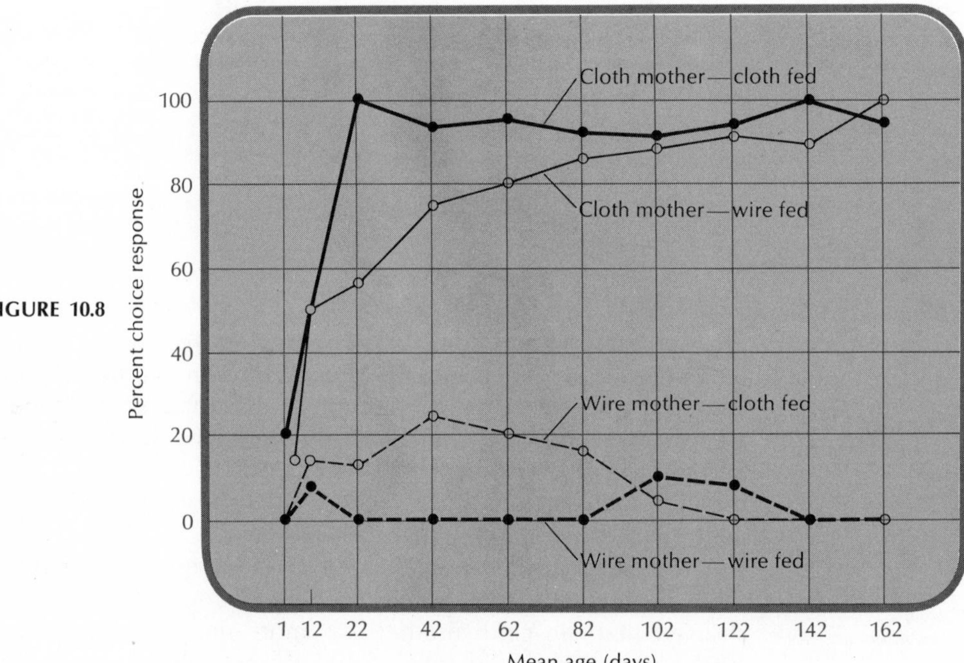

Percentage of time infant monkeys spent on each surrogate when both the wire and cloth mothers were available. All infants, no matter what their feeding situation, preferred the cloth mother surrogate. (From Harlow, 1958.)

on time spent with the mother surrogate, observation of the infants' response to fear shows that after rubbing their bodies against the cloth mother—they became less fearful. Within a few minutes they were visually exploring the object of fear, and the bravest of the babies actually left his mother to touch the monster.

Infants with cloth mothers learn to control their anxieties; infants with wire mothers do not.

In a series of open-field studies, monkeys raised on mother surrogates were compared with monkeys raised in a wire cage containing a cheesecloth blanket during the first 14 days of their life. The infants were introduced into an unfamiliar room measuring six feet on a side. The infants raised with single mother surrogates were placed in the situation two times a week for eight weeks, no mother surrogate being present during one session and the appropriate mother surrogate (the kind on which the infant lived) in the other sessions. Four monkeys were used in each group; the results are shown in Figures 10.9, 10.10, and 10.11. The infants raised with cloth mothers rushed to their mother surrogate when she was present and clutched her tenaciously. Following several minutes of contact the infants relaxed and began to demonstrate positive signs of manipulating and climbing on the mother. After several sessions the monkeys began to use the mother as a base from

FIGURE 10.9

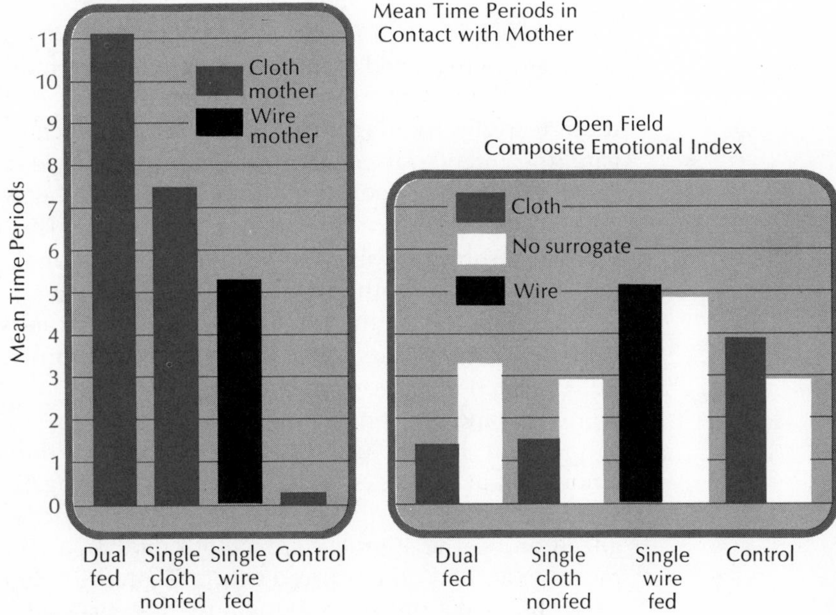

(Left) Responsiveness to mother surrogates in the open-field test. *(Right)* Emotionality index in testing with and without the mother surrogates. (From Harlow & Zimmerman, 1959.)

FIGURE 10.10

Subsequent response to cloth mother and stimulus in the open-field test. (After Harlow & Zimmerman, 1959.)

which to explore the fearful room. When monkeys raised on the cloth surrogate were placed in the room without their mothers, they crouched in the middle of the room and did not move, or they ran about the room fearfully (see Figure 10.11). In the presence of the mother surrogate, the infants raised with the wire mother were different from the other group; they spent little time on the mother surrogate; the presence of the wire mother did not relax them. The four infants raised without a surrogate had about the same emotionality scores as infants raised on a wire mother.

Infants raised with cloth mothers are more curious than those raised with wire mothers.

Another test of the cloth or wire-mother care was obtained from exploratory or curious behavior of the infant monkey. Some years ago Butler (1953) showed that monkeys enclosed in a dimly lighted box will open and reopen a window in the box for no other reason than to look out. Harlow used this box to measure differences in curiosity among infant monkeys raised with mother surrogates. The test involved showing the infant monkeys four stimuli on successive days in a balanced order. The stimuli were a cloth mother, a wire mother, an infant monkey, and an empty box, each presented for 30 minutes a day. The data obtained from the groups raised on wire and cloth mothers are shown in Figure 10.12. The groups raised on the cloth mother showed high responsiveness to the cloth mother; the infants raised with the wire mother and those in the control group showed more responsive-

FIGURE 10.11

Response in the open-field test in the absence of the mother surrogate. (After Harlow & Zimmerman, 1959.)

FIGURE 10.12

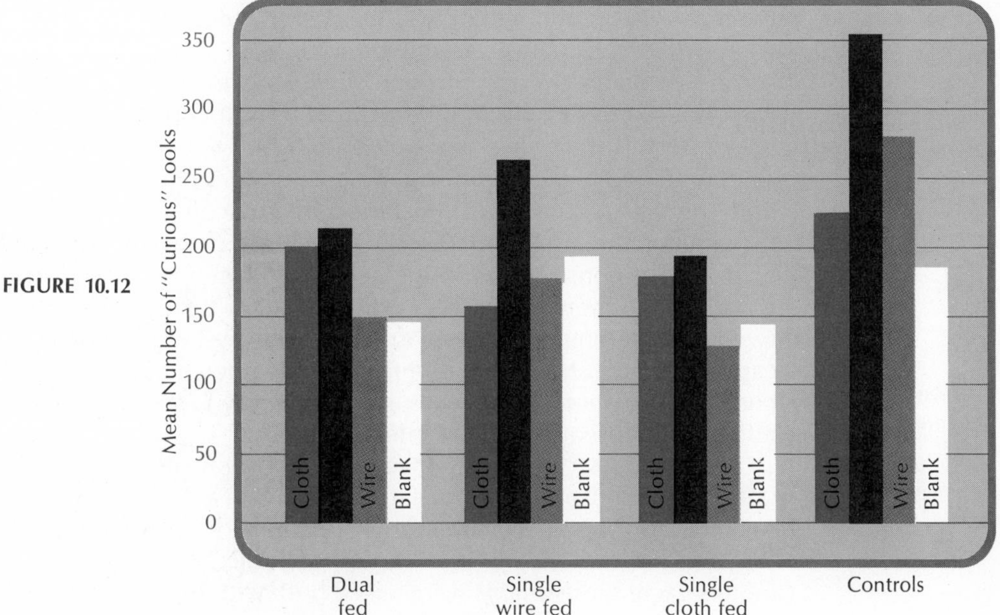

Differential responses to visual exploration. (From Harlow, 1958.)

ness to the infant monkey. The group raised on the wire mother showed a higher response rate to the blank field than to the wire mother—Hate? Body contact has a strong influence on the formation of mother-infant attachment. Nursing plays a relatively minor role in the attachment formation; feeding is neither a necessary nor sufficient condition for attachment.

Group psychotherapy did not help maternally deprived monkeys.

Harlow (1958) reported in another study that he had devised a group psychotherapy situation for nine male and 10 female monkeys who had endured maternal deprivation early in their lives; he used them to stock a monkey island of the Madison, Wisconsin, zoo. This was their first experience outside the laboratory. They had to learn to eat and drink from an open trough. Within a few days they made many necessary adjustments. Fighting was severe but decreased as dominance relations were established. Normal grooming appeared and a limited amount of inadequate infantile sexual behavior appeared. Harlow introduced his largest, strongest, most productive male onto the island in midsummer. The new male immediately established himself at the head of the order; however, he did not succeed in starting a single pregnancy. Apparently the animals that had not received early mother-child and peer relations could not develop normal sexual and other social relations later in their life. Even with considerable assistance from the more experienced male, they showed infantile patterns of interaction; fear and withdrawal were characteristic.

Monkeys raised in maximum isolation (consistent with survival) are very anxious and asocial.

Harlow (1958) also reared two monkeys in a situation of maximum social deprivation consistent with survival. A male and a female were each housed from birth in their own solid-wall cubicle. Their behavior was observed through a one-way mirror. The animals had adapted to solid food and had developed good coats when removed from the box. Both animals responded to liberation by crouching, a typical reaction to extreme threat. When placed together they again crouched and made no response. When approached by a monkey raised in partial isolation, the monkeys raised in total isolation froze or fled. Even after two years, during which the isolated monkeys were kept in a large cage, they still showed abnormal fear of other monkeys. Apparently complete isolation during early stages of growth produced irreversible effects on subsequent social interaction.

Peer interaction is sufficient to overcome most of these difficulties.

In Harlow's early isolation experiments animals were deprived of both peers and mothers. He later performed a series of experiments to compare the effects of mother-infant and infant-infant relations separately. His most privileged group of subjects was two sets of four infants each; these infants were raised both with their mothers and with peers. They were able to play together in pairs or in foursomes during scheduled sessions and could return to their mothers at any time. In parallel with these groups, he raised another set of four infant monkeys in a playpen with a terrycloth surrogate in each cage. Harlow reported that after 20–30 days, the infant monkeys with natural mothers entered into more lively and consistent social relations and increasingly complex play than did the four infants with surrogate mothers. At the end of the second year all 12 animals were living together in one playpen, with each original group occupying one living cage. All were observed in daily interaction. Early differences between them disappeared. Seven of the eight "mothered" animals engaged in normal social activities and assumed correct sexual postures. The deviant was a male social reject. Of the two "motherless" males, one achieved full sexual posture and the other approached full posture. Observations of the three groups of infant monkeys raised in close association indicate that the opportunity for infant-infant interaction may compensate to a large extent for a lack of mothering. This is particularly true in the case of social and sexual relations.

Studies on monkeys are relevant to human development.

Research with monkeys may never completely resolve the complex rôle of early experience in the development of human cognition and personality. However, important theoretical and practical questions can be answered by the use of lower primates.

Infants vary in the amount of cuddling enjoyed.

Schaffer and Emerson (1964) report that not all human infants are attracted to contact comfort; from a sample of 37 infants they reported that 19 "cuddlers" enjoyed handling and nine rejected close contact. The remainder of the sample were intermediate—sometimes accepting and other times rejecting close contact. These differences might arise from the parent's interaction or from the infant's genetic disposition to reject contact.

Ribble was one of the first to suggest mothering is important for infant health.

One of the first investigators to deal with the question of maternal factors in infant development was Margaret Ribble (1943). She observed 600 infants in three different institutions to study their early development and its relation to later personality disorders. She particularly noted signs of withdrawal, regression, negativism, and exaggerated reactions to frustration; she attempted to determine whether these reactions were inborn or developed as a result of early infantile experience. She followed the children longitudinally (over several months) taking motion pictures and notes for case histories. Ribble reported that the mother-child relation depends on three types of stimulation—tactile, kinesthetic, and auditory. She found that the neonate is particularly sensitive to touch around the head and face and shows evidence of satisfaction after vigorous sucking (by improved breathing and digestion). Ribble also felt that the infant derives a sense of security from adequate mothering, receives pleasure from being held and fondled by the mother, and finds the sound of the mother's voice (when it is soft) soothing and pleasurable. She also noted several reactions to inadequate mothering; the most prevalent were negativism and regression. Negativism was evidenced by refusal to suck, rigidity of body, shallow breathing, and constipation; regression was shown by quiescence, stuporous sleep, and gastro-intestinal disturbances. She argued strongly in her conclusions that good mothering and considerable handling during the first three months contribute greatly to the positive development of an infant. Ribble also argued that a minimal amount of "mothering" (handling and attention) is necessary for adequate development.

Pinneau attacked her methods and results. Her explanations were wrong but her data are correct.

Pinneau (1955) attacked Ribble's conclusions on several grounds, the main one being her claim that the infant needs mothering and attention to stabilize his physiological reactions. Pinneau showed that the infant's breathing and urination become physiologically stable during the first two days of life. He said there is no evidence for Ribble's claim that crying is a response to suffocation on the part of the infant. In general, Pinneau's criticisms were correct, but he discarded the facts along with Ribble's explanations of her findings. Simply because Ribble advanced the wrong explanations is no justification to discard observations validated by many others and conclude that infantile experience is of no great importance in the development of personality. There is good evidence that early experience with the mother has strong effects on later development (Harlow & Zimmerman, 1959).

Extra caretaking can increase infants' social responsiveness.

Institutionalization provides a setting for many studies on maternal deprivation. Rheingold and Bayley (1959) explored the effects of mothering on institutionalized infants during their first eight months of life. One group was cared for by the experimenter alone for daily periods of seven and one-half hours. A control group was cared for in the usual hospital manner, which included frequent changing of "mothers." The experimenter performed many more caretaking acts than did the institutional mothers. Infants under the normal hospital routine were often without a caretaker; they spent more time alone in their cribs. Both groups were given sets of infant tests to measure social responsiveness, postural development, cube manipulation, and development. The experimenters supposed that the group which received more attention would become more socially responsive and also improve more in their test scores than the control infants. Results showed that infants who receive more maternal attention become more socially responsive. Rheingold's impression was that this responsiveness developed through day-by-day byplay between the experimenter and the babies outside the regular caretaking duties. The investigators followed their original study with a reexamination of the infants one year later. At that time the experimental infants were slightly more vocal than the control children, but not more socially responsive. The additional maternal care affected the social behavior of the infants immediately after the intervention, but was not strong enough to maintain the differences for a year.

Inadequate early caretaking results in retarded perceptual and sensory-motor coordination.

Dennis and Najarian (1957) studied the effects of institutionalization on infants in Lebanon. Because of inadequate financial support, the facility they examined was able to provide few caretakers for their infant wards. The investigators explored the development of children between one year and four and one-half years of age. For comparison they used children at the well baby clinic of the American University in Beirut Hospital. Infants under one year were given the Cattell Infant Intelligence Tests; those at four and one-half were given the Goodenough Draw-a-Man Test and a maze test. The results showed that at two months there was little difference between the experimental and control groups. At one year, children in the institution were retarded in comparison with the control group living at home. By the age of four and one-half the groups were again comparable in measured abilities. During the first year of life the environment has strong effects upon the development of the child (at least on those items measured). An analysis of the Cattell Scale shows that the items which differentiated the two groups required manual skills and adjustment to visually presented objects. Dennis suggested that the differences were the result of restricted experience with the environment, due to lack of social interaction, on the part of the institutionalized children. The older children were apparently able to compensate for their early lack of experience by moving about the institution on their own; they therefore overcame their early deficiency. The authors had no doubt that on other tests the older children would exhibit retardation in comparison with the control children, especially on tests involving language comprehension and use.

Adequate institutions produce infants almost comparable to normal infants; inadequate institutions produce retarded infants.

A second study by Dennis (1960) investigated infant development in three Tehran institutions. Conditions in the first two institutions were poor and infant retardation was marked. The third institution was a model of institutional care; the attendants were trained in child-care methods and responsible to only four children. They handled the children, placed them upright in their cribs, put them in playpens, and gave them toys. Observations of motor coordination and social and emotional behavior were made. In the first two institutions 123 children were tested; in the third institution 51 children were examined. Children in the first two institutions seldom had visitors and were fearful of the experimenter. Children in the model institution showed little fear of strangers and only limited attention-seeking. Only half the children in the first institution (between one and two years of age) could sit alone; none could walk alone. Between two and three years of age only eight percent of these children could walk alone. Fifteen percent of the three- to four-year-old children from the second institution could walk unsupported. In the model institution all children between two and three years of age could walk unaided. However, children in the model institution did not equal the performance of children in their own homes. Dennis concluded that it is not primarily institutionalization which handicaps a child's motor development; the handicap is caused by lack of locomotor activities, lack of experience in the prone and sitting positions, paucity of handling, and restriction of learning opportunities. These restrictions occur because of space limitations and lack of caretakers.

We know enough about maternal deprivation to insist on early adoption and adequate caretaking.

What do we know from studies of maternal deprivation? Enough to insist on the earliest possible adoption of infants placed in foundling homes and institutions. Some adoption agencies are now allowing parents to risk getting infants with imperfections on the grounds that early family care is a major safeguard against abnormal development. Also, on these same grounds, adoption agencies have relaxed the more stringent requirements on adoptive parents (for example, large family income and middle or upper class status). Sensory stimulation and human relations are prerequisites to normal growth.

Institutional children need someone who is free to play with them.

Institutional care is necessary for various reasons, but we now know some of the dangers. We must provide people who are free to play with the institutionalized infant. It is difficult to make other firm generalizations. The level of observation in these studies is usually superficial and few objective methods are available to study the effects of separation and deprivation.

THE ROLE OF INFANT EXPERIENCE IN PSYCHOSEXUAL DEVELOPMENT

Freud proposed that we pass through three stages: (1) oral, (2) anal, and (3) genital.

Freud's (1949) theory of psychosexual development contains three stages—oral, anal, and genital. In the oral stage our zones of pleasure include the lips, mouth, and gums. Characteristic behavior is incorporation (taking things in); the infant has a passive relation with the world. During this stage a child acquires trust or mistrust of the world. Fixation at the oral stage can result from too much gratification, which makes the infant reluctant to abandon oral satisfaction, or too much frustration, which leads to later regression. The child moves from the oral stage during weaning; Freud assumed weaning was necessarily a painful experience.

Fixation at the anal stage leads to a concern for possessions.

During the anal stage our zones of pleasure include the anus, urethra, and large muscles. Typical behavior includes control of the sphincter; this action gives the infant some power over his environment. Later, the child takes pleasure in muscular expression. The main goal of the anal phase is autonomy and control, leading to a capacity for decision, choice, love, and hate. Conflict occurs between autonomy and shame. The anal stage contains the beginnings of our ego. Fixation at the anal phase can result from too much pampering or frustration. Anal fixation makes a person concerned with possessions, preserving things, and keeping order; anal fixation also makes the person intolerant of frustration.

Freud believed the ego develops from interaction with reality.

The ego is Freud's label for the self-awareness of one's own actions and their consequences. He believed the ego develops from reality; children must learn to control their impulses and delay gratification to avoid constant frustration. The ego's function is to plan impulse gratification or to delay and sublimate impulses that cannot be gratified directly. The ego mediates between libidinal impulses and the superego. In Freud's scheme of man, the ego is caught between desire and restriction—damned if it does and damned if it does not. Remarkably similar to Victorian notions!

During the genital phase we learn to interact.

The genital stage contains two phases: (1) a phallic or infantile genital phase, which terminates at the beginning of the latency period (the period during which all sexual expression is repressed), and (2) the adult genital phase, which emerges with the solving of the conflicts of puberty, the development of heterosexual relations, and growth of a concern for others as well as for oneself. The zone of pleasure is the phallic region in particular and locomotion in general. The basic behavior is intrusion; locomotion, curiosity, aggression, and loud speech characterize the phallic child.

Boys' and girls' tasks are different during the genital phase; they must achieve appropriate sex-role identification.

During the genital stage boys and girls differentiate. The boy's developmental task is easier, because intrusion is the appropriate sexual behavior. However, sexual interest in his mother puts the little boy in conflict with his more powerful father. The father's power and the boy's fear of castration lead to sexual repression, manifested in a latent period in which no overt sexual behavior occurs.

During the Oedipal situation a boy lusts after his mother.

The Oedipal situation (a son's lust for his mother) derives its name from a Greek myth in which Oedipus was doomed to marry his mother and kill his father. Freud believed that all little boys want to possess their mother and kill their father. This conflict between desire and obvious inability is solved by suppressing sexual desires and identifying with the father. Identification protects the little boy from castration fears and enhances his development of a mature sex role.

Freud believed little girls have a difficult time solving the Electra complex—attraction to their father and fear of their mother.

In the girl, intrusive activity conflicts with her feminine tendency to be incorporative and passive in social-sexual relations. This conflict produces a continuing problem for the female; to compete or submit is the constant question. The girl also desires her mother at first, but is frustrated by her during weaning and toilet training. As a consequence, Freud postulated the castration complex (the girl blames her mother and desires her father's penis). The girl's desire for her father (Electra complex) produces conflict with her mother. Thus, in the little girl, a feeling of castration prepares the way for sexual conflict which is repressed during the latency period.

Fixation at various stages produces different neurotic tendencies.

The various stages of development were assumed to be prototypical situations for various neurotic disorders. Fixation at the oral phase was assumed to produce ulcers in people who are basically passive and incorporative: When the situation demands activity and decision they remain passive; the flow of digestive juices, which forms part of the oral complex, is exaggerated as a reaction to this frustration and anger, and the walls of the stomach are digested. Fixation at the anal stage makes a person selfish. The child who stops at the first genital phase is a showoff who intrudes upon others. Only the person who develops into the second genital phase functions fully.

Studies of Freudian theory confound verbal reinforcement and Freud.

The "organ" language of Freud's theory was symbolic; he used it for easy communication and shock effect. Studies to test Freudian theory have been conducted by psychiatrists and psychologists engaged in the treatment of patients. Using the method of free association, they had their patients recall past experiences. Since there is no independent assessment of the antecedent conditions of the neuroses except those talked about in the therapy situation, these "tests" of Freudian theory are full of social reinforcement—the experimenter is likely to pay attention to and thus reinforce those responses which confirm his theory. This does not mean that psychoanalytic theory is incorrect; it simply means the theory cannot be tested in the therapy situation itself. It is an open question whether psychoanalytic theory is correct or not. There is a common sense appeal about the stages, but they need to be more carefully defined and studied before we can begin to understand the processes that occur in infantile experience and personality development.

Dollard and Miller translated Freud into learning theory.

Dollard and Miller (1950) systematically reformulated psychoanalytic concepts in learning theory terms; they emphasized four early conflicts: feeding, toilet training, sexual expression, and the control of aggression and anger. There are six situations in which these conflicts have been studied: (1) the effects on later behavior of breast or bottle-feeding, (2) feeding on a self-demand schedule or on a predetermined schedule, (3) early or late weaning, (4) abrupt or gradual weaning,

(5) early or late toilet training, and (6) lenience or severity in the management of infantile sexual expression. These areas are outlined and conclusions about their effects on later child behavior considered.

Breast or bottle feeding makes no difference in later personality development.

Breast feeding was advocated for centuries to preserve interaction with the mother; the breast was supposed to satisfy not only hunger but the need for tactual stimulation of the infant's erogenous zones. Many studies have compared general health, personality traits, and items such as thumb sucking in children who were breast or bottle fed. The comparisons have been universally retrospective; they take existing characteristics of children selected because they were either breast or bottle fed. Seldom are other factors adequately controlled (socioeconomic level, intelligence, and type of mother-infant relation). Differences between the two groups are always slight, and as more factors are controlled, the differences become smaller. Thus, no evidence exists that one method of feeding is superior to another in terms of later personality development.

Children fed on schedule are more integrated into groups than those fed on demand.

Allowing a child to nurse when he wishes should produce more gratification of oral needs. (However, recall that excessive gratification can produce bad effects.) Several studies have looked for relations between characteristics reflecting emotional stability and the degree to which feeding was self-regulated. Children fed on schedule are more integrated and attached to groups than those fed on demand (Sewell, Mussen, & Harris, 1955).

Weaning trauma and neurotic difficulties are unrelated.

The trauma of weaning is inevitable, according to psychoanalytic theory, but more abrupt weaning should produce more frustration. Strong frustration should lead to finger sucking, temper tantrums, and sensitive feelings in abruptly weaned children, since they have not had the opportunity to learn alternate means of gratifying their desires. A study comparing groups who had been weaned quickly or gradually tested various traits like finger sucking, nail biting, and so on; no significant differences occurred between the two groups (Sewell, Mussen, & Harris, 1955). Too much gratification or frustration may produce fixation. Thus, the duration of breast feeding should be related in a curvilinear fashion to personality development—very short and very long durations should produce early fixation and poor later development. Studies in this area are contradictory and inconclusive.

Fixation at the anal stage leads to rigidity if the mother is cold and undemonstrative.

Psychoanalytic theorists are quite confident about the effects of fixation during the anal stage. When the management of toilet training is considerate and sufficient time is allowed for learning, the child should adjust adequately. But if the transformation is demanded early and quickly, we may get fixation at the early anal stage. Sears, Maccoby, and Levin (1957) showed that five-year-old children who are emotionally upset over toilet training received early toilet training, but this was true only when the mothers were cold and undemonstrative. When the mothers were warm and demonstrative, early training was not related to emotional upset. In general, the character of parent-child relations is more important than the timing of toilet training—or any other activity, for that matter!

Permissiveness about sexuality is correlated with permissiveness about aggression.

There are no reliable data on the control of modesty training. Sears, Maccoby, and Levin (1957) found that permissiveness about sexual play is highly correlated with permissiveness toward aggression, while severity concerning sexual play accompanies harshness toward aggression, independence, and cleanliness.

The general character of parent-child relations is more important than the particular way training is handled.

The conclusion from studies of child management is that psychoanalytic predictions are not often substantiated. The general character of parent-child interactions (warm-cold or controlling-independent) is more important than what happens in toilet training. We will see when considering parent-child interaction that the control and emotional responses of parents toward their children are the important determinants of development; they control whether children are neurotic, delinquent, spoiled, or merely normal.

SUMMARY

1 Animals are important in developmental work because they are cheap, they can be manipulated easily without ethical problems, they mature quickly, and they are interesting.

2 Difficult delivery can result in anoxia, brain damage, and decreased intellectual development.

3 The early visual environment of a monkey or human being has profound effects on his later development. Studies show that rats who receive enriched stimulation perform more complex discriminations than rats reared in the dark.

4 Maternal separation can occur after the child and the mother have developed a lasting relation (about seven months) while maternal deprivation can occur from birth. Maternal deprivation is difficult to separate from sensory deprivation.

5 Studies using infant monkeys separated from their mothers and raised on surrogate caretakers show that feeding has little to do with infant-maternal attachment. Only if it is correlated with contact comfort does feeding make a difference. Infant monkeys separated from their mothers develop abnormally unless they have a mother surrogate to supply contact comfort. Peers seem able to supplant maternal interaction to some extent; infants raised with peers develop normal sexual behavior in contrast to the inadequate sexual behavior of maternally deprived monkeys.

6 Modification of mothering between three and eight months has little effect on human infants' social and intellective behavior one year later. There was some indication that number of vocalizations is affected by the increased caretaking.

7 Studies of institutionalized infants in Tehran show that they develop motor deficiencies early in their lives from restricted experience and poor maternal care; this retardation is overcome when they move about on their own.

8 The statements of Freudian theory that infantile experience in toilet training, breast feeding, weaning, and modesty management should have profound effects on later personality development are only partially substantiated. There is good evidence that the type of mother-child relation is much more important than the management of these specific areas.

FURTHER READINGS

Ainsworth, M. D. The effects of maternal deprivation: A review of findings and controversy in the context of research strategy. Deprivation of maternal care: A reassessment of its effects. *Public Health Papers,* **14,** 1962, World Health Organization, Geneva.

REFERENCES

Butler, R. A. Discrimination learning by rhesus monkeys to visual exploration motivation. *Journal of comparative and physiological Psychology,* 1953, **46,** 95-98.

Chow, K. L., & Nissen, H. W. Interocular transfer of learning in visually naive and experienced infant chimpanzees. *Journal of comparative and physiological Psychology,* 1955, **48,** 229-237.

Dennis, W. Causes of retardation among institutional children: Iran. *Journal of genetic Psychology,* 1960, **96,** 47-59.

Dennis, W., & Najarian, P. Infant development under environmental handicap. *Psychological Monographs,* 1957, **71** (Whole Number 436).

Dollard, J., & Miller, N. E. *Personality and psychotherapy.* New York: McGraw-Hill, 1950.

Forgays, D. G., & Forgays, J. W. The nature of the effect of free-environmental experience in the rat. *Journal of comparative and physiological Psychology,* 1952, **45,** 322-328.

Forgus, R. H. The effect of early perceptual learning on the behavioral organization of adult rats. *Journal of comparative and physiological Psychology,* 1954, **47,** 331-336.

Forgus, R. H. Early visual and motor experience as determiners of complex maze-learning ability under rich and reduced stimulation. *Journal of comparative and physiological Psychology,* 1955, **48,** 215–220.

Forgus, R. H. Advantage of early over late perceptual experience in improving form discrimination. *Canadian Journal of Psychology,* 1956, **10,** 147–155.

Freud, S. *An outline of psychoanalysis.* New York: Norton, 1949.

Gibson, E. J., & Walk, R. D. The effect of prolonged exposure to visually presented patterns on learning to discriminate them. *Journal of comparative and physiological Psychology,* 1956, **49,** 239–242.

Graham, F. G., Matarazzo, R. G., & Caldwell, B. M. Behavioral differences between normal and traumatized newborns. *Psychological Monographs,* 1956, **70.**

Harlow, H. F. The nature of love. *American Psychologist,* 1958, **13,** 673–685.

Harlow, H. F., & Zimmerman, R. R. Affectional responses in the infant monkey. *Science,* 1959, **130,** 421–432.

Hebb, D. O. The innate organization of visual activity: II. Transfer of response in the discrimination of brightness and size by rats reared in total darkness. *Journal of comparative and physiological Psychology,* 1937, **24,** 277–299.

Hebb, D. O. Effects of early experience on problem-solving at maturity. *American Psychologist,* 1947, **2,** 306–307.

Hebb, D. O. *The organization of behavior,* New York: John Wiley & Sons, 1949.

Hebb, D. O., & Williams, K. A method of rating animal intelligence. *Journal of genetic Psychology,* 1946, **34,** 59–65.

Hess, E. H. Imprinting. *Science,* 1959, **130,** 130–141.

Hymovitch, B. The effects of experimental variations on problem solving in the rat. *Journal of comparative and physiological Psychology,* 1952, **45,** 313–321.

Page, E. I. Haptic perception: A consideration of one of the investigations of Piaget and Inhelder. *Education Review,* 1959, 115–124.

Piaget, J. *The psychology of intelligence.* (Trans. by M. Piercy and D. E. Berlyne) New York: Harcourt, Brace & World, 1950.

Pinneau, S. R. The infantile disorders of hospitalism and anaclitic depression. *Psychological Bulletin,* 1955, **52,** 429.

Reisen, A. H. The development of visual perception in man and chimpanzees. *Science,* 1947, **106,** 107–108.

Rheingold, H., & Bayley, N. The later effects of an experimental modification of mothering. *Child Development,* 1959, **30,** 363–372.

Ribble, M. A. *The rights of infants.* New York: Columbia University Press, 1943.

Schaffer, H. R., & Callender, W. M. Psychological effects of hospitalization in infancy. *Pediatrics,* 1959, **24,** 538.

Schaffer, H. R., & Emerson, P. E. Patterns of response to physical contact in early human development. *Journal of Child Psychology and Psychiatry,* 1964, **5,** 1–13.

Scott, J. P. Critical periods in the development of social behavior in puppies. *Psychosomatic Medicine,* 1958, **20,** 42–54.

Sears, R. R., Maccoby, E. E., & Levin, H. *Patterns of child rearing.* New York: Harper & Row, 1957.

Sewell, W. H., Mussen, P., & Harris, C. W. Relationships among child training practices. *American Sociological Review,* 1955, **20,** 137-148.

Spitz, R. A., & Wolf, K. M. Anaclitic depression. In *Psychoanalytic study of the child.* Vol. 2. New York: International Universities Press, 1946.

Thompson, W. R., & Heron, W. The effects of restricting early experience on the problem solving capacity of dogs. *Canadian Journal of Psychology,* 1954, **8,** 17-32.

Von Senden, M. *Space and sight.* (Trans. by Peter Heath) Glencoe, Ill.: The Free Press, 1960 (1932).

Walk, R. D. Visual and visual-motor experience: A replication. *Journal of comparative and physiological Psychology,* 1958, **51,** 785-787.

11 SENSORY-MOTOR INTEGRATION

> In my stars I am above thee; but be not afraid of greatness; some are born great, some achieve greatness and some have greatness thrust upon 'em.
>
> TWELFTH NIGHT

There is no well-articulated model of how the infant makes common sense of his inputs. However, there exist fascinating, and very tentative, notions of how he builds simple sensory-motor units into complex systems of behavior and thought. The notions draw heavily on Piaget's observations of his own three children. These observations represent theoretical landmarks concerning sensory integration, object perception, and intelligence.

Piaget believes the early sensory-motor activities of infants profoundly influence later cognitions.

Piaget [1950 (1947)] suggests that the child's early sensory-motor experiences have profound and probably irreversible effects on his later intellective and perceptual abilities. When Piaget observed his own children in their first few years of life, he assumed that an infant starts with a small set of innate reflexes from which come sensory-motor functions and then sophisticated cognitive operations. These early sensory-motor coordinations of the infant (the binding together of simple sensory inputs and response productions to reach an external goal) lead gradually to the development of symbolic processes. Once symbolic processes become available, the child can actively search, manipulate, and test his environment. This active searching stands in sharp contrast to his earlier passive registration of memory traces. The child is seen as an inquiring scientist; given certain simple tools, he builds a complex and accurate model of the world.

Piaget came to study perception and thought through an interest in how we know.

Piaget came to the study of children through an interest in genetic epistemology—the study of how we come to know our world. How children know has profound implications for the theory of knowledge. In his writings Piaget distinguishes structure, function, and content. Structure is the set of integrated connections among various ideas, abilities, or habits of the infant, which change over time and experience. In contrast, functions are unchanging processes present in the early makeup of the organism; they are responsible for modifications in structure. Examples of functions are assimilation and accommodation. The contents of the mind are the raw data from which we may infer structure and function. The content is irrelevant in itself and becomes important only when we interpret it within the theory.

The neonate has two basic functions—assimilation and accommodation.

Piaget believes that the newborn possesses two processes by which he organizes the world and maintains his mind in equilibrium (balance). The first process is "assimilation," by which the infant fits environmental events into already existing cognitive structures. Assimilation produces no new cognitive structure, no matter how inappropriate the classification. "Accommodation," on the other hand, forces the infant to develop new cognitive structure. Accommodation occurs when the repertory of the infant contains no category appropriate to handle a given sensory input. When the infant is presented new sensory input, he must either develop a new category for it (accommodation) or distort the sensory information to fit existing categories (assimilation).

Assimilation is the use of an existing operation; accommodation is the development of a new one.

To illustrate: A child familiar with flying animals will have available the category bird. The first time this child sees a flying squirrel, he is quite likely to call it a bird; he assimilates the flying squirrel into his already existing category of bird. He obviously distorts some properties of the object in making this classification. Later he may learn that it has no feathers or wings and is actually gliding. The child should then develop a new cognitive structure (through accommodation) in which to classify flying animals other than birds. Consider an example from a younger age. The first time an infant comes into contact with a ring, he will make a series of exploratory assimilations—he will stick it in his mouth, chew it, and suck on it. The ring is categorized under the class of things to be sucked and chewed. Later the infant will begin to develop new ways of responding to the ring—throwing and twirling, for instance. At first the young infant approaches every new object according to his category of "things to be mouthed." By a series of trials he gradually accommodates new systems of behavior to encompass the ring.

A schema is a structure, a class of similar actions, or a category underlying a set of operations.

A third major notion of Piaget's theoretical system is the "schema." A schema is (1) a cognitive structure, (2) a class of similar actions or thoughts, and (3) a category or underlying operation that subsumes a collection of similar action sequences. A schema may be all the means by which one can take a cookie from a jar, or it may be the class of dogs. Schemata are developed through experience. During a primary circular reaction the child repeats the same act over and over; the action seems to generate itself (for example, sucking). Later such simple events become linked and form a set of more complex operations (means) which the infant or child may use to order and understand his world. Piaget believes that schemata may be developed separately to a point and then combined to form a superordinate schema through a process he calls reciprocal assimilation. Piaget stresses the integration of sensory-motor abilities in the development of intellect. This does not mean that Piaget is interested in motor skills; he is primarily concerned with the coordination of information from the various senses into a common picture of the world. Sensory-motor means the coordination of visual and kinesthetic information.

Assimilation and accommodation form a balance which Piaget calls equilibrium.

In Piaget's "grand design" assimilation and accommodation are always interrelated. These two processes form an equilibrium (cognitive balance) in the developing organism. The functions of assimilation and accommodation do not change with the growth of the organism; only their relations change systematically with age and experience. Piaget

REMARKS: THEORY

Recent experiments suggest that our ability to understand changing perceptual information requires feedback from the muscles and motor components of our central nervous system (Held, 1965). If a subject wearing distorting lenses (glasses that displace or invert the visual field) walks freely, he gradually makes adjustments to the distortions; however, another subject who is wearing the lenses and is pushed around in a wheelchair does not adjust to the changes. Both see the same visual stimuli, but only the subject who actively walks in the environment receives feedback and can adjust.

Held has performed experiments to support these speculations about the requirement of active participation in sensory-motor adjustment. Kittens reared in the dark with their mother and littermates were given visual stimulation only in the apparatus shown in Figure 11.1 for three hours each day. One kitten could move more or less normally; his gross movements were transmitted by a system of gears and pulleys to a second kitten who was transported in a basket. Both kittens received essentially the same visual stimulation because the pattern on the walls and the center post of the apparatus were unvarying. Eight pairs of kittens were raised in this manner. After an average of 30 hours in the apparatus, the active member of each pair showed normal behavior in a series of visual tests. It blinked at an approaching object, put up its paws to avoid collision when carried toward a surface, and avoided the deep side of a visual cliff. The passive kittens, on the other hand, failed to show normal behavior; they did develop appropriate behavior, however, after being allowed to run freely for several days. The sensory feedback accompanying active movement seems necessary for normal development of sensory-motor coordination and perceptual functions.

FIGURE 11.1

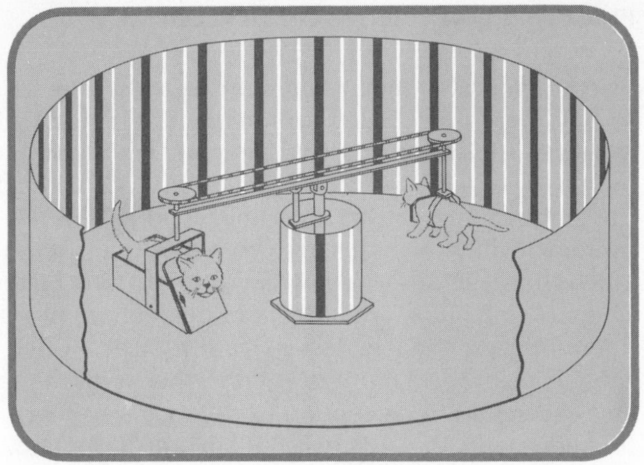

Apparatus for determining effect of active versus passive movements on spatial orientation. The gross movements of the "active" kitten, who moves about more or less freely are transmitted by means of the chain and bar to the "passive" kitten who is conveyed in a gondola. Both kittens are reared in the dark, except for their daily experience in the apparatus, and are subsequently tested for visual-motor coordination.

sees the basic development of the child shifting gradually from an early egocentric involvement in self, (where the process of assimilation is superordinate) to a final stage of equilibrium and objectivity (in which assimilation and accommodation are separate and complementary).

Sucking and looking are prewired schemata in the neonate.

Piaget feels that the infant is born with a simple set of prewired schemata, the most important of which is sucking. Almost all objects in the early life of the infant are approached through this schema (assimilated). As the infant develops, he organizes two classes—those things that are to be sucked and everything else in the world (first accommodation). The very young infant is indeed the original solipsist; he is aware neither of his unique perception of the world nor of alternative views.

Development is not a continuum, but a series of new rules and dimensions added to past abilities.

Piaget's stages of infant growth should not be viewed as a unidimensional progression toward maturity. Instead, they may be seen as the addition of new dimensions to the experience and ability of the child. Shifting from one stage to another does not represent simple growth along a continuum but rather an expansion of the dimensions of mind so the child can function in entirely different ways.

PIAGET'S CONCEPTION OF DEVELOPMENT

Piaget orders the sensory-motor period into six stages.

Piaget organizes the sensory-motor period into six stages. From birth to one month the infant is primarily concerned with the reflexive activities of sucking, crying, and sleeping. The second stage, which covers months one to four, treats the child's first acquired adaptation. Through the primary circular reaction the child begins to integrate sensory-motor activities. A third stage, from four to eight months of age, Piaget labels the stage of secondary circular reactions. Here we see the beginnings of intention and the development of procedures for making interesting experiences last. A fourth stage, which has age limits of roughly eight to 12 months, is concerned with the separation of means and ends and the perception of object permanence. The infant begins to understand the existence of an outside world, and he gradually separates goals and the means for obtaining those goals. The fifth stage, which covers roughly the period from 12 to 18 months, treats tertiary circular reactions. This stage is characterized by the discovery of new means through active experimentation and by an interest in novel and unfamiliar things. The child shows trial-and-error learning. The sixth stage of Piaget treats the child's invention of new means through mental combinations. This final stage of the sensory-motor period spans the growth of the child from 18 months to about two years. Now active thinking and problem-solving replace the more mechanistic trial-and-error learning of earlier ages. Following the sensory-motor period is another domain of intellective activity for the child, the period of concrete operations (see Chapter 6). This period starts around two years of age and ends at ten; it includes the development of symbolic functioning, logic, and language.

Piaget is interested not in the ages of stages but in their sequence.

The reader should not attribute a rigid schedule to the ages given for various stages. Piaget is perfectly willing to allow age variation. His only constraint is that the child must pass through all earlier stages before he can achieve a later one. This rule is inviolate in Piaget's system of cognitive development, while the particular age at which the infant achieves a stage is unimportant. Previous stages through which the infant has passed determine his present ability, because the present stage is constituted of those earlier abilities. For example, the child cannot throw a ball unless he has first learned to grasp it and to move his arm, both activities which occur in earlier stages. "Stage" is an ordinal notion.

Stage 1—Reflex activity: Birth to one month

Stage 1 is characterized by reflexive behavior.

A newborn's behavior is quite limited. He sucks, cries, swallows, thrashes about, and moves his eyes. Although he can orient, there is good evidence that he is unable to focus his vision once it is directed at a particular object (Haynes, White, & Held, 1965). This first stage is characterized by an absence of even the most elementary intellectual behavior. Although behavior is very primitive during this early stage, it is extremely important, since these early reflexive responses form the base of the child's subsequent intellective development. The neonate's simple reflexes show orderly changes following environmental contact. His reflexes constitute the primitive building blocks of all subsequent sensory-motor and intellectual development. They are the infant's first contact with the world.

Most activity during the first month is assimilation.

Within Piaget's theoretical system the infant's early reflexive behavior is assumed to contain the primitive outlines of functional invariants—the assimilation and accommodation processes which will lead to the gradual development of mature intellective capacities. Piaget believes that most activity during this first period requires assimilation. However, accommodation is present to some extent in two ways. First, reflexive sucking requires objects in order to continue its functioning; objects consolidate and strengthen the reflex. This strengthening is a first example of accommodation. Other limited evidence of accommodation exists. For example, Piaget wrote that his son Laurent showed some progress in distinguishing and localizing his mother's nipple as opposed to the surrounding skin area. It should be noted that the pattern of sucking itself (the form of the response) is not modified; rather, the stimuli that instigate the activity become more differentiated. Moreover, Piaget cites evidence that sucking seems to maintain itself; sucking induces further sucking, which strengthens and consolidates the reflexive schema. These changes constitute the limit of accommodation in this first stage, and their shortcomings (as accommodations) should be clearly understood. The sucking reflex is almost invariant; it is instigated and exercised as a rigid totality, knowing nothing of the object it uses. The infant at this stage exists in a state Piaget calls complete and utter egocentrism.

Stage 2—Primary circular reactions: One to four months

Stage 2 brings some modification of reflexes into primary circular reactions (chains).

During the second stage of acquired adaptations and primary circular reactions the neonatal reflexes are modified as a function of experience. During this period the first simple habits are acquired; the most elementary of sensory-motor acquisitions occur. Piaget (1952, p. 48) writes:

> At any given moment . . . the child's activity retains something external to itself, that is to say, it is transformed into a function of experience; in this respect there is acquired accommodation. For instance, when the

> child systematically sucks his thumb, no longer due to chance contacts but through coordination between hand and mouth, this may be called acquired accommodation. Neither the reflexes of the mouth nor of the hand can be provided such coordination by heredity (there is no instinct to suck the thumb!) and experience alone explains this formation.

These early changes are quite primitive; despite their advances they lack the goal-oriented characteristics of later stages. The circular reaction (series of repetitions of a sensory-motor sequence) is the essence of Stage 2. The initial response in the circular series is usually a new one for the child. Generally, the specific results were not anticipated nor intended before the response was made. The principal feature of the reaction, and the one that gives it its name, concerns what follows the first response. After the initial event, the infant repeats the happy accident over and over. Through these repetitions, the "accidental" response sequence becomes consolidated into a schema. This is similar to what happens following reinforcement, except that in Piaget's model reinforcement is provided by the child interacting with his environment. There is no need for external agents to administer reinforcement.

There are three types of circular reactions—primary (chains), secondary (relations between infant and world), and tertiary (new combinations of means and goals).

Piaget lists three types of circular reactions—primary, secondary, and tertiary. They are classified on the basis of what the response accomplishes and how it is repeated. Primary circular reactions are centered on and around the infant's own body (for example, sucking) instead of being directed toward manipulation of surroundings. Secondary circular reactions concern the relation between the child's body and outside events (pushing). Secondary circular reactions develop new goals for existing motor responses. Finally, tertiary circular reactions combine existing reactions and goals in new ways (using a stick to reach something). Observation of the infant's own body is a landmark of Stage 2 (see Figure 11.2). When he begins to watch his hand, the infant is then concerned with the integration of input from different sensory modalities. Things heard become things to look at; things seen become things to grasp; things grasped become things to suck. Intersensory integration has begun.

Stage 3—Secondary circular reactions: Four to eight months

Stage 3 is characterized by a shift from stimulus-response to intention-response action.

Of these Piaget says (1952, pp. 185–186):

> The facts hitherto studied constitute essentially phenomena of reproductive assimilation; through repetition rediscovering a fortuitous result. Before seeing how this behavior is extended into generalizing assimilation and thus gives rise to "procedures to make interesting sights last,"

FIGURE 11.2

Hand watching by a Stage 2 infant (age about three months).

> let us once more emphasize a group of facts, which no longer constitute circular reactions in themselves but which are derived from secondary reactions, in the capacity of recognitory assimilations. What happens, in effect, is that the child, confronted by objects or sights which habitually set in motion his secondary circular reactions, limits himself to outlining the customary movements instead of actually performing them. Everything takes place as though the child were satisfied to recognize these objects or sights and to make a note of this recognition, but could not recognize them except by working, rather than thinking, the schema helpful to recognition. Now this schema is none other than that of the secondary circular reaction corresponding to the object in question.

The child now distinguishes goals and response sequences, and he may be able to reverse the direction of an act. He goes from stimulus-response instigation of activities to intention-response, and he is beginning to develop symbolic representations. Instead of being governed by his past (by passive repetition of acts) his behavior is directed toward new goals. During Stage 3, behavior is controlled by the results it produces.

Secondary circular reactions are movements of the body in relation to external events.

Piaget gives examples of secondary circular reactions observed in his own children. Lucianne (at four months) was lying in her bassinet. Piaget hung a doll over her feet. Immediately the infant started shaking back and forth. During the shaking her feet reached the doll and gave it a violent movement. Lucianne surveyed this with delight. She looked

FIGURE 11.3

A Stage 3 infant (age about six months) attending to an external object.

at her motionless foot for a second, then kicked again. There was no visual control of the foot. The movements were the same when Lucianne only looked at the doll or when the doll was placed over her head.

Secondary circular reactions are primitive trial-and-error problem-solving.

Two things are important about secondary circular reactions. First, the infant's developing attention to external events (see Figure 11.3) gives rise to the sensory-motor analogues of classes. The rattle is seen as something to shake, the doll as something to push and move. In addition, the secondary circular reaction is fundamental to intellectual development throughout life. Piaget suggests that adults, when they face a new situation, resort again to secondary circular reactions. They push this and pull that, repeating the acts that bring interesting consequences. However, there are several differences between the infant and adult. The secondary circular reaction represents the limit of the infant's capabilities, whereas the adult possesses many exploratory and experimental techniques. Moreover, the adult is systematically trying to make new adaptations, but the Stage 3 infant is not.

Secondary circular reactions mark the beginning of intentionality—the deliberate pursuit of a goal.

Secondary circular reactions are of fundamental importance for Piaget's theory, since they represent a landmark in the development of intentional thinking. For Piaget, intentionality (the deliberate pursuit of a goal by means of instrumental behavior subordinate to that goal) is the distinguishing characteristic of intelligence. However, we must know how to measure it. The assessment of intentionality is not difficult when we look at a newborn or a two-year-old child. However, sensible standards are needed to help us decide whether a particular act of a six- or eight-month-old infant is intentional. Piaget suggests that we use several interrelated criteria to establish the intentionality of an act. (1) To what extent is an act oriented toward a goal rather than being sheer exercise for exercise's sake? Only acts concerned with objects and their interrelations contain a distinction between means and ends and thus are eligible for the label "intention." (2) The complexity of the intermediate links between the stimulus for an action and action itself may be a second criterion, with a longer chain considered more intentional. (3) Finally, an intentional act would show adaptation to a new situation rather than simple repetition of a habitual response.

Stage 4—The coordination of secondary schemata and their application to new situations: Eight to 12 months

Stage 4 is characterized by the coordination of schema developed during Stage 3.

Near the end of the first year the infant shows several new intellectual accomplishments. Secondary circular reactions developed in Stage 3 are coordinated with each other to form new behavior patterns. These new patterns show unquestionable intentionality (see Figure 11.4A). Simultaneously the infant begins to use signs to anticipate events. As we have seen, the infant's early circular reactions show only simple means-end differentiation and a primitive intentionality. This may be illustrated by his attempt to bring a rod through the bars of his playpen. If the rod is long, the child must learn first to rotate it so he will not pull the rod against the vertical bars. With successive trials his actions gradually change to a pattern which succeeds smoothly. During Stage 4, these previously independent response systems are coördinated into a superordinate schema; the original schemata may serve as means or goals. Through this coordination of schemata, goals are established and means are called into play to reach these goals (Figure 11.4A). For example, the infant will now push aside an object to reach another desired object (Figure 11.4B).

A good example of Stage 4 behavior involves removal of a barrier to gain an object; infants of 8–12 months will persist as long as they can see the goal.

The development of the pattern of moving an obstruction to reach a goal is complex. At first the child ignores his objective if an obstacle intervenes, or he may inaugurate irrelevant habits in magical attempts to reach the goal. Later, Piaget observed in his own children, the infant hits at the intervening object. From this striking, a successful act of pushing the object aside develops. During Stage 4, part of the infant's goal must be visible behind the obstacle before he will seek it. In subsequent stages (12 to 18 months), this restriction disappears. The child develops a symbolic ability; he will then pursue a goal that is out of sight.

FIGURE 11.4

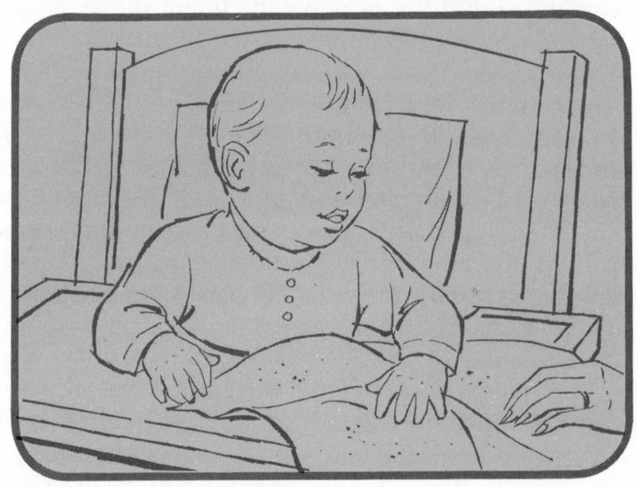

(*Top*) Illustration of a secondary circular reaction in a Stage 4 infant (about 10 months). The earlier behaviors are being coordinated into a new pattern which shows intentionality. (*Bottom*) Child moving an object aside to reach a desired goal. This also shows intentionality.

Stage 5—Tertiary circular reactions; the discovery of new means by active experimentation: Twelve to 18 months

The tertiary circular reaction produces new combinations of means and ends by active experimentation.

During the stage of tertiary circular reactions, the infant approaches a new object with old familiar response patterns. He then develops variations of these older patterns to fit the new object. Dropping or letting something go becomes throwing by a series of variations in the

FIGURE 11.5

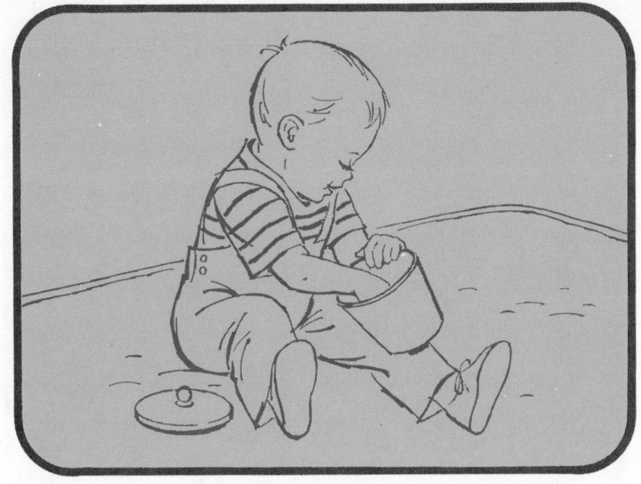

A Stage 5 infant (about 14 months) finding a hidden object.

original act. The infant observes his throwing with interest; he develops new behaviors through active experimentation.

The 12–18-month-old infant possesses object permanence—when an object disappears from view, he continues to search for it.

Another basic characteristic of Stage 5 is the permanence of objects for the infant. By this time the child will follow the movements of a hidden object. When an object disappears, he does not go back to the original spot where he first found it (as he would have done in earlier stages) but extrapolates to where the object is likely to be next (see Figure 11.5). The child during Stages 4 and 5 experiments to see what will happen. The difference is that the Stage 5 child's groping is a function of the goal itself. The infant is now an active, deliberate experimenter, not just a random explorer.

Stage 6—Invention of new means through mental combinations: 18 months to two years

The Stage 6 child can develop new means through thought.

For the first time we see elements of what may later be called productive thinking. This major new pattern of behavior may be illustrated as follows. The infant has a goal but no habitual response to serve as a means for obtaining his goal. The beginning of our sequence is like a behavior from Stage 5. No available means exist, so one must be discovered. Now, however, instead of fumbling randomly for a solution through a series of trial-and-error actions, the child can produce new means through mental combinations.

As an example, consider the infant in a playpen with a stick. Piaget's first child, Lucianne, learned to get the stick out by trial-and-error groping. However, Laurent, at 18½ months, learned the same

FIGURE 11.6

A Stage 6 infant (20 months) inventing new means by thinking.

trick by mental combinations. He was in a playpen and wanted a duck, which was outside his reach. A stick was between him and the duck. He looked at the situation, immediately grasped the stick and directed it to the duck, gradually pulling the toy within his reach. This phenomenon is insight (see Figure 11.6).

Children between 18 months and 2 years can follow objects through invisible spatial transformations and predict their path.

Another important characteristic of the sixth stage concerns the child's ability to follow objects through unseen spatial displacements (see Figure 11.7). For example, suppose an object is put in a box and the box is transported behind a screen. There the experimenter may take the object from the box and then return the empty box to the child. If the infant has reached Stage 6 in his development, he immediately goes to the place where the box was last seen to retrieve the desired object. He will not sit and look helplessly into the empty box as he would have done during previous stages of development.

Development includes the incorporation of earlier stages and structures into later schemata.

In summary, Piaget's landmarks of transition show an essential incorporation of earlier stages into later ones. This process of incorporation produces the hierarchical nature of later intelligence. The dominant feature of the sensory-motor period is the integration of various sensory inputs into a coherent picture of the world. During this period the infant develops object concepts, an idea of time and space, play, imitation, and a notion of causality. These all represent the interaction of the child with his immediate physical environment.

During the next period (from two to about ten years of age), the child develops intellectual abilities. The period of concrete operations covers the development of language, logic, conservation, and transitivity, relations which have no immediate perceptual referent. The sensory-motor infant is bound by his immediate sensory input, while the child of concrete operations may symbolically represent and manipulate his world.

Piaget believes development comes from organism-environment interaction.

Piaget pictures development as entirely dependent on an organism-environment interaction. This view is in marked contrast to the theories of G. S. Hall (1883), who saw all development as the result of intrinsic factors laid down in the genes. This predeterminist was interested in describing age-characteristic behaviors. Piaget tries to describe the process whereby the organism's interaction with circumstances forces developmental change. A third position—that of extreme environmentalism—is represented by the writings of J. B. Watson (1919). This issue is covered in detail in Chapter 1.

THE SENSORY-MOTOR PERIOD: SPECIAL DEVELOPMENTS

There are six areas of interest in the sensory-motor period: (1) play,

Six special developments occur during the early stages of the infant's development; as we outline these areas, keep in mind that achievement in one area is completely confounded with and dependent on develop-

FIGURE 11.7

A Stage 6 infant (about 2 years) finding a hidden object after it was placed in a box behind a pillow

(2) space, (3) time, (4) imitation, (5) causality, and (6) object conception.

ments in the other five. This interdependency of the areas will be presented within the six stages of development of the sensory-motor period. The six special developments are (1) play, (2) the conception of space, (3) the conception of time, (4) imitation, (5) causality, and (6) the object concept.

Play

The early stages of play are difficult to differentiate.

As with all the special developments, the early stages are difficult to differentiate with any confidence, and it is only later, when more well-formed characteristics appear, that we can classify them in detail. Piaget describes assimilation for assimilation's sake as the primary characteristic of play behavior.

During Stage 1 the infant engages in empty sucking.

Stage 1 All that can be said about play in Stage 1 is that the child sometimes indulges in empty sucking movements without either the breast or bottle present, he looks around when there are stimuli in the environment, he kicks and moves his arms.

Primary circular reactions are sometimes pursued for pleasure instead of practice.

Stage 2 There is little behavior that we can say unambiguously represents play rather than adaptation. We do see the pattern of primary circular reactions pursued first for stability and then for sheer pleasure. As an example, Laurent at two months threw his head back to look at familiar things from a new position. After a few repetitions this movement was performed with increasing enjoyment and ever-decreasing interest in the actual external result. He just brought his head back to an upright position and jerked it time and again, laughing loudly.

At about four months the infant acts for pleasure rather than coordination.

Stage 3 The differentiation between play and serious learning becomes much easier by Stage 3. At about three months Laurent studied the phenomenon of swinging an object over the top of his crib, without smiling. He had the appearance of intense interest, as though he were studying it. However, at about four months he indulged in this activity with a great show of joy. In other words, his action was no longer accompanied by accommodation; it was no longer an effort at comprehension. There was merely assimilation to the activity itself—use of the phenomenon for its own pleasure. This is play.

During Stage 4 the infant may abandon a goal to play with the barrier.

Stage 4 The differentiation of play from learning and adaptation or accommodation becomes simple by Stage 4. Now we see the child abandon a goal in favor of playing with a particular behavior (which might reach that goal). For example, at seven months infants remove an object to gain an objective. Then they begin to enjoy this kind of exercise. When Piaget put his hand or a piece of cardboard between the child and the toy, the child reached the stage of momentarily forgetting the toy and pushing aside the obstacle, bursting into laughter (again a transfer from accommodation to assimilation). Once accommodation is achieved, actions are used for their own pleasure.

During Stages 5 and 6 the infant turns almost all new behavior into play.

We now begin to see a new adaptation turned into a ritual of play as soon as it is discovered. The child has developed a set to play with each new behavior. Finally, as the child grows older, we see the emergence of symbolization. The child is now capable of make-believe. Instead of requiring stimuli that will elicit a schema and then using the behavior that the stimuli call out for play, the child in Stage 6 can re-enact an existing schema without external stimulation. He can also treat acts as symbols of other acts. For example, Piaget's 18-month-old said "soap," and she rubbed her hands together and pretended to wash them without water. The following day she pretended that she was eating various things (a piece of paper), saying "very nice."

Piaget describes further stages in his book Play, dreams, and imitation in childhood.

Piaget, of course, has not stopped his treatment of dreams, play, imitation, and related phenomena with Stage 6 in the sensory-motor period. He developed his notions through the stage of preoperational thought. We do not have space to cover these later parts; the interested student may go to *Play, dreams, and imitation in childhood* (1951) for more detail.

The conception of space

Concepts of space are related to groupings.

The infant's conception of space is intimately connected with his conceptions of groupings. Since this topic has been treated in some detail in Chapter 6, only a brief summary of the sensory-motor period is included here.

Space begins as several spaces; only later does the infant know that things seen are things felt.

For the infant, space is initially a collection of separate spaces, each entirely centered on its own activity with few interconnections. However, during later stages (near the end of the sensory-motor period), the infant generates a single space within which all objects (including himself) are contained and interrelated. The infant's development of a conception of space seems to involve the externalization of things as different from the self. During Stages 1 and 2 the infant's conceptions of space are many. A space around the mouth, a visual space, an auditory space, and a tactual space all exist separately rather than as one common reference onto which all things may be mapped. During Stage 3, with the growing coordination between different schemata (particularly between vision and prehension) the infant collects his many spaces into one.

During Stages 4 and 5 the infant begins to integrate information from all his senses; things touched become things to see.

The integration of sensory spaces begins with the simultaneous visual search for and manipulation of objects. Beginning in Stage 4 and continuing on into Stage 5, the infant discovers interrelations among objects. At first he considers only the interrelations among sensations and movements, but later he begins to discover the interrelations among objects of the world as well. Finally, the infant relates the different spaces in which the object appears and the different sense modalities from which he receives information about an object into a single system. The Stage 6 infant develops a unique new ability. He can keep a running tabulation of his own movements in space, representing his own displacements in relation to other bodies. (This is no easy feat—as our space teams discovered.) He is able to keep track of the displacements of other objects. As an example, consider an 18-month-old who throws a ball under the sofa. Instead of bending over and searching for it at once on the floor at the base of the sofa (as a younger infant would have done), she looks at it, realizes that the ball must have crossed under the sofa, and sets out to go behind it to retrieve her ball; good example of a complex system of tabulation and spatial representation at work.

The conception of time

The infant's conception of time is little understood.

In the writings of Piaget, few pages are devoted to the special development of time, probably for the good reason that information is exceptionally difficult to find. He draws heavily on analogies to the development of other concepts, such as causality and object. The area of time perception seems particularly ambiguous and shaky. However, Piaget seems willing to tolerate this ambiguity to gain some simple information about how temporal phenomena are understood by the infant.

During Stages 1 and 2 we believe sequences of perceptions occur.

Stages 1 and 2 All that we can say about the Stage 1 and 2 infant's conceptions of time is that sequences of perceptions do occur. These are the raw material from which he might develop a notion of ordering. They are available, but this does not necessarily imply that the infant in fact perceives events as sequential. Idle speculation seems pointless.

During later stages the ordered sequence of action and result occurs.

Stage 3 The closest thing to a pre-post (before and after) sequence at Stage 3 probably comes in the form of an action-result or means-end relation. The seriation of events is understood by the Stage 3 infant only if his own action intervenes in the sequence.

By Stage 4 the infant knows that goals follow means.

Stage 4 During Stage 4 the infant begins to relate an object that occurs first in time to another object or behavior that occurs second. The first object is conceived as the means and the second as the goal. This is a clear instance of sequentiality.

The Stage 5 infant is able to follow sequences of movements.

Stage 5 During Stage 5 the seriation of events independent of the infant's own behavior becomes much stronger. For example, when an object is hidden under *A* and then moved to *B,* the infant can follow its path. He is able to seriate events without the necessity of acting.

By Stage 6 Piaget believes the infant has some concep-

Stage 6 In Stage 6 the child is able to represent events outside his immediate perception and to recall past events which did not occur in his own behavior. Piaget believes that during Stage 6 the child is *tion of time (independent of his own experiences).*

finally beginning to conceptualize time as a generalized medium, much like space, and in this medium of time self and objects are located in relation to one another.

Imitation

Imitation is accommodation; play is assimilation.

This is the opposite of play (almost all imitation is accommodation). During Stage 1 the child is socially independent; there are equivocal examples of an infant being stimulated to cry by hearing the crying of others, but for the most part he seems sensitive only to his own internal states.

Stage 2 infants show little imitation.

During Stage 2 we see weak isolated instances in which the child may perform a particular behavioral pattern after seeing another person enact that pattern. For example, Piaget's son Laurent imitated him when Piaget uttered a sound. He sometimes smiled with his mouth open and would produce the sound that Piaget had made. During this stage the infant cannot imitate sounds that are new to him. He must first produce the sound, have a model reproduce it, and then he can imitate the model's sound. However, if the model presents a new sound, the Stage 2 infant will not imitate it.

The Stage 3 infant systematically imitates sounds and movements.

At Stage 3 we see more progress toward the development of imitation. The infant will systematically imitate sounds and movements made by a model. Piaget describes an experiment he performed on his four-month-old daughter in which he first put his hand in front of her, opening and closing it slowly. He noted that the child did essentially the same thing. She opened and closed her hand whenever her father moved his. To test whether the infant was merely trying to grasp his hand, Piaget put a carrot in front of the child. Instead of merely opening and closing her hand (as she had done with Piaget's hand in front of her), she immediately reached out and grasped the carrot.

By Stage 4 the infant develops a generalized ability to imitate.

During Stage 4 the infant learns to coordinate visual, auditory, tactual, and kinesthetic information. The infant can now imitate new behaviors. Imitation begins to separate itself from the general learning repertory and become a special tool for the acquisition of new acts.

Stage 5 infants imitate with purpose.

During Stage 5 the infant's imitative behavior becomes much more frequent and purposeful. For example, Piaget swung a watch on a chain in front of his one-year-old daughter. Piaget then put down the watch. The child picked it up, but she held the chain too close to the watch to allow it to swing properly. She immediately put the watch down and picked up the chain again, this time taking care to increase the distance between her hand and the watch to the point where it would actually swing, a clear case of imitation.

Stage 6 infants symbolically imi-

During Stage 6 the child has developed primitive symbolic representation. He is now able to imitate behaviors without having either *tate; they copy a model who is not there; this may be the development of conscience.*

to perform them first or to see them performed. Second, the child in Stage 6 begins to imitate the actions of objects as well as of persons. Furthermore, the Stage 6 child begins to show something of great significance—deferred imitation. The child is now able to imitate an absent model. This may be how he develops a conscience; the ability to imitate a model who is not present suggests that the infant has an internal representation of the model, a notion quite analogous to conscience.

Conceptions of causality

Causality is undifferentiated during early stages.

During the first three stages causality is an undifferentiated phenomenalism for the infant—a phenomenalism in the sense that temporal (but not necessarily spatial) continuity between any two events means that one caused the other. During these early stages the infant believes his own actions are the actual causes of events. He believes objects move because he puts his hand on them. For example, one of Piaget's children placed his hand on his father's to make his father's hand close.

By Stage 4 the infant believes all events are caused by his own efforts.

Even by Stage 4 the infant still believes that external sources can be causal only when his own actions intervene (for example, when he pushes the adult's hand to move an object). During Stage 5, when the infant develops new means through active experimentation, he seems to acquire a simple objectification of causality. He will place an object in a position from which it will set itself in motion. For example, he may put a ball on a slight incline and sit back to watch it roll. During this stage people and objects are seen as causal centers, completely independent of the child's own action. The child's world has become less egocentric.

The Stage 6 infant can predict the cause given an effect.

During Stage 6 not only does the child understand something of our conception of causality but he can (by representation of cause-effect relations) infer a cause from its effect. He can also predict an effect, given its cause. For example, Laurent was seated in his carriage and Piaget was in a chair beside him. While reading, and without paying any attention to the child, Piaget put his foot on the carriage and moved it slowly. Without hesitation, Laurent leaned over the edge of the carriage and looked in the direction of the wheels. Seeing that his father had his foot on it, he smiled.

The object concept

The object is an entity that moves in a common space and has unity.

To understand the development of "Object," we must first appreciate Piaget's conception of a mature object concept. For him a mature conception of objects demands that a group of sensations be seen as an entity in their own right. The entity must exist and move in a space common to it and the person. Second, the existence of the object must be construed as separate from and independent of activities the person applies to the object. When the infant achieves an object concept, he must know that the object has an existence of its own, even when he is no longer acting upon it or looking at it.

During the first two stages of sensory-motor development, Piaget believes, the infant has no conception of an object. At most, the infant tries to prolong a pleasing image by continuing to look, listen, or grasp.

By Stage 3 the infant is beginning to develop object permanence.

During Stage 3 the infant first tries to maintain or recapture sensory-motor relations with objects. With his growing ability to assimilate (predict) movement, the child begins to anticipate where an object will be next. For example, an infant in Stage 3 who sees an object drop to the floor will lean over to look for it, whereas an infant at an earlier period would stare at the place where it had been. By Stage 3, the infant can also free his own perception of the object from an obstruction (by removing a blanket resting on his own face). However, he is unable to free an object from this same sort of obstruction. If the blanket is put over the object, the infant will not remove it. He wants to see, and thus he will remove any obstruction to seeing. But this same infant apparently has no permanent conception of an object as something that exists when he cannot see it (as something to search after).

The Stage 4 infant searches actively for hidden objects.

During Stage 4 the infant has developed a good object concept. He begins to search actively for hidden objects, with one interesting restriction. He will search behind a screen for a hidden object only if he has been reaching for the object at the moment it is hidden. Only later will the infant search for an object, even if he was only looking at it when it was hidden. During Stage 5 the infant overcomes his dependence on motor searching and external stimulus supports. He learns to search in a place where the object was last seen. However, if the object's journey to a hiding place is not perceptible to the Stage 5 infant, he will fail to find it. It is only during Stage 6, with his mastery of invisible displacements, that the infant is capable of representational and symbolic adaptations. He is now able to follow an invisible path of the object through the environment, and he can find an object he did not see hidden.

Our conceptions of sensory-motor development are primitive.

These summary remarks about our conceptions of the sensory-motor infant should leave the reader with two notions. First, we know almost nothing about how the child comes to develop object perceptions, conceptions of time and space, or other cognitive abilities. Second, these observations of Piaget represent a very promising body of insights and intuitions on intellective growth. The crudeness of the models reflects the state of the field and not the ability of the theorist. Piaget is an extremely capable and articulate proponent of a position—when his observations suggest that one class of models is much more appropriate than others to describe a set of data. Without exception, he is interested in applying techniques and models that are appropriate to our state of knowledge about an area. He is firmly convinced that too quick an application of sophisticated methods will lead to rigid thinking and unproductive model building. His advice is to suit the tool to the task and not to use whatever tools are at hand, however powerful they may seem.

SUMMARY

1 Piaget came to the study of children through an interest in genetic epistemology—the study of how we come to know our world. He is interested in how children build a model of reality.

2 The newborn is given, genetically, two basic functions: Assimilation and accommodation. Assimilation is the performance of already learned acts and behavior sequences, while accommodation is the development of new acts and ideas.

3 The sequencing of stages in the development of the child is invariant; however, the particular ages of the stages are not critical. Only the ordering is assumed to remain constant.

4 Stage 1 is characterized by reflex activity; it lasts from birth through the first month of life.

5 The primary circular reaction—chaining of a sequence of responses that are genetically determined—dominates Stage 2. This period in the development of the infant begins at one month and is finished by the age of four months.

6 Stage 3, the secondary circular reaction—the development of differentiated means and goals—develops between four and eight months of age.

7 The coordination of schemata into new combinations occupies the child during Stage 4, from eight months to one year of age.

8 The tertiary circular reaction—the discovery of new means through active experimentation—occupies the child during Stage 5, from 12 to 18 months of age.

9 Stage 6 is characterized by insight—the development of new means through mental combinations. The child is about two years of age when this sensory-motor period is finished and he develops into the preoperational period (see Chapter 6).

FURTHER READINGS

Baldwin, A. *Theories of child development.* New York: Wiley, 1967.

Flavell, J. *The developmental psychology of Jean Piaget.* Princeton, N.J.: Van Nostrand, 1963.

REFERENCES

Hall, G. S. The contents of children's minds. *Princeton Review,* 1883, 249–272.

Haynes, H., White, B. L., & Held, R. Visual accommodation in human infants. *Science,* 1965, **148,** 528–530.

Held, R. Plasticity in sensory-motor systems. *Scientific American,* 1965, **213,** 84–97.

Piaget, J. *The psychology of intelligence.* London: Routledge & Kegan Paul, 1950 [1947].

Piaget, J. *Play, dreams, and imitation in childhood.* New York: Norton, 1951.

Piaget, J. *The origins of intelligence in children.* New York: International Universities Press, 1952.

Watson, J. B. *Psychology from the standpoint of a behaviorist.* Philadelphia: Lippincott, 1919.

12 PARENT-CHILD RELATIONS

It is a wise father that knows his own child.
MERCHANT OF VENICE

There is little doubt that parental control directly affects the child's personal development. However, there is considerable uncertainty about how this influence occurs; we know little about which parental controls cause various children's personalities. Once we understand how parents influence their children, we can suggest how people should or should not raise their children (depending on the type of child they want). Broad statements about good or bad parental relations ignore both the large variation in parental values and the genetic predispositions that occur among children. Some parents want aggressive and self-sufficient children; we should not tell these particular families to be warm and controlling. Aggressive children can be produced most easily by giving them a model of aggression, some autonomy, and a good deal of frustration. Again, if parents want quiet, modest children, then they should train them with little love, infinite control, and high moral standards.

Parent-child relations interact with genetic predispositions.

The point in understanding parent-child interactions is to allow predictions about what types of children different parental procedures produce. Yet two factors must be recalled: (1) children come into the world with strong genetic predispositions and (2) parents interact with their child; children are not simply the innocent victims of adults. Parents who find their child calm, loving, and happy can afford to be democratic, warm, and charming in their discipline. However, parents who find their infant hostile, irritable, and difficult to manage may try many different tactics to control him.

Interest in parent-child relations

Literally hundreds of studies have measured parental attitudes toward their children; however, the patterns derived from these studies *comes from learning theory and Freud.*

are often contradictory and inconclusive. Interest in parent-child relations comes from a focus on early learning processes, the interest of psychoanalytic theory in early development, and the high incidence of atypical disciplinary practices in clinical populations.

Parents of delinquents and disturbed children use atypical child-training procedures.

Early studies showed that parents of delinquents do not interact with their children the way more typical parents do. Longitudinal studies were introduced in several developmental centers across the country, notably at the University of California, Berkeley, and at the Fels Research Institute. Relations between child behavior and parental discipline were explored in detail. Following the introduction of better computing facilities, more representative samples of parent and child interaction appeared. Many variables contribute to the complex interaction of parent and child.

DIMENSIONS OF PARENT-CHILD INTERACTION

Three variables describe parent-child relations—love, control, and consistency.

Three main variables emerge as major factors of parent-child interaction. The most important is whether parents use love-oriented or physical discipline to control the child. A second significant variable for understanding parent-child interaction is the strictness or permissiveness of parental control. Finally, the parents' consistency in applying discipline affects children's personality development.

Schaefer proposed that the dimensions of autonomy-control and hostility-love describe how parents treat their children.

Schaefer (1961) summarized several studies which showed that two dimensions account for much of the consistent effects of parents on their children. He proposed a model to account for the findings (Figure 12.1). It suggests that autonomy versus control and hostility versus love are the bipolar (opposite-valued) dimensions of parent-child interaction. For example, parents who control cannot give their child autonomy; the two procedures are incompatible. The same is true, of course, for love and hostility. Notice the several points plotted around the perimeter of Figure 12.1. For example, the combination of love and autonomy produces an atmosphere that is free, democratic, and accepting of the child. These characteristics of the parent are copied by the child (through imitation) and become part of his personality. The other combinations produce different atmospheres in the home; for example, hostility and autonomy produce a rejecting, indifferent, detached atmosphere. This milieu is likely to produce character disorders; the child tends to become delinquent.

Love versus hostility

The loving parent is warm, accepting

The warm, accepting, affectionate mother is approving, understanding, child-centered, uses frequent examples and explanations in her disci-

FIGURE 12.1

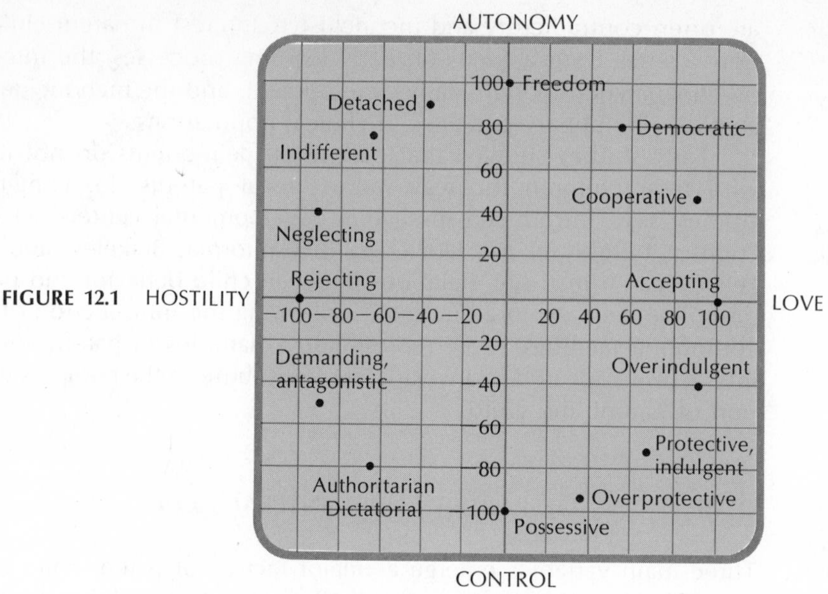

A two-dimensional model of parent-child interactions as proposed by Schaefer. The four combinations of love-hostility and autonomy-control produce very different children. The types of parental attitudes characteristic of the various combinations are outlined along the perimeter of the figure. (From Schaefer, 1961.)

and affectionate; the hostile parent is rejecting, critical, and cold.

pline, gives a positive response to dependency, uses reason in discipline, is low in the use of physical punishment, and does not criticize her husband. On the other hand, a hostile mother is rejecting, cold, disapproving, and is centered around herself; she uses negative reinforcement, little or no reasoning, physical punishment, and is critical of her husband.

Control versus autonomy

The controlling parent is restrictive; the autonomous parent places few restrictions on a child's behavior.

The second set of opposing categories is independent of the first. The controlling parent places many restrictions on the child and strictly enforces them. The child who is controlled displays excessive modesty, has good table manners, is neat and orderly, makes little noise, and is not aggressive toward siblings, parents, or peers. The more permissive parent places few restrictions on the child and does not enforce even these modest demands. The child of permissive parents shows little modesty behavior or table manners, no orderliness, and is quite aggressive toward siblings and parents.

Implications of the categories

We want to understand the effects of various combinations of these two bipolar dimensions.

Some categories of parent-child relations are independent; restrictive or permissive parents are neither predominantly hostile nor warm but can show various degrees of warmth or hostility. We want to understand the effects of various combinations of love-hostility and control-autonomy on other behaviors of the young child. There are four possible combinations of these bipolar factors: love-control, love-autonomy, hostile-control, and hostile-autonomy. Discussion of various parent-child relations and their consequences in a systematic manner follows (see Table 12.1 for a summary of the four factors).

Control and love

Parents who control and love their children produce neat, polite, obedient little boys and girls.

Parents who control and love their children produce submissive, dependent, polite, neat, and obedient little moppets who are seen and not heard. These children are considered ideal by parents, teachers, and little girls. However, boys tend to see these children as sissies. Both boys and girls of controlling and loving parents display little outward aggression; if they are boys, they insist on following the rules themselves, and they want others to follow them, too. Children of loving and controlling parents are dependent, unfriendly to others, show little creativity, and comply with the wishes and demands of almost everybody. They are the overprotected little boys and girls we see hovering around their mothers' skirts long after other children have gone to explore the world. They are anxious when outside their mothers' control; they tend to believe they cannot survive without her help (and the mother encourages this notion).

TABLE 12.1 Children's Personality Traits Resulting from Love versus Hostility and Control versus Autonomy in the Home

	Control	*Autonomy*
Love	Submissive, dependent, polite, neat, obedient Minimal aggression Dependent, not friendly, not creative Maximal compliance Maximum rule enforcement, boys	Active, socially outgoing, creative, successfully aggressive Minimal rule enforcement, boys Facilitates adult role-taking Minimal self-aggression, boys Independent, friendly, creative, low projective hostility
Hostility	"Neurotic" problems More quarreling and shyness with peers Socially withdrawn Low in adult role-taking Maximal self-aggression, boys	Delinquency Noncompliance Maximal aggression

Hostility and control

Parents who control and are hostile produce neurotic children.

This combination of parental characteristics produces clinical problems; children of these parents become neurotic. The children are socially withdrawn, do not take adult roles well, show little aggression toward others, and much aggression toward themselves. Children raised in hostility and under the control of dominant parents tend to quarrel with and withdraw from their peers; their self-image is low and they feel guilty most of the time. These children are seen as quiet, shy, ideal children by parents and teachers. However, while children raised with love and control feel they are worthwhile (but not very capable) children raised in an atmosphere of hostility and control feel worthless (but tend to be capable). They become depressed easily and withdraw from frustrating situations instead of finding solutions to their problems. These children experience great difficulties adjusting to the adult world. However, they are not viewed as "problem" children and are frequently overlooked by teachers and others. Neurotic children may function quite well in the school situation; however, they do it at a cost in happiness and well-being which can only lead to serious adjustment problems later in their lives.

Autonomy and love

Parents who practice autonomy and love produce open, affectionate, and happily aggressive children.

The child raised by "ideal" parents—those who fill their home with love and permissiveness—becomes socially outgoing, creative, active, and successfully aggressive. Boys raised in this environment feel little need to enforce rules; they can easily take the role of adults in their environment (they imitate significant others) and incorporate adult characteristics into their own personality structure. Boys raised in a milieu of love and permissiveness develop minimal self-aggression; they become independent, friendly, creative, and interesting little creatures. This is the "ideal" child most people want to raise; he is noisy, interested in others, and well adjusted enough to tolerate frustration. He stays in a situation long enough to solve it. He is successfully aggressive, but not hostile toward himself or others; he is a happy child with open feelings. He is also rare!

Hostility and autonomy

Parents who practice autonomy and hostility produce delinquents.

Family atmospheres that combine hostility and lack of control produce children who receive considerable attention from authorities: They become delinquent. This child is maximally aggressive to all save his parents; he has little respect for authority, is noncompliant in almost all situations, and is primarily interested in social interaction and freedom from authority. He is hostile and vents his hostility against all external authority. He lacks internal controls and feels the world is trying to keep him from expressing himself. There is little or no guilt associated with transgressions among these children; however, they develop a feeling of shame when caught. Their moral code is power over others and freedom for themselves. They are constantly frustrated because society does not permit the autonomy they were allowed in the home.

REMARKS: METHOD

The most discouraging fact about parent-child relations is that different measures yield different results. The most common reaction is to look accusingly at the measures, but usually these failures result from the assumption of no interaction between people and the measurement situation. Interaction may occur between persons and the stimulus situation (people behave differently in different situations), between persons and the observer (observer and observed react to each other), or among persons, stimulus conditions, and the observer.

A particularly complex problem arises when we allow parents or children to evaluate their own attitudes or those of the family (the interview or questionnaire asking for recall of past experiences). The attitudes of parents toward childrearing practices are usually investigated through questionnaires, interviews, paper and pencil tests, and sometimes by direct observations of the parents' behavior. The attitudes of parents are one step removed from their actual behavior, but they are much easier to measure (they require only paper and pencil interviews) than actual behavior. Mothers, fathers, and children do not observe each other in the same situations, and there are no precise methods for separating the contribution of the observer from that of the person observed. Self-ratings reflect the person's ideal evaluation; they are not necessarily related to his actual behavior. It is little wonder that few systematic relations are found between self-ratings and ratings by others, but these problems do not mean that self-report data are useless. It is assumed that direct observation leads to more useful results because interaction effects can be more readily controlled or evaluated in this situation.

Three studies have related ratings based on home observation and interviews to those procedures requiring self-report. Patterson (1943) correlated scores from a personality inventory with ratings made from home observations. He found modest positive relations between a negative self-image on personality inventories and high ratings of autocratic behavior among mothers of three- to five-year-old children. An examination of the relation between self-ratings and observer ratings also was made by Crandall and Preston (1955). Forty-four mothers of children between two and four were rated by home visitors and then were asked to rate themselves on 24 scales which paralleled those used by the home observer. Agreement was good on scales concerned with warmth and adjustment but poor on scales concerned with protectiveness, democracy, and strictness.

The most ambitious attempt to compare direct observation of parent and child with other methods was made by Becker, Peterson, Luria, Shoemaker, and Hellmer (1962). They examined the relative effectiveness of observations and self-report in predicting child behavior in different situations. Each parent of 58 five-year-olds was observed for 30 minutes in a playroom with his child. The situation was structured so that the parent and child had to work together in making up a creative story with the materials presented. Two observers coded the behavior of the parents and the children, and a number of personality tests were completed by the parents and children. Data on the parents were available from interviews and from parent self-ratings and ratings of each other. Teacher ratings, parent ratings, and observation ratings were available on the children to permit comparison of the various methods in predicting child behavior.

The results of the various comparisons support the following conclusions: The highest relation was found between interview ratings and parent self-ratings; mothers' self-perceptions and fathers' perceptions of mothers showed modest relations. If an interviewer sees a mother as hostile, the mother will rate herself as nervous and emotional; the father is likely to agree with the interviewer. The mother who is hostile toward the child usually had a self-concept of, "Of course I love my child; I just can't stand the way he gets me upset all the time." Child behavior in school was best predicted by the interview ratings and poorest by parent ratings. Considerable caution must be exercised in concluding that measures of maternal behavior gathered by different methods have similar implications.

Several studies have tried to assess the distortions that occur when parents are asked to give developmental histories of their children. Macfarlane (1938) interviewed mothers of 21-month-old infants. She found that birth weight was accurately reported but that physical condition during pregnancy, use of instruments, duration of labor, and children's illnesses were not. Mothers tended to err in the direction of precocity, especially mothers of first-born children. However, Goddard, Broder, and Wenar (1961) reported that details of motor development and difficulty in labor are reliably reported, but the details of feeding are not. Wenar and Coulter (1962) reinterviewed 25 mothers who had brought their children to a therapeutic nursery school three to six years earlier. An interview was conducted to reproduce information they had gathered earlier. Forty-three percent of the second statements were judged to be different from the mothers' first reports. The most reliable reports concerned whether the child was wanted, sex preference, breast or bottle feeding, motor development, problems in toilet training, illnesses, and amount of sleep in infancy. The least reliable reports concerned health during pregnancy, use of discipline, relations of the child to mother and father, and attitudes toward interpersonal problems.

Wenar and Coulter also examined the personality attributes of mothers who produced reliable and unreliable reports; they found a pattern for unreliable mothers: They tend to be anxious, talkative, intense, and controlling. The affective content of the material recalled was very important; the mothers did not simply have difficulty recalling all anxiety-arousing material. Some anxiety-laden material was recalled well. It was their own feelings about events which were poorly recalled. In retrospective interviews we are dealing with a reconstructive process subject to modification by experience and with a social interaction situation where neurotic defenses operate. In this emotionally involved situation, which the mothers often see as threatening to their own self-concepts, it is little wonder that truth suffers. Indeed, the types of distortions of parent-child interactions that appear in the parents' self-reports should produce valuable information about the discrepancies between what parents think they should be doing and what they are actually doing. If the discrepancies are great, we have a strong suggestion that the parent-child situation is unhealthy; if there is little discrepancy, then the parents at least see reality.

ANTECEDENTS OF AGGRESSION

Aggression is designed to hurt, bluff, or disturb another.

Fighting, yelling, and other aggressive activities of children have received considerable study; they disturb parents and command attention from teachers, psychologists, and others. In contrast to a neurotic, withdrawn child, the aggressive individual receives more than his share of attention. Aggression activities are those designed to hurt, bluff, remove, or disturb another.

Freud proposed the death wish to explain aggression.

Several theories of aggression have been postulated. The earliest theory was proposed by Freud; he believed we all possess a death instinct. He proposed that the death instinct (as opposed to the libido) wishes to destroy others and ourselves. The theory was never articulated in detail, and others have proposed alternative conceptions which are more compelling.

Dollard et al. *believed aggression is an instinctive reaction to frustration.*

The notion that aggression is an instinctive reaction to frustration was proposed by Dollard *et al.* (1939). Their assumption received considerable support from work with animals. It is now clear, however, that their simple conception of aggression and frustration is incomplete. Children's aggression is multidetermined; frustration, reinforcement, general drive level, amount of guilt associated with aggression and types of models to which the child has been exposed all contribute to children's aggressive behavior.

Models of aggression

Parents often are models for children's aggressions.

Parents have a large effect upon the child's aggression. If parents provide a model of aggression for the child, or reinforce him for aggression, he will produce abundant aggressive behavior. There is a positive relation between parental punitiveness and amount of overt aggression in school for boys. However, this relation is curvilinear for girls; girls of both very high and very low punitive families show little aggression, while the intermediate group shows more. Cross-cultural studies support the positive relation between parents' use of power (punishment) in their childrearing and the amount of children's aggression. More punishment is used in societies in which the gods are perceived as aggressive compared to societies in which the gods are seen as passive. Punishment is frustrating; it instigates anger, and thus aggression. The punitive parent is also an effective model of aggression for the child. The child is punished, his drive level is increased, and he has a model of effective aggression. Hostile parents also dispense a good deal of positive reinforcement for aggression outside the home. It is not surprising that delinquency and aggressiveness are difficult to control in this type of home.

Mothers who are punitive demand that their children fight back and they reward fighting.

An often-quoted study was conducted by Sears, Maccoby, and Levin (1957); they interviewed (recall the problems with interview data) 379 mothers of five-year-old children concerning their childrearing practices. One of the areas they studied was the child's aggressiveness, the mother's punitiveness, and the pattern of control she used. Mothers who were rated high in punitiveness and aggressiveness demanded that their children aggress toward other children and were quite permissive of children's hostility. Punitive mothers used much more physical punishment and were more aggressive toward their children.

Dependency among boys disappears during adolescence, while it is a continuing trait for girls.

Restrictiveness is associated with early hostility by the mother—the mother rejects her child. Restricted children are more dependent, conforming, and submissive than their less-controlled peers. For girls this pattern of dependency continues into adulthood, while for boys it stops during adolescence; they become aggressive and hostile. Girls with very restrictive parents become quite dependent and submissive as they approach adolescence; they then acquire appropriate sex characteristics for females. Early restriction is most effective in generating submission, and the effects are longer lasting. If parents become restrictive later, they only produce aggression and hostility, since older children sense the unfairness and retaliate.

Physical punishment makes children dependent on adults.

Physical punishment tends to orient the child away from his environment and make him dependent upon adults. Children who are allowed to make their own mistakes and to learn from these mistakes possess more attractive personalities than children who experience adult interference and punishment. Dependent children experience great difficulty adjusting to school and community. They avoid other nursery school children. Children of restrictive parents are more inhibited and withdrawn and are less popular with others. Permissive childrearing results in boisterous children who are aggressive and popular.

Friendly children are produced by warm mothers; aggressive children are produced by hostile, rejecting mothers.

A longitudinal study of aggressive parental behavior and its effects on children is found in the Berkeley Growth Study (Bayley & Schaefer, 1960), which recorded personality evaluations from birth to adulthood. They report that friendly, cooperative, and attentive children are produced by mothers who score high in autonomy, positive self-evaluation, equalitarian treatment, and expression of affection. Hostile mothers produce children who score much lower in friendliness, cooperation, and attention. On the other hand, mothers who are excessively involved with and controlling toward infant sons produce rude, irritable, impulsive, dependent children. These observations are consistent with conclusions from previous studies.

Aggressive boys are raised in a punitive fashion; they have few controls imposed on them and they are often involved in conflict.

A year after results from the Berkeley Growth Study were released McCord, McCord, and Howard (1961) published their findings in cooperation with the Cambridge-Somerville Youth Study program. They examined 174 nondelinquent boys by direct observation over a period of five and three-quarter years. At least three counselors observed each child; none was aware that his observations would be used to study aggression. The results showed that aggressive boys are raised by parents who (1) treat the boys in a rejecting, punitive fashion, (2) fail to impose direct controls on their behavior, (3) offer them an example of deviance, and (4) are often involved in intense conflict. On the other hand, they found that nonaggressive boys come from contrasting homes in which they are (1) treated in an affectionate, nonpunitive manner, (2) guided by a stable set of controls, (3) exposed to examples of social conformity, and (4) reared by affectionate, satisfied parents.

Mothers and fathers of problem children are not well adjusted, sociable, or democratic.

Another approach was tried by Peterson *et al.* (1959); they studied the parental characteristics of normal and "disturbed" children. The subjects were parents of children undergoing clinical evaluations in a child guidance center; they used a group of "normal" parents for comparison. Their results showed that mothers and fathers of problem children were not well adjusted, sociable, or democratic and that they were more strict with their children. The children's personality problems in the clinical group were relatively independent of maternal attitudes but were related to autocratic attitudes and lack of parental concern among fathers. Similarly, conduct problems were associated with general maladjustment among mothers in the clinical group and with permissiveness and ineffectuality on the part of fathers.

Love and positive reinforcement of the child produce guilt when he transgresses.

The child trained with love and positive reinforcement feels guilty when he transgresses against social rules; the child who receives hostility, control, and negative reinforcement feels guilty all the time, no matter what his behavior! There are several explanations of the association between love and guilt: (1) Withdrawal of love is more effective where love exists. (2) The love-oriented parent provides a model of good behavior for the child. (3) Love-oriented parents are more likely to use reason in their discipline, thus giving the child an understanding of what he did wrong. Explanations provide internal sources for the child's evaluation of his behavior, and he gains explicit training in moral judgments. In a cross-cultural study, Whiting and Child (1953) asked groups of natives to list their causes for illnesses. Attribution of the causes of illness to the person rather than to external agents was assumed to reflect high guilt and personal responsibility. This causal explanation was more prominent in cultures that use love-oriented techniques of training than in those which use other types of child-training techniques. (See Figure 12.2 for a summary of parent-child behaviors which are related.)

FIGURE 12.2

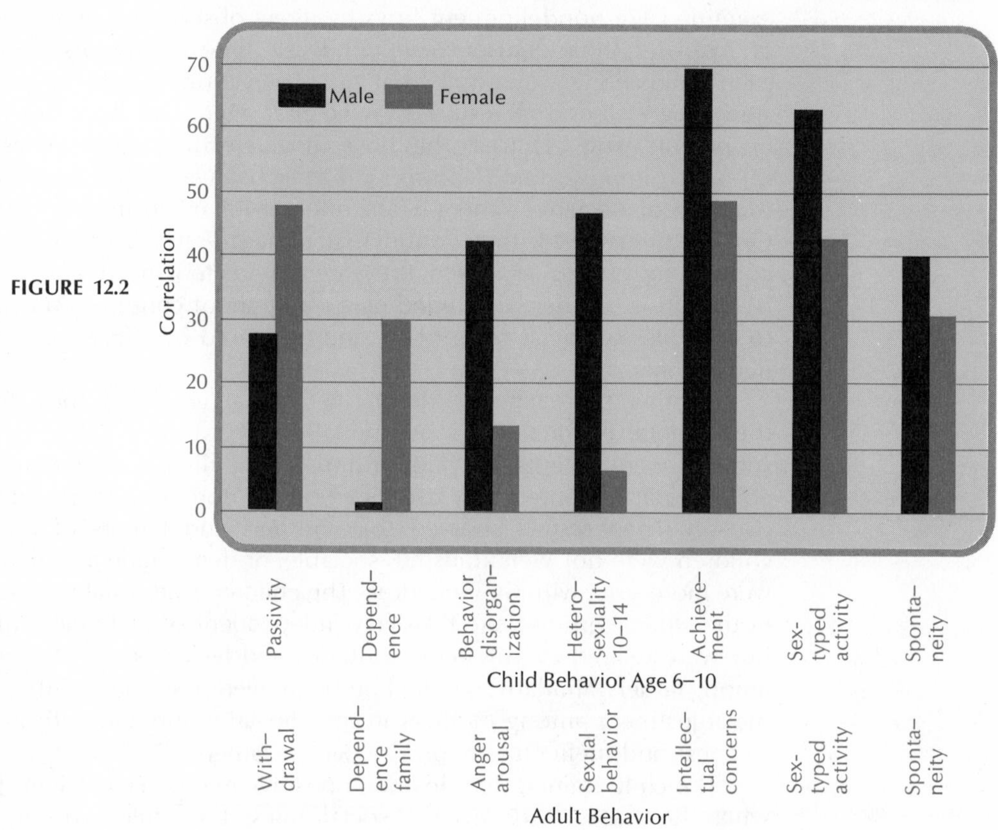

Summary of relations between selected child behaviors (6–10 years of age) and similar adult behaviors. (From Kagan & Moss, 1962.)

Parental inconsistency

Inconsistency produces aggressive, hostile children.

Children's behavior which is permitted at one time and not at another reflects parental inconsistency. Inconsistency may result from the parents' psychological and physical well-being—they are tired or sick—or their pattern of rewards and punishments (the parents may threaten punishment and not carry through, or they may reward at one time and punish at another time). Children who are delinquent have a history of inconsistent disciplinary action by their parents. Parents who are consistent produce more docile children, while inconsistent parents raise aggressive children. If one parent is strict and the other permissive, very aggressive child behavior results, much more than when both parents are either strict or permissive. In general, warm, permissive, consistent, supporting families produce friendly, healthy children, while parental hostility and inconsistency are debilitating to the child.

Children's attitudes

Children's attitudes toward their parents generalize to other authority figures.

The attitudes children develop toward their parents are important; children generalize these attitudes to others. The boy who is hostile and resentful toward his parents tends to resent all authority—the boss, the policeman, the judge. Boys who see themselves as similar to their fathers show favorable personality and social adjustment and are less anxious. Boys who view their parents as authoritarian and rejecting are more delinquent than boys who have a high evaluation of their parents. Mothers are seen in a more positive light than fathers, although girls, as they grow older, develop a positive attitude toward their fathers.

SOCIAL CLASS DIFFERENCES

Social class and urban-rural differences occur in childrearing practices.

The process of socialization of the child varies within subgroups of American society (see Figure 12.3). The child from a lower class home differs in important ways from the middle class child. Americans growing up in a rural community would have quite different experiences than those growing up in an urban environment, particularly in terms of mores and values.

The middle class shows more variation in childrearing because it has access to books and magazines; the lower class is more stable.

Social classes differ in the way they train children. However, we have conflicting reports on these differences. Davis and Havighurst (1946) reported that middle class parents are more strict with their children, train them earlier, and cause their children to suffer more frustration than do lower class parents. On the other hand, Sears, Maccoby, and Levin (1957) published a study of childrearing practices

FIGURE 12.3

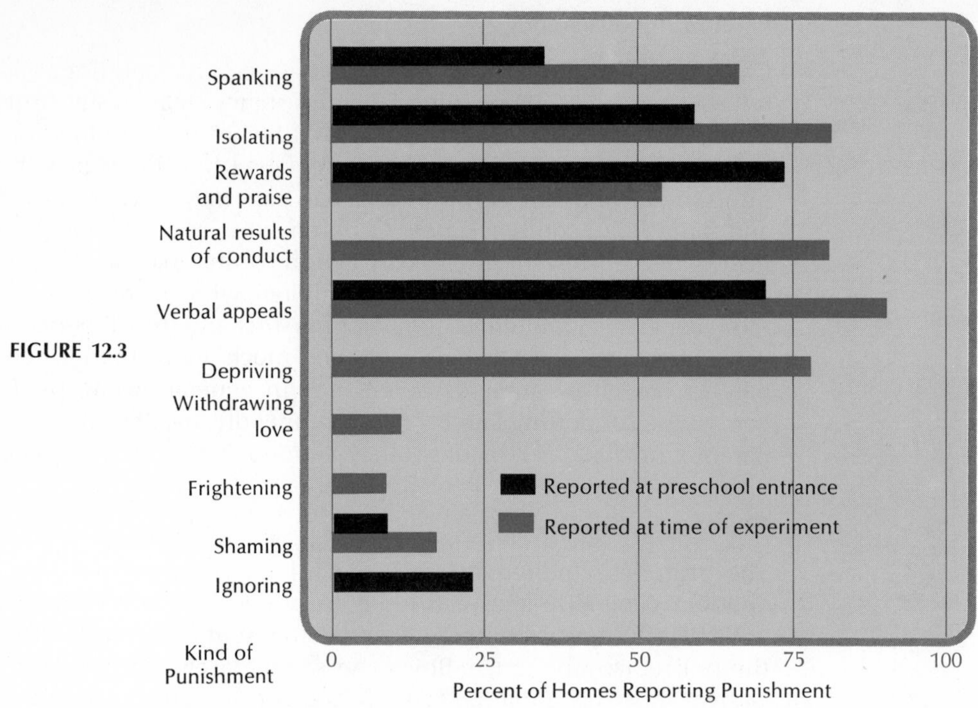

The kinds of punishment reported by a group of parents who were superior in socioeconomic status. The discrepancies between preschool-entrance and time-of-experiment reports may have been partially due to differences in the age of the children on the two occasions and differences in data-gathering procedures. (Redrawn from Radke, 1946.)

which contradicted the Davis-Havighurst findings. Sears *et al.* found that middle class mothers are generally more permissive than lower class mothers, although middle class mothers are more severe in toilet training and sex education. The findings of these two studies reflect changing socialization processes in the American family. The Havighurst and Davis study was conducted prior to World War II, when lower class mothers were more permissive than middle class mothers with respect to feeding, weaning, and toilet training. A revolution in child-training recommendations began in the early 1950s. Spock (1957), among others, advocated permissive childrearing. Since childrearing practices change most quickly in those segments of society that have access to child-training literature, physicians, and counselors, the revolution was most noticeable in the middle class. Comparison of maternal behaviors over a 20-year period from 1940 to 1960 shows that before 1940 middle class mothers were quite strict with their children; a period of permissiveness followed during the 1950s, when baby care books suggested permissiveness as the best method of rearing children. More recently there has been a swing toward a middle ground in which the limits of behavior are outlined, but severe restrictions are not used (Spock, 1957). Throughout this cycle lower class mothers maintained a more stable pattern of childrearing practices than did middle class mothers.

Lower class children receive more punishment while middle class children receive more reasoning and praise.

Currently, lower class children receive physical punishment, deprivation of privileges, and ridicule from their parents; middle class children are more likely to experience reasoning, praise, and warmth. Middle class families allow their children to express aggression toward the parents while lower class parents do not. Well-educated mothers are more likely to have approving attitudes toward childrearing than are lower class mothers. The middle class child has high expectations placed on him when compared to the lower class child; this is particularly true of academic achievement. Middle class parents expect their children to go through college, while lower class parents hope their children will finish high school. Lower class children become aware of sex role patterns earlier than middle class children. Middle class families permit more variation in child behavior; they do not define appropriate sexual behavior as rigidly as do lower class families. In addition, sex education occurs earlier among lower class children (through informal peer groups) since lower class parents are not so anxious about children's sexual curiosity. Lower class children explore and learn more about sex and they have less anxiety associated with sexual subjects.

MOTHER-CHILD RELATIONS

Mothers are important in the early development of the infant, while the father becomes more influential when the child reaches four years of age.

During the first years of a child's life, relations with his mother are very important in his development. The father becomes more important when the child is around four years of age; he then begins to identify with his father. This is when the Oedipal situation appears. In this country, early childrearing is primarily the mother's responsibility.

> It is generally accepted that the most potent of all influences on social behavior is derived from the primary social experience with the mother. If a mother maintains toward the child a consistent attitude of, let us say, indifference and hostility, the assumption is made that the child's personality is greatly affected by the maternal attitude. Life under a

regime of maternal indifference develops a psychic pattern of quite a different mold than under a regime of maternal overprotection. Psychiatrists regard the difference as great as though the children concerned lived in entirely different worlds. Indeed, two children of the same parents, whose mother exhibits a different attitude toward each, manifest on that basis alone profound differences in personality. (Levy, 1943, pp. 3–4.)

Mothers can damage their children's development by giving them too much or too little attention. Too much attention produces an overprotected child, while too little attention produces a rejected child.

The overprotected child

The overprotected child is dependent, nursed too long, and has difficulty breaking away from his mother.

The overprotected child receives excessive maternal care; he has excessive contact with his mother—she will not let him out of her sight. She treats him like a baby and will not let him grow up. Overprotection prevents the development of independent behavior—he's eight, but he cannot take any risks; she will not let him cross the street by himself. Overprotective mothers spend an enormous amount of time with their children and give them prolonged nursing care. If the child is ill, the mother will fondle him excessively. She also will encourage the child to sleep with her long past infancy (contributing to his Oedipal problems and fears of castration). She seeks and acts on medical advice more often than other mothers. Overprotected children are ill twice as often and undergo three times as many operations as other children. The overprotected child is not less healthy than his peers; he is simply overexposed to preventative medicine. A characteristic sign of overprotection is prolonged breast feeding; overprotected children average 14 months of breast feeding compared with about four or five months for other children. Maturity is also blocked by limiting the child's social contacts; his friendships with other children are discouraged or prevented.

Overprotection can come from overindulgence and domination.

There are two kinds of overprotective parents—indulgent and domineering. The indulgent, overprotective parent satisfies the child's every need and pays attention to his every whim. This child is rebellious, aggressive, disrespectful, and disobedient. He is a little tyrant who may hit or kick his mother and throw food on the floor; he may even make mother sleep in a particular bed. The domineering mother, on the other hand, produces a submissive, dependent child. Typically, a dominated, overprotected child is timid and seclusive, clean, neat, obedient, and polite. He does not fight with other children and is usually regarded as a sissy. The dominated child is as submissive in school as he is at home.

The rejected child

The rejected child may look overprotected because of the mother's guilt about hating her infant.

The rejected child is a little more difficult to identify, and he appears similar to the overprotected child. In our society parents are supposed to love their children. To hate one's child is considered inhuman; therefore, parental rejection of children exists only in disguised forms. The rejecting mother may dress her child very well, look after his physical comfort solicitously, and appear to be a very good parent. Yet, she may deny her child what he needs most—acceptance and affection. Overprotection may stem from guilt feelings because of this unconscious rejection.

The rejecting parent has high expectations of achievement and uses excess criticism.

Maternal rejection appears in several ways; excessive physical or verbal punishment of the child may result from the parent's underlying hostility. Some rejecting parents constantly expect too much of the child intellectually or developmentally, making him feel inadequate. The child is never good enough for the rejecting parent no matter how hard he tries. Since the healthy development of a child depends on parents accepting his real accomplishments, the personality of the rejected child suffers severe damage. Often, rejected children refuse to grow up; their speech remains unintelligible and their manners infantile. Some rejected children become hostile and aggressive, while others withdraw into a shell of anxiety.

Working mothers

The mother's working is not harmful to the older child; it may even be helpful if the mother-infant relation is poor.

More and more mothers are working; however, the effects of maternal employment are difficult to assess. Two factors affect the results: the child's age when his mother begins work and the type of substitute care provided. In some families the husband and wife share child-rearing tasks. They have an arrangement that allows one to work while the other is home. The father interacts with his child much more in this situation and can exert a positive influence on the child's adjustment. Also, many mothers return to child care with better attitudes after an absence from household routines. On the other hand, parents who are trying to do two jobs often lack patience with their children. Finally, the father's self-esteem may be challenged if he is required to do housework. He may feel inadequate, and the resulting tension can cause emotional strain.

The substitute care is important in determining the effects of a mother's working.

Turning child care over to another person raises other problems. In lower class homes this substitute care is often haphazard; children may be left with a neighbor or someone who may be responsible for many children in the neighborhood. Often, older children are free to roam the streets by themselves. The success of any arrangement depends on the attitude of the caretaker. Children need security and comfort; if the substitute mother provides these, it may sometimes be desirable to separate mother and child. This is particularly true if the mother has neurotic needs—if she encourages dependency or is punishing or rejecting; in these cases the child will benefit from a reliable caretaker.

FAMILY COMPOSITION

Family size affects parent-child relations; first children overachieve, second-born males are more dependent, and boys with older brothers are more competitive.

The typical American family is small; it usually includes the father and mother and their children. Family size and ordinal position of children within the family influence children's growth. "Only" children receive their parents' undivided attention (positive or negative) and the first-born child is alone with his parents for a year or two before a rival appears. Koch (1956) studied correlates of ordinal position in families with two children. She examined the effects of being the first or second child, the sex of both children, and the interval between the first and second child. All three variables interact; they cannot be understood independently. The first-born child develops differently according to his sex, when his younger sibling comes along, and the sex of his younger sibling. Second-born males with an older sister are more dependent than first-born males. Boys with older brothers are more competitive than boys with older sisters. Only children and second members of a family are not indulged; they receive the same infant discipline as their peers. The mother with one child is more likely to supervise his activities than is a mother with more children.

Children with one parent

Whether the father or mother is absent differentially affects the child.

The typical American family includes two socializing influences, the mother and the father. What happens if one agent is removed from the home by death, divorce, or separation? Loss of the mother is quite different from the effects of losing the father. A father who is responsible for preschool children will continue his role and hire a new caretaker to take over housekeeping duties and care of his children. The new agent is a substitute mother. However, when the father is missing from a family, the mother usually works; she may or may not hire a substitute caretaker.

Fathers are important for boys and girls because they are influential in producing sex-role identification.

To understand growing up without a father, we need to consider what a father means to a growing child. Most young children see their fathers as a source of strength and security. To a growing boy the father is a model, a most important source of sex-appropriate behaviors. The boy must identify with a model and also have him available as a source of information. For a boy to develop sex-appropriate behavior, he requires a good relation with someone who has practical knowledge of correct sex-linked behavior.

Masculine mothers inhibit their sons' identification with males.

Not all father-son relations are adequate; masculine mothers often inhibit their son's identification with his father. These boys tend to show feminine characteristics. A boy who is rejected by his father has difficulty learning to be a man. If his father prefers a daughter, the boy may become feminine to win acceptance. The father can reinforce femininity in the growing girl. He can admire her clothes, comment on her hair, and treat her as a young woman. However, if he admires tomboys, a father can encourage his daughter to act like a boy; this will make her task of becoming a woman very difficult.

How the mother feels about the absent father influences a child's reaction.

How the mother feels about an absent father significantly affects the child's feelings toward his missing father. Studies of children's fantasies in homes where the father is absent show that children of mothers who are antagonistic toward the children's father are more aggressive than children whose mothers are affectionate and miss the absent father.

Women who live alone may be hostile and rejecting, thus keeping the boy from identifying with his father.

There are many problems associated with not having a father; often the children become excessively dependent on their mother. They may be rebellious and difficult to control; boys may start to steal. However, boys from homes with no fathers display less aggression than do boys whose fathers are present. This puzzling fact is not true for girls. Sears, Pintler, and Sears (1946) suggested that during the preschool years the father contributes to the sex typing of boys and serves as a model for aggression. However, an equally tenable hypothesis would suggest that women who live alone are rejecting, hostile, and masculine; these women would tend to keep a boy from identifying with his father. The result would be less masculinity on the part of the boy. The hostile, rejecting woman is also most likely to lose her husband.

Divorce and the child

Divorce can be good or bad for the child. If it helps his parents overcome their conflicts, it is therapeutic.

Divorce affects a child's development; however, its precise influences are difficult to know. How much influence may be attributed to divorce and how much is the result of conflict and tension prior to the divorce is impossible to say. However, adolescents from broken homes show much less psychosomatic illness, less delinquent behavior, and better adjustment than those from unhappy, unbroken homes (Nye & Hoffman, 1963). Often separation and divorce are desirable; a broken home is better than an atmosphere of hate and conflict.

Adolescents who remember their homes as happy resent divorce; those who remember their homes as unhappy see divorce as a healthy step.

Divorce does not have the same effect on all children; adolescents who recall their family as happy before the divorce react quite differently from those who feel their homes were unhappy. Children who saw their homes as happy feel divorce is an unhappy, traumatic experience. However, these same children admit to little change in their feelings of security and personal happiness following divorce, strongly suggesting adjustment by denial of their own feelings and the reality of their situation. However, those children who viewed their homes as unhappy feel more secure and happy following a divorce. Children from both groups say they feel no loss of security after a divorce (perhaps denial?).

The unhappy child may be denying reality.

Their true feelings are hard to know, but it seems likely that those children who saw their families as happy before a divorce either possess very thick skins or strongly deny reality. The admission of unhappiness is a giant step toward better adjustment. Those children who say they were unhappy before the divorce have a better grasp on reality and some chance to overcome their unhappiness.

Children must adjust at several stages during a divorce.

There are several facts that must be accepted by the child. First, he must accept that a divorce is going to happen. Then he must adjust to the divorce itself. During the period of pre- or postdivorce, one of the parents may use the child as a weapon, with traumatic effects on the child. The child must learn to establish new relations with his parents and make new adjustments in his peer group. And, finally, there are the problems of adjustment for the child if the parents remarry. Divorced women report that the greater their trauma from a divorce, the more difficult their children are to manage.

The child may feel guilt, he may have to move, and he usually will not have a father in the house.

There are various other factors: The child may feel guilty about the parents' separation; psychological tension and anxiety on the part of the parents may lead to emotional instability in the child. Following divorce, many families must move. This adds to the adjustment problem facing the child, particularly if he is in school. In approximately 90 percent of divorce cases, the mother receives custody of the children. This affects a boy's identification with a father figure.

Children who realistically see their homes as unhappy before a divorce are much better adjusted following the separation.

All in all, there is good evidence that children who see their homes as unhappy before the divorce are much better off following the divorce; the tension and conflict are gone. These children now have a more relaxed atmosphere in which to develop. If the parents seek guidance during or following their separation, both may come to realize that the children need not suffer from their mistake. Both parents can establish a warm relation with the children and help them grow into mature, productive adults. The effect of divorce is primarily contingent on what both parents do with their second chance. If they remain hateful and use the children as weapons in the battle over who

REMARKS: THEORY

In parent-child relations the balance between permissiveness and demands for independence cannot be answered by a flat statement about how the child must be handled. The treatment of an infant must be vastly different from the expectations one has for the five-year-old, who in turn should be treated more permissively than the older child. The principle is that treatment accorded the child should be appropriate to his developmental level. When the child is very young, he should be nurtured; as he develops, his competence must be rewarded and gradually developed. The scheduling of weaning, how quickly it is accomplished, and the expectations of parents toward their children must be tempered by some consideration of the level of competence reached by the child. The optimum parent-child relation should include a great deal of indulgence during his early formative period when the child is weak and dependent. However, once a basic feeling of security is established, a schedule of independence training should be started; the older child should be shifted toward more and more independence as he progresses toward competence in handling his own affairs. A simple prescription of permissiveness or restriction must be replaced by the more subtle notion of early permissiveness which is gradually shifted toward expectations of competence as the child grows. The relation between the child's competence and the parents' expectations is crucial; only by proper scheduling of tasks and the structuring of situations so that the child can develop competence will the task of childrearing be accomplished with a maximum of security and a minimum of dependence.

was right, the divorce has accomplished nothing; however, if they achieve a new maturity through separation, the divorce has been the right surgery for a poor personal relation.

SUMMARY

1 Two bipolar dimensions describe most home atmospheres. One dimension centers about love or hostility toward children while the other concerns the amount of parental control over children. Parents who are loving and controlling produce submissive, dependent, polite, and neat children. Children who grow in an atmosphere of love and autonomy are active, socially outgoing, creative, and successfully aggressive. Parents who control their children and are hostile produce neurotics who withdraw from difficult situations, are shy, and are maximally self-aggressive. Children raised in an atmosphere of autonomy and hostility become delinquent.

2 Several factors contribute to the aggressive tendencies of children. Among these are the model of aggression which parents provide, the amount of frustration the child experiences, the amount of guilt attached to aggression, and the amount of reinforcement the child receives from his parents for aggressive behavior.

3 Parents who are inconsistent handicap their children; delinquent children show a history of inconsistent parental discipline. Inconsistency also produces aggressive children.

4 Parent-child relations are fairly consistent among the lower classes, but the middle class runs in cycles. In the early 1930s the middle class was more strict with children; during the 1940s there was a trend toward permissiveness, while now child-care experts are saying that children need some guides and too much permissiveness is as bad as too much control. The lower classes have been fairly strict, physical, and consistent in their training.

5 Mother-child relations have a profound effect on young children. The mother may either pay too much attention to the child (overprotection) or too little attention to him (rejection). The overprotected child is a sissy; he cannot be without his mother. She keeps him in infancy much too long. The rejected child feels insecure, withdrawn, and unloved.

6 The working mother may improve or destroy a mother-child relation; we need to know the previous relation, the type of substitute care, and the attitude of her husband before we can judge how working affects childrearing.

7 Families without fathers tend to produce boys with poor masculine self-images who idealize the masculine role.

8 Divorce may be a healthy act; if the home was hostile and filled with conflict, the resulting calm may produce better adjustment among children and parents.

FURTHER READINGS

Becker, W. C. Consequences of different kinds of parental discipline. In M. L. Hoffman & Lois Hoffman (Eds.), *Review of child development.* Vol. 1. New York: Russell Sage Foundation, 1963.

Sears, R. R., Maccoby, E. E., & Levin, H. *Patterns of child rearing.* New York: Harper & Row, 1957.

REFERENCES

Bayley, N., & Schaefer, E. S. Maternal behavior and personality development data from the Berkeley Growth Study. *Psychiatric Research Reports,* 1960, **13,** 155–173.

Becker, W. C., Peterson, D. R., Luria, Z., Shoemaker, D. J., & Hellmer, L. A. Relations of factors derived from parent-interview ratings to behavior problems of five-year-olds. *Child Development,* 1962, **33,** 509-535.

Crandall, V. J., & Preston, A. Patterns and levels of maternal behavior. *Child Development,* 1955, **26,** 267-277.

Davis, W. A., & Havighurst, R. J. Social class and color differences in child-rearing. *American Sociological Review,* 1946, **11,** 698-710.

Dollard, J., Doob, L. W., Miller, N. E., Mowrer, O. H., & Sears, R. *Frustration and aggression.* New Haven, Conn.: Yale University Press, 1939.

Goddard, K. E., Broder, G., & Wenar, C. Special article—reliability of pediatric histories, a preliminary study. *Pediatrics,* 1961, **28,** No. 6.

Kagan, J., & Moss, H. *Birth to maturity.* New York: Wiley, 1962.

Koch, H. L. Attitudes of young children toward their peers as related to certain characteristics of their siblings. *Psychological Monographs,* 1956, **70,** No. 19.

Levy, D. M. *Maternal overprotection.* New York: Columbia University Press, 1943.

Macfarlane, J. W. Studies in child guidance: I. Methodology of data collection and organization. *Monograph of the Society for Research in Child Development,* 1938, **3,** No. 6.

McCord, W., McCord, J., & Howard, A. Familial correlates of aggression in non-delinquent male children. *Journal of abnormal and social Psychology,* 1961, **62,** 79-93.

Nye, F. I., & Hoffman, L. *The employed mother in America.* Chicago: Rand-McNally, 1963.

Patterson, C. H. A note on the Bernreuter personality of mothers and some measures of child personality. *Journal of social Psychology,* 1943, **17,** 89-92.

Peterson, D. R., Becker, W. C., Hellmer, L. A., Shoemaker, D. J., & Quay, H. C. Parental attitudes and child adjustment. *Child Development,* 1959, **30,** 119-130.

Radke, M. J. The relation of parental authority to children's behavior and attitudes. *University of Minnesota Child Welfare Monographs Series.* 1946, **22.**

Schaefer, E. S. Converging conceptual models for maternal behavior and for child behavior. In J. C. Glidewell (Ed.), *Parental attitudes and child behavior.* Springfield, Ill.: Charles C Thomas, 1961.

Sears, R. R., Maccoby, E. E., & Levin, H. *Patterns of child rearing.* New York: Harper & Row, 1957.

Sears, R. R., Pintler, M. H., & Sears, P. S. Effect of father separation on preschool children's doll play aggression. *Child Development,* 1946, **17,** 219-243.

Spock, B. *Baby and child care.* New York: Pocket Books, 1957.

Wenar, C., & Coulter, J. B. A reliability study of developmental histories. *Child Development,* 1962, **33,** 453-462.

Whiting, J. W. M., & Child, I. L. *Child training and personality.* New Haven: Conn.: Yale University Press, 1953.

13 LANGUAGE

You taught me language; and my profit on't
Is, I know how to curse. The red plague rid you
For learning me your language.

THE TEMPEST

This chapter sketches the early vocalizations of infants, the development of phonological groupings, some empirical work on first grammar learning (with a consideration of the abilities a child needs to learn a language), and three elementary linguistic theories. The three linguistic theories describe adult language; they are not developmental. No model of language development exists. Linguists have proposed various adult grammars; their theories include a Markov model, a phrase-structure grammar, and a grammar with transformational rules.

Language enables a child with limited abilities to transmit information in a noisy world.

Language has certain features that enable a child with limited discrimination and memory to transmit and receive large amounts of information in the midst of many distractions. In designing a language we could assign a unique sound to each message. However, this procedure would use up our sounds long before we had a reasonable set of messages. We would do better to design our language along the principles of phonemes. Phonemes are vowels and consonants which correspond roughly to letters. They are semantically empty (they have no meaning) and only a few exist in any language. English uses 45; the range in all languages is from 10 to 70 (Greenberg, Osgood, & Jenkins, 1966). With these 45 phonemes we can build all the morphemes (words) of a standard dictionary without making any word very long. Furthermore, we need use only about half the possible combinations of phonemes to generate our morphemes. This redundancy allows the listener to correct errors in transmission without distorting the message (Brown, 1965).

Four levels of language analysis exist: phonemes,

Phonemes are the raw material of speech, while morphemes represent a higher level of language. Following his development of phonemes and morphemes (letters and words), the child must learn to *morphemes, grammar, and semantics.*

group words on the basis of grammatical structure (write sentences). The production of words (strings of letters) is a problem for morphological analysis; the generation of sentences (strings of words) is a problem in grammatical analysis, and semantics is the study of meaning.

Early explanations of language assumed man invented speech because he found it convenient to communicate.

Early explanations of language development were based on the principle of discovery and the rational utilization of inarticulate sounds. These explanations supposed that someone discovered the advantages of vocalization and this discovery was incorporated into a communication system. Since verbal ability increased the rate of survival, humans evolved who used language and were endowed with enlarged intellectual capacities. Lenneberg (1967) assumed that reason, discovery, and intellect are irrelevant to an explanation of language. His explanation is biological and assumes that we have innate abilities to learn language.

EARLY VOCALIZATIONS

Infants produce all the sounds of most languages.

In general, infants produce similar sound patterns across different language groups, cultures, and races; the basic phonemes (sounds of languages) are present in these early babblings. Systematic repetition of sounds (in Piaget's terms, secondary circular reactions) occurs early in the life of the child and has aroused interest among some theoreticians. They have speculated that babbling represents a primary basis for all later speech.

Infants generate vowels and then consonants.

Most of the psychological work on the development of speech sounds has concentrated on the frequencies with which various vowels and consonants are produced by children at various ages. Experimenters have often taken time samples of infant babbling. One study of phonemic development was carried out by Velten (1943) on his daughter. Velten recorded (in order of appearance) the meaningful speech forms used by his daughter. He considered a form meaningful if it was used with consistency of reference. Velten concluded that "ba," "da," and "za" were meaningful forms for "bottle," "down," and "that." This distributional analysis alone is not very interesting. We should try to teach the infant to differentiate among the several phonemes that are not available in his repertoire. Procedures for training and the limitations of the child are of great interest. Chen and Irwin (1946) looked at the growth of vowels and consonants over age (see Figure 13.1).

Another theory of language suggests infants learn sounds which match their linguistic community.

Other theories of language learning have been founded on the ability of the infant to match his early vocalizations to those of the community. This match is assumed to reinforce selectively certain classes of grammar while others are extinguished. The rules of grammar which are learned could grow either through an active process of model

FIGURE 13.1

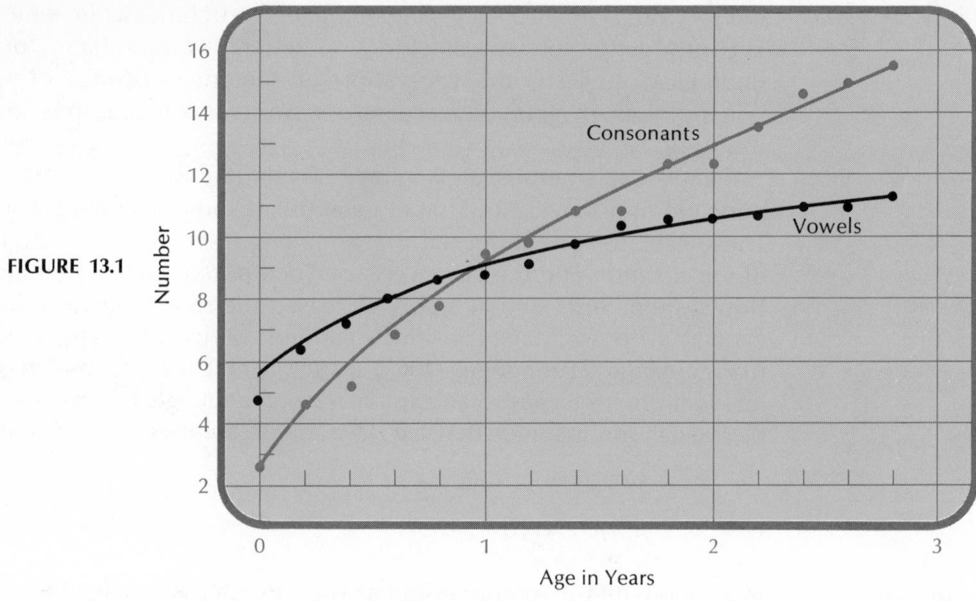

The increase in mean number of different vowels and consonants with age. Note the greater number of vowels during the first year of life. (From Chen, & Irwin, 1946.)

building, by genetically programmed development, or by the joint action of these processes. However, babbling is independent of later language growth; age of babbling is related neither to age of speech acquisition nor to intelligence (Lenneberg, 1967).

THE ACQUISITION OF LANGUAGE

Children begin to speak at about 18 months of age.

Children normally begin to speak between 18 and 20 months of age. Surely this is not because all mothers initiate language training; in fact, there is no evidence that any conscious training takes place. The most important influences originate within the child—he matures. The hallmarks of maturationally controlled behavior are (1) a regular sequence of appearance of abilities correlated with age, (2) environmental stimulation is available throughout his development, but as he matures the infant makes differential use of the stimulation, (3) emergence of the behavior before it is of immediate use to the individual, and (4) evidence that early abilities are not goal directed. The acquisition of language satisfies all these criteria!

Language, like imprinting, may be elicited during a critical period.

It is tempting to relate language acquisition to other animal behaviors that require stimulation during a critical period. A typical example is imprinting (which has been investigated most closely in birds). Imprinting occurs in early infancy, usually a few hours after hatching. The chick follows that moving object to which it is exposed during its critical period; the chick continues to follow that object during most of its young life (Hess, 1959). The response is established rapidly and indiscriminately to anything that moves at a given speed and fits certain size limitations. The response resists extinction, but it is not completely irreversible. However, simply because critical periods for the acquisition of some behaviors exist does not imply critical periods for all behaviors. Some skills are better learned during the late teens than in early childhood, and for a great deal of learning no age limitation exists. In the case of language, the limiting factor is cerebral maturity.

The role of experience in language acquisition is not clear.

Of course, a child cannot learn a language unless he is exposed to it, but aside from this trivial point, the role of environment in language acquisition is not at all clear. There are two problems here: How is the infant's eventual language ability affected by environmental variations and what influence does the environment have upon the age at which language ability appears? In general, a poor early language environment does not cripple the child's potential forever. If the social environment is enriched, he will begin to improve his language habits. The age of onset of language use is similarly influenced (Lenneberg, 1967).

The infant babbles; the child produces one-word sentences and then learns the complex rules of grammar.

The young infant produces single-word sentences, and even before that he babbles. Following these simple utterances, he slowly learns to generate two-word sentences that are organized around the place of a word as a marker of grammatical class. Finally, following a process that we are only beginning to understand, the child formulates a grammar which controls the generation of complex meaningful sentences. Finding the rules of speech and understanding how he learns these rules remain major problems in child psychology.

The empiricist believes experience is necessary for language acquisition; the rationalist believes speech is predetermined.

Historically there have been two basic approaches to grammar acquisition. The *empiricist* (see Osgood, 1966) assumes that we have processing mechanisms of a very simple sort (for example, generalization, association). Under this system all knowledge is acquired by the application of the processing mechanisms to elementary sensory data. The primary process of language acquisition was assumed to be association. The *rationalist* (see Chomsky, 1957, 1965), on the other hand, holds that besides sensory processing mechanisms the infant has innate ideas which determine the form of knowledge. Innate ideas are assumed to remain dormant until stimulated by appropriate experiences.

It is impossible for a child to learn all the sentences of English by association; however, he may learn rules of grammar.

Is it possible for a child working within the constraints of an empirical theory to learn a grammar? Can the processes postulated (association and generalization) generate a grammar within the child's time, memory, and attentional constraints? The simple process of association seems incapable of generating the types of sentences that any three-year-old child can produce. On the other hand, the rational approach (represented by recent developments in transformational grammar) can easily produce the language of a native speaker. We explore transformational grammars to see how they solve the memory and attentional problems which plague the associationistic language learner.

The development of morphemes

Morphemes (the smallest meaningful unit of language) are of three types—free, bound, and combined.

Roughly, morphemes are the minimal meaningful forms of a language. As an example, "the," "man," and "bought" are all morphemes. "Apple/s" contains a morpheme and a plural ending. There are three classes of morphemes: (1) free morphemes, (2) bound morphemes, and (3) combinations of these (Brown, 1965). Free morphemes may occur alone, whereas bound morphemes may occur only in conjunction with another morpheme. "Cat" is a free morpheme, and "cats" is a combination of the free morpheme "cat" and the bound morpheme "s." Other bound morphemes include prefixes, suffixes, and tense endings.

Grammatical competence and vocabulary size grow concurrently; however, they are not the same process.

The correct use of words in sentences and the size of the child's vocabulary grow concurrently, but this does not necessarily mean they reflect the same process. In general, by the age of two, the average child spontaneously uses about 40 different items. However, his vocabulary of use is much smaller than the number of words he can understand; he comprehends around 250 words. An experiment on the joint development of word associations and grammar was performed by Brown and Berko (1960). They presented words to children and adults and asked them for their primary associations. The expectations were that children would produce associations to the words on the basis of contiguity in sentences, while adults would generate associated words on the basis of grammatical class. For example, if the stimulus word was "table," a child should say "eat" whereas an adult should produce another word of the same grammatical class ("chair"). In response to the word "man," children were expected to produce a verb (such as "works"), while adults were expected to produce another noun ("woman"). The results confirmed these postulations. Adults produced associations on the basis of grammatical class, while children produced associations on the basis of sequential occurrence in a sentence.

Using names for objects helps in their discrimination.

Several investigators have suggested that naming stimuli would aid children's discrimination. In a study by Weir and Stevenson (1959) groups of three-, five-, seven-, and nine-year-old children learned to discriminate animals. The results show that naming helps discrimination at all age levels. However, correct discrimination performance increased from three to five years and then decreased from five to nine years. The investigators suggested that older children develop complex strategies which interfere with their learning of a simple task. These results imply that we must take into account the general ability of the child *and* his problem-solving strategy if we want to understand behavior. Once the child acquires language, all other learning and problem-solving is affected. Both his approach to problems and his ability to solve them are a function of his language ability.

FIGURE 13.2

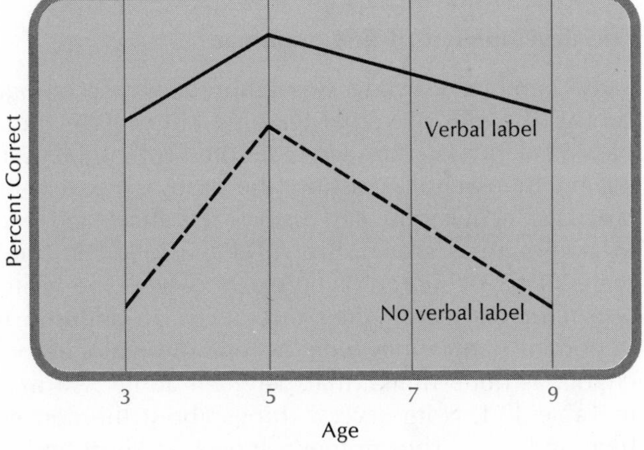

Results of a discrimination-learning study in which some children were given verbal labels associated with the correct discrimination and others were simply given the stimuli. Two effects are of note. First, discrimination ability increased from 3 to 5 years and then decreased. Second, verbal labels helped the children discriminate. The decrease in ability with age probably reflects complex strategies which interfere with the simple discrimination for older children. A verbal label helps discrimination because language is a convenient code for perceptual inputs. (From Weir, & Stevenson, 1959.)

REMARKS: THEORY

Language universals are characteristics of language shared by all human speakers. They constitute the strongest principles of a science of linguistics. For example, all languages have at least two vowels, and the number of phonemes is not fewer than 10 or more than 70 (Greenberg, Osgood, & Jenkins, 1966). Chomsky (1957) believes that all languages are characterized by levels of organization.

Any theory of grammar that tries to explain the performance of language users must consider the problem of universals and say something about how the child might come to know them. Most theorists assume the child does possess some universals. Language learning would probably be impossible otherwise. The question is, What are the initial assumptions about universals that can be made, and how detailed and specific must they be for the child to learn a language? At the moment, we have no model of the child that is rich enough to explain how he learns a language or what universals of language are necessary and sufficient for the learning of grammar.

The development of first grammar

Brown followed children around to record their utterances and develop grammars for them.

Early grammar learning was ignored by psychologists until quite recently. Theories of verbal learning either gave the area of grammar a passing glance or completely ignored the problem. However, since the advent of psycholinguistics (the study of psychological processes of language acquisition and use), theoretical and experimental interest in grammar has grown. Brown (1965) followed the language development of two children. Every second week he visited the children for two hours to record their utterances. In addition to tape recordings, important happenings were noted. The dialogue between mother and child was quite unlike that between adults. An example may be seen in Table 13.1. Note several things about the conversation. It is in the here and now. The mother's speech is short and simple and models what her child will produce a year later. The mother's sentences are perfectly grammatical. It may be that these simple, grammatically perfect sentences are necessary for the development of syntax by the child; we do not know.

The order of sentences is preserved when a child reproduces an adult's sentence.

Consider sentences in which the child imitates what his mother says. In general, these imitations preserve the word order of the original sentence. Several words of the model sentences may be missing, but those present are correctly ordered. We do not know why the order is preserved. Perhaps it is because the child understands the sentence and wants to communicate with the parent, or it may be that the brain is built to preserve the ordering of words as they are input.

TABLE 13.1 A Section from Adam's First Record

Adam	*Mother*
See truck, Mommy. See truck.	
	Did you see the truck?
No I see truck.	
	No, you didn't see it? There goes one.
There go one.	
	Yes, there goes one.
See a truck. See truck, Mommy. See truck. Truck. Put truck, Mommy.	
	Put the truck where?
Put truck window.	
	I think that one's too large to go in the window.

SOURCE: From Brown, 1965.

Children produce telegraphic replications of adults' model sentences.

Notice that when model sentences grow larger, there is no corresponding increase in the length of the child's reproductions. His imitations always contain two to four morphemes (words). This constraint is not on the number of words the child knows (see Figure 13.3) but on the number he can plan or program at once. The words most likely to be retained are nouns and verbs (which have semantic meaning) and, less often, adjectives. The forms omitted are inflections, auxiliary verbs, articles, prepositions, and conjunctions. Why should the young child omit the connectors ("the," "and," "but," and so on) and keep the open parts of syntax (nouns, verbs)? Probably because the open parts have referents. When we operate with a constraint on words (such as when writing a telegram), our own language becomes much like the child's. We tend to use verbs, nouns, and adjectives. A telegraphic message communicates well because it contains all the highly meaningful words in the language and leaves out most of the connectives (which the receiver can replace). There is another possible explanation of this happening. If you say a sentence aloud, you stress those words which the child tends to retain in his utterances. However, McNeill (1966) showed that in foreign languages, where the stress is on other parts of the sentence, young children show the same telegraphic speech—suggesting strongly that vocal stress is not the indicator.

FIGURE 13.3

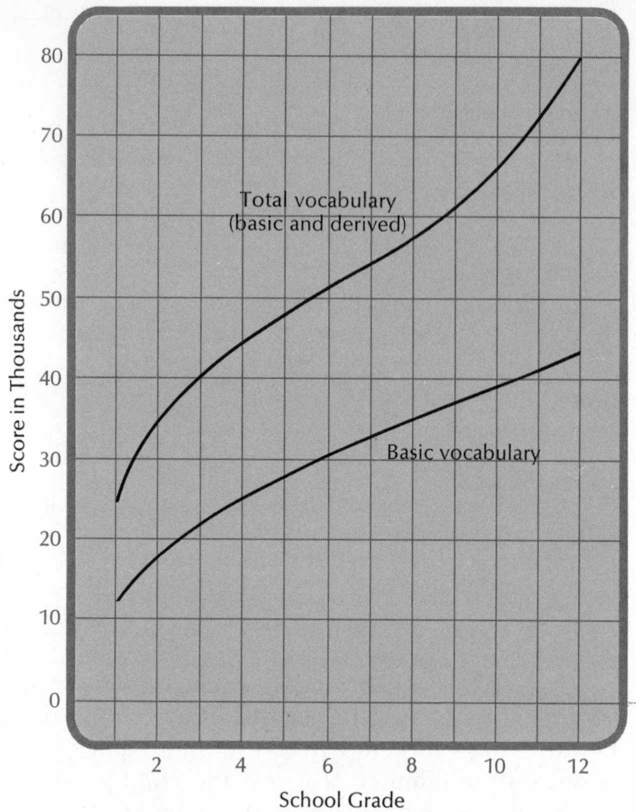

The average reading-recognition vocabulary of children from grades 1 through 12. Basic terms include words like "loyal"; derived terms, which extend the total vocabulary, include words like "loyalize," and "loyal legion." (Adapted from Smith, 1941.)

Adults tend to expand a child's speech into correct grammar.

Another feature of parent-child language is imitation with expansion. In the course of a brief conversation the child will say, "There go one," to which the mother may reply, "Yes, there goes one." She expands the sentence to more correct grammatical form and preserves the order of the child's words. From the mother's view the expansion is a communication check ("Is this what you mean?"). The mother expands words by adding the auxiliary verbs, the prepositions, the articles, and the pronouns—the words the child has left out of his telegraphic sentence. The interaction between mother and child is a cycle of reductions and expansions. How does the mother choose the correct expansion of a child's simple utterance? Primarily from the context in which it is uttered. If the child is holding a ball and says, "John ball," it is likely he means, "John has the ball." We do not know that expansions help learning of grammar or that they are even necessary for grammar learning. We know that expansions do occur between educated mothers and their children.

Learning the latent structure of grammar

Children learn more than associations between words—they learn the latent structure of past tenses, possessives, and plurals.

If the expansions are necessary for grammar learning, is the child learning only the particular expansion or is he learning something more general and pervasive about his language? Consider the learning of the latent structure of English grammar. The clearest example a child can give that he is working out the latent structure of English grammar is the production of a nongrammatical utterance of a particular type. Suppose the child comes into the house and says, "I digged a hole," or, "We saw some sheeps." "Digged" and "sheeps" are not proper utterances in English; they are natural extensions of the rules for forming past tense of verbs and plurals of nouns. The two children Brown (1965) followed overgeneralized English grammar by the age of three.

Association theorists believe grammar is independent of language development.

Psychologists working in areas not directly concerned with linguistics seem to think of grammar as a discipline taught throughout the grades and, at best, unrelated to the child's acquisition of language. Psychological theorists show an almost universal tendency to view the acquisition of grammar as not a very special case of learning in general. Association theorists discuss learning quite independent of grammar, grammar being in effect a nonfunctional system superimposed on language learning by the educator. Such a simple conclusion is unwarranted; no one could ever learn the language of the adult on the basis of association, for the simple reason that the learner would have to be exposed to every sentence in the language before he could utter it. The memory requirement is fantastic. Obviously, some system of generating and using rules must be available. The nature of these rules and how they are acquired must be the primary concern of psychologists studying the development of grammar.

Brown showed that children know the grammatical class of totally strange words.

There seems to be little doubt that children build elementary grammars that enable them to differentiate among words of different language functions. An interesting illustration of this process was provided by Brown (1957). Using subjects ranging from age three to five, he presented words that were totally strange to them. However, the children were able to understand the grammatical category of each word. Specifically, they were presented a single word (either a noun or verb) and asked to point to the picture of the same functional cate-

This is a wug.

FIGURE 13.4

Now there is another one.
There are two of them.
There are two——.

Illustration of Jean Berko's method for eliciting inflections. (From Brown, 1965.)

gory as the presented word. Even at age three, the children were able to reliably select the correct picture. Given a strange "thing" word, the children could point to a "thing" picture rather than to an "action" picture. It is obvious, of course, that the children did not have the adult category "noun," but they were apparently aware of the functional nature of the word. Figure 13.4 shows how Berko (Brown, 1965) tested young children for their morphological (word-forming) rules.

Braine believes children learn grammar from the position of words in sentences.

Braine (1963) has published a biographical account of the development of grammar in three small children. Although the study briefly touched on the sequential appearance of types of speech (that is, vowel, vowel-consonant pairs, morphemes, and word combinations), he was primarily interested in examining the development of children's use of words. Within the obvious limitations of the sample size, Braine noted consistent evidence for the generalizations of position in sentences. He claims that children learn two classes of words: pivot words and other words. As the vocabulary of the child develops, he begins on some unknown basis to select certain morphemes as pivot words and anchor them in a fixed position relative to all other words. In these early stages the children combine no more than two words to generate semisentences. The position of the pivot words becomes invariant. If placed first in the child's two-word grammar, then the word remains there in subsequent utterances and combinations. These words (a small number in relation to the active vocabulary of the child) become the pivot words. Braine says children experimentally manipulate various combinations of words to test their legality in the language community. They develop an active process of generating and testing grammars against those of the community. Having tested and accepted or rejected various combinations of words, the child's vocabulary building continues. Now, however, the child tests each new word within the context of his primitive grammar.

Special problems in language acquisition

Deaf children do not speak without special training.

The environments of normal children and children of congenitally deaf parents differ enormously. The amount and nature of adult vocalizations vary, and the baby's own vocalizations are not returned by the deaf mother. The babies of deaf parents make as much noise, but they produce it at random intervals. Deaf children cannot learn to speak without special training. Thus, there must be a connection between hearing and the development of speech. There are similarities between hearing and deaf children; they all babble at an early age, and they receive feedback from their vocalizations through sensory channels other than hearing. Maturation occurs and social experience expands for both the hearing and the deaf child. Because they live in groups, all children need communication.

The deaf child does not hear; he learns meanings only from facial expressions, and he can use only visual symbols in thought.

There are, of course, basic differences between a hearing and a deaf child. The normal child hears the sounds he and others produce; the deaf child can hear neither his own vocalizations nor the voices of others. The normal child learns to associate meaning with sounds; he gathers messages from his mother's voice as well as from her expressions and gestures. The deaf child learns to associate meanings only with facial expressions and gestures. The hearing child has frequent opportunity to say distinctly the same word over and over and to associate the word with its contextual meaning; the deaf child sees only glimpses of words on the lips of others. These glimpses are too vague for him to attach meanings. The normal child begins to use words in his thinking. The deaf child, because he cannot attach meanings to sounds, probably thinks in visual symbols.

Deaf children must be trained as early as possible and given hearing aids early if they will help.

As the normal child begins to talk, the deaf child's need for communication is also urgent. He begins to use gestures to express his wants, and he looks for gestures from other people. For the normal child, the comprehension of speech develops through his contact with other people. It brings him new knowledge and an active interest in the world. His ability to use words stimulates his social development. The deaf child's social development is handicapped, since sign language is his only means of communication. A wide gap develops between a deaf child and his peers. Gestures alone are not adequate signs, either for intellectual development or for social relations. The deaf child's communication by gestures and signs becomes more limited as he matures; he becomes isolated. By the age of three, the normal child can understand a good deal of what others say. A deaf child of three can express only his immediate needs; he is understood only by people familiar with his particular code. This isolation can be stopped, certainly by one year of age, by giving hearing aids to those children who can be helped by these devices. Special instruction must be given to the totally deaf child by the time he is two. The earlier training is started, the better.

The acquisition of language occurs before puberty. In aphasia, the child relearns while the adult may only recover.

When is it too late to acquire speech and language? The primary acquisition of language occurs before puberty. This is shown dramatically in the effects of age upon recovery from traumatic aphasia (Lenneberg, 1967). Aphasia is not at all like the usual memory loss. In aphasia, language is not lost; its proper organization is just disrupted. An aphasic person cannot organize his activities to integrate or inhibit his language. In contrast to children, the adult aphasic cannot relearn his language; adults either recover within three months or they do not recover at all. With children between four and ten years of age, the early symptoms are similar but the prognosis is very different. Almost all young children recover with no residual effects, although their recovery takes much longer than does the adult's, since children regain language by relearning. Children continue to improve through puberty. In the infant, we find still another pattern. If the very young child has lost his speech, he will go back to very early stages and retrace all of the earlier phases of infant language organization—babbling, single words, two-word phrases, and then speech. In the very young, recovery is by reacquisition; in the adolescent or adult, language returns only to the extent of brain recovery.

The brains of infants are equipotential; only after structure is developed can damage lead to permanent impairment.

This probably results from lateralization and organization of speech functioning in the human brain. If trauma occurs or a tumor is present in the infant or child, a normally left-dominant brain becomes right dominant; speech functions are carried out on the right side (Lenneberg, 1967). However, as the child moves closer and closer to puberty, left or right dominance and total brain organization are more firmly established; if he acquires a trauma or a tumor on the left side, he will become partially or completely aphasic (depending on how complete is the organization).

THEORIES OF SYNTAX

Although models of adult grammar are probably inappropriate, they are the only ones we have to describe children's speech.

Most research deals with models of grammar appropriate only for adult language. Considerable evidence suggests that these models cannot adequately describe the grammar of children. For example, the protocols gathered by Piaget (Flavell, 1963) argue strongly for a sequential staging of mental development, which would place grammar learning prior to the logical operations of adults. Thus, to argue that the learning processes and the grammatical utterances of adults are similar to those of children is hasty. Nevertheless, we will do exactly that, for the simple reason that no model of language development exists. We will look

REMARKS: THEORY—COMPETENCE AND PERFORMANCE

There are two levels of interest in language behavior: (1) competence (the knowledge of a language the individual has without considering memory limitations, shifts in attention, false starts, and so on), and (2) performance (the actual ability of the language user to produce strings of words). Only when we are dealing with ideal language users (with no human limitations) do these two levels directly correspond. Most modern linguists take the ideal user as their starting point. They feel we must know something of the structure and underlying grammar of the ideal individual before we can make statements about how he comes to produce the sounds of sentences.

Correspondingly, there are two sets of criteria by which sentences are judged. If we are interested in competence, then the grammaticalness of the sentence is the important aspect for us to consider—how a sentence compares with the possible sentences that may be generated by the syntactic rules of our grammar. However, if we are interested in performance, then we should use acceptability as our criterion for judging sentences. Acceptability of sentences concerns their pronounceability and comprehensibility—characteristics that interact with the native speaker's memory and attention limitations (Chomsky, 1957).

Recall that syntax is the study of the rules by which sentences are constructed. Syntactic investigation has as its goal the development of a grammar—a system for producing sentences of a language. In general, a language is considered to be an infinite set of sentences, each finite in length and constructed from a finite set of elements. All natural languages meet these criteria. The primary aim of a linguistic analysis is to separate the grammatical sequences (which are sentences of the language) from the ungrammatical sequences (which are not sentences in the language).

A successful model of a language should be a device that generates all the grammatical sequences of a language and none of the ungrammatical ones. A simple way to test the adequacy of a model is to determine whether or not the sequences it generates seem grammatical (to a native speaker). How do we go about separating grammatical sequences from ungrammatical ones? Some answers that suggest themselves cannot be correct (Chomsky, 1965). For example, (1) the grammar cannot be identified with any particular set of utterances; (2) our notion of grammatical sentences cannot be identified with meaning or significance in a systematic sense. Sentences can be nonsensical but grammatical. For example, "Colorless, green ideas sleep furiously" is a grammatically correct, nonsensical sentence, whereas, "Furious sleep ideas green colorless" is equally nonsensical and also ungrammatical. In summary, grammar is autonomous, independent of meaning, and is not related directly to the particular body of sentences used in its construction or test.

Currently, the acceptability and grammaticalness of utterances is based on the judgment of a native speaker. This leads to no serious problems, since usually the judgment is not difficult to make.

at descriptions of adult language and make what inferences we can about how children come to use grammar.

A Markov model (Chomsky, 1957; Miller, 1962)

Linguists generate meaningful grammatical sentences at the level of morphemes; phonemic representation is too difficult.

Assume that the grammatical sentences of English are strings of symbols we want to produce. What sort of device will produce this set of utterances? Language is an enormously complex system. Thus, it seems clear that any attempt to develop correct phonemic sequences directly (one letter at a time) would require many complex rules. Because direct phonemic description requires many complex rules, linguistic description proceeds through levels of representation. Instead of starting with the phonemic structure of sentences directly, the linguist starts at a higher level of organization, such as morphemes (words). He first states the morphemic structure of sentences (grammar) and then the phonemic structure of morphemes (spelling, speech). The use of two levels will produce simpler rules than a direct description of the phonemic structure (letter by letter) of sentences.

A simple device with finite states and transitional probabilities will produce some but not all of the sentences of English.

What type of grammar will generate the sequences of morphemes that constitute a grammatical English sentence? The grammar must be finite, so it cannot be a simple listing of morphemes; there are infinitely many of these strings. A simple communication-theory model suggests a way out of this difficulty. Assume we have a device which may be in any one of several finite states and suppose the machine changes from one state to another by producing a symbol. Thus, our machine begins in an initial state, runs through a sequence of states (producing a word with each transition), and ends in a final state. We may call the sequence of words that were produced a sentence. Thus, the machine defines a language, and any language that can be produced by a machine of this sort is a finite-state language. The grammar that produces just two sentences, "The boy comes" and "The boys come," can be represented by the state diagram in Figure 13.5. We may extend this grammar to produce an infinite number of sentences by adding closed loops. Thus, in the finite-state grammar contained in the sentences, "The boy comes" and "The boys come," we add the

FIGURE 13.5

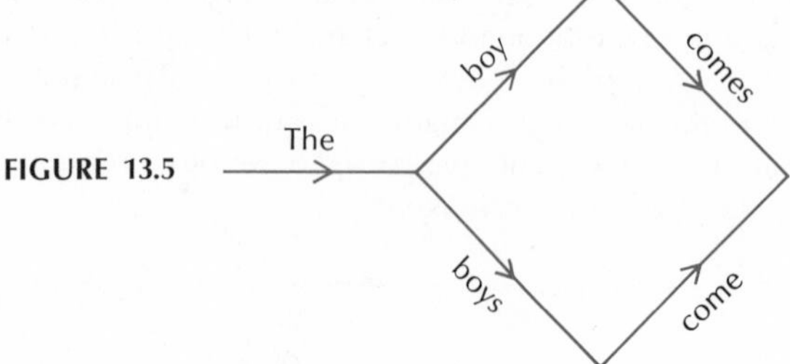

This state diagram shows the paths that can be taken to produce either of two sentences. By taking the upper path the sentence is "The boy comes," while taking the lower path produces the sentence "The boys come." (From Chomsky, 1954.)

FIGURE 13.6

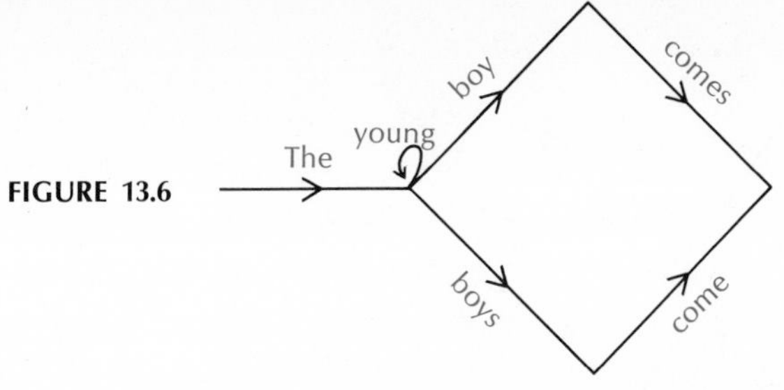

State diagram. By adding the closed loop ("young") we are now able to produce four sentences. By using the loop we can produce the two sentences "The young boy comes" and "The young boys come," and by not using the loop we can produce the two sentences "The boy comes" and "The boys come." (From Chomsky, 1957.)

closed loop "young" to produce "The young boy comes," "The young, young boy comes," "The young boys come," "The young, young boys come." All these sentences can be represented by the state diagram in Figure 13.6. This conception of language is extremely general. If we adopt it, we view the speaker as a device of the type described. However, any attempt to construct a finite-state grammar of English runs into serious difficulties, since English is not a finite-state language; there are an infinite number of possible sentences in the English language. One can show that English is *not* a finite language by embedding: Theoretically, *one* sentence can be very long—just keep adding descriptive phrases—and there are an infinite number of possible sentences. It is impossible, not just difficult, for the device described above to produce all the grammatical sentences of English.

A phrase-structure model

A phrase-structure grammar describes English more adequately.

The basic units of a sentence are individual morphemes; larger parts of a sentence are called intermediate constituents. Table 13.2 shows a constituent-structure analysis of a sentence. The hierarchical analysis of a sentence into constituent structures suggests a new rule: Instead of trying to generate the sentence from left to right, we might move from the top down.

Constituent structure includes several levels of analysis.

Linguistic descriptions may be formulated in terms of constituent phrase structures (Chomsky, 1957). This new type of grammar is much more powerful than the finite-state model. Constituent-structure gram-

TABLE 13.2 Constituent-Structure Analysis of a Sentence

Sentence	The man bought the apples				
Subject-predicate	The man		bought the apples		
Subject-verb-object	The man		bought	the apples	
Words	The	man	bought	the	apples
Morphemes	The	man	bought	the	apple s
Phonemes	T h e m a n b o u g h t t h e a p p l e s				

FIGURE 13.7

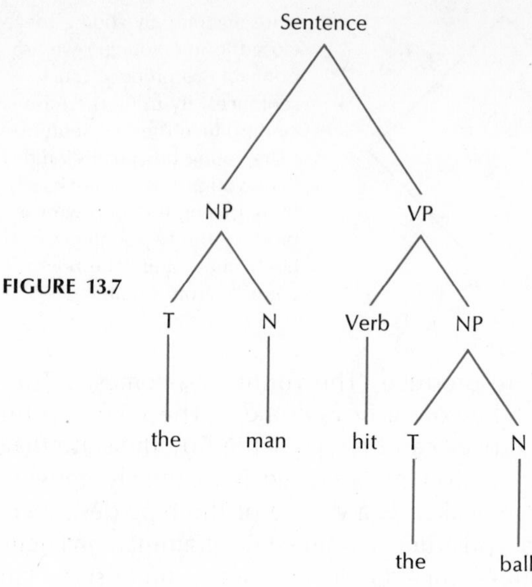

Derivation diagram. (From Chomsky, 1957.)

mars assume several levels of organization. Suppose we take a sentence as the top level (see Figure 13.7 and Table 13.2). At the next level we find two constituents, a noun phrase and a verb phrase (a subject and a predicate). Each of these parts can be separated further. The noun phrase contains an article (for example, "a," "the") and a subject (noun); the verb phrase usually contains a verb (for example, "hit," "fall") and often another noun phrase (the object). The second noun phrase, contained in the verb phrase, can be further separated into an article and a noun. Thus, in Table 13.2 we see the sentence "The man bought the apples" contains first a noun phrase ("the man") and a verb phrase ("bought the apples"). The noun phrase contains an article ("the") and a noun ("man"). The verb phrase contains a verb ("bought") and another noun phrase ("the apples") and the second noun phrase contains an article ("the") and another noun ("apples"). This type of analysis produces the tree shown in Figure 13.7 and follows the rules of constituent-structure grammar:

(i)	Sentence → *NP* + *VP*	(a sentence contains a noun phrase and a verb phrase)
(ii)	*NP* → *T* + *N*	(a noun phrase contains an article and a noun)
(iii)	*VP* → *Verb* + *NP*	(a verb phrase contains a verb and a noun phrase)
(iv)	*T* → *the*	(*T* is an article)
(v)	*N* → *man, ball,* and so on	(*N* is a noun)
(vi)	*V* → *hit, took,* and so on	(*V* is a verb)

Next, we run through these rules in the *derivation* of a sentence: "The man hit the ball." The numbers at the right of each line of the derivation refer to the rule of our "grammar" used in constructing that line from the preceding line.

Sentence Operation	*Rule Used*
NP + *VP*	(i)
T + *N* + *VP*	(ii)
T + *N* + *Verb* + *NP*	(iii)
the + *N* + *Verb* + *NP*	(iv)
the + *man* + *Verb* + *NP*	(v)
the + *man* + *hit* + *NP*	(vi)
the + *man* + *hit* + *T* + *N*	(ii)
the + *man* + *hit* + *the* + *N*	(iv)
the + *man* + *hit* + *the* + *ball*	(v)

Thus the second line is formed from the first by rewriting *Sentence* → *NP* + *VP* in accordance with rule (i); the third line is formed from the second line by rewriting *NP* as *T* + *N* in accordance with rule (ii), etc.

A transformational grammar (Chomsky, 1957)

In addition to phrase structure, we need transformations to generate the passive voice, interrogation, plurality, and so on.

We have outlined two models for the construction of language, a communication theory model based on a notion of language as a statistical process (finite state) and a phrase-structure model based on structural analysis. The first is inadequate as a model of English and the second, although more powerful, also has limitations. The theory of phrase structure has difficulty describing all the grammar of English. In the phrase-structure grammar described above, we had only one way of analyzing the verb element (*hit*). And even if the verb root is fixed (*take*), there are many forms this element may assume (*takes, has* + *taken, will* + *take, has* + *been* + *taken,* and so on). How to generate auxiliary verbs is crucial to the development of an English grammar. We can more easily define the occurrence of auxiliary verbs in declarative sentences by adding to phrase-structure grammar some transformation rules that handle verb forms, interrogation, tense, negation, and the like.

The combination of phrase structure and transformational grammar is more powerful than either alone.

A phrase-structure grammar adequately handles part of the language; the remainder may be derived by repeated application of a simple set of transformations to the strings produced by the phrase-structure grammar. If we attempt to extend phrase-structure grammar to cover the entire language, we lose the simplicity of a limited phrase-structure grammar combined with the transformational development. The extension of phrase-structure grammar to cover the entire language would negate the whole point of level construction. What we want to do is rebuild the vast complexity of the actual language corpus simply and systematically. We may do this by abstracting several linguistic levels, each of which is simple in itself, and combining these levels with rules to form the total complex language corpus. We call these supplementary rules transformations.

Transformations have an obligatory order, and some must be applied.

The main properties of a transformational grammar are (1) the order of application of transformations and (2) certain transformations are obligatory while others are optional. Thus, we have a grammar with a natural three-way arrangement. Corresponding to the level of phrase structure, a grammar has a sequence of rules of the form $X \rightarrow Y$. Corresponding to lower levels, it has the sequence of morphological rules (which dictate how letters go into words) and, linking these two levels, it has a sequence of transformational rules (how to ask a question, negate a sentence, and so on).

To produce an utterance, we take a kernel sentence and derive a particular form by applying transformations.

To generate a sentence from such a grammar, we must perform an extended derivation. We begin with the ideas of the sentence (meaning). Then we apply rules to construct a sequence of morphemes (not necessarily in their proper order). We then apply the sequence of transformations, using each obligatory one and sometimes optional ones. These transformations rearrange, add, or delete morphemes. For example, in asking a question we reverse the order of verb and object (declaration—*we can;* question—*can we?*). Next, we use phonemic rules to convert the string of morphemes into a string of phonemes. When this transformational analysis is correctly formulated, it is more powerful than description in terms of phrase structure, just as the latter was more powerful than description in terms of a finite-state process.

Grammar is independent of semantics (meaning); sentences can be grammatical and nonsensical.

The study of grammar is independent of semantics. The notion of grammaticalness should not be identified with meaningfulness. In following this independent study, we saw that a simple model of language as a finite-state Markov process, which produces sentences from left to right, is not adequate. We introduced more abstract levels of analysis, phrase-structure and transformational rules, to aid our description of language and to gain important insights into its structure. We have limited our description in terms of phrase structure to a kernel sentence (simple, declarative, active, with no complex verb or noun phrases) and derived all other sentences from these kernel sentences, or, more properly, from the strings that underlie them. We carry out the derivation by transformations (that is, passive, negative). Having found the set of transformations that carries grammatical sentences into other grammatical sentences, we can determine the constituent structure of particular sentences by investigating their behavior under these transformations.

Studies of transformational grammar

Mehler showed that we store kernel sentences in memory and make errors which lose the transformation code.

The notion that grammar is comprised of a structural component that formulates simple sentences and another that transforms these into more complex forms by rules of combining, permuting, and deleting has generated several experiments. Mehler (1963) tested the notion that in storing a complex sentence in memory we recode it into its simplest declarative form to which we add a syntactic footnote specifying its particular grammatical complexity. He had his subjects memorize sentences that varied systematically in grammatical form (simple declarative, passive, negative, and interrogative sentences). Recall of the sentences was marked by two effects. Most of the errors were due to syntactical confusions; the meaning was correct, but the subject could not remember whether the sentence was a declaration or a question. Errors were much rarer in the kernel content of the sentences (declarative) than in their more complex forms (questions, negations, passive). Moreover, the recalled form of the sentences tended toward simpler syntactical form (declarative). Mehler also tested the hypothesis that the recall of any one syntactic footnote is independent of recalling any other. If his assumption was correct, then errors for none, one, two, or three of the transformations should be distributed binomially. Within tolerable limits, that was the distribution he found.

Slobin tested linguistic notions about transformations; he showed that the ability to handle linguistic complexity increases with age, and that most transformations are available by the age of six.

On the development of grammar, Slobin (1963) studied several interesting notions derived from the transformational grammar of Chomsky. Children between six and 12 years of age were presented a number of spoken sentence-picture pairs, one pair at a time. Their task was to say whether the sentence was true or false in describing the picture. Errors and the time required to decide in each instance were recorded. The sentences were of four grammatical types—kernel, passive, negative, and negative passive. The pictures also were of two kinds—reversible and nonreversible, the former permitting reversibility of subject and object (a dog chasing a cat) and the latter not permitting it (a boy raking the grass). The findings point to limitations on our formal grammar as a model of language development. The passive sentences took the children longer to decide upon than kernels, and the passive negatives more time than the negatives. But one must introduce semantic and psychological considerations to account for the fact that negative sentences require more time to evaluate than passive ones. On the basis of syntax alone, it should not be so (both are single transformations). If anything, the syntactic complexity of the passive form should produce slower evaluation time than the simpler negative form. But, as we know from several sources, negative information is difficult for children to process. Recall, however, that the transformational grammar is supposed to describe the ideal speaker, (without limitations of memory, attention, articulation, etc.); the distinction between competence and performance is relevant here. Only when the psycholinguist formulates performance rules can we test his theory of language. At the moment, grammar describes only the competence of an ideal speaker; it says nothing about the difficulties a native speaker might have with different transformations. On the other hand, we should be unhappy if the complexity of transformations is not related to performance difficulty.

Formal language theory is not directly related to language performance.

A hint at what was going on was contained in the reversible and nonreversible pictures. For irreversible pictures, the difference in evaluation time between passive and kernel sentences vanished; passive-negatives were no more difficult than plain negative sentences. Slobin suggested that when the picture carries an irreversible message, the order of the two nouns does not matter. Only when there is some semantic reversibility does the order marker of the passive require time to compute. Slobin also had the children repeat stories in their own words. He told the stories in two forms—full passive and passive without the actor. It is a procedure that tests for the kernelization hypothesis (in comprehending a complex sentence it is translated back into a kernel form, taking note of the transformations used). The regular passive sentence was often repeated in kernel (active) form, although this happened rarely with the passive form from which the actor had been deleted ("The cake was eaten by the boy" versus "The cake was eaten"). The results suggest that while skill in dealing with syntactical complexity increases with age, the abilities mentioned above are present by six years. The syntactically more complex passives are easier to deal with correctly than the simpler negative. It can hardly be said that the formal linguistic theory easily generates a psychological theory of language development, but it was not intended to do such; it does give us hints about the processes going on.

INDIVIDUAL VARIATION IN LANGUAGE SKILLS

Children from middle class homes are superior in language ability to children from lower class homes.

Although all children learn their native tongue, there are vast differences in competence. Children from professional homes, from middle class homes, only children, and girls tend to have superior language abilities when compared with children from laborers' homes, lower class homes, children from large families, and boys. Twins develop a native language but also communicate between themselves with a private language. This private language can often retard their development of conventional communication.

Language is one of man's most unique characteristics.

Language is one of man's unique characteristics; how he comes to speak and comprehend these sounds remains one of the great problems for developmental psychology.

SUMMARY

1 There are three levels of language analysis: phonemic, morphemic, and grammatical. Phonemes are the raw materials of language; they correspond roughly to letters. Morphemes are the building blocks of sentences; they correspond roughly to words, while grammar comprises the rules for arranging words into sentences.

2 The early babbling of infants has attracted considerable attention; they produce all the sounds of language during this time. However, their babbling is unrelated to later language abilities.

3 The acquisition of language seems to be largely maturational; it fits the main criteria of a genetic process; however, there must be experience.

4 Two theories of language acquisition have been proposed. The empiricist suggests that association and generalization can explain how the child comes to talk. However, the child would have to be exposed to every sentence in the language before he could speak—an unlikely situation. The rationalist believes a child is endowed with genetic propensities for speech; he need only be stimulated by the environment to develop these devices.

5 Early grammar learning focuses on nouns and verbs; the connectives come later. The child's interaction with his mother is different from adult-adult conversation; however, there is no evidence that this interaction is necessary for speech development.

6 Children learn the latent structure of language. They do not memorize sentences; they analyze a language. Early grammars consist of single words. Later they choose pivot words, with all other words following the pivot word. Position is the keeper of early grammar. Next, the child comes to understand language as a threefold system.

FURTHER READINGS

Brown, R. *Social psychology.* New York: The Free Press, 1965.

Chomsky, N. *Aspects of the theory of syntax.* Cambridge, Mass.: M.I.T. Press, 1965.

REFERENCES

Braine, M. D. S. The ontogeny of English phrase structure: The first phase. *Language,* 1963, **39,** 1-13.

Brown, R. W. Linguistic determinism and the parts of speech. *Journal of abnormal and social Psychology,* 1957, **55,** 1-5.

Brown, R. W. *Social psychology.* New York: The Free Press, 1965.

Brown, R. W., & Berko, J. Word association and the acquisition of grammar. *Child Development,* 1960, **31,** 1-14.

Chen, H. P., & Irwin, O. C. Infant speech vowel and consonant types. *Journal of Speech Disorders,* 1946, **11,** 27-29.

Chomsky, N. *Syntactic structures.* The Hague: Mouton, 1957.

Chomsky, N. *Aspects of the theory of syntax.* Cambridge, Mass.: M.I.T. Press, 1965.

Flavell, J. *The developmental psychology of Jean Piaget.* Princeton, N.J.: Van Nostrand, 1963.

Greenberg, J. H., Osgood, C. E., & Jenkins, J. J. Memorandum concerning language universals. In J. H. Greenberg (Ed.), *Universals of language.* Cambridge, Mass.: M.I.T. Press, 1966. Pp. xv-xxvii. Paperback edition.

Hess, E. H. Imprinting. *Science,* 1959, **130,** 133-141.

Lenneberg, E. *Biological foundations of language.* New York: Wiley, 1967.

McNeill, D. Developmental linguistics. In F. Smith & G. A. Miller (Eds.), *The genesis of language. A psycholinguistic approach.* Cambridge, Mass.: M.I.T. Press, 1966.

Mehler, J. *How some sentences are remembered.* Unpublished doctoral dissertation, Harvard University, 1963.

Miller, G. A. Some logical aspects of grammar. *American Psychologist,* 1962, **17,** 748-762.

Osgood, C. E. Language universals and psycholinguistics. In J. H. Greenberg (Ed.), *Universals of language.* Cambridge, Mass.: M.I.T. Press, 1966. Pp. 299-322. Paperback edition.

Slobin, D. I. Grammatical transformations in childhood and adulthood. Unpublished doctoral dissertation, Harvard University, 1963.

Smith, M. K. Measurement of the size of general English vocabulary through the elementary grades and high school. *Genetic Psychology Monographs,* 1941, **24,** 311-345.

Velten, H. V. The growth of phonemic and lexical patterns in infant language. *Language,* 1943, **19,** 281-292.

Weir, M. W., & Stevenson, H. W. The effect of verbalization in children's learning as a function of chronological age. *Child Development,* 1959, **30,** 143-149.

14 INTELLIGENCE AND CREATIVITY

Not Hercules
Could have knock'd out his brains, for he had none.
CYMBELINE

A major achievement of nineteenth-century psychology was the ability to assign numbers reflecting a person's intellectual capacity. Binet initiated the first successful measurement of intelligence by devising problems which required a child to use past experiences in their solutions. These were phrased as standard questions which could be answered and scored objectively.

Intelligence tests measure the relative standing of children and their peers.

Intelligence tests tell us the relative standing of a child compared with his peers. This chapter examines the early history of intelligence testing, various definitions of intelligence, the reliability and validity of tests, and the controversy over constancy of IQ. A brief summary of several different intelligence tests (including infant, preschool, adult, and special-purpose tests), and the case for "culture-fair" and "culture-free" tests follows. A section on productive thinking, an important and often neglected part of intelligence, concludes the chapter.

THE DEVELOPMENT OF INTELLIGENCE TESTS

Some view intelligence as a global trait while others see it as a collection of separate abilities.

Definitions of intelligence revolve about two poles: (1) intelligence is a general, global trait which permeates all behavior, and (2) intelligence is an aggregate of simple skills which combine to give us intellect. Binet (1905), who was commissioned by the Paris public school system to find a test for predicting academic achievement, defined intelligence as the ability to carry out abstract thinking in the solution of problems. He assumed that intelligence increases with age. Once he had developed a set of questions related to age (older children more often passed

FIGURE 14.1

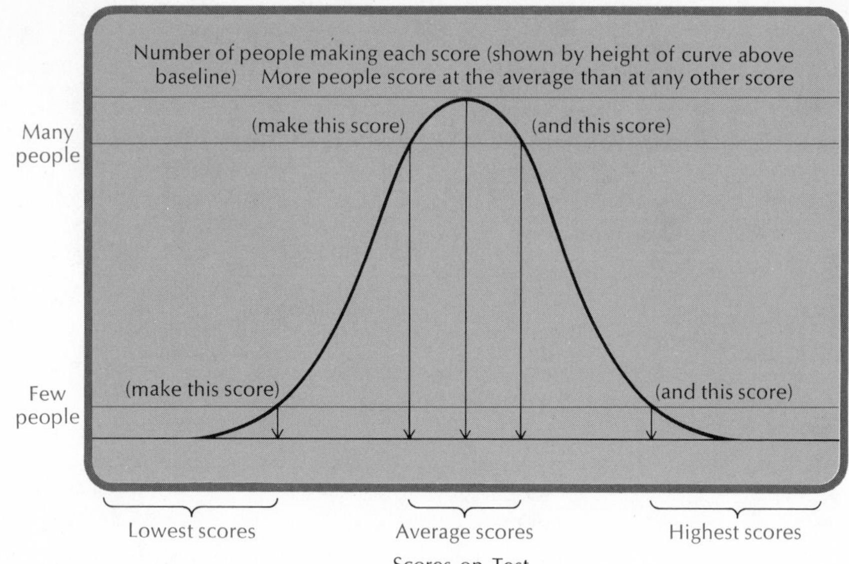

The curve of intelligence.

an item than younger children) he began refining his test to make it more reliable and valid. One step was to pick items that correlated with each other and with the child's total score. Those items with the highest relation to the total score were retained. By a series of steps—(1) assuming an external criterion (age), (2) developing a set of items that correlated with age, and (3) selecting an internally consistent set—Binet and Simon (1905) developed the first, and one of the best, tests of intelligence.

Terman believed intelligence is the ability to use abstract symbols to solve problems.

Terman (1916), who brought the Binet-Simon Intelligence Scale to the United States, believed IQ is the ability to carry out abstract thinking and to use abstract symbols in the solution of problems. Wechsler (1949), on the other hand, defined intelligence as an aggregate of specific capacities. He set out to measure a person's ability to act purposefully, think rationally, and deal effectively with his environment.

TABLE 14.1 Terman's (1916) IQ Classification

Dullness, rarely classifiable as feeble-mindedness	80–90
Borderline deficiency, sometimes classifiable as dullness, often as feeble-mindedness	70–80
Moron	50–70
Imbecile	20–50
Idiot	Below 20

TABLE 14.2 Percentile Values of Various IQ Scores

The Child Whose IQ Is	Is Equalled or Excelled by
160	1 out of 10,000
156	3 out of 10,000
152	8 out of 10,000
148	2 out of 1,000
144	4 out of 1,000
140	7 out of 1,000

The Child Whose IQ Is	*Equals or Exceeds*	*The Child Whose IQ Is*	*Equals or Exceeds*
136	99 percent	99	48 percent
135	98	98	45
134	98	97	43
133	98	96	40
132	97	95	38
131	97	94	36
130	97	93	34
129	96	92	31
128	96	91	29
127	95	90	27
126	94	89	25
125	94	88	23
124	93	87	21
123	92	86	20
122	91	85	18
121	90	84	16
120	89	83	15
119	88	82	14
118	86	81	12
117	85	80	11
116	84	79	10
115	82	78	9
114	80	77	8
113	79	76	8
112	77	75	6
111	75	74	6
110	73	73	5
109	71	72	4
108	69	71	4
107	66	70	3
106	64	69	3
105	62	68	3
104	60	67	2
103	57	66	2
102	55	65	2
101	52	64	1
100	50	63	1
		62	1

REMARKS: THEORY

What is an average IQ? This question was answered by Binet; he picked the round number 100. Dividing mental age by chronological age to obtain the child's rate of intellectual growth was first used by Terman (1916) when he introduced the Binet-Simon Intelligence Scale in the United States. Notice that the child who is performing "normally" has the same mental age(*MA*) and chronological age (*CA*). This means his IQ is 1. Since Terman did not like fractions he multiplied *MA*/*CA* by 100. Thus, the average child receives an IQ score of 100. Deviations from this average follow a bell-shaped normal curve (see Figure 14.1). This distribution describes the result of many processes interacting in a random fashion. Individuals of below average IQ were classified by Terman (see Table 14.1) into five categories. Table 14.2 shows the number of individuals below persons receiving various scores on the Binet IQ test.

The particular score is completely arbitrary; only the relative ranking of individuals is invariant. The usual practice is to define intervals between scores in terms of the variability of a test. These statistics (called standard deviations) are estimates of the test's sensitivity. A test that produces a large standard deviation is insensitive when compared with another which generates a small standard deviation. Scores are expressed in terms of deviations from the mean. The purpose of this standardization is to achieve equality of intervals—so that the difference between 90 and 100 is the same as the difference between 40 and 50. If the units are equal, then the difference of ten points is the same in both cases. It is doubtful that strict equality of units exists, but IQ tests have a reasonable approximation to equality.

The Wechsler test measures several different traits which, collectively, enable the person to function in his environment. Thorndike *et al.* (1927) and Thurstone (1952) devised tests for children and adults to measure various elementary abilities (for example, spatial concepts, counting ability, and perceptual speed). However, Spearman (1927) felt intelligence is a single factor (*g*) which influences all behavior. Although these two definitions of intelligence seem quite different, the correlation between a person's score on the Binet test and his score on the Wechsler test is high. The correlation reflects the pragmatic history of both tests: They were designed to differentiate people, and they do that quite well.

RELIABILITY AND VALIDITY

An intelligence test should be valid and reliable.

There are two methodological problems every test maker must solve—the problem of reliability (how to obtain the same score when measuring a single trait several times) and the problem of validity (how to know that we are measuring what we want to measure). A test is reliable if it produces the same score for the same individual over different testing sessions. A test is valid if it measures what it is supposed to measure and we can predict other performance from scores on the test.

Test reliability is assessed by measuring the same person twice, by dividing the test into parts, or by producing separate forms.

The reliability of a test is estimated by administering it on two separate occasions and computing the correlation between the scores of several children on occasions one and two. If the relation is high and positive, the test is reliable. Reliability of a test may also be estimated by correlating the child's score on one half of the test with his score on the other half. This "split-half" reliability is legitimate only if we believe the test is measuring a single general factor of intelligence; if we are measuring specific abilities, there is no reason to believe, for example, that a high score on numerical items will be related to a high score on language items. The most reasonable estimate of reliability is to measure the same group on two occasions. The main problem with this approach is that some children may recall answers from the first session, and this will give them a higher score on their second test. If we are interested only in the test's reliability, this is no problem; the child's relative *rank* is important, not the average score of the group. As long as each child remembers a comparable amount, either the same for all children or, more likely, some amount proportional to their IQs, their relative ranks will not be changed, and the

FIGURE 14.2

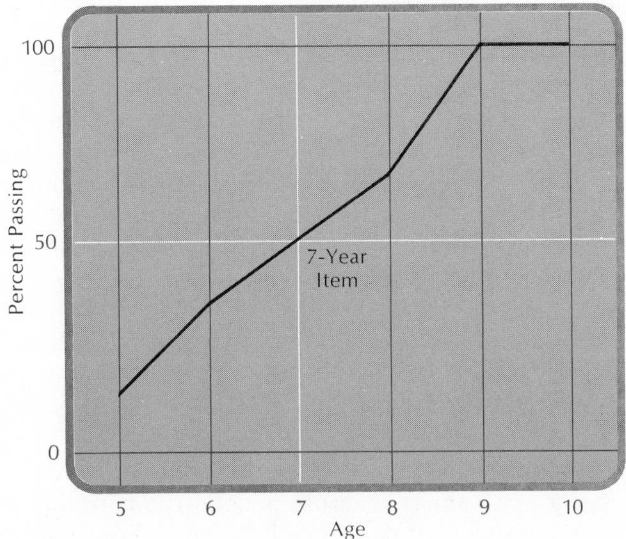

The percentage of children at various ages who pass a seven-year-item from the Stanford-Binet Intelligence Scale.

FIGURE 14.3

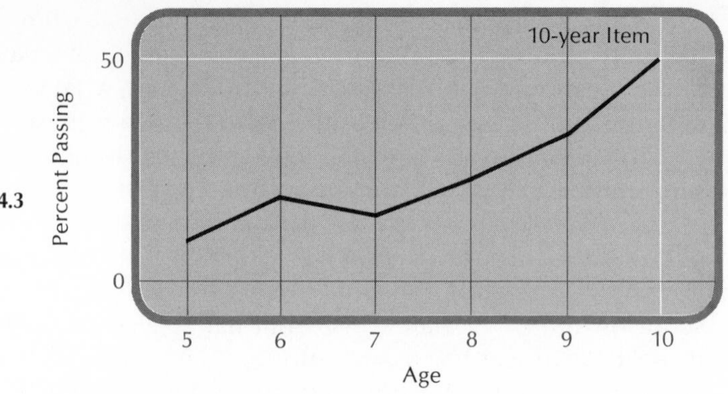

The percentage of children at various ages who pass a ten-year-item from the Stanford-Binet Intelligence Scale.

correlation between sessions one and two will reflect reliability unconfounded by memory.

The main problem in assessing validity is the selection of a criterion.

Our main concern about validity is in the selection of a criterion with which to compare our test of intelligence. After we have solved the criterion problem, any item that correlates with the criterion is a good candidate for our test.

Binet used age and internal consistency as his criteria of intelligence.

Our conceptions of intelligence are criteria against which items may be evaluated. For example, Binet and Simon assumed that amount of intelligence increases with age. The number of children passing an item was used to decide whether the item should be included in the test (see Figures 14.2 and 14.3). The assumption was that older children possess more intelligence than younger children, and so more older children should pass an item than younger children. Binet used other criteria: intercorrelation of items and correlation of a particular item with the total score. In addition, Binet used two other characteristics in evaluating test items. The item had to be easy to administer and it had to be reliably scored.

THE CONSTANCY OF IQ

Fixed or variable intelligence can best be understood in the context of genetic-environment interaction.

Terman (1916) assumed that intelligence tests measure the genetic capacity of the individual. However, if we take seriously the notion of interaction between genetic endowment and environmental influences, then a test cannot measure genetic capacity directly; it can measure the joint effects of nature and nurture expressed in the phenotype. We must be able to specify both the environmental influence and genotype before we can say whether the child has reached his potential.

Consider an example. Suppose we have a three-by-three matrix (Figure 14.4). Along one axis of this matrix we place three levels of genetically endowed intelligence—low, medium, and high. Along the other axis we place three levels of environmental influence—again, for convenience, called low, medium, and high. If we take interaction seriously, then the particular genetic endowment the organism receives and the environmental influences to which he is exposed both have to be specified before we can know whether or not the child is growing at an optimum rate.

There is optimal stimulation for any given genetic endowment.

As a simple example, consider the low genetically endowed individual. The child who receives low endowment may develop optimally under low environmental stimulation while exposure to either medium or high environmental stimulation will overload him and retard development. In the case of the child with moderate genetic endowment, medium stimulation from the environment might be optimal, and either too little or too much environmental input would be detrimental; little environmental input would not be stimulating enough, while high input could confuse him. Finally, in the case of the high genetically endowed child, low and medium environmental stimulation would be dull; he should receive rich stimulation. Notice that the main diagonal of the three-by-three matrix defines optimum interaction between genetic endowment and the environmental influences to which children are exposed; any deviation from the main diagonal is probably detrimental to development.

FIGURE 14.4

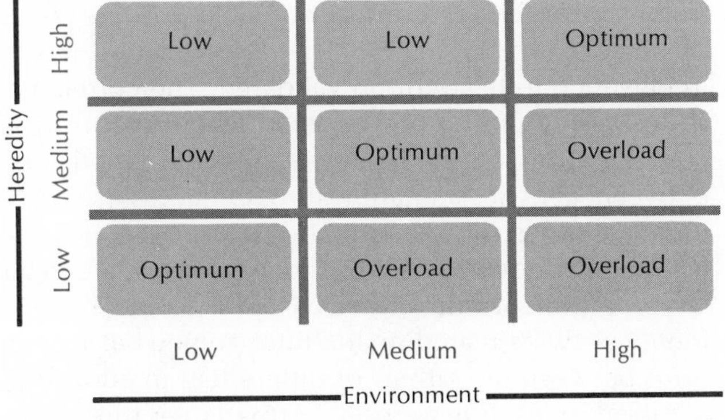

A matrix showing three levels of genetically endowed intelligence (low, medium, and high) and three levels of environmental conditions (low, medium, and high). The main diagonal shows the optimum interaction between genetic endowment and environmental influences.

Finding the optimum environment for each child is the main problem of education.

Finding an optimum match between genetic endowment and environmental stimulation is difficult; we cannot solve these complexities by exposing all children to a constant environment. Talk about optimal intellectual growth is useless unless we can specify the child's genetic endowment. However, the direct measurement of genetic endowment is confounded with environmental influences. One way to solve this problem is to present a variety of environmental influences to each child and see under which level of stimulation he grows optimally. For example, we could expose a child to various levels of environmental stimulation (low, medium, and enriched) for specified intervals and measure his intellectual growth. In this way we should find his optimum level of environmental stimulation. Another method is to measure the parents' IQ which will give us a fair estimate of the child's genetic endowment.

Terman, who introduced intelligence testing to the United States, believed intelligence is predetermined.

Neither Binet nor Simon supported predeterminism, but the man who introduced intelligence tests to the United States saw genetics as the primary cause of intelligence (Terman, 1916). He pointed out that individual children show good IQ constancy through the school years. This may be because schools standardize the child's environment. Also, some children's IQ scores change dramatically over time, due to either adverse or improved environmental conditions. Proponents of predetermined intelligence also point out that scores from various tests of intelligence are closely related. However, they are related because intelligence tests are developed to generate scores that correlate with the Stanford-Binet IQ test, or the same external criteria.

IQ scores are highly correlated with school performance.

Another argument for predetermined intelligence is that scores from various tests of intelligence yield positive correlations with quality of performance in school. These scores are the criteria against which intelligence tests are often validated. The correlation with school work shows only that the test does, in fact, measure what we define as IQ.

The best evidence for genetic determination of intelligence comes from twin studies (see Chapter 1).

The strongest evidence for predetermined IQ is the high relation between genetic similarity and IQ scores (see Chapter 1). Scores of identical twins show minimal differences. A high relation between the IQ scores of identical twins means that we are dealing with an hereditary component and that environment and heredity are confounded. Identical twins reared apart differ somewhat in measured IQ; correlations between the ratings of differences in educational opportunity and identical twins' IQs were +.79 (the larger the difference in educational opportunity, the larger the IQ difference) in a study by Newman, Freeman, & Holzinger (1937). This means that the type of education given a twin influences his intellectual development.

IQ scores for individuals show variation with age.

The Berkeley Growth Study (Macfarlane, 1939) showed large variations of individual scores on tests given at different ages. This may be because the same items are not given to children of different ages, a fact that constitutes a basic problem facing anyone trying to predict intelligence—we use different items to estimate the "same" ability.

Foundling children who are stimulated grow intellectually.

Evidence against predetermined IQ comes from the effects of orphanages and foundling homes upon the intellectual and cultural development of children. Apathy and retardation occur in orphanages. Observations suggest that the absence of a single *active* caretaker contributes to the apathy and retardation observed in such institutions. Much of the early apathy may come from sensory impoverishment and not simply the absence of a single caretaker.

Studies show that early environmental conditions affect the later performance of rats.

In contrast to the ambiguous findings with children, results from lower animals are relatively clear. Hebb (1947), using a complex maze as a test of intelligence, compared rats raised by his own children with litter mates reared in laboratory cages. The rats raised as pets were consistently faster at solving the maze, suggesting that variety of experience (or lack of experience) affects intellectual functioning even in the rat. Puppies reared as pets for their first eight months after weaning showed higher scores on a complex alley maze than did litter mates raised in laboratory cages for eight months. Finally, Riesen (1947) showed that monkeys are perceptually handicapped after being reared in darkness for 19 months.

Varied environmental stimulation may produce higher intelligence.

Encounters with a variety of environmental circumstances may enhance perceptual and intellectual abilities, while perceptual isolation or deprivation certainly has a debilitating effect on development. Varied early experience may be more important for more complex animals.

The particular unit to use in determining the growth of intelligence is ambiguous.

Hundreds of studies have been conducted to estimate the growth and decline of intellect. A major difficulty in relating intellectual growth to age is the selection of a unit. To use the year as an equal unit does not make sense in terms of what we know about the developmental sequence. A year at age two is much more important than a year at age 20. We probably ought to use the logarithm of age and relate this transformed score to mental age changes. We find a generally linear function relating intellectual development (mental age) and the logarithm of chronological age (see Figure 14.5).

Mature men who continue in college, live in cities, or major in science show significant IQ gains over peers who drop out, live in the country, or major in agricultural engineering.

Owens (1953) administered the same IQ test to 127 men as college freshmen and again 30 years later. Those who were not available for the follow-up test were not conspicuously different in general characteristics from those who took part in the second test. The mature men were significantly higher in average IQ than they had been as entering college freshmen. Their gain was greatest in those abilities labeled practical judgment, synonyms-antonyms, disarranged sentences, and information analogies. Ability to follow directions, handle arithmetic, and manage numbers was constant or decreased slightly. Men who

FIGURE 14.5

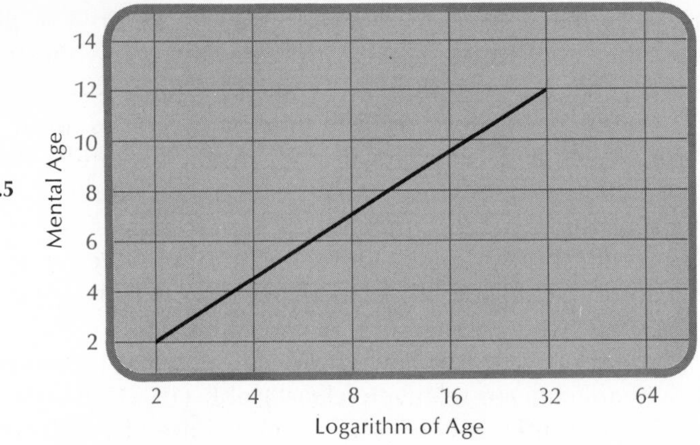

A proposed relation between mental age and chronological age.

were under 50 years of age gained slightly more than those who were over 50. The men who had completed more college work gained more than those with less education. Science majors showed more gain than agricultural engineering majors; men who moved from rural to urban settings gained more than those who had other patterns of residence. All these results suggest that measured IQ is influenced by the experiences to which a person is exposed.

Pettigrew believes that cultural and educational differences between whites and blacks contribute to IQ differences.

A comprehensive review of black American intelligence was presented by Pettigrew (1964). He stated that the old nature-nurture controversy is outdated and has been replaced by studies of how heredity and environment combine. He believes that the initial establishment and subsequent development of intellectual abilities is rooted in the earliest experiences of children. He feels that phenotypic intelligence is nowhere near the limits of genetic endowment. The intellectually damaging consequences of deprived environments are well documented. Studies of canal-boat children (Anastasi, 1965) and isolated mountain children (Sherman & Key, 1932) show that cultural deprivation lowers IQ; also, the IQs of isolated children differentially decline as they mature. This is not the case among children from more privileged or stimulating environments.

The black child is exposed to poor maternal diet, prematurity, inferior education, poor achievement motivation, and discrimination.

Pettigrew discussed the mediators of black children's intellectual underdevelopment: First is an inadequate diet for the mother; this factor accounts for many neurological defects and premature births among blacks. Black children show larger deficits in IQ as they age; this result may come from higher weighting of tests with verbal items or the schools to which black children are exposed. Pettigrew believes that the black's self-concept affects his performance. He often feels inferior in White America, and he may act in a self-fulfilling way.

Blacks who move north improve their IQ scores either by better education or self-selection.

Two well-known studies have demonstrated that blacks who move North improve their IQs; although there is reason to believe that motivational and genetic selection may be operating here along with better schools (Klineberg, 1935; Lee, 1951). Changes in self-concept, school environment, and early experience are necessary before blacks can attain equal standing in American society.

Jensen proposed the hypothesis that black-white IQ differences reflect genetic and not simply environmental differences.

Jensen (1969) has proposed an alternative hypothesis to explain the difference of 12-15 IQ points typically found between blacks and whites; he suggests the black community constitutes a closed breeding population biased in favor of lower IQ. He presents evidence from four sources in support of this hypothesis: (1) the strong heritability of IQ; (2) the impermanence of IQ gains from enrichment programs; (3) the filial regression of middle class black populations to white lower class IQ; and (4) the differential reproductive rate of lower class blacks compared with lower class whites. This hypothesis has produced considerable political rhetoric, some scientific interest, and a strong need for objective study.

INTELLIGENCE TESTS

The four main types of intelligence tests are (1) infant, (2) children, (3) adult, and (4) specialized.

There are four general types of intelligence tests—infant tests (birth to two years), children's tests (two to 12 years), adult tests, and more specialized placement tests like the Graduate Record Examination for superior adults. Tests for infants and children must be administered individually; for children below the age of five they contain mainly performance items. The infant is usually tested while he is lying down or supported on a person's lap; the preschool child sits, uses his hands to manipulate objects, and communicates by language; he is much more responsive to the experimenter (good rapport is thus more important). Adult intelligence tests are administered either individually or in a group. They are primarily verbal and test intellectual abilities like memory, information integration, perceptual completion, and vocabulary. Adult tests are the most reliable and valid of all intelligence scales. The final category includes tests for superior adults (such as the Graduate Record Examination) and tests of special abilities (such as clerical exams). The tests for superior adults differentiate among very bright individuals applying for advanced training in graduate schools. The tests are designed to differentiate among individuals who score at the upper limits of regular intelligence tests.

Infant tests

Widely used infant tests include the Gesell and the Cattell.

The most widely used developmental tests for infants are those of Gesell (1947) and Cattell (1947). Finding test items which tap the problem-solving ability of an infant is quite difficult. A problem involves a goal, and the infant is tested on his ability to obtain that goal. However, the goals of young infants are primitive; they want only to be full and warm. The infant has no direct means of reaching goals; he is dependent upon adults. Most infant intelligence scales concentrate on sensory-motor responses to changes in the environment; they also measure sensory-motor alertness (turning the head in the direction of a bell or light, or dropping one of two cubes to take a third and different one). A child who is advanced in sensory-motor coordination earns a high score while one who is not alert earns a low score. We believe that sensory-motor coordination plays some part in later intellectual growth (Piaget); however, correlations with later tests of intelligence are very low.

Gesell followed the development of 107 infants through their first year.

Gesell developed an extensive series of measures of infant and child behavior at the Yale Clinic of Child Development. He obtained data on 107 normal infants selected from parents whose socioeconomic status was about average, examining the children at four, six, and eight weeks of age, and then every four weeks through the first year. Follow-up studies were made at 18 months, two, three, four, five, and six years of age, with a re-examination every ten years thereafter. The studies were designed to determine the level of development the children had obtained in four areas (see Table 14.3).

TABLE 14.3 Four Areas of Behavior Measured by the Gesell Infant Test

1. *Motor behavior:* covers both gross bodily control and finer motor coordination. This category includes postural reactions, head balance, sitting, standing, creeping, walking, reaching for and grasping objects, and the manipulation of things.
2. *Adaptive behavior:* includes eye-hand coordination in reaching for and handling objects, solution of practical problems, and exploration. Examples of behavior in this category include reactions to toy cubes, a ringing bell, a dangling ring, and the solution of simple form boards.
3. *Language behavior:* includes all means of communication—facial expression, gesture, postural movements, prelinguistic vocalizations, and speech. The comprehension of communication by others is also included.
4. *Personal-social behavior:* covers the child's personal reactions to his culture Among the behaviors in this category are feeding, toilet training, play, smiling and other responses to persons, and reaction to a mirror.

Most items on the Gesell test are observational.

The Yale Developmental Examination is a standardized procedure for evaluating the course of development. Most of the items are purely observational. No overall score is computed for the infant; instead, his

FIGURE 14.6

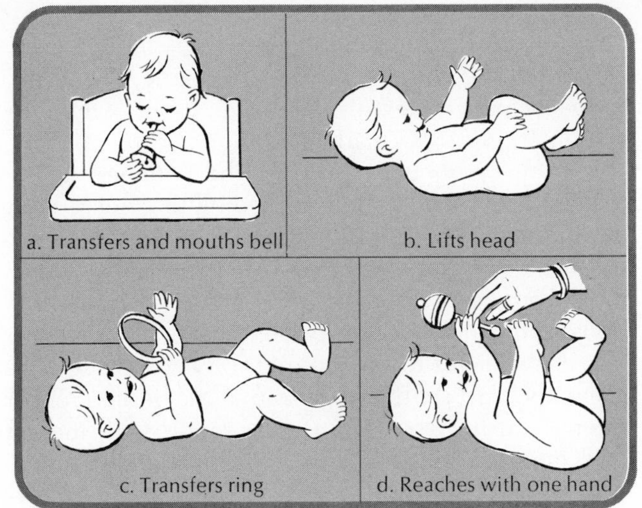

Drawings illustrating the Yale Developmental Examination. They show typical behavior at 28 weeks of age. Note the predominance of sensory-motor abilities. (From Gesell & Amatruda, 1947).

record indicates the approximate level (in months) he has reached in each of the four areas. Items in each of the scales are classified as *increasing* (behaviors whose frequency of occurrence increases with age, such as vocalizations), *decreasing* (behaviors that decrease with age, such as sucking), or *focal* (behaviors that increase to a point and then decrease with age, such as prelinguistic vocalizations). Increasing and decreasing behavior items are assigned to the age level where it occurs one half the time. Focal items are assigned to the age levels where they occur most frequently.

The more satisfactory Cattell test is essentially an extension of the Binet intelligence test into infancy.

The Cattell Infant Intelligence Scale is much more satisfactory than the Gesell scales for infant testing. It was developed as an extension of the Stanford-Binet Intelligence Scale and utilizes items from the Yale Developmental Examination and other infant tests together with original items. Items are grouped according to age levels, and IQ is computed in the same manner as the Stanford-Binet test. The Cattell scale was standardized on a group of 274 children tested at 3, 6, 9, 12, 18, 24, 30, and 36 months of age. The statistical criterion employed was the same as that used with the Stanford-Binet test; the item was retained if more children passed it from one age to the next. If the percentage passing the item decreased with age, the item was not included. Other criteria were also applied in retaining or discarding items. Items that were difficult to administer or score, involved undue subjectivity, required cumbersome apparatus, or failed to hold the attention of the young child were discarded. No time limit is used in the Cattell scale. The test usually takes about 30 minutes, and the order of presentation of the material is modified to suit the interests and abilities of the particular child. At the youngest ages, the test items are largely perceptual, such as attending to a bell, following a ring, looking at a spoon, or inspecting one's own fingers. Motor items such as lifting the head and transferring objects are also included. As age increases, more complex items and verbal material are used. Form boards, cups, dolls, and other toys are presented for discrimination and naming.

Difficulties in infant testing include inability to use instructions, short attention span, lack of motivation, and difficult scoring of items.

It is difficult to test an infant. Oral directions cannot be used; the examiner must set the stage so that the desired response will be elicited. Interest in the test stimuli and rapport with the experimenter are the sole means available to motivate the infant, since he is hardly concerned with doing his best on the test. Scoring of items is difficult because we lack any objective record of the infant's responses. We cannot know if he really lifted his head or if his eyes really followed the moving object. Normative samples are smaller and less representative than those used to standardize tests for older children. A longitudinal method of measurement has been followed in the construction of infant tests. This is in contrast to the cross-sectional approach used in the standardization of tests for older children. However, we find lower reliability with infant tests than among tests of older children.

Measuring the validity of infant tests is difficult because we have no suitable external criterion.

Measuring the validity of an infant test is hampered by the lack of suitable criteria; independent estimates of infants' intelligence are not available. Infants do not have school grades or job records, although in some cases independent evidence can be obtained (feebleminded or very bright children). Also, the parent's IQ can be used as a criterion. Babies tested when they are in a good mood score at about the same level later, but infants who are fussy during testing score substantially higher if they are retested in a better mood. Validation of infant tests is based largely on two criteria—age differentiation and prediction of subsequent status on other tests of intellect. One practical use of infant intelligence tests is to predict the intelligence of school-age children. We find low validity coefficients among infant, preschool, and later adult tests. Two reasons explain this fact: (1) the long interval between infant and adult testing and (2) the different types of items on infant and adult tests. Correlations between infants' scores at various ages on the Cattell test and scores at age three on the Stanford-Binet test are shown in Table 14.4. Below the age of 12 months the correlations are little better than chance and indicate that the tests have no predictive validity for the three-year-old IQ. However, after one year of age, the correlations are considerably higher with IQ at age three.

TABLE 14.4 Validity Coefficients of the Cattell Infant Intelligence Scale

Age in Months	*Number of Cases*	*Correlation with Stanford-Binet IQ at Age 3 Years*
3	42	.10
6	49	.34
9	44	.18
12	57	.56
18	52	.67
24	52	.71
30	42	.83

SOURCE: Adapted from Cattell, 1947.

However, intelligence tests at this age do not predict adult IQ.

Infant tests can detect special disabilities; however, they are not good predictors of future IQ scores.

In the hands of a sensitive, well-trained tester, infant tests can detect special disabilities, such as deficiency in social responsiveness or in hearing. They provide a moderately accurate picture of the infant's intellectual functioning. Infant tests show that (1) mentally defective babies can be distinguished from normal infants, (2) babies who live in institutions score lower than babies in homes, and (3) scores on tests given to infants under 12 months have no relation to IQ scores earned later.

Preschool tests and their evaluation

Preschool tests are more reliable and valid than infant tests.

Among tests specifically designed for the preschool level, the best known are the Merrill-Palmer Scale and the Minnesota Preschool Scale. The Merrill-Palmer Scale, standardized on 631 children between the ages of 18 and 77 months, is scored on a point basis. Tests are arranged in order of difficulty and contain few language items; most of the test is performance. The language items deal with simple words or questions, such as, "What is this?" "What is it for?" Many items measure sensory-motor coordination—throwing a ball, pulling a string, standing on one foot, cutting with scissors, buttoning, building with blocks, and fitting cubes into a block. Testing is begun at a level within the child's chronological age; it is carried down until the child passes all items and up until half or more of the items are failed. The child's score is determined by crediting one point for each item passed, including all test items below the base level (where the child passes all items). Test validity was determined by selecting items on the basis of age differentiation. The major weakness of the Merrill-Palmer Scale is its emphasis on motor skills and speed. Its principal asset is the undoubted appeal of many items to young children; the tasks are interesting and they are presented in attractive, gaily colored boxes.

The Minnesota Preschool Scale uses untimed verbal questions.

The Minnesota Preschool Scale contains almost no motor items and none of the test is timed. The scale is part verbal and part nonverbal; each yields a separate score. Verbal items include pointing at parts of the body, pointing to objects, naming things, telling what a picture is about, following directions, and answering simple questions such as, "What should you do if you're hungry?" Also included are naming objects from memory, naming colors, identifying incomplete pictures, using vocabulary, and the number of words in the child's longest sentence. The nonverbal items include drawing pictures of a circle, a triangle, and a diamond, drawing vertical and horizontal cross strokes, block building, form discrimination, form recognition, tracing, rearranging cut-out puzzles, paper folding, and indicating the missing parts of pictures. The child's score for the verbal and nonverbal scales is found by adding the number of points earned in each task. Validity of the Minnesota Preschool Scale was determined by the criteria of age differentiation and internal consistency of items. Also, the correlation of test scores with father's occupational level is further evidence of the test's validity.

Problems include motivation, short attention span, and fatigue.

The problems encountered in administering infant tests also occur at the preschool level. Oral directions can be used, but we still have the problem of motivation, short attention span, and susceptibility to fatigue. Subjectivity of scoring is also encountered. Shy children have trouble with preschool tests. The preschool child's mother should remain in the examination room or even hold the child to reassure him. On the other hand, standardization and follow-up studies are more adequate for the preschool than the infant tests. Although correlations are still too low to permit good predictions, they show substantial stability of test performance over a ten-year period. The predictive subtests emphasize spatial relations, controlled attention, memory, and logical operations. Examples include incomplete pictures, block building, discrimination of color and form, definitions, detection of verbal absurdities, and vocabulary. Preschool and infant tests face the same problems encountered in cross-cultural testing. Unlike the school child, infants and preschool children have not been exposed to a standardized set of experiences.

The school-age test

The Wechsler Intelligence Scale for Children (WISC) contains verbal and motor parts; it is a model of test construction.

The Wechsler Intelligence Scale for Children (WISC) is an individual schedule divided into subtests; the items are arranged in order of difficulty. The tests contain an equal number of verbal and performance items from which separate verbal and performance IQs are computed. Brief descriptions of each of the subtests are included in Table 14.5.

TABLE 14.5 The Weschler Intelligence Scale for Children

Verbal Scale

1. *General Information.* The child may be asked 30 questions covering a wide variety of information which he has presumably had an opportunity to acquire in our culture. An effort was made to avoid specialized or academic knowledge. It might be added that questions of general information have been used for a long time in informal psychiatric examinations to establish the individual's intellectual level and his practical orientation.

2. *General Comprehension.* Designed to measure practical judgment and common sense, this test is similar to the Stanford-Binet comprehension items, but its specific content was chosen so as to be more consonant with the interests and activities of children. It consists of 14 items, in each of which the child is requested to explain what should be done under certain circumstances or why certain practices are followed.

3. *Arithmetical Reasoning.* This test consists of 16 arithmetic problems similar to those encountered in elementary school arithmetic. Each problem is orally presented and is to be solved without the use of paper and pencil. Speed and correctness of response determine the score.

4. *Similarities.* In each of the 16 items of this test, the child is asked to state in what way the two things named are alike. The resemblance to certain Stanford-Binet items is again apparent.

5. *Vocabulary.* A list of 40 words, steeply graded in difficulty, is presented orally. The child is asked to state what each word means.

5a. *Digit Span* (optional). This is a memory span test for orally presented lists of digits, ranging from three to nine digits. In the second part of this test, the subject is instructed to reproduce each list (two to eight digits) in reverse order.

Performance Scale

6. *Picture Completion.* The child is shown 20 cards, each containing a picture from which there is a part missing. He must state (or show) what is missing from each picture.

7. *Picture Arrangement.* Each item consists of a set of cards containing pictures that are to be rearranged in the proper temporal sequence so as to tell a story. One set of cards is used for preliminary demonstration only (a dog in three parts) and is followed by the seven sets in the test proper. Both time and accuracy are scored.

8. *Block Design.* In the Wechsler adaptation of the block design test, the patterns use only the red, white, and red-and-white sides of the cubes. Two simple demonstration items are followed by seven designs of increasing complexity requiring from 4 to 16 cubes each. Both time and accuracy are scored.

9. *Object Assembly.* Modeled after the Pintner-Paterson Manikin and Feature Profile, this test includes improved versions of both of these objects (a boy and a face) together with a horse and an auto (four in all). In each part the task is essentially similar to that in a jigsaw puzzle. Both time and accuracy are scored.

10. *Coding.* This is a version of the familiar code-substitution test which dates back to the early Woodworth-Wells Association Tests and has often been included in non-language intelligence scales. There are two codes: the more difficult set contains nine symbols paired with the nine digits. The simpler code contains five figures (star, circle, triangle, cross, and square). The subject's score is the number of symbols correctly written in 1½ minutes.

10a. *Mazes* (optional). Five paper-and-pencil mazes are provided on a separate sheet to measure the child's ability to plan his moves in advance.

The WISC contains 12 subtests, two of which—the digit span and the mazes—are alternate or supplementary tests. Raw scores on each subtest are transformed into standard scores, which are summed to give a verbal IQ, a performance IQ, and a full-scale IQ. Two hundred children between 5 and 15 years of age (a total of 2200 children) were used in the standardization of the WISC. Split-half reliability of the test is between .92 and .94. In general, the correlations between verbal and performance scores are quite high. However, the performance scores show smaller differences between rural and urban groups and between different occupational groups than do the verbal scores. Several studies report correlations ranging from .60 to .90 between the WISC and the Stanford-Binet, the verbal scale of the WISC correlating most highly with the Stanford-Binet. The WISC is a well standardized, very adequate test; the establishment of norms and reliability are models of test constructions.

Adult and special tests

Adult tests stop increasing chronological age in their IQ formula at age 15.

Statements about school-age tests hold for adult tests. The main differences include increased difficulty of items and increased reliability of measurement. The only feature of adult tests that is clearly different from school tests is the limit of chronological age used in adult testing. The chronological age used to compute IQ in the equation $IQ = MA/CA$ does *not* increase after the adult reaches age 15.

The Graduate Record Examinations are constructed annually to evaluate adults of superior intelligence for professional school admission.

Almost all applicants to professional and graduate schools are tested prior to acceptance. Good examples of the tests used to differentiate these bright individuals are the Graduate Record Examinations. These tests are constructed each year by the Educational Testing Service of Princeton, New Jersey. The tests include aptitude examinations in verbal and mathematical ability and advanced scales in such areas as Spanish, English, history, psychology, and physics. Reliability ranges from .85–.95; predictive validity has been checked by correlation with teachers' ratings. The results show that scores on the Graduate Record Examination are about as effective in predicting graduate school success as are grades from undergraduate work. However, when combined, the predictive ability of undergraduate grades and Graduate Record Examination grades is much higher (middle .60s).

LEARNING ABILITY AND INTELLIGENCE

For simple tasks, learning and intelligence are independent; for more

Uncertainty exists about the effects of IQ on learning ability. Some students of behavior suggest that IQ is independent of ability to learn. Others have found that certain types of learning are directly related to complex tasks, they are correlated.

intelligence while others are not. A third group holds that all learning is related to intelligence. Studies in which simple discrimination problems are used or in which simple materials must be associated show little relation between learning ability and intelligence. However, more complex discrimination learning (in which the child must learn how to learn) shows a high correlation between IQ and learning rate. Intelligence is not related to the child's ability to associate two simple items in a rote memory task; however, intelligence is related to the child's ability to use past experience in solving complex problems. Those children who bring a large range of abilities to a new problem are more intelligent. The simple ability to form a rote connection between two events is not related to what we generally call intelligence.

A simple learning task might be discrimination among common objects.

A typical study (Eisman, 1958) of simple discrimination included children of low, average, and high intelligence. The discrimination was among common objects such as jacks, hammers, and baskets. These were presented until a criterion of four correct trials was reached. The results showed no significant differences among low-, intermediate-, and high-intelligence groups on any measure of learning, generalization, or retention. Educable mentally retarded and normal subjects develop new associations at about the same rate.

A more complex learning situation might be learning to learn.

Other studies have looked at the effect of IQ on learning set formation. Harter (1965) gave children a series of ten problems with four trials per problem until they reached the criterion for "learning set" of five successive problems in which no more than one error was made on trials two, three, and four. They were also given pairs of objects to connect in a simple association. The learning-to-learn curves of the children showed they were at chance on the early problems and then climbed abruptly to criterion after several different problems. The number of trials to reach criterion in the learning set problems decreased as IQ increased. Older children learned faster and so did brighter children. Simple paired-associate learning was not affected by IQ or mental age, but learning to learn is related to intellect.

"CULTURE-FAIR" INTELLIGENCE TESTS

Culture-fair tests were developed to overcome biases assumed to exist in middle class white intelligence tests.

A major problem with intelligence tests, according to some critics, is that they were developed by, and are most appropriate for, the middle class Western European child. All other groups are judged against the performance of these children. Articulate and influential critics of IQ tests maintain that children of lower socioeconomic classes and children of other cultures are discriminated against. These critics say that IQ tests abound in abstract verbal conventions which form part of the Western European middle class culture but which are foreign to lower class children and children from other cultures. The world is one of harsh reality for the lower class child, and the future an uncertain thing. The lower class child lives in the here and now; he has neither much use for, nor familiarity with, abstract symbols. These children understand the concrete and tangible.

Culture-fair tests reword items in the natural language of the examinee.

Critics of standard intelligence tests have developed "culture-fair" intelligence tests in which conventional abstract items are rewritten in familiar, concrete language. A conventional item might read, "Cub is to bear as gosling is to ____," and the alternative choices would be "fox," "grouse," "goose," "rabbit," "duck." The culture-fair item might be, "Puppy goes with dog like kitten goes with 'fox,' 'goose,' 'cat,' 'rabbit,' 'duck.'" Another example might be a conventional item which reads, "*A* weighs less than *B*, *B* weighs less than *C*," with choices, "*B* weighs more than *C*"; "*A*'s weight is equal to *B* and *C*'s"; "*A* weighs less than *C*." The analogous-culture fair item might be, "Jim can hit harder than Bill; Bill can hit harder than Ted," with choices, "Ted can hit harder than Bill"; "Bill can hit as hard as Ted and Jim"; "Jim can hit harder than Ted."

However, the reliability and validity of culture-fair tests is much lower than their standard counterparts.

Haggard (1954) measured 671 10–12-year-old children to see how they performed on the two types of tests under different conditions. He expected that lower class children would score higher on the culture-fair form of the test than on the conventional form but that there should be little change for the middle class children. Familiarity and interest should help the lower class children more than the middle class children, particularly on the culture-fair test. However, he found that both the middle and lower class children made larger gains on the culture-fair than on the standard intelligence test. Haggard was correct in assuming that lower class children would do better on the culture-fair than on the standard test. However, the middle class children also did better! The class differences were just as marked on the culture-fair as on the conventional test. Also, culture-fair intelligence tests do *not* predict school success as well as standard IQ tests; in other words, the culture-fair tests are not as valid as the conventional tests. Conventional IQ tests sample more operations that are common to school work.

Lower class children achieve below their intellectual potential and middle class children achieve near their potential.

On the basis of test score differences between social classes, we would expect differences in school performance. Middle and upper class children do better in school than lower class children, but the difference is much greater than we would expect on the basis of intellectual level alone. Lower class children achieve below their intellectual potential, while middle and upper class children approach their potential more closely. This serious problem, is partly due to the middle class bias of teachers, curricula, and textbooks (see Chapter 15). This bias makes classroom experiences difficult for lower class youngsters. The differential achievement also results from lower motivation to achieve and lower intellectual ability among lower class children.

Theoretical notions about intelligence have fallen behind our empirical measurement of the trait.

Intelligence testing is a well-developed area of psychology; however, theoretical notions about the development of intelligence are scarce. Some believe general intelligence is all important; others feel that specific abilities exist. These arguments are primarily about the type of statistical analyses that should be used. In a strict sense, there are no theoretical statements about "intelligence." Up to now we have relied on pragmatic rules and empirical findings. The most promising notions to date concerning a theory of intellect come from the speculations and experiments of Piaget on the growth of children's thinking (see Chapters 6 and 11).

CREATIVITY AND PRODUCTIVE THINKING

Productive thinking is difficult to measure.

Productive thinking is the process and result of our operating on sensory or perceptual input to produce something different. The essence of creativity is the development of novel *and* clever ideas. This ability is neglected in our usual tests of intelligence. A minimum level of intelligence is required before one can be creative; above that minimum level there is good reason to believe that creativity is independent of intellectual power.

Our conception of intelligence as a single trait made us ignore divergent thought.

Three conceptions dominated early work on productive thinking: (1) A good test of intelligence was supposed to measure everything of importance about thinking; (2) the fact that there might be more than one dimension to thought escaped consideration; and (3) many believed the child's capacities for thought developed by maturation. Now we think IQ is multidimensional. In addition, motivation and personality are relevant. This last notion has received particular attention in the Head Start programs, which hope to bring the disadvantaged child into school on a fairer basis by giving him many of the everyday experiences of the middle class child.

Guilford believes intelligence has three aspects: content, operations, and products.

Guilford (1956) developed a model of creativity and intelligence. He proposed three dimensions of intelligence: The first he called content—the particular medium in which the child happens to be operating at the moment. It may be symbolic, graphic, semantic, or motor. The second dimension of intelligence is labeled operations; this refers to the particular cognitive process the child is using. Examples of operations are cognition, memory, and divergent or convergent production of ideas. The final dimension of intellect is products—the results of operations and content. Examples of these are classes, relations, transforma-

FIGURE 14.7

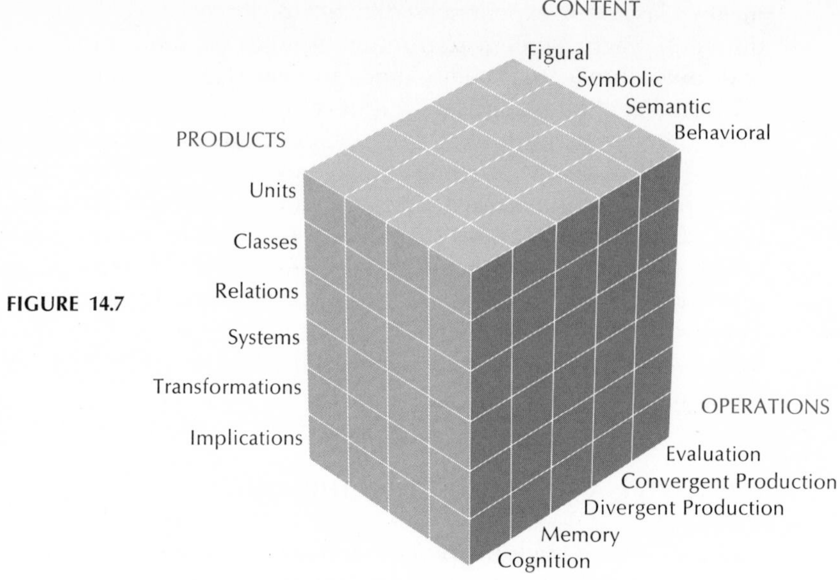

Theoretical model for the complete "structure of intellect." Note the three types of intelligence proposed. (From Guilford, 1956.)

tions, and evaluations. The connections among these three dimensions are shown in Figure 14.7, and some examples of how these relations might work are given in Table 14.6.

Guilford believes intelligence and creativity are separate abilities.

This complex picture of thought reflects Guilford's concern for the richness and diversity of mind. He believes creativity and intelligence are separate abilities. Within the area of creativity he finds two quite different sorts of productive thought. Convergent thinking occurs when the child follows rules to formulate a product. Divergent thinking, on the other hand, is the production of novel ideas. There are four criteria of divergent thinking: (1) A person who is able to think creatively should produce many ideas; (2) he should understand the implications of questions; (3) he should produce original ideas; and (4) he should be able to shift easily from one category of thought to another.

Creativity requires preparation, incubation, insight, and confirmation.

Many famous men of science have introspected about the process of creating an idea. They uniformly report four steps in their thinking (see Table 14.7). First comes the stage of intense preparation—they learn as much as possible about the subject in which they are interested. Following this intense period of instruction, they report a period of incubation, when there is little or nothing going on. However,

TABLE 14.6 Classified Problems in Three Content Areas

CONTENT—the medium in which thought takes place
OPERATIONS—the particular mental operation or process performed on the material
PRODUCTS—the results of the operation on the particular content dimensions

A. Figural
Which figure does not belong?

B. Symbolic
Which letter group does not belong?

XECM PVAA QXIN VTRO

C. Semantic
Which object does not belong?

CLAM TREE OVEN ROSE

The tasks are given in three content areas: figural, symbolic, and semantic. All of these would fall in the cognition dimension of operations and in the classes subcategory in the products area.

during this period there is intense activity at the unconscious level. The person may be puzzled about how to solve a problem, but after some incubation he will usually find a new way of looking at the task; a final solution may result from this insight. This is the third stage. The final stage of creative thought is to verify the insight by going into the laboratory.

TABLE 14.7 Different Expectations for Different Stages of the Creative Process

Stages of the Creative Process	*Expected Form*	*Predominant Thinking Operation*	*Personality Factor or Attitude Required*
Preparation	Neat Well organized Well stated	Cognitive memory	Studiousness Sustained attention
Incubation	Sloppy Often confused	Divergent thinking	Intellectual freedom Risk-taking Tolerance of failure and ambiguity
Insight	Incoherent		
Verification	Neat Well organized Clearly stated	Convergent thinking Evaluative thinking	Intellectual discipline Following logical sequence

SOURCE: From Gallagher, 1964.

Creativity is hard work. It comes to the prepared person.

The first period requires intense dedication and long hours of work. No great discovery is made by an ignorant man. Tedious work is absolutely necessary for creation. The second period can be most frustrating; during this time there is little apparent progress, and the solution seems to slip further and further from the inquiring grasp. However, the creative person will often experience an insight just after he has given up thinking about the problem for a while. Incubation seems to break a particular set and make possible a new approach to the problem. The insight comes in a flash, and only the details remain to be elaborated. The process of verification may require days and days of painstaking work—but it is an anticlimax if the idea is correct.

FACILITATING AND INHIBITING FACTORS IN CREATIVITY

Personality, cognitive style, social environment, and sex affect creativity.

Several factors affect the individual's creativity. Among these are his personality characteristics, the cognitive style with which he attacks problems, the social environment in which he works and grows, and his sex.

Personality

Geniuses are self-assured.

The creative scientist is less sociable than his peers. He seems to require little social interaction, to be more interested in ideas and things than in people. This reputation has earned him both respect and ridicule. Terman *et al.* (1925) studied several very bright children who scored above 145 on the Stanford-Binet Intelligence Scale. One of the outstanding characteristics of successful children in this class of geniuses was their self-assurance, feeling of perseverence, and lack of inferiority feelings. Successful adults from Terman's group showed these characteristics during early adolescence, and they reported a more integrated set of goals than their less successful but equally bright peers. In general, creative people are less repressed and neurotic than non-creative individuals. Creative people use other mechanisms of adjustment than denial, repression, and suppression in dealing with their feelings. Repressed individuals produce few ideas; they are busy keeping themselves together.

Cognitive style

Some children are analytic in their problem-solving style while others use relations.

Kagan and Moss (1962) showed that children have characteristic ways in which they approach problems. Some children are analytic—they pick a small part of the stimulus and solve the problem on that basis. Others are more conceptually oriented—they pick relations among items and pay less attention to details.

Social environment

Families of highly creative children support their divergence.

The family of a highly creative individual tends to support his divergent ideas, to respect his individuality, and to allow for risks in everyday life. They tolerate the ambiguities and frustrations of new ideas. However, the creative child's peer group is not supportive; ratings by his peers suggest that the one who contributes most good ideas in a group problem-solving situation receives little credit or support from other members. His peers rate a creative person low in producing ideas, not producing many good ideas, and being silly and scatterbrained. In addition, the middle class teacher prefers the high IQ child to the equally bright but creative child. All the pressure from peers and teachers may be why the creative person is often stifled; the grade grabber is rewarded while the creative individual is regarded as silly.

SUMMARY

1 Definitions of intelligence form two sets: One suggests intelligence is an aggregate of simple abilities which together produce what we call IQ, while another sees intelligence as the ability to think symbolically in solving problems.

2 The two most important factors about intelligence tests are their reliability and validity. The reliability of a test is an estimate of its error of measurement. The more reliable a test, the more likely a child will receive the same score on two separate occasions. The validity of a test tells us whether it measures what it was designed to assess. For example, do intelligence tests predict school success?

3 Much controversy has centered on determinants of IQ—is it predetermined or can it be manipulated by environmental influences? Older evidence on predetermined IQ was based on the same criteria used to measure IQ. Later evidence shows that identical twins reared apart produce IQ differences related to their different educational opportunities. The greater their educational opportunity, the higher their IQ. In addition, studies of environmental deprivation of animals suggest lack of stimulation slows intellectual growth.

4 There are four types of intelligence tests. The infant test is designed to measure sensory-motor development; it has little relation to later tests of intelligence. Preschool tests are better predictors of later IQ. However, they still suffer from a preponderance of performance tasks; they contain too few vocabulary and problem-solving items. This limitation results from the child's limited abilities. School and adult tests of intelligence are reliable, valid, and easy to administer. However, for very bright individuals we must use special tests, for example, the Miller Analogies or the Graduate Record Examination.

5 The relation between simple learning abilities (for example, rote learning) and intelligence is small; the relation between complex learning and intelligence (for example, learning how to learn) is high and positive.

6 "Culture-fair" tests of intelligence are unreliable and do not accurately predict academic performance.

7 Productive thinking is a neglected part of intelligence testing. Until quite recently tests of thought ignored the production of novel ideas. However, there is renewed interest in individuals who can produce new, varied, and unusual ideas.

FURTHER READINGS

Anastasi, A. *Psychological testing.* (2nd ed.). New York: Macmillan, 1968.

Kogan, N., & Wallach, M. *Risk taking: A study in cognition and personality.* New York: Holt, Rinehart and Winston, 1964.

REFERENCES

Anastasi, A. *Individual differences.* New York: Wiley, 1965.

Binet, A., & Simon, T. Upon the necessity of establishing a scientific diagnosis of inferior states of intelligence. *L'Anée Psychologique,* 1905, **11,** 163-190.

Cattell, P. *The measurement of intelligence of infants and young children.* New York: Psychological Corporation, 1947.

Eisman, B. Paired associate learning, generalization, and retention as a function of intelligence. *American Journal of Mental Deficiency,* 1958, **63,** 481-489.

Gallagher, J. J. *Teaching the gifted child.* Boston: Allyn and Bacon, 1964.

Gesell, A., & Amatruda, C. *Developmental diagnosis* (2nd ed.). New York: Hoeber, 1947.

Guilford, J. P. The structure of intellect. *Psychological Bulletin,* 1956, **53,** 267-293.

Haggard, E. A. Social-status and intelligence: An experimental study of certain cultural determinants of measured intelligence. *Genetic Psychology Monographs,* 1954, **49,** 141-186.

Harter, S. Discrimination learning set in children as a function of IQ and MA. *Journal of Experimental Child Psychology,* 1965, **2,** 31-43.

Hebb, D. O. The effect of early experience on problem-solving at maturity. *American Psychologist,* 1947, **2,** 306-307.

Jensen, A. How much can we boost IQ and scholastic achievement? *Harvard Educational Review,* 1969, **39,** No. 1, 1-123.

Kagan, J., & Moss, H. A. *Birth to maturity.* New York: Wiley, 1962.

Klineberg, O. *Negro intelligence and selective migration.* New York: Columbia University Press, 1935.

Lee, E. Negro intelligence and selective migration: A Philadelphia test of the Klineberg hypothesis. *American Sociological Review,* 1951, **16,** 227–233.

Macfarlane, J. W. The guidance study. *Sociometry,* **2,** 1939.

Newman, H. H., Freeman, F. N., & Holzinger, K. H. *Twins: A study of heredity and environment.* Chicago: University of Chicago Press, 1937.

Owens, W. A., Jr. Age and mental abilities: A longitudinal study. *Genetic Psychological Monographs,* 1953, **14,** 3–54.

Pettigrew, T. *A profile of the Negro American.* Princeton, N. J.: Van Nostrand, 1964.

Riesen, A. H. The development of visual perception in man and chimpanzee. *Science,* 1947, **106,** 107–108.

Sherman, M., & Key, C. B. The intelligence of isolated mountain children. *Child Development,* 1932, **3,** 279–290.

Spearman, C. *The abilities of man.* New York: Macmillan, 1927.

Terman, L. M. *The measurement of intelligence.* Boston: Houghton Mifflin, 1916.

Terman, L. M., *et al.* Genetic studies of genius. *The mental and physical characteristics of a thousand gifted children.* Vol. 1. Stanford, Calif. Stanford University Press, 1925.

Thorndike, E. L., *et al. The measurement of intelligence.* New York: Bureau of Publications, Teachers College, Columbia University, 1927.

Thurstone, T. G., & Thurstone, L. L. *Thurstone tests of mental alertness: Examiner manual.* Chicago: Science Research Associates, 1952.

Wechsler, D. *Wechsler intelligence scale for children: Manual.* New York: Psychological Corporation, 1949.

15 SOCIAL RELATIONS

I weigh my friend's affection with mine own.
TIMON OF ATHENS

How infants and children relate to and affect others has fundamental implications for their later development. The infant's social attitude develops through relations with his mother. The family shapes his social interactions for a few years, and then his peer group dominates. Factors that control social acceptance or rejection, social affiliation or withdrawal, and social competence are covered in this chapter. It begins with some notes about infant-mother attachment, covers Freud and Piaget on play, outlines the child's relations with his peers, and then considers the influences of mass media and school on a child's social relations.

INFANT SOCIAL RELATIONS

Early conceptions of social interaction centered about feeding.

Early theorists assumed that infant social responsiveness evolves from oral activity; the feeding situation was emphasized by both psychoanalytic and learning theory. Freud proposed that each developmental stage is characterized by a particular bodily zone; oral activities dominate infancy. He assumed that sucking and related oral stimulation is innately pleasurable; thus, the infant's early social attachment (most often his mother) derives from the association of mother with oral pleasure. Early learning theories also emphasized feeding; however, they argued that the mother acquires positive value by association with hunger reduction.

Causes of infant attachment

Recent studies show contact is more important than feeding in the formation of infant-mother attachment.

Recent studies have changed the view that feeding is crucial for the development of infant attachment. Harlow (1958), using infant rhesus monkeys, showed that feeding is much less important than "contact comfort" in the development of attachment (see Chapters 7 and 10). Infant monkeys were raised on inanimate surrogate mothers of wire or terrycloth. Half the infants were fed on a wire mother and the remainder on a cloth mother. Infants fed on the wire mother spent little time with her; they stayed with the cloth mother, "a finding completely contrary to any intepretation of derived-drive in terms of which the mother-form becomes conditioned to hunger-thirst reduction" (Harlow, 1958, p. 676). Also, infant monkeys preferred the cloth mother when they were anxious. They used her as a safe base from which to explore the environment. These findings support the notions of Ribble (1944) that tactile stimulation is important for early infant development. However, physical contact may not be necessary for human infant attachment; mothers who preferred physical contact with their infants produced no more intensely attached infants than mothers who preferred nonphysical interaction. The amount of mother-child interaction and the mother's response to infant crying are strongly related to children's attachment.

Modern theorists think imprinting is also important.

According to imprinting notions, animals form social attachments with any perceptually salient object to which they are exposed during a critical period. Direct physical contact is not necessary for attachment in sheep, although it may facilitate attachment. However, species-specific differences may account for this variance of sheep from Harlow's data.

Satisfaction of physical needs is not necessary for attachment.

Studies of attachment formation using human infants have also contradicted the drive-reduction position. Schaffer and Emerson (1964) reported in a longitudinal investigation of infant social attachments during the first year and a half of life that "satisfaction of physical needs does not appear to be a necessary precondition to the development of attachments, the latter taking place independently and without obvious regard to the experiences that the child encounters in physical care situations." Most theories of infant social relations assume that first attachments must be to the mother; later attachments can occur only after the mother-child relation is firmly established. Schaffer and Emerson found that some infants develop multiple attachments immediately; for these infants, mother was never the principal object of attachment.

During feeding mothers provide auditory, tactual,

The fact that oral gratification is not the most important cause of social responsiveness does not imply that feeding has no importance for the development of attachment. During feeding mothers provide *and kinesthetic stimulation.*

auditory and visual stimulation and physical contact. However, attachment is multiply determined, and feeding is only one factor.

Stranger anxiety

Fear of strangers develops during the latter half of the first year.

Infants develop attachments to familiar figures and show fear of strangers during the latter half of the first year. Stranger anxiety is well known (Preyer, 1888; Bridges, 1932; Spitz, 1950) but not understood. Two views exist: Some favor an incongruity hypothesis—stranger anxiety is fear evoked by stimuli which contain both familiar and unfamiliar parts (Hebb, 1946; Freedman, 1961; Schaffer, 1966). Others give a psychoanalytic interpretation—fear of losing a loved one is the main cause of fear of strangers (Spitz, 1950). Several factors affect the age of onset of stranger anxiety. Schaffer (1966) showed that the more people an infant encounters in his daily life, the later he will develop fear of strangers. Also, strong mother-infant attachment increases the fear reaction to strangers.

Positive social reactions

Smiling is often used as an index of positive social responsiveness.

Smiling, vocalizing, and play have all been used as indices of social responsiveness. Smiling is most often used as an index of infant social interaction. Studies have explored the stimuli that elicit smiling at various ages. Smiling during the first week of life is controlled by the infant's internal state; it has no social significance. However, by the third or fourth week social smiling begins; infants respond to a variety of external (sometimes social) stimuli. Early explanations of smiling assumed the existence of an innate releasing stimulus. Many thought that a smiling adult face was the best elicitor. However, recent work shows that many different stimuli are effective (including auditory, tactual, and visual inputs). The earliest elicitor of infant smiling is a high-pitched human voice (Wolff, 1963); however, a voice and face (particularly a moving face) is the most reliable elicitor of smiling during the first six months of life.

There is a positive relation between early linguistic stimulation and later vocabulary and sentence length.

Infant vocalization has received recent attention. Early infant vocalizations are assumed to be both a means of rudimentary communication and the beginnings of later language. Studies of early language development show a relation between the infant's early language *stimulation* and his later vocabulary and sentence length (Day, 1932). Moreover, severe language retardation is found in institutionalized children; their early vocalizations receive little attention. External social reinforcement can modify the frequency of infant vocalizations (Rheingold, Gewirtz, & Ross, 1959).

PLAY

Children's play was a neglected area before 1915.

Children's play was a neglected activity until Karl Groos (1915) published *The play of animals* and *The play of man.* He proposed that play in man and animals provides early training for adult life. This doctrine flourished during the late nineteenth century.

Groos differentiated five theories of play: (1) physiological, (2) biological, (3) psychological, (4) aesthetic, and (5) sociological.

Groos differentiated five theories of play:

Physiological—play is a necessary discharge of energy. Play affords relaxation and conservation of energy; it is an attempt to recapture a pleasurable stimulus.

Biological—play is instinctual and derives from biological needs.

Psychological—play is a reproduction of pleasure; play is repetitive, conscious, and accompanied by attention and enjoyment; play has a dream quality. Pleasure in play comes from the satisfaction of inborn impulses; psychological play involves self-deception. Play involves freedom, creativity, and mastery.

Aesthetic—The pleasures of play may lead to aesthetics and art. The skills in artistic endeavor resemble those in play.

Sociological—The cheering and harmonizing effect of play strengthens social ties.

Early theories of play relied on the notion of instinct.

How does play develop, and why do children choose one toy rather than another? Early theories relied on the notion of instinct. Play was assigned the dual function of discharging surplus energy and preparing the infant for later life. But is all such activity play? Baldwin (1906) thought not. He wrote that repetition is necessary for an act to be play. The infant must be aware that he is the creator of the act and must repeat it over and over. His position is very close to the assimilation notion proposed by Piaget (1951).

The transition to problem-solving was explained by an instinct for discovery.

The progression from disorganized activity to structured games is apparent to anyone who has watched children. Early explanations proposed that play instincts are supplanted by instincts of problem-solving and discovery. For example, when the child is problem-oriented (taking the lid off a can) he is learning abilities necessary for later life.

Explanations of fantasy were given by Freud (controlling anxiety) and Piaget (cognitive structure).

Following the period of sensory-motor play (after 18 months) the infant begins to daydream. Why does the child use fantasy? He now uses a stick as a horse, a cloth as a doll, or dreams about giants and dwarfs. He needs no toys for play; he is delighted with fantasies and their course. Early theories of play could not explain daydreaming. Freud (1949) and Piaget (1951) proposed that fantasies are necessary to handle anxiety (Freud) or are the results of developing symbolic abilities (Piaget).

Freud on play

Freud proposed that children play with toys to handle mild amounts of anxiety and avoid toys associated with high anxiety.

Psychoanalytic theories of play assume that each stage of life produces anxieties and deprivations; play is used to deny, distort, or work through these anxieties and deprivations. Children avoid—if the anxiety is too great—or play with—if the anxiety is manageable—objects related to their fears. Freud proposed that children play to master their fears (counterphobic behavior); children prefer play materials related to their fears and deprivations.

Freud proposed four phases of children's play: (1) substitutes for the body, (2) mother-child relations, (3) Oedipal conflicts, and (4) team games.

Freud outlined four phases through which children's play grows:

Phase 1 The infant experiences general anxiety because he feels deficient and helpless. Toys are used during this period as substitute or improved versions of his body. Infants experience fantasies of great skill and potency.

Phase 2 During the second phase, play is related to mother-child relations. The central theme of the child's play is, "I can do to you what mother did to me," or, "I can leave you as she left me." Play becomes repetitive, serious, and sober.

Phase 3 During Phase 3, beginning around three years of age, play stems from attempts to solve Oedipal conflicts; it is controlled by rules. Children start to plan their play, and interest in tricks, jokes, riddles, and puns begins. Play during earlier phases may have included another person, and there may have been a semblance of rules or order of activity. However, play in Phase 3 is more social. It serves to release the child from the painful disappointments of family attachments.

Phase 4 In the post-Oedipal phase (about six years) team games dominate. The group is all important. Strict rules emerge and are followed; they give some sense of independence from external authority. Games begin, follow a prescribed course, and end, suggesting to the child that problems have a solution.

Piaget on play and imitation

Piaget sees play as another example of cognition.

For Piaget (1951) development involves changes in cognitive structures; changes come through the action of two invariant processes, assimilation and accommodation. He assumed that play involves primarily assimilation while imitation involves accommodation. A longitudinal survey of imitation and play will serve as a review of early child development from Piaget's view. (See Chapter 11 for a more complete account.)

Stage 1 behavior is reflexive.

Stage 1 (0–1 month) Behavior during this stage is reflexive; we find neither imitation nor play.

Imitation occurs only occasionally while play is strong by Stage 2.

Stage 2 (1–4 months) *Imitation:* Isolated instances of pseudo-imitation appear. If a model repeats an act that the child has just performed, the child will often repeat the act. This is merely assimilation of the model's action as if it were the child's.

Play: Once a primary circular reaction is mastered through assimilation and accommodation, it can become "autonomous." For example, once the child has learned to throw his head back to look at familiar things from this new position, he begins to throw his head back without concern for what he can *see*.

By Stage 3 we see the beginning of imitation of sounds; play involves an environment but not a partner.

Stage 3 (4–8 months) *Imitation:* In Stage 3 we find the beginnings of imitation of sounds and movements already in the infant's repertoire. He can now reproduce another's actions even though he was not engaged in that action a moment before. However, the infant can imitate only familiar patterns.

Play: Play remains essentially the same as in Stage 2, but it becomes easier to differentiate play and adaptive assimilation. For example, one of Piaget's children found that she could make the objects hanging from the top of her cot swing. At three and one half months she studied this phenomenon seriously. At four months, however, she performed this activity with great joy. The serious work of comprehension has been accomplished; play now reigns.

Between four and eight months the infant pays more attention to his immediate environment than to a partner or specific play materials. Attempts by another child to interact with him are ignored. Friendly contacts, when they occur, are limited to looking at, smiling at, and grasping the other infant. Games are unsystematic and short; they consist of manipulations of an object. The partner receives little attention. Fights are equally impersonal, with both participants trying to get hold of the same play materials.

The Stage 4 infant can imitate actions not already in his repertory; by this time he can play with means separate from goals.

Stage 4 (8–12 months) *Imitation:* A Stage 3 child can imitate only patterns already in his repertoire. However, by Stage 4 he overcomes these limitations; he will now reproduce new responses. Also, the Stage 3 child confuses his own responses with those of the model; imitation is not very different from circular reactions, and the child continues the model's action as though it were his own. By Stage 4 the child's view of a model's actions is quite different; subject and object are differentiated. Instead of becoming incorporated into the child's own activity, the model is now viewed as an independent entity. Once differentiation of model and child has occurred, the child develops an interest in novel actions; he begins to imitate new patterns.

Play: The distinction between play and adaptive behavior is more clear in Stage 4 following the child's differentiation of means from ends. When the child pursues a "means" for its own sake, he is obviously engaged in play. Early in Stage 4 the child will attack a barrier (means) to reach an object (goal) beyond it. Later, the same child forgets all about the goal object in his zeal over attacking the barrier; he is now playing.

The Stage 4 child still responds to play material in preference to another child. If the partner gets in the way, fighting will flare. Conflicts are more personal, though not really hostile; other play materials—his own toys and clothing—are still preferred over fighting.

The year-old child can imitate anything; he has elaborate rituals for play.

Stage 5 (12–18 months) *Imitation:* During Stage 5 the child becomes more adept at imitation; he can reproduce patterns that are less similar to established schemata, and his productions are more precise than before.

Play: Stage 5 play is noteworthy for its elaboration of rituals. For example, when a child's hand slips from his head and splashes into the bath water, he will repeat the sequence with great glee; he varies the height (as if it were a tertiary circular reaction) but always grasps his hair first, which, of course, has no effect whatever on the splash. Or when the child sets an orange peel to rocking on a table immediately after having looked at its convex side, this becomes a ritual; he will rock the orange peel many times, each time looking at its underside before proceeding further.

Stage 5 is a transitional period. The infant is shifting his attention from play materials to his partner. There is less fighting for play materials and more social interaction.

The Stage 6 child can imitate absent models; his play is characterized by make-believe.

Stage 6 (18–24 months) *Imitation:* Stage 6 is marked by three advances: (1) the child can imitate complex new behavior without extensive trial and error, (2) he can imitate nonhuman—even nonliving—objects, and (3) he can now imitate absent objects.

During Stage 5 the child must produce an external response and then modify it; by Stage 6 the experimentation is internal (a pattern is worked out internally before he makes a move). The imitation of absent objects shows that the child is now capable of symbolic representation.

> When Jacqueline's doll got caught by its feet in the top of her dress, she extricated it, with difficulty, but as soon as she got it out, she tried to put it back again, apparently in an effort to understand what had happened. Failing this, she crooked her forefinger into the shape of the doll's foot and placed that into the neck of her dress. After pulling briefly with the imprisoned finger, she removed it, apparently satisfied. Piaget interpreted this as the construction of an active representation of the thing that had just happened and that she did not understand (Flavell, 1963, p. 7).

The Stage 6 child imitates models who are not physically present when he first reproduces the act. "Deferred imitation" mirrors the general intellectual growth during Stage 6 and is very important in the development of play.

Play: The distinctive characteristic of Stage 6 is symbolism. Earlier the child could produce only simple motor games; now he is capable of representing previous experiences in "make believe." For example: Lucianne accidentally fell backward while sitting on her cot. Seeing a pillow, she seized it and pressed it against her face as though sleeping on it. Then after a moment she "sat up delightedly." This procedure was repeated many times during the day, even in places other than the cot and with no pillow available. Each time, she would first smile and then throw herself back and press her hands against her face as though the pillow were there. The symbolic basis of this behavior should be clear to any thoughtful observer. It is at this stage that play and imitation become fused, with the former dominating the latter. The advances of representational processes make possible "internal" or "deferred" imitation (Flavell, 1963).

The infant integrates his social interest in a partner with his interest in the playthings. Games show a considerable increase in frequency and length. The play becomes personal with much looking, smiling, and grasping, with a modification of his behavior in adjustment to that of his partner.

Piaget sees play as a means of learning about the world; Freud views play in terms of anxiety.

Theorists differ in their interpretation of play's function. Piaget views play as a means of learning about novel or complex objects and events, but Freud sees play primarily in terms of motivational factors. Psychoanalytic theory suggests that when a child is anxious he will play with toys on the basis of their relevance to the source of his anxiety, while Piaget believes the child plays with toys on the basis of their relative novelty or complexity (see Chapter 7). Children about to undergo surgery and a matched group of school children showed the following effects (Gilmore, 1966): (1) novelty does *not* interact with anxiety to determine toy preferences; (2) anxiety does affect a child's preferences for toys, but (3) anxiety is by no means as strong a determinant as the relative novelty of the toys.

Classes of infant play

Parten developed six categories of children's play: (1) unoccupied, (2) solitary, (3) onlooker, (4) parallel, (5) associative, and (6) cooperative.

Social interaction becomes more varied and complex as the child becomes cooperative. Parten (1932) studied the size of groups in which children played and the nature of their play by sampling children's activities at specific intervals. She found that children play in groups of two 30 percent of the time at age two and a half years; groups of five or more occur only nine percent of the time. Children aged four to four and a half spend 25 percent of their play time in groups of five

FIGURE 15.1

(A) Solitary play–the child is alone. (B) Parallel play–the children are beside each other but do not interact. (C) Cooperative play–the children form a socially interacting group.

or more. Parten also classified the play behavior of the children into the following categories: (1) unoccupied, (2) solitary (independent play), (3) onlooker, (4) parallel activity (playing alongside, but not with other children), (5) associative activity (common activity with borrowing, lending, and taking turns), and (6) cooperative (working toward some common goal, different roles that supplement one another taken by various members). Very young children engage in either solitary or parallel play, while older children engage in associative or cooperative play to a much greater extent (see Figure 15.1). To summarize the relation of play and age, each category was given an arbitrary score for cooperativeness. The highest category (cooperative play) was given the highest score, while unoccupied play was given the lowest score on cooperativeness. The cooperativeness score was positively correlated with age of the children ($r = 0.61$). Older preschool children engage more in associative and cooperative play and less in solitary play. The frequency of parallel play does not change with age.

REMARKS: THEORY

A LEARNING MODEL OF TWO-PERSON INTERACTION (ATKINSON, BOWER, & CROTHERS, 1965)

We define each play of the game as a trial and assume that the child chooses a strategy on each trial. Both players must exhibit their choice simultaneously, and the trial terminates when each player is told whether he has won or lost. Whether a child wins or loses depends jointly on what he *and* his opponent do.

We may symbolize the two players as R and C and let R_i (where $i = 1, \cdots, n$) and C_j (where $j = 1, \cdots, n$) stand for the strategies available to the players on each trial. The possible responses may be placed in the form of a "payoff matrix," where the number R_{ij} represents the probability that player R wins on any trial, given the responses R_iC_j, and similarly C_{ij} is the probability that player C will win, given the response pair R_iC_j. Each player has two responses, and the game is described by the following simple matrix (Atkinson, Bower & Crothers, 1965).

$$\begin{array}{cc} & \begin{array}{cc} C_1 & \qquad C_2 \end{array} \\ \begin{array}{c} R_1 \\ \\ R_2 \end{array} & \begin{bmatrix} (0, 0) & (a, 1-a) \\ & \\ (1-a, a) & (\tfrac{1}{2}, \tfrac{1}{2}) \end{bmatrix} \end{array}$$

This matrix says that if both players make response 1, they will both lose; if both players make response 2, then each player independently has probability ½ of winning. When the players disagree on their responses (R_1C_2 and R_2C_1), then the player making response 1 will win with probability *a*, and, independently, the player making response 2 will win with probability $1-a$. If *a* is greater than ½, then our two-person interaction game resembles that class of games known as prisoner's dilemma.[1] If one player cooperates, (for example, he makes response R_2), his opponent should never cooperate (he should make response C_1). The danger to *C* in responding C_1 is that player *R* will retaliate by making response R_1, thus making it impossible for either player to win.

MATRIX GAMES

If we assume that the child must arrive at a game strategy by thinking, how might he go about this? Consider a simple example (Kemeny, Snell, & Thompson, 1957). Suppose two children, *R* and *C*, are playing a card game. Player *R* has a hand that contains a black 5 and a red 5, while player *C* is given a black 5 and a red 2. The rules are as follows: At a given signal the children simultaneously expose one of their two cards; if the cards match in color, player *R* wins the difference between the numbers on the cards, whereas if the cards do not match in color, player *C* wins the difference between the numbers on the two cards. A convenient way to represent this game is by the matrix shown in Figure 15.2. The rows represent the possible choices of player *R* and the columns the possible choices of player *C*. The numbers represent the gains or losses to player *R* under the four possible combinations of plays.

To understand the payoff outcomes, consider the situation in which *R* chooses row one (black 5) and *C* chooses column one (black 5). Here the net outcome is zero. If *R* chooses row one (black 5) but *C* chooses column two (red 2), then *C* wins the difference of 3, which is indicated by the -3 entry in the matrix (*R* loses 3). Any two-person game may be represented as a matrix by letting one player control the rows and the other player the columns and defining the payoffs to be the various matrix entries.

How should the children play the game? Player *C* would like the -3 entry of the matrix. However, the only way he may receive it is to play the second column of the matrix, in which case *R* will choose the second row, which will cause *C* to lose 3 instead of gain 3. If *C* chooses the first column, he assures himself of breaking even no matter what *R* does. It is clear that *R*

[1] The term "prisoner's dilemma" is used because of its analogy to the following situation (Luce & Raiffa, 1957, p. 95). "Two suspects are taken into custody and separated. The district attorney is certain that they are guilty of a specific crime, but he does not have adequate evidence to convict them at a trial. He points out to each prisoner that each has two alternatives, to confess to the crime the police are sure they have done, or not to confess. If neither suspect confesses, then the district attorney states he will book them on some very minor trumped-up charge such as petty larceny and illegal possession of a weapon, and they will both receive minor punishment; if they both confess they will be prosecuted, but he will recommend less than the most severe sentence. But if one confesses and the other does not, then the confessor will receive lenient treatment for turning state's evidence whereas the latter will get 'the book' thrown at him."

FIGURE 15.2

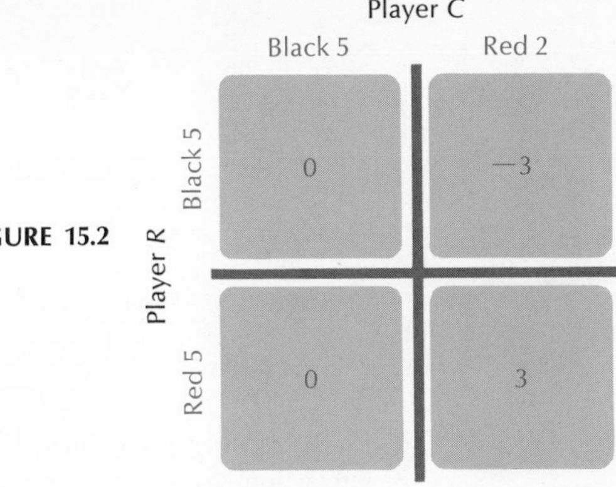

Game matrix.

has nothing to lose and may possibly gain by choosing the second row; hence, he will do that. If player *R* uses the strategy of choosing row two, then regardless of what *C* does he assures himself of at least a payoff of zero. Also, if *C* uses the strategy of choosing column one, he assures himself of gaining, at most, zero. These are optimum strategies.

We may use the proposed solutions to determine any strictly determined game as normative models of optimal strategies. These strategies may be compared with the actual sets of strategies used by children at various ages to see if they are able to compute optimal solutions and use them. Deviations from the optimal strategies should suggest the type of computations actually carried out by children. In addition, the theory of games and two-person interaction may have useful application in the field of social interaction. Interactions between children and their parents may be represented as a matrix game. The types of payoffs and reward structures used by the parent might well benefit from a strict application of the procedures outlined here. The strategies used and their relative values may clarify which payoff structures could lead to cooperation and which are likely to lead to undesirable behavior by either member of the game. Recall that cooperative behavior may more easily be obtained in a situation in which the child is not faced with some variant of the prisoner's dilemma (you lose in either case, but one loss is less than another).

Suppose we represent by a matrix game a typical parent-child situation in which the parent asks the child to clean up his room or he will not allow the child to watch television. We need an estimate of the values of the various alternatives for the child. We may do this by asking him to rate each of the items; assume a rank of 1 indicates dislike for the item and a rank of 5 indicates preference for the item. Figure 15.3 shows the matrix of the child's preferences. The optimum solution of this game becomes the entry which is simultaneously the minimum of the row in which it occurs and the maximum of the column in which it occurs. Note that the intersection of no TV and dirty room satisfies this condition. Game theory predicts that this cell will be picked by the child if he perceives the parent-child interaction as competition.

FIGURE 15.3

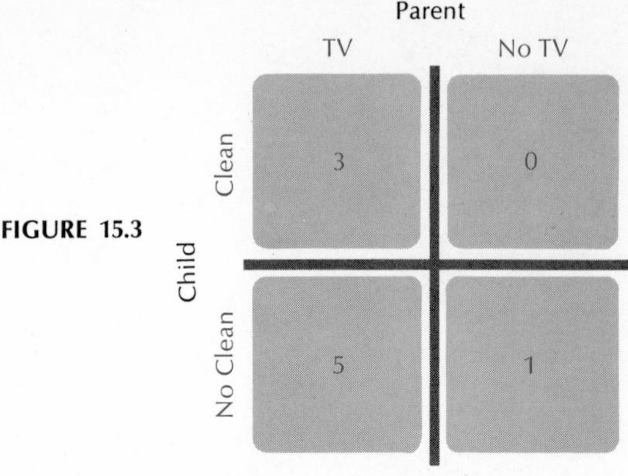

Game matrix of parent-child interaction.

CHILDREN'S PEER RELATIONS

Children live in a world of parents and of peers.

Children live in two worlds. One is managed by their parents while the other is influenced by their peers, the mass media, and teachers. The child's second world becomes more important as he matures. To understand the child we need to review his relations with peers and study the influence of television, books, movies, newspapers, and teachers on his social relations.

Problems in studying peer relations

Samples of subjects and measuring instruments are inadequate in many peer studies.

Two limitations plague studies of peer relations—the samples of subjects are not representative and the measuring instruments are crude. Results from one group of children often cannot be applied to another group; information relevant to middle class children is not appropriate for lower class homes. In addition, the particular manner in which the data are collected often affects the outcome. Results obtained in the laboratory may be quite different from those involving long-term peer relations in the real world.

Interviews and questionnaires are the major sources of information.

The primary measurement techniques include verbal reports and direct observation. An interview or questionnaire is easier to use, but the results are ambiguous, since verbal statements of what the child will do often do not coincide with his actual behavior (see Remarks, Chapter 12). Methodological problems are characteristic of the behavioral sciences; the reader should be aware of the problems but not be paralyzed by them. We do know something about how children interact and how the mass media and the classroom affect their behavior.

Although methodological problems account for some confusions and inconsistencies in the results, these problems don't negate the findings.

Early studies of children's groups

Peers exert more influence on older children than do parents.

One of the earliest studies of peer relations concerned the effects of group influences on boys' sympathy, ambition, and honor. Cooley (1909) showed that peers exert more influence than his family upon a boy's choices and actions after 12 years of age. Terman (1904) studied leadership and suggestibility among school-age children; he contributed much needed methodological sophistication to the study of social relations among children. During the 1930s research on groups increased rapidly. Thomas and her co-workers (1933) introduced the notion of rating categories for classifying children's social behavior. At about the same time, Moreno's (1934) sociometric method was introduced. In this technique individuals nominate those with whom they prefer to associate in a variety of specific activities. Examination of the patterns of choice yields a picture of the relations within a group. Figures 15.4A and B show examples of social networks. Both rating categories and sociograms are used extensively in current research.

A democratic group atmosphere produces more activity and satisfaction than either a laissez-faire or an authoritarian atmosphere.

Lippitt and White (1947) used experimental methods to study the effect of differing social climates on group productivity and satisfaction among members. They organized democratic groups with no leadership, and groups controlled by authoritarian leaders. They found that by setting group goals the democratic process leads to both high production and satisfaction; authoritarian methods produce high group production and dissatisfaction. The laissez-faire organization produced neither activities nor satisfaction.

Group ties form through contacts, common goals, and fear of an outside group.

How group ties develop was studied by Sherif *et al.* (1961) at a summer camp; they waited until the boys knew each other and had formed temporary friendships before beginning the experiment. Once early friendships had developed, the boys were divided into two experimental groups so that friends were separated. The two groups saw little of each other except during competition. The friendships that had developed before the experiment began soon deteriorated into bitter rivalry and hostility under the heat of competition. New ties were quickly established within each experimental group. As the two experimental groups were about to fight, the experimenters introduced a problem of great importance to both groups, which could only be solved by cooperation among all the boys. Cooperation decreased the animosity and rivalry; the early friendships reappeared. In-groups are very important during competition. However, forced cooperation quickly leads to new ties.

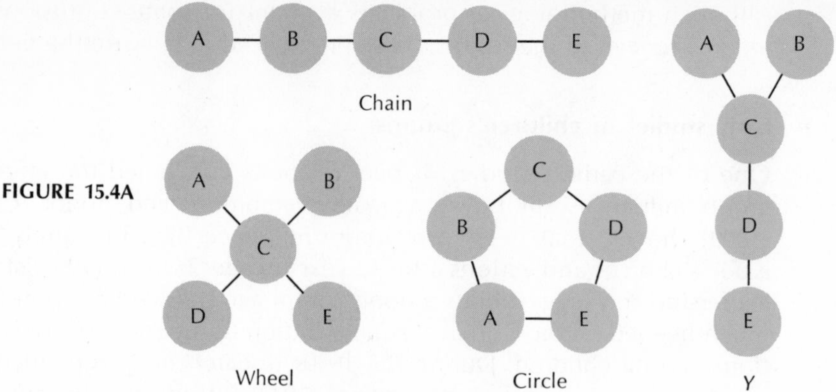

FIGURE 15.4A

Four different social networks. Members of each group are designated by circles. The lines between them represent interaction. The wheel, chain, and Y are centralized; one position, C, has access to more information than any of the others. The circle is decentralized because all positions receive equivalent information. None of these networks accurately describes the typical peer group; children usually form more unstructured groups in the beginning, and only later, when they mature, do leaders, strict lines of communication, and chains develop.

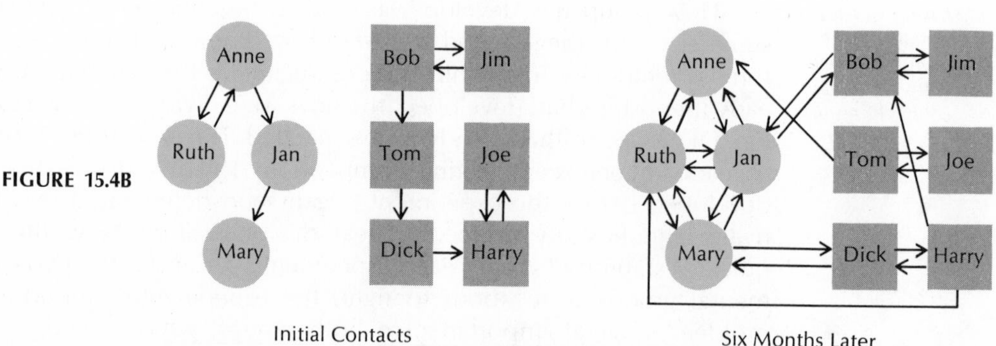

FIGURE 15.4B

Changes in social contact following brief and prolonged contact. Note the relatively simple lines of communication established during the initial contacts and the more complex and cross-sexed lines of communication established after about four months of play together.

Class and cultural variations in peer relations

Children choose their peers on the basis of social and economic factors.

A child's social class and cultural traditions affect his peer relations; different patterns appear among middle and lower class children as well as among various ethnic subcultures (Psathas, 1957). The generation gap is created primarily by rapid changes in social interaction patterns; children learn their social behaviors from peers. In contrast to our own school system, Soviet education relies to a marked extent on peer relations for control of the child. The Israeli kibbutz also uses peer groups for primary socialization. Cultural variation in peer group influence occurs between American and Mexican children. Mexican children live more within a family and as a result are not under such strong social pressures from their peers. American youth often are abandoned to the morals and mores of their peer group. After 13 years of age parental control of the child is small (particularly of boys) compared to peer influence. The amount of conformity among children is amazing. Young children need an opportunity to explore various modes of behavior; they also need the sanction, support, and control of a peer group. New patterns of acting are easier to assimilate with support from others. Children sever the umbilical cord by establishing other bonds; they form a mutual support society to survive detachment from the family. This peer group exerts enormous influence on the child during his school years.

Children discriminate on the basis of social class, race, and money.

How does parental social class affect children's peer relations? Hollingshead (1949) showed that group membership tends to be homogeneous within social classes. Children discriminate on the basis of class, race, and economic advantage. Frequency of contact, physical separation, and differences in values probably account for most social class variation in friendships (Macdonald, McGuire, & Havighurst, 1949).

Children's sex and age determine the remainder of peer-relation variation.

The sex and age of a child control the remainder of his peer relations; children are segregated according to age and sex throughout the latency period (five to 12 years of age). The child's sex and age contribute substantially to his choice of group membership. Older children develop heterogeneous sex groupings. Peer groups are the primary source of models; children copy the accepted activities of peers. They learn some sex-appropriate behaviors from the peer group. Boys who are popular with their peers are more aggressive than boys not accepted by their peers. However, among girls aggression is not popular. Children's social roles become more differentiated, and the peer group becomes more effective in controlling individual members as they mature. The importance of group membership increases with age from nursery school through college (Smith, 1960).

Family influences on peer relations

Children tend to choose peers on the basis of their own family composition.

Family structure also affects a child's peer relations; children pattern peer relations after their family interactions. Firstborn children choose younger peers for companions, while children who have opposite-sexed siblings prefer opposite-sexed playmates more than children with no siblings or children with siblings of the same sex (Koch, 1957). The relations among family members also affect a child's social interactions. Well-adjusted children interact more adequately with their peers than do children who have a poor home adjustment.

Peer acceptance and rejection

Peers value friendliness and sociability; they don't like children who withdraw or show hostility.

The criteria for acceptance or rejection by one's peers are well known. Children accept or reject others on the basis of judgments about personality characteristics, skills, and abilities. Personality characteristics which lead to acceptance include friendliness and sociability; children who withdraw or show hostility are often rejected. Skills in creative areas and athletics rate high with peers, while physical immaturity produces low social status.

Children's social relations are established quickly and remain stable for some time.

Social relations are established soon after a group of children come together, and they show remarkable stability over time. Hunt and Solomon (1942) showed that during the earliest days of a summer camp group structure was formed. The structure remained stable over several weeks. Stability of relations is positively related to age; older children have more stable criteria of acceptance and rejection and more reliably judge their peers on these criteria.

The child's self-concept is affected by his peer relations.

A child's self-concept is affected by his peer relations; less popular children consider themselves inferior to their more popular peers. Whether rejection causes feelings of inferiority or the inferior feelings cause children to withdraw from social relations (and thus be rejected) is unknown. Most likely, a vicious circle develops: The insecure child withdraws and his withdrawal insures rejection. Because he is rejected, he becomes more insecure and withdraws more. One way to break this cycle is to teach the child an activity the group values (such as karate); he will be accepted, and withdrawal will not be reinforced.

Children's suggestibility

Children who are older and more secure are less suggestible than other children.

Some children are more resistant to peer influences than others. Older children and boys tend to resist pressures more than younger children and girls (Berenda, 1950). Also, the extent to which a child is influenced by others relates to his status in the group. Children accorded low status are more likely to change their judgments when confronted

TABLE 15.1 Conditions That Determine Whether a Particular Act Will Spread Among a Group of Children

1. *The group status of the initiator:* A boy who ranks high in leadership among a group of children is more likely to be imitated than a child not accepted by the group.

2. *Closeness of the behavior to the group code:* If the act "counts" with the group (e.g., a reference to elimination among young children) the behavior will spread.

3. *Commonality of basic emotions:* Suppressed hostility in a group may flare if an act occurs which appeals to that latent frustration.

4. *Size, structure, and organizational pattern of the group:* If there are no subgroups, contagion is more likely to occur. If a class is organized into small groups working around tables, contagion is less likely to occur than if the whole group is in a circle.

5. *Group atmosphere:* A disturbed child is less apt to be noticed in a democratic atmosphere, although a particular group, no matter what the atmosphere, can absorb only a few disturbed children.

SOURCE: Adapted from Redl & Wineman, 1951.

by peer pressure than are children high in leadership and social status. Dependent children are more likely to be influenced by others than are their independent peers.

Athletic, independent children tend to be leaders of peer groups.

The child who is athletic, independent of adults, and relatively free from social pressures exerts the most influence on his peer group; however, there are exceptions. The impulsive child who produces an "appropriate" action at the right moment may produce behavioral contagion. Behavioral contagion results when members of a group share common attitudes and frustrations and they copy the violent behavior of a single member. The particular pattern of behavior spreads through the group like plague. The behavior is often violent and disruptive (see Table 15.1).

Peer groups control tastes and behaviors among their members; they may be cruel, but children are honest in their evaluations.

The peer group often controls tastes and attitudes by pointing out acceptable actions among its members. The peer group is often cruel, but seldom biased; unlike the emotionally involved parent (who projects his own fears onto the child) the peer group accepts a child for himself. They quickly tell the offending child what he is doing wrong and reject him if he is unable or unwilling to meet their standards of behavior. Peer acceptance is a good predictor of future personal adjustment. Among children rejected by their peers, adjustment problems are high.

The generation gap

Parents exert early control over their children and influence their choice of peers.

Both adults and children contribute to the development of a child; but which group controls him? The issue can be posed as a conflict between the world of children and adults; however, this is too simple. Young children are certainly controlled by parents. Parents influence a

FIGURE 15.5

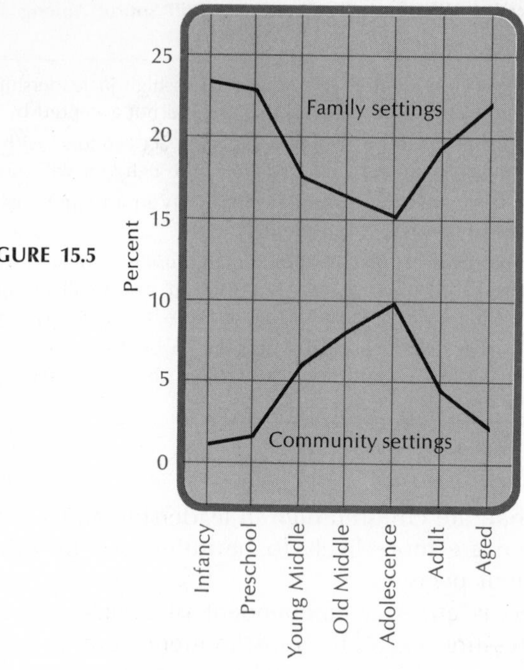

Average percent of time spent in family and community settings. (From Wright, 1956.)

child's choice of peers and his adjustment to them. Indirectly the adult has enormous influence on the child, even through his peers, since the adult guides children in peer selection. The power of a peer group over the child increases with age, while adult authority decreases as the child becomes more mature and capable of independent action (see Figure 15.5).

MASS MEDIA AND CHILDREN

Mass media occupy as much time as school.

Television, comic books, radio, and movies absorb a substantial part of our children's attention; children are attracted by the mass media very early and they learn social patterns from what they see and hear. Their attachment to entertainment is often more compelling than dinner or social interactions (ask any mother who tries to pull Johnny from his favorite program). What are the effects of exposure to mass media? Is the child primarily entertained, or does he receive ideas which affect his later actions and attitudes? Early critics suggested that even fairy tales are too violent; defenders say that some excitement is necessary to arouse interest, to entertain, and to allow the child an opportunity to deal with new thoughts and social patterns vicariously.

Systematic research into the mass media was started in the 1920s.

Systematic research into the effect of movies on children's attitudes and actions was started in the 1920s. The Payne fund (Charters, 1933) studied the effects of movies on social attitudes, delinquency, and emotional responsiveness. Current concern over the mass media stems from fears that delinquency is related to violence on television and in the comic strips. It is true that young delinquents are addicted to the mass media; but to conclude that the mass media are responsible for violence is premature.

Some possible effects

Mass media may take children from other activities or suppress their emotions.

Mass media might exert their influences either by indirect means (taking the child away from other activities) or directly (through emotional reactions or learning new attitudes and beliefs). The major content of mass media is not documentary; but children learn a great deal from movies and television. Children are attracted to mass media because they entertain; they allow escape from reality into a world of vicarious experience.

Boys are excited by violence while girls are stimulated by romantic encounters on the screen.

We assume that children identify with the hero and vicariously experience his actions. Physiological measures of children's emotions while viewing movies show that boys are aroused during fights while girls are aroused by romantic encounters. Of course, mass media do not influence all children in the same manner. Children are not passive; each has different interests, and the hero must be relevant to those interests before identification and learning can occur.

Methods of study

To study the effects of mass media we should measure children before and after the introduction of the new entertainment.

How can we study the mass media? It is tempting to look for any changes that occur after the introduction of a new entertainment source and ascribe the changes to that introduction. However, other things could cause the change. To study the effects of mass media we must find two situations with comparable changes in all variables except the introduction of a new media. The best way to study the effects of mass media is to measure children in a community before the medium is introduced and then remeasure the same children following the introduction of new entertainment.

Children watch television rather than look at comic books or listen to the radio.

Children spend 15 to 18 hours a week viewing television—almost as much time as they spend in school! What activities are displaced by television? Following the introduction of television into their homes, children go to bed later, they listen to the radio less, they read fewer comic books, and they see fewer movies. Also, what is the effect of mass media on school performance? Schramm *et al.* (1961) showed that children who grow up with television are a year ahead of children without television (in vocabulary size when they enter school). However, this difference disappears by the sixth grade. There is a negative relation between IQ and amount of time spent viewing television. When IQ is matched among children who watch television, there is no relation between amount of television viewing and school performance (Himmelweit, *et al.*, 1958).

Does vicarious aggression change our desire to be violent?

Many people are concerned about violence that might occur after watching television programs. Do children learn to be aggressive by watching fights on television? Are there hostile feelings that last after the viewing is over? Do the emotional reactions to a fight dissipate or do they last for some time? Does it make a difference who is violent? Early theories postulated that aggressive experiences reduce our need to be aggressive. While it may be true that children experience a release of tension when they are aggressive, is that same release available when they experience aggression vicariously?

Bandura, Ross, and Ross showed that fantasy aggression increases the probability of aggression following frustration.

Work with children shows interesting results of fantasy aggression. Bandura, Ross, and Ross (1963) showed children aggressive film scenes and then frustrated them. These children imitated the filmed aggression. However, when adults are frustrated and then allowed to write stories about their aggressive feelings, they experience less hostility. Why are these two results so different? The children were frustrated after they had seen the movies, and they expressed their hostility. Perhaps if the children were frustrated *before* seeing the movies, their aggressive impulses would be diminished by the film. Such a study would prove interesting and is badly needed.

Mass media and affective behavior of the child

Viewing violent programs makes children deny their feelings.

What are the moods and feelings of a child following encounters with mass media? Does the child feel less secure, less afraid, or less childish following a particular scene? Do Westerns help the child control his impulses and gain mastery of his environment? Is the child learning to control his antisocial impulses by watching the hero defeat the bad guys? Thomson (1959) showed that viewing violent programs has other effects than transmitting specific information. He found that children repress their feelings if they constantly watch violent movies. They become insensitive to social realities.

Individual variation in television viewing

Children who are rejected watch more television.

All children do not watch television. The effects of viewing a particular program are individual. What characteristics contribute to watching television? What makes children who watch susceptible to influence?

Children who are rejected or punished by their parents and children from homes with conflict view television most often. They are trying to escape a difficult situation by withdrawing into a world of fantasy. Fantasy may be the most important effect of television, and its most dangerous product.

Shy children watch more television than their more social peers.

Shy, withdrawn children who have few friends spend a great deal of time watching television. The example that parents set contributes substantially to children's viewing habits. The shy, withdrawn child may daydream about a movie after he has seen it, while a better-integrated child may simply gain information from the picture which helps his interactions with peers.

THE CHILD IN SCHOOL

On entering school

Most children look forward to school.

Children change when they enter school; they are removed from their mothers and placed in close contact with children their own age and an adult who makes demands on them and enforces these demands with power. How do children feel about entering school? Most mothers report that their children look forward to school. The school is represented to the child—particularly the middle class child—as a nice place where he will learn to read, write, and do numbers. Mothers report, however, that their children meet some problems on entering school. Chief among these is the aggressive behavior of other children. How to handle peer aggression is a recurring problem. Also, the child's relation to his teacher is important.

The teacher

Teachers strongly influence the classroom atmosphere.

A child's teacher exerts strong influences over his early behavior; a pupil spends many hours in her classroom. She directs his learning and sets the stage for many pleasant or uncomfortable experiences. The young child learns values and attitudes from his teachers. Her rules and the manner in which these rules are enforced convey information. Teachers help determine the child's future attitude toward work and a career. The teacher replaces the mother (at least for young children). It is no accident that teachers in the lower grades are women; it is also no accident that schools try to place men in classrooms around the fourth or fifth grade. Teachers can substitute for neglectful or irrational parents, offering a stabilizing and maturing influence. However, this stabilizing influence on any particular child is limited by responsibility to 25 or 30 children. The teacher cannot be intimate with every child in the room.

Teachers select their occupation for prestige, parental interests, security, and power.

Teachers select their occupation for the same irrational reasons others use—personality factors, half-forgotten memories of their own teachers, social class background, interests, and parental pressures. Teachers generally come from the middle class; they want security, social position, and power. Sometimes they are unable to meet the requirements of other professions. Most enter teaching because it offers security and respectability. Some hope to help the growing youngster.

Teachers are becoming more liberal about children's behavior; they are more concerned with withdrawal and less with aggression.

Teacher attitudes toward child behavior Teachers must maintain an atmosphere conducive to learning. However, their own needs often determine the atmosphere they feel is most appropriate. What are teachers' attitudes toward children's behavior? A classic study by Wickman (1938) showed large differences between the rated seriousness of children's behavior problems as viewed by teachers and mental hygienists (see Table 15.2). The hygienists rated withdrawal and regressive behaviors as most serious, while the teachers felt that sexual problems and transgression against authority are the most serious problems faced in the classroom. Wickman believed that teachers should pay more attention to asocial behavior and be less concerned with antisocial behavior. Asocial behavior indicates serious emotional or social maladjustment.

TABLE 15.2 **Comparison of Mean Ratings[a] by Teachers in 1955 and by Teachers and Mental Hygienists in 1926 of the Relative Seriousness of 50 Behavior Problems**

Behavior Problems	*Teachers (1955) N = 308*	*Teachers (1926) N = 511*	*Mental Hygienists (1926) N = 30*
1. Heterosexual activity	12.9	17.3	9.9
2. Stealing	14.9	17.0	12.5
3. Masturbation	10.7	16.7	6.4
4. Obscene notes, talk	11.5	16.6	8.8
5. Untruthfulness	13.3	15.8	10.3
6. Truancy	13.6	15.6	10.3
7. Impertinence, defiance	13.4	15.0	7.1
8. Cruelty, bullying	13.5	14.8	13.5
9. Cheating	11.9	14.7	10.3
10. Destroying school materials	13.7	14.3	5.1
11. Disobedience	13.0	14.1	6.4
12. Unreliableness	13.1	13.9	10.4
13. Temper tantrums	11.7	13.0	11.7
14. Lack of interest in work	12.1	12.8	9.6
15. Profanity	10.5	12.3	2.9
16. Impudence, rudeness	12.4	12.2	7.6
17. Laziness	11.6	12.2	7.2

TABLE 15.2 Comparison of Mean Ratings[a] by Teachers in 1955 and by Teachers and Mental Hygienists in 1926 of the Relative Seriousness of 50 Behavior Problems *(Continued)*

Behavior Problems	*Teachers (1955) N = 308*	*Teachers (1926) N = 511*	*Mental Hygienists (1926) N = 30*
18. Smoking	7.3	12.0	2.3
19. Enuresis	9.2	11.8	9.2
20. Nervousness	11.1	11.7	3.4
21. Disorderliness in class	11.5	11.7	3.4
22. Unhappy, depressed	13.4	11.5	16.2
23. Easily discouraged	11.9	11.5	13.4
24. Selfishness	11.6	11.3	11.8
25. Carelessness in work	11.8	11.3	7.1
26. Inattention	11.1	11.2	7.3
27. Quarrelsomeness	12.0	11.1	8.3
28. Suggestible	11.4	11.0	13.3
29. Resentfulness	12.5	10.8	14.1
30. Tardiness	9.7	10.5	5.6
31. Physical cowardice	9.8	10.4	12.0
32. Stubbornness	10.1	10.3	10.9
33. Domineering	11.2	10.3	13.0
34. Slovenly in appearance	9.7	10.1	7.2
35. Sullenness	10.2	9.9	12.6
36. Fearfulness	10.4	9.7	14.0
37. Suspiciousness	9.5	9.1	16.4
38. Thoughtlessness	9.7	8.7	6.8
39. Attracting attention	10.2	8.5	8.5
40. Unsocial, withdrawing	11.6	8.3	17.3
41. Dreaminess	8.8	8.3	11.3
42. Imaginative lying	8.0	8.1	7.5
43. Interrupting	9.0	8.0	2.8
44. Inquisitiveness	8.8	8.0	5.3
45. Overcritical of others	9.8	7.9	13.2
46. Tattling	8.1	7.5	8.8
47. Whispering	6.3	7.5	0.8
48. Sensitiveness	9.6	7.0	13.1
49. Restlessness	8.6	6.9	6.4
50. Shyness	9.5	5.4	12.5
Average	10.9	11.3	9.5

[a] Rating chart: slight consequence, 5.0; considerable difficulty, 12.0; extremely grave problem, 20.0.

The differences between teachers and mental health experts probably reflect the teachers' desire to instruct.

Many reasons have been expressed for these differences between clinical judgments and teachers' judgments of behavior. The teacher, after all, must teach; her primary responsibility is to develop academic skills. The withdrawn child presents little threat to this goal, while antisocial behavior disrupts the class, making effective teaching difficult.

The psychologist has had a clear influence on the teacher—the comparisons of Table 15.2 show that teacher attitudes have shifted toward those of the mental hygienists in the last 25 years. This shift reflects an increased awareness of and concern with the problems of withdrawal and personality development. The teacher is coming to understand that disruptions within the classroom are less disturbing than disruptions within the student.

Teachers are concerned about their colleagues, the administration, and paperwork; they are not bothered by children.

The problems of the teacher What are the main irritations with which a teacher must contend? The list is long: First come a series of complaints about colleagues, the school administration, paperwork, inadequate pay, and the interpersonal conflicts teachers endure. Classroom discipline is not a major concern of most teachers, except in ghetto schools; they are more unhappy about other aspects of their job.

A teacher's attitude toward children determines the attitude of children toward school.

Teacher-child relations The feedback a teacher gives her pupils determines their emotional adjustment and self-concept in the classroom. The student who receives praise and good marks from the teacher cannot help but grow in emotional security and self-confidence. However, what about the perpetual failure? He is doomed to negative judgments every day of his school life. Is it any wonder we see dropouts from our competitive school situation? The child who receives only negative reinforcement from a middle class teacher is not likely to identify with or stay in that situation.

Teachers approve and disapprove of a few children; the rest are mostly ignored.

DeGroat and Thompson (1949) studied the pattern of approval and disapproval in sixth-grade classrooms. They asked children to nominate peers who fit certain descriptive categories (for example, someone whose work is often called neat, or someone who is often scolded). They found an uneven distribution of teacher attention. Relatively few students were singled out by the teacher for approval or disapproval (Figure 15.6). Approved students were bright, high in achievement motivation, and scored high on personality adjustment. In contrast, students who received disapproval were less intelligent, lower in academic achievement, and scored below average on a test of personality adjustment. Teachers form closer ties with middle and upper class children and experience most difficulties with lower class boys. This fact is related to the low academic achievement found among lower class boys.

Boys are disapproved more than girls.

Meyer and Thompson (1956) found that boys receive more disapproval than do girls in the classroom. Boys are more active and aggressive than girls; males find it difficult to sit still in the classroom. When their natural impulses break through, a teacher is likely to disapprove. Disapproval tends to evoke resentment, which in turn leads to revolt

FIGURE 15.6

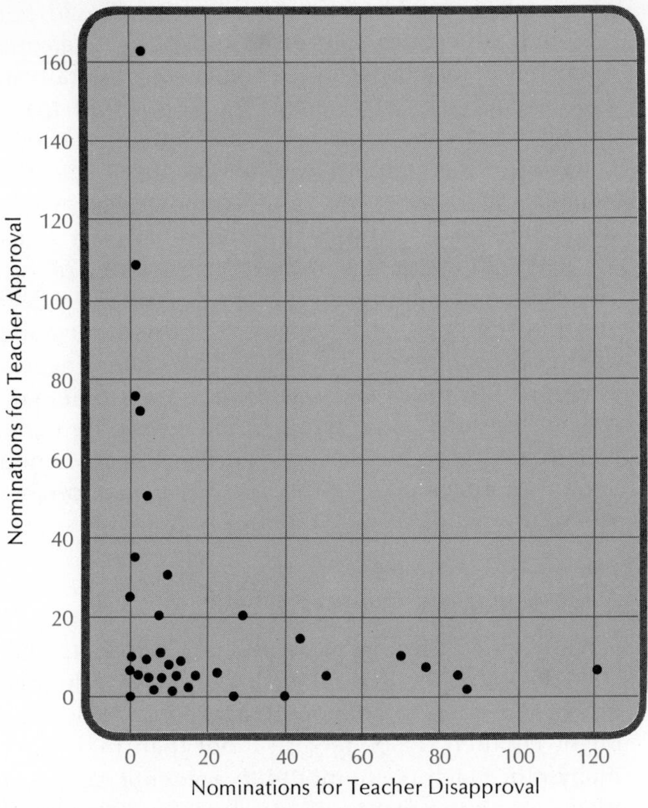

The distribution of teacher approval-disapproval in a sixth-grade classroom as indicated by pupils' responses to a "guess who?" inventory. This distribution is very similar to one obtained by the recordings of an outside observer during 30 one-hour samples of teacher-pupil interactions. Note that one pupil received over 160 nominations for teacher approval, whereas another pupil received over 120 nominations for teacher disapproval. Is it any wonder that some children dislike school? (From DeGroat & Thompson, 1949.)

and more activity in the classroom. A gulf forms between the active boy and his teacher. Most boys are interested in action and exercise, not in learning and academic success. Disinterest may result from the passive classroom. More active participation might produce more interest and better learning.

Some teachers are oriented toward the student; others are concerned with themselves.

Teachers may be classified into two broad sets: Some are pupil-oriented, others teacher-oriented. The teacher-oriented classroom is rigid; these teachers can't recognize or tolerate individuality among children. On the other hand, pupil-oriented teachers cultivate individuality and variation among their students. They try to integrate the behavior of the child, to give him feedback and influence his thoughts indirectly by praise and reinforcement. The teacher-oriented person directs the child and tries to impress her own goals on the class.

A pupil-oriented approach leads to satisfaction and learning.

These differing approaches reflect varying philosophies of teaching. The democratic approach (Lippitt & White, 1947) allows choice and a voice in the goals of the group. On the other hand, the authoritarian approach produces frustration with resultant aggression or regression. The apparent order and control in an authoritarian classroom reflects hidden tensions. Little group spirit exists. The democratic style makes high demands on the teacher to understand the child, while the authoritarian approach allows the teacher to act on her own wishes and ignore the needs of her students.

Achievement and failure in school

Bright children do better in school; independence is also important.

School is for learning; thus, it's not surprising that achievement has been explored by school systems and psychologists. As one might expect, the best predictor of academic achievement is intelligence! Bright children do better in school than their duller peers. However, many other factors contribute to academic success or failure. Achievement during the first years of school may be hampered by immaturity in otherwise bright children. Physiological maturity contributes to school achievement, even with IQ matched among groups of children. The amount of independence encouraged in the home also contributes to academic achievement.

Personality factors in school achievement

Emotional stability contributes to school achievement.

The relation between emotional problems and academic achievement is complex; often academic underachievement contributes to emotional instability. Emotional instability certainly results in underachievement, and this is particularly true among boys with poor father identification. These boys develop a poor concept of self, have low self-esteem, and lack the security to achieve according to their abilities. High-achievement children are responsive to the socialization pressures of their parents, while children who underachieve have a history of disturbed interpersonal relations. The overachiever conforms to the demands of his parents. But by the time he reaches the fifth or sixth grade, signs of hostility and resentment toward parents appear among many overachievers. They are anxious to please, but overachievement does not soothe their anxiety. By contrast, underachievers actively fight the demands of parents. The active disruption of interpersonal relations among the underachievers is healthier for the child's personal adjustment, but he misses academic skills in the process.

Failure breeds fear; fear breeds further failure.

Failure breeds demoralization and fear of further failure. Children with a history of failure set unrealistically high or low goals, while children with a history of success set more realistic goals in their striving for attainment. This result may come from better information feedback to the successful child; it may be that successful children are brighter and can understand the consequences of over- or under-expectations, or it may be that fear of failure frightens the unsuccessful child so much that he will perform any irrational act to finish the task quickly.

SUMMARY

1 Early explanations of infant social attachment emphasized the association of feeding with mother. Later work shows that feeding is of minor importance; the amount of "contact comfort" available determines the infant's attachment to his mother.

2 Infants' anxiety of strangers develops about six months following birth. Infants exposed to many people develop stranger anxiety later. Psychoanalytic theorists believe stranger anxiety results from fear of losing the mother; however, perceptually oriented theories of development (Hebb) suggest that a combination of novel and familiar stimuli elicits fear.

3 Smiling, vocalizations, and play are positive social relations. Smiling can be evoked by social stimuli (face and voice) at about the sixth week. Infant vocalizations can be conditioned during the first three months of life, and play occurs early in the child's life. Two explanations of play exist: Freud proposed that children choose toys on the basis of anxiety, while Piaget wrote that children are attracted to various play materials by their growing cognitive abilities.

4 Children live in two worlds, the world of their parents and that of their peers. Parents are important early in the life of the child, but as he matures, more and more influence is exerted by his peers. Children choose peers on the basis of their social, cultural, and intellectual status. Also, age and sex help determine their choice of friends.

5 Television affects children's activities. The first things that suffer are movies, comic books, and reading. There is no relation between amount of television viewing and school performance when the contribution of intelligence is controlled. However, there are subtle effects of television viewing on the child's sensitivity to other persons. Children who watch violent television programs grow less sensitive to their own and others' feelings.

6 Children approach school with positive feelings. However, they report that teachers often make them dislike school. The attitude of a teacher and her response to the child (either dominating or integrative) determines the school atmosphere and the child's attitude toward school. Teachers' attitudes toward child behavior have changed over the years, becoming more like the attitudes of mental hygienists.

FURTHER READINGS

Kagan, J., & Moss, H. A. *Birth to maturity.* New York: Wiley, 1962.

Kohlberg, L. The development of children's orientations toward a moral order: I. Sequence in the development of moral thought. *Vita Humana,* 1963, **6,** 11-33.

Piaget, J. *Play, dreams, and imitation in childhood.* New York: Norton, 1962.

Winterbottom, M. R. The relation of need for achievement to learning experience in independence and mastery. In J. W. Atkinson (Ed.), *Motives in fantasy, action and society.* Princeton, N.J.: Van Nostrand, 1958. Pp. 453-478.

REFERENCES

Anderson, H. H. The measurement of domination and socially integrative behavior in teachers' contacts with children. *Child Development,* 1939, **10,** 73-89.

Atkinson, R. C., Bower, G. H., & Crothers, E. *An introduction to mathematical learning theory.* New York: Wiley, 1965.

Baldwin, J. M. *Mental development in the child and the race.* (3rd ed.) New York: Macmillan, 1906.

Bandura, A., Ross, D., & Ross, S. A. Imitation of film-mediated aggressive models. *Journal of Abnormal and Social Psychology,* 1963, **66,** 3-11.

Berenda, R. W. *The influence of the group on the judgments of children.* New York: King's Crown Press, 1950.

Bridges, K. M. B. Emotional development in early infancy. *Child Development,* 1932, **3,** 324-341.

Charters, W. W. *Motion pictures and youth: A summary.* New York: Macmillan, 1933.

Cooley, C. H. *Social organization, and human nature and the social order.* 1909, 2 Vols. in 1. New York: The Free Press, 1955.

Day, E. J. The development of language in twins: I. A comparison of twins and single children. *Child Development,* 1932, **3,** 179-199.

DeGroat, A. F., & Thompson, G. G. A study of the distribution of teacher approval and disapproval among sixth-grade children. *Journal of Experimental Education,* 1949, **18,** 57–75.

Flavell, J. H. *The developmental psychology of Jean Piaget.* Princeton, N.J.: Van Nostrand, 1963.

Freedman, D. G. The infant's fear of strangers and the flight response. *Journal of Child Psychology and Psychiatry,* 1961, **2,** 242–248.

Freud, S. *An outline of psychoanalysis.* New York: Norton, 1949.

Gilmore, J. B. Play: A special behavior. In R. N. Haber (ed.), *Current research in motivation.* New York: Holt, Rinehart and Winston, 1966.

Groos, K. *The play of animals.* New York: Appleton-Century, 1915.

Harlow, H. F. The nature of love. *American Psychologist,* 1958, **13,** 673–685.

Hebb, D. O. On the nature of fear. *Psychological Review,* 1946, **53,** 259–276.

Himmelweit, H. T., Oppenheim, A. N., & Vince, P. *Television and the child.* Published for the Nuffield Foundation. New York: Oxford, 1958.

Hollingshead, A. B. *Elmstown's youth.* New York: Wiley, 1949.

Hunt, J. McV., & Solomon, R. L. The stability and some correlates of group-status in a summer-camp group of young boys. *American Journal of Psychology,* 1942, **55,** 33–45.

Kemeny, J. G., Snell, J. L., & Thompson, G. L. *Introduction to finite mathematics.* Englewood Cliffs, N.J.: Prentice-Hall, 1957.

Koch, H. L. The relation in young children between characteristics of their playmates and certain attributes of their siblings. *Child Development,* 1957, **28,** 175–202.

Lippitt, R., & White, R. K. An experimental study of leadership and group life. In T. M. Newcomb and E. L. Hartley (Eds.), *Readings in social psychology.* New York: Holt, Rinehart & Winston, 1947. Pp. 315–330.

Luce, R. D., & Raiffa, H. *Games and decisions.* New York: Wiley, 1957.

Macdonald, M., McGuire, C., & Havighurst, R. J. Leisure activities and the socioeconomic status of children. *American Journal of Sociology,* 1949, **54,** 505–519.

Meyer, W. J., & Thompson, G. G. Sex differences in the distribution of teacher approval and disapproval among sixth-grade children. *Journal of Educational Psychology,* 1956, **47,** 385–396.

Moreno, J. L. *Who shall survive?* Washington, D.C.: Nervous and Mental Disease Publishing Company, 1934.

Parten, M. B. Social participation among preschool children. *Journal of Abnormal Social Psychology,* 1932, **27,** 243–270.

Psathas, G. Ethnicity, social class and adolescent independence from parental control. *American Sociological Review,* 1957, **22,** 415–423.

Piaget, J. *Play, dreams, and imitation in childhood* (1954). London: Heinemann, 1951.

Preyer, W. T. *The mind of the child.* Vol. 1. New York: Appleton, 1888.

Redl, F., & Wineman, D. *Children who hate.* Glencoe, Ill.: The Free Press, 1951.

Rheingold, H. L., Gewirtz, J. L., & Ross, H. W. Social conditioning of vocalizations in the infant. *Journal of Comparative and Physiological Psychology,* 1959, **52,** 68–73.

Ribble, M. A. Infantile experiences in relation to personality development. In J. McV. Hunt (Ed.), *Personality and the behavior disorders,* II. New York: Ronald Press, 1944. Pp. 621-651.

Schaffer, H. R. The onset of fear of strangers and the incongruity hypothesis. *Journal of Child Psychology and Psychiatry,* 1966, **7,** 95-106.

Schaffer, H. R., & Emerson, P. E. The development of social attachments in infancy. *Monograph of the Society for Research in Child Development,* 1964, **29,** No. 3 (Serial No. 94).

Sherif, M., Harvey, O. J., White, B. J., Hood, D. R., & Sherif, C. W. *Intergroup conflict and cooperation: The robbers' cave experiment.* Norman, Okla.: University of Oklahoma Press, 1961.

Schramm, W., Lyle, J., & Parker, E. B. *Television in the lives of our children.* Stanford, Calif.: Stanford University Press, 1961.

Smith, A. J. A developmental study of group processes. *Journal of Genetic Psychology,* 1960, **97,** 29-30.

Spitz, R. A. Anxiety in infancy. *International Journal of Psycho-Analysis,* 1950, **31,** 138-143.

Terman, L. M. A preliminary study of the psychology and pedagogy of leadership. *Pedagogical Seminary,* 1904, **11,** 413-451.

Thomas, D. S., Loomis, A. M., & Arrington, R. E. *Observational studies of social behavior.* Vol. 1. *Social behavior patterns.* New Haven, Conn.: Institute of Human Relations, Yale University, 1933.

Thomson, R. J. *Television crime drama.* Melbourne: Department of Audio-Visual Aids, University of Melbourne, 1959.

Wickman, E. K. *Teachers and behavior problems.* New York: Commonwealth Fund, 1928.

Wolff, P. H. Observations on the early development of smiling. In B. M. Foss (Ed.), *Determinants of infant behavior.* II. New York: Wiley, 1963. Pp. 113-167.

Wright, H. F. Psychological development in the Midwest. *Child Development,* 1956, **27,** 265-286.

16 PERSONALITY

> Men should be what they seem;
> Or those that be not, would they might seem none!
>
> OTHELLO

Personal growth comes from interaction between children and their environment; each makes demands on the other. Sometimes adjustment occurs when the environment yields to the child; at other times, the child must yield to his environment (if he cannot change the conditions in which he finds himself). Most often, adaptation is a compromise between domination by environment and mastery of it. Adaptation is a process, not a state of happiness. The adapted child is not always a happy, confident little boy with no problems. Sometimes the best possible solution entails discouragement, sorrow, and frustration. Adjustment occurs when a child's compromise between demands—the environment—and desires—physical needs and personal wishes—is satisfactory. Maladjustment occurs when the bargain is not as satisfactory as it might be (because of fear or withdrawal). Personality results from varying environmental demands, unequal genetic potentials, and their complex interactions within the particular person. Two theories articulate this view most clearly: The work of Erikson (1950) and the writings of Freud (1949). Their notions are presented following a discussion of some problems in personality development. An environmental alternative (social reinforcement) is also discussed.

Personality development is usually studied by reviewing single clinical cases.

Personality development has been studied by reviewing single cases—the idiographic method. However, studying one person gives a confused impression of normal growth; we need to describe in detail the general notions of personality. Information about personality is now gathered primarily by standardized testing procedures. These methods promise to supplant the single clinical case as a main data source. There are two types of tests (see Remarks: Method); variation on a theme has produced numerous inventories.

TESTS OF PERSONALITY

There are two basic personality tests: the projective (in which the child is shown an ambiguous stimulus and asked what he sees), and the objective (in which the child is asked to answer yes or no to a series of simple questions). Each test has various strengths and weaknesses.

Projective tests

Projective devices are disguised; the child is usually unaware that he is being tested or what the test is about. Projective tests make the assumption that a child is guided by his unconscious wishes and desires in an ambiguous situation: His responses should mirror unconscious thoughts and desires.

The best-known projective test was invented by Hermann Rorschach (1942), who was the first to use inkblots for systematically studying personality. Five of his blots contain shades of grey, two include bright red, and the remaining three have several colors. The child is asked to look at each blot and tell what he sees. The tester keeps a verbatim record of the child's responses and latencies. Following presentation of all ten cards, the child is questioned about the location and meaning of each response. The major scoring categories of the Rorschach include location (part of the blot used) determinant (form, color, or shading), content (human, animal, anatomical diagrams, landscapes, food, art, or abstractions), and popularity of a response (its frequency among people taking the test). On the basis of these categories and the particular theory used by the psychologist, a detailed description of the child's personality can be produced.

There are several problems associated with the Rorschach test; the most critical concerns the number of responses. Because of variation in the number of responses produced, we can't use simple frequency of response in the various categories as a score. Proportion of responses is also misleading; if there are many responses, then the proportion of whole responses cannot be large, since there are usually ten for the entire test. Also, the total number of responses is related to age (older children produce more responses) and intelligence (brighter individuals give more responses). The Holtzman Rorschach Test (Holtzman, *et al.,* 1961), which requires only one response to each of a large number of cards, is a solution to this problem. It should be more reliable and easier to score.

Objective tests

A variety of self-report inventories have been used to test personality objectively. Some require the child to admit he has a variety of symptoms, others ask him to check adjectives which describe his personality. More recent tests have been developed by factor analysis, a correlation technique used to determine the minimum number of dimensions which can be used to describe personality (Guilford & Zimmerman, 1956). Table 16.1 shows a list of factors found in a variety of tests.

There is a growing tendency not to interpret single-trait scores but the total pattern. For example, a high score in emotional stability is favorable if coupled with a high score in general activity, but the same score is unfavorable if connected with low general activity. In the latter case the individual may be lazy, sluggish, or withdrawn.

Two problems plague objective personality testing. One is the ambiguity of test items and the other concerns children's response set. Many children (and some adults) simply say yes or no to everything. They cannot be tested by standard techniques; instead, we must ask them to choose between two contradictory items. In this way their predominant tendency to say yes or no won't affect the outcome. The social desirability of test items must also be matched ("Would you rather murder someone or rob a bank?"). The social desirability of both items is low, but one must still choose. Ambiguities can be solved by writing better questions. Test-makers are often empirical; they use any question that differentiates two groups. The typical procedure is to gather hundreds of items and present them to various groups. Questions that differentiate among the groups are retained, while questions that do not are eliminated. The empirical approach has been successful, but it limits our understanding of personality.

PROBLEMS OF DEVELOPMENT

There are four problems associated with early development: (1) dependence, (2) discipline, (3) sex, and (4) aggression.

There are four main problems of early personal development: (1) dependence and deprivation, (2) autonomy versus discipline, (3) sexual development, and (4) the management of aggression. These are particularly strong emotional problems, and they tax the adaptive processes of a young child. Deprivation and dependence occur early in development (during the first year). Next, the child struggles with discipline—the development of a compromise between his own requirements for autonomy and socialization by society (in the second and third years). Sexual development has three distinct phases in our society: (1) the fourth and fifth years, when sex reaches a peak in childhood, (2) a long latency period, and (3) puberty, when mature sexual reproduction develops and strengthens the sexual urge. Aggression is a constant problem; the young child must learn to accept his aggressive impulses, channel them into productive activities, and overcome the fear and hurt which come from the aggression of others. Frustration leads instinctively to aggression; however, other factors contribute to the strength and frequency of this antisocial response.

TABLE 16.1 Factors of Personality

G. *General activity:* hurrying, liking for speed, liveliness, vitality, production, efficiency versus slow and deliberate, easily fatigued, inefficient.
R. *Restraint:* serious-minded, deliberate, persistent versus carefree, impulsive, excitement-loving.
A. *Ascendance:* leadership, speaking in public, bluffing versus submissiveness, hesitation, avoiding conspicuousness.
S. *Sociability:* having many friends, seeking social contacts and limelight versus few friends and shyness.
E. *Emotional stability:* evenness of moods, optimism, composure versus fluctuation of moods, pessimism, daydreaming, excitability, feelings of guilt, worry, loneliness, and ill health.
O. *Objectivity:* thick-skinned versus hypersensitive, self-centered, suspicious.
F. *Friendliness:* toleration of hostile action, acceptance of domination, respect for others versus belligerence, hostility, resentment, desire to dominate, and contempt for others.
T. *Thoughtfulness:* reflective, observing of self and others, mental poise versus interest in overt activity.
P. *Personal relations:* tolerance of people, faith in social institutions versus fault-finding, critical of institutions, suspicious, self-pitying.
M. *Masculinity:* interest in masculine activities, not easily disgusted, hard-boiled, inhibits emotional expression, little interest in clothes and style versus interest in feminine activities and vocations, easily disgusted, fearful, romantic, emotionally expressive.

The items in the Guilford-Zimmerman Temperament Survey (1956) are expressed in the form of affirmative statements rather than questions. Most concern the examinee directly. A few represent generalizations about other persons. Three examples are given below:

You start work on a new project with a great deal of enthusiasm.	YES	NO
You are often in low spirits.	YES	NO
Most people use politeness to cover up what is really "cutthroat" competition.	YES	NO

Childhood dependency

Early handling of infant dependence determines whether the child's world is happy or sad.

The young infant is virtually helpless; he is completely dependent on adults. For the first six or eight months, the infant is primarily involved in his own drives and pleasures—thirst, the satisfaction of hunger, and oral pleasure through sucking. The infant's early experiences tell him the world is a place where (1) you cry a little and get what you want or (2) you cry forever and get nothing.

Deprivation and rejection during the first stage leads to mistrust, withdrawal, and pessimism.

There are various maladaptive possibilities in the oral phase. Freud (1949) wrote that a child who is gratified during the oral stage would be optimistic, while frequent deprivation should lead to pessimism. Erikson (1950) calls this the stage of trust and mistrust. If the infant develops a sense of trust, he can become independent and self-reliant with no feeling of bitterness or isolation. However, if he mistrusts others and somehow still becomes independent and self-reliant, the independence and self-reliance will be accompanied by feelings of alienation and hate. Early deprivation and rejection form an insecure base for the development of independence. A complete loss of trust may lead to infant autism; he may show no responsiveness to other human beings. The effects of early experience in the oral stage (with particular reference to early maternal and sensory deprivation) are discussed in Chapter 10.

Dependency can be either task-oriented or person-oriented.

Two types of dependency may be distinguished: task-oriented and person-oriented (Bandura & Walters, 1963). In the case of task-oriented dependency, a child seeks help in order to reach a goal. The infant, for example, is dependent on his mother for warmth. Of more interest is person-oriented dependence; here others' social responses are the *goal* and not merely a means. Task-oriented dependence (the mother-child relation) often leads to person-oriented dependency. Some emotional dependence on others is necessary for a satisfactory social adjustment; children without emotional dependence, such as institutionalized infants, show poor personality growth.

Dependency is a feminine characteristic seldom allowed in males.

Males are not supposed to be dependent and females often do not want to be, but aside from these social value judgments, what is dependent behavior, how does it develop, and how stable is it from childhood into adult life?

Experimental studies use fearful situations which elicit dependent reactions.

The experimental study of dependency uses situations likely to elicit dependent responses. Novel, fear-inducing situations are good candidates (as are tasks difficult for children to perform). Different child-rearing practices produce variations in dependency. Child-centered homes produce more dependent children than do adult-centered homes. Many mothers reinforce dependency in their children (overprotection).

Positive reinforcement and rejection contribute to dependency.

In addition to positive reinforcement, parental rejection is an important antecedent of dependency. Sears, Maccoby, and Levin (1957) reported a positive relation between maternal punitiveness for dependency behavior and the strength of the child's dependency (when dependency was also frequently rewarded). If dependency was not reinforced, rejection accounted for little variation in the child's behavior. Withdrawal of attention leads to an increase in dependency; the effects are most marked in girls and very dependent boys.

Children who are dependent are also suggestible.

What are the correlates of dependency? Jakubezak and Walters (1959) noted that suggestibility may be another form of dependency. They proposed that dependent children should conform more than their independent peers and results confirmed that hypothesis.

Dependency is stable over age among females but not among males.

The stability of dependent behavior was studied longitudinally by Kagan and Moss (1960). They reported it is relatively stable for girls, but they found no relation between child and adult dependency among boys. In our culture, dependency is a feminine behavior pattern; the differential stability probably results from encouragement of dependency in females and its discouragement in older males. Changes do occur with age in the *form* of dependent responses and the persons toward whom dependent responses are aimed. Clinging and affection-seeking decline with age relative to attention or approval-seeking. Similarly, as the child matures, emotional dependence on adults declines while dependence on his peers increases. Older peers provide social reinforcers to their classmates more frequently than do younger, preschool-age children (Charlesworth & Hartup, 1967).

Autonomy versus discipline

Infants are spontaneously curious; this curiosity must be preserved while the child is socialized.

The young infant is spontaneously active—following things with his eyes, exploring and experimenting with his hands, looking at his hands, and trying to integrate sensory-motor activity. By the time the infant is one year old, he spends more of his time exploring and playing than satisfying his physical needs. Now he learns manipulations for the joy of manipulating. In the chapters on motivation and sensory-motor integration, we discussed the development of active experimentation. This shift from dependency to independence may often conflict with the mother's need to control. However, for normal personal growth the child must develop a sense of his own efficacy. This feeling can come only from producing an intended result through his own effort. If the child is denied this feeling, he will become insecure and remain dependent.

The two- and three-year-old child learns the value of "no!" during his competence training.

During his second and third years the child begins to emerge from his condition of helplessness; he learns the usefulness of "no!" He can now control the human part of his environment. Negativism is characteristic of the two-year-old. He sees himself as a living entity with power and wishes of his own. The young child must somehow come to terms with parental rules and regulations and at the same time salvage his own wishes. A typical example concerns toilet training. There is a strong natural connection between pressure in the bowels and evacuation. This automatic response must be inhibited; the child must learn to go to the bathroom, unbutton, and sit on the toilet. This complex behavior may be learned when the child only *partly* understands verbal cues (for those children trained early). Parents in their own childhood were often trained to feel disgust toward evacuation, and they have little patience during their child's toilet training. Strong emotions get involved which set the tone for later encounters with authority.

Children must learn what to do, when to do it, and how to do it.

Also, a child must learn the appropriate times (he may play in the morning but not at nap time), places (he may eat at the table but not in the living room), means (he may push other children but not hit them), and objects (he may ask his mother for money but he may not ask a stranger) for the satisfaction of his needs. In learning autonomy and discipline, the child must accept discipline while retaining his own sense of autonomy.

Children who receive no restrictions (permissiveness) or who are inhibited (repressed) suffer most.

There are two possible problems with autonomy and discipline. The child may receive no restrictions or he may be subjected to total control. Extreme permissiveness produces an unruly brat. Overindulgence can fixate the child in a dependent relationship. Even more serious problems spring from the opposite course—overcontrol. The child who is tricked, ridiculed, shamed, or threatened with pain and terrible punishments if he does not conform can find no middle ground between hopeless resistance and unconditional surrender. Excessive control produces two distinct patterns: *Anxious conformity* (resentments and desires are suppressed and the child becomes a model of cleanliness and outward propriety) or *negativism* (resentment against all demands even when overt resistance is impossible).

Although competition increases with age, cross-cultural studies show this is not inevitable.

Independence, competition, and motivation for achievement increase with age (see Figure 16.1). Cross-cultural studies show that competition is not inevitable; many American Indian tribes cooperate. Among these groups it is almost impossible to establish the usual competitive grading system. Early experiences and cultural demands mold cooperation *or* competition. Dependency decreases. Part of this shift comes from decreased reinforcement of dependency; however, independence is more than the lack of dependent needs. Achievement implies that the child is trying to perform well; self-evaluation against a standard of excellence is the main characteristic of achievement. While achievement and independence are not exactly the same thing, many studies have found them to be highly correlated (Sontag, Baker, & Nelson, 1958).

Independence must be gained early (by the time the child is five) if at all.

Winterbottom (1958), in her pioneering study of childrearing and achievement motivation, found that high-achievement boys receive strong early independence training. Mothers of nine-year-old boys (rated high in achievement motivation) expected self-reliant behavior relatively early and placed few restrictions on their sons' spontaneous activities. Also, these mothers gave large and frequent reinforcements to their sons for successful independent behavior. The result of this training was explored by Field (1959); he found that early independence training is strongly related to boys' achievement motivations in adoles-

FIGURE 16.1

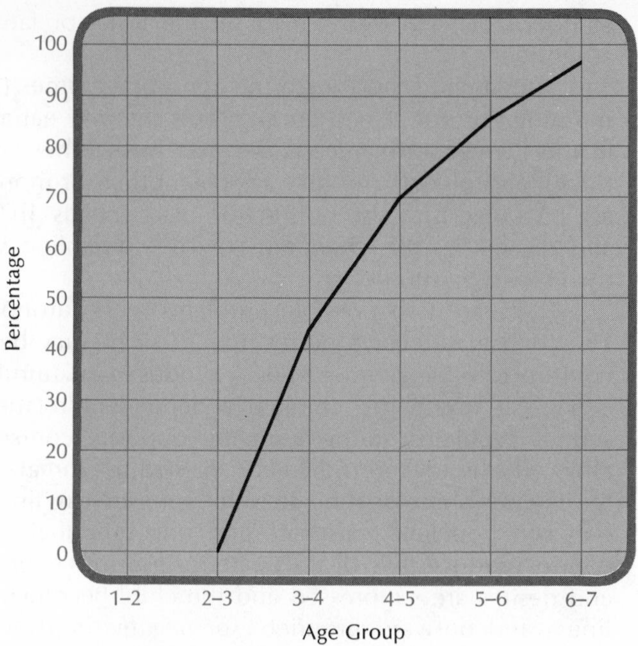

Percentage of children showing competitive responses at various ages. (After Greenberg, 1932.)

cence. By contrast, encouragement of independence during adolescence was negatively related to boys' achievement motivation. Early independence training is therefore necessary for the child's growth of competence.

Children who believe they will be successful try harder, work longer, and succeed more.

Several characteristics distinguish high- and low-achieving children. Children who show intellectual success expect to do well (not surprising, since they have successful past experiences to guide them). Moreover, children who expect to do well persist longer, try harder, and thus succeed more often than children who do not expect to perform well (Crandall & McGhee, 1967). Low achievers believe other people rather than themselves are responsible for their academic successes and failures. On the other hand, high achievers feel that control resides within themselves.

Children who achieve learn well with delayed reinforcement.

High achievers perform well under delayed reinforcement conditions and prefer to delay immediate gratification to receive a larger reward later. Academic success requires the ability to work for a long-range goal with little or no immediate reinforcement. High-achievement children prefer moderately difficult tasks which involve a challenge rather than very easy or very difficult tasks. Successful children are not necessarily gamblers; in fact, they prefer tasks where skill or ability is involved. They choose moderate risks rather than certainty or extreme risks.

Sexual development

Children are curious about sex.

Young children are fascinated by sex; Freud's (1949) great contribution was calling our attention to these early sexual interests. Many aspects of children's behavior are sexually oriented. An important example is masturbation, practiced by most children of both sexes during their fourth and fifth years. The activity grows from curiosity about sexual organs and anatomical differences. Despite recent changes in our culture, we remain generally hostile toward childhood sexuality. Many parents feel uneasy about children's masturbation.

Young children are sexually interested in their parents.

A child's early sexual experiences are attached to members of his own family. Children of four and five have an erotic interest in their parents. Freud called the little boy's interest in his mother Oedipal; the interest of the little girl in her father and her jealousy of the mother he called the Electra complex. The relative importance of these early attachments has been vigorously debated. Surely, love and sex are not the same! A young infant's love for his mother is grounded in dependency. The Oedipal situation develops when the child becomes aware of himself and wants to be treated like an adult; however, his desire for esteem is imperiled by his parents' interest in each other, producing feelings of jealousy in the child. He becomes aware for the first time of a human triangle. One of the triangle's members must be demoted. It is not surprising that the child's first brush with jealousy demands difficult adjustments.

Sexual latency develops from social pressure, not physiological changes.

The child's acceptance of an inferior position in the triangle brings on the latency period. Sexual latency comes from cultural pressures; it has no physiological basis. Latency does not appear among some other cultures or among many lower class children in our own society. During latency sexuality is suppressed; boys associate with boys and girls with girls. This arrangement collapses rather suddenly at puberty, requiring extensive relearning. The management of a strengthened, unruly sexual impulse produces new conflicts and requires new adjustments. Early sexual desires were connected with forbidden objects—parents, siblings, or friends of the same sex. As a result, the young adolescent often feels that sex is dirty, dangerous, and disgusting; he certainly has strong conflict over his increased interest. However, there are positive processes at work. Among his peers, the adolescent finds support for channeling his urges toward members of the opposite sex.

Sexual repression is more harmful than sexual permissiveness.

What are some possible maladaptive influences during sexual development? Indulgence has no particularly bad effects; it certainly does not cause fixation. Masturbation does not injure the child or make later heterosexual adjustment more difficult. The outstanding problem in sexual growth is the association of guilt, disgust, and fear with sexual feelings. Sexual feelings then are suppressed and denied because of shame or guilt. The consequence is a general inhibition; in extreme cases the person may never dare venture into an erotic relation. Often, interference is incomplete, but sex is seen as shameful and demeaning. Sometimes sexual inhibitions are opposed by a reaction formation (reacting against shame by overindulgence), which can produce vigorous demonstrations of sexual freedom. However, the need to prove potency and seductive capabilities interferes with warm mutual relations.

Aggression

Children become aggressive at the beginning of their second year.

Aggression aims at injury and destruction; it is accompanied by feelings of anger and hate. In the infant's early responses to unpleasant situations, it is impossible to distinguish rage from anxiety. Rage emerges later as a general struggling and flailing of the arms. During the second year of life there is a clear emergence of aggressive acts; striking and kicking are carried out with mischievous facial expressions (particularly if the child is attacking his younger sibling). There are two distinct views of aggression: According to one view, aggression is an instinctive response to frustration; aggression is always instigated by outside events that prevent gratification (Dollard, Doob, Miller, Mowrer, & Sears, 1939). In another conceptualization (Freud, 1949), aggression is seen as the product of instinctive energies growing from the death wish. Dollard *et al.* suggested that permissiveness will reduce aggression while Freud believed that aggression occurs unless controlled and channeled into productive activities (sublimated).

The child must learn to accept and handle his feelings of hostility.

The child must learn to handle aggression. Tantrums are a forceful way to obtain what a child wants, but his mother must eventually exercise restrictions. In the course of time, children learn to control frustrations and anger; losing one's temper in an argument makes one ridiculous and ineffective. Children's aggressive outbursts follow a daily pattern: Most episodes occur right before lunch and dinner (see Figure 16.2).

Frustration and aggression bring possible loss of love; the child must learn to handle this ambivalence.

Of those things which complicate human relations, ambivalence (the alternation between love and hate) is the most difficult to understand and control. Frustration brings aggression, but aggression brings a loss of security; what can a child do? There are three typical reactions to frustration: extrapunitive (outward), intrapunitive (inward), and

FIGURE 16.2

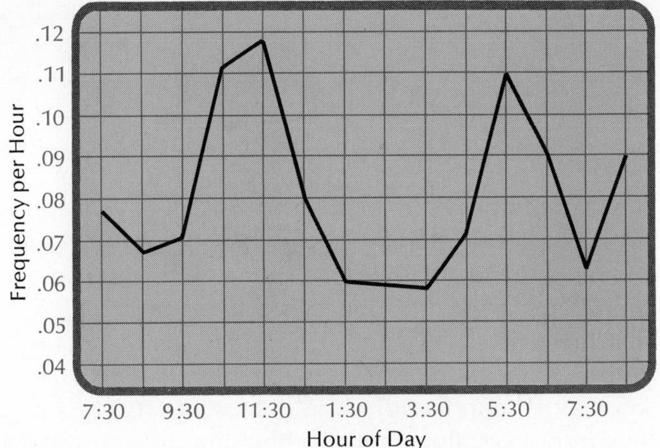

Variations in frequency of anger outbursts among children as a function of time of day. Note the high frequency of episodes just before lunch and dinner. (From Goodenough, 1931.)

impunitive (withdrawal). In an extrapunitive reaction hostility is directed outward; the objects of aggression are those people to blame for the frustrating experience. An intrapunitive reaction directs blame and anger toward oneself: "It's my fault," "I acted unwisely," "I provoked the anger." An impunitive reaction seeks to minimize the aggressive elements; the episode is forgotten or not taken seriously. Each way of handling aggressive impulses is appropriate under particular situations. The child will take his cues from the family; he may adopt one mode to the exclusion of others. One mode of handling aggression will often be inappropriate, with resultant frustration and anger. Learning to handle love *and* hate within a family is well illustrated by sibling rivalry. Sibling relations can be positive if children feel their parents love them.

Maladaptation comes from total repression or total encouragement of aggression.

Maladaptive aggression comes from two quite divergent directions—(1) where little attempt is made to curb aggression and (2) where the attempt to control aggression is so strenuous that no outlets are available. The latter may *appear* to be a better solution. Adults who get angry and smash furniture or hurt people are hardly pleasant. However, the person who can never express aggression or even admit to hostile feelings is in serious trouble. He must avoid aggression by a wide margin; he cannot express desires with which aggression might be connected. The intrapunitive reaction brings self-hate and feelings of unworthiness; anger is bottled up, resulting in rising blood pressure and other psychosomatic illnesses (ulcers, headaches). The person who stifles aggression is placed in a very weak position. He cannot demand justice for himself; unfair punishment must be accepted, otherwise he would need to admit that aggressive impulses exist in himself.

Aggression is controlled by drive, frustration, anxiety, imitation, and reinforcement.

Aggression is controlled by five factors: (1) the child's general drive level; (2) the degree to which the environment is frustrating; (3) the amount of anxiety associated with aggressive responses; (4) the models of aggression available for the child to imitate; and (5) reinforcement. A child's general drive level affects the intensity of all behavior; the amplitude of any response is greater under high when compared to low drive. In lower animals and man, an instinctive reaction to frustration is aggression. Anyone who has tried to take a bone from a dog knows this connection. The degree of anxiety associated with aggressive responses also controls their amount (Buss, 1961). Children in one kindergarten group were told, "Nice boys don't do that" whenever they were aggressive, while other children were told nothing. Ratings of amount of aggression over the four sessions for the experimental and the control group are shown in Figure 16.3. Both the experimental and control children produced a comparable amount of aggressive behavior during the first session. Being told "Nice boys don't do that" maintained the experimental group's inhibitions; as a consequence, they did not change their level of aggressive behavior. The control children, on the other hand, increased their aggressive responses during

FIGURE 16.3

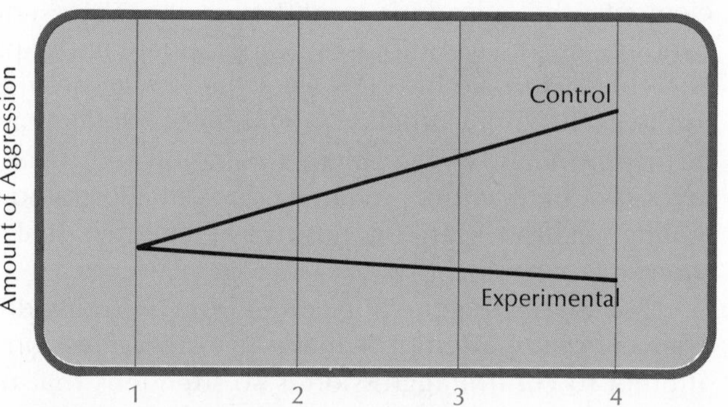

Amount of aggression over a four-day period in nursery school children; the experimental children were told, "Nice boys don't do that" whenever they were aggressive, while the control children received no feedback about aggression. The results show that permissiveness reduces inhibitions associated with aggressiveness and increases its frequency.

all four sessions. Apparently, their anxiety was reduced through extinction in the permissive situation.

Children imitate an aggressive model following frustration.

That children imitate aggressive models has been demonstrated in a long series of studies (Bandura, Ross, & Ross, 1963). In their first study, Bandura *et al.* demonstrated that children imitate specific aggressive behavior exhibited by a model. They tried to determine the extent to which film-mediated aggressive models can serve as sources of imitative aggression. The subjects were 48 boys and 48 girls from a nursery school. A male or a female adult served as the model. There were three experimental groups: One group observed an aggressive model in a "real life" situation; a second experimental group saw the same model portraying aggression on film; and a third group saw an aggressive cartoon. The groups were further subdivided into boys and girls. Half the children were exposed to a same-sex model and the other children to an opposite-sex model. A control group of children who were given no experience in the aggressive modeling situation was included.

Both comic and real life models produce imitative aggression in children.

In the real life situation the child was brought into a room at the beginning of an experimental session and asked to play with some toys. The model also played with some toys for about a minute. Then the model became very aggressive toward a Bo-Bo doll in the room, sitting on the doll and punching it repeatedly in the nose, raising it above his head, hitting it with a mallet, tossing it in the air, and kicking it about the room. The model also verbalized—"Sock him, hit him in the nose, kick him down, pow." Children exposed to the film session were brought into the room, seated, and shown ten minutes of movies involving the model performing the acts just described (Figure 16.4). The cartoon setting included the female experimenter in the costume of a cat; colored glass was spread on the floor. The same aggressive behaviors were performed. Following experience with the model and prior to a test phase, each child was exposed to mild frustration in another room: Each child was shown some beautiful toys and allowed to play with them for a short while; once the child became interested, he was taken from the toys into a testing room. The child was told that the interesting toys he had been playing with were reserved for others, since they were the best toys. Instead, he was told to play with the toys in the test room—a Bo-Bo doll, a mallet, and other toys just like the model had used. Each child played for 20 minutes in this test session.

Boys produce more imitative aggression than girls.

Two observers judged the amount of aggression each child expressed. They found little difference between the influence of the real life aggressive model, the human film aggressive model, and the cartoon aggression; all produced significantly more aggressive responses than did the control group. Boys produced many more aggressive

FIGURE 16.4

The top row shows a model portraying aggression, the other two rows show children imitating the model. (From Bandura, Ross, & Ross, 1963.)

responses in all categories than did girls. In the real life aggression situation the male experimenter was a better model for the boys; however, in the film aggression situation the female model was more effective in eliciting aggression from both boys and girls—a puzzling finding. Girls produced more aggressive responses after viewing a female model than after viewing a male model.

We know almost nothing about how to stop aggression. Punishment increases it.

Although we know a good deal about how to increase aggression, there is little information on ways to inhibit it. Only a few studies of the effects of punishment on aggression exist. Hollenberg and Sperry (1951) showed that verbal punishment decreased temporarily the amount of aggression in a doll-play situation. Bandura and Walters (1963) also reported that punishment of children's aggression inhibited parentally aimed aggression. However, that same punishment increased the child's aggression in other situations. Hollenberg and Sperry found that children who were punished for aggression at home produced *more* aggressive doll play than children receiving little punishment for aggression in the home.

One effective way to decrease aggression is to reinforce positive responses.

An effective way of inhibiting aggressive behavior is to reinforce positive social behaviors. Brown and Elliott (1965) used this technique to control aggression in a nursery school; teachers ignored aggressive acts and encouraged cooperative, nonaggressive actions. The procedure significantly decreased the frequency of aggression. The technique is important because it avoids the undesirable consequences of punishment and at the same time controls aggression.

THE SELF-CONCEPT

The self-concept is difficult to understand but necessary for personal development.

Between 1870 and 1940, psychology was fascinated by the strict methods of the physical sciences; most psychological experiments studied simple processes. However, if we are to understand personality, some concept of self is necessary. The self is difficult to understand; but despite its dangers, we need the notion. The self includes an interrelated pattern of motivations unique to one person, organized to develop a single living organism—to help him live and grow. The definition of self implies an ordered hierarchy of goals.

Freud believed the ego (self) mediates between libido and reality.

Freud defined the self (the ego which mediates between desire and reality) in terms of the libido; Erikson, on the other hand, saw personality growth in terms of crises (the interaction between behavior and environment). The self develops as an experience of "I" or "me" as opposed to "others" or "not-me." Theories of social learning try to predict and control human behavior without recourse to the self-concept.

Knowledge about oneself is affected by social interaction.

Knowledge about oneself is influenced by social interaction. The self is a concept built jointly from the reflections of others and one's own desires and abilities. Parents' attitudes are mirrored in the child's feelings toward himself; if his parents are hostile, the child will feel hostile and debasing toward himself. The child must identify with significant others—a boy with his father and other men, a girl with her mother and other women.

The self is strengthened by competence.

Ego identity depends on a child's relation with reality; his sense of identity is strengthened by learning to walk, talk, or read. The self may evoke positive or negative emotions. If the child is competent in play, intelligent, or gifted in athletics, he is likely to feel confident. If he is not, he may develop feelings of inferiority. We are all inferior in a great many ways, but failure means little if we are compensated by success in another area. But we must find success somewhere!

THEORIES OF PERSONALITY DEVELOPMENT

Erikson

Erikson outlined eight stages.

Erikson (1950) outlined eight stages in the development of personality. Each stage is a set of demands imposed on the individual by his environment.

During the period of infancy we must learn to trust others.

Trust versus mistrust Chronologically, this is the period of infancy—if the baby is well handled and loved, he will develop trust, security, and a basic optimism. If badly handled, he will become insecure and mistrustful.

Between two and three years the child must learn independence or shame.

Autonomy versus shame The second stage occurs during early childhood (between 18 months and three years). In our culture the first major control-learning involves toilet training. The child may emerge from his early training elated with his control and proud of his body; or he may feel dirty, ashamed, and insecure. Autonomy means not only self-possession and initiative but also tantrums, stubbornness, and negativism. The "terrible twos" fold their arms to prevent mother from holding their hand to cross the street. The sound of "No!" becomes monotonous.

During the three- to six-year period a child must learn initiative or guilt.

Initiative versus guilt Erikson proposed a third psychosocial stage for the preschool years (from three to six). During this stage the child learns new skills through active play—how to imagine, to use fantasy, to cooperate with others, and to lead as well as follow. However, if immobilized by guilt through parental control and hostility, he remains fearful, hangs on the fringes of groups, depends on adults, and learns few new skills.

During school the child must learn to be industrious and not to feel inferior.

Industry versus inferiority The fourth psychosocial stage occurs during the school years (through junior high school). Now the child must learn to master the formal skills of life—relating to peers by rules, progressing from free play to structured teamwork (such as in baseball) and mastering social studies, reading, and mathematics. Homework is required and the need for self-discipline increases. The child who possesses autonomy and initiative should learn easily, but the mistrusting child may doubt his future; shame and guilt may drive the child to defeat and to feelings of inferiority.

In adolescence the child must integrate his personal identity.

Identity versus identity diffusion The fifth psychosocial stage (adolescence to about 20) requires the person to ask, "Who am I?" During early adolescence, a mature time perspective is developed; the well-adjusted young person should feel self-confident, not self-conscious. During this period he should experiment with different roles; the well-adjusted adolescent may even dabble in minor delinquency. Rebellion flourishes. The healthy youngster should anticipate adulthood rather than feel "paralyzed" by insecurity and a short time perspective. In late adolescence, clear sexual identity must be established. The adolescent looks for leadership (someone to inspire him), and tests his ideals. In our culture adolescence affords (particularly for middle and upper class children) a time to experiment, to try various roles, and to find a suitable style in which to grow.

The young adult needs intimacy.

Intimacy versus isolation The young adult needs intimacy to make possible a good marriage or friendship.

The adult should be productive.

Generativity versus self-absorption Adulthood requires generativity in marriage, parenthood, and work.

If other stages are handled well, the mature individual can face the last years of his life with integrity, not despair.

Integrity versus despair If the previous psychosocial stages have been resolved, the mature adult may reach the peak of adjustment—integrity. The integrated person is successful, trusting, independent, and dares to try anew. He works hard, has a well-defined role, and maintains a balanced self-concept. He can be intimate without strain, guilt, regret, or lack of realism, and he is proud of what he creates—his children, his work, or his hobbies. However, if earlier psychosocial crises have not been resolved, he may view himself and his life with disgust and despair.

Freud

Freud also viewed development as a series of stages: the oral, anal, and genital periods.

What is the proper course of personality development? Freud (1949) proposed several stages: In the beginning an infant is without ego; he is only a set of instinctive reactions. The neonate is id. This completely asocial creature must (by developing an ego and a superego) learn a complex system of social responses and values. He must sort out the relations between id (desiring), ego (executive), and superego (values). Freud viewed personality development as a series of stages, fixed in sequence, which occur at appropriate times in the life of every individual. The determining characteristic of each stage is the object to which the child attends (invests with his energy). Freud believed that each infant is endowed with a store of psychic energy to transfer from one object to another. This transfer of energy (of interest and desire) among objects accounts for personality development. By desiring various objects the child comes to terms with reality. He learns what he may possess and what is not possible. Early the child sees himself as the only proper object for energy investment. Later he becomes fascinated by inanimate objects; finally, people become the main objects of his interest. Table 16.2 summarizes these stages.

The infant develops by identification with others.

However, the infant does not come into the world interested in others; he is concerned only with himself. The neonate is interested in simple pleasures: sucking, warmth, food, and petting. As the infant

TABLE 16.2 Freudian Stages of Personality Development

Stage	*Natural Mode of Pleasure*	*Object Relation*	*Personality Structure*	*Mechanisms Operating*
Oral Stage (0–8 months)				
Early oral phase	Sucking, swallowing	Dependence	Id and beginning of ego	Fixation by gratification or deprivation
Late oral phase	Biting	Ambivalence	Id and ego	Regression
Anal Stage (8–18 months)				
Early anal phase	Expelling	Ambivalence	Ego strengthened	Denial
Late anal phase	Retaining	Competence	Anxiety (superego)	Guilt
Phallic Stage (2–6 years)	Touching and looking at genitals	Oedipus complex	Superego and ego emerge in full form	Beginning of ego defense mechanisms Sublimation Repression Reaction formation Displacement
Latency (6–11 years)	Loss of sexual interest	Sublimation	Consolidation of ego, superego, id	Reaction formation present
Genital Stage (11–18 years)				
Prepubertal phase	Revival of infantile modes of pleasure	Reactivation of childhood	Disruption of organization	Intellectualization
Pubertal phase, heterosexual-genital	Adult modes of pleasure finding	New sexual relations	Reorganization into adult personality	

begins to realize he is incompetent, he learns to identify with another who is stronger. Identification meets two needs: security and competence (by modeling, the infant learns new responses).

The early infant is interested only in himself.

Infantile egocentrism During the first stage of development an infant does not differentiate himself from the world; they are one. Instinctive impulses determine his behavior. Later, when he differentiates himself from the world, an ego is born. The child becomes aware of himself as "I." This stage of development is characterized by narcissism (an intense interest in oneself). The emerging infant is a tyrant; he has no consideration of parents or siblings. At some point parents (and certainly siblings) object and begin to control his behavior. During socialization, the infant loves his parents because they place limits on him and at the same time give him security and comfort. The child trades complete independence for security and guidance.

Children solve the Oedipal and Electra situation by identification with their same-sexed parent.

Oedipus and identification At about four the child becomes attracted to his opposite-sexed parent. This attraction encounters a universal taboo against incest. Children are allowed to express affection only indirectly: If the little girl *becomes* like her mother, she can vicariously enjoy her father; if the little boy *becomes* like his father, then he can vicariously enjoy his mother. There are other motives for identification with the same-sexed parent: fear of the more powerful competing adult and desire for the opposite-sexed parent both compel the boy to identify with his father and the girl with her mother. Identification leads to the latency period (during which sexual feelings are repressed).

Identification with the same-sexed parent occurs during latency.

The latency period Following identification, boys associate with boys and girls with girls; they fight with and run from the opposite sex for several years (through elementary school). The child suppresses his sexual feelings and becomes interested in sports, games, and intellectual pursuits. Then comes sexual reawakening—puberty.

During puberty the sexual urge emerges; adolescents must learn to handle their feelings.

Puberty During puberty, sexual feelings recur; they are strong and cannot be ignored. However, it is still unacceptable for the pubertal child to possess his opposite-sexed parent; he must seek other relations. He enters a homosexual stage—in particular, he is likely to form a very close attachment with one or two significant peers. Friends replace parents in socialization. New issues develop, and the child begins to make his own decisions and to assume more responsibility for his life.

The homosexual relation of latency must give way to heterosexual interactions.

However, homosexual relations bring incomplete satisfaction. Sooner or later, the normal individual seeks sexual relations with members of the opposite sex. The ultimate purpose of a mature sexual relation is to express love and to produce and raise children. Thus, we begin the cycle again. In the choice of mates the little girl usually seeks the characteristics of her father (or, more accurately, her ideal father), while the little boy is attracted by characteristics of his ideal mother. If the relation between mother and boy and father and girl has been warm and open, there is little problem in using these criteria; however, if the parent-child relations were poor, the marriage may be destructive.

SOCIAL LEARNING AND IMITATION

Two types of identification occur: nurturant and defensive.

How can a little boy or girl develop appropriate behaviors? Most attempts to understand this process rely on the notion of identification. Two types of identification may be distinguished—nurturant and defensive identification. In the case of nurturant identification the child accepts the characteristic of a parent because he fears withdrawal of parental affection. Learning theorists (Mowrer, 1950; Sears, 1957) have suggested that parental warmth and nurturance support parent-child identification. Both boys and girls initially form a nurturant bond with their mothers; however, this form of identification is more important for girls than for boys. Girls are able to maintain their identification with the mother, but boys must shift to the father as a sex-role model. Defensive identification (adoption of parental behaviors through fear of punishment) and nurturance control the boy's identification with his father. Freud thought defensive identification results from resolution of the Oedipus complex (in which a boy adopts his rival's characteristics and thereby reduces his fear of punishment by the father).

The conditions that promote identification include: (1) warmth, (2) nurturance, (3) masculinity of the father, and (4) femininity of the mother.

Identification theories assume that the adoption of a same-sexed parent as a model facilitates the acquisition of appropriate sex-typed behaviors. Consequently, research has focused on the conditions that promote identification. Children identify with and imitate a parent who is warm and nurturant. Payne and Mussen (1956) found that high school boys who identified with their fathers possessed a good sex-role and viewed their fathers as nurturant; minimally identified boys saw their fathers as cold and rejecting. Fathers also play a large role in the development of their daughters' sex-role. Feminine girls have masculine fathers who encourage feminine activities. By contrast, mothers' femininity and encouragement are unrelated to their daughters' sex-typing. Boys' sex-role appropriateness is less affected by their family; Hetherington (1968) showed that many more family factors are related to femininity in girls than to masculinity in boys. This is probably because girls sustain their family ties while boys seek outside attachments.

Boys identify with the more powerful member of a family; hopefully, that is the father.

In addition to warmth and nurturance, the power relations among family members affect sex-role identifications. Masculine boys see their fathers as more powerful and competent than do feminine boys. A dominant father accentuates his daughter's femininity and at the same time makes his son masculine. In a mother-dominant home the boy is more feminine and the girl more masculine and dominating. Having a dominant father in the house is crucial for male sex-role identification because the little boy must shift his identification from his mother to his father; the little girl merely keeps her mother as her role model and learns to interact with her father.

Lack of a father during the boy's early years hinders his sex-role development.

The father's role in sex-typing has also been studied by looking at the consequences of father absence. If the father is necessary for the boy to acquire appropriate sex-typed behaviors, then boys who have no father in the home should be less masculine. The results of a variety of studies do not clearly support this prediction. For example, Bach (1946) compared boys from father-absent and father-present homes during World War II; he found less aggressive fantasy in the doll play of father-absent boys. If we assume that aggression is a male characteristic, then this study supports the hypothesis. Also, the loss of a father model should be more disruptive during the child's early years, when father-identification is incomplete, than later when his masculine behaviors are already developed. To test this notion, Hetherington (1966) compared boys from homes where the father was present with boys from homes where the father was absent. In addition, she compared boys whose fathers left before the child was five years old with boys whose fathers left after five years. Only when the father-son separation occurred during the first four years of the boy's life did disruption of sex-typing occur. Sex-typing and aggression of the late-separated boys were identical to those of father-present boys.

Direct imitation of another's behavior helps sex-role learning.

Social behaviors and personality characteristics develop through the interaction of social reinforcement and genetic endowment; however, direct imitation of another's behavior may accelerate the cumbersome learning process. By imitating characteristics of a person similar to himself, the young child can acquire personality characteristics much faster than through trial and error searching. The child who imitates has available a large repertory of responses from which he can select the most appropriate set.

Children imitate responses which are followed by reinforcement.

A child models those responses which are (1) followed by reinforcement when the model performs them, (2) seen as similar to behaviors the child has in his repertory or has accidentally performed, and (3) performed by a significant other.

Attempts to explain imitation assume the child learns to imitate.

A number of attempts to account for imitation exist. The instrumental learning situation has received the most attention. Miller and Dollard (1941) presented a classic statement of the position in *Social Learning and Imitation.* They described a form of imitation called matched-dependent behavior. As an example of matched-dependent behavior, consider a two-choice discrimination situation in which the child simultaneously makes a choice, sees the choice made by a model, and sees the outcome of the model's choice (reinforcement or nonreinforcement). When the child matches the model during his task he is reinforced; nonmatching results in nonreinforcement. Children easily learn to follow the model's choice to gain reinforcement. In this way, Miller and Dollard argued, children could be taught to imitate a model. They showed that imitation acquired in this manner would generalize across situations, models, and motivational states.

The consequences of a model's response determine whether the child will perform them, but not whether he learns them.

Bandura (1965) also showed that the consequences of a model's responses are important in determining whether the child imitates a particular response. Children imitate a model more frequently when the model's responses are reinforced. However, reinforcements given the model affect only the child's *performance;* they have little effect on his *learning* of the responses. All children (whether they were exposed to a rewarded or punished model) could accurately perform the model's responses.

The child learns to imitate after many trials.

A general tendency to imitate can be produced by reinforcement contingent on the child's making responses similar to those of a model. Following many matching responses, matching itself can acquire secondary reinforcement value. Thus, the set to imitate others' behavior develops through experience. Mowrer (1950) believes that when a model performs an action and at the same time rewards the child, the model's behavior acquires secondary reinforcing value for the child. He is motivated to reproduce the model's behavior, even in the model's absence, to secure the secondary reinforcing feedback from imitation.

Children imitate models who are similar to themselves.

Children imitate models that are similar to themselves. Once imitation starts, the model and the child become more and more alike because the child is acquiring new behaviors from the model. Modeling is based on perceptions of similarities, a warm relation, and love for the model. The more nurturant and warm the relation between a model and child, the more imitation occurs. The effectiveness of a model's responses is also relevant. The more successful a model is, the more a child will imitate him.

MECHANISMS OF DEFENSE

Defense mechanisms handle stress situations; if they are used constantly, the child is not adjusting.

When a child is buffeted by difficulties, frustrations, and conflicts, mechanisms of defense begin to operate against these stresses. If his defense mechanisms are used only occasionally, the child is healthy and reacting adequately to his environment. However, if a child habitually uses defense mechanisms to cope with his environment, he is developing abnormally. Reliance on defense mechanisms to maintain personal stability means the child has few healthy reactions to his world; he is maintaining stability only through constant struggle. The defense mechanisms commonly employed in dealing with crises include repression, projection, sublimation, and regression to more infantile stages of development.

Repression

Repression is the most common form of defense (pressing things out of one's mind).

If a child cannot tolerate thinking about something, the most common solution is to push it into his unconscious. Painful or anxiety-provoking thoughts are relegated to unconsciousness and kept there. Blocking thoughts from consciousness (particularly emotionally laden thoughts) requires a great deal of psychic energy. For example, assume that a little boy has just been spanked by his mother; he immediately hates his mother. However, he also recognizes the danger of saying that he hates his mother, since he is dependent on her for love, security, and comfort. The child may feel that if his mother saw the hate she would desert him. Children usually express their feelings of hate and anger; however, many mothers can't tolerate rejection by their child, so these mothers discourage all expressions of anger or hate. The only alternative for the child is to repress his feelings.

Repression leads to segregation of the child's thoughts. He becomes anxious when he thinks about "bad" things.

The repression of unwanted thoughts can become a way of life; many children segregate feelings into two compartments—Those that are "good," and the "dirty," "naughty" things they think about. The second set of thoughts and feelings is repressed. Repression keeps the child from feeling anxious, but he spends a lot of time feeling guilty about his thoughts of hate and anger. He really wants to be a good boy. The guilt and self-rejection associated with having "bad" thoughts keep the child in a constant state of anxiety and depression.

Repressed hate and fear are the major causes of psychosomatic disorders.

Repressed feelings of anger and hate are the major cause of psychosomatic and hysteric disorders. When anger and hate are repressed, the physiological processes which accompany these feelings are still present. The stomach still secretes extra acid, the heart still beats faster; the entire system is geared for fight or flight. Repressed feelings cause tension, ulcers, and high blood pressure. The young child can be started on the path of repression and subsequent psychosomatic disorder by being forced to inhibit his feelings instead of expressing them. When they are expressed, they can be handled.

Projection

Projecting repressed feelings onto others is another defense.

There are other ways for a child to handle unacceptable thoughts and feelings. Instead of repressing his hate, the child may transfer it to another person. However, since he has been taught not to attack others who have done nothing to him, the child must somehow make the other person the aggressor. He can attack another only when he has been attacked first. The child wants to attack another but cannot; he may repress his wishes and come to believe (through projection of his own repressed desires) that the other person is about to attack him. Now that the other person is about to attack him, the child can be aggressive in return. He attributes his own motives to those around him; as a result of this projection, he no longer feels guilty about wanting to attack. After all, the other is the aggressor; the child is only defending himself by being aggressive in return. (Notice the similarities to international relations.)

Projection is unconscious.

Projection is an unconscious process; the child is not aware that he is projecting his own feelings onto another. He is completely sincere when he claims that the other child attacked him first. How do we know when a child is projecting and when he is telling a lie? One way is to place the child in a play situation and watch how he handles a wide variety of aggressive interactions. If he consistently shifts the blame for aggression, you know he is projecting; the child who is conscious of his actions would not lie about something you have just witnessed. He will lie only when you don't know the truth.

Sublimation

Sublimation requires that an impulse be satisfied in another, socially acceptable way.

Sublimation is another mechanism of defense. Here the child seeks a substitute satisfaction for his needs and desires. To understand what the child is substituting, we need to remember that his basic needs are satisfied by instinctive action patterns early in his life. However, these early instincts often conflict with social taboos or family power. Socialization requires that the child learn new means of gratifying his basic instincts. Changing from one mode of satisfaction to another requires the child to give up old pleasurable ways and gain new ones. When a primitive mode of satisfaction is blocked, other means of expression must be found. The substitution of a new mode of satisfaction for the instinctive pattern is sublimation. Sublimation converts primitive instinctive response patterns into socially acceptable systems of behavior.

Severe socialization leads to repression and guilt; too little socialization leads to delinquency.

Sublimation of the destructive and sexual impulses is called socialization in our culture. Too severe socialization can lead to emotional problems because we usually associate anxiety or guilt with the instinctive pattern and then substitute another activity. In the case of sexual drives, this anxiety cripples many individuals when they finally attempt to develop sexual relations. The frigid woman and impotent man result from complete socialization of early sexual impulses. A more relaxed expression of sexual feelings without guilt and fear would produce more wholesome feelings about sex.

ABNORMAL DEVELOPMENT

Information about personality problems comes primarily from disturbed families.

Our thoughts about the development of abnormal personalities are based primarily on studies of troubled families. Families undergoing psychological treatment develop intensive relations with a clinician; these case studies provide detailed information. However, studies of troubled families contain problems: (1) No adequate battery of tests exists; (2) the classifications used are often inappropriate; and (3) the samples are small and not randomly selected. Considering these difficulties, some systematic findings emerge.

Families of problem children behave abnormally.

Divergent parent-child and parent-parent interaction is obviously associated with the development of abnormal behavior (Hodgkiss, 1932–1933). A higher incidence of separation and divorce, disagreement about childrearing practices, and faulty discipline characterize the parents of problem children.

Delinquency

Delinquency involves hostility toward authority, property, and people.

The study of delinquent children's families originated in the Chicago juvenile courts (Hewitt & Jenkins, 1946). Delinquency means many things; typically, it involves hostility toward authority and little control over one's own behavior. The family background of delinquent children is marked by extreme marital discord and/or the absence of parents. The incidence of broken homes (either through divorce, death, separation, desertion, or prolonged absence of one parent) is twice as high among delinquent children as among nondelinquents.

Separation of the child from his family increases delinquency.

In trying to understand the effects of a broken home, Bowlby (1944) looked at 44 juvenile delinquents and 44 children referred for other problems. He also studied groups in which the child had been separated from his parents before or after one year of age. He found no systematic relation between age of separation and the development of delinquency; it is not when separation occurs but the fact of separation that is important (unlike sex-role identification). However, studies of broken homes imply that the parents' methods of child training are the primary cause of delinquency.

Discipline and affectional relations interact in producing delinquency.

The discipline used and the types of affectional relations established are strongly associated with the development of deviant behavior. The joint effects of discipline and affectional relations must be studied, since these variables are not independent. Some methods of discipline and some attitudes force the child away from his parent; they hinder the development of affectional ties which can mediate self-control. Delinquents run away from home to escape punishment.

Parents of delinquents exercise little or no control.

Healy and Bronner (1926) studied 4000 children from the Chicago and Boston courts; they were among the first to stress the relation between parental discipline and delinquency. Forty percent of the parents in their study exercised no discipline. The mothers in particular showed extreme laxity, particularly with delinquent boys, although a significant number of the fathers also imposed no discipline on their sons. On the other hand, another group of delinquent boys received very strict and hostile discipline from their fathers. Bandura and Walters (1963), in a study of 26 aggressive antisocial adolescent boys, also found that mothers of aggressive boys are ineffective socializing agents. The mothers required no obedience, were inconsistent, placed few restrictions on their sons, and made few achievement demands. In contrast to this laxity on the mothers' part, fathers of these delinquent boys were very strict. They used physical punishment and deprivation to control their sons. Hostile, aggressive fathers provide a model of uncontrolled hostility which is overlooked or encouraged by the mother. Bandura and Walters also showed that certain styles of discipline are related to a high incidence of delinquency. Physical punishment and little reasoning are used by mothers and fathers of delinquents. A hostile home with little control over the child produces delinquent behavior (see Chapter 12).

Parents of delinquents are hostile and rejecting.

A second factor affecting delinquency is the affectional relations among members of the family. Loving mothers tend to marry loving fathers while rejecting mothers marry cruel and negligent fathers. Boys raised by passive fathers are not delinquent; imitation of a timid, withdrawn father produces a timid, withdrawn boy. If both parents reject a child, he is likely to turn to crime, while rejection by one parent does not always foster delinquency. Bandura and Walters (1963) also found that parents of delinquents are cold with children; delinquent families have no "we" feelings. Few delinquent boys see their father as a model. Little love is lost.

Homes of delinquents contain immorality, cruelty, alcoholism, and fighting.

Other aspects of a delinquent's home are also undesirable; there is marked immorality, cruelty, alcoholism, and quarreling among parents. A more severe home background is required to produce a delinquent girl than a delinquent boy. Disruptive factors that contribute to delinquency occur twice as often in the homes of delinquent girls as in the homes of delinquent boys. Factors that contribute to female delinquency are immorality, sexual molesting of the child, an unmarried parent, and drunkenness. Girls commit sexual offenses (prostitution), while boys are likely to be detained for stealing or violence.

Delinquents lack play materials, and they associate with other delinquents.

Conditions outside the home (type of companions and availability of play facilities) are also related to delinquency. Delinquent companions and lack of play facilities are associated with antisocial behavior. Although delinquent behavior has a multitude of antecedent conditions, parents contribute a great deal to the problem. Becker *et al.* (1962) suggested that when one parent is punitive and frustrating toward the child and the other parent is lax about discipline, conditions are optimum for the development of aggression and delinquency.

Clinical syndromes and parent behavior

Parents of psychotic children employ unusual training techniques.

There is a large and active literature relating family variables to clinical problems such as schizophrenia, psychosomatic disorders, stuttering, enuresis, and alcoholism. There are no experimental studies showing a direct link between childrearing practices and the occurrence of psychoses; however, childrearing practices and attitudes differ between parents of psychotic and parents of nonpsychotic children.

These unique child-rearing techniques may be a reaction to the baby.

The parents of schizophrenic children typically have "undesirable" attitudes; frequently the parents use deviant childrearing practices. However, these attitudes and practices *may* be reactions to a difficult child; they may not be related directly to the development of childhood schizophrenia. Mednick and Schulsinger (1965) examined 207 children whose mothers had severe chronic schizophrenia. These children were compared with 104 control children matched with the experimental group for age, sex, father's occupational status, rural or urban residence, number of years of formal education, and institutional or family rearing conditions. The main purpose of the study was to determine the characteristics that distinguished those children who developed schizophrenia from those who did not and to look at the interaction of these characteristics with the circumstances that surround the onset of psychosis. Because of the enormous difficulty in getting enough children who become schizophrenic from the normal population, the investigators picked a group of high-risk children (offspring of schizophrenic parents). Several characteristics distinguish a schizophrenic mother. She is dominant in the home and her influence is not benign. Children see her as scolding, unreliable, and not worthy of confidence. Home life is marked by frequent parental quarrels. Since the autonomic system of children with schizophrenic mothers is highly labile, their autonomic reaction is quick and violent. To make things still more difficult, their reactions are overgeneralized, greatly increasing the range of stimuli that provoke an already sensitive system. In school, teachers recognize the tendency of these children from schizophrenic homes to become upset easily. The children of schizophrenics react to excitement by withdrawing and handle peer relations and classroom challenges by passivity. Once they begin to use avoidance to handle anxiety, it is difficult to stop, since it takes them away from social situations in which they might learn more direct ways of dealing with anxiety. They withdraw, feel rejected, and withdraw still more; the cycle gets harder to break. However, despite the use of withdrawal and passivity, the children perform relatively adequately. They have learned to withdraw when pressure builds up; on tasks that require continuous concentration their performance slips. They are alone much of the time and do not share associations with a peer group. In addition, they learn to escape from autonomic arousal by drifting off into idiosyncratic thoughts. These children withdraw from threat—a clear example of how genetic endowments interact with the environment to make the child more likely to become psychotic.

Overprotection results from (1) waiting for the child, (2) physical handicaps, (3) sexual incompatibility, (4) isolation, (5) unhappy childhood for the mother, (6) the mother's dominating characteristics, (7) thwarted maternal ambitions.

Various parental activities have been related to abnormal child behavior. Studies of "maternal overprotection" (Levy, 1943) suggest that many factors are involved in this syndrome: (1) a long period of waiting for the child, (2) physical handicaps that make the child less likely to survive, (3) the mother's sexual incompatibility with her husband, (4) isolation between husband and wife, (5) an unhappy childhood for the mother, (6) the mother's development of dominating characteristics through the assumption of undue responsibility in childhood, and, finally, (7) thwarted maternal ambitions. An indulgent mother produces a rebellious, aggressive "brat," while a dominating mother produces a submissive, dependent, and timid child.

Experimental studies group children on the basis of undesirable characteristics.

One way to study abnormal personality development is to group children on the basis of their behavior (aggressive or dependent) and compare their home experiences. We assume that those behaviors which occur together can be used as criteria in forming a group. Grouping problem behaviors allows systematic study of home backgrounds associated with the problems.

Anxiety is associated with later alcoholism.

Factors which make children anxious are associated with later alcoholism [parental conflict and negative maternal attitudes (Hall, 1930)]. The alcoholic has a low tolerance for delay of reinforcement; he uses escapist approaches when faced with conflict. Mothers of alcoholics show three distinct reactions to a crisis: Some find a rational solution; others become aggressive and attack the source of frustration; a third group withdraws and evades the situation. This last group is promiscuous and drinks excessively. Alcoholism among offspring of these three groups are, respectively, 15, 14, and 40 percent. Similar reactions by the fathers are also related to children's later alcoholism (McCord, McCord, & Gademan, 1960).

Alcoholics do not usually commit crimes.

How are alcoholism and crime related? Crime and alcohol rates are available on the same sample of subjects, so we can see how alcoholics and criminals differ. Alcoholics and criminals possess several common background features: Both have neural disorders, parents with poor personalities, and they have been neglected. However, criminals are usually reared in an aggressive home environment in which dependency is discouraged, while alcoholics are raised in homes which reinforce dependency. Alcoholism is most likely if the father was present and the mother cold.

The middle class produces alcoholics and neurotics; the lower class develops criminals and psychotics.

The relation of delinquency and abnormal behavior to social class is complex. If our sample is divided into middle class (father holds a professional or white collar job) and lower class (the family lives in a transitional neighborhood), sharp differences in types of deviations occur. Noncriminal alcoholics come from the middle class, while criminals and criminal-alcoholics derive from the lower class.

Early experience, punishment, reinforcement schedules, and heredity all affect the child's personality.

We have very little definitive evidence on the effects of early child interaction on personality development. Before a systematic statement can be made, we need to know more about the effects of early experience, early learning, punishment, reinforcement schedules, and, of course, how heredity and environment interact.

THE TREATMENT OF PERSONALITY DISORDERS

Quacks looking for money and crackpots with religious missions abound; insist that your therapist have an advanced degree from a recognized institution.

Many charlatans exist in the field of personal diagnosis and treatment. Two types predominate—the crackpot who has a divine cure and the quack looking for money. How can one avoid these destructive types? The safest route is to insist that a therapist possess an advanced degree (either a PhD in clinical psychology, an MD in psychiatry, or a master's degree in psychiatric social work). In addition, one should know the institution that granted the degree; it should be recognized by the American Psychological Association or the American Medical Association. Recently, state legislatures have begun to establish licensing practices for psychologists, social workers, and counselors. The last category in particular has little formal regulation and is an easy mark for the charlatan. Another reason for confusion on the part of patients is that many types of therapists exist, and it is difficult to evaluate the outcome of psychotherapy. No adequate method of evaluation exists. The only way to protect oneself is to visit a licensed professional and follow his advice.

Therapists

There are four classes of legitimate therapists.

Psychiatrists are MDs with postdoctoral training in psychotherapy.

Psychiatrists These therapists are MDs who have taken psychiatric training during postdoctoral residency. Psychiatrists use physical treatment (such as drugs) in combination with psychotherapy. Some follow Freud's psychoanalytic theory; others are eclectic. Therapy tends to be directive.

Psychoanalysts are MDs or PhDs with training in analysis.

Psychoanalysts This category contains MDs plus occasional PhDs, (known as lay analysts). Their main therapeutic qualification is self-analysis. They believe that therapists without self-analysis act out their own neurotic problems in dealing with patients. Following self-analysis, the psychoanalyst performs training analyses under the supervision of an experienced psychoanalyst before entering his own practice. Most analysts have their patients recall childhood incidents associated with the present problems. Insight under adult conditions is the first step toward recovery.

Clinical psychologists are PhDs trained in diagnosis and treatment of mental illnesses.

Psychologists They have a PhD in clinical psychology. Their therapy is often nondirective and based on the notion that our knowledge of psychological disturbances is incomplete. The psychologist is supportive; by planning, the patient gains insight into his problems and thus heals himself. Psychologists do not administer drugs. Of the various therapists, they are more fully trained in diagnostic testing.

Psychiatric social workers are tuned to the family background.

Psychiatric social workers The social worker began his career by searching the patient's history. He then moved into group therapy, where a number of individuals interact with the therapist and with one another. Training includes psychiatric social work and group experience. Many psychiatric social workers are trained in psychoanalytic techniques.

The therapy used depends on the therapist, the patient, and the theory of personality.

Forms of therapy How can a therapist change behavior? How can he relieve anxieties and help a patient adjust to his life? Approaches to these problems depend on the therapist's conception of personality development, the nature of the psychiatric problem, and how he believes change can occur. Directive therapists believe they know the basis of a patient's problem. Their main goal is to convey this insight to the patient. Freudian theory finds the Oedipal situation (early parent-child relations) at the root of most problems. Psychoanalysts try to teach their patients self-awareness and insight. The nondirective therapist feels he knows little about the roots of behavior. He supports the patient and hopes that the patient will gain some insights and cure himself. A third position believes that maladaptive behavior comes from the adoption of poor social roles; these therapists teach the patient more adequate social roles.

Directive therapy includes active intervention in and interpretation of a patient's problems.

A good example of directive therapy exists in the daily activities of psychiatrists. They are interested in the here and now problems of the patient; psychiatrists use drug therapy, electro-convulsive shock, direct suggestion, hypnosis, and social engineering to change behavior. They typically see patients one at a time for about 50 minutes each.

Sessions vary from once a week to every day. Treatment focuses on current emotional problems—(anxieties, hates, ambivalences, frustrations) and the particular technique varies with the therapist and patient. Psychiatrists are reality oriented with their patients; they believe that facts must be dealt with if a patient is to function effectively. Psychiatrists believe support is only a crutch. They foster dependency, love, or hate and then work through the emotion with the patient. They try to uncover repressed emotions (in the neurotic), gain control of behavior (in the delinquent), and suppress anxiety and orient to reality (in the psychotic). Treatment lasts from a few months to several years.

Clinical psychologists use primarily nondirective therapy.

Clinical psychologists typically practice nondirective therapy; they seem less secure (they are somewhat lower in the pecking order than psychiatrists and neurologists). The psychologist is strong in diagnostic ability based on psychological testing. However, many psychologists practice individual and group therapy. Their techniques include an occasional supportive remark, conditioning therapy (based on social-learning) and support. Psychologists cannot use drugs.

Psychoanalysis is based on the notion that a patient is fixated at an early stage of development.

Psychoanalytic technique is based on the following assumptions: (1) the patient is disturbed because he has not progressed through early stages of development; (2) the most effective method of treatment is to uncover these early fixations and relive them; (3) the method of choice for uncovering early childhood conflicts is free association; and (4) the emotional relation will be relived with the therapist as a principle participant (as the mother, the father, the wife, or the husband). Transference (either positive or negative) is based on a revival of suppressed emotions being relived in the therapeutic situation. Psychoanalysts are ambitious—they want to change the patient's fundamental personality structure. They require daily sessions for years, and the criterion of cure is positive mental health rather than elimination of symptoms.

Play therapy often works with children.

Play therapy is a popular treatment for children. It can help a child deal with his environment and emotions. Play provides an opportunity for the child's thoughts and actions to be expressed. In the case of children, inappropriate social roles are often the source of problems. The therapist can serve as an effective model for the child to imitate. Often groups of six to eight boys and girls are formed. These groups are carefully balanced: An aggressive boy is placed with an effeminate one, for example. Each can then learn the consequences of various acts.

Psychodrama helps people try different roles.

Psychodrama also tries to teach new social roles (Moreno, 1946). The assumption is made that playing roles in an artificial environment will help change behavior in real life. Children can gain experience in various roles, especially those important for their later development.

Personality is the result of many processes interacting.

The personality of an individual is the result of interactions among many processes. Our understanding of the child is deeper in areas of learning, perception, cognition, and emotion. By knowing these individual functions (and how they interact) we can begin to understand the person. Both the various processes *and* the integrated self are important. This text has presented the child through the development of his basic processes (sensation, perception, learning) and as an integrated self (in school, in the home, and in society). Appreciation of both levels is necessary. Neither view is more important; both reflect complementary conceptions of the child.

SUMMARY

1 Four major problems recur in the course of human development: (1) The child must either become trusting or paranoid; (2) he must learn autonomy or be controlled by his parents; (3) he must form an adequate sex role; (4) he must learn to manage and express his aggressive impulses or they will become self-destructive.

2 Erikson believes children and adults face eight challenges in their development. These stages concern the growth of trust, autonomy, initiative, industry, identity, intimacy, generativity, integrity, and the self-concept. If these challenges are handled well, the child's personality will grow; however, if they are handled by withdrawal, fear, and hostility, the resulting person will be narrow, mean, and fearful.

3 Freud outlined four stages of child development. The oral stage involves incorporation of things into the body; the anal stage requires that the child develop competence; the latency period is a time when he must suppress his sexual activities. The final stage is genital; it requires the child to develop intimate heterosexual relations.

4 The main personality defense mechanisms are repression, in which unwanted events or thoughts are suppressed into the unconscious; projection, in which our own impulses of hate and destruction are transferred to others; and sublimation, in which destructive and sexual impulses are channeled into more socially acceptable modes of expression.

5 Two kinds of abnormal development have been studied in detail. Delinquency results primarily from lax maternal care and punitive paternal attention. Children from hostile, uncontrolled homes develop little respect for authority; the home presents good models of aggression with few controls. The mothers often reinforce their sons' aggression. Neurotic and psychotic children result from different home environments. Neurotic children are overprotected or rejected. However, psychotic children generally live in homes with excessive conflict, hostility, and inconsistent discipline.

6 There are four legitimate types of therapists: the psychiatrist (MD with postgraduate training in psychiatry); the psychologist (PhD with postgraduate training in psychotherapy); the psychiatric social worker (MS with training in group and individual therapy); and the analyst (who has undergone personal analysis). Numerous quacks (who are out to make money from their patients) and misguided "do-gooders" (who believe it is their mission to save the world) exist. They must be avoided.

FURTHER READINGS

Bandura, A., & Walters, R. H. *Social learning and personality development.* New York: Holt, Rinehart and Winston, 1963.

Kagan, J. & Moss, H. A. *Birth to maturity.* New York: Wiley, 1962.

Miller, N. E., & Dollard, J. *Social learning and imitation.* New Haven, Conn.: Yale University Press, 1941.

Sears, R. R., Maccoby, E., & Levin, H. *Patterns of child rearing.* New York: Harper & Row, 1957.

REFERENCES

Bach, G. R. Father-fantasies and father-typing in father-separated children. *Child Development,* 1946, **17,** 63-80.

Bandura, A. Influence of models' reinforcement contingencies on the acquisition of imitative responses. *Journal of Personality and Social Psychology,* 1965, **1,** 589-595.

Bandura, A., Ross, D., & Ross, S. A. Imitation of film-mediated aggressive models. *Journal of Abnormal and Social Psychology,* 1963, **66,** 3-11.

Bandura, A., & Walters, R. H. *Social learning and personality development.* New York: Holt, Rinehart and Winston, 1963.

Becker, W. C., Peterson, D. R., Luria, Z., Shoemaker, D. J., & Hellmer, L. A. Relations of factors derived from parent-interview ratings to behavior problems of five-year-olds. *Child Development,* 1962, **33,** 509-535.

Bowlby, J. Forty-four juvenile thieves: Their characters and home life. (I) *International Journal of Psychoanalysis,* 1944, **25,** 19-53.

Brown, P., & Elliott, R. Control of aggression in a nursery school class. *Journal of Experimental Child Psychology,* 1965, **2,** 103-107.

Buss, A. H. *The psychology of aggression.* New York: Wiley, 1961.

Charlesworth, R., & Hartup, W. W. Positive social reinforcement in the nursery school peer group. *Child Development,* 1967, **38(4),** 993-1002.

Crandall, V. C., & McGhee, P. E. Expectancy of reinforcement as a determinant of academic competence. Unpublished manuscript, Fels Research Institute, 1967.

Dollard, J., Doob, L. W., Miller, N. E., Mowrer, O. H., & Sears, R. R. *Frustration and aggression.* New Haven, Conn.: Yale University Press, 1939.

Erikson, E. H. *Childhood and society.* New York: Norton, 1950.

Field, S. C. Studies in the origins of achievement strivings. Unpublished doctoral dissertation, University of Michigan, 1959.

Freud, S. *An outline of psychoanalysis.* New York: Norton, 1949.

Goodenough, F. L. *Anger in young children.* Minneapolis: University of Minnesota Press, 1931.

Greenberg, P. J. Competition in children: An experimental study. *American Journal of Psychology,* 1932, **44,** 221-248.

Guilford, J. P., & Zimmerman, W. S. Fourteen dimensions of temperament. *Psychological Monographs,* 1956, **70,** No. 10.

Hall, D. E. Domestic conflict and its effect on children. *Smith College Studies in Social Work,* 1930, **1,** 403-404.

Healy, W., & Bronner, A. L. *Delinquents and criminals: Their making and unmaking.* New York: Macmillan, 1926.

Hetherington, E. M. Effects of paternal absence on sex-typed behaviors in Negro and white preadolescent males. *Journal of Personality and Social Psychology,* 1966, **4,** 87-91.

Hetherington, E. M. The effects of familial variables on sex role typing, parent-child similarity and imitation in children. In J. P. Hill (Ed.), *Minnesota symposia on child psychology.* Vol. I. Minneapolis: University of Minnesota Press, 1968.

Hewitt, L. E., & Jenkins, R. L. *Fundamental patterns of maladjustment: The dynamics of their origin.* Springfield, Ill.: State of Illinois, 1946.

Hodgkiss, M. The influence of broken homes and working mothers. *Smith College Studies in Social Work,* 1932-33, **3,** 259-274.

Hollenberg, E., & Sperry, M. Some antecedents of aggression and effects of frustration in doll play. *Personality,* 1951, **1,** 32-43.

Holtzman, W. H., *et al. Inkblot perception and personality—Holtzman inkblot technique.* Austin, Tex.: University of Texas, 1961.

Jakubezak, L. F., & Walters, R. H. Suggestibility as dependency behavior. *Journal of abnormal and social Psychology,* 1959, **59,** 102-107.

Kagan, J., & Moss, H. A. The stability of passive and dependent behavior from childhood to adulthood. *Child Development,* 1960, **31,** 577-591.

Levy, D. M. *Maternal overprotection.* New York: Columbia University Press, 1943.

McCord, W., McCord, J., & Gudeman, J. *Origins of alcoholism.* Stanford, Calif.: Stanford University Press, 1960.

Mednick, S., & Schulsinger, F. Children of schizophrenic mothers. *Bulletin de l'association Internationale de Psychologie Appliquee,* 1965, **14,** 11-27.

Miller, N. E., & Dollard, J. *Social learning and imitation.* New Haven, Conn.: Yale University Press, 1941.

Moreno, J. L. *Psychodrama.* New York: Beacon House, 1946.

Mowrer, O. H. *Learning theory and personality dynamics.* New York: Ronald Press, 1950.

Payne, D. B., & Mussen, P. M. Parent-child relations and father identification among adolescent boys. *Journal of abnormal and social Psychology,* 1956, **52,** 358-362.

Piaget, J. *The psychology of intelligence.* London: Routledge & Kegan Paul, 1947.

Rorschach, H. (Trans. by P. Lemkau and B. Kronenberg.) *Psychodiagnostics: A diagnostic test based on perception.* Berne: Huber, 1942.

Sears, R. R. Identification as a form of behavioral development. In D. B. Harris (Ed.), *The concept of development.* Minneapolis: University of Minnesota Press, 1957. Pp. 149-161.

Sears, R. R., Maccoby, E. E., & Levin. H. *Patterns of child rearing.* New York: Harper & Row, 1957.

Sontag, L. W., Baker, C. T., & Nelson, V. L. Mental growth and personality development: A longitudinal study. *Monograph of the society for research in Child Development,* 1958, **23(2).**

Winterbottom, M. The relation of need for achievement in learning experiences in independence and mastery. In J. Atkinson (Ed.), *Motives in fantasy, action and society.* Princeton, N.J.: Van Nostrand, 1958. Pp. 453-478.

GLOSSARY

Accommodation. Adjustments that prepare a sense organ for receiving impressions distinctly. The effect of a new experience in modifying the schema by which a person perceives or thinks.

Adaptation. Originally, a change in structure or behavior that has survival value; now, more generally, any beneficial change to meet environmental demand.

Aggression. Hostile action; hostility against the person or object producing frustration; action that causes fear or flight in another, or that—failing such effect—brings the aggressor into forceful contact with the other; or any psychological equivalent for such attack.

All-or-none learning. A theoretical position concerning the process of association; the theory assumes that an association is either formed completely in one trial or there is no learning at all.

Allele. Either of two genes that alternate in Mendelian inheritance, a given mature cell receiving one or the other but not both. Brown or blue eyes are allelomorphic characteristics.

Amnion. A thin membrane forming a closed sac about the embryo and containing a fluid in which the embryo is immersed.

Anaclitic depression. Severe depression found in young infants who are deprived of maternal care during their early months of life.

Many of the above definitions have been reprinted or adapted from English, H. B., & English, A. C. *A comprehensive dictionary of psychological and psychoanalytical terms.* New York: David McKay Company, Inc., 1958. Reprinted by permission of authors and publisher.

Anal stage. The period in an infant's life when he is supposed to be preoccupied with the pleasurable feelings connected with the anus and defecation.

Animism. An implicit belief that many objects in the environment are living or manifest purpose.

Anoxia. A deficiency in the supply of oxygen to the tissues.

Anti-Semitism. Hostility toward Jews as a minority group.

Aphasia. Loss or impairment of the ability to use language because of lesions in the brain. Aphasia may be sensory (inability to understand words) or motor (inability to speak or to speak the words intended).

Approach-approach. A conflict arising when an individual is drawn toward two goals, both satisfying but at least partially incompatible.

Approach-avoidance. A situation in which there are both positive and negative aspects to the same goal.

Associative play. Partial interaction in a play situation—not yet real cooperation.

Association. A functional relation between psychological phenomena established in the course of individual experience, such that the presence of one tends to evoke the other; or the process whereby the relation is established.

Asymmetrical relation. One that does not hold when the terms are inverted: *A* is father of *B; x* is larger than *y.*

Attitude. An enduring, learned predisposition to behave in a consistent way toward a given class of objects; a persistent mental and/or neural state of readiness to react to a certain object or class of objects not as they are but as they are conceived to be.

Audition. The sense, or act, of hearing. Properly, *audition* is the sense or capacity, *hearing* the act or process, but the distinction is not observed.

Authoritarian. One who craves and demands unquestioning obedience and subordination. This is the defining quality, but various other qualities are believed to be generally associated with it, such as a servile acceptance of superior authority, scorn for weakness, rigidity, rejection of out-groups, conventionality, desire to have everything clearly marked off and determined, cynicism.

Avoidance-avoidance. The situation in which an animal, if he moves away from one undesirable situation, moves toward another undesirable one. The closer the animal approaches one situation, the higher becomes the avoidance gradient toward that situation and the lower the avoidance gradient toward the other.

Axones. One of two fibers extending from the central portion (cell body) of the neuron (the fundamental unit of structure of nerve tissue). Axones are usually longer than the other fiber (dendrite), often have branches called collaterals, and end in much smaller end brushes than the dendrites. The end brushes of the axon may transmit excitation by acting directly on muscle or gland or may transmit excitation to the dendrite of another neuron.

Babbling. Speech sounds without meaning, as found in the vocalization of infants.

Baby biography. A daily diary of the activities and growth patterns of a single child.

Balance (kinesthesis). The sense of where the body is. Consists of feedback from the muscles and joints. The balance sense is also composed of feedback from the semicircular canals in the inner ear which inform the person of acceleration and deceleration of the head.

Behavioral contagion. The spontaneous imitation by other persons of a behavior initiated by one person but without overt intention to stimulate such imitation.

Binocular vision. Seeing with both eyes fixated on the same point in space.

Bipolar dimension. Characterizing a variable, trait, or factor that extends from an extreme or maximum value through zero to an extreme opposite: for example, from a maximum of self-effacement to a maximum of exhibitionism by way of a zero or neutral value. Tending to behave in opposed ways—to love and to hate someone, either simultaneously or in alternation.

Bound morpheme. A morpheme, or word, that cannot occur alone (prefixes, suffixes).

Brightness. The intensity attribute of all visual sense data; the correlate of luminosity.

Centration. When a child, during preoperational thought, concentrates on one aspect of an object to the neglect of others—for example, when he attends to the height of a glass and neglects the width in making his judgment of equality for conservation.

Cephalocaudal. Pertaining to, or extending between, the head and the tail.

Cerebral dominance. Control of the activity of one organ by another, especially cerebral or cortical dominance, that is, control of lower centers in the brain and cord by the cerebrum or cortex, respectively. *Hemispherical dominance:* The fact that one cerebral hemisphere generally leads the other in control of bodily movement, resulting in laterality (handedness).

Choice. Selection among two or more alternative objects or acts, usually after a period of deliberation. It is implied that the alternatives are effectively presented and are perceived or thought of as possible.

Classical conditioning. The experimental procedure wherein two stimuli are presented in close temporal proximity. One of them has a reflex or previously acquired connection with a certain response, whereas the other is not an adequate stimulus to the response. Following many presentations of the two stimuli, the second stimulus acquires the potentiality of evoking a response.

Cognitive style. The typical way in which a person approaches a problem. An example is that some children analyze relations among items while others look for detail similarities.

Color saturation. The degree to which any color possessing a hue differs from a gray of the same brightness.

Competence. The ability for a particular job, vocation, or skill.

Complementary color. Pairs of colors which, mixed in a given proportion, yield gray.

Computer simulation. The use of computer programs to simulate (produce a model which behaves in the same manner) human thought. The notion is that if the computer operates on the input to produce the same output as a human, the set of mechanisms which perform the operations must be similar to, or more strongly, identical to the operations the human performs during thinking. The more nearly the computer output resembles the output of the human, the closer is simulation.

Concept. Any object of awareness together with its significance or meaning; anything one can think about that can be distinguished from other "things." A general meaning, an idea, or a property that can be stated about two or more individual items.
Knowledge that is not directly perceived through the senses but is the result of the manipulation of sensory impressions.

Concrete-operational. The stage of symbolic representation according to Piaget—characterized by flexible cognitive systems on the part of schoolchildren.

Conditioned response. The new or modified response that is elicited by a stimulus after conditioning.

Conditioned stimulus. An originally ineffective stimulus for a given response that, by the experimental procedure of conditioning, is capable of eliciting that response.

Conflict. The simultaneous functioning of opposing or mutually exclusive impulses, desires, or tendencies; or the state of a person when opposed impulses or response tendencies have been activated.

Constant-ratio rule. A notion from Luce's choice theory which says that the ratio between two choices should be the same no matter what the subset from which the set is taken. It means that one should prefer steak to chicken no matter what the other items on the menu happen to be. The ratio of one's choices for steak over chicken should remain independent of the particular menu from which one makes the selections.

Constituent-structure analysis. The analysis of language into the components which produce it. The aim is to produce the language with a minimum of effort and computing. The usual structure turns out to include verb and noun phrases.

Contact comfort. The sense of peace, security, and well-being obtained from being in close proximity to or touching a trusted person or thing.

Convergent thinking. Thought which follows rules in solving a problem. An example is the application of multiplication procedures to a set of numbers.

Cooperative play. Play in which each member takes a complementary part.

Correlation. The tendency to concomitant variation; the degree to which two (or more) variables change together.

Correlation, negative. A correlation between two variables which indicates that large values of one variable tend to be associated with small values of the other variable, and vice versa.

Correlation, positive. A relation between two variables such that large values of one variable tend to be associated with large values of the other variable, and small values of the one tend to be associated with small values of the other.

Counterphobic. Deliberate experiencing of fear in a situation in which it can be overcome.

Cretinism. A condition arising from thyroid insufficiency in foetal life or early infancy, marked by great retardation in mental and physical growth.

Criterion. A comparison object or a rule, standard, or test for making a judgment, especially a qualitative judgment; the basis for assignment to a class or category.

Critical flicker frequency. The rate of change at which a rapid periodic stimulation is extinguished and a smooth fusion takes its place. This rate increases with changes in absolute brightness or differences between the two phases.

Cross-cultural studies. The attempt to discover the effects on behavior of a particular environmental stimulus by observing more than one culture.

Cross-section method. The study of a large number of variables—persons, anatomical structures, psychological functions—as they all are at a single period of time.

Crossing-over. The process whereby some of the linked genes separate and enter into different sex cells and thus generate new combinations.

Curvilinear relation. A relation of two variable quantities portrayed by some curve other than a straight line.

Defense mechanisms. Any enduring structure of the psyche that enables a person to avoid awareness of the unpleasant or the anxiety-arousing.

Delinquency. A relatively minor violation of legal or moral codes, especially by children or adolescents.

Dendrite. The receiving fiber or branch of the neuron, usually very short in lenth and ending in a complicated branching effect (end brush). Excitation starts with the end brush of the *dendrite* and is transmitted to the ends of the axon (the other fiber of the neuron).

Denial. Refusal to admit reality; disavowal.

Dependency. Habitual reliance upon another person for comfort, guidance, and decision; a lack of self-reliance; the tendency to seek the help of others in making decisions or in carrying out difficult actions.

Developmental norm. The average behavior expected of children at various ages. Based on predetermined maturation.

Discrimination. (1) The process of detecting differences in objects; especially sensory discrimination, the detecting of sensory differences. (2) Reacting differently to different objects. (3) Prejudicial treatment; any difference in action premised upon a *prejudice* or upon the class or category by which an individual is typed rather than upon his relevant characteristics.

Distorting lenses. Lenses in eyeglasses made so that they change the retinal or the visual images of the wearer.

Distribution. A systematic grouping of data into classes or categories according to the frequency of occurrence of each successive value or range of values.

Distributional analysis. The frequency with which words appear in a particular language.

Divergent thinking. Creative problem-solving; an example is the number of ways one can use a brick.

Domination. Control of the behavior of others, especially by coercion.

Down's syndrome. *Mongolism:* a congenital condition characterized by a flat skull, oblique eye slits, stubby fingers and thumbs, and a fissured tongue. Severe mental deficiency at imbecile or idiot level is an invariable accompaniment.

Drive reduction. The sequence of events within the organism that results in lessening the specific activity called a drive (the feeling of need).

Ectoderm. The outermost of the three cell layers in the embryo. It develops into the ectomorphic structures of the skin and nervous system.

Ectomorphic type. Relatively thin, with a large skin surface in comparison with weight.

Ego. The I, self, person, or individual, as distinguished from others; that which is postulated as the center to which all a person's psychological activities and qualities are referred. That aspect of the psyche which is conscious and most in touch with external reality.

Ego ideal. A part of the ego closely related to, but *also* to be distinguished from, the superego. The *ego ideal* represents the sum of positive identifications with loving, reassuring parents (or parent substitutes, including society and God so far as these are *positively* identified with). In the main, the *ego ideal* provides positive striving for ideals.

Egocentric. Concerned with oneself; preoccupied with one's own concerns and relatively insensitive to the concerns of others, though not necessarily selfish. Behavior, especially speech, that is controlled by one's own concerns and is characterized by a lack of sensitivity to the needs, expressions, or reactions of others.

Eidetic imagery. A peculiarly vivid type of imagery: it is practically as if the subject were actually perceiving, although in general he realizes that the imaged object is not literally present to the senses. It is common in childhood and is gradually lost by most persons.

Electra complex. The repressed desire of a female for incestuous relations with her father. Held by Freudians to be nearly universal.

Embryonic phase. In mammals the embryonic phase precedes the time the organism begins to resemble its adult form. In man it is conventionally the six weeks after implantation (eight weeks from conception).

Empiricism. The doctrine that all development is controlled by environmental influences.

Endoderm. The innermost of the three cellular layers of the embryo that develops into the digestive tract and most of the viscera.

Endomorphic type. Relatively heavy, with highly developed viscera and relatively weak muscular and bony structure.

Epinephrine. Properly, the hormone secreted by the adrenal glands, lying just above the kidneys; adrenalin and adrenin are names of proprietary products, but the three terms are often used interchangeably.

Ethnocentric. A hypothesized syndrome of underlying attitudes that involve the following: division of the social world into in-groups with which one identifies and to which one submits and out-groups to which one is hostile; positive stereotypy of the former and negative stereotypy of the latter; and the arrangement of the in-groups and out-groups into an evaluative hierarchy in which the former are always dominant and the latter always subordinate.

Eugenics. The attempt to improve the inborn qualities of a race or breed, especially of men. *Positive eugenics* seeks to increase propagation of the specially fit, *negative eugenics* to prevent propagation of the unfit. Though sometimes called a science, eugenics is properly an application of the science of *genetics.*

Extinction. The progressive reduction in the conditioned responses consequent upon either of two experimental procedures: (1) the repeated presentation of the CS (conditioned stimulus) without the US: (unconditioned stimulus); or (2) the withholding of reward after the emission of a conditioned instrumental response.

Fantasy. Imagining a complex object or event in concrete symbols or images, whether or not the object or event exists; or the symbols or images themselves: for example, a daydream. Fantasy is usually pleasant and represents a sort of wish fulfillment. Originally synonymous with imagination, it is now distinguished by the fact that, if it represents reality at all, it is whimsical or visionary, not primarily either constructive or reproductive. Yet it is not necessarily delusive or pathological.

Finite state. A model of grammar which suggests that the child develops his sentences on the basis of statistical rules concerning the occurrences of words. The model can produce sentences of finite length and therefore is not a proper model for language.

Foetal period. The stage of development of the embryo in its more advanced period; especially the human embryo after the eighth week of pregnancy.

Free morpheme. A word that may occur alone, without a bound morpheme.

Frustration. The blocking of, or interference with, an ongoing goal-directed activity.
The *motivational* and/or *affective* state resulting from being blocked, thwarted, disappointed, or defeated.

Gene. An inferred submicroscopic structure in the chromosomes which is the physical unit of heredity.

General Problem Solver. A computer program that has operations in it to solve very general problems; for example, it will solve logic problems, puzzles, and games. The program was developed to simulate the basic processes that seem important in human problem-solving.

Genital stage. The culminating phase of development in respect to sex in which the person has a genuinely affectionate relation with the sex partner. It does *not* mean, as the term might be interpreted, a phase with strong emphasis upon the genitals (phallic stage), nor a phase in which the interest lies primarily in coitus (genital primacy), though these distinctions are often not observed.

Genotype. The qualities or traits, shared by members of a biologically defined group, that form the basis for its classification; or a hypothetical animal or plant embodying those traits; a type organism. The sum of all the traits that an individual is capable of *transmitting* biologically; or a single such trait.

Germinal phase. In human beings, the first two weeks of prenatal life.

Gestalt. A form, a configuration, or a totality that has, as a unified whole, properties which cannot be derived by summation from the parts and their relations. The term is now naturalized in English and often spelled without initial capital. It may refer to physical structures, to physiological and psychological functions, or to symbolic units.

Global. Total; taken as a whole without attempt to distinguish separate parts of functions.

Gradient of reinforcement. The generalization that in a series of acts the closer an act is to the reward, the more it is strengthened.

Grammar. A study of the classes of words, their inflections, and their functions and relations in the sentence—what is to be preferred and what avoided in inflection and *syntax*.

Groupings. Things classified into classes, categories, or ranks.

Heterozygous. An individual who has, with respect to a given trait, a gene pair containing both a dominant and a recessive gene. Such an individual may transmit either of the two genes to offspring.

Homozygous. An individual who has, with respect to a given trait, a gene pair containing either two dominant or two recessive genes.

Hospitalism. A term introduced by Ribble and Spitz to describe their observations that unattended young infants withdraw, lose interest in their surroundings, do not mature properly, and finally die. They proposed that the effect was due to lack of mothering.

Id. That division of the psyche from which come blind, impersonal, instinctual impulses that lead to immediate gratification of primitive needs. The *id* is conceived as the true unconscious, or the deepest part of the psyche. It is in contact not with the world but only with the body, and in its relations with the body it is dominated by the pleasure principle. While descriptions of the *id* and its functions are couched in personalized terms, it is explicitly held that the *id* is not an entity but is merely a description of a system of actions.

Identification. Becoming identical through affiliation; associating or affiliating oneself closely with a person or group. Accepting as one's own the purposes and values of another person (or of a group); merging or submerging one's own purposes and values with the other. Imitation of outward behavior and sympathy or empathy with the other's feelings are frequent correlates.

Imitation. Action that copies the action of another more or less exactly, with or without intent to copy.

Implantation. The attachment of the fertilized ovum to the wall of the uterus.

Imprinting. A particular kind of learning characterized by occurrence in very early life, rapidity of acquisition, and relative insusceptibility to forgetting or extinction. Imprinted behavior includes some behavior commonly called instinctive.

Inbreeding. The breeding of close relatives. The so-called inbred lines of genetics are established and maintained by unbroken brother-sister matings.

Incremental learning. The gradual strengthening of the association or connection between a stimulus and a response. This is in opposition to all-or-none learning.

Infant attachment. The emotional bond that exists between caretaker and infant.

Information. Knowledge of facts gained through investigation, observation, study, or instruction. In behavioral theory, that aspect of a stimulus situation which is a *cue* or a *clue;* the nonintensive aspect of the stimulus. Technically, the reduction of uncertainty.

Innate releasing stimulus. A stimulus that is genetically programed to produce a sequence of behavior.

Instinct. A predetermined tendency or disposition to act in an organized and biologically adaptive way that is characteristic of a given species.

Institution. An enduring organization of some aspect of collective life (social, political, economic, religious) controlled by rules, customs, rituals, or laws.

Institutionalization. Such degree of habituation to the routine of an institution that one is anxious or even incapable of living without.

Integration. The process or result of bringing together and unifying parts into a whole; the production of units of a higher order. In integration, though the parts may be distinguished, they lose their separate identity.

Interaction. Mutual or reciprocal influence between two or more systems; especially social interaction, that relation between animals in which the behavior of either one is stimulus to the behavior of the other. A broader term than *communication.* Two animals may be in the same situation without significant interaction.

Intersection. The act or process of intersecting, of meeting and crossing at a point and thereby sharing a common area.
A place or area where two or more things intersect.

Invariance. The property of remaining constant while other conditions are changing.

Iterative. A trial-and-error process for achieving a known goal.

Kernel sentence. The simple declarative sentence; the base structure from which all transformations are produced.

Kinesthesis. The sense that yields knowledge of the movements of the body or of its several members. Its chief divisions are: (1) muscle sense, (2) tendon sense, (3) joint sense, and (4) static sense, having sensors in the labyrinth of the inner ear (often not classified as kinesthetic).

Lamarckianism. A theory of evolution that maintains the possibility that changes resulting from the use or disuse of an organ during an organism's life may be transmitted genetically.

Language universals. The rules or principles of the science of linguistics; statements about characteristics, tendencies, or rules of language shared by all human speakers.

Latency. The interval between the onset of a stimulus and the onset of the associated reaction.

Laterality. Sidedness; the preferential use of one side of the body, especially in tasks demanding the use of only one hand, one eye, or one foot.

Learning set. A generalized approach to problems as if the animal recognizes that they are to be solved by learning an instrumental response. The animal, whether human or subhuman, reacts on the implicit hypothesis that a means to the end is to be discovered. The learning set is itself believed to be a result of learning.

Libido. Any *instinctual* manifestation that tends toward life rather than death, integration rather than disintegration.

Likelihood ratio. The probability of the alternative hypothesis being considered, divided by that of the null hypothesis. This is the basic quantity computed after each set of observations in a sequential analysis.

Linkage. The tendency for certain characters of an organism to be inherited together, the offspring showing either both or neither. The linked traits are believed to be transmitted by genes located in the same chromosome.

Longitudinal method. The study of a large number of variables in the same person over a considerable period of time.

Loudness. The heard attribute of a tone that corresponds to physical intensity.

Major gene. A single gene that produces a large effect on the variability of a trait.

Maternal overprotection. Providing greater care for an infant or child than is necessary. The term has a very inclusive reference: pampering, indulgence, excessive physical contact, prevention of independent behavior, oversolicitude, shielding from competition, etc.

Maternal separation. The loss of a mother-child relation after the child has experienced a good relation. Maternal separation can occur following the child's recognition of his mother as a caretaker—usually after six months of age.

Mean. An average calculated by dividing the sum of all the values by the number of cases in a statistical series. Unless qualified, *mean* always refers to the arithmetic mean.

Mediation. The intervening of an object or process between two items or terms. In a chain of events, any event is in mediation between those before it and those after it.

Meiosis. The process of sex cell production. Alleles are separated so only one member of each pair of chromosomes goes to each cell.

Mesoderm. The middle of the three cellular layers of the embryo, which develops into the bones and muscles.

Mesomorphic type. A highly developed skeletal structure, thick skin, sturdy upright posture.

Mitosis. The process of normal cellular reproduction.

Monocular vision. Usable vision in only one eye; seeing, permanently or for long periods, with only one eye.

Moral realism. The tendency to judge acts in terms of their consequences.

Morality. That quality of conduct which makes it right or wrong.

Morphemes. The smallest linguistic unit with a meaning of its own. It is composed of one or more *phonemes.*

Mother surrogate. A person or thing that functions in another's life as a substitute for the mother. The surrogate need not be consciously recognized as a substitute.

Mutation. An abrupt change in the nature of a gene so that it thenceforth reduplicates itself in a new form. It may or may not be immediately observable as a change in phenotype.

Neurotic behavior. Characterizing behavior that resembles neurosis; erratic and excessively emotional behavior. *Neurosis:* a mental disorder ill-defined in character but milder than psychosis.

Noise. The sensory effect of irregular (aperiodic) sound waves; a sound that lacks tone, that is composed of conflicting pitches. Undesired sound.

Nonsense form (nonsense figure). A figure that neither closely resembles any familiar thing nor conforms exactly to any simple geometric or regular form.

Novelty. Something new or unusual.

Object. Any phase, aspect, or part of the environment in the widest sense; a unit of the situation that has a relatively constant meaning for a person.

Objective personality test. A means of measuring individual differences in behavior that eliminates, as far as possible, the influence of the examiner's bias or opinion. A test that can be routinely scored by the application of simple rules requiring a minimum of judgment.

Oedipal complex. The repressed desire of a male for incestuous relations with his mother. It is held by Freudians to be nearly universal.

Oedipal period. The time during the young child's life when he lusts after his opposite-sexed parent; in particular, the boy for his mother.

Olfaction. The sense of smell.

Open field. A test situation for fear and curiosity; it consists of an open area that contains markings on the floor so that the path of the animal can be traced for later study.

Operant conditioning. Instrumental conditioning: the experimental procedure wherein a response that brings into view a rewarding stimulus thereafter is more likely to occur.

Operations. An *empirical operation* alters the nature or relations among facts; a *logical* or *mathematical operation* changes the relations between symbols according to the rules of logic or mathematics.

Oral stage. The infantile period in which desire has not been differentiated into desire for nourishment and desire for sexual activity, and, hence, taking food has something of a sexual nature.

Ordinal measure (ordinal position). One indicating place in a succession. Ordinal position is usually indicated by the number series—first, second, third, and so on.

Overachievement. Better performance than predicted from a measure of aptitude; specifically, receiving higher marks in school, or making better scores on school achievement tests, than predicted from a test of general intelligence or of academic aptitude.

Overprotection. Providing greater care for an infant or child than is necessary. The term has a very inclusive reference: pampering, indulgence, excessive physical contact, prevention of independent behavior, oversolicitude, shielding from competition, and so on.

Pain. The opposite of pleasure: The sensation that results when the skin or any sense organ is too intensely stimulated.

Pair-comparison. A procedure in which objects are compared with each other in pairs, each with each, until all combinations are given. It is often used for the study of emotional and aesthetic values.

Parallel play. The side-by-side independent play of two or more children (or occasionally adults) doing much the same things but without active cooperation and yet with heightened interest because of each other's presence and activity.

Performance. What a person does when faced with a task, whether self- or other-imposed. Examples are approach, avoidance, escape, going to class, answering a test item.

Phase sequence. A theory that conceives of the neural correlates of behavior and/or conscious process as consisting of a number of cell assemblies joined serially (Hebb, 1949).

Phonemes. Groups of similar speech sounds in a given language.

Phrase structure. The analysis of sentences into phrases—verb phrases and noun phrases—from which the sentence is built. As an example, the sentence, "The man hit the ball" can be broken into a noun phrase and a verb phrase.

Pitch. The character of a tone as high or low, determined chiefly by the vibration frequency.

Placenta. In mammals, the vascular structure within the uterus to which the foetus is attached by the umbilical cord and through which it is nourished.

Placental barrier. A function of the placenta; it prevents some harmful substances from reaching the embryo and foetus.

Play. Voluntary activity pursued without ulterior purpose and, on the whole, with enjoyment or expectation of enjoyment. (Certain elements of play may not be enjoyed.)

Polygenes. Genes having such small quantitative effect on the variability of a trait that they are known only collectively. They cannot be isolated by classic genetic techniques.

Predeterminism. The doctrine that all development is controlled by pre-set biological mechanisms.

Preference. The turning toward, or accepting, one stimulus object rather than another. Preference is shown by doing the one thing sooner, more often, or with more vigor or zeal—but not always better.

Preformationism. The doctrine that organismic development is but the unfolding of certain patterns or powers, present in rudimentary and latent form from the start.

Prehension. The act of grasping an object. In the human infant, the gradual refinement of prehension is considered one of the most significant signs of development.

Prejudice. A favorable or unfavorable belief or judgment, made without adequate evidence and not easily alterable by the presentation of contrary evidence.

Prematurity. In pregnancy, a period of time before the end of normal gestation in which a viable foetus is delivered.

Preoperational. Piaget's second period of development in children's thinking, characterized by the dominance of perceptual events over conceptual processes (centration).

Primacy. The notion that first events are most important.

Primary circular reaction. A reflexive circle of behavior that keeps running once the original link is activated—for example, sucking.

Primary drive. A drive that in its major form is determined by the animal's heredity; a drive that depends upon a physiological need and that, independent of prior learning, instigates a special class of behavior.

Primary reinforcement. The presentation of a stimulus situation that reinforces or rewards any animal of a given species without need of prior training; or the state of affairs that so reinforces.

Prisoner's dilemma. A forced choice between two distasteful alternatives.

Projection. The process of unwittingly attributing one's own traits, attitudes, or subjective processes to others. For example, the child's naive assumption that adults feel as he does. The process of ascribing to others one's own unacknowledged desires or faults.

Projective technique. A procedure for discovering a person's characteristic modes of behavior, his attitudes, motivations, or dynamic traits, by observing his behavior in response to a situation that does not elicit or compel a particular response—that is, in a relatively unstructured, ambiguous, or vague situation.

Proximodistal progression. From the middle outward to the ends or sides.

Pseudoconditioning. The eliciting of a response to a previously neutral stimulus by presenting the neutral stimulus after a series of effective stimuli. The neutral stimulus is not paired, as in true conditioning, with the unconditioned stimulus or unconditioned response.

Psychiatrist. A person, licensed to practice medicine, who is engaged professionally in the prevention, diagnosis, treatment, and care of *psychic* or mental illness. Under existing laws in most states, the medical license is the only *legally* necessary qualification.

Psychotic behavior. Pertaining to a psychotic disorder or psychosis; characterizing a certain behavior pattern as symptomatic of psychotic disorder or (at least) as strongly resembling the behavior of such a disorder.

Punishment. The infliction of a penalty by one animal upon another because the second has done something disapproved by the first or has failed to do something. The penalty may be any kind of dissatisfaction: a painful stimulus, physical or social, or denial or removal of a satisfaction.

Punitive. Characterizing the tendency to enforce obedience by means of punishment.

Realism. Any of a number of philosophical doctrines which assert that objects have an independent existence—i.e., are not dependent for their existence upon the knower.
An attitude of being sensitive to, and guided by, things as they are rather than as one wishes they were.

Recency. The notion that recent events are most important.

Redundancy. That property of a message which reduces the error of prediction for a given event to less than chance because the message contains information about what will come next. If a message begins, "Hurry h—," it contains some information about what will (probably) follow, hence the error of prediction is less than a chance level. Such a message contains redundancy. The message "Hurry h—" is redundant not only about its own continuation but about the event it may lead to; for example, there is an above-chance probability that the recipient will go home.

Regression. Moving backward; a return to earlier and less mature behavior; or, manifestation of more primitive behaviors after having learned mature forms, whether or not the immature or primitive behavior had actually formed part of the person's earlier behavior.

Rejection. The process of regarding something as worthless, of throwing something away, or of refusing to admit it to a certain category. In interpersonal relations rejection is seldom absolute or complete, and usually it shows itself indirectly: by excessive criticism of the person rejected, by invidious comparisons, by signs of hostility, crossness, or refusal to pay attention to the other person.

Relation. The bearing or influence one object may have upon another.

Relational. Characterized or constituted by relations; of or relating to kinship.

Reliability. Accuracy; dependability; trustworthiness; the quality or qualities of a person or thing in virtue of which it can be counted on. In test theory, the reproducibility of a score.

Representation. Standing for, or in the place of, something else; specifically, for psychology, an experience, a psychic activity, or a mental content that in some essential way represents an earlier experience.

Representative sample. Taking a sample that accurately depicts what is true of the population from which the sample is drawn; taking a sample that includes in due proportion or frequency every relevant or required characteristic of the whole; drawing a sample that has the same distribution of scores as the entire population. All samples are by definition designed to be representative. If it is not to be redundant, representative sampling must refer to the extent to which a sample is truly representative.

Repression. The exclusion of specific psychological activities or contents from conscious awareness by a process of which the individual is not directly aware. Exclusion includes preventing entry into, forcing out of, or continuously preventing return to, consciousness. A common implication of this definition is that repression is a defense mechanism against anxiety or guilt.

Reversibility. The ability to retrace a thought sequence. Thought is distinguished from a stimulus-response chain by this property.

Rh factor. An agglutinating factor present in the blood of about 85 percent of human beings. It causes antibody formation if introduced into blood lacking it. An Rh positive foetus causes antibody formation in an Rh negative mother (during the birth process).

Schema. A number of ideas or concepts combined into a coherent plan or outline; a plan or model that displays the essential or important relations between concepts; a model.
A framework for the systematic recording of data; an outline showing the interrelations of data, especially one that subordinates detail.

Secondary circular reaction. The development of differentiated means and goals.

Secondary drive (acquired drive). A drive aroused and/or satisfied in ways acquired by experience or learning.

Secondary reinforcement. Any reinforcing or rewarding event or state that derives its effectiveness from a previous process of learning or conditioning; or the operation of bringing about that event or state.

Segregation. In sexual reproduction, the breaking up of gene pairs so that only one gene from each pair appears in the gamete (sperm or ovum). When two gametes combine to form a new organism, gene pairs are reformed, one gene of each pair being derived from each parent. The genes are not affected by their previous association with other genes.

Selective breeding. The mating of animals selected because they display a desired trait, followed by the further mating of those among their offspring that show the same trait.

Self-concept. A person's view of himself; the fullest description of himself of which a person is capable at any given time. Emphasis is upon the person as object of his own self-knowledge, but his feeling about what he conceives himself to be is usually included.

Semantics. The science of meanings of words or other signs; the rules that describe the way signs relate to objects (interpreting objects in a very broad sense). The study of meanings; the historical and psychological study and the classification of changes in the signification of words or forms viewed as factors in linguistic development.

Sensation. The elementary unanalyzable and uninterpreted item or unit of that which one apprehends when certain receptors are excited. Colors, sounds, odors, tastes, warmth, cool, and pressures are familiar and relatively unquestioned examples of such items. The process or activity of apprehending colors, sounds, tastes, and so on.

Sensitization in conditioning. The process of becoming, or the state of being, sensitive or oversensitive to a conditioning stimulus or stimuli.

Sensory deprivation. The lack of sensory stimulation—this deprivation can lead to impaired sensory and perceptual abilities and probably accounts for some early difficulties of the child (during the first six months of his life) as opposed to maternal deprivation and separation.

Sequential dependencies. A statistical notion that measures the amount of predictability (the probability that given one item, the next one will be known) among a set of items in sequential order; for example, the sequential dependency among letters of the alphabet is very high if they appear in their alphabetical order. However, if they are in a random order, there is no sequential dependency among them.

Sex role. The pattern of attitudes and behavior that in any society is deemed appropriate to one sex rather than the other. The role is taught by precept and example. There is no act except childbearing and suckling that is not, in some society, part of the male role; none that is not, in some society, part of the female role.

Shape constancy. The tendency to see an object as of the same shape regardless of the viewing angle.

Signal. A sign communicated by one person to another in order to indicate that the time and place for a certain action are at hand.

Size constancy. The tendency to perceive a familiar object as of a certain standard size, despite moderate variation in its distance from the observer or in other viewing conditions.

Social learning. A learning process in which social demands are the determining conditions.

Social reinforcement. The strengthening of a response or response tendency by *social stimuli;* strengthening the tendency to make a given response by insuring that it wins a social reward such as approval, a parent's love, attention.

Socialization. The process whereby a person, especially a child acquires sensitivity to social stimuli, particularly the pressures and obligations of group life, and learns to get along with, and to behave like, others in his group or culture; the process of becoming a social being; or the result of those processes.

Sociometric network. The diagram of communication networks among individuals.

Solipsist. One holding the philosophical view that he can be certain of nothing except his own experience, thus, that only experiences exist. This is an extreme form of idealism.

Solitary play. Play activity by oneself.

Specific nerve energies. The notion that sensory qualities are genetically coded by specific nerves.

Spontaneous recovery. When a conditioned response has been extinguished, it can often be elicited again after rest, though its strength is diminished.

Standard deviation. A measure of the dispersion or variability of a distribution.

Stranger anxiety. The infant's fear or apprehension of unknown persons. Appears around six to eight months of age in human infants.

Sublimation. Refinement or redirection of the energy belonging to a primitive tendency into new, noninherited channels; somewhat more broadly, such alteration in instinctive behavior as will bring it within the boundaries of conventional approval and yet allow partial satisfaction. In Freudian theory, altered sexual striving.

Superego. A system within the total psyche developed by incorporating the parental standards as perceived by the ego; or, somewhat more broadly, by incorporating the moral standards of society as perceived by the ego. The superego has two parts: *ego ideal* and *conscience.* (It has been quipped to be that part of the psyche most readily soluble in alcohol.)

Swaddle. To wrap an infant with narrow strips of cloth to restrict movement.

Symmetrical relation. A relation that holds when the terms are inverted: $x = y$.

Syntax. The way in which words are put together to form phrases, clauses, and sentences; the part of *grammar* dealing with this. The study of the rules by which sentences are constructed.

Tachistoscope. An instrument for providing a very brief timed exposure of visual material such as pictures, letters, or digits. The exposure may be regulated by a shutter, a falling screen, or an interrupted illumination.

Tautology. Needless repetition of the same or equivalent words, as if to add to the thought or feeling: e.g., necessary essentials.

Tertiary circular reaction. The discovery of new means through active experimentation.

Thermal sensitivity. Responsiveness to temperature changes; the sensing of warmth and cool.

Threshold. The statistically determined point at which a stimulus is just barely adequate to elicit a specified organismic response (absolute threshold) or at which it differs enough from another stimulus to elicit a different response (difference or differential threshold).

Transformation. A linguistic operation that changes a particular part of grammar into another state. For example, negation and passive voice are transformations of sentences and verbs.

Transitivity. A relationship such that if *A* stands in a certain relation to *B,* and *B* stands in the same sort of relation to *C,* then *A* stands in that relation to *C.* Ordinary physical qualities are transitive, but psychological qualities or activities are not necessarily so. One may prefer *A* to *B* as a dinner guest, and *B* to *C,* but not *A* to *C.*

Triad. A group of three.

Tropism. An automatic or forced orienting movement toward or away from a source of stimulation whose direction and extent is a direct function of the stimulus.

Unconditioned response. A response evoked by a certain stimulus before learning.

Unconditioned stimulus. A stimulus that at the beginning of a given learning or conditioning period evokes a certain response.

Underachievement. Performance poorer than predicted from an aptitude measurement.

Univocal. A term that refers to only one object or class of objects; a term that does not refer to objects from different classes as if they belonged to the same class.

Unoccupied play. Doing nothing in a play situation; withdrawal.

Validity. The quality of being founded on truth, fact, or law. A property of the whole measuring or testing process, but especially of the test instrument, which insures that the obtained test scores correctly measure the variable they are supposed to measure; the property of the measurement process that makes the obtained scores useful in predicting a given variable.

Vicarious aggression. The experience of seeing another aggress and its effects on the individual's feelings of hate and frustration.

Villi. Rootlike fingers on the amniotic sac to collect food from the uterine wall and deliver it to the foetus through a primitive tube or stalk. Later in the embryonic period most of the *villi* degenerate; the remainder develop into the placenta.

Visual angle. The angle subtended by an object in the visual field at the nodal point of the eye. This angle determines the size of the image on the retina. Objects of different sizes or distances have the same-sized image on the retina if they subtend the same angle.

Will. The capacity for voluntary activity; the ability to hold in check certain impulses and to release others.

INDEX

A

Abnormal behavior, 413–417
  and genetics, 24–25
Accommodation (Piaget), 123, 124, 265, 267
Accommodation, newborn, 85–86
Achievement, 395
  and failure, 384
  and personality, 384–385
Achievement motivation, 186
Acquired characteristics, 10
Acquired distinctiveness of cues, 81
Acuity, visual, 66
Adam's first record, 315
Addition of asymmetrical relations, 144
Additive model of genetic-environment interaction, 9
Adorno, T. W., 209, *212*
Adrenaline, 178
Adult tests, 348
Aggression, 293, 398–403
  control, 400
  and dependency, 294
  maladaptive, 399
  and mass media, 378
  models, 293–294
  and punishment, 294, 402
Ainsworth, M. D., *261*
Albert, 168
Alcohol and crime, 416–417
All-or-none learning, 110, 115
Ambivalence, 398
Anal stage, 257
  fixation, 259
Anastasi, A., 340, *356*
Anderson, H. H., *386*
"Anger-in," 178
Animalcules, 4
Animals as subjects, 19, 238
Animism, 130
Anoxia, 239
Anxiety, 169, 171
  and IQ, 171
Anxiety, novelty, and play, 365
Anxious conformity, 395
Aphasia, 320
A priori probability, 58
Aronson, E., 201, *212*
Assimilation (Piaget), 123, 124, 260, 267
Association, 104, 106
Atkinson, R. C., 113, *127*, 150, *158*, 367, *386*
Attachment and feeding, 359
Attention, selective, 91
Audition, 67
Authoritarian group, 371
Authoritarian personality, 207, 210
  See also Puritan ethic
Autonomy, 394–397
  problems of, 395
Autonomy versus control, 287–291
Autonomy versus shame stage (Erikson), 404

B

Babbling, 309
Baby biography, 48
Bach, G. R., 409, *421*
Baldwin, A., *285*
Baldwin, J. M., 361, *386*
Bandura, A., 206, *212*, 378, *386*, 393, 401, 402, 410, 414, *421*
Barker, R. G., 48, *51*, 163, *189*
Bartley, S. H., 54, *75*, *101*
Bayley, N., *51*, 295, 306
Becker, W. C., 292, *306–307*, 415, *421*
Behavioral contagion, 375
Behavioral embryology, 220
Berenda, R. W., 374, *386*
Bias, response, 195
Bijou, S. W., 116, *127*
Binet, A., 331, 332, *356*
Bipolar dimensions, 287
  autonomy versus control, 287–291
  hostility versus love, 287–291
Birth, 231, 232, 239
Birth cry, 233
Black intelligence, 340–341
Blindness, congenital, 241
Body build and personality, 45
Body proportion, 32

NOTE: Page entries in italics indicate complete reference citations.

Bower, G. H., 112, *128*
Bower, T. G. R., 89, *101*
Bowlby, J., 413, *421*
Brackbill, Y., 120, *128*, 173, *189*
Brain localization, 320
Braine, M., 318, *330*
Breast-bottle feeding, 259
Breeding, selective, 16, 19-20
Bridges, K. M., 176, *189*, 360, *386*
Brightness sensitivity, newborn, 62-63
Brodsky, C. M., 46, *51*
Brown, P., 402, *421*
Brown, R., 308, 312, 314, 315, 317, 318, *329*, *330*
Bruner, J. S., 98, 99, *101*, 133, *158*
Burke, B. S., 228, *235*
Buss, A. H., *421*
Butler, R. A., 180, *189*, 250, *261*

C

Cannibals and missionaries, problem of, 156
Cantril, H., 177, *189*
Carmichael, L., 217, 219, *235*
Castanada, A., 171, *189*
Cattell, P., 342, *356*
Cattell Infant Test, 343-345
Causality, 282
Centration (Piaget), 135
Cephalo-caudal development, 30, 216
  of touch, 70
Cerebral dominance, 39
Charlesworth, R., 394, *421*
Charters, W. W., 377, *386*
Chase, W. P., 64, *75*
Cheating, 205
Chen, H. P., 309, *330*
Children, attitudes of, 297
  in groups, 371-373
  schizophrenic, 415-416
Choice, 192, 193, 196
  axiom, 195
Chomsky, N., 311, 314, 321, 322, 323, 324, *329-330*
Chow, K. L., 241, *261*
Class (social), and peer relation, 373
Class multiplication, 142
Classes of play, 365-367
Classical conditioning, 105, 107, 108
Classification ability, 146
Classification of IQ, 332-333
Claus, Santa, 168
Cliff, visual, 87
Closure, 91
Coghill, G. E., 216, *235*
Cognition and emotion, 176-178
Cognitive behavior, groupings in (Piaget), 140-146
Cognitive dissonance, 199, 200, 201, 202
Cognitive style, 354
Color vision, 62, 64, 65
"Colorless green ideas sleep furiously," 321
Competence and performance, 321
Competition, 395
Components of learning, 106
Computer chess, 155
Computer simulation, 154
Concept attainment, 150
  and IQ, 154
Concept formation, 126
Conceptual style, 153
Concordance, 22
Concrete operations (Piaget), 137, 138
Conditioning, social, 119-120
Conflict, 197, 198
  approach-approach, 197
  approach-avoidance, 197-198
  avoidance-avoidance, 197
  double approach-avoidance, 197, 198
Conflict situations, early feeding, 258-259
  hostility, 258-259
  sexuality, 258-259
  toileting, 258-259
Congenital blindness, 241
Consciousness, 131
Constancy, 89
Constant ratio rule, 195
Constituent structure analysis, 323-325
Contact comfort, 247
Content (Piaget), 122, 264
Control of aggression, 400
Control versus autonomy, 287-291
Convergent thinking, 352
Cooley, C. H., 371, *386*
Correct rejection, 59
Correction for guessing, 60
Correlation, 49, 50
Co-univocal multiplication of classes, 143
Crandall, U. C., 291, *307*, 396, *421*
Creativity, 351-355
  and personality, 354
Cretinism, 227, 228
Crick, F., 14, 15
Crime and alcohol, 416-417
Criteria of a sense, 60, 61
Criterion (perception), 56
Critical fusion frequency (CFF), 65
Critical period, 236, 237, 238
  for language, 311
Cross-sectional method, 48, 49
Crossing-over, 12, 13, 19
Culture-fair intelligence tests, 349-351
Curiosity, 134, 160, 179-180
Curve of intelligence, 332

D

Darwin, C., 5, *27*
Davis, W. A., 297, *307*
Day, E. S., 360, *386*
Deaf children, 319-320
Death wish, 398
Decision criteria, 55
Decision rule, 56, 57
Defense mechanisms, 410-412
DeGroat, A. F., 382, *387*
Delay of reinforcement, 117, 118
Delinquency, 413
Democratic group, 371
Dennis, W., 45, *51*, 255, *261*
Dependency, 392-394
  and aggression, 294
Depth perception, 87, 88
Descartes, R., 79, *101*
Detection, yes-no, 55
Development, problems of, 391
Developmental norm, 29
Diagram, tree, 324
Difference threshold, 55
Dimension of perception, 82, 83
Directive therapy, 418-419
Discipline, inconsistent, 297
Discrimination, 193
  and language, 313
  learning, 125
  reversal-shift, 148
Distorting lenses, 99
Divergent thinking, 352
Divorce, effect on child, 303-304
DNA (deoxyribonucleic acid), 14, 15
Dobzhansky, T., 15, *27*
Dollard, J., 163, *189*, 258, *261*, 293, *307*, 398, *422*

Dominance, 15, 18
Double helix, 14, 15
Dreams, 131
Drugs, influence on foetus, 228

E

Early experience, 236
  enrichment of, 240
  factors, 237
  perceptual deprivation, 241
  perceptual development, 240
  and problem-solving, 241
Early maturing, 45
Early vocalizations, 309
Ectomorph body type, 46
Effects of media, 377
Egocentrism, 130, 134, 406
Eidetic imagery, 93, 94, 95
Eisman, B., 349, *356*
Electra complex, 203, 258
Elkind, D., 92, *101*
Embryonic behavior, 218
Embryonic phase, 220
Emotion, 175
  and cognition, 176-178
  pseudo ("as-if"), 177
Empiricism, 311
Endomorph body type, 46
Environmentalism, 3, 5, 78, 217
Epistemology, 140
Equilibrium, 137, 266
Erikson, E. H., 389, 392, 403, *422*
Erlenmeyer-Kimling, 23, *27*
Estes, W. K., 118, *128,* 172, *189*
Ethic, Puritan, 201
Expansion and check, 316
Experimental caretaking, 254
Extinction, 109, 116

F

Factors, of intelligence, 331
  of personality, 392
Failure and achievement, in school, 384
False alarms, in decision-making, 59
Family size, 302
  and peer relations, 374
Fantz, R. L., 64, 67, *75, 76,* 78, 83, 86, *101*
Father-daughter relations, 303
Father-son relations, 303
Feeding and attachment, 359
Festinger, L., 192, 200, *211, 212*
Field, S., 395, *422*
First grammar learning, 314-316
Flavell, J. H., 131, 134, 140, *158, 285,* 320, *330,* 365, *387*
Foetal behavior, 215, 219
  methods of studying, 216
Foetal development, timing of influences, 230-231
Foetal period, 221
Foetus and smoking, 228
Forgays, D., 240, *261*
Forgus, R. H., 240, *261*
Forman, J. J., 66, *76*
Freedman, D. G., 360, *387*
Frenkel-Brunswik, E., 209, *212*
Freud, S., 166, *189,* 202, 203, *212,* 236, 256, *262,* 293, 358, 361, *387,* 389, 392, 397-398, 403, 405-407, *422*
  on play, 362
Fromm, E., 166, *189*
Frustration-aggression hypothesis, 163, 165, 293
Fuller, J. L., *27*
Function (Piaget), 122, 264
Funkenstein, H., 178, *189*

G

G factor, 334
Gallagher, J. J., 353, *356*
Geldard, F. A., *75*
Gene(s), 9
General Problem Solver, 155
Generation gap, 375-376
Generativity versus self-absorption stage (Erikson), 405
Genetic(s), 3
  and abnormal behavior, 24-25
  code, 14
  environmental influences and, 11, 22
  epistemology, 264
  and intelligence, 22-23, 236-241
  and language, 310-311
Genital stage, 257
Genotype, 6
Germinal phase, 220
Gesell, A., 5, *27,* 30, *51,* 342, *356*
Gesell Infant Test, 342-343
Gestalt school, 79
Gewirtz, J. L., 120, *128,* 167, *189*
Ghent, L., 91, *101*
Gibson, E. J., 82, 96, *101,* 241, *262*
Gilmore, J. B., 365, *387*
Global intelligence, 331
Goal gradients, 198, 199
Goddard, K. E., 292, *307*
Graduate Record Exam (GRE), 348
Graham, F., 33, *52,* 239, *262*
Graham, G. E., 232, *235*
Grammar, development of, 309
Grasp reflex, 40
Grasping, 41
Green, D. M., 59, *76*
Greenberg, J., 308, 314, *330*
Greenberg, P. J., 396, *422*
Groos, K., 361, *387*
Growth patterns, 34-36
Guilford, J. P., 351, *356,* 391, *422*
Guilt, 295
Guthrie, E. R., 106, *128*
Gutteridge, M., 43, *52*

H

Haber, R. N., 94, 95, *101*
Haggard, E. A., 350, *356*
Haley, W., 414, *422*
Hall, D. E., 416, *422*
Hall, G., 5, *27,* 277, *285*
Hamilton, W. J., 221, *235*
Harlow, H., 162, 180, *190,* 244, 250-252, 254, *262,* 359, *387*
Harter, S., 349, *356*
Hartshorne, H., 205, 212
Haynes, H., 85, *101,* 269, *285*
Hebb, D. O., 6, *27,* 80, *102,* 133, *158,* 236, 239, 240, *262,* 339, *356,* 360, *387*
Held, R., 266, *285*
Hershenson, M., 62, *76,* 84, 86, *102*
Hess, E. H., 243, *262,* 311, *330*
Heterozygous genetic transmission, 15, 16
Hetherington, E. M., 408-409, *422*
Hewitt, L. E., 413, *422*
Hilgard, R., *127*
Himmelweit, H. T., 378, *387*
Hits, 59
Hobbes, T., 80, *102*
Hodgkiss, M., 413, *422*
Hollenberg, E., 402, *422*
Hollingshead, A., 25, *27,* 373, *387*
Holtzman, W. H., 390, *422*
Homeostatic need, 160
Homozygous genetic transmission, 15, 16
Hooker, D., 70, 76, 218, 219, 221, *234-235*
Horney, K., 166, *190*
Horowitz, E., 208, *212*
Hostility versus love, 287-291
Hubel, D. H., 81, *102*

Hull, C. L., 106, *128*
Hunt, E. B., *158*
Hunt, J. McV., 98, *102*, 374, *387*
Hymovitch, B., 240, *262*

I

Identification and Oedipus, 407
Identity versus diffusion stage (Erikson), 404
Idiographic method, 389
Imitation, 281, 408
Imprinting, 243, 359
Inbreeding, 19, 20
Inconsistent discipline, 297
Independent assortment, 12
Individual differences, 24
  in language, 328
Industry versus inferiority stage (Erikson), 404
Infant attachment, 359
Infant Scale of Motor Development, 37
Infant social relations, 358
Infant tests, 342
Ingalls, T. H., 231, *235*
Initiative versus guilt stage (Erikson), 404
Insight, 276
Institutionalization, 255, 256
Instrumental learning, 105
Integrity versus despair stage (Erikson), 405
Intelligence, factors, 331
  and genetics, 22-23, 336-341
  and maturity, 339-340
  tests, types of, 341-348
  See also IQ
Intentionality, 272-273
  barrier removal, 273
Interactionism, 3, 6, 8, 10, 18
  with limits, 7
Intimacy versus isolation stage (Erikson), 405
IQ, and anxiety, 171
  and concept attainment, 154
  definition of, 334
  and learning, 348-349
  See also Intelligence

J

Jakubezak, L. F., 393, *422*
James, W., 175, 176, *190*, 192, 212
Jeffrey, W. E., 125, *128*
Jensen, A., 341, *356*
Jensen, K., 72, *76*
Jersild, A. T., 170, *190*
Jones, M. C., 62, *76*
Judgment, 192, 193

K

Kagan, J., 153, *158*, 296, *307*, 354, 356, 386, 394, *421-422*
Kallman, F., 25, *27*
Kant, E., 79, *102*
Kemeny, J. G., 368, *387*
Kendler, H. H., 147, 148, *158*
Kendler, T. S., 126, *128*
Kernal sentence, 326
Kessen, W., 139, *159*, 161, *190*
Kinesthesis, 70
Kleinberg, O., 341, *356*
Koch, H., 41, *52*, 302, *307*, 374, *387*
Kogan, N., 356
Kohlberg, L., 204, 205, *212*, *386*
Kohler, I., 99, *102*, 218, *235*
Kuo, Z. Y., 217, *235*

L

Laissez-faire atmosphere, 371
Lamarck, J., 10, *27*
Lambert, W. W., 99, *102*
Landis, L., 177, *190*
Language, acquisition, 310-317
  critical period, 311
  and discrimination, 313
  and genetics, 310-311
  individual differences in, 328
  loss and recovery of, 320
  and reinforcement, 309
  universals, 314
Late maturing, 45
Latency, 407
Latent structure, 317-318
Laterality, 39
Learning, all-or-none, 110-115
  instrumental, 105
  and IQ, 348-349
  operant, 105, 116
  paired-associate, 112
  perceptual, 95
  set and intelligence, 349
  to learn, 124
Lee, E., 341, *357*
Lee, J. C., 153, *159*
Lenneberg, E., 309, 311, 320, *330*
Letter-word perception, 96
Levy, D. M., 300, *307*, 416, *422*
Libido theory, 166
Likelihood ratio, 56, 57, 58
Line detecting mechanisms, 81
Ling, B., 62, *76*
Linkage, 13
Lippitt, R., 371, 384, *387*
Lipsitt, L. P., 68, *76*, 108, 117, *128*
Locke, J., 80, *102*
Longitudinal method, 48, 49
Love, 178-179
Love versus hostility, 289-291
Lubchenco, L., 223, 232, *235*
Luce, R., 192, 195, *211*, *212*, 368, *387*

M

Maccoby, E. E., 91, *102*
Macdonald, M., 373, 387
Macfarlane, J. W., 292, *307*, 338, *357*
Major-gene transmission, 14
Maladaptive aggression, 399
Mandler, G., 179, *190*
Markov chain, 322-323
Marquis, D. P., 161, *190*
Marum, K. D., 109, *128*
Mass media, 376-379
  and aggression, 378
  and school, 378
Maternal influences, age, 230
  deprivation, 242
  emotionality, 227
  on foetus, 225-230
  infections, 229
  nutrition, 227
  overprotection, 416
  separation, 242
    monkey, 244
  See also Mother-child relations
Matrix games, 368-370
Matthews, S. A., 217, *235*
Maturity and intelligence, 339-340
McClelland, D., 186, *190*
McCord, W., 295, 307, 416, *422*
McDougall, W., 178, *190*
McFarland, R. A., 66, *76*
McGinnis, J. M., 62, *76*
McGraw, M. B., 43, *52*, 71, *76*
McNeill, D., 315, *330*
Mediation, 149
Mednick, S., 415, *422*
Mehler, J., 327, *330*
Meiosis, 11, 12, 13
Mendel, G., 9, *27*
Mental retardation, 24
Merrill-Palmer Scale, 345-346
Mesomorph body type, 46, 47

Meyer, W. J., 173, *190*, 382, *387*
Miller, G. A., 180–181, *190*, 332, *330*
Miller, N. E., 168, 170, *190*, 409, *421*, *422*
Minnesota Preschool Scale, 346
Mischel, W., 205, 206, *212*
Misses, in decision-making, 59
Missionaries and cannibals, problem of, 156
Mitosis, 11, 12
Mixed design, 48, 49
Modeling, behavior, 206, 401–402
Models of aggression, 293–294
Mongolism, 230
Monkeys, studies of, 244
  isolation, 252–253
  therapy, 252
Montague, A., 226, 227, 228, 230, *234–235*
Moore, O. K., 98, *102*
Moral rules, 204
Morality, 202
  See also Puritan ethic
Moreno, J. L., 371, *387*, 419, *422*
Morgan, S. S., 62, *76*
Morpheme, 308, 312
Mother attachment, 163
Mother-child relations, 299–302
  See also Maternal influences
Mother surrogate, 245, 246
  and curiosity, 249, 250
  and infant anxiety, 249
Motor abilities, interrelations among, 41
  stages of, 35
Motor development scale, 37
Movement perception, 67
Mowrer, O. H., 106, *128*, *189*, 408, 410, *422*
Mueller, J., 79, *102*
Multiplication, of classes, 142
  of relations, 145–146
Munsinger, H., 95, 96, *102*, 134, *159*, 183, 184–185, *190*
Murphy, G., 69, *76*
Mussen, P., 30, 45, *52*
Mutation, 13, 14, 18

N

Natural selection, 18
Needham, J., 4, 27
Negativism, 395
Neural conductance rate, 42
Newborn, accommodation, 85, 86
  brightness sensitivity, 62–63
Newborn *(Continued)*
  perception, 83
  preference for brightness, 87
  responses, 31–33
Newell, A., 155, *159*
Newman, H. H., 338, *357*
Noise, 57, 58
Nondirective therapy, 419
Noradrenaline, 178
Novelty, anxiety, and play, 365
Nye, F. I., 303, *307*

O

Object concept, 282–283
  permanence, 275
Objective test, 390–391
Ocular orientation, 82
Oedipal situation, 173, 174, 203, 257
  See also Puritan ethic
Oedipus, 257
  and identification, 407
Olfaction, 68
One-element model, 112
Only child, 302
Operant learning, 105, 116
Optimum interaction, 337
  in parent-child relations, 305
Optokinetic nystagmus, 66
Oral stage, 256
Orientation of figures, 91
Osgood, C. E., 311, *330*
Osler, S., 126, *128*, 154, *159*
Overprotected child, 300
Owens, W. A., 339, *357*

P

Page, E. I., 241, *262*
Pain, 71
Paired-associate learning, 112
Paradoxical cold, 72
Parent attitude measures, 291–292
Parent-child interaction, 260
Parten, M. B., 365, *387*
Partial reinforcement, 116
Patterson, C. H., 291, *307*
Payoff, 55
  matrix, 58
Payne, D. B., 408, *422*
Pearson, K., 24, 25, *27*
Peer acceptance and rejection, 374
Peer relations, 370–375
  and class, 373
  and family size, 374
Perception, criterion, 56
  letter-word, 96
  newborn, 83
  response theory, 81
  and value, 99
  whole-part, 92
Perceptual deprivation, 241
Perceptual learning, 95
Perceptual set, 90
Performance and competence, 321
Permissive child-rearing, 298–299
Personality, and achievement, 384–385
  and body build, 45
  and creativity, 354
  factors, 392
  stage, 304–305
  therapy, 417
Peterson, D., 295, *307*
Peterson, F., 62, *76*
Pettigrew, T., 340, *357*
Pfaffmann, C., 69, *76*
Phenotype, 10
Phoneme, 308
Phrase-structure model, 323
Phylogenetic skill, 43
Piaget, J., 80, *102*, 122, 123, *128*, 131, 132, 139, 142, 143, 144, 146, *159*, 194, 202, 203, 211, *212*, 236, *262*, 264–284, *285*, 361, *386*, *387*
  on imitation, 362–365
  on play, 362–365
Pinneau, S. R., 254, *262*
Pivot words, 310
Play, 278–279, 361–370
  novelty, anxiety, and, 365
  therapy, 419
Pollack, R. H., 73, *76*
Polygene transmission, 18
Positive social relations, 360
Postman, L., 110, *128*
Potter, M. C., 91, *102*
Power relations, 408
Pratt, K. C., 62, 64, 67, 68, 69, 72, *76*
Predeterminism, 3–5, 7, 78, 215, 217
Preference, 192, 193
  for brightness (newborn), 87
  for complexity, 87, 182–186
  for human face, 84, 86–87
Preformationism, 3, 4, 5
Prejudice, 207, 210
Prematurity, 232, 239
Prenatal development, timetable of, 223–224

Preoperational thought, 132, 134
Preschool tests, 345-346
Presolution behavior, 151
Preyer, W. T., 360, *387*
Primary addition of classes, 141
Primary drive, 161
Prisoner's dilemma, 368
Probability, a priori, 58
Problems of development, 391
Process of creativity, 352-353
Processing limit, 180-181
Projection, 411-412
Projective test, 390
Proximo-distal development, 30
Psathas, G., 373, *387*
Pseudo ("as-if") emotions, 177
Psychiatric social worker, 418
Psychiatrists, 417
Psychoanalysis, 419
Psychoanalyst, 418
Psychodrama, 419
Psychologist, 418
Puberty, 407
Punishment, 118, 119, 171, 172, 173, 203
  and aggression, 294, 402
Puritan ethic, 201
  See also Will

R

Radke, M. J., 298, *307*
Rationalism, 311
Reaction to frustration, 398-399
Reading difficulty, 94
Realism, 130
Recognition, and redundancy, 96
  tachistoscopic, 95
Redl, F., 375, *387*
Redundancy, and recognition, 96
Reese, H. E., 90, *102*
Regeneration, of retinal fiber, 218
Reinforcement, 105, 116
  and language, 309
  social, 117, 173
Rejected child, 301
Relevant-irrelevant clues, 98
Reliability, of intelligence tests, 334-335
Repression, 411
Response bias, 195
  theory of perception, 81
Responses, newborn, 31-33
Retardation, mental, 24
Retinal fiber regeneration, 218
Reversal shift discrimination, 148
Reversibility, 137
Rh sensitization, 229
Rheingold, H. L., 120, *128,* 180, *190,* 254, 262, 360, *387*
Ribble, M. A., 253, *262,* 359, *388*
Riesen, A. H., 9, *27, 75,* 241, *262,* 339, *357*
Rock, I., 110, *128*
Rorschach, H., 390, *423*
Rosen, B. C., 188, *190*
Ross, R. T., 85, *102,* 193, *212*
Ruebush, B. K., 172, *190*
Rules, development of, 181
  moral, 204

S

Santa Claus, 168
Sarason, I. G., 172, *190*
Schachter, S., 177, *190*
Schaefer, E. S., 287, 307
Schaffer, H. R., 242, 253, *262,* 359, 360, *388*
Schedule, feeding on, 259
Schema (Piaget), 123, 265
Schizophrenic children, 415-416
School, 379-385
  effect of entering, 379
  and mass media, 378
School-age tests, 346-348
Schramm, W., 377, *388*
Scott, J. P., 237, *262*
Sears, R. R., 203, 212, 259, 260, *262,* 294, 297, 303, *306, 307,* 393, 408, *421, 422*
Secondary addition of classes, 142
Secondary drive, 166, 168
Secondary reinforcement, 167
Segregation, 12
Selective attention, 91
Selective breeding, 16, 19, 20
Self-concept, 403
Semantics, 326
Sensitization, Rh, 229
Sensory abilities, 53
Sensory enrichment, 81
Sensory-motor functions, 122
  coordination, 266
  and early experience, 264
Sensory-motor stages (Piaget), 268-277
  Stage 1 (reflex), 268
  Stage 2 (primary circular), 269
  Stage 3 (secondary circular), 270
  Stage 4 (coordinating), 273
  Stage 5 (tertiary circular), 274
  Stage 6 (productive), 275
Sensory systems (eight) in children, 61
Sequential dependency, 194
Sewell, W. H., 259, *263*
Sex, determination of, 16
  development of, 397-398
  ratio, 17
  type, 409
Shame versus autonomy stage (Erikson), 404
Sheldon, W., 46, *52*
Sherif, M., 371, *388*
Sherman, M., 63, 73, *76,* 175, *190,* 233, *235,* 340, *357*
Signal-to-noise ratio, 55, 58
Siipola, E. M., 94, *102*
Silfen, C., 67, *76*
Skinner, B. F., 117, *128,* 180, *190*
Slater, E., 25, *27*
Sleep, 233
Slobin, D. I., 327, *330*
Smiley, S. S., 150, *159*
Smiling, 25, 360
Smith, A. S., 373, *388*
Smith, J. M., *76*
Smith, M. K., 316, *330*
Smock, C. D., 91, *102*
Smoking, influence on foetus, 228
Social class, and abnormal behavior, 25
  and parent-child relations, 297-299
  and peer relations, 373
Social conditioning, 119, 120
Social reinforcement, 117, 173
Social relations, infant, 358
Sociometric method, 371-372
Sontag, L. W., 395, *423*
Space, 279-280
Spatial displacement, 276
Spearman, C., 334, *357*
Specific nerve energies, 69
Spectral sensitivity, 65
Sperry, R. W., 217, *235*
Spiker, C. C., *127*
Spitz, R. A., 243, *263,* 360, *388*
Spock, B., 298, *307*
Spontaneous recovery, 109
Stage theory, 268
Stages of personality (Erikson), 403-405
Staples, R., 64, *76*
Stevenson, H. W., 173, *190-191*
Stimulus-preference method, 85, 86
Stranger anxiety, 242, 360
Street, R. F., 93, *102*
Structure (Piaget), 122, 264
Stubbs, E. M., 67, *77*
Sublimation, 398, 412
Sucking, 161

Suggestibility, 374
Superego, 202, 203
Suppes, P., 112, 114, *128,* 152, *159*
Surrogate mother, 162, 163
Swaddling, 44
Symbolic representation, 132, 133
Symmetrical relations, 145
  See also Oedipal situation

T

Tabula rasa, 80
Tachistoscopic recognition, 95
Talbot-Plateau effect, 65
"Talking typewriter," 98
Tanner, J. M., 47, *52*
Target-seeking growth, 47
Taste, 68, 69
TAT, 46
Teacher(s), 379–383
  and approval-disapproval, 382–383
  attitudes of, 380–381
  problems of, 382
Teidemann, D., 48, *52*
Telegraphic speech, 315
Terman, L. M., 5, *27,* 332, 338, 354, *357,* 371, *388*
Test(s), infant, 342
  intelligence, 341–348
  preschool, 345–346
  projective, 390
  school-age, 346–348
Thematic Apperception Test (TAT), 46
Theories of play, 361
Thermal sensitivity, 72
Thomas, D. S., 371, *388*
Thompson, H., *51*
Thompson, W. R., 241, *263*
Thomson, R. J., 378, *388*
Thorndike, E. L., 334, *357*
Thought, preoperational, 132–134
Threshold, 54
Thurstone, T., 334, *357*
Time, 280
Tolman, E. C., 106, *128*
Torgerson, W. S., 85, *102*
Touch, 70
Transformations, 136, 317–318, 325–328
Transitivity, 144, 194, 196
Tree diagram (derivation diagram), 324
Trust versus mistrust stage (Erikson), 404
Tryon, R., 20, 21, *27*
Twins, 20, 22
Two-person interaction, 367–368

V

Validity, 336
Value and perception, 99
Van Leeuwenhoek, A., 4, *27*
Velten, H. V., 309, *330*
Victorian notions, 257
  See also Puritan ethic
Visual acuity, 66
Visual cliff, 87
Von Senden, M., 241, *263*

W

Walk, R. D., 87, 88, *103,* 241, 263
Walker, R., 47, *52*
Walking, 36
  stages of, 38, 39
Walters, R. H., 120, *129,* 168, *191*
Watson, J. B., 5, *27,* 71, *77,* 107, *129,* 139, 159, 167, 168, *191,* *277,* *285*
Watson, J. D., 14, 15, *27*
Weaning, 259
Wechsler, D., 332, 357
Wechsler Intelligence Scale for Children, 346–348
Weir, M. W., 127, *129,* 313, *330*
Weisberg, P., 121, *129*
Weismann, A., 10, *27*
Wenar, C., 292, *307*
Wertheimer, M., 79, *103*
White, B. L., 87, *103*
Whiting, J. M., 296, *307*
Whole-part perception, 92
Wickman, E. K., 380, *388*
Will, 192
  See also Puritan ethic
Winterbottom, M. R., 187, *191,* *386,* 395, *423*
WISC, 346–348
Wolff, K., 4, *27*
Wolff, P. H., 360, 388
Woodworth, R. S., 70, *77*
Working mothers, 301
Wright, H. F., 376, *388*
Wug, 318

XYZ

X-rays, influence on foetus, 230
Yes-no detection, 55
Zelhart, P., 94, *103*

THE MathML HANDBOOK

LIMITED WARRANTY AND DISCLAIMER OF LIABILITY

THE MATHML HANDBOOK

PAVI SANDHU

CHARLES RIVER MEDIA, INC.
Hingham, Massachusetts

Publisher: David Pallai
Production: Devi Information Systems
Cover Design: The Printed Image

CHARLES RIVER MEDIA, INC.
20 Downer Avenue, Suite 3
Hingham, Massachusetts 02043
781-740-0400
781-740-8816 (FAX)
info@charlesriver.com
www.charlesriver.com

This book is printed on acid-free paper.

Pavi Sandhu. *The MathML Handbook*.
ISBN: 1-58450-249-5

Library of Congress Cataloging-in-Publication Data

Sandhu, Pavi.
The MathML handbook / Pavi Sandhu.–1st ed.
p. cm.
ISBN 1-58450-249-5 (pbk. : acid-free paper)
1. MathML (Document markup language) I. Title.
QA41.6 .S36 2002
510'.285'572–dc21
2002012912

Printed in the United States of America
02 7 6 5 4 3 2 First Edition

CHARLES RIVER MEDIA titles are available for site license or bulk purchase by institutions, user groups, corporations, etc. For additional information, please contact the Special Sales Department at 781-740-0400.

Requests for replacement of a defective CD-ROM must be accompanied by the original disc, your mailing address, telephone number, date of purchase and purchase price. Please state the nature of the problem, and send the information to CHARLES RIVER MEDIA, INC., 20 Downer Avenue, Suite 3, Hingham, Massachusetts 02043. CRM's sole obligation to the purchaser is to replace the disc, based on defective materials or faulty workmanship, but not on the operation or functionality of the product.

CONTENTS

Acknowledgments		ix
Preface		xi
Foreword		xvii
Part I MathML Concepts		**1**
Chapter 1	**Introduction to MathML**	**3**
1.1	What is MathML?	4
1.2	A History of MathML	5
1.3	Other Methods of Displaying Mathematics on the Web	7
1.4	The Design of MathML	9
1.5	Applications of MathML	12
Chapter 2	**XML Primer**	**17**
2.1	XML and HTML	18
2.2	Elements and Attributes	21
2.3	Other Types of Markup	24
2.4	DTDs	25
2.5	Entities	28
2.6	Namespaces	31
2.7	XML and Unicode	32
Chapter 3	**Fundamentals of MathML**	**35**
3.1	MathML and XML	36
3.2	Presentation and Content	38
3.3	MathML Attributes	49
3.4	MathML Characters	52
Chapter 4	**Presentation Markup**	**59**
4.1	Introduction	60
4.2	Token Elements	64
4.3	General Layout Elements	77
4.4	Scripts and Limits	87

4.5	Tables and Matrices	92
4.6	Other Elements	99
Chapter 5	**Content Markup**	**103**
5.1	Introduction	104
5.2	Token Elements	107
5.3	Constructor Elements	109
5.4	Operators and Functions	120
5.5	Qualifier Elements	131
5.6	Constants and Symbols	131
5.7	Semantic Mapping Elements	131
5.8	Content Element Attributes	134
Chapter 6	**Combining Presentation and Content Markup**	**139**
6.1	Introduction	140
6.2	Mixed Markup	141
6.3	Parallel Markup	146
Part II	**Working with MathML**	**153**
Chapter 7	**Displaying MathML in Web Browsers**	**155**
7.1	Introduction	156
7.2	The Universal MathML Stylesheet	160
7.3	MathML-enabled Browsers	164
7.4	Add-on Software	172
7.5	Choosing a Display Method	189
Chapter 8	**Applying Styles and Transformations**	**193**
8.1	Introduction	194
8.2	CSS Primer	195
8.3	Using CSS with MathML	197
8.4	XSLT Primer	204
8.5	Using XSLT with MathML	212
Chapter 9	**Authoring and Editing MathML**	**231**
9.1	Introduction	232
9.2	*MathType*	233
9.3	*WebEQ*	238
9.4	*Mathematica*	244
9.5	*Publicon*	250
9.6	*Scientific Word*	254
9.7	*Amaya*	257
9.8	*EzMath*	262
9.9	Choosing an Authoring Tool	265

Chapter 10 Converting Between TEX and MathML **269**
10.1 Introduction 270
10.2 Entering Formulas in LATEX 273
10.3 Converting Individual Formulas 277
10.4 Converting Complete Documents 286
10.5 Converting XML+MathML to TEX 294

Chapter 11 Using MathML for Computations **307**
11.1 Introduction 308
11.2 *Mathematica* 309
11.3 *Maple* 327

Chapter 12 Creating Dynamic Math Web Pages **339**
12.1 Introduction 340
12.2 JavaScript and HTML 342
12.3 *WebEQ* 345
12.4 IBM *techexplorer* 369
12.5 Doing Computations on the Server 375
12.6 web*Mathematica* 377
12.7 *MapleNET* 390

Part III References **397**

Chapter 13 Presentation Elements **399**
13.1 Introduction 400
13.2 Listing of Presentation Elements 400

Chapter 14 Content Elements **427**
14.1 Introduction 428
14.2 Listing of Content Elements 429

Chapter 15 MathML Characters **477**
15.1 Introduction 478
15.2 Character Tables 478

Appendix A About the CD-ROM **491**

Appendix B MathML Resources **497**

Index **503**

ACKNOWLEDGMENTS

I am indebted to many people for making this book possible. First and foremost, I want to thank the members of the W3C Math Working Group for applying their talent and hard work in creating the MathML specification.

Stephen Wolfram and George Beck encouraged and supported the project from the very beginning. The following people gave freely of their time in answering my questions or providing feedback on specific parts of the manuscript: Amy Young, Bobby Hoggard, Brendan Elli, Chris Hill, David Arcoleo, Jeff Bryant, Greg Martel, Michael Trott, Sebastian Rahtz, Shaun McCance, and Shreya Mago. I owe a special thanks to Andy Hunt for his help with generating the character tables.

Laurent Bernard of Waterloo Maple, Robert Miner of Design Science, and Samuel Dooley of IBM provided information on prerelease versions of software. The technical reviewers—Eric Lengyel, Neil Soiffer, and Robert Miner—helped eliminate errors and provided valuable suggestions for improving the manuscript. Any errors that remain are, of course, entirely my responsibility.

I am grateful to Vicki Harding and David Rogelberg for their role in initiating this project, to David Pallai for taking a chance on a first-time author, and to the staff at Charles River Media for their fine work in editing, designing, and producing the book.

Finally, I would like to thank my wife Anu for her love and support at all stages of this project. Her advice and encouragement were invaluable during the long months it took to complete this book.

PREFACE

MathML is a markup language for describing the visual structure and meaning of mathematical formulas. It was developed by the World Wide Web Consortium (W3C) primarily for displaying mathematics in Web pages. The goal of MathML is to do for mathematics what Hypertext Markup Language (HTML) did for text; that is, to allow equations to be freely exchanged, processed, and displayed over the Web. This has long been an important goal for scientific communication, but it has proved impossible to do with existing techniques.

MathML can describe the symbolic meaning of mathematics, not just its notation. As a result, equations expressed in MathML can be searched, indexed, archived, interpreted, and evaluated by software applications designed for that purpose. This makes MathML an ideal format for exchanging mathematical content between applications such as Web browsers, equation editors, computer algebra systems, and other scientific software.

It is already possible to view MathML equations in most Web browsers, either directly or using free add-on software. In addition, a wide variety of software tools are available for authoring MathML and for converting mathematical content in other formats into MathML. After many years of development, MathML is finally ready for widespread adoption by a mainstream audience. However, at this time the only reliable source for learning about MathML is the W3C specification, which is intended mainly as a reference for specialists. There is, hence, a need for a clear and comprehensive account of MathML that will make the details of this language and its use accessible to the average user. This book was written to fill that need.

WHO THIS BOOK IS FOR

This book will be useful to anybody interested in learning about MathML and its potential for communicating mathematics on the

Web. Some of this book's specific audiences—which are overlapping rather than mutually exclusive—are listed below:

- Researchers in technical fields like mathematics, physics, and engineering who wish to share their work with colleagues and distribute content over the Web
- Educators and students at universities, colleges, and high schools who have a special interest in developing courseware and other instructional materials for use over the Web
- Web developers who want to create dynamic Web sites for displaying interactive mathematical content
- Programmers who need to develop new MathML-based applications or modify existing applications to support MathML
- Managers who need to understand the significance of MathML to evaluate whether it should play a role in their company's documentation strategy
- Users of computer algebra systems such as *Mathematica, Maple,* and *Mathcad*
- Users of mathematical typesetting systems such as $\TeX$ and $\LaTeX$
- Academic and commercial publishers who need to archive and distribute technical documents in electronic form

This book is both a primer that introduces the fundamental concepts of MathML as well as a detailed and comprehensive reference guide. It includes the following elements:

- An overview of MathML—its origin, importance, and practical applications.
- A tutorial introduction to MathML with detailed examples to illustrate the syntax.
- A review of free and commercial software for viewing and authoring MathML. This includes browsers, plug-ins, authoring tools, and mathematical software.
- A discussion of how to use Cascading Style Sheets (CSS) and Extensible Stylesheet Language for Transformations (XSLT) in rendering MathML for display.
- Practical information on converting $\TeX$ documents to MathML.
- A complete listing of all tags and attributes organized in a systematic way for ready reference.

The discussion of MathML syntax in this book closely follows the W3C specification but with some important differences. Some technical details, such as the concept of embellished operators or the algorithm for determining alignment in tables, have been omitted since they are not essential for a general understanding of MathML.

To make the material more accessible, discussion of many topics has been simplified and a number of additional examples have been provided.

Athough a basic familiarity with HTML and XML is useful, you do not need to know programming to understand the material in this book. To make the book as self-contained as possible, Chapter 2 briefly describes all XML concepts you do need to know in order to understand MathML.

HOW THIS BOOK IS ORGANIZED

The book consists of 15 chapters divided into three parts:

- Part I explains the key features of MathML syntax.
- Part II provides information on using MathML for specific tasks.
- Part III contains reference information on MathML.

A brief description of the contents of each chapter is given below.

Part I MathML Concepts

Chapter 1, "Introduction to MathML," gives the background needed to understand the origin, goals, and benefits of MathML.
Chapter 2, "XML Primer," reviews the XML concepts needed for understanding MathML.
Chapter 3, "Fundamentals of MathML," explains the basic features of presentation and content markup. It also gives an overview of the character entities defined by the MathML Document Type Definition (DTD).
Chapter 4, "Presentation Markup," describes the different types of presentation elements and gives examples of their use.
Chapter 5, "Content Markup," describes the different types of content elements and gives examples of their use.
Chapter 6, "Combining Presentation and Content Markup," explains the reasons and rules for combining presentation and content markup.

Part II Working with MathML

Chapter 7, "Displaying MathML in Web Browsers," gives an overview of the current support for MathML in Web browsers and provides information on how to author MathML documents for display on the Web.

Chapter 8, "Applying Styles and Transformations," summarizes the basic principles and syntax of CSS and XSLT stylesheets and gives examples of their applications to MathML documents.

Chapter 9, "Authoring and Editing MathML," reviews the software tools available for authoring and editing MathML content.

Chapter 10, "Converting between TEX and MathML," reviews the tools and techniques available for converting TEX documents into XHTML and MathML, and vice versa.

Chapter 11, "Using MathML for Computations," provides an overview of the two major computer algebra systems—*Mathematica* and *Maple*—that can perform computations using MathML.

Chapter 12, "Developing Dynamic MathWeb Pages," provides detailed information on using MathML to create dynamic Web pages that feature interactive mathematical content.

Part III Reference

Chapter 13, "Presentation Elements," gives an alphabetical listing of all presentation elements with a description of each element's usage, syntax, and attributes.

Chapter 14, "Content Elements," gives an alphabetical listing of all content elements with a description of each element's usage, syntax, and attributes.

Chapter 15, "MathML Characters," contains a set of character tables that show glyphs for all the characters defined in the MathML DTD and their position in Unicode.

Appendix A, "About the CD-ROM," contains a list of software included with the book, along with system requirements and installation information.

Appendix B, "MathML Resources," provides a list of resources relevant for MathML users such as Web sites, software products, e-mail discussion lists, and books.

Style Conventions

Names of all elements and attributes as well as all examples of XML, MathML, and HTML markup are shown in a `monospaced` font. URLs and product names are shown in *italics*.

REQUEST FOR COMMENTS

We welcome feedback on this book from readers. We invite you to contribute comments, report errors, or suggest topics you would like to see covered in future editions. You can contact us by any of the following means:

Mail: Charles River Media, 20 Downer Ave., Suite 3, Hingham, MA 02043
Phone: 781-740-0400
E-mail: *info@charlesriver.com*

Please consult the Web site for this book at *www.charlesriver.com/titles/mathml.html* for the latest updates and errata.

FOREWORD

I got involved with the Math Activity at the World Wide Web Consortium (W3C) in 1995. Ever since, I have attended two or three meetings a year on the topic of MathML. At nearly every one of those meetings, the need for a book on MathML has come up in one way or another. Anyone who has slogged through the MathML specification will know that it is neither an enjoyable read, nor a very good way to learn about using MathML. So the topic of an accessible book on MathML kept coming up, and the anxiety and hand-wringing it provoked became more and more intense as the MathML community continued to grow. Thus, I was relieved when I learned that Pavi Sandhu was writing a book on MathML. And after looking at a draft and discovering it was actually a good book on MathML, I was positively delighted!

It couldn't come at a better time. When the *MathML Recommendation* was first published in 1998, there was an initial surge in interest, and expectations were high. A number of specialized tools soon added MathML support. But rendering MathML in browsers proved to be a harder problem and only in the last few months has it really become practical on a large scale. In the intervening time, the lack of browser support had a distinctly chilling effect on the use and usefulness of MathML.

Now, however, MathML support is finally there in browsers, and there are clear signs of a resurgence. Publishers are again looking at MathML as a way of moving to XML work flows for their math and science materials, and as a means of unifying production streams for paper and electronic media. Distance learning vendors have begun embracing MathML as a solution for archiving, displaying, and manipulating mathematics on the Web. Makers of XML authoring tools and content management systems are starting to add MathML support. And most important, thousands of teachers, students and researchers are beginning to wonder if Math on the Web has finally come far enough to take a second look.

I confidently predict that with resources such as *The MathML Handbook* to guide them, many people will find that the time is indeed ripe for Math on the Web. And I look eagerly forward to the outpouring of creativity that will inevitably flow from that happy discovery.

Robert Miner
MathML 2.0 Recommendation Editor

PART

I

MathML Concepts

CHAPTER

1

INTRODUCTION TO MATHML

This chapter gives the background you need to understand the origin, goals, and benefits of MathML. It explains the problems with current ways of representing mathematics on the Web and shows why MathML is an effective solution to these problems. It describes the history of MathML and explains its relation to other Web standards such as HTML and XML. Finally, it describes the various practical uses of MathML such as Web publishing and interchange of mathematical content between applications.

1.1 What Is MathML?

MathML, the Mathematical Markup Language, is an XML application for encoding mathematics on the Web. It provides a simple but precise syntax for encoding both the visual structure and the symbolic meaning of mathematics. Using MathML, you can display even the most complex mathematical notation in a Web page with a high degree of fidelity and clarity. At the same time, the meaning of the notation can be preserved so that, for example, you can copy and paste an equation from a Web page into a computer algebra system for evaluation.

MathML was the first XML application endorsed by the W3C and is supported by major software vendors (including IBM, HP, Microsoft, and Sun) as well as by professional organizations such as the American Mathematical Society (AMS). Currently, a major development effort to create tools for authoring, rendering, and processing MathML is underway. This includes support for displaying MathML in leading Web browsers including *Internet Explorer* (*IE*), *Netscape*, and *Mozilla*.

As a common and widely accepted standard for representing mathematics, MathML provides the foundation for many interesting and useful applications. For example, using MathML you can develop dynamic math Web sites that feature interactive equations; create a database of technical documents whose contents can be easily searched, indexed, and archived; or develop speech synthesis software for the aural rendering of mathematics.

MathML is simple enough to be readable by humans but is also well suited for being generated and processed by software. It is also flexible and extensible—it includes methods for modifying the meaning of existing notation and for describing new notation that the current syntax does not support. This is important since mathematical notation is continually evolving, making it impossible for any fixed set of constructs to describe all possible notations.

MathML was specifically designed to work well with existing Web technologies. MathML equations can be dynamically processed using JavaScript and Java, styled using CSS and XSLT, or hooked up to HTML controls like buttons and pull-down menus. The combination of scripting and MathML makes it possible to create interactive Web sites that can display and manipulate mathematical content. This is an important requirement for teaching, research, and anywhere else that mathematics is important.

Since MathML is an XML application, general XML tools such as XML editors and parsers can process it. In particular, mathematical notation from a single MathML source file can be rendered in diverse media such as Web pages, print, and audio by using different CSS or XSLT stylesheets, each optimized for a specific medium.

Because it is written in plain text, MathML is portable and platform independent. This makes it a convenient medium for exchanging mathematical content between diverse applications such as Web browsers, word processors, equation editors, as well as computer algebra systems and other scientific software. MathML is thus well suited to becoming a standard format for storing and communicating mathematical information.

1.2 A History of MathML

Since its inception in the early 1990s, the World Wide Web has transformed the way people exchange and receive information. With the rapid development of browser technology, the varied enhancements to the HTML language, and the advent of stylesheet mechanisms, the Web has evolved into a rich and versatile medium. It is now possible to create Web pages that contain frames, buttons, and forms; include rich content in the form of animations, sound, and video; as well as respond dynamically to user actions using applets and scripting languages.

Despite all these impressive developments, current Web technology still has its share of weaknesses. Notable among these is the lack of adequate support for displaying mathematical content. Most current methods for representing mathematics in Web pages have severe limitations. This situation is all the more surprising given that the Web was invented by scientists for the exchange of scientific information, which typically makes intensive use of mathematical notation.

With the overwhelming success and popularity of the Web in the 1990s, the need for a suitable method to represent mathematics on the Web became increasingly acute. Some mathematicians and programmers recognized that a markup language was needed, one that would overcome the limitations of HTML and allow mathematical notation to be displayed on the Web in all its richness and complexity.

After the W3C was formed in 1994, it began looking into the issue of representing mathematics on the Web. The W3C's initial efforts focused on developing a special set of tags that could be incorporated into a future version of HTML. In 1994, Dave Raggett submitted a proposal for HTML Math, which was to be included in the HTML 3.0 working draft. In 1996, formal support for the new mathematical tags was added as part of HTML 3.2. However, due to lack of interest from major browser vendors, this approach failed to get wide acceptance.

In 1997, the W3C Math Working Group was formed. By this time, XML had emerged as a widely accepted standard for extending HTML. The Math Working Group therefore decided to create a new XML-based language, separate from HTML, to be called Mathematical Markup Language (or MathML). The first version of this language, MathML 1.0, was released as a W3C recommendation in April 1998.

An extended and refined version, MathML 2.0 was released on February 21, 2001. This version added some new tags and attributes as well as deprecated a few existing features. Its goal was to provide greater consistency and compatibility with other Web technologies, including CSS, Extensible Stylesheet Language (XSL), and Document Object Model (DOM). MathML 2.0 also supports a larger range of extended characters than MathML 1.0. Version 2.0 defines named entity references for about 2,500 special characters and symbols.

The W3C's *Amaya* and the open-source browser *Mozilla*, were the first browsers to include native support for MathML. Over the last year (that is, in 2002), there has been important progress in making MathML viewable on a wide variety of browsers and platforms. The release of *Netscape* 7.0 means that MathML display is now natively supported in at least one mainstream browser. *IE* and older versions of *Netscape* can display MathML using freely available add-on software. The W3C has also provided a Universal MathML stylesheet that eliminates many of the incompatibility issues between different browsers and add-on software. Many free and commercial tools for authoring and editing MathML content are available. Several leading mathematical software applications, such as *Mathematica* and *Maple*, support MathML as a format for importing or exporting formulas. All of these developments mean that it is easier than ever before to create and display MathML on the Web.

1.3 Other Methods of Displaying Mathematics on the Web

Despite the importance of mathematics for scientific communication, few effective solutions to the problem of displaying mathematical notation in Web pages have been put forth. Most mathematical content currently available on the Web is based on using either images or Portable Document Format (PDF) files. However, both of these methods have severe limitations.

Images

The simplest way to include mathematical formulas in a Web page is to represent each formula as an image, typically in GIF or JPEG format. However, this approach has some severe drawbacks:

- If a page has many equations, each of them must be stored as a separate image. This leads to large file sizes and long download times.
- The quality of the images is poor, which is undesirable for both viewing online and printing. Images typically have a resolution of 72 or 96 dpi while the surrounding text has a resolution of 300 or 600 dpi. This disparity in resolution makes the images difficult to read.
- Equations displayed as images cannot be integrated with the surrounding text. For example, the spacing and alignment of the equations cannot be adjusted to be correct relative to the adjacent text. Further, the font size, style, and color used to display the equation are fixed and cannot be updated to reflect changes in the display environment.
- When you save an equation as an image, all information about the meaning of the equation is lost. This makes it impossible to search, archive, index, or otherwise process mathematical information. For example, consider the following equation: $x^n + y^n = z^n$. If this equation is encoded textually using an appropriate markup language, you can search through a database and retrieve all documents containing the equation. If the equation is stored as an image, however, there is no way to search for the equation.
- Equations stored as images cannot be copied and pasted from one application to another, limiting your ability to reuse the information.

PDF Files

Another popular method for communicating mathematical content on the Web is using PDF files. The needed mathematical fonts are embedded in the PDF file, which leads to a high-quality, high-resolution document suitable for viewing and printing. However, PDF files suffer from several problems:

- The display of PDF files requires a special viewer application, which must be specially installed and takes extra time to launch.
- PDF files cannot be well integrated with the Web environment. Since the PDF reader takes over the entire browser window, you cannot combine equations in PDF form with other Web content such as HTML markup and images.
- Mathematical content in PDF files cannot be copied and pasted into other applications and still retain its structure. This makes the information less portable and reusable.

For these reasons, PDF files are at best a workaround to the problem and not a complete solution.

Other Markup Languages

Before the advent of the Web, scientists were already using markup languages to encode mathematics. In particular, the TEX system invented by Donald Knuth in the 1970s was widely adopted by the phys ics and mathematics communities. However, TEX documents cannot be displayed on the Web without complex processing. Although, several tools and utilities to automatically convert TEX documents into HTML exist, they are difficult to use. Also, the equations are, in any case, stored as images so you encounter all the problems discussed earlier.

In addition, TEX is primarily a formatting language. It is designed only to encode information about the visual appearance of mathematics, not its meaning. TEX is therefore unsuitable for applications where the meaning of mathematics is important, such as computer algebra systems.

Other markup languages besides TEX have been developed to represent mathematics. The two most notable ones are ISO 12083 and OpenMath. ISO 12083 is a Standard Generalized Markup Language (SGML) application for representing mathematical notation. Like TEX, ISO 12083 is a presentational language only and does not directly encode the meaning of mathematical expressions.

OpenMath, on the other hand, is a standard specifically developed for encoding the semantic meaning of mathematics (*www.openmath.org*). OpenMath uses content dictionaries written in a special XML format for defining the meaning of mathematical objects. In fact, MathML makes use of the OpenMath specification to define the logical meaning of all content elements that represent operators and functions. However, the focus of OpenMath is on describing semantics and it does not address the issue of representing mathematical notation at all. In a sense, OpenMath is like the converse of presentational languages like TEX and ISO 12083.

1.4 The Design of MathML

Creating a markup language to faithfully render mathematical notation is an extremely complex problem, for several reasons. First, unlike text, mathematics has a two-dimensional structure. This means that the markup language has to indicate information about the relative positioning of characters along both the horizontal and vertical axes.

Second, mathematics makes use of a very large number of special characters and symbols, each of which has a precise meaning depending on the context. Any language for representing mathematics must therefore find a way to deal with several thousand special characters and the fonts that represent them.

Third, mathematical notation relies upon a large number of typesetting conventions that have evolved over centuries of use. For example, variables that denote numbers are usually displayed in an italic font that is different from the usual italic text font. Also, the spacing around operators, such as + and =, is different from that of text, to reflect conventions about operator precedence.

There are many other conventions, such as the rules for choosing the size of parentheses and the proper alignment of subscripts and superscripts, as well as more specialized conventions used in specific sub-fields of mathematics. Any markup language that seeks to represent mathematical notation faithfully must respect all these conventions.

These conventions of mathematical notation are relevant both in authoring the markup and rendering it. The markup must be sufficiently detailed to store complete information about the two-dimensional structure of a formula. At the same time, the rendering application must be aware of all rules and conventions for translating the markup back into the corresponding visual representation.

MathML solves the first problem, namely how to encode the information about mathematical notation. The tasks of rendering the notation or interpreting its mathematical meaning are left to supporting software such as a browser, an equation editor, or a computer algebra system. MathML specifies guidelines for how specific elements should be rendered but, in general, rendering applications are free to use their own rules as long as the basic conventions of mathematical typesetting are observed.

The W3C's Math Working Group gave itself several challenging design goals in developing the specifications for MathML:

- MathML should encode both mathematical notation and mathematical meaning.
- MathML should be readable by humans but simple enough for software to generate and process.
- MathML should be extensible.
- MathML should provide a convenient medium for exchanging mathematical content between diverse software applications such as computer algebra systems and equation editors.
- MathML should integrate well with the existing Web environment.
- It should be possible to embed MathML in HTML markup so that it is accessible to browsers, search engines, and other Web applications that manipulate HTML.
- It should be possible to render MathML embedded in HTML in current Web browsers.
- It should be easy to convert between MathML and existing mathematical markup languages such as TEX.
- It should be possible to easily modify existing authoring tools to generate MathML.
- It should be easy to render MathML in multiple media such as print, Braille, and speech.

When MathML's creators made it an application of XML, most of these design goals were achieved. XML is an extremely flexible and powerful language, ideally suited for creating structured documents that can be used across multiple platforms. Owing to the rapid growth in the popularity of XML in the last few years, many tools for processing and rendering XML documents are available. These include: editors and parsers for creating and validating XML documents, application programming interface (API) libraries—like Simple API for XML (SAX) and DOM—for manipulating XML, stylesheet mechanisms (like CSS and XSLT) for controlling the display and formatting of XML, as well as support for displaying XML documents in Web browsers. These tools can be used to develop applications for editing, importing, exporting, rendering, and processing MathML. Hence, developers of MathML applications do not have to start from scratch.

The only downside of making MathML an XML application is that XML syntax is extremely verbose. The MathML markup for even a simple one-line equation can extend for over half a page. As a result, MathML is difficult and error prone to edit by hand. However, this is not a serious problem since MathML's creators did not intend for humans to author MathML directly. Rather, most people are expected to use software applications such as equation editors to generate MathML. There are several what-you-see-is-what-you-get (WYSIWYG) equation editors that support MathML as an output format. Typically, you can create a formula by clicking a series of buttons on a palette and then, using an appropriate menu command, convert the formula to MathML for pasting into an HTML document.

MathML is designed to serve as the bottom layer in a two-layer architecture. The top layer consists of software applications that the user directly interacts with (such as equation editors, Web browsers, or computer algebra systems). These applications provide a convenient interface for creating and displaying MathML, while automatically translating the user input into the low-level MathML markup. This arrangement is convenient because the user is insulated from the details of the low-level markup. At the same time, software behind the scenes can easily handle the conversion, since MathML is well suited for automated processing.

Although MathML markup is difficult to author by hand, it is still relatively easy to read and understand. Users with a basic familiarity with the syntax can open a MathML document in a text editor to examine or debug the markup, even if they choose not to author it directly for large-scale applications. In this way, MathML strikes a good balance between the demands of automated processing and human legibility.

This situation is analogous to that with HTML, which can be created by hand. However, the majority of professional Web developers use specialized Web authoring applications to generate the HTML. This allows developers to concentrate on creating the content and shifts the task of generating the underlying markup to the software. However, as with HTML, it is still worthwhile to understand the syntax of MathML so you can debug and modify documents by hand if the need arises.

1.5 APPLICATIONS OF MATHML

The applications of MathML can be divided into five main categories.

- Displaying mathematics in Web pages
- Creating dynamic math Web sites
- Publishing technical information electronically
- Exchanging mathematical data between applications
- Rendering mathematics in non-visual media

Some more details of each of these applications are provided below.

Displaying Mathematics in Web Pages

Using MathML, you can display even the most complicated mathematical notation in a Web browser, and it will be properly formatted according to the standard conventions of mathematical typesetting. Equations can be properly integrated with the surrounding text and can automatically inherit information about fonts and alignment from their environment. Thus, MathML is well suited for scientists, engineers, and other researchers who want to post technical documents on the Web without compromising on the quality of the presentation. At the same time, the equations are "live" and can be copied and pasted from a Web page into another application, allowing formulas to be exchanged and re-used as easily as text or allowing them to be evaluated by mathematical software.

MathML is a convenient medium for educators who want to post assignments and quizzes to support their teaching efforts. MathML is also useful for universities and corporations that provide Web-based instructional courseware. For example, many universities now offer calculus courses over the Web, and many corporations provide technical training to their employees using instructional materials over the Web.

Creating Dynamic Math Web Sites

The above uses of MathML involved the passive display of mathematical content on a Web page. However, MathML can also be used to add interactivity to Web sites. The display of interactive equations is of great importance for applications like educational courseware, online testing, or mathematical bulletin boards, which are useful in a wide variety of academic and professional contexts.

In the last few years, many sophisticated tools have become available for developing dynamic Web sites, which respond to user input. Such Web sites make use of scripting languages like JavaScript or Java applets that can be embedded in Web pages to perform actions in response to specific user actions such as clicking or moving the cursor over some piece of text. It is possible to connect scriptable actions to HTML controls like buttons, text fields, and pull-down menus.

MathML, being a fully Web-compliant language, is well suited for integration with these technologies. Using MathML in concert with scripting languages and applets creates many interesting possibilities for delivering dynamic mathematical content. Some possibilities for interactive behavior are:

- Changing the size or appearance of an equation
- Bringing up a pop-up window or a menu to let the user to choose from various options, such as changing the display size or color
- Toggling between different displays, for example, to expand or collapse a large expression
- Using formulas as hyperlinks to jump to a different document or location
- Clicking a button to bring up the next step in a solution
- Entering the solution to a problem in a text field, and then clicking a button to find out if the solution is right or wrong

You get an additional level of control and flexibility by adding scripts and programs to process mathematical input on the servers. For example, a user can click a button to send mathematical input to a computer algebra system running on the server, which then evaluates the input and returns the result for display on the user's Web page. Such applications are already possible using specialized proprietary software like *WebEQ* or web*Mathematica*. The use of MathML can provide a common standard for implementing such solutions, which will lead to greater interoperability between software from different vendors, as well as for existing programming languages such as Perl, PHP, and Java.

Publishing Technical Information Electronically

A significant feature of scientific publishing in the last few years has been a gradual shift towards archiving and distributing documents in electronic form. Two notable examples are the physics preprint server arXiv (*www.arxiv.org*), housed at Cornell University, and the database maintained by the AMS (*www.ams.org*), which contains over a million mathematical documents.

Almost every major publisher of scientific journals is moving towards providing access to journals in electronic form via a Web site. As a result, the number and size of databases of scientific information, both commercial and academic, are steadily growing. It is vital to have a way of searching, archiving, and indexing the information stored in these databases, and the information needs to be as useful and accessible as possible. Because of its ability to encode the content of equations as well as their appearance, MathML provides an ideal data format for storing mathematical information.

There is also a growing demand for electronic versions of print books that can serve as interactive textbooks. MathML meets the needs of commercial publishers since it provides high-quality rendering of mathematics, is robust enough for large-scale use, and is compatible with SGML-based production systems that are currently in use.

Exchanging Mathematical Data between Applications

MathML can encode both the appearance and meaning of equations, so it can provide a complete and detailed description of all aspects of mathematics. It is thus an ideal format for exchanging mathematical content between applications such as Web browsers, equation editors, computer algebra systems, statistical and data analysis packages, and other scientific software. As the importance of MathML grows and as it is used more frequently, most applications will likely be able to at least import and export mathematical formulas in MathML.

Rendering Mathematics in Non-visual Media

All the applications of MathML discussed above focus on printed and online documents. However, MathML also provides excellent support for rendering mathematics in other media, such as sound and Braille. Being able to support aural rendering of mathematical notation was an important criterion in the design of MathML. Hence, many of the notational conventions of presentation markup were designed to provide enough information to software for creating sensible audio rendering of equations.

For example, proper MathML usage requires that character entities such as `⁢` and `&FunctionApply;` be used in presentation markup to indicate common operations (such as multiplication or function application) that are not readily apparent from the visual display. This provides information about the meaning of the notation that can be reflected in the corresponding audio rendering by changes in intonation or rhythm or the length of pauses.

There has also been a great deal of effort in converting mathematical equations into Braille. For example, using a system called MAVIS developed at the University of New Mexico, you can convert equations in LaTeX into digital instructions for embossing Braille documents. MathML provides enough information about an equation that it should be possible to create software tools that can convert the MathML markup for any given equation directly into Braille output. Such tools do not currently exist, though MathML provides a good foundation for their development in the future.

The Future of MathML

MathML has the potential to transform the publishing, processing, and distribution of technical information. However, the extent to which its potential can be realized depends on the number and quality of available software tools. As we saw earlier in this chapter, MathML is not suitable for direct authoring by users. Instead, it is a low-level format that will typically be generated by specialized software tools, such as equation editors or computer algebra systems.

MathML is still in its early stages of development. Its adoption by a large number of users is limited by the lack of available software, and the development of the required software is limited by the small size of the user base. Several excellent applications for authoring, editing, and viewing MathML documents are already available. However, most of the applications are still evolving and vary considerably in their level of support for MathML and the exact details of implementation.

As with other Web technologies, the initial use of MathML is likely to be confined to specific groups and organizations that have a pressing need to take advantage of the benefits it provides. For example, a college instructor may start using MathML to circulate quizzes and assignments to students of a mathematical course. Or a publisher of research journals may decide to use MathML internally for archiving articles. Such individuals will have a stronger motivation than the average person to invest the time and effort needed to implement customized solutions based on MathML. Also, the small and focused nature of the target audience means that all of the potential users can be guided to install the browsers or other add-on software needed to view MathML.

Modern versions of most browsers already support the display of MathML either directly or with the help of add-on software. However, until the newer browsers become more widely deployed, it will be necessary to support older ones as well. During the initial transitional period, individuals and organizations that post technical documents on the Web can also provide both a MathML version and an image-based version of the same document so that users can choose the version they are comfortable with. This is analogous to Web sites that offer users the option of viewing content with and without frames, a scenario that was very common during the late 1990s.

Initially, MathML use will therefore be confined to small pockets of people who are willing to experiment with this new and developing technology. However, as the number of users grows, the network effect is bound to kick in. The larger number of users will stimulate the development of more software tools, which in turn will provide greater incentive for more people and organizations to adopt MathML as the medium of choice for displaying mathematics on the Web. Once that happens, MathML will finally be able to fulfil its potential. By facilitating the free exchange of mathematical information over the Web and between applications, MathML promises to open up many new possibilities for scientific research, education, and publishing.

CHAPTER

2

XML PRIMER

MathML is an application of XML that is a markup language constructed using the rules of XML. Hence, to properly understand MathML you need to know some XML concepts. This chapter reviews the key features of XML such as elements, attributes, entities, DTDs, and namespaces. If you are already familiar with XML, you can skip ahead to the next chapter.

2.1 XML AND HTML

It is helpful to understand XML by contrasting it with HTML, the markup language that is most familiar to people. An HTML document consists of text marked up by tags that provide information about the text they contain. Each tag can also include attributes that provide additional information about the enclosed text. A Web browser can then use the tags and attributes to display the content in the document. HTML consists of about a hundred different tags with names like `h1`, `h2`, and `p` that provide formatting and layout information. Here is what a typical HTML fragment looks like:

```
<h1>This is a heading.</h1>
 <h2>This is a subheading.</h2>
   <p>Here is a paragraph of text.</p>
```

In contrast to HTML, XML, is a metamarkup language. This means that XML does not specify a fixed set of allowed tags or attributes. Instead, it allows users to define any tags they wish that make sense in the context of what they want to accomplish. For example, a stock transaction could be expressed in XML as:

```
<Stock>
 <Company>Acme Corporation</Company>
   <Ticker>ACME</Ticker>
   <Price>$43.57</Price>
   <Shares>10</Shares>
</Stock>
```

Here, the user specifically defined the `Stock`, `Company`, `Ticker`, `Price`, and `Shares` tag names for this document. The great strength of XML is that it provides a standard framework for constructing new markup languages. A company, organization, professional body, or any other group can use the syntax of XML to define tag names that are meaningful for a specific purpose. This makes XML an extremely flexible and open-ended language that can easily be tailored to fit a wide range of applications.

As you saw in the stock example, XML tag names are usually chosen to describe the meaning of the data they enclose. This allows processing applications to interpret and search the semantic content of the information. For example, you can design search engines to locate specific types of information instead of just looking for literal keywords or strings, greatly increasing the precision and relevance of the results they return. This is not possible with HTML since most HTML tags provide information about the formatting of their content, not its meaning.

Although XML is flexible in its vocabulary, its rules of syntax (which determine how tags and attributes can be combined) are very strictly enforced. An XML document that violates any of these syntax rules is automatically rejected by XML processing tools. In contrast, applications that process HTML are relatively tolerant of minor errors in syntax. For example, an HTML document can contain some overlapping elements as well as elements whose start tag is not followed by an end tag. A typical Web browser will try to guess the correct form for any content that has a nonstandard syntax. If the browser cannot guess the correct form, it will ignore the offending tags and continue processing the rest of the document. This tolerance, though convenient in some ways, is also problematic, since it can lead to different processors treating the same document differently.

The strictness of XML's syntax is a great advantage over HTML because it ensures that XML documents behave in a predictable and orderly fashion. This makes it easier to develop software tools for processing XML. XML's combination of flexibility in its vocabulary and inflexibility in its syntax makes it a much more powerful and versatile language than HTML.

XML and HTML are both derived from another metamarkup language called SGML, which became popular during the 1970s and 1980s. SGML is an extremely powerful language, well suited for creating and maintaining large collections of documents in a format independent of specific software and hardware systems. However, SGML is a very complex language, so it is difficult to understand and implement. As a result, the use of SGML was mainly confined to a few large corporations and government organizations that could afford the huge expense of developing and maintaining SGML-based systems. SGML's biggest success was HTML, which is an application of SGML; that is, a markup language defined according to the syntax rules specified by SGML.

In the early 1990s, Tim-Berners Lee and Anders Berglund at CERN (European Laboratory for Nuclear Research) in Geneva developed HTML. Their goal was to create a compact and efficient way of encoding hypertext documents for exchanging scientific information. However, HTML's impact was felt far beyond the scientific community. Since HTML is a simple language to learn and write software for, it facilitated the development of freely available browser software for viewing HTML documents. Thousands of people all over the world learned HTML and used it to create their own Web pages. HTML thus served as a key catalyst in the emergence of the Web as a revolutionary new medium for mass communication.

However, HTML's greatest strength—its compactness and simplicity—was also its biggest weakness. Despite new extensions to the language in its subsequent versions, HTML was just not powerful enough to support all the complex functionality that browser vendors wanted to implement. The various browser vendors created their own additions and modifications to the language, and the resulting proliferation of incompatible standards became a serious threat to the growth of the Web.

In 1994, the W3C was formed, with participation from both corporate and academic organizations. Its mission was to oversee the development of new standards and technologies for the Web. The W3C's initial efforts focused on adding new features to HTML and creating the specifications for new versions of the language, the last of them being HTML 4.0, released in 1997. However, as the limitations of HTML became more apparent, the W3C decided on an alternative approach.

In 1996, the W3C began work on creating a simplified version of SGML specifically for use on the Web. This "lite" version of SGML was intended to retain most of SGML's strengths while eliminating aspects of the language that were unduly complex or had not proved very useful in practice. The resulting language was XML, and its first official specification was released by the W3C in February 1998.

XML was readily adopted by developers all over the world who had long needed a convenient format for creating structured documents but who had been unwilling to adopt SGML on account of its complexity. In the years following its release, XML has become an extremely popular standard for creating structured documents and data, for Web applications and otherwise. Hundreds of books are devoted to XML, and dozens of free and commercial tools for creating, editing, and manipulating XML documents are available. The popularity of XML has also spawned a whole family of related standards, such as XSL (for formatting and transforming XML documents), XLink (for linking XML documents), and XPath (for specifying parts of an XML document). Taken together, they promise to define the future of the Web platform.

XML has several convenient features:

- It is extensible.
- It is a non-proprietary (or open) standard.
- Being a text-based format, it is platform independent.
- It is based on Unicode, which makes it well suited for internationalization.
- It is widely supported.

Although, users can create an XML document containing any tags they wish, in practice, most XML documents are written in a particular XML application; that is, a specific markup language defined according to the rules of XML, with its own fixed set of tags and attributes. MathML is an application of XML in the same way that HTML is an application of SGML. A large number of XML applications have been defined for specialized purposes in different industries and organizations.

Some prominent examples of XML applications are:

- DocBook: for describing documents such as books, articles, and manuals.
- Chemical Markup Language (CML): for describing the structure of molecules.
- Wireless Markup Language (WML): for describing wireless data. It is part of the Wireless Application Protocol (WAP) specification developed by a consortium of companies including Ericsson, Nokia, and Motorola.
- Scalable Vector Graphics (SVG): for describing two-dimensional graphics. It includes primitives for points, lines, curves, and so on.
- Extensible Business Reporting Language (XBRL): for describing financial statements produced by companies.
- XSL: for formatting and transforming XML documents.
- XHTML: for aiding the transition from HTML to XML. XHTML is an XML version of HTML developed by the W3C. XHTML has the same tags and attributes as HTML, so that XHTML documents can be displayed in any Web browser.

2.2 Elements and Attributes

An XML document consists of text organized into one or more elements. There are two types of elements: *container elements* and *empty elements*. Here is a simple XML document consisting of a single container element:

```
<author>Mark Twain</author>
```

Each container element consists of a start tag followed by some data followed by an end tag. The data enclosed between the start and end tags is called the element's *content*. The start and end tags consist of angle brackets enclosing the name of the element. This syntax is similar to that used in HTML. However, unlike in HTML, XML element names are case sensitive. Hence, the element `title` is different from `Title` and `TITLE`. Element names can contain any number of letters, numbers, underscores, hyphens, or periods but they must start with a letter or underscore.

The second type of XML element is called a canonically empty element, because it cannot contain any content. An empty element has the syntax `<blank/>`. This can also be written in the equivalent form `<blank></blank>`; that is, like a container element without any content. Both forms can be used interchangeably, but the single-tag form, `<blank/>`, is more common, since it is more compact and it emphasizes that this is an empty element.

Although they do not contain any data, empty elements can still provide useful information based on the position in which they occur and the value of their attributes.

Each element can have one or more attributes. An *attribute* is a parameter that describes some property of the element in which it occurs. The attributes for an element are always specified in the start tag after the element name, as shown in this example:

```
<author country="U.S.">Mark Twain</author>
```

The value of an attribute is always enclosed in either single quotation marks or double quotation marks. Here the attribute `country` has the value `"U.S."`. Attributes can be set up to have a default value that is automatically assumed if you do not explicitly specify a value.

An element can have any number of attributes as long as each attribute has a unique name. Here is an example of an element with three attributes:

```
<point xcoord="1.2" ycoord="3.1" zcoord="6.0">
```

When you are constructing an XML document, you can often describe the same information either by using an element or an attribute. For instance, the information in the three-element example can also be described in XML in the following way:

```
<point>
 <xcoord>1.2</xcoord>
 <ycoord>3.1</ycoord>
 <zcoord>6.0</zcoord>
</point>
```

Here, information about each coordinate is given in a separate element instead of as an attribute to the `point` element. There is no hard and fast rule for deciding when to use elements or attributes. In general, your own taste and judgment mainly determine whether you choose one or the other. However, elements are usually preferable in the following two situations:

- When you are encoding a parameter that can take multiple values such as a person's name, phone number, or occupation. Attributes are unsuitable for this purpose, since a given attribute can take only one value.
- When you are encoding information that has a complex structure, such as a name. This is because the substructure of the name (that is, the first name, last name, and middle initial) can be encoded by additional elements. It is not possible to do this using attributes, since an attribute value can only be a simple text string.

The content of an element can be character data, other XML elements, or a mixture of the two. Here is an example of an XML document showing an element that contains other elements:

```
<book>
 <title>Huckleberry Finn</title>
 <author>Mark Twain</author>
</book>
```

We say that the `book` element is the *parent* of the `title` and `author` elements. Conversely, the `title` and `author` elements are called *children* of the `book` element and *siblings* of each other. XML documents have a tree structure with each element corresponding to a single node of the tree. The root of the document tree in the above example is the `book` element, and the branches of the tree are the `author` and `title` elements.

Each XML document must have exactly one root element. However, the tree can contain any number of branches, nested however deep you like. Here is a slightly more complicated XML document, with three levels of parent-child relationships:

```
<library>
 <book>
   <title>Huckleberry Finn</title>
   <author>Mark Twain
     <born>1835</born>
     <died>1910</died>
   </author>
 </book>
 <book>
   <title>Moby Dick</title>
   <author>Herman Melville
     <born>1819</born>
     <died>1891</died>
   </author>
 </book>
</library>
```

2.3 Other Types of Markup

The document tree is where the bulk of the useful information in an XML document resides. However, some information (such as the XML *declaration*) appears outside the document tree as well. The XML declaration is a statement that identifies the document as being written in XML. It appears at the beginning of the document before the root element. An XML declaration is not required but it is a good practice to include one. Here is what a typical XML declaration looks like:

```
<?xml version="1.0" encoding="US-ASCII" standalone="yes"?>
```

The XML declaration accepts the following three attributes. The first attribute is required while the other two are optional:

- `version`—This specifies the version of XML the document conforms to. This attribute must always have the value 1.0 since that is the only version of XML currently defined. Other values may become possible if and when the W3C releases a later XML version.
- `standalone`—This has the value `no` if the document references an external DTD and the value `yes` if the XML document does not refer to a DTD or refers to an internal DTD (that is, a DTD included in the document itself). See Section 2.4 for an explanation of DTDs.
- `encoding`—This specifies the character encoding used for the text in the XML document. By default, the text in any XML document is assumed to be in the UTF-8 encoding of the

Unicode character set. However, you can specify a different encoding scheme using this attribute.

Two other types of markup that can occur in an XML document are *comments* and *processing instructions*. These can occur either as part of an element's content or before or after the root element. However, they cannot appear inside a tag; that is, within the angled brackets containing the tag name.

Authors typically use comments to provide information about the document (such as the date it was last modified) or what changes were made to it. Any text that is enclosed by the delimiters `<!--` and `-->` is regarded as a comment and is ignored by XML processors. Here is an example:

```
<?xml version="1.0"?>
<!-- The document tree starts here.-->
 <client>
   <name>Jim Jones</name> <!-- The client's name -->
   <number>217-352-3717</number>
   <!-- The client's number -->
 </client>
<!-- The document tree ends here.-->
```

Processing instructions contain information that a processing application can use to decide how to handle specific parts of the XML document. One important use of processing instructions is for specifying a stylesheet to be used with the document. Here is an example:

```
<?xml-stylesheet type="text/xsl"
href="http://www.w3.org/Math/XSL/mathml.xsl"?>
```

The `type` attribute specifies the format of the stylesheet, while the `href` attribute gives its location, either as an absolute or relative Universal Resource Locator (URL). We'll see examples of using stylesheet-processing instructions with MathML documents in Chapters 7 and 8.

2.4 DTDs

A document that conforms to the basic rules of XML syntax is said to be well formed. Some typical rules a well-formed document must follow are:

- It must have exactly one root element.
- Every start tag must have a matching end tag.
- Elements cannot overlap.

- Attribute values must be enclosed in quotation marks.
- No element can have two attributes with the same name.
- The character data of an element or attribute cannot contain any literal < or & signs.
- Comments cannot appear inside tags.

When creating an XML document, you can define your own tags and attributes to create what is called *free-form XML*. As long as your document is well formed, standard XML tools such as parsers can accept and process it.

Free-form XML offers the greatest flexibility since you can create your own tag names and assign to them any meaning you choose. However, free-form XML documents are not very useful as a medium for communicating information. If you exchange your document with other people, they may not know the specific meaning of the tag names you used. Hence, they cannot easily search, modify, or manipulate the information contained in your document.

For documents to be publicly exchanged, it is important that they be composed according to an agreed-upon standard. For this reason, most XML documents used for real-world applications are restricted to using a specific set of tags and attributes, whose meaning and usage are clearly defined. Such documents are said to conform to a specific document type.

The document type determines the list of tags and attributes that can be used in a document as well as other details (such as which elements can be nested inside other elements and in what order). In XML, information of this type is specified using a special document called a Document Type Definition (DTD). A DTD is written in a formal syntax, defined by the XML specification. The DTD syntax is hard for humans to read because it is intended mainly for use by XML processors. Also, the DTD provides only the bare minimum information needed to define a particular document format. To explain the meaning and usage of the various elements and attributes, some additional documentation is usually necessary to supplement the information in the DTD.

You can define your own DTDs to formalize the structure and vocabulary of any XML document that you create. Various groups have defined a large number of public DTDs to provide a standard XML document format for a specific purpose. Each XML format defined by a specific DTD is called an *XML application*, because it is an application of XML to a specific field, such as mathematics, music, or vector graphics.

A well-formed XML document that conforms to the rules specified by a particular DTD is said to be a *valid* document. Validity is a stronger requirement than being well formed since a document can be well formed without being valid. Note that since validity is defined with respect to a specific DTD, a document can be valid with respect to one DTD but invalid with respect to another.

A valid document must include a reference to the DTD to which it conforms. This is done using a *document type declaration*, which is a statement that appears at the beginning of the document, before the root element. Here is an example of a document type declaration for a MathML document:

```
<!DOCTYPE math SYSTEM
 "http://www.w3.org/TR/MathML2/dtd/mathml2.dtd">
```

This declaration says the document's root element is `math` and the DTD for the document can be found at the URL *http://www.w3.org/TR/MathML2/dtd/mathml2.dtd*.

You can also specify the DTD using a relative URL (if it is in the same file system as the document) or just the filename (if it is in the same directory as the document), as shown here:

```
<!DOCTYPE math PUBLIC "-//W3C//DTD MathML 2.0//EN"
 "http://www.w3.org/TR/MathML2/dtd/mathml2.dtd">
```

The two declarations above are examples of external DTDs, in which the DTD being specified is a separate document specified as an external URL. XML documents can also have internal DTDs; that is, the DTD is included in the content of the XML document itself. The declaration for an internal DTD is similar to that of an external DTD, except that instead of a URL, you explicitly include the contents of the DTD enclosed in square brackets. For example:

```
 <!DOCTYPE library [
<!ELEMENT author (#PCDATA, born, died)>
<!ELEMENT born (#PCDATA)>
<!ELEMENT died (#PCDATA)>
<!ELEMENT title (#PCDATA)>
<!ELEMENT book (title, author+)>
<!ELEMENT library (book*)>
]>
```

Each `<!ELEMENT ...>` statement defines the name of a specific element (and the content it can have) using a specific syntax defined for use in DTDs. For example:

`<!ELEMENT title (#PCDATA)>` means that a `title` element can contain any parsed character data, that is ordinary text, possibly containing entity references but not containing any tags or child elements.

`<!ELEMENT author (#PCDATA, born, died)>` means that each `author` element can contain ordinary text as well as a `born` and `died` element.

`<!ELEMENT book (title, author+)>` means that each `book` element can contain one `<title>` element and one or more `author` elements.

`<!ELEMENT library book*>` means that each `library` element can contain zero or more `book` elements.

An XML document can also have both an external and internal DTD. That is, a part of the DTD is in an external file and the rest is specified explicitly inside the document. The external part is called the *external DTD subset*, and the internal part is called the *internal DTD subset*. For example, the following DTD declaration includes both an external DTD subset and an internal DTD subset (the declarations for the `author`, `born`, and `died` elements are made in the internal subset, while the remaining elements are declared in the external subset):

```
<!DOCTYPE library SYSTEM "library.dtd" [
<!ELEMENT author (#PCDATA, born, died)>
<!ELEMENT born (#PCDATA)>
<!ELEMENT died (#PCDATA)>
]>
```

Combining an internal and external DTD is useful when you want to use an existing DTD but if you want to modify it slightly for a specific document (say to add declarations for a small number of extra elements). The two parts of the DTD must be consistent; that is, the element and attribute declarations in one part must not conflict with the declarations in the other part. In case of a conflict, the declarations in the internal subset override the declarations in the external subset.

2.5 ENTITIES

We saw earlier that the value of an attribute must be enclosed in quotation marks. However, if the value of an attribute itself contains a quotation mark, the XML processor may interpret the quotation mark as indicating the end of the attribute value. The appearance of a quotation mark in an attribute value is therefore an XML error, as shown here:

```
<person relation='Alice's friend'>
```

To prevent errors of this type, you can use one type of quotation mark inside the attribute value and the other type of quotation mark to enclose the entire value, as shown here:

```
<person relation="Alice's friend">
```

An alternative solution to the problem is to replace the quotation mark in the attribute value with the entity reference '. When the XML document is processed, the single quotation mark character replaces this entity reference, and there is no confusion about the start and end quotation marks that enclose the attribute value itself, as you can see here:

```
<person relation='Alice&apos;s friend;>
```

Another common use of an entity reference is to replace the < character when it occurs as part of an element's content. For example, a processor could interpret the < in the content of the inequality element here as the start of a new element (this leads to an XML error since there is no matching > to close the tag):

```
<inequality>x<2</inequality>
```

In cases like this, when the character data in an element includes a <, you must use the entity reference < to avoid inadvertently indicating the start of another element. For the above element to be interpreted correctly, you must represent it as follows:

```
<inequality>x&lt;2</inequality>
```

XML includes five predefined entities that can be used to represent characters that have a special meaning in XML syntax (Table 2.1).

TABLE 2.1 Entities That Represent Characters with a Special Meaning

Entity Name	Character
'	'
"	"
&	&
>	>
<	<

Each entity reference consists of an ampersand (&) followed by a keyword followed by a semicolon (;). To include any of the characters in the right column in your document, you can insert the corresponding entity reference (in the left column) instead.

The use of entities in XML is not confined to these five characters. You can define your own entities to serve as an abbreviation for any piece of data, whether it be a single character or an entire file. Entities provide a convenient way to refer to any data that occurs frequently in a given document. The proper use of entities can make complex documents easier to read, write, and maintain.

For each entity that you wish to use, there must be a corresponding entity declaration in the DTD referenced by the document. An entity declaration is a special type of statement that associates a keyword with the piece of data that you want to represent. Each entity declaration has the following syntax:

```
<!ENTITY name string>
```

This associates the keyword *name* with the data specified by *string*. Then, anytime that data occurs in your document, you can use the text &*name*; in place of the actual data. Here is an example of an entity declaration:

```
<!ENTITY crm www.charlesriver.com>
```

This statement defines a named entity called crm to represent the URL of the Charles River Media Web site. You can then include a reference to this URL in an XML document, as shown below:

```
<message>For more information, visit &crm;.</message>
```

An XML processor will then interpret this markup as the following text.

```
<message>For more information, visit
 www.charlesriver.com.</message>
```

There are two ways to include an entity declaration for a given document:

- Add it to the external DTD referenced by the document. Doing this is appropriate if the entity is going to be used in many documents that use that DTD.
- Add it to the internal DTD subset declared in the body of the document itself. Doing this is appropriate if the entity reference is to be used in that particular document only.

The entities discussed in this section, which are used in ordinary XML documents, are called *general entities*. XML also defines another set of entities called *parameter entities,* which serve the same function but are used only in XML DTDs. We're not discussing parameter entities since they are not relevant to the main theme of this book.

2.6 NAMESPACES

It is often necessary to combine markup from two different XML applications in a single document. If the same element name is used in both XML applications, the interpretation of that element name becomes ambiguous.

For example, both MathML and SVG define an element called `set`. If you include a MathML equation and an SVG graphic in an XHTML document, an XML processor reading that document has no way of knowing whether a given `set` element is a MathML element or an SVG element. This can lead to problems in validating the document and interpreting its meaning.

XML uses the concept of *namespaces* to distinguish elements with the same name belonging to different XML formats. Each namespace associates a collection of element and attribute names with a specific URL. So, for example, all MathML elements are placed in the MathML namespace, and all SVG elements in the SVG namespace. Since each URL is a unique string, two elements that have the same name but belong to different XML applications can always be distinguished.

There are two ways to specify the namespace for a particular element. The first is to specify the namespace explicitly on each element, using a namespace prefix. To do this, you use an attribute declaration of the form `xmlns:` *prefix-name* `="`*url*`"` to associate a prefix name with a specific namespace URL. This prefix declaration must occur either on or before the outermost element belonging to that namespace. You then replace the name of each element belonging to that namespace by a qualified name of the form, *prefix-name*:*element-name*. Here is an example:

```
<m:math xmlns:m="http://www.w3.org/1998/Math/MathML">
 <m:set>
   <m:ci>b</m:ci>
   <m:ci>a</m:ci>
 </m:set>
</m:math>
```

The URL *http://www.w3.org/1998/Math/MathML* is a unique identifier for the MathML namespace. If you associate the prefix `m` with this URL using the `xmlns:m` attribute, all element and attribute names of the form m:*name* are interpreted as names defined by MathML.

The second way is to specify a default namespace using an xmlns attribute. This provides an alternative to using a namespace prefix for each element. For example:

```
<math xmlns="http://www.w3.org/1998/Math/MathML">
 <set>
   <ci> b </ci>
   <ci> a </ci>
 </set>
</math>
```

Here, the math element contains an xmlns attribute whose value is set to the URL that defines the MathML namespace. By default, all element names that appear inside the math element (such as set and ci) are then assumed to lie within the namespace defined by that URL. This distinguishes them from any other set elements in the document belonging to another XML application.

2.7 XML and Unicode

An XML document can contain any Unicode text. Unicode is an international standard for representing multilingual text. It defines a very large character set that includes characters from most of the world's languages as well as many mathematical and technical symbols.

A character set defines a mapping between a set of characters and a set of numbers, which are called *code points*. For example, in Unicode, the Greek letter α is represented by the code point 945 (in decimal notation), or x3B1 (in hexadecimal notation).

Unicode is a superset of American Standard Code for Information Interchange (ASCII), a widely used character set that includes all the letters and common punctuation marks used in English. ASCII consists of 128 characters with code points from 0 to 127. The first 128 characters of Unicode are identical to ASCII. For example, the letter A has the code point 65 in both ASCII and Unicode. However, Unicode goes well beyond ASCII by including many more characters. The current version of the standard, Unicode 3.2, defines code points for approximately 95,000 characters.

In an XML document, the names of elements and attributes, as well as the character data contained in an element, can all be written in Unicode. The advantage of using Unicode is that it allows you to use a single character set for text containing multiple languages and many different types of symbols. This avoids the problems caused by conflicting character sets, in which a single code point might be assigned to more than one character or a single character might have more than one code point, depending on the type of computer being used. Many software applications and operating systems now support Unicode. Unicode thus provides a standard way of encoding multilingual text so it can be exchanged and interpreted reliably across a wide variety of computer systems.

You can include a Unicode character in an XML document in the form of a character entity reference. For example, to include the Greek character α, you would type `α`. If the document includes a DTD declaration with entity names defined for specific characters, you can also insert the character using a named entity reference. For example, suppose you include a reference to the MathML DTD, as shown here:

```
<!DOCTYPE math SYSTEM
 "http://www.w3.org/TR/MathML2/dtd/mathml2.dtd">
```

You can then insert the α character in this document by using the named entity reference, `α` because the MathML DTD includes an entity declaration that associates the entity name alpha with the corresponding Unicode character code. We shall learn more about named characters in MathML in Section 3.4.

CHAPTER

3

FUNDAMENTALS OF MATHML

This chapter introduces the key concepts of MathML. It explains the differences between presentation and content markup, with the help of examples. It also discusses the syntax of MathML attributes and gives an overview of the character entities defined by the MathML DTD.

3.1 MathML and XML

MathML is an application of XML. This means that the syntax of MathML—that is, its rules for using elements and attributes—is determined by the rules of XML. The vocabulary of MathML (the elements and attributes allowed) is determined by an XML DTD.

Each instance of MathML markup consists of Unicode characters organized into a nested tree of elements. MathML is case sensitive, but all element and attribute names are defined in lowercase for simplicity. MathML includes both container elements, such as `mrow` or `apply`, and empty elements, such as `mspace` or `sin`.

As explained in Section 2.2, a container element consists of a start tag, an end tag, and the content included between them. An empty element consists of a single start tag, and has no content or end tag. Strictly speaking, XML makes a clear distinction between elements and tags. However, it is customary to refer to the `mrow` element, for example, to mean the element whose start tag is `mrow`. This convention is followed throughout this book.

MathML also contains some additional syntax rules that go beyond those specified by XML. These additional rules fall into two categories:

1. MathML places restrictions on the type of value that certain attributes can take. For example, the content token element, `cn`, which is used to represent numbers has an attribute called `base`, which specifies the base of the number encoded. This attribute can take integer values between 2 and 36 only.
2. MathML places restrictions on the number of child elements of certain elements and assigns a special meaning to those child elements based on their order. Child elements of this type are called arguments. For example, the `msup` element always has two arguments; the first one is interpreted as the base and the other as the superscript.

XML syntax does not provide a way of specifying these two types of constraints. Hence, these rules are not specified in the MathML DTD and an XML processor does not recognize their violation as an error. However, violation of these rules is a MathML error and will be recognized as such by applications that process MathML.

The Root Element

We saw earlier that every XML document must have exactly one root element. For a MathML document, the root element must be a `math` element. In addition, whenever a MathML document is embedded in another XML or HTML document, it is a good practice to declare the namespace of the `math` element. This ensures that the `math` element as well as all other elements contained within it are recognized as being MathML elements.

Every example of MathML markup must be enclosed by a single top-level `math` element. This means that if you copy part of a MathML expression from an existing MathML document, you must add an outer `math` element to the expression before it can be used as a valid piece of free-standing MathML markup. Conversely, if you take a MathML expression and paste it into an existing MathML document, the outer `math` tags of the expression being pasted must be removed, so that the destination document does not contain more than one `math` element. This behavior is automatically built into all applications for copying, pasting, and processing MathML, such as equation editors.

The most important attribute of the `math` element is `display`. This can take two values, `inline` or `block`. The default setting `display="inline"` is suitable for equations that are to be displayed inside a paragraph of text. With this setting, some operators such as the integral and summation symbols are shown in a smaller size. In addition, their limits are shown as subscripts and superscripts, so the equation takes up less room vertically. The setting `display="block"` is used when equations are to be displayed in a separate line, by themselves. With this setting, symbols such as integral and summation signs are shown in a larger size and their limits are shown as underscripts and overscripts.

For MathML equations to be integrated into a Web page, the MathML markup must be inserted at appropriate places in the HTML (or XHTML) document that defines the Web page. When the browser processes the HTML document and comes across the MathML islands, it either renders them directly or passes them to the plug-in for processing. See Chapter 6 of this book for detailed information on how to embed MathML equations in an HTML for display by specific browsers and plug-ins.

At present, the following browsers can natively display MathML: *Amaya, Mozilla* and *Netscape* 7.0. *Amaya* is the test browser provided by the W3C for testing new Web technologies. It is available for Windows and various Unix platforms but not for Macintosh. *Mozilla* is an open-source browser that will serve as the basis for the next version of *Netscape*. It is available for all major platforms.

IE and *Netscape* support the display of MathML using special add-on software, such as IBM's *techexplorer* or Design Science's *MathPlayer* or *WebEQ*.

ON THE CD

You can install Amaya or MathPlayer on your computer using the CD-ROM included with this book. It is recommended that you install one of these applications so you can test and modify the examples in this book. For details of how to embed MathML markup in an HTML document and information on configuring specific browsers to view MathML, see Chapter 7.

3.2 Presentation and Content

The appearance of mathematical notation and its conceptual meaning have a complex relationship. The same notation can express two completely different mathematical meanings, depending on the context. For example, the expression $f(x + y)$ can be interpreted in two ways:

- The value of a function f with the arguments x and y
- The variable f multiplied by the sum of x and y

Conversely, a given mathematical concept can be expressed by more than one notation. For example, the notations $\frac{df}{dx}$ and $f'(x)$ both have the same mathematical meaning; that is, the derivative of the function f with respect to x. Yet the two notations are distinct in their visual appearance. Similarly, the operation of dividing a by b can be represented in at least three different ways: a/b, $\frac{a}{b}$, or ab^{-1}.

Due to such ambiguity, it is important to have some way of independently specifying the appearance and meaning of a given type of mathematical notation. The solution adopted in MathML is to use two separate sets of tags for these two purposes. *Presentation tags* are used to encode the appearance of mathematical notation—that is, its visual two-dimensional structure. *Content tags*, on the other hand, are used to encode the symbolic meaning conveyed by the notation.

Hence, any mathematical expression can be represented in several different ways in MathML:

- Using only presentation tags. This type of markup is called *presentation markup*. It is useful in situations where the primary goal is to display mathematical notation, without regard to its meaning. This is the case, for example, when you include equations in a document that is intended only for display on the Web.
- Using only content tags. This type of markup is called *content markup*. It is useful in situations where it is important to encode mathematical meaning; for example, if you want to post an equation on a Web page that readers can copy and paste into *Mathematica* for evaluation.
- Using a combination of presentation and content tags. This type of markup is called *combined markup* and is used when you want to encode both the appearance and meaning of equations. For example, you can use combined markup to specify a nonstandard notation for a common mathematical construct or to associate a specific mathematical meaning with a certain type of notation that usually has a different meaning.

Presentation Markup

MathML presentation markup consists of about 30 elements and 50 attributes. The most important presentation elements are the so-called *token elements*—`mo`, `mn`, and `mi`—which are used to represent operators (such as + or −), numbers (such as 3.14 or −27), and identifiers (that is, variables like x or y), respectively.

Token elements are the only presentation elements that can directly contain character data. All other elements can only contain other MathML elements. The reason for using separate elements to represent operators, numbers, and identifiers is so that each type of item can be rendered according to its own typesetting conventions. For example, operators have extra spacing around them, numbers are usually shown in an upright font, and identifiers are typically italicized.

This simple example of presentation markup encodes the expression $x + y$:

$$x + y$$

```
<math>
 <mrow>
   <mi>x</mi>
   <mo>+</mo>
   <mi>y</mi>
 </mrow>
</math>
```

The outermost element of the expression is a math element, as required for any piece of MathML markup. The rest of the markup consists of two mi elements for representing the identifiers x and y and an mo element representing the operator +. These are all enclosed in an mrow element, which causes its child elements to be displayed in a horizontal row.

Here is the presentation markup for a slightly more complicated expression:

$$(x+y)^2$$

```
<math>
 <msup>
   <mrow>
     <mo>(</mo>
     <mrow>
       <mi>x</mi>
       <mo>+</mo>
       <mi>y</mi>
     </mrow>
     <mo>)</mo>
   </mrow>
   <mn>2</mn>
 </msup>
</math>
```

The first element in the markup after the math element is msup, which reflects the fact that the encoded expression consists of a base with a superscript. The msup element has two arguments, which represent the base expression and the superscript, respectively. That is, it has the syntax: <msup> *base index* </msup>. The *base* and *index* terms can either be token elements or more complicated expressions consisting of other MathML elements.

In the above example, the base consists of a single mrow element that is used to encode the expression $x + y$. The superscript (that is, the second argument of the msup element) is the number 2 enclosed in an mn element to indicate that it is a number.

This example indicates some general principles that you can use to determine the presentation markup for any mathematical expression. Each expression is decomposed into its constituent subexpressions, and the process is continued recursively until one reaches the fundamental or atomic units of the expression, namely numbers, operators, or identifiers. The atomic units are represented by the appropriate token elements. All other subexpressions are then represented by the corresponding MathML presentation elements, so that the recursive structure of the MathML tree exactly duplicates the recursive structure of the original expression.

Here is the presentation markup for a simple quadratic polynomial:

$$x^2 - 2x + 1$$

```
<math>
 <mrow>
   <msup>
     <mi>x</mi>
     <mn>2</mn>
   </msup>
   <mo>-</mo>
   <mrow>
     <mn>2</mn>
     <mo>&InvisibleTimes;</mo>
     <mi>x</mi>
   </mrow>
   <mo>+</mo>
   <mn>1</mn>
 </mrow>
</math>
```

This example uses the `mrow` and `msup` elements introduced in the previous example, along with the token elements `mi`, `mn`, and `mo`. The additional feature here is the use of the entity reference `⁢` to indicate that the 2 and the *x* are being multiplied together. The use of this entity reference is not required, since the visual display of the equation is unaffected if the `<mo>⁢</mo>` element is omitted altogether.

However, if you explicitly include the entity reference, the markup gives additional information about the meaning of the equation. This information is useful, for example, when you are evaluating the markup in a computer algebra system or converting it to an audio rendering. Hence, the use of such entities is strongly encouraged in presentation MathML. Note that for applications in which interpreting the meaning of an equation is important, the use of content MathML would be preferable.

The following example illustrates how you can use presentation markup to represent fractions and square roots:

$$\frac{1+\sqrt{5}}{2}$$

```
<math>
 <mrow>
   <mfrac>
```

```
      <mrow>
        <mn>1</mn>
        <mo>+</mo>
        <msqrt>
          <mn>5</mn>
        </msqrt>
      </mrow>
        <mn>2</mn>
    </mfrac>
  </mrow>
</math>
```

The mfrac and msqrt elements are used to represent fractions and square roots, respectively. The mfrac element has the syntax: <mfrac> *num denom* </mfrac>, where the first argument is the numerator and the second argument is the denominator.

Here is the presentation markup for the solution of a general quadratic equation:

$$x = \frac{-b \pm \sqrt{b^2 - 4ac}}{2a}$$

```
<math>
  <mrow>
    <mi>x</mi>
    <mo>=</mo>
    <mfrac>
      <mrow>
        <mo>-</mo>
        <mi>b</mi>
        <mo>&PlusMinus;</mo>
        <msqrt>
          <mrow>
            <msup>
              <mi>b</mi>
              <mn>2</mn>
            </msup>
            <mo>-</mo>
            <mrow>
              <mn>4</mn>
              <mo>&InvisibleTimes;</mo>
              <mi>a</mi>
              <mo>&InvisibleTimes;</mo>
              <mi>c</mi>
            </mrow>
          </mrow>
        </msqrt>
      </mrow>
```

```
        <mrow>
          <mn>2</mn>
          <mo>&InvisibleTimes;</mo>
          <mi>a</mi>
        </mrow>
      </mfrac>
    </mrow>
  </math>
```

This example uses several of the presentation elements introduced so far: mrow, msqrt, msup, and mfrac. It differs from the previous example only in the complexity of the nesting: the markup has a larger number of elements that reflect the complexity of the layout tree from which the expression is composed. Note the use of the entity reference ⁢ to explicitly indicate multiplication. The example also uses the entity reference ± to represent the ± symbol.

Here is the presentation markup for a simple matrix:

$$\begin{pmatrix} a & b \\ c & d \end{pmatrix}$$

```
<math>
 <mrow>
   <mo>(</mo>
   <mtable>
     <mtr>
       <mtd><mi>a</mi></mtd>
       <mtd><mi>b</mi></mtd>
     </mtr>
     <mtr>
       <mtd><mi>c</mi></mtd>
       <mtd><mi>d</mi></mtd>
     </mtr>
   </mtable>
   <mo>)</mo>
 </mrow>
</math>
```

The outermost element of the matrix is an mtable element, which is used to represent any type of table or array. Each row of the table is enclosed in an mtr element, and each entry or cell in a row is enclosed in an mtd element. The parentheses surrounding the matrix are indicated explicitly using mo elements.

Here is the presentation markup for an equation involving an integral:

$$\int_0^\infty e^{-x} dx = 1$$

```
<math>
 <mrow>
   <mrow>
     <msubsup>
       <mo>&int;</mo>
       <mn>0</mn>
       <mi>&infin;</mi>
     </msubsup>
     <mrow>
       <msup>
         <mi>&ExponentialE;</mi>
         <mrow>
           <mo>-</mo>
           <mi>x</mi>
         </mrow>
       </msup>
       <mo>&InvisibleTimes;</mo>
       <mrow>
         <mo>&DifferentialD;</mo>
         <mi>x</mi>
       </mrow>
     </mrow>
   </mrow>
   <mo>=</mo>
   <mn>1</mn>
 </mrow>
</math>
```

The only new element introduced in this example is `msubsup`, which has the syntax: `<msubsup>` *base subscript superscript* `</msup>`. This element is used to position a subscript and superscript symmetrically about a base expression. Note the use of the named entity references `∫`, `ⅇ`, and `ⅆ` to represent the integral, exponential, and differential d symbols, respectively. As with the use of `⁢`, the use of these named character references provides useful information about the meaning of the expression.

Content Markup

MathML content markup consists of about 150 elements and 12 attributes. The majority of content elements are empty elements that represent a specific operator, function, or relation. Examples of such elements are `plus`, `power`, `log`, and `sin`.

Content markup also contains three different token elements, cn, ci, and csymbol, which are used to encode numbers, identifiers, and user-defined symbols, respectively. Content token elements are the only content elements that can directly contain character data. All other content elements are either empty elements or can contain only other content elements.

The single most important content element is the apply element, which is used to apply operators or functions to expressions. The first argument of the apply element is typically an element that represents an operator or function. The remaining arguments represent one or more expressions to which the first argument is applied.

Content markup is based on the concept of prefix notation, a convention for writing mathematical expressions that is used in programming languages like LISP. In prefix notation, any expression is written as an operator followed by the objects it operates on, namely its operands. For example, to represent $x + y$ in prefix notation, you would write something like $+xy$. Similarly, to represent x^2, you would write Power x 2. You can represent more complicated expressions in prefix notation by nesting and combining smaller subexpressions.

To get the content markup for an expressions, you first write the expression in prefix notation; then you replace each operator and operand by the corresponding content elements. Here is a simple example of content markup:

x^2

```
<math>
 <apply>
   <power/>
   <ci>x</ci>
   <cn>2</cn>
 </apply>
</math>
```

The markup consists of a single apply element, followed by three elements that each represent an argument of the apply element. The first element is the empty element power, which represents the function to be applied. The next two elements, ci and cn, represent the arguments to which the power function is applied. The ci element represents the base and the cn element the power.

Here is the content markup for the expression: $x + y$:

$x + y$

```
<math>
 <apply>
```

```
      <plus/>
      <ci>x</ci>
      <ci>y</ci>
    </apply>
  </math>
```

The markup consists of a single apply element followed by a plus element (which represents the function to be applied) and two ci elements (which represent the arguments to which the plus function is applied).

Here is the content markup for a slightly more complicated expression:

$$(x+y)^2$$

```
<math>
  <apply>
    <power/>
    <apply>
      <plus/>
      <ci>x</ci>
      <ci>y</ci>
    </apply>
    <cn>2</cn>
  </apply>
</math>
```

This markup combines elements of both the previous examples. It uses two nested apply elements. The inner apply element is used to encode the sum $x+y$, and the outer apply element is used to raise the summed expression to the power of two.

Here is the content markup for a simple algebraic expression:

$$x^2 - 2x + 1$$

```
<math>
  <apply>
    <plus/>
    <apply>
      <minus/>
      <apply>
        <power/>
        <ci>x</ci>
        <cn>2</cn>
      </apply>
      <apply>
        <times/>
        <cn>2</cn>
        <ci>x</ci>
```

```
      </apply>
    </apply>
    <cn>1</cn>
  </apply>
</math>
```

This example uses the `apply`, `plus`, and `power` elements that we saw in combination with the `minus` and `times` elements. The last two elements represent subtraction and multiplication, respectively.

The following example illustrates how to represent fractions and square roots using content markup:

$$\frac{1+\sqrt{5}}{2}$$

```
<math>
  <apply>
    <divide/>
    <apply>
      <plus/>
      <cn>1</cn>
      <apply>
        <root/>
        <cn>5</cn>
      </apply>
    </apply>
    <cn>2</cn>
  </apply>
</math>
```

The square root is encoded using the `root` element. You can also use this element to represent radicals by specifying the degree of the radical as the second argument. As you can see, more complicated expressions are built up in a straightforward way by combining and nesting smaller subexpressions, as required.

Here is the content markup for a simple matrix:

$$\begin{pmatrix} a & b \\ c & d \end{pmatrix}$$

```
<math>
  <matrix>
    <matrixrow>
      <ci>a</ci>
      <ci>b</ci>
    </matrixrow>
    <matrixrow >
      <ci>c</ci>
      <ci>d</ci>
```

```
    </matrixrow >
  </matrix>
</math>
```

Here is the content markup for an equation involving an integral:

$$\int_0^\infty e^{-x}dx = 1$$

```
<math>
 <apply>
   <eq/>
   <apply>
     <int/>
     <bvar><ci>x</ci></bvar>
     <lowlimit><cn>0</cn></lowlimit>
     <uplimit><infinity/></uplimit>
     <apply>
       <power/>
       <exponentiale/>
       <apply>
         <minus/>
         <ci>x</ci>
       </apply>
     </apply>
   </apply>
   <cn>1</cn>
 </apply>
</math>
```

In the above example, the `int` element is used to represent an integral. The `lowlimit`, `uplimit`, and `bvar` elements are used to represent the upper limit, lower limit, and variable of integration, respectively. The constants ∞ and e are represented using the content elements `infinity` and `exponentiale`, respectively.

Handling Whitespace

MathML ignores all whitespace (spaces, tabs, new lines, or carriage returns) that occurs outside of token elements. Whitespace occurring within token elements is trimmed from the ends; that is, all whitespace at the beginning and end of the content is removed Whitespace internal to MathML elements is collapsed so that each sequence of one or more spaces is replaced by exactly one blank space.

If you need to explicitly encode whitespace characters at the start or end of the content of a token element or in sequences other than a single space, you can do so by using the ` ` entity reference or the whitespace character entities (such as ` `, ` `, and ` `). For whitespace that occurs outside of token elements, you should use an `mspace` element instead of an `mtext` element that contains whitespace entities.

3.3 MATHML ATTRIBUTES

Each MathML element has a number of attributes. The attribute for an element is specified after the element name in the start tag of the element, using the syntax: *attribute-name*="*value*". The value of the attribute must be enclosed in either single quotation marks or double quotation marks. The following six attributes are accepted by all MathML elements:

- `class`, `style`, and `id`: to facilitate use of CSS and XSL stylesheets
- `xlink:href`: used for setting up links
- `xref`: for use in parallel markup
- `other`: used for specifying nonstandard attributes that are not defined in MathML but may be supported by specific processing applications

In addition, each content or presentation element may have other attributes based on its specific role. For example, the `mfrac` element has an attribute called `linethickness`, as shown here:

$$\binom{n}{m}$$

```
<mrow>
 <mo>(</mo>
 <mfrac linethickness="0">
   <mi>n</mi>
   <mi>m</mi>
 </mfrac>
 <mo>)</mo>
</mrow>
```

The `linethickness` attribute determines the thickness of the line that separates the numerator and denominator of the fraction. The default value of this attribute is `1`, which corresponds to a line of normal thickness. In the above example, `linethickness` is set to `0`, which corresponds to the line being invisible.

MathML attributes can be set in two ways:

- They can be explicitly set in the start tag of an element, as in the above example.

- They can take the default value if not specified explicitly. The default value can be specified in the DTD, or it can be *automatic* (specified by the MathML rendering software) or *inherited* (from the surrounding environment).

An example of an inherited value that overrides a default value is shown here:

$x + y$

```
<math>
 <mrow>
   <mstyle mathsize="18 pt">
     <mi>x</mi>
     <mo>+</mo>
   </mstyle>
   <mi>y</mi>
 </mrow>
</math>
```

The example uses the presentation element `mstyle`, which you use to set style attributes for presentation markup. The value of all this element's attributes is automatically inherited by all its child elements. Here, the `mi` element containing the x and the `mo` element containing the + both inherit the value of the `mathsize` attribute, even though this attribute is not specified explicitly on either of the two elements.

MathML restricts the types of values certain attributes can take. These restrictions may be specified in the MathML DTD or may be additional rules that are enforced by MathML processors even if they are not explicitly described in the DTD. The allowed values for each type of attribute are described in the discussion of individual elements in Chapters 4 and 5. The following syntax is used to specify the possible values an attribute can take:

attribute-name value 1 | value 2 .... | value N

The allowed values are separated by a vertical bar indicating that any one of them can be used as a value for *attribute-name*. For example, the `form` attribute of the `mo` element can take three possible values:

```
form  prefix|infix|postfix
```

Certain attribute values may be indicated with a + (which means the value can occur 1 or more times) or with a * (which means the value can occur 0 or more times). Here is an example:

```
columnalign (left|center|right)+
```

This means that the `columnalign` attribute of the `mtable` element can take a set of values, each controlling the alignment of a specific column of the table. If fewer values than the number of columns are specified, the last value is repeated as many times as necessary. If there are more values than the number of columns, the extra values are ignored.

The notation used to indicate allowed values of attributes in the MathML specification is summarized in Table 3.1. For compactness, the same notation is used later in the book when we describe the attributes in the discussion of individual elements.

Some attributes are specified with a unit in addition to a numerical value. In this case, the attribute value typically consists of a number followed by a unit. For example, the allowed values of the `mathsize` attribute are specified as:

```
mathsize small|normal|big|number v-unit
```

Here, *v-unit* denotes a unit of vertical length. The example below shows the use of an attribute value that includes a unit (it causes the identifier *x* to be displayed in a 24-point font size):

```
<mi mathsize="24 pt">x</mi>
```

Possible units and the identifiers used to denote units in attribute values are listed in Table 3.2.

TABLE 3.1 Notation Used to Indicate Allowed Values of MathML Attributes

Notation	Meaning
x|*y*	Either *x* or *y* is allowed.
*x**	*x* can occur zero or more times.
x+	*x* can occur one or more times.
(*x*|*y*)+	Either *x* or *y* can occur one or more times.
[*x*]	*x* is optional.
h-unit	Unit of horizontal distance.
v-unit	Unit of vertical distance.
%	Percentage of the default value.
#rgb	Color in Red Green Blue (RGB) units with one digit for each color component.
#rrggbb	Color in RGB units with two digits for each color component.

TABLE 3.2 Possible Units and the Identifiers Used to Denote Units in Attribute Values

Identifier	Description
`em`	Width of the letter "m" in the font being used
`ex`	Height of the letter "x" in the font being used
`px`	Pixels
`in`	Inches
`cm`	Centimeters
`mm`	Millimeters
`pt`	Points
`pc`	Picas
`%`	Percentage

If an attribute values is specified as a percentage, it is usually a percentage of the default value of that attribute. For example:

```
<mfrac linethickness="2"><mi>x</mi><mi>y</mi></mfrac>
```

is equivalent to

```
<mfrac linethickness="200 %"><mi>x</mi><mi>y</mi></mfrac><
```

3.4 MathML Characters

Mathematical notation makes extensive use of special characters and symbols. Any language for representing mathematics must therefore provide a way of displaying the many extended characters that are widely used in various sub-fields of mathematics. In addition, the language must be open-ended enough to allow for display of new characters and symbols that may be invented in the future.

MathML enables you to directly include most of the extended characters that are important in mathematical notation. You can include character data in a MathML document, in three different ways:

- Type in characters directly from the keyboard. This is the most common way for entering common characters, such as those belonging to the ASCII character set.
- Use numeric Unicode character references; for example, the letter A can be entered by typing `A` or `A`, and the Greek letter α can be entered by typing `α`. (See Section 2.7 for more information on Unicode.)
- Use named entity references defined in the MathML DTD. For example, you can enter the character α by typing `α`.

The MathML DTD includes entity declarations for over 2,500 special characters. Each entity declaration associates an entity name for a particular character with its Unicode numeric code. The various MathML characters are divided into groups according to the ISO character set they belong to (Table 3.3). To see a listing of all the MathML characters arranged according to the Unicode blocks they occupy, see Chapter 15.

The list of characters included in the MathML DTD is large and comprehensive enough to be sufficient for most practical purposes. However, in special cases it may be necessary to encode characters that are not defined in the DTD. For this purpose, MathML provides the `mglyph` element. See Section 4.2 for a description of this element and an example of how it can be used to include nonstandard symbols in a MathML document.

Plane 1 Characters

The characters in Unicode can be divided into two planes, called the Basic Multilingual Plane (BMP), or plane 0, and the Secondary Mul-

TABLE 3.3 MathML Characters Divided into Groups According to the ISO Character Set

ISO Group	Description
ISOAMSA	Added mathematical symbols: arrows
ISOAMSB	Mathematical symbols: binary operators
ISOAMSC	Mathematical symbols: delimiters
ISOAMSN	Mathematical symbols: negated relations
ISOAMSO	Mathematical symbols: ordinary
ISOAMSR	Mathematical symbols: relations
ISOBOX	Box and line drawing
ISOCYR1	Cyrillic 1
ISOCYR2	Cyrillic 2
ISODIA	Diacritical marks
ISOGRK3	Greek-3
ISOLAT1	Latin-1
ISOLAT2	Latin-2
ISOMFRK	Mathematical Fraktur
ISOMOPF	Mathematical Openface (Double-struck)
ISOMSCR	Mathematical script
ISONUM	Numerical and special graphic
ISOPUB	Publishing
ISOTECH	General technical
MMLEXTRA	Extra names added by MathML

tilingual Plane (SMP), or plane 1. Each plane has space for 2^{16} or 65,536 characters. Most of the code points in plane 0 have already been assigned to specific characters, while the majority of code points in plane 1 are still unassigned.

The MathML DTD includes entity references for characters in both plane 0 and plane 1. However, most browsers do not currently support the display of plane 1 characters. Hence, if you include an entity reference corresponding to a plane 1 character in a MathML document, most browsers will display a ? symbol in place of that character. As a workaround to this problem, the W3C has created an interim version of the MathML DTD in which all entity references to plane 1 characters have been replaced with references to code points that belong to the private use area of plane 0.

The private use area of plane 0 consists of code points that have not been assigned to any characters in the official Unicode standard. Therefore, specific applications can use these code points to create private encodings for characters that are needed for special purposes.

For example, `𝔄` is a MathML character that represents the Fraktur Capital A. In the MathML DTD, this reference is replaced by the character reference `&x1D504;`, which belongs to plane 1. However, in the modified MathML DTD, `𝔄` would be replaced by the character reference `&xE504;`, which belongs to the private use area of plane 0. Similarly, any plane 1 character reference of the form `&x1D`*nnn*`;` will get replaced by a plane 0 reference of the form `&xE`*nnn*`;` instead.

The modified DTD for MathML allows you to include references to MathML characters that belong to plane 1 and have them interpreted and displayed by browsers. It is therefore preferable to use the modified DTD instead of the real MathML DTD until native support for plane 1 characters becomes available in browsers. Since most MathML content displayed in browsers will be embedded in an XHTML document, the W3C has provided a DTD that merges the DTD for XHTML and the modified DTD for MathML. To include a reference to this combined XHTML+MathML DTD, you would need to include the following declaration in your document:

```
<!DOCTYPE html PUBLIC "-//W3C//DTD XHTML 1.1 plus
MathML 2.0//EN" "http://www.w3.org/Math/DTD/mathml2/xhtml-
math11-f.dtd">
```

For more information on this topic and other issues involved in displaying MathML in Web browsers, see Section 7.3.

Fonts

Of course, it is not enough to define entity references for all extended characters that are likely to be needed for mathematical notation. If you want to be able to use these characters in a document and have them display properly in a Web browser or other rendering application, you must install on your system special fonts that contain glyphs for all the characters.

There is considerable effort underway to develop fonts for all the MathML characters. In particular, a consortium of academic organizations and technical publishers called STIX (*www.stix.org*) is working to develop a set of glyphs for each of the MathML characters. In the meantime, however, the number of fonts available for displaying mathematical symbols is relatively small, and the few that do exist are proprietary and are not widely distributed. The two products with the largest selection of fonts for displaying mathematical characters are the equation editor *MathType* and the computer algebra system *Mathematica*. The Computer Modern fonts, which are widely used in TEX/LATEX documents, are another widely used set of fonts.

ON THE CD

These fonts are all present in the CD-ROM included with this book. See Appendix A for information on installing these fonts in your system.

Non-marking Characters and Special Constants

The majority of MathML characters are associated with specific glyphs and provide a visual representation of a particular operator, symbol, or identifier. However, a small number of MathML characters provide information about the meaning or structure of the markup in which they occur. These characters can be divided into two groups: *non-marking characters* and *special constants*.

The MathML characters listed in Table 3.4 are used to represent operators or identifiers that do not have any glyphs associated with them. They are called non-marking characters since they do not leave any visible marks when displayed in a document. There are several other non-marking characters for representing whitespace that are not listed in this table.

The MathML characters listed in Table 3.5 are used to represent special constants that are ordinarily represented by conventional letters. If you use the named entity reference instead of the more common letter, the specific mathematical meaning of the constant can be included in the markup.

TABLE 3.4 MathML Characters Used to Represent Operators or Identifiers Unassociated with Glyphs

Character Name	Description
`⁢`	Indicates multiplication
`⁣`	Indicates separation between indices
`⁡`	Indicates function application in presentation markup
` `	Tabulator stop; horizontal tabulation
`
`	Forces a line break; line feed
` `	Space that is not a legal breakpoint
``	Space of no width at all
` `	Space of width 1/18 em
` `	Space of width 3/18 em
` `	Space of width 4/18 em
` `	Space of width 5/18 em

TABLE 3.5 MathML Characters Used to Represent Special Constants That Are Ordinarily Represented by Conventional Letters

Entity Name	Description
`ⅅ`	*D* for use in differentials; e.g., within integrals
`ⅆ`	*d* for use in differentials; e.g., within integrals
`ⅇ`	*e* for use for the exponential base of the natural log
`ⅈ`	*i* for use as a square root of −1

It is desirable to use these entity references whenever possible because they provide meaningful information that processing applications can use. This information can have specific consequences on the precise visual or aural rendering of the expression or its interpretation by a computer algebra system. For example, the characters `⁢` and `⁡` denote the operation of multiplication and function application, respectively. Consider the following example:

f(*xy*)

```
<math>
 <mrow>
   <mi>f</mi>
   <mo>&ApplyFunction;</mo>
   <mrow>
     <mo>(</mo>
     <mrow>
       <mi>x</mi>
       <mo>&InvisibleTimes;</mo>
       <mi>y</mi>
     </mrow>
     <mo>)</mo>
   </mrow>
 </mrow>
</math>
```

This markup may be spoken in an audio rendering system as "f of x times y." This rendering is more faithful to the meaning of the markup than just "f x y", which is how the markup might be spoken if the named entity references were omitted.

CHAPTER

4

PRESENTATION MARKUP

This chapter provides detailed information on the syntax of MathML presentation markup. It includes descriptions and examples of the major types of presentation elements, such as token elements, general layout elements, and elements for representing scripts, indices, tables, and matrices.

4.1 INTRODUCTION

Some simple examples of presentation markup were discussed in Section 3.2. We saw there that presentation markup consists of approximately 30 elements and 50 attributes that describe the visual structure of mathematical notation. Most presentation elements can be divided into two categories: *token elements* and *layout schemata*. Token elements represent the smallest building blocks of mathematical notation; that is, numbers, operators, and identifiers used to denote names of variables and functions. There are also separate token elements for representing text, blank space, strings, and character glyphs. Table 4.1 summarizes the different types of token elements.

Numbers, operators, and identifiers are each represented by a different token element (`mn`, `mo`, and `mi`, respectively) because each of these types of items has slightly different notational conventions. For example, numbers are usually rendered in an upright font, whereas variables are usually rendered in an italic font. Further, the space left around operators is different from that left around numbers or variables.

Token elements are the only presentation elements that can directly contain character data. They can contain any sequence of zero or more Unicode characters as well as entity references. Token elements can include whitespace, but any whitespace in the content

TABLE 4.1 Types of Token Elements

Element	Role
`mn`	Number
`mo`	Operator, fence, separator, or accent
`mi`	Identifier
`mtext`	Text
`mspace`	Blank space
`ms`	String
`mglyph`	Character glyph

is trimmed from the ends, as explained in Section 3.2. In general, token elements cannot contain other elements. However, there are two exceptions. The `mglyph` element, used for representing non-standard characters, and the `malignmark` element, used for aligning parts of an expression, can appear inside token elements.

Layout schemata specify templates for constructing expressions out of smaller parts. Table 4.2 summarizes the different types of layout schemata.

Layout schemata can contain only other elements as content; they cannot contain character data except for whitespace, which they ignore. The rules for rendering layout schemata are more complex than those for token elements since layout schemata specify how to construct a two-dimensional notational structure out of

TABLE 4.2 Types of Layout Schemata

Element	Role
`mrow`	Horizontal row
`mfrac`	Fraction
`msqrt`	Square root
`mroot`	Root
`mstyle`	Apply style
`mspace`	Blank space
`mphantom`	Make content invisible
`mfenced`	Add fences around content
`menclose`	Enclose content in a stretchy symbol
`merror`	Error messages
`msub`	Add subscript to a base
`msup`	Add superscript to a base
`msubsup`	Add subscript-superscript pair to a base
`munder`	Add underscript to a base
`mover`	Add overscript to a base
`munderover`	Add underscript-overscript pair to a base
`mmultiscripts`	Add multiple prescripts and postscripts to a base
`mtable`	Table or matrix
`mtr`	Row of a table
`mlabeledtr`	Labeled row of a table
`mtd`	Cell in a table
`maligngroup`	Alignment group
`malignmark`	Alignment marker

smaller subexpressions. MathML suggests rules for rendering each type of layout schemata but these rules are only suggestions, not requirements. In general, each processing application can choose its own rendering rules for different MathML elements as long as the rules are consistent with the basic conventions of mathematical typesetting.

In addition to token elements and layout schemata, there are a few other elements that do not belong to either category. These include the elements `none` and `prescripts` (which are empty elements used inside other layout schemata) and the `maction` element (which is used to add interactivity to MathML equations).

Note that in this and all subsequent chapters of the book, the `math` *element is omitted from all examples for the sake of brevity. However, this element is implied by the context; that is, each instance of MathML markup should be thought of as being enclosed in an outer* `math` *element.*

Number of Arguments

MathML specifies constraints on the number of child elements that certain layout schemata are allowed to contain. Child elements subject to such constraints are called *arguments*. Some arguments may also have a special meaning based on their position within the parent element. For example, an `msub` element must have exactly two arguments, the first of which is interpreted as the base and the second as the subscript attached to that base.

The MathML DTD does not specify either the number of arguments a given element has or their interpretation. The restrictions placed on arguments is an example of the additional rules specified by MathML that go beyond the basic syntax of XML.

Table 4.3 lists the number of arguments for each presentation element as well as any special meaning attached to the argument based on its position.

The elements in Table 4.3 whose required number of arguments is listed as 1^* have a special property. They are always interpreted as having a single argument even if they are written with a different number of arguments. In other words, if any of these elements occurs with either zero arguments or more than one argument, the contents of the element are interpreted as being enclosed in an `mrow` element. Such an `mrow` element is called an *inferred* `mrow` since its presence is inferred from the context. The elements that place an inferred `mrow` around their arguments are: `msqrt`, `mstyle`, `merror`, `mpadded`, `mphantom`, `menclose`, and `mtd`.

TABLE 4.3 Arguments for Each Presentation Element

Element	Number of Arguments	Argument Role
mrow	0 or more	
mfrac	2	*numerator denominator*
msqrt	1*	
mroot	2	*base root*
mstyle	1*	
merror	1*	
mpadded	1*	
mphantom	1*	
mfenced	0 or more	
menclose	1*	
msub	2	*base subscript*
msup	2	*base superscript*
msubsup	3	*base subscript superscript*
munder	2	*base underscript*
mover	2	*base overscript*
munderover	3	*base underscript overscript*
mmultiscripts	1 or more	*base* (*underscript overscript*)* [<mprescripts/>(*underscript overscript*)*]
mtable	0 or more	0 or more mtr or <mlabeledtr> elements
mtr	0 or more	0 or more mtd elements
mlabeledtr	2	A label and 0 or more mtd elements
mtd	1*	
maction	1 or more	Depends on the actiontype attribute

The advantage of this behavior is that you can omit a large number of mrow elements that would otherwise be necessary. This allows MathML expressions to be written more compactly. For example, the msqrt element below has 2 arguments:

```
<msqrt>
 <mo>-</mo>
 <mn>1</mn>
</msqrt>
```

Hence, the above expression is automatically interpreted as:

```
<msqrt>
 <mrow>
   <mo>-</mo>
   <mn>1</mn>
 </mrow>
</msqrt>
```

4.2 TOKEN ELEMENTS

There are three different types of token elements in presentation markup: mi, mn, and mo. This section discusses these elements in more detail.

Style Attributes

A set of style attributes controls the precise way in which the content of token elements is rendered. There are nine style attributes that all token elements accept. These attributes can be divided into two groups, depending on which version of MathML they were introduced in (Tables 4.4 and 4.5).

The use of the second set of attributes is deprecated in MathML 2.0 since they conflict with properties of the same name defined in CSS. Having the same attribute names in MathML and CSS can lead to problems. For example, the meaning of an equation may be altered by system-wide style changes applied using

TABLE 4.4 Style Attributes Introduced in MathML 2.0

Name	Property Specified	Allowed Value
mathbackground	Background color	*#rgb* | *#rrggbb* | *html-colorname*
mathcolor	Text color	*#rgb* | #rrggbb | *html-colorname*
mathsize	Font size	small | normal | big | *number v-unit*
mathvariant	Style variant	normal | bold | italic | script | bold-script | double-struck | fraktur | bold-fraktur | sans-serif | bold-sans-serif | sans-serif-italic | monospace

html-color-name refers to one of the named color keywords defined in HTML 4 (that is, aqua, black, blue, fuchsia, gray, green, lime, maroon, navy, olive, purple, red, silver, teal, white, and yellow).

TABLE 4.5 Style Attributes Introduced in MathML 1.0

Name	Property Specified	Allowed Value
`color`	Text color	*#rgb* | *#rrggbb* | *html-colorname*
`fontfamily`	Font family	*string* | *css-fontfamily*
`fontsize`	Font size	*number v-unit*
`fontstyle`	Font style	*normal* | `italic`
`fontweight`	Font weight	*normal* | `bold`

a CSS stylesheet. These attributes are still supported for backward compatibility and because they provide a simple way to directly specify common style properties. For some examples of how these attributes can be used in a CSS stylesheet, to control the rendering of MathML equations, see Section 8.2.

There is some overlap between the style attributes introduced in MathML 2.0 and the older ones from MathML 1.0. For example, you can specify the color of an equation using either the `color` or `mathcolor` attributes. Similarly, you can cause an equation to be displayed in bold font using either `fontweight` or `mathvariant`. In case of a conflict between the new attributes (from MathML 2.0) and the deprecated attributes (MathML 1.0), the former take precedence. For example, the following expression should render in a bold font.

ABC

```
<mi fontweight="normal" mathvariant="bold">ABC</mi>
```

The following expression should render in an italic sans-serif font.

ABC

```
<mi fontweight='bold' mathvariant= 'sans-serif-italic'>
ABC</mi>
```

In practice, most MathML expressions are likely to be embedded in another XML data format such as XHTML. In such cases, it is desirable for the displayed equations to have the same style attributes as the surrounding text, so that the font styles and sizes, for example, are compatible with the environment. For this reason, the default values of most of the above style attributes are inherited from the environment.

The meaning and usage of most of the style attributes listed above are evident from their names. However, the `mathvariant` attribute requires some further explanation. This attribute specifies that a character should be displayed in a particular font variant, such as Fraktur, Bold, Italic, Script, Bold-Script, Double-struck, and so on. In mathematical notation, each of these style variants often has a specific meaning associated with it. For example, an italic g might indicate a function name, a bold g might indicate a vector, and a Fraktur $\mathfrak{g}$ might indicate a Lie algebra. Hence, you should not use the `mathvariant` style attribute to specify styles unless the meaning implied by that style is specifically intended.

The MathML DTD includes a set of character entities that directly represent styled characters described by different values of the `mathvariant` attribute. However, these characters are in plane 1 of Unicode and plane 1 characters cannot be displayed in current browsers. Hence, in many cases it is preferable to use the `mathvariant` attribute in combination with a plane 0 character instead of the corresponding plane 1 character. (The meaning of plane 0 and plane 1 characters was explained in Section 3.4.)

For example, if you want to include a Fraktur g in a mathematical expression, you can do so using the character entity reference to the plane 1 Unicode character for this symbol, as shown here:

$\mathfrak{g}$

```
 <mi>&gfr;</mi>
<mi>&1D524;</mi>
```

Alternatively, you can use the `mathvariant` attribute applied to the ordinary letter g, as shown below:

$\mathfrak{g}$

```
<mi mathvariant="fraktur">g</mi>
```

The fact that the same character can be represented in two different ways can cause problems for applications where the semantic meaning of the markup is important, such as when you are searching or indexing mathematical content. To avoid such problems, the MathML specification requires that processing applications treat plane 0 characters with the `mathvariant` attribute specified as equivalent to the corresponding plane 1 characters.

Numbers

The `mn` element is used to represent numbers, or more precisely numeric literals. A *numeric literal* is any sequence of characters that represents an unsigned integer or real number. Here are some examples:

```
<mn>1</mn>
<mn>6.67</mn>
<mn>2002</mn>
<mn>1.6e-19</mn>
<mn>0xAEFF</mn>
<mn>1100101</mn>
```

Negative numbers can be represented by including a "-" sign before the numeric literal in the same <mn> element, as shown below:

```
<mn>-1</mn>
```

However, it is preferable to place the minus sign in a separate mo element so that you provide additional information about the meaning of the markup for use by processing applications, as shown here:

```
<mo>-</mo><mn>1</mn>
```

An mn element is rendered as the characters in its content with no extra spacing around them. By default, the content is rendered in an unslanted font. However, you can specify a different rendering using the style attributes available for token elements.

Not all numbers should be represented using mn. For example, fractions are represented using the mfrac element, as shown here:

$$\frac{1}{2}$$

```
<mfrac><mn>1</mn><mn>2</mn></mfrac>
```

A named symbolic constant, such as π, is represented by an entity reference enclosed in an mi element, as shown below:

```
<mi>&pi;</mi>
```

Complex numbers are represented as an mrow element, which contains separate arguments for the real part, the imaginary part, and the operator between them, as shown here (note the use of the entity reference ⁢ to denote multiplication between the imaginary part and the symbolic number i):

$$3.4 + 5i$$

```
<mrow>
 <mn>3.4</mn>
 <mo>+</mo>
```

```
  <mrow>
    <mn>5</mn>
    <mo>&InvisibleTimes;</mo>
    <mi>&ImaginaryI;</mi>
  </mrow>
</mrow>
```

Identifiers

The mi element is used to represent identifiers; that is, names of variables and functions. Examples are:

```
<mi>x</mi>
<mi>sin</mi>
<mi>F</mi>
```

Symbolic constants such as π, e, and i are also represented using an mi element, as shown here:

```
<mi>&pi;</mi>
<mi>&ExponentialE;</mi>
<mi>&ImaginaryI;</mi>
```

Not every identifier is represented using an mi element. For example, subscripted or primed variables are represented using an msub or msup element, respectively. Conversely, you can include any text in a mi element, if it is to be rendered as an identifier. A typical example is an ellipsis that represents a term in a series, as shown below:

$$1 + 2 + \cdots + n$$

```
<mrow>
  <mn>1</mn>
  <mo>+</mo>
  <mn>2</mn>
  <mo>+</mo>
  <mi>&ctdot;</mi>
  <mo>+</mo>
  <mi>n</mi>
</mrow>
```

The mi element accepts all the common style attributes defined for token elements. However, the mathvariant and fontstyle attributes have a different default value for mi elements. The default value is italic if the content of the mi element is a single character, and normal otherwise. This reflects the convention that variables and functions represented by single letters are typeset in an italic font.

Operators

The `mo` element is used for representing operators as well as other symbols that should render as operators. This includes fence characters (such as braces, parentheses, or absolute value bars), separators (such as commas or semicolons), and accents (such as a bar or tilde over a character). Here are some examples:

```
<mo>+</mo>
<mo>&lt;</mo>
<mo>=</mo>
<mo>&int;</mo>
<mo>and</mo>
<mo>(</mo>
<mo>}</mo>
```

Invisible Operators

As discussed in Section 3.2, some operators that are invisible in traditional notation should be specified using explicit named entity references in an `mo` element. These include `⁢`, `⁣`, and `⁡`. The advantage of using these entity references is that they provide semantic information about the markup. This information can then be used by rendering applications to achieve better results in visual and audio rendering or by computer algebra systems to evaluate an equation. Some examples of expressions involving invisible operators follow.

The following markup could be spoken as "x times y" instead of just "xy":

xy

```
<mrow>
  <mi>x</mi>
  <mo>&InvisibleTimes;</mo>
  <mi>y</mi>
</mrow>
```

The following markup could be spoken as "A sub one, two" instead of "A sub twelve":

A_{12}

```
<msub>
  <mi>A</mi>
  <mrow>
    <mn>1</mn>
    <mo>&InvisibleComma;</mo>
```

```
    <mn>2</mn>
  </mrow>
</msub>
```

The following markup could be spoken as "f of x" instead of "f times x":

$f(x)$

```
<mrow>
  <mi>f</mi>
  <mo>&ApplyFunction;</mo>
  <mrow>
    <mo>(</mo>
    <mi>x</mi>
    <mo>)</mo>
  </mrow>
</mrow>
```

Attributes

The attributes of the mo element determine the precise details of how individual operators and symbols are rendered. The mo element has the unique property that the default values of its attributes are determined based on its content, using an operator dictionary (described in the "Operator Dictionary" section later in this chapter).

Table 4.6 summarizes the various attributes of the mo element and their default values. Each default value is shown with an

TABLE 4.6 Attributes of the mo Element

Attribute	Values	Default
fence	true | false	false*
separator	true | false	false*
accent	true | false	false*
form	prefix | infix | postfix	Determined by position in mrow
lspace	*number h-unit* | *namedspace*	thickmathspace*
rspace	*number h-unit* | *namedspace*	thickmathspace*
stretchy	true | false	false*
symmetric	true | false	true*
maxsize	*number* [*v-unit* | *h-unit*] | *namedspace* |	infinity infinity*
minsize	*number* | *namedspace*	1*
largeop	true | false	false*
movablelimits	true | false	false*

asterisk to indicate that it is a generic default, which is used only if no match is found for that attribute in the operator dictionary.

The meaning of these attributes is given here:

- `fence`, `separator`, and `accent`: specify if the content of the `mo` element should be interpreted as a fence, separator, or accent, respectively. If any of these attributes is set to `true`, the rendering conventions relevant to that type of object are applied to the operator.
- `form`: specifies the position in which an operator occurs.
- `lspace` and `rspace`: determine the amount of space that should be inserted to the left or right of an operator, respectively.
- `stretchy`: specifies if an operator should expand or shrink to accommodate the elements it encloses.
- `symmetric`: specifies if a stretchy operator should stretch in such a way that its height above and depth below the baseline is always the same.
- `maxsize`: specifies the maximum size to which a stretchy operator can grow.
- `minsize`: specifies the minimum size to which a stretchy operator can shrink.

The MathML specification defines detailed rules for how stretchy operators should grow in size both vertically and horizontally, based on the context in which the `mo` element occurs. Here is an example of an operator that stretches vertically:

$$\left(\frac{x}{y}\right)$$

```
<mrow>
  <mo>(</mo>
  <mfrac>
    <mi>x</mi>
    <mi>y</mi>
  </mfrac>
  <mo>)</mo>
</mrow>
```

Compare this example to the case where the parentheses are prevented from stretching if you set the attribute `maxsize` to `1` (this forces the operators to stay at their default size):

$$(\frac{x}{y})$$

```
<mrow>
  <mo maxsize="1">(</mo>
```

```
  <mfrac>
    <mi>a</mi>
    <mi>b</mi>
  </mfrac>
  <mo maxsize="1">)</mo>
</mrow>
```

Here is an example of an operator that stretches horizontally:

$$x \xrightarrow{\textit{tends to}} a$$

```
<mrow>
  <mi>x</mi>
  <mover>
    <mo>&RightArrow;</mo>
    <mtext>tends to</mtext>
  </mover>
  <mi>a</mi>
</mrow>
```

The following two attributes affect the rendering of an operator based on the value of the `displaystyle` attribute of the `mstyle` element:

- `largeop`: specifies if an operator should be drawn larger than normal when `displaystyle="true"` is in its environment.
- `movablelimits`: specifies if the limits of an operator should be moved to the subscript and superscript positions when `displaystyle="false"` is in its environment.

Each presentation element inherits a default value of `displaystyle` from its environment. This attribute specifies if a given expression should be rendered in *inline* mode or *display* mode. Inline expressions are typically rendered in a smaller size and with underscripts and overscripts drawn in the subscript and superscript position. Display expressions are typically rendered in a larger size and with any underscripts and overscripts shown in their normal position.

The `largeop` and `movablelimits` attributes are used in MathML to control the two key properties that distinguish the inline and display mode of an operator, namely its size and the position of its limits.

Some typical examples of operators for which `largeop` and `movablelimits` are both `true` by default are the integral, summation, and product symbols. Here is an example of an expression for which `displaystyle="true"`:

$$\sum_{a}^{b} f(x)$$

```
<mstyle displaystyle="true">
 <munderover>
   <mo>&sum;</mo>
   <mi>a</mi>
   <mi>b</mi>
 </munderover>
 <mrow>
   <mi>f</mi>
   <mi>&ApplyFunction;</mi>
   <mrow>
     <mi>(</mi>
     <mo>x</mo>
     <mo>)</mo>
   </mrow>
 </mrow>
</mstyle>
```

Here is how the same expression might look if rendered with `displaystyle="false"`:

$\sum_a^b f(x)$

Notice that the summation symbol is shown in a smaller size and the underscripts and overscript have moved to the subscript and overscript position. These changes are a consequence of the fact that the `largeop` and `movablelimits` are both `true` by default for the `mo` element that contains the `∑` operator.

Operator Dictionary

Most mathematical operators and symbols have special rendering properties that must be handled on a case-by-case basis. For example, prefix operators are typically rendered with extra space on the left, postfix operators have extra space on the right, and infix operators have extra space on both sides. The mechanism used in presentation markup to respect such rendering conventions is to determine the default attribute values for each operator from an operator dictionary.

The *operator dictionary* is a table that lists attribute values for a large collection of common operators and symbols. When displaying an `mo` element containing a particular operator, the renderer first checks to see if that operator is listed in the operator dictionary. If so, the default attribute values for that `mo` element are taken from the entry for that operator in the dictionary. If the operator is not listed in the dictionary (or if it is listed but all of its attributes are not assigned explicit values), then the values of all unmatched attributes are determined from their generic defaults.

For example, the entry in the operator dictionary for the "=" operator is shown below:

```
"=" form="infix" lspace = "thickmathspace" rspace =
"thickmathspace"
```

This entry specifies default values for the `form`, `lspace`, and `rspace` attributes in an `mo` element that contains the "=" operator as its content. All other attributes of this `mo` element take their generic default values, since these attributes are not specified explicitly in the operator dictionary entry. In other words, the following markup:

```
<mo>=</mo>
```

is automatically interpreted as the following:

```
<mo form="infix" lspace = "thickmathspace" rspace =
"thickmathspace">=</mo>
```

This operator dictionary entry applies the typesetting convention that the "=" operator is typically used in the infix position and that it should be rendered with extra space on either side.

Here is the operator dictionary entry for the "(" operator:

```
"(" form="prefix" fence = "true" stretchy = "true"
    lspace = "0em" rspace = "0em"
```

This entry reflects the fact that the "(" character is typically used in an expression as a fence, it is normally stretched to accommodate its contents, and it does not have extra space around it.

The operator dictionary thus provides a way to automatically apply the typesetting conventions associated with each type of operator that might occur inside an `mo` element. Of course, you can always override the default behavior and change the rendering properties of any operator by explicitly specifying one or more attributes.

Text

The `mtext` element is used to represent ordinary text that appears inside a mathematical expression. This element is useful for mixing text and mathematical notation, as in the following example:

Theorem 1: If $x > 0$ and $y > 0$, then $xy > 0$

```
<mrow>
 <mtext>Theorem 1:If</mtext>
 <mi>x</mi><mo>&gt;</mo><mn>0</mn>
 <mtext>and</mtext>
 <mi>y</mi><mo>&gt;</mo><mn>0</mn>
 <mtext>then</mtext><mi>,</mi>
 <mi>x</mi><mo>&InvisibleTimes;</mo><mi>y</mi>
 <mo>&gt;</mo><mn>0</mn>
</mrow>
```

Another common use of `mtext` elements is for including literal whitespace, since MathML automatically removes whitespace that is included directly. You can include whitespace of varying widths using the named character entities such as ` `, ` `, ` `, or ` `, as shown here:

```
<mtext> </mtext>
<mtext>  </mtext>
```

Alternatively, you can insert whitespace of arbitrary width, height, and depth, using the `mspace` element, as discussed below.

Blank Space

The empty element `mspace` is used to explicitly insert a blank space of any desired size. The size and position of the space inserted depends on the value of the following three attributes:

- `width`: specifies the width of the bounding box that contains the `mspace` element
- `height`: specifies the distance from the baseline of the text to the top edge of the bounding box
- `depth`: specifies the distance from the baseline of the text to the bottom edge of the bounding box

The default values of all these attributes are chosen to make the `mspace` element have no effect on visual rendering. Hence, if you want to include a visible blank space, you must explicitly specify one or more attributes, as shown here:

```
<mspace width="5 em" height="2 ex" depth="2 ex"/>
```

The `mspace` element also takes an attribute called `linebreak`, which can be used to provide suggestions for linebreaking to a visual renderer. Possible values of this attribute and their meaning are given in Table 4.7.

TABLE 4.7 Possible Values of the `linebreak` Attribute

Value	Meaning
`auto`	There is no effect on linebreaking; the renderer uses its default linebreaking behavior.
`newline`	This is a new line and do not indent.
`indentingnewline`	This is a new line and do indent.
`nobreak`	A linebreak is not allowed here.
`goodbreak`	A linebreak is needed on the line; here is a good spot.
`badbreak`	A linebreak is needed on the line; try to avoid breaking here.

Strings

Most programming languages include strings as a fundamental data type for representing sequences of characters. In order to communicate with other programming applications such as computer algebra systems, MathML provides the `ms` element for representing strings.

The content of an `ms` element is typically rendered with a quotation mark character at the beginning and end. By default, the left and right quotation mark characters are the standard double quotation mark character, `"`, but using the attributes `lquote` and `rquote` you can substitute either of these with a different character, as shown here:

```
 "This is a string"
<ms>This is a string</ms>

 'This is a string'
<ms lquote="&apos;" rquote="&apos;">This is a string</ms>
```

As with any other token element, whitespace that occurs within the content of an `ms` element is automatically trimmed from the ends and collapsed. Hence, any whitespace that you must include when representing a string should be explicitly encoded using one of the named space characters such as ` ` or ` `.

Character Glyphs

A MathML expression can contain any character included in the Unicode character set. In particular, technical symbols and other extended characters can be included either using a named entity reference defined in the MathML DTD or, more generally, using the numeric character entity reference defined in Unicode.

However, in special cases, you might need to use a character that is not available in Unicode. Alternatively, you might wish to use a Unicode character but represent it using a variant of the standard glyph associated with the character. MathML provides the `mglyph` element specifically for use in such situations. It allows you insert a particular glyph from a particular font family at any place in your document.

The `mglyph` element accepts the following three attributes:

- `fontfamily`: specifies the font family that contains the glyph.
- `index`: is a number that specifies the position of the glyph in a particular font family.
- `alt`: provides an alternate name for the glyph. This name can be used by an audio renderer or by a visual renderer if it cannot find the specified font family for rendering the glyph. If using this, you should choose a descriptive name for it.

These are all required attributes; that is, they do not have a default value and must be explicitly specified in every `mglyph` element.

Here is an example that shows the use of the `mglyph` element:

$\mathfrak{R} = \mathfrak{A} + \mathfrak{B}$

```
<mrow>
 <mi><mglyph fontfamily="Mathematica 6" index="82"
   alt="GothicCapitalR"/></mi>
 <mo>=</mo>
 <mi><mglyph fontfamily="Mathematica 6" index="65"
   alt="GothicCapitalA"/></mi>
 <mo>+</mo>
 <mi><mglyph fontfamily="Mathematica 6" index="66"
 alt="GothicCapitalB"/></mi>
</mrow>
```

This explicitly specifies that the characters in positions R, A, and B from the *Mathematica* 6 font family should be used to display certain capital letters in a Gothic script.

4.3 General Layout Elements

General layout elements, also known as *layout schemata*, specify templates for constructing expressions out of smaller parts. In this section, we look at the different types of layout schemata in more detail.

Rows

The mrow element is used to group together any number of related subexpressions. The arguments of the mrow element are visually rendered in a horizontal row from left to right, in the order they occur. This element is important because:

- It provides guidance for proper spacing between its arguments.
- It provides information about linebreaking and indentation.
- It provides information on the meaning of the markup that is useful for audio renderers or computer algebra systems.
- It specifies the grouping of subexpressions into arguments.
- It specifies the scope of stretchable operators.

In general, multiple mrow elements are nested inside each other to reflect the tree structure of the expression being represented. Typically, each mrow element has as its arguments a single operator along with the operands that are being acted upon, as shown here:

$$x + 2y - 1$$

```
<mrow>
  <mi>x</mi>
  <mo>+</mo>
  <mrow>
    <mn>2</mn>
    <mo>&InvisibleTimes;</mo>
    <mi>y</mi>
  </mrow>
  <mo>−</mo>
  <mn>1</mn>
</mrow>
```

The presence of an mrow element is automatically inferred around the content of certain presentation elements, if they occur with a number of arguments different from 1, as explained in Section 4.1.

It is possible to add additional mrow elements to an expression without changing its meaning. This is not a MathML error and does not affect the validity of the expression. However, to avoid any additional overhead in processing the markup it is a good practice in general to use the smallest number of mrow elements that are necessary. This is because each extra mrow element adds another level in the document tree and requires you to create an extra bounding box; for example, when you apply a CSS stylesheet to the expression.

Fractions

The mfrac element is used to represent fractions and has the following syntax:

```
<mfrac> numerator denominator </mfrac>
```

The mfrac element has four attributes: linethickness, bevelled, numalign, and denomalign.

The linethickness attribute specifies the thickness of the line that separates the numerator and denominator. The default setting of 1 causes the line to be drawn in the standard thickness of lines for the font style being used. A setting of 0 causes the line to be invisible and can be used to represent binomial coefficients, as shown here:

$$\binom{n}{r}$$

```
<mrow>
 <mo>(</mo>
 <mfrac linethickness="0">
   <mi>n</mi>
   <mi>r</mi>
 </mfrac>
 <mo>)</mo>
</mrow>
```

When the bevelled attribute is set to false, the numerator is shown above the denominator with a horizontal line between them. When it's set to true, a slightly raised numerator is shown to the left of a slightly lowered denominator with a diagonal line between them, as shown in the following example:

$$^{1}/_{x+y}$$

```
<mrow>
<mfrac bevelled="true">
 <mn>1</mn>
 <mrow>
   <mi>x</mi>
   <mo>+</mo>
   <mi>y</mi>
 </mrow>
 </mfrac>
</mrow>
```

The numalign and denomalign–attributes specify the horizontal alignment of the numerator and denominator, respectively. They can take values `left`, `right`, and `center`. The default is to be centered, but it may be more appropriate for a very long numerator or denominator that stretches along multiple line to be aligned at left.

In the following example, you can left-align the numerator with the denominator by setting the value of `numalign="left"`:

$$\frac{a+b}{a+b+c}$$

```
<mfrac numalign="left">
 <mrow>
   <mi>a</mi><mo>+</mo><mi>b</mi>
 </mrow>
 <mrow>
   <mi>a</mi><mo>+</mo><mi>b</mi>
   <mo>+</mo><mi>c</mi>
 </mrow>
</mfrac>
```

It is conventional for the numerator and denominator to appear in a smaller font when a fraction is displayed as an inline expression; that is, surrounded by text. To satisfy this convention, the `mfrac` element automatically changes the value of two attributes of the `mstyle` element: `displaystyle` and `scriptlevel`, which are normally inherited from the environment. The `mfrac` element sets `displaystyle` to `false`, or if it was already set to `false` it increments `scriptlevel` by 1, within *numerator* and *denominator*. For more details about the `displaystyle` and `scriptlevel` attributes, see the description of the `mstyle` element later in this chapter.

Roots and Radicals

The `msqrt` element is used for representing square roots, as shown here:

$$\sqrt{2}$$

```
<msqrt><mn>2</mn></msqrt>
```

An `msqrt` element accepts any number of arguments. However, if the number of arguments is other than 1, they are interpreted as lying within an inferred `mrow`.

More generally, roots are represented using the `mroot` element. Each `mroot` element must contain exactly two arguments with the following syntax:

```
<mroot> base index </mroot>
```

Here is an example:

$$\sqrt[3]{x}$$

```
<mroot>
  <mi>x</mi>
  <mn>3</mn>
</mroot>
```

An `mroot` element increments `scriptlevel` by 2 and sets `displaystyle` to `false` within *index* but leaves both attributes unchanged within *base*. This causes the index of the radical to be displayed in a smaller size, as required by convention. For more details about the `displaystyle` and `scriptlevel` attributes, see the description of the `mstyle` element below.

Applying Styles

The `mstyle` element is used to apply style changes throughout a given piece of presentation markup. If an attribute is specified explicitly on an `mstyle` element, the value of that attribute is inherited by all elements contained within that `mstyle` element, either directly or indirectly. The net effect is to reset the default value of that attribute everywhere in the environment defined by that `mstyle` element. The `mstyle` element therefore provides a general mechanism for applying style changes selectively to specific parts of an expression.

Suppose you want an attribute to have a particular value everywhere in a given piece of markup. Instead of specifying that attribute explicitly on each element, you can just specify the attribute once on an `mstyle` element that encloses the markup where you want the changes to apply. Of course, you can still override the default setting applied by the `mstyle` element by explicitly specifying an attribute on any element in the environment.

For example, if you want a certain subexpression within a larger expression to be rendered in a 24-point font size, you can use the following markup:

$$x + 1$$

```
<mrow>
  <mi mathsize="24 pt">x</mi>
  <mo mathsize="24 pt">+</mo>
  <mn mathsize="24 pt">1</mn>
</mrow>
```

A simpler way to achieve the same result is shown here (this markup is equivalent to the markup in the above example):

```
<mstyle mathsize="24 pt">
 <mrow>
   <mi>x</mi>
   <mo>+</mo>
   <mn>1</mn>
 </mrow>
</mstyle>
```

Each mstyle element can accept any attribute for any presentation element that does not have a required value. This means that any attribute with either a default value or a value that is inherited or computed can be specified using the mstyle element. In addition, several style attributes are specifically defined for use with the mstyle element. Each of these attributes has a default value that is inherited by every presentation element, even if the element is not explicitly enclosed in an mstyle element.

Script Size Attributes

Many common notational structures require characters to be displayed in a reduced size relative to the surrounding text. For example, the numerator and denominator of a fraction that appears in a line of text are typically shown in a reduced size. Similarly, subscripts and superscripts are typically shown in a smaller size than the base to which they are attached. The reduction in size of characters that occur in such special positions is controlled by two attributes of the mstyle element: scriptlevel and scriptsizemultiplier.

The scriptlevel attribute takes integer values. It has a value of 0 for normal text, 1 for subscripts, 2 for subscripts of subscripts, and so on. Each increase in the value of scriptlevel leads to a corresponding decrease in the font size, according to the following algorithm. The current font size is multiplied by the value of scriptsizemultiplier raised to the power of the change in the value of scriptlevel. The default value of scriptsizemultiplier is 0.71. This value, as well as the algorithm for calculating the reduction in font size, is based on typesetting conventions chosen because they produce acceptable-looking results in practice. There is also an additional attribute called scriptminsize, which specifies a minimum value below which the font size cannot be reduced, regardless of the value of scriptsizemultiplier.

Another important attribute of the mstyle element is displaystyle. This attribute specifies whether an expression should be rendered in display mode or inline mode. It achieves this by affecting the rendering of the mo element, based on the values of its largeop and movablelimits, as explained in the discussion of the mo element in Section 4.1.

A setting of displaystyle="false" is used for inline mathematical expressions, which typically appear embedded in a paragraph of text. Such expressions are typically rendered in a smaller size and with underscripts and overscripts moved to the subscript and superscript position, respectively. This causes the mathematical expression to be vertically compressed so that it does not disrupt the spacing between lines.

A setting of displaystyle="true" is used for mathematical expressions that are to be rendered in display mode; that is, in a line by themselves. Such expressions are typically rendered in a larger size and with any underscripts and overscripts in their normal positions.

Certain presentation elements, such as mfrac, mroot, msub, msup, and so on, automatically change the values of scriptlevel and displaysize in one or more of their arguments. Details of this behavior are provided in the discussion of these individual elements in this chapter.

Color and Background Attributes

The mstyle attribute also accepts the color and background attributes, which determine the color of the font and background, respectively. These attributes can be set directly on token elements only. Hence, the mstyle element provides a way to specify the color and background of elements other than token elements.

The color and background attributes can both be specified in either RGB notation or as an HTML color name, as shown in the examples below.

This markup displays some text in a red color with a yellow background:

```
<mstyle mathcolor="red" mathbackground="yellow">
 <mtext>Here is some colored text.</mtext>
</mstyle>
```

This displays an expression in red color with a white background:

```
<mstyle mathcolor="#FF0000"
mathbackground="#FFFFFF">
 <mrow>
   <mi>x</mi>
   <mo>+</mo>
   <mn>1</mn>
 </mrow>
</mstyle>
```

Spacing Attributes

The following seven attributes of the `mstyle` element set the size of the various named spaces defined in MathML:

- `veryverythinmathspace`
- `verythinmathspace`
- `thinmathspace`
- `mediummathspace`
- `thickmathspace`
- `verythickmathspace`
- `veryverythickmathspace`

Each of these attributes defines a fixed horizontal space, with the default value ranging between 1/18 em and 7/18 em. Since the spacing between operators in the operator dictionary is defined in terms of these values, setting these values to a larger or smaller value can make the spacing between all operators looser or tighter.

Fenced Expressions

The `mfenced` element surrounds its content with a pair of fences (such as brackets or parentheses) and automatically inserts a separator between each pair of arguments. It provides a compact way of expressing markup involving fences and separators.

Consider the following expression:

$f(x, y)$

```
<mrow>
 <mi>f</mi>
 <mo>&ApplyFunction;</mo>
 <mrow>
   <mo>(</mo>
   <mi>x</mi>
   <mo>,</mo>
   <mi>y</mi>
   <mo>)</mo>
 </mrow>
</mrow>
```

The same expression can also be represented more compactly by the following markup:

$f(x, y)$

```
<mrow>
 <mi>f</mi>
 <mo>&ApplyFunction;</mo>
 <mfenced><mi>x</mi><mi>y</mi></mfenced>
</mrow>
```

The characters used as the opening and closing fence are determined by the value of the attributes, `open` and `close`. The default values of these attributes are the opening and closing parentheses. The attribute `separators` determine the character used as the separator. This can be specified as a sequence of zero or more characters. If there are too many separators, the extra ones are ignored. If there are too few separators, the last one is repeated as many times as required.

Here are two more examples that show the use of these attributes:

$(a + b + c)$

```
<mfenced separator="+">
 <mi>a</mi>
 <mi>b</mi>
 <mi>c</mi>
</mfenced>
```

$[0, 1)$

```
<mfenced open="[">
 <mn>0</mn>
 <mn>1</mn>
</mfenced>
```

Padding Expressions

The `mpadded` element provides a way to add extra space or "padding" around its content. It works by modifying the apparent size and position of the bounding box in which its content is rendered. The bounding box of the content is surrounded by an extra bounding box. The attributes of the `mpadded` element determine the size and position of this extra box.

The `mpadded` element has four attributes:

- `width`: determines the horizontal length of the bounding box. The bounding box of the mpadded element is rendered flush left with the bounding box of its contents. Hence, when you increase the width, you add space to the right of the box's contents.
- `lspace`: specifies the amount of space between the left edge of the bounding box and the left edge of the bounding box of its contents.
- `height`: specifies the vertical space between the baseline of the contents (the line along the bottom of most letter glyphs in normal text rendering) and the top of the bounding box of the `mpadded` element

- `depth`: specifies the vertical space between the baseline of the contents and the bottom of the bounding box of the `mpadded` element.

You can specify each of these attributes in several different ways: as a number followed by a unit, as a percentage, or as a multiple of the default value or a named space. Here are some examples of the `mpadded` element that show different ways of specifying the attribute values:

```
<mpadded width="+0em"> ... </mpadded>
<mpadded width="+75%"> ... </mpadded>
<mpadded width="100%"> ... </mpadded>
<mpadded width="1.0 width"> ... </mpadded>
```

Each attribute value can take positive or negative values. You can use negative values of the attributes to fake the appearance of certain characters. For example, the open-face R character used to represent the set of all real numbers would normally be indicated using the character entity reference, as shown below:

$\mathbb{R}$

```
<mi>&#x211D; </mi>
```

Alternatively, you could use the named entity reference for this character, `ℝ`. However, on a system where the appropriate font to display the open-face character is not available, you could approximate the appearance of this character using the following markup:

$\mathbb{R}$

```
<mrow>
 <mpadded width="0"> <mi>R</mi> </mpadded>
 <mspace width="0.3em"/>
 <mtext>|</mtext>
</mrow>
```

However, this type of markup alters the meaning of the expression and hinders its interpretation by audio renderers and computer algebra systems. Hence, MathML specifically discourages the use of spacing to convey meaning.

Making Expressions Invisible

The `mphantom` element makes its content invisible while preserving the size and position of the bounding box of its contents. This element is useful for aligning parts of an expression.

For example, in the expression below the x in the numerator is aligned with the x in the denominator if you explicitly add a "$+x^2$" term enclosed in an `mphantom` element, in the numerator:

$$\frac{1+x}{1+x+x^2}$$

```
<mfrac>
 <mrow>
   <mn>1</mn><mo>+</mo><mi>x</mi>
   <mphantom>
     <mo>+</mo>
     <msup>
       <mi>x</mi>
       <mn>2</mn>
     </msup>
   </mphantom>
 </mrow>
 <mrow>
   <mn>1</mn><mo>+</mo><mi>x</mi><mo>+</mo>
   <msup>
     <mi>x</mi>
     <mn>2</mn>
   </msup>
 </mrow>
</mfrac>
```

Special Notations

The `menclose` element renders its content inside an enclosing notation, determined by the value of its `notation` attribute. This attribute can take three values, `longdiv`, `actuarial`, and `radical`, each corresponding to a specific type of notation. The following example shows what the rendering for `notation="longdiv"` looks like:

$$37\overline{)1456}$$

```
<mrow>
 <mn>37</mn>
 <menclose notation="longdiv">
   <mn>1456</mn>
 </menclose>
</mrow>
```

4.4 Scripts and Limits

Presentation markup includes several elements to represent expressions involving scripts and limits. This section provides a detailed description of all such elements.

Subscripts and Superscripts

Subscripts and superscripts are indicated using the `msub` and `msup` elements, respectively. The syntax of `msub` is:

<msub> *base subscript* </msub>

Here is an example of a subscript:

a_i

```
<msub>
 <mi>a</mi>
 <mi>i</mi>
</msub>
```

The `msub` element has one attribute called `subscriptshift`. This specifies the minimum amount by which the subscript should be shifted down relative to the baseline of the base expression.

The syntax of `msup` is:

<msup> *base superscript* </msup>

Here is an example of a superscript:

x^2

```
<msup>
 <mi>x</mi>
 <mn>2</mn>
</msup>
```

The `msup` element has one attribute called `superscriptshift`. This specifies the minimum amount by which the superscript should be shifted up relative to the baseline of the base expression.

MathML also provides an additional element called `msubsup`. This is used to attach both a subscript and a superscript to a base expression. It has the following syntax:

<msubsup> *base subscript superscript* </msubsup>

The `msubsup` element accepts both `subscriptshift` and `superscriptshift` as attributes. Here is an example of `msubsup`'s use:

A_i^j

```
<msubsup>
 <mi>A</mi>
 <mi>i</mi>
 <mi>j</mi>
</msubsup>
```

Underscripts and Overscripts

Underscripts and overscripts are represented using the `munder` and `mover` elements, respectively. The syntax of `munder` is as follows:

<munder> *base underscript* </munder>

The `munder` element has one attribute called `accentunder`. If this is set to `true`, the underscript is treated like an accent and if `false` like a limit. Accents are rendered in normal size and closer to the base; on the other hand, limits are rendered in a smaller size and farther away from the base. The following example shows an underscript rendered as an accent:

$$\underbrace{1+2+\cdots+n}$$

```
<mrow>
  <munder accentunder="true">
    <mrow>
      <mn>1</mn>
      <mo>+</mo>
      <mn>2</mn>
      <mo>+</mo>
      <mo>&ctdot;</mo>
      <mi>n</mi>
    </mrow>
    <mo>&UnderBrace;</mo>
  </munder>
</mrow>
```

If the base is an `mo` element with `movablelimits="true"` and `displaystyle="false"`, then the underscript is rendered as a subscript and the `accentunder` attribute is ignored.

The syntax of `mover` is:

<mover> *base overscript* </mover>

The `mover` element has one attribute: `accent`. If this is set to `true`, the overscript is treated like an accent and if `false` like a limit. Accents are rendered in normal size and closer to the base, whereas limits are rendered in a smaller size and farther away from the base. The following example shows an overscript rendered as an accent:

$$\hat{x}$$

```
<mover accent="true">
  <mi>x</mi>
  <mo>&Hat;</mo>
</mover>
```

The following example shows an overscript rendered as a limit:

$$\hat{x}$$

```
<mover accent="false">
 <mi>x</mi>
 <mo>&Hat;</mo>
</mover>
```

If *base* is an operator with `movablelimits="true"` and `displaystyle="false"`, then the overscript is rendered as a superscript and the accent attribute is ignored.

In addition, MathML provides the `munderover` element for attaching both an underscript and overscript to a base expression. This produces a better visual appearance than if you use separate `munder` and `mover` elements. This is because the vertical spacing of the underscript and overscript is more symmetrical relative to the base and both the scripts follow the slant of the base. This element has the following syntax:

`<munderover>` *base underscript overscript* `</munderover>`

Here is an example of its use:

$$\int\limits_a^b f(x)\, dx$$

```
<mrow>
 <munderover>
   <mo>&int;</mo>
   <mi>a</mi>
   <mi>b</mi>
 </munderover>
 <mi>f</mi>
 <mo>&ApplyFunction;</mo>
 <mrow>
   <mo>(</mo><mi>x</mi><mo>)</mo>
 </mrow>
 <mo>&DifferentialD;</mo><mi>x</mi>
</mrow>
```

The `munderover` element accepts both `accent` and `accentunder` as attributes. If the base is an operator with `movablelimits="true"` and `displaystyle="false"`, then the underscript is rendered as a subscript, the overscript is rendered as a superscript, and the `accent` attribute is ignored.

Multiscripts

Another common type of notation involves objects that have multiple subscripts and superscripts attached to the base expression. This type of notation is used, for example, to represent tensors such as T^a_{bc}. MathML provides the `mmultiscripts` element specially for this type of notation. This element can be used to attach any number of vertically aligned pairs of subscripts and superscripts to a base expression. It allows you to attach both prescripts and postscripts—notation to the left and right of the base expression, respectively.

The syntax for this element is:

```
<mmultiscripts>
base (subscript superscript)*
[<mprescripts/> (presubscript presuperscript)*]
</mmultiscripts>
```

The important points to note about the `mmultiscripts` element are as follows:

- Subscripts are always listed before the corresponding superscript in each subscript-superscript pair.
- If one of the members of a subscript-superscript pair is missing, its position must be explicitly indicated using the empty element `none`.
- The empty element `mprescripts` must be inserted before you specify any subscript-superscript pairs that occur in the prescript position.
- Prescripts are specified after postscripts since prescripts are relatively uncommon.
- Both prescript and postscript pairs are listed in left-to-right order.

Here is an example:

$${}_{12}^{\;3}T^a_{bc}$$

```
<mmultiscripts>
 <mi>T</mi>
 <mi>b</mi><mi>a</mi>
 <mi>c</mi><none/>
 <mprescripts/>
 <mi>1</mi><none/>
 <mi>2</mi><mi>3</mi>
</mmultiscripts>
```

The `mmultiscripts` element has two attributes: `subscriptshift` and `superscriptshift`. These specify the minimum amount by which a superscript or subscript should be shifted up or down relative to the baseline of the base expression, respectively.

Changes to `displaystyle` and `scriptlevel`

It is conventional for characters placed in a script position to appear in a smaller font than the base expression. To satisfy this convention, the presentation elements that represent scripts automatically change the value of two attributes of the `mstyle` element, `displaystyle` and `scriptlevel`. Normally, these are inherited from the environment. These changes are summarized here:

- The `msub` element sets `displaystyle` to `false` and increments `scriptlevel` by 1 in *subscript* but leaves both attributes unchanged within *base*.
- The `msup` element sets `displaystyle` to `false` and increments `scriptlevel` by 1 in *superscript* but leaves both attributes unchanged within *base*.
- The `msubsup` element sets `displaystyle` to `false` and increments `scriptlevel` by 1 in both *subscript* and *superscript* but leaves both attributes unchanged within *base*.
- The `munder` element sets `displaystyle` to `false` in *underscript* and increments `scriptlevel` by 1 only when `accentunder="false"`. It leaves both attributes unchanged within *base*.
- The `mover` element sets `displaystyle` to `false`in *overscript* and increments `scriptlevel` by 1 only when `accent="false"`. It leaves both attributes unchanged within *base*.
- The `munderover` element sets `displaystyle` to `false` in *overscript* and increments `scriptlevel` by 1 only when `accent="false"`. It sets `displaystyle` to `false` in *underscript* and increments `scriptlevel` by 1 only when `accentunder="false"`. It leaves both attributes unchanged within *base*.
- The `mmultiscripts` element increments `scriptlevel` by 1 and sets `displaystyle` to `false` in all its arguments except the base.

For more details about the `displaystyle` and `scriptlevel` attributes, see the discussion of the `mstyle` element in Section 4.3.

4.5 TABLES AND MATRICES

The next section discusses the structure of tables in MathML.

The Structure of Tables

In MathML, tables and matrices can be represented using the `mtable`, `mtr`, and `mtd` elements. These correspond roughly to the table, tr, and td elements used for tables in HTML. The mtable element represents an entire table, the mtr element represents a single row of the table, and each mtd element represents a single cell within a row.

In addition, MathML includes an mlabeledtr element that can be used in place of any mtr element to specify a labeled row. The first argument of the mlabeledtr element specifies a label, and each subsequent argument specifies a specific cell of the row.

Here is a simple example that shows the presentation markup for a 2 by 2 matrix:

$$\begin{pmatrix} 1 & 2 \\ 3 & 4 \end{pmatrix}$$

```
<mrow>
 <mo>(</mo>
 <mtable>
   <mtr>
     <mtd><mn>1</mn></mtd>
     <mtd><mn>2</mn></mtd>
   </mtr>
   <mtr>
     <mtd><mn>3</mn></mtd>
     <mtd><mn>4</mn></mtd>
   </mtr>
 </mtable>
 <mo>)</mo>
</mrow>
```

The mtable element accepts a large collection of attributes for adjusting various properties of the rows and columns, such as their spacing and alignment. There are 18 attributes in all (Table 4.8).

For several of these attributes, the value can be a sequence of zero or more entries. In such cases, the first entry applies to the first row/column, the second entry to the second row/column, and so on. If there are fewer entries than rows/columns in the table, the last entry is repeated as many times as necessary. If there are more entries than rows/columns, the extra entries are ignored.

The meaning of most of these attributes is evident from their name. For a detailed description of each attribute, see Chapter 13.

The mtr element takes the attributes rowalign, columnalign, and groupalign. The values are normally inherited from the surrounding mtable element. You can override the inherited value by setting the attribute explicitly.

TABLE 4.8 Attributes of the `mtable` Element

<table>
<tr><th>Attribute</th><th>Values</th><th>Default</th></tr>
<tr><td><code>align</code></td><td><code>(top | bottom | center | baseline | axis)</code></td><td>[rownumber] <code>axis</code></td></tr>
<tr><td><code>rowalign</code></td><td><code>(top | bottom | center | baseline | axis)+ baseline</code></td><td></td></tr>
<tr><td><code>columnalign</code></td><td><code>(left | center | right)+ center</code></td><td></td></tr>
<tr><td><code>columnwidth</code></td><td><code>(auto</code> | number h-unit | namedspace | <code>fit</code>) +</td><td><code>auto</code></td></tr>
<tr><td><code>width</code></td><td><code>auto</code> | number h-unit</td><td><code>auto</code></td></tr>
<tr><td><code>rowspacing</code></td><td>(number v-unit) +</td><td><code>1.0 ex</code></td></tr>
<tr><td><code>columnspacing</code></td><td>(number h-unit | namedspace)+</td><td><code>0.8 em</code></td></tr>
<tr><td><code>rowlines</code></td><td><code>(none | solid | dashed) +</code></td><td><code>none</code></td></tr>
<tr><td><code>columnlines</code></td><td><code>(none | solid | dashed) +</code></td><td><code>none</code></td></tr>
<tr><td><code>equalrows</code></td><td><code>true | false false</code></td><td></td></tr>
<tr><td><code>equalcolumns</code></td><td><code>true | false false</code></td><td></td></tr>
<tr><td><code>frame</code></td><td><code>(none | solid | dashed) +</code></td><td><code>none</code></td></tr>
<tr><td><code>framespacing</code></td><td>(number h-unit | namedspace) (number v-unit | namedspace) <code>0.4 em 0.5 ex</code></td><td></td></tr>
<tr><td><code>displaystyle</code></td><td><code>true | false false</code></td><td></td></tr>
<tr><td><code>side</code></td><td><code>left | right | left-overlap | rightoverlap right</code></td><td></td></tr>
<tr><td><code>minlabelspacing</code></td><td>number h-unit</td><td><code>0.8 em</code></td></tr>
<tr><td><code>groupalign</code></td><td>groupalignment-list-list</td><td><code>{left}</code></td></tr>
<tr><td><code>alignmentscope</code></td><td><code>true | false true</code></td><td></td></tr>
</table>

The `mlabeledtr` element has the same attributes as the `mtr` element. The only difference is that the attributes of the `mlabeledtr` element apply to the label as well as the individual cells in the row. To apply an attribute only to a label, you must set the attribute in the `<mtd>` element that surrounds the label.

The `mtd` element also takes the `rowalign`, `columnalign`, and `groupalign` attributes. The values of these attributes are normally inherited from the surrounding `mtr` element. You can override the inherited value by setting the attribute explicitly. In addition, the mtd element takes two other attributes: rowspan and columnspan. These can be set to an integer and allow a cell in the table to occupy a specified number of rows or columns.

Here is an example of a simple table with several attributes specified explicitly:

1	$1+x+y$
$1+x$	$1+y$
$1+x+y$	y

```
<mtable columnalign='left' rowlines='solid'
columnlines='solid' frame='solid'>
 <mtr>
   <mtd>
     <mn>1</mn>
   </mtd>
   <mtd>
     <mn>1</mn><mo>+</mo><mi>x</mi>
     <mo>+</mo><mi>y</mi>
   </mtd>
 </mtr>
 <mtr>
   <mtd>
     <mn>1</mn><mo>+</mo><mi>x</mi>
   </mtd>
   <mtd>
     <mn>1</mn><mo>+</mo><mi>y</mi>
   </mtd>
 </mtr>
 <mtr>
   <mtd>
     <mn>1</mn><mo>+</mo><mi>x</mi>
     <mo>+</mo><mi>y</mi>
   </mtd>
   <mtd>
     <mi>y</mi>
   </mtd>
 </mtr>
</mtable>
```

Labeled Rows and Numbered Equations

The mlabeledtr element can be used to implement cross-referencing and automatic numbering of equations in conjunction with XSLT processing (even though these features are not directly supported in MathML). Here is an example:

$$y = x^2 + 1 \qquad (1.7)$$

```
<mtable>
 <mlabeledtr id="parabola">
   <mtd>
     <mtext>(1.7)</mtext>
   </mtd>
   <mtd>
     <mrow>
       <mi>y</mi>
       <mo>=</mo>
       <mrow>
       <msup>
         <mi>x</mi>
         <mn>2</mn>
       </msup>
       <mo>+</mo>
       <mn>1</mn>
     </mrow>
   </mtd>
 </mlabeledtr>
</mtable>
```

More information on using the `id` attribute to implement cross-referencing is provided in Section 6.3.

Controlling Alignment

MathML provides a sophisticated mechanism for controlling the alignment of expressions that appear in a table. You can align the content of any cell with that of other cells in the same column. Each cell can contain any number of subexpressions that can be aligned independently, along the right, left, or center, or along a decimal point.

To specify the alignment, you must take the following steps:

1. Create alignment groups within each expression that you want to align. An *alignment group* is defined as any content between the start of one `maligngroup` element and the next `maligngroup` element or the end of the cell, whichever comes first.
2. Specify a point of alignment for each alignment group. You can do this either by inserting a `malignmark` element or using the `groupalign` attribute. This attribute can be specified for an entire table or for a specific row or cell.

Let's look at a simple example. Suppose you want to display a pair of simultaneous equations so that the following items in one equation are each aligned with the corresponding items in the other equation:

- The variables "x" and "y"
- The operators "+" or "-"
- The "=" sign
- The number on the right-hand side

Here is the markup for this example:

$$\begin{aligned} 2x + \;\; y &= -5 \\ x - 2y &= \;\;\; 1 \end{aligned}$$

```
<mtable>
 <mtr>
   <mtd>
     <mrow>
       <mn>2</mn>
       <mo>&InvisibleTimes;</mo>
       <maligngroup/><mi><malignmark/>x</mi>
       <maligngroup/><mo><malignmark/>+</mo>
       <maligngroup/><mi><malignmark/>y</mi>
       <maligngroup/><mo><malignmark/>=</mo>
       <mo>-</mo>
       <maligngroup/><mn><malignmark/>5</mn>
     </mrow>
   </mtd>
 </mtr>
 <mtr>
   <mtd>
     <mrow>
       <maligngroup/><mi><malignmark/>x</mi>
       <maligngroup/><mo><malignmark/>-</mo>
       <mn>2</mn>
       <mo>&InvisibleTimes;</mo>
       <maligngroup/><mi><malignmark/>y</mi>
       <maligngroup/><mo><malignmark/>=</mo>
       <maligngroup/><mn><malignmark/>1</mn>
     </mrow>
   </mtd>
 </mtr>
</mtable>
```

Notice that each equation is placed in a separate cell of a table that consists of two rows and one column. In each equation, five different parts must be aligned independently. Hence, each equation contains five alignment groups, each defined using a single `maligngroup` element.

For each alignment group, you specify the alignment point by inserting a `malignmark` element in the content of the token element that contains the character to be aligned. Recall that `malignmark` is one of only two elements that can occur as the content of a token element (the other is `mglyph`).

The `malignmark` element takes a single attribute called `edge`, which defines the position of the alignment point. With the default setting `edge="left"`, the alignment point is the left edge of the character immediately to the right of the `malignmark` element. With the setting `edge="right"`, the alignment point is the right edge of the character immediately to the left of the `malignmark` element.

For complex expressions with a large number of alignment points, it is verbose to specify each alignment point using an explicit `malignmark` element. As an alternative, you can use the `groupalign` attribute to specify the alignment point for each alignment group.

The following markup represents the same set of equations as above but with the alignment specified using the `groupalign` attribute on the top-level `mtable` element:

$$\begin{array}{rcl} 2x+y &=& -5 \\ x-2y &=& 1 \end{array}$$

```
<mtable>
 <mtr groupalign="{left}">
   <mtd>
     <mrow>
       <mn>2</mn>
       <mo>&InvisibleTimes;</mo>
       <maligngroup/><mi>x</mi>
       <maligngroup/><mo>+</mo>
       <maligngroup/><mi>y</mi>
       <maligngroup/><mo>=</mo>
       <mo>-</mo>
       <maligngroup/><mn>5</mn>
     </mrow>
   </mtd>
 </mtr>
 <mtr>
   <mtd>
     <mrow>
       <maligngroup/><mi>x</mi>
       <maligngroup/><mo>-</mo>
       <mn>2</mn>
       <mo>&InvisibleTimes;</mo>
       <maligngroup/><mi>y</mi>
       <maligngroup/><mo>=</mo>
       <maligngroup/><mn>1</mn>
```

```
        </mrow>
      </mtd>
    </mtr>
  </mtable>
```

You can specify the `groupalign` attribute on an `mtable` element (for the entire table), on an `mtr` or `mlabeledtr` element (for a single row), or on an `mtd` element (for a single cell). If this attribute is not specified explicitly, it is inherited from the environment. Note that an alignment point specified by a `malignmark` element overrides the automatic specification defined by the `groupalign` attribute.

The alignment position for each alignment group can be specified as one of four values: `left`, `right`, `center`, and `decimalpoint`. Since each cell can contain multiple alignment groups, the `groupalign` attribute on an `mtd` element is set to a list of alignment values, each value applying to a specific alignment group. If there are more alignment groups than alignment values in the list, the last element in the list is applied to all the remaining groups. Here is an example:

```
<mtd groupalign="right decimalpoint left">
```

When you specify `groupalign` on an `mtr`, `mlabeledtr`, or `mtable` element, the attribute is set to a list of list of alignment values. Each list is enclosed in curly braces to separate it from other lists. Here is an example:

```
<mtr groupalign="{right decimalpoint left}
                 {right left}">
```

The `mtable` element also takes an attribute called `alignmentscope`. If you set this to `false`, all `maligngroup` and `malignmark` elements in the table are ignored. This attribute is useful when you are representing nested tables. For example, you can use it to prevent alignment information intended for the outer table from being applied to the inner table.

In general, `alignmentscope` is specified as a list of Boolean values, each applying to one column of the table. For example, with the following markup, alignment elements would be recognized in the first two columns of the table but ignored in the last column:

```
<mtable alignmentscope="true true false">
```

4.6 Other Elements

For most of the presentation elements discussed in this chapter, the rendering rules are determined by the standard conventions of mathematical notation. However, two presentation elements, maction and merror, do not correspond to any type of mathematical notation. This section explains the meaning and usage of these two elements.

Setting up Actions

The maction element provides a mechanism for adding interactivity to MathML equations. This element associates a type of action with an MathML expression. You can then program a processing application to perform the specified action in response to a user event (such as clicking or moving the mouse over the MathML expression).

An maction element can contain any other MathML elements and can have any number of arguments. This element has the following two attributes:

- selection : is an integer that identifies one of the arguments of the maction element. The value 1 refers to the first argument, 2 to the second argument, and so on. This attribute provides a way to refer to subexpressions of the maction element—for example, in cases where the intended action is to toggle between different subexpressions. The argument of the maction element that corresponds to the specified value of the selection attribute is called the *selected subexpression.*
- actiontype : specifies the action to be performed. The allowed values of this attribute are not defined by the MathML specification. Instead, each MathML application is expected to define its own values depending on the type of actions it supports.

Some examples of possible values of actiontype along with the actions associated with them are given below. Note that all these examples are hypothetical. They are provided only to illustrate the concept. For these values of the actiontype attribute to work as indicated, they must first be implemented by a specific application. A MathML application that does not recognize a value specified for actiontype will just render the selected subexpression without performing the action.

With actiontype="toggle", a rendering application would display one of a given series of subexpressions. Each time the user clicks the displayed subexpression, the renderer would update the value of selection by 1 and cause the next expression in the series to be displayed. Here is an example illustrating this behavior:

```
<maction actiontype=toggle selection=1>
 (expression1)
 (expression2)
</maction>
```

With `actiontype="statusline"`, clicking or moving the mouse over an expression would cause the specified message to appear in the status line of the browser, as shown here:

```
<maction actiontype="statusline">
 (expression)
 (message)
</maction>
```

With `actiontype="tooltip"`, clicking or moving the mouse over an expression would cause the message to be displayed in a pop-up tooltip box near the expression, as follows:

```
<maction actiontype="tooltip">
 (expression)
 (message)
</maction>
```

With `actiontype="highlight"`, clicking or moving the mouse over an expression would cause the message to be displayed in a different color and/or with a different background, as shown here:

```
<maction actiontype="highlight" xhtml:color="red"
    xhtml:background="yellow">
 expression
</maction>
```

In the above example, the color and background are specified by two other attributes from a different namespace.

With `actiontype="menu"`, clicking or moving the mouse over an expression would cause a pop-up menu to be displayed. A typical MathML expression using this attribute would have the following structure:

```
<maction actiontype="menu" selection="1">
 (menu item 1)
 (menu item 2)
</maction>
```

The items in the menu above are determined by the arguments of the `<maction>` element. Since a `<maction>` element can contain any other MathML elements, each menu item could itself be a MathML expression, to allow a user to choose from different forms of an expression.

Displaying Error Messages

The `merror` element displays its contents as an error message. It is intended as a way of displaying syntax errors encountered when an application is generating MathML from some other form of input. Each application can choose its own style for displaying the contents of the merror element so they are easy to distinguish from the surrounding text (for example, in a different color or with a different background).

The suggested use of the merror element is for an application to replace the erroneous part of the input with an merror element that contains a description of the error. The application then continues processing the surrounding input as normally as possible. This way, the error message appears at the location where the erroneous input would have appeared, making it easier to identify the cause of the error.

The merror element can contain any arbitrary MathML expression. Typically the text of the error message is enclosed in an mtext element. If the erroneous input contains fragments that are correctly formatted, then these can be processed normally and included in the contents of the error message.

For example, suppose a user includes the MathML element mssub instead of the MathML element msub because of a typing error, as shown in the following markup:

```
<mssub>
 <mi>&ExponentialE;</mi>
 <mrow>
   <mi>&ImaginaryI;</mi>
   <mi>&InvisibleTimes;</mi>
   <mi>&pi;</mi>
 </mrow>
</mssub>
```

When this markup is processed by an application that checks for MathML syntax, an error message like the following might be produced:

```
<merror>
 <mtext>Unrecognized element at line
   17:mssub;arguments were:</mtext>
     <mi>&ExponentialE;</mi>
 <mtext>and</mtext>
   <mrow>
     <mi>&ImaginaryI;</mi>
     <mi>&InvisibleTimes;</mi>
     <mi>&pi;</mi>
 </mrow>
</merror>
```

CHAPTER

5

CONTENT MARKUP

This chapter provides detailed information on the syntax of MathML content markup. It explains the different categories into which content elements can be classified and gives examples of typical elements from each category. It also discusses the meaning and values of all the attributes defined for content markup.

5.1 INTRODUCTION

Some simple examples of content markup were discussed in Section 3.2. We saw there that content markup consists of approximately 150 elements and 12 attributes that are used to encode the logical meaning of mathematical expressions. Most content elements can be broadly divided into the following categories:

- Token elements
- Constructor elements
- Operators and functions
- Qualifier elements
- Constants and symbols
- Semantic mapping elements

Token elements are the only content elements that can directly contain character data. All other elements can contain only other elements. There are three token elements: `cn`, `ci`, and `csymbol`. These are used to represent numbers, identifiers, and user-defined symbols, respectively.

Constructor elements are used to construct expressions by combining token elements and elements that represent operators and functions. The most important constructor element is `apply`, which represents the operation of applying a function or operator to one or more arguments. By recursively nesting constructor elements, you can build up the content markup to represent an expression of any complexity. Token elements and constructor elements are collectively called *container elements* because they act as containers for mathematical objects.

The majority of content elements are empty elements that directly represent common *operators* and *functions*. Some elements that correspond to most operators and functions are encountered at the level of high school and college mathematics. For example, the `plus`, `sin`, and `int` elements represent addition, the trigonometric sine function, and integration, respectively.

Some content elements provide additional information needed to fully specify the meaning of other elements. For example, the `uplimit`, `lowlimit`, and `bvar` elements are used to specify the upper limit, lower limit, and variable of integration of a definite integral that is represented using the `int` element. These elements are called *qualifier elements* since they qualify the meaning of other elements.

A small number of content elements are used to directly represent specific *constants* and *symbols* that are important in mathematics. For example, the elements `pi`, `exponentiale`, `imaginaryi`, and `infinity` are used to represent the constants π, e, i, and ∞, respectively.

Semantic mapping elements are used to provide additional information, such as comments and annotations, about a given piece of content markup. For example, you can use the `annotation` element to give the encoding of a given MathML expression in another format such as TEX or *Mathematica*.

Table 5.1 lists all the content elements, organized into categories according to the type of element.

For the sake of brevity, the `math` element is omitted from all examples in this chapter. However, this element is implied by the context; that is, you should think of each instance of MathML markup as being enclosed in an outer `math` element.

Modifying the Default Semantics

Each content element has a default semantic meaning. However, you can modify the meaning of any of these elements using the following two attributes, which most content elements accept:

- `definitionURL`: specifies a URL that contains information on the semantics of the symbol
- `encoding`: specifies the form in which the semantic information is encoded

For example, the content element `times` by default represents the operation of multiplying two numbers. However, you can modify its semantics so that it refers to the cross product of two vectors, as in the following example:

$A \times B$

```
<apply>
 <times encoding="text" definitionURL=
   "http://www.example.org/vectorcrossproduct.html />
 <ci type="vector"> A </ci>
 <ci type="vector"> B </ci>
</apply>
```

Here, the URL specified as the value of `definitionURL` must contain a definition of the vector product encoded as plain text. Note

TABLE 5.1 Content Elements

Category	Elements
Token elements	ci, cn, csymbol
Basic content elements	apply, lambda, declare, reln, fn, set, list, vector, matrix, matrixrow, interval, piecewise, piece, otherwise, domain, codomain, image, inverse, ident
Arithmetic, algebra, and logic	plus, minus, times, divide, power, root, quotient, rem, exp, factorial, max, min, gcd, abs, conjugate, arg, real, imaginary, lcm, floor, ceiling, and, or, xor, not, implies, forall, exists
Relations	eq, neq, gt, lt, geq, leq, equivalent, approx, factorof, tendsto, in, notin, subset, prsubset, notsubset, notprsubset
Elementary functions	exp, ln, log, sin, cos, tan, sec, cosec, cot, sinh, cosh, tanh, sech, cosech, coth, arcsin, arccos, arctan, arcsec, arccosec, arccot, arcsinh, arccosh, arctanh, arcsech, arccosech, arccoth
Theory of sets	set, list, union, intersect, setdiff, card, cartesianproduct
Sequences and series	sum, product, limit
Linear algebra	determinant, transpose, selector, vectorproduct, scalarproduct, outerproduct
Calculus	int, diff, partialdiff, grad, divergence, curl, laplacian
Statistics	mean, median, mode, var, sdev
Qualifier elements	bvar, lowlimit, uplimit, degree, logbase, domainofapplication, momentabout
Constants and symbols	pi, exponentiale, eulergamma, infinity, imaginaryi, true, false, emptyset, notanumber, integers, reals, rationals, complexes, primes, naturalnumbers
Semantic mapping elements	semantics, annotation, annotation-xml

that the `type` attribute of the `ci` element is used to specify that the identifiers *A* and *B* represent vectors.

5.2 Token Elements

Content markup contains three token elements: `cn`, `ci`, and `csymbol`. The `cn` and `ci` elements are analogous to the `mn` and `mi` elements in presentation markup; that is, they are used to represent numbers and identifiers, respectively. The `csymbol` element is used to associate a specific mathematical meaning with a particular symbol. Token elements have a special status since they are the only content elements that can directly contain character data. Token elements can also contain arbitrary presentation markup, which allows you to have greater control over how they are rendered.

Numbers

The `cn` element is used to represent numbers. Its content consists of an optional '+' or '−' sign followed by a string of digits, possibly containing a decimal point. Alternatively, the `cn` element can contain one of the named entity references that represent a numerical constant, such as `π` or `ⅇ`. By default, the contents of the `cn` element are interpreted as a signed real number in base 10. However, you can specify a different type of number or a different base, using the `type` and `base` attributes.

The `type` attribute of the `cn` element describes the type of number encoded. It can take the values `real`, `integer`, `rational`, `complex-polar`, `complex-cartesian`, `e-notation`, and `constant`. The empty element `sep` is used to separate different parts of a number (such as the numerator and denominator of a fraction or the real and imaginary parts of a complex number). For example, a fraction is represented as shown here:

$$\frac{1}{2}$$

```
<cn type="rational">1<sep/>2</cn>
```

A complex number is represented as shown here:

$$3 + 4i$$

```
<cn type="complex-cartesian">3<sep/>4</cn>
```

The `base` attribute of the `cn` element specifies the base of the number being encoded. It can be any number between 2 and 36. For example, a hexadecimal number would be represented as shown here:

$$\mathrm{EF2}_{16}$$

```
<cn type="integer" base="16">EF2</cn>
```

Table 5.2 gives a few examples of some other types of numbers that can be represented using the cn element.

In addition to type and base, the cn element takes the definitionURL and encoding attributes, which can be used to modify its default semantics, as explained in Section 5.1.

Identifiers

The ci element is used to represent identifiers such as the names of variables or functions. Each ci element represents a single mathematical object. However, you can make its appearance as complex as you want by including any type of presentation markup inside it. For example, the following markup can be used to represent the second component of a vector ***x***:

x_2

```
<ci>
  <msub>
    <mi>x</mi>
    <mn>2</mn>
  </msub>
</ci>
```

You can indicate the type of object represented by using the type attribute, which can take values real, integer, rational, complex-polar, complex-cartesian, and constant. In addition, you can set the type attribute to the names of container elements in content markup, such as vector, matrix, set, and fn. An application can use the information in the type attribute to determine how the content should be rendered. For example, the following markup might be rendered in a bold font to indicate that it represents a vector:

```
<ci type="vector">A</ci>
```

Symbols

The csymbol element is used to associate a specific mathematical meaning with a particular symbol. It can contain any presentation

TABLE 5.2 Types of Numbers Represented by the cn Element

Number	Content Markup
765.43	`<cn type="real">765.43</cn>`
2002	`<cn type="integer">2002</cn>`
Polar(5, 3.14)	`<cn type="complex-polar">5<sep/>3.14</cn>`
π	`<cn type="constant">π</cn>`

markup inside it, so you can specify the rendering of the symbol precisely.

This element is provided as an extension mechanism. In effect, it enables you to create a new symbol with a specific user-defined meaning. You can then use that symbol to represent any operator, function, or constant that is not described by any of the existing content elements. The meaning associated with the symbol is specified using the `definitionURL` and `encoding` attributes, as explained in Section 5.1.

For example, the following markup associates the symbol N_A with the value of Avogadro's constant, used in chemistry:

N_A

```
<csymbol encoding="text" definitionURL=
"www.example.org/universalconstants/Avogadro.htm" >
 <msub>
   <mi>N</mi>
   <mi>A</mi>
 </msub>
</csymbol>
```

The following example defines the notational unit P_1 to mean the first Legendre polynomial function:

$P_1(x)$

```
<apply>
 <csymbol encoding="OpenMath" definitionURL=
   "http://www.openmath.org/cd/LegendrePolynomial.ocd">
   <msub><mi>P</mi><mn>1</mn></msub>
 </csymbol>
 <ci>x</ci>
</apply>
```

Here, the rendering of the symbol is specified using presentation markup and its meaning is specified in terms of the OpenMath convention, using the attributes of the `csymbol` element. You can then use this element as the first argument of an `apply` function.

5.3 Constructor Elements

Constructor elements are the building blocks of content markup. They are so called because they construct complete expressions out of more basic components such as operators, functions, variables, and numbers. They are also used to create compound objects such as lists, sets, vectors, or matrices. They accomplish this by providing a framework for combining other content elements that represent more basic mathematical objects such as numbers, identifiers, operators, and functions. In this section, we look at some important constructor elements and give simple examples to illustrate their meaning and usage.

The `apply` Element

We saw several examples of the `apply` element in Section 3.2. This is by far the most common content element, since it represents one of the most basic mathematical concepts, that of applying an operator or function to its arguments.

The first child element of the `apply` element is the operator or function to be applied. The subsequent elements are the arguments of the function sor the operands of the operator. The number of subsequent child elements allowed depends on the operator or function specified as the first child element. For example, the `plus` element can be followed by zero or more child elements while the `minus` element must have either one or two child elements after it.

The operator or function specified as the first child element of the `apply` element can be represented in three ways:

- Using one of the existing content elements that represent specific operators or functions
- Using the `csymbol` element, as explained in Section 5.2
- Using the `ci` element; for example, you can specify the function *f* as `<ci type="function">f<ci>`

Here is a simple example of using the `apply` element:

$$\sin(x)$$

```
<apply>
 <sin/>
 <ci>x</ci>
</apply>
```

You can easily distinguish two different expressions that look similar but have different mathematical meanings by the number and position of `apply` elements used in the content markup. For example, the following markup represents the result of applying the sum of two functions f and g to the argument x:

$$(f+g)(x)$$

```
<apply>
 <apply>
   <plus/>
```

```
      <ci>f</ci>
      <ci>g</ci>
    </apply>
    <ci>x</ci>
  </apply>
```

The following markup represents the multiplication of the sum of two variables *f* and *g* with *x*:

$$(f+g)(x)$$

```
<apply>
  <times/>
  <apply>
    <plus/>
    <ci>f</ci>
    <ci>g</ci>
  </apply>
  <ci>x</ci>
</apply>
```

The `declare` Element

The `declare` element is used in content markup to associate a specific property or meaning with a mathematical object. For example, you can indicate that a certain identifier A represents a vector using this markup:

```
<declare type="vector"><ci>A</ci></declare>
```

The `declare` element is always placed at the beginning of a `math` element, and the scope of the declaration is the entire `math` element. This element is not rendered visually or aurally but it does affect the semantic interpretation of the identifier it encloses. The `declare` element is used whenever you need to specify that a given symbol represents a particular type of object such as a vector, matrix, list, set, or function. This information is specified using the `type` attribute of the `declare` element, which can be set to the name of any content element. By setting this attribute to the name of a container element such as `cn`, `list`, `set`, `vector`, `matrix`, or `fn`, you can declare any identifier to be an object of the specified type.

For example, the following declaration states that *x* is a real number with the value 3.75:

```
<declare>
  <ci>x</ci>
  <cn>3.75</cn>
</declare>
```

The following declares A to be a vector with three components a, b, and c:

```
<declare>
 <ci>A</ci>
 <vector>
   <ci>a</ci>
   <ci>b</ci>
   <ci>c</ci>
 </vector>
</declare>
```

Subsequent uses of A can then take into account that A is a vector. For example, if three identifiers, R, A, and B, are all declared to be vectors, an equation like the following could be interpreted as vector addition (by a particular MathML processor):

$$R = A + B$$

You can declare an identifier to be of a specified type without providing a complete description of it. For example, the declaration

```
<declare type="function">
 <ci>F</ci>
</declare>
```

specifies that F is a function without indicating the exact meaning of the function or the number of arguments it takes.

The `lambda` Element

The `lambda` element is used to represent the concept of a lambda function, used in calculus. The lambda calculus provides a formal syntax for specifying a statement of the form "let f be a function that takes x to x^2". A typical notation for the above statement looks like $f = \lambda(x, x^2)$.

In content markup, the concept of a lambda function is expressed using the `lambda` element. A function having n variables is specified using a `lambda` element with $n + 1$ child elements. Each of the first n child elements is a `bvar` element that represents one of the variables of the function. The $(n+1)$th element is an expression that defines the function itself. Here is an example:

$$f = \lambda(x, x^2)$$

```
<lambda>
 <bvar><ci>x</ci></bvar>
 <apply>
   <power/>
   <ci>x</ci>
```

```
    <cn>2</cn>
  </apply>
</lambda>
```

The following markup uses the `declare` and `lambda` elements to construct a function f for which $f(x, y) = x^2 + y^2 + xy$:

$$f = \lambda(x, y, x^2 + y^2 + xy)$$

```
<declare type="fn">
 <ci> f </ci>
 <lambda>
   <bvar><ci>x</ci></bvar>
   <bvar><ci>y</ci></bvar>
   <apply>
     <plus/>
     <apply>
       <power/>
       <ci>x</ci>
       <cn>2</cn>
     </apply>
     <apply>
       <power/>
       <ci>y</ci>
       <cn>2</cn>
     </apply>
     <apply>
       <times/>
       <ci>x</ci>
       <cn>y</cn>
     </apply>
   </apply>
 </lambda>
</declare>
```

Intervals

The `interval` element is used to represent intervals of real numbers. Here is an example of a closed interval:

$$[0, 1]$$

```
<interval>
 <cn>0</cn>
 <cn>1</cn>
</interval>
```

The `interval` element takes an attribute called `closure`, which specifies whether the interval is open or closed at each end. This attribute can take values that correspond to the four types of intervals: open, closed, open-closed, and closed-open. The default value is closed. Here is an example of an interval where the closure is specified explicitly:

$[0, \infty)$

```
<interval closure="closed-open">
 <cn>0</cn>
 <infinity/>
</interval>
```

One common use of the interval element is with the int element to specify the limits of a definite integral. Here is an example:

$$\int_{0}^{\pi} \sin(x)dx$$

```
<apply>
 <int/>
 <bvar><ci>x</ci></bvar>
 <interval>
   <cn>0</cn>
   <pi/>
 </interval>
 <apply>
   <sin/>
   <ci>x</ci>
 </apply>
</apply>
```

Relations

A relation such as equality or inequality is expressed in content markup by using a relational content element as the first argument of an apply element. The apply element is appropriate for this purpose because you can think of a relational expression as the result of applying a function to a set of arguments to yield the Boolean values True or False.

Here is an example of an inequality:

$x < y$

```
<apply>
 <lt/>
 <ci>x</ci>
 <ci>y</ci>
</apply>
```

In MathML 1.0, the same relation was expressed using the reln element, as shown below:

```
<reln>
 <lt/>
 <ci>x</ci>
 <ci>y</ci>
</reln>
```

The reln element is still supported in MathML 2.0 for backward compatibility. However, its use is deprecated. Instead, MathML 2.0 specifies that relations be expressed using the apply element to reflect that each relational expression is equivalent to applying a Boolean function.

Functions

The fn element is used to indicate that a particular MathML expression should be interpreted as a function. This element has exactly one argument, which specifies the name or symbol used to represent the function. For example, the following markup can be used to represent a function called *f*:

```
<fn><ci>f</ci></fn>
```

A function defined in this manner can then be used as the first child element of an apply element in the same way as the existing elements that represent functions, such as times or cos. Here is an example:

$$f(x)$$

```
<apply>
 <fn><ci>f</ci></fn>
 <ci>x</ci>
</apply>
```

You can indicate the meaning of the function by using the definitionURL or encoding attributes. In MathML 1.0, this was the only way to extend content markup to represent user-defined function. In MathML 2.0, the csymbol element is provided for the same purpose and is the preferred way to specify user-defined functions.

Conditions

The condition element is used to encode expressions that make use of the "such that" construct used in mathematical statements. Here is an example:

$$\exists\ x \mid x^2 = -1$$

```
<apply>
 <exists/>
```

```
 <bvar><ci>x</ci></bvar>
 <condition>
   <apply>
     <eq/>
     <apply>
       <power/>
       <ci>x</ci>
       <cn>2</cn>
     </apply>
     <apply><minus/><cn>1</cn></apply>
   </apply>
 </condition>
</apply>
```

A condition element has the following properties:

- It is typically used together with an exists or forall element to define a logical expression, as in the example above.
- It is always preceded by one or more bvar elements, each of which specifies a bound variable whose values are restricted by a relation.
- It always has one child element that must be an apply or reln element specifying the relation used for defining the condition.

One common use of the condition element is to specify the range of integration in conjunction with an int element, as seen in the following example:

$$\int_{x \in D} f(x)dx$$

```
<apply>
 <int/>
 <bvar>
   <ci>x</ci>
 </bvar>
 <condition>
   <apply><in/>
     <ci> x </ci>
     <ci type="set">D</ci>
   </apply>
 </condition>
 <apply><ci type="fn">f</ci>
   <ci>x</ci>
 </apply>
</apply>
```

You can use the condition element to define the elements of a list or set as well. You do so by specifying a condition that the elements must satisfy. Two examples of this are given in the "Sets and Lists" section.

Sets and Lists

Sets and lists are represented using the `set` and `list` elements, respectively. Sets and lists are both used to represent a collection of elements that can be numbers, identifiers, or expressions. However, lists differ from sets in two important respects:

- In a list, the order of elements is significant. In contrast, two sets with the same elements are equivalent, regardless of the order in which the elements are written.
- In a list, each element can occur only once, whereas a set can contain repeated elements. The `set` element accepts the `type` attribute, which can take values `normal` or `multiset`, depending on whether repeated elements are allowed or not.

You can specify the elements of a set either by explicitly listing the elements or by using the `bvar` and `condition` elements to define a condition that elements of the set must satisfy. Here is an example of a set in which the elements are listed explicitly:

$$\{0,\ 1,\ 2,\ 3\}$$

```
<set>
 <cn>0</cn>
 <cn>1</cn>
 <cn>2</cn>
 <cn>3</cn>
</set>
```

Here is an example of the same set defined using a condition:

$$\{x \mid x < 4 \wedge x \in N\}$$

```
<set>
 <bvar><ci>x</ci></bvar>
 <condition>
   <apply>
     <and/>
     <apply>
       <lt/>
       <ci>x</ci>
       <cn>4</cn>
     </apply>
     <apply>
       <in/>
       <ci>x</ci>
       <naturalnumbers/>
```

```
      </apply>
    </apply>
  </condition>
  <ci>x</ci>
</set>
```

As with sets, you can describe lists either by explicitly listing their elements or by using a condition. Here is an example of a list in which the elements are listed explicitly:

[0, 1, 2, 3]

```
<list>
  <cn>0</cn>
  <cn>1</cn>
  <cn>2</cn>
  <cn>3</cn>
</list>
```

Here is an example of the same list defined using a condition:

$\{x \mid x < 4\}$

```
<list order="numeric">
  <bvar><ci> x </ci></bvar>
  <condition>
    <apply><lt/>
      <ci>x</ci>
      <cn>5</cn>
    </apply>
  </condition>
  <ci>x</ci>
</list>
```

You specify the ordering of the list elements by using the `order` attribute. This can take two values: `numeric` (which orders the elements in increasing numeric order) and `lexicographic` (which corresponds to an alphabetic ordering).

Vectors and Matrices

The `vector` element is used to represent vectors. A vector from an n-dimensional vector space is represented by a `vector` element that contains n child elements, each of which represents one scalar component of the vector. For example, a three-dimensional vector, (1, 0, 2), can be represented as shown below:

```
<vector>
  <cn>1</cn>
  <cn>0</cn>
  <cn>2</cn>
</vector>
```

The `matrix` element is used to represent matrices. It contains zero or more `matrixrow` elements, each of which represents a single row of the matrix. Every `matrixrow` element, in turn, has zero or more child elements, each of which must be a number, symbol, or algebraic expression. For example, the 3 × 3 identity matrix can be represented as shown below:

$$\begin{pmatrix} 1 & 0 & 0 \\ 0 & 1 & 0 \\ 0 & 0 & 1 \end{pmatrix}$$

```
<matrix>
 <matrixrow>
   <cn>1</cn><cn>0</cn><cn>0</cn>
 </matrixrow>
 <matrixrow>
   <cn>0</cn><cn>1</cn><cn>0</cn>
 </matrixrow>
 <matrixrow>
   <cn>0</cn><cn>0</cn><cn>1</cn>
 </matrixrow>
</matrix>
```

Piecewise Declarations

Piecewise declarations are used in mathematics to describe a function that has a different definition in different intervals. In content markup, piecewise declarations are represented using the three constructor elements: `piecewise`, `piece`, and `otherwise`. The entire declaration is enclosed in a single `piecewise` element, and each piece of the declaration is enclosed in a separate `piece` element. Each `piece` element takes two child elements: the first one gives the value and the second argument gives the condition or interval in which that value is taken. That is, it has the form:

```
<piecewise>
 <piece> value condition </piece>
   ....
 <piece> value condition </piece>
 <otherwise> value </otherwise>
</piecewise>
```

Each occurrence of *value* and *condition* is itself indicated by other content elements. For example, the definition of the absolute function and its representation in content markup are shown below:

$$|x| = \begin{cases} -x & \text{if} \quad x < 0 \\ 0 & \text{if} \quad x = 0 \\ x & \text{if} \quad x > 0 \end{cases}$$

```
<piecewise>
 <piece>
   <apply><minus/><ci>x</ci></apply>
   <apply><lt/><ci>x</ci><cn>0</cn></apply>
 </piece>
 <piece>
   <cn>0</cn>
   <apply><eq/><ci>x</ci> <cn>0</cn></apply>
 </piece>
 <otherwise>
   <ci>x</ci>
 </otherwise>
</piecewise>
```

5.4 Operators and Functions

The majority of content elements are empty elements that represent specific operators or functions. They are organized into groups named after specific subfields of mathematics, as shown below:

- Arithmetic, algebra, and logic
- Relations
- Elementary functions
- Calculus
- Linear algebra
- Theory of sets
- Sequences and series
- Statistics

In MathML, there is no distinction between operators, functions, and relations because, viewed in an abstract sense, an operator or relation is just a special type of function. For example, the operator + can be thought of as a function that maps pairs of real numbers to real numbers. Similarly, you can think of the relation $x < y$ as a Boolean function that maps pairs of real numbers to the logical values True or False. However, operators and functions are grouped in separate categories in the MathML DTD for the purposes of convenience and consistency with historical usage.

The rest of this section contains examples of selected elements from each category to illustrate how they are used.

Arithmetic, Algebra, and Logic

Several content elements represent common operators and functions used in arithmetic, algebra, and logic. For example, the `plus`, `minus`, `divide`, and `times` elements represent the basic arithmetic operations of addition, subtraction, division, and multiplication, respectively.

The `power` and `root` elements are used to represent taking a power or root. You can encode a fractional power using either of these elements, but the default rendering is typically different in each case. For example, you could encode the cube root of x using the `power` element as shown here (this element is followed by two child elements, the first of which represents the base and the second the power):

$$x^{\frac{1}{3}}$$

```
<apply>
 <power/>
 <ci>x</ci>
 <cn type="rational">1<sep/>3</cn>
</apply>
```

Alternatively, you can use the `root` element to encode the same expression. By default, this would be rendered with a radical sign around the base expression. The first element following the `root` element is the qualifier element `degree`, which specifies the kind of root. It must contain the number 2 for square roots, 3 for cube roots, and so on. If no `degree` element is specified, a default value of 2 is assumed. Here is the relevant markup:

$$\sqrt[3]{x}$$

```
<apply>
 <root/>
   <degree><cn>3</cn></degree>
 <ci>x</ci>
</apply>
```

Here are some other important content elements:

- The `factorial` element is used to represent the factorial of a number.
- The `real` and `imaginary` elements represent the real and imaginary parts of a complex number.
- The `and`, `or`, `xor`, and `not` elements represent the corresponding operators in Boolean logic.

Relations

Several content elements have been defined for representing various types of arithmetic and logical relations, such as $a = b$ or $x < y$. You express a relation in content markup by using a relational content element as the first argument of an apply element. You do it this way because you can think of a relational expression as the result of applying a function to a set of arguments. The result of applying the function is one of the logical values, True or False.

The following content elements represent the common types of relational operators: eq, neq, gt, lt, geq, leq, equivalent, approx, factorof, implies, and tendsto.

Here is an example of a simple equality:

$$2 + 2 = 4$$

```
<apply>
 <eq/>
 <apply>
   <plus/>
     <cn>2</cn>
     <cn>2</cn>
 </apply>
 <cn>4</cn>
</apply>
```

The number of child elements in the apply element is determined by the type of relational element that occurs as the first argument. Some relational elements such as neq act as binary operators since they always express a relation between two quantities. Other relational elements such as eq, leq, lt, gt, and geq act as n-ary operators; that is, they can be followed by an arbitrary number of elements to express compound relations, such as in the markup below:

$$a < b < c < d$$

```
<apply>
 <lt/>
 <ci>a</ci>
 <ci>b</ci>
 <ci>c</ci>
 <ci>d</ci>
</apply>
```

Elementary Functions

Several content elements represent classical elementary functions, such as the exponential and logarithmic functions as well as the trigonometric and hyperbolic functions. Here is an example involving the exponential and natural logarithmic functions:

$$\ln(e^x) = x$$

```
<apply>
 <eq/>
 <apply>
   <ln/>
   <apply>
     <exp/>
     <ci>x</ci>
   </apply>
 </apply>
 <ci>x</ci>
</apply>
```

The `log` element is used to represent the natural logarithmic function. You can use the qualifier element `logbase` to specify the base of the logarithm. If no `logbase` element is present, a default value of 10 is assumed for the base, as shown here:

$$\log_2(x)$$

```
<apply>
 <log/>
 <logbase><cn>2</cn></logbase>
 <ci>x</ci>
</apply>
```

Here is an example of a simple trigonometric formula:

$$\sin(2x) = 2\sin(x)\cos(x)$$

```
<apply>
 <eq/>
 <apply>
   <sin/>
   <apply><times/><cn>2</cn><ci>x</ci></apply>
 </apply>
 <apply>
   <times/>
   <cn>2</cn>
   <apply><sin/><ci>x</ci></apply>
   <apply><cos/><ci>x</ci></apply>
 </apply>
</apply>
```

Calculus

The following content elements represent various operators or functions used in calculus: `int`, `diff`, `partialdiff`, `grad`, `divergence`, `curl`, and `laplacian`. The following sections provide examples of how these elements are used.

Integrals

Integrals are represented using the `int` element. The variable of integration is specified using the qualifier element `bvar`. Here is an example:

$$\int x dx$$

```
<apply>
 <int/>
 <bvar><ci>x</ci></bvar>
 <ci>x</ci>
</apply>
```

For definite integrals, the upper and lower limits of integration can be represented using the qualifier elements `lowlimit` and `uplimit`, as shown here:

$$\int_0^\pi \sin(x) dx$$

```
<apply>
 <int/>
   <bvar><ci>x</ci></bvar>
   <lowlimit><cn>0</cn></lowlimit>
   <uplimit><pi/></uplimit>
   <apply><sin/><ci>x</ci></apply>
</apply>
```

The limits of integration can also be specified using the `interval` element, while integration over a general domain can be specified using the `condition` element. Examples of using the `interval` and `condition` elements to represent the range of integration are provided in the discussion of these elements in Section 5.3.

Derivatives

The `diff` element is used to represent derivatives of functions of a single variable, as shown below:

$$f'$$

```
<diff>
 <ci>f</ci>
</diff>
```

The qualifier element bvar is used to specify the variable of integration. The bvar element can include a degree element to specify the degree of differentiation, as shown below:

$$\frac{d^2 f(x)}{dx^2}$$

```
<apply>
 <diff/>
 <bvar><ci>x</ci></bvar>
 <degree><cn>2</cn></degree>
 <apply>
   <ci type="fn">f</ci>
   <ci>x</ci>
 </apply>
</apply>
```

Partial Derivatives

The partialdiff element is used to represent partial derivatives of multivariable functions. Here is an example:

$$\frac{\partial^2 f(x, y)}{\partial x \partial y}$$

```
<apply>
 <partialdiff/>
   <bvar><ci>x</ci></bvar>
   <bvar><ci>y</ci></bvar>
   <apply><ci type="fn">f</ci>
     <ci>x</ci>
     <ci>y</ci>
   </apply>
</apply>
```

You can specify the degree of differentiation with respect to any of the variables by including a degree element inside the bvar element that corresponds to that variable. You can also include a degree element directly as a child element of the enclosing apply element to specify the total degree of differentiation, as shown here:

$$\frac{\partial^{m+n} f(x, y)}{\partial x^m \partial y^n}$$

```
<apply>
 <partialdiff/>
   <bvar><ci>x</ci>
```

```
      <degree><ci>m</ci></degree>
    </bvar>
    <bvar><ci>y</ci>
      <degree><ci>n</ci></degree>
    </bvar>
    <apply><ci type="fn">f</ci>
      <ci>x</ci>
      <ci>y</ci>
    </apply>
</apply>
```

Vector Calculus

The elements grad, divergence, curl, and laplacian represent the gradient, divergence, curl, and Laplacian operators of vector calculus, respectively. For example, here is one of Maxwell's equations of electrodynamics; it describes the divergence of the magnetic field:

$$\nabla \cdot \vec{B} = 0$$

```
<apply>
 <eq/>
 <apply>
   <divergence/>
   <ci type="vector">B</ci>
 </apply>
 <cn>0</cn>
</apply>
```

Linear Algebra

The following content elements represent various operators or functions used in linear algebra: determinant, transpose, selector, vectorproduct, scalarproduct, and outerproduct.

The determinant and transpose elements represent the determinant and transpose of a matrix, respectively. The matrix itself is represented using the matrix and matrixrow elements, as discussed in Section 5.3.

For example, given a matrix:

$$\mathbf{A} = \begin{pmatrix} 1 & 2 \\ 3 & 4 \end{pmatrix}$$

the equations that describe the transpose and determinant of A are given below:

$$\mathbf{A}^T = \begin{pmatrix} 1 & 3 \\ 2 & 4 \end{pmatrix}$$

```
<apply>
 <eq/>
   <apply>
     <transpose/>
     <ci type="matrix">A</ci></apply>
 <matrix>
   <matrixrow><cn>1</cn><cn>3</cn></matrixrow>
   <matrixrow><cn>2</cn><cn>4</cn></matrixrow>
 </matrix>
</apply>
```

$$\det(\mathbf{A}) = 2$$

```
<apply>
 <eq/>
   <apply>
     <determinant/>
     <ci type="matrix">A</ci>
   </apply>
 <cn>2</cn>
</apply>
```

The `selector` element is used to select a specific part of a list, vector, or matrix. This element can take one, two, or three arguments. The first argument identifies the object whose element is being selected. The remaining arguments specify the index number of the item in that object.

For matrices, the second argument specifies the row and the third argument specifies the column. For example, the element in the first row and second column of a matrix **A** is represented as shown below:

$$\mathbf{A}_{12}$$

```
<apply>
 <selector/>
 <ci type="matrix">A</ci>
 <cn>1</cn>
 <cn>2</cn>
</apply>
```

If the `selector` element is given with three arguments and the first argument identifies a vector or list, the third argument is ignored.

The `vectorproduct`, `scalarproduct`, and `outerproduct` elements represent the vector product, the scalar product, and the outerproduct of vectors, respectively. Here is an example showing the scalar product of two vectors:

$$\mathbf{A} . \mathbf{B} = ab \cos(\theta)$$

```
<apply>
 <eq/>
 <apply><scalarproduct/>
   <ci type="vector"> A </ci>
   <ci type="vector"> B </ci>
 </apply>
 <apply><times/>
   <ci>a</ci>
   <ci>b</ci>
   <apply><cos/>
     <ci>&theta;</ci>
   </apply>
 </apply>
</apply>
```

Theory of Sets

We have already seen the use of the constructor elements `set` and `list` to represent sets and lists. There are several content elements that represent various operators and functions used in the theory of sets.

The elements `union` and `intersect` are used to represent the union and intersection of two sets, as seen in the following example:

$$A \cup (B \cap C)$$

```
<apply>
 <union/>
 <ci type="set">A</ci>
 <apply>
   <intersect/>
   <ci type="set">B</ci>
   <ci type="set">C</ci>
 </apply>
</apply>
```

The elements `in`, `notin`, `subset`, `prsubset`, `notsubset`, `notprsubset`, and `setdiff` are used for representing various types of relationships between sets, as seen in the following examples:

$$a \in A$$

```
<apply>
 <in/>
```

```
  <ci>a</ci>
  <ci type="set">A</ci>
</apply>
```

$A \subseteq B$

```
<apply>
  <subset/>
  <ci type="set">A</ci>
  <ci type="set">B</ci>
</apply>
```

The `card` element represents the cardinality of a set; that is, the number of elements it contains. Here is an example that uses this element:

$\mathbb{Z} = \aleph_0$

```
<apply>
  <eq/>
  <apply>
    <card/>
    <integers/>
  </apply>
  <cn><msub><mn>&aleph;</mn><mn>0</mn></msub></cn>
  </apply>
</apply>
```

The `setdiff` element represents the difference of two sets. The `cartesianproduct` element represents the Cartesian product of two sets; that is, the set of all pairs (a, b) with $a \in A$ and $b \in B$. Using the elements described in this subsection, you can represent most mathematical statements encountered in the elementary theory of sets.

Sequences and Series

The following content elements can be used to represent limits, sequences, and series: `sum`, `product`, `limit`, and `tendsto`.

The `sum` and `product` elements are used to represent the summation and product operators. You can indicate the range over which the summation or product occurs either by using the `uplimit` and `lowlimit` qualifier elements, or more generally by using the `condition` element. Here is an example of using the `sum` element:

$$\prod_{a}^{b} f(x)$$

```
<apply>
  <sum/>
```

```
  <bvar><ci>x</ci></bvar>
  <lowlimit><ci>a</ci></lowlimit>
  <uplimit><ci>b</ci></uplimit>
  <apply>
    <ci type="fn">f</ci>
    <ci>x</ci>
  </apply>
</apply>
```

The `limit` element is used to represent the operation of taking a limit. The qualifier elements `bvar` and `lowlimit` are used to indicate the variable and the value it is approaching. Here is an example:

$$\lim_{x \to 0} \frac{\sin(x)}{x}$$

```
<apply>
  <limit/>
    <bvar><ci>x</ci></bvar>
    <lowlimit><cn>0</cn></lowlimit>
  <apply>
    <divide/>
      <apply>
        <sin/>
        <ci>x</ci>
      </apply>
      <ci>x</ci>
  </apply>
</apply>
```

The `tendsto` element is used to indicate that a quantity is tending to a specified value. Here is an example:

$$x \to 0$$

```
<apply>
  <tendsto/>
  <ci>x</ci>
  <cn>0</cn>
</apply>
```

Statistics

The content elements `mean`, `median`, `mode`, `var`, `sdev`, and `moment` represent the statistical concepts of mean, median, mode, variance, standard deviation, and moment, respectively.

For example, the mean of a distribution denoted by X would be represented as shown below:

$\overline{X}$

```
<apply>
 <mean/>
 <ci>X</ci>
</apply>
```

The standard deviation of the same distribution would be represented as shown below:

$\sigma(X)$

```
<apply>
   <sdev/>
   <ci>X</ci>
</apply>
```

5.5 Qualifier Elements

A small number of content elements are used to provide additional information needed to fully specify the meaning of other content elements. These qualifier elements act as parameters that qualify the meaning of the content element with which they are associated. We have seen examples of many of these qualifier elements in the discussion of other content elements in this chapter.

Table 5.3 lists the various qualifier elements along with their meaning and the other content elements they are typically used with.

5.6 Constants and Symbols

Several elements represent commonly used constants (such as π, ∞, e, or i) and symbols (such as those used to denote the set of all integers or the set of all complex numbers). A list of all content elements of this type is given in Table 5.4.

5.7 Semantic Mapping Elements

Content markup describes the logical meaning of mathematical expressions. However, there are many situations in which it is useful to supplement the content markup with additional information. For example, you might want to include the presentation markup for an expression along with the content markup to specify that the expression be rendered in a special form that is different from the

TABLE 5.3 Qualifier Elements

Qualifier Element	What It Represents	Elements It's Used With
`bvar`	Bound variable	`int, sum, product, min, max, diff, partialdiff, limit, condition, forall, exists`
`lowlimit`	Lower limit	`int, sum, product, limit`
`uplimit`	Upper limit	`int, sum, product, limit`
`interval`	Interval	`int, sum, product`
`condition`	Condition	`int, min, max, exists, sum, product, limit`
`domainofapplication`	Domain	`int, sum, product`
`degree`	Degree of root, differentiation, or moment	`root, diff, partialdiff, moment`
`momentabout`	Statistical moment	`moment`
`logbase`	Base of logarithm	`log`

default rendering that would be used if the content markup alone were specified by itself.

Alternatively, you might want to include the representation of a mathematical expression in another computer language (such as $\TeX$, C, or *Mathematica*) for use by particular applications that recognize those languages. This type of additional information is called a *semantic mapping*. MathML provides three content elements for specifying semantic mappings: `semantics`, `annotation`, and `annotation-xml`.

The `semantics` element is used as a container element for the MathML expression and all its semantic mappings. This element takes one or more child elements. The first element is the MathML expression for which semantic mappings are to be specified, and the subsequent arguments are the semantic mappings themselves. Each semantic mapping is enclosed in an `annotation` or `annotation-xml` element.

The `semantics` element accepts a `definitionURL` attribute you can use to specify a URL that contains the semantic mapping for the expression. The presence of the `annotation` and `annotation-xml`

TABLE 5.4 Content Elements That Represent Constants and Symbols

Element	Default Rendering	Meaning
`pi`	π	The ratio of a circle's circumference to its diameter (approx. 3.141592653)
`exponentiale`	e	The base of the natural logarithm
`imaginaryi`	i	The (imaginary) square root of −1
`notanumber`	NaN	Not a number
`true`	True	The Boolean value True
`false`	False	The Boolean value False
`emptyset`	$\emptyset$	An empty set
`eulergamma`	γ	Euler's constant (approx. 0.5772156649)
`infinity`	∞	Infinity
`integers`	$\mathbb{Z}$	The set of all integers
`reals`	$\mathbb{R}$	The set of all real numbers
`rationals`	$\mathbb{Q}$	The set of all rational numbers
`naturalnumbers`	$\mathbb{N}$	The set of all natural numbers
`complexes`	$\mathbb{C}$	The set of all complex numbers
`primes`	$\mathbb{P}$	The set of all prime numbers

elements is optional since you can specify the semantic mapping completely by using only the `definitionURL` attribute.

The `annotation` element can contain any arbitrary character data. The format of the data is indicated using the value of the `encoding` attribute. For example, you could include the *Mathematica* command that corresponds to a given MathML expression by specifying `encoding="mathematica"` or you could give the TEX equivalent by specifying `encoding="TeX"`.

The `annotation-xml` element also specifies a semantic mapping but with the additional constraint that its content must be a well-formed XML expression. The format of the mapping is specified using the `encoding` attribute. Typical values of this attribute are `Presentation-MathML` (for presentation markup), `Content-MathML` (for content markup), or `OpenMath`. The OpenMath consortium is a regulatory body that has developed a platform-independent and vendor-neutral standard for specifying the semantic meaning of mathematical expressions. The OpenMath specification of any mathematical expression is written in XML; hence, OpenMath statements are suitable for inclusion in an `annotation-xml` element.

The following example shows a content MathML expression with three semantic mappings specified:

$$\int_0^{\pi} \sin(x) dx$$

```
<semantics>
 <apply>
   <int/>
     <bvar><ci>x</ci></bvar>
     <lowlimit><cn>0</cn></lowlimit>
     <uplimit><pi/></uplimit>
     <apply><sin/><ci>x</ci></apply>
 </apply>
 <annotation-xml encoding="MathML-Presentation">
   <mrow>
     <munderover>
     <mo>&int;</mo><mn>0</mn><mi>&pi;</mi>
     </munderover>
     <mrow>
       <mrow><mi>sin</mi><mo>&ApplyFunction;</mo>
       <mo>(</mo><mi>x</mi><mo>)</mo></mrow>
       <mo>&InvisibleTimes;</mo><mrow>
       <mo>&DifferentialD;</mo><mi>x</mi></mrow>
     </mrow>
   </mrow>
 </annotation-xml>
 <annotation encoding="TeX">
   $$\int_0^pi {\sin(x)dx}$$
 </annotation>
 <annotation encoding="Mathematica">
   Integrate[Sin[x], {x, 0, Pi}]
 </annotation>
</semantics>
```

Above, the presentation markup encodings are included in an `annotation-xml` element, while the TEX and *Mathematica* encodings are each included in an `annotation` element. The original expression, along with all three semantic mappings, is enclosed in a `semantics` element.

5.8 Content Element Attributes

Content markup supports about a dozen attributes. The relatively small number of attributes reflects the fact that content markup does not provide detailed information about rendering. This is in contrast to presentation markup, which requires a relatively large number of attributes (about 50), to properly describe the numerous subtle details of how notation should be visually rendered.

As discussed in Section 3.3, six attributes are accepted by all content elements:

- `class`, `style`, and `id`: facilitate use of CSS and XSL stylesheets
- `xlink:href`: is used for setting up links
- `xref`: is used in parallel markup
- `other`: is used for specifying nonstandard attributes that are not defined in MathML but may be supported by specific processing applications

The `other` attribute has a special role in content markup. It can be used to tell rendering applications to favor one type of notation over another when they render specific types of content markup. You can use this attribute to indicate that a particular expression should be rendered in display style instead of inline style. Alternatively, you could use it to specify that the derivative of a function should be rendered as $f'(x)$ instead of $\frac{df}{dx}$. This type of information cannot be described using existing content elements and attributes, but specific rendering applications can still recognize and interpret it.

For example, if a specific renderer recognizes a `display` attribute, an author could indicate that an expression be displayed in inline style using the following markup:

```
<apply other='display="inline"'>
 <divide/>
 <mn>1</mn>
 <mi>x</mi>
</apply>
```

In addition to the six common attributes that are accepted by all content elements, nine other attributes are accepted by specific content elements only. A brief description of each attribute is given below.

`base`

This attribute is used with the `cn` element to specify the base of the number being encoded. It can be set to any number and has a default value of 10. For example, the following markup specifies the number 18 in binary notation:

```
<cn base="2">10010</cn>
```

`closure`

This attribute is used with the `interval` element to specify the type of interval being encoded. It can take the values `open`, `closed`, `open-closed`, or `closed-open`. Its default value is `closed`. For example, the interval [0, 1) can be specified as:

```
<interval closure="open-closed">
 <cn>0</cn>
 <cn>1</cn>
</interval>
```

`definitionURL`

This attribute is accepted by the `csymbol`, `declare`, and `semantics` elements as well as by every content element that represents an operator or function. It specifies a URL that contains semantic information about the meaning of the object being constructed.

`encoding`

This attribute is accepted by the `semantics`, `annotation`, `annotation-xml`, and `csymbol` elements as well as by every content element that represents an operator or function. It specifies the format used to encode semantic information about the meaning of the object being constructed.

`nargs`

This attribute is used with the `declare` element to specify the number of arguments taken by the function being declared. For example, the following expression declares a function *f* with two arguments:

```
<declare type="fn" nargs="2">
 <ci>f</ci>
</declare>
```

`occurrence`

This attribute is used with the `declare` element to specify the position in which an operator being declared can occur. Possible values are `prefix`, `infix`, and `function-model`, with the latter being the default value.

`order`

This attribute is used with the `list` element to specify the criterion used for ordering the elements of a list. Possible values are `lexicographic` and `numeric`, which correspond to the list elements being ordered alphabetically or numerically, respectively. The default value is `numeric`.

`scope`

This attribute is used with the `declare` element to indicate the scope of the declaration. Possible values are `local` and `global`. In MathML 2.0, this attribute is deprecated and there is no difference between its two possible values.

`type`

This attribute has a slightly different meaning—allowed values and default value—depending on the type of element with which it is used. It can be used with the following five content elements: `cn`, `ci`, `declare`, `set`, and `tendsto`.

When used with the `cn` element, it specifies the type of the number being encoded. Possible values are `real`, `integer`, `float`, `rational`, `complex-polar`, `complex-cartesian`, `e-notation`, or `constant`. The default value is `real`.

When used with the `ci` element, it specifies the type of identifier being encoded. In addition to all the above values that it can take when specified in the `cn` element, it can be set to the name of a container content element such as `list`, `set`, `vector`, `matrix`, or `fn`.

When used with the `declare` element, it declares an object to be of a specified type. It can be set to the name of any container content element such as `list`, `set`, `vector`, `matrix`, or `fn`.

When used with the `set` element, it indicates the type of set. Possible values are `multiset` (which indicates that repeated values are allowed) and `normal` (which indicates that repeated values are not allowed). The default value is `normal`.

When used with the `tendsto` element, it indicates the direction in which one quantity is approaching another. Possible values are `above`, `below`, and `two-sided`. The default value is `above`.

CHAPTER

6

COMBINING PRESENTATION AND CONTENT MARKUP

This chapter explains the rules for combining presentation and content tags and the situations in which combining them is useful. It also explains the difference between mixed and parallel markup, and shows how you can use cross-references for expressing parallel markup more compactly.

6.1 INTRODUCTION

As we saw in Chapters 3, 4, and 5, MathML consist of two different markup schemes, each with its own set of tags and attributes. Presentation markup describes the visual structure of mathematical notation. It is useful in contexts that emphasize the visual aspects of mathematics; for example, displaying a technical paper in a Web page. Content markup, on the other hand, describes the symbolic meaning of a mathematical expression. It is useful in contexts where the precise meaning of a mathematical expression has to be communicated; for example, when you are evaluating an equation in a computer algebra system.

In many cases, there is a natural correspondence between the notation for a mathematical expression and its symbolic meaning. Hence, given the presentation encoding for an expression, you can infer its meaning—and therefore its content encoding. However, the correspondence between mathematical notation and meaning is imperfect. As we saw in Section 3.3, the same notation may express more than one mathematical concept; conversely, a given concept can be expressed by different notations. In such cases, there is no simple relationship between the presentation markup and content markup for an expression.

Presentation markup and content markup thus play a complementary role, with each providing a different type of information about a mathematical expression. When authoring a document containing MathML, you can use either presentation or content markup exclusively, depending on the audience for the document and the purpose for which it will be used. However, each of these options has certain limitations. If you use presentation markup, you are limited in the amount of information you can provide about the meaning of the encoded expression. If you use content markup, you cannot directly control how a given expression will be rendered.

To overcome these limitations, MathML also allows a third option, mixing presentation and content tags inside the same `math` element. This type of markup is called *combined markup*. It provides a way to specify information about both the presentational and semantic aspects of mathematics, in a single MathML expression, thus allowing a more complete description of any mathematical construct.

Combined markup can be classified into two main types, depending on the structure of the expression tree. If presentation and content tags are mixed together within a single branch of the expression tree, the resulting markup is called *mixed markup*. If the expression tree contains both content and presentation encodings of the same expression, enclosed in parallel within a `semantics` element, the resulting markup is called *parallel markup*. In the rest of this chapter we shall see examples of both types of markup, the situations in which they are useful, and the rules that govern them.

6.2 Mixed Markup

Mixed markup itself can be of two types, depending on whether the outermost element is a presentation element or a content element:

1. You can embed content markup inside presentation markup. This allows you to specify additional information about the meaning of the presentation markup, and processing applications can use this information to provide a more meaningful rendering of the encoded expression.
2. You can embed presentation markup inside content markup. This allows you to specify how a particular piece of content markup should be rendered. You can, for example, specify a nonstandard rendering for a particular content expression. You can also specify a rendering for a content expression that does not have a well-defined default rendering.

Here is an example of content markup embedded in a presentation expression:

x^2

```
<mrow>
 <apply>
   <power/>
   <ci>x</ci>
   <cn>2</cn>
 </apply>
</mrow>
```

A processing application can use this content markup to provide a better rendering of the mixed expression. For example, in an audio rendering, the markup might be spoken as "x square" to clearly indicate its logical meaning. If pure presentation markup were used instead, the exponent would have to be represented using an msup element. This element does not contain enough information for a renderer to distinguish a power from a plain superscript.

Here is an example of presentation markup embedded in a content expression:

$\vec{\mathbf{A}}$

```
<ci type="vector">
 <mover>
   <mi mathvariant="bold">A</mi>
   <mo>&RightArrow;</mo>
 </mover>
</ci>
```

Here, presentation markup is used to specify that the identifier **A** should be rendered in a bold font and with an arrow in the overscript position, to indicate that it represents a vector.

Rules for Mixing Markup

Of course, you cannot freely mix presentation and content tags in any order. For any instance of combined markup to be valid, it must satisfy some additional rules beyond those required for presentation or content markup alone. The exact rules that apply depend on whether you are including content tags in a presentation expression or vice versa.

If the combined markup is contained in a presentation expression, that expression must have a well-defined rendering. Similarly, if the combined markup is contained in a content expression, that expression must have a precise and unambiguous semantic meaning. Both of these requirements are a consequence of the general principle that any expression containing combined markup must have a sensible interpretation as a whole. Some specific rules that result as a consequence of this general principle are discussed below.

Content Markup in Presentation Markup

The main requirement for content markup contained within a presentation expression is that the content markup be self-contained and have a well-defined semantic meaning. The reason for this is that any content expression whose semantic meaning is well defined also has a well-defined rendering, in the sense that the corresponding presentation markup can be inferred.

One consequence of this requirement is that certain content elements, such as bvar, uplimit, or lowlimit, cannot be directly included as children of a presentation element. The reason for this is that each of these content elements derives its meaning from the context in which it occurs. For example, the bvar element has a different meaning depending on whether it occurs inside an integral, derivative, root, or lambda expression. Similarly, the meaning of the degree element depends on whether it is qualifying a derivative, a root, or a statistical moment. Hence, to be meaningful, each of these elements must be enclosed in an appropriate content element.

The following markup is illegal, since the qualifier element degree has been directly included as a child of the presentation element mroot:

```
<mroot>
 <mi><x></mi>
 <degree>3</degree >
</mroot>
```

The enclosing presentation expression therefore does not have a well-defined rendering. Hence, this type of markup is not allowed.

Another example of an illegal expression is given below (in this case the <bvar> element has been wrongly inserted as the child of an <mrow> element):

```
<mrow>
 <bvar>x</bvar>
 <mo>+</mo>
 <mi>1</mi>
</mrow>
```

The complete list of content elements that cannot be directly included as children of a presentation element is as follows: bvar, uplimit, lowlimit, degree, logbase, condition, domainofapplication, momentabout, declare, sep, annotation, and annotation-xml.

This list includes all the qualifier elements like bvar and degree since these exist only to qualify the meaning of other elements and are not meaningful on their own. In addition, the list includes some other elements that require a specific context to be meaningful. For example, the sep element can occur only inside a cn element. Similarly, the annotation and annotation-xml elements must be enclosed in a semantics element.

In general, content elements that represent operators, relations, containers, constants, and symbols have a meaning on their own and can be directly included in a presentation expression. However, content markup cannot occur inside the presentation token elements, namely mi, mn, and mo. The reason is that the token elements of presentation markup are allowed to contain only character data or a specific set of presentation elements.

Presentation Markup in Content Markup

Presentation markup placed within a content expression must be semantically meaningful. An expression like the following is not allowed, since it does not have a well-defined semantic interpretation:

```
<apply>
 <ci>x</ci><mo>+</mo><ci>y</ci>
</apply>
```

To prevent ill-defined expressions like the one above, presentation markup is allowed to occur in content markup in only one of four elements: `ci`, `cn`, `csymbol`, and `semantics`.

Each `ci` or `cn` element serves as an indivisible notational unit that represents an identifier or number. The `ci` and `cn` elements can contain any sequence of presentation elements freely interspersed with MathML characters. The role of the included presentation elements is only to specify a rendering for the particular object that is represented by the `ci` or `cn` element.

The following markup represents the second component of a vector, **X** (the presentation tags indicate that the expression should be rendered in a bold font and the 2 should be rendered in the subscript position):

X_2

```
<ci>
 <msub>
    <mi>X</mi>
    <mn>2</mn>
 </msub>
</ci>
```

The following example uses presentation tags to specify a rendering for a rational number:

${}^{2}/_{3}$

```
<cn>
 <mfrac bevelled="true">
    <mn>2</mn>
    <mn>3</mn>
 </mfrac>
</cn>
```

A MathML application that recognizes both presentation and content tags could, in principle, parse the above markup so that it is rendered as a bevelled fraction, while still retaining the mathematical meaning associated with the number 2/3.

The csymbol element is provided as an extension mechanism for content markup. It can be used to describe concepts for which existing content elements are inadequate. This element can contain any valid presentation markup or any valid content markup. However, it cannot contain both presentation and content markup.

Here is an example of mixed markup using the csymbol element:

C^1

```
<csymbol encoding="text" definitionURL =
"http://www.example.org/ContDiffFunc.htm">
 <msup>
   <mi>C</mi>
   <mn>1</mn>
 </msup>
</csymbol>
```

This markup defines a symbol to represent the space of continuously differentiable functions. The enclosed presentation markup is used to specify the conventional notation for this symbol.

The embedded presentation markup can be as elaborate as desired. Here is an example of a symbol with a slightly more complex rendering than the previous example:

Γ_{ij}^{k}

```
<csymbol encoding="text" definitionURL =
"http://www.example.org/ChristoffelSymbol.htm">
 <mmultiscripts>
   <mi>&Gamma;</mi>
   <mi>i</mi>
   <mi>k</mi>
   <mi>j</mi>
   <none/>
 </mmultiscripts>
</csymbol>
```

Finally, presentation markup can occur inside a semantics element, in the form of parallel markup. A detailed discussion of parallel markup is given in Section 6.3.

6.3 Parallel Markup

In many cases, it is desirable to encode both the presentation and content markup for a mathematical expression. A MathML processing application can then use one type of markup or the other, depending on the context. For example, the presentation markup could be used for displaying the expression in a Web page while the content markup could be used for copying and pasting the expression into a computer algebra system for evaluation. This type of combined markup is called parallel markup because it contains multiple encodings of the same expression, in parallel branches of the main expression tree.

The mechanism used in MathML for providing multiple encodings of the same expression is the `semantics` element. The syntax of the `semantics` element was discussed in Section 5.7. The first child of this element is a complete content markup or presentation markup expression. The second child can be an `annotation-xml` element that contains the same expression encoded in a different form. The form of the annotation is specified using the `encoding` attribute of the `annotation-xml` element. This attribute has the value `MathML-Content` for content markup and `MathML-Presentation` for presentation markup.

Top-level Parallel Markup

Parallel markup that consists of a single `semantics` element is called *top-level parallel markup*. This is because it establishes a correspondence between the content encoding and presentation encoding of the main top-level expression.

To specify a particular rendering for a given piece of content markup, you would specify a content expression as the first argument of the `semantics` element and the corresponding presentation expression as the second argument. Here is an example:

$f'(x)$

```
<semantics>
 <apply>
   <diff/>
     <bvar><ci>x</ci></bvar>
     <apply>
       <ci type="fn">f</ci>
       <ci>x</ci>
     </apply>
 </apply>
```

```
  <annotation-xml encoding="MathML-Presentation">
    <mrow>
      <msup>
        <mi>f</mi><mo>&prime;</mo>
      </msup>
      <mo>(</mo><mi>x</mi><mo>)</mo>
    </mrow>
  </annotation-xml>
</semantics>
```

By default, a particular MathML application might render the content expression in the above markup as $\frac{df(x)}{dx}$. By using presentation markup as an annotation, you can specify that the content expression be rendered as $f'(x)$ instead.

Alternatively, you can specify the presentation encoding as the first argument and place the content encoding in the second argument. Here is the same example as the one just shown; this time, however, the order of presentation and content markup is reversed:

$f'(x)$

```
<semantics>
 <mrow>
   <msup>
     <mi>f</mi><mo>&prime;</mo>
   </msup>
   <mo>(</mo><mi>x</mi><mo>)</mo>
 </mrow>
<annotation-xml encoding="MathML-Content">
 <apply>
   <diff/>
     <bvar><ci>x</ci></bvar>
     <apply>
       <ci type="fn">f</ci>
       <ci>x</ci>
     </apply>
 </apply>
</annotation-xml>
</semantics>
```

Notice that the `encoding` attribute of the `annotation-xml` element is set to `MathML-Content` in this case (as opposed to `MathML-Presentation` in the earlier example).

The type of markup shown in the previous example is useful for applications that are primarily presentation based but that can benefit from additional information provided by the content markup annotation.

Fine-grained Parallel Markup

In top-level parallel markup, the content and presentation markup for the entire expression are each contained in a different branch of a single `semantics` element. Thus, the correspondence between the presentation and content encodings is for the entire expression as a whole. However, in some contexts, you need to specify the correspondence between presentation and content encodings of subexpressions of the main expression as well. One way to accomplish this is to use nested `semantics` elements, thereby creating what is called *fine-grained parallel markup*.

This type of markup can be useful, for example, in an equation editor that allows a user to build up complicated expressions by nesting and combining smaller, simpler subexpressions. Suppose the application internally stores a representation of each expression in MathML form. Since a user might select a particular fragment of a large expression for copying and pasting, it is desirable for both the content and presentation markup of the selected fragment to be included in the content copied to the clipboard.

Consider the following example of top-level parallel markup:

$$x^2 + \sin(x)$$

```
<semantics>
 <mrow>
   <msup><mi>x</mi><mn>2</mn></msup>
   <mo>+</mo>
   <mrow>
     <mi>sin</mi><mo>&ApplyFunction;</mo>
     <mo>(</mo><mi>x</mi><mo>)</mo>
   </mrow>
 </mrow>
<annotation-xml encoding='MathML-Content'>
 <apply>
   <plus/>
   <apply><power/><ci>x</ci><cn>2</cn></apply>
     <apply><sin/><ci>x</ci></apply>
 </apply>
</annotation-xml>
</semantics>
```

Here is the same expression represented using fine-grained parallel markup, involving two nested `semantics` elements:

$x^2 + \sin(x)$

```
<semantics>
 <mrow>
   <semantics>
     <msup><mi>x</mi><mn>2</mn></msup>
     <annotation-xml encoding="MathML-Content">
       <apply><power/><ci>x</ci><cn>2</cn></apply>
     </annotation-xml>
   </semantics>
   <mo>+</mo>
   <semantics>
     <mrow>
       <mi>sin</mi><mo>&ApplyFunction;</mo>
       <mo>(</mo><mi>x</mi><mo>)</mo>
     </mrow>
     <annotation-xml encoding="MathML-Content">
       <apply><sin/><ci>x</ci></apply>
     </annotation-xml>
   </semantics>s
 </mrow>
<annotation-xml encoding="MathML-Content">
 <apply>
   <plus/>
   <apply><power/><ci>x</ci><cn>2</cn></apply>
   <apply><sin/><ci>x</ci></apply>
 </apply>
</annotation-xml>
</semantics>
```

This markup provides separate content and presentation encodings of the two terms x^2 and $\sin(x)$, as well as for the top-level expression, $x^2 + \sin(x)$.

Using Cross-References

By using a sufficient number of `semantics` elements, you can explicitly specify down to as small a level as desired the correspondence between content and presentation encodings of sub-expressions of the main expression. However, the limitation of this approach is that the markup quickly becomes very verbose, which leads to a large increase in the size of the document.

A more efficient way to specify fine-grained markup is to use the `id` and `xref` tags, which all MathML elements support. These tags provide a compact way to create cross-references between different parts of the expression tree. You can then use cross-references to associate content elements with the corresponding presentation elements, down to the level of the individual token elements that represent the leaves of the expression tree—namely, numbers, operators, and identifiers.

The `id` and `xref` attributes can be set to any arbitrary value, as long as that value is unique within the document. Any element with an `id` attribute then defines a target, which is referenced by all elements that have an `xref` attribute with the same value. The following markup uses cross-references to represent the same expression used in the last example:

$x^2 + \sin(x)$

```
<semantics>
 <mrow id="A">
   <msup id="A.1">
     <mi id="A.1.1">x</mi>
     <mn id="A.1.2">2</mn>
   </msup>
   <mo id="A.2">+</mo>
   <mrow id="A.3">
     <mi id="A.3.1">sin</mi>
     <mo id="A.3.2">&ApplyFunction;</mo>
     <mo id="A.3.3">(</mo>
     <mi id="A.3.4">x</mi>
     <mo id="A.3.5">)</mo>
   </mrow>
 </mrow>
<annotation-xml encoding='MathML-Content'>
 <apply xref="A">
   <plus xref="A.2"/>
   <apply xref="A.1">
   <power/>
     <ci xref="A.1.1">x</ci>
     <cn xref="A.1.2">2</cn>
   </apply>
     <apply xref="A.3.2">
   <sin xref="A.3.1"/>
   <ci xref="A.3.4">x</ci>
   </apply>
   </apply>
</annotation-xml>
</semantics>
```

Notice that the content and presentation encodings of the entire expression, $x^2 + \sin(x)$, are associated using `id` and `xref` attributes with the value `A`. Moving one level down the expression tree, the two encodings of the term x^2 are identified using the `id` and `xref` pairs having the value `A.1`. Finally, the token elements in the content and presentation markup, describing the identifier x and the number 2 in the first term, are identified using the values `A.1.1` and `A.1.2`.

PART II

WORKING WITH MATHML

CHAPTER

7

DISPLAYING MATHML IN WEB BROWSERS

This chapter gives an overview of the current support for MathML in Web browsers and provides information on authoring MathML documents for display on the Web. It also reviews the features of the leading Web browsers and add-on software available for rendering MathML.

7.1 INTRODUCTION

It is currently possible to view MathML in most major Web browsers, either directly or using freely available add-on software. The MathML markup must be embedded in an HTML (or XHTML) document that is then displayed in the browser window. For the MathML markup to be interpreted and displayed as properly formatted mathematical notation, there are two main options.

The first option is to use a MathML-aware browser that can interpret and render MathML natively, without the need to install any additional components. Currently, the main browsers that fit this description are *Mozilla* 1.0, *Netscape* 7.0, and *Amaya*. The second option is to use Microsoft *IE* or *Netscape* in combination with suitable add-on software. The add-on software can be in the form of a plug-in or ActiveX control like IBM *techexplorer*, an *IE* Behavior like *MathPlayer*, or a tool for rendering MathML with Java applets, like *WebEQ*.

For an author of a Web document containing MathML, the main consideration is that the document should be viewable on as wide a variety of browsers and platforms as possible and using any of the standard add-ons available for rendering MathML. Unfortunately, the exact form of the MathML markup and the details of how it is embedded in the HTML document vary depending on the type of browser and add-on to be used.

Until recently, this lack of uniformity was a serious problem. It effectively meant that a MathML document had to be written specifically to target a particular type of browser or add-on. Once this was done, the same document would not be viewable on any other browser or even in the same browser using a different add-on. This problem has now been eliminated—at least for newer versions of the most popular browsers—thanks to an ingenious solution by David Carlisle, a member of the W3C and a co-editor of the MathML specification.

His solution involves the use of a special XSLT stylesheet called the *Universal MathML stylesheet*. This stylesheet can automatically transform the original source document and insert the specific markup needed to view the document in the environment available on the client machine. (For more information on XSLT and it how it can be used to transform MathML, see Section 8.3.) The Universal MathML stylesheet makes it possible to create a single MathML document that can be displayed on various platforms using a variety of browsers and add-ons. All that's required is for the browser being used to support XSLT transformations. Recent versions of the most popular browsers, including *IE* 5.0 and later or *Netscape* 6.1 and later, support these transformations. At the moment, however, XSLT-capable browsers are not widely deployed. Until they are, it will be necessary in the short term to support MathML display on older browsers as well.

This chapter is organized as follows. Section 7.1 describes the various compatibility problems that prevent a given MathML document from being displayed in a variety of environments. Section 7.2 explains how the Universal MathML stylesheet provides an effective solution to these compatibility problems and gives instructions on authoring documents to take advantage of this stylesheet. Sections 7.3 and 7.4 review the features of the different browsers and add-ons available for displaying MathML. These sections include detailed information on the type of markup required to render MathML using a specific browser or add-on. This information is useful when you are authoring documents for older browsers, which do not support XSLT and therefore cannot use the Universal MathML stylesheet. Finally, Section 7.5 summarizes the strengths and limitations of the different display methods to help you choose between them.

Compatibility Issues

The various browsers and add-ons for displaying MathML have different requirements for how a document that contains MathML should be authored because each application requires a different set of answers to the following four questions:

- What is the Multipurpose Internet Mail Extensions (MIME) type of the document?
- What DOCTYPE declarations does the document include?
- How is the namespace of the MathML markup specified?
- Are any additional tags required to embed the MathML markup in the document?

In the following sections, we will briefly consider each of these issues. Although this information can be confusing, keep in mind that the Universal MathML stylesheet makes it unnecessary for you to know any of these details. If your main interest is in just authoring Web documents that contain MathML, you can skip ahead to Section 7.2, which explains how to use the Universal MathML stylesheet.

MIME Types

The MIME type of a file describes the type of content that the file contains. The browser uses this information to decide how the file should be processed. The MIME type is usually specified by the server (for files downloaded over the Web), but it can also be inferred from the file extension (for local files). For an XHTML+MathML document to be displayed by *IE*, the document's MIME type must be specified as text/html. On the other hand, for an XHTML+MathML document to be displayed by *Mozilla*, the document must have a MIME type of text/xml. This effectively means that the same document cannot be viewed in both *IE* and *Mozilla*.

One solution to this problem is to configure the Web server so it recognizes the type of browser that is requesting the document and then sets the MIME type accordingly. In other words, the server would send the same document with a MIME type of text/html to *IE* and text/xml to *Mozilla*. This requires you to know something about server programming, and you must have access to the server; both of these can be problematic for a potential author. A simpler solution is to include a reference to the Universal MathML stylesheet in the XHTML+MathML document. The stylesheet automatically specifies the MIME type for both *IE* and *Mozilla* correctly, using XSLT transformations on the client side.

DOCTYPE Declarations

The second issue involves what DOCTYPE declarations should be included in the document. The DOCTYPE declaration specifies the DTD to which the document conforms (as explained in Section 2.4). *Mozilla* requires an XHTML+MathML document to include a DOCTYPE declaration that specifies the XHTML DTD. *IE* does not require a DOCTYPE declaration but will read and interpret one if it is included. This would imply that to create a document that is viewable in both *Mozilla* and *IE*, you should include a DTD declaration.

However, the problem is that *IE* will give an error if you attempt to view a document containing a DTD declaration to the real MathML DTD. This is because *IE* cannot handle named character entities corresponding to MathML characters that belong to plane 1 of Unicode. The solution to this is to use a modified XHTML

+MathML DTD in which the entity declarations for all plane 1 characters have been replaced by alternative declarations that map all plane 1 characters to the private-use area of plane 0. (See Section 3.4 for more details.)

The modified DTD can be specified via the following declaration:

```
<!DOCTYPE html PUBLIC "-//W3C//DTD XHTML 1.1 plus
MathML 2.0//EN" "http://www.w3.org/Math/DTD/mathml2/xhtml-
math11-f.dtd">
```

You can use this declaration in a document to make it viewable in both *IE* and *Mozilla*. Of course, if you are using the Universal MathML stylesheet, this issue is irrelevant, since no DOCTYPE needs to be specified. The stylesheet automatically adds a suitable DOCTYPE declaration, if needed, based on the type of browser being used.

Namespaces

The third issue is how the namespace of the MathML markup should be specified. Specifying the namespace is important so that you can distinguish the MathML element and attribute names from those in the containing document. One way to specify the namespace of MathML elements is to use the `xmlns` attribute on the outer `math` element, as shown below:

```
<math xmlns="http://www.w3.org/1998/Math/MathML">
 <mrow>
   <mi>x</mi><mo>+</mo><mn>1</mn>
 </mrow>
<math>
```

Alternatively, you can use a namespace prefix for each element and attribute, as shown below:

```
<m:math xmlns:m="http://www.w3.org/1998/Math/MathML">
 <m:mrow>
   <m:mi>x</m:mi><m:mo>+</m:mo><m:mn>1</m:mn>
 </m:mrow>
<m:math>
```

This form is required when you are using *MathPlayer* or IBM *techexplorer* as a Behavior in *IE*. For more information on Behavior in *IE*, see Section 7.4.

Additional Tags

The fourth issue to consider is whether any extra tags are required to embed the MathML markup in the HTML/XHTML document. In *Mozilla* and *Amaya*, the MathML markup can be included directly in the XHTML document; no additional tags are required. IBM *techexplorer* requires each instance of the MathML markup to be enclosed in an `object` or `embed` tag (depending on whether the MathML is to be viewed using *IE* or *Netscape*), and *WebEQ* requires an `applet` tag. *MathPlayer* does not require a tag around each MathML expression, but it requires an `object` tag to be inserted in the `head` tag of the HTML document. We shall see some examples of the markup required for specific browsers and add-ons in Sections 7.3 and 7.4. But first, let's look at the stylesheet that resolves most of these compatibility issues.

7.2 The Universal MathML Stylesheet

The Universal MathML stylesheet specifies how to transform a document that contains MathML into a form suitable for the browser or MathML add-on available on the client machine. This stylesheet can be used with modern browsers that include support for CSS and XSLT,(such as *IE* 5.0 and later or *Netscape* 6.1 and later). The stylesheet can also be used with *Mozilla*. However, you can't use the stylesheet with *Amaya* since *Amaya* does not support XSLT transformations.

The Universal MathML stylesheet works as follows:

1. When a document that contains MathML content is downloaded, the stylesheet checks to see what browser is being used on the client machine and if a suitable add-on to render the MathML is available.
2. If the browser can render MathML natively, the browser's native rendering capabilities are used.
3. If the browser cannot render MathML directly but an add-on for rendering MathML is present on the machine, the stylesheet adds the appropriate markup needed in the document to render it with that add-on.
4. If more than one add-on is present, the stylesheet chooses one based on a set of preferences that the author can specify.
5. Finally, if none of the required add-ons are installed, at least on *IE*, the stylesheet can still render the MathML using a combination of CSS and JavaScript. The quality of this rendering is not as good as with a dedicated plug-in. However, since the rendering uses standard built-in features of the browser, the equations can be rendered quickly and with acceptable quality, both for viewing and printing.

The Universal MathML stylesheet resolves the problem of *IE* and *Mozilla/Netscape* having conflicting MIME type and DOCTYPE requirements for an XHTML+MathML document.

The beauty of the Universal MathML stylesheet is that all these transformations are performed automatically; the person authoring the document doesn't have to do anything other than including a reference to the stylesheet, as explained later in this chapter. Using this stylesheet, an author can create a MathML document that will be viewable on any browser, with or without a special plug-in. This eliminates the need to author documents tailored to specific rendering environments and goes a long way towards achieving the goal of "write once, read everywhere," which is essential for MathML documents to be accessible to a broad audience.

Another important feature of the stylesheet is that it allows content MathML to be displayed even on browsers that support only the display of presentation MathML. Most add-on software for rendering MathML, including *MathPlayer* and *techexplorer*, support the display of content markup as well as presentation markup. However, browsers like *Mozilla* and *Amaya* can only render presentation markup. To allow content markup to be displayed on such browsers, the Universal MathML stylesheet includes code for transforming all content markup in the input document into a corresponding presentation markup expression. The resulting document contains only presentation markup and can therefore be displayed in *Mozilla* or *Amaya* using their native rendering capabilities.

Using the Stylesheet

To display MathML in a browser using the Universal MathML stylesheet, you need to do two things. First, embed the MathML markup in an XHTML document, with each instance of MathML enclosed in a `math` tag. The MathML namespace must be specified for each MathML element, either using a namespace prefix or via a declaration on the outer `math` tag.

Note that the requirements for an XHTML document are more stringent than those for an HTML one. Some guidelines on creating valid XHTML documents are given in the discussion of Mozilla in Section 7.3.

After embedding the MathML markup in an XHTML document, you must include the following processing instruction at the start of the XHTML document, before the opening `html` tag but after the XML declaration:

```
<?xml-stylesheet type="text/xsl"
  href="http://www.w3.org/Math/XSL/mathml.xsl"?>
```

This statement tells the browser to download an XSLT stylesheet called `mathml.xsl` from the specified URL and apply it to the document. The stylesheet contains transformation rules that provide a proper rendering for presentation elements. As explained earlier in this chapter, any content MathML present in the document is first converted into presentation MathML. Hence, the transformation rules appropriate to presentation markup can be used for rendering content elements as well.

Example 7.1 shows a template for a typical document that observes these guidelines.

Example 7.1 A template document that contains a reference to the Universal MathML stylesheet.

```
 <?xml version="1.0">
<?xml-stylesheet type="text/xsl"
href="http://www.w3.org/Math/XSL/mathml.xsl"?>
<html xmlns="http://www.w3.org/1999/xhtml">
 <head><title> ... </title></head>
   <body>
   <math xmlns="http://www.w3.org/1998/Math/MathML">
     <mrow>
       <msqrt><mi>x</mi></msqrt>
     </mrow>
   </math>
 </body>
</html>
```

If the XHTML document contains only presentation markup, the `mathml.xsl` stylesheet can be replaced by a simpler version called `pmathml.xsl`. In other words, the processing instruction to be inserted in the document should be the following:

```
<?xml-stylesheet type="text/xsl"
  href="http://www.w3.org/Math/XSL/pmathml.xsl"?>
```

The `pmathml.xsl` stylesheet is much smaller than the `mathml.xsl` stylesheet because it contains only the transformation rules needed for presentation elements. Hence, the document can be displayed faster.

IE Security Issues

The method of referencing a stylesheet at its public location on the W3C Web site, as shown in Example 7.1, will not work for *IE* when you use its default security settings. This is because, with its default settings, *IE* will not accept a stylesheet that is on a different server from the one that contains the document to be viewed. One solution to this problem would be to change *IE*'s security settings. However, this requires some customization on each individual client machine, which is not a practical option.

A better solution is to place a local copy of the stylesheet on the server. The stylesheet-processing instruction should then specify the location of the stylesheet on your server using a relative URL, as in the example below:

```
<?xml-stylesheet type="text/xsl"
  href="styles/mathml.xsl"?>
```

As discussed earlier, if the document contains only presentation markup, the `mathml.xsl` stylesheet can be replaced by `pmathml.xsl` instead.

If you specify a local URL, the stylesheet is downloaded from the server along with the XHTML+MathML document. This ensures that your document is viewable on *IE* as well as on *Netscape/Mozilla*. Hence, to make your documents accessible to the widest possible audience, it is advisable to use a local copy of the stylesheet instead of the public copy.

The Universal MathML stylesheet consists of the following four files, which can be accessed from the URL *www.w3.org/Math/XSL*:

- `pmathml.xsl`: is the main stylesheet for presentation MathML. It detects the browser and add-on available on the client machine and sets up an appropriate transformation.
- `mathml.xsl`: is identical to `pmathml.xsl` except that it first uses `ctop.xsl` to transform content MathML t presentation MathML on *Mozilla/Netscape*.
- `ctop.xsl`: transforms content MathML to presentation MathML.
- `pmathmlcss.xsl`: transforms presentation MathML to XHTML using CSS and JavaScript, so MathML can be rendered using the browser's native capabilities.

If you are going to make the stylesheet accessible locally, you must copy all four files to your server.

Specifying Preferences

If the browser on the local machine has more than one way of displaying MathML, you can use the `pref:renderer` attribute to specify which method should be used. This attribute belongs to a private namespace and must be specified in the `html` tag, as shown here:

```
 <?xml-stylesheet type="text/xsl" href="pmathml.xsl"?>
<html xmlns="http://www.w3.org/1999/xhtml"
 xmlns:pref="http://www.w3.org/2002/Math/preference"
 pref:renderer="css">
 <head>...</head>
 <body>...</body>
</html>
```

The `renderer` attribute can take the following values, each corresponding to a specific method of rendering MathML:

- `css`: uses the browser's native CSS capabilities
- `mathplayer`: uses *MathPlayer*
- `mathplayer-dl`: uses *MathPlayer* if it is installed, or prompts the user to install it
- `techexplorer-plugin`: uses the *techexplorer* plug-in
- `techexplorer`: uses the *techexplorer* Behavior (see Section 7.4 for details)

Supported Browsers

Table 7.1 provides a partial list of the different browsers and add-ons that can be used to render MathML, with the help of the Universal MathML stylesheet, on different platforms. For a more detailed and up-to-date listing, see the following URL: *http://www.w3.org/Math/XSL*.

7.3 MathML-enabled Browsers

This section provides information on viewing MathML in specific browsers. The browsers that support native display of MathML are *Mozilla* 1.0, *Netscape* 7.0, and *Amaya*. All of these browsers can display presentation MathML directly. They can also be used to render content MathML, provided the document contains a reference to the Universal MathML stylesheet, as explained in Section 7.2.

Mozilla/Netscape

Mozilla is the open-source version of the *Netscape* browser. Version 1.0 of *Mozilla* was released in June 2002 and supports native display of MathML 2.0 presentation elements, on Windows and Unix/Linux. MathML support for Macintosh was added starting with *Mozilla* 1.1. *Netscape* 7.0, released in September 2002, uses the same rendering

TABLE 7.1 Browsers That Can Render MathML

Platform	Browser
Windows	*IE* 5.0 with *techexplorer*
	IE 5.5 with either *MathPlayer* or *techexplorer*
	IE 6.0 with either *MathPlayer* or *techexplorer*
	Netscape 6.1 or later with *techexplorer*
	Netscape 7.0 either directly or with *techexplorer*
	Mozilla 1.0 or later
	Amaya
Macintosh	*IE* 5.0 or later with *techexplorer*
	Netscape 6.1 or later with *techexplorer*
	Mozilla 1.1 or later
Linux/Unix	*Netscape* 6.1 or later with *techexplorer*
	Netscape 7.0 either directly or with *techexplorer*
	Mozilla 1.0 or later
	Amaya

engine as *Mozilla* 1.0 and also supports native display of MathML on Windows and Linux only. If you include a reference to the Universal MathML stylesheet, you can also display content MathML on recent versions of *Mozilla/Netscape*.

Creating XHTML Documents

Mozilla cannot render MathML included in an HTML file. To be properly displayed, the MathML markup must be embedded in an XHTML document. XHTML is a reformulation of HTML to make it consistent with the rules of XML syntax. An XHTML document has the same tags and attributes as an HTML document and can therefore be displayed in any standard Web browser. But there are some important differences between XHTML and HTML arising from the fact that an XHTML document must be a well-formed and valid XML document.

Some of the important features of XHTML documents are:

- All tag names, attribute names, and attribute values must be written in lower case. For example, `<H2 ALIGN="Center">...</H2>` is not allowed but `<h2 align="center">...</h2>` is.
- All non-empty elements must have a closing tag. For example, `<p>Some text` is not allowed but `<p>Some text</p>` is.

- All empty elements must have a trailing slash. For example, `<hr>` is not allowed but `<hr/>` is.
- No two elements should overlap. For example, `<p>Here is some <b><i>styled text.</b></i></p>` is not allowed but `<p>Here is some <b><i>styled text</i></b></p>`.
- All attribute values must be quoted. For example, `<table align=left>` is not allowed but `<table align="left">` is.
- Attribute value pairs must be written in full. For example, `<td nowrap>` is not allowed but `<td nowrap="nowrap">` is.
- The root element must be an `html` element, with the XHTML namespace specified, as in `<html xmlns="http://www.w3.org/1999/xhtml">`.

Making all these changes to an existing HTML document takes a great deal of time and labor. You can greatly simplify this task by using a special utility called Tidy, written specifically for this purpose by Dave Raggett. Tidy is a C program that takes an HTML document as input and returns an XHTML document as output, automatically making all the necessary changes and substitutions described above. The program can fix most common mistakes in an HTML document. However, if there are mistakes it cannot fix, it issues a warning so you can fix them yourself. You can download a copy of Tidy from */www.w3.org/People/Raggett/Tidy*.

Mozilla also requires each XHTML document to have an explicit DOCTYPE declaration that references the XHTML DTD. The W3C has supplied three separate DTDs for XHTML, called the *strict, transitional,* and *frameset* versions. For XHTML documents that contain MathML, you can use any of these three DTDs. However, the best choice is to use the following declaration, which refers to a combined DTD that merges the DTD for XHTML with a modified DTD for MathML:

```
<!DOCTYPE html PUBLIC "-//W3C//DTD XHTML 1.1 plus
MathML 2.0//EN" "http://www.w3.org/Math/DTD/mathml2/
 xhtml-math11-f.dtd">
```

Note that even if you include a reference to an external MathML DTD, *Mozilla* still refers to a local copy of the DTD installed in its cache. In other words, the DTD declaration is required but it is ignored.

Example 7.2 shows a simple document that can be displayed in *Mozilla*; it contains an MathML equation. The document must be valid and well-formed XHTML, and the filename must end with the extension .xml. This is to ensure that the server specifies the MIME type of the file as text/xml when sending the file to the browser.

Note also the use of the DOCTYPE declaration to declare the DTDs for XHTML and MathML, and the namespace declaration on both the `html` element and the `math` element.

Example 7.2 An XHTML+MathML document suitable for display by *Mozilla*.

```
<?xml version="1.0"?>
 <!DOCTYPE html PUBLIC "-//W3C//DTD XHTML 1.1 plus
 MathML 2.0//EN"
 "http://www.w3.org/Math/DTD/mathml2/xhtml-math11-f.dtd">
   <html xmlns="http://www.w3.org/1999/xhtml">
     <head><title> MathML Example </title></head>
     <body>
       <p> Here is a simple equation. </p>
       <p><math xmlns=
   "http://www.w3.org/1998/Math/MathML">
 <mrow>
 <msup><mi>x</mi><mn>2</mn></msup>
 <mo>-</mo>
 <mrow>
 <mn>2</mn><mo>&InvisibleTimes;</mo><mi>x</mi>
 </mrow>
 <mo>+</mo><mn>1</mn>
 </mrow>
 </math>
 </p>
 </body>
</html>
```

Figure 7.1 shows the above document as displayed in *Mozilla*. If you right-click on the equation, a pop-up menu that contains the command `View MathML Source` appears. Choosing this command opens another window that contains the MathML markup for the equation. You can copy the markup from this window and paste it into another application, if desired. Of course, you can also view the MathML markup embedded in the source for the XHTML document by choosing the `View ▶ Page Source` menu command.

Installing and Customizing Fonts

An important issue in displaying MathML in a browser is that the appropriate fonts for mathematical symbols and other special characters must be available. The two main add-ons for rendering MathML, *MathPlayer* and *techexplorer*, both come with their own set of mathematical fonts, and these are installed automatically when you install the software. *Mozilla*, however, does not include any

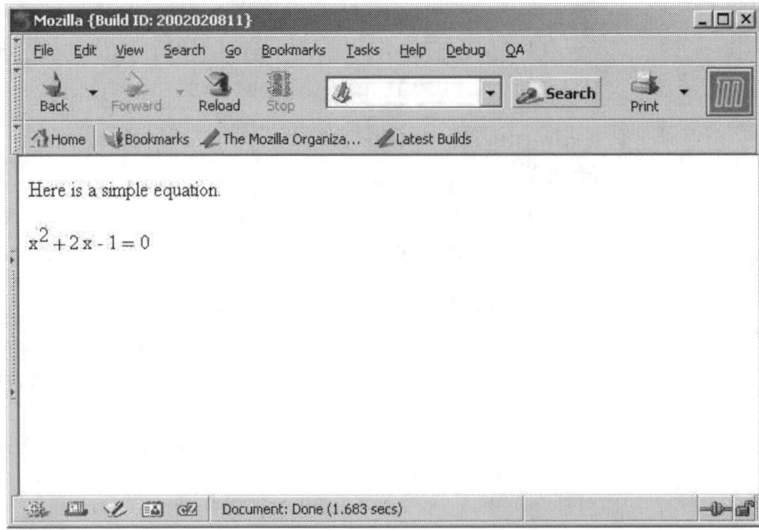

FIGURE 7.1 An XHTML document that contains MathML markup, as displayed by *Mozilla*.

special fonts for displaying mathematics. Hence, to properly view MathML using *Mozilla* or *Netscape*, you must install some additional fonts yourself. Otherwise, some mathematical symbols will not render properly.

One popular set of mathematical fonts are the Computer Modern fonts, which are typically part of any TEX or LATEX distribution. These fonts are maintained by the AMS and are available for free download from their Web site: http://www.ams.org. They are also included on the CD-ROM that comes with this book.

To install the Computer Modern fonts, you must copy them onto your machine and then place them in the appropriate location for your operating system. Here are the instructions for installing these fonts on Windows NT/2000/XP:

1. Copy the font files (called CMEX10, CMSY10, CMM10, and CMR10) on to your machine.
2. These fonts are stored in the form of compressed archives. Use a program like *WinZip* to extract the files from the archives.
3. Open the Fonts control panel using the Windows Start menu.
4. In the File menu of the Fonts control panel, choose Install New Font.
5. In the dialog that appears, specify the location of the font files on your machine and click OK.

The Computer Modern fonts are then installed on your machine and will be automatically used by *Mozilla*, if required.

Alternatively, you can install and use the Mathematica fonts, developed by Wolfram Research for use in that company's technical computing software of the same name. These fonts are available free for non-commercial use. To use these fonts, you can install the trial version of Mathematica included on the CD-ROM that comes with this book. The Mathematica fonts are installed automatically on your machine when you install Mathematica.

You can tell *Mozilla* to use one font in preference to another. When you view a page that contains MathML, the `View ▶ Use Style` submenu is automatically updated to show the following three choices, each corresponding to a specific set of mathematical fonts:

- `Basic Page Style`
- `TEX`
- `Mathematica`

The `Basic Page Style` setting uses the default fonts present on the system. By switching to `TEX` or `Mathematica`, you can force *Mozilla* to use the Computer Modern or *Mathematica* fonts, respectively, if these are installed on your system.

You can also customize *Mozilla*'s font preferences at a much lower level by setting up your own font-encoding tables. These allow you to associate particular fonts to be used for particular characters. For more information on how to do this, see the following URL: *http://www.mozilla.org/projects/mathml/fonts/encoding*.

Amaya

Amaya is the test browser developed by the W3C for demonstrating new Web technologies. It is available for Windows and some Unix platforms. Like *Mozilla, Amaya* supports only native display of presentation MathML. However, unlike *Mozilla, Amaya* does not include support for XSLT transformations. Hence, it cannot be used to display content MathML using the Universal MathML stylesheet.

To view MathML content in *Amaya*, you must enclose each instance of MathML in an outer `math` element, as required by the MathML specification. However, there is no need to use a namespace prefix or any additional HTML elements to embed the markup in the HTML document. This allows you to freely mix MathML markup along with the usual HTML tags for displaying text and images. Example 7.3 shows a simple document that contains

MathML, suitable for display in *Amaya*. Figure 7.2 shows how the document appears when viewed in *Amaya*.

Example 7.3 A sample document for displaying MathML in *Amaya*.

```
<html>
 <head><title>MathML Example</title></head>
 <body>
   <p>Here is a simple equation.</p>
   <p><math>
     <mrow>
       <msup><mi>x</mi><mn>2</mn></msup>
       <mo>-</mo>
       <mrow>
         <mn>2</mn><mo>
         <mo>&InvisibleTimes;</mo>
         <mi>x</mi>
       </mrow>
       <mo>+</mo>
       <mn>1</mn>
     </mrow>
   </math></p>
 </body>
</html>
```

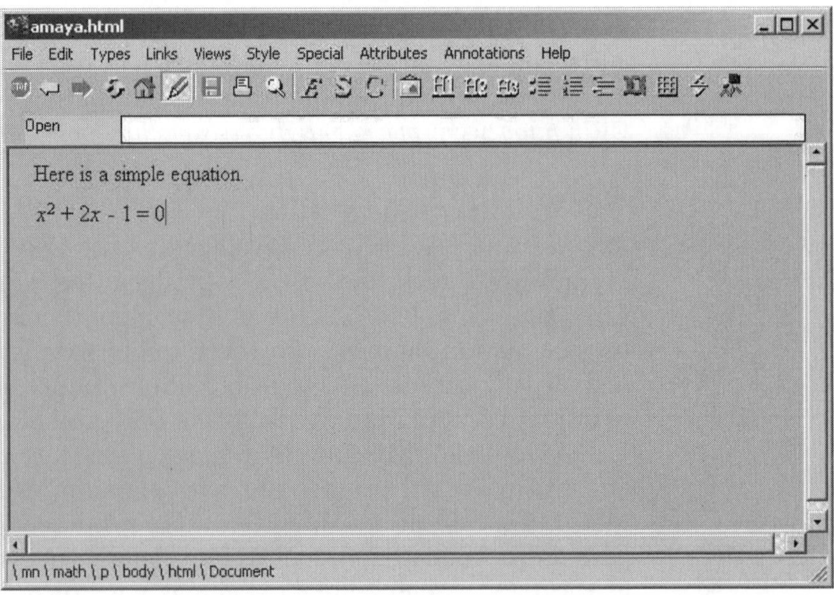

FIGURE 7.2 An HTML document that contains MathML markup, as displayed by *Amaya*.

Amaya also provides a Structure view (Figure 7.3), which reveals the hierarchical structure of the markup for the document being displayed. To see this view, choose `Show structure` from the Views menu. This feature is particularly useful for MathML equations, since you can see the relationship between the various MathML elements.

Since *Amaya* does not contain any special fonts for mathematical symbols, it has only limited support for displaying extended characters. The only extended characters that can be displayed are those found in the Symbol font. A question mark (?) is displayed in place of any character entities for which fonts are not available.

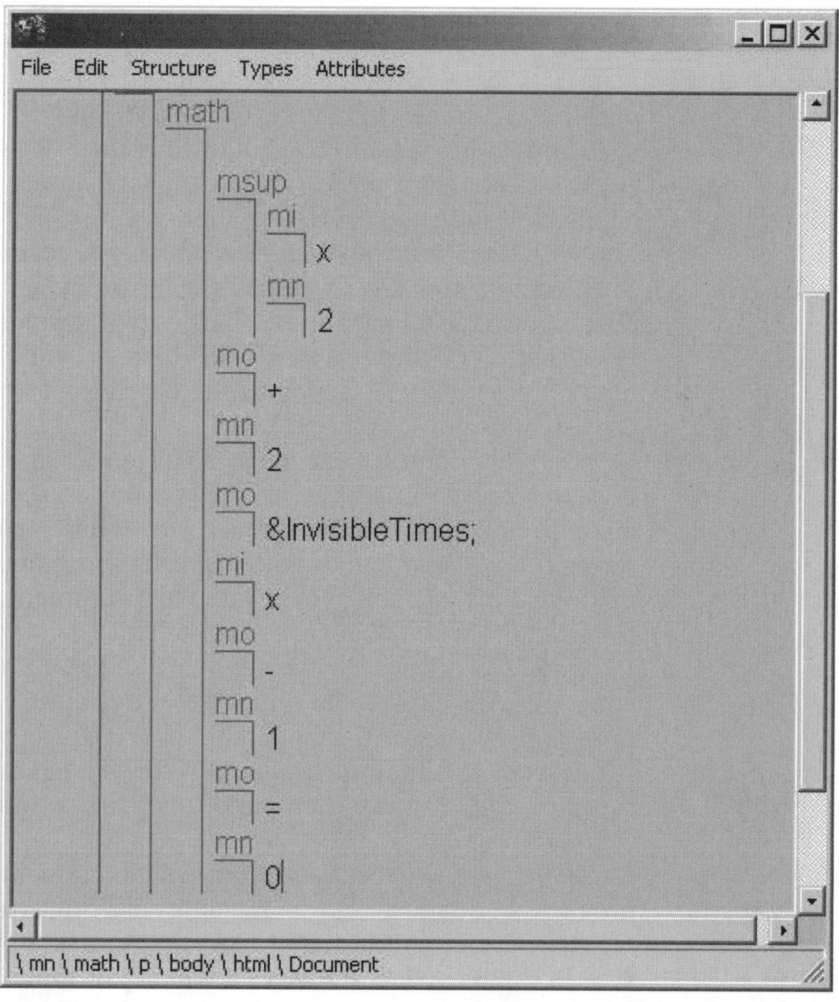

FIGURE 7.3 The same document as in Figure 7.2 seen in *Amaya*'s Structure view.

Amaya also provides limited support for authoring and editing MathML equations. To build up MathML expressions you can either use templates from a palette or use menu commands. *Amaya* automatically inserts the appropriate presentation tags around your input. Details of using *Amaya* for authoring MathML are given in Section 9.7.

7.4 ADD-ON SOFTWARE

This section provides information on the three different types of add-ons available for viewing MathML in *IE* and *Netscape*, namely *MathPlayer*, IBM *techexplorer*, and *WebEQ*.

MathPlayer

MathPlayer is a free plug-in developed by Design Science Inc. It enables high-quality rendering of MathML on Versions 5.5 and later of *IE* on Windows. *MathPlayer* takes advantage of a special feature of *IE* called Behaviors, which allows low-level integration of a helper application with the browser. When you use the Behaviors functionality, *MathPlayer* can query the browser to get information about the font style and size, as well as spacing and alignment of text in a document. This information is then used to render MathML equations that are well integrated with their environment; that is, the font styles and sizes, as well as the baseline of the equations, are consistent with the adjacent text.

MathPlayer does an excellent job of rendering both content and presentation markup. It is written entirely in C++, making it fast and efficient. It can render hundreds of equations in a fraction of a second. *MathPlayer* comes with a special set of fonts for displaying mathematical symbols. These fonts are automatically installed on the machine when *MathPlayer* is installed.

MathPlayer also allows you to access the MathML source for any equation it displays. To do this, right-click on the equation to bring up a pop-up menu. If you then choose the Copy MathML command from this menu, the markup for the equation is copied to the clipboard. You can then paste this markup into another application, if desired.

MathPlayer supports some limited functionality for displaying interactive equations, such as toggling between two displays, changing the color or background of an equation, and displaying a message in the browser's status area when you move the mouse over it. For this type of interactivity, the equations must be authored using the *WebEQ* Editor application, details of which are provided in Section 8.3.

At this time, *MathPlayer* is not available for Macintosh. This is because the Behaviors functionality that it relies on is not implemented in *IE* for Macintosh.

Authoring Documents for *MathPlayer*

Example 7.4 shows the source of a typical document that contains an equation to be displayed by *MathPlayer*.

Example 7.4 A sample document for displaying MathML in *IE* using *MathPlayer*.

```
<html xmlns:m="http://www.w3.org/1998/Math/MathML">
 <head>
 <object id=MathPlayer
 classid="clsid:32F66A20-7614-11D4-BD11-00104BD3F987">"
 </object>
 <?import namespace="m" implementation="#MathPlayer" >
 </head>
   <body>
   <p>Here is a simple equation.</p>
   <p>
   <m:math>
   <m:mrow>
       <m:msup><m:mi>x</m:mi><m:mn>2</m:mn></m:msup>
       <m:mo>-</m:mo>
       <m:mrow>
       <m:mn>2</m:mn>
       <m:mo>&InvisibleTimes;</m:mo>
       <m:mi>x</m:mi>
     </m:mrow>
     <m:mo>+</m:mo>
     <m:mn>1</m:mn>
   </m:mrow>
   </m:math>
   </p>
 </body>
</html>
```

The above document has the various key features that are explained next.

The `xmlns:m` attribute in the `html` tag associates the prefix `m:` with the MathML 2.0 namespace. This specifies that any tag of the form `m:`*name* in the document should be interpreted as the *name* tag defined by MathML 2.0.

The `object` element associates the *MathPlayer* ID with the *MathPlayer* software. This association is established through the values of three attributes:

- `id`: defines a keyword for referring to the software.
- `classid`: is a unique label that identifies *MathPlayer* in the Windows registry. It tells *IE* where *MathPlayer* is installed on the local machine.

The import processing instruction says that any element with the namespace prefix `m:` should be displayed using the software whose ID is *MathPlayer*.

The MathML expression is included in the document with each MathML element in the form of a qualified name with the `m:` prefix.

Using the above guidelines, you can author by hand Web pages that contain MathML to be displayed by *MathPlayer*. Alternatively, you can use the translation mechanism provided in products like *MathType* or *WebEQ* to save an equation in the desired form and directly paste it into the HTML document. Details of how to do this are provided in Sections 8.2 and 8.3. Figure 7.4 shows how the document in Example 7.4 looks, when viewed in *IE*.

Since *MathPlayer* is implemented as an *IE* Behavior, it has access to information about the various display settings of the browser (such as the font style, size and color). Hence, *MathPlayer* can automatically adjust the display of all equations to match the default

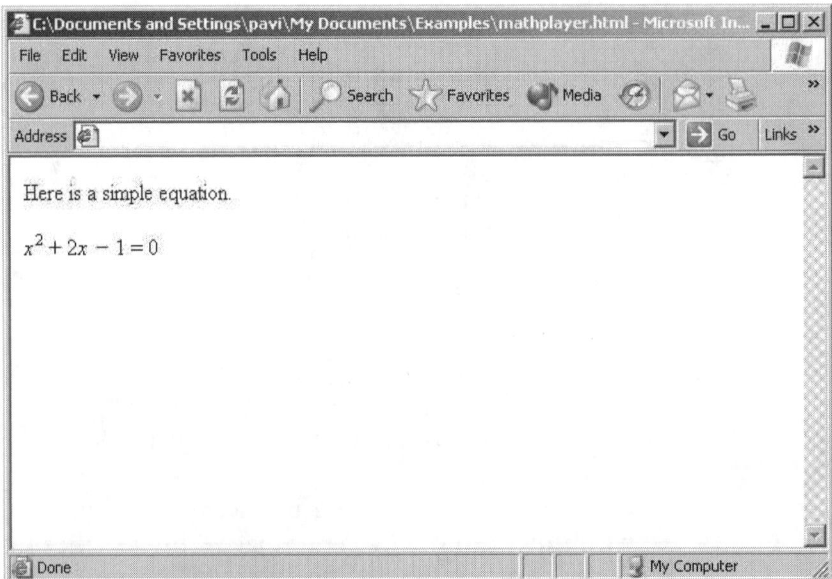

FIGURE 7.4 A simple MathML equation as displayed in *IE* using *MathPlayer*.

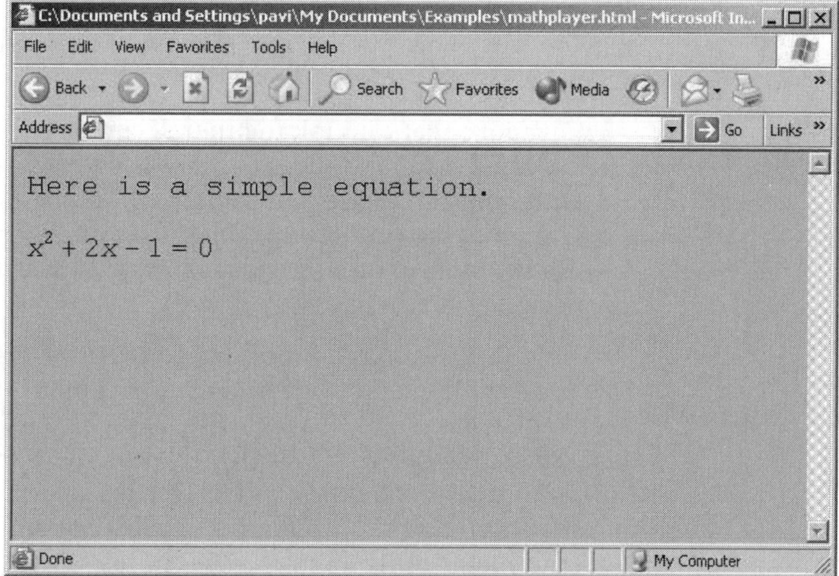

FIGURE 7.5 The same equation as in Figure 7.4 but using different default settings for the font style, font size, and background color.

settings of the browser. Figure 7.5 shows the result of viewing the same document as in Figure 7.4 but with the default font style set to Courier, a larger font size, and the background color set to gray. Note that all these changes are automatically applied to the display of the equation.

IBM *techexplorer*

IBM's *techexplorer* was one of the first tools released that enabled users to display MathML in Web browsers. It can directly render MathML, as well as $\TeX$ and $\LaTeX$ markup, in both *IE* and *Netscape*. *techexplorer* works as a plug-in for *Netscape* and as an ActiveX control for *IE*. Versions of *techexplorer* are available for most platforms, including Windows, Macintosh, and Unix. The current release, Version 3.1, supports most of the presentation and content tags defined in MathML 2.0. You can also use *techexplorer* as an ActiveX control to display interactive equations in Microsoft applications such as *Word*, *Excel*, and *PowerPoint*.

techexplorer is available in two versions: a free Introductory edition (which has the basic features needed for viewing scientific documents) and a Professional edition (which adds some extra features such as support for printing as well as scripting using JavaScript and Java). *techexplorer* is much more than a viewer for scientific documents. It supports a special set of commands that can be included as markup in a document to implement various features, such as the following:

- Equations that can link to other documents
- Links that can play audio or video files
- Links that can toggle between two different displays
- Links that open a pop-up window for displaying footnotes
- A programming interface that allows *techexplorer* to be controlled using JavaScript or Java

These features make it possible to use *techexplorer* for creating Web pages with interactive mathematical content. The Professional version of *techexplorer* includes a special set of class libraries and an implementation of the W3C's DOM. You can use these to manipulate various parts of a document in response to user events such as mouse clicks by writing appropriate JavaScript and Java programs. Some examples of using *techexplorer* to display interactive mathematical content are given in Section 12.4.

Viewing Documents

Once you install *techexplorer*, your browser is automatically configured to view files with the extensions `.mml`, `.tex`, `.ltx`, and `.tcx` (for MathML, $\TeX$, $\LaTeX$, and *techexplorer* documents, respectively). Whenever you open any document with these file extensions, *techexplorer* will be used to display the entire document. Alternatively, you can include instances of MathML, $\TeX$, or $\LaTeX$ markup in an HTML document.

You can use *techexplorer* in either full-screen mode or window. In full-screen mode, the entire browser window is taken up by *techexplorer* for displaying the content of a document. This mode is used when you load a document that has one of the extensions or file types noted above for which *techexplorer* is defined as the helper application.

In window mode, *techexplorer* displays an embedded expression in an HTML document in a small window within the main browser window. The size of the *techexplorer* window is typically specified via the attributes of the `embed` tag or `object` tag, used for inserting the displayed expression in the HTML document.

If you right-click in a blank area inside the *techexplorer* window (or control-click on Macintosh) a context menu (Figure 7.6) appears. This menu gives you access to several basic features of *techexplorer* such as navigating within a document, printing (available in the Professional edition only), and changing options.

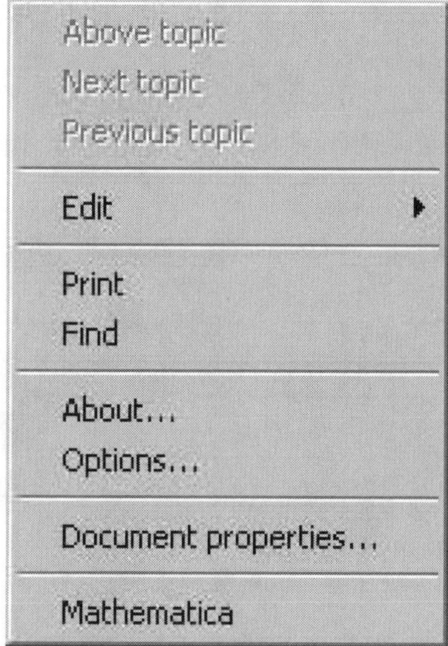

FIGURE 7.6 The *techexplorer* document context menu.

If you click on the Options menu, the dialog shown in Figure 7.7 appears. This lets you set options to control various features of how a document is displayed (such as colors, fonts, and so on). You can specify different option settings for regular text and mathematical expressions. For example, using the MathAutoColor tab, you can cause mathematical expressions to be displayed with a different background and foreground color from the surrounding text. You can also set operators, delimiters, and numbers to each appear in a different color.

If you have multiple fonts installed for displaying mathematical symbols, you can specify a given set of fonts as a default by using the Math and Symbols section of the Options dialog.

The following sections provide information on how to author HTML documents containing MathML content that can be displayed by *techexplorer*. The details of how MathML markup should be embedded in the HTML document vary depending on whether the document is to be viewed in *Netscape* or *IE* and whether you wish to use *techexplorer* as a plug-in, an ActiveX control, or an *IE* Behavior.

Authoring Documents for *Netscape*

In *Netscape*, content to be rendered by *techexplorer* must be included in an HTML document using the `embed` tag. This element is used

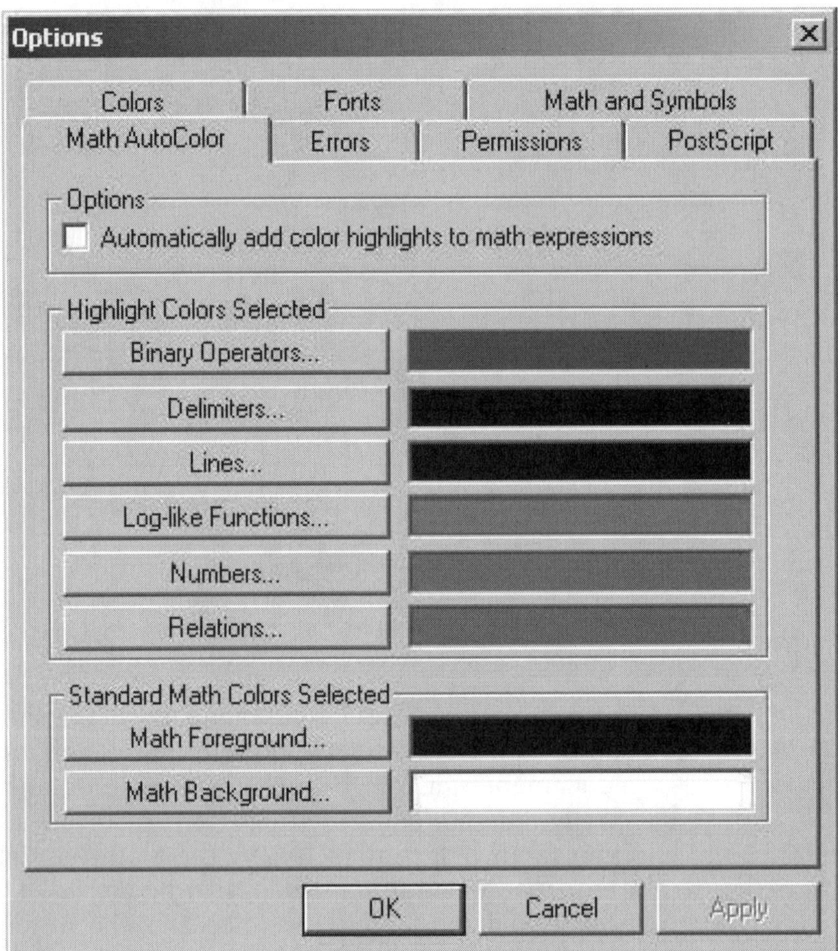

FIGURE 7.7 The MathAutoColor section of the Options dialog.

in HTML to enclose any content that should be rendered using a plug-in. Some of the important attributes of the `embed` element are:

- `type`: is the MIME type of the embedded object. For *techexplorer*, this is always set to `application/x-techexplorer`.
- `src`: gives the location of the file to be displayed, either as an absolute or relative URL.
- `width` and `height`: give the size of the plug-in display window, in pixels or as a percentage of the screen size.
- `name`: allows you to name the embedded object so that it can be referred to by a Java or JavaScript program or another plug-in.

- `pluginspage`: specifies the URL of the Web site for the plug-in that should be used to display the content. For *techexplorer*, this is always set to `http://www.software.ibm.com/techexplorer/`.
- `alt`: allows you to specify alternate text that should be displayed as a fallback in case the plug-in cannot render the embedded content.

You can directly insert the MathML markup into the `embed` element using the `mmldata` attribute. The value of this attribute is a string that contains the MathML markup to be rendered. Example 7.5 shows the source for an HTML document that contains content to be rendered by *techexplorer*. Figure 7.8 shows the document of Example 7.5 displayed in *Netscape*.

Example 7.5 A sample document for displaying MathML in *Netscape* using *techexplorer*.

```
<html>
 <head></head>
 <body>
   <p>Here is a simple equation.
     <embed type="application/x-techexplorer" mmldata=
   "<math xmlns='http://www.w3.org/1998/Math/MathML'>
   <mrow>
```

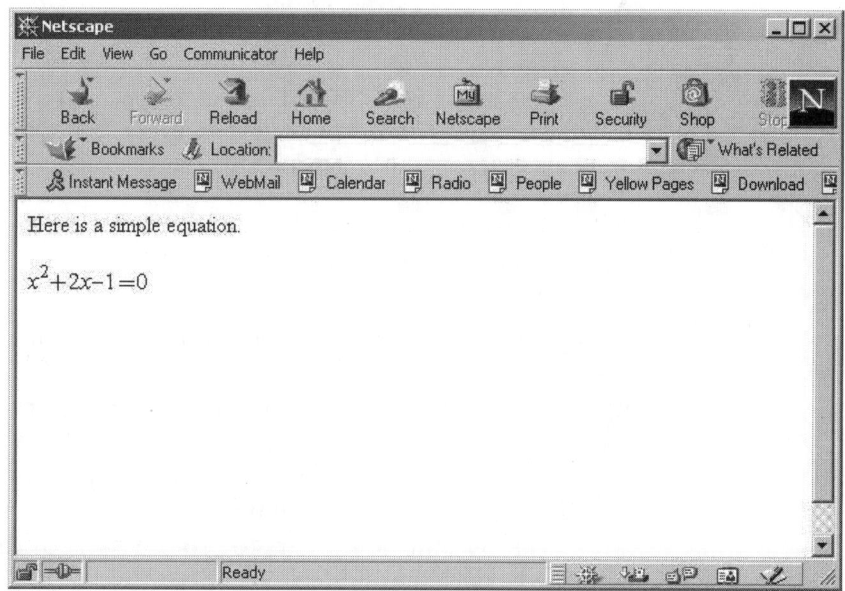

FIGURE 7.8 A simple MathML equation displayed in *Netscape* using *techexplorer*.

```
        <msup><mi>x</mi><mn>2</mn></msup>
        <mo>-</mo>
        <mrow>
          <mn>2</mn>
          <mo>&InvisibleTimes;</mo>
          <mi>x</mi>
        </mrow>
        <mo>+</mo>
        <mn>1</mn>
      </mrow>
 </math>"
pluginspage='http://www.software.ibm.com/techexplorer/'
 height=100 width=200 name="equation">
 </embed>
 </p>
 </body>
</html>
```

Alternatively, you can include the MathML markup in a separate document and refer to the document using the `src` attribute of the `embed` tag. In Example 7.6, the MathML content is placed in a file called `equation.mml`, which is in the same directory as the HTML document.

Example 7.6 Using the `src` attribute to specify a MathML equation in a separate file.

```
<html>
 <head></head>
   <body>
     <embed type="application/x-techexplorer"
pluginspage="http://www.software.ibm.com/techexplorer/"
src="equation.mml" height=100 width=200
name="equation">
     </embed>
 </body>
</html>
```

Note that for each MathML equation in your document, you must explicitly specify the size of the window in which it will be displayed. If you specify a window size that is too small to display the equation, the parts of the equation that don't fit in the window will get cut off. However, in such a case, *techexplorer* automatically places scroll bars around the display window, as shown in Figure 7.9. You can then move the scroll bars to see the parts of the equation that would otherwise be hidden. When you use *techexplorer* with *IE* on

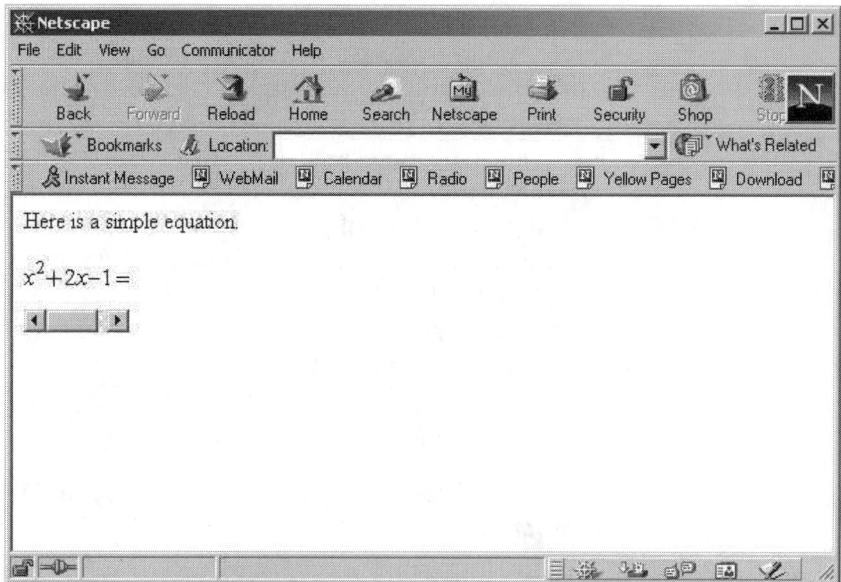

FIGURE 7.9 An equation rendered by *techexplorer* with too small a window size specified. The equation gets clipped because it is too long to fit in the window.

Windows, it is possible to have the size of the window calculated automatically, as explained in the next subsection.

Authoring Documents for *IE*

For *IE* on Windows, *techexplorer* is also implemented as an ActiveX control. Hence, to view MathML content you can enclose the MathML data in an `object` element instead of the `embed` element. Some of the important attributes of the `object` element are listed here:

- `classid`: is a unique label used in the Windows registry to tell *IE* where the helper application is installed on the local machine. For *techexplorer*, this is always set to: `clsid:5AFAB315-AD87-11D3-98BB-002035EFB1A4`.
- `width` and `height`: give the size of the ActiveX control window, in pixels or percentage of the screen size.
- `autosize`: specifies if *techexplorer* should allow the minimum space needed for the displayed expression. If set to `true`, the expression is shown without a scroll bar. If this parameter is not specified or if it is set to `false` and the *techexplorer* window is not large enough to fit the entire expression, the expression is displayed with scroll bars.

- name: allows you to name the embedded object so that it can be referred to by a Java or JavaScript program or another plug-in.
- param: provides a way to specify additional properties of the embedded object. It lets you specify values for a number of named parameters, using the syntax: <param name="*name*" value="*value*">. For viewing MathML using *techexplorer*, the important values of *name* are datatype and data.
- data: specifies the URL or the actual data of the document to be displayed.
- datatype: specifies the type of data to be displayed. It can take the values shown in Table 7.2.

Example 7.7 shows the same document as in Example 7.5, modified for viewing in *IE*.

Example 7.7 A sample document for displaying MathML in *IE* using *techexplorer*.

```
<html>
 <head></head>
   <body>
     <p>Here is a simple equation.
   <object ID="eqn" height=100 width=200
   classid="clsid:5AFAB315-AD87-11D3-98BB-002035EFB1A4">
     <param name="autosize" value="true">
     <param name="datatype" value="1">
     <param name="data" value=
   "<math xmlns='http://www.w3.org/1998/Math/MathML'>
     <mrow>
       <msup><mi>x</mi><mn>2</mn></msup>
         <mo>-</mo>
         <mrow>
         <mn>2</mn><mo>&InvisibleTimes;</mo>
         <mi>x</mi>
         </mrow>
         <mo>+</mo><mn>1</mn>
       </mrow>
```

TABLE 7.2 datatype **Values**

Value of datatype attribute	Type of Data
0	TeX or LaTeX data
1	MathML data
2	URL to a TeX or LaTeX document
3	URL to a MathML document

```
        </math>">
      </object>
    </p>
  </body>
</html>
```

Notice that the `width` and `height` attributes are not specified explicitly in the `object` tag. The `autosize` parameter is set to `true`, so *techexplorer* automatically sets the window to the size needed for displaying the equation. Since *techexplorer* is used here as an ActiveX control, it can get information about the equation's size from the browser and adjust the size of the display window accordingly. This makes authoring easier and produces better-looking output than if you used *techexplorer* as a plug-in with *Netscape*.

For content that can be rendered by both *Netscape* and *IE*, you can use the `object` tag to enclose an `embed` tag, as shown in Example 7.8. This is a more robust method than using either the `object` or `embed` tag alone, because it allows *techexplorer* to be used as an ActiveX control by *IE* and as a plug-in by *Netscape*.

Example 7.8 An `object` tag that contains an embed tag. This allows the MathML markup to be rendered by both *IE* and *Netscape*.

```
 <object ID="eqn" height=100 width=200
classid="clsid:5AFAB315-AD87-11D3-98BB-002035EFB1A4">
 <param name="datatype" value="1">
 <param name="data" value=
 "<math>
   <msup><mi>x</mi><mn>2</mn></msup>
 </math>">
 <embed type="application/x-techexplorer"
 mmldata=
   "<math>
   <msup><mi>x</mi><mn>2</mn></msup>
 </math>"
pluginspage="http://www.software.ibm.com/techexplorer/"
height=100 width=200 name="eqn">
 </embed>
</object>
```

Although you can use the `AutoSize` parameter to solve the problem of adjusting the window size to fit the equation, another limitation of *techexplorer* remains: it renders all equations with an opaque background. If you change the default background color of your document using the browser's option settings, the background of the *techexplorer* window can be explicitly seen since it appears in a contrasting color (Figure 7.10). You can overcome this problem by using *techexplorer* as a Behavior, as explained in the next section.

IE Behaviors

IBM *techexplorer* can also be used as a Behavior for *IE*. As explained in the discussion of *MathPlayer*, *IE* Behaviors allow you to associate a given type of embedded content with a specific rendering application. Moreover, the application has access to the APIs of the browser, and can thus get more information about the Web page, which allows for better integration of the plug-in content with the surrounding HTML data.

To use *techexplorer* as a Behavior, you have to author the document as shown in Example 7.9.

Example 7.9 A sample document for displaying MathML in *IE* using *techexplorer* as a Behavior.

```
 <html xmlns:m="http://www.w3.org/1998/Math/MathML">
<head>
 <object id="techexplorer"
 classid="clsid:0E76D59A-C088-11D4-9920-
```

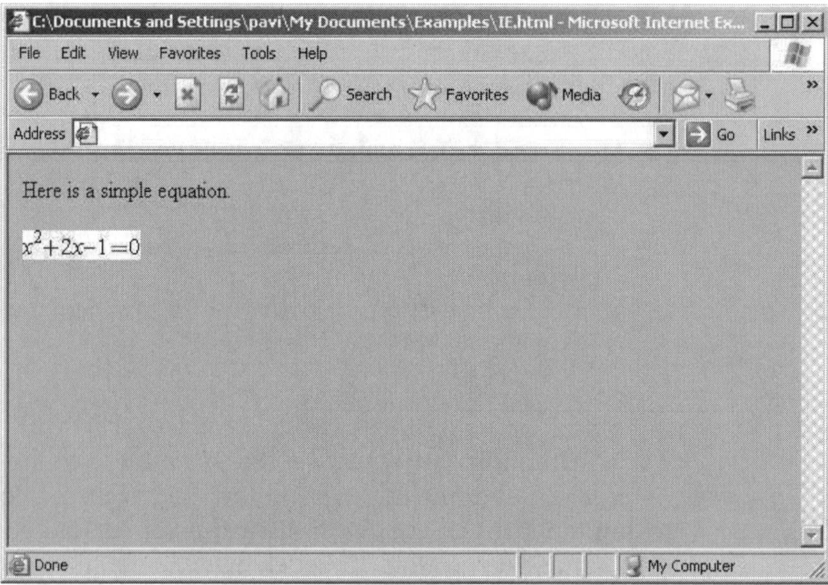

FIGURE 7.10 A MathML equation displayed in *IE* that shows a mismatch between the background color of the document and the *techexplorer* window.

```
    002035EFB1A4">
    </object> <?import namespace="mml"
    implementation ="#techexplorer"/>
  </head>
    <body>
      <p>Here is a simple equation.</p>
      <p>
      <m:math>
      <m:mrow>
        <m:msup>
          <m:mi>x</m:mi><m:mn>2</m:mn>
        </msup>
        <m:mo>-</m:mo>
        <m:mrow>
        <m:mn>2</m:mn>
        <m:mo>&InvisibleTimes;</m:mo>
        <m:mi>x</m:mi>
        </m:mrow>
        <m:mo>+</m:mo>
        <m:mn>1</m:mn>
      </m:mrow>
    </m:math>
    </body>
  </html>
```

The `object` element associates the *techexplorer* ID with the *techexplorer* software. This association is established through the values of three attributes:

- `id`: defines a keyword for referring to the software.
- `classid`: is a unique label that identifies *techexplorer* in the Windows registry. It tells *IE* where *techexplorer* is installed on the local machine.
- `codebase`: tells *IE* where to find the *techexplorer* software if it is not present on the local machine.

The import processing instruction says that any element with the namespace prefix `m:` should be displayed using the software whose ID is *techexplorer*. The MathML expression is then included in the document with each MathML element in the form of a qualified name with the `m:` prefix. A namespace declaration in the `html` element associates this prefix with the MathML namespace.

Figure 7.11 shows an equation rendered in *IE* as a *techexplorer* Behavior. Notice that the background color of the *techexplorer* window is automatically adjusted to match that of the entire document, instead of rendering the equation with an opaque background.

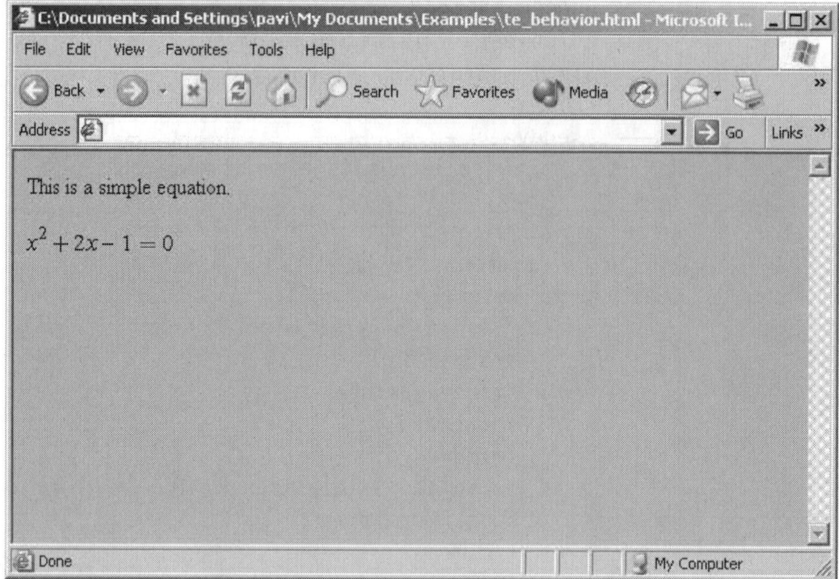

FIGURE 7.11 A MathML equation displayed in *IE* as a *techexplorer* Behavior.

WebEQ

WebEQ is a suite of Java-based software tools for authoring and displaying mathematical equations in a Web page. *WebEQ* consists of five components:

- Editor: is a WYSIWYG tool for authoring equations using template-based palettes similar to those available in *MathType*.
- Publisher: is a tool for processing an HTML document that contains mathematics so it can be directly placed on a Web server.
- Equation Server: is a command-based version of Publisher to enable batch processing of documents; for example, using scripts on a server.
- Viewer Control: is a Java applet for displaying mathematical notation in a Web browser. The equations must be enclosed in an `applet` tag in either MathML or WebTEX form. WebTEX is a markup language for mathematics whose syntax is very similar to that of LaTEX.
- Input Control: is a Java applet that enables a user to create and edit equations interactively by clicking buttons on a Web page. The equations can then be transmitted to a server for processing. For example, the Input Control can be used as part of a mathematical bulletin board. Students can graphically input equations that are then converted to images by the server and posted on a Web page.

WebEQ Input Control is primarily useful in setting up dynamic mathematical Web sites that allow users to interactively manipulate mathematical equations. The details of installing and using the Input Control are relatively complex, since it requires some knowledge of using JavaScript and Common Gateway Interface (CGI) programming on Web servers. A detailed discussion of the Input Control is deferred to Chapter 12, which specifically deals with dynamic mathematical features. A discussion of the Editor and Publisher is provided in Chapter 9, which deals with MathML authoring tools. In this section, we confine ourselves to discussing the features of the Viewer Control, since that is the component relevant for displaying equations.

WebEQ Viewer Control provides a way of displaying interactive MathML equations in a Web browser. For the equations to be displayed in a browser, the user must have access to a set of Viewer Control class files. These files can be either installed locally on the client machine or automatically downloaded from the server each time you view a Web page that contains an equation. For details of how to make the class files available on a Web server or to install them on a client machine, see the *WebEQ* product documentation.

Viewer Control Applets

To be displayed by the Viewer Control, each equation must be enclosed in an `applet` tag. This tag is used in HTML to indicate an applet call and has the following important attributes:

- `codebase`: specifies the location of the required *WebEQ* class files.
- `code`: specifies the applet to be run. For *WebEQ* Viewer Control applets, this attribute is always set to the value `"webeq3.ViewerControl"`.
- `width` and `height`: specify the size of the window in which the applet is displayed.
- `name`: assigns to the applet a name that can be used to control it using a JavaScript or Java program.
- `param`: specifies additional properties of the applet. This attribute is always specified using the syntax: `<param name="`*name*`" value="`*value*`">`.

The *WebEQ* Viewer Control recognizes a number of parameters that can be used to control specific aspects of how *WebEQ* should display the equation. Some of the important parameters are:

- `name=eq`: specifies the equation to be displayed in the form of MathML or WebT$_E$X markup.

- `name=src`: specifies the URL of file that contains the equation to be. This is an alternative to specifying the equation directly using `name=eq`.
- `name=parser`: specifies the markup language used for representing the equation. The allowed values are `mathml` and `webtex`.

Several other input parameters control various aspects of the equation's appearance (such as its font size, color, alignment, or padding). However, you do not have to know the names of all the parameters since in most cases you will not be authoring Viewer Control applet tags by hand. You can instead create applet tags for any equation using either *WebEQ* Editor or Publisher. These applications allow you to specify the properties of an equation using menus or dialogs, and they automatically generate the applet tag for the equation with the appropriate parameter values included.

Example 7.10 shows a simple document that contains a Viewer Control applet tag.

Example 7.10 A sample document for displaying MathML using the *WebEQ* Viewer Control.

```
<html>
<head><title> MathML Example </title></head>
 <body>
   <p>Here is a simple equation.</p>

     <applet codebase="../../classes"
     code="webeq3.ViewerControl"
     width=200 height=100>
     <param name=size value=12>
     <param name=eq value=
     "<math xmlns='http://www.w3.org/1998/Math/MathML'>
     <mrow>
       <msup>
         <mi>x</mi><mn>2</mn>
       </msup>
       <mo>-</mo>
       <mrow>
         <mn>2</mn>
         <mo>&InvisibleTimes;</mo>
         <mi>x</mi>
       </mrow>
       <mo>+</mo>
       <mn>1</mn>
     </mrow>
```

```
    </math>">
    </applet>
    </body>
</html>
```

Figure 7.12 shows a typical document that contains *WebEQ* Viewer Control applets as displayed in *IE*.

7.5 Choosing a Display Method

We have examined a variety of browsers and add-on applications that can be used for viewing MathML. In this section, we briefly compare the various rendering options available and evaluate their relative strengths and limitations.

The most important consideration in choosing a display method is the nature of your target audience and the browsers or add-on software they will be using. As far as browsers with native support for MathML are concerned, *Mozilla* 1.0 and *Netscape* 7.0 are better choices than *Amaya*, since they are more mature, fully developed browsers with a more complete set of features. Moreover, *Amaya* does not support XSLT transformations and therefore cannot be used to render content markup, even with the Universal MathML stylesheet. The two nice features of *Amaya* are its Structure

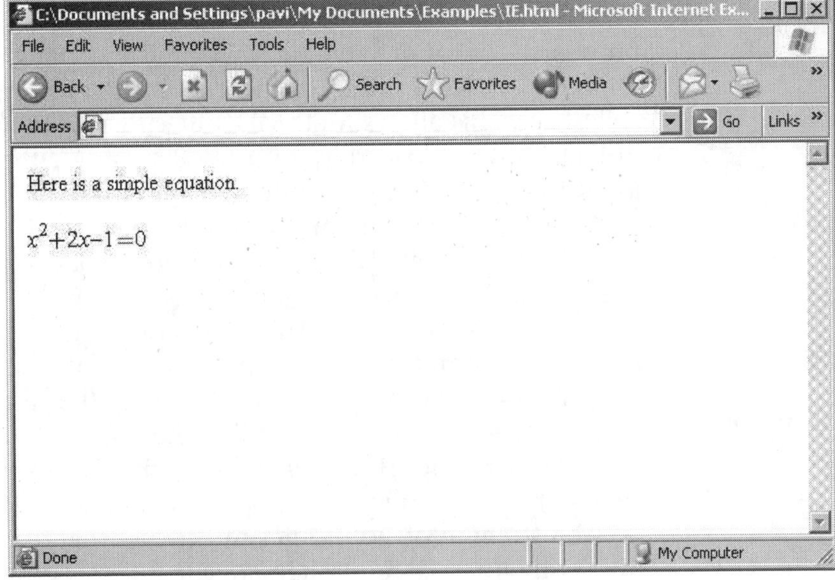

FIGURE 7.12 Displaying a MathML equation as a *WebEQ* applet.

view, which is useful for viewing the tree structure of a MathML expression, and its support for authoring basic presentation MathML.

Since a very large majority of users have access to *IE*, it is clearly important to support display of MathML on this browser. This can be done using either *MathPlayer* or IBM *techexplorer* as an add-on. Both provide a good-quality rendering of content and presentation markup and come with their own fonts for mathematical symbols.

MathPlayer has some advantages over *techexplorer* since it is under active development and is slightly easier to download and install. It is compact, fast, and efficient and provides a high-quality rendering. *MathPlayer* also provides a pop-up menu for copying the MathML source for any equation. This is a useful feature for pasting MathML into other applications. Finally, *MathPlayer* is distributed free of charge, so it is easily accessible to a large audience.

The only downside of *MathPlayer* is that it works only on Windows and only with *IE* 5.5 or later. IBM *techexplorer*, in contrast, supports display of MathML on Windows, Macintosh, and Linux and works on newer and older versions of both *IE* and *Netscape*. Hence, if you want your content to be viewable on a wider variety of platforms and on older browsers, then *techexplorer* is a better option. The downside of *techexplorer* is that only the Introductory version is free, and this version lacks some basic features, including the ability to print equations.

Of course, these two options are not mutually exclusive. As explained in Section 7.2, if your target audience has access to newer browsers (*IE* 5.0 or later or *Netscape* 6.1 or later), then the best option by far is to author documents using the Universal MathML stylesheet. This allows MathML content to be viewed on a variety of platforms and a variety of browsers using either *MathPlayer* or *techexplorer* or the native rendering abilities of the browser itself.

The third add-on mentioned in this chapter, *WebEQ*, is less useful than either *MathPlayer* or *techexplorer* as far as displaying static equations. This is because *WebEQ* displays MathML equations as Java applets, which are relatively slow to download and run. Hence, a page that contains a large number of equations can take a long time to load. You can significantly reduce the time taken for displaying *WebEQ* applets by installing the required Java class files on the local machine. However, this requires an extra configuration step on the user's side, which is an obstacle to large-scale use.

The strength of *WebEQ* lies in the fact that it is well suited for displaying interactive mathematical content. Using *WebEQ* applets is therefore a good choice if you want to create a large Web site that makes extensive use of interactive mathematical content. This is because the other tools in the *WebEQ* suite provide powerful support for authoring such sites. These features include automatic batch processing of Web documents, support for authoring mathematical notation in a Web page for sending input to the server, and integration with JavaScript and Java for creating scriptable content. Hence, *WebEQ* applets are a useful display method in an integrated Web site developed and maintained using the other tools in the *WebEQ* suite.

CHAPTER

8

APPLYING STYLES AND TRANSFORMATIONS

This chapter provides an overview of CSS and XSLT, two stylesheet languages of special importance for MathML. It summarizes the basic principles and syntax of both stylesheet languages and gives examples of their applications to MathML documents.

8.1 INTRODUCTION

When you are posting an HTML (or XHTML) document that contains MathML on a Web site, it is important to have a way of controlling the exact style in which the document will be displayed. The style of the document includes information about properties such as font size, style, color, page margins, alignment, and so on. For displaying mathematics, there are also additional style considerations, such as the size of subscripts and superscripts relative to the base or whether fractions, integrals, and sums should be shown in display or inline form.

You can use the tags and attributes provided in MathML presentation markup to specify the precise rendering for any mathematical formula in a document. However, instead of specifying styles locally for each individual expression, it is a good practice to collect style information that applies to the entire document in a separate stylesheet. The stylesheet can then be stored in a central location where multiple documents on a Web site can reference it. This makes it possible to assign a consistent appearance to a related set of documents. Also, by editing the stylesheet, you can apply style changes to an entire collection of documents without having to edit each document individually.

For HTML and XML documents, two stylesheet languages are of particular importance: CSS and XSLT. These are both recommendations of the W3C and are supported by most modern browsers. A key reason for their popularity is that since they are open standards, they are not tied to a specific vendor or platform.

CSS specifies a simple syntax that allows you to associate style properties with specific elements in a document. XSLT, in contrast, is a more complex but also more powerful language. In addition to its role in specifying styles, XSLT provides a general mechanism for transforming XML documents. In particular, XSLT has a variety of useful applications in the context of MathML, such as creating macros to abbreviate complex notation, defining new tags to represent concepts that are not supported by the existing MathML specification, or even translating content markup to presentation markup. We shall see examples of these uses of XSLT in Section 8.5 of this chapter.

8.2 CSS PRIMER

CSS is the most popular way of specifying styles in HTML documents. A CSS stylesheet consists of a set of style rules of the form shown below:

```
h2 {font-family:"Helvetica"; font-size:16pt}
```

The effect of this style rule is to display the content of all `h2` elements in the document in a 16-point Helvetica font.

Each style rule consists of a selector (such as an element name) followed by a list of properties enclosed in braces. Each property consists of a property name and a value separated by a colon. A semicolon separates different properties in the style rule.

A property name can also be followed by more than one value, with the different values being separated by a comma, as shown below:

```
h2 { font-family:"Helvetica", "Geneva", sans-serif}
```

This rule means that the content of an `h2` element should be shown in a Helvetica font. If that font is not available, the next value—Geneva—is used. If that font is not available either, then any sans-serif font can be used instead.

You can apply a style rule to multiple elements by separating them with commas. The following rule applies to all `h1`, `h2`, and `h3` elements:

```
h1, h2, h3 {color:red}
```

Referencing a CSS Stylesheet

A CSS stylesheet can be referenced in an XML document using a processing instruction, as shown below:

```
<?xml-stylesheet href="report.css" type="text/css"?>
```

In the above markup, the `href` attribute specifies the name and location of the stylesheet, and the `type` attribute specifies its format.

In an HTML document, the same stylesheet can be specified using a link element:

```
<link href="report.css" type="text/css">
```

including a reference to an external stylesheet is a good practice, since doing so allows documents to be modular and separates information about style and content, in keeping with the spirit of XML. However, in the case of HTML documents, there are two other ways of specifying CSS styles. The first way is to directly embed the stylesheet within the document itself, using a `style` element, as shown below:

```
<style>
 h2 {font-family:"Helvetica"; font-size:16pt}
</style>
```

Alternatively, you can include CSS style rules as the value of the `style` attribute in any HTML element, as shown here (in this case, the curly braces around the properties are omitted):

```
<h2 style="font-family:"Helvetica"; font-size:16pt">
 ...
</h2>
```

Style rules specified directly in an element override any other rules that might be specified in an embedded or external stylesheet.

Other Types of Selectors

The first part of any style rule is a *selector*. This is an expression that identifies the parts of the document to which the style rule is applied. In the examples shown above, the selector is either a single element name or a list of element names. CSS also provides some other types of selectors for picking out different parts of a document. You can, for example, select elements based on their relationship to other elements or the value of their attributes.

The wildcard character (`*`) acts as a universal selector. The following rule therefore applies to all elements in the document:

```
* {color:black; background-color:white}
```

If one element name is followed by another, the second element must be contained in the first element. The following rule applies only to `p` elements that are contained in a `div` element:

```
div p {display:block}
```

A > sign is used to specify that one element must be a direct descendant of another. The following rule applies only to `p` elements that occur as direct children of a `div` element:

```
div > p {color:red}
```

A + sign is used to specify that one element must occur immediately after another. The following rule applies only to tables that immediately follow a paragraph:

```
para + table {font-size:14pt}
```

Square brackets are used to select elements with particular attributes or attribute values. The following rule selects all `p` elements that have the `lang` attribute specified explicitly:

```
p[lang] {font-style:italic}
```

This rule selects only those `p` elements in which the `lang` attribute has the value `french`:

```
p[lang='french'] {font-style:italic}
```

You can use the wildcard character along with square brackets to select all elements with a particular attribute. The following rule applies to all elements in the document in which the `id` attribute is specified:

```
*[id] {font-family:Courier}
```

Another important selector uses the keyword `first-child` to select elements according to the name of their first child element. The following rule causes all elements whose first child is a paragraph element to be shown in a separate block:

```
p:first-child {display:block}
```

8.3 Using CSS with MathML

All the examples used in the previous section used HTML element and attribute names, for the purpose of illustration. However, you can use a CSS stylesheet to control the appearance of any type of XML document. All that is needed is to define appropriate style rules that refer to the element and attribute names used in that document. In particular, you can use CSS style rules to specify how MathML expressions should be rendered. Style rules for MathML and XHTML can then be combined in a single stylesheet that can be used, for example, to control the appearance of an XHTML document that contains embedded MathML equations.

Some examples of effects you can achieve with a custom CSS stylesheet, include the following:

- Display all equations in a document in a different font size or color
- Choose a different scaling factor for the size of subscripts and superscripts
- Assign a different meaning to the `big` and `small` values of the `mathsize` attribute
- Associate a particular font family that contains the relevant glyphs with particular values of the `mathvariant` attribute

In this section, we give some examples of CSS rules involving MathML presentation markup. These rules illustrate how you can use a CSS stylesheet to control specific aspects of the display of MathML.

Display and Inline Mode

Mathematical formulas can be displayed in a Web page, in either *inline* or *display* form. Inline equations are integrated with the surrounding text, while display equations are typically shown in a separate block and aligned with the center of the page. These two modes are distinguished in MathML using the `display` attribute of the `math` element. This attribute has the value `inline` for inline equations, and `block` for display equations.

The following rule sets some style properties that are characteristic of inline equations:

```
math[display="inline"] {
   display: inline;
     font-family: cmsy10, cmex10, Symbol, Times; }
```

This rule specifies that the contents of a `math` element whose `display` attribute has the value `inline` should be displayed using the cmsy10 or cmex10 fonts. These are part of the Computer Modern family of fonts, which is widely used in TEX and LATEX documents. These fonts contain glyphs for a large number of symbols and special characters used in mathematical expressions. If these fonts are not available, then the Symbol font is used instead. This font also contains glyphs for Greek letters and other special characters. If the Symbol font is also not available, the Times font is used.

The following rule sets some style properties characteristic of display equations:

```
math[display="block"] {
 display: block;
```

```
text-align: center;
  font-family: cmsy, cmex, Symbol, Times;}
```

In addition to specifying the font family, this rule assigns suitable values to the CSS properties `display` and `text-align`.

Style Attributes of Token Elements

There is a potential problem with using CSS stylesheets to control the appearance of Web documents that contain MathML. This is because the meaning carried by many mathematical symbols is closely related to the style in which they are rendered. For example, an italic letter might be used to indicate a variable or function name, a bold letter might indicate a vector, and a letter displayed in a Fraktur font might indicate a Lie algebra. As a result, style changes that are applied to a document purely for formatting reasons and inherited by the embedded MathML markup can change the meaning of the mathematical expression.

To avoid such unintended consequences of document-wide style changes, it is desirable to maintain a clean separation between the properties used to control the style of MathML expressions and the style of other content in an HTML document. To facilitate this goal, the MathML 2.0 specification introduces four new style attributes that can be used to set style properties in presentation markup (Table 8.1).

Of these, the `mathsize`, `mathcolor`, and `mathbackground` attributes correspond closely to the `font-size`, `color`, and `background-color` property names in CSS. The `mathvariant` attribute is a composite of the CSS properties `font-family`, `font-weight`, and

TABLE 8.1 New Style Attributes That Can Be Used to Set Style Properties in Presentation Markup

Name	Property Specified	Allowed Value
`mathbackground`	Background color	*#rgb* | *#rrggbb* | *html-color name*
`mathcolor`	Text color	*#rgb* | *#rrggbb* | *html-color name*
`mathsize`	Font size	`small` | `normal` | `big` | *number v-unit*
`mathvariant`	Style variant	*#rgb* | *#rrggbb* | *html-color name*

font-style. Some examples of CSS style rules involving these attributes are given in the sections that follow.

Size

The following rules define the mathsize attribute in terms of the CSS property font-size:

```
math *.[mathsize="small"] {font-size: 80%}
math *.[mathsize="normal"] {font-size: 100%}
math *.[mathsize="big"] {font-size: 125%}
```

Each rule, in effect, implements a particular value of the mathsize attribute by specifying its effect on the font size. The numbers 80% and 125% are typical values for the change in font size corresponding to mathsize="small" and mathsize="big", respectively.

Color and Background

The following rules define the mathcolor attribute in terms of the CSS property color:

```
math *.[mathcolor="black"] {color: black}
math *.[mathcolor="white"] {color: white}
math *.[mathcolor="red"] {color: red}
math *.[mathcolor="blue"] {color: blue }
math *.[mathcolor="green"] {color: green }
```

The following rules define the mathbackground attribute in terms of the CSS property background-color:

```
math *.[mathbackground="black"] {
      background-color: black}
math *.[mathbackground ="white"] {
      background-color:white}
math *.[mathbackground ="red"] {
      background-color:red}
```

You can include similar style rules for the other HTML color keywords, such as gray, yellow, maroon, purple, teal, and aqua.

Font Variants

The mathvariant attribute is defined in terms of its cumulative effect on the three CSS properties font-family, font-weight, and font-style. Here is a typical CSS rule for a particular value of mathvariant:

```
math *.[mathvariant="bold-italic"] {
font-family: "Times", "Courier", serif;
font-weight: bold;
font-style: italic;}
```

This rule specifies the effect of setting `mathvariant="sans-serif"` on any MathML element:

```
math *.[mathvariant="sans-serif"] {
font-family: "Helvetica", "Arial", sans-serif;
font-weight: normal;
font-style: normal;}
```

This rule uses the msbm font, which is part of the AMS font collection and includes double-struck characters:

```
math *.[mathvariant="double-struck"] {
font-family: msbm;
font-weight: normal;
font-style: normal;}
```

This rule uses the eusb font, which is part of the AMS font collection and includes bold script characters:

```
math *.[mathvariant="bold-script"] {
font-family: eusb;
font-weight: bold;
font-style: normal;}
```

This rule uses the eufb font, which is included in the AMS font collection and includes medium Fraktur characters:

```
math *.[mathvariant="fraktur"] {
font-family: eufb;
font-weight: bold;
font-style: italic;}
```

Similar rules can be defined for all other values of the `mathvariant` attribute: `normal`, `bold`, `italic`, `script`, `fraktur`, `bold-sans-serif`, `sans-serif-italic`, and `monospace`.

Fractions and Radicals

When a fraction occurs in an inline position, its numerator and denominator are shown in a reduced size, typically 71% of the font size of the surrounding text. This behavior can be implemented using the following CSS style rule, which sets the font size for child elements of any `mfrac` element that is itself contained in a `math` element whose `display` attribute is set to `inline`. Here's an example:

```
math[display="inline"] mfrac>* {font-size: 71%}
```

The following two rules show the effect of specifying the `mathsize` attribute inside an `mfrac` element (the statements enclosed in the `/* ... */` signs are CSS comments that explain how the values of the font size are calculated):

```
 math[display="inline"] mfrac>* [mathsize="big"]{
font-size: 80%}/* .80 = 71 times 1.25 */


math[display="inline"] mfrac>* [mathsize="small"]{
 font-size: 57%}/* .57 = 71 times .80 */
```

The index of the root (the terms that appear outside the radical sign) is usually drawn at half the size of the base expression. This behavior can be implemented using the following style rules:

```
mroot > *:first-child{font-size: 100%}


mroot > *{font-size: 50%}
```

The first rule applies to the first child of the `mroot` element; that is, the expression that appears inside the radical sign. The second rule then reduces the size of all children of the `mroot` element by 50%. The first rule overrides the second. Hence, the net result of both rules is to reduce the size of the expression outside the radical sign, while keeping the font size of the base expression unchanged.

The following set of rules defines how the contents of the `mroot` element should be scaled in response to different settings of the `mathsize` attribute:

```
mroot > *:first-child[mathsize="big"]{font-size: 125%}


mroot > *[mathsize="big"]{
font-size: 62%}/* .62 = .5 times 1.25 */


mroot > *:first-child[mathsize="small"]{
font-size: 80%}


mroot > *[mathsize="small"]{
font-size: 40%}/* .40 = .5 times 0.80 */
```

Scripts and Limits

By convention, expressions that appear in a superscript position are typically shown in a reduced size, typically 71% of the font size of the base expression. You can use the following two CSS rules to implement this behavior in any MathML document:

```
msub > *:first-child{font-size: 100%}

msub > *{font-size: 71%}
```

The first rule applies to the first child of the msub element, that is, the base expression. The second rule then reduces the size of all children of the msub element by 71%. The first rule overrides the second. Hence, the net result of both rules is to reduce the size of the superscript, while keeping the font size of the base expression unchanged.

The following rules define how the contents of the msub element should be scaled in response to different settings of the mathsize attribute:

```
msub > *:first-child[mathsize="big"]{font-size: 125%}

msub > *[mathsize="big"]{
font-size: 89%}/*(.71 times 1.25)*/

msub > *:first-child[mathsize="small"]{font-size: 80%}

msub > *[mathsize="small"]{
font-size: 57%}/*(.71 times .80)*/
```

Similar rules can be defined for all the other script and limit elements, namely msup, msubsup, munder, mover, munderover, and mmultiscripts. For several MathML elements, the font size changes automatically as a consequence of a change in the value of the scriptlevel attribute. As discussed in Section 4.3, this is an attribute of the mstyle element, and a default value for it is inherited from its environment by every presentation element.

The default value of scriptlevel for most elements is 0. However, some elements, such as those representing scripts and limits, increase the value of scriptlevel in some of their child elements. Each increase in the value of scriptlevel by one reduces the font size of the expression by a constant amount, which is determined by the value of the scriptsizemultiplier attribute. The default value of this attribute is 0.71. This means that an element for which scriptlevel="1" will display its contents at a font size 71% smaller than normal text. Similarly, if scriptlevel="2", the font size will be reduced by 0.71 times 0.71, which is 50%. This behavior can be implemented by the following style rules:

```
math *[scriptlevel="+1"]{font-size: 71%}

math *[scriptlevel="+2"]{font-size: 50%}
```

The following rules define the combined effect of changing the `scriptlevel` and `mathsize` attributes simultaneously:

```
math *[scriptlevel="+1"][mathsize="big"] {
font-size: 89%}/*(.71 times 1.25)*/

math *[scriptlevel="+1"][mathsize="small"] {
font-size: 57%}/*(.71 times .80)*/

math *[scriptlevel="+2"][mathsize="big"] {
font-size: 62%}/*(.71 times .71 times 1.25)*/

math *[scriptlevel="+2"][mathsize="small"] {
font-size: 40%}/*(.71 times .71 times .80)*/
```

The examples in this section illustrate how you can use CSS style rules to control the details of how a MathML expression is rendered. Any good MathML rendering application will, of course, already have some basic style rules of the type shown here built in and will apply them automatically when displaying any document that contains MathML. But if you want to change the default behavior and customize the display of mathematical formulas for special contexts, it's useful to know how to control these rendering properties explicitly by means of a CSS stylesheet.

8.4 XSLT PRIMER

XSLT is a flexible and powerful language for transforming XML documents. An XSLT stylesheet contains detailed instructions on how to process the different types of elements in an XML document. The instructions in the stylesheet are then interpreted by a special program, called an XSLT processor, which applies them to the input document to produce another document as output.

XSLT is part of the XSL family of standards developed by the W3C for expressing style information in XML documents. In addition to XSLT, XSL consists of two other standards: XPath and

XSL Formatting Objects (XSL-FO). *XPath* is a special syntax for referring to specific parts of an XML document. XPath syntax is used extensively in XSLT stylesheets for specifying what parts of an input document should be selected.

XSL-FO is an XML vocabulary for specifying the detailed layout and formatting of a document. XSLT was originally developed as a means for applying styles to arbitrary XML documents by translating them into XSL-FO documents. However, XSLT has turned out to be much more broadly useful and is now used as a general-purpose transformation language for XML documents.

The primary purpose of XSLT is for converting one type of XML document into another. For example, there are XSLT stylesheets for converting DocBook documents into XHTML or for converting MathML expressions into Scalable Vector Graphics (SVG) graphics. However, the output is not restricted to being in XML format. By using an appropriate stylesheet, you can convert XML documents into other document formats, such as HTML or PDF.

XSLT is, in fact, widely used for converting XML documents into HTML so they can be displayed by Web browsers. A Web browser cannot properly interpret an arbitrary XML document since the document can contain tag names that are not defined in HTML. The solution is to write an XSLT stylesheet that replaces the document-specific element names with standard HTML elements. The resulting HTML document can even include CSS commands for specifying how different elements should be formatted. XSLT and CSS are therefore complementary and can be used effectively in combination with each other.

XSLT is powerful because it allows you to select specific parts of the XML document tree in any desired order and perform arbitrary transformations on them. An XSLT processor can select and manipulate an element based on various criteria such its position in the document tree, the text it contains, or the names and values of its attributes. It is possible to write an XSLT stylesheet, for example, to extract all elements with a certain name, and then rename them, combine them with additional text, and insert them into the output document in a different order.

XSLT stylesheets have a variety of uses in MathML documents, from specifying styles for particular types of notation to creating macros for complicated markup. In the rest of this chapter, we give a brief overview of the key concepts of XSLT and then provide some simple examples of how it can be used in the context of MathML.

XSLT Processors

To view the results of applying XSLT transformations on an XML document, you must have access to an XSLT processor. Two widely used XSLT processors include Apache Xalan and Saxon. (See Appendix B for URLs from where you can download these processors.) If you have one of these processors installed, you can generate an input document by applying a stylesheet to an output document. For example, in Saxon, the command for doing such a transformation is as shown below:

```
java -jar saxon.jar -o output.xml input.xml test.xsl
```

This generates an output document called `output.xml` from an input document called `input.xml` by applying a stylesheet called `test.xsl`.

The alternative to using a standalone XSLT processor is to use the built-in XSLT capabilities of a Web browser. Recent versions of most popular browsers, including *IE* 5.0 or later and *Netscape* 6.1 or later, have an XSLT processor already built in and can automatically transform XML documents before displaying them. This allows you to display arbitrary XML documents on the Web, with their content automatically formatted in any desired style. All that is needed is to write an appropriate stylesheet that specifies how to transform the XML document into an HTML one.

Suppose you want to apply a stylesheet called `test.xsl` to an XML document to convert it into an HTML document. You can perform the XSLT transformation and view the results using any XSLT-capable browser, such as *IE* 6.0 or *Netscape* 7.0. To do this, you first need to edit the input XML document by adding the following processing instruction at the start:

```
<?xml-stylesheet href="test.xsl" type="text/xsl"?>
```

In this instruction, the `href` attribute specifies the name and location of the stylesheet and the `type` attribute specifies its format. If you then open the XML document in a suitable browser, the specified XSL stylesheet is automatically applied to the document and the HTML document resulting from the transformation is displayed in the browser.

Applying Templates

An XSLT stylesheet must be a well-formed and valid XML document. All XSLT element and attribute names in the document should be associated with the XSL namespace, which is usually indicated by the prefix xsl. The root element of the document is called xsl:stylesheet. A typical XSLT stylesheet therefore has the following structure:

```
<xsl:stylesheet version="1.0" xmlns:xsl=
   "http://www.w3.org/1999/XSL/Transform">
 ...
</xsl: stylesheet>
```

The most important part of any XSLT stylesheet is its templates. Each template specifies a set of instructions about how to process a particular type of element in the input document. A template has the following structure:

```
<xsl:template match="expression">
 ...
</xsl:template>
```

The value of the match attribute in the xsl:template element is an XPath pattern. This is a specific type of XPath expression that specifies the type of content in the input document to which the template should be applied. For example, a template with match= "title" contains instructions to be applied to all elements called title in the current context. The current context depends on what node in the document is being processed by the XSLT processor when the template is matched. Let's look at a simple example of an XML document (Example 8.1).

Example 8.1 A simple XML document.

```
<book>
 <title>The MathML Handbook</title>
</book>
```

Example 8.2 shows a simple XSLT stylesheet that converts the above document into HTML.

Example 8.2 An XSLT stylesheet that contains a single template.

```
<xsl:stylesheet version="1.0"
xmlns:xsl="http://www.w3.org/1999/XSL/Transform">

 <xsl:template match="book">
   <html><body>
   <h1><xsl:value-of select="title"/></h1>
   </body></html>
 </xsl:template>

</xsl:stylesheet>
```

Here is the result of applying the above stylesheet to the document in Example 8.1:

```
<html>
 <body>
   <h1>The MathML Handbook</h1>
 </body>
</html>
```

The stylesheet in Example 8.2 consists of a single template that picks out the `book` element in the input document and then does the following things:

- It first copies into the output the literal text that corresponds to the opening tags for the `html`, `body`, and `h1` elements.
- Next, the `<xsl:value-of select="title">` element is applied. The effect of this element is to copy into the output document the text of any `title` element in the current context.
- Finally, the template writes out the closing tags for the `html`, `body`, and `h1` elements.

Example 8.3 shows a slightly more complicated XML document than the one in Example 8.1.

Example 8.3 An XML document with several nested elements.

```
<book>
 <title>The MathML Handbook</title>
 <author>Pavi Sandhu</author>
 <publisher>
   <name>Charles River Media</name>
   <address>20 Downer Ave., Hingham, MA 02043</address>
   <phone>781-740-0400</phone>
 </publisher>
</book>
```

Example 8.4 shows a stylesheet written for the document in Example 8.3. It is possible to write a simpler stylesheet to do the same transformation, but the one shown here is useful for the purposes of illustration.

Example 8.4 An XSLT stylesheet that uses *`xsl:apply-templates`*.

```
 <xsl:stylesheet version="1.0"
xmlns:xsl="http://www.w3.org/1999/XSL/Transform">

   <xsl:template match="book">
     <html><body><xsl:apply-templates/></body></html>
   </xsl:template>
```

```
  <xsl:template match="title">
    <h1><xsl:value-of select="."/></h1>
  </xsl:template>

  <xsl:template match="author">
    <h2><xsl:value-of select="."/></h2>
  </xsl:template>

  <xsl:template match="name">
    <h3><xsl:value-of select="."/></h3>
  </xsl:template>

  <xsl:template match="address">
    <p><xsl:value-of select="."/></p>
  </xsl:template>

  <xsl:template match="phone">
    <p><xsl:value-of select="."/></p>
  </xsl:template>

</xsl:stylesheet>
```

Here is the output that results from applying the above stylesheet to the document in Example 8.3:

```
<html>
 <body>

   <h1>The MathML Handbook</h1>

   <h2>Pavi Sandhu</h2>


   <h3>Charles River Media</h3>

     <p>20 Downer Avenue, Hingham, MA 02043</p>

     <p>781-740-0400</p>


 </body>
</html>
```

The stylesheet in Example 8.4 contains templates for many of the elements in the original XML document. Each template contains some literal text to be copied to the output document as well as an XSLT element that specifies a particular instruction to be executed. The `xsl:apply-templates` element in the template for the `book` element specifies that any templates found for all child elements of the current element should be applied. All the other templates contain an `<xsl:value select=".">` element. The `.` in the attribute value is an XPath pattern that refers to the current element being processed.

To understand the order in which templates are applied, it is useful to know how the input document is processed. The XSLT processor represents the input document as a tree consisting of nodes. Different types of nodes represent elements, attributes, text, comments, and so on. The XSLT processor then traverses the document tree from top to bottom. For each node in the document, the processor checks to see if a matching template is defined in the stylesheet. If a template matching that node is found, the instructions contained in that template are executed. If more than one template matching that node is found, the more specific template is used. After a template is executed, the processor moves on to the next node in the document tree.

One consequence of this traversal order is that the order in which the templates are written in the stylesheet is not important. A specific template is applied when it matches an element in the document tree, regardless of where that template occurs in the stylesheet. Hence, if you edit a stylesheet to change the order of some of its templates, this does not affect the output document that is produced.

Note that more than one template can be active at any given time because when a template for an element is applied, the template remains active until templates for all the child elements have been applied. Hence, one template can call another template, which can call another template, and so on. The processing of templates can therefore occur in a recursive manner, reflecting the nested structure of the document tree.

Default Templates

The stylesheet shown in Example 8.4 did not contain a template for the `publisher` element. Yet, the output from this stylesheet includes the text contained in the child elements of the `publisher` element, namely `name`, `address`, and `phone`. The reason for this is that XSLT defines a default template that is automatically applied to any elements in the document for which no explicit template is given. The default template looks like the following:

```
<xsl:template match="*|/">
 <xsl:apply-templates/>
</xsl:template>
```

The value of the match attribute in the template element is an XPath expression that identifies a specific part of the document. In XPath syntax, the * refers to any element in the current context, while / refers to the root element. The vertical bar is used to separate two choices. Hence, the default template shown above means that the xsl:apply-templates element should be applied to all child elements as well as the root element in the document.

If this default template is applied to any element in the document, its effect is to write out into the output document any text contained in that element. This is because XSLT also defines the following default template for the text or attributes of elements:

```
<xsl:template match="text()|@*">
 <xsl:value-of select="."/>
</xsl:template>
```

The match attribute here is set to the XPath pattern text()|@*. In XPath syntax, text() stands for all text in the current context. and @* stands for any attribute.

Example 8.5 shows a simple XSLT stylesheet that illustrates the effect of the default templates:

Example 8.5 An XSLT stylesheet that illustrates the concept of default templates.

```
<xsl:stylesheet version="1.0"
xmlns:xsl="http://www.w3.org/1999/XSL/Transform">

 <xsl:template match="book">
   <html><body><p>
   <xsl:apply-templates/>
   </p></body></html>
 </xsl:template>

</xsl:stylesheet>
```

When the stylesheet in Example 8.5 is applied to the document in Example 8.3, the following output document is obtained:

```
<html>
 <body>
   <p>
     The MathML Handbook
     Pavi Sandhu

     Charles River Media
     20 Downer Avenue, Hingham, MA 02043
     781-740-0400
```

```
    </p>
  </body>
</html>
```

Notice that the text of the `title`, `author`, `publisher`, `name`, `address`, and `phone` elements appears in the output document, even though the stylesheet does not contain explicit templates for these elements. This behavior is a result of the XSLT processor applying the default templates for these elements.

Although the examples discussed so far are very simple, they illustrate some of the key features common to any XSLT stylesheet. A more elaborate XSLT stylesheet has the same basic structure. It would differ only in the number of templates and the complexity of the processing rules defined in each template.

8.5 USING XSLT WITH MATHML

All the examples in Section 8.4 involved the conversion of an XML document into HTML format. In this section, we will see some simple examples of how XSLT can be used to transform MathML documents.

Specifying Notation

An important issue in displaying mathematics is that different notations may be used for the same concept, depending on the context. XSLT transformations provide a good way to convert one notational form into another.

The Tangent Function

For example, the trigonometric function tan(x), is written as tg(x) in some countries. An author in such a country can create an XSLT stylesheet that will detect the occurrence of the `<mi>tan <mi>` element in a MathML document and convert it into a `<mi>tg</mi>` element instead. A browser will then render the element as tg(x). Hence, any MathML document that contains presentation markup involving the tangent function, such as the one in Example 8.6, can be modified to use the notational form that the author prefers.

Example 8.6 A simple MathML document with presentation markup for the tan function.

```
<math>
 <mrow>
   <mi>tan</mi>
```

```
    <mrow><mo>(</mo><mi>x</mi><mo>)</mo> </mrow>
  </mrow>
</math>
```

Example 8.7 shows an XSLT stylesheet that transforms a presentation MathML document by replacing all occurrences of tan with tg.

Example 8.7 An XSLT stylesheet that changes the name of the tangent function.

```
<xsl:stylesheet version="1.0"
xmlns:xsl="http://www.w3.org/1999/XSL/Transform">


   <xsl:template match="math">
     <math><xsl:apply-templates/></math>
   </xsl:template>

   <xsl:template match="mrow">
     <mrow><xsl:apply-templates/></mrow>
   </xsl:template>

   <xsl:template match="mo">
     <mo><xsl:apply-templates/></mo>
   </xsl:template>

   <xsl:template match="mi">
     <xsl:choose>
       <xsl:when test="text()='tan'">
         <mi>tg</mi>
       </xsl:when>
       <xsl:otherwise>
         <mi><xsl:value-of select="."/></mi>
       </xsl:otherwise>
     </xsl:choose>
   </xsl:template>

</xsl:stylesheet>
```

This stylesheet contains templates for the `math`, `mrow`, and `mo` elements that simply implement an identity transformation; that is, they copy the content of any element they match into the output, without making any changes. Each of these templates also adds to the output explicit tags to replace the tags in the input document that are stripped away by the XSLT processor.

The key template in this stylesheet is the one that matches the `mi` element. This contains an `xsl:choose` element, which is the XSLT equivalent of a switch or case statement in programming. This element can contain any number of xsl:when elements and a single xsl:otherwise element. Each xsl:when element has a match attribute, which specifies a test condition. If the condition is true, the contents of that xsl:when element are processed; otherwise, the condition in the next xsl:when element is evaluated. If none of the xsl:when elements contains a match attribute that evaluates to true, then the statements in the xsl:otherwise element are processed.

In the stylesheet of Example 8.7, the first xsl:when element checks to see if the text contained in the mi element being processed is "tan." If so, the processor writes out the text "tg" to the output file. Otherwise, the xsl:otherwise element is processed. This element encloses the content of the mi element with a pair of mi tags and copies it to the output document. The net result of this template is therefore to replace any mi element that contains the text tan with an equivalent element that contains the text tg . All other mi elements are copied to the output document unchanged.

The result of applying the stylesheet in Example 8.7 to the MathML document in Example 8.6 is given below (the XML declaration at the start of the output is added automatically by the XSLT processor):

```
<?xml version="1.0" encoding="utf-8"?>
<math>
 <mrow>
   <mi>tg</mi>
   <mrow>
     <mo>(</mo>
     <mi>x</mi>
     <mo>)</mo>
   </mrow>
 </mrow>
</math>
```

Binomial Coefficients

Another common mathematical concept for which there are several different notations is the binomial coefficient, $\binom{n}{r}$. This is also represented as C_r^n in France and C_n^r in Germany. An author who prefers one of these notations can use an XSLT transformation to detect the presence of any alternate notation for this concept, in a MathML document, and convert it into the desired form. Example 8.8 shows a simple MathML document to illustrate this behavior.

Example 8.8 A MathML document that contains the presentation markup for a binomial coefficient.

```
<math>
 <mrow>
   <mo>(</mo>
   <mfrac linethickness="0">
     <mi>n</mi>
     <mi>m</mi>
   </mfrac>
   <mo<)</mo>
 </mrow>
</math>
```

The stylesheet shown in Example 8.9 will convert all instances of the markup for $\binom{n}{r}$ in a presentation MathML document into the markup for C_r^n.

Example 8.9 An XSLT stylesheet that changes the notation for a binomial coefficient.

```
<xsl:stylesheet version="1.0"
xmlns:xsl="http://www.w3.org/1999/XSL/Transform">

   <xsl:template match="math">
     <math><xsl:apply-templates/></math>
   </xsl:template>

   <xsl:template match="mrow">
     <mrow><xsl:apply-templates select="mfrac"/></mrow>
   </xsl:template>

   <xsl:template match="mo">
     <mo><xsl:apply-templates/></mo>
   </xsl:template>

   <xsl:template match="mi">
     <mi><xsl:apply-templates/></mi>
   </xsl:template>

   <xsl:template match="mn">
     <mn><xsl:apply-templates/></mn>
   </xsl:template>

   <xsl:template match="mfrac">
     <xsl:choose>
```

```
        <xsl:when test="@linethickness='0'">
          <msubsup>
            <mi>C</mi>
            <xsl:apply-templates select="*[2]"/>
            <xsl:apply-templates select="*[1]"/>
          </msubsup>
        </xsl:when>
        <xsl:otherwise>
          <mfrac><xsl:apply-templates/></mfrac>
        </xsl:otherwise>
      </xsl:choose>
    </xsl:template>

</xsl:stylesheet>
</math>
```

The stylesheet shown in Example 8.9 contains templates for the `math`, `mrow`, `mn`, `mi`, and `mo` elements. These templates simply copy the content of the matching element to the output document (after enclosing them in the appropriate tags). The key template in the stylesheet is the one that matches the `mfrac` element. This template uses the `xsl:choose` element to check if the currently selected `mfrac` element has the attribute `linethickness` set to 0. This condition is implemented by the `<xsl:when test="@linethickness='0'>` element. Recall that `@linethickness='0'` is the XPath syntax for specifying an attribute called `linethickness`, whose value is 0.

If the `mfrac` element for which the template is being evaluated matches this condition, the statements inside the `xsl:when` element are evaluated. These statements replace the `mfrac` element with an `msubsup` element. The three arguments of the `msubsup` element are constructed using three separate statements. First, the literal text `<mi>C</mi>` is copied to the output document to serve as the first argument.

Next, the `<xsl:apply-templates select="*[1]/>` element is called. This element applies all templates in the current context that match the value specified by the `select` attribute. This attribute has the value `*[1]`, which is the XPath syntax for the first child element of the current node. Hence, the net effect of this statement is to copy the first argument of the `mfrac` element into the output document to serve as the third argument of the `msubsup` element.

Finally, the `<xsl:apply-templates select="*[2]/>` element is called. This element takes the second argument of the `mfrac` element in the input document and copies it as the second argument of the `msubsup` element in the output document.

Applying the stylesheet in Example 8.9 to the MathML document in Example 8.8 yields the following output:

```
<?xml version="1.0" encoding="utf-8"?><math>
 <mrow><msubsup><mi>C</mi><mi>m</mi><mi>n</mi>
   </msubsup></mrow>
```

Hence, the net effect of the stylesheet is to convert the markup for $\binom{n}{r}$ into the markup for C_r^n. You can easily modify the same stylesheet to produce the markup for the alternative notational form, C_n^r, if desired. To do so, you would just reverse the order of two statements in the template for the mfrac element, as shown below:

```
<xsl:apply-templates select="*[1]"/>
<xsl:apply-templates select="*[2]"/>
```

This causes the first and second arguments of the `mfrac` element in the input document to become the second and third arguments of the `msubsup` element in the output, respectively.

Note that if the input document does not contain an `<mfrac linethickness="0">` attribute, then the condition in the `xsl:when` element of the stylesheet evaluates to `false`, and the statements in the `xsl:otherwise` element are applied instead. This has the effect of simply copying the `mfrac` element unchanged into the output, which is what you want to happen.

Translating between Content and Presentation Markup

In the XSLT transformations discussed so far, both the input and the output were in the form of presentation MathML. However, XSLT is also an effective tool for transforming content MathML into presentation MathML, or vice versa.

Converting presentation MathML to content MathML is useful in situations where the mathematical meaning of the markup is important. For example, a student might want to copy a mathematical formula displayed in a Web page (using presentation MathML) and then paste the markup into a computer algebra system for evaluation. For many types of formulas, the mathematical meaning can be inferred from the notation and so a stylesheet can apply simple heuristic rules for transforming presentation markup into content markup.

For example, a superscript, as in x^2, can be interpreted as a power. However, this is not always accurate. There could be some cases, for example, where an author uses x^2 to denote the second component of a vector x. In general, any notation described using presentation MathML can have more than one meaning or sometimes no meaning at all. Hence, it is impossible to write a single stylesheet that is general enough to convert any arbitrary presentation MathML into content MathML, even though such a conversion is possible in specific cases.

A more realistic goal is to do the reverse transformation; that is, convert content markup into presentation markup. Since content markup specifies mathematical meaning unambiguously, this type of conversion is always possible. In principle, one can create a single stylesheet that is general enough to take almost any type of valid content markup expression and convert it into the corresponding presentation markup. Such a stylesheet can be very useful since it allows you to specify the notation for a formula independently of its mathematical meaning. For example, an author can create a technical paper in which all the formulas are specified using content MathML. A publisher can then use an XSLT stylesheet to convert the content MathML in the document into presentation MathML while applying specific notational rules that enforce the style of a particular journal.

The conversion of content markup into presentation markup is also of great importance when you are displaying MathML in Web browsers. Most browsers that support native display of MathML, such as *Amaya*, *Mozilla* 1.0, and *Netscape* 7.0, can recognize only MathML presentation tags. They cannot render content MathML. However, *Mozilla* 1.0 and *Netscape* 7.0 do have built-in support for XSLT transformations. Hence, one possible strategy for rendering content MathML in such browsers is to use an XSLT stylesheet that will convert any content MathML expression into presentation MathML. This can then be displayed using the browser's native rendering abilities.

David Carlisle, as part of his work on the Universal MathML stylesheet, has successfully implemented this approach. As we saw in Section 7.2, this is a large and complex XSLT stylesheet that allows both content and presentation MathML to be displayed on a wide variety of browsers and using a variety of plug-ins. One feature of this stylesheet is that it includes templates for all the different types of content elements. When applied to any document that contains content MathML, the stylesheet automatically transforms each instance of content MathML in the document into an equivalent presentation MathML expression.

In this section, we focus on giving some simple examples of XSLT transformations for converting content MathML to presentation MathML. Of course, you do not need to write such a stylesheet from scratch; for most purposes, you can use the stylesheet already created by David Carlisle. The purpose of this section is to illustrate some of the general techniques and issues involved in doing such conversions. You can then use these techniques to customize the existing stylesheet, for example, to implement a different set of notational preferences.

Factorials

As the first example, let's write a stylesheet that will transform a content MathML document involving the factorial operator into presentation MathML. Example 8.10 shows a simple MathML document that we can use to illustrate this behavior.

Example 8.10 A content MathML document that uses the *`factorial`* element.

```
<math>
 <apply>
   <factorial/>
   <ci>n</ci>
 </apply>
</math>
```

The factorial operator is typically indicated by an exclamation mark after its operand; that is, the factorial of n is shown as $n!$. Example 8.11 shows a simple stylesheet that generates presentation markup using this notation.

Example 8.11 An XSLT stylesheet for transforming content MathML expressions involving the factorial operator.

```
<xsl:stylesheet version="1.0"
xmlns:xsl="http://www.w3.org/1999/XSL/Transform">

   <xsl:template match="math">
     <math><xsl:apply-templates/></math>
   </xsl:template>

   <xsl:template match="ci">
     <mi><xsl:apply-templates/></mi>
     </xsl:template>

   <xsl:template match="apply[factorial]">
     <mrow><xsl:apply-templates select="*[2]"/>
     <mo>!</mo></mrow>
   </xsl:template>

</xsl:stylesheet>
```

The key template in the stylesheet is the one for the `apply` element. The `select` attribute of this template has the value `apply[factorial]`, which is the XPath expression for an `apply` element having a `factorial` element as one of its children. When this template is matched, it first writes an opening `mrow` tag to the output. It then triggers all templates that match the second child of the `apply` element, which happens to be a `ci` element. This triggers the template for the `ci` element, which simply copies the content of the matched `ci` element into the output and replaces the `ci` tags with `mi` tags. The template for the `apply` element then resumes and copies the literal text `<mo>!</mo>` to the output, followed by a closing `mrow` tag.

Applying the stylesheet in Example 8.11 to the document in Example 8.10 yields the following output:

```
<?xml version="1.0" encoding="utf-8"?><math>
 <mrow><mi>n</mi><mo>!</mo></mrow>
</math>
```

The stylesheet in Example 8.11 is a relatively simple one and is not general enough to accommodate all the different contexts in which a factorial element might occur in a content MathML expression. It is easy to construct cases where the stylesheet breaks down. For example, suppose you used the content MathML expression for the factorial of $2n$ as the input expression instead of n, as shown in Example 8.12.

Example 8.12 A MathML document that contains the content markup for $(2n)!$

```
<math>
 <apply>
   <factorial/>
   <apply><mn>2</mn><ci>n</ci></apply>
 </apply>
</math>
```

Applying the same stylesheet to this expression yields the following output:

```
<?xml version="1.0" encoding="utf-8"?><math>
 <mrow>2
   <mi>n</mi><mo>!</mo></mrow>
</math>
```

This output is not valid presentation markup since the 2 is not enclosed in an `mn` element, as required by MathML. The reason for this is that the stylesheet in Example 8.11 does not contain a template for the `cn` element. Hence, when a `cn` element is encountered, the default template for it is used, which has the effect of simply copying the element's content without wrapping it in any tags. For `cn` elements to be processed properly, we can add the following template to the stylesheet:

```
<xsl:template match="cn">
  <mn><xsl:apply-templates/></mn>
</xsl:template>
```

With the addition of this template to the stylesheet in Example 8.11, processing the document in Example 8.12 yields the following output:

```
<?xml version="1.0" encoding="utf-8"?><math>
 <mrow><mn>2</mn>
   <mi>n</mi><mo>!</mo></mrow>
</math>
```

This is better than before since now at least the 2 is properly enclosed in the tags for the `mn` element. However, there is still a problem with the output expression. If it is rendered in a browser, it will appear as $2n!$, which is ambiguous, since it could represent either the factorial of $2n$ or two times the factorial of n. Of course, presentation markup specifically provides the entity reference `⁢` to distinguish such cases. We could, of course, modify our stylesheet to insert this reference in cases where multiplication is intended. But it would be better still to use parentheses to explicitly indicate all complex operands to which the factorial operator is applied, as in $(2n)!$. You can achieve this by modifying the template for the `apply` element in Example 8.11 to the form shown below:

```
<xsl:template match="apply[factorial]">
 <mrow>
 <xsl:choose>
   <xsl:when test="(*2=(ci or cn))">
     <xsl:apply-templates select="*[2]"/>
       <mo>!</mo></mrow>
   </xsl:when>
   <xsl:otherwise>
     <mrow><mo>(</mo>
     <xsl:apply-templates select="*[2]"/>
     <mo>)</mo></mrow><mo>!</mo></mrow>
   </xsl:otherwise>
```

```
  </xsl:choose>
  </mrow>
</xsl:template>
```

The difference between this and the template shown in Example 8.11 is that now we have included an `xsl:when` element for conditional processing. When the child element immediately following the factorial element is either a `ci` or `cn` element, the same processing is done as in Example 8.11. Otherwise, parentheses are placed around the expression. The revised template therefore takes into account information about the context in which the factorial element occurs. Example 8.13 shows the stylesheet of Example 8.11 modified to include the more complex template shown above as well as a template for the `cn` element.

Example 8.13 An XSLT stylesheet that causes parentheses to be placed around complex operands of the factorial operator.

```
<xsl:stylesheet version="1.0"
 xmlns:xsl="http://www.w3.org/1999/XSL/Transform">

   <xsl:template match="math">
     <math><xsl:apply-templates/></math>
   </xsl:template>

   <xsl:template match="ci">
     <mi><xsl:apply-templates/></mi>
   </xsl:template>

   <xsl:template match="cn">
     <mn><xsl:apply-templates/></mn>
   </xsl:template>

   <xsl:template match="apply[factorial]">
     <mrow>
     <xsl:choose>
       <xsl:when test="(*2=(ci or cn))">
         <xsl:apply-templates select="*[2]"/>
           <mo>!</mo></mrow>
       </xsl:when>
       <xsl:otherwise>
         <mrow><mo>(</mo>
         <xsl:apply-templates select="*[2]"/>
         <mo>)</mo></mrow><mo>!</mo></mrow>
       </xsl:otherwise>
     </xsl:choose>
```

```
      </mrow>
    </xsl:template>

  </xsl:stylesheet>
```

Applying the stylesheet of Example 8.13 to the document in Example 8.10 yields the following output, which renders correctly as $(2n)!$:

```
  <?xml version="1.0" encoding="utf-8"?><math>

   <mrow><mo>(</mo><mn>2</mn><mi>n</mi><mo>)</mo></mrow>
   <mo>!</mo></mrow>
  </math>
```

Integrals

The last example demonstrated the importance of writing templates that take into account the context in which specific elements might occur in the input document. It is not enough to write a stylesheet that works as intended for a specific document. For the stylesheet to be generally useful, the template for any element must be sufficiently robust to work properly in all the possible contexts that the element could occur. Also, since templates can be called recursively, it is important to ensure that the templates for different elements do not interact in unintended ways. Clearly, writing a stylesheet that is general enough to work for all documents that could be written in a particular XML format, such as MathML, is a challenging task and requires a great deal of testing and fine-tuning.

The importance of making templates that are as general as possible is illustrated in the next example. Suppose we want to create a stylesheet that will convert the content markup for an integral into the corresponding presentation markup. Example 8.14 shows the content markup for a simple integral: $\int_a^b \sin(x)\,dx$. Notice that the limits of the integral are specified using the qualifier elements `lowlimit` and `uplimit`.

Example 8.14 A MathML document showing the content markup for an integral.

```
  <math>
   <apply>
     <int/>
     <bvar><ci>x</ci></bvar>
     <lowlimit><ci>a</ci></lowlimit>
     <uplimit><ci>b</ci></uplimit>
```

```
    <apply>
    <ci>sin</ci>
    <ci>x</ci>
    </apply>
  </apply>
</math>
```

Example 8.15 shows an XSLT stylesheet for transforming expressions like Example 8.14 into presentation markup.

Example 8.15 An XSLT stylesheet for transforming the content markup for an integral into presentation markup.

```
<xsl:stylesheet version="1.0"
xmlns:xsl="http://www.w3.org/1999/XSL/Transform">

   <xsl:template match="math">
     <math><xsl:apply-templates/></math>
   </xsl:template>

   <xsl:template match="ci">
     <mi><xsl:apply-templates/></mi>
   </xsl:template>

   <xsl:template match="apply[sin]">
     <mrow><mi>sin</mi><mo>(</mo>
     <xsl:apply-templates/><mo>)</mo></mrow>
   </xsl:template>

   <xsl:template match="apply[int]">
     <mrow>
       <msubsup>
         <mo>&#8747;</mo>
         <mrow>
           <xsl:apply-templates select="lowlimit"/>
         </mrow>

         <mrow>
           <xsl:apply-templates select="uplimit"/>
         </mrow>
       </msubsup>
       <xsl:apply-templates select="last()"/>
       <mo>d</mo>
       <xsl:apply-templates select="bvar"/>

     </mrow>
   </xsl:template>

</xsl:stylesheet>
```

The key template in this stylesheet is the one whose `select` attribute is set to `apply[int]`. This template is matched by any `apply` element that contains an `int` element. The three important statements in this template are:

```
<xsl:apply-templates select="lowlimit"/>
<xsl:apply-templates select="uplimit"/>
<xsl:apply-templates select="last()"/>
```

These statements apply all templates that match a `lowlimit`, `uplimit`, and the last child element in the `apply` element, respectively. `last()` is an XPath expression that refers to the last child element in the current context.

Applying the stylesheet of Example 8.15 to the document in Example 8.14 results in the following output:

```
<?xml version="1.0" encoding="utf-8"?><math>


 <mrow><msubsup><mo>&8747;</mo><mi>a</mi><mi>b</mi>
 </msubsup><mrow><mi><sin></mi><mi>x</mi><mo>d</mo>
 <mi>x</mi></mrow></mrow>
</math>
```

If this presentation markup is viewed in a MathML-enabled browser, it renders as $\int_a^b \sin(x)dx$, indicating that the transformation was indeed successful.

However, the template used for the `int` element in Example 8.15 is not very general. Recall that in content markup, the limits of a definite integral can also be represented using other content elements, such as `interval` and `condition`. For example, the integral of Example 8.15 can also be represented using the content markup shown in Example 8.16.

Example 8.16 A content MathML document that represents an integral using the `interval` element.

```
<math>
 <apply>
   <int/>
   <bvar><ci>x</ci></bvar>
   <interval><ci>a</ci><ci>b</ci></interval>
   <apply>
     <ci>sin</ci>
     <ci>x</ci>
```

```
    </apply>
  </apply>
</math>
```

You can extend the stylesheet in Example 8.15 to take into account this alternative method of representing the limits of an integral. The only template that needs to be changed is the one that matches the `apply[int]` element. You can generalize the `xsl:apply-templates` elements that match the `lowlimit` and `uplimit` elements by modifying the value of their `select` attribute. The modified elements look as follows:

```
<xsl:apply-templates select="lowlimit|interval/*[1]"/>

<xsl:apply-templates select="uplimit|interval/*[2]"/>
```

Here, `lowlimit|interval/*[1]` is an XPath expression that matches either a `lowlimit` element or the first child of the `interval` element. Similarly, `uplimit|interval/*[2]` matches either the `uplimit` element or the second child of the `interval` element. The modified stylesheet with these generalized elements is shown in Example 8.17.

Example 8.17 A modified XSLT stylesheet for converting integrals from content markup to presentation markup.

```
<xsl:stylesheet version="1.0"
xmlns:xsl="http://www.w3.org/1999/XSL/Transform">

   <xsl:template match="math">
     <math><xsl:apply-templates/></math>
   </xsl:template>

   <xsl:template match="ci">
     <mi><xsl:apply-templates/></mi>
   </xsl:template>
   <xsl:template match="apply[sin]">
     <mrow><mi>sin</mi><mo>(</mo>
     <xsl:apply-templates/><mo>)</mo></mrow>
   </xsl:template>

   <xsl:template match="apply[int]">
     <mrow>
       <msubsup>
         <mo>&#8747;</mo>
         <mrow>
           <xsl:apply-templates
```

```
                select="lowlimit|interval/*[1]"/>
            </mrow>
            <mrow>
                <xsl:apply-templates
                select="uplimit|interval/*[2]"/>
            </mrow>
        </msubsup>
        <xsl:apply-templates select="last()"/>
        <mo>d</mo>
        <xsl:apply-templates select="bvar"/>
    </mrow>
</xsl:template>

</xsl:stylesheet>
```

Applying the stylesheet of Example 8.17 to the document in Example 8.16 results in the following output:

```
<?xml version="1.0" encoding="utf-8"?><math>
 <mrow><msubsup><mo>&8747;</mo><mi>a</mi><mi>b</mi>
 </msubsup><mrow><mi><sin></mi><mi>x</mi><mo>d</mo>
 <mi>x</mi></mrow></mrow>
</math>
```

It is easy to generalize the stylesheet further so it can handle integrals in which the limits are represented using the `condition` element, as well as the `interval` or `lowlimit` and `uplimit` elements. This would require adding templates for all elements that can occur as child elements of the `condition` element.

Creating Macros

Another important use of XSLT in working with MathML is for creating macros to abbreviate complex notation. For example, suppose you are authoring a document in which a complicated expression is repeated frequently. Instead of writing out the full expression each time, you can use an XSLT stylesheet to define a new element to represent the whole expression. This allows you to write out the entire document in a much more compact form. Once the document is finished, you can replace each occurrence of the macro with the corresponding MathML expression by using the XSLT stylesheet that contains the definition for the macro.

This technique is particularly useful when you are defining new elements to represent concepts not covered in the existing MathML specification. For example, content MathML does not include any element that correspond to the concept of the trace of matrix.

Hence, suppose we wanted to encode a statement like the one below:

$\mathrm{Tr}(A + B) = \mathrm{Tr}(A) + \mathrm{Tr}(B)$

You could define a new element called `x:trace` to represent this concept. You can specify the notation and meaning of this element in terms of standard MathML elements by using a `semantics` element. In other words, you can define `x:trace` to be equivalent to the following expression:

```
<semantics>
 <mi>Tr</mi>
 <annotation-xml encoding="OpenMath">
   <function name="Trace" cd="linalg3"
   xmlns="http://www.openmath.org/OpenMath"/>
 <annotation-xml>
</semantics>
```

If you then wanted to encode a statement like Tr`(A + B) = Tr(A) + Tr(B)`, you could use the following markup:

```
<apply>
 <eq/>
   <apply>
     <x:trace/>
     <apply><plus/><ci>A</ci><ci>B</ci></apply>

   </apply>
   <apply>
     <plus/>
     <apply><x:trace/><ci>A</ci></apply>
     <apply><x:trace/><ci>B</ci></apply>
   </apply>
</apply>
```

This is much more compact than having to use the full `semantics` element in place of each occurrence of `x:trace`. Of course, the `x:trace` element exists only in a private namespace and would not be recognized by other MathML processing applications. Hence, before processing the document further, you can replace all macros with their full form by applying an XSLT stylesheet that contains a template of the form shown below:

```
<xsl:template match="x:trace">
 <semantics>
 <mi>Tr</mi>
 <annotation-xml encoding="OpenMath">
```

```
    <function name="Trace" cd="linalg3"
    xmlns="http://www.openmath.org/OpenMath"/>
  <annotation-xml>
  </semantics>
</xsl:template>
```

Of course, in practice, most MathML markup will not be authored by hand but rather generated by special authoring software. Hence, the strategy described here for defining, inserting, and replacing macros is best implemented by a particular software application. The point here is that XSLT transformations provide a convenient mechanism for carrying out this kind of replacement procedure, even if the actual details are concealed under a more high-level interface.

CHAPTER

9

AUTHORING AND EDITING MathML

This chapter reviews some of the leading software tools available for authoring and editing MathML. The tools discussed include equation editors, like *MathType* and *WebEQ*, as well as full-featured document processing applications like *Mathematica*, *Publicon*, and *Scientific Word*.

9.1 INTRODUCTION

Most technical documents displayed on the Web currently are produced using one of two methods. The first method is to use a word-processing application like Microsoft *Word* for the text and to insert equations using the built-in *Equation Editor*, or its professional version, *MathType*. The *Word* document can then be converted into HTML using *Word*'s `Save As HTML` feature, which converts all the equations into images. Users who have *MathType*, the professional version of *Equation Editor*, also have the option of using its *MathPage* feature to do the HTML conversion. This gives better results than *Word*'s built-in HTML conversion, especially in the matter of integrating equations with the surrounding text. Alternatively, the *Word* document can be converted to PDF using *Adobe Acrobat Distiller*.

The second method, which is popular in the mathematical research community, is to use a TEX-based macro package such as LATEX to author documents, freely mixing text and equations as desired. TEX offers a high degree of control over the final output and allows authors to produce publication-quality typesetting of mathematics. The finished document can then be converted to HTML using programs like LATEX2HTML or TEX4ht, which convert all equations into images. Alternatively, you can use the `pdftex` utility to convert TEX documents into PDF files.

However, as discussed in Section 1.3, both images and PDF files have severe limitations for representing equations. These include poor image quality for viewing and printing, longer download time, lack of integration with the surrounding text, and inability to reuse the equations in another context. MathML was, of course, specially designed to overcome all these limitations. Now that all the major browsers support MathML display, the use of MathML to replace traditional methods of displaying mathematics on the Web is bound to increase.

Since MathML is highly verbose, it is tedious and error-prone to author by hand, and the task of authoring MathML is best handled by software. With the growth of interest in MathML in the last few years, several authoring applications have begun to support

MathML as an output format. Typically, these applications provide an equation editor-type interface for authoring mathematical notation. The resulting formula can then be converted into MathML using a translation mechanism, usually implemented through a menu command.

This chapter reviews the main features of some of the leading applications available for authoring MathML. These applications are of two main types:

- Dedicated equation editors, such as *MathType* or *WebEQ*, that focus on authoring formulas and are intended to be used in combination with another word-processing program.
- Full-featured authoring applications that can be used for creating complete documents, such as *Mathematica, Publicon,* or *Scientific Word.*

Of course, a significant number of technical documents are authored by TEX and LATEX users, who are accustomed to writing mathematical notation by hand in a plain text document. Such authors may prefer to retain a TEX-based system for authoring and then use a conversion program to produce a document for display on the Web. For a discussion of the various tools and methods available for translating TEX/LATEX documents to XHTML+MathML, see Chapter 10.

9.2 *MathType*

MathType is a powerful equation editor that provides a simple graphical interface for authoring equations of any complexity. The resulting equations can be converted into several different formats for insertion into Web pages and other documents. You can choose from both image-based formats and text-based markup (such as LATEX or MathML).

MathType is the professional version of the *Equation Editor* program that is included with Microsoft *Word* and Corel *WordPerfect*. The principal differences between *MathType* and *Equation Editor* are that *MathType* has:

- More fonts and templates for displaying special characters and symbols
- Customizable toolbars and keyboard shortcuts
- *MathPage* technology for creating Web pages from *Word* documents
- Support for automatic numbering of equations and references in *Word*

The *MathType* Interface

The *MathType* interface (Figure 9.1) consists of a series of palettes for pasting symbols and equation templates into a document. The symbols and templates are organized into groups that you can access on the taskbar via pop-up menus. There are templates for creating all the major types of mathematical notation, including fractions, radicals, subscripts, superscripts, sums, products, integrals, and matrices.

To construct an equation, you click the button for the desired template from the taskbar. Doing so inserts the template into the *MathType* window with empty placeholders for content, which you can fill by typing text from the keyboard or inserting other templates. You can construct equations of any complexity using the templates as building blocks, adding and nesting templates as desired. *MathType* automatically applies common typesetting conventions for font style, size, spacing, alignment, and other parameters, based on the context. If needed, you can also adjust any of these parameters manually.

When you have finished creating an equation, you can either paste it into another application like a word processor or convert

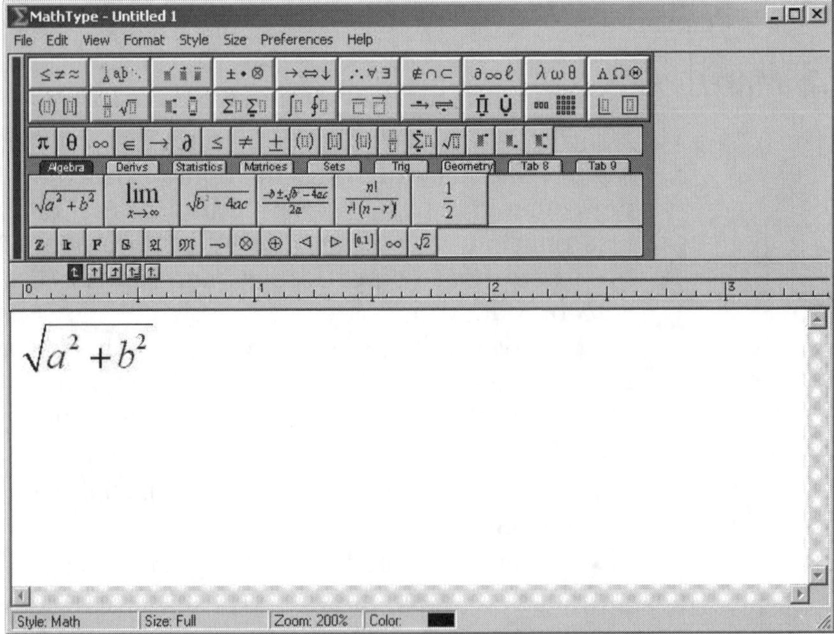

FIGURE 9.1 The *MathType* window, which shows the different symbol and template palettes.

the equation into an image (in EPS, GIF, or other formats) or a text markup language like MathML or LaTeX.

MathType also provides good support for including mathematical symbols and other extended characters in equations. It includes fonts for representing several hundred of the most commonly used extended characters. In addition to the standard Symbol font, *MathType* includes the Euclid family of fonts, which are similar to the Computer Modern fonts that are widely used for TeX and LaTeX documents. *MathType* also includes a proprietary font called MTExtra. You can search for a specific symbol using the Insert Symbol command under the Edit menu. This brings up a dialog (Figure 9.2) that lets you browse all characters for all fonts installed on your computer. You can also search for characters (in any font) whose name matches a specified keyword.

Converting Equations to MathML

The latest version of *MathType* for Windows, Version 5.1, includes complete support for MathML 2.0. Using the Translators dialog (Figure 9.3) to specify a suitable translator, you can copy the

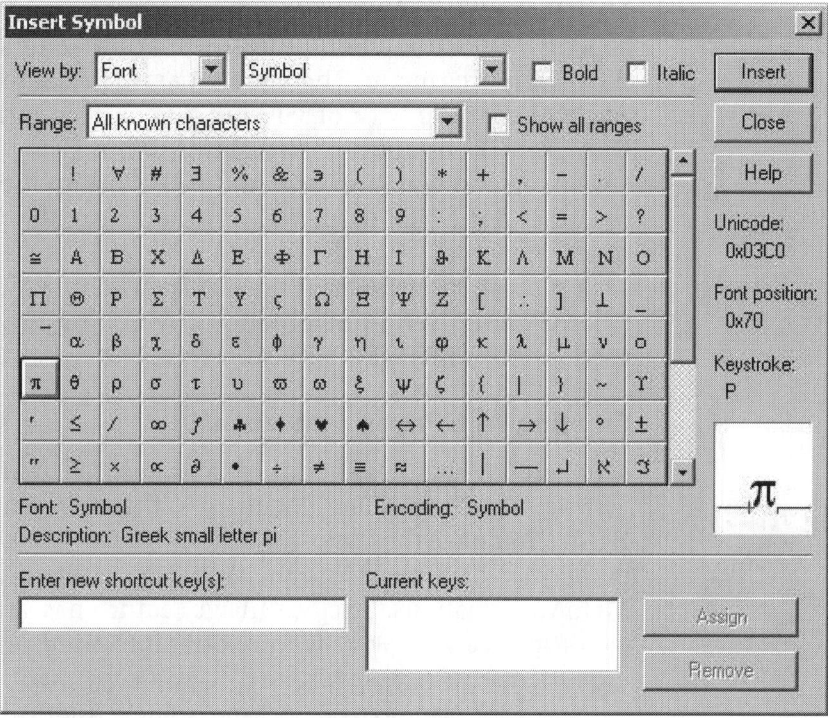

FIGURE 9.2 The Insert Symbol dialog for choosing extended characters.

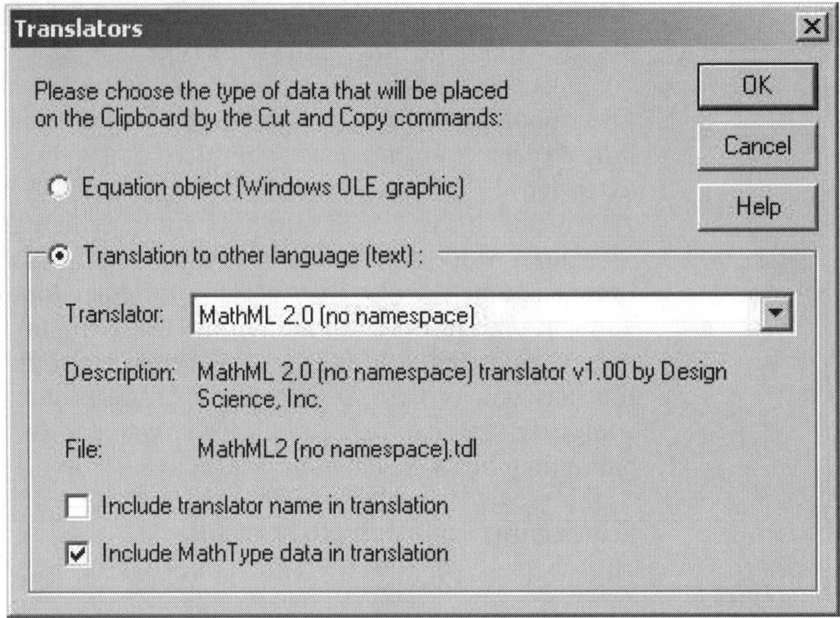

FIGURE 9.3 The dialog for converting equations into MathML.

MathML markup for any equation into the clipboard . This dialog appears when you choose the `Translators` command listed under the Preferences menu. There are separate translators for generating MathML markup with or without a namespace attribute or prefix. Once you choose any of the MathML translators, each time you cut or copy an equation, the MathML markup for that equation is copied into the clipboard. You can then paste the markup into any other document or application. A separate translation file handles each type of conversion. If needed, you can further customize the type of MathML output produced by editing the translation files used for the conversion.

Creating Web Pages with MathML

MathType 5.0 includes a special technology called MathPage for converting Microsoft *Word* documents that contain equations into HTML. You have the option of including *MathType* equations present in the *Word* document into the Web page, either as GIF images or as MathML equations. The MathPage feature has several advantages over the `Save As ▶ HTML` feature built into *Word*:

- The equations are better integrated with the surrounding text since *MathType* automatically adjusts the baseline, font styles, and sizes of the equations.

- The type of MathML produced can be automatically tailored for a specific rendering application.
- The resulting HTML is much cleaner than that produced by *Word* and is easier to edit and modify by hand.
- The MathZoom feature enables you to magnify any equation in a Web page by clicking it. This enables you to more clearly view the details of an equation such as subscripts and superscripts.

To save a *Word* document as an HTML file using the MathPage feature, choose the `Export to MathPage` command from the MathType menu in *Word*. This brings up a dialog (Figure 9.4) that allows you to set various export options. You can generate MathML adapted for viewing using *techexplorer*, *WebEQ*, *MathPlayer*, *Amaya*, and *Mozilla*. For each type of rendering environment, *MathType* automatically adds any extra markup needed and generates elements with the proper namespace. Version 5.1 of *MathType* (which was in beta testing at the time this book was written) also includes as an export option the ability to include a declaration for the Universal MathML stylesheet. As discussed in Section 7.2, this is the best way to author MathML documents that are viewable on a wide variety of platforms and browsers.

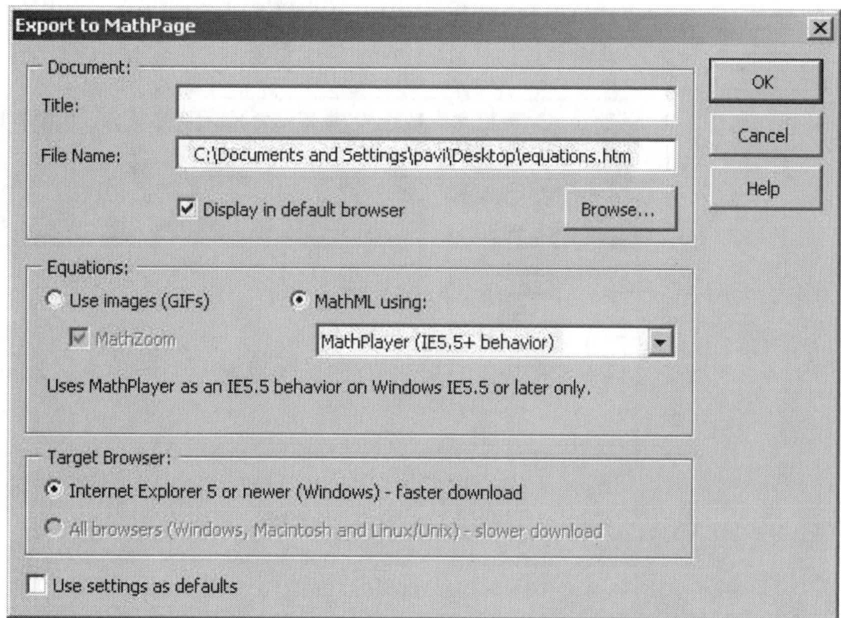

FIGURE 9.4 The Export to MathPage dialog, which shows the different options for translating MathML.

9.3 *WEBEQ*

WebEQ is a suite of Java-based software tools for authoring and displaying mathematical equations in a Web page. See Section 7.4 for an overview of the different components of *WebEQ*. In this section, we provide some more details about the two components of *WebEQ* that are most relevant to authoring MathML: Editor and Publisher.

Editor

WebEQ Editor is a Java application that provides a graphical interface for authoring equations. The interface of *WebEQ* Editor is very similar to that of *MathType*, which is not surprising considering they are both made by the same company, Design Science. The main difference is that *MathType* is a plug-in application that is typically used in combination with a word processing application like Microsoft *Word*. *WebEQ* Editor, instead, is a simpler version of *MathType*. It does not have many of the word-processing type features of *MathType* (such as automatic number of equations and alignment control). However, *WebEQ* supports a much wider range of MathML features, including attributes and actions.

As in *MathType*, you enter equations by inserting equation templates and symbols into the Editor window (Figure 9.5), by clicking

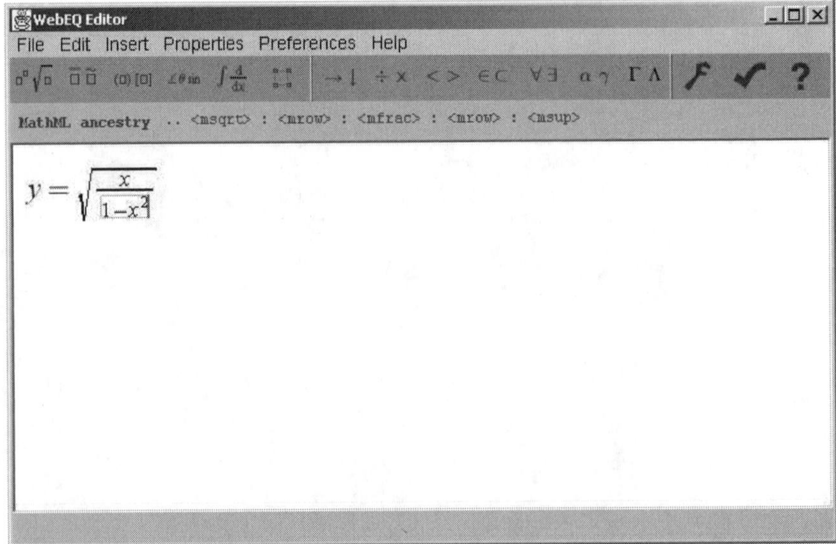

FIGURE 9.5 Using *WebEQ* Editor to create an equation.

buttons from the toolbar. There are templates corresponding to the basic building blocks of mathematical notation, such as fractions, square roots, subscripts, superscripts, and integrals. The toolbar is customizable. Using the Preferences menu you can create a configuration file to add or remove buttons for specific symbols or templates. There are also menu commands and keyboard shortcuts for entering the most common types of templates.

Each equation template contains one or more empty slots or placeholders, which you can fill in by typing text and numbers from the keyboard. You can quickly build up complex equations by nesting and combining templates, or by copying and pasting fragments of equations. You can also import MathML equations saved as external documents. The Editor automatically recognizes the MathML tags and displays the corresponding notation in the window for you to edit.

As you build up an equation, its MathML ancestry is displayed at the top of the window, providing a convenient visual cue to the type of elements being created behind the scenes. The Editor also provides a syntax-checking feature to verify if the notation you have entered is meaningful for conversion to content markup. To test the syntax of an equation, you can select it and click the checkmark button in the toolbar. If the equation is malformed in any way, either because some template slots are unfilled or because some notation does not have a clear interpretation, a dialog that tells you about the type of problem appears.

Once you have finished entering an equation, you can save it in one of three formats: an image (in JPG or PNG format), a MathML equation, or a *WebEQ* Viewer Control applet. For each format, the *WebEQ* Editor automatically generates the tag for pasting the equation into an HTML document. If you choose to export as MathML or Viewer Control applets, you can also copy and paste equations directly into another application.

For each type of export format, several options are available. When exporting as MathML, you can generate either content or presentation MathML. By default, equations are exported as presentation MathML, but you can change the default using the Preferences menu. You can also add a particular namespace prefix to all tags and attributes in the markup generated. This is useful when you are authoring MathML equations meant to be displayed with a specific rendering application. Figure 9.6 shows the dialog for specifying MathML export options. This dialog appears each time you try to export an equation as MathML, either by copying the

FIGURE 9.6 Setting the export options when you are exporting equations in MathML format.

equation or using the `File ▶ Save as MathML` menu. The dialog can also be accessed from the Preferences menu.

WebEQ Editor also lets you create interactive equations, which perform some action in response to user events (such as moving the cursor over an equation or clicking it). Three types of actions are supported:

- Toggle: clicking on an equation causes it to alternate between two different displays.
- Link: this turns an equation into a hyperlink that points to a specified URL.
- Mouseover: moving the cursor over an equation highlights it by changing the background and foreground colors.

To create any of these types of actions, you choose the corresponding command from the `Insert ▶ Actions` menu. This brings up a dialog with fields for specifying the various parameters that define the action. These actions are all implemented using the `maction` element of presentation MathML, which is currently not supported by most MathML display engines. However, the *WebEQ* Viewer Control Java applet does include support for the `maction` tag for the above three types of actions. Hence, if it is important to retain the interactive behavior when viewing an equation, you should save the equation as an HTML applet tag and view it using the *WebEQ* Viewer Control applet.

You can specify various properties for the equations, each of which corresponds to specific MathML attributes. The properties you can set belong to five categories:

- Font properties such as font color, font variant, font size, and background color
- Operator properties such as the form of the operator
- Layout properties such as script level, foreground, and background color

- Matrix properties such as alignment and spacing of rows and columns
- Action properties such as a change in color or a message displayed in the status line of a browser when an action is performed

Figure 9.7 shows the dialog used for specifying operator properties. Most of the properties correspond directly to various attributes of the `mo` presentation element, such as `form`, `stretchy`, `symmetric`, or `accent`.

Publisher

WebEQ Publisher is a Java application for processing an HTML document that contains equations to make it suitable for viewing in a browser. The source document can contain equations in either MathML or WebTEX, a markup language developed by Design Science that is similar to LaTeX in its syntax. *WebEQ* Publisher converts all equations present in the input document into HTML tags for displaying images, MathML equations, or *WebEQ* applet code, depend-

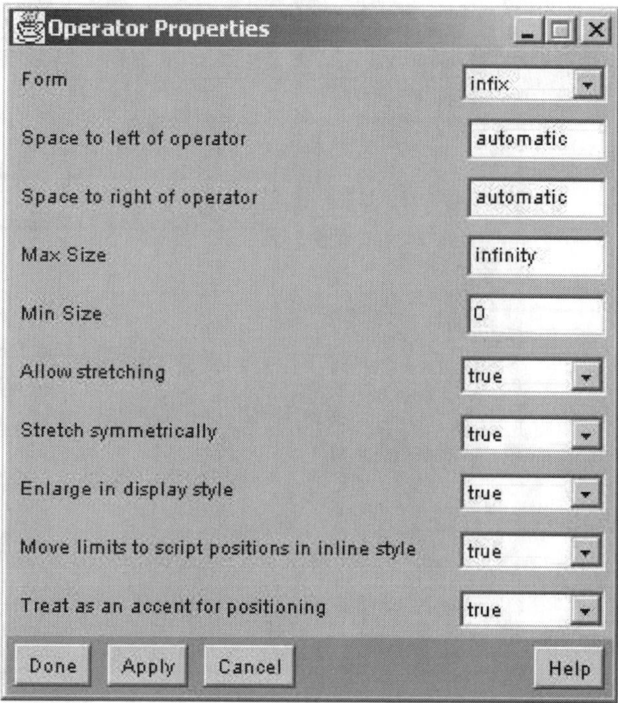

FIGURE 9.7 The dialog for setting operator properties in *WebEQ*.

ing on the user's preferences. The main advantage of using *WebEQ* Publisher to generate MathML documents is that it automatically handles the namespace and header declarations needed for viewing equations with specific rendering applications. Figure 9.8 shows the main window of *WebEQ* Publisher.

Typically, you specify a source file as input and *WebEQ* Publisher writes the output to another file. But you can also enter input for conversion directly into the Publisher window and then view the output in a separate window on the screen (Figure 9.9). Viewing input and output directly on the screen is useful for debugging. For example, you can vary the different translation options and see how the output changes. Once you are satisfied that the conversion is taking place exactly as you want it, you can then write the output to a file by checking the appropriate box in the *WebEQ* Publisher window.

For each type of export format, you can set various options from the Options menu. Using the Appearance Options dialog, you can control various aspects of the equation's appearance, such as the

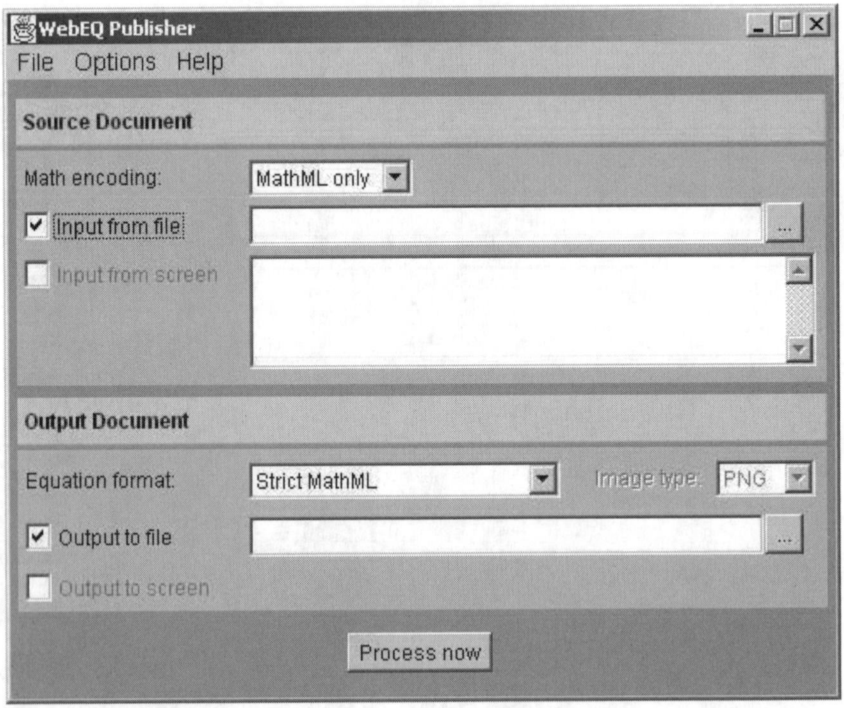

FIGURE 9.8 Using *WebEQ* Publisher to transform a source document into a form suitable for viewing in a Web browser.

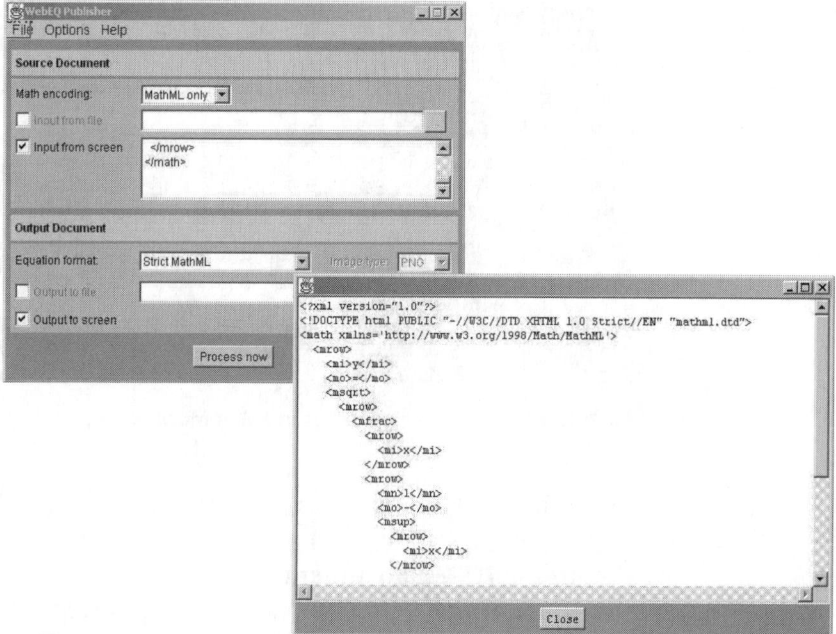

FIGURE 9.9 Viewing the output on the screen instead of writing to a file.

font size, font color, background color, and vertical alignment relative to the surrounding text. When exporting equations as MathML, you can use the Translation Options dialog (Figure 9.10) to specify a namespace prefix and add header declarations that correspond to specific rendering applications such as *techexplorer*, *MathPlayer*, *Mozilla*, and *WebEQ* Viewer Control. You can also choose to insert a reference to the Universal MathML stylesheet. The Options dialog also lets you specify whether symbol names in the source document should be converted to named entity references, numerical entity references, or binary Unicode characters.

WebEQ Editor and *WebEQ* Publisher complement each other. The combination of the two applications provides you with a convenient and flexible method for authoring documents that contain MathML. To create a technical document for display on the Web, you would take the following steps:

1. Construct an HTML version of your document using your usual method of creating Web pages.
2. Author each equation that you want to include in the document using the symbol and template palettes provided by *WebEQ* Editor.

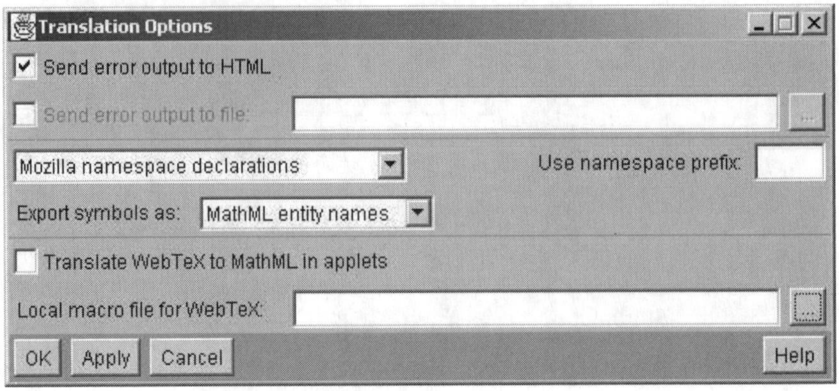

FIGURE 9.10 The dialog for setting MathML export options.

3. Copy each equation as MathML (using content tags or presentation tags as desired) and paste them at the appropriate places in the HTML document.
4. Once all the equations have been inserted into the HTML document, make it the source document for *WebEQ* Publisher.
5. Use the Translation Options dialog in *WebEQ* Publisher to control the namespace declarations. You should also add a prefix to each equation, based on the rendering application that will be used to view the document. You can also control the style in which the equations will be displayed using the Appearance Options dialog.
6. Process the document to generate an HTML document with embedded MathML equations.

9.4 *MATHEMATICA*

Mathematica is best known as a powerful application for doing mathematical computations. However, in addition to its computational abilities, *Mathematica* provides a rich WYSIWYG environment for authoring technical documents. Section 11.2 discusses *Mathematica*'s computational abilities in the context of MathML. In this section, we focus on *Mathematica*'s notebook interface and how you can use it as an environment for authoring MathML content.

The Notebook Interface

Mathematica consists of two separate applications: the front end, which provides the user interface for creating and editing documents, and the kernel, which acts as the computational engine.

The front end provides the standard word-processing features such as formatting, outlining, spell checking, and stylesheets. It also includes a sophisticated mathematical typesetting system that allows you to create complex mathematical notation quickly and easily, using palettes, menu commands, or keyboard shortcuts. The front end automatically handles the details of adjusting spacing, font size and style, linebreaking, and other properties according to the normal conventions of mathematical typesetting. But you can also control these properties explicitly using the large number of options provided.

Mathematica documents are called *notebooks*. Notebooks can contain text, typeset equations, graphics, and programs as well as active elements such as buttons and hyperlinks. When you start *Mathematica*, a blank notebook appears on the screen along with some palettes for entering input. Each notebook consists of a series of cells, indicated by brackets on the right. Cells are a generalization of paragraphs and in addition to text can contain equations, graphics, or commands for evaluation. Each cell has a specific style, such as Text, Input, Output, Graphics, Section, or Subsection, which determines the default properties of its contents. You can create a cell of a specific style using the `Format ▶ Style` menu.

Authoring Mathematical Formulas

You can enter mathematical notation in a notebook in three ways: using palettes, menu commands, or keyboard shortcuts. For somebody new to *Mathematica*, palettes are the most convenient method since they are easy to use. However, for experienced users, the menu and keyboard shortcuts provide a much faster and more efficient way of entering equations.

Palettes

When you first launch *Mathematica*, the Basic Input palette appears on the left of the screen (Figure 9.11). This contains buttons for about two dozen commonly used symbols and equation templates. Clicking a button on the palette causes the corresponding symbol or template to be pasted into your notebook at the position of the cursor. You can quickly construct the desired equation by combining templates and symbols and then filling in the placeholders by typing text from the keyboard.

In addition to the Basic Input palette, you can access the Basic Typesetting, Complete Characters, and International Characters palettes using the `File ▶ Palette` menu. The Complete Characters

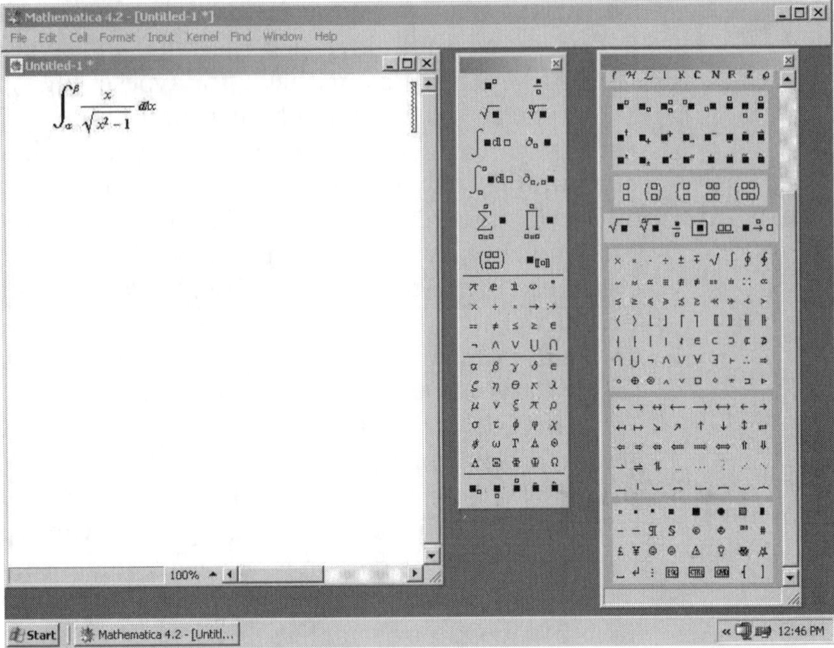

FIGURE 9.11 The *Mathematica* front end, which shows a notebook and some palettes for entering mathematical notation and special characters.

palette has a much wider selection of technical symbols and other special characters than the Basic Input palette. The characters are arranged into groups, such as Letters, Letter-like Symbols, and Operators. Each group is further divided into subgroups, such as Shapes and Icons, Textual Forms, and Keyboard Characters. You can click the triangle to the left of any group or sub-group to display or hide its contents.

Menus and Keyboard Shortcuts

The `Edit ▶ Expression Input` menu (Figure 9.12) contains commands for creating common mathematical constructs, such as subscripts, superscripts, fractions, and radicals. Each of these menu commands has a corresponding keyboard shortcut. For example, on Windows, you would press Ctrl+6 to create a subscript or Ctrl+/ to create a fraction. If you use one of the keyboard shortcuts for entering a mathematical expression while in a text cell, *Mathematica* automatically places the equation in an inline cell for better integration with the surrounding text.

The keyboard shortcuts are optimized so it is possible to enter complicated equations using only a small number of keystrokes.

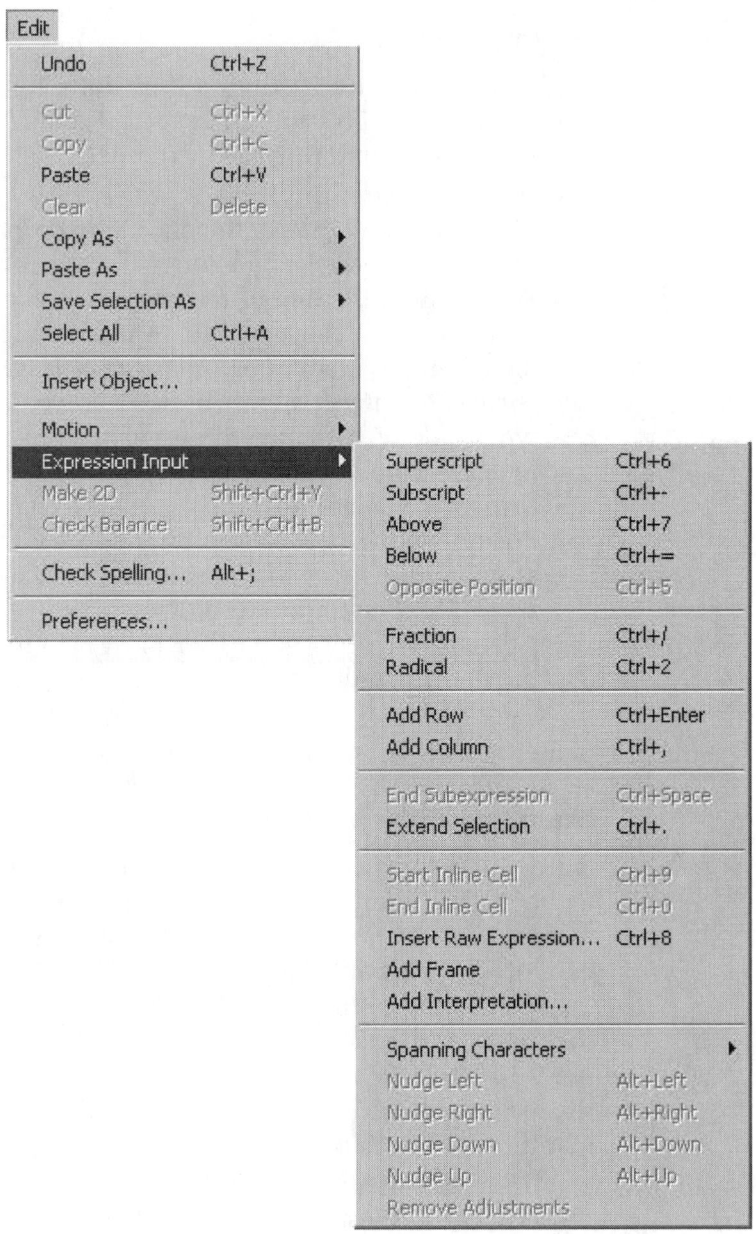

FIGURE 9.12 The `Edit` ▶ `Expression Input` menu.

Using these shortcuts, you can enter equations entirely from the keyboard, as you would, for example, in a text-based markup language such as TeX or LaTeX. However, unlike in TeX or LaTeX, the equations are immediately displayed in properly formatted two-dimensional notation.

Entering Special Characters

Mathematica includes its own set of fonts for over five hundred mathematical symbols and other special characters. There are three different ways of entering each extended character:

- Using a palette: the Basic Input, Basic Typesetting, Complete Characters, and International Characters palettes have a broad selection of special characters.
- Typing the full name of the character: each extended character has a name (for example, Alpha for alpha and Integral for the integral symbol). For any extended character, you can type \[*name*] to enter it into the notebook. So, for example, you can type \[Alpha] to enter the α character, or \[Integral] for the integral symbol, ∫.
- Using a keyboard alias: to enter any character, you type the Escape key (Esc) followed by a short name of the character and then the Escape key again. So, for example, you can type Esc-a-Esc to enter the α character, or Esc-int-Esc for the integral symbol. The short names for most characters are the same as the names used in TEX.

For a complete list of the supported characters and their full names and keyboard aliases, consult the product documentation.

Exporting and Importing MathML

Once you have used the techniques described so far in this chapter to author formulas, you can then convert the formulas into MathML for display on the Web. There are several ways to export mathematical formulas from a notebook as MathML.

To export a specific formula as MathML, select the formula and then choose the `Edit ▶ Copy As ▶ MathML` menu command (Figure 9.13). This copies the selected expression into the clipboard in the form of MathML presentation markup. You can then paste the markup into another application.

You can also export an entire notebook as HTML with MathML included. To do this, open the notebook and choose the `File ▶ Save As Special ▶ XML (XHTML+MathML)` menu command (Figure 9.14). This produces a well-formed and valid XHTML version of the notebook with all mathematical formulas in the notebook automatically converted into MathML. The resulting document can then be displayed in any suitably configured Web browser, including *Mozilla* or *IE* with *MathPlayer*. Note that you should save the file with a .xml extension for it to be viewable in the widest range of browsers.

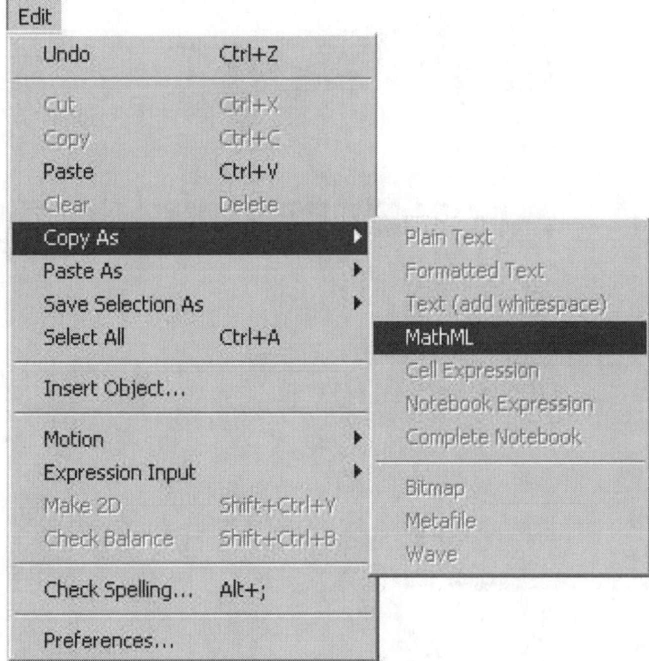

FIGURE 9.13 The `Edit` menu showing the `Copy As` ▶ `MathML` command.

Mathematica automatically inserts a reference to the Universal MathML stylesheet into the XHTML+MathML document. A local copy of this stylesheet is placed in a folder called HTMLFiles in the same directory as the XHTML+MathML file. This overcomes the limitation of *IE* not being able to use XSLT stylesheets from a remote location (see Section 7.2 for details).

Mathematica 4.2 also introduces an option for saving notebooks in an XML format called *NotebookML*. This allows notebooks to be saved as well-formed and valid XML documents so they can be used as part of an XML-based production process. Files in other XML formats, such as XHTML or DocBook, can also be imported into *Mathematica* as notebooks if you first transform them to NotebookML. To save a notebook in NotebookML format, simply choose the `File` ▶ `Save As Special` ▶ `XML (NotebookML)` menu command. You can also specify that all mathematical formulas in the notebook be embedded in the NotebookML document in MathML format by choosing `File` ▶ `Save As Special` ▶ `XML (NotebookML+MathML)`.

You can also copy and paste MathML content from another application directly into a notebook. When you paste a valid MathML expression into a notebook, *Mathematica* brings up a

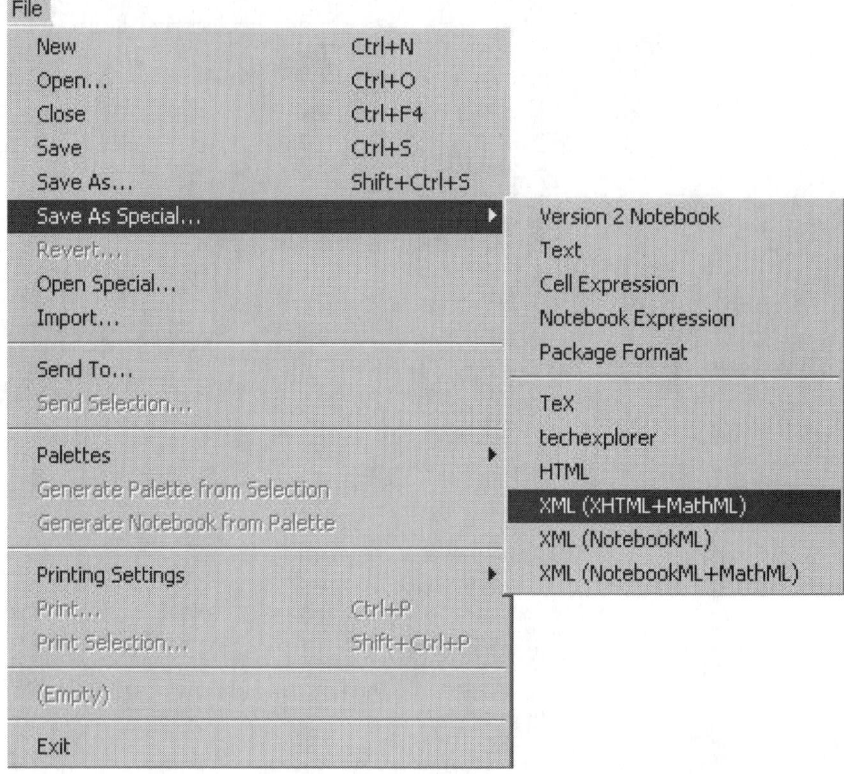

FIGURE 9.14 The `File` ▶ `Save As Special` submenu showing the commands for saving notebooks in HTML or XML format with embedded MathML.

dialog asking if you want to paste the literal markup or interpret it. If you choose to interpret the markup, it is pasted into the notebook as mathematical notation.

9.5 *PUBLICON*

Publicon is an application for authoring structured technical documents, and was developed by Wolfram Research, the same company that makes *Mathematica*. *Publicon* uses much of the same technology as *Mathematica* for authoring and editing documents. The two applications share the same typesetting system as well as the same document format, namely notebooks. In *Publicon*, too, you can enter mathematical notation quickly and easily using palettes, menus, or keyboard shortcuts.

The main difference is that *Publicon* lacks any computational abilities, since its focus is on creating documents. At the same time,

Publicon also goes beyond *Mathematica* in some respects. It has a more elaborate graphical interface with special palettes for creating various document styles and inserting formatted input such as lists, tables, and numbered equations. In addition, *Publicon* provides support for adding notes, citations, and cross-references and for creating a bibliography.

Publicon also includes a series of document palettes for authoring documents in specific TEX or XML formats. For example, there are separate palettes for creating documents in the style of *Physical Review*, the journals of the AMS, and the BioMed XML format used for authoring biomedical research papers. *Publicon* is thus a convenient tool for authors who want to create technical papers for submission to specific journals, or to produce documents that are interoperable with TEX and XML.

Figure 9.15 shows the *Publicon* interface. When you start *Publicon*, you see a blank notebook as well as two palettes: the Typesetting palette and the Default document palette. The Typesetting palette contains buttons for entering mathematical notation and applying formatting changes. The Default document palette allows you to create a document formatted according to the default stylesheet.

The Typesetting Palette

The Typesetting palette is a master palette that is composed of seven subpalettes. Each subpalette contains buttons for entering input in one of the following categories:

- Mathematical notation
- Shapes and symbols
- Relational operators and arrows
- Latin and Greek letters
- Script, gothic, and double-struck letters
- Fonts, alignment, and spacing
- Lists and value display objects (for inserting the current date, time, and so on)

Only one subpalette can be displayed at any given time. You can easily switch between the different subpalettes by clicking a button at the top of the Typesetting palette. The button that corresponds to the currently selected palette appears in a darker color.

Document Palettes

To author a document in a specific style, you use a document palette. Each document palette provides a point-and-click interface for

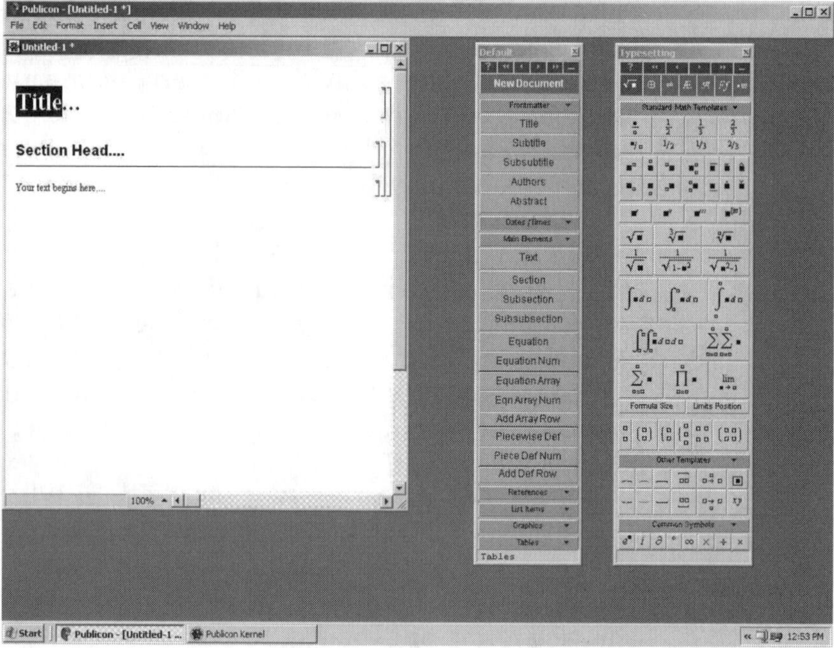

FIGURE 9.15 The *Publicon* interface showing the Typesetting palette and the Default document palette.

implementing the styles defined in a specific stylesheet. There are different document palettes, for example, to implement a set of predefined styles suitable for articles, reports, or books. These palettes are all listed under the `File ▶ Standard Palettes` menu.

In addition, *Publicon* includes a set of customized palettes, each of which implements the style of a specific journal. Some of the supported journal styles are listed below:

- RevTeX: for journals of the American Physical Society (APS)
- AMS-TeX: for journals of the AMS
- BioMed Central: for biomedical research papers
- arXiv: for physics and mathematics papers submitted to the arXiv preprint server

There are also three different document palettes that implement the LaTeX book, article, and report styles. These palettes are all listed under the `File ▶ Custom Palettes` menu.

Clicking the `New Document` button at the top of any of these custom palettes creates a template document, with headings and front matter already formatted in the particular style. Thus, you can quickly create a document with the style and structure required by a particular journal. Once you have finished authoring your document, you can export the notebook as a TeX or XML file, in the submission format appropriate for that journal. For example, you can author a physics paper using the Physical Review document palette (Figure 9.16) and then use the `File ▶ Save As ▶ TeX` menu to automatically produce a TeX file formatted according to the RevTeX macro package.

Exporting and Importing MathML

Once you have created a document, you can save it in several formats using the `File ▶ Save As` submenu. For MathML, the relevant format is XHTML+MathML. This saves the entire document in NotebookML format with all equations embedded in the form of MathML.

You can copy specific equations to the clipboard as presentation MathML and paste them into another application. To do this, select the equation and choose the `Edit ▶ Copy As MathML` menu command.

You can also copy MathML equations from another application, such as a Web browser, and paste them into a *Publicon* notebook. When you do this, *Publicon* brings up a dialog asking if you want

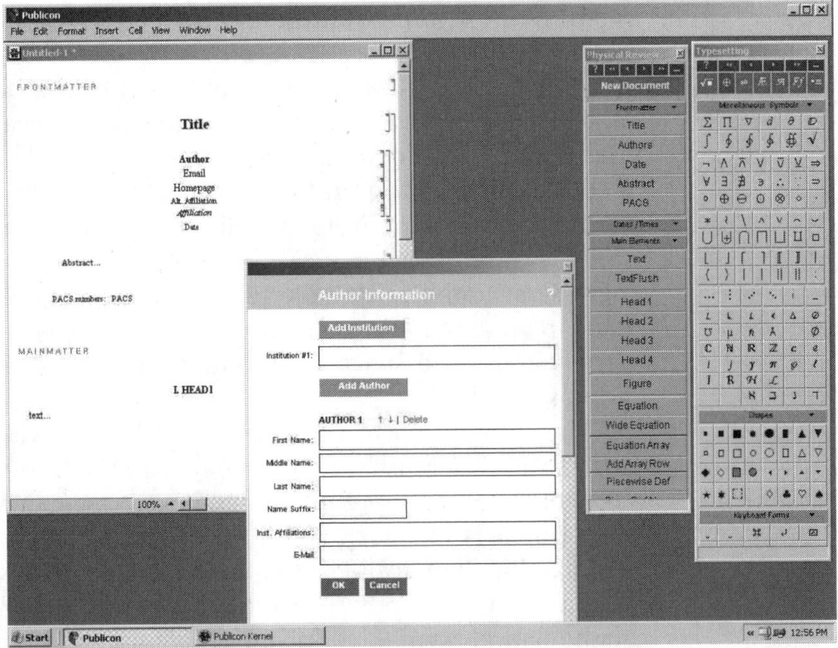

FIGURE 9.16 Authoring a paper in the style of an APS journal using the Physical Review document palette.

to paste the markup literally (as a MathML string) or interpret it. If you choose to interpret the markup, it is automatically displayed in the form of mathematical notation.

9.6 *Scientific Word*

Scientific Word is a mathematical word processor produced by MacKichan Software, Inc. It is part of a family of products that also includes *Scientific Notebook* and *Scientific Workplace*. *Scientific Notebook* and *Scientific Workplace* contain a computational engine for doing mathematical calculations. On the other hand, *Scientific Word* is a dedicated authoring tool for technical documents. It includes all the document processing and mathematical typesetting features of *Scientific Notebook* and *Scientific Workplace* but without any computational abilities.

Scientific Word offers a WYSIWYG environment for creating technical documents that contain typeset equations integrated with text. Text formatting and mathematical typesetting features are both integrated within a single application. One advantage of this is that the resulting document can be automatically converted into LaTeX, which is convenient for scientists and researchers who need to prepare articles in LaTeX for submission to a journal. Version 4.0 of *Scientific Word* includes support for exporting documents as HTML with MathML. Most presentation tags defined in MathML 2.0 are supported, but content tags aren't.

A *Scientific Word* document can be in one of two modes: Text mode, which is used for entering ordinary text, and Math mode, used for entering equations. You can toggle between Text and Math modes using a button on the toolbar. When you type text in Math mode, *Scientific Word* automatically recognizes operators, numbers, variables, and mathematical functions, and formats them accordingly. For example, alphabetic characters are italicized, names of standard mathematical functions and numbers are shown in an upright font, and space is automatically added around operators such as + and =.

The user interface of *Scientific Word* is shown in Figure 9.17. There are two Math toolbars that contain buttons and palettes for entering equation templates and extended characters. There are also templates for most common mathematical constructs, including fractions, radicals, subscripts, superscripts, sums, products, integrals, and derivatives. There are also palettes for most common mathematical symbols, including Greek and Latin characters,

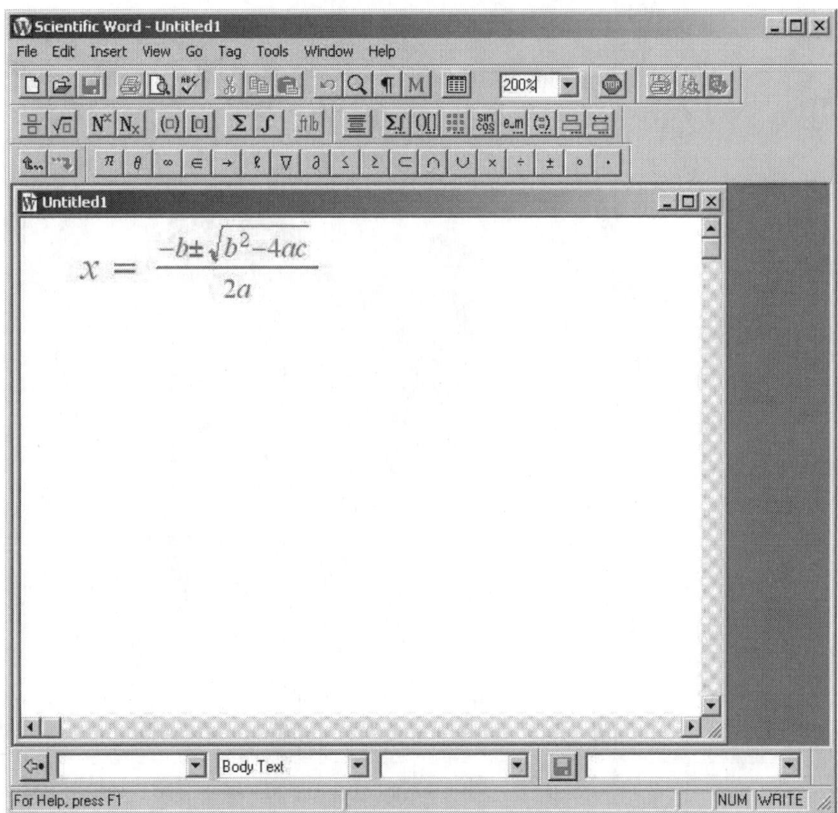

FIGURE 9.17 The *Scientific Word* interface showing the Math toolbars for entering equations.

operators, arrows, delimiters, and other technical symbols. Some of these palettes are shown in Figure 9.18.

Clicking one of the buttons in the Math toolbar inserts the corresponding symbol or equation template in the document. You can then construct expressions by typing text in the placeholders. By default, equations are entered in inline form, but you can switch to display form by clicking a button on the toolbar. Inline equations have various features optimized for better integration with the surrounding text. For example, numerators and denominators in a fraction have a smaller font size, and the limits of integrals are shown as subscripts and superscripts. Display equations, on the other hand, are shown centered and in a larger font size with the limits of integrals shown as underscripts and overscripts. You can control the display properties using the Operator dialog, accessible by clicking the button with the $\sum \int$ icon in the Math toolbar.

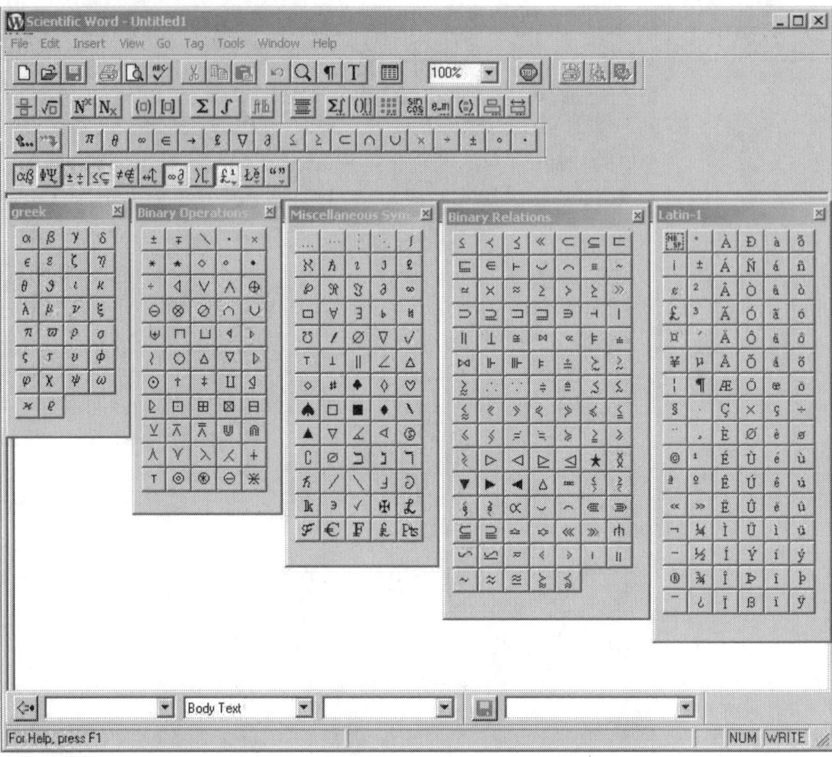

FIGURE 9.18 The Symbol toolbar along with some of the palettes for entering extended characters.

Scientific Word contains fonts for most common mathematical symbols, including the Computer Modern fonts that are widely used with TEX documents. You can enter a wide variety of extended characters, including Greek and Latin letters, operators, arrows, delimiters, and other mathematical symbols using a set of palettes accessible from the Symbol toolbar. To access the Symbol toolbar, choose the Toolbars command from the Views menu and click the checkbox marked Symbol. Clicking any of the buttons on the Symbol toolbar brings up a palette with buttons for entering symbols of a certain type. The Symbol toolbar along with some of the palettes available are shown in Figure 9.18.

Once you have created a document, you can convert it to LATEX format by using the built-in LATEX typesetting features. You can also convert the document to HTML with the equations saved as MathML using the `File ▶ Save As ▶ HTML + MathML` command. However, there is no support for importing MathML equations from another application, unless the imported document was also created using *Scientific Word*.

9.7 AMAYA

The W3C's *Amaya* browser includes native support for displaying MathML equations embedded in an HTML document, as discussed in Section 7.3. *Amaya* includes limited support for creating and editing presentation MathML. Support for authoring content MathML is yet to be included, but it may be added in a future release. *Amaya*'s authoring features are fairly rudimentary, and it is not an ideal authoring solution for somebody who wants to create a large number of complex technical documents. Its main virtue is that it is a free product and provides an integrated environment for authoring HTML documents containing MathML equations and SVG graphics.

There are two ways of authoring an equation in *Amaya*: using the menu commands listed in the `Math` submenu of the `Types` menu or using the Math palette, which is accessible from the toolbar. All the commands listed in the Math menu also have keyboard shortcuts, and these provide a much faster way of entering equations.

The Math Menu

In *Amaya*, a document can be viewed in two modes: Editor mode, which allows you to edit the document, and Browser mode, which only permits viewing. You can switch between the two modes by clicking a button on the toolbar or by choosing the `Editor Mode` command under the `Edit` menu. When you first start *Amaya* and open a new document, by default the document is shown in Editor mode.

The commands for authoring MathML equations are located in the `Types ▶ Math` submenu (Figure 9.19). Most commands in this submenu correspond to a specific presentation tag. There are also commands for entering the commonly used character references `⁢` and `⁡`.

To start entering an equation, you must first choose `Math ▶ New formula`. This creates the top-level `math` element, where the text you type subsequently is placed. When you type any characters inside a `math` element, *Amaya* parses the characters and automatically places the text in `mo`, `mi`, `mn`, and `mtext` elements, based on the type of characters you enter. Hence, you can create an equation without having to explicitly specify whether you are entering an operator, identifier, number, or literal text.

For example, to enter the expression, $y = x^2$ follow these steps:

1. From the `Types` menu, click `Math ▶ New formula`.
2. Type the character "y". *Amaya* automatically places this in an `mi` element.

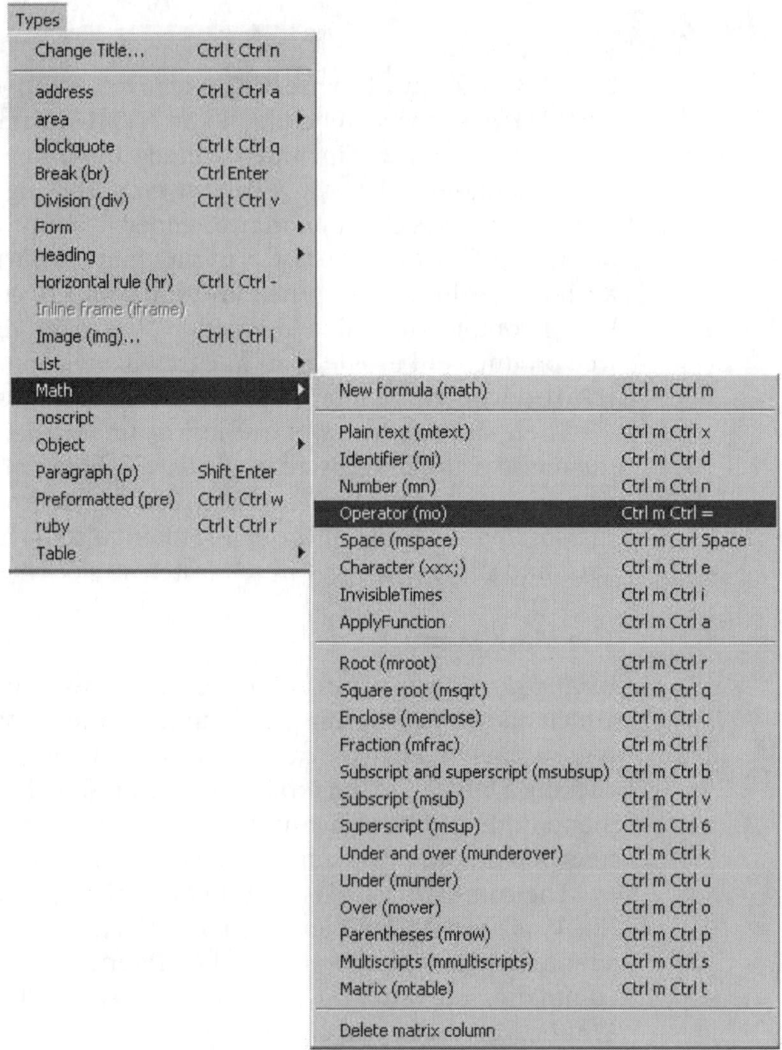

FIGURE 9.19 Authoring an equation in *Amaya* using the `Types` ▶ `Math` menu.

3. Type the character "=". *Amaya* automatically places this in an `mo` element.
4. From the `Types` menu, click `Math` ▶ `Superscript`. *Amaya* creates an `msup` element.
5. Type "x". *Amaya* automatically places this in an `mo` element and interprets it as the base, or first argument, of the `msup` element.
6. Type "2". *Amaya* automatically places this in an `mn` element and interprets it as the superscript, or second argument, of the `msup` element.

The status bar of the browser window displays the structure of the equation based on the current position of the cursor. If any of the elements created automatically by *Amaya* are not of the type you intended, you can explicitly change the element by selecting the text and then choosing the desired element (such as `mtext`, `mi`, `mn`, or `mo`) from the `Types ▶ Math` menu. You can also monitor the nested structure of the elements by viewing your document in the Structures view. This view is displayed in a separate window when you choose `Show structure` from the Views menu.

Each command listed in the Math submenu also has a keyboard shortcut associated with it. Once you become familiar with the various key combinations, it is much faster to enter an equation by using the keyboard shortcuts. For example, you can type Ctrl-m Ctrl-6 to create a superscript.

The Maths Palette

Amaya also provides a Maths palette (Figure 9.20) for creating equations by clicking buttons. You can access this palette by clicking the button marked $\frac{x}{y}$ on the toolbar. The Maths palette contains buttons with templates for creating the common types of mathematical notation, such as square roots, fractions, radicals, subscripts, superscripts, limits, tables, and matrices. To start entering an equation, you first click the Math button in the top left corner of the palette. This creates a `math` element for enclosing the text you enter.

To enter a specific type of template, you can click any of the buttons and then enter text from the keyboard to fill the placeholders in the template.

Extended Characters

To enter extended characters such as Greek letters and technical symbols, you can use the `Types ▶ Math ▶ Character` menu command (or press Ctrl+m Ctrl+e). This brings up a dialog in which you can enter the keyword for the special character; for example, omega or theta, to enter ω or θ. Alternatively, you can type the Unicode character code for the character in the dialog. For example, to insert the Greek letter α, you can type in either "alpha" or "x3B1" in the dialog and then click OK.

Another way to enter extended characters is by using the Math palette. Clicking a button at the bottom right corner of the Math palette brings up a Greek alphabet palette (Figure 9.21) that shows

FIGURE 9.20 The Maths palette for entering equations in *Amaya.*

a collection of special characters. You can click any of the buttons in this palette to paste the corresponding character into the document.

Amaya's support for displaying extended characters is fairly limited. It does not have any special fonts for mathematical symbols apart from the standard ISO-Latin 1 and Adobe Symbol font. As a result, some values of the `mathvariant` attribute (`script`, `double-struck` and `fraktur`) cannot be rendered. *Amaya* displays any character for which the font is not available using a "?" character. However, when creating a document, you can enter extended characters as either numeric or named entity references. These entity references are preserved in the internal representation and can thus be used when you export a document created in *Amaya* to another application that has better support for fonts.

Linking MathML Equations

Amaya supports linking in MathML equations using a draft version of the XML Linking Language (XLink). You can turn any MathML formula or a part of it into a hyperlink by specifying the target of the hyperlink as the value of the `xlink:href` attribute. For example, the following code defines a fraction that acts as a hyperlink to the W3C Math home page:

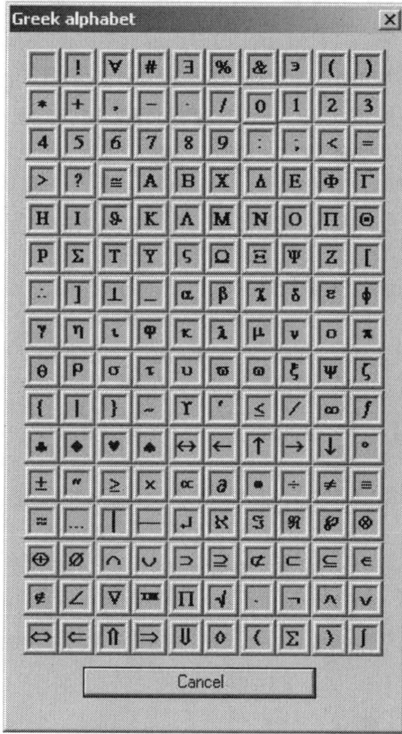

FIGURE 9.21 The Greek alphabet palette for entering special characters.

```
<math xmlns="http://www.w3.org/1998/Math/MathML">
<mfrac xmlns="http://www.w3.org/1999/xlink"
 xlink:href="http://www.w3.org/Math">
   <mi>x</mi>
   <mi>y</mi>
   </mfrac>
</math>
```

To convert an equation into a hyperlink, follow these steps:

1. Select the equation or the part of the equation from which you wish to link.
2. Click the `Link` button on the toolbar and choose `Links` ▶ `Create or change link` from the menu.
3. Enter the URL you wish to link to and click `Confirm`.

You can also turn an equation into the target of a link by selecting it, choosing `Links` ▶ `Create target`, and then entering a keyword to identify the equation in the dialog. This automatically assigns the `id` attribute to the equation so it can be the target of another hyperlink.

9.8 *EZMATH*

EzMath is a markup language for equations that corresponds closely to the way mathematics is spoken. It was developed by Dave Raggett and Davy Batsalle. *EzMath* is closely related to content MathML in its structure and can be used as a convenient input method for authoring content MathML. As with content MathML, *EzMath* notation covers most mathematical concepts covered in high schools in the United States.

The *EzMath* markup for any equation is based on the English language transliteration of the corresponding content MathML. For example, here is the *EzMath* markup for the solution of the quadratic equation:

$$\frac{-b \pm \sqrt{b^2 - 4ac}}{2a}$$

```
x = {-b plus or minus square root of
{b squared - 4ac}}/2a
```

An integral would be represented in *EzMath* markup as shown below.

$$\int_0^\pi \sin(x)\, dx$$

```
integral from 0 to pi of sin x wrt x
```

Compared to MathML, *EzMath* is much more concise as well as easier to write and understand. You can download a plug-in for displaying *EzMath* markup in a browser as well as the *EzMath* Editor application. Just go to *www.w3.org/People/Raggett/ezmath1_1.zip*. The plug-in is no longer very useful now that other methods are available for viewing MathML in browsers. However, the *EzMath* language is still useful as a way of authoring MathML. This is because the *EzMath* Editor can generate the content MathML encoding for any piece of *EzMath* markup. Thus, using the *EzMath* notation as an input language and the Editor as a translation mechanism is a simple and convenient method for authoring content MathML equations.

The *EzMath* Editor window (Figure 9.22) has three menus: `Math`, `Edit`, and `Help`. The Math menu contains examples of mathematical notation organized under several submenus, such as Arithmetic and Algebra, Theory of Sets, Trigonometry, Linear Algebra, and Calculus. If you choose one of these examples, the corresponding formula is displayed in the *EzMath* window. You can view the *EzMath*

FIGURE 9.22 The *EzMath* Editor window.

markup for the example by choosing `View expression` from the Edit window or by clicking a button in the taskbar.

This opens an Expression Editor window (Figure 9.23), which shows the markup for the equation. You can directly edit the markup in the window and then click `OK`. The notation displayed in the main window is automatically updated.

When you have finished editing the equation, you can import it as content MathML. To do this, follow these steps:

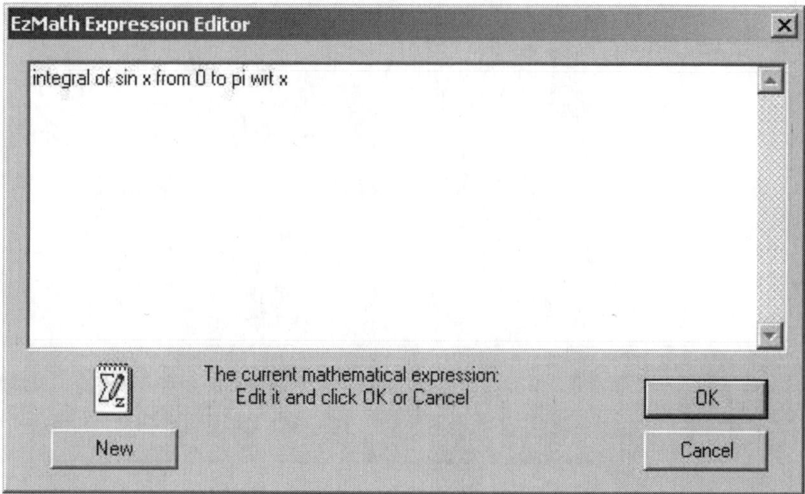

FIGURE 9.23 The *EzMath* Expression Editor window.

1. Set the clipboard format to MathML by clicking the appropriate button on the toolbar.
2. Choose `Copy to Clipboard` from the Edit menu (or click the Copy button on the toolbar). This copies the equation to the clipboard in the format you specified.
3. Choose `View Clipboard` from the Edit menu (or click the Clipboard button on the toolbar) to view the contents of the clipboard.
4. Copy the HTML tag or the content MathML encoding from the Clipboard window (Figure 9.24) and paste it into your HTML document.

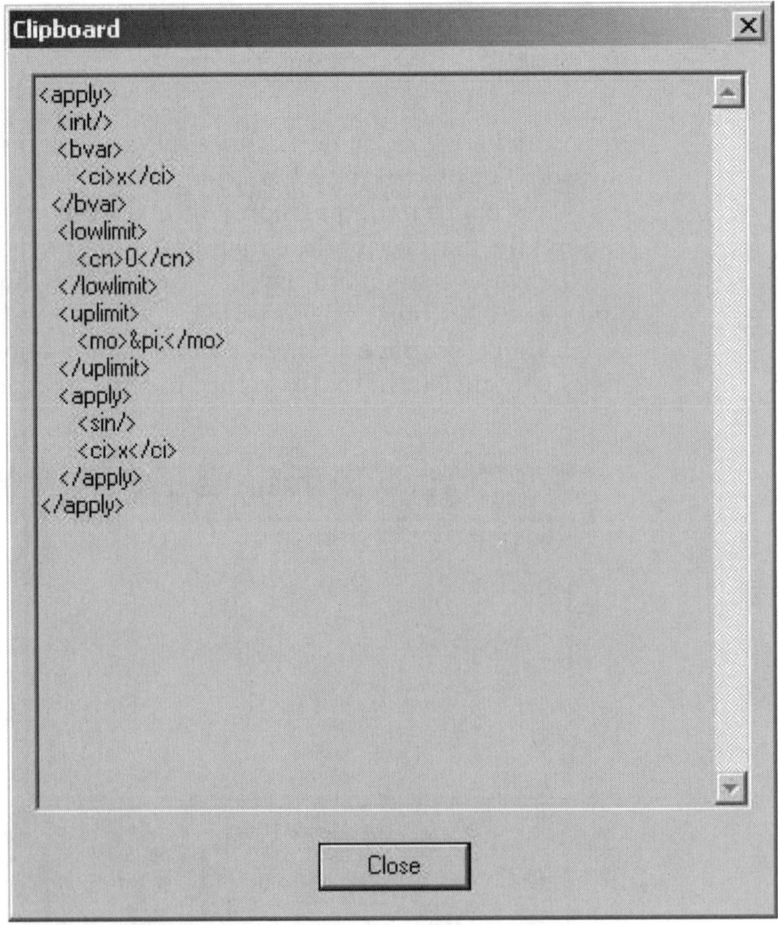

FIGURE 9.24 The *EzMath* Clipboard window.

9.9 CHOOSING AN AUTHORING TOOL

We have described the features of several different applications that you can use to author MathML. However, this variety can be confusing for an author trying to decide which application to use. This section evaluates the strengths and limitations of the different MathML authoring applications, so you can decide which one is best suited to your needs.

The MathML authoring tools can be broadly classified into three groups, in increasing order of complexity and cost. At the low end of the spectrum are *Amaya* and *EzMath*, which offer minimal features but are freely available. *Amaya* can be used for authoring presentation MathML and *EzMath* for content MathML. These applications don't provide many frills and features, but they are simple low-cost options for somebody who just wants to experiment with MathML and does not need to author a large number of equations.

The next category of tools is suitable for authors who produce a greater volume of technical content and already have a familiar application for producing their documents such as Microsoft *Word*. For such authors, *MathType* and *WebEQ* are good solutions. *MathType* is, of course, ideal for *Word* users, both for inserting individual formulas into a document and for converting the eventual document into HTML+MathML format for displaying on the Web. *MathType* provides excellent support for controlling the fine details of typeset equations in a *Word* document, such as alignment, spacing, and automatic numbering. However, *MathType* cannot produce content MathML and is unsuitable for large-scale processing of multiple documents.

WebEQ is more versatile and powerful than *MathType*, at least as far as their MathML capabilities are concerned. *WebEQ* lacks some features, found in *MathType*, specifically for integrating equations into a word-processing document. However, it is well suited for Web developers who want to create and maintain interactive Web sites that feature mathematical content. This is because *WebEQ* offers a whole suite of tools not just for authoring MathML but for processing documents and for adding interactive equations to a Web site. In addition to the Editor and Publisher applications discussed in this chapter, *WebEQ* includes two Java applets called Viewer Control and Input Control for displaying interactive equations and authoring mathematical notation in a Web page, respectively. The Viewer Control and Input Control components of *WebEQ* are covered in detail in Section 12.3.

The last category of MathML authoring tools consists of applications like *Mathematica*, *Publicon*, and *Scientific Word*, which provide a full-featured document-authoring solution. They can be used to create complete documents that integrate text, equations, graphics, and other elements. Using a menu command, you can then convert the document into HTML+MathML format for display on the Web.

Publicon and *Mathematica* both provide support for authoring individual MathML expressions as well as complete documents. *Publicon* includes document palettes for authoring papers in the style of specific journals and has a more elaborate graphical interface for applying styles and creating mathematical notation. *Mathematica*, on the other hand, is a full-fledged computer algebra system, and using it just for authoring MathML is like using a sledgehammer to crack a nut. However, *Mathematica* is an excellent authoring tool for people who create a large volume of technical documents. The only downside of *Mathematica* is that it is relatively expensive. It is, however, available on more affordable terms through a company-wide

TABLE 9.1 Features of MathML Authoring Tools

Product	Presentation MathML	Content MathML	Customizable Output[1]	Individual Formulas	Complete Documents	Price[2]
MathType	√	×	√	√	×	$129
WebEQ	√	√	√	√	×	$495
Mathematica	√	√	√	√	√	$1895
Publicon	√	√	×	√	√	$150
Scientific Word	√	×	×	×	√	$550
Amaya	√	×	×	√	×	Free
EzMath	×	√	×	√	×	Free

1. The Customizable Output column indicates whether a given application can be used to create MathML output with specific namespace information or declarations, so the output can be tailored to a specific rendering application, like *Mozilla* or *IE* with *MathPlayer*.

2. The prices listed are suggested retail prices for an individual commercial license. Most of these products are also available at lower prices for academic users or under volume discounts. Check with the specific vendors for details.

or campus-wide license and is hence a good solution for adoption by an entire organization.

Table 9.1 summarizes the various features of all the products discussed in this chapter.

CHAPTER

10

CONVERTING BETWEEN TEX AND MATHML

This chapter reviews the tools and techniques available for converting TEX-based documents into XHTML+MathML and vice versa. The tools discussed include *WebEQ*, itex2mml, TEX4ht, TtM, and xmltex.

10.1 Introduction

TEX (pronounced "tek") is a text-processing system that makes it easy to create professionally formatted documents. Donald Knuth, a computer scientist at Stanford University, created TEX. Knuth was dissatisfied with the quality of the typesetting in his published book, *The Art of Computer Programming*. To remedy the limitations of the manual typesetting processes in use at the time (the middle 1970s), Knuth resolved to create a program that would allow documents to be typeset electronically. He first started work on TEX in 1977, and the first version was completed in 1979. Knuth continued to develop and refine TEX until 1990, when he officially declared the source code to be frozen.

Today, TEX is widely used in many contexts where high-quality printed output is important. TEX provides a set of commands for specifying the precise details of a document's typeset appearance. There are commands, for example, to insert a fixed amount of vertical or horizontal space, to determine the indentation of paragraphs or the alignment of text, to specify the font style, and so on. TEX automatically handles many subtle details of typesetting, such as the kerning or ligature of fonts, hyphenation, and linebreaking. However, the author can also control each of these properties explicitly by using specific TEX commands.

The process of creating a document using TEX involves several steps. The author first creates a plain text document called the source file, which contains TEX commands along with the content of the document. This source file is then processed by the TEX program, which interprets then TEX commands in the file to produce a device-independent (DVI) file as the output. DVI is a page-description language, similar to PostScript, for specifying the exact details of how text should be laid out on the page. The DVI file can be either rendered on the screen, using a viewer program, or converted to PostScript for printing. This process can be less convenient than using a word processor with a WYSIWYG graphical interface for formatting documents. However, the extra steps involved in creating documents with TEX are more than justified by the greater degree of control and flexibility a user has over the form of the printed output.

A given TEX source file produces exactly the same output regardless of the type of computer or operating system the author uses. This makes TEX highly portable and platform independent, which is one key reason it appeals to technical authors. Implementations of TEX are freely available for all major computer platforms. In addition, many free and commercial applications for working with TEX, including editors, viewers, and font utilities, are available.

TEX is a large and complex system with a number of files and utility programs that interact with each other in complicated ways. An experienced TEX user can customize the system to create virtually any typographic effect or style desired. In practice, most TEX authors use a standard macro package, such as Plain TEX or LATEX for authoring documents. Each of these packages uses the primitives or low-level commands of TEX to implement a set of high-level commands that provide an easier interface for creating specific types of formatted output.

LATEX, for example, includes commands for creating tables of contents, indexes, citations, cross-references, numbered sections, numbered equations, and so on. TEX does not directly support these types of elements. An individual author or publisher can also create specific style files to define the style of a particular type of document. By using a macro package in combination with one or more style files, a user can create complex documents formatted according to a specific style, without having to know the technical details of TEX. In the rest of this chapter, we use the term TEX to refer to documents authored using any TEX package, such as Plain TEX, LATEX, or AMS-TEX. The term "LATEX" is used when we make comments that apply specifically to LATEX documents.

TEX and MathML

TEX provides special commands for entering many different types of mathematical constructs, such as fractions, square roots, subscripts, and superscripts, as well as the large number of special characters and symbols important in mathematical notation. TEX automatically applies the various rules and conventions of mathematical typesetting, such as using different styles and spacing for numbers, identifiers, and operators.

Using TEX, an author can type in complicated mathematical formulas quickly and easily using characters present on any standard keyboard. Then, the TEX program processes the formulas and converts them into beautiful-looking typeset equations. This combination of simplicity in authoring and excellence in typographic output has made TEX a popular tool among the majority of physicists, mathematicians, and other researchers who produce complex technical documents. Most physics and mathematics journals specify TEX as their preferred submission format and use TEX extensively in their internal production processes.

Although TEX and MathML can both be used as markup languages for describing mathematics, they have many points of contrast. TEX is compact, while MathML is verbose. TEX is intended for authoring by humans, while MathML is best generated using software tools. TEX can describe only the appearance of mathematical formulas, while MathML can also describe their symbolic meaning. TEX is intended for producing printed output, while MathML is primarily for displaying mathematics in Web pages.

For all these reasons, TEX and MathML have a complementary role, and authors can use one or the other depending on the context. As MathML use becomes more widespread, conversion between TEX and MathML will become increasingly important. In particular, authors and publishers will need to convert the vast number of TEX-based documents stored in scientific databases into HTML or XHTML (with embedded MathML) for deployment on the Web.

An author who wants to convert a TEX document into a Web document that contains MathML has two main options:

- Convert individual mathematical formulas in the document from TEX to MathML. The resulting MathML markup can then be pasted into an HTML document (produced using some other application) to produce a complete document that can be displayed in a Web browser.
- Convert the entire TEX document into HTML or XHTML with all formulas converted into MathML. This approach is clearly convenient for large-scale conversion of complete documents.

We shall see examples of both types of conversions in this chapter.

Most TEX constructs can be easily mapped to equivalent presentation MathML elements. For example, the `\frac` and `\sqrt` commands in LATEX correspond to the `mfrac` and `msqrt` elements in MathML. However, there are two types of problems in using software for translating TEX to MathML. One is that complicated TEX constructs, especially those involving user-defined macros, are not so easy to interpret. Another problem arises with scripted expressions like `$(a+b)^2$`. When a program that parses formulas in linear order encounters a superscript, the program may no longer have information about where the base expression begins. Hence, the program might not be able to translate an expression like `$(a+b)^2$` into the corresponding `<msup>...</msup>` element in MathML.

It is useful to keep these issues in mind while you are trying out the software tools discussed in the rest of this chapter. Most of the tools for converting between TEX and MathML are still at an early stage of development, mainly because MathML itself is relatively new. Hence, you may need to do some trial and error to fine-tune your results and get documents that are viewable on the Web in the way you want. However, these tools are under active development, so you can expect rapid progress as far as the range of TEX constructs that can be translated and in the quality of the output.

10.2 ENTERING FORMULAS IN LATEX

As mentioned earlier in this chapter, most authors use a macro package such as LATEX for preparing documents. LATEX provides a number of high-level commands for entering mathematical notation. These commands make LATEX a very compact and expressive markup language for describing mathematical expressions. This section provides a quick review of the LATEX syntax for entering formulas.

In LATEX, there are two main modes for displaying mathematics:

- Math mode: for formulas embedded in text. To enter formulas in this mode, you enclose them in `$...$`, `\(...\)`, or `\begin{math}...\end{math}`.
- Display math mode: for formulas shown in a separate paragraph and in the center of the page. To enter formulas in this mode, you enclose them in `$$...$$`, `\[...\]`, or `\begin{displaymath}...\end{displaymath}`.

In addition, a variant of the display math mode, called equation mode, automatically adds a number to the equation. In this mode, you indicate formulas by wrapping them in the text `\begin{equation}...\end{equation}`.

The following sections cover some of the commands for common mathematical constructs.

Scripts and Indices

The caret (^) is used for superscripts, and the underscore (_) for subscripts:

$r^2 = x_1^2 + x_2^2 + x_3^2$

```
$r^2 = x_1^2 + x_2^2 + x_3^2$
```

You can display multiple script indices as shown below:

T^{a}_{bc}

`$T^{a}_{bc}$`

In the above expression, the base is followed by pairs of matched subscripts and superscripts. The members of each pair appear vertically aligned in the displayed expression.

The order of the subscript or superscript within the pair is not relevant. For example, the above tensor can also be represented as follows:

T_{bc}^{a}

`$T_{bc}^{a}$`

Fractions and Radicals

Fractions are represented by the command `\frac{} {}`, where the first argument is the numerator and the second is the denominator. Here is an example:

$$\frac{x}{y}$$

`$\frac{x}{y}$`

Square roots are represented by `\sqrt{}`, as shown here:

$\sqrt{x+1}$

`$\sqrt{x+1}$`

The optional argument can be used to indicate roots other than square roots. For example, a cube root would be written as shown below:

$\sqrt[3]{x+1}$

`$\sqrt[3]{x+1}$`

Operators and Symbols

A large number of extended characters and mathematical symbols have special names. They can be inserted using a command of the form *name*. The list of supported characters includes uppercase and lowercase Greek letters as well as operators, arrows, and other symbols. Table 10.1 shows some examples of LaTeX commands for special characters.

Several packages, such as `amsymb`, define additional symbols used in specialized areas of mathematics. You can insert these symbols in a document by loading the appropriate package.

TABLE 10.1 LATEX Commands for Special Characters

Character	LATEX Command
π	`\pi`
Γ	`\Gamma`
∞	`\infty`
$\rightarrow$	`\rightarrow`
$\leq$	`\leq`
$\cup$	`\cup`
$\bigcup$	`\bigcup`
$\subseteq$	`\subseteq`

LATEX includes commands, such as `\sin`, `\cos`, `\exp`, and `\log`, to represent common functions. The names of such functions are displayed in an upright font and an extra space is added before their arguments.

The commands `\int`, `\sum`, and `\product` represent the integral, summation, and product symbols, respectively. You can specify the upper and lower limits for these symbols using the standard ^ and _ notation used for subscripts and superscripts. These operators are displayed differently depending on whether you choose math mode or display math mode. In math mode, the symbol appears smaller and the limits are shown as subscripts and superscripts. In display math mode, the symbol is shown in a slightly larger size and the limits are shown as underscripts and overscripts.

Here is an example of an integral in math mode:

$\int_0^\pi \sin(x)\,dx$

```
$\int_0^\pi {\sin(x)\thinsp dx}$
```

Here is the same integral shown in display math mode:

$$\int_0^\pi \sin(x)\,dx$$

```
$$\int_0^\pi {\sin(x)\thinsp dx}$$
```

In the above examples, the `\thinsp` command inserts a thin space between the function and the differential, which is conventional for integrals. You can insert blank spaces of specified sizes using the commands `\negthinsp`, `\thinsp`, `\medsp`, `\thicksp`, `\quad`, and `\qquad`. The first four of these can also be entered using the equivalent shorthand notation `\!`, `\,`, `\:`, and `\;`.

The command `\space`{h} {d} {w} inserts a blank space of height h, depth d, and width w. The command `\phantom` renders its contents invisibly. The `\space` and `\phantom` commands correspond to the MathML elements `mspace` and `mphantom`, respectively.

Delimiters and Accents

You can use the commands `\left` and `\right` before delimiters, such as parentheses, brackets, and braces. This makes the delimiters stretchable, so they automatically expand to cover their contents. Note that to use curly brackets as delimiters, you must escape them as \{ and \}, since by default they are interpreted as enclosing arguments.

The following example uses `\left` and `\right` to indicate delimiters:

$$\left(\frac{1}{1+x^2}\right)^5$$

```
$\left(\frac{1}{1+x^2}\right )^5$
```

The commands `\bar`, `\hat`, `\check`, `\tilde`, `\vec`, and `\dot` place an accent with a one-character width over their argument, as shown here:

$\bar{A}$	`\bar{A}`
$\hat{A}$	`\hat{A}`
$\check{A}$	`\check{A}`
$\tilde{A}$	`\tilde{A}`
$\vec{A}$	`\vec{A}`
$\dot{A}$	`\dot{A}`

To make the first five of these accents stretchable, use their wide versions: `\widebar{}`, `\widehat{}`, `\widecheck{}`, `\widetilde{}`, and `\widevec{}`.

To place a stretchable brace over or under an expression, use the commands `\overbrace{}` and `\underbrace{}`. The commands `\overset{}{}` and `\underset{}{}` place the first argument over the second argument. You can also enter lowered, centered, diagonal, and vertical ellipses using the commands `\ldots`, `\cdots`, `\ddots`, and `\vdots`, respectively.

Here is an example involving a centered ellipse:

$$\overset{n\ terms}{\overbrace{1+2+\cdots+n}}$$

```
\overset{\text{$n$terms}}{\overbrace{1+2+\cdots+n}}
```

TABLE 10.2 Commands Used in Math Mode

Style	TEX Name	Rendering
Roman	\mathrm{ABC}	ABC
Italic	\mathit{ABC}	ABC
Bold	\mathbf{ABC}	$\mathbf{ABC}$
Fraktur	\mathfr{ABC}	$\mathfrak{ABC}$
Sans serif	\mathsf{ABC}	ABC
Typewriter	\mathtt{ABC}	$\mathtt{ABC}$
Calligraphic	\mathcal{ABC}	$\mathcal{ABC}$

Entering Text

You can enter text in math mode in a specific style by using one of the commands shown in Table 10.2.

You can also insert text in the middle of an equation using the `\text{}` command, which is similar to the MathML element `mtext`.

Matrices, Tables, and Arrays

Matrices, tables, and arrays are represented using the `\array{}` command. The elements of the array are specified in its argument using a double backslash (`\\`) to separate rows and an ampersand (`&`) to separate any two entries in a row, as you can see here:

$$\begin{pmatrix} a & b \\ c & d \end{pmatrix}$$

```
$\left(\array{a & b \\c & d}\right$
```

In the above example, the `\left` and `\right` commands are used to place stretchable brackets around the elements of the matrix.

10.3 Converting Individual Formulas

Now that we have reviewed the basic features of LATEX syntax and noted some similarities and differences with MathML, let's look at specific tools for converting LATEX formulas into MathML.

WebEQ

The *WebEQ* Publisher application provides a convenient way of creating Web pages that contain MathML. This application allows you to use the WebTEX language for authoring mathematical notation. WebTEX is a markup language for describing mathematics that was developed by Design Science. WebTEX markup is simple enough to author directly by hand and can be readily converted into MathML. This makes WebTEX a convenient input method for authoring MathML, especially for users who are already familiar with the LATEX syntax for mathematical formulas.

For information on how to create an HTML+MathML file starting with a document that contains WebTEX markup, see the description of *WebEQ* Publisher in Section 9.3. *WebEQ* Publisher is a Java application that takes a source file that contains WebTEX equations and produces an HTML file with all the equations automatically converted either to Viewer Control applet tags or to MathML, depending on your preference.

The WebTEX Language

The syntax of WebTEX is almost identical to that of LATEX. However, there are some differences. For example, in LATEX the `\sqrt` command is used to indicate any type of root or radical. Hence, the cube root of x would be indicated as shown below:

$$\sqrt[3]{x}$$

```
$\sqrt[3]{x+1}$
```

In WebTEX, the same expression would be written as:

```
$\root{x}{3}$
```

The WebTEX expression is clearly much easier to translate into MathML since it has the same structure as the MathML `mroot` element.

Another area in which WebTEX commands differ from those of LATEX is when you are entering tables and matrices. In WebTEX, as in LATEX, matrices are entered using the `\array` command, as shown below:

$$\begin{pmatrix} 1 & 2 \\ 3 & 4 \end{pmatrix}$$

```
$\left(\array{1 & 2 \\3 & 4}\right$
```

However, WebTEX provides a set of options that make it easier to control various features of the array. To use these options, you must specify the command `\arrayopts{}` as the first argument of `\array{}`. The `\arrayopts{}` command can have as arguments one or more options, each controlling a specific property of the array.

For example, the options `\colalign` and `\rowalign` determine the alignment of columns and rows, respectively. Possible values for

`\colalign` are `left`, `right`, and `center`. Possible values for `\rowalign` are `top`, `bottom`, `center`, and `axis`. Here is an example:

$$\begin{pmatrix} 1 & x+1 & x^2+1 \\ x^2-1 & x-1 & 1 \end{pmatrix}$$

```
\array{\arrayopts{\colalign{left left right}}
1 & x+1 & x^2+1 \\x^2-1 & x-1 & 1}
```

The option `\equalrows{true}` causes all rows in the array to have the same height, while `\equalcolumns{true}` causes all columns to have the same width. However, if either of these options is set to the default value, `false`, each row or column is adjusted to fit the entry with the largest height or width. The options `\rowlines{}` and `\collines{}` determine if a line is drawn between any two rows or columns, while `\frame` determines if a frame is drawn around the entire array. The possible values for all these options are `solid`, `dashed`, and `none`.

These array options in WebTEX correspond directly to attributes of the `mtable`, `mtr`, and `mtd` elements in MathML—namely `rowalign`, `columnalign`, `rowspacing`, `columnspacing`, `rowlines`, `columnlines`, and `frame`. This makes it easy to translate tables in WebTEX syntax into MathML. In contrast, specifying properties of tables in LATEX requires more complicated commands that do not fit well with the structure of MathML.

WebTEX also includes a few commands that allow for interactivity in equations:

- The command `\href`{*url*} {*expr*} can be used to turn an equation into a hyperlink. The first argument is the URL to be followed, and the second is the expression that should appear as a link.
- The command `\statusline`{*message*} {*expr*} causes the text of *message* to be displayed in the status line of the browser when the cursor is moved over the expression *expr*.
- The command `\fghighlight`{*color*} {*expr*} causes the expression *expr* to be displayed in a different color when the cursor is moved over it. The color is specified in six-digit hexadecimal notation; for example, `#ff0000` for red.
- The command `\toggle`{*expr1*} {*expr2*} {*prompt1*} {*prompt2*} can be used to toggle between two different expressions. Initially, *expr1* is displayed in the Web page and *prompt1* appears in the browser status line; however, clicking the expression using the left mouse button causes *expr2* to be displayed in the browser window and *prompt2* in the status line.

When you translate WebT$_E$X markup into MathML using *WebEQ* Publisher, as explained in Section 9.3, these commands get converted into `maction` elements. They can then be displayed in browsers as *WebEQ* applets. For details on using `maction` elements in *WebEQ* to get interactive behavior, see Section 12.3.

WebT$_E$X also allows you to define macros to create shorthand notation for commands that you use frequently. A macro is specified using the command

```
\define{expr1}{expr2}
```

where the first argument is the name of the macro and the second argument is the expression that the macro represents.

Example 10.1 shows a simple HTML file that contains WebTeX markup.

Example 10.1 An HTML document called calculus.html that contains WebT$_E$X equations.

```
<html>
 <head ><title>Calculus</title></head>
   <body>
     <h1>Fundamental Theorems of Calculus</h1>
<p>The first fundamental theorem of calculus states that,
if $f$is continuous on the closed interval $[a, b]$and
$F$is the antiderivative (indefinite integral) of $f$on
$[a, b]$, then </p>

<p>\[\int _{a}^{b}f(x) \DifferentialD x=F(b)−F(a)\]</p>

<p>The second fundamental theorem of calculus holds that if
$f$is a continuous function on an open interval $I$$a$any
point in $I$, and if $F$is defined by </p>

<p>\[\int _{a}^{b}f(x)\DifferentialD x=F(b)−F(a)\]</p>

<p>then $F(x)=f(x)$at each point in $I$. </p>

<p>The fundamental theorem of calculus along curves states
that if $f(z)$has a continuous antiderivative $F(z)$in
a region $R$containing a parameterized curve $\gamma:
z=z(t)$for $\alpha \leq t \leq \beta$, then</p>

<p>\[{{\int}_{\gamma}}f(z)\DifferentialD z=F(z(\beta))
−F(z(\alpha))\]</p>

   </body>
</html>
```

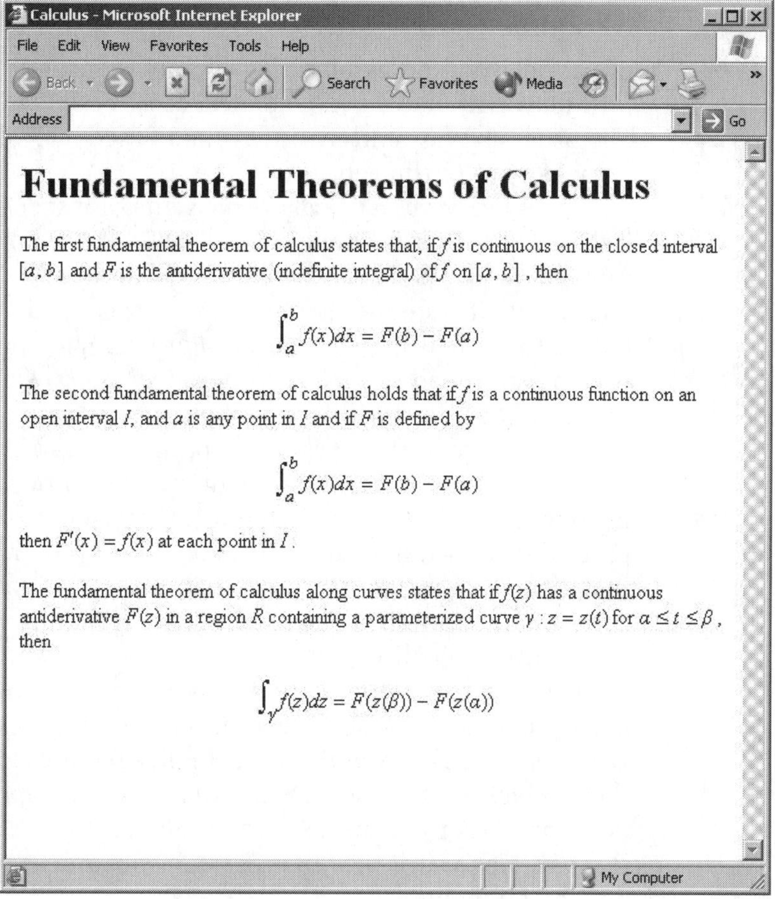

FIGURE 10.1 Viewing the document produced by processing calculus.html in *IE*.

If you process this file using *WebEQ* Publisher, you get an output document in which all the WebTEX equations have been translated to MathML. You can also set an option to automatically insert a reference to the Universal MathML stylesheet. The resulting output file can then be viewed in *IE*.

Note that the output file may not contain well-formed XHTML, so it cannot be viewed in *Mozilla*. In order to view the file in *Mozilla*, you may have to first convert the file into XHTML using the free utility Tidy. As discussed in Section 7.3, Tidy is a C program for converting HTML files into XHTML.

Figure 10.1 shows the document produced by processing the document calculus.html in *WebEQ* Publisher. The resulting document contains MathML equations that can be rendered in *IE* using *MathPlayer*.

itex2mml

itex2mml is a freely available C program that converts mathematical formulas written in a special dialect of TEX called itex into MathML. The program was written and is maintained by Paul Gartside of the University of Pittsburgh.

itex is like WebTEX, a LATEX-like syntax for specifying mathematical notation. itex is a superset of WebTEX; any command that you can use in WebTEX is also a valid itex command. The main difference is that itex defines some extra commands that use the natural names for some LATEX commands. For example, in itex you can use `\infinity` instead of `\infty` to describe the ∞ symbol and `\Union` instead of `\bigcup` for the $\cup$ symbol.

To create a Web page that contains MathML using itex2mml, you first prepare the HTML document as you normally would and include all mathematical formulas using the itex syntax. You then process this document using the itex2mml program. This program replaces every instance of itex markup in the document into the corresponding MathML equation, leaving all other text in the document unchanged.

You can download an archive that contains the files for itex2mml from the following URL: *http://pear.math.pitt.edu/mathzilla/itex2mml.html*. This contains precompiled binaries for the Linux platform as well as raw C source files that can be compiled for any other platform. To convert an HTML document into an XHTML document that contains MathML, you process the document using a command like the following:

```
itex2MML < input.xml > output.xml
```

This reads input from a file called input.xml and writes the output to a file called output.xml. In order to view the document in *Mozilla*, you might need to run Tidy on the document to convert it into a well-formed XHTML document, as discussed in Section 7.3.

Since itex2mml is a C program, you can easily configure it to run on a Web server and to process input submitted to it from a Web page. This type of setup has been implemented at the following URL: *http://pear.math.pitt.edu/mathzilla/itex2mmlFrag.html*. This Web page contains a text area in which you can paste a sample HTML document that contains itex equations. When you click a button, the text you entered is submitted to the server, it's processed using itex2mml, and the resulting output is returned back to the Web page. You can either see the source of the resulting HTML+MathML

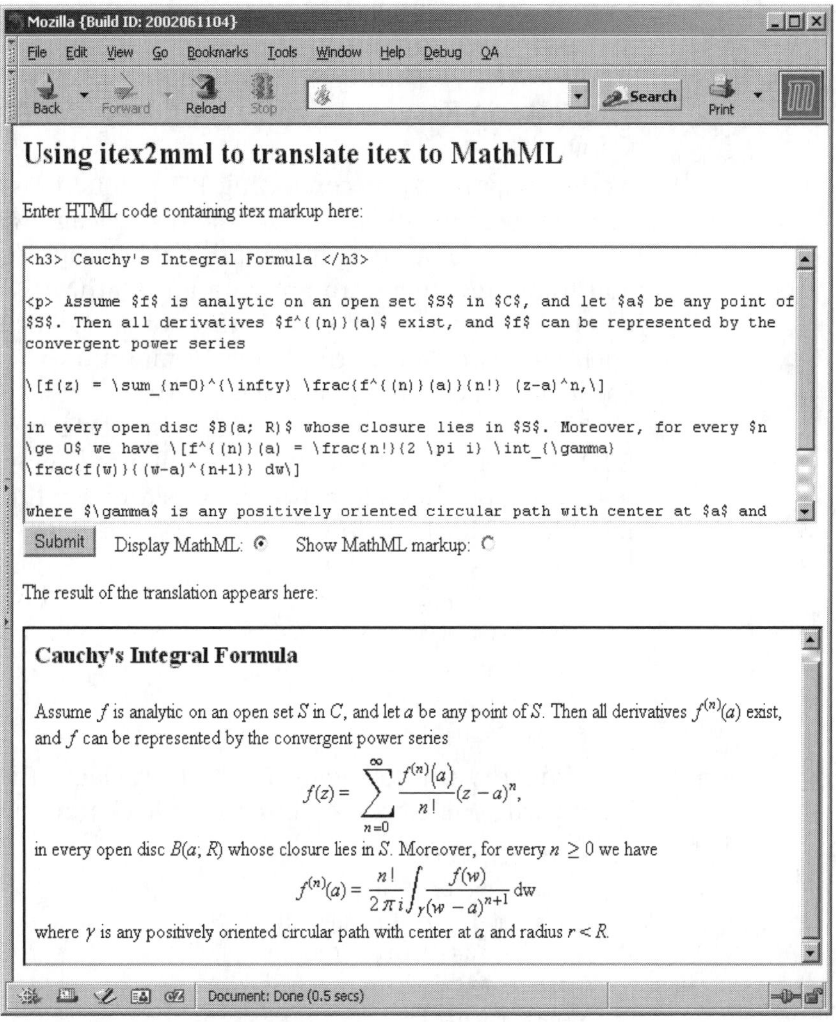

FIGURE 10.2 Submitting the text of an HTML file that contains itex equations for processing using itex2mml.

file or display the file in the same Web page. This process is demonstrated in Figure 10.2.

Alternatively, you can upload your input document and submit it to the server from the following Web page: *http://pear.math.pitt.edu/mathzilla/itex2mmlFile.html*. This page allows you specify a sample HTML file, which contains itex markup, located on your computer. When you click a button, the file is uploaded to the server, it's processed using itex2mml, and the resulting output is returned back to the Web page. You can either see the raw text of the resulting

XHTML+MathML file in the same Web page or download the file and save it on your computer.

The Ontario Research Centre for Computer Algebra (ORCCA) Converter

Another approach to converting LaTeX equations to MathML has been adopted by Stephen Watt and his colleagues at ORCCA. They have developed a Java program that takes LaTeX equations as input and translates them into presentation MathML. The translation is determined by a map file, which contains a collection of templates. Each template defines the MathML markup that corresponds to a particular type of TeX construct.

The map file is written in a specific XML syntax, for which a DTD is provided. For example, the following template replaces the opening parenthesis in a TeX expression with the `<mo>(</mo>` element in MathML:

```
<pat:template>
 <pat:tex op="("/>
 <pat:mml op="(">
   <mo>(</mo>
 </pat:mml>
</pat:template>
```

Similarly, the following template replaces the TeX command `\alpha` with the corresponding Unicode character:

```
<pat:template>
 <pat:tex op="\alpha"/>
 <pat:mml op="&#x03B1;">
   <mo> &#x03B1; </mo>
 </pat:mml>
</pat:template>
```

All the elements defined for use in the map file have the namespace prefix `pat`. Each template is represented by a `pat:template` element. The `pat:tex` element, via its `op` attribute, specifies a particular TeX command to which the template applies. The `pat:mml` element defines the MathML markup that corresponds to a TeX command. A user can edit the templates in the map file, for example, to specify a different set of notational preference. Details about the syntax of the map file and the various elements and attributes it can contain are given at *www.orcca.on.ca/mathml/texmml/MapSpecWeb.html.*

This conversion process is very similar to the XSLT transformations discussed in Chapter 8. The map file plays the role of the XSLT stylesheet, and the Java program that does the transformations is

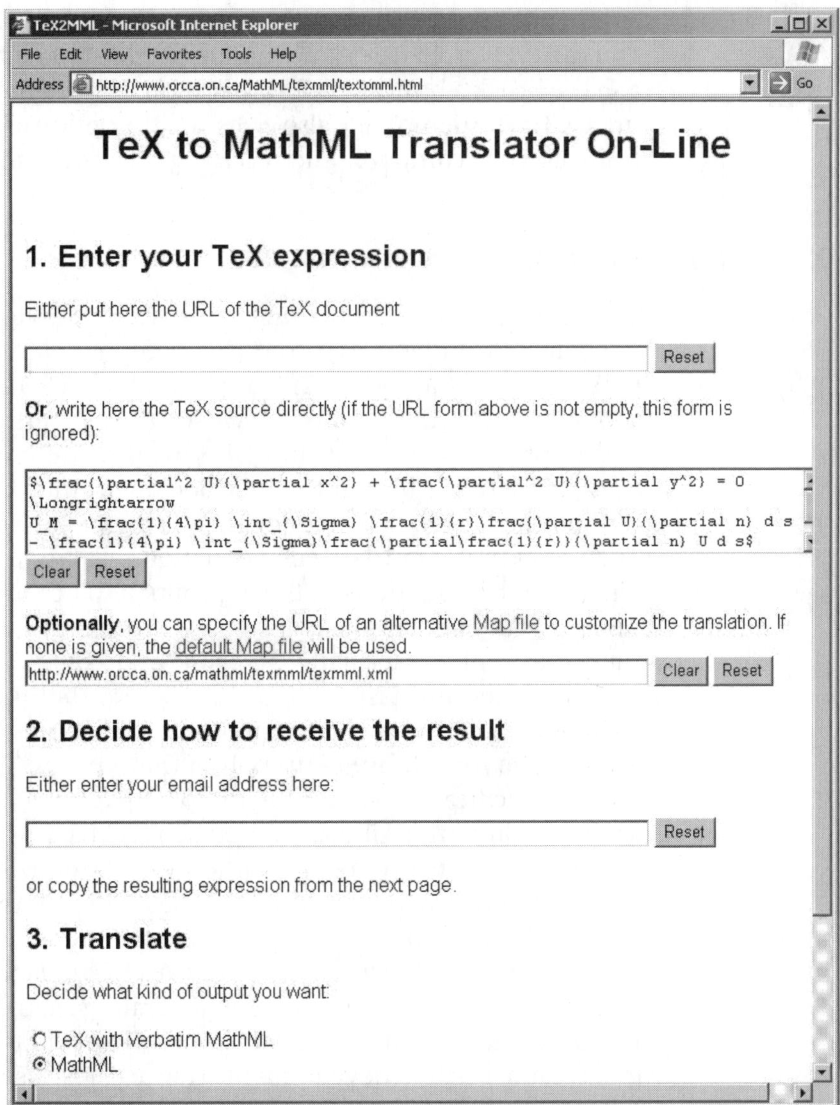

FIGURE 10.3 Converting LaTeX equations into MathML using the online converter at ORCCA.

like an XSLT processor. The difference is, of course, that XSLT stylesheets can be applied only to well-formed XML documents, while the map file and Java program used here have been specially defined for use with TEX documents, which do not conform to XML syntax.

By specifying an appropriate map file, you can use a Java program to process LaTeX equations and translate them into the corresponding MathML. An online demo of the ORCCA converter is available at the following URL: *www.orcca.on.ca/mathml/texmml/textomml.html*. You can type in a particular equation in TEX syntax into the text area and then click a button to view the result in the same Web page (Figure 10.3). The demo page also gives you the option of uploading a TEX file from your computer and receiving the output in a separate file.

10.4 Converting Complete Documents

The tools discussed so far make it easy to convert into MathML individual formulas in TEX or LATEX syntax. You can use any of these tools to convert an entire TEX paper into an HTML document that contains MathML equations. However, the conversion involves several steps, each of which must be handled differently. First, you must convert the text in the TEX document into HTML using one of the other tools available for this purpose, such as LATEX2HTML. Then, you must translate each equation into MathML individually and paste the equations at the appropriate place in the HTML document. Following all the steps in the process can be laborious and time-consuming, especially for large and complex documents. A much simpler and faster option is to use a tool that can translate a complete TEX or LATEX document into HTML and MathML in one go. The two most prominent tools of this type are TEX4ht and TtM.

We specifically omit discussion of LATEX2HTML, a popular program for converting LATEX documents to HTML. This is because there is currently no ready-made solution for customizing LATEX2HTML, so it converts mathematical formulas into MathML instead of images. A trial project for doing this was initiated by Russ Moore in 1998 (see *www.geom.umn.edu/~ross/webtex/webtex* for details). He developed a prototype method for generating MathML output from LATEX2HTML, by using Perl subroutines. However, this project is no longer under active development. Hence, most users who want to convert LATEX documents into HTML+MathML will find it much easier to use TEX4ht or TtM instead.

TEX4ht

TEX4ht, developed by Eitan Gurari of Ohio State University, is a powerful and versatile system for converting TEX documents into HTML or XML formats. In its default mode, TEX4ht converts a TEX or LATEX document into HTML with all mathematical formulas saved as images. However, TEX4ht can be readily configured to produce other document types such as XHTML, DocBook, or Text Encoding

Initiative (TEI). It can also convert formulas present in the original document into MathML instead of images.

The TEX4ht system has two main components: a set of style files and a postprocessor. The process of converting a TEX document takes place in two stages: first, TEX processes the original document using the style files provided by TEX4ht. The result is a DVI file that contains "hooks" or special instructions meant for the TEX4ht postprocessor. In the next stage, the postprocessor acts on the DVI file and interprets the hooks in the file to produce the final output.

Since TEX itself handles the conversion from the original TEX document to the DVI file, TEX4ht has access to the full power of TEX for typesetting the document. In particular, TEX4ht can use TEX's capabilities for handling fonts, macros, variables, and so on to control the form of the output. TEX4ht can also handle most user-defined macros that occur in a LATEX document.

TEX4ht has a number of nice features. You can place separate sections of the LATEX document on separate Web pages, with appropriate hyperlinks connecting them. You can also create HTML versions of tables of contents, bibliographies, and so on. *The LATEX Web Companion* by Michel Goossens and Sebastian Rahtz (see Appendix B for details) provides detailed instructions on customizing the output of TEX4ht.

For converting TEX documents into XHTML+MathML documents, you do not have to customize TEX4ht yourself, since most of the work has already been done. Paul Gartside of the University of Pittsburgh has created a modified form of TEX4ht called TEX4moz. This contains some additional scripts and configuration files that customize the output of TEX4ht to produce XHTML+MathML files that can be displayed by *Mozilla*. More information on TEX4moz is given on Gartside's Mathzilla Web site: *http://pear.math.pitt.edu/mathzilla*.

Installing TEX4ht

Since TEX4ht uses TEX to handle the first stage of processing the source document, you must have a working installation of TEX already present on your system. If you do not already have TEX installed, you can download all the relevant files from the TEX User's Group Web site: *www.tug.org*. This site also contains a wealth of information on all aspects of TEX, ranging from tutorials for beginners to specialized information for more advanced users.

On Windows

To install TEX4moz on Windows, follow these steps:

1. Download $\TeX$4moz. You can get the Windows version in zipped form at the following URL: *http://pear.math.pitt.edu/mathzilla/tex4mozDownload.html.*
2. Create a directory called `c:\tex4ht` and unzip all the files into this directory.
3. Modify the files `tex4ht.env` and `moz4ht.env` by editing the lines starting with `tc:\path\tfm!` to specify the directories in which the `tfm` files of $\TeX$ are located on your machine. For example, if you are using Mik$\TeX$, which has `tfm` files in `c:/texmf/fonts/tfm`, change the above line in each `.env` file to `tc:\texmf\fonts\tfm\!`. The ! at the end of the line indicates that $\TeX$4ht should search all subdirectories of the specified path for the font metric files.
4. Rename the `htlatex.tab`, `httex.tab`, `mztex.tab`, and `mzlatex.tab` files to change the file extension from `.tab` to `.bat`.
5. Add the `c:\tex4ht` directory to your path. To do this on Windows 2000/XP, open the System control panel, click the Advanced tab, click the Environment Variables button, select Path in the list of system variables, and click Edit. In the dialog that comes up, add `c:\tex4ht` as one of the values of the Path variable, and then click OK.
6. Move `tex4ht.sty` and all the '.4ht' files to the `c:\tex4ht` directory. Alternatively, you can modify the environment variable TEXINPUTS to point to `c:\tex4ht`, using the same procedure outlined in Step 5.

On Unix

There are two ways of installing $\TeX$4ht on Unix. You can install it in your local directory, in which case it is available for use only by you. Alternatively, if you have root access, you can do a root installation, in which case the program will be available to all users who have access to that machine. The installation on Unix requires the following steps:

1. Download the archive that contains the package files.
2. Untar and decompress the archive.
3. Run the installer.

For a local installation, one additional step is required. You need to modify the value of the environment variables PATH and TEXINPUTS so that they point to the directory in which the $\TeX$4moz files are installed. You can change the value of these variables by editing your configuration file.

Unlike on Windows, there is no need to change the file extensions of any files. You can get the zipped files as well as the detailed installation instructions at the following URL: *http://pear.math.pitt.edu/mathzilla/tex4mozDownload.html*.

Running TEX4ht

To process a document using TEX4ht, you run a command of the following form:

```
mzlatex filename
```

The output file is specially optimized for viewing in *Mozilla*. It is an XHTML file, contains a DOCTYPE declaration to the XHTML DTD, and has a .xml file extension. Hence, this file cannot be rendered in *IE*. However, you can easily modify the file so it is viewable in *IE* using either *MathPlayer* or IBM *techexplorer*. Just add a statement that references the Universal MathML stylesheet, as explained in Section 7.2.

Let us look at an example of using TEX4ht to translate a TEX document into XHTML+MathML. Example 10.2 shows a LATEX document that contains some mathematical formulas.

Example 10.2 A LATEX document called article.tex that contains inline and display equations.

```
\documentclass{article}
\begin{document}
\title{Electronic Structure of a Two-Dimensional Metal}
\maketitle
The effect of the magnetic field can be included in
the electronic structure calculation by using the
Peierls substitution $$t_l\rightarrow t_l e^{i{2\pi \over
\phi_o}\int_{i,j}^{i',j'}{\bf A}\cdot d{\bf l}}$$
where $\phi_o=hc/e$and $\bf A$are the flux quantum and the
vector potential, respectively.

For simplicity, we choose the Landau gauge ${\bf
A}=-B(y,0,0)$. By following a standard procedure, we
rewrite the Hamiltonian as a function of magnetic field
in {\bf k}-space. It is straightforward to compute the
thermodynamic quantities from the field $$\Omega=-{2
\over \beta}\sum_{i=1}^{4 \tilde q}\sum_{\bf k}{\rm
ln}[1+e^{-\beta (E_i({\bf k})-\mu)}]$$where $\beta$,
$E_i({\bf k})$and $\mu$denote the inverse temperature,
the dispersion relation of the $i$-th magnetic subband and
the chemical potential, respectively.
```

```
The field dependence of the chemical potential is calcu-
lated by inverting the constraint equation for occupation
$$N=2\sum_{i=1}^{4\tilde q}\sum_{\bf k}{1 \\over e^{\beta
(E_i({\bf k})-\mu)}+1}$$where the factor 2 comes from
the spin degeneracy. Because there are six electrons per
unit cell distributed among four bands at zero magnetic
field, the total occupancy factor $N/N_{max}$is 3/4 where
$N_{max}=2\sum_{\bf k}\sum_{i=1}^{4\tilde q}1$. Once the
chemical potential and thermodynamic potential are cal-
culated as a function of fields, it is straightforward to
compute the magnetization $M=-dF/dB$from the free energy
$F=\Omega+\mu N$.
\end{document}
```

To process this document using TEX4moz, run the following command:

```
mzlatex article.tex
```

Several auxiliary files are created in the same directory as the input file and a large number of messages are displayed on the screen, just like when you are processing the document using TEX. This is, of course, because TEX4ht itself calls TEX. Once the TEX processing is over, the final output document called article.xml is created. This is an XHTML+MathML document that contains the appropriate DOCTYPE declarations needed so it can be viewed in *Mozilla*. Figure 10.4 shows how article.xml, looks when viewed in *Mozilla*.

Compare this with the output produced by processing the same input document using LATEX. This is shown in Figure 10.5. You can see that the quality of the rendering produced by *Mozilla* is comparable to that of the TEX output.

TtM

TtM is a commercial program for converting TEX or LATEX documents into HTML+MathML documents. It was developed and is maintained by Ian Hutchinson of MIT. TtM is available for Linux and Windows. The Linux version is available for free, while the Windows version sells for $40.

TtM is a modified version of another program, called TtH, which converts LATEX documents into HTML. The difference between the two is that TtH converts formulas in the original LATEX document into images, while TtM converts the formulas into MathML. Both TtM and TtH use the Symbol font, available to most browsers, to represent special characters and symbols.

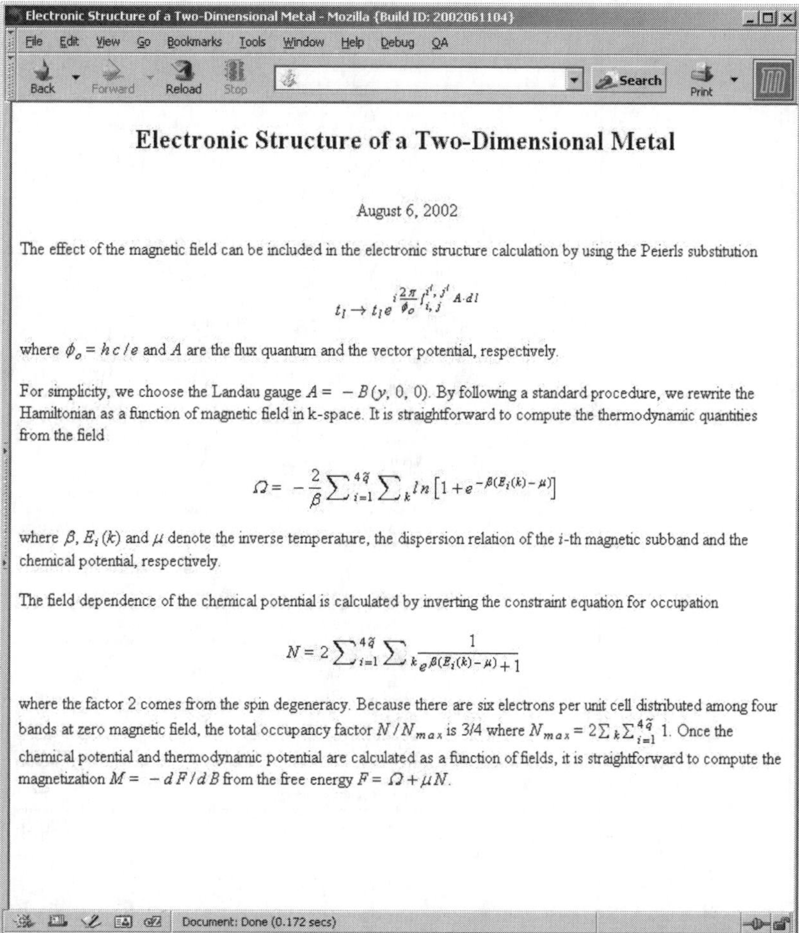

FIGURE 10.4 Converting the LATEX document article.tex into XHTML+MathML using TEX4ht.

TtM supports many of the complex features of LATEX, including macros, tables, and bibliographies. Some special types of TEX input that do not have a clear counterpart in HTML are not translated. TtM will generate a warning or error message if it encounters any TEX or LATEX constructs it does not recognize. These messages are directed to `stderr`, which typically means they are displayed on the terminal. However, on Unix systems, these messages can also be redirected to a file.

Installing TtM

You can get the source for TtM as a zipped archive from the following URL: *http://hutchinson.belmont.ma.us/tth/mml/*. You must extract

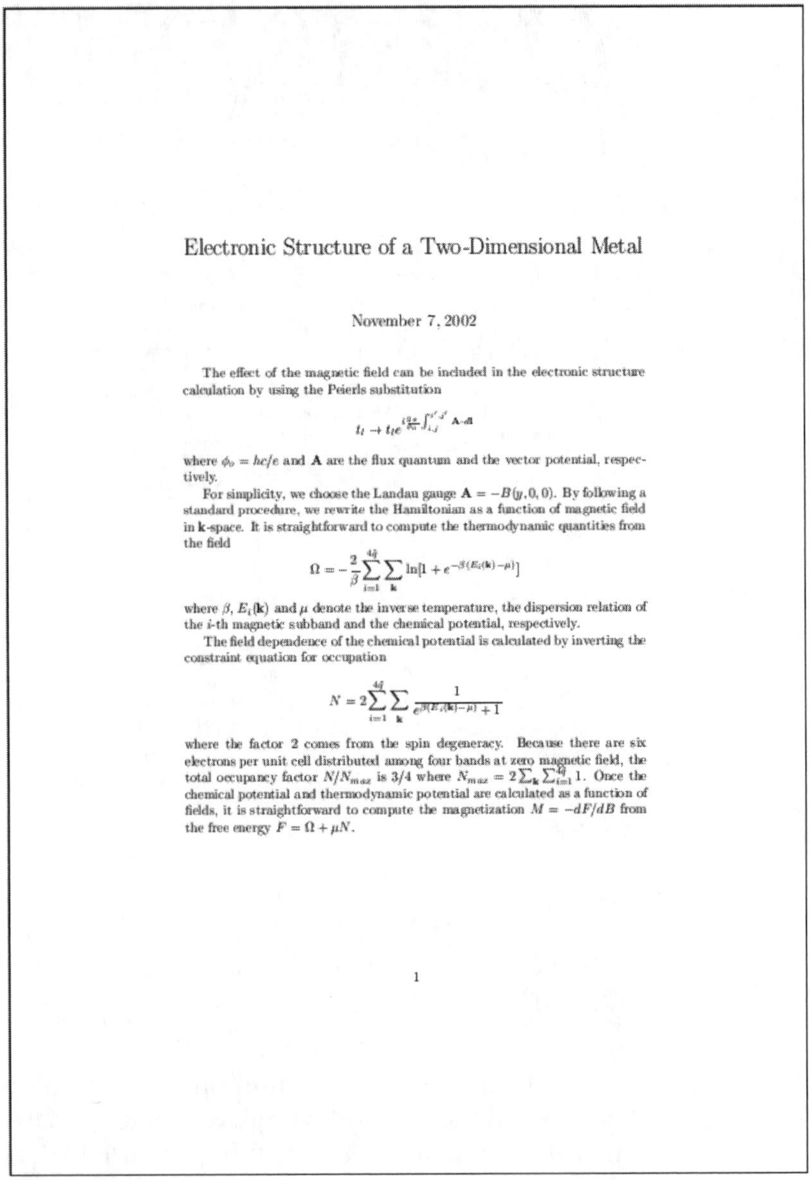

Electronic Structure of a Two-Dimensional Metal

November 7, 2002

The effect of the magnetic field can be included in the electronic structure calculation by using the Peierls substitution

$$t_l \to t_l e^{i\frac{2\pi}{\phi_0}\int_{i,j}^{i',j'} \mathbf{A}\cdot d\mathbf{l}}$$

where $\phi_0 = hc/e$ and $\mathbf{A}$ are the flux quantum and the vector potential, respectively.

For simplicity, we choose the Landau gauge $\mathbf{A} = -B(y, 0, 0)$. By following a standard procedure, we rewrite the Hamiltonian as a function of magnetic field in $\mathbf{k}$-space. It is straightforward to compute the thermodynamic quantities from the field

$$\Omega = -\frac{2}{\beta}\sum_{i=1}^{4\bar{q}}\sum_{\mathbf{k}} \ln[1 + e^{-\beta(E_i(\mathbf{k})-\mu)}]$$

where β, $E_i(\mathbf{k})$ and μ denote the inverse temperature, the dispersion relation of the i-th magnetic subband and the chemical potential, respectively.

The field dependence of the chemical potential is calculated by inverting the constraint equation for occupation

$$N = 2\sum_{i=1}^{4\bar{q}}\sum_{\mathbf{k}} \frac{1}{e^{\beta(E_i(\mathbf{k})-\mu)} + 1}$$

where the factor 2 comes from the spin degeneracy. Because there are six electrons per unit cell distributed among four bands at zero magnetic field, the total occupancy factor N/N_{max} is 3/4 where $N_{max} = 2\sum_{\mathbf{k}}\sum_{i=1}^{4\bar{q}} 1$. Once the chemical potential and thermodynamic potential are calculated as a function of fields, it is straightforward to compute the magnetization $M = -dF/dB$ from the free energy $F = \Omega + \mu N$.

1

FIGURE 10.5 The DVI file produced by processing article.tex using TEX.

the files from this archive and then run the installer program to get the executable file. You can then place the executable file in any directory located on your path. Detailed installation instructions are provided with the product.

Running TtM

To convert a given TEX or LATEX document into HTML, you run the following command:

```
ttm < test.tex
```

By default, the output is written to a file with the same name as the input file but with the extension `.html`. Hence, the above command would produce an output file called `test.html`. You can explicitly specify a different name for the output file using the redirection operator >, as shown here:

```
ttm < test.tex > output.html
```

TtM provides various "switches" or command-line options to customize the output. Some of the important options are:

- `-w*`: determines the style of HTML that is produced. If the option is `-w0`, a `title` element is not added to the output. If the option is specified as `-w1`, `head` and `body` tags are inserted into the output.
- `-c`: adds the prefix head "Content type: text/HTML" for specifying the MIME type of the file.
- `-e*`: determines how PostScript figures in the original LATEX document are handled. If the option is specified as `-e1`, all figures in the input document are converted to GIF images using the `ps2gif` utility, which must be present on the user's machine. If the option is specified as `-e2`, images are converted to inline GIF images. If the option is specified as `-e0`, the conversion to GIF does not take place and the figures are omitted from the output document.
- `-v`: causes warnings and error messages to be produced in a more verbose format, which is useful for debugging.
- `-L` *filename*: identifies the input document as LATEX and specifies the name of auxiliary files for generating tables of contents and bibliographies.

Unlike TEX4ht and other tools for converting TEX to HTML, such as LATEX2HTML, TtM does not require a TEX or LATEX installation to be present on the user's machine. This makes TtM much more self-contained and portable. It is, however, still advisable to run TEX or LATEX on the input file before the TtM translation so that you can ensure the file is free of syntax errors. If you do not have access to a TEX installation, you can debug the input document using the error messages produced by TtM alone. However, this can be difficult for users who do not have much experience with TEX.

A LaTeX installation is necessary if you are translating a LaTeX document that includes tables of contents or bibliographies. If you want to generate content of this type in LaTeX, the source file has to be processed multiple times. In the first pass, the TeX program generates forward references that are stored in auxiliary files. The information in the auxiliary files is then read by TeX in subsequent passes to generate the final table of contents or bibliography.

TtM can use the auxiliary files generated by LaTeX to generate hypertext versions of a table of contents and bibliography present in the input document. TtM looks for the auxiliary files in the same directory as the input file. By default, TtM expects each auxiliary file to have the same name as the input file but with a different extension. However, you can specify a different name for the auxiliary files by using the command-line option `-L` *filename*. You can also use the `-L` option without a filename to instruct TtM that the input file is in LaTeX format. This enables TtM to interpret LaTeX constructs in the input document even if the document lacks a `\documentclass` line to identify itself as a LaTeX document.

Figure 10.6 shows the HTML+MathML document obtained by processing the document of Example 10.2 using TtM when viewed in *Amaya*. Compare this with the output produced by TeX4ht and LaTeX from the same document, shown in Figures 10.4 and Figure 10.5.

TtM is extremely fast and efficient. Conversion of even large TeX files takes less than a second. As mentioned earlier, TtM is self-contained and does not call TeX or LaTeX when processing a document. Because it is fast and self-contained, you can run TtM on a server via a CGI script to do real-time conversion of LaTeX documents over the Web. You can see examples of such conversion at the following URL: *http://hutchinson.belmont.ma.us/tth/mml/ttmform.html* (Figure 10.7). This page contains a text area for entering arbitrary LaTeX input. You can then click a button to submit the input to the server, where it is processed using TtM. The output produced by TtM is then displayed on the same Web page. You can try out this Web page for experimenting with different types of TeX and LaTeX input and seeing what types of output TtM generates.

10.5 Converting XML+MathML to TeX

MathML and TeX play a complementary role as formats for representing mathematics. MathML is ideal for displaying formulas in Web pages, while TeX is a superior solution for creating high-quality

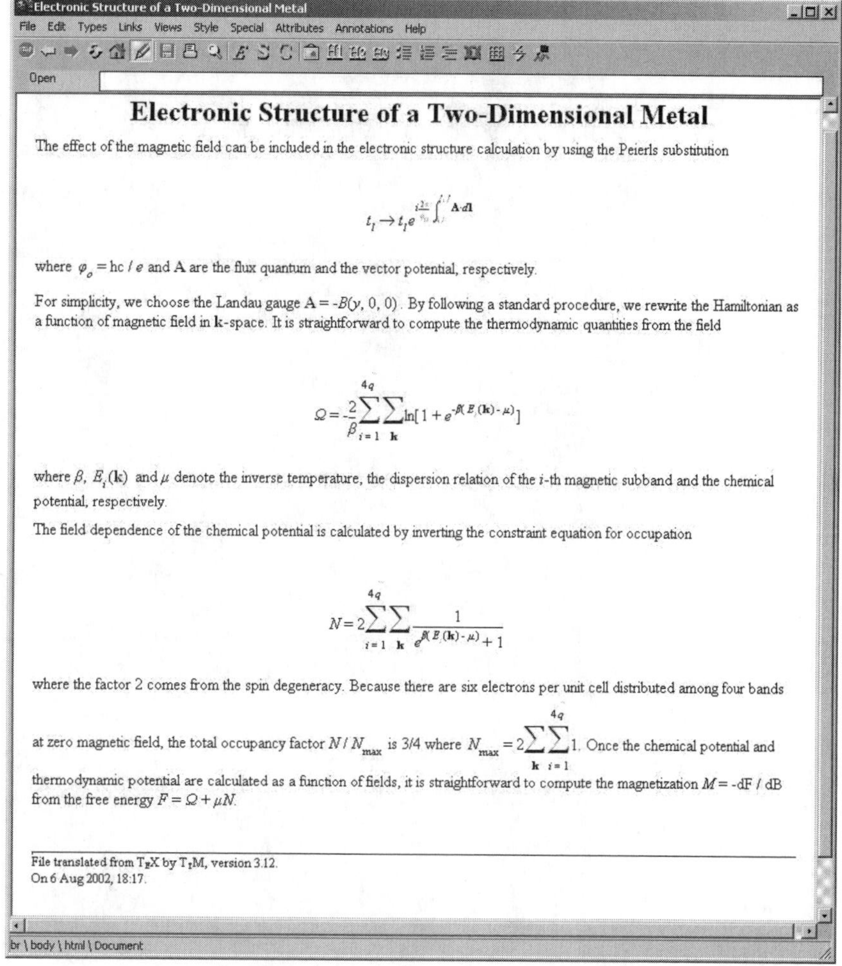

FIGURE 10.6 The HTML+MathML file produced by translating article.tex using TtM. The resulting file is viewed here in *Amaya.*

printed output. Ideally, an author should be able to switch easily between TEX and MathML, going back and forth between the two formats, as needed.

In the majority of cases, authors will be translating existing TEX and LATEX documents for display on the Web. Some of the tools available for this type of translation were described in Section 10.4. However, there are also situations in which the reverse transformation, that is converting MathML into TEX, can be useful. This allows authors to use TEX as a formatting engine for typesetting mathematical documents that were originally created for display on the Web. In this section, we briefly look at some techniques for

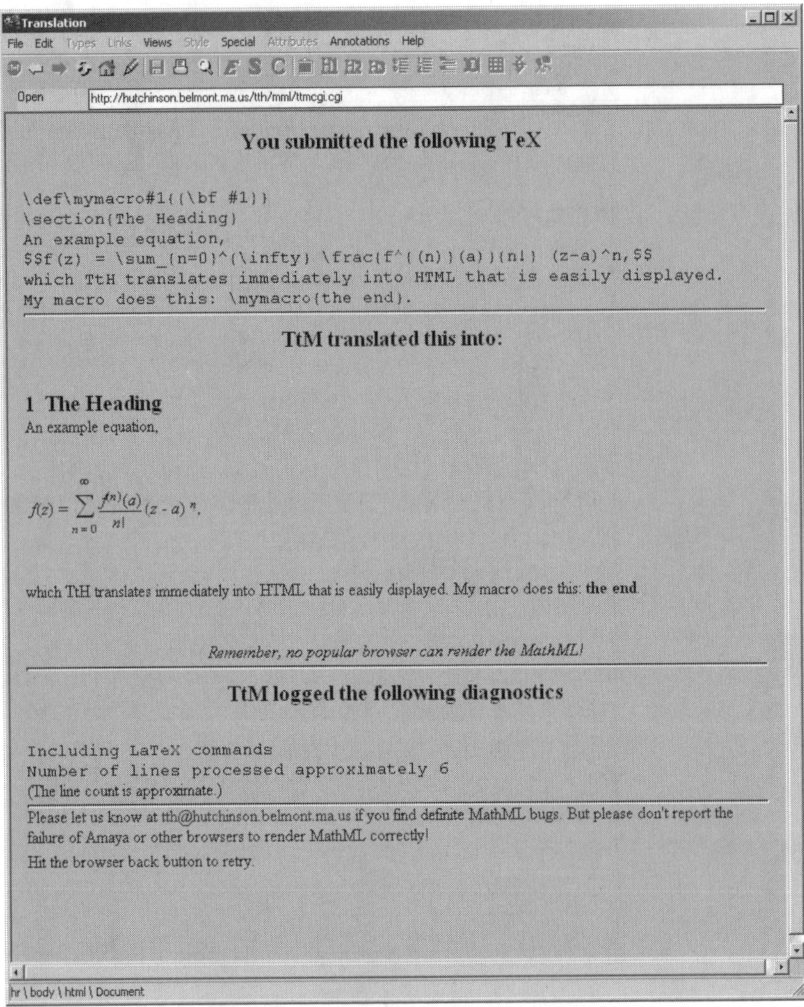

FIGURE 10.7 A conversion Web page for translating LaTeX documents using TtM.

converting MathML equations, either individually or embedded in another XML document type (such as XHTML), into TeX.

XSLT Stylesheets

As discussed in Section 8.4, XSLT transformations provide a flexible and powerful method for converting arbitrary XML data into other formats. In particular, you can use XSLT for transforming MathML equations into LaTeX. Vasil Yaroshevich has implemented this approach in the form of an XSLT MathML Library. This is a collection of six XSLT stylesheets that together specify how to translate any arbitrary presentation MathML expression into LaTeX. Currently, the stylesheets handle conversion from presentation MathML only, but support for content MathML is likely to be added in the future.

The XSLT MathML library consists of the following six stylesheets:

- `mmltex.xsl`
- `tokens.xsl`
- `glayout.xsl`
- `scripts.xsl`
- `tables.xsl`
- `entities.xsl`

The templates for transforming token elements, layout schemata, scripts, tables, and entities are placed in separate stylesheets for the sake of modularity. However, for transforming a given MathML document, you only need to refer to a top-level stylesheet called `mmltex.xsl`. This contains commands for importing the template definitions from all the other stylesheets.

To use the XSLT MathML Library for translating MathML into LaTeX, you have two options. You can do interactive trials on the Web page set up by the author of the library: *www.raleigh.ru/MathML/mmltex/online.php* (Figure 10.8). You can enter any MathML expression in the text area provided and then click a button to view the corresponding LaTeX markup in the same page. This is useful for translating individual equations and experimenting with how the stylesheets work.

If you are processing a larger volume of files, you can also download all the stylesheets in zipped form from the following URL: *www.raleigh.ru/MathML/mmltex/mmltex.zip*. Once you unzip the files, you can use an XSLT processor, such as Xalan or Saxon, to do the transformations locally on your own machine.

The ORCCA Converter

Another approach for translating MathML equations into LaTeX is to use a custom program written in a low-level language such as Java. In Section 10.3, we discussed the online TeX to MathML converter created by Stephen Watt's group at ORCCA. This uses a map file containing templates that define the correspondence between specific TeX constructs and their MathML counterparts. A Java program is then used to apply the templates in the map file to any arbitrary LaTeX equation and produce MathML as output.

The ORCCA group has also created a converter that uses the same methodology for doing the reverse transformation. This too uses a map file but this time for translating presentation MathML into LaTeX. An online demo of this converter is available at the fol-

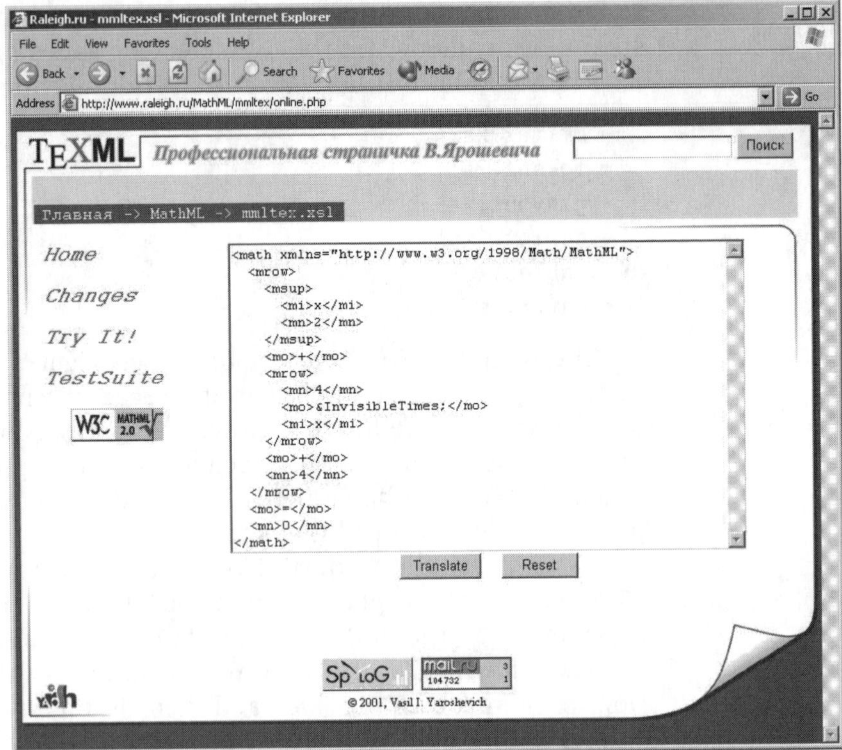

FIGURE 10.8 Converting presentation MathML into LaTeX using XSLT transformations.

lowing URL: *www.orcca.on.ca/MathML/texmml/mmltotex.html*. You can type in any arbitrary presentation MathML as input in a text area and then click a button to view the LaTeX output (Figure 10.9) in the same Web page. The demo page also gives you the option of uploading a MathML file from your computer and receiving the LaTeX output in a separate file.

xmltex

The ORCCA converter and the XSLT MathML library, discussed above, are both limited to translating individual MathML expressions into LaTeX. For large-scale document-processing, for example as part of a publisher's workflow, it is useful to have a way of processing entire XML documents that contain embedded MathML while still using TeX as a formatting engine. This is clearly a much more challenging task than converting individual formulas. However, the foundation for this type of conversion has been provided by David Carlisle, in the form of a program called xmltex.

xmltex is a parser for XML documents and is written entirely in $\TeX$. You can configure xmltex to trigger specific $\TeX$ commands when it encounters a particular type of element, attribute, processing instruction, or entity in the input XML document. xmltex thus

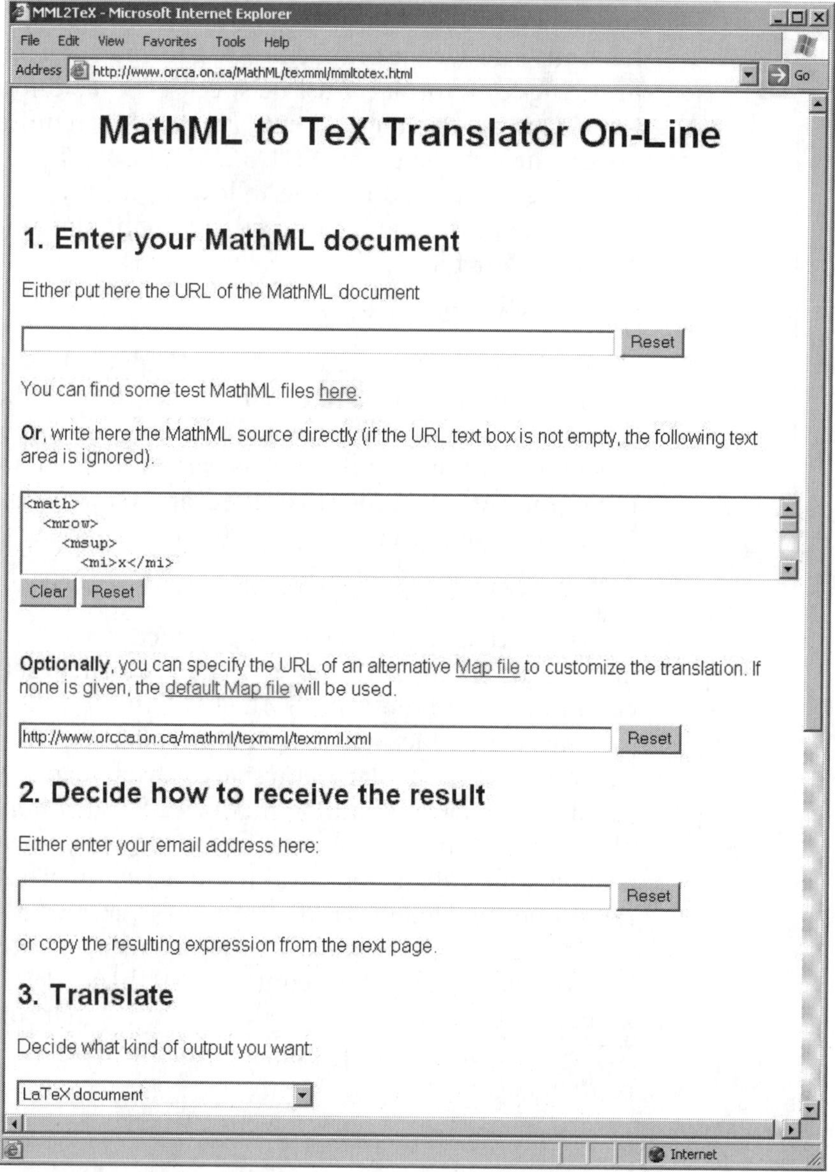

FIGURE 10.9 Converting presentation MathML into $\LaTeX$ using the online converter at ORCCA.

serves as a valuable bridge that connects the worlds of TEX and XML. It allows TEX's powerful typesetting capabilities to be applied not just to TEX documents but to arbitrary XML documents. You can download the xmltex program along with documentation for it at the following URL: *www.dcarlisle.demon.co.uk/xmltex/manual.html.*

xmltex can process XML documents that combine elements from different namespaces; for example, XHTML documents that contain embedded MathML. The xmltex program by itself does not have any knowledge of specific XML formats. All information about a specific XML format must be specified in additional package files (with a `.xmt` extension). A separate `xmt` file is required for each XML document type, such as XHTML, DocBook, TEI, or MathML. By including a command of the following form in a catalog file, you can associate the namespace for a specific document type with a particular `xmt` file:

```
\NAMESPACE{URL}{xmt-file}
```

When xmltex processes an XML document and encounters elements from a particular namespace, it loads the `xmt` file corresponding to that namespace. For example, the following command specifies that the `mathml2.xmt` package should be loaded whenever the input XML document contains an element that belongs to the MathML namespace:

```
\NAMESPACE{http://www.w3.org/1998/Math/MathML}{mathml2.xmt}
```

The `mathml2.xmt` package is included with the standard xmltex distribution. It contains TEX commands for typesetting most of the common presentation MathML elements.

The catalog file, which specifies which `xmt` file should be associated with a particular namespace, has a `.cfg` file extension. You can define a specific catalog file for each document. So, for example, to typeset an XML document called `test.xml`, you would create a catalog file called `test.cfg`. If a document-specific catalog file is not found, the default configuration file `xmltex.cfg` is used.

Let's look at a simple example of using xmltex to typeset an XHTML document that contains MathML. We can set up an `xhtml.xmt` file that defines LATEX commands that correspond to each XHTML element used in this document. Example 10.3 shows the contents of this file.

Example 10.3 An `xmt` package that defines LATEX commands for specific XHTML elements.

```
\DeclareNamespace{xhtml}{http://www.w3.org/ 1999/xhtml}

\XMLelement{xhtml:html}
{}
 {\documentclass{article}
   \begin{document}
 }
 {\end{document}}

\XMLelement{xhtml:head}
{}
 {}{}

\XMLelement{xhtml:body}
{}
 {}{}

\XMLelement{xhtml:h1}
{}
 {\xmlgrab}
 {\title{#1}
   \maketitle}

\XMLelement{xhtml:p}
 {}
 {\par}
   {\par}
```

The first line in the `xhtml.xmt` file specifies the namespace associated with all XHTML elements in the file. Each `\XMLelement`{*name*} defines LATEX commands to be used when an element called *name* is encountered. The file contains LATEX commands that correspond to the XHTML elements `html`, `head`, `body`, `h1`, and `p`. Example 10.4 shows an XHTML+MathML document called `test.xml`, which uses only these XHTML elements. Figure 10.10 shows how this file looks when displayed by *Mozilla*.

Example 10.4 An XHTML+MathML document called *test.xml*.

```
<html xmlns="http://www.w3.org/1999/xhtml">
<head></head>
<body>
<h1>Using TEX to Typeset MathML</h1>
<h2>Subscript and Superscript</h2>
<p>
```

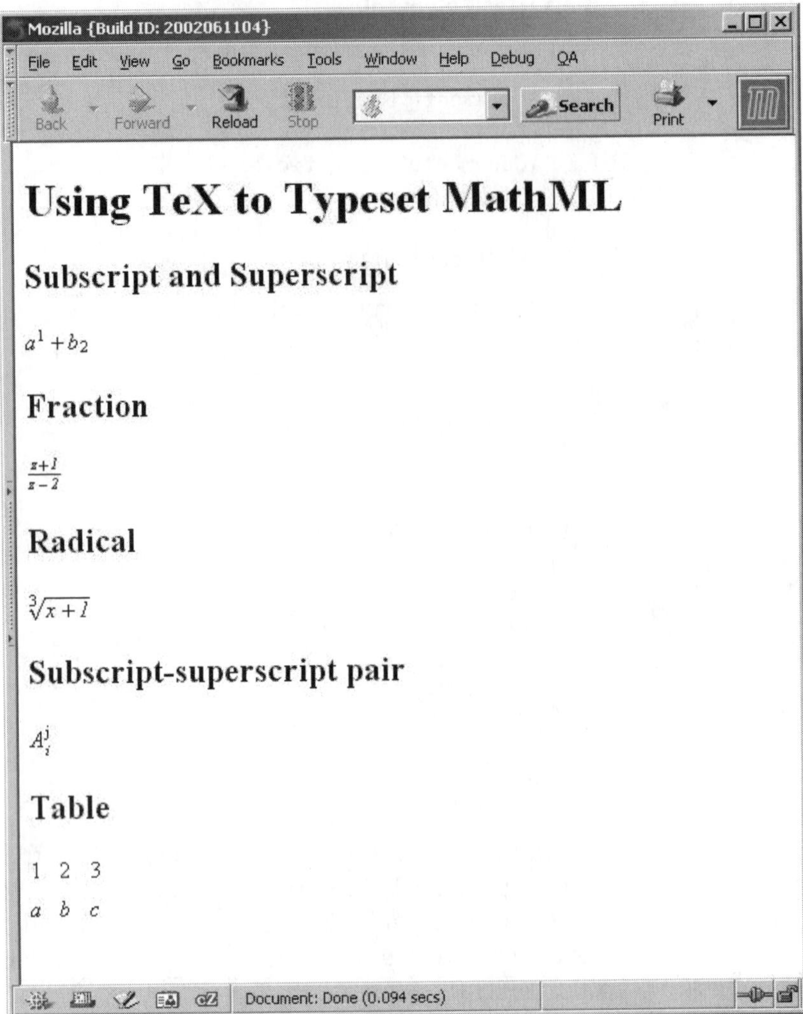

FIGURE 10.10 The file `test.xml` viewed in *Mozilla*.

```
<math xmlns="http://www.w3.org/1998/Math/MathML">
 <mrow>
   <msup><mi>a</mi><mn>1</mn></msup>
   <mo>+</mo>
   <msub><mi>b</mi><mn>2</mn></msub>
 </mrow>
</math>
</p>
```

```
<h2>Fraction</h2>
<p>
<math xmlns="http://www.w3.org/1998/Math/MathML">
 <mfrac>
    <mrow><mi>z</mi><mo>+</mo><mi>1</mi></mrow>
    <mrow><mi>z</mi><mo>-</mo><mi>2</mi></mrow>
 </mfrac>
</math>
</p>

<h2>Radical</h2>
<p>
<math xmlns="http://www.w3.org/1998/Math/MathML">
 <mroot>
    <mrow><mi>x</mi><mo>+</mo><mi>1</mi></mrow>
    <mn>3</mn>
 </mroot>
</math>
</p>

<h2>Subscript-superscript pair</h2>
<p>
<math xmlns="http://www.w3.org/1998/Math/MathML">
 <msubsup>
    <mi>A</mi>
    <mi>i</mi>
    <mn>j</mn>
 </msubsup>
</math>
</p>

<h2>Table</h2>
<p>
<math xmlns="http://www.w3.org/1998/Math/MathML">
 <mtable>
    <mtr><mtd><mn>1</mn></mtd><mtd><mn>2</mn></mtd>
    <mtd><mn>3</mn></mtd></mtr>
    <mtr><mtd><mi>a</mi></mtd><mtd><mi>b</mi></mtd>
    <mtd><mi>c</mi></mtd></mtr>
 </mtable>
</math>
</p>

</body>
</html>
```

TEX cannot process XML files directly, only TEX files. Hence, to run xmltex on the XML document shown in Example 10.4, you first need to create a text file, called `test.tex`, with the following lines in it:

```
\def\xmlfile{test.xml}
\input xmltex.tex
```

For the `xhtml.xmt` file to be automatically loaded whenever the XHTML namespace is encountered, you must create a catalog file called `test.cfg` that contains the following line:

```
\NAMESPACE{http://www.w3.org/1999/xhtml}{xhtml.xmt}
```

You can then run the following command in your LaTeX installation to parse the XML file using xmltex:

```
latex test.tex
```

The result is a DVI file (Figure 10.11) called `test.dvi` that contains the typeset output produced by TeX. Alternatively, you can run the `pdflatex` command to generate a PDF file of the typeset output, as shown here:

```
pdflatex test.tex
```

By suitably defining `xmt` package files for specific document types, you can typeset any XML document using TeX's formatting capabilities. A good example of this approach is the PassiveTeX project of Sebastian Rahtz. He has created a `fotex.xmt` package and a style file that provides a fairly complete implementation of the XSL-FO format. As discussed in Section 8.4, XSL-FO is a W3C standard for specifying the detailed layout and formatting of XML documents. You can use an XSLT stylesheet for transforming a document in any arbitrary XML format, such as XHTML or DocBook, into XSL-FO. Once an XSL-FO document is obtained, you can use Rahtz's package to typeset the document in TeX and directly create PDF files from the typeset output.

You can find more information about PassiveTeX at the following URL: *www.tei-c.org.uk/Software/passivetex/*. This site provides sample input files and XSLT stylesheets for converting XML documents in TEI format into XSL-FO and then processing them with TeX to get PDF files as output. The site also provides an example of typesetting a fairly complex XML document that contains MathML.

The PassiveTeX project is a good prototype for how TeX can be used for typesetting arbitrary XML documents. The same approach can be applied to any other XML format, including XHTML +MathML. Of course, the task of writing a macro package that will translate all elements of a given XML format into their TeX equivalents can be quite challenging. However, once the initial

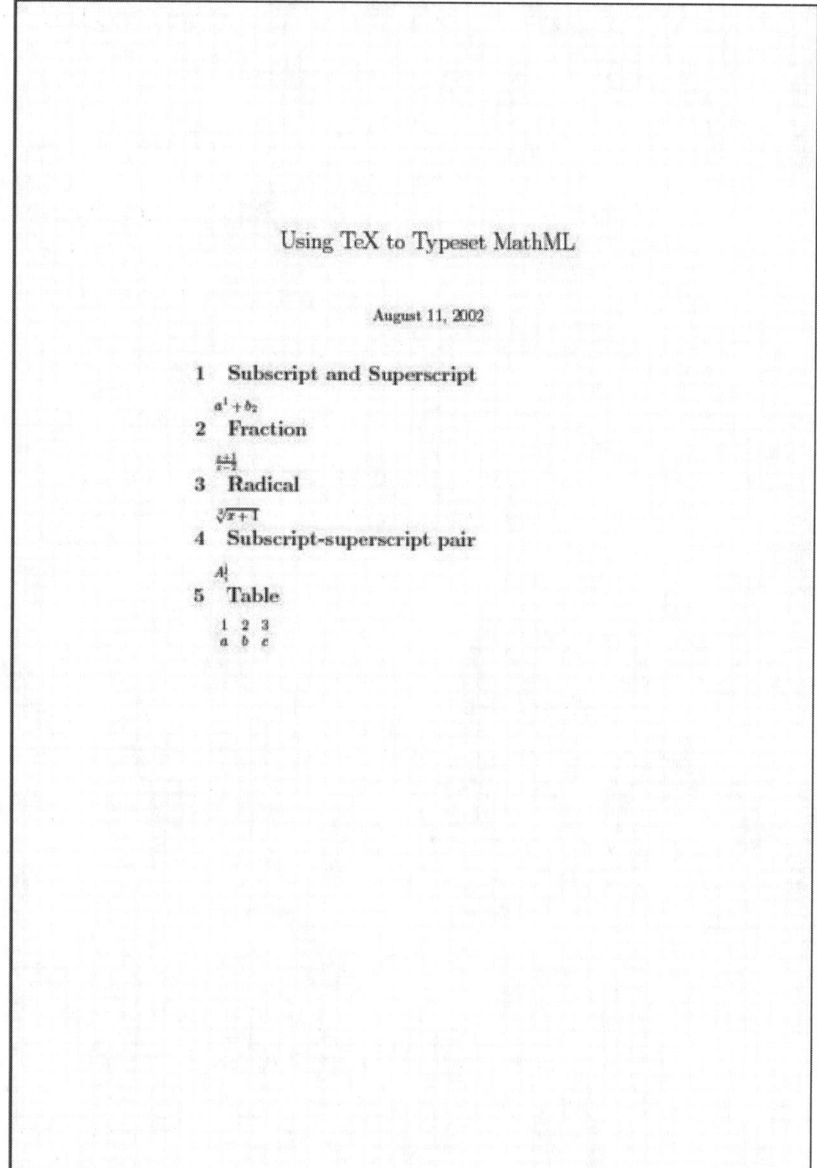

FIGURE 10.11 The DVI file produced by typesetting `test.xml` using xmltex.

implementation is done, the process is flexible and robust enough for large-scale adoption as part of a publisher's production workflow. This discussion shows that TEX can continue to play an important role for generating high-quality printed output, using XHTML +MathML documents as a source.

CHAPTER

11

USING MATHML FOR COMPUTATIONS

This chapter provides an overview of the two major computer algebra systems that can perform computations using MathML: *Mathematica* and *Maple*. It includes detailed information on the support for importing, exporting, and evaluating MathML in both of these systems.

11.1 INTRODUCTION

MathML is an ideal format for mathematical software applications to communicate with each other and with other applications (such as Web browsers, word processors, and e-mail clients). This is hardly surprising since MathML was specifically designed to facilitate the exchange and reuse of mathematical content between such applications. As support for MathML becomes more widespread, it should soon be possible to copy and paste mathematical notation between different applications as routinely and easily as one can do for text.

Most of the leading mathematical software applications, such as *Mathematica*, *Maple*, *Mathcad*, and *Scientific Workplace*, already include support for MathML in some form. You can export a document that's in the native file format of any of these applications into HTML and automatically convert any mathematical formulas in the document into MathML. This allows technical documents authored using any of these applications to be displayed in Web browsers that support the display of MathML.

In the past, each of these applications could use only its own proprietary format for encoding mathematics. Hence, users of different applications could not easily share their work with each other. This situation is starting to change with the advent of MathML. For example, using MathML, you can now directly copy equations out of *Maple* and e-mail them to another user, who can then paste and evaluate them in *Mathematica*.

Recent versions of *Mathematica* (Version 4.2 or later) and *Maple* (Version 7 or later) include menu commands and functions that allow users to freely convert between their native syntax for mathematical expressions and MathML. This makes it possible to perform a wide variety of computations on MathML-encoded input (such as calculating integrals, solving equations, or plotting graphs). *Mathematica* and *Maple* thus provide a good model for how you can use MathML to facilitate mathematical communication.

Mathcad and *Scientific Workplace*, in contrast, do not currently allow you to import MathML equations for evaluation or to manipulate and transform MathML. The rest of this chapter, therefore, focuses on *Mathematica* and *Maple*, since these are the two applications that currently provide the most sophisticated support for MathML.

11.2 *MATHEMATICA*

Mathematica is a versatile application for technical computing. It includes support for numerical and symbolic calculations, graphics, data analysis, and programming using its own built-in language. In addition to these computational abilities, *Mathematica* provides a rich environment for authoring technical documents. We discussed the use of *Mathematica* as an authoring application for MathML in Section 9.4. In this chapter, we focus on *Mathematica*'s computational abilities as they pertain to MathML.

The *Mathematica* Interface

Mathematica consists of two separate applications that work closely together: the front end, which provides the user interface for creating and editing documents, and the kernel, which acts as the computational engine. The kernel works behind the scenes, receiving input from the front end and returning the results of its calculations back to the front end for display. You can thus use *Mathematica* both for doing computations and for presenting the results in the form of publication-quality typeset documents. The advantage of combining document creation and computation in the same application is that the formulas and programs in the document are "live" and can be evaluated to get new results.

Mathematica is available for Windows, Macintosh (including a native Mac OS X version), and most Unix platforms. The latest release of *Mathematica*, Version 4.2, also offers excellent support for MathML 2.0, both presentation and content markup. You can directly copy and paste MathML equations both into and out of *Mathematica*. For example, you can create complicated equations in a notebook, and then copy them as MathML to insert into an HTML document that can be displayed on the Web. Conversely, you can copy MathML equations from a Web page, and then paste them into a *Mathematica* notebook and evaluate them. There are also several functions for translating MathML into *Mathematica* syntax and vice versa. Details of these features are given later in this chapter.

When you start *Mathematica*, a blank notebook appears on the screen along with some palettes for entering input. Each notebook consists of a series of cells, indicated by brackets on the right. Cells are a generalization of paragraphs and, in addition to text, can contain equations, graphics, or commands for evaluation. Each cell has a specific style (such as Text, Input, Output, Graphics, Section, or Subsection) that determines the default properties of its contents. You can create a cell of a specific style using the `Format ▶ Style` menu.

To perform a calculation, you must type a *Mathematica* command into an input cell. By default, when you type into a new notebook, an input cell is automatically created. When you have finished entering the command, press Shift-Enter to evaluate it. The result of the evaluation is displayed in the notebook in an output cell, just below the input cell you evaluated (Figure 11.1). The front end automatically adds In and Out labels to the input and output cells, and numbers them in the order of evaluation.

Mathematica commands are entered in a special syntax that corresponds closely to the way an expression is normally spoken. All function names start with an uppercase letter, and function arguments are enclosed in square brackets. For example, here is the *Mathematica* command for evaluating the definite integral of $\sin(x)$ from 0 to π:

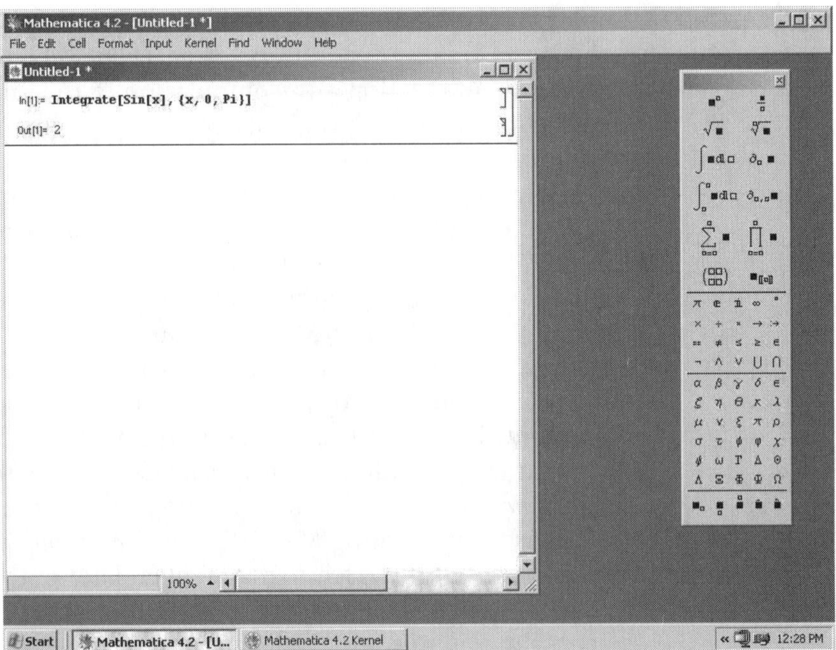

FIGURE 11.1 A *Mathematica* notebook that shows an input and output cell.

```
In[1]:= Integrate[Sin[x], {x, 0, Pi}]
Out[1]= 2
```

The terms `Integrate` and `Sin` are *Mathematica* functions. There are over two thousand built-in functions for performing a wide variety of calculations in fields such as algebra, calculus, statistics, number theory, and graphics.

Mathematica Syntax

There is a close correspondence between MathML and the syntax used internally by *Mathematica* to represent mathematical formulas. The *Mathematica* syntax is, in effect, a text-based markup language for representing mathematical formulas and capturing both their notation and meaning. Because it provides a flexible and powerful system for describing mathematics, *Mathematica* was an important influence in the design of MathML. There are many points of similarity between the structure of MathML and the syntax of *Mathematica* expressions. In this section, we briefly review some details of *Mathematica* syntax and see how it compares with MathML.

Like MathML, *Mathematica* makes a distinction between the semantic meaning of a mathematical formula and its visual structure. The semantic meaning of any formula is represented internally using what is called its *full form*. This is a symbolic expression built up from standard *Mathematica* function names. The full form of a formula is closely analogous to MathML content markup. The appearance of mathematical notation, on the other hand, is described using a series of box structures, which are analogous to MathML presentation markup. *Mathematica* can freely convert between full-form expressions and boxes, using the former for performing computations and the latter for displaying mathematics in a notebook.

`FullForm` and Content MathML

The underlying logical structure of any mathematical formula, which determines its semantic interpretation, is called its full form. You can see the full form, of any expression *expr* by evaluating the command `FullForm[`*expr*`]`. For example, the following command shows the full form of the expression $x^2 + y$:

```
In[1]:= FullForm[x^2+y]
Out[2]// FullForm= Plus[Power[x, 2], y]
```

The `//FullForm` annotation is added to the Out label to indicate that the output is being displayed in FullForm.

The content markup representation for the same expression would be as follows:

```
<apply>
<plus/>
<apply>
 <power/><ci>x</ci> <cn>2</cn>
</apply><ci>y</ci>
</apply>
```

You can see that the *Mathematica* full form of an expression and its content markup representation are very similar. Both use prefix functional notation to recursively build up complicated expressions out of smaller building blocks. The main difference is that in *Mathematica*, function application is indicated as $f[x]$, where f is a specific *Mathematica* command such as `Plus`, `Power`, `Sin`, or `Integrate`. In content MathML, on the other hand, function application is indicated as `<apply>` $f\,x$ `</apply>`, where f is a content markup element that represents a specific operator or function, such as `plus`, `power`, `sin`, or `int`. Also, the atomic units of mathematical notation (numbers, operators, and identifiers) are all denoted by a separate element in MathML, while *Mathematica* does not make any distinction between these different types of objects, encoding them all as strings.

Boxes and Presentation MathML

To describe the two-dimensional appearance of mathematical notation, *Mathematica* uses a series of box structures. There are different types of boxes for describing subscripts, superscripts, or fractions. Each of these box structures is in the form of a symbolic expression that can take one or more arguments. For example, the formula $x^2 + y$ is represented in *Mathematica* by the following symbolic expression:

```
RowBox[{SuperscriptBox["x", "2"], "+", "y"}]
```

There is a close correspondence between the box structures used in *Mathematica* and the presentation elements of MathML. For example, the above expression would be represented in presentation markup as shown below:

```
<mrow>
 <msup><mi>x</mi><mn>2</mn></msup>
 <mo>+</mo><mi>y</mi>
</mrow>
```

TABLE 11.1 ***Mathematica*** **Notational Structures and Their MathML Counterparts**

Mathematica	MathML	Notation
`RowBox[x, y]`	`<mrow>...</mrow>`	xy
`FractionBox[x, y]`	`<mfrac>...</mfrac>`	$\frac{x}{y}$
`SqrtBox[x]`	`<msqrt>...</msqrt>`	$\sqrt{x}$
`RadicalBox[x, y]`	`<mroot>...</mroot>`	$\sqrt[y]{x}$
`SubscriptBox[x, y]`	`<msub>...</msub>`	x_y
`SuperscriptBox[x, y]`	`<msup>...</msup>`	x^y
`SubsupercriptBox[x, y,z]`	`<msubsup>...</msubsup>`	x_y^z
`UnderscriptBox[x, y]`	`<munder>...</munder>`	$\underset{y}{x}$
`OverscriptBox[x, y]`	`<mover>...</mover>`	$\overset{y}{x}$
`UnderoverscriptBox[x, y,z]`	`<munderover>... </munderover>`	$\overset{z}{\underset{y}{x}}$
`GridBox[{x, y}]`	`<mtable>...</mtable>`	$(x y)$

You can see that the `RowBox[...]` and `SuperscriptBox[...]` constructs in *Mathematica* are equivalent to the `<mrow>...</mrow>` and `<msup>...</msup>` constructs in MathML. In each case, the child elements of the MathML presentation element are equivalent to the arguments of the *Mathematica* box expression. In the box expressions, as with full form, numbers, operators, and identifiers are all represented as strings.

A more complete listing of some *Mathematica* notational structures and their MathML counterparts is given in Table 11.1. The different types of boxes can be nested and combined, as necessary, to represent more complicated expressions.

You can see the underlying structure of any mathematical formula in a notebook by selecting the expression and choosing `Format ▶ Show Expression` from the menu. Figure 11.2 shows a formula in a notebook. Figure 11.3 shows the underlying expression for the formula.

Display Forms

Mathematica supports several different forms for the display of mathematics. A given formula can have several different textual representations, each corresponding to a different way of displaying the expression in a notebook. Some of the important display forms are:

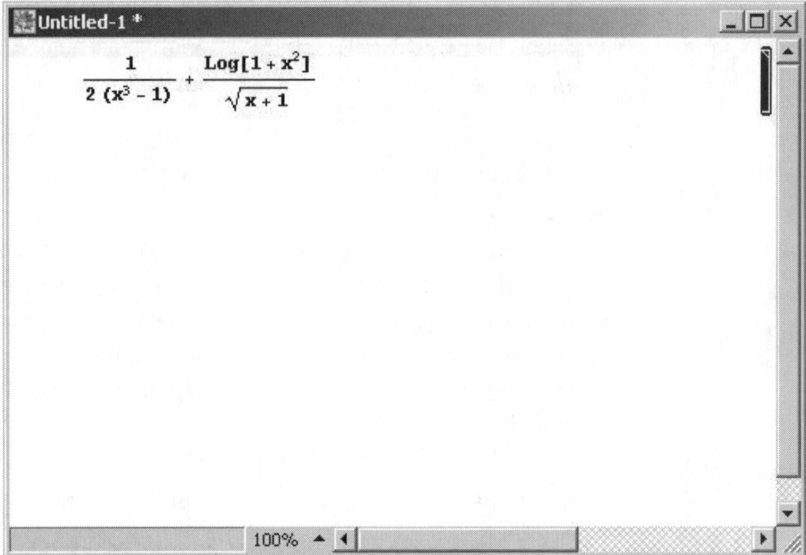

FIGURE 11.2 A mathematical formula in a notebook.

Untitled-1 *

```
Cell[BoxData[
    RowBox[{
      FractionBox["1",
        RowBox[{"2",
          RowBox[{"(",
            RowBox[{
              SuperscriptBox["x", "3"], "-", "1"}], ")"}]}]],
      "+",
      FractionBox[
        RowBox[{"Log", "[",
          RowBox[{"1", "+",
            SuperscriptBox["x", "2"]}], "]"}],
        SqrtBox[
          RowBox[{"x", "+", "1"}]]]}]], "Input"]
```

100%

FIGURE 11.3 The underlying box structure of the formula shown in Figure 11.2 as displayed by using the Format ▶ Show Expression command.

- InputForm: is a linear text-based form that can be typed directly using only the characters on a standard keyboard.
- TraditionalForm: can display special characters and two-dimensional positioning to closely approximate traditional

mathematical notation. It is not well-suited for computation since its mathematical meaning can be ambiguous.

- StandardForm: is a compromise between InputForm and TraditionalForm. It can display special characters and two-dimensional layout while still preserving an unambiguous mathematical meaning. By default, input and output in *Mathematica* notebooks are displayed in StandardForm.
- MathMLForm: displays the MathML markup for a mathematical expression. The markup is indented and formatted to reveal the hierarchical structure of the MathML expression.

Several other display forms (such as TEXForm and CForm) use the syntax of TEX and the C programming language, respectively. Forms that display expressions as a linear sequence of characters, such as FullForm and InputForm, are represented in *Mathematica* as simple strings. Forms that display two-dimensional notation, such as StandardForm and TraditionalForm, are represented using the box structures described earlier in this chapter.

To see an expression, *expr*, displayed in a particular form, you can type and evaluate the command *form*[*expr*]. Here are some examples of the same expression displayed in several different forms.

In StandardForm, the text is in a monospaced font, and square brackets are used for function application:

```
In[1]:= StandardForm[x^2+1/Log[x]]
```

Out[1]//StandardForm= $x^2 + \frac{1}{\mathrm{Log}[x]}$

In TraditionalForm, variables are shown in italics, and parentheses are used for function application:

```
In[2]:= TraditionalForm[x^2+1/Log[x]]
```

Out[2]//TraditionalForm= $x^2 + \frac{1}{\log(x)}$

InputForm does not support two-dimensional display, so information about fractions and powers, for example, is shown in a linear syntax:

```
In[3]:= InputForm[x^2+1/Log[x]]
Out[3]//InputForm= x^2 + Log[x]^(-1)
```

You can also convert a formula from one display form to another by selecting the formula and choosing the appropriate form in the `Cell ▶ Convert To` menu (Figure 11.4).

Figure 11.5 shows a notebook that contains an integral. Both the input and output are in StandardForm by default. `ArcSin` and

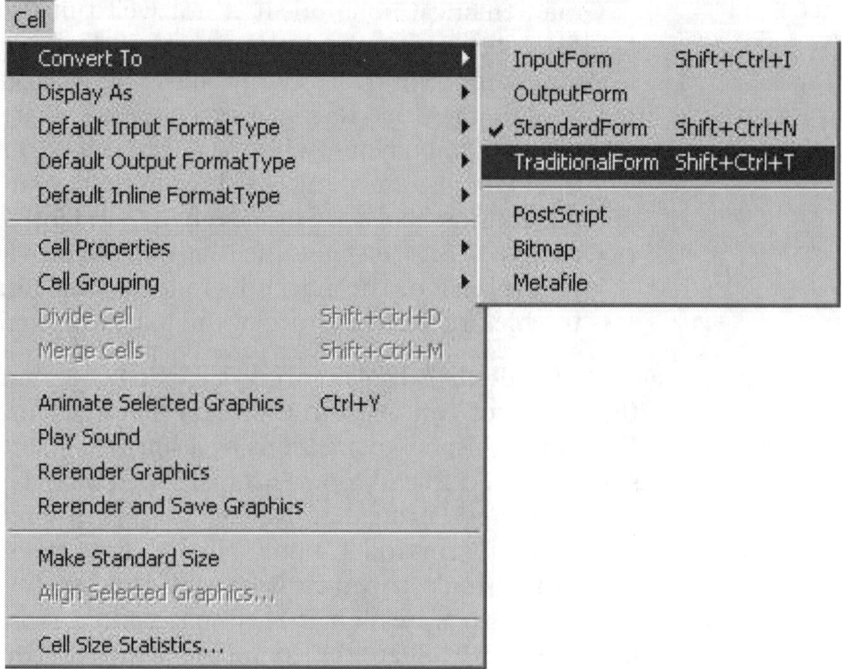

FIGURE 11.4 The Cell ▶ Convert To menu for changing between different display formats.

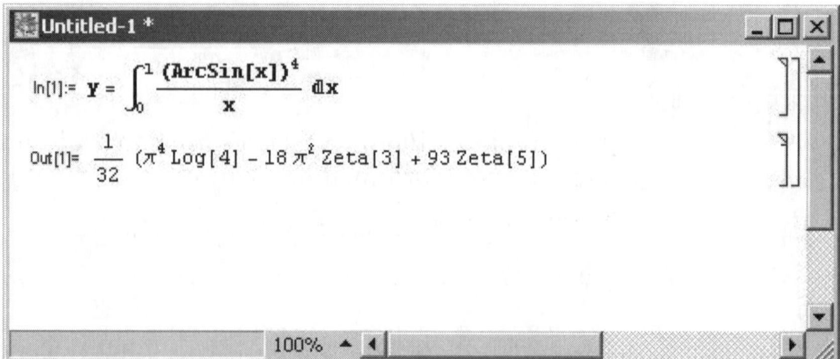

FIGURE 11.5 A mathematical formula, displayed in StandardForm, in a notebook.

`Zeta` are built-in *Mathematica* commands that represent the inverse sine and Riemann zeta functions, respectively.

Figure 11.6 shows the same input and output cells from Figure 11.5 after they are converted to TraditionalForm using the `Cell` ▶ `Convert To` ▶ `TraditionalForm` menu. Notice that the `ArcSin` and `Zeta` functions are automatically displayed in the traditional notation for these functions.

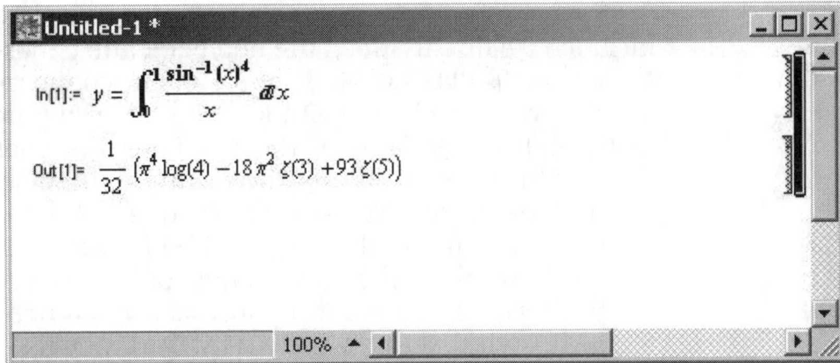

FIGURE 11.6 The same formula as in Figure 11.5 after conversion to TraditionalForm.

There are also several functions for converting between full form expressions and the various display forms (based on strings and boxes):

- `ToString`[*expr, form*]: creates a string that represents the specified textual form of *expr*
- `ToBoxes`[*expr, form*]: creates boxes that represent the specified textual form of *expr*
- `ToExpression`[*input, form*]: creates an expression by interpreting a string or boxes as input in the specified textual form

The aim of this section is to provide an overview of the syntax used in *Mathematica* for representing the meaning and appearance of mathematical notation. If you want more details about the different types of expressions and display forms, you should consult the *Mathematica* documentation.

Exporting MathML from *Mathematica*

This section discusses the various methods available in *Mathematica* for exporting mathematical formulas as MathML.

Menu Commands

You can use *Mathematica*'s typesetting capabilities to create nice-looking equations in a notebook, and then convert them into MathML for display on the Web. There are several ways to export mathematical expressions from a notebook as MathML.

To export a specific expression as MathML, select the expression and then choose the `Edit` ▶ `Copy As` ▶ `MathML` menu command. This copies the selected expression into the clipboard in the form of MathML presentation markup. You can then paste the markup into another application.

You can also export an entire notebook as HTML with MathML included. To do this, open the notebook and choose the `File ▶ Save As Special ▶ XML (XHTML+MathML)` menu command. This produces a well-formed and valid XHTML version of the notebook, with all mathematical formulas in the notebook automatically converted into MathML. The resulting document can then be displayed in any suitably configured Web browser, including *Mozilla* or *IE* with *MathPlayer*. Note that you should save the file with a .xml extension, for it to be viewable in the widest range of browsers.

Mathematica automatically inserts a reference to the Universal MathML stylesheet into the XHTML+MathML document. A local copy of this stylesheet is placed in a folder called HTMLFiles in the same directory as the XHTML+MathML file. This overcomes the limitation of *IE* not being able to use XSLT stylesheets from a remote location (see Section 7.2 for details on the Universal MathML stylesheet).

The `Export` Function

You can also export MathML to an external file using the built-in *Mathematica* function `Export`. This function takes various conversion options that you can use to customize the type of MathML generated. For example, you can choose to generate either presentation or content markup, add an XML declaration and a DOCTYPE declaration to the file, or add a specific namespace prefix to all the element and attribute names.

This function has the following syntax:

`Export [`*file*`,` *expr*`,` *format*`]`

The first argument specifies the name of the file to which the data should be exported. The second argument specifies the data to be exported, and the third specifies the export format. `Export` is a versatile function that can be used to export text, graphics, typeset equations, and other content from *Mathematica* in a variety of formats. If you specify the export format as `"MathML"`, the resulting output is in the form of MathML. Here is an example:

```
In[3]:= Export["test.mml", x^2+y, "MathML"]
Out[3]= test.mml
```

When you evaluate this command, *Mathematica* places the MathML representation of the expression $x^2 + y$ into a file called `test.mml`. You can examine the contents of this file by evaluating the `!!test.mml` command. This prints the contents of the specified file in the notebook, giving the output shown below:

```
In[4]:= !!test.mml
Out[4]= <math xmlns='http://www.w3.org/1998/Math/MathML'>
<semantics>
 <mrow>
   <msup>
     <mi>x</mi>
     <mn>2</mn>
   </msup>
   <mo>+</mo>
   <mi>y</mi>
 </mrow>
 <annotation-xml encoding='MathML-Content'>
   <apply>
     <plus/>
     <apply>
       <power/>
       <ci>x</ci>
       <cn type='integer'>2</cn>
     </apply>
     <ci>y</ci>
   </apply>
 </annotation-xml>
</semantics>
</math>
```

By default, the file contains both presentation markup and content markup for the expression, which is enclosed in a `semantics` element. The `xmlns` attribute is added to the top-level `math` element to provide information about the namespace of the enclosed elements.

The `ExportString` Function

Another useful built-in function is `ExportString`. This works in the same way as `Export` except that it returns output in the form of a string instead of writing to an external file. This behavior is useful if you want to translate a *Mathematica* expression into MathML and get the output in the same notebook for subsequent manipulation. This function has the following syntax:

`ExportString [`*expr*`,` *format*`]`

Here is an example:

```
In[5]:= ExportString[x+1, "MathML"]
Out[5]= <math xmlns='http://www.w3.org/1998/Math/MathML'>
<semantics>
 <mrow>
```

```
    <mi>x</mi>
    <mo>+</mo>
    <mn>1</mn>
  </mrow>
  <annotation-xml encoding='MathML-Content'>
    <apply>
      <plus/>
      <ci>x</ci>
      <cn type='integer'>1</cn>
    </apply>
  </annotation-xml>
</semantics>
</math>
```

Export Conversion Options

You can modify the default behavior of the `Export` and `ExportString` functions by explicitly specifying one or more conversion options. The syntax for specifying a conversion option is given below:

```
Export [file, expr, format, ConversionOptions ->
      {option -> value}]

ExportString [expr, format, ConversionOptions ->
      {option -> value}]
```

The following five conversion options are especially useful for exporting MathML:

- `"Formats"`: specifies the type of MathML generated. It is specified as a list whose elements can be `"PresentationMathML"` for presentation markup, and `"ContentMathML"` for content markup. The default value of this option is {`"PresentationMathML"`, `"ContentMathML"`}, which generates combined parallel markup.
- `"NamespacePrefixes"`: specifies a namespace prefix that should be added to each element and attribute name in the generated MathML. It is specified in the form {*url* -> *value*}, where *url* is the URL associated with the namespace and *value* is the namespace prefix.
- `"Annotations"`: specifies whether an XML declaration or a DTD declaration should be added before the exported MathML expression. The option is specified as a list whose elements can be `"DocumentHeader"`, `"XMLDeclaration"`, and/or `"DOCTYPEDeclaration"`. `"DocumentHeader"` is an overall switch that determines whether the other two values should take effect or not.

- "Entities": specifies whether character entities are written out using names or numeric codes. The possible settings are "XML", "HTML", and "MathML". Each setting defines a set of named characters that are written out with their full names instead of the corresponding character codes.
- "ElementFormatting": specifies the formatting of the MathML markup. If this option is set to "All", special indentation and linebreaking is used to indicate the tree structure of the markup. With a setting of "None", no special formatting is used.

Let's look at some examples of using these conversion options to control the form of the MathML generated.

The following command uses the "Formats" option to generate pure presentation markup:

```
In[6]:= ExportString[x^2+y, "MathML",
   ConversionOptions->{"Formats"->
   {"PresentationMathML"}}]
Out[6]= <math xmlns='http://www.w3.org/1998/Math/MathML'>
 <mrow>
   <msup>
     <mi>x</mi>
     <mn>2</mn>
   </msup>
   <mo>+</mo>
   <mi>y</mi>
 </mrow>
</math>
```

The following command generates pure content markup, and uses conversion options to add the namespace prefix mml to each element and attribute name and to add a declaration for the MathML DTD at the start of the exported expression:

```
In[7]:= ExportString[x^2+y, "MathML",
   ConversionOptions->{"Formats"->{"ContentMathML"},
   "Annotations"->{"DocumentHeader",
   "DOCTYPEDeclaration"}, "NamespacePrefixes"->
   {"http://www.w3.org/1998/Math/MathML"->"mml"}}]
Out[7]= <!DOCTYPE math PUBLIC '-//W3C//DTD MathML 2.0//EN'\
'http://www.w3.org/TR/MathML2/dtd/mathml2.dtd'>
<mml:math
xmlns:mml='http://www.w3.org/1998/Math/MathML'
xmlns='http://www.w3.org/1998/Math/MathML'>
 <mml:apply>
   <mml:plus/>
```

```
    <mml:apply>
      <mml:power/>
      <mml:ci>x</mml:ci>
      <mml:cn mml:type='integer'>2</mml:cn>
    </mml:apply>
    <mml:ci>y</mml:ci>
  </mml:apply>
</mml:math>
```

By default, whenever *Mathematica* produces any MathML as output, character entities are specified using their Unicode values. This is to make the output readable in Web browsers, such as *IE*, that do not recognize MathML entity names.

Here is an example:

```
In[8]:= ExportString[x*Sin[x],"MathML",
    ConversionOptions->{"Formats"->
    {"PresentationMathML"}}]
Out[8]:= "<math xmlns='http://www.w3.org/1998/Math/MathML'>
 <mrow>
    <mi>&#945;</mi>
    <mo>&#8290;</mo>
    <mrow>
      <mi>sin</mi>
        <mo>&#8289;</mo>
        <mo>(</mo>
        <mi>x</mi>
        <mo>)</mo>
    </mrow>
 </mrow>
</math>"
```

However, by setting the conversion option, `"Entities"->"MathML"`, you can tell *Mathematica* to write out the named entities instead, as shown here:

```
In[8]:= ExportString[x*Sin[x],"MathML",
    ConversionOptions->{"Formats"->
    {"PresentationMathML"}, "Entities"->"MathML"}]
Out[8]:= "<math xmlns='http://www.w3.org/1998/Math/MathML'>
 <mrow>
    <mi>&alpha;</mi>
    <mo>&InvisibleTimes;</mo>
    <mrow>
      <mi>sin</mi>
        <mo>&ApplyFunction;</mo>
        <mo>(</mo>
        <mi>x</mi>
```

```
            <mo>)</mo>
        </mrow>
    </mrow>
  </math>"
```

All the above examples automatically apply indentation and linebreaking to the MathML output, so it is nicely formatted to display its tree structure. This behavior is controlled by the conversion option `"ElementFormatting"`, whose default value is `"All"`. If you prefer to get the MathML output without any extra formatting, you can set this option to `"None"`. This produces more compact output, which is useful when you are exchanging data for machine processing, where the visual formatting is not important. Here is an example:

```
In[8]:= ExportString[x*Sin[x],"MathML",
   ConversionOptions->{"Formats"->
   {"PresentationMathML"},"ElementFormatting"->"None"}]
In[8]:= "<math xmlns='http://www.w3.org/1998/Math/MathML'>
<mrow>
 <mi>x</mi><mo>&#8290;</mo><mrow><mi>sin</mi><mo>&#8289;
 </mo><mo>(</mo><mi>x</mi><mo>)</mo></mrow></mrow></math>"
```

For more details about the available conversion options and their allowed values, you should consult the product documentation.

Importing MathML into *Mathematica*

There are two ways to import MathML equations into *Mathematica*. The first way is to copy and paste MathML equations from another application directly into a notebook. When you paste a valid MathML expression into a notebook, *Mathematica* brings up a dialog that asks if you want to paste the literal markup or interpret it (Figure 11.7). If you choose to interpret the markup, it is automatically converted into *Mathematica* syntax.

Another way to import MathML expressions into a notebook is by evaluating the built-in *Mathematica* function, `Import`. This function has the following syntax:

```
Import [file]
Import [file, format]
```

The first argument specifies the name of the file from which the data should be imported. *Mathematica* can use the file extension to identify the type of data in the file and to treat it accordingly. For example, any file with a `.mml` extension is automatically

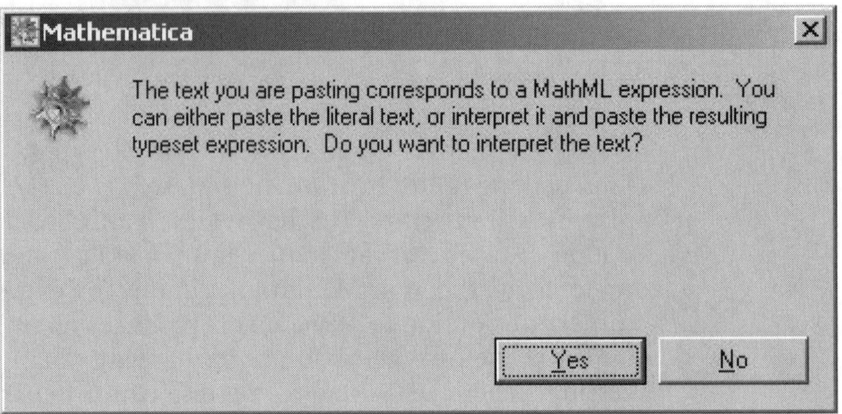

FIGURE 11.7 This dialog appears when you paste MathML markup into a *Mathematica notebook.*

recognized as a MathML file and is converted into a *Mathematica* box expression. You can use the optional second argument to specify the export format explicitly. For importing MathML, the relevant import format is `"MathML"`.

The following command creates a file called `test.mml` that contains the MathML markup corresponding to the expression, x^2:

```
In[1]:= Export["test.mml", x^2, "MathML"]
Out[1]= test.mml
```

The file `test.mml` contains the following MathML expression:

```
<math xmlns='http://www.w3.org/1998/Math/MathML'>
 <semantics>
   <msup>
     <mi>x</mi>
     <mn>2</mn>
   </msup>
   <annotation-xml encoding='MathML-Content'>
     <apply>
       <power/>
       <ci>x</ci>
       <cn type='integer'>2</cn>
     </apply>
   </annotation-xml>
 </semantics>
</math>
```

However, when the file is imported back into *Mathematica*, the MathML is automatically converted into a symbolic expression consisting of boxes, as shown here:

```
In[2]:= Import["test.mml"]
Out[2]= FormBox[TagBox[TagBox[SuperscriptBox["x", "2"],
    "MathMLPresentationTag", AutoDelete -> True],
    "AnnotationsTagWrapper"[TagBox[SuperscriptBox[
    "x", "2"],
    "MathMLContentTag", AutoDelete -> True]], AutoDelete ->
    True], TraditionalForm]
```

The output of the last example is the *Mathematica* equivalent of the MathML expression. It contains information about both the appearance and meaning of the expression that was imported. You can convert this box expression into a mathematical expression using the function `ToExpression`, as shown here:

```
In[3]:= ToExpression[%]
Out[3]= x^2
```

MathML Conversion Functions

Mathematica 4.2 contains several functions for converting between MathML and the boxes and expressions used internally to represent mathematical formulas. Some of the important MathML functions are listed in Table 11.2.

These functions are all found in the context `` XML`MathML` ``. Hence, to evaluate any of these functions, you must add this context name as a prefix to the name of the function. Here is an example that shows how these functions work:

```
In[1]:= XML`MathML`ExpressionToMathML[x^2]
Out[1]= <math xmlns='http://www.w3.org/1998/Math/MathML'>
 <semantics>
   <msup>
     <mi>x</mi>
     <mn>2</mn>
```

TABLE 11.2 Important MathML Functions

Function	Description
`MathMLToExpression`	Converts a MathML string to a *Mathematica* expression
`ExpressionToMathML`	Converts a *Mathematica* expression to a MathML string
`MathMLToBoxes`	Converts a MathML string to a box expression
`BoxesToMathML`	Converts a box expression into MathML

```
    </msup>
    <annotation-xml encoding='MathML-Content'>
      <apply>
        <power/>
        <ci>x</ci>
        <cn type='integer'>2</cn>
      </apply>
    </annotation-xml>
  </semantics>
</math>
```

You can specify any of the export conversion options listed earlier in this chapter directly in the functions that produce MathML. For example, the function `` XML`MathML`ExpressionToMathML `` yields both presentation and content markup enclosed in a `semantics` tag. But you can get either presentation or content markup alone by specifying the `"Formats"` conversion option. Here is an example:

```
In[2]:= XML`MathML`ExpressionToMathML[x+1,"Formats"->
    "PresentationMathML"]
Out[2]= <math xmlns='http://www.w3.org/1998/Math/MathML'>
 <msup>
   <mi>x</mi>
   <mn>2</mn>
 </msup>
</math>
```

You can add a namespace prefix to the output using the option `"NamespacePrefixes"`, as shown here:

```
In[3]:= XML`MathML`ExpressionToMathML[x+1,"Formats"->
    "ContentMathML""NamespacePrefixes"->
    {"http://www.w3.org/1998/Math/MathML"->"mml"}]
Out[3]= <math xmlns='http://www.w3.org/1998/Math/MathML'>
 <m:apply>
   <m:power/>
   <m:ci>x</m:ci>
   <m:cn m:type='integer'>2</m:cn>
 </m:apply>
</math>
```

The `%` command represents the result of the last calculation that you did in the notebook. The following command converts the MathML string back to a *Mathematica* expression:

```
In[4]:= XML`MathML`MathMLToExpression[%]
Out[4]= x^2
```

The following command converts a *Mathematica* box expression into the corresponding presentation MathML:

```
In[5]:= XML`MathML`BoxesToMathML[SuperscriptBox["x","2"]]
Out[5]= <math xmlns='http://www.w3.org/1998/Math/MathML'>
 <msup>
   <mi>x</mi>
   <mn>2</mn>
 </msup>
</math>
```

You can transform the MathML back into a box expression as shown here:

```
In[3]:= XML`MathML`MathMLToBoxes[%]
Out[3]= FormBox[TagBox[SuperscriptBox[x,2],
 MathMLPresentationTag, AutoDelete->True],TraditionalForm]
```

These examples demonstrate how closely MathML support is integrated into *Mathematica*. You can seamlessly and automatically convert mathematical expressions from *Mathematica*'s syntax to MathML and vice versa. This makes it easy to integrate *Mathematica* with other applications using MathML as the format for exchanging mathematical information. In Section 12.5, we shall see some specific examples of how *Mathematica* and MathML can be combined to do computations in a Web browser.

The functions outlined above, for importing, exporting, and transforming MathML, are a special case of the more general XML processing capabilities available in *Mathematica* 4.2. You can import any arbitrary XML documents into *Mathematica* and then transform them using SymbolicXML. This is a format for representing XML documents as *Mathematica* expressions while preserving their tree structure. The advantage of converting XML documents into SymbolicXML is that you can apply to XML data any of *Mathematica*'s built-in functions for numerical, symbolic, and graphical computations as well as functional programming. The MathML conversion functions discussed in this chapter are all implemented internally using SymbolicXML. The combination of SymbolicXML and *Mathematica* programming provides a useful alternative to other techniques for manipulating XML documents, such as XSLT transformations or the SAX or DOM APIs used with a low-level programming language such as Java.

11.3 *MAPLE*

Maple is, like *Mathematica*, a general-purpose technical computing package that offers support for numerical and symbolic calculations, graphics, data analysis, and programming. The main difference is that *Maple*'s front end is not as flexible and configurable as *Mathematica*'s. *Maple* does not include as much support for document processing and typesetting, such as the ability to edit the expression structure of mathematical notation or to create programmable documents. *Maple* is available for Windows and most Unix platforms but not for Macintosh.

The *Maple* Interface

The native file format in *Maple* is called a worksheet. When you first launch *Maple*, a new worksheet that shows a command prompt (>) enclosed in an execution group appears. Each execution group is indicated by a square bracket on the left of the worksheet and contains a group of input commands that are to be evaluated as a group. To get a new execution group with a command prompt, choose `Insert` ▶ `Execution Group` ▶ `After Cursor`.

Doing Calculations

To do a calculation, you type a command followed by a semicolon after the command prompt, and then press Enter to evaluate the input. The result of the calculation is returned as output immediately below the input. A typical *Maple* command consists of a *Maple* function name followed by one or more arguments for the function enclosed in parentheses. All function names start with a lowercase letter. Here is an example of a *Maple* command:

```
int(sin(x), x=0..Pi);
```

Here, `int` and `sin` are *Maple* functions that represent the integration and the sine function, respectively. Pressing Enter causes *Maple* to evaluate the command, and the resulting output is printed just below the input. Figure 11.8 shows an example of *Maple* input and output in a worksheet.

Entering Mathematical Notation

You can enter input for evaluation in two forms:

- *Maple* input: consists of plain-text commands written in a *Maple*-specific syntax
- Standard mathematical notation: simulates the two-dimensional layout of traditional mathematical notation

To enter input in *Maple* syntax, choose `Insert` ▶ `Maple Input`. When you are in *Maple* input mode, any text you type appears directly in the worksheet after the command prompt.

FIGURE 11.8 The *Maple* interface showing a worksheet, toolbars, and palettes.

Figure 11.9 shows an example of *Maple* input in an execution group, with the corresponding output displayed below it.

You can toggle between *Maple* input and standard mathematical notation by clicking the **x** button in the toolbar at the top of the application window. For example, you can use this button to convert the *Maple* input of Figure 11.9 into standard mathematical notation, shown in Figure 11.10.

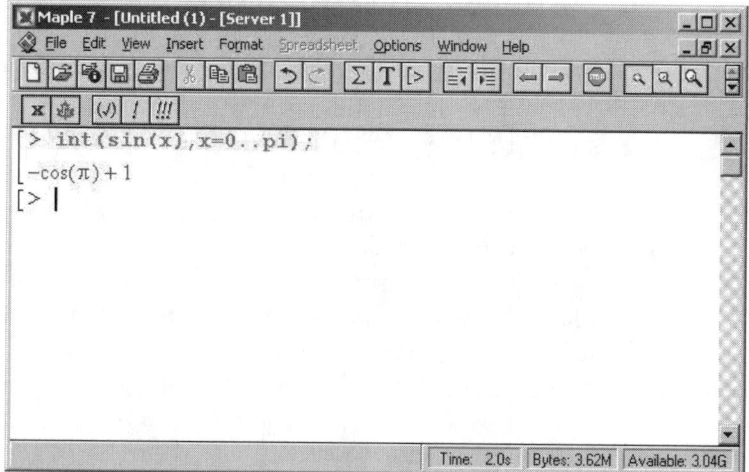

FIGURE 11.9 A worksheet that shows the result of evaluating a command in *Maple* input.

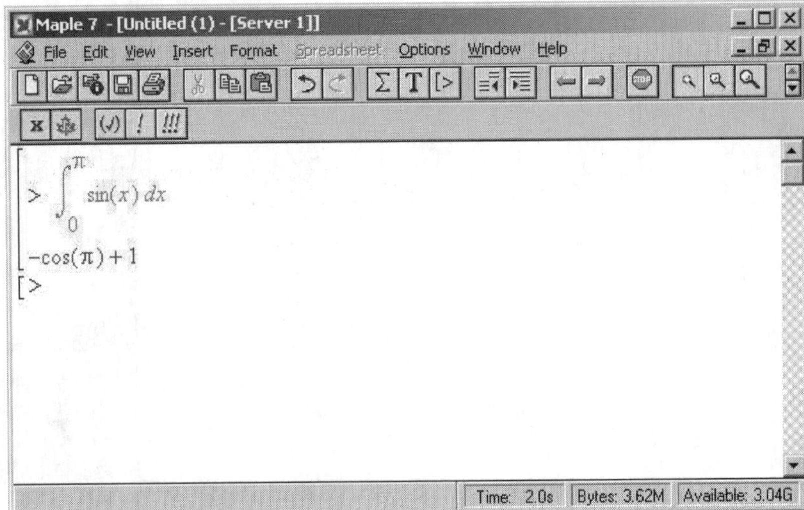

FIGURE 11.10 The same input as in Figure 11.9 shown in standard mathematical notation instead of *Maple* input.

To directly enter executable input in standard mathematical notation, choose `Insert ▶ Standard Math Input`. When you are in this mode, a question mark (?) appears in the input area, and a text editing window appears at the top of the screen. Any text you type first appears in this editing window. If you then press Enter, the text in the editing window is copied into the worksheet at the position of the ? sign.

Figure 11.11 shows the Insert menu, which contains commands for entering text, standard mathematical notation, and *Maple* input and standard mathematical input.

You can then construct the mathematical notation you want using the templates from the Expression palette as building blocks. The Expression palette contains buttons for entering most of the standard types of mathematical notation, such as subscripts, superscripts, fractions, square roots, or integrals. There are also separate palettes for entering vectors, matrices, and symbols such as Greek characters.

If you press any of the buttons on the Expression palette, a template for the corresponding notation appears in the worksheet, with the different parts of the template indicated by ? signs. You can move between the different ? positions by pressing Tab.

Entering Text and Inline Equations

You can intersperse text with the input and output by creating text areas. To enter text, choose `Insert ▶ Text` or click the **T** button

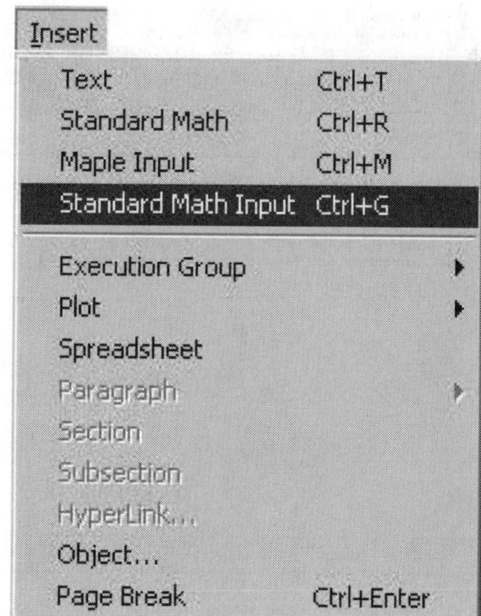

FIGURE 11.11 The *Maple* Insert menu, which shows the different types of input formats.

in the toolbar. Any text you type then appears in a text region of the worksheet. You can format paragraphs in a specific style (such as that of a heading, subheading, or normal text) by choosing one of the predefined styles from the `Format ▶ Style` menu. By combining text in specific styles with execution groups that contain input-output pairs, you can create nicely formatted technical docu ments.

You can include mathematical notation in a text cell in the form of inline equations (Figure 11.12). To do this in a text region, choose `Insert ▶ Standard Math` or click Σ in the tool bar. This inserts a ? sign at the position of the cursor. You can type in the notation in the text box at the top of the document and then press Enter for the corresponding notation to be inserted into the text cell to replace the ? sign.

Copying and Pasting MathML

Version 7 and later versions of *Maple* include full support for MathML 2.0. Both presentation and content tags are supported. You can import, evaluate, and export MathML functions using either copying and pasting, menu commands, or specialized package functions.

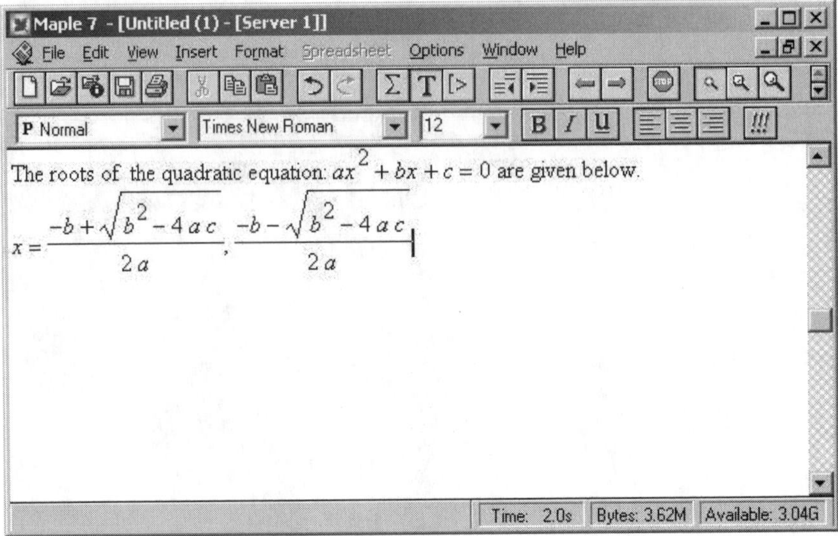

FIGURE 11.12 Entering an inline equation in a text region using the Expression palette.

To copy mathematical output as MathML, follow these steps:

1. Select the expression you wish to convert into MathML in the *Maple* worksheet.
2. Right-click with the mouse. This brings up a contextual menu of the type shown in Figure 11.13.
3. From the menu choose `Conversions` ▶ `MathML`.

A MathML version of the selected expression is returned as an output string. You can then copy the MathML expression from the output and paste it into another application.

You can also copy MathML equations from another application and paste them into *Maple* in the form of a valid *Maple* expression. When you attempt to paste a MathML expression into a worksheet, you will get a dialog that asks if you wish to interpret the expression or paste it literally (Figure 11.14). If you click Yes, the corresponding Maple expression will be pasted into the worksheet.

Exporting a Worksheet As HTML+MathML

You can export a worksheet to HTML and automatically convert all mathematical output into MathML. To do this, follow these steps:

1. Open the worksheet that you want to export.
2. Choose `File` ▶ `Export As` ▶ `HTML with MathML`.
3. In the `Save As` dialog that appears, specify a name and location for the file, and then click `OK`.

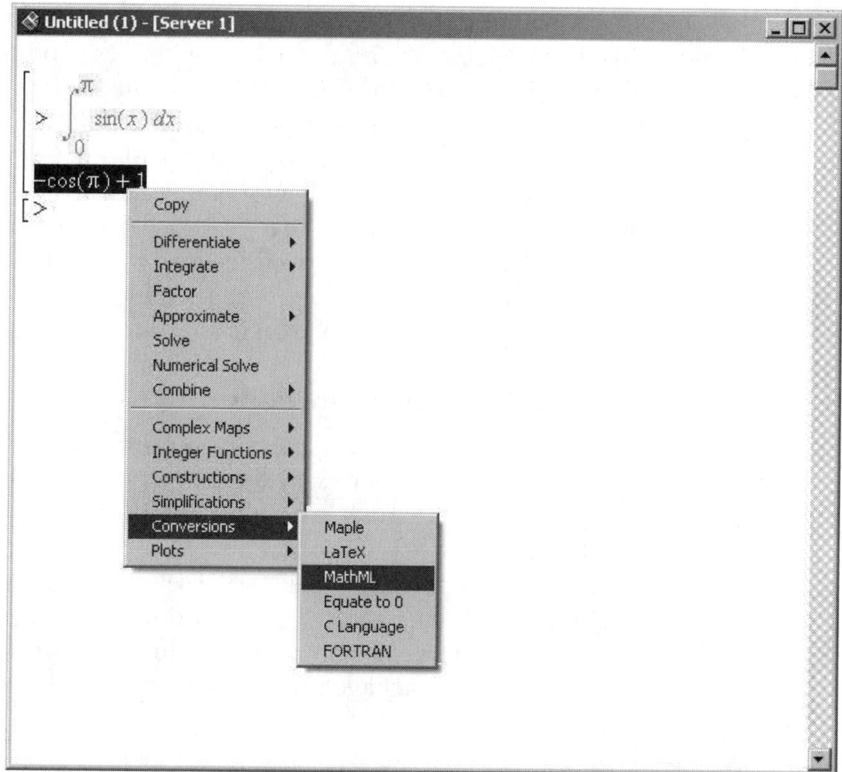

FIGURE 11.13 The contextual menu for converting output into MathML.

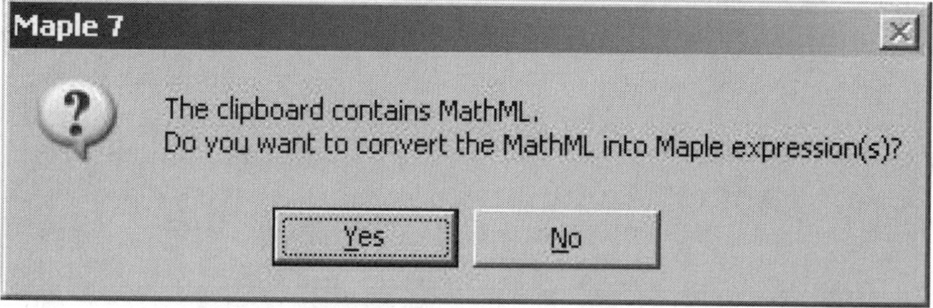

FIGURE 11.14 The dialog that appears when you paste a MathML expression into a worksheet.

4. The HTML options dialog is displayed. Use the `Save Mathematical Expressions As` pop-up menu to specify the type of MathML you want to produce.
5. Click `OK`.

An HTML version of the worksheet that contains embedded MathML equations is saved in the location you specified. Parts of the worksheet that cannot be saved as HTML (such as graphics) are saved as GIF images. By default, any images produced are saved in an images directory located in the same directory as the HTML document. You can choose the particular type of MathML in which to save formulas using the HTML Options dialog (Figure 11.15).

Conversion from *Maple* worksheets to HTML+MathML documents is not reversible. That is, you cannot import an HTML +MathML document produced in this way into *Maple* and convert it back into a worksheet for doing further calculations. This type of two-way conversion, however, is supported in *Mathcad*.

MathML Conversion Functions

Maple (Version 7 or later) contains a number of functions for converting *Maple* expressions to different types of MathML and vice versa. These functions are all contained in a package called `MathML`.

Each *Maple* package consists of a set of specialized functions that deal with a specific topic. Unlike the top-level functions (such as `integrate` or `sin`, which can be evaluated if you just specify the function name), package functions must be prefaced with the name of the package.

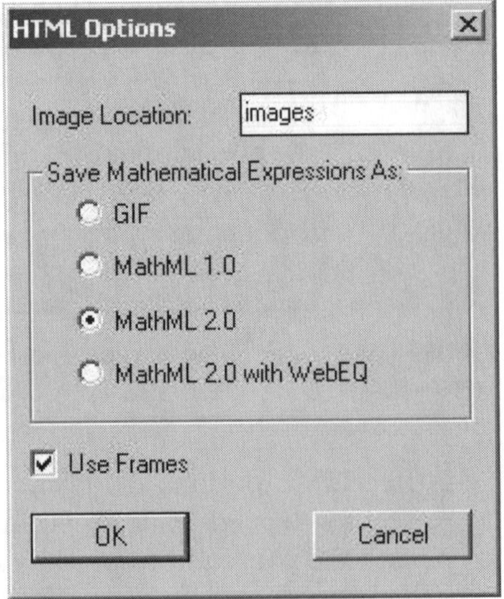

FIGURE 11.15 The HTML Options dialog, which shows the options available for saving formulas in a worksheet as MathML.

For example, the `MathML` package contains a function called `Export`, which converts a *Maple* expression into MathML. Hence, to evaluate this function, the *Maple* command would be:

```
MathML[Export](arg);
```

This is called the *long form* of the function name. Alternatively, you can first load the package using the `with` command. You can then refer to functions in the package using their short names; that is, without using the package name as a prefix. Doing this is useful when you intend to use one or more functions from a package repeatedly in the same *Maple* session.

The following two commands are equivalent to the single command just given:

```
with(MathML); Export(arg);
```

Converting *Maple* Syntax to MathML

The `MathML` package contains three functions for converting a *Maple* expression into a MathML:

- `MathML[Export]`(*expr*): converts a *Maple* expression into a MathML string. The resulting MathML is in the form of combined markup with three separate encodings enclosed in parallel in a `semantics` tag: presentation markup followed by content markup enclosed in an `annotation-xml` followed by a textual representation of the *Maple* syntax for the input expression enclosed in an `annotation` element. This allows *Maple* to recover the original input if it encounters the same MathML expression.
- `MathML[ExportContent]`(*expr*): converts a *Maple* expression into content MathML. This is faster and more efficient than using the `MathML[Export]` function, which must produce three separate encodings of the same expression.
- `MathML[ExportPresentation]`(*expr*): converts a *Maple* expression into presentation MathML. This works by first generating a full parallel encoding for the specified expression and then stripping off the content MathML and *Maple* annotations. Hence, it is not more efficient or faster than using `MathML[Export]`.

Here are some examples showing how these functions work.

The following command produces combined markup, with both presentation and content markup representations of the *Maple* expression, enclosed in a `semantics` tag:

```
MathML[Export](x^2 + sqrt(x));
"<math mlns='http://www.w3.org/1998/Math/MathML'>
<semantics><mrow xref='id6'><mrow xref='id3'><msup>
<mi xref='id1'>x</mi><mn xref='id2'>2</mn></msup>
</mrow><mo>+</mo><mrow xref='id5'><msqrt>
<mi xref='id4'>x</mi></msqrt></mrow></mrow>
<annotation-xml encoding='MathML-Content'><apply id='id6'>
<plus/><apply id='id3'><power/><ci id='id1'>x</ci>
<cn id='id2'type='integer'>2</cn></apply><apply id='id5'>
<root/><ci id='id4'>x</ci></apply></apply></annotation-
xml><annotation encoding='Maple'>x^2+x^(1/2)</annotation>
</semantics></math>"
```

Notice that the output elements contain the id and xref attributes for fine-grained cross-referencing. As explained in Section 6.3, the purposes of these attributes is to establish a correspondence between the content and presentation markup for each subexpression of the overall expression.

The following command produces content markup only:

```
MathML[ExportContent](x^2 + sqrt(x));
"<math xmlns='http://www.w3.org/1998/Math/MathML'>
<apply id='id6\'><plus/><apply id='id3'><power/>
<ci id='id1'>x</ci><cn id\='id2'type='integer'>2</cn>
</apply><apply id='id5'><root/><ci id='id4'>x</ci>
</apply></apply></math>"
```

The following command produces presentation markup only:

```
MathML[ExportPresentation](x^2+sqrt(x));
"<math xmlns = 'http://www.w3.org/1998/Math/MathML'>
<mrow><msup><mi>x</mi><mn>2</mn></msup><mo>+</mo>
<msqrt><mi>x</mi></msqrt></mrow></math>"
```

You can use the Print function contained in the XMLTools package to print the output in a tab-indented form in the worksheet, or XMLTools[PrintToFile](*filename*, %) to print the tab-indented output to a file. The % symbol is the *Maple* notation to represent the result of the last calculation you did in the worksheet. Here is an example showing the output from XMLTools:

```
XMLTools[Print](%)
<math xmlns='http://www.w3.org/1998/Math/MathML'>
 <mrow>
    <msup>
       <mi>x</mi>
       <mn>2</mn>
```

```
      </msup>
      <mo>+</mo>
      <msqrt>
        <mi>x</mi>
      </msqrt>
    </mrow>
  </math>
```

Converting MathML to *Maple* Syntax

The `MathML` package contains two functions for converting a MathML expression into a *Maple* expression. Both functions take as their argument a MathML expression specified as a string. The first is:

`MathML[Import](`*`mmlstring`*`)` -

This converts into a *Maple* expression parallel combined markup that contains both the presentation MathML and content MathML representation of an expression. This function will also attempt a conversion on presentation markup in cases where it is possible to do so unambiguously. If the conversion fails, the function returns an error message. Here is an example showing the effect of `MathML[Import]`:

```
MathML[Import]("<math><msup><mi>x</mi><mn>2</mn>
</msup></math>");
```

x^2

The second function is:

`MathML[ImportContent](`*`mmlstring`*`)` -

This converts a content MathML expression into a *Maple* expression. If the conversion fails, *Maple* produces an error message. Here is an example showing the effect of `MathML[ImportContent]`:

```
MathML[ImportContent]("<math><apply><power/>
<ci>x</ci><cn>2</cn></apply></math>");
```

x^2

CHAPTER

12

CREATING DYNAMIC MATH WEB PAGES

This chapter provides information on using MathML to create dynamic Web pages that feature interactive mathematical content. It starts with an overview of how to use HTML controls and JavaScript. It then provides detailed examples of how to implement various types of interactivity in Web pages using the MathML-specific features of products like *WebEQ*, *techexplorer*, and web*Mathematica*.

12.1 INTRODUCTION

The rapid development of HTML and related standards over the last few years has made the Web a rich and flexible medium for communication. Web pages are no longer static and passive, as was the case in the early days of the Internet. Instead, Web pages can respond to user input, execute programs, and deliver interactive content in a variety of formats, including text, images, animations, sounds, and video.

This evolution has been made possible by the emergence of a standard framework of technologies for describing and transforming Web content. This framework includes W3C specifications such as HTML, CSS, XSLT, and DOM for describing the detailed structure and layout of Web pages. These are supplemented by programming and scripting languages, such as JavaScript or Java applets on the client side, and CGI, ASP, Java, Perl, or PHP on the server side—that can be used to dynamically update Web pages in response to user input. The combined use of these technologies for delivering interactive content on the Web is collectively referred to by the term *dynamic HTML*.

In the past, it was not possible to apply the techniques of dynamic HTML to mathematical formulas, since there was no standard format for representing mathematics on the Web. For example, when mathematical notation is represented using images, there is no way to interactively transform the content or appearance of the formulas displayed. The advent of MathML provides a simple and effective way to overcome such limitations. Because it is an XML-based language, MathML is fully compatible with other Web technologies, such as HTML, CSS, JavaScript, Java, and DOM.

By making equations embedded in Web pages just as scriptable and easy to process as text, MathML provides a solid basis for delivering dynamic mathematical content on the Web. This opens up many interesting possibilities for communicating mathematical information, in both educational and professional contexts. Some applications of interactive MathML content on the Web include online demos, courseware, assignments, quizzes, or other instructional material, as well as services such as online testing and e-mail message boards.

Types of Interactivity

The term *dynamic math* refers to the display of interactive mathematical content that changes in some way in response to an action by the user. The types of interactivity possible can be divided into three broad categories.

First, you can use equation actions to change some aspect of an equation's display in response to an event like clicking or moving the mouse. For example, you can change color of an equation, turn it into a hyperlink, toggle between two different displays, or display a message in the browser's status bar. MathML provides the `maction` element for implementing such changes. However, the type of actions supported and the method of encoding them depends on the specific rendering application. These simple types of interactivity are easy to set up using a suitable tool that supports actions; for example, *WebEQ* or *techexplorer*.

Second, you can use HTML controls in combination with JavaScript programs or Java applets. This involves inserting HTML controls such as buttons, text boxes, or menus in a Web page. The controls are hooked up to a JavaScript or Java function that does some processing in response to user input and displays the result in the same Web page or in a separate window. You can use this technique to implement a much wider variety of interactive behavior than you can if you use simple actions, but the user has to have some basic knowledge of Web programming.

These two types of interactivity both involve transformations on the client side. You can achieve a greater degree of control by doing transformations on the Web server. This involves configuring a Web page to accept input from a user and send it to a server, which processes the input and returns the result back to the client. You can specify the input either by entering text in an HTML form or by authoring arbitrary mathematical notation in the Web page using an equation editor applet. By running suitable scripts and programs in the server, in any standard language, such as Java, Perl, or PHP, you can perform a wide variety of operations. You can even run specialized software like *Mathematica* or *Maple* on the server to perform computations on MathML equations and display the results in the client's browser. Server-side programming can be used to implement some very sophisticated applications, but it is also the most technically demanding.

We will see simple examples of each of these types of interactivity in this chapter. Since most MathML-content will be created and rendered by specific applications, we provide examples of developing interactive content using specific applications, such as *WebEQ*, *techexplorer*, and web*Mathematica*.

The source code for all examples in this chapter is included in the CD-ROM, so you can run the examples on your computer and use them as templates for creating your own interactive Web pages.

This chapter assumes some basic familiarity with Web programming concepts such as HTML, JavaScript, and Java applets. For detailed information on these topics, you can refer to one of the many books available on dynamic HTML. The focus of this chapter is not to give an exhaustive treatment of Web programming techniques but to give you a broad idea of the kinds of interactivity possible using MathML.

12.2 JAVASCRIPT AND HTML

Most client-side interactivity in Web pages involves the use of a scripting language, such as JavaScript or VBScript, to control the browser and modify its contents. In this section, we provide some simple examples of using JavaScript in combination with HTML controls to dynamically update the contents of a Web page. This is a basic technique that is common to many of the examples discussed in the rest of this chapter.

JavaScript is a scripting language that is widely used to implement interactive behavior in Web browsers. You can directly embed JavaScript code in a Web page to be executed by the browser either when the page is displayed or when the user performs some action, such as moving the mouse or pressing a button. JavaScript is supported by most modern Web browsers, including recent versions of *IE* and *Netscape*. However, the details of implementation differ slightly from one browser to another.

Example 12.1 shows a simple HTML document that contains some JavaScript code.

Example 12.1 An HTML document that contains JavaScript code.

```
<html>
 <head>
   <title>JavaScript example</title>
 </head>
 <body>
   <h1>JavaScript example</h1>
   <script language="javascript">
     document.write("This text was written by
     JavaScript.")
   </script>
 </body>
</html>
```

The JavaScript code is enclosed in an HTML `script` tag with the attribute `language` set to `javascript`. The command `document.write` is a JavaScript function that writes the text specified as its argument into a Web page when that Web page is loaded into a browser. Figure 12.1 shows the result of viewing the above HTML document in *IE*.

Objects and Methods

JavaScript is an object-oriented language. It defines a set of objects that represent various aspects of a document or the browser. For

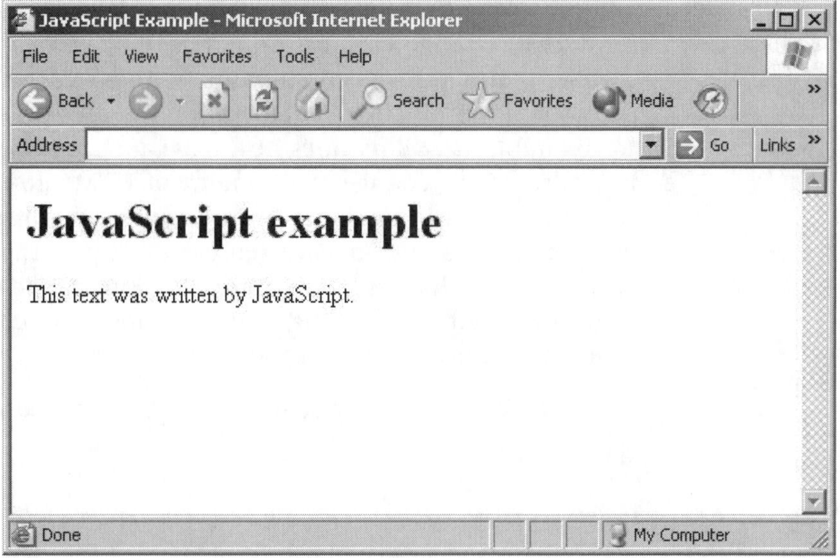

FIGURE 12.1 An HTML document viewed in *IE* that contains JavaScript.

example, the document object represents the entire document currently displayed in the browser. Some other important objects defined in JavaScript are window, which represents the current browser window; history, which keeps a record of the pages viewed in the browser before the current page; and navigator, which represents the specific browser application being used.

Each object has a set of methods that are functions for performing specific actions. For example, the document.write command used in Example 12.1 represents the write method associated with the document object. Each object also has a set of properties associated with it. For example, the document.fgcolor and document.bgcolor commands represent the foreground color and background color properties of the current document, respectively.

Forms and Controls

The most common way for users to interact with Web pages is through HTML *forms* and *controls*. Forms allow users to enter some input and send it to the Web server for processing. Each form is represented in HTML using a form element. A form can contain interactive items called controls for specifying input. There are many different types of controls such as buttons, checkboxes, radio buttons, menus, and text boxes. These are represented by HTML elements such as input, selection, and textarea.

JavaScript includes objects that correspond to each form or control in a Web page. You can use these objects and the methods and properties associated with them to control the behavior of the browser or change various properties of a Web page. Hence, using JavaScript programs in combination with HTML forms and controls allows you to implement many different types of interactivity.

Example 12.2 illustrates how a JavaScript function can receive input from and change the content of HTML forms. It shows an HTML document that contains three different controls; that is, two text boxes and a button, each represented by an input element. The input element has two important attributes: type, which specifies the type of control, and name, which assigns a name that a JavaScript function can use to refer to the control.

Example 12.2 An HTML document that contains controls.

```
<html>
 <head>
 <title>JavaScript Example</title>
 <script language="javascript">
```

```
      function displayText() {
        document.form2.text2.value =
        document.form1.text1.value
      }
      </script>
   </head>
  <body>
  <h1>Using controls with JavaScript</h1>
  <p>Enter some text here:
   <form name="form1">
   <input type="text" name="text1" size=50></input>
   </form>
   <p><input type="button" name="button1"
     value="Click" onclick="displayText()">
   <p>The text you typed appears here:
   <form name="form2">
   <input type="text" name="text2" size=50></input>
   </form>
   </body>
  </html>
```

When the above HTML document is first loaded into a browser, two blank text boxes are displayed with a button in between them. If you type some text into the first text box and then click the button, the same text is displayed in the second text box, as shown in Figure 12.2. The process by which this happens is as follows. When the user clicks the button, the `onclick` attribute of the `input` element for the button causes the JavaScript function `displayText` to be executed. This function sets the `value` attribute of the second text box to have the same value as the `value` attribute of the first text box. The `value` attribute determines the text displayed in the text box. Hence, the net effect of the function is to cause the same text to be displayed in the second text box.

This section reviewed some general principles involved in using JavaScript with forms and controls to add interactive behavior in Web pages. We shall apply these principles to the special case of creating interactive mathematical content by combining the techniques discussed here with the additional MathML-specific functionality provided by MathML tools such as *WebEQ*, *techexplorer*, and web*Mathematica*.

12.3 *WebEQ*

As we saw in Section 7.4, *WebEQ* is a Java-based suite of programs for authoring and displaying mathematics on the Web. In

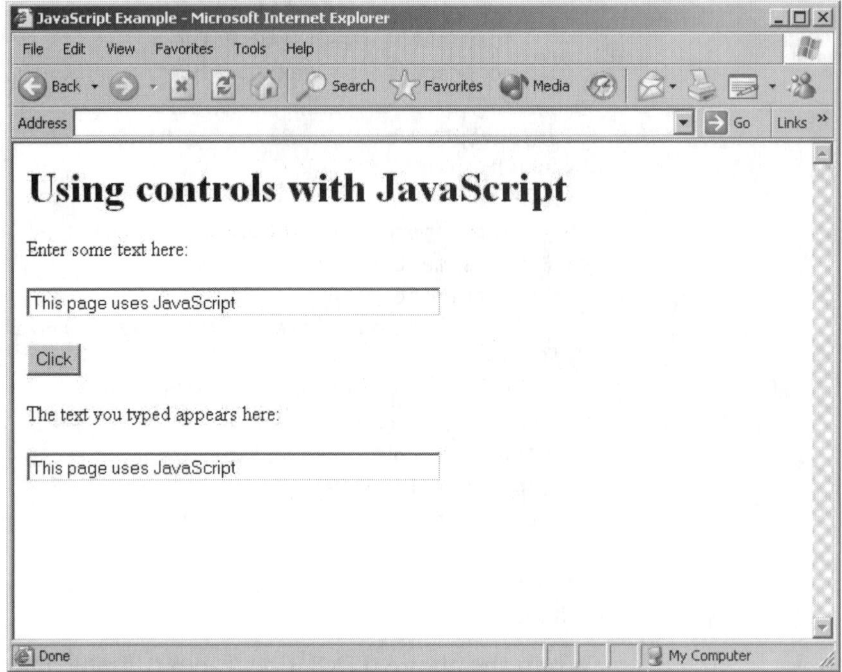

FIGURE 12.2 Using JavaScript with HTML forms and controls.

Section 9.3, we discussed the use of the *WebEQ* Editor (for authoring MathML equations) and the *WebEQ* Viewer Control (for displaying the equations in a Web page). In this section, we look at some additional features of the Editor and Viewer Control that are relevant for creating interactive mathematical content. We also discuss a third component of the *WebEQ* suite, the Input Control, which is an applet for authoring and editing equations in a Web page.

A key feature of *WebEQ* is that it includes a set of JavaScript and DOM APIs for scripting the Viewer Control and Input Control applets. Using the API functions, you can create scriptable mathematical content in Web pages.

Viewer Control

The *WebEQ* Viewer Control is a Java applet for displaying mathematical formulas in Web pages. As discussed in Section 7.4, the equations to be displayed are embedded in an HTML document in an `applet` tag, in either MathML or WebTEX format. The display of the applet requires a special set of class files that can either be installed locally on the client machine or downloaded directly from the server along with the document to be viewed. The location of these files is specified using the `codebase` and `code` attributes.

A typical Viewer Control applet tag has the following structure:

```
<applet codebase="classes"
 code="webeq3.ViewerControl"
 width=200 height=100>
 <param name=eq value=mml_string>
</applet>
```

Here, *mml_string* is a string that specifies the MathML markup for the equation to be displayed. Alternatively, you can place the MathML markup in a separate file, whose location you can specify via an absolute or relative URL using the parameter *src*, as shown below:

```
<applet codebase="classes"
 code="webeq3.ViewerControl"
 width=200 height=100>
 <param name=src value=url>
</applet>
```

The Viewer Control applet supports various parameters for controlling the appearance of an equation, such as its font size, color, and alignment. One of the parameters is `controls`, which can take the values `true` or `false`. If this parameter is set to `true`, as shown in the following code fragment, right-clicking the displayed equation opens a dialog that allows the user to change the font size of the equation:

```
<applet codebase="classes"
 code="webeq3.ViewerControl"
 width=200 height=100>
 <param name=src value=url>
 <param name=controls value=true>
</applet>
```

Figure 12.3 shows a Viewer Control applet displayed in *IE*, along with the font size control panel that appears when you right-click the equation.

Actions in *WebEQ*

For authoring formulas to be displayed using the Viewer Control, you can use the *WebEQ* Editor, as explained in Section 9.3. Once you have created an equation using the Editor, you can export the equation as a *WebEQ* Viewer Control applet tag, which is suitable for pasting into an HTML document that can be displayed in a browser.

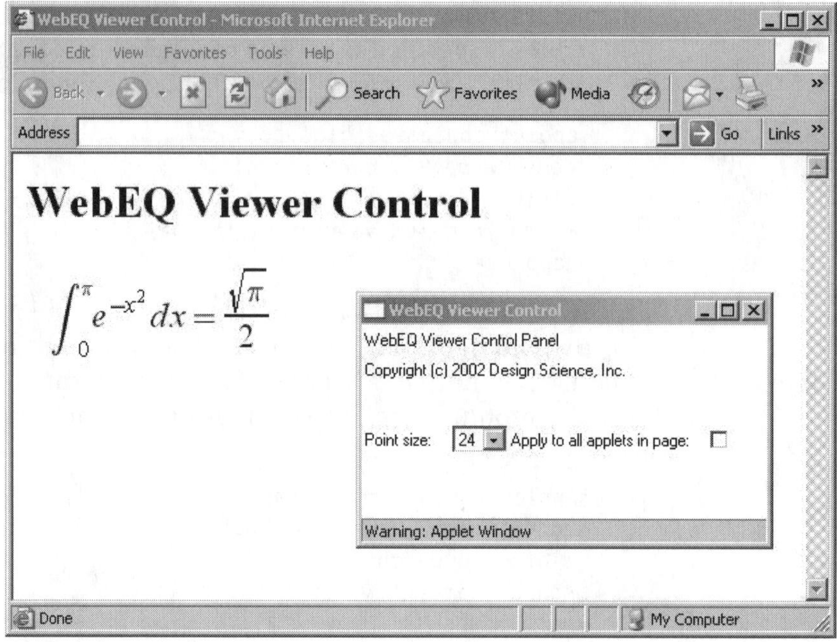

FIGURE 12.3 A Viewer Control applet displayed in *IE* that shows the pop-up menu for changing the font size of the displayed equation.

WebEQ provides support for three types of interactive actions in equations:

- Mouseover: moving the cursor over an equation changes the background and foreground colors, to highlight it.
- Link: this turns an equation into a hyperlink that points to a specified URL.
- Toggle: clicking on an equation causes it to alternate between two different displays.

To create any of these types of actions, you choose the corresponding command from the `Insert` ▶ `Actions` menu in the *WebEQ* Editor window (Figure 12.4). This opens a dialog with fields for specifying the various parameters that define the action. These actions are all implemented using the `maction` element of presentation MathML. In other words, a `maction` tag with the appropriate attribute values set is automatically added in the underlying markup for the equation you are authoring. This tag can then be interpreted by the Viewer Control when it displays the markup. Thus you can author interactive equations using the *WebEQ* Editor and display them in a Web page using the *WebEQ* Viewer Control.

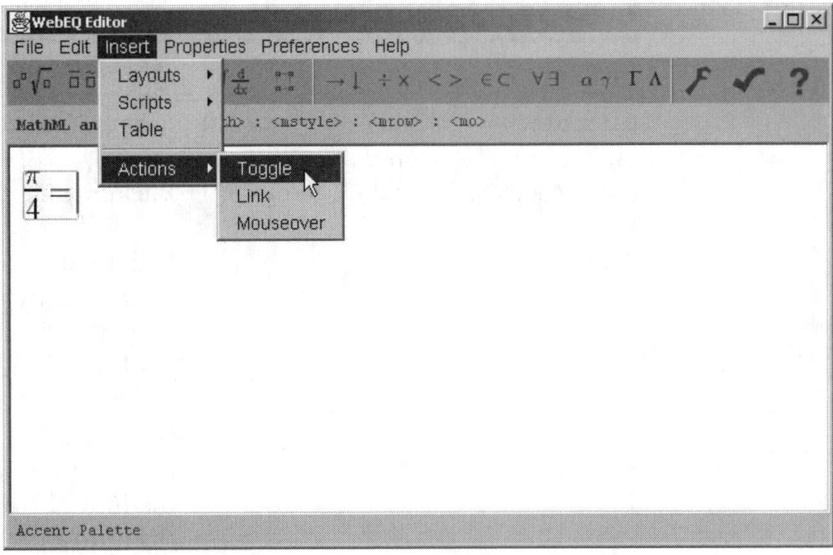

FIGURE 12.4 Authoring an equation with an action in *WebEQ* Editor.

As we saw in Section 4.6, the `maction` element takes an attribute called `actiontype`, which defines the type of interactivity in the equation. In *WebEQ*, this attribute can take one of three values: `mouseover`, `link`, or `toggle`, which correspond to the three types of actions supported. In addition, for each type of action, some "pseudo-attributes" specify additional information about the action. These attributes are not part of the MathML specification. They are supported by *WebEQ* only for implementing specific actions and have the namespace prefix `dsi`. These attributes are listed in Table 12.1.

Here is the `applet` tag for an equation with a mouseover action:

```
<applet codebase="classes"
 code="webeq3.ViewerControl" height=100 width=200>
 <param name="eq" value="
 <math>
   <mrow>
     <maction actiontype='mouseover'dsi:color='red'
     dsi:background='blue'dsi:cue1='Mouseover effect'>
       <mrow>
         <mi>x</mi>
         <mo>+</mo>
         <mn>1</mn>
       </mrow>
     </maction>
```

TABLE 12.1 Pseudo-Attributes

Attribute	Values	Meaning
dsi:color	*#rgb* | *#rrggbb* | *html-color name*	Foreground color of equation
dsi:background	*#rgb* | *#rrggbb* | html-color name	Background color
dsi:href	*string*	URL to link to (for `actiontype ='link'` only)
dsi:cue1	*string*	Message displayed in the status line of the browser when the mouse is moved over the equation
dsi:cue2	*string*	Message displayed in the status line of the browser when the mouse is moved over the alternate equation (for `actiontype = 'toggle'` only)

```
    </mrow>
  </math>">
</applet>
```

When the cursor is moved over the applet, the equation's text color becomes red, the background color becomes blue, and a message is displayed in the browser's status bar. These properties are specified using the *WebEQ* pseudo-attributes that we saw in Table 12.1.

The `applet` tag for the same equation to act as a link is shown below:

```
<applet codebase="classes"
 code="webeq3.ViewerControl" height=100 width=200>
 <param name="eq" value="
 <math>
   <mrow>
     <maction actiontype='link'dsi:color='red'
     dsi:background='blue'dsi:cue1='integral'
     dsi:href='http://www.examples.org/webeq_link'>
       <mrow>
         <mi>x</mi>
         <mo>+</mo>
         <mn>1</mn>
       </mrow>
```

```
      </maction>
    </mrow>
  </math>">
</applet>
```

The main differences between this markup and the previous one are that here, the `actiontype` attribute has the value `link` instead of `mouseover` and the extra attribute `dsi:href` is used to specify the destination URL.

To create a toggle action, the `maction` element has two arguments, which represent the two expressions to alternate between. In other words, the element has the following syntax:

```
<maction actiontype="toggle"
 dsi:cue1=message1 dsi:cue2=message2>
   expr1
   expr1
<maction>
```

Here is the `applet` tag for an equation with a toggle:

```
<applet codebase="classes"
 code="webeq3.ViewerControl" height=100 width=400>
 <param name="eq" value=
   "<math><mstyle displaystyle='true'>
   <mrow><mrow><mfrac><mrow><mi>&pi;</mi></mrow>
   <mrow><mn>4</mn></mrow></mfrac></mrow><mo>=</mo>
   <maction actiontype='toggle'dsi:cue1='Leibniz
   formula'dsi:cue2='first few terms in the series'>
   <mrow><mrow><munderover><mo>&sum;</mo><mrow>
   <mi>n</mi><mo>=</mo><mn>1</mn></mrow><mrow>
   <mi>&infin;</mi></mrow></munderover><mrow><mfrac>
   <mrow><mo>(</mo> <mo>-</mo><mn>1</mn><msup><mrow>
   <mo>)</mo></mrow><mrow><mi>n</mi><mo>+</mo>
   <mn>1</mn></mrow></msup></mrow><mrow><mo>(</mo>
   <mn>2</mn> <mi>n</mi><mo>-/mo><mn>1</mn><mo>)
   </mo></mrow></mfrac></mrow></mrow></mrow><mrow>
   <mn>1</mn><mo>-</mo><mfrac><mrow><mn>1</mn>
   </mrow><mrow><mn>3</mn></mrow></mfrac><mo>+</mo>
   <mfrac><mrow><mn>1</mn></mrow><mrow><mn>5</mn>
   </mrow></mfrac><mo>-</mo><mfrac><mrow><mn>1</mn>
   </mrow><mrow><mn>7</mn></mrow></mfrac><mo>+</mo>
   <mn>...</mn></mrow></maction></mstyle></math>">
</applet>
```

The MathML markup in this example is shown without the normal indentation and linebreaking (to save space). Although the markup is verbose, remember that the entire `applet` tag along with the MathML markup inside it can be generated automatically using the *WebEQ* Editor. Hence, you will rarely need to author such expressions by hand. The purpose of this example is mainly to explain the structure of the underlying markup, so you can see how toggle actions work.

Inserting this applet into a Web page causes the display to switch between the two expressions shown in Figures 12.5 and 12.6. You can switch between the two views by clicking anywhere on the right-hand side of the equation. The message in the status line of the browser window also changes with the equation being displayed.

Scripting the Viewer Control

WebEQ includes a set of APIs for scripting the Viewer Control applet. The APIs contain high-level functions that can be called by other Java applets or JavaScript programs to access or change various properties of the displayed equation. This allows you to create various types of interactive behavior; for example, changing the display of an equation when the user clicks a button or chooses an item from a menu. Table 12.2 shows a few of the functions included in the Viewer Control API.

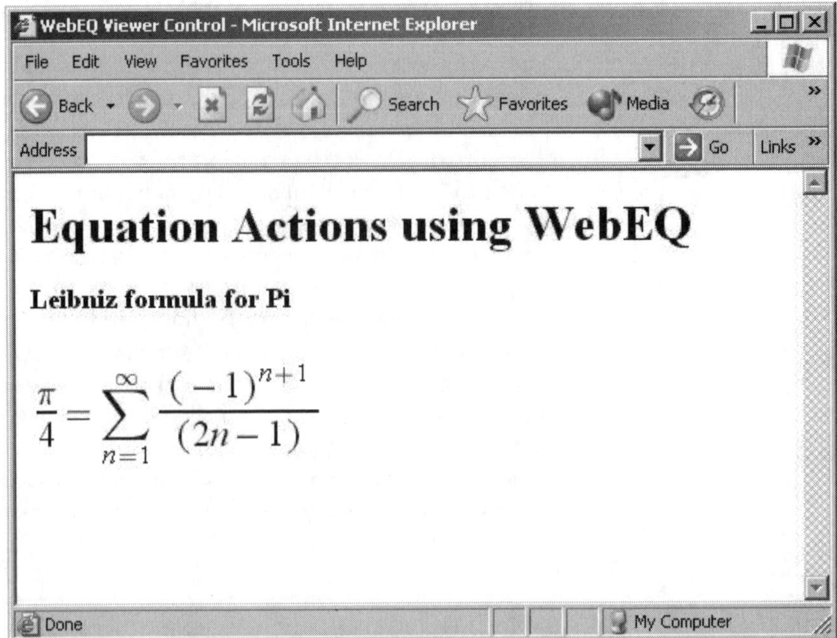

FIGURE 12.5 A Web page that contains a Viewer Control applet with a toggle action.

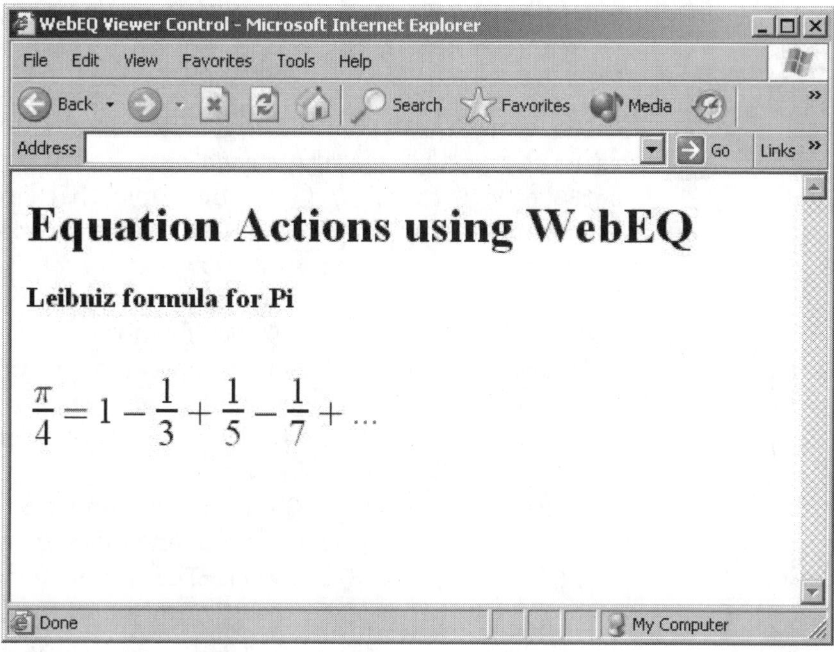

FIGURE 12.6 The same Web page as in Figure 12.5, but this one shows the alternate display you get when you click the equation.

Le's look at some examples of using these functions to implement some simple interactive behavior.

Example 12.3 sets up a Web page (Figure 12.7) with a text area in which a user can type in any MathML expression When the user clicks the "Display" button, the Viewer Control renders the MathML as an applet embedded in the page.

Example 12.3 An HTML document for rendering a specified MathML expression.

```
<html>
<head>
 <title>WebEQ Viewer Control</title>
   <script language="javascript">
     function showMath( ) {
       var expr = document.MMLForm.MMLString.value;
       document.mathapplet.setEquation(expr);
     }
   </script>
</head>
<body bgcolor="white">
 <h1>WebEQ scripting example</h1>
   <p>Enter MathML string:
```

TABLE 12.2 Functions Included in the Viewer Control API

Method	Description
`setEquation(String neweq)`	Changes the value of the `eq` parameter to `neweq`.
`setBGColor(String newcolor)`	Sets the applet background color to `newcolor`, where `newcolor` is of the form "*#rrggbb*", "*#rgb*", or a predefined color keyword (as defined in the HTML 4.0 specification).
`setFGColor(String newcolor)`	Sets the applet foreground color to `newcolor`, where `newcolor` is of the form "*#rrggbb*", "*#rgb*", or a predefined color keyword.
`setSize(int size)`	Changes the point size of the characters in a single instance of the *WebEQ* applet. The point size is set to the largest number on the list (36, 30, 24, 18, 16, 14, 12, 10, 8) that is less than or equal to size.
`preferredHeight()`	Returns the height of the rendered equation. This is also the value to which the `height` parameter in the `applet` tag should be set.
`preferredWidth()`	Returns the width of the rendered equation. This is also the value to which the `width` parameter in the `applet` tag should be set.

```
   <p><form name="MMLForm">
     <textarea name="MMLString" rows=10
         cols=30></textarea>
   </form>
 <p><form><input type="button" name="MMLSend"
 value="Display" onclick="showMath()">
       </form>
 <applet codeBase="../../classes"
     code="webeq3.ViewerControl"
     align="middle" width="400" height="50"
     name="mathapplet" mayscript>
```

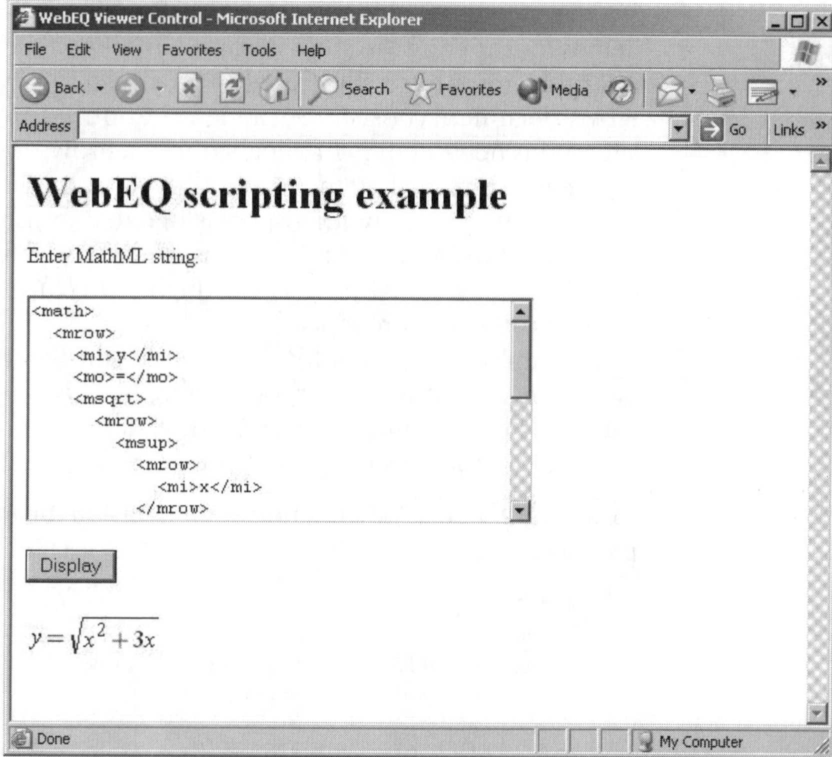

FIGURE 12.7 A Web page that renders an arbitrary MathML expression as a Viewer Control applet.

```
            <param name="parser" value="mathml">
            <param name="eq" value="">
        </applet>
    </body>
</html>
```

Example 12.3 works in the following way. When the user clicks the "Display" button, the JavaScript function `showMath` is called. This function consists of two statements. The first statement retrieves the MathML expression typed by the user and assigns it as the value of the variable `expr`, as shown here:

```
var expr = document.MMLForm.MMLString.value;
```

The second statement updates the display of the Viewer Control applet, called `mathapplet`, by using the function `setEquation`, as shown here:

```
document.mathapplet.setEquation(expr);
```

You can also use the setEquation function to create interactive demos for showing the steps involved in solving specific mathematical problems. This is illustrated in Example 12.4, which shows an HTML document consisting of a Viewer Control applet and a button. When this document is first loaded into a browser, a mathematical problem is displayed by the applet (Figure 12.8). Each time the user clicks a button, the applet display is updated to show the next step in the solution of the problem. This continues until the problem is completely solved. After this, clicking the button again causes the original problem to reappear.

Example 12.4 works like a toggle action but with a repeating cycle that can be of any arbitrary length. This type of behavior is useful for educational Web sites, for example, to demonstrate the solution of problems in an assignment.

Example 12.4 An HTML document for showing the steps in solving a problem.

```
<html>
 <head>
   <title>WebEQ Viewer Control</title>
   <script language="javascript">
```

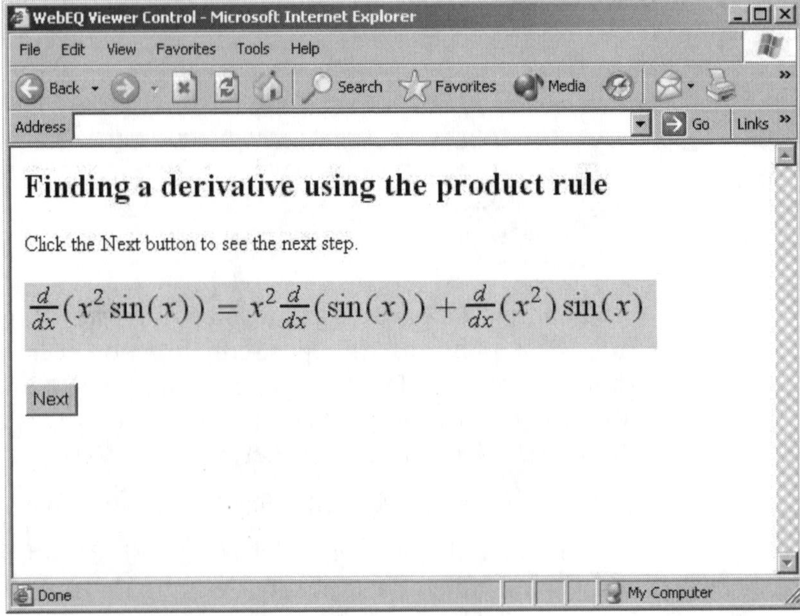

FIGURE 12.8 An interactive Web page that shows the steps in the solution of a calculus problem.

```
    var i=1;
    function nextStep() {
    i++;
    if (i==1) {
    document.mathapplet.setEquation(mml_string1);}
    if (i==2) {
      document.mathapplet.setEquation(mml_string2);}
    if (i==3) {
      document.mathapplet.setEquation(mml_string3);}
    if (i==4) {
      document.mathapplet.setEquation(mml_string4);
      i=-1;}
    }
    </script>
  </head>
  <body bgcolor="#ffffff">
    <h2>Finding a derivative using the product rule</h2>
    <p>Click the Next button to see the next step.</p>
      <applet codebase="classes"
        code="webeq3.ViewerControl" height=50 width=400
        name="mathapplet" mayscript>
        <param name="parser" value="mathml">
        <param name="color" value="#dddddd">
        <param name="size" value="18">
        <param name="align" value="left">
        <param name="eq"
        value="mml_string1">
  </applet>
  <form><input type="button" value="Next"
      onclick="nextStep();">
  </form>
  </body>
</html>
```

Example 12.4 works as follows. Each time the user clicks the "Next" button, the JavaScript function `nextStep` is called. This function increments the value of the counter `i` by 1 and calls the `setEquation` function to change the equation displayed in the Viewer Control applet. The various steps in the solution are hard coded as MathML expressions. A different MathML string is specified as the argument of the `setEquation` function for each value of `i`. Hence, with each click of the button, the applet displays successive steps in the equation until the original equation reappears and the cycle starts again.

In Example 12.4, the MathML expression that corresponds to the mathematical problem to be solved is denoted by *mml_string1*, and the three steps involved in the solution of the problem are denoted by *mml_string2, mml_string3,* and *mml_string4.* In a working implementation of this example, these would be replaced with the MathML strings for the specific mathematical expressions to be displayed.

WebEQ and the DOM

The DOM is a W3C recommendation designed to simplify the processing of XML documents. The DOM defines a set of objects and methods for selecting and modifying any part of the XML document tree. These objects and methods are specified as abstract interfaces that any application can implement. For example, many Web browsers define an object hierarchy that is based on the DOM. The DOM is useful because it provides a standard way of working with XML documents that is independent of any specific platform, programming language, or application.

The *WebEQ* API implements many of the standard interfaces defined in the W3C specification of the DOM. *WebEQ* also implements some parts of the MathML DOM, which is defined in the MathML 2.0 specification. The MathML DOM extends the generic DOM by adding some extra interfaces for handling specific types of MathML expressions.

Using the objects and methods defined in the *WebEQ* DOM API, you can navigate the MathML tree to select a specific node and change its attributes. You can also add or delete nodes to interactively modify a part of the displayed equation. This is illustrated in Example 12.5, which shows an HTML document that contains a Viewer Control applet. You can update the color of the equation by choosing a color from a pull-down menu. Figure 12.9 shows how this document looks when viewed in a browser.

Example 12.5 An HTML document with a menu for changing the color of an equation.

```
<html>
 <head>
   <title>Using the WebEQ DOM API</title>
     <script language="javascript">
       function colorText() {
         var i = document.form1.menu1.selectedIndex;
         var item = document.form1.menu1.options[i];
         var fgcolor = item.text;
     var appletNode=document.equation
     var mathDocument=appletNode.getMathMLDocument();
```

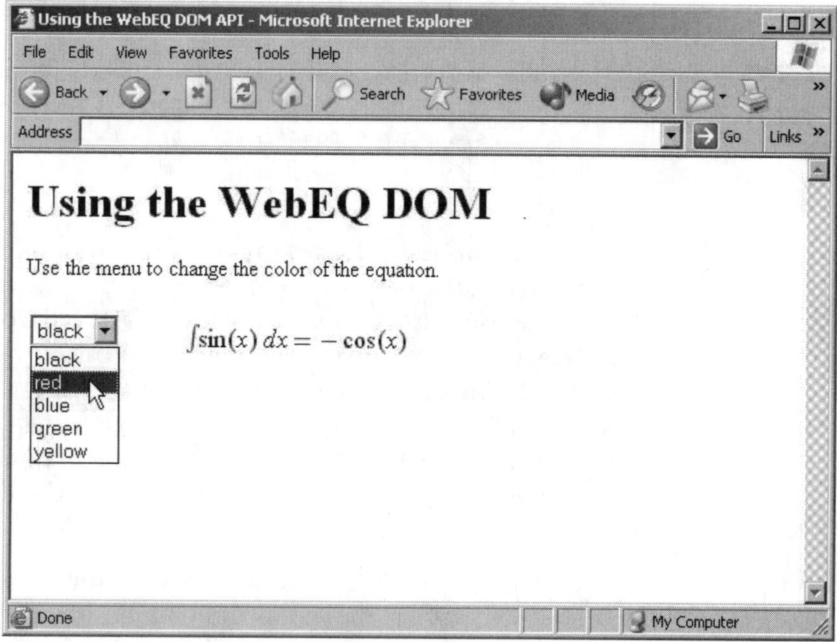

FIGURE 12.9 Using the *WebEQ* DOM API to access a specific node of an equation and change its attributes.

```
        var mathnode= mathDocument.getFirstChild();
        var mstylenode=mathnode.getFirstChild();
        mstylenode.setAttribute("mathcolor", fgcolor);
        }
        </script>
    </head>
    <body bgcolor="white">
      <h1>Using the WebEQ DOM</h1>
        <p>Use the menu to change the color of the
equation.</p>
      <table><tr><td>
        <form name="form1">
          <select onChange="colorText()" name="menu1">
            <option>black
            <option>red
            <option>blue
            <option>green
            <option>yellow
            </select>
        </form></td>
        <td><applet codebase="classes"
          code="webeq3.ViewerControl" width=250
          height=50 align="middle" name="equation" mayscript>
```

```
            <param name="parser" value="mathml">
            <param name="eq" value="
            <math><mstyle mathcolor='black'><mrow><mi><x></mi>
            <mo>+</mo><mn>1</mn></mrow></mstyle></math>">
            </applet></td></tr></table>
</body>
</html>
```

In Example 12.5, the `select` tag is used to indicate a pull-down menu, with each item in the menu specified using an `option` tag. When the user changes the currently displayed item in the menu, an `onChange` event occurs, which calls the JavaScript function `colorText`. This function reads the currently selected color and assigns it as the value of the variable `fgcolor`. The function then uses the following three methods from *WebEQ*'s implementation of the DOM to pick out a specific element in the MathML expression and change it:

- `getMathMLDocument()`: returns the complete MathML expression tree, when applied to the Viewer Control applet node
- `getFirstChild()`: returns the first child of the node it is applied to
- `setAttribute(`*attr*, *value*`)`: changes the attribute value of a particular node

By applying these methods in sequence, the `colorText` function first selects out the `mstyle` tag that encloses the MathML expression. It then sets the value of the `mathcolor` attribute of this element to that stored in the `fgcolor` variable. This causes the color of the equation displayed in the Viewer Control applet to be updated to the item that the user selects in the menu.

Input Control

The *WebEQ* Input Control is a Java applet that acts as an interactive graphical equation editor that can be embedded in a Web page. Its interface and operation are very similar to those for the *WebEQ* Editor. However, there are some important differences between them. The Editor is a standalone application with a standard menu-drive interface. It allows you to export equations in a variety of formats (including images) or MathML markup tailored to a variety of rendering applications (such as *MathPlayer*, *Mozilla*, or *WebEQ* Viewer Control applets).

The Input Control, on the other hand, is an applet that is intended only for use in a Web page. It does not have any menus and is more limited in its export options. You can think of the Input

Control as a simplified version of the Editor. The main advantage of the Input Control is that it provides a way to interactively author mathematical notation in a Web page.

To embed the Input Control in a Web page, you simply add the following `applet` tag to an HTML document, as shown here:

```
<applet codebase="classes"
code="webeq3.editor.InputControl"
name="output" height=200 width=525 mayscript>
<param name=eq value="<math><mrow></mrow></math>">
</applet>
```

The `applet` tag used here is very similar to the `applet` tag for the Viewer Control, the main difference being the value of the `code` attribute. The Input Control also supports a slightly different set of parameters than the Viewer Control. For example, you can use the `toolbar` parameter to customize the toolbar displayed at the top of the Input Control. The value of this parameter is a string that specifies the exact configuration of the toolbar. You specify the toolbar's configuration, in terms of a special XML-based language that includes keywords for the different types of palettes and symbols available. By using the `toolbar` parameter, you can create a customized toolbar that contains only the palettes and symbols relevant to a particular type of problem.

The *WebEQ* JavaScript and DOM APIs include a number of methods for manipulating the Input Control. You can use these methods to interactively access and modify the equations created using the Input Control. Table 12.3 shows a selection of the functions included in the JavaScript API for Input Control.

Scripting the Input Control

This section illustrates how you can use the Input Control API functions to extract information about the equation authored using the Input Control. This information can then be used in concert with JavaScript programs or Java applets to implement various kinds of interactive behavior.

Example 12.6 shows an HTML document that contains the Input Control applet along with two buttons. The user can author an equation using the Input Control and then click a button to get either the presentation markup or content markup that corresponds to that equation. Figure 12.10 shows how this document looks in a browser.

TABLE 12.3 Functions Included in the JavaScript API for Input Control

Method	Description
`getMathML()`	Returns a string that contains formatted presentation markup for the current equation.
`getContent-MathML()`	Returns a string that contains formatted content markup for the current equation.
`getEscaped-MathML()`	Returns a string that contains presentation markup for the current equation in which unnecessary characters have been escaped in order for the string to be safely transmitted as CGI data.
`getEscapedContent-MathML()`	Returns a string that contains content markup-for the current equation in which unnecessary characters have been escaped in order for the string to be safely transmitted as CGI data.
`getPackedMathML()`	Returns a string that contains unformatted presentation markup for the current equation. The markup is stripped of extra white space (including linefeeds and indenting) and is much more compact than formatted MathML.
`getPackedContent-MathML()`	Returns a string that contains unformatted content markup for the current equation. The markup is stripped of extra white space (including linefeeds and indenting) and is much more compact than formatted MathML.
`getSelection()`	Returns a string that contains formatted presentation markup for the current on-screen selection.
`getContent-Selection()`	Returns a string that contains formatted content markup for the current selection as above.
`setMathML(String-mml_str)`	Replaces the current equation with the equation described by `mml_str`.
`getEquation-Image()`	Returns a Java AWT (Abstract Window Toolkit) image of the current equation for use by another Java applet.
`getEquation-Image(int n)`	Returns a Java AWT image of the current equation rendered in a specified font size.
`getEquation-Image(int n, String color)`	Returns a Java AWT image of the current equation in a specified point size and with the background set to a specified color.

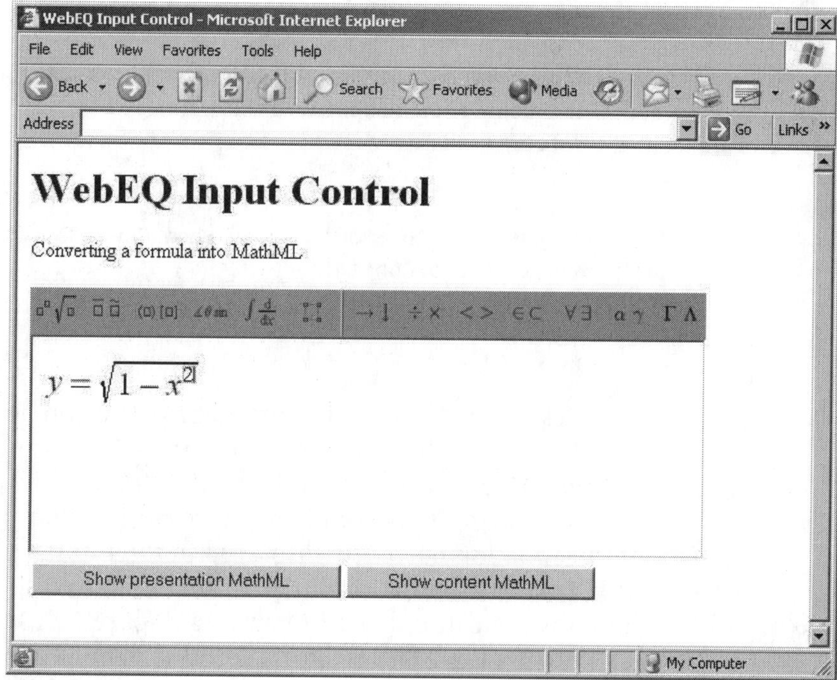

FIGURE 12.10 Using the *WebEQ* Input Control to enter a formula and view its MathML representation.

Example 12.6 An HTML document that contains the *WebEQ* Input Control.

```
<html>
 <head>
   <title>WebEQ Input Control</title>
   <script language="javascript">
   function showPresentation() {
   mml_data = document.output.getMathML();
   alert(mml_data);}
   function showContent() {
   mml_data = document.output.getContentMathML();
   alert(mml_data);}
   </script>
 </head>
 <body bgcolor="white">
 <h1>Converting a Formula into MathML</h1>
 <applet codebase="classes"
   code="webeq3.editor.InputControl"
   name="output" height=200 width=525 mayscript>
   <param name=eq value="<math><mrow></mrow></math>">
   </applet>
```

```
<p><tr><td>
<form>
<input type="button" value="Show Presentation MathML"
onclick="showPresentation()">
</form></td>
<td>
<form>
<input type="button" value="Show Content MathML"
onclick="showContent()">
</form></td></tr>
</body>
</html>
```

Clicking the "Show content MathML" button, for example, runs the JavaScript function `showContent`. This function uses the `getContentMathML` function from the Input Control API, which returns a string that contains the content markup representation of the equation currently displayed in the Input Control. The standard JavaScript function `alert` is then used to display a dialog that contains the content MathML string (Figure 12.11).

Viewing the MathML for a formula is not very useful by itself. The Input Control becomes much more useful if you process the MathML output in some way to return a result to the user. You can do this on the client side by using JavaScript or Java applets. Alternatively, you can send the MathML string to the server and perform some computations on it, using, for example, mathematical software like *Mathematica* or *Maple*. We will discuss examples of doing server-side computations on user input in Sections 12.6 and 12.7. However, for now, we confine ourselves to examples of how the data provided by the Input Control can be processed on the client machine.

One important use of the Input Control is to create courseware for educational or training purposes. For example, you can use it to set up Web pages for online testing. Each Web page would display a mathematical problem and require a user to enter the answer to the problem via the Input Control. You can then use a JavaScript function to check the answer and return a message saying whether the answer was right or wrong. Example 12.7 shows an HTML document of this type.

Example 12.7 An HTML document for entering and checking the answer to a problem.

```
<html>
<head>
```

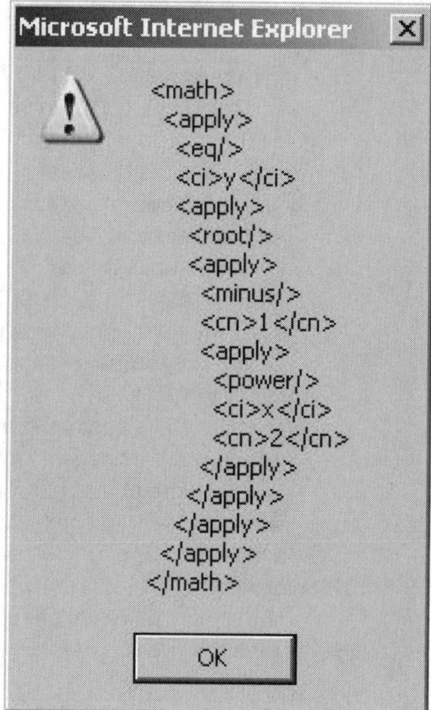

FIGURE 12.11 Using the *WebEQ* Input Control to get the MathML representation of a formula.

```
<title>Input Control Example</title>
   <script language="javascript">
   function checkAnswer() {
   var mml_string =
   document.answer.getPackedContentMathML();
   var solution = "<math><apply><plus/><apply><times/>
   <cn>2</cn><ci>x</ci></apply><apply><divide/><cn>1
   </cn><apply><times/><cn>2</cn><apply><root/><ci>x
   </ci></apply></apply></apply></apply></math>";
   if (mml_string==solution)
        {alert("Correct answer.");}
   else
        {alert("Wrong answer. Try again.");}}
   </script>
</head>
<body bgcolor="white">
   <h1>Calculus Test</h1>
```

```
        <p><b>Problem 1 </b>Calculate the following
        derivative: </p>
        <applet codeBase="../../classes"
          code="webeq3.ViewerControl"
          align="middle" width="100" height="50">
          <param name="parser" value="mathml">
          <param name ="selection" value="true">
          <param name ="eq" value=
          "<math><apply><diff/><bvar>
          <ci>x</ci></bvar><apply><plus/><apply><power/><ci>x
          </ci><cn>2</cn></apply><apply><root/><ci>x</ci>
          </apply></apply></apply></math>">
        </applet>
        <p>Enter your answer here:</p>
        <applet name="answer" codeBase="../../classes"
          code="webeq3.editor.InputControl"
          width="525" height="200" mayscript>
        </applet>
        <form>
        <input onclick="checkAnswer()" type="button"
        value="Check Answer">
        </form>
</body>
</html>
```

The HTML document described in Example 12.7 displays a calculus problem that involves finding the derivative of a particular function. The mathematical notation for the problem is displayed using a Viewer Control applet (Figure 12.12). The user can enter the answer to the problem in standard mathematical notation using the Input Control, and then click the "Check Answer" button. This launches the JavaScript function `checkAnswer`, which retrieves the MathML markup that corresponds to the answer and then compares it with the solution for that particular problem, which is hard coded as a string. If the user's answer matches the solution, an alert saying the answer is correct is produced; otherwise, an alert prompting the user to try again is produced.

Another useful thing to do with the input received from the Input Control is to convert the MathML expression into an image that can be displayed in any standard Web browser. You can use the Input Control as one component of an e-mail discussion group or bulletin board for posting messages on mathematical topics. For example, students in a mathematical course can author and submit formulas (using the Input Control) that are automatically converted to images for displaying in a Web page. Other students can then

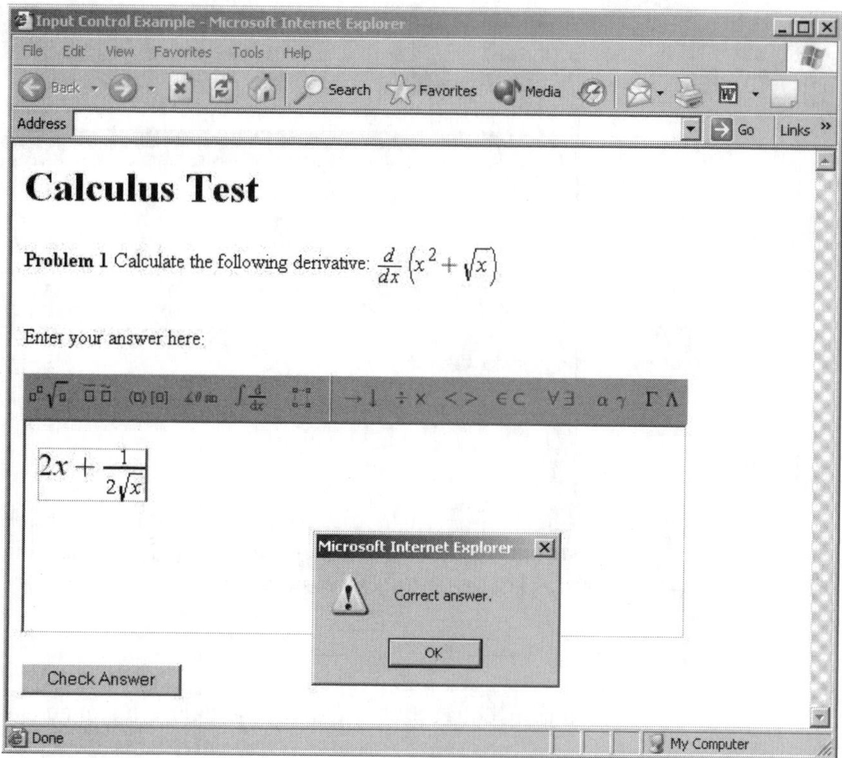

FIGURE 12.12 Using the *WebEQ* Input Control API to check the answer to a mathematical problem.

view the message and respond to it, authoring and submitting other formulas as part of their response.

Example 12.8 shows an HTML document that converts the formula displayed in the Input Control into an image, which is then displayed in the same Web page using a Java applet. Figure 12.13 shows how this document looks when viewed in a browser.

Example 12.8 An HTML document that uses a Java program to convert an equation into an image.

```
<html>
<head>
   <title>Displaying a java.awt.Image from the WebEQ
    Input Control</title>
 </head>
 <body>
 <applet code="webeq3.editor.InputControl"
 codebase="classes" height=200 width=600
```

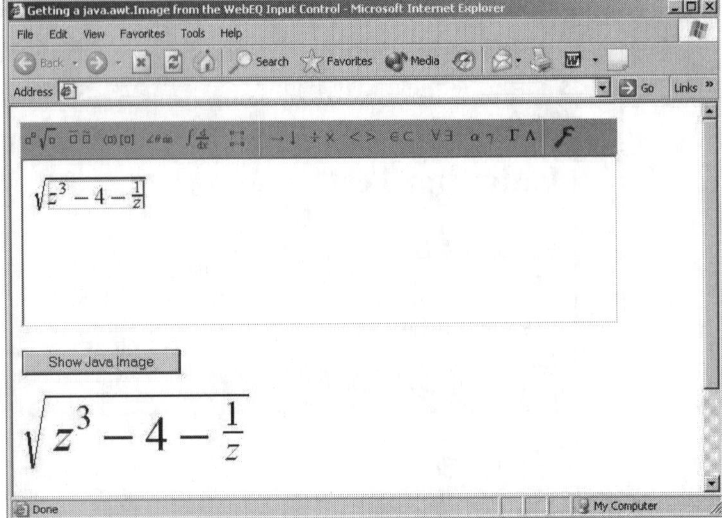

FIGURE 12.13 Converting equations authored using the Input Control to an image using another Java applet.

```
name="Equation" mayscript><param name=eq value=
"<math><msqrt><msup><mrow><mi>z</mi></mrow><mrow>
  <mn>3</mn></mrow></msup><mo>-</mo><mn>4</mn>
  <mo>-</mo><mfrac><mn>1</mn><mi>z</mi></mfrac>
  </msqrt></math>">
</applet>
   <p /><input type="button" value="Show Java Image"
    onclick="document.ImageApplet.setImage(
    document.Equation.getEquationImage(36));"><p/>
<applet code="ImageApplet" height="200" width="600"
name="ImageApplet"></applet>
</body>
</html>
```

Example 12.8 uses the `getEquationImage` function from the InputControl API to convert the MathML representation of an equation into a Java AWT image. When the user clicks the "Show Java Image" button, this image is passed on to another Java applet for displaying in a different window. Here is the Java code for the `setImage` function used in Example 12.8:

```
import java.applet.*;
import java.awt.*;
import java.awt.image.*;
public class ImageApplet extends Applet {
```

```
    private Image myImage;
    public void setImage(Image newImage){
      myImage = newImage;
      repaint();
    }
    public void update(Graphics g){
      paint(g);
    }
    public void paint(Graphics g){
      g.setColor(Color.white);
      g.fillRect(0,0,getSize().width,getSize().height);
      if(myImage != null)
      g.drawImage(myImage, 0, 0, null);
}}
```

This code defines a class called `ImageApplet` that extends the standard Applet class. It then uses the standard Java graphics functions, `paint`, `setColor`, `fillRect`, and `drawImage`, to first draw a rectangle of the desired size and then render the image of the equation produced by the Input Control in that rectangle. This example illustrates how the *WebEQ* API functions can be accessed from Java applets as well as JavaScript functions.

Another technique for converting MathML equations into images is to use GtkMathView, an open-source MathML rendering engine written by Luca Padovani. This consists of a set of libraries that can be used either as a standalone widget or as part of another application. You can download the GtkMathView package as well as instructions for installing and using it from the following Web site: *http://le.cs.unibo.it/helm/mml-widget/*.

Drew Bowering has written a program called mathmlrender that uses GtkMathView in combination with PHP to translate MathML into JPEG or PNG images. PHP is a general-purpose scripting language that is widely used for Web development. PHP scripts can, like JavaScript programs, be directly embedded in an HTML document. mathmlrender is a module for PHP. You can download the files for mathmlrender at the following URL: *www.math.mcgill.ca/~drew/athmlrender*.

12.4 IBM *TECHEXPLORER*

IBM *techexplorer* is designed to be a general purpose rendering application for scientific documents that can interpret and display TEX and LATEX markup as well as MathML. As discussed in Section 7.4, the markup to be rendered by *techexplorer* is inserted into an HTML document using either an `embed` tag (for *Netscape*) or `object` tag (for *IE*). A better solution is to place the `embed` tag inside the `object` tag,. This ensures that the markup can be rendered in both *Netscape* and *IE*. Here is an example:

```
<object name="techexplorer"
classid="clsid:5AFAB315-AD87-11D3-98BB- 002035EFB1A4"
width=200 height=100>
<param name="DataType" value="1">
<param name="Data" value=string >
     <embed name="techexplorer"
      type="application/x-techexplorer"
      mmldata=string
      width=200 height=100>
</embed>
</object>
```

techexplorer also provides support for interactivity in two ways. You can directly author a number of equation actions (such as toggling between two displays or creating links) using built-in *techexplorer* commands. In addition, you can use the built-in class libraries and API functions in conjunction with JavaScript or Java programs to interactively control *techexplorer* in response to user input. We shall see some examples of both types of interactivity in this section.

Actions in *techexplorer*

techexplorer supports a number of special commands that you can insert into a document to implement specific features, such as creating hyperlinks, opening pop-up windows or menus, and toggling between two different expressions. The name and syntax of *techexplorer* commands are modeled on those of LaTeX. Most commands take the form *commandname*{*arg1*}..{{*argn*}. The name of the command is preceded by a slash(\\ ) and followed by one or more arguments, each of which is enclosed in curly brackets.

Here are some of the important *techexplorer* commands for implementing actions:

- `\doclink`{*url*}{*expression*}: creates a hyperlink to the URL specified by *url*. Here, *expression* specifies the content to be rendered by *techexplorer*.
- `\doclink`{*url*}{*label*}{*expression*}: links to the specified URL and causes the window to scroll to the position indicated by *label*. If the label is not found, the window is positioned at the top of the document.

- `\labellink`{*label*} {*expression*}: creates a hyperlink to another part of the same document.
- `\labellink`{*label*}: defines the target of the links defined by `\doclink`{*url*}{*label*} {*expression*} and `\labellink`{*label*} {*expression*}.
- `\popuplink`{*popupText*}{*caption*} {*expression*}: causes a pop-up window to appear with *popupText* displayed in the window and *caption* in its title bar. This feature is useful for adding footnotes in a document.
- `\altlink`{*expression1*} {*expression2*}: toggles between the display of *expression1* and *expression2* each time a user clicks the displayed expression.

These commands can be freely interspersed with the markup to be rendered by *techexplorer*. However, most of these commands do not work with MathML markup. If you want to implement equation actions using these commands, you must encode all mathematical expressions in LaTeX format.

Scripting *techexplorer*

The Professional version of *techexplorer* contains a set of APIs. These consist of several class libraries with functions that JavaScript and Java programs can access to control *techexplorer* and implement interactive behavior. Table 12.4 shows a selected list of the API functions that *techexplorer* makes available to external programs.

Example 12.9 illustrates the use of the *techexplorer* API functions to implement interactive behavior in a Web page. It shows an HTML document that contains a text area and a button. A user can enter a MathML expression in the text area and then click the button to render the MathML using *techexplorer*.

Example 12.9 An HTML document for rendering MathML expressions using *techexplorer*.

```
<html>
 <head>
   <title>IBM techexplorer</title>
   <script language="JavaScript">
   function displayMML( ) {
     var expr = document.MMLForm.MMLString.value
     document.te.reloadFromMMLString(expr);
     document.MMLForm.MMLString.value=
     document.te.getMMLString();
     }
   </script>
```

TABLE 12.4 API Functions That *techexplorer* Makes Available to External Programs

Method	Description
`getMMLString()`	Returns the MathML data displayed in the *techexplorer* window
`reloadFromMMLString (String mmlSource)`	Replaces the document with the supplied MathML source
`getWidthFromMMLString (String mmlSource)`	Returns the width of a MathML expression
`getHeightFromMMLString (String mmlSource)`	Returns the height of a MathML expression
`getDepthFromMMLString (String mmlSource)`	Returns the depth of a MathML expression
`convertMMLtoTeX()`	Converts the document from MathML source to $\TeX$
`convertTeXtoMML()`	Converts the document from $\TeX$ source to MathML

```
    </head>
    <body bgcolor="white">
  <h1>techexplorer scripting example</h1>
  <p>Enter MathML string:
    <p><form name="MMLForm">
      <textarea name="MMLString" rows=10
    cols=30></textarea>
      </form>
        <p><input type="button" name="MMLSend"
         value="Display in techexplorer"
            onClick="displayMML()">
    <p><object name="te"
    classid="clsid:5AFAB315-AD87-11D3-98BB- 002035EFB1A4"
    width=500 height=80>
    <param name="DataType" value="0">
    <param name="Data" value="Equation will be
    displayed here.">
        <embed name="te"
          type="application/x-techexplorer"
          mmldata="Equation will be displayed here"
          width=400 height=100>
        </embed>
      </object>
  <body>
 </html>
```

The HTML document of Example 12.9 has the following features. The "Display in techexplorer" button calls the JavaScript function `displayMML`. This function reads the MathML expression entered by the user and passes it as the argument of the `reload-FromMMLString` function. This function causes the *techexplorer* window in the Web page to be redrawn so that the MathML markup entered by the user is rendered in the page (Figure 12.14). Example 12.9 is the *techexplorer* equivalent of Example 12.3, which also renders a MathML expression but using the *WebEQ* Viewer Control. The `reloadfromMMLString` function in *techexplorer* is analogous to the `setEquation` function in the *WebEQ* Viewer Control.

One of the useful features of *techexplorer* is that it can interpret and render LaTeX markup in addition to MathML. The *techexplorer* API includes functions for converting between LaTeX and MathML. Thus, you can easily modify Example 12.9 to set up a Web page that allows users to type in the LaTeX markup for a formula and convert it to MathML, or the other way around. For example, LaTeX users who want to convert existing equations in their documents into MathML for posting on the Web can use this type of tool. Example 12.10 shows an HTML document that implements this type of conversion.

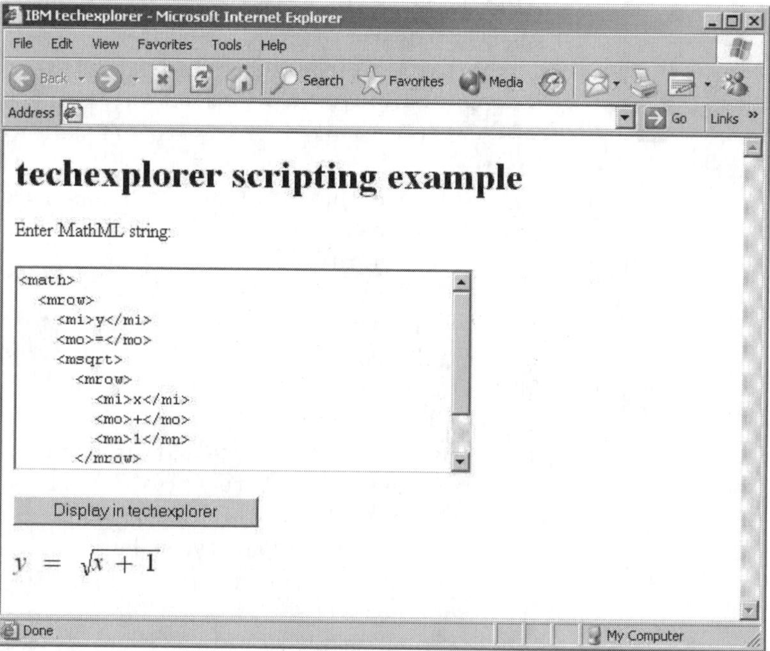

FIGURE 12.14 Viewing the *techexplorer* rendering of an arbitrary MathML expression.

Example 12.10 An HTML document for converting between MathML and LATEX.

```
<html>
<head>
   <title>IBM techexplorer</title>
   <script language="javascript">
    function submitMML( ) {
     document.te.reloadFromMMLString(
     document.MMLForm.MMLString.value);
     document.MMLForm.MMLString.value=
     document.te.getMMLString()
     document.TeXForm.TeXString.value=
     document.te.convertMMLtoTeX()
   }
   function submitTeX( ) {
     document.te.reloadFromTeXString(
     document.TeXForm.TeXString.value);
     document.TeXForm.TeXString.value=
     document.te.getTeXString()
     document.MMLForm.MMLString.value=
     document.te.convertTeXtoMML()
     }
   </script>
 </head>
 <body bgcolor="white">
   <h1>techexplorer scripting example</h1>
   <table><tr><td>Enter MathML string:</td>
   <td>Enter LaTeX string:</td></tr>
   <tr><td><form name="MMLForm">
     <textarea name="MMLString" rows=10 cols=30>
     </textarea>
     </form></td>
     <td><form name="TeXForm">
     <textarea name="TeXString" rows=10 cols=30>
     </textarea>
     </form></td></tr>
     <tr><td>
       <form><input type="button" name="MMLSend"
       value="Convert to LaTeX" onclick="submitMML()">
       </form></td>
       <td><form><input type="button" name="TeXSend"
       value="Convert to MathML" onclick="submitTeX()">
       </form></td></tr></table>
     <object name="te" classid="clsid:5AFAB315-AD87-
       11D3-98BB-002035EFB1A4">
     <param name="AutoSize" value="true">
```

```
        <param name="DataType" value="1">
        <param name="Data"
        value="<math><mrow></mrow></math>">
        <embed name="te"
          type="application/x-techexplorer"
          mmldata="<math><mrow></mrow></math>"
          width=200 height=100>
        </embed>
      </object>
    </body>
  </html>
```

The document in Example 12.10 contains two text areas, two buttons, and a *techexplorer* window. One of the text areas is for entering MathML markup, and the other is for entering LaTeX markup. Below each text area is a button for converting the markup contained in that text area from one format to the other. For example, suppose you type in a LaTeX expression in the text area with the name `TeXString` and then click the button marked "Convert to MathML" . This calls the JavaScript function `submitTeX`, which uses the `convertTeXtoMML` function to translate the LaTeX markup into MathML. The resulting MathML expression is then displayed in the MathML text area, and the equation is rendered in the *techexplorer* window as well (Figure 12.15).

12.5 Doing Computations on the Server

All the examples discussed in this chapter so far have involved programs running on the client machine. We saw that by using one of the MathML rendering applications in combination with JavaScript and HTML, you can implement many different types of interactive behavior. However, client-side processing has its limitations. It is hard to do any serious mathematical operations (such as solving equations, calculating integrals, or plotting graphs) on the client side since this is beyond the scope of simple scripting languages that can be run in a browser. If you want to do any type of advanced computation on mathematical content, it is necessary to do some processing on the server side.

There are many well-established technologies for server-side programming, such as CGI scripting, Active Server Pages, Perl, Python, PHP, and Java servlets. However, the focus of these scripting and programming languages is on processing textual data, not on doing mathematical computations. These languages play a key role in any type of server-side programming, since they are well suited

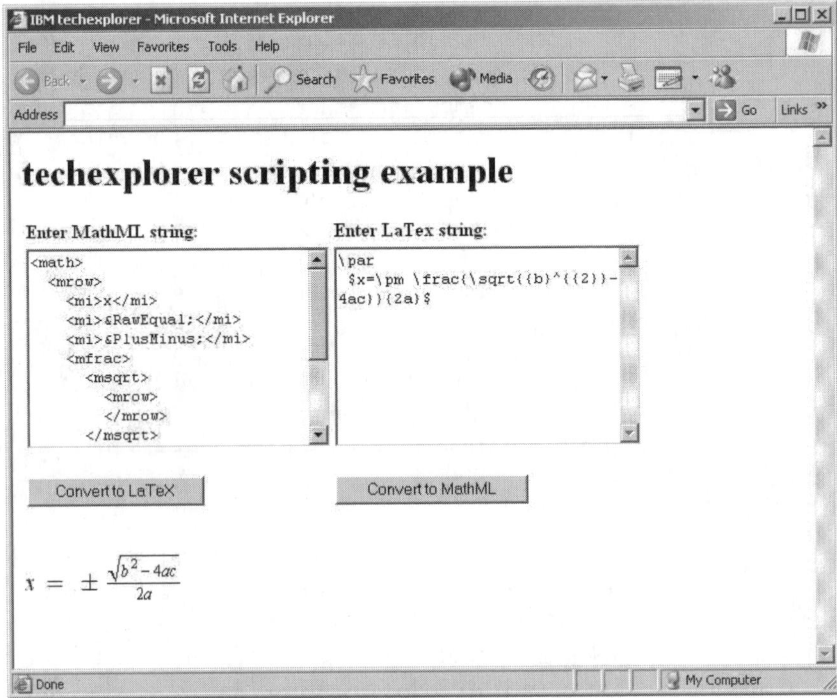

FIGURE 12.15 Converting between MathML and LaTeX encodings of a formula using *techexplorer.*

for the tasks of receiving input from the client, launching executable programs, and then transforming and returning output back to the client. However, the task of doing the core computations is best left to a dedicated mathematical software package, such as *Mathematica* or *Maple*. The advantage of having the mathematical software application do the work is that you have access to the full computational power of the application, and you can use this power for performing a wide range of symbolic, numeric, or graphical calculations.

As we saw in Chapter 11, both *Mathematica* and *Maple* offer excellent support for MathML. Both can import data in the form of MathML, do arbitrary computations on the data, and then return the result back as MathML. This makes *Mathematica* and *Maple* well suited for integration with the Web. They can act as back-end applications that run on the Web server and perform computations in response to requests from client machines. Of course, some initial work has to be done to connect the various processes on the client and server sides. The typical steps involved in implementing this type of behavior are as follows:

1. Create a Web page that allows a user to enter the data for a specific mathematical problem. You can specify the user input either via a forms-based interface that involves text areas, buttons, or menus, or via an equation editor-type applet (such as *WebEQ* Input Control) that can translate mathematical notation entered by the user into MathML.
2. Set up the Web page so that the mathematical data is submitted to a Web server when the user performs some action such as clicking a button.
3. Install a mathematical software application such as *Mathematica* or *Maple* on the server. You then configure the application to receive the data submitted by the client and perform the desired computations on it. Some preprocessing may have to be done on the data to turn it into a form suitable for evaluation by *Mathematica* or *Maple*.
4. Return the result of the evaluation back to the client in a form suitable for display in a browser. Before the output received from the mathematical software can be displayed, some post-processing may have to be done on it. For example, if the result of the computation is a mathematical expression, the expression may have to be converted into MathML for display in the browser. Alternatively, if the computation involves generating a plot, the resulting graphic may have to be converted into a GIF or JPEG image and a link to the image inserted into the Web page.

Developing a Web site that allows users to do general mathematical computations is clearly a challenging task. Implementing all these steps starting from scratch would require a great deal of complex programming. A simpler option is to use a product such as web*Mathematica* or *MapleNET* that provides a pre-built solution for delivering mathematical computations over the Web. These products provide a simple way to integrate an existing mathematical software package with a Web server to make computations accessible via a Web browser. The next two sections provide detailed examples of how to set up interactive Web pages using these products.

12.6 WEB*MATHEMATICA*

web*Mathematica* is a Java-based application that provides interactive access to *Mathematica* computations over the Web. The underlying technology behind web*Mathematica* is called *Mathematica* Server Pages (MSP), which is an application of Java servlet technology.

Servlets are Java programs that run on a Web server, either directly or through a separate plug-in program called a *servlet container*. The details of installing and configuring web*Mathematica* on a server can be somewhat complicated. However, once the initial installation is done, it is relatively easy to write Web pages that can interact with the server to produce live mathematical content.

The basic idea is that you can insert *Mathematica* commands into a standard HTML document in the form of special `Mathlet` tags. When a Web page enhanced in this way is submitted to a suitably configured Web server, each `Mathlet` tag is interpreted and its contents evaluated by a copy of *Mathematica* running on the server. The results of the evaluation are then inserted into the HTML document, replacing the original `Mathlet` tag. The new Web page is then returned back to the client and displayed in the browser.

web*Mathematica* thus provides a simple way to integrate *Mathematica* input and output into a standard Web page. The Web server can run multiple *Mathematica* sessions simultaneously and can manage multiple requests, queuing and assigning evaluations as a new session becomes available. Users can purchase a license for any desired number of sessions, depending on the level of demand expected on the Web site. The configuration is scalable, and you can easily modify it for high levels of usage by increasing the number of *Mathematica* sessions available.

HTML documents enhanced by the addition of `Mathlet` tags are called *MSP scripts*. They must have the file extension .msp. A typical `Mathlet` tag has the following structure:

```
<% Mathlet expr %>
```

Here, *expr* can be any command or sequence of commands that is valid as input to *Mathematica*. In addition to ordinary *Mathematica* commands, `Mathlet` tags can contain a small set of commands, with the prefix MSP, that are defined exclusively for use in MSP scripts. These handle various details of the interaction between the Web page and *Mathematica*. Let's see look at a few examples of MSP scripts to illustrate how such pages work.

Integrating a Function

Example 12.11 shows a simple MSP script that sets up a Web page for calculating integrals. The page includes a text field and a button. A user can enter a function of one variable in the text field, and then click the "Integrate" button to see the result in the same Web page (Figure 12.16). The function must be entered using *Mathematica*'s input syntax, which means that all function names must

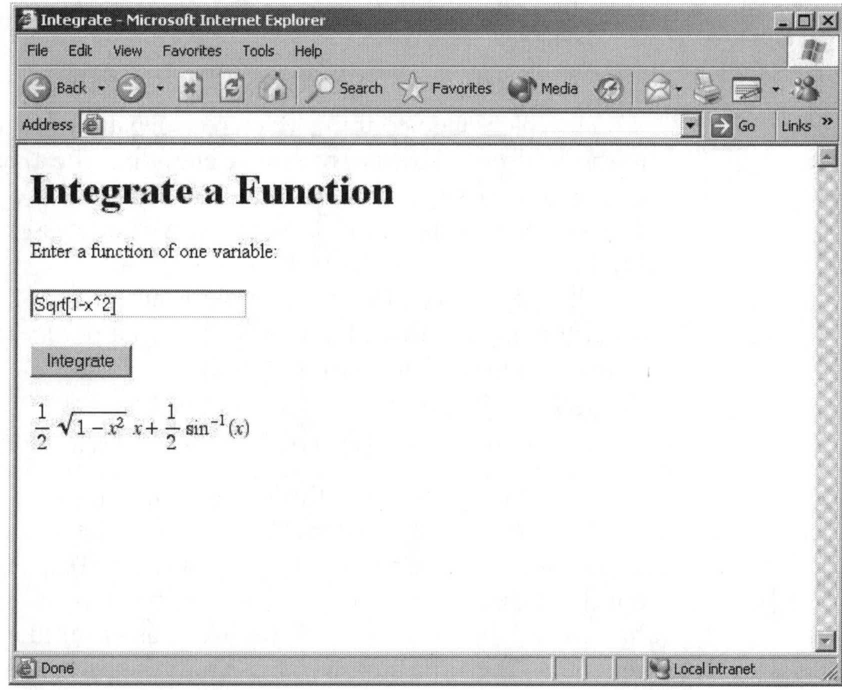

FIGURE 12.16 A Web page for calculating integrals using *Mathematica*.

be capitalized and arguments must be enclosed in square brackets, as in `Sqrt[x]`, `Sin[x]`, or `Log[x, 2]`.

Example 12.11 An HTML document for calculating the integral of a function using web*Mathematica*.

```
<html>
<head><title>Integration</title></head>
 <body bgcolor="white" >
   <h1>Integrate a Function</h1>
   <form method="post">
     <p>Enter a function of one variable:
   <input type="text" name="fn" align="left"
     size="24" %>">
   </p>
   <p>
     <input type="submit" name="inputButton"
     value="Integrate"> </p>
     <p><%Mathlet MSPBlock[{$$fn},
     MSPFormat[Integrate[$$fn, x],TraditionalForm]] %>
     </p>
```

```
    </form>
  </body>
</html>
```

This Web page contains two controls, a text field and a button, each represented by its own `input` element. The `input` elements are enclosed in a `form` element that has the attribute `method="post"`. This attribute determines how the server processes the contents of the form.

The page also contains a single Mathlet tag. This tag contains the following command that will be passed to *Mathematica* for evaluation when the form is submitted:

```
MSPBlock[{$$fn},
MSPFormat[Integrate[$$fn, x], TraditionalForm]]
```

Here `$$fn` represents the value of the `input` element with the attribute `name="fn"`. All variables that are to be sent to the *Mathematica* session must be prefaced with a `$$` sign. The `MSPBlock` function checks the value of its first argument, namely `$$fn`. If this variable has a valid value—that is, if the user has entered a function in the text box—then the command given in the second argument is executed. Otherwise, `MSPBlock` returns a null string, which does not lead to any visible output in the Web page. The `MSPBlock` command is thus a way of ensuring that the evaluation proceeds only when a valid input is available. Otherwise, *Mathematica* will generate an error message that will be displayed in the Web page.

The second function in the Mathlet tag is `MSPFormat`, which formats the result obtained after evaluating its first argument and displays it in the Web page. By default, the result is displayed in StandardForm, which is a two-dimensional output format used by *Mathematica* for displaying mathematical expressions. You can specify a different display format by specifying the format as the second argument of `MSPFormat`. For example, to display an expression in traditional mathematical notation, you would use the command `MSPFormat[`*expr*`, TraditionalForm]`. See Section 11.2 for more information about the different display forms in *Mathematica*.

When the user specifies a function in the text box and clicks the button, the contents of the text box are assigned to the variable `$$fn` and submitted to the server. *Mathematica* then evaluates the command `Integrate[$$fn, x]`. The result of the evaluation replaces the `Mathlet` tag in the original Web page. The result is displayed in the form of a GIF image that is stored in the browser's cache, and a link to the image is automatically inserted into the Web page. The `MSPFormat` function automatically handles these steps.

Plotting a Function

Example 12.12 shows an MSP for plotting functions. A user can enter a function along with a range, and then click a button to see a plot of the function over the specified range (Figure 12.17).

Example 12.12 An HTML document for plotting a function using web-*Mathematica*.

```
<html>
 <head><title>Plot</title></head>
 <body bgcolor="white" >
   <h1>Plot a Function</h1>
   <form method="post">
     <p>Enter a function of one variable:
     <input type="text" name="f" size="20" value=
     "<%Mathlet MSPValue[ $$f, "Sin[x^2]"] %>"> </p>
     <p>Enter the start of the range:
```

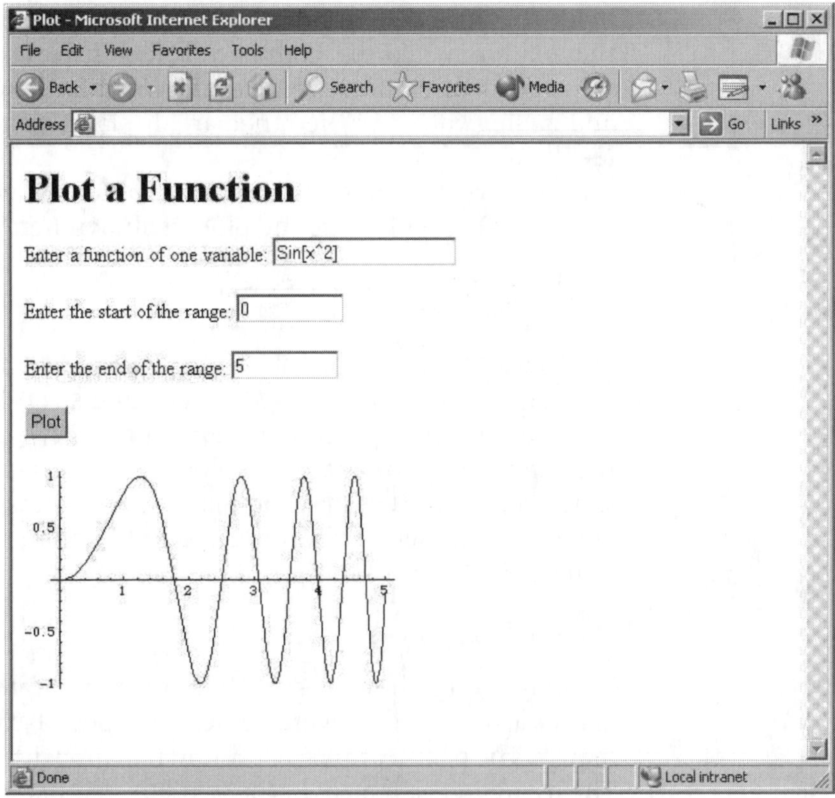

FIGURE 12.17 A Web page for plotting functions using *Mathematica*.

```
            <input type="text" name="x1" size="10" value=
            "<%Mathlet MSPValue[ $$x1, "0"] %>"> </p>
            <p> Enter the end of the range:
            <input type="text" name="x2" size="10" value=
            "<%Mathlet MSPValue[ $$x2, "5"] %>"> </p>
            <p><input type="submit" name="inputButton"
            value="Plot"></p>
            <%Mathlet MSPBlock[ {$$f, $$x1, $$x2},
            MSPShow[ Plot[$$f, {x,$$x1,$$x2}]]] %>
        </form>
    </body>
</html>
```

This page is a straightforward generalization of the page shown in Example 12.11. It contains a `form` element that contains four different controls: three text boxes and one button. Notice that each text box has its `value` attribute set to a Mathlet tag that contains the command `MSPValue[$$`*name, value*`]`. This command displays the variable contained in the first argument if that variable has been assigned a value. Otherwise, it displays the second argument. Specifying a second argument is thus a way to include a default value in the text box when the Web page is first displayed. When the page is first loaded, a default value of the function as well as the starting and ending values of the range are displayed in the corresponding text boxes.

The page also contains a fourth Mathlet tag, which encloses the command for generating the plot, as shown here:

```
MSPBlock[{$$f, $$x1, $$x2},
MSPShow[Plot[$$f, {x, $$x1, $$x2}]
```

The `MSPBlock` command, as in Example 12.11, first checks to see that all three variables (`$$f`, `$$x1`, and `$$x2`) have valid values. Then, it executes its second argument, `Plot[`*f*`, {`*x*`, `*a*`, `*b*`]`. This is the *Mathematica* command for plotting a function of *x* in the range from *a* and *b*. The `MSPShow` command saves an image of the resulting graphic on the server and returns a link to that image for insertion into the Web page.

Matrix Operations

Example 12.13 shows a slightly more complicated Web page that allows a user to do several different types of computations on a matrix. The page features a pull-down menu with a list of functions. The user enters a matrix in the text box using standard *Mathematica* syntax, and then chooses a particular function from the pull-down menu. Clicking the Evaluate button causes the result of the computation to be displayed in the Web page, as shown in Figure 12.18.

Example 12.13 An HTML document for doing matrix calculations using web*Mathematica*.

```
<html>
 <head><title>Matrix Operations</title></head>
   <h1>Matrix Operations</h1>
   <form method="post">
   <p>Enter a matrix:
   <input type="text" name="matrix" align="left"
   size="24" value = "<%Mathlet MSPValue[$$matrix,
   "{{1, 2}, {3, 4}}"] %>"></p>
   <p>Choose an operation from the menu:
   <%Mathlet MSPSetDefault[$$fn, "Transpose"]; %>
   <select name="fn" size=1>
     <option value="Transpose"
```

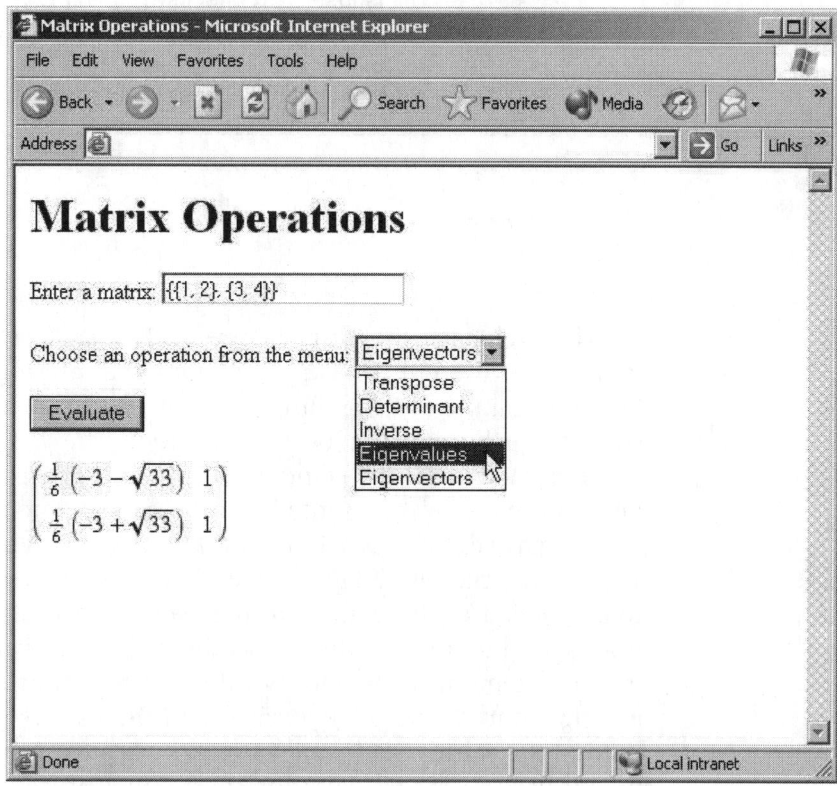

FIGURE 12.18 A Web page for doing matrix calculations.

```
    <%Mathlet If[$$fn=="Transpose", "selected"]%>>
      Transpose </option>
    <option value="Inverse"
    <%Mathlet If[$$fn=="Transpose", "selected"]%>>
      Transpose </option>
    <option value="Determinant"
    <%Mathlet If[$$fn=="Transpose", "selected"]%>>
      Transpose </option>
    <option value="Eigenvectors"
    <%Mathlet If[$$fn=="Transpose", "selected"]%>>
      Transpose </option>
    <option value=" Eigenvectors "
    <%Mathlet If[$$fn=="Eigenvectors", selected"]%>>
    Eigenvectors </option>
  </select></p>

    <p><input type="submit" name="Submit"
    value="Evaluate"> </p>
    <p><%Mathlet MSPBlock[$$matrix, MSPFormat[Which[
    $$fn=="Inverse", Inverse[$$matrix],
    $$fn=="Transpose", Transpose[$$matrix],
    $$fn=="Determinant", Det[$$matrix],
    $$fn =="Eigenvalues", Eigenvalues[$$matrix],
    $$fn =="Eigenvectors", Eigenvectors[$$matrix],
    True, $$matrix], TraditionalForm]]%>
  </p>

  </form>
 </body>
</html>
```

The Web page shown in Figure 12.18 works as follows. It contains three different controls: a text box for entering input, a menu for choosing the type of computation to perform, and a button for submitting the information to the server. The pull-down menu is implemented using the standard HTML `select` element, with each item in the menu represented by an `option` element.

The page defines two variables, `$$matrix` and `$$fn`, which represent the matrix entered by the user in the text box and the function to be applied to the matrix, respectively. The `MSPSetDefault` function is used to assign a default value to the `$$fn` variable. Depending on the menu item selected, the corresponding function name is assigned to the variable `$$fn`. When the user clicks the Evaluate button, the value of `$$fn` and `$$matrix` are passed to the `Which` command, used in *Mathematica* for conditional processing. Depending on the value of `$$fn`, the corresponding computation is performed on `$$matrix`, and the result is displayed in the Web page using `MSPFormat`.

Converting Expressions to MathML

As we saw in Section 11.2, *Mathematica* includes many commands for working with MathML. In particular, you can convert expressions in *Mathematica* syntax into MathML and vice versa. Example 12.14 shows an MSP script that displays the MathML representation for any expression in *Mathematica* syntax. Figure 12.19 shows how this script looks when viewed in *IE*.

Example 12.14 An HTML document for converting an expression into MathML.

```
<html>
 <head><title>Conversion to MathML</title></head>
 <body bgcolor = "white">
```

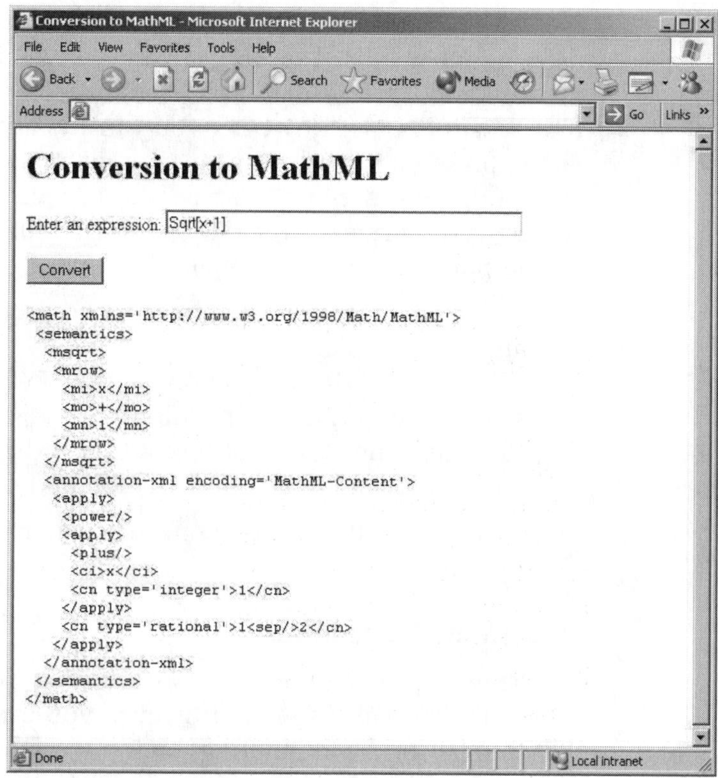

FIGURE 12.19 Translating mathematical expressions into MathML.

```
    <h1>Conversion to MathML</h1>
      <form method="post">
      Enter an expression:
      <input type="text" name="input" align="left"
      size="50" value =
    "<%Mathlet MSPValue[ $$input, "Sqrt[x+1]"] %>">
    <p><input type="submit" name="inputButton"
    value="Convert"> </p>
    <p><%Mathlet MSPBlock[{$$input}, MSPFormat[
    XML`MathML`ExpressionToMathML[$$input]]] %></p>
    </form>
  </body>
</html>
```

This script is similar to the previous ones in that it uses `Mathlet` tags along with the standard functions: `MSPValue`, `MSPBlock`, and `MSPFormat`. The *Mathematica* function `XML`MathML`ExpressionToMathML` is used to translate the expression entered by the user into MathML.

You can use the conversion options discussed in Section 11.2 to control various aspects of the MathML produced, such as the type of markup or the declarations added to it. For example, by default, `XML`MathML`ExpressionToMathML` yields both presentation markup and content markup encodings of its argument, enclosed in a `semantics` tag. However, you can modify the function to get either presentation markup or content markup alone by setting the option `"Formats"` to `"PresentationMathML"` or `"ContentMathML"`, respectively. Other conversion options for customizing the form of the output include, for example:

- Adding a namespace declaration and prefix to all the element and attribute names
- Adding an XML declaration or DOCTYPE declaration at the start of the MathML expression
- Changing the format of the output to be a continuous string without any additional indentation and linebreaking

See Section 11.2 for more information on the available conversion options.

Using MathML as Input

All the examples of MSP scripts shown so far require you to specify input in *Mathematica* syntax. However, you can also use web*Mathematica* to perform computations on input specified as MathML. This allows you, for example, to copy a MathML expression from another application, paste it into a form in a Web page, and then perform some computation on it (such as differentiating the expression or generating a plot).

The basic procedure for doing this is to convert the MathML string supplied as input into the equivalent *Mathematica* expression. You can do this by using the function `XML`MathML`MathMLToExpression`, which is the converse of the `XML`MathML`ExpressionToMathML'` function used in Example 12.14. Once a *Mathematica* expression is obtained, you can perform a wide variety of computations on it by applying any of the *Mathematica* functions for algebra, calculus, graphics, and so on. Example 12.15 shows an MSP script for calculating the integral of a function of one variable. Figure 12.20 shows how this script looks when viewed in *IE*.

Example 12.15 An HTML document for integrating a function specified in MathML form.

```
<html>
 <head>
     <title>Integrating MathML</title>
```

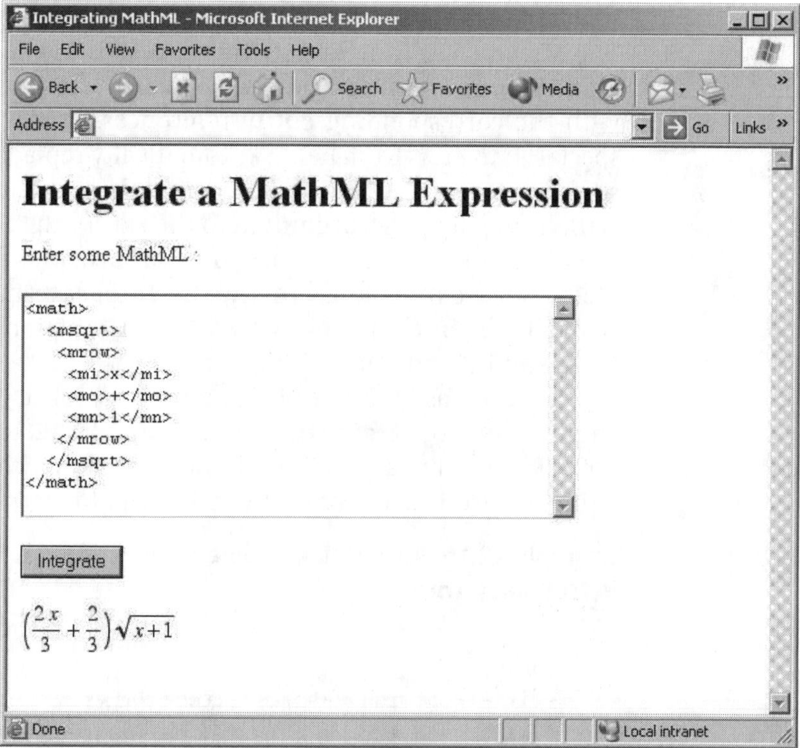

FIGURE 12.20 Calculating the integral of a function specified in MathML.

```
</head>
<body>
<h1>Integrating a MathML Expression</h1>
<form method="post">
<p>Enter some MathML:</p>
<p><textarea name="input" rows="10" cols="50" >
<%Mathlet StringReplace[MSPValue[$$input,
"<math><msup><mi>x</mi><mn>2</mn></msup></math>"],
{"\n"->"","&" -> "&amp;", "<" -> "&lt;",
">" -> "&gt;", "'"->"&#39;", "\""->"&quot;"}]%>
</textarea></p>
<input type="submit" name="inputButton"
  value="Integrate">
<p><%Mathlet MSPFormat[Integrate[
    XML`MathML`MathMLToExpression[$$input],x],
    TraditionalForm] %></p>
    </form>

</body>
</html>
```

Example 12.15 works as follows. The user enters a MathML string in the text box provided and then clicks the Integrate button. The *Mathematica* function `StringReplace` is applied to the MathML string to remove linebreaks and replace various special characters with the corresponding entity references. This is to prevent these special characters from being automatically replaced in certain browsers. The MathML string obtained after these substitutions are made is then supplied as an argument to the `XML`MathML`MathMLToExpression` function, which translates the MathML into the corresponding *Mathematica* expression. Finally, the `Integrate` function is used to calculate the integral, and the `MSPFormat` function is used to display the result in TraditionalForm.

You can easily modify Example 12.15 for doing other types of computation on MathML input. Example 12.16 shows an MSP script for plotting a function of one variable specified as a MathML string. Figure 12.21 shows how this script looks when viewed in *IE*.

Example 12.16 An HTML document for plotting a function specified in MathML form.

```
<html>
 <head>
 <title>Plotting MathML</title>
 </head>
 <body>
```

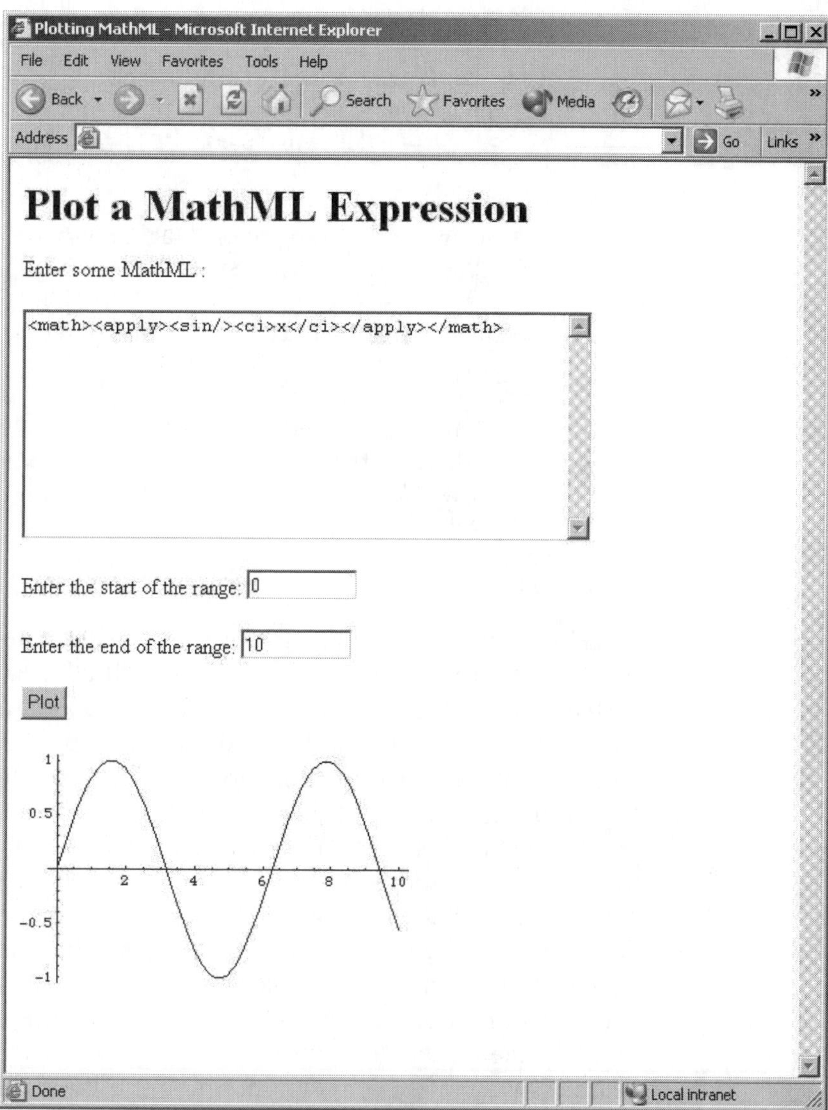

FIGURE 12.21 Plotting a function specified in MathML.

```
<h1>Plotting a MathML Expression</h1>
<form method="post">
  <p>Enter some MathML :</p>
  <p><textarea name="input" rows="10" cols="50" >
  <%Mathlet StringReplace[MSPValue[$$input,
  "<math><apply><sin/><ci>x</ci></apply></math>"],
  {"\n"->"","&" -> "&amp;", "<" -> "&lt;", ">" ->
  "&gt;", "'"->"&#39;", "\""->"&quot;"}] %>
```

```
            </textarea></p>

            <p>Enter the start of the range:
            <input type="text" name="x1" size="10" value =
            "<%Mathlet MSPValue[$$x1, "0"] %>"></p>

            <p> Enter the end of the range:
            <input type="text" name="x2" size="10" value =
            "<%Mathlet MSPValue[ $$x2, "10"] %>"></p>

            <input type="submit" name="inputButton"
            value="Plot">

            <p><%Mathlet MSPBlock[{$$x1,$$x2}, MSPShow[
            Plot[XML`MathML`MathMLToExpression[$$input],
            {x,$$x1,$$x2}]]]%></p>
        </form>
    </body>
  </html>
```

This example is similar to Example 12.12. The only difference is that the function to be plotted is specified as a MathML string instead of a *Mathematica* expression. As in Example 12.14, the MathML string is processed and converted into a *Mathematica* expression. The `Plot` function then produces the plot, and the `MSPShow` function displays an image of the plot in the Web browser.

The examples given here can be readily extended to provide access to calculations of any degree of complexity directly from a Web page. All the details for sending input to *Mathematica* and returning output back to the Web page are handled automatically by web*Mathematica*, so the user does not have to worry about the low-level implementation details. Also, since the Mathlet tags can be embedded directly in the HTML document in a fairly natural and seamless way, whoever is maintaining the Web site can choose the tools for generating and maintaining Web pages.

12.7 *MapleNET*

MapleNET is a system for doing interactive calculations on the Web using *Maple* as a computational engine. It provides a way of setting up *Maple* on a Web server to receive input and return output to a standard Web browser. *MapleNET* is to *Maple* what web*Mathematica* is to *Mathematica*—namely, a solution for delivering interactive computations over the Web. However, the design and interface of *MapleNET* are completely different from those of web*Mathematica*.

In the web*Mathematica* examples we saw earlier in this chapter, all controls such as text boxes, buttons, and menus are represented using standard HTML elements. In a Web page that communicates with the *MapleNET* server, however, all the interactive elements must be in the form of Java applets. To create such a Web page, you can write your own Java applets for sending input to the server and displaying output in the Web page. This requires some knowledge of Java programming.

However, a simpler alternative is to use the `Maplets` package, available in *Maple* Version 7 and later. This package provides a way to create custom user interfaces, called *maplets*, to access *Maple*'s computational abilities. Each maplet consists of a window that can contain text boxes, buttons, menus, sliders, and other types of interactive elements. Maplets are like Java applets but they are created using high-level *Maple* commands present in the `Maplets` package. Maplets therefore give you a way to get applet-like functionality without having to know Java programming.

To create a Web page that can perform computations using *Maple*, you first use the `Maplets` package to create maplets that correspond to the user interface elements (such as text boxes, buttons, or menus) that you want to include in the Web page. You can then insert a reference to the maplet in the Web page by embedding some *Maple*-specific markup in the HTML document.

This markup must be in the form of an `object` element (for *IE*) or an `embed` element (for *Netscape*). To make the Web page viewable by both browsers, you can include the `embed` element inside the `object` element. This is similar to the technique we used in Section 7.4 for embedding content to be rendered by *techexplorer* in a Web page. Here is the typical markup for displaying a maplet in a Web page:

```
<object classid="clsid:8AD9C840-044E-11D1-B3E9-
00805F499D93" width="1" height="1" align="middle" >
<param name="codebase" value = "." />
<param name="code" value =
"com.maplesoft.client.maplets.MapletLoader.class"/>
<param name="archive" value =
"../jar/mapletloader.jar" />
<param name="mapleFile" value="Plot.maplet" />
<comment>
<embed width="1" height="1" align="middle"
type="application/x-java-applet"
```

```
code="com.maplesoft.client.maplets.MapletLoader.class"
archive="../jar/mapletloader.jar"
mapleFile="Plot.maplet">
</embed>
</comment>
</object>
```

The `object` tag must have the following parameters:

- `codebase`: specifies the location of the class files.
- `code`:specifies the class that handles the maplets. It is always set to `com.maplesoft.client.maplets.MapletLoader.class`.
- `archive`:specifies the name of a jar file. It must be set to `jar/mapletloader.jar`.
- `mapleFile`:specifies the name of a file that contains the code for the maplet.

In the `embed` tag, the `codebase`, `code`, and `archive` parameters are replaced by attributes of the same name.

We illustrate this process using some simple examples.

Integrating a Function

Here is a simple maplet that implements a dialog for evaluating integrals:

```
with(Maplets[Elements]);
 m:=Maplet([
 ["Enter an expression to be integrated"],
 ["Integrand: ", TextField['fn']()],
 ["Enter a variable of Integration:",
 TextField['x'](3)],
 MathMLViewer['Result'](),
 [Button("Integrate", Evaluate('Result'=
 'MathML[Export](int(fn, x))'))]
 ]):
Maplets[Display](m);
```

The maplet contains a text box for entering a function, a button for doing the evaluation, and an area for displaying the results. This file consists of three commands. The first command, `with(Maplets [Elements]);`, loads the *Maple* package called `Maplets[Elements]`. The last command uses the `Display` function to cause the maplet to be displayed.

The most important command is the second one. This command defines a maplet by giving a series of commands as arguments to the `Maplet` function that is defined in the `Maplets` package. Each argument of the `Maplet` function defines a particular element in the maplet window using predefined keywords from the `Maplets` package. For example:

- `[`*text*`]`: writes a line of text in the maplet window.
- `TextField['`*name*`']`: defines a text box called *name* in which a user can enter input.
- `MathMLViewer['`*name*`']`: defines a rectangular box called *name* in which the result of an evaluation can be displayed. *Maple* uses the *WebEQ* Viewer Control Java applet for displaying results as properly formatted mathematical notation.
- `Button("Integrate",` *command*`)`: defines a button bearing the text "Integrate". Clicking the button executes the *Maple* command specified as the second argument. In this example, the *Maple* command used is
    - `Evaluate('Result' = 'MathML[Export](int(fn, x))'`

This evaluates the integral of the function specified in the text box called `fn` with respect to the variable `x` and displays the result in the rectangular area called `result`. Figure 12.22 shows what this maplet looks like with some input and output displayed.

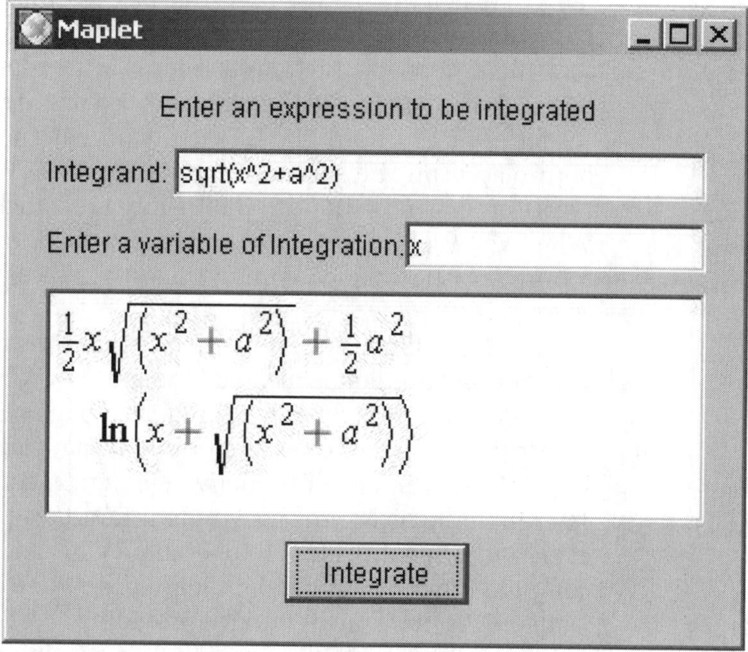

FIGURE 12.22 Integrating a function using *Maple*.

Plotting a Function

Here is a simple maplet that implements a dialog for plotting a function:

```
with(Maplets[Elements]);
 m:=Maplet([
 ["Enter a function of one variable:",]
 TextField['fn'](),
 ["Enter the start of the range:",
 TextField['x1'](3)],
 ["Enter the end of the range:",
 TextField['x2'](3)],
 [Plotter['Figure']()],
 [Button("Plot", Evaluate('Figure'=
 'plot(fn, x=x1..x2)'))]
 ]):
Maplets[Display](m);
```

This maplet contains a text box for entering a function, a button for doing the evaluation, and an area for displaying the results. Figure 12.23 shows what the maplet looks like after you use it to create a plot.

These examples illustrate how you can use *MapleNET* to perform interactive calculations from a Web site. Once you have written a maplet to define the user interface for your calculation and the particular *Maple* computation to be performed, you save the maplet as a file. Then you include a reference to that maplet file in the HTML document in the form of an `embed` or `object` tag, as explained earlier in this section. The HTML document and the maplet file are both placed on the server, either using an FTP (File Transfer Protocol) process or using the publishing tools included in *MapleNET*. When the Web page that contains this extra markup is viewed in a browser, the maplet window is automatically displayed on the screen.

The main limitation of maplets is that they appear in a separate window and are hence not well integrated with the rest of the Web page. You can directly embed in a Web page inline interactive elements (such as text boxes and buttons) that can communicate with *Maple*. However, each interactive element must be in the form of a Java applet, which requires you to know Java programming. However, once these hurdles are overcome you can, in principle, do any computations over the Web that are possible to do directly in *Maple*. *MapleNET* is thus one option for providing access to interactive computations over the Web, especially for existing users of *Maple*, who

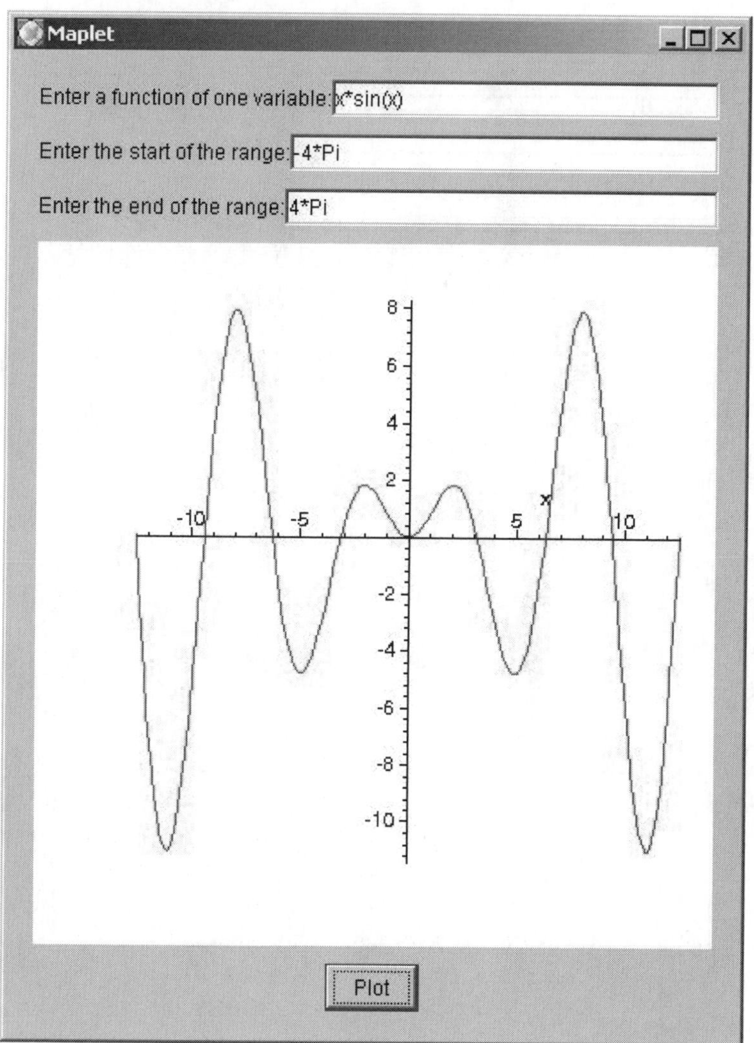

FIGURE 12.23 Plotting a function using *Maple*.

already have an investment in the system and are familiar with the syntax of *Maple* commands.

PART III

REFERENCES

CHAPTER

13

PRESENTATION ELEMENTS

This chapter gives an alphabetical listing of all presentation elements and describes each element's syntax, description, and attributes.

13.1 Introduction

The entry for each element has the following parts:

- Syntax: gives the syntax of the element showing the type of content it can contain.
- Description: gives the meaning of the element and summarizes any additional information relevant to its use.
- Attributes: gives the name of each attribute, its allowed values, and default value. For brevity, attributes common to all presentation elements are not included explicitly in the entry for each element. They are listed only once, in this introduction.

Common Attributes

The following five attributes are accepted by all MathML presentation elements:

- `class`, `style`, and `id`: are used with CSS and XSL stylesheets.
- `xlink:href`: is used for setting up links. (See Section 6.3 for more details.)
- `other`: is used for specifying nonstandard attributes that are not defined in MathML but may be supported by specific processing applications.

These attributes are not included in the entry for each element but are implied.

13.2 Listing of Presentation Elements

For brevity, attributes common to all token elements are listed only once, in this section. They are not included in the list of attributes for each token element but are implied. Table 13.1 shows the style attributes of token elements.

`maction`

Syntax

```
<maction>(child)*</maction>
```

TABLE 13.1 Style Attributes of Token Elements

Attribute	Values	Default
mathbackground	*#rgb* | *#rrggbb* | *html-color name*	inherited
mathcolor	*#rgb* | *#rrggbb* | *html-color name*	inherited
mathsize	small | normal | big | *number v-unit*	inherited
mathvariant	normal | bold | italic | script | bold-fraktur | double-struck | bold-script | fraktur | sans-serif | bold-sans-serif | sans-serif-italic | sans-serif-bold-italic | monospace	normal (except on mi)
fontsize	*number* v-unit	inherited
fontweight	normal | bold	inherited
fontstyle	normal | italic	normal (except on mi)
fontfamily	*string* | *css-fontfamily*	inherited
color	*#rgb* | *#rrggbb* | *html-color name*	inherited

Description

The maction element is used to associate interactive actions with specific parts of a MathML expression. This element is provided as a means of hooking up interactivity features implemented in a specific application to a MathML expression. Hence, the type of actions supported, if any, depend on the rendering application.

Attributes

This element accepts the two attributes shown in Table 13.2.

These attributes have the following meaning:

- selection: is an integer that identifies one of the arguments of the maction element. The value 1 refers to the first argument, 2 to the second argument, and so on. The purpose of

TABLE 13.2 Attributes of maction

Attribute	Values	Default
selection,	*number*	1
actiontype	Depends on application	Depends on application

this attribute is to provide a way to refer to subexpressions of the `maction` element; for example, in cases where the intended action is to toggle between different subexpressions.

- `actiontype`: specifies the action to be performed. The allowed values of this attribute are not defined by the MathML specification. Instead, each MathML application is expected to define its own values, depending on the type of actions it supports. Some examples of possible values that may be supported are: `toggle`, `statusline`, `highlight`, and `tooltip`.

maligngroup

Syntax

```
<maligngroup/>
```

Description

The `maligngroup` element is used to indicate the start of a new alignment group in a table column.

Attributes

None.

malignmark

Syntax

```
<malignmark/>
```

Description

The `malignmark` element is used to indicate an alignment point inside an alignment group in a table column.

Attributes

This element accepts the one attribute shown in Table 13.3.

If `edge="left"`, the alignment point is the left edge of the nearest element to the right of the `malignmark` element. If `edge="right"`, the alignment point is the right edge of the nearest element to the left of the `malignmark` element.

TABLE 13.3 Attributes of `malignmark`

Attribute	Values	Default
`edge`	`left` | `right`	{`left`}

`menclose`

Syntax

```
<menclose>(child)</menclose>
```

Description

The `menclose` element encloses its contents inside a notational symbol of a type specified by the value of its `notation` attribute.

Attributes

This element accepts the one attribute shown in Table 13.4.

The `notation` attribute determines the type of symbol placed around the contents.

`merror`

Syntax

```
<merror>(child)*</merror>
```

Description

The `merror` element is used to enclose information about syntax errors found when MathML markup is processed. The contents of the element are typically rendered in a different color or font style, to distinguish them from the surrounding text. The exact details of rendering depend on the specific processing application.

Attributes

None.

`mfenced`

Syntax

```
<mfenced>(child)*</mfenced>
```

Description

The `mfenced` element is used as a compact way to express common notational constructs involving fences, such as braces, brackets, or

TABLE 13.4 Attributes of `menclose`

Attribute	Values	Default
`notation`	`longdiv` | `actuarial` | `radical`	`radical`

parentheses. By default, this element renders its contents enclosed in parentheses with arguments separated by commas.

Attributes

This element accepts the three attributes shown in Table 13.5.

These attributes have the following meaning:

- `open`: specifies the character used as the opening fence.
- `close`: specifies the character used as the closing fence.
- `separators`: specifies the characters used to separate the arguments. The value of this attribute is a list of characters, with successive members of the list used to separate successive pairs of arguments. If there are fewer characters than needed, the last one is repeated as many times as necessary. If there are more characters than needed, the extra ones are ignored.

`mfrac`

Syntax

`<mfrac>`*numerator denominator*`</mfrac>`

Description

The `mfrac` element is used to display fractions or fraction-like notation, such as binomial coefficients.

Attributes

This element accepts the four attributes shown in Table 13.6.

These attributes have the following meaning:

- `linethickness`: specifies the thickness of the line that separates the numerator and denominator
- `numalign`: specifies the horizontal alignment of the numerator
- `denomalign`: specifies the horizontal alignment of the denominator

TABLE 13.5 Attributes of `mfenced`

Attribute	Values	Default
`open`	*string*	(
`close`	*string*	)
`separators`	*character**	,

TABLE 13.6 Attributes of `mfrac`

Attribute	Values	Default
`linethickness`	*number* [*v-unit*] | `thin` | `medium` | `thick`	`axis`
`numalign`	`left` | `center` | `right`	`center`
`denomalign`	(`left` | `center` | `right`)+	`center`
`bevelled`	`true` | `false`	`false`

- `bevelled`: when `false`, the numerator is shown above the denominator with a horizontal line between them; when `true`, a slightly raised numerator is shown to the left of a slightly lowered denominator with a diagonal line between them

`mglyph`

Syntax

```
<mglyph fontfamily="..." index="..." alt="..."/>
```

Description

The `mglyph` element is provided as an extension mechanism to allow arbitrary symbols and other extended characters to be displayed. It is displayed as a specific glyph in a specific font, the values of which are determined by its attributes.

Attributes

This element accepts the nine attributes common to all token elements. In addition, it accepts the three attributes shown in Table 13.7.

These attributes have the following meaning:

- `fontfamily`: specifies the font in which the desired glyph appears
- `index`: is an integer that specifies the position of the desired glyph in the font

TABLE 13.7 Attributes of `mglyph`

Attribute	Values	Default
`fontfamily`	*string* | *css-fontfamily*	required
`index`	*integer*	required
`alt`	*string*	required

- `alt`: specifies some alternative text that is displayed as a fallback if the glyph specified by the other two attributes is not found

mi

Syntax

```
<mi>PCDATA</mi>
```

Description

This element is used to represent identifiers such as names of variables and functions. The content of an `mi` element is displayed in italics if it is a single character and in an upright font otherwise.

Attributes

This element accepts the nine attributes common to all token elements.

mlabeledtr

Syntax

<mlabeledtr>*label* (<mtd>)*</mlabeledtr>

Description

The `mlabeledtr` element is used to represent a single labeled row in a table or matrix. It can occur only as a child element of an `mtable` element. It takes zero or more `mtd` elements, each of which corresponds to a single cell of the table or matrix.

Attributes

This element accepts the three attributes shown in Table 13.8.

These attributes have the same meaning as in the `mtable` element.

TABLE 13.8 Attributes of `mlabeledtr`

Attribute	Values	Default
`rowalign`	`(top | bottom | center | baseline | axis)+`	`baseline`
`columnalign`	`(left | center | right)+`	`center`
`groupalign`	*groupalignment-list-list*	`{left}`

mmultiscripts

Syntax

```
<mmultiscripts>
  base
  (subscript superscript)*
  [<mprescripts/> (presubscript presuperscript)*]
</mmultiscripts>
```

Description

The mmultiscripts element is used to attach prescripts and tensor indices to a base. It increments scriptlevel by 1, and sets displaystyle to false, within each of its arguments except *base*. It leaves both attributes unchanged within *base*.

Attributes

This element has the two attributes shown in Table 13.9.

These attributes have the following meaning:

- subscriptshift: specifies the minimum amount by which the subscript should be shifted down relative to the baseline of the base expression
- superscriptshift: specifies the minimum amount by which the superscript should be shifted up relative to the baseline of the base expression

mn

Syntax

```
<mn>PCDATA</mn>
```

Description

The mn element is used to represent a numeric literal; that is, a string that represents a number. A numeric literal can consist of an optional "+" or "−" sign followed by an arbitrary number of digits, possibly separated by a decimal point. The number can be in any base and any standard notation. The contents of the mn element are typically displayed in an upright font.

TABLE 13.9 Attributes of mmultiscripts

Attribute	Values	Default
subscriptshift	*number v-unit*	automatic
superscriptshift	*number v-unit*	automatic

Numbers that have some structure (such as negative numbers, complex numbers, fractions, and symbolic constants) cannot be specified as simple `mn` elements and require additional presentation elements.

Attributes

The `mn` element accepts the nine attributes common to all token elements.

`mo`

Syntax

```
<mo>PCDATA</mo>
```

Description

The `mo` element is used to represent operators, fences, separators, and accents. Fences include all characters used as delimiters such as braces, brackets, parentheses, and absolute value bars.

This element has a large collection of attributes that affect the details of how it is rendered. An operator dictionary, which specifies the values of attributes for most common operators, determines the default value of the attributes. If an attribute value is not specified in the operator dictionary, the attribute takes a generic default value, specified in Table 13.10.

Attributes

The `mo` element accepts the nine attributes common to all token elements. In addition, it has twelve other attributes, shown in Table 13.10. The default values for most of these attributes are typically determined from the operator dictionary. Some default values in Table 13.10 are shown with an asterisk to indicate that they are generic default values, to be used only if no match is found for that attribute in the operator dictionary.

These attributes have the following meaning:

- `form`: specifies whether the operator occurs in the prefix, postfix, or infix position. This, in turn, determines the amount of space rendered on either side of the operator by default.
- `lspace`: specifies the amount of space that should be added to the left of an operator. It is usually specified as a number followed by a unit of horizontal distance. If no unit is specified, a value in ems is assumed.
- `rspace`: specifies the amount of space that should be added to the right of an operator. It is usually specified as a number

TABLE 13.10 Attributes of `mo`

Attribute	Values	Default
`form`	`prefix` | `infix` | `postfix`	Determined by position in `mrow`
`lspace`	*number h-unit* | *namedspace*	`thickmathspace`*
`rspace`	*number h-unit* | *namedspace*	`thickmathspace`*
`stretchy`	`true` | `false`	`false`*
`symmetric`	`true` | `false`	`true`*
`maxsize`	*number* [*v-unit* | *h-unit*] | *namedspace* |	`infinity infinity`*
`minsize`	*number* | *namedspace*	`1`*
`largeop`	`true` | `false`	`false`*
`movablelimits`	`true` | `false`	`false`*
`fence`	`true` | `false`	`false`*
`separator`	`true` | `false`	`false`*
`accent`	`true` | `false`	`false`*

followed by a unit of horizontal distance. If no unit is specified, a value in ems is assumed.

- `stretchy`: specifies whether an operator should stretch to accommodate its contents.
- `symmetric`: specifies whether an operator for which `stretchy="true"` should always remain vertically symmetric with respect to its contents. That is, when `symmetric="true"`, the height of the operator above and the depth below its contents are always kept equal.
- `maxsize`: specifies the maximum size an operator can stretch to accommodate its contents. This attribute is either specified in absolute terms (that is, as a number with a unit) or in relative terms (that is, as a number). If it is specified as a number, the number is multiplied by the normal size of the operator to determine the maximum size.
- `minsize`: specifies the minimum size an operator can stretch to accommodate its contents. This attribute is either specified in absolute terms (that is, as a number with a unit) or in relative terms (that is, as a number). If it is set to a number, the number is multiplied by the normal size of the operator to determine the maximum size.
- `largeop`: specifies whether the operator should be drawn in a larger size when `displaystyle="true"` in that operator's environment. The operators that represent integrals, sums, and

products, for example, typically have `largeop` set to `true` by default.

- `movablelimits`: specifies whether underscripts and overscripts attached to an operator should be rendered as subscripts and superscripts when `displaystyle="false"` in that operator's environment. The operators that represent integrals, sums, and products, for example, typically have `movablelimits` set to `true` by default.
- `fence`: specifies whether the operator should be treated as if it were a fence. A fence is any character that plays the role of a delimiter, such as braces, brackets, parentheses, and absolute value bars. This attribute has no effect on the visual rendering of the operator. It is provided only as way of passing this information to applications that need to interpret the semantic meaning of the presentation markup.
- `separator`: specifies whether an operator should be treated as a separator for the purposes of rendering. It is provided as a means of giving linebreaking information to rendering applications. Setting `separator="true"` for an operator indicates that a linebreak should be avoided after the operator; that is, it is preferable to place the operator at the beginning of a broken line rather than at the end.
- `accent`: specifies whether an operator should be treated as an accent (or diacritical mark) when used as an underscript or overscript. Accents are typically rendered in normal size and closer to the base, while limits are rendered in a smaller size and farther away from the base.

mover

Syntax

`<mover>` *base overscript* `</mover>`

Description

The `mover` element is used for representing an overscript attached to a base.

By default, the `mover` element sets `displaystyle` to `false` in *overscript* and increments `scriptlevel` by 1 if `accent="false"`. It leaves both attributes unchanged within *base*.

Attributes

This element has the one attribute shown in Table 13.11.

TABLE 13.11 Attributes of `mover`

Attribute	Values	Default
`accent`	`true` | `false`	automatic

The `accent` attribute specifies whether the expression that appears in the overscript position should be treated as an accent or a limit. Accents are rendered in normal size and closer to the base, while limits are rendered in a smaller size and farther away from the base.

mpadded

Syntax

<mpadded>(*child*)*</mpadded>

Description

The `mpadded` element is used to make precise adjustments to the position of an expression relative to its surrounding elements. It changes the position of the bounding box used for rendering its contents by an amount determined by its attributes.

Attributes

This element accepts the four attributes shown in Table 13.12.

These attributes have the following meaning:

- `width`: specifies the horizontal width of the bounding box
- `lspace`: specifies the amount of blank space inserted before the left edge of the bounding box

TABLE 13.12 Attributes of `mpadded`

Attribute	Values	Default
`width`	[+ | –] *number* | (%[*pseudo-unit*] | *pseudo-unit* | *h-unit* | *namedspace*)	same as content
`lspace`	[+ | –] *number* | (%[*pseudo-unit*] | *pseudo-unit* | *h*-unit)	same as the element's content
`height`	[+ | –] *number* | (%[*pseudo-unit*] | *pseudo-unit* | *h-unit*)	same as the element's content
`depth`	[+ | –] *number* | (%[*pseudo-unit*] | *pseudo-unit* | *h-unit*)	same as the element's content

- `height`: specifies the vertical distance between the baseline and the top of the bounding box
- `depth`: specifies the vertical distance between the baseline and the bottom of the bounding box

mphantom

Syntax

```
<mphantom>(child)*</mphantom>
```

Description

The `mphantom` element is used to render an expression invisibly. It inserts an amount of blank space equal to the space that would have been needed to render its contents if they were not enclosed in an `mphantom` element. This property is useful in aligning certain types of expressions.

Attributes

None.

mprescripts

Syntax

```
<mmultiscripts>
 base (subscript superscript)*
 [<mprescripts/> (presubscript presuperscript)*]
</mmultiscripts>
```

Description

This is an empty element used as a child element of the `<mmultiscripts>` element to indicate that the elements after it should be displayed in the prescript position.

Attributes

None.

mroot

Syntax

```
<mroot>base index</mroot>
```

Description

The `mroot` element is used to display arbitrary roots. The base is displayed enclosed in a radical sign with the index placed outside the radical sign, which is the conventional notation for roots.

Attributes

None.

mrow

Syntax

```
<mrow>(child)*</mrow>
```

Description

The `mrow` element is used to group any number of subexpressions. Its elements are displayed in a horizontal row, from left to right.

Attributes

None.

ms

Syntax

```
<ms>PCDATA</ms>
```

Description

The `ms` element is used to represent string literals, a concept of importance for programming languages and computer algebra systems. By default, its contents are rendered enclosed in quotation marks.

Attributes

This element accepts the nine attributes common to all token elements. In addition, it accepts the two attributes shown in Table 13.13.

These attributes have the following meaning:

- `lquote`: specifies the character that appears at the start of the string
- `rquote`: specifies the character that appears at the end of the string

TABLE 13.13 Attributes of `ms`

Attribute	Values	Default
`lquote`	*character*	`"`
`rquote`	*character*	`"`

`mspace`

Syntax

```
<mspace/>
```

Description

The `mspace` element is used to insert a blank space of arbitrary size. The size of the space inserted is determined by the value of its attributes. The default values of the attributes are chosen to have no effect on visual rendering. Hence, to insert any additional space, you must use this element with explicit attribute values specified.

Attributes

This element accepts the nine attributes common to all token elements. In addition, it accepts the three attributes shown in Table 13.14.

These attributes have the following meaning:

- `width`: is the distance from the left edge of the bounding box that defines the space
- `height`: is the distance from the baseline to the top of the bounding box
- `depth`: is the distance from the baseline to the bottom of the bounding box

`msqrt`

Syntax

```
<msqrt>base</msqrt>
```

Description

The `msqrt` element is used to display square roots. It takes a single child element, which is displayed with a square root sign around its contents. If it is written with more than one child element, an `mrow` element is inferred around the contents.

TABLE 13.14 Attributes of `mspace`

Attribute	Values	Default
`width`	*number h-unit* | *namedspace*	`0 em`
`height`	*number v-unit*	`0 ex`
`depth`	*number v-unit*	`0 ex`

Attributes

None.

mstyle

Syntax

```
<mstyle>(child)*</mstyle>
```

Description

The mstyle element is used to set the default value of an attribute throughout a given piece of presentation markup. If an attribute is specified explicitly on an mstyle element, the specified value is inherited by all elements contained within the mstyle element directly or indirectly. In other words, that value will be used as the default on every element contained within that mstyle element, unless the value is explicitly changed by another attribute specification.

The mstyle element displays its children in a horizontal row aligned along the baseline, similar to the mrow element.

Attributes

This element accepts the thirteen attributes shown in Table 13.15. In addition, it accepts all attributes of all other presentation elements, except for those attributes that have a required value.

TABLE 13.15 Attributes of mstyle

Attribute	Values	Default
scriptlevel	[+|-] *unsigned-integer*	inherited
displaystyle	true | false	inherited
scriptsizemultiplier	*number*	0.71
scriptminsize	*number v-unit*	8 pt
color	*#rgb*|*#rrggbb*|transparent| *html-color-name*	inherited
background	#rgb|*#rrggbb*|transparent| *html-color-name*	transparent
veryverythinmathspace	*number h-unit*	1/18 em
verythinmathspace	*number h-unit*	1/9 em
thinmathspace	*number h-unit*	1/6 em
mediummathspace	*number h-unit*	2/9 em
thickmathspace	*number h-unit*	5/18 em
verythickmathspace	*number h-unit*	1/3 em
veryverythickmathspace	*number h-unit*	7/18 em

The first six of these attributes have the following meaning:

- `scriptlevel`: controls the font size. The higher the script level, the smaller the font size. The change in the font size depends on the value of the attribute `scriptsizemultiplier`.
- `displaystyle`: controls the value of two other attributes in `mo` elements, namely `largeop` and `movablescripts`. These attributes can take one of several values, depending on the value of the `displaystyle` attribute in their environment. In general, the `displaystyle` attribute has the value `true` for equations intended for display and `false` for equations that occur inline as well as for tables, fractions, or scripts. Presentation elements that typically cause their content to be displayed in a smaller size or with less vertical spacing (such as subscripts, superscripts, fractions, square roots, and tables) typically set `displaystyle` to false and increase the value of `scriptlevel`. Ten elements change the value of either `displaystyle` or `scriptlevel`: `msub`, `msup`, `msubsup`, `munder`, `mover`, `munderover`, `mmultiscripts`, `mfrac`, `mroot`, and `mtable`.
- `scriptsizemultiplier`: is a number that determines the change in font size caused by `scriptlevel`. The new font size is equal to the old font size multiplied by the `scriptsizemultiplier` to the power of the change in `scriptlevel`.
- `scriptminsize`: is the minimum size to which a font can be reduced as a consequence of changes in `scriptlevel`.
- `color`: specifies the color in which the markup is rendered in RGB notation.
- `background`: specifies the background color in RGB notation.

Spacing between operators is typically one of a small set of values. The `<mstyle>` element has the following seven named attributes that set the size of these values:

- `veryverythinmathspace`
- `verythinmathspace`
- `thinmathspace`
- `mediummathspace`
- `thickmathspace`
- `verythickmathspace`
- `veryverythickmathspace`

Each of these attributes defines a fixed horizontal space, with the default value ranging between 1/18 em to 7/18 em. Since the spacing between operators in the operator dictionary is defined in terms of these values, setting these values to a larger or smaller value can make the spacing between all operators looser or tighter.

msub

Syntax

<msub>*base subscript*</msub>

Description

The msub element is used for representing a subscript attached to a base.

By default, the msub element automatically increments scriptlevel by 1 and sets displaystyle to false in *subscript* but leaves both attributes unchanged within *base*.

Attributes

This element has the one attribute shown in Table 13.16.

The subscriptshift attribute specifies the minimum amount by which the subscript should be shifted down relative to the baseline of the base expression.

msubsup

Syntax

<msubsup>*base subscript superscript*</msubsup>

Description

The msubsup element is used for representing a subscript attached to a base.

By default, the msubsup element automatically increments scriptlevel by 1 and sets displaystyle to false in both *subscript* and *superscript* but leaves both attributes unchanged within *base*.

Attributes

This element has the two attributes shown in Table 13.17.

These attributes have the following meaning:

- subscriptshift: specifies the minimum amount by which the subscript should be shifted down relative to the baseline of the base expression

TABLE 13.16 Attributes of msub

Attribute	Values	Default
subscriptshift	*number v-unit*	automatic

TABLE 13.17 Attributes of `msubsup`

Attribute	Values	Default
`subscriptshift`	*number v-unit*	automatic
`superscriptshift`	*number v-unit*	automatic

- `superscriptshift`: specifies the minimum amount by which the superscript should be shifted up relative to the baseline of the base expression

`msup`

Syntax

`<msup>`*base superscript*`</msup>`

Description

The `msup` element is used for representing a superscript attached to a base.

By default, the `msup` element automatically increments `scriptlevel` by 1 and sets `displaystyle` to `false` in *superscript* but leaves both attributes unchanged within *base*.

Attributes

This element has the one attribute shown in Table 13.18.

The `superscriptshift` attribute specifies the minimum amount by which the superscript should be shifted up relative to the baseline of the base expression.

`mtable`

Syntax

`<mtable>(`*child*`)*</mtable>`

Description

The `mtable` element is used to represent tables or matrices. It takes zero or more `mtr` or `mlabeledtr` elements, each of which corresponds to a single row of the table or matrix.

TABLE 13.18 Attributes of `msup`

Attribute	Values	Default
`superscriptshift`	*number v-unit*	automatic

Attributes

This element accepts the eighteen attributes shown in Table 13.19.

For several of these attributes, the value can be a sequence of zero or more entries. In such cases, the first entry applies to the first row or column, the second entry to the second row/column, and so on. If there are fewer entries than rows/columns in the table, the last entry is repeated as many times as necessary. If there are more entries than rows/columns, the extra entries are ignored.

These attributes have the following meaning:

- `align`: specifies where to align the table with respect to its environment. If the value of this attribute ends with a number between 1 and n (for a table with n rows), the value of that entry is applied to that row of the table only. The top row is

TABLE 13.19 Attributes of `mtable`

Attribute	Values	Default
`align`	(`top` | `bottom` | `center` | `baseline` | `axis`)	[*rownumber*] `axis`
`rowalign`	(`top` | `bottom` | `center` | `baseline` | `axis`)+	`baseline`
`columnalign`	(`left` | `center` | `right`)+	`center`
`columnwidth`	(`auto` | *number h-unit* | *namedspace* | `fit`) +	`auto`
`width`	`auto` | *number h-unit*	`auto`
`rowspacing`	(*number v-unit*) +	`1.0 ex`
`columnspacing`	(*number h-unit* | *namedspace*) +	`0.8 em`
`rowlines`	(`none` | `solid` | `dashed`) +	`none`
`columnlines`	(`none` | `solid` | `dashed`) +	`none`
`equalrows`	`true` | `false`	`false`
`equalcolumns`	`true` | `false`	`false`
`frame`	(`none` | `solid` | `dashed`) +	`none`
`framespacing`	(*number h-unit* | *namedspace*) (*number v-unit* | *namedspace*)	`0.4 em 0.5 ex`
`displaystyle`	`true` | `false`	`false`
`side`	`left` | `right` | `leftoverlap` | `rightoverlap`	`right`
`minlabelspacing`	*number h-unit*	`0.8 em`
`groupalign`	*groupalignment-list-list*	{`left`}
`alignmentscope`	`true` | `false`	`true`

numbered 1 and the bottom row is numbered n. Alternatively, you can use a negative number between −1 and −n, in which case the top row is referred to as −n and the bottom row as −1. Possible values of this attribute are:

  - `top`: aligns the top of the table along the environment's baseline
  - `bottom`: aligns the bottom of the table along the environment's baseline
  - `center`: aligns the center of the table (that is, the midpoint of the table's vertical extent) along the environment's baseline
  - `baseline`: same as `center`
  - `axis`: aligns the center of the table along the environment's axis (that is, the line on which the minus sign typically lies)

- `rowalign`: specifies how the entries in each row should be aligned. Possible values are:
  - `top`: specifies that the top of all entries in the row should be aligned
  - `bottom`: specifies that the bottom of all entries in the row should be aligned
  - `center`: specifies that the center of all entries in the row should be aligned
  - `baseline`: specifies that the baseline of all entries in the row should be aligned
  - `axis`: specifies that the axis of all entries in the row should be aligned
- `columnalign`: specifies how the entries in each column should be aligned. Possible values are:
  - `left`: specifies that the left edge of all entries in the column should be aligned
  - `center`: specifies that the center of all entries in the column should be aligned
  - `right`: specifies that the right edge of all entries in the column should be aligned
- `columnwidth`: specifies how wide a column should be. Possible values are:
  - `auto`: specifies that the column is as wide as needed to accommodate its contents
  - *number h-unit* or *namedspace*: specifies a fixed width either by giving a number and a unit or any of the seven named

spaces, each of which define a fixed width between 1/18 em and 7/18 em
    - `fit`: adjusts the width of the columns so the table spans the width of the page; the width of each column that is set to a fixed width or `auto` is subtracted from the page width and the resulting number is divided by the remaining number of columns

- `width`: specifies the width of the entire table. It can be set to a fixed number or `auto`, which means that the renderer should adjust the width of the table, depending on its contents.
- `rowspacing`: specifies the amount of space between any two rows. The spacing before the first row and after the last row is determined by the attribute `framespacing`.
- `columnspacing`: specifies the amount of space between any two columns. The spacing before the first column and after the last column is determined by the attribute `framespacing`.
- `rowlines`: specifies the type of line to be drawn between any two rows, if any.
- `columnlines`: specifies the type of line to be drawn between any two columns, if any.
- `equalrows`: if `true`, forces all the rows to have the same height.
- `equalcolumns`: if `true`, forces all the columns to have the same width.
- `frame`: specifies if a frame should be drawn around the table.
- `framespacing`: if `frame` is set to either `solid` or `dashed`, determines how much space should be left between the frame and the first and last row or column. It is given as a sequence of two numbers; the first one determines the spacing between the frame and the first and last row, and the second determines the spacing between the frame and the first and last column.
- `displaystyle`: specifies the display mode for each cell of the table. The default value is `false` and is appropriate when the table is embedded in a block of text. A value of `true` is appropriate if the table is displayed in a separate block by itself. In either case, the value of `scriptlevel` in the cells of the table is unchanged.
- `side`: specifies on what side of the table the label for a labeled row should be displayed. The label is displayed on the left if set to `left` and on the right if set to `right`. If the table fits on the page without the label but does not fit when the label is added, the label overlaps the row and is shown above the row if `rowalign` for that row is `top` and below the row otherwise.

- `minlabelspacing`: specifies the minimum space allowed between a label and the adjacent entry in the corresponding row.
- `groupalign`: specifies the alignment point for alignment groups defined using the `maligngroup` element.
- `alignmentscope`: specifies if alignment information defined using the `maligngroup` and `malignmark` elements should be interpreted or ignored.

mtd

Syntax

```
<mtd>(child)*</mtd>
```

Description

The `mtd` element is used to represent a single cell in a table or matrix. It can occur only as a child element of an `mtr` or `mlabeledtr` element.

Attributes

This element accepts the five attributes shown in Table 13.20.

These attributes have the following meaning:

- `rowalign`, `columnalign`, and `groupalign`: have the same meaning as in the `mtable` element
- `rowspan`: allows a given cell in the table to occupy the specified number of rows
- `columnspan`: allows a given cell in the table to occupy the specified number of columns

mtext

Syntax

```
<mtext>PCDATA</mtext>
```

TABLE 13.20 Attributes of `mtd`

Attribute	Values	Default
rowalign	(top | bottom | center | baseline | axis)+	baseline
columnalign	(left | center | right)+	center
groupalign	*groupalignment-list-list*	{left}
rowspan	*number*	1
columnspan	*number*	1

Description

The mtext element is used to represent plain text that must be included literally in a mathematical expression.

Attributes

The mtext element accepts the nine attributes common to all token elements.

mtr

Syntax

```
<mtr>(<mtd>)*</mtr>
```

Description

The mtr element is used to represent a single row in a table or matrix. It takes zero or more mtd elements, each of which corresponds to a single cell of the table or matrix.

Attributes

This element accepts the three attributes shown in Table 13.21.

These attributes have the same meaning as in the mtable element.

munder

Syntax

<munder>*base underscript*</munder>

Description

The munder element is used for representing an underscript attached to a base.

By default, the munder element sets displaystyle to false in *underscript* and increments scriptlevel by 1 if accentunder="false". It leaves both attributes unchanged within *base*.

TABLE 13.21 Attributes of mtr

Attribute	Values	Default
rowalign	(top | bottom | center | baseline | axis)+	baseline
columnalign	(left | center | right)+	center
groupalign	*groupalignment-list-list*	{left}

TABLE 13.22 Attributes of munder

Attribute	Values	Default
accentunder	true | false	automatic

Attributes

This element has the one attribute shown in Table 13.22.

The accentunder attribute specifies whether the expression that appears in the underscript position should be treated as an accent or a limit. Accents are rendered in normal size and closer to the base, while limits are rendered in a smaller size and farther away from the base.

munderover

Syntax

<munderover>*base underscript overscript*</munderover>

Description

The munderover element is used for representing an underscript and overscript attached to a base.

By default, the munderover element sets displaystyle to false in *underscript* and *overscript* and increments scriptlevel by 1 only when accentunder="false". It leaves both attributes unchanged within *base*.

Attributes

This element has the two attributes shown in Table 13.23.

These attributes have the following meaning:

- accentunder: specifies whether the expression that appears in the underscript position should be treated as an accent or a limit. Accents are rendered in normal size and closer to the base, while limits are rendered in a smaller size and farther away from the base.

TABLE 13.23 Attributes of munderover

Attribute	Values	Default
accentunder	true | false	automatic
accent	true | false	automatic

- `accent`: specifies whether the expression that appears in the overscript position should be treated as an accent or a limit. Accents are rendered in normal size and closer to the base, while limits are rendered in a smaller size and farther away from the base.

none

Syntax

```
<mmultiscripts>  base
 (subscript|<none/>superscript|<none/>)*
 [<mprescripts/> (presubscript|<none/>
 presuperscript|<none/>)*]
</mmultiscripts>
```

Description

The `none` element is used as a child element of the `mmultiscripts` element to indicate that the position opposite to a particular subscript or superscript is blank.

Attributes

None.

CHAPTER

14

CONTENT ELEMENTS

This chapter contains an alphabetical listing of all the content elements and describes each element's syntax, description, and attributes.

14.1 INTRODUCTION

The entry for each element has the following parts:

- Syntax: gives the syntax of the element showing the type of content it can contain.
- Description: gives the meaning of the element and any additional information relevant to its use.
- Attributes: gives the name of each attribute, its allowed values, and default value. For brevity, attributes common to all content elements are not listed explicitly in the entry for each element. They are listed only once, in this introduction, and implied everywhere else.

Common Attributes

The following six attributes are accepted by all content elements:

- `class`, `style`, and `id`: are used with CSS and XSL stylesheets.
- `xref`: is used in parallel markup. (See Section 6.3 for more details.)
- `xlink:href`: is used for defining links.
- `other`: is used for specifying nonstandard attributes that are not part of the MathML specification but may be supported by specific processing applications.

These attributes are not included in the entry for each element but are implied.

Changing the Default Semantics

The attributes `definitionURL` and `encoding` are used to modify the semantic meaning of a content element. These attributes are accepted by all content elements that represent operators or functions as well as by the elements `csymbol`, `declare`, and `semantics`. The syntax and usage of these two attributes are explained in this section so that they can be omitted in the entry for each element.

The value of the `definitionURL` attribute is a URL that contains information about the semantic meaning to be associated with a particular content element. The `encoding` attribute specifies the format in which the semantic information is given.

For example, the content element `times` by default represents the operation of multiplying two numbers. However, by using the following markup, you can modify its semantics so that it refers to the cross-product of two vectors:

$A \times B$

```
<apply>
  <times definitionURL=
  "http://www.example.org/vectorcrossproduct.html"
  encoding="text"/>
  <ci type="vector">A</ci>
  <ci type="vector">B</ci>
</apply>
```

Here, the URL specified as the value of `definitionURL` must contain a definition of the vector product encoded as plain text. Note that the `type` attribute of the `<ci>` element is used to specify that the identifiers *A* and *B* represent vectors.

14.2 Listing of Content Elements

abs

Syntax

```
<apply><abs/>arg1</apply>
```

Description

The `abs` element represents the absolute value of the number specified as an argument.

Attributes

This element accepts the attributes `definitionURL` and `encoding`.

and

Syntax

```
<apply><and/>...</apply>
```

Description

The `and` element represents the logical AND operator. It evaluates to the value True when all of its arguments are True, and False otherwise. It can take any number of arguments.

Attributes

This element accepts the attributes `definitionURL` and `encoding`.

annotation

Syntax

```
<annotation>...</annotation>
```

Description

The `annotation` element is used as a container for alternative representations of a MathML expression, specified in a format different from XML. Each `annotation` element must be enclosed in a `semantics` element.

Attributes

This element accepts the attributes `definitionURL` and `encoding`.

annotation-xml

Syntax

```
<annotation-xml>...</annotation-xml>
```

Description

The `annotation-xml` element is used as a container for additional information about the meaning of an expression, specified using an XML-based format different from MathML. Each `annotation-xml` element must be enclosed in a `semantics` element.

Attributes

This element accepts the attributes `definitionURL` and `encoding`.

apply

Syntax

```
<apply>operator (argument) * </apply>
```

Description

The `apply` element represents the result of applying an operator or function to one or more arguments. The first child element of the `apply` element is the operator or function to be applied, and the subsequent child elements are the arguments of that operator or function. The type of operator or function used as the first child element determines the number of child elements.

Attributes

This element accepts the attributes `definitionURL` and `encoding`.

approx

Syntax

```
<apply><approx/>arg1 arg2...</apply>
```

Description

The approx element is used to indicate that two or more quantities are approximately equal.

Attributes

This element accepts the attributes definitionURL and encoding.

arccos

Syntax

```
<apply><arccos/>arg</apply>
```

Description

The arccos element represents the inverse cosine function.

Attributes

This element accepts the attributes definitionURL and encoding.

arccosec

Syntax

```
<apply><arccosec/>arg</apply>
```

Description

The arccosec element represents the inverse cosecant function.

Attributes

This element accepts the attributes definitionURL and encoding.

arccosh

Syntax

```
<apply><arccosh/>arg</apply>
```

Description

The arccosh element represents the inverse hyperbolic cosine function.

Attributes

This element accepts the attributes `definitionURL` and `encoding`.

`arccosech`

Syntax

```
<apply><arccosech/>arg</apply>
```

Description

The `arccosech` element represents the inverse hyperbolic cosecant function.

Attributes

This element accepts the attributes `definitionURL` and `encoding`.

`arccot`

Syntax

```
<apply><arccot/>arg</apply>
```

Description

The `arccot` element represents the inverse cotangent function.

Attributes

This element accepts the attributes `definitionURL` and `encoding`.

`arccoth`

Syntax

```
<apply><arccoth/>arg</apply>
```

Description

The `arccoth` element represents the inverse hyperbolic cotangent function.

Attributes

This element accepts the attributes `definitionURL` and `encoding`.

`arcsec`

Syntax

```
<apply><arcsec/>arg</apply>
```

Description

The `arcsec` element represents the inverse secant function.

Attributes

This element accepts the attributes `definitionURL` and `encoding`.

arcsech

Syntax

```
<apply><arcsech/>arg</apply>
```

Description

The `arcsech` element represents the inverse hyperbolic secant function.

Attributes

This element accepts the attributes `definitionURL` and `encoding`.

arcsin

Syntax

```
<apply><arcsin/>arg</apply>
```

Description

The `arcsin` element represents the inverse sine function.

Attributes

This element accepts the attributes `definitionURL` and `encoding`.

arcsinh

Syntax

```
<apply><arcsinh/>arg</apply>
```

Description

The `arcsinh` element represents the inverse hyperbolic sine function.

Attributes

This element accepts the attributes `definitionURL` and `encoding`.

arctan

Syntax

```
<apply><arctan/>arg</apply>
```

Description

The arctan element represents the inverse tangent function.

Attributes

This element accepts the attributes definitionURL and encoding.

arctanh

Syntax

```
<apply><arctanh/>arg</apply>
```

Description

The arctanh element represents the inverse hyperbolic tangent function.

Attributes

This element accepts the attributes definitionURL and encoding.

arg

Syntax

```
<apply><arg/>arg1</apply>
```

Description

The arg element represents the argument of a complex number specified as an argument.

Attributes

This element accepts the attributes definitionURL and encoding.

bvar

Syntax

```
<bvar>variable</bvar>
```

Description

The bvar element is a qualifier element that is used in conjunction with the `int`, `diff`, and `partialdiff` elements to represent a bound variable.

Attributes

This element accepts the attributes `definitionURL` and `encoding`.

card

Syntax

<apply><card/>*set*</apply>

Description

The `card` element represents the cardinality of a set; that is, the number of elements contained in the set.

Attributes

This element accepts the attributes `definitionURL` and `encoding`.

cartesianproduct

Syntax

<apply><cartesianproduct/>*set1 set2*</apply>

Description

The `cartesianproduct` element represents the Cartesian product of two or more sets.

Attributes

This element accepts the attributes `definitionURL` and `encoding`.

ceiling

Syntax

<apply><ceiling/>*number*</apply>

Description

The `ceiling` element represents the smallest integer greater than or equal to the number specified as an argument.

Attributes

This element accepts the attributes `definitionURL` and `encoding`.

ci

Syntax

```
<ci>...</ci>
```

Description

The ci element is used to represent objects such as functions, variables, and symbolic constants. The type of the object is specified using an attribute. To allow precise control over rendering, this element can contain any arbitrary presentation markup.

Attributes

This element accepts the attributes `definitionURL` and `encoding`. In addition, it accepts the one attribute shown in Table 14.1.

The `type` attribute specifies the type of object encoded. It can be set to any string, including the names of MathML container elements (such as `set`, `list`, `vector`, `matrix`, and `fn`).

cn

Syntax

```
<cn>...</cn>
```

Description

The `cn` element is used to represent numerical constants. The type of the number and its base are specified via attributes. Rational, complex, and floating-point numbers require the different parts of the number to be separated by a `sep` element.

Attributes

This element accepts the attributes `definitionURL` and `encoding`. In addition, it accepts the two attributes shown in Table 14.2. These attributes have the following meaning:

- `type`: specifies the type of number encoded
- `base`: specifies the base of the number being encoded

TABLE 14.1 Attributes of `ci`

Name	Values	Default
`type`	*string*	`real`

TABLE 14.2 Attributes of `cn`

Name	Values	Default
type	real | integer | rational | floating-point | constant real complex-polar | complex-cartesian | e-notation	
base	Integer between 2 and 36	10

codomain

Syntax

```
<apply><codomain/>function</apply>
```

Description

The `codomain` element represents the codomain of a function; that is, a set that contains all values taken by the function. The codomain is also referred to as the range.

Attributes

This element accepts the attributes `definitionURL` and `encoding`.

complexes

Syntax

```
<complexes/>
```

Description

The `complexes` element represents the set of all complex numbers. It has the default rendering C.

Attributes

This element accepts the attributes `definitionURL` and `encoding`.

compose

Syntax

```
<apply><compose/>(function) + </apply>
```

Description

The `compose` element is used for composing two functions. The result is a new function whose range is the same as the range of the first function and whose domain is the same as the domain of the second function.

Attributes

This element accepts the attributes `definitionURL` and `encoding`.

condition

Syntax

```
<condition><apply>...</apply></condition>
```

or

```
<condition><reln>...</reln></condition>
```

Description

The `condition` element is used to encode conditional statements; that is, statements involving the phrase "such that."

Attributes

This element accepts the attributes `definitionURL` and `encoding`.

conjugate

Syntax

```
<apply><conjugate/>arg1</apply>
```

Description

The `conjugate` element represents the complex conjugate of a complex number specified as an argument.

Attributes

This element accepts the attributes `definitionURL` and `encoding`.

cos

Syntax

```
<apply><cos/>arg</apply>
```

Description

The `cos` element represents the trigonometric cosine function.

Attributes

This element accepts the attributes `definitionURL` and `encoding`.

cosec

Syntax

```
<apply><cosec/>arg</apply>
```

Description

The cosec element represents the trigonometric cosecant function.

Attributes

This element accepts the attributes definitionURL and encoding.

cosech

Syntax

```
<apply><cosech/>arg</apply>
```

Description

The cosech element represents the hyperbolic cosecant function.

Attributes

This element accepts the attributes definitionURL and encoding.

cosh

Syntax

```
<apply><cosh/>arg</apply>
```

Description

The cosh element represents the hyperbolic cosine function.

Attributes

This element accepts the attributes definitionURL and encoding.

cot

Syntax

```
<apply><cot/>arg</apply>
```

Description

The cot element represents the trigonometric cotangent function.

Attributes

This element accepts the attributes `definitionURL` and `encoding`.

coth

Syntax

```
<apply><coth/>arg</apply>
```

Description

The `coth` element represents the hyperbolic cotangent function.

Attributes

This element accepts the attributes `definitionURL` and `encoding`.

csymbol

Syntax

```
<csymbol>...</csymbol>
```

Description

The `csymbol` element is used to define new objects such as constants and functions, which cannot be represented using the existing content elements. To allow precise control over rendering, it can contain any arbitrary presentation markup. The meaning of the object is defined using the `definitionURL` and `encoding` attributes.

Attributes

This element accepts the attributes `definitionURL` and `encoding`.

curl

Syntax

```
<apply><curl/>function</apply>
```

Description

The `curl` element represents the curl operator of vector calculus.

Attributes

This element accepts the attributes `definitionURL` and `encoding`.

declare

Syntax

<declare>*identifier definition*</declare>

Description

The `declare` element is used for declaring that a given identifier is an object of a certain type and for assigning that object a specific value.

Attributes

This element accepts the attributes `definitionURL` and `encoding`. In addition, it accepts the three attributes shown in Table 14.3.

These attributes have the following meaning:

- `type`: specifies the type of object being declared. Typical values of this attribute are `set`, `list`, `vector`, `matrix`, or `function`.
- `nargs`: specifies the number of arguments when you are declaring an operator or function.
- `occurrence`: specifies the position in which an operator being declared occurs.

degree

Syntax

<degree>*variable*</degree>

Description

The `degree` element is a qualifier element that is used in conjunction with the `diff` and `partialdiff` elements to specify the order of differentiation, with the `root` element to specify the degree of a root, and with the `moment` element to specify the type of a statistical moment.

TABLE 14.3 Attributes of `declare`

Name	Values	Default
`type`	Any MathML content element	real
`nargs`	`integer`	none
`occurrence`	`infix` | `prefix`	`infix`

Attributes

This element accepts the attributes `definitionURL` and `encoding`.

determinant

Syntax

```
<apply><determinant/>matrix</apply>
```

Description

The `determinant` element represents the operator for the determinant of a matrix.

Attributes

This element accepts the attributes `definitionURL` and `encoding`.

diff

Syntax

```
<apply><diff/><bvar>...</bvar><degree>...</degree>
 <apply>function<ci>var</ci></apply>
</apply>
```

Description

The `diff` element represents the operation of taking a derivative. The variable of differentiation is specified using a `bvar` element. The order of differentiation is specified using a `degree` element.

Attributes

This element accepts the attributes `definitionURL` and `encoding`.

divergence

Syntax

```
<apply><divergence/>function</apply>
```

Description

The `divergence` element represents the divergence operator of vector calculus.

Attributes

This element accepts the attributes `definitionURL` and `encoding`.

divide

Syntax

```
<apply><divide/>dividend divisor</apply>
```

Description

The `divide` element represents the operation of division. It must have two arguments.

Attributes

This element accepts the attributes `definitionURL` and `encoding`.

domain

Syntax

```
<apply><domain/>function</apply>
```

Description

The `domain` element represents the domain of a function; that is, the set of values over which that function can be applied.

Attributes

This element accepts the attributes `definitionURL` and `encoding`.

emptyset

Syntax

```
<emptyset/>
```

Description

The `emptyset` element represents a set without any elements. It has the default rendering $\emptyset$.

Attributes

This element accepts the attributes `definitionURL` and `encoding`.

eq

Syntax

```
<apply><eq/>arg1 arg2...</apply>
```

Description

The eq element is used to indicate that two or more expressions are equal. It must have at least two arguments.

Attributes

This element accepts the attributes definitionURL and encoding.

equivalent

Syntax

```
<apply><equivalent/>arg1 arg2</apply>
```

Description

The equivalent element represents the logical equivalence function. Two Boolean expressions are equivalent if their values are equal for all values of the Boolean variables they contain. This element can take two or more arguments.

Attributes

This element accepts the attributes definitionURL and encoding.

eulergamma

Syntax

```
<eulergamma/>
```

Description

The eulergamma element represents the Euler-Gamma constant γ (approx. 0.5772156649), which occurs as the limiting value of certain series.

Attributes

This element accepts the attributes definitionURL and encoding.

exists

Syntax

```
<apply>
 <exists/>(optional <bvar> or <condition>)
 <apply>...</apply>
</apply>
```

or

```
<apply>
 <exists/>(optional <bvar> or <condition>)
 <reln>...</reln>
</apply>
```

Description

The `exists` element is used to indicate the existence of an element that satisfies a certain condition. It represents the mathematical concept normally denoted by the symbol ∃.

Attributes

This element accepts the attributes `definitionURL` and `encoding`.

exp

Syntax

```
<apply><exp/>exponent</apply>
```

Description

The `exp` element represents the exponential function, e^x, where e is the base of the natural logarithm (2.71828....).

Attributes

This element accepts the attributes `definitionURL` and `encoding`.

exponentiale

Syntax

```
<exponentiale/>
```

Description

The `exponentiale` element represents the numerical constant e (approx. 2.71828); that is, the base of the natural logarithm.

Attributes

This element accepts the attributes `definitionURL` and `encoding`.

factorial

Syntax

```
<apply><factorial/>argument</apply>
```

Description

The `factorial` element represents the unary operator used to construct factorials. Factorials are defined by $n! = n * (n - 1) * (n - 2) * \ldots * 1$.

Attributes

This element accepts the attributes `definitionURL` and `encoding`.

factorof

Syntax

```
<apply><factorof/>m n</apply>
```

Description

The `factorof` element is used to indicate that one number is a factor of the other. An integer m is a factor of another integer n if m mod $n = 0$.

Attributes

This element accepts the attributes `definitionURL` and `encoding`.

false

Syntax

```
<false/>
```

Description

The `false` element represents the Boolean constant "false."

Attributes

This element accepts the attributes `definitionURL` and `encoding`.

floor

Syntax

```
<apply><floor/>number</apply>
```

Description

The `floor` element represents the greatest integer less than or equal to the number specified as an argument.

Attributes

This element accepts the attributes `definitionURL` and `encoding`.

fn

Syntax

```
<fn>...</fn>
```

Description

The fn element is used to build a new function definition. This element is deprecated in MathML 2.0 since its function is now taken over by the apply and declare elements.

Attributes

This element accepts the attributes definitionURL and encoding.

forall

Syntax

```
<apply>
 <forall/>(optional <bvar> or <condition>)
 <apply>...</apply>
</apply>
```

or

```
<apply>
 <forall/>(optional <bvar> or <condition>)
 <reln>...</reln>
</apply>
```

Description

The forall element is used to indicate that some condition is true for all members of a certain set. It represents the mathematical concept normally denoted by the symbol ∀.

Attributes

This element accepts the attributes definitionURL and encoding.

gcd

Syntax

```
<apply><gcd/>...</apply>
```

Description

The gcd element represents the greatest common divisor of a set of integers, specified as arguments.

Attributes

This element accepts the attributes `definitionURL` and `encoding`.

geq

Syntax

```
<apply><geq/>arg1 arg2</apply>
```

Description

The `geq` element is used to indicate that one element is greater than or equal to another. It can take two or more arguments.

Attributes

This element accepts the attributes `definitionURL` and `encoding`.

grad

Syntax

```
<apply><grad/>function</apply>
```

Description

The `grad` element represents the gradient operator of vector calculus.

Attributes

This element accepts the attributes `definitionURL` and `encoding`.

gt

Syntax

```
<apply><gt/>arg1 arg2</apply>
```

Description

The `gt` element is used to indicate that one element is greater than another. It can take two or more arguments.

Attributes

This element accepts the attributes `definitionURL` and `encoding`.

ident

Syntax

```
<ident/>
```

Description

The `ident` element represents the identity function. The domain and range of the identity function, as well as the type of operation it represents, all depend on the context in which the function is used. For example, if the `ident` element is used in the context of matrix multiplication, it will be interpreted as the identity matrix.

Attributes

This element accepts the attributes `definitionURL` and `encoding`.

image

Syntax

```
<apply><image/>function</apply>
```

Description

The `image` element represents the image of a function; that is, the set of values that results from applying the function to all points in its domain.

Attributes

This element accepts the attributes `definitionURL` and `encoding`.

imaginary

Syntax

```
<apply><imaginary/>arg1</apply>
```

Description

The `imaginary` element represents the imaginary part of a complex number specified as an argument.

Attributes

This element accepts the attributes `definitionURL` and `encoding`.

imaginaryi

Syntax

```
<imaginaryi/>
```

Description

The imaginaryi element represents the number *i*; that is, the complex square root of -1.

Attributes

This element accepts the attributes definitionURL and encoding.

implies

Syntax

```
<apply><implies/>arg1 arg2</apply>
```

Description

The implies element is used to indicate that one expression implies another.

Attributes

This element accepts the attributes definitionURL and encoding.

in

Syntax

```
<apply><in/>element set</apply>
```

Description

The in element represents the relation that an element is a member of a set.

Attributes

This element accepts the attributes definitionURL and encoding.

infinity

Syntax

```
<infinity/>
```

Description

The `infinity` element represents the concept of infinity. It has the default rendering ∞.

Attributes

This element accepts the attributes `definitionURL` and `encoding`.

int

Syntax

<apply><int/>*variable expression*</apply>

or

<apply><int/>*variable limits expression*</apply>

Description

The `int` element represents the operation of integration. Each variable of integration is specified using the qualifier element `bvar`. For definite integrals, you can indicate the region of integration in three different ways: using a pair of `lowlimit` and `uplimit` elements, using an `interval` element, or using a `condition` element.

Attributes

This element accepts the attributes `definitionURL` and `encoding`.

integers

Syntax

<apply><in/>*expression*<integers/></apply>

Description

The `integers` element represents the set of all integers, typically denoted by Z.

Attributes

This element accepts the attributes `definitionURL` and `encoding`.

intersect

Syntax

<apply><intersect/>*set1 set2*...</apply>

Description

The intersect element represents the intersection of two or more sets.

Attributes

This element accepts the attributes definitionURL and encoding.

interval

Syntax

<interval>*left-boundary right-boundary*</interval>

Description

The interval element is used to define intervals on the real line. It has two child elements, which specify the left and right boundaries of the interval.

Attributes

This element accepts the attributes definitionURL and encoding. In addition, it accepts the attribute shown in Table 14.4.

The closure attribute specifies the closure of an interval on the real line.

inverse

Syntax

<apply><inverse/>*function*</apply>

Description

The inverse element represents the inverse of a function.

Attributes

This element accepts the attributes definitionURL and encoding.

TABLE 14.4 Attributes of interval

Name	Values	Default
closure	open | closed | open-closed | closed-open	closed

lambda

Syntax

<lambda>(*variable*) + <apply>*definition*</apply></lambda>

Description

The `lambda` element represents the definition of a lambda function. A lambda function with *n* arguments is represented as a `lambda` element with *n* + 1 child elements. The first *n* elements are the arguments, each enclosed in a `bvar` element, and the last child element is the definition of the function, typically specified using an `apply` element.

Attributes

This element accepts the attributes `definitionURL` and `encoding`.

laplacian

Syntax

<apply><laplacian/>*function*</apply>

Description

The `laplacian` element represents the Laplacian operator of vector calculus.

Attributes

This element accepts the attributes `definitionURL` and `encoding`.

lcm

Syntax

<apply><lcm/>(*number*) * </apply>

Description

The `lcm` element represents the lowest common multiple of a set of integers, specified as arguments.

Attributes

This element accepts the attributes `definitionURL` and `encoding`.

leq

Syntax

```
<apply><leq/>arg1 arg2</apply>
```

Description

The `leq` element is used to indicate that one element is less than or equal to another. It can take two or more arguments.

Attributes

This element accepts the attributes `definitionURL` and `encoding`.

limit

Syntax

```
<apply><limit/>variable limit function</apply>
```

Description

The `limit` element represents the operator for the limit of a sequence or function. You can specify the limit point either by using a pair of `bvar` and `lowlimit` elements or by using a `condition` element.

Attributes

This element accepts the attributes `definitionURL` and `encoding`.

list

Syntax

```
<list>elements</list>
```

or

```
<list>
 (<bvar>...</bvar>)*
 <condition>...</condition>
</list>
```

Description

The `list` element is used to represent a set of elements. The elements can either be specified explicitly or by using `bvar` and `condition` elements. This element is similar to the `set` element, the only difference being that in a list, the order of elements is relevant.

Attributes

This element accepts the attributes `definitionURL` and `encoding`. In addition, it accepts the attribute shown in Table 14.5.

The `order` attribute specifies the criterion used for ordering the elements of the list. With the setting `lexicographic`, the elements are ordered alphabetically; with the setting `numeric`, the elements are ordered numerically.

`ln`

Syntax

```
<apply><ln/>arg</apply>
```

Description

The `ln` element represents the natural logarithmic function.

Attributes

This element accepts the attributes `definitionURL` and `encoding`.

`log`

Syntax

```
<apply><log/>arg</apply>
```

Description

The `log` element represents the logarithm function.

Attributes

This element accepts the attributes `definitionURL` and `encoding`.

`lowlimit`

Syntax

```
<lowlimit>limit</lowlimit>
```

TABLE 14.5 Attributes of `list`

Name	Values	Default
`order`	`lexicographic` | `numeric`	`lexicographic`

Description

The `lowlimit` element is a qualifier element that is used in conjunction with the `int` element to represent the lower limit of a definite integral.

Attributes

This element accepts the attributes `definitionURL` and `encoding`.

lt

Syntax

```
<apply><lt/>arg1 arg2</apply>
```

Description

The `lt` element is used to indicate that one element is less than another. It can take two or more arguments.

Attributes

This element accepts the attributes `definitionURL` and `encoding`.

matrix

Syntax

```
<matrix>(<matrixrow>...<matrixrow/>)*</matrix>
```

Description

The `matrix` element is used to represent a table or matrix. It contains a sequence of `matrixrow` elements, each corresponding to a single row of the table or matrix.

Attributes

This element accepts the attributes `definitionURL` and `encoding`.

matrixrow

Syntax

```
<matrixrow>(<mtd>...<mtd/>)*</matrixrow>
```

Description

The `matrixrow` element is used to represent a row of a table or matrix. It always occurs as a child element of a `matrix` element and contains a sequence of mtd child elements, each corresponding to a single cell of the table or matrix.

Attributes

This element accepts the attributes definitionURL and encoding.

max

Syntax

```
<apply><max/>...</apply>
```

Description

The max element represents the maximum of a set of numbers. You can specify the numbers as arguments or by using a condition.

Attributes

This element accepts the attributes definitionURL and encoding.

mean

Syntax

```
<apply><mean/>distribution</apply>
```

Description

The mean element represents the mean of a distribution or set of elements.

Attributes

This element accepts the attributes definitionURL and encoding.

median

Syntax

```
<apply><median/>distribution</apply>
```

Description

The median element represents the median of a distribution or set of elements.

Attributes

This element accepts the attributes definitionURL and encoding.

`min`

Syntax

```
<apply><min/>...</apply>
```

Description

The `min` element represents the minimum of a set of numbers. You can specify the numbers as arguments or by using a condition.

Attributes

This element accepts the attributes `definitionURL` and `encoding`.

`minus`

Syntax

```
<apply><minus/>...</apply>
```

Description

The `minus` element represents subtraction. It can take one or two arguments. By default, the subtraction is assumed to be over a real field, but the default semantics of the element can be modified using attributes, for example, to represent vector subtraction.

Attributes

This element accepts the attributes `definitionURL` and `encoding`.

`mode`

Syntax

```
<apply><mode/>distribution</apply>
```

Description

The `mode` element represents the mean of a distribution or set of elements.

Attributes

This element accepts the attributes `definitionURL` and `encoding`.

moment

Syntax

```
<apply>
 <moment/>[<degree>...</degree>]
 [<momentabout>...</momentabout>]distribution
</apply>
```

Description

The moment element represents the statistical moment of a distribution or set of elements about a point. The qualifier element degree is used to indicate the type of moment, and the momentabout element is used to specify the point about which the moment is taken. If these elements are omitted, the default values, 1 and 0, are assumed.

Attributes

This element accepts the attributes definitionURL and encoding.

momentabout

Syntax

```
<apply>
 <moment/>[<degree>...</degree>]
 [<momentabout>...</momentabout>]distribution
</apply>
```

Description

The momentabout element represents the point about which the moment of a distribution or set of elements is taken. This element is always used as a qualifier element in conjunction with the moment element.

Attributes

This element accepts the attributes definitionURL and encoding.

naturalnumbers

Syntax

```
<naturalnumbers/>
```

Description

The `naturalnumbers` element represents the set of all natural numbers, typically denoted by the symbol `N`.

Attributes

This element accepts the attributes `definitionURL` and `encoding`.

neq

Syntax

```
<apply> <neq/>arg1 arg2</apply>
```

Description

The `neq` element is used to indicate that two expressions are not equal. It must have two arguments.

Attributes

This element accepts the attributes `definitionURL` and `encoding`.

notanumber

Syntax

```
<notanumber/>
```

Description

The `notanumber` element represents the constant, typically denoted by NaN; that is, returned as the result of an ill-defined floating-point operation, such as division by zero.

Attributes

This element accepts the attributes `definitionURL` and `encoding`.

notin

Syntax

```
<apply><notin/>element set</apply>
```

Description

The `notin` element represents the relation that an element is not a member of a set.

Attributes

This element accepts the attributes `definitionURL` and `encoding`.

notprsubset

Syntax

```
<apply><notprsubset/>subset set</apply>
```

Description

The `notprsubset` element represents the relation that one set is not a proper subset of another set.

Attributes

This element accepts the attributes `definitionURL` and `encoding`.

notsubset

Syntax

```
<apply><notsubset/>subset set</apply>
```

Description

The `notsubset` element represents the relation that one set is not a subset of another set.

Attributes

This element accepts the attributes `definitionURL` and `encoding`.

or

Syntax

```
<apply><or/>...</apply>
```

Description

The `or` element represents the logical OR operator. It evaluates to the value True if any of its arguments are True. It can take any number of arguments.

Attributes

This element accepts the attributes `definitionURL` and `encoding`.

otherwise

Syntax

```
<otherwise>definition domain</otherwise>
```

Description

The otherwise element represents a specific part of a piecewise declaration. It always occurs as a child element of a piecewise element.

Attributes

This element accepts the attributes definitionURL and encoding.

outerproduct

Syntax

```
<apply><outerproduct/>vector1 vector2</apply>
```

Description

The outerproduct element represents the outer product of two vectors.

Attributes

This element accepts the attributes definitionURL and encoding.

partialdiff

Syntax

```
<apply>
 <partialdiff/> (<bvar>...</bvar>)*
 (<degree>...</degree>)*
 <apply>function (<ci>var</ci>)* </apply>
</apply>
```

Description

The partialdiff element represents the operation of taking a partial derivative. Each variables of differentiation is specified using a bvar element. The order of differentiation with respect to each variable is specified using a degree element.

Attributes

This element accepts the attributes definitionURL and encoding.

pi

Syntax

```
<pi/>
```

Description

The `pi` element represents the numerical constant π (approx. 3.14159), the ratio of the circumference of a circle to its diameter.

Attributes

This element accepts the attributes `definitionURL` and `encoding`.

piece

Syntax

```
<piece>definition domain</piece>
```

Description

The `piece` element represents a specific part of a piecewise declaration. It always occurs as a child element of a `piecewise` element.

Attributes

This element accepts the attributes `definitionURL` and `encoding`.

piecewise

Syntax

```
<piecewise>(<piece>) + <otherwise></apply>
```

Description

The `piecewise` element, in association with the `piece` and `otherwise` elements, represents piecewise declarations of the form $f(x) = 0$ if $x < 0$, $f(x) = 1$ if $x \geq 0$.

Attributes

This element accepts the attributes `definitionURL` and `encoding`.

plus

Syntax

```
<apply><plus/>...</apply>
```

Description

The `plus` element represents addition. It can take any number of arguments. By default, the addition is assumed to be over a scalar field, but the default semantics of the element can be modified using attributes, for example, to represent vector addition.

Attributes

This element accepts the attributes `definitionURL` and `encoding`. In addition, it accepts the attribute shown in Table 14.6.

The `type` attribute specifies the type of the operand(s).

power

Syntax

`<apply><power/>`*base exponent*`</apply>`

Description

The `power` element represents the operation of raising a number or expression to a power. It must have two arguments.

Attributes

This element accepts the attributes `definitionURL` and `encoding`.

primes

Syntax

```
<primes/>
```

Description

The `primes` element represents the set of all prime numbers, typically denoted by P.

Attributes

This element accepts the attributes `definitionURL` and `encoding`.

TABLE 14.6 Attributes of `plus`

Name	Values	Default
`type`	MathML type	`real`

product

Syntax

`<apply><product/>`*index limits expression*`</apply>`

Description

The `product` element represents the product operator. Each index of the product is specified using a single `bvar` element. The limits of the product can be indicated in several different ways: by using a pair of `lowlimit` and `uplimit` elements or by using a `condition` element.

Attributes

This element accepts the attributes `definitionURL` and `encoding`.

prsubset

Syntax

`<apply><prsubset/>`*subset set*`</apply>`

Description

The `prsubset` element represents the relation that one set is a proper subset of another set.

Attributes

This element accepts the attributes `definitionURL` and `encoding`.

quotient

Syntax

`<apply><quotient/>`*numerator denominator*`</apply>`

Description

The `quotient` element represents the quotient of integer division. In other words, if m and n are integers, the quotient is the integer q, such that $m = n * q + r$, where $|r| < |m|$ and $m * r > 0$.

Attributes

This element accepts the attributes `definitionURL` and `encoding`.

rationals

Syntax

```
<rationals/>
```

Description

The <rationals/> element represents the set of all rational numbers, typically denoted by Q.

Attributes

This element accepts the attributes definitionURL and encoding.

real

Syntax

```
<apply><real/>arg1</apply>
```

Description

The real element represents the real part of a complex number specified as an argument.

Attributes

This element accepts the attributes definitionURL and encoding.

reals

Syntax

```
<apply><in/>expression<reals/></apply>
```

Description

The reals element represents the set of all real numbers, typically denoted by R.

Attributes

This element accepts the attributes definitionURL and encoding.

reln

Syntax

```
<reln>operator (argument) + </reln>
```

Description

The `reln` element is used to specify a mathematical relation, such as $a = b$, $a < b$, and $a \geq b$. It contains as its first child element one of the content elements that represent relations, such as `eq`, `lt`, or `geq`. The `reln` element is deprecated in MathML 2.0 since its role is now taken over by the `apply` element.

Attributes

This element accepts the attributes `definitionURL` and `encoding`.

rem

Syntax

```
<apply><rem/>dividend divisor</apply>
```

Description

The `rem` element represents the remainder of integer division. In other words, if m and n are integers, the remainder is the integer r, such that $m = n * q + r$, where $|r| < |m|$ and $m * r > 0$.

Attributes

This element accepts the attributes `definitionURL` and `encoding`.

root

Syntax

```
<apply>
 <root/><degree>degree</degree>
 radical
</apply>
```

Description

The `root` element is used to take the root of a number or expression. It has two arguments. The first argument is a `degree` element that specifies the degree of the root. If this is omitted, a default value of 2 is assumed.

Attributes

This element accepts the attributes `definitionURL` and `encoding`.

scalarproduct

Syntax

```
<apply><scalarproduct/>vector1 vector2</apply>
```

Description

The scalarproduct element represents the scalar product of two vectors.

Attributes

This element accepts the attributes definitionURL and encoding.

sdev

Syntax

```
<apply><sdev/>distribution</apply>
```

Description

The sdev element represents the standard deviation of a distribution or set of elements.

Attributes

This element accepts the attributes definitionURL and encoding.

sech

Syntax

```
<apply><sech/>arg</apply>
```

Description

The sech element represents the hyperbolic secant function.

Attributes

This element accepts the attributes definitionURL and encoding.

selector

Syntax

```
<apply><selector/>vector index</apply>
```

or

```
<apply><selector/>matrix index</apply>
```

or

```
<apply><selector/>matrix index1 index2</apply>
```

Description

The `selector` element represents the operator for selecting a specific component of a vector, list, or matrix. The first argument following the selector element identifies the vector or matrix. This can be followed by one or two other arguments, which specify the position of the selected component. For a matrix, if two more arguments are given, they are interpreted as specifying the position of a row and column, respectively. In the case of a vector or list, if a second argument is given, it is ignored.

Attributes

This element accepts the attributes `definitionURL` and `encoding`.

semantics

Syntax

```
<semantics>...</semantics>
```

Description

The `semantics` element is used as a container for alternative representations of a given MathML expression. Each `semantics` element can contain any number of `annotation-xml` and `annotation` elements. XML-based representations are enclosed in an `annotation-xml` element, and non-XML representations are stored in an `annotation` element. The most common use of the `semantics` element is for combining presentation and content markup.

Attributes

This element accepts the attributes `definitionURL` and `encoding`.

sep

Syntax

```
<cn>...<sep/>...</cn>
```

Description

The sep element is used inside a cn element as a separator for the different parts of a rational, complex, or floating-point number.

Attributes

This element accepts the attributes definitionURL and encoding.

set

Syntax

```
<set>elements</set>
```

or

```
<set>
 (<bvar>...</bvar>)*<condition>...</condition>
</set>
```

Description

The set element is used to represent a set of elements. The elements can either be specified explicitly or by using bvar and condition elements.

Attributes

This element accepts the attributes definitionURL and encoding.

setdiff

Syntax

```
<apply><setdiff/>set1 set2</apply>
```

Description

The setdiff element represents the set-theoretic difference between two sets.

Attributes

This element accepts the attributes definitionURL and encoding.

sin

Syntax

```
<apply><sin/>arg</apply>
```

Description

The `sin` element represents the trigonometric sine function.

Attributes

This element accepts the attributes `definitionURL` and `encoding`.

sinh

Syntax

```
<apply><sinh/>arg</apply>
```

Description

The `sinh` element represents the hyperbolic sine function.

Attributes

This element accepts the attributes `definitionURL` and `encoding`.

subset

Syntax

```
<apply><subset/>subset set</apply>
```

Description

The `subset` element represents the relation that one set is a subset of another set.

Attributes

This element accepts the attributes `definitionURL` and `encoding`.

sum

Syntax

```
<apply><sum/>index limits expression</apply>
```

Description

The `sum` element represents the summation operator. Each index of the summation is specified using a single `bvar` element. The limits of summation can be indicated in several different ways: using a pair of `lowlimit` and `uplimit` elements, using an `interval` element, or using a `condition` element.

Attributes

This element accepts the attributes `definitionURL` and `encoding`.

tan

Syntax

```
<apply><tan/>arg</apply>
```

Description

The `tan` element represents the trigonometric tangent function.

Attributes

This element accepts the attributes `definitionURL` and `encoding`.

tanh

Syntax

```
<apply><tanh/>arg</apply>
```

Description

The `tanh` element represents the hyperbolic tangent function.

Attributes

This element accepts the attributes `definitionURL` and `encoding`.

tendsto

Syntax

```
<apply><tendsto/>variable value</apply>
```

Description

The `tendsto` element represents the operation of a variable that approaches a certain limiting value.

Attributes

This element accepts the attributes `definitionURL` and `encoding`. In addition, it accepts the attribute shown in Table 14.7.

The `type` attribute specifies the direction from which the limiting value is approached.

TABLE 14.7 Attributes of `tendsto`

Name	Values	Default
`type`	`above` | `below`	`above`

`times`

Syntax

```
<apply><times/>...</apply>
```

Description

The `times` element represents multiplication. It can accept any number of arguments.

Attributes

This element accepts the attributes `definitionURL` and `encoding`.

`transpose`

Syntax

```
<apply><transpose/>matrix</apply>
```

Description

The `transpose` element represents the transpose of a matrix.

Attributes

This element accepts the attributes `definitionURL` and `encoding`.

`true`

Syntax

```
<true/>
```

Description

The `true` element represents the Boolean constant True.

Attributes

This element accepts the attributes `definitionURL` and `encoding`.

union

Syntax

```
<apply><union/>set1 set2...</apply>
```

Description

The union element represents the union of two or more sets.

Attributes

This element accepts the attributes definitionURL and encoding.

uplimit

Syntax

```
<uplimit>limit</uplimit>
```

Description

The uplimit element is a qualifier element that is used in conjunction with the <int/> element to represent the upper limit of a definite integral.

Attributes

This element accepts the attributes definitionURL and encoding.

var

Syntax

```
<apply><var/>distribution</apply>
```

Description

The var element represents the variance of a distribution or set of elements.

Attributes

This element accepts the attributes definitionURL and encoding.

vector

Syntax

```
<vector>components</vector>
```

Description

The `vector` element is a container element used to represent a vector. It contains a sequence of child elements, each corresponding to one component of the vector.

Attributes

This element accepts the attributes `definitionURL` and `encoding`.

vectorproduct

Syntax

```
<apply><vectorproduct/>vector1 vector2</apply>
```

Description

The `vectorproduct` element represents the vector product of two vectors.

Attributes

This element accepts the attributes `definitionURL` and `encoding`.

xor

Syntax

```
<apply><xor/>...</apply>
```

Description

The `xor` element is used to represent the logical XOR (or exclusive OR) operator. It evaluates to the value True if an odd number of its arguments are True. It can take any number of arguments.

Attributes

This element accepts the attributes `definitionURL` and `encoding`.

CHAPTER

15

MATHML CHARACTERS

The MathML DTD defines about 2,500 character entities, which cover most characters and symbols that are widely used in mathematics. This chapter contains a set of character tables that show glyphs for all the MathML characters and their position in Unicode.

15.1 INTRODUCTION

Each block of Unicode consists of 256 characters arranged in a 16 by 16 grid. The MathML characters are distributed over 22 different blocks of Unicode. Each of these blocks is shown in a separate table in the following pages. By glancing through these tables, you can get a quick overview of all the different types of characters available for use in MathML.

You can determine the hexadecimal numeric character code for each character from the number of the row and column in which that character occurs. For example, the Greek letter Ω occurs in the row numbered 03A and the column numbered 9. Hence, to insert this character, you must type the character entity `Ω`. The entity names associated with each character are not listed here due to space restrictions. You can look up the entity name for each character at the following URL: *www.w3.org/Math/characters*.

15.2 CHARACTER TABLES

	0	1	2	3	4	5	6	7	8	9	A	B	C	D	E	F
000																
001																
002		!	"	#	$	%	&	'	(	)	*	+	,		.	/
003											:	;	<	=	>	?
004	@															
005												[	\	]	^	_
006	`										j					
007												{	|	}		
008																
009																
00A		¡	¢	£	¤	¥	¦	§	¨	©	ª	«	¬	-	®	¯
00B	°	±	²	³	´	µ	¶	·	¸	¹	º	»	¼	½	¾	¿
00C	À	Á	Â	Ã	Ä	Å	Æ	Ç	È	É	Ê	Ë	Ì	Í	Î	Ï
00D	Đ	Ñ	Ò	Ó	Ô	Õ	Ö	×	Ø	Ù	Ú	Û	Ü	Ý	Þ	ß
00E	à	á	â	ã	ä	å	æ	ç	è	é	ê	ë	ì	í	î	ï
00F	ð	ñ	ò	ó	ô	õ	ö	÷	ø	ù	ú	û	ü	ý	þ	ÿ

Figure 15.1 Controls and Basic Latin, and Latin-1 Supplement. Unicode range: 0000-00FF.

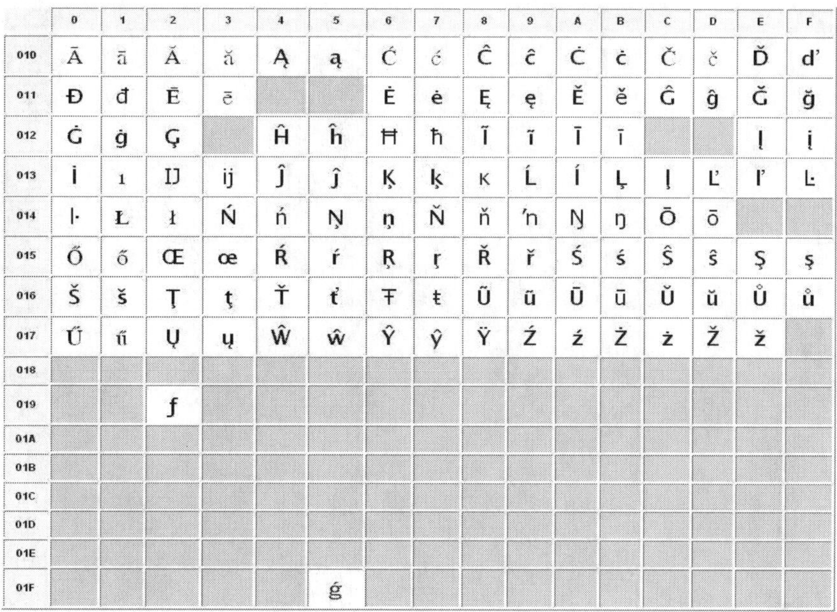

Figure 15.2 Latin Extended-A and Latin Extended-B. Unicode range: 00100-001FF.

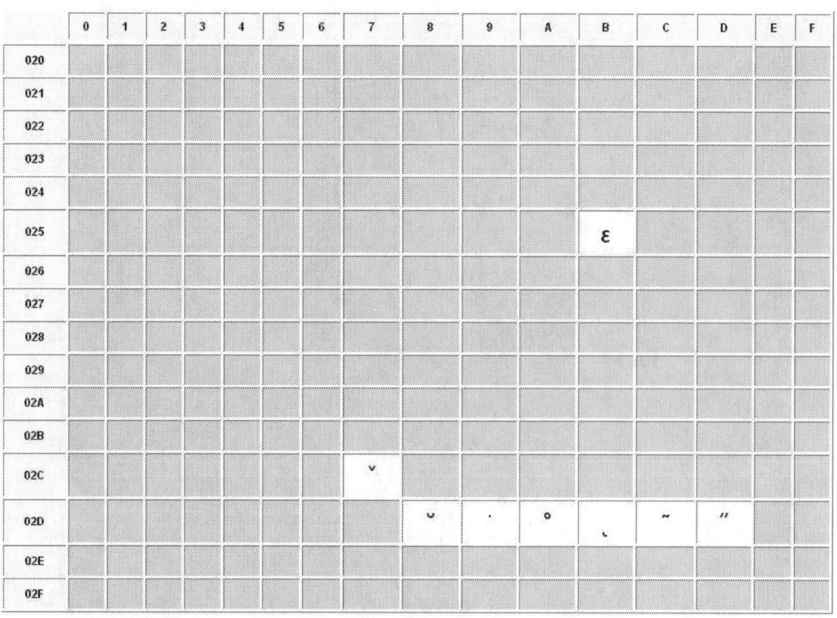

Figure 15.3 International Phonetic Alphabet (IPA) Extensions and Spacing Modifier Letters. Unicode range: 00200-002FF.

	0	1	2	3	4	5	6	7	8	9	A	B	C	D	E	F
030																
031		⌢														
032																
033																
034																
035																
036																
037																
038																
039				Γ	Δ				Θ			Λ			Ξ	
03A	Π			Σ		ϒ	Φ		Ψ	Ω						
03B		α	β	γ	δ	ε	ζ	η	θ	ι	κ	λ	μ	ν	ξ	
03C	π	ρ	ς	σ	τ	υ	φ	χ	ψ	ω						
03D		ϑ	ϒ			ϕ	ϖ						Ϝ			
03E																
03F	ϰ	ϱ					϶									

Figure 15.4 Combining Diacritical Marks and Greek [and Coptic]. Unicode range: 00300-003FF.

	0	1	2	3	4	5	6	7	8	9	A	B	C	D	E	F
040		Ё	Ђ	Ѓ	Є	Ѕ	І	Ї	Ј	Љ	Њ	Ћ	Ќ		Ў	Џ
041	А	Б	В	Г	Д	Е	Ж	З	И	Й	К	Л	М	Н	О	П
042	Р	С	Т	У	Ф	Х	Ц	Ч	Ш	Щ	Ъ	Ы	Ь	Э	Ю	Я
043	а	б	в	г	д	е	ж	з	и	й	к	л	м	н	о	п
044	р	с	т	у	ф	х	ц	ч	ш	щ	ъ	ы	ь	э	ю	я
045		ё	ђ	ѓ	є	ѕ	і	ї	ј	љ	њ	ћ	ќ		ў	џ
046																
047																
048																
049																
04A																
04B																
04C																
04D																
04E																
04F																

Figure 15.5 Cyrillic. Unicode range: 00400-004FF.

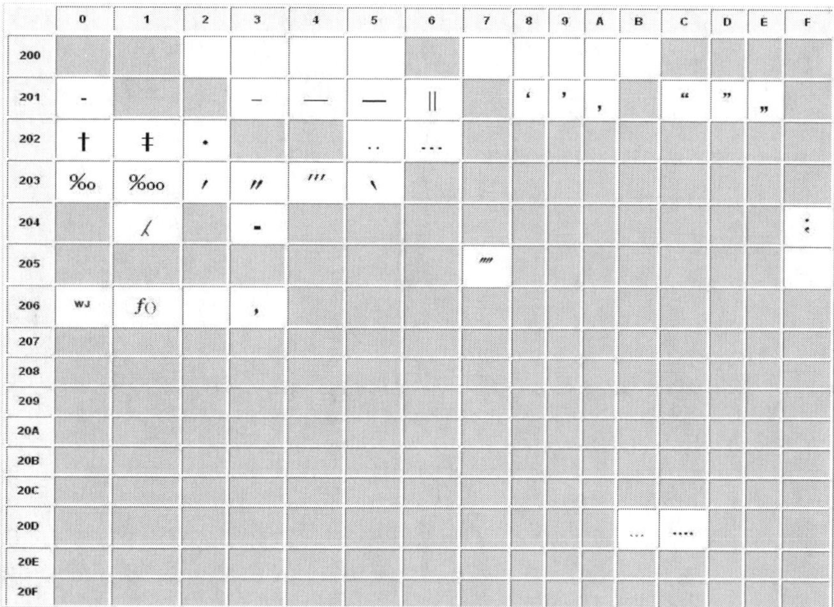

Figure 15.6 General Punctuation, Superscripts and Subscripts, Currency Symbols, and Combining Diacritical Marks for Symbols. Unicode range: 02000-020FF.

	0	1	2	3	4	5	6	7	8	9	A	B	C	D	E	F
210			ℂ			℅					ℊ	ℋ	ℌ	ℍ	ℎ	ℏ
211	ℐ	ℑ	ℒ	ℓ		ℕ	№	℗	℘	ℙ	ℚ	ℛ	ℜ	ℝ	℞	
212			™		ℤ		Ω	℧	ℨ	℩		Å	ℬ	ℭ		ℯ
213	ℰ	ℱ		ℳ	ℴ	ℵ	ℶ	ℷ	ℸ							
214						ⅅ	ⅆ	ⅇ	ⅈ							
215				⅓	⅔	⅕	⅖	⅗	⅘	⅙	⅚	⅛	⅜	⅝	⅞	
216																
217																
218																
219	←	↑	→	↓	↔	↕	↖	↗	↘	↙	↚	↛		↝	↞	↟
21A	↠	↡	↢	↣	↤	↥	↦	↧		↩	↪	↫	↬	↭	↮	
21B	↰	↱	↲	↳			↶	↷			↺	↻	↼	↽	↾	↿
21C	⇀	⇁	⇂	⇃	⇄	⇅	⇆	⇇	⇈	⇉	⇊	⇋	⇌	⇍	⇎	⇏
21D	⇐	⇑	⇒	⇓	⇔	⇕	⇖	⇗	⇘	⇙	⇚	⇛		⇝		
21E					⇤	⇥										
21F						⇵								⇽	⇾	⇿

Figure 15.7 Letter-like Symbols, Number Forms, and Arrows. Unicode range: 02100-021FF.

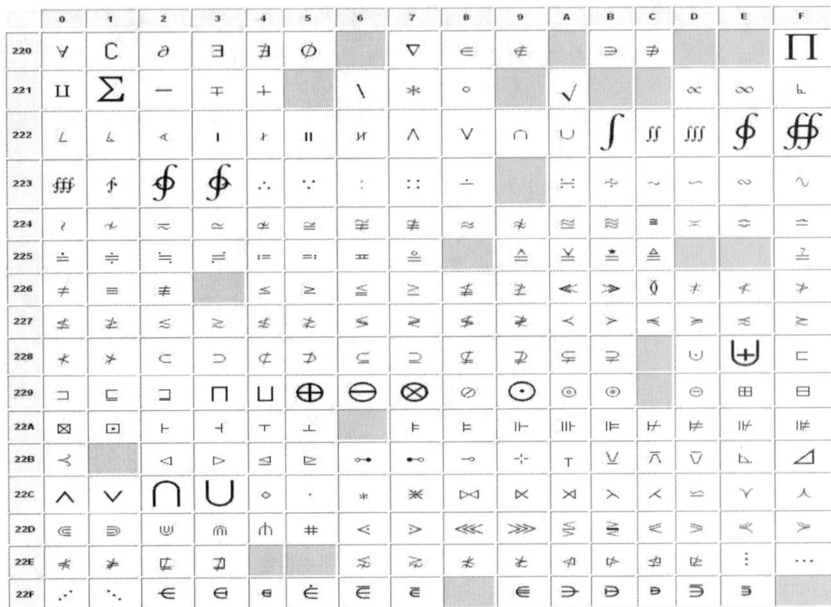

Figure 15.8 Mathematical Operators. Unicode range: 02200-022FF.

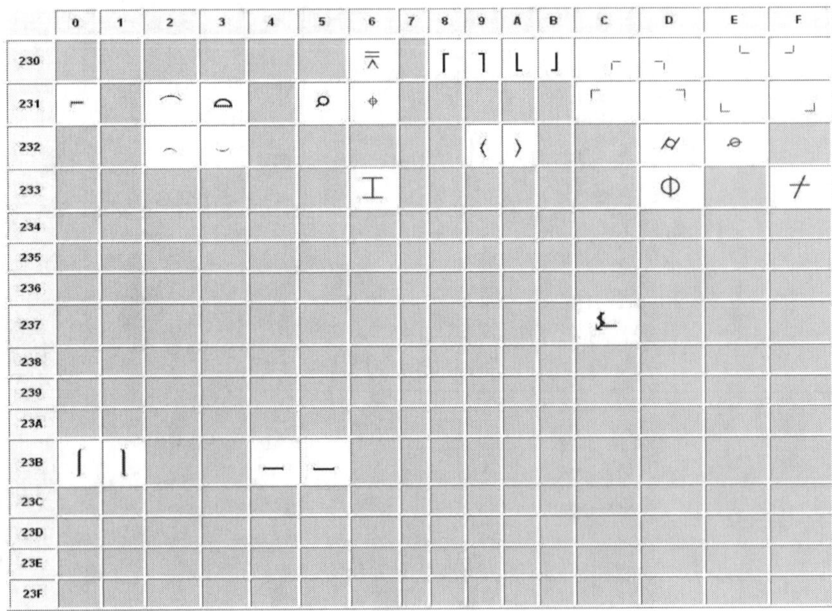

Figure 15.9 Miscellaneous Technical. Unicode range: 02300-023FF.

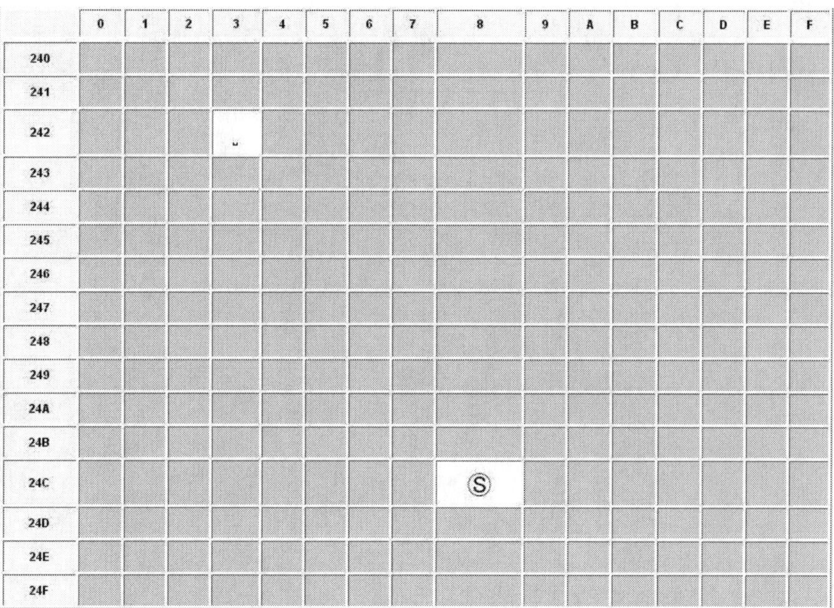

Figure 15.10 Control Pictures, Optical Character Recognition, and Enclosed Alphanumerics. Unicode range: 02400-024FF.

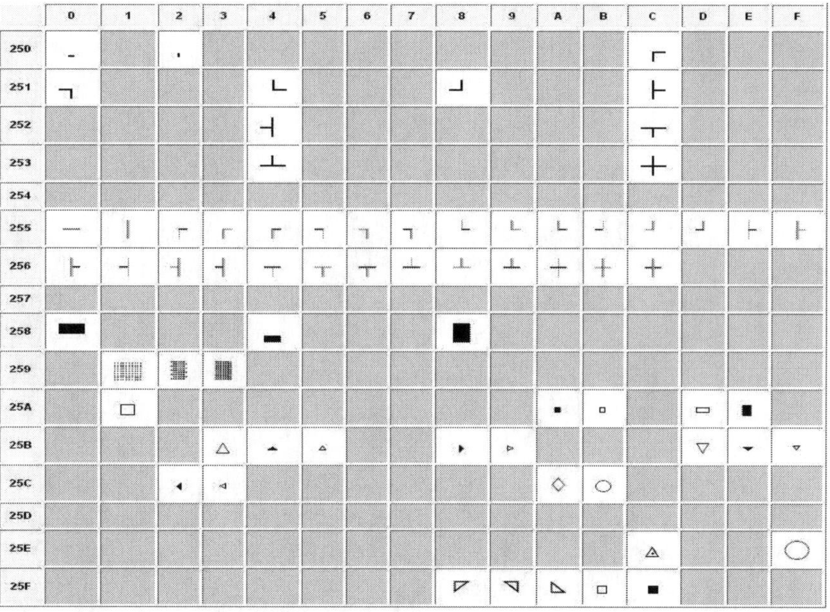

Figure 15.11 Box Drawing, Block Elements, and Geometric Shapes. Unicode range: 02500-025FF.

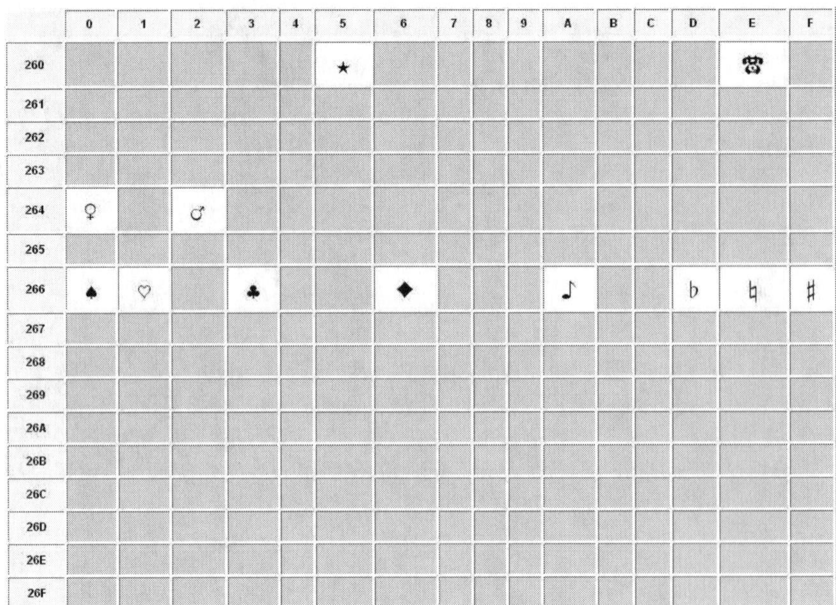

Figure 15.12 Miscellaneous Symbols. Unicode range: 02600-026FF.

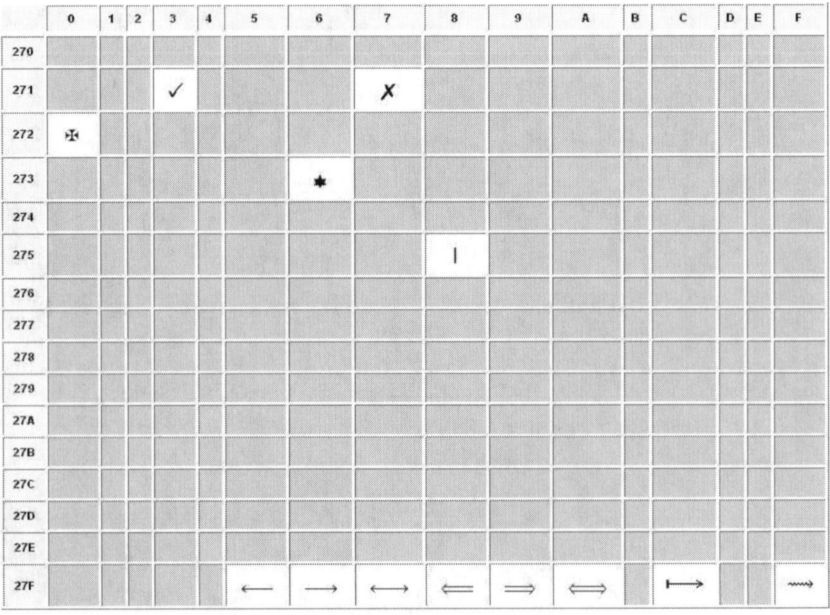

Figure 15.13 Dingbats, Miscellaneous Mathematical Symbols-A, and Supplemental Arrows-A. Unicode range: 02700-027FF.

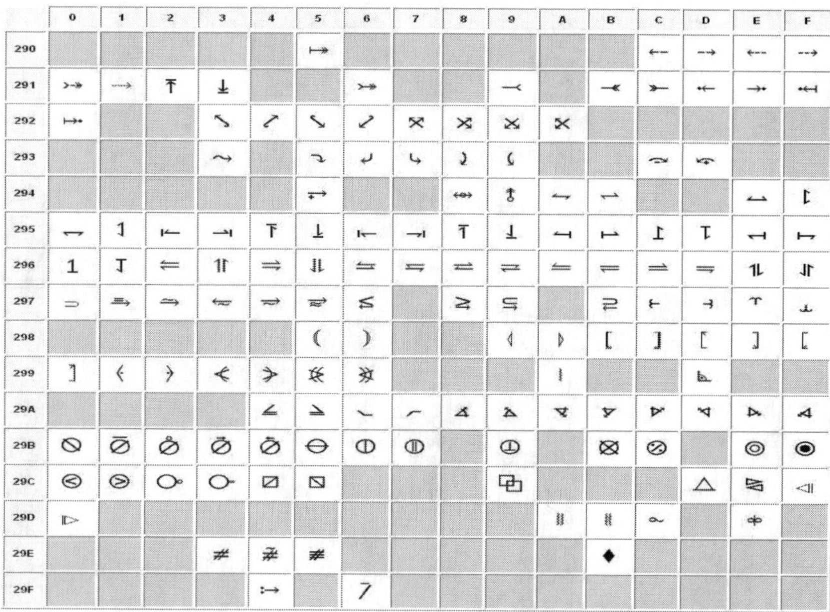

	0	1	2	3	4	5	6	7	8	9	A	B	C	D	E	F
290						⤅							⤌	⤍	⤎	⤏
291	⤐	⤑	⤒	⤓			⤖			⤙		⤛	⤜	⤝	⤞	⤟
292	⤠			⤣	⤤	⤥	⤦	⤧	⤨	⤩	⤪					
293				⤳		⤵	⤶	⤷	⤸	⤹			⤼	⤽		
294						⥅			⥈	⥉	⥊	⥋			⥎	⥏
295	⥐	⥑	⥒	⥓	⥔	⥕	⥖	⥗	⥘	⥙	⥚	⥛	⥜	⥝	⥞	⥟
296	⥠	⥡	⥢	⥣	⥤	⥥	⥦	⥧	⥨	⥩	⥪	⥫	⥬	⥭	⥮	⥯
297	⥰	⥱	⥲	⥳	⥴	⥵	⥶		⥸	⥹		⥻	⥼	⥽	⥾	⥿
298						⦅	⦆			⦉	⦊	⦋	⦌	⦍	⦎	⦏
299	⦐	⦑	⦒	⦓	⦔	⦕	⦖				⦚			⦝		
29A					⦤	⦥	⦦	⦧	⦨	⦩	⦪	⦫	⦬	⦭	⦮	⦯
29B	⦰	⦱	⦲	⦳	⦴	⦵	⦶	⦷		⦹		⦻	⦼		⦾	⦿
29C	⧀	⧁	⧂	⧃	⧄	⧅				⧉				⧍	⧎	⧏
29D	⧐										⧚	⧛	⧜		⧞	
29E				⧣	⧤	⧥						⧫				
29F					⧴		⧶									

Figure 15.14 Supplemental Arrows-B and Miscellaneous Mathematical Symbols-B. Unicode range: 02900-029FF.

	0	1	2	3	4	5	6	7	8	9	A	B	C	D	E	F
2A0													⨌	⨍		
2A1	⨐	⨑	⨒	⨓	⨔	⨕	⨖	⨗								
2A2			⨢	⨣	⨤	⨥	⨦	⨧		⨩	⨪			⨭	⨮	⨯
2A3	⨰	⨱		⨳	⨴	⨵	⨶	⨷	⨸	⨹	⨺	⨻	⨼			⨿
2A4	⩀		⩂	⩃	⩄	⩅	⩆	⩇	⩈	⩉	⩊	⩋	⩌	⩍		
2A5	⩐			⩓	⩔	⩕	⩖	⩗	⩘		⩚	⩛	⩜	⩝		⩟
2A6							⩦				⩪			⩭		⩯
2A7		⩱	⩲	⩳	⩴	⩵		⩷	⩸	⩹	⩺	⩻	⩼	⩽	⩾	⩿
2A8	⪀	⪁	⪂	⪃	⪄					⪉	⪊			⪍	⪎	⪏
2A9	⪐	⪑	⪒	⪓	⪔			⪗	⪘	⪙	⪚			⪝	⪞	⪟
2AA	⪠	⪡	⪢		⪤	⪥	⪦	⪧	⪨	⪩	⪪	⪫	⪬	⪭	⪮	⪯
2AB						⪵	⪶					⪻	⪼	⪽	⪾	⪿
2AC	⫀	⫁	⫂	⫃	⫄			⫇	⫈							⫏
2AD	⫐	⫑	⫒	⫓	⫔	⫕	⫖	⫗	⫘	⫙	⫚	⫛				
2AE					⫤		⫦	⫧	⫨	⫩		⫫	⫬	⫭	⫮	⫯
2AF	⫰	⫱	⫲	⫳												

Figure 15.15 Supplemental Mathematical Operators. Unicode range: 02A00-02AFF.

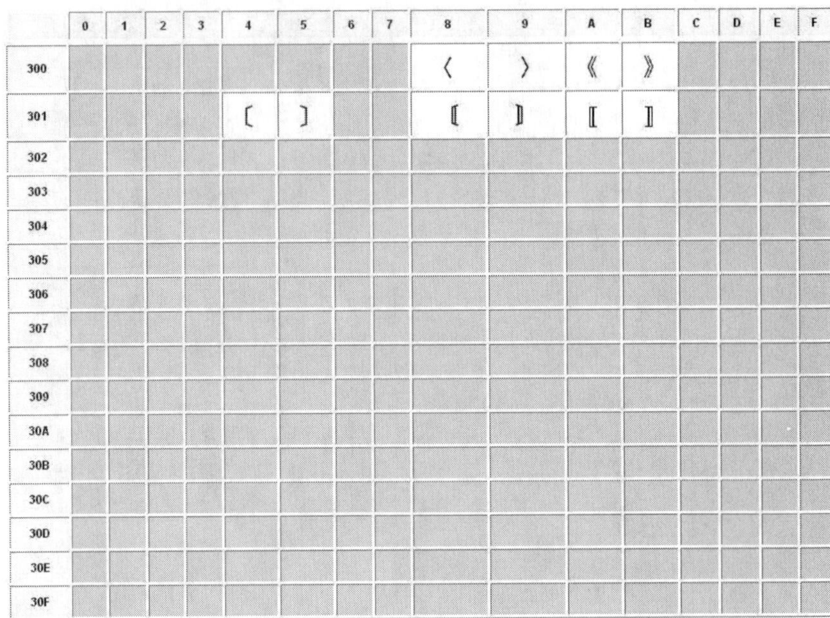

Figure 15.16 Chinese Japanese Korean (CJK) Symbols and Punctuation, Hiragana, and Katakana. Unicode range: 03000-030FF.

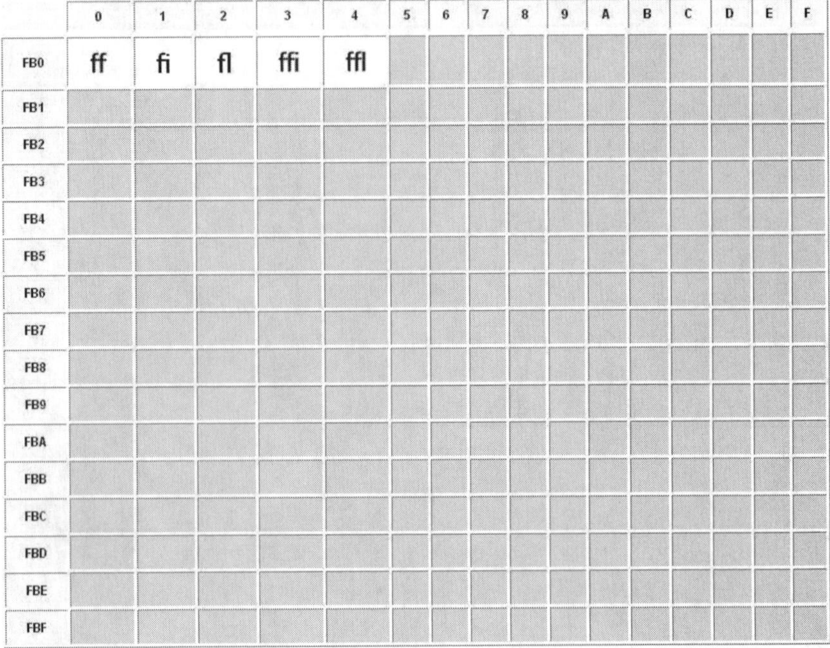

Figure 15.17 Alphabetic Presentation Forms. Unicode range: 0FB00-0FBFF.

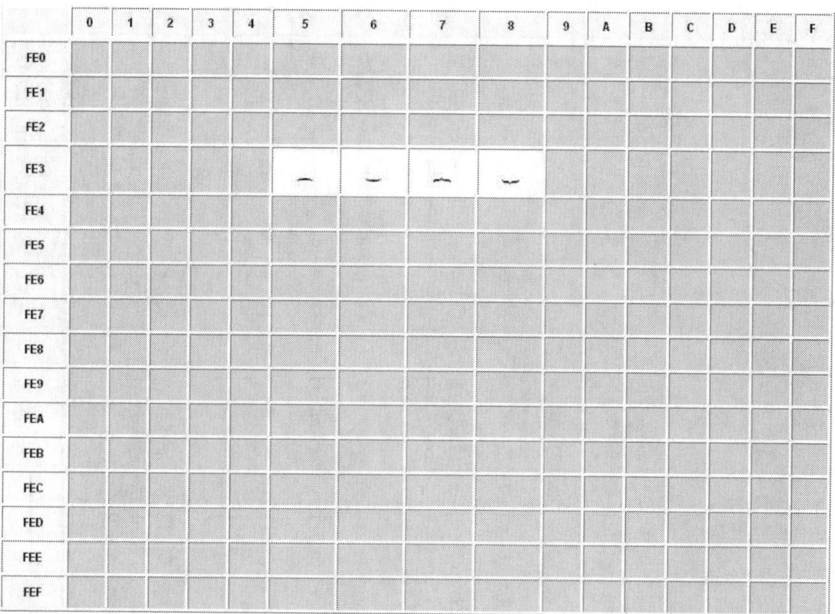

Figure 15.18 Variation Selectors, Combining Half Marks, CJK Compatibility Forms, Small Form Variants, and Arabic Presentation Forms-B. Unicode range: 0FE00-0FEFF.

	0	1	2	3	4	5	6	7	8	9	A	B	C	D	E	F
1D40	𝐀	𝐁	𝐂	𝐃	𝐄	𝐅	𝐆	𝐇	𝐈	𝐉	𝐊	𝐋	𝐌	𝐍	𝐎	𝐏
1D41	𝐐	𝐑	𝐒	𝐓	𝐔	𝐕	𝐖	𝐗	𝐘	𝐙	𝐚	𝐛	𝐜	𝐝	𝐞	𝐟
1D42	𝐠	𝐡	𝐢	𝐣	𝐤	𝐥	𝐦	𝐧	𝐨	𝐩	𝐪	𝐫	𝐬	𝐭	𝐮	𝐯
1D43	𝐰	𝐱	𝐲	𝐳	𝐴	𝐵	𝐶	𝐷	𝐸	𝐹	𝐺	𝐻	𝐼	𝐽	𝐾	𝐿
1D44	𝑀	𝑁	𝑂	𝑃	𝑄	𝑅	𝑆	𝑇	𝑈	𝑉	𝑊	𝑋	𝑌	𝑍	𝑎	𝑏
1D45	𝑐	𝑑	𝑒	𝑓	𝑔		𝑖	𝑗	𝑘	𝑙	𝑚	𝑛	𝑜	𝑝	𝑞	𝑟
1D46	𝑠	𝑡	𝑢	𝑣	𝑤	𝑥	𝑦	𝑧	𝑨	𝑩	𝑪	𝑫	𝑬	𝑭	𝑮	𝑯
1D47	𝑰	𝑱	𝑲	𝑳	𝑴	𝑵	𝑶	𝑷	𝑸	𝑹	𝑺	𝑻	𝑼	𝑽	𝑾	𝑿
1D48	𝒀	𝒁	𝒂	𝒃	𝒄	𝒅	𝒆	𝒇	𝒈	𝒉	𝒊	𝒋	𝒌	𝒍	𝒎	𝒏
1D49	𝒐	𝒑	𝒒	𝒓	𝒔	𝒕	𝒖	𝒗	𝒘	𝒙	𝒚	𝒛	𝒜		𝒞	𝒟
1D4A			𝒢		ℐ	𝒥	𝒦			𝒩	𝒪	𝒫	𝒬		𝒮	𝒯
1D4B	𝒰	𝒱	𝒲	𝒳	𝒴	𝒵	𝒶	𝒷	𝒸	𝒹		𝒻		𝒽	𝒾	𝒿
1D4C	𝓀		𝓂	𝓃		𝓅	𝓆	𝓇	𝓈	𝓉	𝓊	𝓋	𝓌	𝓍	𝓎	𝓏
1D4D	𝓐	𝓑	𝓒	𝓓	𝓔	𝓕	𝓖	𝓗	𝓘	𝓙	𝓚	𝓛	𝓜	𝓝	𝓞	𝓟
1D4E	𝓠	𝓡	𝓢	𝓣	𝓤	𝓥	𝓦	𝓧	𝓨	𝓩	𝓪	𝓫	𝓬	𝓭	𝓮	𝓯
1D4F	𝓰	𝓱	𝓲	𝓳	𝓴	𝓵	𝓶	𝓷	𝓸	𝓹	𝓺	𝓻	𝓼	𝓽	𝓾	𝓿

Figure 15.19 Mathematical Styled Latin (Bold, Italic, Bold Italic, and Script; Bold Script begins). Unicode range: 1D400-1D4FF.

	0	1	2	3	4	5	6	7	8	9	A	B	C	D	E	F
1D50	𝔀	𝔁	𝔂	𝔃	𝔄	𝔅		𝔇	𝔈	𝔉	𝔊			𝔍	𝔎	𝔏
1D51	𝔐	𝔑	𝔒	𝔓	𝔔		𝔖	𝔗	𝔘	𝔙	𝔚	𝔛	𝔜		𝔞	𝔟
1D52	𝔠	𝔡	𝔢	𝔣	𝔤	𝔥	𝔦	𝔧	𝔨	𝔩	𝔪	𝔫	𝔬	𝔭	𝔮	𝔯
1D53	𝔰	𝔱	𝔲	𝔳	𝔴	𝔵	𝔶	𝔷	𝔸	𝔹		𝔻	𝔼	𝔽	𝔾	ℍ
1D54	𝕀	𝕁	𝕂	𝕃	𝕄		𝕆				𝕊	𝕋	𝕌	𝕍	𝕎	𝕏
1D55	𝕐		𝕒	𝕓	𝕔	𝕕	𝕖	𝕗	𝕘	𝕙	𝕚	𝕛	𝕜	𝕝	𝕞	𝕟
1D56	𝕠	𝕡	𝕢	𝕣	𝕤	𝕥	𝕦	𝕧	𝕨	𝕩	𝕪	𝕫	𝕬	𝕭	𝕮	𝕯
1D57	𝕰	𝕱	𝕲	𝕳	𝕴	𝕵	𝕶	𝕷	𝕸	𝕹	𝕺	𝕻	𝕼	𝕽	𝕾	𝕿
1D58	𝖀	𝖁	𝖂	𝖃	𝖄	𝖅	𝖆	𝖇	𝖈	𝖉	𝖊	𝖋	𝖌	𝖍	𝖎	𝖏
1D59	𝖐	𝖑	𝖒	𝖓	𝖔	𝖕	𝖖	𝖗	𝖘	𝖙	𝖚	𝖛	𝖜	𝖝	𝖞	𝖟
1D5A	𝖠	𝖡	𝖢	𝖣	𝖤	𝖥	𝖦	𝖧	𝖨	𝖩	𝖪	𝖫	𝖬	𝖭	𝖮	𝖯
1D5B	𝖰	𝖱	𝖲	𝖳	𝖴	𝖵	𝖶	𝖷	𝖸	𝖹	𝖺	𝖻	𝖼	𝖽	𝖾	𝖿
1D5C	𝗀	𝗁	𝗂	𝗃	𝗄	𝗅	𝗆	𝗇	𝗈	𝗉	𝗊	𝗋	𝗌	𝗍	𝗎	𝗏
1D5D	𝗐	𝗑	𝗒	𝗓	𝗔	𝗕	𝗖	𝗗	𝗘	𝗙	𝗚	𝗛	𝗜	𝗝	𝗞	𝗟
1D5E	𝗠	𝗡	𝗢	𝗣	𝗤	𝗥	𝗦	𝗧	𝗨	𝗩	𝗪	𝗫	𝗬	𝗭	𝗮	𝗯
1D5F	𝗰	𝗱	𝗲	𝗳	𝗴	𝗵	𝗶	𝗷	𝗸	𝗹	𝗺	𝗻	𝗼	𝗽	𝗾	𝗿

Figure 15.20 Mathematical Styled Latin (Bold Script ends; Fraktur, Double-struck, Bold Fraktur, and Sans-serif; Sans-serif Bold begins). Unicode range: 1D500-1D5FF.

	0	1	2	3	4	5	6	7	8	9	A	B	C	D	E	F
1D60	𝘀	𝘁	𝘂	𝘃	𝘄	𝘅	𝘆	𝘇	𝘈	𝘉	𝘊	𝘋	𝘌	𝘍	𝘎	𝘏
1D61	𝘐	𝘑	𝘒	𝘓	𝘔	𝘕	𝘖	𝘗	𝘘	𝘙	𝘚	𝘛	𝘜	𝘝	𝘞	𝘟
1D62	𝘠	𝘡	𝘢	𝘣	𝘤	𝘥	𝘦	𝘧	𝘨	𝘩	𝘪	𝘫	𝘬	𝘭	𝘮	𝘯
1D63	𝘰	𝘱	𝘲	𝘳	𝘴	𝘵	𝘶	𝘷	𝘸	𝘹	𝘺	𝘻	𝘼	𝘽	𝘾	𝘿
1D64	𝙀	𝙁	𝙂	𝙃	𝙄	𝙅	𝙆	𝙇	𝙈	𝙉	𝙊	𝙋	𝙌	𝙍	𝙎	𝙏
1D65	𝙐	𝙑	𝙒	𝙓	𝙔	𝙕	𝙖	𝙗	𝙘	𝙙	𝙚	𝙛	𝙜	𝙝	𝙞	𝙟
1D66	𝙠	𝙡	𝙢	𝙣	𝙤	𝙥	𝙦	𝙧	𝙨	𝙩	𝙪	𝙫	𝙬	𝙭	𝙮	𝙯
1D67	𝙰	𝙱	𝙲	𝙳	𝙴	𝙵	𝙶	𝙷	𝙸	𝙹	𝙺	𝙻	𝙼	𝙽	𝙾	𝙿
1D68	𝚀	𝚁	𝚂	𝚃	𝚄	𝚅	𝚆	𝚇	𝚈	𝚉	𝚊	𝚋	𝚌	𝚍	𝚎	𝚏
1D69	𝚐	𝚑	𝚒	𝚓	𝚔	𝚕	𝚖	𝚗	𝚘	𝚙	𝚚	𝚛	𝚜	𝚝	𝚞	𝚟
1D6A	𝚠	𝚡	𝚢	𝚣					𝚨	𝚩	𝚪	𝚫	𝚬	𝚭	𝚮	𝚯
1D6B	𝚰	𝚱	𝚲	𝚳	𝚴	𝚵	𝚶	𝚷	𝚸	𝚹	𝚺	𝚻	𝚼	𝚽	𝚾	𝚿
1D6C	𝛀	𝛁	𝛂	𝛃	𝛄	𝛅	𝛆	𝛇	𝛈	𝛉	𝛊	𝛋	𝛌	𝛍	𝛎	𝛏
1D6D	𝛐	𝛑	𝛒	𝛓	𝛔	𝛕	𝛖	𝛗	𝛘	𝛙	𝛚	𝛛	𝛜	𝛝	𝛞	𝛟
1D6E	𝛠	𝛡	𝛢	𝛣	𝛤	𝛥	𝛦	𝛧	𝛨	𝛩	𝛪	𝛫	𝛬	𝛭	𝛮	𝛯
1D6F	𝛰	𝛱	𝛲	𝛳	𝛴	𝛵	𝛶	𝛷	𝛸	𝛹	𝛺	𝛻	𝛼	𝛽	𝛾	𝛿

Figure 15.21 Mathematical Styled Latin (Sans-serif Bold ends; Sans-serif Italic, Sans-serif Bold Italic, Monospace, and Bold) and Mathematical Styled Greek (Bold; Italic begins). Unicode range: 1D600-1D6FF.

	0	1	2	3	4	5	6	7	8	9	A	B	C	D	E	F
1D70	𝜀	𝜁	𝜂	𝜃	𝜄	𝜅	𝜆	𝜇	𝜈	𝜉	𝜊	𝜋	𝜌	𝜍	𝜎	𝜏
1D71	𝜐	𝜑	𝜒	𝜓	𝜔	𝜕	𝜖	𝜗	𝜘	𝜙	𝜚	𝜛	𝜜	𝜝	𝜞	𝜟
1D72	𝜠	𝜡	𝜢	𝜣	𝜤	𝜥	𝜦	𝜧	𝜨	𝜩	𝜪	𝜫	𝜬	𝜭	𝜮	𝜯
1D73	𝜰	𝜱	𝜲	𝜳	𝜴	𝜵	𝜶	𝜷	𝜸	𝜹	𝜺	𝜻	𝜼	𝜽	𝜾	𝜿
1D74	𝝀	𝝁	𝝂	𝝃	𝝄	𝝅	𝝆	𝝇	𝝈	𝝉	𝝊	𝝋	𝝌	𝝍	𝝎	𝝏
1D75	𝝐	𝝑	𝝒	𝝓	𝝔	𝝕	𝝖	𝝗	𝝘	𝝙	𝝚	𝝛	𝝜	𝝝	𝝞	𝝟
1D76	𝝠	𝝡	𝝢	𝝣	𝝤	𝝥	𝝦	𝝧	𝝨	𝝩	𝝪	𝝫	𝝬	𝝭	𝝮	𝝯
1D77	𝝰	𝝱	𝝲	𝝳	𝝴	𝝵	𝝶	𝝷	𝝸	𝝹	𝝺	𝝻	𝝼	𝝽	𝝾	𝝿
1D78	𝞀	𝞁	𝞂	𝞃	𝞄	𝞅	𝞆	𝞇	𝞈	𝞉	𝞊	𝞋	𝞌	𝞍	𝞎	𝞏
1D79	𝞐	𝞑	𝞒	𝞓	𝞔	𝞕	𝞖	𝞗	𝞘	𝞙	𝞚	𝞛	𝞜	𝞝	𝞞	𝞟
1D7A	𝞠	𝞡	𝞢	𝞣	𝞤	𝞥	𝞦	𝞧	𝞨	𝞩	𝞪	𝞫	𝞬	𝞭	𝞮	𝞯
1D7B	𝞰	𝞱	𝞲	𝞳	𝞴	𝞵	𝞶	𝞷	𝞸	𝞹	𝞺	𝞻	𝞼	𝞽	𝞾	𝞿
1D7C	𝟀	𝟁	𝟂	𝟃	𝟄	𝟅	𝟆	𝟇	𝟈	𝟉					𝟎	𝟏
1D7D	𝟐	𝟑	𝟒	𝟓	𝟔	𝟕	𝟖	𝟗	𝟘	𝟙	𝟚	𝟛	𝟜	𝟝	𝟞	𝟟
1D7E	𝟠	𝟡	𝟢	𝟣	𝟤	𝟥	𝟦	𝟧	𝟨	𝟩	𝟪	𝟫	𝟬	𝟭	𝟮	𝟯
1D7F	𝟰	𝟱	𝟲	𝟳	𝟴	𝟵	𝟶	𝟷	𝟸	𝟹	𝟺	𝟻	𝟼	𝟽	𝟾	𝟿

Figure 15.22 Mathematical Styled Greek (Italic continued; Bold Italic, Sans-serif Bold) and Mathematical Styled Digits. Unicode range: 1D700-1D7FF.

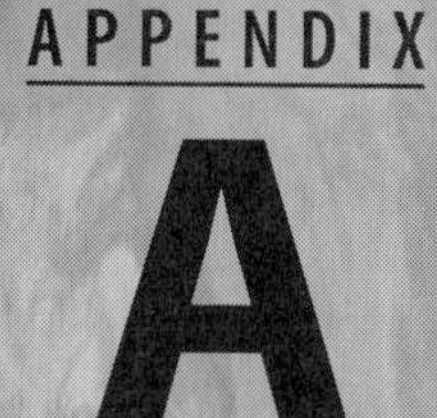

ABOUT THE CD-ROM

The CD-ROM included with the book contains three folders with the following contents:

- **Applications:** software tools for working with MathML
- **Fonts:** fonts for displaying mathematics
- **Examples:** source code for examples from the book

Table A.1 summarizes the software applications included on the CD-ROM and the system requirements for each.

Mathematica is a registered trademark of Wolfram Research, Inc. MathPlayer, MathType, and WebEQ are registered trademarks of Design Science, Inc.

All the applications on the CD-ROM will work with Windows 95/98/ME/2000/XP. In addition *WebEQ* 3.0 and *Mathematica* 4.2 can be used on Macintosh systems running Mac OS 8.1 or later. More detailed information on each application, along with installation instructions, is provided below.

Amaya 6.2

This is the W3C's test browser for new Web technologies. It can render presentation MathML and includes menu commands and palettes for authoring MathML. You can find more information about *Amaya* at the following URL: *www.w3.org/Amaya*.

Installation Instructions

1. Insert the CD-ROM into your CD-ROM drive.
2. Open the Applications: *Amaya* folder on the CD-ROM.
3. Double-click the installer file amaya-WinNT-6.2.exe.
4. Follow the instructions on your screen.

EzMath 1.1

This is an application for authoring content MathML using *EzMath* markup as an input language. Dave Raggett created it. You can find more information about *EzMath* at *www.w3.org/People/Raggett/EzMath*.

Installation Instructions

1. Insert the CD-ROM into your CD-ROM drive.
2. Open the Applications folder on the CD-ROM.
3. Copy the *EzMath* folder on to your hard disk.

TABLE A.1 Software Applications Included on the CD-ROM

Product	Operating System System	Hard Disk Space Space	RAM
Amaya 6.2	Windows	10 MB	-
EzMath 1.1	Windows	-	-
Mathematica 4.2	Windows or Macintosh	235 MB (full)	64 MB
		130 MB (minimal)	64 MB
MathPlayer 1.0	Windows	-	-
MathType 5.1	Windows	9 MB	-
WebEQ 3.0	Windows or Macintosh	14 MB	-

Mathematica 4.2 (Thirty-Day Trial Version)

Mathematica 4.2 is the latest version of the powerful technical computing application from Wolfram Research. The CD-ROM includes installers for a 30-day save-disabled trial version of *Mathematica* 4.2. The trial version has all the functionality of the original product except that you cannot save files.

Installation Instructions

1. Insert the CD-ROM into your CD-ROM drive.
2. Open the Applications:*Mathematica* folder on the CD-ROM.
3. Double-click the appropriate installer for your platform. The CD-ROM includes separate installers for Windows, Mac OS 8-9, and Mac OS X.
4. Follow the instructions on your screen. You will need to enter a license number and password during the installation process. Use the following license number: 3006-3320. Go to *register.wolfram.com* to get a password.

Contact Information

Wolfram Research, Inc.
100 Trade Center Drive
Champaign, IL 61820
1-800-WOLFRAM
www.wolfram.com
info@wolfram.com

MathPlayer 1.0

MathPlayer, from Design Science, Inc., is an application for rendering MathML in *IE* on Windows.

Installation Instructions

1. Insert the CD-ROM into your CD-ROM drive.
2. Open the Applications:MathPlayer folder on the CD-ROM.
3. Double-click the installer file MathPlayerSetup.exe.
4. Follow the instructions on your screen.

Contact Information

Design Science, Inc.
4028 Broadway Ave.
Long Beach, CA 90803
1-562-433-0685
www.dessci.com/webmath/mathplayer
info@dessci.com

MathType 5.1 (Thirty-Day Trial Version)

MathType, from Design Science, Inc., is an equation editor that can be used with a word processor such as Microsoft *Word*.

Installation Instructions

1. Insert the CD-ROM into your CD-ROM drive.
2. Open the Applications:*MathType* folder on the CD-ROM.
3. Double-click the installer file mtw50.exe.
4. Follow the instructions on your screen.

WebEQ 3.0 (Thirty-Day Trial Version)

WebEQ, from Design Science, Inc., is a suite of Java-based tools for authoring and displaying mathematics in Web pages.

Installation Instructions

1. Insert the CD-ROM into your CD-ROM drive.
2. Open the Applications:*WebEQ* folder on the CD-ROM.
3. Double-click the file install.exe (for Windows) or install (for Macintosh).
4. Follow the instructions on your screen.

You do not need to install any other software. A Java virtual machine is included with the installer.

Fonts

Mathematica

The Fonts/*Mathematica* folder on the CD-ROM includes the *Mathematica* fonts in TrueType format for both Windows and Macintosh. To install the fonts, simply copy the fonts into the appropriate Fonts folder on your system.

TEX

The Fonts/TEX folder on the CD-ROM includes the Computer Modern fonts and the AMS fonts, which are typically used with TEX. The fonts are in Type 1 (PostScript) format. To install the fonts, simply copy them into the appropriate Fonts folder on your system.

APPENDIX

B

MATHML RESOURCES

This appendix provides a list of useful resources for MathML users. The resources include Web sites with informative content, software products, e-mail discussion lists, and books on topics relevant to MathML.

B.1 Web Resources

W3C Math Working Group: *www.w3.org/Math*

The official Web site of the W3C Math Working Group. The site includes links to the official MathML 2.0 specification, products that support MathML, as well as the latest news and updates.

Universal MathML Stylesheet: *www.w3.org/Math/XSL*

This Web site provides information on the Universal MathML stylesheet along with a current list of browsers that can render MathML using this stylesheet.

Mozilla: *www.mozilla.org/projects/mathml*

This is the official Web site of the *Mozilla* MathML project. It includes instructions for authoring documents for *Mozilla*, sample pages for testing if your browser can render MathML, tips on installing and configuring mathematical fonts, and other information.

MathML Central: *www.mathmlcentral.com*

This is a nicely designed site with configurable interactive tools for experimenting with MathML. You can render MathML equations as images, convert mathematical expressions into MathML, validate MathML, and process XHTML documents that contain MathML. You can also create plots and evaluate integrals of functions specified as MathML. The site is hosted by Wolfram Research, the makers of *Mathematica*.

Mathematical Functions: *http://functions.wolfram.com*

This is one of the largest repositories of MathML content on the Web. You can see the MathML markup for several thousand formulas dealing with mathematical functions. This site is also maintained by Wolfram Research.

Zvon: *www.zvon.org/xxl/MathML/Output/index.html*

This Web site provides detailed reference information on all MathML elements and attributes. You can download the source code for examples of all MathML elements. The source code is available as MathML fragments or embedded in an XHTML file for viewing in a browser.

MathML Information Center: *www.webeq.com/mathml*

This Web site offers an introductory tutorial on MathML, reference information on elements and attributes, sample documents, and links to more information. This site is hosted by Design Science, the makers of *MathPlayer*, *MathType*, and *WebEQ*.

ORCCA MathML page: *www.orcca.on.ca/mathml*

This Web site provides information on MathML-related projects at the Ontario Research Center for Computer Algebra. This site includes links to online converters for translating LaTeX to MathML and vice versa.

Mathzilla: *http://pear.math.pitt.edu/mathzilla*

This Web site contains information on converting TeX documents into XHTML+MathML so they can be rendered in *Mozilla*.

MathML Conference: *www.mathmlconference.org/2002*

This Web site offers downloadable talks and presentations given at the Second International MathML conference, which was held in Chicago, IL, in June 2002.

B.2 Software

Amaya: *www.w3.org/Amaya*

This is the W3C's test browser for new Web technologies. It can render presentation MathML and includes menu commands and palettes for authoring MathML.

EzMath: *www.w3.org/People/Raggett/EzMath*

This is a plug-in for *Netscape* and an application for authoring content MathML.

GtkMathView: *http://le.cs.unibo.it/helm/mml-widget*

This is an open-source MathML rendering engine written by Luca Padovani. It can be used either as a standalone widget or as part of another application.

IBM *techexplorer*: *www.software.ibm.com/techexplorer*

This is a plug-in, ActiveX control, and Behavior for rendering presentation or content MathML in a variety of browsers and on a variety of platforms.

Maple: *www.maplesoft.com*

This is a technical computing application with support for MathML, from Waterloo Maple.

Mathematica: *www.wolfram.com/products/mathematica*

This is a technical computing application with support for MathML, from Wolfram Research.

MathPlayer: *www.mathtype.com/webmath/mathplayer*

This is a tool for rendering MathML in *IE* on Windows.

MathType: *www.mathtype.com*

This is the Professional version of the Equation Editor included with Microsoft *Word*. It can export equations as MathML and convert *Word* documents into Web pages that contain MathML.

Mozilla: *www.mozilla.org*

This is the open source version of the *Netscape* browser. It includes native support for rendering presentation MathML.

Netscape: *http://channels.netscape.com/ns/browsers/download.jsp*

The latest version of this popular browser, *Netscape* 7.0, includes native support for rendering presentation MathML.

Publicon: *www.publicon.com*

This is an application for authoring technical documents, from Wolfram Research.

Saxon: *http://saxon.sourceforge.net*

This is an XSLT processor created by Michael Kay.

Scientific Word: *www.mackichan.com*

This is an application for authoring technical documents, from MacKichan Software, Inc.

TeX4ht: *www.cis.ohio-state.edu/~gurari/TeX4ht/mn.html*

This is a configurable system for converting TeX documents into hypertext, created by Eitan Gurari.

Tidy: *www.w3.org/People/Raggett/Tidy*

This is Dave Raggett's utility for converting HTML documents into well-formed XHTML documents.

TtM: *http://hutchinson.belmont.ma.us/tth/mml*

This is Ian Hutchinson's program for converting TeX documents into HTML with embedded MathML.

WebEQ: *www.mathtype.com/webmath/webeq*

This is a suite of Java-based tools from Design Science for authoring and displaying interactive equations on the Web.

web*Mathematica*: *www.wolfram.com/products/webmathematica*

This is a system for delivering interactive computations over the Web using *Mathematica*.

Xalan: *http://xml.apache.org/xalan-j/index.html*

This is an XSLT processor created as part of the Apache XML project.

B.3 Mailing Lists

The following mailing lists provide a good forum for discussion of MathML-related issues:

- *http://lists.w3.org/Archives/Public/www-math*: a mailing list for MathML maintained by the W3C Math Working Group
- *netscape.public.mozilla.mathml*: a public mailing list for discussion of MathML issues in Mozilla. You can view the messages in this list by using your favorite newsgroup viewer or by going to a Web site such as *groups.google.com* that archives newsgroups
- *http://camel.math.ca/mail/webmath*: a mailing list for topics related to mathematics on the Web

B.4 Books

Few books directly deal with MathML. The titles listed below contain useful information on topics relevant to MathML, such as XML, XSLT, JavaScript, and LaTeX.

Neil Bradley. *The XSL Companion*. Addison Wesley Longman, Inc., Reading, MA (2000)

David Flanagan. *JavaScript: The Definitive Guide*, 4th ed. O'Reilly and Associates, Sebastopol, CA (2001)

Danny Goodman. *Dynamic HTML: The Definitive Reference*, 2nd ed. O'Reilly and Associates, Sebastopol, CA (2002)

Michel Goossens and Sebastian Rahtz. *The LaTeX Web Companion*. Addison Wesley Longman, Inc., Reading, MA (1999)

Elliot Rusty Harold and W. Scott Means. *XML in a Nutshell*, 2nd ed. O'Reilly and Associates, Sebastopol, CA (2002)

Steve Holzner. *Inside XML* . New Riders Publishing, Indianapolis, IN (2000)

Doug Tidwell. *XSLT*. O'Reilly and Associates, Sebastopol, CA (2001)

INDEX

A

abs element, 429
accent attribute
  application, 89, 90, 241
  discussion of, 70, 71, 409, 410–411
accents, rendering, 276
accentunder attribute, 90, 423–424
action properties, 241
actions
  techexplorer, 370–371
  WebEQ, 347–352
actiontype attribute, 100–101, 349, 351, 401–402
Active Server Pages, 375
actuarial value, 87
Adobe Acrobat Distiller, 232
algebra content elements, 121
align attribute, 94, 419–420
alignment, controlling, 96–99
alignmentscope attribute, 94, 99, 419, 422
alphabetic presentation forms, 486, 487
alt attribute, 77, 179, 405–406
\altlink(*expression1*) (*expression2*) attribute, 371
Amaya
applications, 38, 156, 169–172, 257–261, 492, 499
discussion of, 6, 159–161, 189–190, 218, 237, 265–266
\name command, 274
American Mathematical Society, 4, 251
AMSTEX, 252
amsymb package, for defining symbols, 274
and element, 121, 429
annotation element, 132, 133, 134, 143, 146, 430
Annotations conversion option, 320
annotation-xml element, 132, 133, 134, 143, 146, 430
API (application programming interface), 10, 352, 354, 358, 361–362, 371–373
applet tag, 187, 346, 350, 361
apply element
  application, 46, 110–111, 220–221
  discussion of, 45, 104, 114–115, 122, 430
⁡, 56, 69, 257
approx element, 122, 431
arccosec element, 431
arccosech element, 432
arccos element, 431
arccosh element, 431–432
arccot element, 432
arccoth element, 432
arcsec element, 432–433
arcsech element, 433
ArcSin command, 315
arcsin element, 433
arcsinh element, 433
arctan element, 434
arctanh element, 434
arg element, 434
arguements, of elements, 36, 40, 62–64
arithmetic content elements, 121
\array () command, 277, 278

\arrayopts command, 278
arrays, rendering, 277
arrows characters, 481, 484, 485
arXiv, 252
ASCII (American Standard Code for Information Interchange), 32
ASP, 340
attributes. *See also* individual attribute by name
MathML, 36–38, 49–52, 64–66
XML, 21–24
authoring tools, choosing, 265–267
automatic attributes, 50
autosize attribute, 181, 183
auto value, 76

B

background attribute, 83, 415, 416
badbreak value, 76
\bar command, 276
base attribute, 107, 135, 436–437
base element, 81
Basic Input palette, *Mathematica*, 245
Basic Multilingual Plane (BMP), 53–54
Basic Page Style setting, 169
Batsalle, Davy, 262
Behaviours functionality, 172, 174, 184–185
Berglund, Anders, 19
bevelled attribute, 79, 404–405
binomial coefficients, rendering, 214–217
Biomed XML format, 251, 252
blank space, 48–49, 75–76
Block Elements characters, 483
Bowering, Drew, 369
box drawing characters, 483
BoxestoMathML function, 325
box expressions in *Mathematica*, 312–313
Braille, conversion to, 14–15
Button("Integrate," command), 393
bvar element
application of, 48, 112, 124, 130
discussion of, 104, 124, 125, 130, 142–143, 434–435

C

C++, 172
calculus, rendering, 124–126
ⅅ, 56
card element, 435
Carlisle, David, 156, 218, 298
cartesianproduct element, 129, 435
\cdots command, 276
ceiling element, 435
CERN (European Laboratory for Nuclear Research), 19
CForm, 315
CGI, 340, 375
character glyphs, rendering, 76–77
characters, MathML, 52–54, 478–489
checkAnswer function, 366
\check command, 276
Chemical Markup Language (CML), 21
child elements, 23, 50
Chinese characters, 486, 487
ci element
application, 46, 110, 222
discussion of, 45, 104, 107–108, 136, 144, 435–436
class attribute, 49, 134, 400, 428
classid attribute, 174, 181, 185
close attribute, 85. 404
closure attribute, 113–114, 135, 452
CML (Chemical Markup Language), 21
cn element
application, 221
discussion, 45, 104, 107–108, 136, 144, 436
\coalign command, 278–279
code attribute, 187, 347, 361
codebase attribute, 185, 187, 347

code points, 32, 54
codomain element, 436–437
\collines command, 279
color attribute, 65, 83, 401, 415, 416
colorText function, 360
columnalign attribute, 93, 94, 406, 419, 420, 422, 423
columnlines attribute, 94, 279, 419, 421
columnspacing attribute, 94, 279, 419, 421
columnspan attribute, 95, 422
columnwidth attribute, 94, 419, 420–421
combined markup, 39, 140–151. *See also* content markup; presentation markup
comments, in an XML document, 25
compatibility issues, 157–160
Complete Characters palette, 245–246
complexes element, 132, 437
compose element, 437–438
condition element, 115–117, 129, 143, 225, 227, 438
conditions, rendering, 115–117
conjugate element, 438
constants, rendering, 131
constructor elements, 104, 109–120
container element, 21–22
content elements, 22, 106, 120–126, 134–137, 428–475
content markup
  application, 140, 217–227, 254
  discussion of, 39, 44–48, 104–137, 311–312 *See also* combined markup; content elements
Content MathML attribute, 133
content tags, in MathML, 38–39
control pictures, 483
controls parameter, 347
conversion functions
  Braille, 14–15
  ElementFormatting conversion option, 321
  Entities conversion option, 321
  individual formulas, 235–236, 277–281, 315
  LaTeX to MathML, 373–375
  Maple to MathML, 334–337
  Mathematica, 320–323, 385–390
  MathML, 294–296, 325–327, 337
  NamespacePrefixes conversion option, 320, 326
  ORCCA, 284–286, 297–298
  TEX4ht, 286–290
  TEX to MathML, 270–305
  Translation Options dialog box, 244
  TtM, 290–294
  xmltex, 298–305
convertMMLtoTEX() API function, 372
convertTEXtoMML() API function, 372
Coptic characters, 480
copying MathML, 331–332
\cos command, 275
cosec element, 439
cosech element, 439
cos element, 438
cosh element, 439
cot element, 439–440
coth element, 440
CSS
  discussion of, 5, 6, 10, 64, 160, 205, 340
  and MathML, 197–204
  pmathmlcss.xsl, 163
  primer, 195–197
css value, 164
csymbol element
  application, 108–109, 110, 144–145
  discussion of, 45, 104, 107, 115, 440
ctop.xsl, 163
curl element, 124, 126, 440
currency symbols, 481
Cyrillic characters, 480

D

data attribute, 182
database creation, 4
datatype attribute, 182
\ddots command, 276
declarations
  document type declaration (DOCTYPE), 27–28, 158–159, 166–167
  header, 243–244
  MathML, 53, 54
  piecewise, 119–120
  XML, 24–25
declare element, 111–112, 136, 137, 143, 441
Default Document palette, 251–252
\define(*expr1*) (*expr2*), 280
definitionURL attribute, 105, 109, 115, 133, 135, 428
degree element, 121, 143, 441–442
delimiters, rendering, 276
denomalign attribute, 79–80, 404–405
depth attribute, 75, 85, 411–412, 414
derivatives, rendering, 254
Design Science Inc., 172, 238, 241
determinant element, 126, 442
Diacritical Marks, 480, 481
diff element, 124, 442
ⅆ, 56
digits, mathematical styled, 489
Dingbats characters, 484
display attribute, 134, 198
display forms, *Mathematica*, 313–317
display method, choosing, 189–191
display mode, 72, 198–199
displaystyle attribute
  application, 80, 82–83
  discussion of, 72, 92, 94, 419, 421
displaytext function, 345
divergence element, 124, 126, 442
divide element, 121, 443
DocBook, 21, 249, 286
\doclink(*url*) (*expression*)command, 370
\doclink(*url*) (*label*) (*expression*) command, 370
DOCTYPE declarations, 27–28, 158–159, 166–167
document.bgcolor command, 344
document.fgcolor command, 344
DocumentHeader element, 320
document object, 344
document type declarations (DOCTYPE), 27–28, 158–159, 166–167
Document Type Definition (DTD)
  application, 158–159
  discussion of, 25–28, 166–167
  MathML, 50, 52–53, 54, 62, 66, 120
document.write command, 343, 344
DOM (Document Object Model), 6, 10, 340, 358–360
domain element, 443
domainofapplication element, 143
\dot command, 276
drawImage function, 369
dsi:background pseudo–attribute, 350
dsi:color pseudo-attribute, 350
dsi:cue1 pseudo-attribute, 350
dsi:cue2 pseudo-attribute, 350
dsi:href pseudo-attribute, 350
DTDs
  application, 158–159
  discussion of, 25–28, 166–167
  MathML, 50, 52–53, 54, 62, 66, 120
DVI (device independent) files, 270, 304

E

edge attribute, 98, 402
Edit/Expression Input menu, 246
Editor, *WebEQ*, 186, 238–241, 352, 360

electronic publishing, 13–14
ElementFormatting conversion option, 321
elements, 21–24, 36–38, 132, 443. *See also* individual elements by name
embed tag, 176, 177
Enclosed Alphanumerics, 483
encoding attribute, 24–25, 105, 109, 115, 133, 135, 147, 428
entities
  entity references, 30, 41, 43, 44, 56, 260
  of MathML, 41, 53
  of XML, 28–31
Entities conversion option, 321
entities.xsl stylesheet, 297
entity references, 30, 41, 43, 44, 56, 260
eq element, 122, 443–444
equalcolumns attribute, 94, 419, 421
\equalcolumns command, 279
equalrows attribute, 94, 419, 421
\equalrows command, 279
Equation Editor, 232
Equation Server, *WebEQ*, 186
equivalent element, 122, 444
Euclid fonts, 235
eulergamma element, 132, 444
European Laboratory for Nuclear Research (CERN), 19
exists element, 444–445
\exp command, 275
exp element, 445
ⅇ, 56
exponentiale element, 105, 132, 445
Export function, 318–319, 320
exporting/ importing
  general discussion, 6–7, 14, 248–250, 253–254, 260, 263
  Maple to HTML+MathML, 332–334
  Mathematica to MathML, 323–325
  MathML to *Mathematica*, 317–325
  WebEQ to MathML, 239–240
ExportString function, 319–320
Export to MathPage commmand, 237
Expression Editor window, *EzMath*, 263
expressions, 80, 84–86, 312–313, 330–331. *See also* individual exp ressions by name
ExpressiontoMathML function, 325
Extensible Business Reporting Language (XBRL), 21
Extensible Stylesheet Language (XSL), 6, 20, 21, 204
external DTD subset, 28
EzMath, 262–264, 265–266, 492, 499

F

factorial element, 121, 220, 445–446
factorials, rendering, 219–223
factorof element, 122, 446
false element, 132, 446
fence attribute, 70, 71, 409, 410
fenced expressions, rendering, 84–85
\fghighlight command, 279
File/Palette menu, *Mathematica*, 245
fillRect function, 369
fine-grained parallel markup, 148–149
floor element, 446
fn element, 115, 447
fontfamily attribute, 65, 77, 401, 405
fonts
  application, 200–201, 240, 243, 248, 347, 495
  discussion of, 55, 167–169, 235, 256, 260
fontsize attribute, 65, 401
fontstyle attribute, 65, 68, 401
fontweight attribute, 65, 401
forall element, 447
Formats conversion option, 320

form attribute, 70, 71, 241, 408–409
form element, 344
form[expr] command, 315
forms and controls, HTML, 344–345
formulas
converting, 277–281
importing/exporting, 6–7, 14
/frac command, 272, 274
FractionBox[x, y]construct, 313
fractions, rendering
  application, 79–80, 201–202, 274
  general discussion, 82, 234, 239, 254, 312, 330
Fraktur characters, 488
frame attribute, 94, 279, 419, 421
\frame command, 279
framespacing attribute, 94, 419, 421
FullForm, 315
full form, of formula, 311–312
functions. *See also* specific function by name
  elementary, 122
  integrating, 378–380, 392–393
  plotting, 381–382, 394–395
  rendering, 115, 120–131

G

Gartside, Paul, 287
gcd element, 447–448
geometric shapes, 483
geq element, 122, 448
getContentMathML(), API function, 362
getContentSelection(), API function, 362
getDepthFromMMLString(String mmlSource), API function, 372
getEquationImage(), API function, 362
getEquationImage(int n), API function, 362
getEquationImage(int n, String color), API function, 362, 368
getEscapedContentMathML(), API function, 362
getEscapedMathML(), API function, 362
getFirstChild() element, 360
getHeightFromMMLString(String mmlSource), API function, 372
getMathML(), API function, 362
getMathMLDocument() element, 360
getMMLString(), API function, 372
getPackedContentMathML(), API function, 362
getPackedMathML(), API function, 362
getSelection(), API function, 362
getWidthFromMMLString(String mmlSource), API function, 372
GIF format, 7, 236
glayout.xsl stylesheet, 297
goodbreak value, 76
Goossens, Michael, 287
grad element, 124, 126, 448
Greek characters, 480, 488, 489
GridBox[]construct, 313
groupalign attribute
  application, 96–99
  discussion of, 93, 94, 406, 419, 422, 423
gt element, 122, 448
GtkMathView, 369, 499
Gurari, Eitan, 286

H

\hat command, 276
header declarations, 243–244
height attribute
  application, 181, 183, 187
  discussion of, 75, 85, 411–412, 414
history object, 344
href attribute, 49, 195, 206
href attribute, of XML, 25
\href command, 279
HTML

and CSS, 196
general discussion, 6, 18, 19, 20, 344–345
MathML, 5, 6, 13, 156, 161, 332–334
Scientific Word, 256
techexplorer, 369–375
Web pages, 342–345, 363–369
Word, 237
XSLT, 205
html-colorname, 64
HTML Math, 6
Hutchinson, Ian, 290

I

IBM *techexplorer*
application, 159, 175–186, 369–375
discussion of, 156, 160, 161, 190, 500
and interactive Web sites, 341
techexplorer-plugin value, 164
techexplorer value, 164
id attribute
application, 149–151, 261, 336
discussion of, 49, 134, 174, 185, 400, 428
ident element, 449
identifiers, 39, 45, 60, 68, 108, 313
IE Behaviours, 172, 174, 184–185
ImageApplet, 369
image element, 449
images, 7, 8, 239
imaginary element, 121, 449
ⅈ, 56
imaginaryi element, 105, 132, 450
implies element, 122, 450
Import function, 323
importing/exporting
general discussion, 6–7, 14, 248–250, 253–254, 260, 263
Maple to HTML+MathML, 332–334
Mathematica to MathML, 323–325
MathML into *Mathematica*, 317–325
MathML to *Mathematica*, 317–325
WebEQ to MathML, 239–240
incompatibility issues, 6
indentingnewline value, 76
index attribute, 77, 81, 405
in element, 128, 450
inferred mrow element, 62
infinity element, 105, 132, 450–451
information, reuse of, 7, 8
inherited attributes, 50
inline expression, display of, 80, 83, 330–331
inline mode, 72, 198–199
Input Control, *WebEQ*, 186–187, 265, 360–369
input element, 344
InputForm, 314, 315
Insert/Actions menu, 240
Insert menu, 330
Insert Symbol command, 235
\int command, 275
integers element, 132, 451
integrals, rendering, 124, 223–227, 234, 239, 254, 330
Integrate function, 388
int element, 48, 104, 114, 124, 328, 451
interactive equations, 4
interactivity, types of, 341–342
internal DTD subset, 28
International Phoenetic Alphabet (IPA) characters, 479
Internet Explorer (*IE*), 4, 6, 157, 158, 162–163, 249, 281. *See also IE* Behaviours
intersect element, 128, 451–452
interval element, 113–114, 124, 225, 227, 452
inverse element, 452
inverse sine, 316
⁣, 56, 69
invisible operators, 69–70, 86–87
⁢, 56, 67, 69, 221, 257

ISO 12083, 8–9
itex2mml, 282–284

J

Japanese characters, 486, 487
Java
  application, 5, 13, 176, 341, 375
  discussion of, 178, 238, 241, 265, 284, 340
JavaScript
  application, 5, 13, 176, 341
  discussion of, 160, 178, 340
JPEG format, 7, 239

K

Kay, Michael, 500
Knuth, Donald, 8, 270
Korean characters, 486, 487

L

\labellink(*label*) command, 371
\labellink(*label*) (*expression*) command, 371, 453
lambda element, 112–113
language attribute, 343
laplacian element, 124, 126, 453
largeop attribute, 70, 72, 73, 82, 409
LaTeX. *See also* TeX
  conversion to MathML, 373–375
  discussion of, 55, 175, 176, 198, 233, 247, 252, 254, 256
  The LaTeX Web Companion (Goossens and Rahtz), 287
  syntax, 273–277
Latin characters, 478–479, 487, 488
layout schemata, 61–62, 77–87, 240
lcm element, 453
\ldots command, 276
Lee, Tim-Berners, 19
\left command, 276, 277
leq element, 122, 454
limitations, 7, 8, 11, 232
limit element, 129, 130, 454
linear algebra, rendering, 126–128
linebreak attribute, 75–76
linethickness attribute, 49, 79, 404–405
links, forming, 240, 261, 348, 349
LISP, 45
list element, 117–118, 128, 454–455
lists, rendering, 117–118
ln element, 455
logbase element, 123, 143
\log command, 275
log element, 44, 123, 455
logic content elements, 121
longdiv value, 87
lowlimit element
  application, 104, 124, 129, 130, 223, 227
  discussion of, 48, 104–105, 142–143, 455–456
lquote attribute, 76, 413
lspace attribute, 70, 71, 85, 408–409, 411
lt element, 122, 456
.ltx extension, 176

M

macros, creating, 227–229, 280
maction element
  application, 99–101, 240, 348–349, 400–402
  discussion of, 62, 63, 341, 400–402
mailing lists, MathML, 501
maligngroup element, 61, 402
malignmark element, 61, 96–99
Maple, 6, 308, 327–337, 500
MapleNet, 390–395
maplet interface, 391
match attribute, 207, 211
mathapplet, 355
MathAutoColor tab, 177
mathbackgroud attribute, 64, 199, 401
Mathcad, 308
mathcolor attribute, 64, 199–200, 401

Mathematica
application, 133, 134, 233, 244–250, 308–327
discussion of, 6, 55, 105, 169, 265–266, 493, 500
Mathematical Functions, 498
mathematical information processing, 7, 8
mathematical notation, 4, 14–15, 245
mathematical operators, 482
mathematical symbols, miscellenous, 484, 485
Mathematica Server Pages (MSP), 377
mathematics, 5–6, 9
Math menu, *EzMath*, 262
MathML
attributes, 36–38, 49–52
characters, 52–54
and CSS, 197–204
fonts, 55
general discussion, 4–7, 9–15, 38–39
mailing lists, 501
and XLST, 212–229
MathML Central, 498
MathML Conference, 499
MathMl[ExportContent](expr), 335
MathML[Export](expr), 335
MathML[ExportPresentation](expr), 335
MathMLForm, 315
MathML[Import](mmlstring), 337
MathML Information Center, 499
mathmlrender, 369
MathMLtoBoxes function, 325
MathMLtoExpression function, 325
MathMLViewer['name'], 393
mathml.xsl, 163
Math mode, 254
MathPage feature, 232
MathPlayer. *See also IE* Behaviours
application, 159, 160, 172–175, 281
discussion of, 156, 161, 190, 237, 494, 500
mathplayer -dl value, 164
mathplayer value, 164
mathsize attribute, 51, 64, 198, 199–200, 202, 401
Maths palette, *Amaya*, 259–260
Math toolbars, *Scientific Word*, 254–255
MathType, 55, 174, 232–236, 265–266, 494, 500
mathvariant attribute, 64, 65–66, 68, 199–201, 260, 401
Mathzilla, 287, 499
MathZoom feature, 237
matrices, rendering
application, 92–99, 119, 227–229, 382–385
general discussion, 234, 241, 277, 330
matrix element, 119, 126, 456–457
matrixrow element, 119, 126
max element, 457
maxsize attribute, 70, 71, 409
mean element, 130, 457
median element, 130, 457
mediummathspace, 84, 415, 416
 , 56, 75
\medsp command, 275
menclose element, 61, 62, 63, 87, 403
merror element, 61, 62, 63, 101–102, 403
mfenced element, 61, 63, 84–85, 403–404
mfrac element
application, 42, 49, 79–80, 201–202
general discussion, 61, 63, 83, 217, 272, 404–405, 416
mglyph element, 53, 60, 61, 77, 98, 405–406
Microsoft Word, 232, 236–237
mi element
application, 41, 50, 257

discussion of, 60, 64, 68, 143, 406
MIME types, 158
min element, 458
minilabelspacing attribute, 94, 419, 422
minisize attribute, 70, 71
minus element, 47, 121, 458
mixed markup, 141–145
mlabeledtr element, 61, 63, 93–96, 99, 406
mmldata attribute, 179
.mml extension, 176
mml_string, 347
mmltex.xsl stylesheet, 297
mmultiscripts element, 61, 63, 91–92, 407, 416
mn element
application, 40, 41, 67, 257
discussion of, 60, 64, 143, 407–408
mode element, 130, 458
mo element
application, 67, 69–74, 82, 89
general discussion, 41, 50, 60, 64, 143, 257, 408–410
momentabout element, 143, 459
moment element, 130, 459
mouseover, 240, 348, 349
movablelimits attribute, 70, 72, 73, 83, 409, 410
mover element, 63, 89–90, 92, 203, 410–411, 416
Mozilla
application, 158, 159–161, 189, 281
general discussion, 4, 6, 38, 156, 164–169, 218, 500
mpadded element, 62, 63, 85–86, 411–412
mphantom element, 61, 62, 63, 86–87, 276, 412
mprescripts element, 91, 412
mroot element, 63, 80–81, 83, 202, 412–413, 416
mrow element, 40, 61, 62, 63, 67, 78, 413
ms element, 60, 76, 413
mspace element, 49, 60, 61, 75, 276, 414
MSPBlock function, 380
MSPFormat function, 380, 385, 388
MSPSetDefault function, 384
MSPShow command, 382, 390
msqrt element, 42, 61, 62, 63, 80, 272, 414–415
mstyle element, 61, 63, 81–84, 92, 203, 415–416
msub element
application, 61, 68, 83, 88, 203, 416, 417
general discussion, 61, 63, 92, 416, 417
msubsup element
application, 88, 203
general discussion, 44, 61, 63, 92, 416, 417–418
msup element
application, 68, 83, 88, 142, 203
general discussion, 40, 61, 63, 92, 416, 418
mtable element
application, 99, 279
general discussion, 43, 61, 63, 92–95, 416, 418–422
mtd element, 61, 62, 63, 92–95, 279, 422
mtext element, 49, 60, 74–75, 257, 422–423
MTExtra font, 235
MathML[ImportContent](mml-string), 337
mtr element, 61, 63, 92–95, 99, 279, 423
multiscripts, rendering, 91–92, 203
munder element, 61, 63, 89–90, 92, 203, 416, 423–424
munderover element, 61, 63, 90, 92, 203, 416, 424
mzlatex command, 289, 290

N

name attribute, 178, 182, 187, 344
name=eq parameter, 187
name=parser parameter, 188
NamespacePrefixes conversion option, 320, 326
namespaces
  application, 159, 161, 167, 185, 243–244, 284
  general discussion, 31–32, 239, 300
\namespace command, 300
name=src parameter, 188
nargs attribute, 136, 441
naturalnumbers element, 132, 459–460
navigator object, 344
\underbrace command, 276
\underset command, 276
\negthinsp command, 275
neq element, 122, 460
Netscape
  application, 156, 157, 164–169
  discussion of, 4, 6, 38, 189, 218, 500

, 56
newline value, 76
nextStep function, 357
nobreak value, 76
 , 56
none element, 62, 425
non-marking characters, 55–57
notanumber element, 132, 460
notation, specifying, 212–217, 328–330
notation attribute, 403
NotebookML, 249, 253
not element, 121
notin element, 128, 460–461
notprsubset element, 128, 461
notsubset element, 128, 461
numalign attribute, 79–80, 404–405
number forms characters, 481
numbers, 39, 45, 60, 66–68, 107–108, 313
numeric literals, rendering, 66

O

object tag, 176, 181, 183
occurrence attribute, 136, 441
onChange event, 360
onclick attribute, 345
op attribute, 284
open attribute, 85, 404
OpenMath, 8–9
OpenMath attribute, 133
Operator dialog box, 255
operator dictionary, 73–74
operators
  application, 69–74, 90, 313
  discussion of, 39, 60, 120–131, 240, 274–276
Optical Character Recognition, 483
Options menu, 177
ORCCA (Ontario Research Center for Computer Algebra), 284–286, 297–298, 499
order attribute, 118, 136, 455
or element, 121, 461
other attribute, 49, 134, 400, 428
otherwise element, 119, 462
outerproduct element, 126, 128, 462
\overbrace command, 276
overscripts, rendering, 89–90
\overset command, 276
OversuperscriptBox[x, y]construct, 313

P

padding expressions, 85–86
Padovani, Luca, 369
paint function, 369
parallel markup, 141, 146–151
param attribute, 182, 187
parameter entities, 31
parent elements, 23
partialdiff element, 124, 125, 462
PassiveTEX Project, 304
pasting MathML, 331–332
pat:mml element, 284
pat:template element, 284
pdf files, 7, 8, 304
pdflatex command, 304

Perl, 13, 340, 341, 375
\phantom command, 276
PHP, 13, 340–341, 369, 375
Physical Review, 251
piece element, 119, 463
piecewise declarations, 119–120
piecewise element, 119, 463
pi element, 105, 463
Plot function, 390
pluginspage attribute, 179
plus element, 44, 46, 104, 121, 463–464
pmathmlcss.xsl, 163
pmathml.xsl, 163
\popuplink(popuptext) (caption) command, 371
power element, 44, 45, 121, 464
preferredHeight() function, 354
preferredWidth() function, 354
prefix notation, 45, 312
pref:renderer attribute, 163
prescripts element, 62
presentation elements, 400–425
presentation markup
- application, 194, 217–227, 312–313
- general discussion, 39–44, 59–102, 60, 140, 199, 254, 312–313 *See also* combined markup; presentation elements

Presentation MathML attribute, 133
presentation tags, in MathML, 38–39
primes element, 132, 464
processing instructions, in XML, 25
\product command, 275
product element, 129, 465
products, rendering, 234, 254
programming, server-side, 375–377
prsubset element, 128, 465
psuedo-attributes, 350
Publicon, 233, 250–254, 265–266, 500
Publisher, *WebEQ*, 186, 241–244
punctuation characters, 481
Python, 375

Q

\qquad command, 275
\quad command, 275
quadratic equations, rendering, 262
qualifier elements, 105, 131
quotient element, 465

R

RadicalBox[x, y]construct, 313
radicals, rendering, 80–81, 201–202, 254, 274
radical value, 87
Raggett, Dave, 6, 166, 262
Rahtz, Sebastian, 287, 304
rational numbers, rendering, 144
rationals element, 132, 466
real element, 121, 466
reals element, 132, 466
relations, rendering, 114–115, 122
relationships between elements and attributes, 23–24
reln element, 115, 116, 466–467
reloadFromMMLString(String mmlSource), API function, 372
rem element, 467
renderer attribute, 164
rendering mathematics into non-visual media, 14–15
resolution, of images, 7
RevT_EX, 252
Rieman zeta functions, 316
\right command, 276
root element, 23, 37, 47, 121, 467
roots, rendering, 80–81
rowalign attribute
- application, 93, 279
- discussion of, 94, 406, 419, 420, 422, 423

\rowalign command, 278
RowBox[x, y]construct, 313
rowlines attribute, 94, 279, 419, 421

\rowlines command, 279
rows, rendering, 78
rowspacing attribute, 94, 279, 419, 421
rowspan attribute, 95, 422
rquote attribute, 76, 413
rspace attribute, 70, 71, 408–409

S

Save As HTML feature, 232, 236
Saxon, 500
Scalable Vector Graphics (SVG), 21
scalarproduct element, 126, 128, 468
Scientific Word, 233, 254–256, 265–266, 500
Scientific Workplace, 308
scope attribute, 136
scriptlevel attribute, 80, 82, 92, 203–204, 415, 416
scriptminisize attribute, 82, 415, 416
scripts, rendering, 202–204, 273–274
script size attributes, 82–83
scriptsizemultiplier attribute, 82, 203, 415, 416
scripts.xsl stylesheet, 297
sdev element, 130, 468
sech element, 468
Secondary Multilingual Plane (SMP), 53–54
select attribute, 100, 220, 360
selection attribute, 344, 401–402
selector element, 126, 127, 468–469
selectors, 196–197
semantic mapping elements, 105, 131–134
semantics, modifying, 105–106, 428–429
semantics element
  application, 144, 145, 146, 148–149, 228
  general discussion, 132, 469
separator attribute, 70, 71, 409, 410
separators attribute, 85, 404
sep element, 107, 143, 469–470
sequences, rendering, 129–130
series, rendering, 129–130
servlet container, 378
servlets, 378
setAttribute() element, 360
setBGColor(Stringnewcolor) function, 354
setColor function, 369
setdiff element, 128, 129, 470
set element, 117–118, 128, 136, 137, 470
setEquation function, 357
setEquation(Stringneweq) function, 354, 355, 356
setFGColor(Stringnewcolor) function, 354
setMathML(String-mml.string), API function, 362
sets, rendering, 117–118
setSize(int size) function, 354
showMath function, 355
sibling elements, 23
side attribute, 94, 419, 421
\sin command, 275
sin element, 44, 104, 328, 470–471
sinh element, 471
\space command, 276
spacing attribute, 84
Spacing Modifier Letters, 479
special constants, 55–57
speech synthesis software development, 4
SqrtBox[x]construct, 313
/sqrt command, 272, 274
square roots, rendering, 239, 330
src attribute, 178, 180, 347
standalone attribute, 24
StandardForm, 315, 380
Standard Generalized Markup Language (SGML), 8, 18, 20
statistics, rendering, 130
\statusline command, 279
STIX, 55
stretchy attribute, 70, 71, 241, 409

StringReplace function, 388
strings, rendering, 76
structure. *See* syntax
style attribute, 49, 134, 196, 400, 428
stylesheets. *See also* templates
  applying, 81–84, 195–197
CSS, 163, 195–196
Universal MathML stylesheet
  application, 160–164, 237
  discussion of, 6, 156–157, 158, 218, 498
  XLST MathML Library, 296, 297
  XSLT, 204–210, 216–217, 296–297
SubscriptBox[x, y]construct, 313
subscripts, 481
subscripts, rendering, 88, 234, 239, 254, 312, 330
subscriptshift attribute, 88, 91–92, 407, 417, 418
subset element, 128, 471
SubsuperscriptBox[x, y]construct, 313
\sum command, 275
sum element, 129, 471–472
sums, rendering, 234, 254
SuperscriptBox[x, y]construct, 313
superscripts, 481
superscripts, rendering, 88, 234, 239, 254, 312, 330
superscriptshift attribute, 88, 91–92, 407, 418
SVG (Scalable Vector Graphics), 21
symbol characters, 481
symbolic constants, rendering, 67, 68, 108–109, 131–132
SymbolicXML, 327
symbols, miscellenous, 484
symbols, rendering, 131, 274–276, 330
symmetric attribute, 241, 409
syntax
  of elements, 42, 44, 400–425
    See also individual elements
  of entity references in XML, 30
  LaTeX, 273–277
  Mathematica, 310–311, 318, 319, 323
  of MathML, 36–38, 49, 50
  of namespaces in XML, 31–32

T

	, 56
tables, rendering, 92–99, 277
tables.xsl stylesheet, 297
tan element, 472
tangent, rendering, 212–214
tanh element, 472
.tcx extension, 176
techexplorer
  application, 159, 175–186, 369–375
  discussion of, 156, 160, 161, 190, 500
  and interactive Web sites, 341
techexplorer-plugin value, 164
techexplorer value, 164
technical symbols, miscellaneous, 482
TEI (Text Encoding Initiative), 286–287
templates. *See also* stylesheets
  applying, 206–210, 239
  default, 210–212
  Mathematica, 245–246
  ORCAA, 284–286
  Publicon, 251, 252
  Scientific Word, 254–255
tendsto element, 122, 129, 130, 136, 137, 472
TeX. *See also* LaTeX
  AMSTeX, 252
  application, 105, 133, 134, 232
  compared to MathML, 271–273
  converting to MathML, 270–305
  general discussion, 8–9, 55, 169, 175, 176, 198, 247
  .tex extension, 176
TeXForm, 315
TeX4ht, 286–290, 501
text, rendering, 74–75, 277

textarea element, 344
[text] command, 393
TextField['name'] command, 393
text integration, 7
Text mode, 254
TEX User's Group Web site, 287
The Art of Computer Programming (Knuth), 270
The LATEX Web Companion (Goossens and Rahtz), 287
theory of sets, rendering, 128–129
thickmathspace, 84, 415, 416
 , 56, 75
\thicksp command, 275
thinmathspace, 84, 415, 416
 , 56, 75
\thinsp command, 275
Tidy, 166, 281, 282, 501
\tilde command, 276
times element, 47, 121, 428–429, 473
ToBoxes[expr, form], 317
ToExpression[input, form], 317
toggle action, 240, 348, 349, 351–352, 356
\toggle(*expr1*) (*expr2*) (*prompt1*) (*prompt2*) command, 279
token elements, 39, 45, 60–61, 64–77, 104, 107–109
tokens.xsl stylesheet, 297
toolbar parameter, 361
top-level parallel markup, 146–148
ToString[expr, form], 317
TraditionalForm, 314
translating equations. *See* conversion functions
Translation Options dialog box, 244
Translators dialog box, *MathType*, 235–236
transpose element, 126, 473
true element, 132, 473
TtM, 290–294, 501
type attribute
  application, 111, 136, 178, 206, 344
  general discussion, 25, 44, 107, 117, 344, 436–437, 464, 472
Typesetting palette, *Publicon*, 251

U

UnderoversuperscriptBox[x, y, z] construct, 313
underscripts, rendering, 89–90
UndersuperscriptBox[x, y]construct, 313
Unicode
  and MathML, 52, 478–489
  and XML, 32–33, 36
union element, 128, 474
Universal MathML stylesheet
  application, 160–164, 237
  general discussion, 6, 156–157, 158, 218, 498
Unix
  installation of TEX4ht, 288–289
  and *Mathematica*, 309
  and TtM, 291
uplimit element, 48
  application, 124, 129, 223, 227
  general discussion, 48, 104–105, 142–143, 474

V

value attribute, 345
var element, 130, 474
\vdots command, 276
\vec command, 276
vector calculus, rendering, 126
vector element, 118, 474–475
vectorproduct element, 126, 128, 475
vectors, rendering, 118–119, 144, 330
version attribute, 24
verythickmathspace, 84, 415, 416
verythinmathspace, 84, 415, 416
 , 56, 75
veryverythickmathspace, 84, 415, 416
veryverythinmathspace, 84, 415, 416
Viewer Control, *WebEQ*, 186, 187, 239, 240, 265, 346–360

view MathML source command, 167
v-unit attribute, 51

W

Watt, Stephen, 284
W3C, 4, 6, 20
W3C Math Working Group, 6, 10, 498
WebEQ
  application, 160, 174, 277–278
  general discussion, 13, 186–191, 233, 237, 238–244, 501
  and interactive Web sites, 341, 345–369
web*Mathematica*, 377–384, 501
Web sites
  creation of, 5, 12–13, 236–237, 279–280, 341–395
  methods of displaying mathematics upon, 7–9, 12
WebTEX, 241, 277–281
whitespace, 48–49, 75–76
width attribute
  application, 178, 181, 183, 187
  discussion of, 75, 85, 94, 411, 414, 419, 421
window object, 344
WML (Wireless Markup Language), 21
Wolfram Research, 169, 250, 493
Word. *See* Microsoft Word
www.ams.org, 13
www.arvix.org, 13
www.openmath.org, 9
www.stix.org, 55

X

Xalan, 501
XBRL (Extensible Business Reporting Language), 21
XHTML
  application, 54, 158–159, 161, 197, 249
  general discussion, 21, 65, 156, 165–166, 286
XLink, 20, 260
xlink attribute, 49, 134, 260
xlink:href attribute, 428
XLST MathML Library, 296, 297, 298
XML
  Biomed XML format, 251
  and CSS, 197–198
  entities, 28–31
  general discussion, 6, 10–11, 18–20, 21–25, 26
  and MathML, 36–38
  SymbolicXML, 327
  and Unicode, 32–33
\XMLelement(name) command, 301
.xml extension, 248, 318
XML`MathML`
  ExpressionToMathML function, 386
  MathMLToExpression function, 387
xmlns attribute, 159
xmlns:m attribute, 173
xmltex, 298–305
xor element, 121, 475
XPath
  application, 207, 210, 211
  discussion of, 20–21, 205, 216, 225
xref attribute, 49, 134, 149–151, 336, 428
XSL, 6, 20, 21, 204
XSL–FO, 205, 304
XSLT
  application, 204–212, 296–297
  MathML, 212–229
  general discussion, 5, 10, 156–157, 160, 194, 340

Y

Yaroshevich, Vasil, 296

Z

, 56
Zeta functions, Rieman, 316
Zvon, 498